DODS PARLIAMENTARY COMPANION

Guide to the General Election 2010

DODS PARLIAMENTARY COMPANION

Guide to the General Election 2010

A division of Huveaux plc

Publishers of
Dods Parliamentary Companion; Dods Civil Service Companion; Dods European Companion;
Dods New Constituency Guide; Who's Who in Public Affairs;
European Public Affairs Directory; Diplomacy.be
www.dodspeople.com

ACKNOWLEDGEMENTS

The publishers would like to thank all the individuals who have spent time and care working with us to ensure that the entries in this book are correct, and everyone who has provided helpful advice and guidance during its publication.

DODS PARLIAMENTARY COMPANION GUIDE TO THE GENERAL ELECTION

EDITOR: MAGGIE SINCLAIR

PRODUCTION MANAGER: ROY HODGKINSON

HEAD OF DATA: AINSLEY GOONASEKERA

DATABASE MANAGER: ELIZABETH NEWTON

SALES MANAGER: MICHAEL MAND

ADVERTISING SALES: MATTHEW HARRIS

PUBLISHING DIRECTOR: RHODRI JOYCE

All electoral calculations are based on the notional results for the 2005 general election as compiled by Colin Rallings and Michael Thrasher, *Media Guide to the New Parliamentary Constituencies* (LGC Elections Centre, University of Plymouth, for BBC, ITN, PA News and Sky News, 2007).

Typesetting by Dods and Dataset Media
Printed in Great Britain by Polestar Wheatons, Exeter, Devon

Westminster Tower, 3 Albert Embankment, London SE1 7SP
Tel: 020 7091 7500 Fax: 020 7091 7555 E-mail: editorial@dods.co.uk
Subscriptions: 020 7091 7540 E-mail: order@dods.co.uk
ISBN: 978-0-905702-94-0

CONTENTS

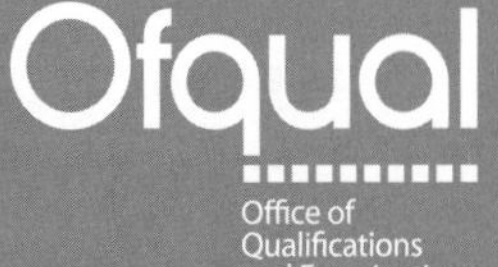

Ofqual is the Office of Qualifications and Examinations Regulation. We regulate qualifications, examinations and assessments in England and vocational qualifications in Northern Ireland. It is our duty to ensure learners get the results their work merits and their qualifications are correctly valued and understood. We are responsible for regulating qualifications taken by learners of all ages, including National Curriculum assessments, GCSEs, A levels, the Diploma, NVQs and vocational qualifications. We also keep assessments taken in the Early Years Foundation Stage (EYFS) under review.

Ofqual was formally established in April 2010 by the Apprenticeships, Skills, Children and Learning Act 2009. We have five objectives which cover qualifications standards, assessments standards, public confidence, awareness and efficiency.

We regulate the qualifications industry on behalf of everyone who uses it. This includes learners, teachers, parents and carers and employers. They all deserve a system of qualifications and assessments that supports the best practice in education, training, and professional development. We want all learners to get the mark their work merits and for the qualifications they take to be worth the same in the future as they are on the day they are taken.

For more information or to get in touch please look at **www.ofqual.gov.uk** or email our **Chief Executive Isabel.Nisbet@ofqual.gov.uk** or our **Director of Communications Francis.Thomas@ofqual.gov.uk** .

Ofqual/10/4750

FOREWORD

Gisela Stuart
MP for Birmingham Edgbaston and Editor of the House Magazine

Any general election brings with it considerable change and this year was certainly no different. In fact, there haven't been so many new faces in parliament since 1997.

The 2010 election gave us our first hung parliament since February 1974 and the new parliamentary session also brings with it a new form of politics, a coalition government – the first since 1918.

This guide will provide a valuable point of reference to the 2010 general election. I am sure this book will be well used.

GENERAL ELECTION 2010

The General Election

The general election of 2010 was unlike any other in modern times, and not just because it led to the unlikely sight of David Cameron and Nick Clegg undergoing the political equivalent of a civil partnership.

For the first time in British history the leaders of the three main political parties agreed to take part in a series of TV debates. They certainly changed the campaign, but arguably the debates had little impact on the final result.

The campaign proper began in January. David Cameron, the Conservative party leader since 2005, was anxious to get things started. On the second day of 2010, he launched his party's election campaign with a pledge to place the country under new economic management, redistribute power "from the political elite to the man and woman in the street". He also promised "the most radical decentralisation of power this country has seen for generations". Cameron had reason to feel confident. The last opinion poll of 2009 by YouGov/Daily Telegraph put the Conservatives on 40 per cent, Labour on 30 per cent and the Lib Dems on 17 per cent. No-one could have predicted the twists and turns of the months leading up to polling day on 6 May. Few grasped what a game-changer the first leaders' debate would be – indeed in January there did not seem to be much stomach for those debates.

The Tories had a bumpy start – an airbrushed photo of Cameron that sprang up on billboards across the country was widely-parodied. Labour tried to hit back with posters of their own, claimed the Tories were using money from Lord Ashcroft to "buy" the election, and pointed to the peer's refusal to clarify his tax status. The Conservatives sought to highlight the financial links between Labour and the Unite union, which was threatening a series of strikes against British Airways. The ill-feeling about 'Ashcroft' and 'union' money became one of the key dividing lines of the election, with the Labour government claiming underdog status.

At the start of the year, the expenses scandal continued to grab headlines. Sir Thomas Legg's report demanded that hundreds of MPs collectively pay back more than £1.1 million. Among them were David Cameron, Gordon Brown and Nick Clegg. In February three Labour MPs and a Tory peer were charged under the Theft Act over some of their expenses claims – parliament had hit rock bottom.

In March chancellor Alistair Darling presented his final Budget before the general election. He said the government would seek to invest in new industries to boost job prospects and warned that a Conservative government that made immediate cuts to public spending would tip the economy back into recession. Labour's decision to intervene to rescue the banks was a "judgement that has proved correct," he said. Darling announced an end to stamp duty on homes up to £250,000 for first time buyers and forecast that the economy would grow by between 1 and 1.5 per cent this year and between 3 and 3.5 per cent in 2011. The Budget set the dividing lines over the key issue of the economy. The Conservatives argued that £6 billion must be cut from public spending this financial year, in order to demonstrate a determination to deal with the country's mounting debt. Labour and the Lib Dems argued such the cuts would be counter-productive and could risk a double-dip recession. While all the main parties agreed on the need for serious cuts in the years ahead, none of them was willing to be specific about which services would suffer.

Despite endless speculation on possible April election dates, the prime minister stuck to 6 May. It had been five years since Tony Blair took Labour to an historic third election victory. Brown visited the Queen on 6 April and asked for the dissolution of parliament. The next day the party leaders clashed at the final prime minister's question time of the 54th parliament. Cameron claimed Labour's planned National Insurance rise, or "jobs tax", would "wreck" the economic recovery. Brown said the electorate was faced with a "clear choice" at the election. "We can put National Insurance up and therefore protect schools, our hospitals and our policing or we can do what the Conservatives do which is put hospitals, police and health services at risk," he said. The argument would be rehearsed over and over again throughout the campaign.

A raft of legislation made it through the wash-up period at the end of the parliament, including the Digital Economy Act, Constitutional Reform and Governance Act, Financial Services Act, Flood and Water Management Act, Personal Care at Home Act, Equality Act and Bribery Act.

Labour launched their manifesto on the day of dissolution, 12 April. Brown promised to secure the recovery by halving the deficit by 2014 through "growth and fair taxes"; 15 hours a week of flexible, free nursery education for three and four-year-olds; new powers for parents to bring in new school leadership teams; guaranteed education or training until 18 and referendums on the alternative vote for the Commons and a democratic second chamber.

On 13 April the Conservatives launched their manifesto at a glitzy event in Battersea Power Station with "an invitation to join the government of Britain". Cameron claimed he was making "no less than the biggest call to arms the country has seen in a generation". "It is an invitation to the whole nation: we'll give you the power, so you can take control," he promised. Key pledges included an emergency Budget within 50 days of taking office; cuts of £6 billion of waste in departmental spending in 2010-11; a freeze public sector pay for one year in 2011 and no National Insurance rise for anyone earning under £35,000 next year. There were also key pledges on reforming schools, the constitution and parliament, and an annual limit on the number of non-EU economic migrants admitted into the UK.

The YouGov/*Sun* poll on the morning of the Tory launch put them on 39 per cent, Labour on 33 per cent and the Liberal Democrats on 20 per cent.

The Lib Dems launched their manifesto on 14 April. Clegg promised a fairer Britain in four steps – fairer taxes, including the promise to raise the income tax threshold to £10,000 paid for by closing loopholes exploited by the wealthy. Economic reform would include the breaking up of giant banks, separating their investment and High Street operations, investment in infrastructure and "honesty" about the "tough choices" to cut the deficit. The Lib Dems also promised reform of the electoral system, an elected House of Lords and a Freedom Bill to restore civil liberties.

After the manifesto launches, the press turned their attention to their new toy, the first-ever election debate between the three main party leaders. ITV News hosted the first debate on 15 April – no-one expected the result, or that it would prove so popular – it attracted an audience of 9.5 million. Nick Clegg surged ahead in public support after an electrifying performance in the 90-minute, advert-free TV debate. He said neither of his opponents was being "straight" with voters about the scale of cuts needed and presented himself as the sensible, no-spin alternative to Labour and the Conservatives.

The next day the country had succumbed to Clegg-mania. In a poll carried out by ComRes for ITV News of 4,032 voters, Clegg was rated the victor, with 43 per cent, against 26 per cent for Cameron and 20 per cent for Brown. The Conservatives quickly changed tactics, cancelling a party political broadcast that would have attacked Labour. Instead Cameron made an appeal to voters not to be seduced by the Lib Dems and claimed a vote for them would leave the country "stuck with" Gordon Brown as prime minister.

In the lead-up to the next debate, the Tories tried to paint the Lib Dems as soft on immigration, as they leaped into second place ahead of Labour. Meanwhile Gordon Brown appealed for a "progressive alliance" of natural Labour and Liberal Democrat supporters.

By Saturday 17 April, a YouGov daily survey for the *Sun* suggested the contest had become a three-horse race, with the Conservatives in the lead on 33 per cent, the Liberal Democrats on 30 per cent and Labour trailing on 28 per cent.

The second debate, hosted by Sky News and watched by more than four million people, was a key moment for Cameron – could he beat Clegg and reassert himself as the prime minister in waiting? In the event all three leaders turned in solid performances, and no-one was declared the winner. They sparred over Europe, nuclear weapons, immigration, political reform and prospects for a hung Parliament. Brown said Clegg was "a risk to our security" because of his opposition to renewing Trident. Cameron attacked the Lib Dem immigration policy and their plans for an amnesty for some illegal immigrants. Clegg remained upbeat and told voters they do not have to choose "the old choices of the past".

The weekend polls showed the Lib Dems holding on at 29 per cent, down one, with the Tories up two on 35 per cent and Labour on 27 per cent, down three. That Saturday the prime minister appeared at Labour event alongside an Elvis impersonator. Some said the campaign could not get any worse for Brown.

Then he met Mrs Duffy, a disheartened Labour supporter who managed to chat to the PM during his visit to her hometown of Rochdale.

What happened next was one of the political gaffes of the century – Brown was caught on an open radio mic declaring Mrs Duffy to be a "bigoted woman" because she had expressed concern about immigration. The prime minister appeared at a radio studio very soon after his comments had been broadcast to the world – he was ashen-faced, crest-fallen and embarrassed. He went to Mrs Duffy's home to apologise in person for his remarks, but the damage had been done. For Gordon Brown, the campaign ended with 'bigot-gate'.

The third and final debate was hosted by the BBC the next day – more than eight million people watched. Like the second debate, all three leaders gave decent, if uninspiring performances.

Cameron's through-the-night campaigning leading up to polling day garnered some good coverage, as the polls showed the Lib Dem surge was fading. The question was by how much – most pundits still expected the third party to win between 75 and 100 seats.

The day of the election was marred by voters in some constituencies unable to cast their ballot due to over-crowding at polling stations. At 10pm, the exit polls were published – Conservatives 307 seats, Labour 255, Lib Dems 59, others 29. The prediction was immediately trashed by commentators on all sides – after the Clegg effect, how could the pollsters predict the Lib Dems would lose seats?

The poll was the first of many surprises that night – not least that Labour, in the final analysis, did better than they feared. Not one cabinet minister lost their seat and Labour fought back in seats like Birmingham Edgbaston, Westminster North and Hammersmith to deny the Tories key victories. Some of Cameron's controversial A-list candidates failed to make the grade, while others sailed into parliament.

As the results poured in, the outcome seemed to become more and more unclear. The Lib Dems won some seats, lost others.

The first Muslim women were elected to parliament, while the first minister of Northern Ireland Peter Robinson lost his seat to the Alliance Party's Naomi Long. Elsewhere in Northern Ireland, the UUP/Conservative coalition failed to win any seats, while Sinn Féin's Michelle Gildernew held Fermanagh and South Tyrone by just four votes.

Labour had a good night in Scotland, winning back two seats lost in by-elections. However, the election outcome in Scotland was interestingly dull – the final result was exactly the same as in 2005.

In Wales the nationalist party Plaid Cymru failed to make any gains, while the Tories picked up four seats.

Across the UK some Labour MPs held on with small majorities. One of the unlucky ones was solicitor general Vera Baird, who lost her Redcar seat to the Lib Dems. Former ministers Jacqui Smith, Charles Clarke, Shahid Malik, Ann Keen and Phil Hope all lost their seats.

In Brighton Pavilion a little bit of history was made when Caroline Lucas became the first ever Green MP.

Many London results were late, but brought more good news for Labour. The BNP was crushed in Barking; George Galloway and the Respect party were dismissed by Labour in Bethnal Green and Bow and Poplar and Limehouse; Glenda Jackson held on in Hampstead and Kilburn; Andy Slaughter defeated A-lister Shaun Bailey in Hammersmith. The key Lib/Con battleground of Richmond Park fell to Tory Zac Goldsmith.

Just before 10am on Friday, the BBC confirmed a "hung parliament" – the Tories would not be able to form a majority government.

On Friday afternoon the Speaker, John Bercow, was comfortably re-elected in Buckingham – his UKIP opponent Nigel Farage was injured in a plane crash on polling day, but suffered only minor injuries.

649 constituencies had declared – the vote in Thirsk and Malton had been postponed due to the death of a candidate.

The final result was: Tories 305; Labour 258; Lib Dem 57; DUP 8; SNP 6; Sinn Féin 5; SDLP 3; Plaid 3; Alliance 1; Green 1; Independent 1; Speaker 1.

Despite a disappointing night at the polls for his party, with the Liberal Democrats actually losing seats rather than gaining them as had been expected, Nick Clegg found himself in the position of kingmaker. Polling day was followed by five days of uncertainty, as both the Conservatives and Labour tried to woo the Lib Dems.

During the campaign Clegg had said he would negotiate first with the party that had the most seats and the most votes, and on the Friday morning Clegg signalled he intended to open negotiations with David Cameron over the shape of a new government. First to respond to Clegg's statement of intent was Gordon Brown, standing outside Number 10 the incumbent prime minister accepted that Clegg would want to speak to Cameron first. But he said he was prepared to hold talks if the Tory-Lib Dem negotiations broke down. Brown's statement was followed by extraordinary press conference that afternoon, where David Cameron offered a "big, open and comprehensive offer" to the Lib Dems that would place him in Downing Street.

On Saturday morning, when the three men stood side-by-side at the Cenotaph to mark 65 years since the end of the Second World War, it was not yet clear which way Clegg would swing.

Over the next four days the formal talks between the three man Lib Dem negotiating team of David Laws, Danny Alexander, Chris Huhne and senior Conservatives George Osborne, William Hague and Oliver Letwin gripped the media as the press pack scurried around Westminster, speculating as to the extent of the deal being hammered out behind closed doors. Rumour and counter-rumour swept Westminster over whether it would be a full coalition or a so called 'supply and confidence' arrangement, where the Lib Dems would prop up a minority Conservative administration.

But while they were conducting formal talks with the Tories, it emerged that informal negotiations were also being carried out with Labour, with Brown slipping out of Number 10 on Saturday evening to meet with Clegg in the Foreign Office. And on Tuesday afternoon, when many felt the Lib Dems and Conservatives pact was a done deal, David Laws emerged from a two hour meeting of the Lib Dem parliamentary party in the Commons to reveal his colleagues were seeking "clarification" from the Conservatives on several policy issues. Less than an hour later, hopes of a "rainbow coalition" of the left appeared to be resurrected, when Brown appeared outside Number 10 to announce Clegg had requested forward formal talks with the Labour party. Apparently conscious of Clegg's reluctance to help him stay in power, he said he would start the process of installing a new Labour leader in order to facilitate talks.

Concerned that Clegg may be wavering, the Tories held a crunch meeting of their MPs in the Commons and decided to make a "final offer" to the Liberal Democrats, a promise them a referendum on changing the voting system – the holy grail of Lib Dem policy demands.

But as quickly as the Left's hopes had been raised they appeared to slip away, as an increasing number of Labour MPs began to voice unease at the prospect of remaining in office, having gained fewer seats than the Tories.

And in the early evening on Tuesday 11 May, Brown emerged from Downing Street to announce his resignation as prime minister. With his wife Sarah at his side Brown said he loved the job "not for its prestige, titles and it's ceremony " but it's potential to create a "fairer, more tolerant, more green, more democratic, more prosperous, more just, truly a Greater Britain."

After five years as leader of the opposition, and five days of uncertainty which nearly saw victory slip through his fingers, David Cameron entered Number 10 as prime minister that evening, with Nick Clegg as his deputy.

Britain had its first coalition government since 1945.

Tony Grew
Editor, ePolitix.com

GOVERNMENT AND OPPOSITION

THE GOVERNMENT

THE CABINET

(Con/Lib Dem coalition)

Prime Minister, First Lord of the Treasury and Minister for the Civil Service	**David Cameron** MP (Con) 130
Deputy Prime Minister, Lord President of the Council (with special responsibility for political and constitutional reform)	**Nick Clegg** MP (Lib Dem) 150
First Secretary of State, Secretary of State for Foreign and Commonwealth Affairs	**William Hague** MP (Con) 292
Chancellor of the Exchequer	**George Osborne** MP (Con) 530
Lord Chancellor and Secretary of State for Justice	**Kenneth Clarke** QC MP (Con) 147
Secretary of State for the Home Department; Minister for Women and Equalities	**Theresa May** MP (Con) 468
Secretary of State for Defence	Dr **Liam Fox** MP (Con) 246
Secretary of State for Business, Innovation and Skills	Dr **Vincent Cable** MP (Lib Dem) 126
Secretary of State for Work and Pensions	**Iain Duncan Smith** MP (Con) 212
Secretary of State for Energy and Climate Change	**Chris Huhne** MP (Lib Dem) 360
Secretary of State for Health	**Andrew Lansley** CBE MP (Con) 405
Secretary of State for Education	**Michael Gove** MP (Con) 274
Secretary of State for Communities and Local Government	**Eric Pickles** MP (Con) 549
Secretary of State for Transport	**Philip Hammond** MP (Con) 300
Secretary of State for Environment, Food and Rural Affairs	**Caroline Spelman** MP (Con) 628
Secretary of State for International Development	**Andrew Mitchell** MP (Con) 486
Secretary of State for Northern Ireland	**Owen Paterson** MP (Con) 539
Secretary of State for Scotland	**Michael Moore** MP (Lib Dem) 490
Secretary of State for Wales	**Cheryl Gillan** MP (Con) 264
Secretary of State for Culture, Olympics, Media and Sport	**Jeremy Hunt** MP (Con) 362
Chief Secretary to the Treasury	**Danny Alexander** MP (Lib Dem) 32
Leader of the House of Lords; Chancellor of the Duchy of Lancaster	**Lord Strathclyde** (Con)*
Minister without portfolio	**Baroness Warsi** (Con)*

ALSO ATTENDING CABINET

Minister for the Cabinet Office; Paymaster General	**Francis Maude** MP (Con) 467
Minister of State, Cabinet Office	**Oliver Letwin** MP (Con) 418
Minister of State for Universities and Science, Department for Business, Innovation and Skills	**David Willetts** MP (Con) 700

*For biography see *Dod's Parliamentary Companion*

Leader of the House of Commons, Lord Privy Seal	Sir **George Young** MP (Con) 725
Parliamentary Secretary to the Treasury; Chief Whip	**Patrick McLoughlin** MP (Con) 456
Chief Parliamentary and Political Adviser to the Deputy Prime Minister	**Norman Lamb** MP (Lib Dem) 402

ATTEND WHEN MINISTERIAL RESPONSIBILITIES ON AGENDA

Attorney General	**Dominic Grieve** MP (Con) 285

Rt Hon David Cameron
Conservative
Prime Minster, First Lord of the Treasury and Minister for the Civil Service

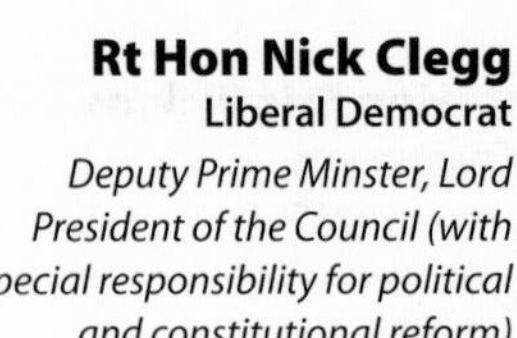

Rt Hon Nick Clegg
Liberal Democrat
Deputy Prime Minster, Lord President of the Council (with special responsibility for political and constitutional reform)

Rt Hon William Hague
Conservative
First Secretary of State, Secretary of State for Foreign and Commonwealth Affairs

Rt Hon George Osborne
Conservative
Chancellor of the Exchequer

Rt Hon Ken Clarke
Conservative
Lord Chancellor and Secretary of State for Justice

Rt Hon Theresa May
Conservative
Secretary of State for the Home Department; Minister for Women and Equalities

Rt Hon Liam Fox
Conservative
Secretary of State for Defence

Rt Hon Vince Cable
Liberal Democrat
Secretary of State for Business, Innovation and Skills; President of the Board of Trade

Rt Hon Iain Duncan Smith
Conservative
Secretary of State for Work and Pensions

Rt Hon Chris Huhne
Liberal Democrat
Secretary of State for Energy and Climate Change

Rt Hon Andrew Lansley
Conservative
Secretary of State for Health

Rt Hon Michael Gove
Conservative
Secretary of State for Education

Rt Hon Eric Pickles
Conservative
Secretary of State for Communities and Local Government

Rt Hon Philip Hammond
Conservative
Secretary of State for Transport

Rt Hon Caroline Spelman
Conservative
Secretary of State for Environment, Food and Rural Affairs

Rt Hon Andrew Mitchell
Conservative
Secretary of State for International Development

Rt Hon Owen Paterson
Conservative
Secretary of State for Northern Ireland

Michael Moore
Liberal Democrat
Secretary of State for Scotland

Rt Hon Cheryl Gillan
Conservative
Secretary of State for Wales

Rt Hon Jeremy Hunt
Conservative
Secretary of State for Culture, Olympics, Media and Sport

Rt Hon Danny Alexander
Liberal Democrat
Chief Secretary to the Treasury

Rt Hon Lord Strathclyde
Conservative
Leader of the House of Lords; Chancellor of the Duchy of Lancaster

Baroness Warsi
Conservative
Minister without Portfolio

ALL MINISTERS

DEPARTMENTAL MINISTERS

DEPARTMENT FOR BUSINESS, INNOVATION AND SKILLS

Secretary of State for Business, Innovation and Skills; President of the Board of Trade	Rt Hon Dr **Vincent Cable** MP (Lib Dem)
Ministers of State	Rt Hon **David Willetts** MP (Con) **Mark Prisk** MP (Con) **John Hayes** MP (Con)
Parliamentary Under-Secretaries of State	**Edward Davey** MP (Lib Dem) **Baroness Wilcox** (Con) Hon **Ed Vaizey** MP (Con)

CABINET OFFICE

Deputy Prime Minister, Lord President of the Council	Rt Hon **Nick Clegg** MP (Lib Dem)
Minister	Rt Hon **Francis Maude** MP (Con)
Minister of State	Rt Hon **Oliver Letwin** MP (Con)
Parliamentary Secretaries	**Mark Harper** MP (Con) **Nick Hurd** MP (Con)
Chief Parliamentary and Political Adviser	**Norman Lamb** MP (Lib Dem)

DEPARTMENT FOR COMMUNITIES AND LOCAL GOVERNMENT

Secretary of State for Communities and Local Government	Rt Hon **Eric Pickles** MP (Con)
Ministers of State	Rt Hon **Greg Clark** MP (Con) Rt Hon **Grant Shapps** MP (Con)
Parliamentary Under-Secretaries of State	**Andrew Stunell** OBE MP (Lib Dem) **Robert Neill** MP (Con) **Baroness Hanham** CBE (Con)

DEPARTMENT FOR CULTURE, MEDIA AND SPORT

Secretary of State for Culture, Olympics, Media and Sport	Rt Hon **Jeremy Hunt** MP (Con)
Parliamentary Under-Secretaries of State	**John Penrose** MP (Con) **Hugh Robertson** MP (Con) Hon **Ed Vaizey** MP (Con)

MINISTRY OF DEFENCE

Secretary of State for Defence	Rt Hon Dr **Liam Fox** MP (Con)
Minister of State	**Nick Harvey** MP (Lib Dem)
Parliamentary Under-Secretaries of State	**Gerald Howarth** MP (Con) **Andrew Robathan** MP (Con) **Lord Astor of Hever** DL (Con) **Peter Luff** MP (Con)

DEPARTMENT FOR EDUCATION

Secretary of State for Education	Rt Hon **Michael Gove** MP (Con)
Ministers of State	**Sarah Teather** MP (Lib Dem) **Nick Gibb** MP (Con)
Parliamentary Under-Secretaries of State	**Tim Loughton** MP (Con) **Jonathan Hill (peerage pending)**

DEPARTMENT OF ENERGY AND CLIMATE CHANGE

Secretary of State for Energy and Climate Change	Rt Hon **Chris Huhne** MP (Lib Dem)
Ministers of State	**Charles Hendry** MP (Con) **Gregory Barker** MP (Con)
Parliamentary Under-Secretary of State	**Lord Marland** (Con)

DEPARTMENT FOR ENVIRONMENT, FOOD AND RURAL AFFAIRS

Secretary of State for Environment, Food and Rural Affairs — Rt Hon **Caroline Spelman** MP (Con)
Minister of State — **Jim Paice** MP (Con)
Parliamentary Under-Secretaries of State — **Richard Benyon** MP (Con); **Lord Henley** (Con)

FOREIGN AND COMMONWEALTH OFFICE

Ministers of State — **David Lidington** MP (Con); **Jeremy Browne** MP (Lib Dem); Rt Hon **Lord Howell of Guildford** (Con)
Parliamentary Under-Secretaries of State — **Henry Bellingham** MP (Con); **Alistair Burt** MP (Con)

GOVERNMENT EQUALITIES OFFICE

Minister — Rt Hon **Theresa May** MP (Con)
Parliamentary Under-Secretary of State — **Lynne Featherstone** MP (Lib Dem)

DEPARTMENT OF HEALTH

Secretary of State for Health — Rt Hon **Andrew Lansley** CBE MP (Con)
Ministers of State — **Paul Burstow** MP (Lib Dem); **Simon Burns** MP (Con)
Parliamentary Under-Secretaries of State — **Anne Milton** MP (Con); **Earl Howe** (Con)

HOME OFFICE

Secretary of State for the Home Department (Home Secretary) — Rt Hon **Theresa May** MP (Con)
Ministers of State — Rt Hon **Baroness Neville-Jones** (Con); **Damian Green** MP (Con); Rt Hon **Nick Herbert** MP (Con)
Parliamentary Under-Secretaries of State — **James Brokenshire** MP (Con); **Lynne Featherstone** MP (Lib Dem)

DEPARTMENT FOR INTERNATIONAL DEVELOPMENT

Secretary of State for International Development — Rt Hon **Andrew Mitchell** MP (Con)
Minister of State — Rt Hon **Alan Duncan** MP (Con)
Parliamentary Under-Secretary of State — **Stephen O'Brien** MP (Con)

MINISTRY OF JUSTICE

Lord Chancellor and Secretary of State for Justice — Rt Hon **Kenneth Clarke** QC MP (Con)
Ministers of State — Rt Hon **Lord McNally** (Lib Dem); Rt Hon **Nick Herbert** MP (Con)
Parliamentary Under-Secretaries of State — **Crispin Blunt** MP (Con); **Jonathan Djanogly** MP (Con)

LAW OFFICERS

Attorney General — Rt Hon **Dominic Grieve** MP (Con)
Solicitor General — **Edward Garnier** QC MP (Con)
Advocate General for Scotland — Rt Hon **Lord Wallace of Tankerness** (Lib Dem)

LEADER OF THE HOUSE OF COMMONS

Leader of the House of Commons — Rt Hon Sir **George Young** MP (Con)
Parliamentary Secretary — **David Heath** CBE MP (Lib Dem)

LEADER OF THE HOUSE OF LORDS

Deputy Leader — Rt Hon **Lord McNally** (Lib Dem)

NORTHERN IRELAND OFFICE

Secretary of State for Northern Ireland — Rt Hon **Owen Paterson** MP (Con)
Minister of State — **Hugo Swire** MP (Con)

PRIVY COUNCIL OFFICE

Lord President of the Council	Rt Hon **Nick Clegg** MP (Lib Dem)

SCOTLAND OFFICE

Secretary of State for Scotland (and provides ministerial support to Deputy Prime Minister)	**Michael Moore** MP (Lib Dem)
Parliamentary Under-Secretary of State	Rt Hon **David Mundell** MP (Con)

DEPARTMENT FOR TRANSPORT

Secretary of State for Transport	Rt Hon **Philip Hammond** MP (Con)
Minister of State	Rt Hon **Theresa Villiers** MP (Con)
Parliamentary Under-Secretaries of State	**Norman Baker** MP (Lib Dem) **Mike Penning** MP (Con)

HM TREASURY

Chancellor of the Exchequer	Rt Hon **George Osborne** MP (Con)
Chief Secretary to the Treasury	Rt Hon **Danny Alexander** MP (Lib Dem)
Financial Secretary	**Mark Hoban** MP (Con)
Exchequer Secretary	**David Gauke** MP (Con)
Economic Secretary	**Justine Greening** MP (Con)
Commercial Secretary	Sir **James Sassoon (peerage pending)**

WALES OFFICE

Secretary of State for Wales	Rt Hon **Cheryl Gillan** MP (Con)
Parliamentary Under-Secretary of State	**David Jones** MP (Con)

DEPARTMENT FOR WORK AND PENSIONS

Secretary of State for Work and Pensions	Rt Hon **Iain Duncan Smith** MP (Con)
Ministers of State	Rt Hon **Chris Grayling** MP (Con) Prof **Steve Webb** MP (Lib Dem)
Parliamentary Under-Secretaries of State	**Maria Miller** MP (Con) **Lord Freud** (Con)

GOVERNMENT WHIPS

COMMONS

CHIEF WHIP

Parliamentary Secretary to the Treasury — Rt Hon **Patrick McLoughlin** (Con)

DEPUTY CHIEF WHIPS

Treasurer of HM Household — Rt Hon **John Randall** (Con)

Comptroller of HM Household — **Alistair Carmichael** (Lib Dem)

WHIPS

VICE-CHAMBERLAIN OF HM HOUSEHOLD

Rt Hon **Mark Francois** (Con)

LORDS COMMISSIONER OF HM TREASURY

James Duddridge (Con)
Michael Fabricant (Con)
Brooks Newmark (Con)
Angela Watkinson (Con)
Jeremy Wright (Con)

ASSISTANT WHIPS

Stephen Crabb (Con)
Philip Dunne (Con)
Robert Goodwill (Con)
Mark Hunter (Lib Dem)
Norman Lamb (Lib Dem)
Chloe Smith (Con)
Shailesh Vara (Con)
Bill Wiggin (Con)

LORDS

CHIEF WHIP

CAPTAIN OF THE HONOURABLE CORPS OF THE GENTLEMEN-AT-ARMS

Rt Hon **Baroness Anelay of St Johns** DBE (Con)

DEPUTY CHIEF WHIP

CAPTAIN OF THE QUEEN'S BODYGUARD OF THE YEOMAN OF THE GUARD

Rt Hon **Lord Shutt of Greetland** OBE (Lib Dem)

WHIPS, LORDS IN WAITING

Lord Astor of Hever DL (Con)
Earl Attlee (Con)
Lord De Mauley TD (Con)
Lord Taylor of Holbeach CBE (Con)
Lord Wallace of Saltaire (Lib Dem)

WHIPS, BARONESSES IN WAITING

Baroness Northover (Lib Dem)
Baroness Rawlings (Con)
Baroness Verma (Con)

ALPHABETICAL LIST OF MINISTERS AND WHIPS

ALEXANDER, Rt Hon **Danny** (Lib Dem)	Chief Secretary to the Treasury
ANELAY OF ST JOHNS, Rt Hon **Baroness** (Con)	Chief Whip
ASTOR OF HEVER, Lord (Con)	Whip
EARL ATTLEE, (Con)	Whip
BAKER, Norman (Lib Dem)	Parliamentary Under-Secretary of State, Department for Transport
BARKER, Gregory (Con)	Minister of State, Department for Energy and Climate Change
BASSAM OF BRIGHTON, Rt Hon **Lord** (Lab)	Opposition Chief Whip
BELLINGHAM, Henry (Con)	Parliamentary Under-Secretary of State, Foreign and Commonwealth Office
BENYON, Richard (Con)	Parliamentary Under-Secretary of State (Natural Environment and Fisheries), Department for Environment, Food and Rural Affairs
BLUNT, Crispin (Con)	Parliamentary Under-Secretary of State, Ministry of Justice
BROKENSHIRE, James (Con)	Parliamentary Under-Secretary of State (Minister for Crime Prevention), Home Office
BROWNE, Jeremy (Lib Dem)	Minister of State, Foreign and Commonwealth Office
BURNS, Simon (Con)	Minister of State for Health, Department of Health
BURSTOW, Paul (Lib Dem)	Minister of State for Care Services, Department of Health
BURT, Alistair (Con)	Deputy chairman Conservative Party; Parliamentary Under-Secretary of State, Foreign and Commonwealth Office
CABLE, Rt Hon Dr **Vincent** (Lib Dem)	Secretary of State for Business, Innovation and Skills; President of the Board of Trade
CAMERON, Rt Hon **David** (Con)	Prime Minister, First Lord of the Treasury and Minister for the Civil Service
CARMICHAEL, Alistair (Lib Dem)	Deputy Chief Whip (Comptroller of HM Household)
CLARK, Rt Hon **Greg** (Con)	Minister of State for Decentralisation, Department for Communities and Local Government
CLARKE, Rt Hon **Kenneth** (Con)	Lord Chancellor and Secretary of State for Justice
CLEGG, Rt Hon **Nick** (Lib Dem)	Leader Liberal Democrats; Deputy Prime Minister, Lord President of the Council
CRABB, Stephen (Con)	Assistant Whip
DAVEY, Edward (Lib Dem)	Parliamentary Under-Secretary of State (Minister for Employment Relations, Consumer and Postal Affairs), Department for Business, Innovation and Skills
DE MAULEY, Lord (Con)	Whip
DJANOGLY, Jonathan (Con)	Parliamentary Under-Secretary of State, Ministry of Justice
DUDDRIDGE, James (Con)	Whip
DUNCAN, Rt Hon **Alan** (Con)	Minister of State, Department for International Development
DUNCAN SMITH, Rt Hon **Iain** (Con)	Secretary of State for Work and Pensions

DUNNE, Philip (Con)	Assistant Whip
FABRICANT, Michael (Con)	Whip
FEATHERSTONE, Lynne (Lib Dem)	Parliamentary Under-Secretary of State (Minister for Equalities), Home Office and Equalities Office
FOX, Rt Hon Dr **Liam** (Con)	Secretary of State for Defence
FRANCOIS, Rt Hon **Mark** (Con)	Whip (Vice-Chamberlain of HM Household)
FREUD, Lord (Con)	Parliamentary Under-Secretary of State (Minister for Welfare Reform) and Spokesperson, Department for Work and Pensions
GARNIER, Edward (Con)	Solicitor General
GAUKE, David (Con)	Exchequer Secretary, HM Treasury
GIBB, Nick (Con)	Minister of State for Schools, Department for Education
GILLAN, Rt Hon **Cheryl** (Con)	Secretary of State for Wales
GOODWILL, Robert (Con)	Assistant Whip
GOVE, Rt Hon **Michael** (Con)	Secretary of State for Education
GRAYLING, Rt Hon **Chris** (Con)	Minister of State, Department for Work and Pensions
GREEN, Damian (Con)	Minister of State for Immigration, Home Office
GREENING, Justine (Con)	Economic Secretary, HM Treasury
GRIEVE, Rt Hon **Dominic** (Con)	Attorney General
HAMMOND, Rt Hon **Philip** (Con)	Secretary of State for Transport
HANHAM, Baroness (Con)	Parliamentary Under-Secretary of State and Spokesperson, Department for Communities and Local Government
HARPER, Mark (Con)	Parliamentary Secretary, Cabinet Office
HARVEY, Nick (Lib Dem)	Minister of State for the Armed Forces
HAYES, John (Con)	Minister of State for Further Education, Skills and Lifelong Learning, Department for Business, Innovation and Skills
HEATH, David (Lib Dem)	Parliamentary Secretary (Deputy Leader of the House of Commons)
HENDRY, Charles (Con)	Minister of State, Department for Energy and Climate Change
HENLEY, Lord (Con)	Parliamentary Under-Secretary of State and Spokesperson, Department for Environment, Food and Rural Affairs
HERBERT, Rt Hon **Nick** (Con)	Minister of State for Police, Home Office and Ministry of Justice
JONATHAN HILL (PEERAGE PENDING),	Parliamentary Under-Secretary of State and Spokesperson, Department for Education
HOBAN, Mark (Con)	Financial Secretary, HM Treasury
HOWARTH, Gerald (Con)	Parliamentary Under-Secretary of State, Ministry of Defence
EARL HOWE, (Con)	Parliamentary Under-Secretary of State and Spokesperson, Department of Health
HOWELL OF GUILDFORD, Rt Hon **Lord** (Con)	Minister of State and Spokesperson, Foreign and Commonwealth Office
HUHNE, Rt Hon **Chris** (Lib Dem)	Secretary of State for Energy and Climate Change

HUNT, Rt Hon **Jeremy** (Con)	Secretary of State for Culture, Olympics, Media and Sport
HUNTER, Mark (Lib Dem)	Assistant Whip
HURD, Nick (Con)	Parliamentary Secretary (Minister for Civil Society), Cabinet Office
JONES, David (Con)	Parliamentary Under-Secretary of State, Wales Office
KNIGHT, Rt Hon **Jim** (Lab)	
LAMB, Norman (Lib Dem)	Chief Parliamentary and Political Adviser to the Deputy Prime Minister; Assistant Whip
LANSLEY, Rt Hon **Andrew** (Con)	Secretary of State for Health
LETWIN, Rt Hon **Oliver** (Con)	Minister of State, Cabinet Office
LIDINGTON, David (Con)	Minister of State, Foreign and Commonwealth Office
LOUGHTON, Tim (Con)	Parliamentary Under-Secretary of State, Department for Education
LUFF, Peter (Con)	Parliamentary Under-Secretary of State, Ministry of Defence
McCARTHY-FRY, Sarah (Lab/Co-op)	Exchequer Secretary, HM Treasury
McLOUGHLIN, Rt Hon **Patrick** (Con)	Parliamentary Secretary to the Treasury; Chief Whip
McNALLY, Rt Hon **Lord** (Lib Dem)	Minister of State and Spokesperson, Ministry of Justice
MARLAND, Lord (Con)	Parliamentary Under-Secretary of State and Spokesperson, Department for Energy and Climate Change
MAUDE, Rt Hon **Francis** (Con)	Minister for the Cabinet Office; Paymaster General
MAY, Rt Hon **Theresa** (Con)	Home Secretary; Minister for Women and Equalities
MILLER, Maria (Con)	Parliamentary Under-Secretary of State, Department for Work and Pensions
MILTON, Anne (Con)	Parliamentary Under-Secretary of State, Department of Health
MITCHELL, Rt Hon **Andrew** (Con)	Secretary of State for International Development
MOLE, Chris (Lab)	
MOORE, Michael (Lib Dem)	Secretary of State for Scotland
MUNDELL, Rt Hon **David** (Con)	Parliamentary Under-Secretary of State, Scotland Office
NEILL, Robert (Con)	Parliamentary Under-Secretary of State, Department for Communities and Local Government
NEVILLE-JONES, Rt Hon **Baroness** (Con)	Minister of State for Security and Spokesperson, Home Office
NEWMARK, Brooks (Con)	Whip
NORTHOVER, Baroness (Lib Dem)	Whip
O'BRIEN, Stephen (Con)	Parliamentary Under-Secretary of State, Department for International Development
OSBORNE, Rt Hon **George** (Con)	Chancellor of the Exchequer
PAICE, Jim (Con)	Minister of State for Agriculture and Food, Department for Environment, Food and Rural Affairs
PATERSON, Rt Hon **Owen** (Con)	Secretary of State for Northern Ireland
PENNING, Mike (Con)	Parliamentary Under-Secretary of State, Department for Transport

PENROSE, John (Con)	Parliamentary Under-Secretary of State (Minister for Tourism and Heritage), Department for Culture, Media and Sport
PICKLES, Rt Hon **Eric** (Con)	Secretary of State for Communities and Local Government
PRISK, Mark (Con)	Minister of State for Business and Enterprise, Department for Business, Innovation and Skills
RANDALL, Rt Hon **John** (Con)	Deputy Chief Whip (Treasurer of HM Household)
RAWLINGS, Baroness (Con)	Whip
ROBATHAN, Andrew (Con)	Parliamentary Under-Secretary of State, Ministry of Defence
ROBERTSON, Hugh (Con)	Parliamentary Under-Secretary of State (Minister for Sport and the Olympics), Department for Culture, Media and Sport
JAMES SASSOON (PEERAGE PENDING), Sir	Commercial Secretary and Spokesperson, HM Treasury
SHAPPS, Rt Hon **Grant** (Con)	Minister of State for Housing and Local Government, Department for Communities and Local Government
SHUTT OF GREETLAND, Rt Hon **Lord** (Lib Dem)	Deputy Chief Whip (Captain of the Queen's Bodyguard of the Yeoman of the Guard)
SMITH, Chloe (Con)	Assistant Whip
SPELMAN, Rt Hon **Caroline** (Con)	Secretary of State for Environment, Food and Rural Affairs
STUNELL, Andrew (Lib Dem)	Parliamentary Under-Secretary of State, Department for Communities and Local Government
SWIRE, Hugo (Con)	Minister of State, Northern Ireland Office
TAYLOR OF HOLBEACH, Lord (Con)	Whip
TEATHER, Sarah (Lib Dem)	Minister of State for Children and Families, Department for Education
VAIZEY, Hon **Ed** (Con)	Parliamentary Under-Secretary of State (Minister for Culture, Communications and Creative Industries), Departments for Business, Innovation and Skills and Culture, Media and Sport
VARA, Shailesh (Con)	Assistant Whip
VERMA, Baroness (Con)	Whip
VILLIERS, Rt Hon **Theresa** (Con)	Minister of State, Department for Transport
WALLACE OF SALTAIRE, Lord (Lib Dem)	Whip
WALLACE OF TANKERNESS, Rt Hon **Lord** (Lib Dem)	Advocate General for Scotland
WARD, Claire (Lab)	
WATKINSON, Angela (Con)	Whip
WEBB, Prof **Steve** (Lib Dem)	Minister of State, Department for Work and Pensions
WIGGIN, Bill (Con)	Assistant Whip
WILCOX, Baroness (Con)	Parliamentary Under-Secretary of State and Spokesperson, Department for Business, Innovation and Skills

WILLETTS, Rt Hon **David** (Con)	Minister of State for Universities and Science, Department for Business, Innovation and Skills
WRIGHT, Jeremy (Con)	Whip
YOUNG, Rt Hon Sir **George** (Con)	Leader of the House of Commons, Lord Privy Seal

THE OPPOSITION

LABOUR (OFFICIAL OPPOSITION)

SHADOW CABINET

Acting Leader of the Opposition	Rt Hon **Harriet Harman** QC MP
Shadow Secretary of State for Foreign and Commonwealth Affairs (Foreign Secretary)	Rt Hon **David Miliband** MP
Shadow Chancellor of the Exchequer	Rt Hon **Alistair Darling** MP
Shadow Lord Chancellor and Secretary of State for Justice	Rt Hon **Jack Straw** MP
Shadow Secretary of State for the Home Office (Home Secretary)	Rt Hon **Alan Johnson** MP
Shadow Secretary of State for Defence	Rt Hon **Bob Ainsworth** MP
Shadow Secretary of State for Business, Innovation and Skills	Rt Hon **Pat McFadden** MP
Shadow Secretary of State for Work and Pensions; Shadow Minister for Women and Equalities	Rt Hon **Yvette Cooper** MP
Shadow Secretary of State for Energy and Climate Change	Rt Hon **Ed Miliband** MP
Shadow Secretary of State for Health	Rt Hon **Andy Burnham** MP
Shadow Secretary of State for Education	Rt Hon **Ed Balls** MP
Shadow Secretary of State for Communities and Local Government	Rt Hon **John Denham** MP
Shadow Secretary of State for Transport	Rt Hon **Sadiq Khan** MP
Shadow Secretary of State for Environment, Food and Rural Affairs	Rt Hon **Hilary Benn** MP
Shadow Secretary of State for International Development	Rt Hon **Douglas Alexander** MP
Shadow Minister for the Cabinet Office	Rt Hon **Tessa Jowell** MP
Shadow Secretary of State for Northern Ireland	Rt Hon **Shaun Woodward** MP
Shadow Secretary of State for Scotland	Rt Hon **Jim Murphy** MP
Shadow Secretary of State for Wales	Rt Hon **Peter Hain** MP
Shadow Secretary of State for Culture, Olympics, Media and Sport	Rt Hon **Ben Bradshaw** MP
Shadow Chief Secretary to the Treasury	Rt Hon **Liam Byrne** MP
Shadow Leader of the House of Lords	Rt Hon **Baroness Royall of Blaisdon**
Shadow Parliamentary Secretary to the Treasury and Opposition Whip	Rt Hon **Nick Brown** MP
Shadow Minister for Housing	Rt Hon **John Healey** MP
Shadow Leader of the House of Commons and Lord Privy Seal	Rt Hon **Rosie Winterton** MP
Opposition Chief Whip in the House of Lords	Rt Hon **Lord Bassam of Brighton**
Opposition Attorney General and Spokesperson for the Law Officers	Rt Hon **Baroness Scotland of Asthal** QC
Shadow Minister for Children	Rt Hon **Dawn Primarolo** MP
Chair, Parliamentary Labour Party	**Tony Lloyd** MP

SHADOW MINISTERS

BUSINESS, INNOVATION AND SKILLS

Shadow Secretary of State	Rt Hon **Pat McFadden** MP
Shadow Ministers	Rt Hon **David Lammy** MP **Kevin Brennan** MP **Ian Lucas** MP Rt Hon **Stephen Timms** MP **Lord Young of Norwood Green**

CABINET OFFICE

Acting Shadow Deputy Prime Minister	Rt Hon **Jack Straw** MP
Shadow Minister for the Cabinet Office	Rt Hon **Tessa Jowell** MP
Shadow Ministers	Rt Hon **Paul Goggins** MP Rt Hon **Lord Hunt of Kings Heath** OBE Rt Hon **Baroness Royall of Blaisdon**

COMMUNITIES AND LOCAL GOVERNMENT

Shadow Secretary of State	Rt Hon **John Denham** MP
Shadow Ministers	Rt Hon **John Healey** MP **Ian Austin** MP **Gordon Marsden** MP **Lord McKenzie of Luton** **Baroness Crawley** **Lord Patel of Bradford**

CULTURE, MEDIA AND SPORT

Shadow Secretary of State	Rt Hon **Ben Bradshaw** MP
Shadow Olympics Minister	Rt Hon **Tessa Jowell** MP
Shadow Ministers	Rt Hon **Margaret Hodge** MBE MP **Gerry Sutcliffe** MP **Lord Evans of Temple Guiting** CBE **Baroness Billingham** **Baroness Jones of Whitchurch**

DEFENCE

Shadow Secretary of State	Rt Hon **Bob Ainsworth** MP
Shadow Ministers	**Kevan Jones** MP **Lord Tunnicliffe**

EDUCATION

Shadow Secretary of State	Rt Hon **Ed Balls** MP
Shadow Ministers	**Vernon Coaker** MP **Iain Wright** MP **Baroness Morgan of Drefelin** Rt Hon **Baroness Royall of Blaisdon**

ENERGY AND CLIMATE CHANGE

Shadow Secretary of State	Rt Hon **Ed Miliband** MP
Shadow Ministers	Rt Hon **Joan Ruddock** MP **Emily Thornberry** MP Rt Hon **Lord Hunt of Kings Heath** OBE

ENVIRONMENT, FOOD AND RURAL AFFAIRS

Shadow Secretary of State	Rt Hon **Hilary Benn** MP
Shadow Ministers	**Jim Fitzpatrick** MP **Huw Irranca-Davies** MP Rt Hon **Baroness Quin**

FOREIGN AND COMMONWEALTH OFFICE

Shadow Foreign Secretary	Rt Hon **David Miliband** MP
Shadow Ministers	**Ivan Lewis** MP **Chris Bryant** MP **Baroness Kinnock of Holyhead** Rt Hon **Baroness Symons of Vernham Dean** **Baroness Crawley**

HEALTH

Shadow Secretary of State	Rt Hon **Andy Burnham** MP
Shadow Ministers	**Barbara Keeley** MP **Diana Johnson** MP **Mary Creagh** MP **Baroness Thornton** **Baroness Crawley** **Baroness Jones of Whitchurch**

HOME OFFICE

Shadow Home Secretary	Rt Hon **Alan Johnson** MP
Shadow Ministers	**Phil Woolas** MP **Meg Hillier** MP **Alan Campbell** MP **Lord Brett**

INTERNATIONAL DEVELOPMENT

Shadow Secretary of State	Rt Hon **Douglas Alexander** MP
Shadow Ministers	**Gareth Thomas** MP **Lord Brett**

JUSTICE

Shadow Secretary of State	Rt Hon **Jack Straw** MP
Shadow Ministers	**Maria Eagle** MP **Helen Jones** MP **Lord Bach**

LAW OFFICERS

Shadow Attorney General	Rt Hon **Baroness Scotland of Asthal** QC
Shadow Solicitor General	**Maria Eagle** MP
Shadow Minister	**Lord Davidson of Glen Clova** QC

LEADER OF THE HOUSE OF COMMONS

Shadow Leader and Minister for Women	Rt Hon **Rosie Winterton** MP
Shadow Deputy Leader	**Barbara Keeley** MP

NORTHERN IRELAND

Shadow Secretary of State	Rt Hon **Shaun Woodward** MP
Shadow Ministers	Rt Hon **Paul Goggins** MP Rt Hon **Baroness Royall of Blaisdon**

SCOTLAND

Shadow Secretary of State	Rt Hon **Jim Murphy** MP
Shadow Ministers	**Ann McKechin** MP **Lord Sewel** CBE

TRANSPORT

Shadow Secretary of State	Rt Hon **Sadiq Khan** MP
Shadow Ministers	**Willie Bain** MP Rt Hon **Lord Davies of Oldham**

TREASURY

Shadow Chancellor of the Exchequer	Rt Hon **Alistair Darling** MP
Shadow Chief Secretary to the Treasury	Rt Hon **Liam Byrne** MP
Shadow Ministers	**Angela Eagle** MP Rt Hon **David Hanson** MP **Gareth Thomas** MP Rt Hon **Stephen Timms** MP **Lord Eatwell** Rt Hon **Lord Davies of Oldham** **Lord Davidson of Glen Clova** QC

WALES

Shadow Secretary of State	Rt Hon **Peter Hain** MP
Shadow Ministers	**Wayne David** MP Rt Hon **Lord Davies of Oldham**

WORK AND PENSIONS

Shadow Secretary of State and Shadow Minister for Women and Equalities	Rt Hon **Yvette Cooper** MP
Shadow Ministers	**Helen Goodman** MP **Kerry McCarthy** MP **Lord McKenzie of Luton** **Baroness Thornton** Rt Hon **Baroness Royall of Blaisdon**

MEMBERS OF PARLIAMENT

Diane Abbott

Hackney North and Stoke Newington ***(returning MP)***

Boundary changes

Tel: 020 7219 4426
E-mail: chalkiasg@parliament.uk
Website: www.dianeabbott.org.uk

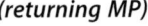

Date of birth: 27 September 1953; Daughter of late Reginald Abbott, welder, and late Mrs Julie Abbott, psychiatric nurse

Education: Harrow County Girls' Grammar School; Newnham College, Cambridge (BA history 1976); Married David Thompson 1991 (divorced 1993) (1 son)

Non-political career: Administration trainee, Home Office 1976-78; Race relations officer, National Council for Civil Liberties 1978-80; Journalist: Thames Television 1980-82, TV AM 1982-84, Freelance 1984-85; Principal press officer, Lambeth Council 1986-87; Equality officer, ACTT 1985-86; Member, RMT Parliamentary Campaigning Group 2002-; Westminster City Councillor 1982-86; Member Greater London Assembly advisory cabinet for women and equality 2000-

Political career: Member for Hackney North and Stoke Newington 1987-2010, for Hackney North and Stoke Newington (revised boundary) since 6 May 2010 general election (First black female MP); *Select Committees:* Member: Treasury and Civil Service 1989-97, Foreign Affairs 1997-2001; Member, Labour Party National Executive Committee 1994-97

Political interests: Small businesses, education; Jamaica, Africa

Other organisations: Founder, Black Women Mean Business 1992-; London Schools and the Black Child; *Spectator* Speech of the Year 2008

Recreations: Reading, cinema

Diane Abbott MP, House of Commons, London SW1A 0AA
Tel: 020 7219 4426 Fax: 020 7219 4964
E-mail: chalkiasg@parliament.uk
Website: www.dianeabbott.org.uk

GENERAL ELECTION RESULT

		%
Abbott, D. (Lab)*	25,553	55.0
Angus, K. (Lib Dem)	11,092	23.9
Caplan, D. (Con)	6,759	14.6
Sellwood, M. (Green)	2,133	4.6
Hargreaves, M. (Christian)	299	0.6
Moore, S. (Ind)	258	0.6
Knapp, K. (Loony)	182	0.4
Shaer, P. (Ind)	96	0.2
Williams, A. (Ind)	61	0.1
Pope-de-Locksley, J. (Magna Carta)	26	0.1
Majority	14,461	31.13
Electorate	73,874	
Turnout	46,459	62.89

**Member of last parliament*

CONSTITUENCY SNAPSHOT

David Weitzman dominated the local political scene for three decades after the Second World War. He was succeeded in 1979 by Ernest Roberts and the seat is currently held by Diane Abbott, who made history in 1987 as the first black woman elected to Parliament.

Her 21,100 majority in 1997 fell to 18,081 in 2001. In 2005 Diane Abbott's majority more than halved to 7,427. Diane Abbot has increased her majority to 14,461 in 2010, taking 55 per cent of the vote.

The seat gained the part-wards of Dalston and Leabridge from Hackney South and Shoreditch, in exchange for Hackney Central.

The seat lies within the north-east London borough of Hackney, stretching from Dalston in the south of the constituency to Stoke Newington in the north.

Increased bus numbers and the expansion of the Overland network has improved transport in the area considerably.

Economically, Hackney will benefit enormously from the infrastructure being created for the 2012 Olympic Games being held in London. Almost one third of the Olympic estate is in the borough, bringing the largest ever regeneration project in the East End of London. Significantly, Hackney is now connected to the tube network via an extension of the East London line.

Gerry Adams

Belfast West ***(returning MP)***

Boundary changes

Tel: 020 7219 8151
E-mail: adamsg@parliament.uk

Sinn Féin

Date of birth: 6 October 1948; Son of late Gerard Adams and Annie Hannaway

Education: St Mary's Christian Brothers' School, Belfast; Married Colette McArdle 1971 (1 son)

Non-political career: Bartender; Founder member of the civil rights movement

Political career: Member for Belfast West 1983-92, 1997-2010, for Belfast West (revised boundary) since 6 May 2010 general election; Member: Northern Ireland Assembly 1982, Northern Ireland Forum for Political Dialogue 1996; MLA for Belfast West 1998-; Sinn Féin: Vice-president 1978-83, President 1983-

Other organisations: Director, Féile an Phobail; Member: PEN, Irish Writers Union; Thorr Peace Prize, Switzerland 1996; Naomh Eoin; *Publications:* Falls Memories (1982); A Pathway to Peace (1988); Cage Eleven (1990); The Street and Other Stories (1992); Before the Dawn (1996); An Irish Voice (1997); The Politics of Irish Freedom and Selected Writings; An Irish Journal; Peace in Ireland – Towards a Lasting Peace; Hope and History (2003); A New Ireland – A Vision for the Future (2005)

Recreations: Gaelic sports, traditional Irish music

Gerry Adams MP, House of Commons, London SW1A 0AA
Tel: 020 7219 8151 E-mail: adamsg@parliament.uk
Constituency: 53 Falls Road, Belfast BT12 4PD Tel: 028 9022 3000
Fax: 028 9034 7360

GENERAL ELECTION RESULT

		%
Adams, G. (Sinn Féin)*	22,840	71.1
Attwood, A. (SDLP)	5,261	16.4
Humphrey, W. (DUP)	2,436	7.6
Manwaring, B. (UCUNF)	1,000	3.1
Hendron, M. (All)	596	1.9
Majority	17,579	54.71
Electorate	59,522	
Turnout	32,133	53.99

**Member of last parliament*

CONSTITUENCY SNAPSHOT

Since 1966, this seat has been held by Nationalist MPs. Apart from a five-year SDLP interlude between 1992 and 1997 Gerry Adams has held this seat since winning it from Gerry Fitt in 1983.

In 2005 a swing of 4.4 per cent from the SDLP handed Adams a 19,315 vote lead, the fourth biggest percentage majority in the UK. Adams retained the seat in 2010 with a slightly reduced 17,579 majority.

The seat gained one ward and part of another from the Lagan Valley constituency, Dunmurry and the part of Derryaghy north of the boundary with Lagmore.

This constituency is overwhelmingly Catholic and nationalist with the highest proportion of Catholics of any Northern Ireland seat.

West Belfast has the highest proportion of unskilled workers in the province, plus the highest number of partly-skilled and of skilled non-manual workers in Belfast as well as the smallest proportion of professionals. The Royal Victoria Hospital is the largest single employer.

The area has placed great emphasis on boosting the local economy through tourism based around its history during the Troubles. Tours around the famous murals of the Falls and Shankill and other political curiosities are popular.

Nigel Adams

Selby and Ainsty

New constituency

Tel: 020 7219 3000
E-mail: nigel.adams.mp@parliament.uk
Website: www.selbyandainsty.com

Conservative

Date of birth: 30 November 1966; Son of Derek Adams, school caretaker, and the late Isabella Adams, home help

Education: Selby Grammar School; Married Claire Louise Robson 1992 (1 son 3 daughters)

Non-political career: Managing Director: Advanced Digital Telecom Ltd 1993-2000, Melgate Ltd 2002-06; Managing Director, NGC Networks Ltd 2006-; Governor: Camblesforth Primary School, Selby 2002-04, Selby High School 2007-; Director, Yorkshire Tourist Board 2005-06

Political career: Contested Rossendale and Darwen 2005 general election. Member for Selby and Ainsty since 6 May 2010 general election; Deputy regional chairman, Yorkshire and Humber Conservatives 2001-03; President, Selby Conservative Association 2002-04; Board member, North of England Conservative Party 2002-03; Conservative Friends of Israel 2007-

Other organisations: Member: Countryside Alliance 2002-, Conservative Rural Action Group 2002-, Yorkshire County Cricket Club Members' Committee 2004-05, Game Conservancy Trust 2006-, York Community Settlement Players 2006-; Member: Carlton, Selby Conservative Club; Member: Yorkshire County Cricket Club, Hovingham Cricket Club

Recreations: Cricket, golf, football, theatre

Nigel Adams MP, House of Commons, London SW1A 0AA
Tel: 020 7219 3000 E-mail: nigel.adams.mp@parliament.uk
Constituency: Tadcaster, 17 High Street, Tadcaster,
North Yorkshire LS24 9AP Tel: 01757 700026 Fax: 01757 213615
Website: www.selbyandainsty.com

GENERAL ELECTION RESULT

		%
Adams, N. (Con)	25,562	49.4
Marshall, J. (Lab)	13,297	25.7
Holvey, T. (Lib Dem)	9,180	17.8
Haley, D. (UKIP)	1,635	3.2
Lorriman, D. (BNP)	1,377	2.7
Glynn, G. (England)	677	1.3
Majority	12,265	23.71
Electorate	72,789	
Turnout	51,728	71.07

CONSTITUENCY SNAPSHOT

This is a new seat based on Selby. Tory MP Michael Alison won Selby at its creation in 1983.

Labour's John Grogan recaptured second place in 1987 and made a further big advance in 1992.

In 1997 Grogan won the seat with a majority of nearly 4,000. Swings in 2001 and 2005 Labour's majority, which was just 467 in 2005. Nigel Adams secured the seat for the Tories in 2010 with a huge majority of 12,265.

The new seat is essentially the old Selby one with the addition of Marston Moor, Ouseburn, Ribston and Spofforth with Lower Wharfedale wards from the abolished Vale of York seat.

Based on the North Yorkshire town of the same name, the constituency extends north to the border with the York council area and south to the M62.

Much of the constituency is rural, with good, flat farming and horticultural land and pleasant villages, criss-crossed by major roads.

There is a major brewing industry in Tadcaster, the only other sizeable centre of population other than Selby itself.

The closure of the Selby coalfield's remaining three pits in the spring of 2004 had a major social and economic impact on the region. The area is home to two huge power stations, Drax and Eggborough. The Drax complex is the biggest coal-fired power station in Western Europe.

Adam Afriyie

Windsor (returning MP)

Boundary changes

Tel: 020 7219 8023
E-mail: afriyiea@parliament.uk
Website: www.adamafriyie.org

Conservative

Date of birth: 4 August 1965

Education: Addey and Stanhope School, New Cross; Imperial College (Wye), London (BSc agricultural economics 1987); Married 2nd Tracy-Jane Newall 2005 (2 sons 1 daughter 1 stepson)

Non-political career: Managing director (now non-executive chair), Connect Support Services 1993-; Chair, DeHavilland Information Services 1998-2005; Board member Policy Exchange 2003-05; Non-executive chair Adfero Ltd 2005-; Governor, Museum of London 1999-2005

Political career: Member for Windsor 2005-10, for Windsor (revised boundary) since 6 May 2010 general election; Shadow Minister for: Innovation, Universities and Skills 2007-09, Innovation and Science 2009-10; *Select Committees:* Member: Science and Technology/Innovation, Universities and Skills 2005-07, Children, Schools and Families 2007-09; Chair, Tonbridge Edenbridge and Malling Association constituency branch 1999-2004

Political interests: Mental health, simpler tax and benefits system, public policy, innovation and science

Other organisations: Chairman (London region): Business for Sterling 1999-2004; No to the Euro campaign 2001-04; Chairman Young Enterprise (North Berkshire) 2005-07, Patron 2008-; Trustee, Museum in Docklands 2003-05; Windsor and Eton Society

Recreations: Distance running

Adam Afriyie MP, House of Commons, London SW1A 0AA
Tel: 020 7219 8023 E-mail: afriyiea@parliament.uk
Constituency: 87 St Leonards Road, Windsor, Berkshire SL4 3BZ
Tel: 01753 678693 Website: www.adamafriyie.org

GENERAL ELECTION RESULT

		%
Afriyie, A. (Con)*	30,172	60.9
Tisi, J. (Lib Dem)	11,118	22.4
Jhund, A. (Lab)	4,910	9.9
Rye, J. (UKIP)	1,612	3.3
Phillips, P. (BNP)	950	1.9
Wall, D. (Green)	628	1.3
Hooper, P. (Ind)	198	0.4
Majority	19,054	38.42
Electorate	69,511	
Turnout	49,588	71.34

**Member of last parliament*

CONSTITUENCY SNAPSHOT

Michael Trend was first elected for Windsor and Maidenhead in 1992 and he held the seat until his retirement in 2005.

Adam Afriyie was selected to defend Trend's 8,889 majority in 2005. At the election he increased the Tory vote-share and won a majority of 10,292 becoming the first black Conservative MP.

The seat was held by Afriyie in 2010 with a 19,054 majority.

The seat gained the wards of Binfield with Warfield, Warfield Harvest Ride and Winkfield and Cranbourne from Bracknell, in exchange for Crownwood and Harmans Water part-wards; Foxborough, Kederminster and Upton part-wards were lost to Slough and Bray part-ward to Maidenhead.

Home to Windsor Castle, Eton College and exclusive suburbs around Windsor, Sunningdale and Ascot, Windsor is one of the wealthiest constituencies in the country.

Tourism is an important industry, and the royal connection ensures a steady stream of visitors to the area. Legoland alone attracts a million and a half visitors a year.

The majority of jobs in Windsor are in the service sector, at companies based along the hi-tech corridor beside the M4. Windsor is situated under the flight-path for Heathrow.

Rt Hon **Bob Ainsworth**

Coventry North East (returning MP)

Boundary changes

Tel: 020 7219 4047
E-mail: ainsworthr@parliament.uk
Website: www.epolitix.com/Bob-Ainsworth

Labour

Date of birth: 19 June 1952; Son of late Stanley and Pearl Ainsworth

Education: Foxford Comprehensive School, Coventry; Married Gloria Sandall 1974 (2 daughters)

Non-political career: Sheet metal worker; Fitter with Jaguar Cars, Coventry 1971-91; Member, MSF/UNITE: Shop steward 1974-80, Senior steward and secretary of joint shop stewards 1980-91, Union Branch President 1983-87; Coventry City Council: Councillor 1984-93, Deputy Leader 1988-91

Political career: Member for Coventry North East 1992-2010, for Coventry North East (revised boundary) since 6 May 2010 general election; Opposition Whip 1995-97; Government Whip 1997-2001; Parliamentary Under-Secretary of State: Department of the Environment, Transport and the Regions 2001, Home Office (Anti-drugs Co-ordination and Organised Crime) 2001-03; Deputy Chief Whip 2003-07; Ministry of Defence 2007-10: Minister of State for the Armed Forces 2007-09, Secretary of State 2009-10; Shadow Secretary of State for Defence 2010-; *Select Committees:* Member: Accommodation and Works 2003-05, Selection 2003-05, 2006-07, Finance and Services 2003-05, Administration 2005-07

Political interests: Industry, environment, taxation; France, India, Pakistan, USA

Other organisations: PC 2005; Bell Green Working Men's; Broad Street Old Boys' Rugby Club

Recreations: Walking, chess, reading, gardening

Rt Hon Bob Ainsworth MP, House of Commons, London SW1A 0AA
Tel: 020 7219 4047 Fax: 020 7219 2889
E-mail: ainsworthr@parliament.uk
Constituency: Bayley House, 22-23 Bayley Lane, Coventry, Warwickshire CV1 5RJ Website: www.epolitix.com/Bob-Ainsworth

GENERAL ELECTION RESULT

		%
Ainsworth, B. (Lab)*	21,384	49.3
Noonan, H. (Con)	9,609	22.2
Field, R. (Lib Dem)	7,210	16.6
Gower, T. (BNP)	1,863	4.3
Nellist, D. (SAP)	1,592	3.7
Forbes, C. (UKIP)	1,291	3.0
Lebar, R. (CMGB)	434	1.0
Majority	11,775	27.14
Electorate	73,035	
Turnout	43,383	59.40

**Member of last parliament*

CONSTITUENCY SNAPSHOT

Coventry North East occupies very similar boundaries to the former Coventry East constituency, represented by Labour's Richard Crossman between 1945 and 1974. Locally-born MP Bob Ainsworth has represented the seat since 1992. Ainsworth beat the sitting Labour MP, John Hughes, for the party's candidacy in the run-up to the 1992 general election. He was re-elected with a slightly reduced, but still very safe, majority of 14,222 in 2005.

Bob Ainsworth held the seat for Labour with a majority of 11,775 despite a swing of 5.5 per cent to the Conservatives.

Four wards within the seat North East were bulked out with part-wards moved into the constituency from Coventry South and Coventry North West. In return, two part-wards were lost to Coventry South.

Coventry North East covers most of the east side of the city. The seat is unified by working-class, industrial characteristics. Reflecting the historic importance of manufacturing in the local economy, the constituency contains an above-average proportion of partly-skilled and non-skilled manual workers.

Both Warwick and Coventry universities, situated in Coventry South, contribute to the local economy. The employment market has diversified in recent years, with the introduction of pharmaceutical and telecommunications companies.

Peter Aldous

Waveney

Boundary changes

Tel: 020 7219 3000
E-mail: peter.aldous.mp@parliament.uk
Website: www.peteraldous.com

Date of birth: 26 August 1961

Education: Harrow School; Reading University (BSc land management 1982); Single

Non-political career: Chartered surveyor, private practice, Norwich and Ipswich 1983-; Councillor, Waveney District Council 1999-2002; Suffolk County Council: Councillor 2001-05, Deputy Leader, Conservative Group 2002-05

Political career: Contested Waveney 2005 general election. Member for Waveney since 6 May 2010 general election; Member, Conservative Party 1998-

Political interests: Employment, transport, broadband, offshore windfarms, education, agriculture, town planning, urban regeneration; USA

Other organisations: Beccles Conservative Club; Beaconsfield Conservative Club; Farmers' Club

Recreations: Squash, Ipswich Town F.C

Peter Aldous MP, House of Commons, London SW1A 0AA
Tel: 020 7219 3000 E-mail: peter.aldous.mp@parliament.uk
Constituency: Waveney Conservative Association, Heathlands, London Road, Kessingland, Suffolk NR33 7PJ Tel: 01502 742495
Fax: 01502 742495 Website: www.peteraldous.com

GENERAL ELECTION RESULT

		%
Aldous, P. (Con)	20,571	40.2
Blizzard, B. (Lab)*	19,802	38.7
Dean, A. (Lib Dem)	6,811	13.3
Tyler, J. (UKIP)	2,684	5.3
Elliott, G. (Green)	1,167	2.3
Barfe, L. (Ind)	106	0.2
Majority	769	1.50
Electorate	78,532	
Turnout	51,141	65.12

**Member of last parliament*

CONSTITUENCY SNAPSHOT

Between 1959 and 1987 the sitting MP was Tory James Prior. David Porter, Prior's Conservative successor, retained the seat in 1987, but his majority fell to 4,376 in 1992.

In 1997, Bob Blizzard, the Labour candidate, was elected with a majority of 12,093, with a 16.2 per cent swing. His majority fell in the elections since and was 5,915 in 2005.

Blizzard was defeated in 2010 with a 6.8 per cent swing to the Conservative candidate, Peter Aldous. The Tories secured a small majority of 769.

Waveney lost the part-ward of Wrentham to Suffolk Coastal in exchange for the part-ward The Saints; they had previously been shared between the two seats.

The most easterly seat in Britain, Waveney is situated in the north-eastern corner of Suffolk. The constituency contains the coastal town of Lowestoft and the market towns of Beccles and Bungay.

Poor transport links have meant that much of the area's manufacturing industry has been relocated. Major employers include Birds Eye, Walls and Bernard Matthews. Boston Putford Offshore providing a significant number of jobs in the offshore gas industry.

Thousands of tourists every year visit the Lowestoft Air Show in July; the two-day seafront show. The air show creates seasonal employment for the area, helped by over 40,000 tourists.

Rt Hon **Danny Alexander**

Inverness, Nairn, Badenoch and Strathspey ***(returning MP)***

No boundary changes

Tel: 020 7219 8328
E-mail: danny.alexander.mp@parliament.uk
Website: www.dannyalexander.org.uk

Date of birth: 15 May 1972; Son of Dion and Jane Alexander

Education: Lochaber High School, Fort William; St Anne's College, Oxford (BA philosophy, politics and economics 1993); Married Rebecca Louise Hoar 2005 (2 daughters)

Non-political career: Researcher Campaign for Freedom of Information 1991; Press officer: Scottish Liberal Democrats 1993-96, European Movement 1996-97; Election aide to Jim Wallace MP 1997; Deputy director and head of communications, European Movement 1997-99; Head of communications: Britain in Europe campaign 1999-2003, Cairngorms National Park 2004-05

Political career: Member for Inverness, Nairn, Badenoch and Strathspey since 5 May 2015 general election; Liberal Democrat: Spokesperson for Work and Pensions, especially disabled people 2005-07, Whip 2006-07, Shadow: Chancellor of the Duchy of Lancaster (Spokesperson for Social Exclusion) 2007, Secretary of State for Work and Pensions 2007-08; Secretary of State for Scotland (and provides ministerial support to Deputy Prime Minister) 2010; Chief Secretary to the Treasury 2010-; *Select Committees:* Member: Scottish Affairs 2005-08; Chief of Staff to Nick Clegg as Leader of the Liberal Democrats 2007-10; Chair Manifesto Group 2007-

Political interests: Highlands and Islands issues, housing, economic policy, Europe, pensions, social security

Other organisations: Director Joseph Rowntree Reform Trust; Advisory Council Demos; PC 2010; Abernethy Angling Improvement Association

Recreations: Hill-walking, fishing, cricket, golf, reading, travel

Rt Hon Danny Alexander MP, House of Commons, London SW1A 0AA Tel: 020 7219 8328 Fax: 020 7219 1438
E-mail: danny.alexander.mp@parliament.uk
Constituency: 45 Huntly Street, Inverness IV3 5HR Tel: 01463 711280 Fax: 01463 714960 Website: www.dannyalexander.org.uk

GENERAL ELECTION RESULT

		%	+/-
Alexander, D. (Lib Dem)*	19,172	40.7	0.5
Robb, M. (Lab)	10,407	22.1	-8.8
Finnie, J. (SNP)	8,803	18.7	5.2
Ferguson, J. (Con)	6,278	13.3	3.0
Boyd, D. (Christian)	835	1.8	
MacLeod, D. (Green)	789	1.7	-0.7
Durrance, R. (UKIP)	574	1.2	
McDonald, G. (TUSC)	135	0.3	
Fraser, C. (JOT)	93	0.2	
Majority	8,765	18.61	
Electorate	72,528		
Turnout	47,086	64.92	

**Member of last parliament*

CONSTITUENCY SNAPSHOT

Inverness, Ross and Cromarty had a Liberal Member until 1950 and again from 1964. By 1992 the seat had been redrawn as Inverness East, Nairn and Lochaber and only 1,741 votes separated the four main parties. Russell Johnston held on with just 458 votes in that year but following his retirement in 1997 the Liberal Democrats were pushed into third place. Labour's David Stewart won with a majority of 2,339. In 2001 Stewart doubled his majority.

The vast majority of Inverness East, Nairn and Lochaber became Inverness, Nairn, Badenoch and Strathspey in the 2005 boundary revision. Lochaber voters were placed with Ross and Skye in Charles Kennedy's seat.

In 2005 the Liberal Democrats won this new seat quite convincingly from Labour. Danny Alexander achieved a majority of 4,148. Alexander doubled his majority to 8,765 in 2010 helped by a 4.6 per cent swing from Labour.

This vast Highland constituency is one of the largest in the UK. The city of Inverness has been transformed and regenerated in the last three decades.

Inverness was granted city status in 2000. The tourist industry is of crucial importance to the local economy: over a third of the workforce is employed in distribution, hotels and restaurants. Inverness is home to the headquarters of the University of the Highlands and Islands.

The constituency includes Loch Ness, the skiing resort of Aviemore, and Culloden, site of the last mainland battle fought in the British Isles.

Rt Hon **Douglas Alexander**

***Paisley and Renfrewshire South** (returning MP)*

No boundary changes

Tel: 020 7219 1345
E-mail: alexanderd@parliament.uk
Website: www.douglasalexander.org.uk

Labour

Date of birth: 26 October 1967; Son of Rev. Douglas Alexander and Dr. Joyce Alexander

Education: Park Mains High School, Erskine, Renfrewshire; Lester B. Pearson College, Vancouver, Canada; Edinburgh University (MA 1990, LLB 1993, Diploma in Legal Practice 1994); University of Pennsylvania, USA; Married Jacqueline Christian 2000 (1 son 1 daughter)

Non-political career: Parliamentary researcher for Gordon Brown MP 1990-91; Solicitor: Brodies W.S. 1994-96, Digby Brown 1996-97; Member, TGWU

Political career: Contested Perth and Kinross 1995 by-election and Perth 1997 general election. Member for Paisley South 6 November 1997 by-election to 2005, for Paisley and Renfrewshire South since 5 May 2005 general election; Minister for E-Commerce and Competitiveness, Department of Trade and Industry 2001-02; Cabinet Office 2002-04: Minister of State 2002-03, Minister for the Cabinet Office and Chancellor of the Duchy of Lancaster 2003-04; Minister of State, Foreign and Commonwealth Office and Department of Trade and Industry (Trade, Investment and Foreign Affairs) 2004-05; Minister of State, Foreign and Commonwealth Office (Europe) 2005-06; Secretary of State for: Transport and for Scotland 2006-07, International Development 2007-10; Shadow Secretary of State for International Development 2010-; General election campaign co-ordinator 1999-2001, 2007-

Political interests: Constitutional reform, economic policy, employment

Other organisations: Member, Muir Society; Rector's Assessor, Edinburgh University 1993-96; PC 2005; Notary Public; *Publications:* Co-author New Scotland, New Britain (1999); Telling it like it could be: the moral force of progressive politics (2005)

Recreations: Running, angling

Rt Hon Douglas Alexander MP, House of Commons, London SW1A 0AA Tel: 020 7219 1345 E-mail: alexanderd@parliament.uk
Constituency: 2014 Mile End Mill, Abbey Mill Business Centre, Paisley, Renfrewshire PA1 1JS Tel: 0141-561 0333
Fax: 0141-561 0334 Website: www.douglasalexander.org.uk

GENERAL ELECTION RESULT

		%	+/-
Alexander, D. (Lab)*	23,842	59.6	7.1
Doig, A. (SNP)	7,228	18.1	0.5
McCaskill, G. (Con)	3,979	10.0	1.5
Ghai, A. (Lib Dem)	3,812	9.5	-8.1
Mack, P. (Ind)	513	1.3	0.8
Kerr, J. (SSP)	375	0.9	-1.1
Hendry, W. (Ind)	249	0.6	0.2
Majority	16,614	41.54	
Electorate	61,197		
Turnout	39,998	65.36	

**Member of last parliament*

CONSTITUENCY SNAPSHOT

In 1983 the Boundary Commission split Paisley in two. Norman Buchan, Labour MP for Renfrewshire West since 1964, took the new Paisley South seat by 6,529 votes.

Two by-elections were held in Paisley on the same day in November 1990, owing to the deaths of Buchan and Paisley North MP Allen Adams. Gordon McMaster, Labour's successful candidate in Paisley South, died shortly after the 1997 general election. Douglas Alexander won the by-election for Labour.

Before the 2005 election the seat was enlarged and renamed, taking in two wards from Paisley North and two wards from West Renfrewshire. Douglas Alexander was returned with a majority of 13,232. He received a small swing from the SNP to win 60 per cent of the vote and a 16,614 majority.

The industrial east of the seat includes the southern half of Paisley and the smaller Clydeside town of Johnstone.

The constituency also covers large tracts of rural Renfrewshire including a number of villages around the many lochs in the area.

Paisley grew up on the linen trade, and textiles is still an important, if declining, industry today. The main sources of employment are in the electronics, communications, food, and oil and micro-technology industries.

The southern division is less prosperous than the north, possibly due to the fact it is further from the motorway and the airport.

Heidi Alexander

Lewisham East

Boundary changes

Tel: 020 7219 3000
E-mail: heidi.alexander.mp@parliament.uk
Website: www.heidialexander.org.uk

Date of birth: 17 April 1975; Daughter of Malcolm Alexander, electrician, and Elaine Alexander

Education: Churchfields Secondary School, Swindon; Durham University (BA geography 1996; MA European urban and regional change 1999); Partner Martin Ballantyne

Non-political career: Researcher to Joan Ruddock MP 1999-2005; Campaigh manager, Clothes Aid 2006; Director and Chair, Greater London Enterprise 2007-09; Director, Lewisham Schools for the Future LEA 2007-09; Member, Unite 2009-; London Borough of Lewisham Council: Councillor 2004-10, Deputy Mayor 2006-10, Cabinet Member for Regeneration 2006-10

Political career: Member for Lewisham East since 6 May 2010 general election

Political interests: Housing

Heidi Alexander MP, House of Commons, London SW1A 0AA
Tel: 020 7219 3000 E-mail: heidi.alexander.mp@parliament.uk
Constituency: c/o Lewisham East Labour Party, 13 Leegate, Eltham Road, London SE12 8SS Website: www.heidialexander.org.uk

GENERAL ELECTION RESULT

		%
Alexander, H. (Lab)	17,966	43.1
Pattisson, P. (Lib Dem)	11,750	28.2
Clamp, J. (Con)	9,850	23.6
Reed, R. (UKIP)	771	1.9
Cotterell, P. (Green)	624	1.5
Rose, J. (England)	426	1.0
Hallam, G. (CNBPG)	332	0.8
Majority	6,216	14.90
Electorate	65,926	
Turnout	41,719	63.28

CONSTITUENCY SNAPSHOT

Roland Moyle won this seat for Labour after its formation in 1974 and held it for nine years until when it was won by the Tories.

However, Labour's Bridget Prentice took the seat from the Conservative Colin Moynihan, in 1992. In 1997 Prentice secured a sizable swing and, a 12,127 majority. In 2005 Prentice was re-elected with a reduced majority of 6,751. Labour's Bridget Prentice retired in 2010 and Heidi Alexander matched the previous MP's performance with a majority of 6,216 and 43 per cent of the vote

The seat gained Rushey Green ward as well as Catford South and Whitepot part-wards. Lewisham Central part-ward moved to Lewisham Deptford.

Lewisham East includes a mix of suburban streets, south-east London estates and leafy Blackheath. The area is mainly residential, and includes the green expanse of Blackheath, surrounded by terraces and large detached houses.

There is no tube but regular rail services into central London and the Docklands Light Railway connect Lewisham to London Docklands and the City.

A £1 million project organised between community groups, the council and agencies in Grove Park has landscaped Chinbrook Meadows for use as a wetlands habitat and an outdoor classroom for school and community groups. Blackheath Village has been given a facelift to make the most of its potential as a shopping centre.

Rushanara Ali

Bethnal Green and Bow

Boundary changes

Tel: 020 7219 3000
E-mail: rushanara.ali.mp@parliament.uk
Website: www.rushanaraali.org

Labour

Education: Mulberry School; Tower Hamlets College; Oxford University (BA philosophy, politics and economics)

Non-political career: Research assistant to Michael Young; Parliamentary assistant to Oona King MP; Research fellow, Institute for Public Policy Research; Foreign and Commonwealth Office; Communities Directorate, Home Office; Associate director, Young Foundation 2005-; Governor, Tower Hamlets College

Political career: Member for Bethnal Green and Bow since 6 May 2010 general election

Other organisations: Commissioner, London Child Poverty Commission; Chair, Tower Hamlets Summer University; Trustee, Paul Hamlyn Foundation; Member, Tate Britain Council

Rushanara Ali MP, House of Commons, London SW1A 0AA
Tel: 020 7219 3000 E-mail: rushanara.ali.mp@parliament.uk
Constituency: 349 Cambridge Heath Road, London E2 9RA
Tel: 020 7729 6682 Website: www.rushanaraali.org

GENERAL ELECTION RESULT

		%
Ali, R. (Lab)	21,784	42.9
Masroor, A. (Lib Dem)	10,210	20.1
Miah, A. (Respect)	8,532	16.8
Khan, Z. (Con)	7,071	13.9
Marshall, J. (BNP)	1,405	2.8
Bakht, F. (Green)	856	1.7
Brooks, P. (Ind)	277	0.6
Van Terheyden, A. (Pirate)	213	0.4
Hikmat, H. (UV)	209	0.4
Choudhury, H. (Ind)	100	0.2
Malik, A. (Ind)	71	0.1
Majority	11,574	22.82
Electorate	81,243	
Turnout	50,728	62.44

CONSTITUENCY SNAPSHOT

This inner city constituency had been a Labour seat since 1945. Oona King was selected as the Labour candidate to replace the long-standing Peter Shore in 1997. Oona King's vote increased by 4 per cent in 2001.

George Galloway's party Respect - The Unity Coalition, formed six months before the 2005 general election and won the seat with a 26.2 per cent swing. The seat was returned to Labour in 2010 as Rushanara Ali won a solid 11,574 majority.

Boundary changes were minimal with part-wards lost to Poplar and Limehouse.

At the heart of the East End, this constituency contains the multi-cultural areas of Whitechapel and Spitalfields in the west and the more traditional areas of Bethnal Green and Bow in the east.

The constituency's ethnic diversity has lent it cultural vibrancy. Spitalfields and Whitechapel are famous for their Asian culture and cuisine, alongside bars and contemporary art galleries.

The Royal London Hospital and the London Chest Hospital are both in the constituency.

Major infrastructure projects in the constituency include the extension of the East London Tube Line, due to open in 2010, the creation of an international rail link through Stratford, and Crossrail, due to open in 2017, all of which will improve transport provision.

Graham Allen

Nottingham North (returning MP)

Boundary changes

Tel: 020 7219 5065
E-mail: allengw@parliament.uk
Website: grahamallenmp.wordpress.com

Labour

Date of birth: 11 January 1953; Son of Bill and Edna Allen

Education: Forest Fields Grammar School, Nottingham; City of London Polytechnic (BA politics and economics 1975); Leeds University (MA political sociology 1977); Married Allyson 1995 (1 daughter)

Non-political career: Warehouseman 1972; Labour Party research officer 1978-83; Local government officer 1983-84; National co-ordinator Political Fund ballots 1984-86; GMBATU research and education officer 1986-87; TGWU

Political career: Member for Nottingham North 1987-2010, for Nottingham North (revised boundary) since 6 May 2010 general election; Shadow Minister for: Social Security 1991-92, Constitutional Affairs 1992-94, Media and Broadcasting 1994-95, Transport 1995-96, Environment 1996-97; Government Whip 1997-2001; *Select Committees:* Member: Public Accounts 1988-91, Selection 2000-01, Reform of the House of Commons 2009-10

Political interests: Economic policy, democratic renewal; China, Russia, USA

Other organisations: Chair One Nottingham the Local Strategic Partnership 2005-; Fellow Industry and Parliament Trust 1995; President Basford Hall Miners Welfare; Vice-President Bulwell Cricket Club; Lords and Commons Cricket XI; Bulwell Forest Golf; *Publications:* Reinventing Democracy (1995); The Last Prime Minister (2001); Co-author (with Iain Duncan Smith MP) Early Intervention (2008)

Recreations: Playing all sports, walking, cooking, oil painting

Graham Allen MP, House of Commons, London SW1A 0AA
Tel: 020 7219 5065 E-mail: allengw@parliament.uk
Constituency: Tel: 0115-975 2377
Website: grahamallenmp.wordpress.com

GENERAL ELECTION RESULT

		%
Allen, G. (Lab)*	16,646	48.6
Curtis, M. (Con)	8,508	24.8
Ball, T. (Lib Dem)	5,849	17.1
Brindley, B. (BNP)	1,944	5.7
Marriott, I. (UKIP)	1,338	3.9
Majority	8,138	23.74
Electorate	63,240	
Turnout	34,285	54.21

**Member of last parliament*

CONSTITUENCY SNAPSHOT

Nottingham North has been won by Labour in all but one general election since the seat's creation in 1955. In the general election of 1983 the Conservatives took the seat when Richard Ottoway won by just 362 votes.

In 1987, however, Nottingham North returned Labour's Graham Allen. Allen's majority has remained relatively strong, and reached its peak in 1997 when he led the Tories by 18,801 votes. In 2001 and 2005 he secured majorities of 12,240 and 12,171 respectively. Graham Allen held the seat with a reduced 8,138 majority in 2010.

Boundary changes moved Basford ward entirely within the seat, having previously been split between the City's three divisions. Part of Bestwood ward moved from Nottingham East, while Leen Valley part-ward moved to Nottingham South.

Manufacturing, while declining, is still the major employment sector. Boots, based in the nearby seat of Broxtowe, is one of the largest employers. Imperial Tobacco also has a number of Nottingham East constituents working in its plant.

The mining industry, while not as crucial to the area's economy as other, more rural Nottinghamshire seats, was also a major employer until its decline in the late 1980s.

David Amess

Southend West (returning MP)

Boundary changes

Tel: 020 7219 3452
E-mail: amessd@parliament.uk
Website: www.epolitix.com/David-Amess

Conservative

Date of birth: 26 March 1952; Son of late James Amess and of Maud Amess

Education: St Bonaventure's Grammar School, Forest Gate, London; Bournemouth College of Technology (BSc economics 1974); Married Julia Arnold 1983 (1 son 4 daughters)

Non-political career: Teacher St John Baptist junior school, Bethnal Green, London 1970-71; Underwriter, Leslie Godwin Agency 1974-76; Accountancy personnel 1976-79; Senior consultant, Executemps Company Agency 1979-81; AA Recruitment Co 1981-87; Chairman and Chief Executive: Accountancy Solutions 1987-90, Accountancy Group 1990-96; Councillor London Borough of Redbridge 1982-86

Political career: Contested Newham North West 1979 general election. Member for Basildon 1983-97, for Southend West 1997-2010, for Southend West (revised boundary) since 6 May 2010 general election; PPS to: Parliamentary under secretaries, DHSS: Edwina Currie 1987-88, Lord Skelmersdale 1988, to Michael Portillo: as Minister of State: Department of Transport 1988-90, Department of Environment 1990-92, as Chief Secretary to the Treasury 1992-94, as Secretary of State: for Employment 1994-95, for Defence 1995-97; Sponsored: Horses and Ponies Bill 1984-85, Members of Parliament (Minimum Age) Bill 1984-85, Horses, Ponies and Donkeys Bill 1987-88, Abortion (Right of Conscience) (Amendment) Bill 1988-89, British Nationality (Hon. Citizenship) Bill 1988-89, Adoption (Amendment) Bill 1989-90, Dogs Bill 1989-90, Pet Animals (Amendment) Bill 1990-91, Protection Against Cruel Tethering Act 1988, Human Fertilisation (Choice) Bill 1992-93, Voluntary Personal Security Cards Bill 1992-93, Football Matches (Violent and Disorderly Conduct) Bill 1992-93, Newly Qualified Drivers Bill 1993-94, Coercion in Family Planning (Prohibition) Bill 1994-95, Freezing of Human Embyros Bill 1995-96, Abortion (Amendment) Bill 1996-97, Reform of Quarantine Regulations Bill 1997-98, Voluntary Personal Security Cards Bill 1997-98, The Warm Homes Act 2000; *Select Committees:* Member: Broadcasting 1994-97, Health 1998-2007, Chairmen's Panel 2001-10; Hon. Secretary, Conservative Friends of Israel 1998-; Member Executive 1922 Committee 2004-

Political interests: Health, education, transport, environment, pro-life movement; USA, European Union, Middle East, Far East, Pacific Basin

Other organisations: Founder Member, Wallenberg Appeal Foundation; President, 1912 Club 1996-; Industry and Parliament Trust: Fellow 1994, Chair Fellowship Committee 2007-; Freeman, City of London; Carlton, St Stephen's Constitutional; Kingswood Squash and Racketball; *Publications:* The Basildon Experience (1995)

Recreations: Socialising, reading, writing, sports, modern music, keeping animals, gardening

David Amess MP, House of Commons, London SW1A 0AA
Tel: 020 7219 3452 Fax: 020 7219 2245
E-mail: amessd@parliament.uk
Constituency: Iveagh Hall, 67 Leigh Road, Leigh-on-Sea, Essex SS9 1JW Tel: 01702 472391 Fax: 01702 480677
Website: www.epolitix.com/David-Amess

GENERAL ELECTION RESULT

		%
Amess, D. (Con)*	20,086	46.1
Welch, P. (Lib Dem)	12,816	29.4
Flynn, T. (Lab)	5,850	13.4
Cockrill, G. (UKIP)	1,714	3.9
Gladwin, T. (BNP)	1,333	3.1
Bolton, B. (Green)	644	1.5
Velmurugan, D. (Ind)	617	1.4
Phillips, T. (England)	546	1.3
Majority	7,270	16.67
Electorate	66,527	
Turnout	43,606	65.55

**Member of last parliament*

CONSTITUENCY SNAPSHOT

In the four successive general elections from 1979 to 1992, Paul (later Lord) Channon always polled well over 50 per cent of the vote and in the three elections from 1983 up to and including 1992, increased his majority. He retired in 1997 and was replaced by David Amess, who had moved from Basildon following boundary changes. Labour and the Liberal Democrats cut his inherited majority of 11,902 votes down to just 2,615.

Amess increased his majority to 7,941 in 2001. In 2005 the Liberal Democrats regained second place, but only by 377 votes. The Tory majority increased by some 1,000 votes to 8,959. Amess held the seat with a reduced majority of 7,270 at the 2010 general election.

Boundary changes were minimal.

Southend West covers the residential areas to the west of the town centre, including popular seafront areas of the Essex town. Southend West covers the more prosperous and affluent parts of Southend.

The town of Southend is a major office and retailing centre, and this plus the number of London commuters is reflected in the high level of skilled non-manual residents in the constituency.

Europe's largest free air show takes place along the seafront with more than half a million visitors attracted to the town every Spring bank holiday.

David Anderson

Blaydon (returning MP)

Boundary changes

Tel: 020 7219 4348
E-mail: andersonda@parliament.uk
Website: www.daveanderson.org.uk

Labour

Date of birth: 2 December 1953; Son of Cyril and Janet Anderson

Education: Maltby Grammar School; Doncaster Technical College; Durham Technical College (mining and mechanical engineering); Moscow Higher Trade Union School 1983; Durham University (DipSocSc 1989); Married Eva Elizabeth Jago 1973

Non-political career: Engineer National Coal Board mines 1969-89; Elderly care worker Newcastle upon Tyne social services 1989-2004; Lay official: NUM 1978-89, UNISON 1989-2005; UNISON NEC board; Member TUC general council 2000-05; President UNISON 2003-04

Political career: Member for Blaydon 2005-10, for Blaydon (revised boundary) since 6 May 2010 general election; PPS to Bill Rammell as Minister of State: Department for Education and Skills/Innovation, Universities and Skills 2006-08, Foreign and Commonwealth Office 2008-09, Ministry of Defence 2009-10; *Select Committees:* Member: Northern Ireland Affairs 2005-10, Procedure 2005-06, Energy and Climate Change 2009-10, North East 2009-10; Chair Labour Friends of Iraq 2005-

Political interests: Public services, employment; Middle East, Northern Ireland, USA, Iraq

Other organisations: Patron: Mick Knighton Mesothelioma Research Fund, Gateshead Visible Ethnic Minorities Group; Director PMR-GCA (Polymyalgia Rheumatica – Giant Cell Arteritis)

Recreations: Walking, travel, football, music, driving

David Anderson MP, House of Commons, London SW1A 0AA
Tel: 020 7219 4348 Fax: 020 7219 8276
E-mail: andersonda@parliament.uk
Constituency: St Cuthbert's Church Hall, Shibdon Road,
Blaydon on Tyne, Tyne and Wear NE21 5PT Tel: 0191-414 2488
Fax: 0191-414 2244 Website: www.daveanderson.org.uk

GENERAL ELECTION RESULT

		%
Anderson, D. (Lab)*	22,297	49.6
Bradbury, N. (Lib Dem)	13,180	29.4
Hall, G. (Con)	7,159	15.9
McFarlane, K. (BNP)	2,277	5.1
Majority	9,117	20.30
Electorate	67,808	
Turnout	44,913	66.24

**Member of last parliament*

CONSTITUENCY SNAPSHOT

Blaydon's electoral history is a story of Labour domination. In the 2001 general election John McWilliam achieved a majority of 7,809, a drop from the 1997 victory of 16,605. Mr McWilliam retired before the 2005 election after serving Blaydon for 26 years, and was replaced by David Anderson. Labour's 2005 majority in Blaydon is at an all-time low at just 5,335, less than the previous low in the 1983 general election, when it stood at 7,222. David Anderson's majority increased to 9,117 due to a sharp reduction in the Liberal Democrat vote.

Boundary changes moved the wards of Dunston Hill and Whickham East (previously part of Gateshead and Washington West), Lamesley (previously part of Tyne Bridge) and Whickham South and Sunniside (previously part of Tyne Bridge) entirely within Blaydon.

The constituency was badly affected by industrialisation trends during the 1980s. However, there are signs of regeneration.

The retail and call-centre sectors in the area are expanding, as are the numbers of small businesses. Major employers within the constituency include AEI Cables, Myson Radiators, Reliance Security Services, NatWest, Allied Bakeries Gateshead, and BAE Systems.

Stuart Andrew

Pudsey

Boundary changes

Tel: 020 7219 3000
E-mail: stuart.andrew.mp@parliament.uk
Website: www.stuartandrew.com

Conservative

Date of birth: 25 November 1971

Education: Ysgol David Hughes, Menai Bridge; Partner

Non-political career: Fundraiser, Hope House Children's Hospice 1998-2000; Head of Fundraising, East Lancashire Hospice 2000-03; Fundraising manager, Martin House Children's Hospice 2003-; Councillor, Leeds City Council 2003-

Political career: Contested Wrexham 1997 general election. Member for Pudsey since 6 May 2010 general election

Political interests: Special needs education, transport, planning, charities

Recreations: DIY

Stuart Andrew MP, House of Commons, London SW1A 0AA
Tel: 020 7219 3000 E-mail: stuart.andrew.mp@parliament.uk
Constituency: Enterprise House, 249 Low Lane, Horsforth, Leeds LS18 5NY Tel: 0113-293 5098
Website: www.stuartandrew.com

GENERAL ELECTION RESULT

		%
Andrew, S. (Con)	18,874	38.5
Hanley, J. (Lab)	17,215	35.1
Matthews, J. (Lib Dem)	10,224	20.8
Gibson, I. (BNP)	1,549	3.2
Dews, D. (UKIP)	1,221	2.5
Majority	1,659	3.38
Electorate	69,257	
Turnout	49,083	70.87

CONSTITUENCY SNAPSHOT

Conservative Sir Giles Shaw was MP from 1974 until his retirement in 1997. When Sir Giles retired, Labour needed a swing of more than 7 per cent to win the seat. In fact, Paul Truswell became Pudsey's first Labour MP with a swing of more than 13 per cent. Truswell held the seat in 2005 with a majority of 5,870.

Labour was defeated in 2010. The Conservative Candidate, Stuart Andrew secured a majority of 1,659.

Pudsey now includes the entirety of the Calverley and Farsley, Guiseley and Rawdon, Horsforth and Pudsey Leeds City Council wards.

This is largely a prosperous suburban seat sandwiched between Leeds and Bradford.

Engineering and textiles are the main local industries. Harry Ramsden's original fish and chip shop is still a popular restaurant in Guiseley.

The constituency is also home to many commuters. Horsforth is one of Leeds's more desirable dormitories, and many people work in Leeds and Bradford.

Leeds Bradford Airport is between Horsforth and Yeadon. Although the airport is not actually in this constituency it is an important employer and economic driver for this part of West Yorkshire.

Rt Hon **James Arbuthnot**

North East Hampshire (returning MP)

Boundary changes

Tel: 020 7219 4649
E-mail: arbuthnotj@parliament.uk
Website: www.jamesarbuthnot.com

Conservative

Date of birth: 4 August 1952; Son of late Sir John Sinclair-Wemyss Arbuthnot, MP for Dover 1950-64, and Lady Arbuthnot. Heir presumptive to baronetcy

Education: Eton College; Trinity College, Cambridge (BA law 1974); Married Emma Broadbent 1984 (1 son 3 daughters)

Non-political career: Called to the Bar, Inner Temple 1975 and Lincoln's Inn 1977; Councillor, Royal Borough of Kensington and Chelsea 1978-87

Political career: Contested Cynon Valley 1983 general election and 1984 by-election. Member for Wanstead and Woodford 1987-97, for North East Hampshire 1997-2010, for North East Hampshire (revised boundary) since 6 May 2010 general election; PPS: to Archie Hamilton as Minister of State for the Armed Forces 1988-90, to Peter Lilley as Secretary of State for Trade and Industry 1990-92; Assistant Government Whip 1992-94; Parliamentary Under-Secretary of State, Department of Social Security 1994-95; Minister of State for Procurement, Ministry of Defence 1995-97; Member, Shadow Cabinet 1997-2001: Opposition Chief Whip 1997-2001; Shadow: Secretary of State for Trade 2003-05, Minister for Trade and Industry 2005; *Select Committees:* Member: Joint Committee on House of Lords Reform 2002-03; Chair: Defence 2005-10; Member: Liaison 2005-10, Joint Committee on National Security Strategy 2010; Branch Chair, Putney Conservative Association 1975-77; Joint Deputy Chair, Chelsea Conservative Association 1980-82; President, Cynon Valley Conservative Association 1983-92

Political interests: Taxation, defence, foreign affairs, law

Other organisations: Fellow Industry and Parliament Trust 1989; PC 1998; Pratts

Recreations: Playing guitar, skiing, cooking

Rt Hon James Arbuthnot MP, House of Commons, London SW1A 0AA Tel: 020 7219 4649 Fax: 020 7219 3910
E-mail: arbuthnotj@parliament.uk
Constituency: North East Hampshire Conservative Association, The Mount, Bounty Road, Basingstoke, Hampshire RG21 3DD
Tel: 01256 471242 Website: www.jamesarbuthnot.com

GENERAL ELECTION RESULT

		%
Arbuthnot, J. (Con)*	32,075	60.6
Coulson, D. (Lib Dem)	13,478	25.5
Jones, B. (Lab)	5,173	9.8
Duffin, R. (UKIP)	2,213	4.2
Majority	18,597	35.13
Electorate	72,196	
Turnout	52,939	73.33

**Member of last parliament*

CONSTITUENCY SNAPSHOT

North East Hampshire was created in 1997, and has been represented by James Arbuthnot since then. Despite an increase in support for Labour and the Liberal Democrats since 1997, Mr Arbuthnot won a majority of 12,549 in 2005.

The seat was held by Arbuthnot in 2010 with a 60.6 per cent vote-share and a 18,597 majority.

The seat gained three wards and a part-ward from Basingstoke and three wards and two part-wards from Aldershot, while losing 11 wards and a part-ward to East Hampshire.

North East Hampshire stretches from the village of Eversley on the Berkshire border through Fleet and Hook to Liphook, Selborne and Whitehill in the south. Fleet, in the northern half of the constituency, is its most urban area, and serves as its administrative, commercial and retail centre.

This constituency is extremely affluent and incomes are higher than the average, even for the South East.

In a constituency where car ownership is high, traffic pressures create serious problems and are invariably cited when opposing new developments.

Ian Austin

***Dudley North** (returning MP)*

Boundary changes

Tel: 020 7219 4811
E-mail: austini@parliament.uk
Website: www.ianaustin.co.uk

Date of birth: 6 March 1965; Son of Alfred and Margaret Austin

Education: Dudley School; Essex University (BA government 1987); Married Catherine Miles 1993 (2 sons 1 daughter)

Non-political career: Communications manager, Focus Housing 1989-94; Regional press officer, West Midlands Labour Party 1995-98; Deputy director of communications, Scottish Labour Party 1998-99; Special adviser to Gordon Brown as Chancellor of the Exchequer 1999-2005; Councillor Dudley Borough Council 1991-95

Political career: Member for Dudley North 2005-10, for Dudley North (revised boundary) since 6 May 2010 general election; PPS to Gordon Brown: as Chancellor of the Exchequer 2007, as Prime Minister 2007-08; Assistant Government Whip 2008-09; Minister for the West Midlands 2008-10; Parliamentary Under-Secretary of State, Department for Communities and Local Government 2009-10

Political interests: Housing, training and skills, employment, manufacturing and trade

Recreations: Football, cycling, reading

Ian Austin MP, House of Commons, London SW1A 0AA
Tel: 020 7219 4811 Fax: 020 7219 4488
E-mail: austini@parliament.uk
Constituency: Turner House, 157-185 Wrens Road, Dudley, West Midlands DY1 3RU Tel: 01384 342503/4 Fax: 01384 342523
Website: www.ianaustin.co.uk

GENERAL ELECTION RESULT

		%
Austin, I. (Lab)*	14,923	38.7
Brown, G. (Con)	14,274	37.0
Beckett, M. (Lib Dem)	4,066	10.5
Davis, M. (UKIP)	3,267	8.5
Griffiths, K. (BNP)	1,899	4.9
Inman, K. (NF)	173	0.5
Majority	649	1.68
Electorate	60,838	
Turnout	38,602	63.45

**Member of last parliament*

CONSTITUENCY SNAPSHOT

Dudley North was a product of boundary changes that amalgamated Dudley East and Dudley West. The seat took five wards from the East division and two more wards from the Dudley West seat that had been Conservative until gained for Labour in a 1994 by-election.

Ross Cranston won in 1997. In 2001 the absence of minor parties meant both Labour and the Conservatives increased their share of the vote but Cranston's majority shrank. In 2005 Cranston's successor Ian Austin's was elected with a 5,432 majority. In 2010 Austin was re-elected with a small majority of 649 following a swing of 4.7 per cent to the Tories.

Boundary changes have moved all of Gornal, St James, and St Thomas wards into Dudley North. The whole of Coseley East ward was transferred into Wolverhampton South East. Coseley East's departure takes a substantial triangular wedge from the north-eastern flank of this constituency. Other readjustments were very minor.

Dudley North contains most of the heart of Dudley, including the town centre, as well as the small towns of Gornal and Sedgley.

The St Thomas and Castle and Priory wards come high on deprivation indices. Gornal and Sedgley are more middle-class, residential suburbs by contrast.

Education provision for primary school pupils is very good, with a falling birth rate resulting in adequate places.

Richard Bacon

South Norfolk (returning MP)

Boundary changes

Tel: 020 7219 8301
E-mail: richardbaconmp@parliament.uk
Website: www.richardbacon.org.uk

Conservative

Date of birth: 3 December 1962

Education: King's School, Worcester; London School of Economics (BSc (Econ) politics and economics 1986); Married Victoria Panton 2006 (1 son)

Non-political career: Investment banker Barclays de Zoete Wedd 1986-89; Financial journalist Euromoney Publications plc 1993-94; Deputy director Management Consultancies Association 1994-96; Brunswick Public Relations 1996-99; Founder English Word Factory 1999-

Political career: Contested Vauxhall 1997 general election. Member for South Norfolk 2001-10, for South Norfolk (revised boundary) since 6 May 2010 general election; Member Public Accounts Commission 2005-; *Select Committees:* Member: Public Accounts 2001-10, European Scrutiny 2003-07; Chair Hammersmith Conservative Association 1995-96; Co-founder Geneva Conservative general election voluntary agency 2000

Political interests: Public expenditure, education, health, agriculture, Europe

Other organisations: Member Amnesty International

Recreations: Music, reading, modern painting

Richard Bacon MP, House of Commons, London SW1A 0AA
Tel: 020 7219 8301 E-mail: richardbaconmp@parliament.uk
Constituency: Grasmere, Denmark Street, Diss, Norfolk IP22 4LE
Tel: 01379 643728 Fax: 01379 642220
Website: www.richardbacon.org.uk

GENERAL ELECTION RESULT

		%
Bacon, R. (Con)*	27,133	49.3
Howe, J. (Lib Dem)	16,193	29.5
Castle, M. (Lab)	7,252	13.2
Heasley, E. (UKIP)	2,329	4.2
Mitchell, H. (BNP)	1,086	2.0
Willcott, J. (Green)	1,000	1.8
Majority	10,940	19.89
Electorate	76,165	
Turnout	54,993	72.20

**Member of last parliament*

CONSTITUENCY SNAPSHOT

South Norfolk has returned a Tory Member since 1950. John MacGregor, the former Cabinet Minister, held the seat for 27 years from 1974.

Richard Bacon became MP for South Norfolk in 2001. He was re-elected in 2005 with an increased majority of 8,782. Bacon held the seat with a majority of 10,940 at the 2010 general election.

The seat lost seven wards to Mid Norfolk and a part-ward to Norwich South. Cringleford is now entirely within the seat's boundaries having previously been shared with Norwich South.

South Norfolk stretches from the southern edge of Norwich to the Suffolk boundary and takes in numerous commuter-laden rural villages.

South Norfolk has an economy split between town and country. To the north, around the towns of Hethersett and Loddon, the constituency is heavily influenced by the city of Norwich, where many residents are employed. To the south, in Roydon and Harleston, the economy becomes more localised.

The agricultural sector is important. Major local companies including B Brooks of Little Melton, Harleston Foods and BOCM Pauls provide employment in the food processing industry. Another major employer is Group Lotus, which manufactures sports cars.

Louise Bagshawe

Corby

No boundary changes

Tel: 020 7219 3000
E-mail: louise.bagshawe.mp@parliament.uk
Website: www.louisebagshawe.net

Conservative

Date of birth: 1971

Education: Oxford University (Anglo saxon and norse); Married Anthony LoCicero (separated) (3 children)

Non-political career: Press officer, EMI records; Marketing, Sony; Full-time writer; Primary school governor

Political career: Member for Corby since 6 May 2010 general election; Member: Young Conservatives 1985, Labour Party 1996, Conservative Party 1997-

Other organisations: Young Poet of the Year 1989; *Publications:* Author of 12 novels

Recreations: Reading

Louise Bagshawe MP, House of Commons, London SW1A 0AA
Tel: 020 7219 3000 E-mail: louise.bagshawe.mp@parliament.uk
Constituency: Corby and East Northamptonshire Conservatives, Cottingham Road, Corby NN17 1SZ Tel: 01536 200255
Fax: 01536 406651 Website: www.louisebagshawe.net

GENERAL ELECTION RESULT

		%	+/-
Bagshawe, L. (Con)	22,886	42.2	2.5
Hope, P. (Lab/Co-op)*	20,935	38.6	-4.3
Wilson, P. (Lib Dem)	7,834	14.5	1.8
Davies, R. (BNP)	2,525	4.7	
Majority	1,951	3.60	
Electorate	78,305		
Turnout	54,180	69.19	

**Member of last parliament*

CONSTITUENCY SNAPSHOT

In 1997 Labour candidate Phil Hope needed only a slight swing in order to take the seat from the Tories. He actually won with a 22 per cent margin, and the Conservative's vote dropped by a quarter as Labour claimed well over half the ballots cast.

In the 2001 general election Mr Hope's majority was halved to 5,700. In 2005 a 4.5 per cent swing to the Conservatives, reduced Hope's majority to a very marginal 1,517.

Hope was defeated in 2010 with a 3.4 per cent swing to the Conservative candidate, Louise Bagshawe.

Centred on a former steel town in Northamptonshire, this constituency is a mix of factory workers and rural dwellers.

Corby's economy was overwhelmingly dependent on the steel industry for much of the twentieth century. Substantial unemployment had ensued after the steelworks here (previously the biggest employer in the area), were closed in 1979, and the town of Corby was granted Enterprise Zone and Assisted Area status in the 1980s, prompting a massive injection of investment across a broad range of industries.

Eurohub, a road-rail interchange connecting Corby with the Continent, has enticed several businesses to set up major regional headquarters in the area. While there is still a residual steel industry and a fairly large rural economy, the largest employers by far are now in the food and service industries.

Adrian Bailey

West Bromwich West ***(returning MP)***

Boundary changes

Tel: 020 7219 6060
E-mail: baileya@parliament.uk
Website: www.adrianbailey.org

Labour/Co-operative

Date of birth: 11 December 1945; Son of Edward Arthur Bailey, fitter and Sylvia Alice, née Bayliss

Education: Cheltenham Grammar School; Exeter University (BA economic history 1967) Loughborough College of Librarianship (postgraduate diploma in librarianship 1971); Married Jill Patricia Millard 1989 (1 stepson)

Non-political career: Librarian, Cheshire County Council 1971-82; Political organiser, Co-operative Party 1982-2000; GMBATU 1982-; Sandwell Borough Council: Councillor 1991-2001, Chair finance 1992-97, Deputy leader 1997-2000

Political career: Contested South Worcester 1970 and Nantwich 1974 general elections and Wirral 1976 by-election. Member for West Bromwich West 23 November 2000 by-election to 2010, for West Bromwich West (revised boundary) since 6 May 2010 general election; PPS: to John Hutton: as Chancellor of the Duchy of Lancaster 2005, as Secretary of State for Work and Pensions 2005-06, to Hilary Armstrong as Chancellor of the Duchy of Lancaster 2006, to Ministers of State, Ministry of Defence: Adam Ingram 2006-07, Bob Ainsworth 2007; *Select Committees:* Member: Northern Ireland Affairs 2001-05, Unopposed Bills (Panel) 2001-10, Business, Enterprise and Regulatory Reform/Business and Enterprise/Business, Innovation and Skills 2007-09, European Scrutiny 2007-10, Quadripartite (Committees on Strategic Export Controls)/Arms Export Controls 2007-10, West Midlands 2009-10; Contested Cheshire West 1979 European Parliament election; Secretary West Bromwich West constituency Labour Party 1993-2000; Chair Parliamentary Group 2004

Political interests: Co-operatives and mutuals, urban regeneration, animal welfare (anti hunting with dogs), taxation, economic policy, child protection policy; China, India, Pakistan

Recreations: football, swimming, walking

Adrian Bailey MP, House of Commons, London SW1A 0AA
Tel: 020 7219 6060 Fax: 020 7219 1202
E-mail: baileya@parliament.uk
Constituency: Terry Duffy House, Thomas Street, West Bromwich, West Midlands BR70 6NT Tel: 01215 691926 Fax: 01215 691936
Website: www.adrianbailey.org

GENERAL ELECTION RESULT

		%
Bailey, A. (Lab/Co-op)*	16,263	45.0
Hardie, A. (Con)	10,612	29.3
Smith, S. (Lib Dem)	4,336	12.0
Green, R. (BNP)	3,394	9.4
Ford, M. (UKIP)	1,566	4.3
Majority	5,651	15.62
Electorate	65,013	
Turnout	36,171	55.64

**Member of last parliament*

CONSTITUENCY SNAPSHOT

Labour has held the advantage in West Bromwich West since 1945 and Betty Boothroyd was the sitting MP for nearly three decades. She recorded victories at each election taking over 50 per cent of the vote.

At the 1997 election Boothroyd was Speaker of the House of Commons, the first woman to have this role. As parliamentary tradition dictates that the seat is uncontested, Boothroyd was elected with a 15,423 majority.

When Betty Boothroyd stood down in 2000, her Labour successor Adrian Bailey won 51 per cent of the vote. Bailey increased his majority in 2001 with an impressive 60.8 per cent of the vote. In 2005 Mr Bailey still had a five-figure majority. In 2010 Bailey was re-elected with 16,263 votes giving him a much-reduced majority of 5,651.

Boundary changes mean Oldbury, Tividale and Wednesbury South wards were consolidated inside this seat. West Bromwich East now makes inroads inside the seat's former south-eastern border (Greets Green and Lyng) while Halesowen has edged up from Rowley in the south.

West Bromwich is typical of the industrial towns of the West Midlands, with a manufacturing and engineering economic base

The area was at the heart of the industrial revolution in mining, engineering, metalwork and manufacturing and in line with regional post-industrial trends, there have been in recent years above-average numbers classified as having never worked or being long-term unemployed.

Willie Bain

Glasgow North East ***(returning MP)***

No boundary changes

Tel: 020 7219 7527
E-mail: bainw@parliament.uk
Website: www.williebain.com

Date of birth: 29 November 1972; Son of William Bain, lift engineer, and Catherine Bain, payroll clerk

Education: St Roch's Secondary School; Strathclyde University (LLM 2004)

Non-political career: Senior lecturer, public law, London South Bank University

Political career: Member for Glasgow North East since 12 November 2009 by-election; PPS to Sadiq Khan as Minister of State, Department for Transport 2010; *Select Committees:* Member: Joint Committee on Tax Law Rewrite Bills 2009-10; Election agent to Michael Martin MP; Secretary, Glasgow North East CLP

Political interests: Crime, anti-social behaviour, pensions

Other organisations: Member, Amnesty International

Willie Bain MP, House of Commons, London SW1A 0AA
Tel: 020 7219 7527 E-mail: bainw@parliament.uk
Constituency: Flemington House, Flemington Street,
Glasgow G21 4BX Tel: 0141-557 2513 Website: www.williebain.com

GENERAL ELECTION RESULT

		%	+/-
Bain, W. (Lab)*	20,100	68.4	
McAllister, B. (SNP)	4,158	14.1	-3.4
Baxendale, E. (Lib Dem)	2,262	7.7	
Davidson, R. (Con)	1,569	5.3	
Hamilton, W. (BNP)	798	2.7	-0.5
McVey, K. (SSP)	179	0.6	-4.3
Berrington, J. (SLP)	156	0.5	-13.6
Majority	15,942	54.21	
Electorate	59,859		
Turnout	29,409	49.13	

**Member of last parliament*

CONSTITUENCY SNAPSHOT

The current seat of Glasgow North East was created in 2005 and included nine wards from Glasgow Springburn and three wards from Glasgow Maryhill.

In this seat's main predessesor, Glasgow Springburn, Michael Martin never polled less than 50 per cent of the vote after taking the seat for Labour in 1979. In 2000 Michael Martin was elected Speaker of the House of Commons.

Martin resigned as Speaker and MP in June 2009 in the wake of his handling of the MPs' expenses controversy. A by-election was held in November and Labour's Willie Bain won the seat comfortably with a 8,111 majority. Turnout was the lowest for any by-election in Scottish history at just 33 per cent. Bain took almost 70 per cent of the vote in 2010 and was re-elected with an absolute majority of 15,942.

This seat extends out towards East Dunbartonshire and contains some of the toughest estates in Glasgow around Springburn.

Dennistoun has some more attractive areas and is home to a number of young professionals and students.

Norman Baker

Lewes (returning MP)

Boundary changes

Tel: 020 7219 2864
E-mail: bakern@parliament.uk
Website: www.normanbaker.org.uk

Date of birth: 26 July 1957

Education: Royal Liberty School, Gidea Park; Royal Holloway College, London University (BA German 1978)

Non-political career: Regional director Our Price Records 1978-83; English as a foreign language teacher/lecturer 1985-97; Lib Dem environment campaigner, House of Commons 1989-90; Councillor: Lewes District Council 1987-99 (Leader 1991-97), East Sussex County Council 1989-97

Political career: Contested Lewes 1992 general election. Member for Lewes 1997-2010, for Lewes (revised boundary) since 6 May 2010 general election; Liberal Democrat: Spokesperson for: Environment, Food and Rural Affairs 1997-99, Millennium Dome 1998-2001, Transport 1998-99, Consumer Affairs and Broadcasting 1999-2001, Home Affairs 2001-02, Shadow: Secretary of State for: Environment 2002-05, Environment, Food and Rural Affairs 2005-06, Minister for the Cabinet Office and Chancellor of the Duchy of Lancaster 2007, Secretary of State for Transport 2007-10; Parliamentary Under-Secretary of State, Department for Transport 2010-; *Select Committees:* Member: Environmental Audit 1997-2000, Broadcasting 2000-01, Joint Committee on Human Rights 2001-03

Political interests: Civil liberties, environment; Tibet, Sweden

Other organisations: Vice President RSPCA; President Tibet Society; Zurich/*Spectator* Parliamentarians of the Year Awards: Best Newcomer MP 1997, *Spectator* Inquisitor of the Year 2001; Channel 4 Opposition MP of the Year 2002; RSPCA Lord Erskine Award 2003; *Publications:* Various environmental texts; The Strange Death of David Kelly (Methuen 2007)

Recreations: Walking, music

Norman Baker MP, House of Commons, London SW1A 0AA
Tel: 020 7219 2864 Fax: 020 7219 0445
E-mail: bakern@parliament.uk
Constituency: 23 East Street, Lewes, East Sussex BN7 2LJ
Tel: 01273 480281 Fax: 01273 480287
Website: www.normanbaker.org.uk

GENERAL ELECTION RESULT

		%
Baker, N. (Lib Dem)*	26,048	52.0
Sugarman, J. (Con)	18,401	36.7
Koundarjian, H. (Lab)	2,508	5.0
Charlton, P. (UKIP)	1,728	3.5
Murray, S. (Green)	729	1.5
Lloyd, D. (BNP)	594	1.2
Soucek, O. (Ind)	80	0.2
Majority	7,647	15.27
Electorate	68,708	
Turnout	50,088	72.90

**Member of last parliament*

CONSTITUENCY SNAPSHOT

Before 1997 this seat had a Tory history, having elected Tory MPs without interruption since 1874, including William Pitt the Elder and George Canning. However, after years of decline in Conservative support, the seat fell to the Lib Dems' Norman Baker in 1997, who built a majority approaching five figures, which was barely dented in 2005.

In 2010 Baker retained the seat for the Lib Dems with a 7,647 majority.

Boundary changes are minimal and relate only to four wards that were shared between the seat and two of its neighbours: Eastbourne and Wealden.

With an interesting past that stretches back to the Norman Conquest, it was in Lewes, East Sussex during the reign of Queen Mary that 17 Protestants were burned to death. The annual Lewes bonfire commemorates this, which draws national attention with its effigy burnings.

The constituency, while not a poor one, is certainly not as wealthy as many others in the London commuter belt.

Agriculture and fishing have been the traditional mainstays of the local economy, but tourism and other industries have become increasingly important.

The working population now is primarily managerial and skilled non-manual workers, and many commute into Lewes as well as to jobs in London or Brighton. The major local employers are the Parker Pen Company, Christian Dior and Roche.

Steve Baker

Wycombe

Boundary changes

Tel: 020 7219 3000
E-mail: steve.baker.mp@parliament.uk
Website: www.stevebaker.info

Conservative

Date of birth: 6 June 1971

Education: Poltair Comprehensive School, St Austell; St Austell Sixth Form College; Southampton University (BEng aerospace systems engineering 1992); St Cross College, Oxford (MSc computer science 2000); Married Beth 1996 (no children)

Non-political career: Engineer officer, Royal Air Force 1989-99; Head of consulting and product manager, DecisionSoft Ltd, Oxford 2000-01; Principal, Ambriel Consulting Ltd 2001-; Chief technology officer, BASDA Ltd, Great Missenden 2002-07; Product development director, Core Filing Ltd Oxford 2005-06; Chief architect, global financing and asset servicing platforms, Lehman Brothers, London 2006-08; Corporate affairs director, The Cobden Centre 2009-

Political career: Member for Wycombe since 6 May 2010 general election

Political interests: Enterprise

Other organisations: Associate consultant, Centre for Social Justice 2008-; Member, Speen Baptist Church; Royal Air Force Club

Recreations: Skydiving, motorcycling, photography, sailing

Steve Baker MP, House of Commons, London SW1A 0AA
Tel: 020 7219 3000 E-mail: steve.baker.mp@parliament.uk
Constituency: c/o Wycombe Conservative Association, 150A West Wycombe Road, High Wycombe, Buckinghamshire HP11 3AE
Tel: 01494 521777 Website: www.stevebaker.info

GENERAL ELECTION RESULT

		%
Baker, S. (Con)	23,423	48.6
Guy, S. (Lib Dem)	13,863	28.8
Lomas, A. (Lab)	8,326	17.3
Wiseman, J. (UKIP)	2,123	4.4
Khokar, M. (Ind)	228	0.5
Fitton, D. (Ind)	188	0.4
Majority	9,560	19.85
Electorate	74,502	
Turnout	48,151	64.63

CONSTITUENCY SNAPSHOT

In 1997 Tory Ray Whitney (MP since 1978) was re-elected with a reduced majority of 2,370 after an increase in support for Labour.

Whitney retired in 2001 and Paul Goodman won the seat with a swing of 1.3 per cent from Labour. In 2005 his majority more than doubled to 7,051.

Goodman retired in 2010 and Steven Baker held the seat for the Conservatives with a 9,560 majority.

The seat gained the part-ward of Hambleden Valley from Aylesbury; Hazlemere North and Hazlemere South wards from Chesham and Amersham; and Tylers Green and Loudwater from Beaconsfield. It lost its part of Greater Hughenden ward to Aylesbury, and Marlow North and West and Marlow South East to Beaconsfield.

This Buckinghamshire constituency is a combination of urban and rural, with around half the seat in the town of High Wycombe, and the rest consisting of the small affluent villages around the Chiltern Hills.

There is a good deal of light industry in Wycombe, and the industrial estate in Cressex is a key employer. One of the largest employers is Dun and Bradstreet, and many local people also work at Air Flow Developments, John Lewis, Wycombe Hospital and the district council. There is also a substantial commuter population.

Tony Baldry

Banbury (returning MP)

Boundary changes

Tel: 020 7219 4491
E-mail: baldryt@parliament.uk
Website: tonybaldry.com

Conservative

Date of birth: 10 July 1950; Son of Peter Baldry, consultant physician, and Oina, neé Paterson

Education: Leighton Park School, Reading; Sussex University (BA social science 1972, LLB 1973, MA international development 2005); Lincoln's Inn (barrister 1975); Married Catherine Weir 1979 (divorced 1996) (1 son 1 daughter); married Pippa Isbell 2001

Non-political career: TA Officer 1971-83; Honorary Colonel RLC (TA); Barrister specialising in construction law, general commercial law and international arbitration 1975-

Political career: Contested Thurrock 1979 general election. Member for Banbury 1983-2010, for Banbury (revised boundary) since 6 May 2010 general election; PA to Margaret Thatcher 1974 general election, served in her private office March-October 1975; PPS: to Lynda Chalker as Minister of State, FCO 1985-87, to John Wakeham: as Lord Privy Seal 1987-88, as Leader of the House 1987-89, as Lord President of The Council 1988-89, as Secretary of State for Energy 1989-90; Parliamentary Under-Secretary of State: Department of Energy 1990, Department of Environment 1990-94, Foreign and Commonwealth Office 1994-95; Minister of State, Ministry of Agriculture, Fisheries and Food 1995-97; *Select Committees:* Member: Trade and Industry 1997-2001, Liaison 2001-05, Standards and Privileges 2001; Chair: International Development 2001-05; Deputy Chair Conservative Group for Europe 1981-83; Chair Conservative Parliamentary Mainstream Group 1997-2001; Member Executive 1992 Committee 2001-02

Political interests: Employment, youth affairs, legal affairs, overseas aid and development, European Union, childcare; Asia, Africa, Caribbean, North America, Middle East

Other organisations: Vice-president National Children's Homes 1981-83; Governor Commonwealth Institute 1997-2005; Member: Council Overseas Development Institute 2003-, Council of Chatham House 2004-; IPU British Group: Executive Committee Member 1997-, Treasurer 2000-01; Robert Schumann Silver Medal 1978; Liveryman: Merchant Taylors Company, Stationers and Newspaper Makers Company, Arbitrators Company, Bowyers Company; Carlton, Farmers', Garrick

Recreations: Walking, cycling, gardening, historical biography

Tony Baldry MP, House of Commons, London SW1A 0AA
Tel: 020 7219 4491 Fax: 020 7219 5826
E-mail: baldryt@parliament.uk
Constituency: Alexandra House, Church Passage, Banbury, Oxfordshire OX16 5JZ Tel: 01295 673873 Fax: 01295 263376
Website: tonybaldry.com

GENERAL ELECTION RESULT

		%
Baldry, T. (Con)*	29,703	52.8
Rundle, D. (Lib Dem)	11,476	20.4
Sibley, L. (Lab)	10,773	19.2
Fairweather, D. (UKIP)	2,806	5.0
White, A. (Green)	959	1.7
Edwards, R. (Ind)	524	0.9
Majority	18,227	32.41
Electorate	86,986	
Turnout	56,241	64.66

**Member of last parliament*

CONSTITUENCY SNAPSHOT

Conservative Tony Baldry has represented this seat since 1983. In 1997 Labour made significant inroads on his notional 1992 majority of 15,731, cutting the Tory lead to 4,737.

He was returned in 2001 with a majority of 5,219. In 2005 the Tory majority more than doubled to 10,797, on a 4.5 per cent swing from Labour.

In 2010 Baldry held the seat with a 18,227 majority.

Boundary changes have adjusted the seat to allow for population growth by moving Kirtlington part-ward, and the entire Otmoor ward into Henley.

Set in North Oxfordshire, this partly rural constituency has experienced significant urban growth in the expanding towns of Banbury and Bicester, where the majority of the electorate now live.

The seat is popular with commuters who favour the area for its fast transport links to Birmingham, Oxford and London, including rail, and proximity to the M40 motorway.

Business ranges from the agricultural to the industrial. In Banbury farming was long the backbone of the Oxfordshire economy, and Banbury was once home to one of the largest livestock markets in Europe, now closed.

New high-tech companies and elements of the racing car industry have been attracted to Banbury and are a large source of employment.

Harriett Baldwin

West Worcestershire

Boundary changes

Tel: 020 7219 3000
E-mail: harriett.baldwin.mp@parliament.uk
Website: www.harriettbaldwin.com

Conservative

Date of birth: 2 May 1960

Education: Friends' school, Saffron Walden; Marlborough College; Lady Margaret Hall, Oxford (BA French and Russian 1982); McGill University, Montreal, Canada (MBA international finance 1985); Married 2nd James Stanley Baldwin 2004 (1 son from previous marriage 2 stepdaughters)

Non-political career: Gradaute trainee, Security Pacific National Bank 1982-83; Treasury analyst, Hewlett-Packard Canada 1985-86; JP Morgan 1986-: Various roles/investor 1986-98, Head of currency management, Asset management division 1998-2006, Managing director 2007-

Political career: Contested Stockton North 2005 general election. Member for West Worcestershire since 6 May 2010 general election

Political interests: Pensions, economics, social enterprise, financial literacy, micro-finance

Other organisations: Member: Countryside Alliance, National Trust, CLA, English Heritage, Ramblers; Carlton Club; *Publications:* Author: Leviathan Is Still At Large (Centre for policy studies 2002), Social Enterprise Zones (Conservative policy review 2007)

Recreations: Canal boats, walking, cycling

Harriett Baldwin MP, House of Commons, London SW1A 0AA
Tel: 020 7219 3000 E-mail: harriett.baldwin.mp@parliament.uk
Constituency: West Worcestershire Conservatives, 209a Worcester Road, Malvern Link, Malvern, Worcestershire WR14 1SP
Tel: 01684 573469 Fax: 01684 575280
Website: www.harriettbaldwin.com

GENERAL ELECTION RESULT

		%
Baldwin, H. (Con)	27,213	50.4
Burt, R. (Lib Dem)	20,409	37.8
Barber, P. (Lab)	3,661	6.8
Bovey, C. (UKIP)	2,119	3.9
Victory, M. (Green)	641	1.2
Majority	6,804	12.59
Electorate	73,270	
Turnout	54,043	73.76

CONSTITUENCY SNAPSHOT

The constituency has been in Conservative hands since its creation in 1997, before which it formed part of the South Worcestershire seat, whose sitting MP, Sir Michael Spicer, it inherited. In the 1980s and 90s Sir Michael won over 50 per cent of the vote, but the boundary changes in 1997, cut his majority to 3,846, and returned him only 45 per cent of the vote. In 2005 Sir Michael's majority was 2,475.

Sir Michael Spicer retired in 2010 and Harriett Baldwin held the seat for the Conservatives with a 6,804 majority.

Boundary changes at the election have expanded the seat northwards to take the remaining districts of Malvern Hills District Council from Leominster. In return, the seat lost one of its wards in Wychavon.

West Worcestershire is a rural constituency on the edge of the Cotswolds. The town of Great Malvern is the major settlement, known for its spring water which is exported across the world.

The river Severn meanders through the constituency, overlooked by the Malvern Hills.

Fruit growing and agriculture are very important to the local economy. The largest town, Great Malvern, is a tourist centre based on its spa town status and connections to Elgar. Transport within the constituency is efficient, enabling Upton-upon-Severn to act as a popular and accessible holiday and boating resort.

Rt Hon **Ed Balls**

Morley and Outwood ***(returning MP)***

New constituency

Tel: 020 7219 4115
E-mail: ballse@parliament.uk
Website: www.edballs.com

Labour/Co-operative

Date of birth: 25 February 1967; Son of Professor Michael and Carolyn Janet Balls

Education: Nottingham High School; Keble College, Oxford (scholarship, BA philosophy, politics and economics 1988); John F Kennedy School of Government, Harvard University (Kennedy scholar MPA 1990); Married Yvette Cooper MP 1998 (2 daughters 1 son)

Non-political career: Teaching fellow Department of Economics, Harvard University 1989-90; Economics leader writer and columnist *Financial Times* 1990-94; Economic adviser to Gordon Brown as Shadow Chancellor of Exchequer 1994-97; Secretary Labour Party Economic Policy Commission 1994-97; Economic adviser to Gordon Brown as Chancellor of Exchequer 1997-99; Chief Economic Adviser HM Treasury 1999-2004; Senior Research Fellow, Smith Institute 2004-05; TGWU; Unison

Political career: Member for Normanton 2005-10, for Morley and Outwood since 6 May 2010 general election; Economic Secretary, HM Treasury 2006-07; Secretary of State for Children, Schools and Families 2007-10; Shadow Secretary of State for Education 2010-

Political interests: Economic, social and international affairs

Other organisations: Chair, Fabian Society 2007-08; PC 2007; Wincott Young Financial Journalist of the Year 1992; *e-politix* Disability Champion 2006; *Publications:* Co-editor Reforming Britain's Economic and Financial Policy (2002); World Bank Development Report (1995); Co-editor Microeconomic Reform in Britain (2004); Co-author Evolution and Devolution in England: how regions strengthen our towns and cities (2006); Britain and Europe: A City Minister's perspective (2007); Contributions to academic journals including Scottish Journal of Political Economy, World Economics and reports by Social Justice Commission and Fabian Society

Recreations: Cooking, playing football with children

Rt Hon Ed Balls MP, House of Commons, London SW1A 0AA
Tel: 020 7219 4115 Fax: 020 7219 3398
E-mail: ballse@parliament.uk
Constituency: 2 Commercial Street, Morley LS27 8HY
Tel: 0113-253 9466 Website: www.edballs.com

GENERAL ELECTION RESULT

		%
Balls, E. (Lab/Co-op)*	18,365	37.6
Calvert, A. (Con)	17,264	35.3
Monaghan, J. (Lib Dem)	8,186	16.8
Beverley, C. (BNP)	3,535	7.2
Daniel, D. (UKIP)	1,506	3.1
Majority	1,101	2.25
Electorate	74,200	
Turnout	48,856	65.84

**Member of last parliament*

CONSTITUENCY SNAPSHOT

The predecessor seat of Morley and Rothwell was itself only created in 1997 as the successor to Morley and Leeds South. Labour's John Gunnell secured a majority of nearly 15,000 in 1997. Ill health forced Gunnell's retirement in 2001. A negligible swing to the Conservatives left his successor Colin Challen with a 12,000 majority.

Despite losing voter share, a slightly increased turnout meant Colin Challen registered a majority of 12,343 in 2005.

Ed Balls moved to this new seat when Normanton was abolished in the boundary review. He faced a strong challenge from the Conservatives but won with a majority of 1,101.

The boundary changes reduced West Yorkshire's representation and this seat is relatively unusual in crossing city boundaries. The Wakefield wards around Outwood that have replaced Rothwell were formerly in Normanton.

This new West Yorkshire seat is made up of the town of Morley and a number of former pit villages either side of the border between the Leeds and Wakefield city council areas.

The area's traditional industries, such as textiles in Morley and mining in Outwood, have all but vanished, but the constituency has made a good recovery, buoyed by a diversified economy and the proximity to the booming city of Leeds.

The constituency is at the crossroads of the M1 and M62 motorways, and employers include engineering and distributive trades, many on industrial estates.

Gordon Banks

Ochil and South Perthshire ***(returning MP)***

No boundary changes

Tel: 020 7219 8275
E-mail: banksgr@parliament.uk
Website: www.gordonbanks.info

Date of birth: 14 June 1955; Son of William and Patricia, née Macknight

Education: Lornshill Academy, Alloa; Glasgow College of Building (City and Guilds construction technology and concrete practice 1976); Stirling University (BA history and politics 2003); Married Lynda Nicol 1981 (1 daughter 1 son)

Non-political career: Chief buyer Barratt Developments 1976-86; Director Cartmore Building Supply Co Ltd 1986-; Parliamentary officer to Dr Richard Simpson MSP 1999-2003; Researcher to Martin O'Neill MP 2003-06; UNITE

Political career: Member for Ochil and South Perthshire since 5 May 2005 general election; PPS to James Purnell: as Minister of State, Department for Work and Pensions 2006-07, as Secretary of State for Culture, Media and Sport 2007-08, as Secretary of State for Work and Pensions 2008-09; *Select Committees:* Member: Northern Ireland Affairs 2005-06, Scottish Affairs 2005-06, Regulatory Reform 2005-10, Unopposed Bills (Panel) 2005-10; Contested Mid Scotland and Fife region 2003 Scottish Parliament election

Political interests: Economy, Europe, environment, international development

Other organisations: Coeliac UK

Recreations: Playing guitar, songwriting, football, motor sport

Gordon Banks MP, House of Commons, London SW1A 0AA
Tel: 020 7219 8275 Fax: 020 7219 8693
E-mail: banksgr@parliament.uk
Constituency: 49-51 High Street, Alloa, Clackmannanshire FK10 1JF
Tel: 01259 214273 Fax: 01259 216761, Penny Lane, Church Street, Crieff, Perthshire PH7 3AE Tel: 01764 654738
Website: www.gordonbanks.info

GENERAL ELECTION RESULT

		%	+/-
Banks, G. (Lab)*	19,131	37.9	6.6
Ewing, A. (SNP)	13,944	27.6	-2.2
Michaluk, G. (Con)	10,342	20.5	-0.9
Littlejohn, G. (Lib Dem)	5,754	11.4	-1.9
Bushby, D. (UKIP)	689	1.4	0.8
Charles, H. (Green)	609	1.2	-0.9
Majority	5,187	10.28	
Electorate	75,115		
Turnout	50,469	67.19	

**Member of last parliament*

CONSTITUENCY SNAPSHOT

In 1939 Labour's Arthur Woodburn won Clackmannan and East Stirlingshire and held it until his retirement in 1970. In that year Dick Douglas held the seat for Labour, but lost in February 1974 to the SNP's George Reid. Martin O'Neill won it back for Labour in 1979 and held it until he retired in 2005.

In 2005 Ochil was enlarged, when its Clackmannanshire and Kinross area was combined with Perth's vast rural hinterland and renamed Ochil and South Perthshire. Annabelle Ewing, who had been MP for Perth, fought the seat for the SNP but lost it by 688 votes to Labour's Gordon Banks. This seat was a key SNP target but Gordon Banks held the seat with a comfortable 5,187.

This largely rural constituency covers the whole of Clackmannanshire council area as well as the southern part of Perthshire.

Hamlets and small villages dot the northern areas while the more populous parts lie in south-east Clackmannanshire, centred on Alloa and Alva. The seat's towns grew up on the wool trade and, in the case of Alva, silver mining.

Tourism and agriculture play a part in the local economy. Beautiful villages such as Auchterarder and Crieff combine with the golfers' paradise at Gleneagles to make this a popular destination.

Rural South Perthshire has a very different social and occupational character from the more urban Ochil area, and accounts for many of the workers employed in agriculture - almost twice the Scottish average.

Steve Barclay

North East Cambridgeshire

Boundary changes

Tel: 020 7219 3000
E-mail: stephen.barclay.mp@parliament.uk
Website: www.stevebarclay.net

Conservative

Date of birth: 1972

Education: King Edward VII School, Lancashire; Royal Military Academy, Sandhurst 1991; Peterhouse College, Cambridge (history 1994); College of Law, Chester (1996); Married Karen

Non-political career: 2nd Lieutenant, Royal Regiment of Fusiliers 1991; Guardian Royal Exchange; Trainee solicitor, Lawrence Graham Solicitors 1996-98; Solicitor, Axa Insurance 1998-2001; Financial Services Authority 2002-06; Special adviser to Liam Fox MP 2005; Director of regulatory affairs, Barclays Bank 2006-

Political career: Contested Manchester Blackley 1997 and Lancaster and Wyre 2001 general elections. Member for North East Cambridgeshire since 6 May 2010 general election; Member, Conservative Party 1994-

Other organisations: Vice-president, March Cricket Club

Recreations: Rugby, playing jazz piano, skydiving

Steve Barclay MP, House of Commons, London SW1A 0AA
Tel: 020 7219 3000 E-mail: stephen.barclay.mp@parliament.uk
Constituency: Cambridgeshire Conservative Association, 111 High Street, March, Cambridgeshire PE15 9LH Tel: 01354 652295
Fax: 01354 660417 Website: www.stevebarclay.net

GENERAL ELECTION RESULT

		%
Barclay, S. (Con)	26,862	51.4
Spenceley, L. (Lib Dem)	10,437	20.0
Roberts, P. (Lab)	9,274	17.7
Talbot, R. (UKIP)	2,991	5.7
Clapp, S. (BNP)	1,747	3.3
Jordan, D. (Ind)	566	1.1
Murphy, G. (England)	387	0.7
Majority	16,425	31.43
Electorate	73,224	
Turnout	52,264	71.38

CONSTITUENCY SNAPSHOT

With the exception of a 14-year Liberal period, the seat has been Conservative in recent history. Malcolm Moss was first elected in 1987. His 1992 majority of 22.6 per cent was more than halved in 1997, but recovered somewhat in 2001.

In 2005 Labour's vote-share fell and Moss's majority increased to 8,901. Moss retired in 2010 and the new Conservative candidate, Stephen Barclay, was elected with a majority of 16,425.

Boundary changes were minor.

The constituency covers a large, flat area known as the Fens, chiefly used for arable farming. Linked to farming is the other major mode of employment for residents of the constituency: haulage. Other major industries include food-processing, warehousing and packing. This is the most rural constituency in the county, and geographically the largest.

One of the largest towns in the constituency, and the only one with a rail link, is March, a pleasant market town popular with tourists, and is bisected by the river Nene. Other market towns include Whittlesey and Chatteris.

Wisbech is Cambridgeshire's only port. It has recently undergone a £1 million renovation, and new facilities include a luxury yacht mooring. This has served to increase tourism in the area, and regenerate a formerly dismal part of the town.

Gregory Barker

Bexhill and Battle (returning MP)

Boundary changes

Tel: 020 7219 1852
E-mail: barkerg@parliament.uk
Website: www.gregorybarker.com

Conservative

Date of birth: 8 March 1966

Education: Steyning Grammar School; Lancing College, West Sussex; Royal Holloway College, London University (BA modern history, economic history, politics 1987); Married Celeste Harrison 1992 (divorced 2008) (1 daughter 2 sons)

Non-political career: Researcher Centre for Policy Studies 1987-89; Equity analyst Gerrard Vivian Gray 1988-90; Director International Pacific Securities 1990-97; Associate partner Brunswick Group Ltd 1997-98; Head investor communications Siberian Oil Company 1998-2000; Director Daric plc (Bartlett Merton) 1998-2001

Political career: Contested Eccles 1997 general election. Member for Bexhill and Battle 2001-10, for Bexhill and Battle (revised boundary) since 6 May 2010 general election; Opposition Whip 2003-05; Shadow Minister for: the Environment 2005-08, Climate Change 2008-10; Minister of State, Department for Energy and Climate Change 2010-; *Select Committees:* Member: Environmental Audit 2001-05, 2007-10, Broadcasting 2003-05; Chair: Shoreham Young Conservatives 1982-83, Holloway Conservative Society 1986-87; Vice-chair: Hammersmith Conservative Association 1993-95, Wandsworth and Tooting Conservative Association 1997-98

Political interests: Environment, education, overseas development; US, Germany, Russia, Australia

Other organisations: Associate Centre for Policy Studies 1988-89; Member British-German Forum; Honourable Artillery Company; Carlton, Bexhill Conservative Club; Bexhill Rowing Club, Aldeburgh Yacht Club

Recreations: Skiing, hunting, horse racing

Gregory Barker MP, House of Commons, London SW1A 0AA
Tel: 020 7219 1852 Fax: 020 7219 1971
E-mail: barkerg@parliament.uk
Constituency: 6a Amherst Road, Bexhill-on-Sea, East Sussex TN40 1QJ
Tel: 01424 736861 Fax: 01424 734910
Website: www.gregorybarker.com

GENERAL ELECTION RESULT

		%
Barker, G. (Con)*	28,147	51.6
Varrall, M. (Lib Dem)	15,267	28.0
Royston, J. (Lab)	6,524	12.0
Wheeler, S. (Trust)	2,699	4.9
Jackson, N. (BNP)	1,950	3.6
Majority	12,880	23.60
Electorate	79,208	
Turnout	54,587	68.92

**Member of last parliament*

CONSTITUENCY SNAPSHOT

The constituency has never seemed likely to slip from Conservative hands since its creation in 1983. When Charles Wardle retired in 2001 the Conservative Association selected Gregory Barker as their candidate. Barker was elected with a 10,503 majority in 2001, and went on to increase it to 13,449 in 2005.

In 2010 the seat was held by Barker with a 12,880 majority.

Boundary changes moved Brede Valley to Hastings and Rye, in exchange for Rother Levels part-ward; the seat also gained two full wards a part-ward from Wealden.

The seaside resort of Bexhill-on-Sea and smaller town of Battle give their names to this semi-rural seat. It was here that the Norman conquest of England began, and the area is rich in significant sites, including Battle Abbey and castles such as Bodiam, Herstmonceaux, and Pevensey. More than a quarter of Bexhill and Battle's population is over 65.

The constituency's geography is undulating, and takes in both coastline and areas of the wooded Weald of Sussex. Farming is a significant industry, while the High Weald, rolling countryside with its many historical sites, and Bexhill's stretches of coastline help to provide employment in the tourist industry.

An insurance call-centre is the biggest single employer, but most work is to be found in the retail trade and various small businesses.

Northern
Gas Networks

John Baron

Basildon and Billericay ***(returning MP)***

New constituency

Tel: 020 7219 8138
E-mail: baronj@parliament.uk
Website: www.johnbaronmp.org

Conservative

Date of birth: 21 June 1959; Son of Raymond Arthur Ernest Baron and Kathleen Ruby, née Whittlestone

Education: Birmingham Grammar School; Wadham Comprehensive, Crewkerne; Queen's College, Taunton, Somerset; Jesus College, Cambridge (BA history and economics 1982); Royal Military College Sandhurst 1984; Married Thalia Anne Mayson, née Laird, 1992 (2 daughters)

Non-political career: Captain Royal Regiment of Fusiliers 1984-87; Director: Henderson Private Investors Ltd 1987-99, Rothschild Asset Management 1999-2001

Political career: Contested Basildon 1997 general election. Member for Billericay 2001-10, for Basildon and Billericay since 6 May 2010 general election; Shadow Minister for: Health 2002-03 (resigned over Iraq War), Health 2003-07; Opposition Whip 2007-10; *Select Committees:* Member: Education and Skills 2001-02

Political interests: Foreign affairs, economy, civil liberties, defence

Other organisations: Member, Securities Institute (MSI)

Recreations: Tennis, walking, history, cycling

John Baron MP, House of Commons, London SW1A 0AA
Tel: 020 7219 8138 Fax: 020 7219 1743
E-mail: baronj@parliament.uk
Constituency: 125 Bramble Tye, Noak Bridge, Basildon, Essex SS15 5GR Tel: 01268 520765 Fax: 01268 524009
Website: www.johnbaronmp.org

GENERAL ELECTION RESULT

		%
Baron, J. (Con)*	21,982	52.8
Davies, A. (Lab)	9,584	23.0
Hibbs, M. (Lib Dem)	6,538	15.7
Bateman, I. (BNP)	1,934	4.7
Broad, A. (UKIP)	1,591	3.8
Majority	12,398	29.78
Electorate	65,482	
Turnout	41,629	63.57

**Member of last parliament*

CONSTITUENCY SNAPSHOT

Formed from parts of the previously separate Basildon and Billericay seats in Essex, this is very much a constituency of two halves, covering the majority of Billericay in the north and Basildon in the south.

Basildon was been a constituency that has reflected the political colour of the Government of the day. Labour's Angela Evans Smith was first elected in 1997 with a majority of 13,280 but it reduced to 3,142 in 2005.

However, most of the new seat is made up of wards from Billericay, which has been represented by the Conservatives since its creation in 1983. In 1997 the Conservative majority of 20,494 was reduced to 1,356. The Conservative vote has since recovered and John Baron (MP since 2001) was re-elected in 2005 with a 11,206 majority.

John Baron was elected to the new seat with a majority of 12,398.

Basildon was designated as a new town in 1949 and grew rapidly with a great deal of investment. It is the commercial centre of south Essex and home to a variety of industries, including engineering, avionics, automotive, distribution and electronics. Ford's Dunton Technical Centre is the largest automotive design and engineering facility in the UK.

Basildon is part of the Thames Gateway regeneration initiative and many areas of the town are scheduled for business and residential regeneration projects.

Rt Hon **Kevin Barron**

Rother Valley (returning MP)

Boundary changes

Tel: 020 7219 4432
E-mail: barronk@parliament.uk
Website: www.kevinbarronmp.com

Date of birth: 26 October 1946; Son of late Richard Barron and Edna Barron

Education: Maltby Hall Secondary Modern, nr. Rotherham; Sheffield University (day release, social sciences); Ruskin College, Oxford (Diploma labour studies 1977); Married Carol McGrath 1969 (died 2008) (1 son 2 daughters)

Non-political career: Colliery electrician and NUM trade union delegate, Maltby 1962-83; AMICUS

Political career: Member for Rother Valley 1983-2010, for Rother Valley (revised boundary) since 6 May 2010 general election; PPS to Neil Kinnock as Leader of the Opposition 1985-88; Sponsor private member's bills: to ban advertising and promotion of tobacco products 1993, 94, Energy efficiency stamp duty rebate; Opposition Spokesperson for: Energy 1988-92, Employment 1993-95, Health 1995-97; Member Intelligence and Security Committee 1997-2005; *Select Committees:* Chair: Health 2005-10; Member: Standards and Privileges 2005-10, Liaison 2005-10

Political interests: Energy, environment, home affairs, health, intelligence and security, international development, British film; Bulgaria, Guyana, Tanzania

Other organisations: Trustee National Coal Mining Museum 2005; Patron Safe@last (charity for runaway children and young people) 2008-; PC 2001; FRCP 2008

Recreations: Family life, football, fly fishing, photography, walking, film

Rt Hon Kevin Barron MP, House of Commons, London SW1A 0AA
Tel: 020 7219 4432; 020 7219 6306 Fax: 020 7219 5952
E-mail: barronk@parliament.uk
Constituency: 9 Lordens Hill, Dinnington, Sheffield,
South Yorkshire S25 2QE Tel: 01909 568611 Fax: 01909 569974
Website: www.kevinbarronmp.com

GENERAL ELECTION RESULT

		%
Barron, K. (Lab)*	19,147	40.9
Donaldson, L. (Con)	13,281	28.4
Paxton, W. (Lib Dem)	8,111	17.3
Blair, W. (BNP)	3,616	7.7
Dowdall, T. (UKIP)	2,613	5.6
Majority	5,866	12.54
Electorate	72,841	
Turnout	46,768	64.21

**Member of last parliament*

CONSTITUENCY SNAPSHOT

The old seat which surrounded the town of Rotherham used to produce sizable majorities for Labour. Of its five MPs since 1918, four have been miners; the exception was Peter Hardy, who served 13 years before moving to Wentworth in 1983.

Kevin Barron became MP in 1983 and by 1997 his majority had reached more than 23,000. Labour support fell in 2001 and again in 2005, nevertheless, Barron was returned with a 14,224 majority.

Barron was re-elected with a much-reduced majority of 5,866 at the 2010 general election.

Boundary changes moved the wards of Hellaby and Sitwell into the seat having previously been shared with Wentworth and Rotherham respectively. Brinsworth and Catcliffe is now completely within Rotherham's boundaries.

This is a semi-rural constituency to the south and east of Rotherham down to the southern tip of South Yorkshire.

Its main towns are the former mining towns Maltby and Dinnington. There are numerous other smaller villages including Thurcroft.

The constituency used to be heavily dependent on its mines. It still has one of the few remaining large pits, at Maltby. The area's other main industry was steel.

New industry includes warehousing, engineering and light industry. LuK make motor clutches at Kiveton Park. The area is helped by being at the M1/M18 junction.

Gavin Barwell

Croydon Central

Boundary changes

Tel: 020 7219 3000
E-mail: gavin.barwell.mp@parliament.uk
Website: www.gavin4croydon.com

Conservative

Education: Trinity School, Croydon; Cambridge University (natural sciences); Married Karen (3 sons)

Non-political career: Conservative Party: Researcher, Special adviser to John Gummer as Secretary of State for the Environment 1997; Chief operating officer, Conservative Party 2003-06; Self-employed consultant; Councillor, Croydon Council 1998-; Chair of governors, Trinity School

Political career: Member for Croydon Central since 6 May 2010 general election

Political interests: NHS, crime

Recreations: Sport, travel

Gavin Barwell MP, House of Commons, London SW1A 0AA
Tel: 020 7219 3000 E-mail: gavin.barwell.mp@parliament.uk
Constituency: 36 Brighton Road, Purley CR8 2LG Tel: 020 8660 0491
Website: www.gavin4croydon.com

GENERAL ELECTION RESULT

		%
Barwell, G. (Con)	19,657	39.5
Ryan, G. (Lab/Co-op)	16,688	33.5
Lambell, P. (Lib Dem)	6,553	13.2
Pelling, A. (Ind)*	3,239	6.5
Le May, C. (BNP)	1,448	2.9
Atkinson, R. (UKIP)	997	2.0
Golberg, B. (Green)	581	1.2
Gitau, J. (Christian)	264	0.5
Cartwright, J. (Loony)	192	0.4
Castle, M. (Ind)	138	0.3
Majority	2,969	5.97
Electorate	78,880	
Turnout	49,757	63.08

**Member of last parliament*

CONSTITUENCY SNAPSHOT

Croydon Central was expanded considerably in 1997 when Geraint Davies won the seat from the Tories with a 3,879 majority. He held on in 2001 but lost to Andrew Pelling in 2005. The Tory whip was withdrawn in 2007 and Pelling sat as an independent. Gavin Barwell gained this seat for the Conservatives on a 3.3 per cent swing from Labour, with a majority of 2,969.

The seat lost two part-wards to both Croydon North and Croydon South.

The seat contains the retail centre and is a popular location for shops and offices outside central London.

The Croydon Gateway development, also known as Ruskin Square, will be situated between East Croydon station and Croydon town centre. Forming part of Croydon Council's regeneration project Vision 2020, the area will include apartments, landscaped open space, office space, cafes, restaurants and a new theatre.

The Border and Immigration Agency employs a large number of people at its Croydon Central headquarters.

Good transport links will be improved when an extension of the Croydon Tramlink from Harrington Road to Anerley and Crystal Palace is opened in 2013.

Hugh Bayley

York Central (returning MP)

New constituency

Tel: 020 7219 6824
E-mail: bayleyh@parliament.uk
Website: www.hughbayley.labour.co.uk

Date of birth: 9 January 1952; Son of Michael Bayley, architect, and Pauline Bayley

Education: Haileybury School; Bristol University (BSc politics 1974); York University (BPhil Southern African studies 1976); Married Fenella Jeffers 1984 (1 son 1 daughter)

Non-political career: District officer, then National officer NALGO 1975-82; General secretary, International Broadcasting Trust 1982-86; York University 1986-92: Lecturer in social policy 1986-97, Research fellow in health economics 1987-92; TGWU 1975-82, BECTU 1982-, RMT 1992-2002; Councillor London Borough of Camden 1980-86; York Health Authority 1988-90; Chair Westminster Foundation for Democracy 2005-09

Political career: Contested York 1987 general election. Member for York 1992-97, for City of York 1997-2010, for York Central since 6 May 2010 general election; PPS to Frank Dobson as Secretary of State for Health 1997-99; Parliamentary Under-Secretary of State, Department of Social Security 1999-2001; *Select Committees:* Member: Health 1992-97, International Development 2001-10, Chairmen's Panel 2005-10

Political interests: Health, economic policy, environment, international development, defence, electoral reform; Africa

Other organisations: Member, Executive Committee: Inter-Parliamentary Union (IPU) UK Branch 1997-99 and 2001-, Commonwealth Parliamentary Association (CPA) UK Branch 1997-99, 2001- (Chair 2006-08); Member UK Delegation to: North Atlantic Assembly 1997-99, NATO Parliamentary Assembly 2001-, Parliamentary Assembly of the Organisation for Security and Co-operation in Europe 2001-07; Chair: Economics and Security Committee 2008-, Parliamentary Network on the World Bank 2008-; *Publications:* The Nation's Health (1995)

Hugh Bayley MP, House of Commons, London SW1A 0AA
Tel: 020 7219 6824 Fax: 020 7219 0346; 020 7219 4293
E-mail: bayleyh@parliament.uk
Constituency: 59 Holgate Road, York YO24 4AA Tel: 01904 623713
Fax: 01904 623260 Website: www.hughbayley.labour.co.uk

GENERAL ELECTION RESULT

		%
Bayley, H. (Lab)*	18,573	40.0
Wade Weeks, S. (Con)	12,122	26.1
Vassie, C. (Lib Dem)	11,694	25.2
Chase, A. (Green)	1,669	3.6
Kelly, J. (BNP)	1,171	2.5
Abbott, P. (UKIP)	1,100	2.4
Vee, E. (Loony)	154	0.3
Majority	6,451	13.88
Electorate	74,908	
Turnout	46,483	62.05

**Member of last parliament*

CONSTITUENCY SNAPSHOT

York was a Conservative seat for most of the first half of the 20th century with Labour tending to win the seat only for brief periods in landslide years.

In 1992 York fell to Labour's Hugh Bayley with a swing of 5 per cent. It was the only Yorkshire seat to change hands that year.

In 1997 Bayley achieved a swing of 12.6 per cent to win with a majority of 20,523. Swings away from Labour in 2001 and 2005 reduced this to 10,472. Bayley won the new seat of York Central with a majority of 6,451 at the 2010 general election.

The new York Central seat is essentially the same as City of York but without two part-wards that are now in York Outer.York manages to amalgamate the ancient and the modern effortlessly. Its incomparable Minster, city walls, quaint streets and world-class museums attract millions of visitors every year.

The traditional industry of confectionery continues in the city. Financial services provide a number of jobs in the city centre. Additionally, York's economy benefits from one of the most highly regarded racecourses in the country, with the Ebor festival in August the highlight. The racecourse is in Micklegate, on the border with York Outer.

Guto Bebb

Aberconwy

New constituency

Tel: 020 7219 3000
E-mail: guto.bebb.mp@parliament.uk

Conservative

Date of birth: 9 October 1968

Education: Ysgol Syr Hugh Owen, Caernarfon; Aberystwyth University (BA history 1990); MIBA 1995; Married Esyllt Penri 1993 (3 sons 2 daughters)

Non-political career: Partner Egin Partnership 1993-

Political career: Contested Ogmore 2002 by-election and Conwy 2005 general election. Member for Aberconwy since 6 May 2010 general election; Contested Conwy constituency 2003 National Assembly for Wales election

Political interests: Europe, taxation, reform of the welfare state, devolution, economy, rural development, regeneration policy; *Publications:* Various in Welsh language

Recreations: Wine, reading, music and family

Guto Bebb MP, House of Commons, London SW1A 0AA
Tel: 020 7219 3000 E-mail: guto.bebb.mp@parliament.uk
Constituency: Aberconwy Conservatives, 12 Ashdown House, Riverside Business Park, Benarth Road, Conwy, Gwynedd LL32 8UB
Tel: 01492 583743 Website: www.aberconwyconservatives.co.uk

GENERAL ELECTION RESULT

		%
Bebb, G. (Con)	10,734	35.8
Hughes, R. (Lab)	7,336	24.5
Priestley, M. (Lib Dem)	5,786	19.3
Edwards, P. (PIC)	5,341	17.8
Wieteska, M. (UKIP)	632	2.1
Wynne Jones, L. (Christian)	137	0.5
Majority	3,398	11.34
Electorate	44,593	
Turnout	29,966	67.20

CONSTITUENCY SNAPSHOT

Sir Wyn Roberts held the old Conwy seat for the Conservatives for 27 years until 1997 when the constituency was lost to Labour. Betty Williams won with a majority of 1,596, which she increased to over 6,000 in 2001.

The partial Tory recovery in Wales halved Betty Williams' lead in the 2005 general election to 3,081. In 2010 the seat gave Conservative Guto Bebb a 3,398 majority on a 7.6 per cent notional swing.

This is a new constituency. Centred on Llandudno and Conwy town, the seat is based on the old Conwy constituency, but without Bangor, which is now within Arfon's boundaries. In addition, Aberconwy has gained the Conwy County wards of the old Meirionnydd Nant Conwy seat.

The economy is largely dependent on tourism. The main resort in the area is Llandudno.

Conwy castle, constructed in the 1280s by Edward I, dominates its town.

Access to the constituency has improved dramatically following the opening of the A55 expressway across North Wales. This key transport artery has helped open up North Wales to the UK road network as a whole and give a boost to the economy in the medium term. The District General Hospital, Ysbyty Gwynedd, Bangor is in the nearby Arfon Constituency while Bryn-y-Neuadd Hospital at Llanfairfechan and Llandudno General Hospital are based in the constituency.

Rt Hon **Margaret Beckett**

Derby South (returning MP)

Boundary changes

Tel: 020 7219 6662
E-mail: beckettm@parliament.uk

Date of birth: 15 January 1943; Daughter of late Cyril Jackson, carpenter, and Winifred Jackson, teacher

Education: Notre Dame High School, Manchester and Norwich; Manchester College of Science and Technology; John Dalton Polytechnic; Married Lionel Arthur Beckett 1979 (2 stepsons)

Non-political career: Student apprentice in metallurgy AEI Manchester 1961-66; Experimental officer Department of Metallurgy, Manchester University 1966-70; Industrial policy researcher, Labour Party 1970-74; Political adviser Ministry of Overseas Development 1974; Principal researcher, Granada Television 1979-83; Member: TGWU 1964-, NUJ, BECTU

Political career: Contested Lincoln February 1974 general election. Member for Lincoln October 1974-79, for Derby South 1983-2010, for Derby South (revised boundary) since 6 May 2010 general election; PPS to Judith Hart as Minister of Overseas Development 1974-75; Assistant Government Whip 1975-76; Parliamentary Under-Secretary of State, Department of Education and Science 1976-79; Shadow: Minister, Social Security 1984-89, Chief Secretary to the Treasury 1989-92, Leader, House of Commons 1992-94; Deputy Leader, Labour Party and Opposition 1992-94; Leader of Opposition May-July 1994; Shadow: Secretary of State for Health 1994-95, President of the Board of Trade 1995-98; Secretary of State for Trade and Industry 1997-98; President of the Council and Leader of the House of Commons 1998-2001; Secretary of State for: Environment, Food and Rural Affairs 2001-06, Foreign and Commonwealth Affairs (Foreign Secretary) 2006-07; Minister for Housing and Planning (attending Cabinet), Department for Communities and Local Government 2008-09; Chair Intelligence and Security Committee 2008-; *Select Committees:* Chair: Modernisation of the House of Commons 1998-2001, Joint Committee on National Security Strategy 2010; Secretary, Trades Council and Labour Party Swinton and Pendlebury 1968-70; Member: Labour Party National Executive Committee 1980-81, 1985-86, 1988-97, Fabian Society, Tribune Group, Socialist Education Committee, Labour Women's Action Committee, Socialist Environment and Resources Association

Political interests: Industry

Other organisations: Member: Amnesty International, Anti-Apartheid Movement; PC 1993; *Publications:* The Need For Consumer Protection (1972); The National Enterprise Board; The Nationalisation of Shipbuilding, Ship Repair and Marine Engineering; Renewing the NHS (1995); Vision for Growth – A New Industrial Strategy for Britain (1996)

Recreations: Cooking, reading, caravanning

Rt Hon Margaret Beckett MP, House of Commons, London SW1A 0AA Tel: 020 7219 6662 Fax: 020 7219 4780
E-mail: beckettm@parliament.uk
Constituency: Tel: 01332 345636 Fax: 01332 371306

GENERAL ELECTION RESULT

		%
Beckett, M. (Lab)*	17,851	43.3
Perschke, J. (Con)	11,729	28.5
Batey, D. (Lib Dem)	8,430	20.5
Fowke, S. (UKIP)	1,821	4.4
Graves, A. (Ind)	1,357	3.3
Majority	6,122	14.86
Electorate	71,012	
Turnout	41,188	58.00

**Member of last parliament*

CONSTITUENCY SNAPSHOT

The seat has a history of long-serving Labour MPs. Twenty years under peace campaigner Philip Noel-Baker (1950 to 1970) were followed by 13 (1970 to 1983) by Walter Johnson. This perhaps belies the sometimes precarious hold Labour has maintained over the seat, however, as Margaret Beckett first won the seat in 1983 with a majority of just 421.

That margin had grown to 13,855 by 2001. However, Beckett's majority was more than halved in 2005, leaving her with only a 5,657 majority.

Beckett held the seat with a 6,122 majority at the 2010 general election.

The seat gained Chellaston ward and a part-ward from South Derbyshire as well as another part-ward from Derby North. Littleover ward was lost to Derby North in addition to four other wards that were previously shared between the two divisions.

Derby South encompasses the working-class heart of Derby. The majority of residents work in the engineering giants who base themselves in this seat.

Many residents work in the several engineering giants which call Derby home, from the Rolls-Royce aerospace factory to the famous railway plant.

The seat is one of the most ethnically diverse in the East Midlands, with large Indian and Pakistani communities in Derby's southern suburbs and significant numbers arriving from Eastern Europe.

Anne Begg

Aberdeen South ***(returning MP)***

No boundary changes

Tel: 020 7219 2140
E-mail: begga@parliament.uk
Website: www.annebegg.info/about.htm

Labour

Date of birth: 6 December 1955; Daughter of late David Begg, MBE, orthotist, and of Margaret Catherine Begg, nurse

Education: Brechin High School; Aberdeen University (MA history and politics 1977); Aberdeen College of Education (Secondary Teaching Certificate 1978); Single

Non-political career: English and history teacher Webster's High School, Kirriemuir 1978-88; English teacher Arbroath Academy 1988-97; Member: Educational Institute of Scotland 1978-, EIS National Council 1990-95, GMB 2004-

Political career: Member for Aberdeen South 1997-2005, for Aberdeen South (revised boundary) since 5 May 2005 general election; *Select Committees:* Member: Scottish Affairs 1997-2001, Work and Pensions 2001-10, Chairmen's Panel 2002-10; Member, Labour Party National Executive Committee 1998-99; Vice-chair, Labour Party National Policy Forum 2006-

Political interests: Disability, broadcasting, welfare reform, social inclusion, genetics, pensions

Other organisations: Patron: Scottish Motor Neuron Society, Angus Special Playscheme, National Federation of Shopmobility, Access to Training and Employment; President Blue Badge Network; Fellow Industry and Parliament Trust 2000; Disabled Scot of the Year 1988

Recreations: Reading, cinema, theatre, public speaking

Anne Begg MP, House of Commons, London SW1A 0AA
Tel: 020 7219 2140 Fax: 020 7219 1264
E-mail: begga@parliament.uk
Constituency: Admiral Court, Poynernook Road, Aberdeen AB11 5QX
Tel: 01224 252704 Fax: 01224 252705
Website: www.annebegg.info/about.htm

GENERAL ELECTION RESULT

		%	+/-
Begg, A. (Lab)*	15,722	36.5	-0.1
Sleigh, J. (Lib Dem)	12,216	28.4	-5.0
Harvie, A. (Con)	8,914	20.7	3.6
McDonald, M. (SNP)	5,102	11.9	2.0
Ross, S. (BNP)	529	1.2	
Reekie, R. (Green)	413	1.0	-0.9
Green, R. (SACL)	138	0.3	
Majority	3,506	8.15	
Electorate	64,031		
Turnout	43,034	67.21	

**Member of last parliament*

CONSTITUENCY SNAPSHOT

Conservative Iain Sproat won Aberdeen South from Donald Dewar in 1970 and held it until boundary changes in 1983 when he stood instead in Roxburgh and Berwickshire. Gerald Malone retained the seat for the Tories. In 1987 the constituency was won by Labour's Frank Doran, who in turn lost it to Conservative Raymond Robertson in 1992.

In 1997, the boundary changes and increased Labour support pushed Robertson into third place behind the Liberal Democrats, as Anne Begg gained the seat for Labour. She increased her vote share in 2001.

Gilcomston, Langstane and Queen's Cross were added from Aberdeen Central for the 2005 election. Labour still had a notional majority of almost 4,000 over the Liberal Democrats. Anne Begg returned with a reduced majority of 1,348. Begg increased Labour's vote following a close election in 2010, returning to Parliament with a 3,506 majority.

Aberdeen South is more prosperous than the northern division, enjoying a higher rate of home ownership and a lower proportion of council tenants. Much of the seat's prosperity is a result of the oil industry.

The old fish processing industry in Torry has declined but this former fishing Royal burgh, now a suburb of the city, is home to a world-renowned food-science and technology research centre.

Rt Hon Sir **Alan Beith**

Berwick-upon-Tweed (returning MP)

Boundary changes

Tel: 020 7219 3540
E-mail: cheesemang@parliament.uk
Website: www.alanbeith.org.uk

Date of birth: 20 April 1943; Son of late James Beith, foreman packer, and Joan Beith

Education: King's School, Macclesfield; Balliol College, Oxford (BA philosophy, politics and economics 1964); Nuffield College, Oxford (BLitt, MA 1966); Married Barbara Jean Ward 1965 (died 1998) (1 son deceased 1 daughter); married Baroness Maddock 2001

Non-political career: Politics lecturer, Newcastle University 1966-73; Association of University Teachers; Councillor: Hexham RDC 1969-74, Tynedale DC 1974-75

Political career: Contested Berwick-upon-Tweed 1970 general election. Member for Berwick-upon-Tweed 8 November 1973 by-election to 2010, for Berwick-upon-Tweed (revised boundary) since 6 May 2010 general election; Chief Whip, Liberal Party 1976-87; Member House of Commons Commission 1979-97; Liberal Spokesperson for Foreign Affairs 1985-87; Alliance Spokesperson for Foreign Affairs 1987; Liberal Spokesperson for Treasury 1987; SLD Spokesperson for Treasury 1988-89; Liberal Democrat: Treasury Spokesperson 1989-94, Home Affairs Spokesperson 1994-95; Member, Intelligence and Security Committee 1994-2008; Liberal Democrat Spokesperson for: Police, Prison and Security Matters 1995-97, Home and Legal Affairs (Home Affairs) 1997-99, Cabinet Office 2001-02; Member: Speaker's Committee on the Electoral Commission 2001-; Deputy chairman Review Committee of Privy Counsellors of the Anti-terrorism, Crime and Security Act 2002-04; *Select Committees:* Member: Procedure 2000-01, Liaison 2003-10; Chair: Constitutional Affairs/Justice 2003-10; Member: Liaison (Liaison Sub-Committee) 2006-10, Joint Committee on National Security Strategy 2010; Deputy Leader: Liberal Party 1985-88, Liberal Democrat Party 1992-2003

Political interests: Parliamentary and constitutional affairs, architectural and artistic heritage; Canada, Scandinavia, Zimbabwe

Other organisations: Local preacher Methodist Church 1965-; President North of England Civic Trust 2005-; Vice-President Northumberland and Newcastle Society 2009-; Chair Historic Chapels Trust; Trustee, Historic Chapels Trust, 1995-: Chair 2002-; PC 1992; Kt 2008; Hon. DCL, Newcastle University 1998; National Liberal; Athenaeum; *Publications:* Co-author Case for Liberal Party and Alliance (1983); Faith and Politics (1987); A View From the North (2008)

Recreations: Music, walking, boating

Rt Hon Sir Alan Beith MP, House of Commons, London SW1A 0AA
Tel: 020 7219 3540 Fax: 020 7219 5890
E-mail: cheesemang@parliament.uk
Constituency: 54 Bondgate Within, Alnwick,
Northumberland NE66 1JD Tel: 01665 602901 Fax: 01665 605702
Website: www.alanbeith.org.uk

GENERAL ELECTION RESULT

		%
Beith, A. (Lib Dem)*	16,806	43.7
Trevelyan, A. (Con)	14,116	36.7
Strickland, A. (Lab)	5,061	13.2
Weatheritt, M. (UKIP)	1,243	3.2
Mailer, P. (BNP)	1,213	3.2
Majority	2,690	7.00
Electorate	57,403	
Turnout	38,439	66.96

**Member of last parliament*

CONSTITUENCY SNAPSHOT

The last, brief, Liberal MP before the current incumbent was Sir William Beveridge, creator of the Welfare State, who took it at an uncontested wartime by-election in 1944, only to lose it to the Conservatives a year later.

The Conservatives held Berwick-upon-Tweed for the next 28 years, and the MP from 1951 to 1973 was Lord Lambton, who resigned from his seat.

The resulting by-election was very closely contested, with the Liberals' Alan Beith winning by 57 votes. He has built up his majority over subsequent elections and was re-elected in 2005 with a 8,632 majority. Alan Beith's majority was much-reduced to 2,690 following a 8.3 per cent swing to the Tories.

Boundary changes were minimal, with Hartburn ward moving entirely within the constituency, having previously been shared with Hexham.

Predominantly agricultural with fishing and tourist industries, the constituency stretches south of the border down the Northumbrian coast, encompassing the county town of Alnwick, as well as sea-ports, and former mining communities. The area is now heavily promoted as the 'Secret Kingdom' of Northumbria.

Most of the population live on or near the coast, from Berwick itself, the largest town, to Alnwick, and its seaport Alnmouth, down to the fishing town of Amble and part of the old Northumberland coalfield near Morpeth.

Sir **Stuart Bell**

Middlesbrough (returning MP)

Boundary changes

Labour

Tel: 020 7219 3577
Website: www.stuartbellmp.org

Date of birth: 16 May 1938; Son of late Ernest Bell, pitman, and late Margaret Rose Bell

Education: Hookergate Grammar School, Co Durham; Pitman's College, London; Council of Legal Education, Gray's Inn 1970; Married Margaret Bruce 1960 (1 son 1 daughter); married Margaret Allan 1980 (1 son)

Non-political career: Barrister, called to the Bar, Gray's Inn 1970; Previously: colliery clerk, newspaper reporter, typist novelist; Conseil Juridique and International Lawyer Paris 1970-77; Member, General Municipal Boilermakers and Allied Trades Union; Councillor, Newcastle City Council 1980-83

Political career: Contested Hexham 1979 general election. Member for Middlesbrough 1983-2010, for Middlesborough (revised boundary) since 6 May 2010 general election; PPS to Roy Hattersley as Deputy Leader of Opposition 1983-84; Second Church Estates Commissioner 1997-; Opposition Frontbench Spokesperson for: Northern Ireland 1984-87, Trade and Industry 1992-97; Member: House of Commons Commission 2000-, Speaker's Committee for the Independent Parliamentary Standards Authority 2009-; *Select Committees:* Member Liaison 2000-01; Chair Finance and Services 2000-05; Member: Liaison 2002-10, Finance and Services 2005-08; Chair Finance and Services 2008-10; Member Ecclesiastical Committee; Member: Fabian Society, Society of Labour Lawyers

Political interests: Economic policy, European Union

Other organisations: Founder member British Irish Inter-Parliamentary Body 1990; Vice-chair British Group, Inter-Parliamentary Union 1992-95; Kt 2004; Chevalier dé la Légion d'Honneur 2006; Freeman, City of London; Beefsteak; *Publications:* Paris 69 (1973); Days That Used to Be (1975); When Salem Came to the Boro (1988); The Children Act 1989 (annotated) (1989); Raising the Standard: The Case for First Past the Post (1998); Where Jenkins Went Wrong: A Further Case for First Past the Post (1999); Tony Really Loves Me (2000); Pathway to the Euro (2002); Binkie's Revolution (2002); The Honoured Society (2003); Lara's Theme (2004); Softly in the Dusk (2004); The Ice Cream Man And Other Stories (2007); The Forward March – An Ever Closer Union (2007)

Recreations: Writing short stories and novels

Sir Stuart Bell MP, House of Commons, London SW1A 0AA
Tel: 020 7219 3577 Fax: 020 7219 4873
Constituency: No constituency office publicised Tel: 01642 851252
Fax: 01642 856170 E-mail: contact@stuartbellmp.org
Website: www.stuartbellmp.org

GENERAL ELECTION RESULT

		%
Bell, S. (Lab)*	15,351	45.9
Foote-Wood, C. (Lib Dem)	6,662	19.9
Walsh, J. (Con)	6,283	18.8
McTigue, J. (Ind)	1,969	5.9
Ferguson, M. (BNP)	1,954	5.8
Parker, R. (UKIP)	1,236	3.7
Majority	8,689	25.97
Electorate	65,148	
Turnout	33,455	51.35

**Member of last parliament*

CONSTITUENCY SNAPSHOT

Labour has held Middlesbrough since 1935, their vote-share never falling below 50 per cent. Stuart Bell won the seat with a majority of over 25,000 in 1997. However, turnout fell by 9 per cent in 1997 and a further 15 per cent in 2001. Nevertheless Bell's majority was still a huge 48 per cent in 2001.

In 2005 the Liberal Democrats made the largest gains of the election, gaining almost 2,500 votes and pushing the Conservatives into third place. Stuart Bell maintained his grip on the seat with a majority of 12,567. Stuart Bell was re-elected with a 8,689 majority in 2010.

At the election, boundary changes will see part-ward Park End move to Middlesbrough South and East Cleveland whilst Beechwood, Brookfield and Kader wards become fully incorporated within this seat.

The great boom industries of steel and chemicals have both declined sharply, and there has been less work for the unskilled and semi-skilled manual workers who make up a sizeable third of the work-force.

Many people do still work in steel and petrochemicals, but now the majority of jobs are in services, in small businesses and the retail sector. Most of the jobs are now in the town centre, and the biggest private employer is HBS. Teesside University is another major employer.

Henry Bellingham

North West Norfolk (returning MP)

Boundary changes

Tel: 020 7219 8234
E-mail: bellinghamh@parliament.uk
Website: www.epolitix.com/EN/MPWebsites/Henry+Bellingham

Conservative

Date of birth: 29 March 1955

Education: Eton College; Magdalene College, Cambridge (BA law 1978); Married Emma Whiteley 1993 (1 son)

Non-political career: Barrister, Middle Temple 1978-84; Company director and business consultant 1997-2001

Political career: Member for Norfolk North West 1983-97. Contested Norfolk North West 1997 general election. Member for North West Norfolk 2001-10, for North West Norfolk (revised boundary) since 6 May 2010 general election; PPS to Malcolm Rifkind as Secretary of State for Transport and for Defence and as Foreign Secretary 1991-97; Shadow Minister for: Trade and Industry 2002-03, Economic Affairs 2003-05; Opposition Whip 2005-06; Shadow Minister for Constitutional Affairs/Justice 2006-10; Parliamentary Under-Secretary of State, Foreign and Commonwealth Office 2010-; Chairman Conservative Council on Eastern Europe 1989-93

Political interests: Small businesses, agriculture, defence, Northern Ireland, tourism; Far East, Eastern Europe

Other organisations: President British Resorts Association 1993-97; Trustee, Russian-European Trust 1994-

Recreations: Country sports, golf, cricket

Henry Bellingham MP, House of Commons, London SW1A 0AA
Tel: 020 7219 8234 Fax: 020 7219 2844
E-mail: bellinghamh@parliament.uk
Constituency: North West Norfolk Conservative Association, Greyfriars Chambers, Tower Street, King's Lynn, Norfolk PE30 5DJ
Tel: 01485 600559 Fax: 01485 600292 Website: www.epolitix.com/EN/MPWebsites/Henry+Bellingham

GENERAL ELECTION RESULT

		%
Bellingham, H. (Con)*	25,916	54.2
Summers, W. (Lib Dem)	11,106	23.2
Sood, M. (Lab)	6,353	13.3
Gray, J. (UKIP)	1,841	3.9
Fleming, D. (BNP)	1,839	3.9
de Whalley, M. (Green)	745	1.6
Majority	14,810	30.98
Electorate	73,207	
Turnout	47,800	65.29

**Member of last parliament*

CONSTITUENCY SNAPSHOT

There has been a history of Labour support in the area dating back to 1945, and Labour remained in the seat until 1970, when Christopher Brocklebank-Fowler took over the King's Lynn division for the Tories. In 1983 he became the only MP to defect from the Conservatives to the Social Democrats. His Conservative replacement, Henry Bellingham, won the seat with a majority of 3,147.

Bellingham lost the seat in 1997 to Labour's George Turner. However, Bellingham returned as MP in 2001 with a 3,485 majority. In 2005 he consolidated his majority to 9,180. The Conservatives increased their majority to 14,810 at the 2010 general election.

The seat lost four of its rural wards to South West Norfolk.

The port town of King's Lynn serves as the economic hub of North West Norfolk. Hunstanton and Castle Rising bring in income with their tourist and wildlife attractions, as is the Queen's residence at Sandringham.

Arable farming forms the basis of the seat's economy. It is estimated that around a fifth of the population are employed in associated manufacturing industries. Major companies in the area include Porvair International, Campbell Grocery Products, Bespak, and Mars Incorporated.

North West Norfolk houses a broad base of light and general engineering firms, including precision engineers and food-grade stainless steel and aluminium fabricators.

Rt Hon **Hilary Benn**

Leeds Central (returning MP)

Boundary changes

Tel: 020 7219 5770
E-mail: bennh@parliament.uk
Website: www.hilarybenn.org

Date of birth: 26 November 1953; Son of Tony Benn and late Caroline Middleton De Camp

Education: Holland Park Comprehensive School; Sussex University (BA Russian and East European studies 1974); Married Rosalind Retey 1973 (died 1979); married Sally Christina Clark 1982 (3 sons 1 daughter)

Non-political career: Research officer and latterly head of policy and communications, MSF 1975-97; Special Adviser to David Blunkett as Secretary of State for Education and Employment 1997-99; Member UNITE; London Borough of Ealing: Councillor 1979-99, Deputy Leader 1986-90, Chair, Education Committee 1986-90; Member Association of Metropolitan Authorities Education Committee 1986-90; Chair Association of London Authorities Education Committee 1989-90

Political career: Contested Ealing North 1983 and 1987 general elections. Member for Leeds Central 10 June 1999 by-election to 2010, for Leeds Central (revised boundary) since 6 May 2010 general election; Parliamentary Under-Secretary of State: Department for International Development 2001-02, Home Office (Community and Custodial Provision) 2002-03; Department for International Development: Minister of State 2003, Secretary of State 2003-07; Secretary of State for Environment, Food and Rural Affairs 2007-10; Shadow Secretary of State for Environment, Food and Rural Affairs 2010-; *Select Committees:* Member: Environment, Transport and Regional Affairs 1999-2001, Environment, Transport and Regional Affairs (Environment Sub-Committee) 1999-2001

Political interests: International development, home affairs, education, employment, trade unions, environment, urban policy

Other organisations: PC 2003; *House Magazine* Minister of the Year 2006, 2007; Channel 4 Politicians' Politician 2006; *Publications:* Contributor: Beyond 2002: Long-term policies for Labour (Profile Books, 1999), The Forces of Conservatism (IPPR, 1999); Men who made Labour (Routledge, 2006); Contributor Politics for a New Generation (IPPR, 2007)

Recreations: Watching sport, gardening

Rt Hon Hilary Benn MP, House of Commons, London SW1A 0AA
Tel: 020 7219 5770 Fax: 020 7219 2639
E-mail: bennh@parliament.uk
Constituency: 2 Blenheim Terrace, Leeds LS2 9JG Tel: 0113-244 1097
Fax: 0113-234 1176 Website: www.hilarybenn.org

GENERAL ELECTION RESULT

		%
Benn, H. (Lab)*	18,434	49.3
Taylor, M. (Lib Dem)	7,789	20.8
Lamb, A. (Con)	7,541	20.2
Meeson, K. (BNP)	3,066	8.2
Procter, D. (Ind)	409	1.1
One-Nil, W. (Ind)	155	0.4
Majority	10,645	28.47
Electorate	64,698	
Turnout	37,394	57.80

**Member of last parliament*

CONSTITUENCY SNAPSHOT

The seat was re-created in 1983 and was won initially by Labour's Derek Fatchett with a majority of more than 8,000. He built up bigger majorities, which in 1997 reached a massive 20,689.

Fatchett died in 1999 and at the by-election a Lib Dem push meant Hilary Benn secured a majority of 2,293 on a low turnout of 19.9 per cent, the lowest in a peace-time by-election since 1918.

In 2005 a 6.5 per cent swing to the Lib Dems reduced Benn's majority to a still very large 11,866. Benn was re-elected in 2010 with a 10,645 majority.

Boundary changes to Leeds Central were numerous, with part-wards being gained and lost from and to the other divisions.

Though the seat includes the financial quarter of the city, the people of Leeds Central have little share in its prosperity. High incomes are rare here, and the majority of families are housed in council or small terraced accommodation.

There is a substantial population of single young people, partly reflecting the presence of the city's two universities.

There are plans to rectify the city's lack of a major sporting and music arena by building a 13,000-seat venue on Claypit Lane. A university building on the site has been demolished to make way for the new arena which is scheduled to be completed in late 2012.

Joe Benton

Bootle (returning MP)

Boundary changes

Tel: 020 7219 6973
E-mail: bentonj@parliament.uk
Website: www.epolitix.com/Joe-Benton

Date of birth: 28 September 1933; Son of late Thomas and Agnes Benton

Education: St Monica's Primary and Secondary School; Bootle Technical College; Married Doris Wynne 1959 (4 daughters)

Non-political career: RAF national service 1955-57; Apprentice fitter and turner 1949; Personnel manager Pacific Steam Navigation Company; Girobank 1982-90; Member, RMT Parliamentary Campaigning Group 2002-; Sefton Borough Council: Councillor 1970-90, Leader, Labour Group 1985-90, JP, Bootle bench 1969

Political career: Member for Bootle 8 November 1990 by-election to 2010, for Bootle (revised boundary) since 6 May 2010 general election; Opposition Whip 1994-97; *Select Committees:* Member: Chairmen's Panel 1997-2010, Education and Employment 1997-99, Education and Employment (Education Sub-Committee) 1997-99, Parliamentary Privilege (Joint Committee) 1997-2000

Political interests: Education, housing, local and regional government, health

Other organisations: Chairman of Governors, Hugh Baird College of Technology 1972-92; Member, Institute of Linguists; Affiliate Member, Institute of Personnel Management

Recreations: Reading, listening to classical music, squash, swimming

Joe Benton MP, House of Commons, London SW1A 0AA
Tel: 020 7219 6973 Fax: 020 7219 3895
E-mail: bentonj@parliament.uk
Constituency: 23A Oxford Road, Bootle, Liverpool,
Merseyside L20 9HJ Tel: 0151-933 8432 Fax: 0151-933 4746
Website: www.epolitix.com/Joe-Benton

GENERAL ELECTION RESULT

		%
Benton, J. (Lab)*	27,426	66.4
Murray, J. (Lib Dem)	6,245	15.1
Qureshi, S. (Con)	3,678	8.9
Nuttall, P. (UKIP)	2,514	6.1
Stewart, C. (BNP)	942	2.3
Glover, P. (TUSC)	472	1.1
Majority	21,181	51.31
Electorate	71,426	
Turnout	41,277	57.79

**Member of last parliament*

CONSTITUENCY SNAPSHOT

Bootle has been Labour since the Second World War. Joe Benton took hold of the seat in 1990 after the untimely deaths of two Labour Members. Allan Roberts, the MP from 1979, died in 1990, and his replacement, Mike Carr, died six months later.

Joe Benton's majority has shrunk in the two elections since 1997: firstly by 9,000 votes in 2001, and then by a further 2,600 votes in 2005. It currently stands at 16,357. In 2010 Benton retained the seat with an increased majority of 21,181.

The seat gained the wards of Church and Victoria from Crosby.

Bootle is situated on the mouth of the river Mersey, to the north of the Liverpool city seats.

The constituency has much in common with the neighbouring Liverpool Walton. Bootle is, like the city to the south, overwhelmingly white and working-class in character.

Regeneration is a key element in the ongoing efforts to lift the area. The seat has benefited from Objective One Funding from the EU, although the Euro-millions for regeneration have now migrated east to the transition communities of Eastern Europe. In addition to EU funding the South Sefton Partnership has stewarded the waves of area-based funding for regeneration.

Richard Benyon

Newbury (returning MP)

Boundary changes

Tel: 020 7219 8319
E-mail: benyonr@parliament.uk
Website: www.richardbenyon.com

Conservative

Date of birth: 21 October 1960; Son of Sir William and Lady Benyon

Education: Bradfield College, Reading; Royal Agricultural College (Diploma real estate managment, land economy 1987); Married Zoe Robinson 2004 (2 sons and 3 sons by previous marriage)

Non-political career: Army officer, Royal Green Jackets 1980-85; Land agent chartered surveyor 1987-; Farmer 1990-; Chairman Rural and Urban Housing Business 2001-; Newbury District Councillor 1991-95: Leader Conservative group 1994-95

Political career: Contested Newbury 1997 and 2001 general elections. Member for Newbury 2005-10, for Newbury (revised boundary) since 6 May 2010 general election; Opposition Whip 2007-09; Shadow Minister for Environment, Food and Rural Affairs 2009-10; Parliamentary Under-Secretary of State (Natural Environment and Fisheries), Department for Environment, Food and Rural Affairs 2010-; *Select Committees:* Member: Home Affairs 2005-07

Political interests: Rural matters, social affairs, defence, health, home affairs; Africa, Northern Ireland

Other organisations: Trustee Help for Heroes

Recreations: Walking, tennis, shooting, fishing, cooking

Richard Benyon MP, House of Commons, London SW1A 0AA
Tel: 020 7219 8319 Fax: 020 7219 4509
E-mail: benyonr@parliament.uk
Constituency: 6 Cheap Street, Newbury, Berkshire RG14 5DD
Tel: 01635 551070 Fax: 01635 569690
Website: www.richardbenyon.com

GENERAL ELECTION RESULT

		%
Benyon, R. (Con)*	33,057	55.5
Rendel, D. (Lib Dem)	20,809	34.9
Cooper, H. (Lab)	2,505	4.2
Black, D. (UKIP)	1,475	2.5
Hollister, A. (Green)	490	0.8
Burgess, B. (Ind)	158	0.3
Yates, D. (Apol Dem)	95	0.2
Majority	12,248	20.90
Electorate	83,411	
Turnout	58,589	70.24

**Member of last parliament*

CONSTITUENCY SNAPSHOT

Newbury was traditionally a Conservative seat. It was held from 1945 to 1964 by Sir Anthony Hurd who passed it on to John Astor; Sir Michael McNair Wilson held the seat from 1974 and Judith Chaplin won it in 1992. Her death in 1993 led to a by-election resulting in a victory for the Liberal Democrats: David Rendel won by over 22,000 votes on a swing of 28.4 per cent.

Rendel held on with a majority of over 8,500 in 1997 and again in 2001 with a 2,415 majority. In 2005 the seat returned to Tory control. A 5.5 per cent swing gave Richard Benyon the votes needed to take the seat, on his third attempt.

In 2010 Benyon held the seat with a strong 12,248 majority.

Boundary changes moved the part-ward of Sulhamstead to Wokingham.

Newbury is a large rural seat in west Berkshire, which covers the market towns of Newbury and Hungerford, the Lambourn valley with its strong horseracing connections, the newer settlement of Thatcham, and large rural areas of the Downlands Area of Outstanding Natural Beauty.

Newbury is a busy market town with low unemployment. The area is home to many large companies including Vodafone, providing much local employment.

Rt Hon **John Bercow**

Buckingham (returning MP)

Boundary changes

Tel: 020 7219 6346
E-mail: bercowj@parliament.uk
Website: www.johnbercow.co.uk

The Speaker

Date of birth: 19 January 1963; Son of Brenda, neé Bailey, and late Charles Bercow

Education: Finchley Manorhill School, London; Essex University (BA government 1985); Married Sally Illman 2002 (2 sons 1 daughter)

Non-political career: Credit analyst, Hambros Bank 1987-88; Public affairs consultant, Rowland Sallingbury Casey, Public Affairs Arm of Saatchi & Saatchi Group 1988-95; Board director, Rowland Company 1994-95; Special adviser to: Jonathan Aitken as Chief Secretary to the Treasury 1995, Virginia Bottomley as Secretary of State for National Heritage 1995-96; London Borough of Lambeth: Councillor 1986-90, Deputy Leader, Conservative Opposition 1987-89; Ex-officio chair: Boundary Commission for England 2009-, Boundary Commission for Northern Ireland 2009-, Boundary Commission for Scotland 2009-, Boundary Commission for Wales 2009-

Political career: Contested Motherwell South 1987 and Bristol South 1992 general elections. Member for Buckingham 1997-2010, for Buckingham (revised boundary) since 6 May 2010 general election (Conservative 1997-2009, Speaker since 2009); Opposition Spokesperson for: Education and Employment 1999-2000, Home Affairs 2000-01; Shadow Chief Secretary to the Treasury 2001-02; Opposition Spokesperson for Work and Pensions 2002; Shadow Secretary of State for International Development 2003-04; Speaker 2009-; Ex-officio chair House of Commons Commission 2009-; Chair: Speaker's Committee on the Electoral Commission 2009-, Speaker's Committee for the Independent Parliamentary Standards Authority 2009-; *Select Committees:* Member: Welsh Affairs 1997-98, Trade and Industry 1998-99, Office of the Deputy Prime Minister 2002-04, Home Affairs 2003, Office of the Deputy Prime Minister (Urban Affairs Sub-Committee) 2003-04, International Development 2004-09, Procedure 2004-05, Chairmen's Panel 2005-09, Joint Committee on Consolidation, Etc, Bills 2005-09, Quadripartite (Committees on Strategic Export Controls)/Arms Export Controls 2006-09; Chair University of Essex Conservative Association 1984-85; National Chair Federation of Conservative Students 1986; Vice-chair Conservative Collegiate Forum 1987; Executive Member 1922 Committee 1998-99

Political interests: Special educational needs, international development, human rights, constitutional reform; Burma, Sudan, Zimbabwe, USA

Other organisations: Hon President: Hansard Society for Parliamentary Government 2009-, Inter-Parliamentary Union, British Group 2009-; President, Commonwealth Parliamentary Association (UK Branch) 2009-; President, Industry and Parliament Trust 2009-; PC 2009; *House Magazine* Backbencher of the Year 2005; Channel 4 / Hansard Society Opposition Politician of the Year 2005; *Publications:* Author of seven books

Recreations: Tennis, squash, reading, swimming, music

Rt Hon John Bercow MP, House of Commons, London SW1A 0AA
Tel: 020 7219 6346 Fax: 020 7219 0981
E-mail: bercowj@parliament.uk
Constituency: Speaker's Office Tel: 020 7219 6346; 020 7219 5300
Fax: 020 7219 6901 Website: www.johnbercow.co.uk

GENERAL ELECTION RESULT

		%
Bercow, J. (Speaker)*	22,860	47.3
Stevens, J. (Ind)	10,331	21.4
Farage, N. (UKIP)	8,410	17.4
Phillips, P. (Ind)	2,394	5.0
Martin, D. (Ind)	1,270	2.6
Mozar, L. (BNP)	980	2.0
Dale, C. (Loony)	856	1.8
Howard, G. (Ind)	435	0.9
Hews, D. (Christian)	369	0.8
Watts, A. (Ind)	332	0.7
Strutt, S. (Deficit)	107	0.2
Majority	12,529	25.92
Electorate	74,996	
Turnout	48,344	64.46

**Member of last parliament*

CONSTITUENCY SNAPSHOT

This seat has been held by the Tories since 1970. In 1997 the Tory share of the vote dropped below 50 per cent for the first time since 1979, but at 49.8 per cent the Conservatives still had more votes than their two rivals combined, as John Bercow became MP.

In 2005 Bercow increased his majority by over 5,000 votes for the second successive election. He was elected Commons Speaker in 2009.

The seat was held by John Bercow in 2010 with a 12,529 majority.

The seat gained the wards of Icknield and The Risboroughs from Aylesbury, in exchange for the part-wards of Coldharbour, Elmhurst and Watermead, Quarendon, and Aston Clinton.

This large and predominantly rural constituency is centred around the small market town of Buckingham.

Most voters are scattered about the large number of affluent villages in the seat, including Grendon Underwood and Newton Longville.

Industries include agriculture and the manufacture of car components. There is a large service sector.

The University of Buckinghamshire is the country's first private university. However, the majority of constituents commute either to nearby Milton Keynes or into central London.

Sir **Paul Beresford**

Mole Valley (returning MP)

Boundary changes

Tel: 020 7219 5018
E-mail: dukem@parliament.uk

Date of birth: 6 April 1946; Son of Raymond and Joan Beresford

Education: Waimea College, New Zealand; Otago University, Dunedin, New Zealand (BDS); Married Julie Haynes (3 sons 1 daughter)

Non-political career: Dental surgeon; London Borough of Wandsworth: Councillor 1978-94, Leader 1983-92

Political career: Member for Croydon Central 1992-97, for Mole Valley 1997-2010, for Mole Valley (revised boundary) since 6 May 2010 general election; Parliamentary Under-Secretary of State, Department of the Environment 1994-97; *Select Committees:* Member: Education 1992-94, Procedure 1997-2001, Environment, Transport and Regional Affairs 2000-01, Environment, Transport and Regional Affairs (Environment Sub-Committee) 2001, Environment, Transport and Regional Affairs (Transport Sub-Committee) 2001, Transport, Local Government and the Regions 2001-02, Transport, Local Government and the Regions (Urban Affairs Sub-Committee) 2001-02, Member ODPM/Communities and Local Government 2002-10, ODPM/Communities and Local Government (Urban Affairs Sub-Committee) 2003-05; 1922 Committee: Secretary 2002-06, Member Executive 2006-07

Political interests: Inner cities, housing, education; Fiji, New Zealand, Samoa, Australia

Other organisations: Fellow Industry and Parliament Trust 2002; Knighted 1990

Recreations: DIY, reading

Sir Paul Beresford MP, House of Commons, London SW1A 0AA
Tel: 020 7219 5018 E-mail: dukem@parliament.uk
Constituency: Mole Valley Conservative Association, 86 South Street, Dorking, Surrey RH4 2EW Tel: 01306 883 312 Fax: 01306 885 194

GENERAL ELECTION RESULT

		%
Beresford, P. (Con)*	31,263	57.6
Humphreys, A. (Lib Dem)	15,610	28.7
Dove, J. (Lab)	3,804	7.0
Jones, L. (UKIP)	2,752	5.1
Sedgwick, R. (Green)	895	1.7
Majority	15,653	28.81
Electorate	72,612	
Turnout	54,324	74.81

**Member of last parliament*

CONSTITUENCY SNAPSHOT

Created in 1983, the area has actually returned Conservative MPs since the Second World War. Sir Paul Beresford was first elected in 1997 with a majority of 10,221. In 2001 little changed and Sir Paul's majority dropped only slightly to 10,153 but four years later it increased to 11,997.

Beresford retained the seat in 2010 with 31,263 votes giving the Conservatives a majority of 15,653 at the 2010 general election.

The seat gained the part-ward of Leatherhead South from Epsom and Ewell, in exchange for the part-wards of Ashtead Common, Ashtead Park and Ashtead Village.

This is a prosperous, middle-class corner of the Home Counties, incorporating the market town of Dorking, Leatherhead and the surrounding Surrey.

There are beauty spots like Box Hill and Leith Hill, and a considerable amount of mixed farming. Dorking attracts visitors to its famous antique shops. The Leatherhead corridor section of the river Mole has become a local nature reserve.

Traditionally, there has been little industry in the constituency itself, but firms have moved to Leatherhead, which is close to the M25 and has good rail links to London; it hosts the national headquarters of Esso and the consultant engineers Halliburton. The National Grid has its research and development base here, and the National Trust its regional headquarters at Polesden Lacey.

Luciana Berger

Liverpool Wavertree

Boundary changes

Tel: 020 7219 3000
E-mail: luciana.berger.mp@parliament.uk
Website: www.lucianaberger.com

Labour/Co-operative

Education: Birmingham University (BA commerce); Birkbeck College (Master's government)

Non-political career: Government strategy unit, Accenture; NHS Confederation; Director, Labour Friends of Israel; School governor

Political career: Member for Liverpool Wavertree since 6 May 2010 general election

Other organisations: Steering group, London Jewish Forum

Recreations: Keeping fit, cinema

Luciana Berger MP, House of Commons, London SW1A 0AA
Tel: 020 7219 3000 E-mail: luciana.berger.mp@parliament.uk
Constituency: 108 Prescott Road, Liverpool L7 0JA
Website: www.lucianaberger.com

GENERAL ELECTION RESULT

		%
Berger, L. (Lab/Co-op)	20,132	53.1
Eldridge, C. (Lib Dem)	12,965	34.2
Garnett, A. (Con)	2,830	7.5
Miney, N. (UKIP)	890	2.4
Lawson, R. (Green)	598	1.6
Singleton, K. (SLP)	200	0.5
McEllenborough, S. (BNP)	150	0.4
Dunne, F. (Ind)	149	0.4
Majority	7,167	18.90
Electorate	62,518	
Turnout	37,914	60.64

CONSTITUENCY SNAPSHOT

Labour's Jane Kennedy won convincingly in 1997 with a 19,701 majority. In the 2001 election her majority fell to 12,319. However, the Liberal Democrats achieved a swing of almost 12 per cent in 2005 and Jane Kennedy's majority was more than halved to 5,173. Kennedy retired in 2010.

In 2010 there was a swing of 5 per cent to Labour. Luciana Berger held the seat for Labour with a 7,167 majority.

The seat gained four part-wards while losing eight part-wards to other Liverpool divisions.

Situated to the east of the city of Liverpool, the constituency of Wavertree is predominantly residential.

Wavertree hosts a large technology park, which has close ties to the university and there is a large student population based here, which helps the local economy.

Like elsewhere in the city, the main issues are of employment and depopulation. However, there are signs that as a result of a decade of investment the city is improving.

Jake Berry

Rossendale and Darwen

Boundary changes

Tel: 020 7219 3000
E-mail: jake.berry.mp@parliament.uk
Website: www.jakeberry.org

Conservative

Date of birth: 1978

Education: Sheffield University (law); Chester College (law finals); Married Charlotte

Non-political career: Property lawyer

Political career: Member for Rossendale and Darwen since 6 May 2010 general election

Recreations: Walking, water-skiing

Jake Berry MP, House of Commons, London SW1A 0AA
Tel: 020 7219 3000 E-mail: jake.berry.mp@parliament.uk
Constituency: 4 Mount Terrace, Rawtenstall, Rossendale, Lancashire BB4 8SF Tel: 01706 215547 Website: www.jakeberry.org

GENERAL ELECTION RESULT

		%
Berry, J. (Con)	19,691	41.8
Anderson, J. (Lab)*	15,198	32.3
Sheffield, B. (Lib Dem)	8,541	18.1
Duthie, D. (UKIP)	1,617	3.4
Bryan, K. (NF)	1,062	2.3
Johnson, M. (England)	663	1.4
Melia, T. (Impact)	243	0.5
Sivieri, M. (Ind)	113	0.2
Majority	4,493	9.53
Electorate	73,003	
Turnout	47,128	64.56

**Member of last parliament*

CONSTITUENCY SNAPSHOT

Conservative Sir David Trippier was the first member for this seat when it was created in 1983. He served as a minister in the Thatcher government before being ousted in the 1992 election. Janet Anderson took the seat in 1992 for Labour, by a mere 121 votes.

Since then Anderson has strengthened her position and won a majority of 3,676 in 2005. This was a reduction from 2001.

Anderson was defeated in 2010 and Jake Berry took the seat for the Conservatives with a majority of 4,493.

The seat gained three part-wards from Blackburn and lost the part-ward of Greenfield to Hyndburn.

This constituency covers the south east part of Lancashire. It covers the districts of Bacup, Rawtenstall and Darwen as well as part of the districts of Haslingdon and Ramsbottom.

Manufacturing is well above the national average for providing jobs in this constituency, albeit it is not as dominant as in other North West seats; distribution, hotels and restaurants are also important. Tourism has increased slightly in recent years but is a minor sector here.

Darwen Academy recently agreed a £45 million investment from the government to improve its facilities. Opened in 2008 on the grounds of the old Darwen Moorland School, it has been completely modernised and caters for 1,600 students.

Clive Betts

Sheffield South East ***(returning MP)***

New constituency

Tel: 020 7219 5114
E-mail: bettsc@parliament.uk
Website: www.clivebetts.com

Labour

Date of birth: 13 January 1950; Son of late Harold and Nellie Betts

Education: King Edward VII School, Sheffield; Pembroke College, Cambridge (BA economics and politics 1971)

Non-political career: Economist, Trades Union Congress 1971-73; Local government economist: Derbyshire County Council 1973-74, South Yorkshire County Council 1974-86, Rotherham Borough Council 1986-91; Member, TGWU; Sheffield City Council: Councillor 1976-92, Chairman: Housing Committee 1980-86, Finance Committee 1986-88, Leader 1987-92

Political career: Contested Sheffield Hallam October 1974 and Louth 1979 general elections. Member for Sheffield Attercliffe 1992-2010, for Sheffield South East since 6 May 2010 general election; Opposition Whip 1996-97; Assistant Government Whip 1997-98; Government Whip 1998-2001; *Select Committees:* Member: Treasury 1996-97, Selection 1997-2001, Transport, Local Government and the Regions (Urban Affairs Sub-Committee) 2001-02, Transport, Local Government and the Regions 2001-02, ODPM/Communities and Local Government 2002-10, ODPM/Communities and Local Government (Urban Affairs Sub-Committee) 2003-05, Finance and Services 2005-10, Chairmen's Panel 2009-10, Yorkshire and the Humber 2009-10, Reform of the House of Commons 2009-10; Member, Labour Leader's Campaign Team with responsibility for Environment and Local Government 1995-96

Political interests: Local and regional government, housing, planning, regeneration, transport; Bosnia, Europe, Iran, Middle East, Netherlands, Serbia, Ukraine

Other organisations: President, South East Sheffield Citizens' Advice Bureau 1998-; Vice-chair, Association of Metropolitan Authorities 1988-91; Vice-president, Local Government Association; Chair, South Yorkshire Pensions Authority 1989-92; Trustee, Parliamentary Pension Scheme; Fellow Industry and Parliament Trust 1997

Recreations: Supporting Sheffield Wednesday FC, playing squash, cricket, walking, real ale, scuba diving

Clive Betts MP, House of Commons, London SW1A 0AA
Tel: 020 7219 5114 Fax: 020 7219 2289
E-mail: bettsc@parliament.uk
Constituency: 2nd Floor, Barkers Pool House, Burgess Street, Sheffield, South Yorkshire S1 2HH Tel: 0114-273 4444
Fax: 0114-273 9666 Website: www.clivebetts.com

GENERAL ELECTION RESULT

		%
Betts, C. (Lab)*	20,169	48.7
Smith, G. (Lib Dem)	9,664	23.3
Bonson, N. (Con)	7,202	17.4
Hartigan, C. (BNP)	2,345	5.7
Arnott, J. (UKIP)	1,889	4.6
Andrew, S. (Comm GB)	139	0.3
Majority	10,505	25.37
Electorate	67,284	
Turnout	41,408	61.54

**Member of last parliament*

CONSTITUENCY SNAPSHOT

This new seat is largely the same as the former Sheffield Attercliffe.

The Attercliffe seat was almost continuously in Labour hands since they first won it in 1909. John Burns Hynd represented the seat for 25 years until 1970, Pat Duffy took over and served for another 22 years and Clive Betts was first elected in 1992.

In 1997 Betts won a 21,818 majority. In 2005, there was a swing of 5.2 per cent to the Liberal Democrats, who took second place from the Tories, however, Betts' majority remained a commanding 15,967. In 2010 Betts held the seat despite a 9 per cent swing to the Lib Dems.

This new South Yorkshire seat stretches through Sheffield's old industrial 'East End' and south to the newer residential areas of Mosborough.

Sheffield's traditional industries of heavy engineering and steel-making, much of which was carried out in the Attercliffe area, were deeply affected in the recessions of the 1980s and 1990s. Most of the steelworks have gone, though some engineering companies remain. But new industries have come to replace the old, not least the huge retail complex of Meadowhall centre.

Leisure, sport and entertainment are also important. The Sheffield Arena, Don Valley Stadium and the English Institute of Sport are at the seat's boundary with Sheffield Central.

Andrew Bingham

High Peak

Boundary changes

Tel: 020 7219 3000
E-mail: andrew.bingham.mp@parliament.uk

Date of birth: 23 June 1962

Education: Long Lane Comprehensive, Chapel-En-Le-Frith; High Peak College of Further Education (catering 1980); Married Jayne Dranfield 1986 (no children)

Non-political career: ARB Sales Ltd: Sales engineer 1981-83, Company director 1983-2004; Freelance engineering consultant 2004-; High Peak Borough Council 1999-: Councillor 1999-, Chair, Social Inclusion Committee 2003-07, Cabinet member, Community and Social Development

Political career: Contested High Peak 2005 general election. Member for High Peak since 6 May 2010 general election; Association deputy chairman 2000-01; Association chairman 2001-04

Political interests: Business, pensions

Recreations: Sports – badminton, football and cricket

Andrew Bingham MP, House of Commons, London SW1A 0AA
Tel: 020 7219 3000 E-mail: andrew.bingham.mp@parliament.uk
Constituency: High Peak Conservative Association, 1A Hardwick Mount, Buxton, Derbyshire SK17 6PP Tel: 01298 22521
Fax: 01298 70785 Website: www.hpca.co.uk

GENERAL ELECTION RESULT

		%
Bingham, A. (Con)	20,587	40.9
Bisknell, C. (Lab)	15,910	31.6
Stevens, A. (Lib Dem)	10,993	21.8
Hall, S. (UKIP)	1,690	3.4
Allen, P. (Green)	922	1.8
Dowson, L. (Ind)	161	0.3
Alves, T. (Ind)	74	0.2
Majority	4,677	9.29
Electorate	71,973	
Turnout	50,337	69.94

CONSTITUENCY SNAPSHOT

This seat stayed Conservative in 1945 but fell to Labour's Peter Jackson in 1966. Jackson enjoyed only one term, losing to Spencer Le Marchant in 1970, the start of 27 more years of Tory representation.

In 1992 Le Marchant's successor, Charles Hendry, maintained the vote-share, but Labour's Tom Levitt halved the Conservative majority. Levitt took the seat in 1997.

The Conservatives fought back in 2001 as the Labour vote fell, however, Levitt was returned with a 4,489 majority. The Conservative advance continued in 2005 as Labour's majority was cut to just 735.

Labour was defeated in 2010 with the Conservative candidate, Andrew Bingham taking the seat with a 4,677 majority.

Boundary changes were minimal.

High Peak is a mixed seat in a wild and beautiful corner of the southern Pennines which also includes some old industrial towns on the edges of Greater Manchester.

The northern part of the Peak District National Park occupies about 90 per cent of this constituency, but contains only 10 per cent of its population. The rest live in small- to medium-sized towns, which house many Greater Manchester commuters.

High Peak is important for limestone quarrying and cement production, and Tarmac Buxton Lime and Cement's Tunstead site is one of the largest limestone quarries in Europe. The other major industry is tourism.

Brian Binley

Northampton South ***(returning MP)***

Boundary changes

Tel: 020 7219 8298
E-mail: binleyb@parliament.uk
Website: www.brianbinley.com

Conservative

Date of birth: 1 April 1942; Son of Phyllis and Frank Binley

Education: Finedon Mulso C of E Secondary Modern, Northamptonshire; Married Jacqueline Denise 1985 (1 son and 1 son by former marriage)

Non-political career: Area manager Courage (central) Ltd 1976-79; National sales manager Phonotas Services Ltd 1980-87; General manager Tele Resources Ltd 1987-89; Managing director and founder BCC Marketing Services Ltd 1989-2001; Chair and co-founder Beechwood House Publishing Ltd 1993-2000; Chair BCC Marketing Services Ltd 2002-; Northamptonshire County Council: Councillor 1997-2005, Chair finance and resources scrutiny committee 2000-05, Member of Cabinet 2005-07

Political career: Member for Northampton South 2005-10, for Northampton South (revised boundary) since 6 May 2010 general election; *Select Committees:* Member: Joint Committee on Consolidation, Etc, Bills 2005-10, Trade and Industry/Business, Enterprise and Regulatory Reform/Business and Enterprise/Business, Innovation and Skills 2006-10, Crossrail Bill 2006-07, Arms Export Controls 2008-10; National Young Conservatives organiser 1965-68; Agent, Kidderminster Conservative Association 1996-98; Member Executive 1922 Committee 2006-; Treasurer Cornerstone Group 2005-; Chair Conservative Parliamentary Enterprise Group 2006-

Political interests: Business, local government; Iran, Israel, India, Maldives, Sri Lanka

Other organisations: Northampton Town and Country; Northampton Conservative; Carlton; *Publications:* Binley Directory of National Health Service Management, Beechwood House 1993-; plus seven other directories

Recreations: Northampton Town FC, Northamptonshire CCC, freemasonry, golf, opera, literature

Brian Binley MP, House of Commons, London SW1A 0AA
Tel: 020 7219 8298 Fax: 020 7219 2265
E-mail: binleyb@parliament.uk
Constituency: Northampton South Conservative Association, White Lodge, 42 Billing Road, Northampton NN1 5DA Tel: 01604 633414 Fax: 01604 250252 Website: www.brianbinley.com

GENERAL ELECTION RESULT

		%
Binley, B. (Con)*	15,917	40.8
Loakes, C. (Lab)	9,913	25.4
Varnsverry, P. (Lib Dem)	7,579	19.4
Clarke, T. (Ind)	2,242	5.8
Clark, D. (UKIP)	1,897	4.9
Sills, K. (England)	618	1.6
Hawkins, J. (Green)	363	0.9
Green, D. (NSOPS)	325	0.8
Willsher, K. (Ind)	65	0.2
Costello, L. (Scrap)	59	0.2
Majority	6,004	15.40
Electorate	66,923	
Turnout	38,978	58.24

**Member of last parliament*

CONSTITUENCY SNAPSHOT

In 1997 Labour swept to power here and overturned the Conservative's 55 per cent share of the vote. However, they were able to gain a majority of only 744. Tony Clarke increased his majority in 2001 to retain the seat for Labour.

This success was short-lived though as, in 2005, the Conservatives' Brian Binley regained the seat by 4,419 votes. In 2010 Binley held the seat for the Tories with a 6,004 majority.

Boundary changes were extensive. The seat lost its part-wards of Harpole and Grange to Daventry, and its part of Abington to Northampton North. In addition the part-wards of Blisworth, Roade, Cosgrove and Grafton, Salcy and Tove, and the full wards of Brafield and Yardley, East Hunsbury, Grange Park, Hackleton, Nene Valley, West Hunsbury moved to the new South Northamptonshire constituency. To compensate, the seat gained Spencer ward and four part-wards from Northampton North.

Outside the town of Northampton itself, the Northampton South constituency takes in the rural and commuter hinterland to the south, including a good deal of green-belt land.

There is a general trend here away from manufacture and towards service industries. Carlsberg's UK base and Barclaycard's headquarters are no longer in the constituency, but MFI, Coca-Cola, Panasonic, Levi-Strauss and Tesco have big distribution centres in the Northampton area.

Gordon Birtwistle

Burnley

No boundary changes

Tel: 020 7219 3000
E-mail: gordon.birtwistle.mp@parliament.uk

Date of birth: 6 September 1943

Education: Accrington College (HNC production engineering; HNC mechanical engineering); Married (2 children)

Non-political career: Apprenticeship, Howard and Bullough, Accrington; Engineering industry; Former Labour councillor 1970s; Burnley Borough Council: Councillor 1983-, Chair, Leadership Scrutiny Committee, Mayor 2002-03, Leader, Liberal Democrat group, Council leader 2006-

Political career: Contested Burnley 1992 and 1997 general elections. Member for Burnley since 6 May 2010 general election

Recreations: Golf, gardening

Gordon Birtwistle MP, House of Commons, London SW1A 0AA
Tel: 020 7219 3000 E-mail: gordon.birtwistle.mp@parliament.uk
Constituency: 19 Glen View Road, Burnley, Lancashire BB11 2QL
Tel: 01282 453749 Website: www.burnleylibdems.org.uk

GENERAL ELECTION RESULT

		%	+/-
Birtwistle, G. (Lib Dem)	14,932	35.7	12.1
Cooper, J. (Lab)	13,114	31.3	-7.0
Ali, R. (Con)	6,950	16.6	5.9
Wilkinson, S. (BNP)	3,747	9.0	-1.3
Brown, A. (Ind)	1,876	4.5	
Wignall, J. (UKIP)	929	2.2	1.3
Hennessey, A. (Ind)	297	0.7	
Majority	1,818	4.34	
Electorate	66,616		
Turnout	41,845	62.82	

CONSTITUENCY SNAPSHOT

Burnley was a Labour seat for the whole of the 20th century, only once falling to another party. That was between 1931 and 1935 when Vice-Admiral Gordon Campbell held the seat for the National Party. In 1997 Peter Pike, the member since 1983, increased his majority to 17,062. This was a big increase on the small majority he attained at his first election, when received a 787 majority.

Peter Pike retired in 2005 and was replaced by Kitty Ussher. She was selected on an all-women shortlist. Her majority in 2005 was 5,778. Ussher stood down in 2010 and the Lib Dem candidate, Gordon Birtwistle took the seat from Labour securing a majority of 1,818.

Burnley is a large Lancashire town situated just east of Blackburn. The constituency also includes some of the surrounding Pennine moors.

It has suffered like many other Lancashire towns from the decline of the textiles and mining industries. Modern-day businesses include high technology, plastics, electronics, manufacturing in aerospace and car components.

Average house prices in Burnley are among the lowest in Lancashire. There is a large Asian community in Burnley but notably smaller than in neighbouring Blackburn.

Bob Blackman

Harrow East

Boundary changes

Tel: 020 7219 3000
E-mail: bob.blackman.mp@parliament.uk

Conservative

Date of birth: 26 April 1956

Education: Preston Manor High School; Liverpool University (Union President); Married to Nicola

Non-political career: Sales, Unisys; British Telecom: Sales, Sales tutor, training college, Former regulatory compliance manager; London Borough of Brent Council 1986-: Councillor 1986-, Conservative Group Leader 1990-, Council Leader 1991-96; Member Greater London Assembly 2004-08; Governor, Preston Manor High School

Political career: Contested Brent South 1992, Bedford 1997 and Brent North 2005 general elections. Member for Harrow East since 6 May 2010 general election

Recreations: Tottenham Hotspur FC, bridge, chess, reading, cricket

Bob Blackman MP, House of Commons, London SW1A 0AA
Tel: 020 7219 3000 E-mail: bob.blackman.mp@parliament.uk
Constituency: Harrow East Conservatives, 10 Village Way, Pinner, Middlesex HA5 5AF Tel: 020 8868 9400 Fax: 020 8868 4412
Website: www.harroweastconservatives.com

GENERAL ELECTION RESULT

		%
Blackman, B. (Con)	21,435	44.7
McNulty, T. (Lab)*	18,032	37.6
Boethe, N. (Lib Dem)	6,850	14.3
Pandya, A. (UKIP)	896	1.9
Atkins, M. (Green)	793	1.7
Majority	3,403	7.09
Electorate	68,554	
Turnout	48,006	70.03

**Member of last parliament*

CONSTITUENCY SNAPSHOT

Since the Second World War Harrow East has alternated between the two major parties broadly corresponding to their alternation in government. From 1970 Tory Hugh Dykes held Harrow East until 1997. Dykes' seat appeared to be secure in 1997, as his share of the vote had been around 50 per cent consistently, and in 1992 his majority was 11,405. However, the Tories lost the seat to Labour's Tony McNulty in 1997 by almost 10,000 votes. McNulty increased his majority in 2001, although it fell to 4,730 in 2005. Labour's Tony McNulty resigned as a minister over his expenses and then lost this seat to Conservative Bob Blackman on a 7 per cent swing.

Harrow East lost the wards of Greenhill and Marlborough (which together comprise the centre of Harrow itself and its 14,000 voters) and one part-ward of Harrow on the Hill to Harrow West.

Harrow East is an ethnically and economically diverse seat situated in the eastern segment of the borough of Harrow, with South Asians making up the largest ethnic group.

Many areas fit the popular perception of a leafy, prosperous suburb.

The seat is easily accessible by several large thoroughfares, and is on national rail and the Bakerloo, Metropolitan and Jubilee Underground lines.

Dr **Roberta Blackman-Woods**

City of Durham (returning MP)

No boundary changes

Tel: 020 7219 4982
Website: www.roberta.org.uk

Date of birth: 16 August 1957; Daughter of late Charles and Eleanor Woods

Education: Methodist College of Belfast; Ulster University (BSc social science 1979, PhD 1989); Married Professor Tim Blackman 1986 (1 daughter)

Non-political career: Welfare rights officer, Newcastle City Council 1982-85; Lecturer in social policy: University of Ulster 1985-90, Newcastle University 1990-95; Dean of labour and social studies, Ruskin College, Oxford 1995-2000; Professor of social policy and associate dean, Northumbria University 2000-05; GMB, UCU; Councillor: Newcastle City Council 1992-95, Oxford City Council 1996-2000

Political career: Member for City of Durham since 5 May 2005 general election; PPS: to Hilary Armstrong as Chancellor of the Duchy of Lancaster 2006-07, to Des Browne as Secretary of State for Defence 2007-08, to David Lammy as Minister of State, Department for Innovation, Universities and Skills/Business, Innovation and Skills 2008-10; Parliamentary assistant to Nick Brown as Minister for the North East 2008-10; *Select Committees:* Member: Joint Committee on Statutory Instruments and Commons Committee on Statutory Instruments 2005-10, Education and Skills 2005-06, Innovation, Universities[, Science] and Skills/Science and Technology 2007-10; Chair CLP: Newcastle East and Wallsend 1991-95, City of Durham 2003-05

Political interests: Education, housing, international development and regeneration; Afghanistan, China, Africa

Recreations: Music, reading

Dr Roberta Blackman-Woods MP, House of Commons, London SW1A 0AA Tel: 020 7219 4982 Fax: 020 7219 8018
Constituency: The Miners' Hall, Redhills, Flass Street, Durham DH1 4BD Tel: 0191-374 1915 Fax: 0191-374 1916
E-mail: mail@roberta.org.uk Website: www.roberta.org.uk

GENERAL ELECTION RESULT

		%	+/-
Blackman-Woods, R. (Lab)*	20,496	44.3	-2.6
Woods, C. (Lib Dem)	17,429	37.7	-1.9
Varley, N. (Con)	6,146	13.3	3.9
Musgrave, R. (BNP)	1,153	2.5	
Coghill-Marshall, N. (UKIP)	856	1.9	
Collings, J. (Ind)	172	0.4	
Majority	3,067	6.63	
Electorate	68,832		
Turnout	46,252	67.20	

**Member of last parliament*

CONSTITUENCY SNAPSHOT

Labour MPs have seen long tenures and large majorities in the City of Durham. In 60 years the constituency was represented by just three men: Charles Grey who was MP for Durham from 1945 to 1970, Mark Hughes up to 1987, and Gerry Steinberg who was MP until 2005.

The Liberal Democrats achieved their best ever performance in 2005, polling 40 per cent of the vote; and reducing Roberta Blackman-Woods' majority to just 3,274 with a 12.5 per cent swing. Roberta Blackman-Woods held on in 2010 with a majority of just 3,067.

At the heart of this constituency is the attractive and ancient city of Durham, with its grand cathedral and esteemed university. The seat also includes ex-mining communities in Brandon and Byshottles, Coxhoe, and the Deerness Valley.

The City of Durham is at the heart of a region whose economy was built on the back of the coal-mining industry, but today the city relies on Durham University, one of the UK's leading research institutions, and a growing tourist industry, centred on landmarks like the magnificent cathedral and Durham Castle.

The presence of the eponymous university has a strong effect on the age structure across the constituency.

The seat is a relatively well-off. The service industry is the largest source of employment in the constituency.

Nicola Blackwood

Oxford West and Abingdon

Boundary changes

Tel: 020 7219 7126
E-mail: nicola.blackwood.mp@parliament.uk
Website: www.nicolablackwood.com

Conservative

Date of birth: 1979

Education: Home schooled; Trinity College of Music; St Anne's College, Cambridge (BA music); Emmanuel College, Cambridge (MPhil musicology); Studying for DPhil in music

Non-political career: Parliamentary researcher to Andrew Mitchell MP -2007

Political career: Member for Oxford West and Abingdon since 6 May 2010 general election; Political Unit, Conservative Research Department, 2005 general election; Member, Conservative Party Human Rights Commission

Political interests: Civil liberties

Nicola Blackwood MP, House of Commons, London SW1A 0AA
Tel: 020 7219 7126 E-mail: nicola.blackwood.mp@parliament.uk
Constituency: 8 Gorwell, Watlington, Oxfordshire OX49 5QE
Tel: 01491 612852 Fax: 01491 612001
Website: www.nicolablackwood.com

GENERAL ELECTION RESULT

		%
Blackwood, N. (Con)	23,906	42.3
Harris, E. (Lib Dem)*	23,730	42.0
Stevens, R. (Lab)	5,999	10.6
Williams, P. (UKIP)	1,518	2.7
Goodall, C. (Green)	1,184	2.1
Mann, K. (Animal)	143	0.3
Majority	176	0.31
Electorate	86,458	
Turnout	56,480	65.33

**Member of last parliament*

CONSTITUENCY SNAPSHOT

Conservative John Patten held the seat from 1983 to 1997. However, Tory support in Oxford West and Abingdon fell enough to allow the Liberal Democrat, Evan Harris, to win in 1997. The Liberal Democrats were able to retain the seat in 2001 and again in 2005. Harris's 2005 majority was reasonably comfortable 7,683.

Evan Harris was defeated in 2010 with a 6.9 per cent swing to the Conservative candidate, Nicola Blackwood.

The seat gained two part-wards from Wantage and a part-ward from Witney. It lost five part-wards in central Oxford to Oxford East, and a part-ward each to Henley and Wantage.

From leafy, affluent north Oxford to the sleepy suburbs of Abingdon, Oxford West and Abingdon encompasses the communities of Abingdon, West Oxford, Kidlington and the villages of Radley, Kennington, Sunningwell, Wootton, Cumnor, and North and South Hinksey.

Both North Oxford and Abingdon are affluent. Due to the academic nature of the town, around a third of jobs are of a professional/managerial nature.

The university is a large employer in this seat and the service sector employs over 64,000 people.

Rt Hon **Hazel Blears**

Salford and Eccles (returning MP)

New constituency

Tel: 020 7219 6595
E-mail: blearsh@parliament.uk
Website: www.hazelblears.co.uk

Labour

Date of birth: 14 May 1956; Daughter of Arthur and Dorothy Blears

Education: Wardley Grammar School; Eccles Sixth Form College; Trent Polytechnic (BA law 1977); Chester College of Law (Law Society part II 1978); Married Michael Halsall 1989

Non-political career: Trainee solicitor, Salford Council 1978-80; Private practice solicitor 1980-81; Solicitor: Rossendale Council 1981-83, Wigan Council 1983-85; Principal solicitor, Manchester City Council 1985-97; Branch Secretary, Unison 1981-85; Member: Unite, USDAW; Councillor, Salford City Council 1984-92

Political career: Contested Tatton 1987 and Bury South 1992 general elections. Member for Salford 1997-2010, for Salford and Eccles since 6 May 2010 general election; PPS to Alan Milburn: as Minister of State, Department of Health 1998, as Chief Secretary, HM Treasury 1999; Parliamentary Under-Secretary of State, Department of Health 2001-03: (Health 2001-02, Public Health 2002-03); Minister of State, Home Office 2003-06: (Crime Reduction, Policing, Community Safety and Counter-Terrorism 2003-05, Policing, Security and Community Safety 2005-06); Minister without Portfolio 2006-07; Secretary of State for Communities and Local Government 2007-09; Member: North West Executive 1997-99, National Policy Forum 1997-2001, Leadership Campaign Team 1997-98; Labour Party Development Co-ordinator and Deputy to Ian McCartney 1998-2001; Leader Parliamentary Campaign Team 2003- Labour Party NEC 2004-; Chair Labour Party 2006-07

Political interests: Employment, health, arts, urban regeneration

Other organisations: Chair Salford Community Health Council 1993-97; PC 2005; *Publications:* Making Healthcare Mutual (Mutuo, 2002); Communities in Control (Fabian Society, 2003); Politics of Decency (Mutuo, 2004)

Recreations: Dance, motorcycling

Rt Hon Hazel Blears MP, House of Commons, London SW1A 0AA
Tel: 020 7219 6595 Fax: 020 7219 0949
E-mail: blearsh@parliament.uk
Constituency: Jubilee House, 51 The Crescent, Salford, Greater Manchester M5 4WX Tel: 0161-925 0705
Fax: 0161-743 9173 Website: www.hazelblears.co.uk

GENERAL ELECTION RESULT

		%
Blears, H. (Lab)*	16,655	40.1
Owen, N. (Lib Dem)	10,930	26.3
Sephton, M. (Con)	8,497	20.5
Wingfield, T. (BNP)	2,632	6.3
O'Dwyer, D. (UKIP)	1,084	2.6
Henry, D. (TUSC)	730	1.8
Morris, S. (England)	621	1.5
Carvath, R. (Ind)	384	0.9
Majority	5,725	13.78
Electorate	75,482	
Turnout	41,533	55.02

**Member of last parliament*

CONSTITUENCY SNAPSHOT

This new constituency is comprised of all but three wards from Salford, with the northern half of Eccles. Broughton and Kessel are now in the new Blackley and Broughton seat, while Barton ward is in Worsley and Eccles.

Salford had been a Labour seat for generations and Hazel Blears held the seat from 1997. In that election Blears was returned with an absolute majority; however, in 2001 her majority fell by 6,000 votes, and fell further in 2005 to 7,945.

In 2010 Blears won the new seat with a majority of 5,725.

Although part of Greater Manchester, Salford, lying on the left bank of the river Irwell, is a city in its own right.

The paintings of Salford's most famous artist, L S Lowry, depict an industrial landscape of terraces and factories. Indeed, Salford is the home of the Working Class Movement Library.

Heavy industry has declined but the terraced communities survive, though depleted in number.

There has been some substantial regeneration, particularly around Salford Quays. It is home to the Daniel Libeskind-designed Imperial War Museum North and the Lowry Arts Centre.

Both Salford and Eccles have benefited from the extension of the Manchester Metrolink tram system.

Tom Blenkinsop

Middlesbrough South and East Cleveland

Boundary changes

Tel: 020 7219 3000
E-mail: tom.blenkinsop.mp@parliament.uk
Website: www.tomblenkinsop.com

Labour

Date of birth: 14 August 1980

Education: Newlands School FCJ Saltersgill, Middlesbrough; St Mary's Sixth Form College, Saltersgill, Middlesbrough; Teesside University (BSc philosophy, politics and economics); Warwick University (MA continental philosophy); TUC Organising Academy; Married Vicki

Non-political career: Constituency researcher to Ashok Kumar MP; Officer, Community trade union, Middlesbrough

Political career: Member for Middlesbrough South and East Cleveland since 6 May 2010 general election

Political interests: Teesside steel industry, public services, Sure Start

Recreations: Middlesbrough F.C

Tom Blenkinsop MP, House of Commons, London SW1A 0AA
Tel: 020 7219 3000 E-mail: tom.blenkinsop.mp@parliament.uk
Constituency: Harry Tout House, 8 Wilson Street,
Guisborough TS14 6NA Tel: 01287 610878 Fax: 01287 631894
Website: www.tomblenkinsop.com

GENERAL ELECTION RESULT

		%
Blenkinsop, T. (Lab)	18,138	39.3
Bristow, P. (Con)	16,461	35.6
Emmerson, N. (Lib Dem)	7,340	15.9
Lightwing, S. (UKIP)	1,881	4.1
Gatley, S. (BNP)	1,576	3.4
Allen, M. (Ind)	818	1.8
Majority	1,677	3.63
Electorate	72,664	
Turnout	46,214	63.60

CONSTITUENCY SNAPSHOT

The seat formerly called Langbaurgh alternated between Labour and the Conservatives until 1997.

Dr Ashok Kumar represented from 1997 until his death in March 2010. He had been re-elected in 2005 with a reduced, but still safe, majority of 8,000. This safe seat has become a marginal with the Conservative advance handing new Labour MP Tom Blenkinsop a majority of just 1,677.

Boundary changes moved part-wards Beechwood, Brookfield and Kader into Middlesborough whilst part-wards Park End and Saltburn become fully incorporated within this seat.

The constituency of Middlesbrough South and East Cleveland is surrounded by the north Yorkshire moors and bordered by the North Sea.

Middlesbrough South and East Cleveland is a large and mixed constituency. The east of the constituency is made up nearly equally of prosperous owner-occupier suburbs, and large peripheral council estates which lie on the southern outskirts of Middlesbrough.

The large market town of Guisborough, acts as the centre core of the constituency; the Victorian resort seaside town of Saltburn and a number of small villages and towns which grew up as part of the ironstone mining boom of Victorian years is collectively known as East Cleveland.

The seat's economy is reliant on a number of industries, notably farming and chemicals. Most constituents work in and on urban Teesside, either in Middlesbrough or Stockton.

Paul Blomfield

Sheffield Central

Boundary changes

Tel: 020 7219 3000
E-mail: paul.blomfield.mp@parliament.uk
Website: www.paulblomfield.co.uk

Education: St John's College, York (theology); Teacher training; Married Linda McAvan MEP 2000 (1 son)

Non-political career: General manager, Sheffield University Students' Union; Former branch secretary, Unison; Member, Amicus/Unite; Former Governor, Sheffield City Polytechnic; Sheffield City Trust: Board member 1994-, Chair 1997-2008

Political career: Member for Sheffield Central since 6 May 2010 general election; Member, Labour Party 1978-; Chair, Sheffield Labour Party 1993-; Member, Co-operative Party

Political interests: Racism, equality

Other organisations: Former member, Anti-Apartheid Movement

Paul Blomfield MP, House of Commons, London SW1A 0AA
Tel: 020 7219 3000 E-mail: paul.blomfield.mp@parliament.uk
Constituency: c/o Sheffield Labour Party, Trades and Labour Club, Talbot Street, Sheffield S2 2TG Tel: 0114-272 4964
Website: www.paulblomfield.co.uk

GENERAL ELECTION RESULT

		%
Blomfield, P. (Lab)	17,138	41.3
Scriven, P. (Lib Dem)	16,973	40.9
Lee, A. (Con)	4,206	10.1
Creasy, J. (Green)	1,556	3.8
Smith, T. (BNP)	903	2.2
Shaw, J. (UKIP)	652	1.6
Rodgers, R. (Ind)	40	0.1
Majority	165	0.40
Electorate	69,519	
Turnout	41,468	59.65

CONSTITUENCY SNAPSHOT

The area has had only two MPs since 1950, both Labour. Fred Mulley, represented the then Sheffield Park for 33 years until 1983 and Richard Caborn since then.

Caborn enjoyed large majorities through all of his general election victories. In 2005 the Liberal Democrats achieved a 9.1 per cent swing in their favour, leaving Labour with a reduced majority of 7,055.

Paul Blomfield held the seat for Labour with a tiny majority of 165 at the 2010 general election.

Boundary changes saw the wards of Broomhill, Nether Edge and Walkley moved entirely within the constituency having previously been shared between the seat and other Sheffield divisions.

Situated in the heart of Sheffield, there have been new developments of commerce and working-class accommodation.

The specialised economy based on skilled labour, heavy engineering, steel, tools and cutlery-making took a heavy blow in the 1980s and 1990s.

The massive restructuring brought an end to an economy largely dependent on a handful of large steel and engineering plants, eventually replacing it with a much more diverse employment base of small and medium-sized businesses. Manufacturing is still important but service industries are now much more so.

Rt Hon **David Blunkett**

Sheffield, Brightside and Hillsborough ***(returning MP)***

New constituency

Tel: 020 7219 4043
E-mail: blunkettd@parliament.uk

Date of birth: 6 June 1947; Son of late Arthur and Doris Blunkett

Education: Royal National Normal College for the Blind; Shrewsbury Technical College; Sheffield Richmond College of Further Education (day release and evening courses); Sheffield University (BA political theory and institutions 1972); Huddersfield College of Education (PGCE 1973); Married Ruth Gwynneth Mitchell 1970 (divorced 1990) (3 sons); 1 son; married Dr Margaret Williams 2009 (3 stepdaughters)

Non-political career: Office work, East Midlands Gas Board 1967-69; Tutor in industrial relations and politics, Barnsley College of Technology 1973-81; Shop steward GMB EMGB 1967-69; Member: NATFHE 1973-87, UNISON 1973-; Councillor, Sheffield City Council 1970-88, Chair, Social Services Committee 1976-80, Seconded as Leader 1980-87; Councillor, South Yorkshire County Council 1973-77; Former Chair, Race Relations Forum

Political career: Contested Sheffield Hallam February 1974 general election. Member for Sheffield Brightside 1987-2010, for Sheffield Brightside and Hillsborough since 6 May 2010 general election; Opposition Spokesperson for Local Government 1988-92; Shadow Secretary of State for: Health 1992-94, Education 1994-95, Education and Employment 1995-97; Secretary of State for Education and Employment 1997-2001; Home Secretary 2001-04; Secretary of State for Work and Pensions 2005; Member, Labour Party National Executive Committee 1983-98; Labour Party: Vice-Chair 1992-93, Chair 1993-94

Political interests: Local government, employment and welfare to work, citizenship and civil renewal; France, USA

Other organisations: Council member Guide Dogs for the Blind Association; Patron several national and local voluntary organisations; Former Trustee Community Service Volunteers; Fellow Industry and Parliament Trust 1991; PC 1997; *Publications:* Building from the Bottom (1983); Democracy in Crisis – the Town Halls Respond (1987); On a Clear Day – (autobiography) (1995, 2002); Politics and Progress (2001); The Blunkett Tapes – My Life in the Bear Pit (2006)

Recreations: Walking, sailing, music, poetry

Rt Hon David Blunkett MP, House of Commons, London SW1A 0AA
Tel: 020 7219 4043 Fax: 020 7219 5903
E-mail: blunkettd@parliament.uk
Constituency: 2nd Floor, MidCity House, 17-21 Furnival Gate, Sheffield, South Yorkshire S1 4QR Tel: 0114-273 5987

GENERAL ELECTION RESULT

		%
Blunkett, D. (Lab)*	21,400	55.0
Harston, J. (Lib Dem)	7,768	20.0
Sharp, J. (Con)	4,468	11.5
Sheldon, J. (BNP)	3,026	7.8
Sullivan, P. (UKIP)	1,596	4.1
Bowler, M. (TUSC)	656	1.7
Majority	13,632	35.03
Electorate	68,186	
Turnout	38,914	57.07

**Member of last parliament*

CONSTITUENCY SNAPSHOT

The new seat of Sheffield, Brightside and Hillsborough has all but two of the wards (Walkley and Darnall) of the Brightside division as well as the Hillsborough ward from the Hillsborough seat.

This part of Sheffield has been held by Labour since 1935. Eddie Griffiths represented the area from 1968 to 1974. He was succeeded by Joan Maynard who held the seat until 1987. David Blunkett was first elected in 1987 on Maynard's retirement with a huge majority of 24,191.

Blunkett's total vote in 2001 was less than his majority four years earlier due to falling turnout. In 2005 David Blunkett was re-elected with a 13,644 majority. At the 2010 general election Blunkett was elected to the new seat with a 55 per cent share of the vote.

This division takes in the northern parts of Sheffield in South Yorkshire. It is made up of a sprawl of mostly pre-Second World War low-rise housing estates and is predominantly urban residential.

A large number of people are employed in manual work as the manufacturing industry remains important, and still provides many jobs in the constituency. Steel and cutlery are still produced in large volumes, but by far fewer people.

Most jobs are now found on industrial parks near the M1 and in the retail areas. The biggest single employer is the Meadowhall retail complex.

Crispin Blunt

Reigate (returning MP)

Boundary changes

Tel: 020 7219 2254
E-mail: crispinbluntmp@parliament.uk
Website: www.crispinbluntmp.com

Conservative

Date of birth: 15 July 1960; Son of late Major-General Peter and Adrienne Blunt

Education: Wellington College, Berkshire; Royal Military Academy, Sandhurst (commissioned 1980); University College, Durham University (BA politics 1984); Cranfield Institute of Technology (MBA 1991); Married Victoria Jenkins 1990 (1 son 1 daughter)

Non-political career: Army Officer 1979-90; Regimental duty 13th/18th Royal Hussars (QMO) in England, Germany and Cyprus; District agent, Forum of Private Business 1991-92; Political consultant, Politics International 1993; Special Adviser to Malcolm Rifkind: as Secretary of State for Defence 1993-95, as Foreign Secretary 1995-97

Political career: Contested West Bromwich East 1992 general election. Member for Reigate 1997-2010, for Reigate (revised boundary) since 6 May 2010 general election; Opposition Spokesperson for Northern Ireland 2001-02; Shadow Minister for Trade and Industry 2002-03; Opposition Whip 2004-09; Shadow Minister for National Security 2009-10; Parliamentary Under-Secretary of State, Ministry of Justice 2010-; *Select Committees:* Member: Defence 1997-2000, Environment, Transport and Regional Affairs 2000-01, Environment, Transport and Regional Affairs (Environment Sub-Committee) 2000-01, Defence 2003-04, Finance and Services 2005-09; Executive member 1922 Committee 2000-01; Treasurer Conservative Parliamentary Friends of India 2001-06; Chairman Conservative Middle East Council 2003-08

Political interests: Defence, foreign affairs, environment, energy; Middle East, India, USA

Other organisations: Reigate Priory Cricket, MCC

Recreations: Cricket, skiing, bridge

Crispin Blunt MP, House of Commons, London SW1A 0AA
Tel: 020 7219 2254 Fax: 020 7219 3373
E-mail: crispinbluntmp@parliament.uk
Constituency: 83 Bell Street, Reigate, Surrey RH2 7AN
Tel: 01737 249740 Website: www.crispinbluntmp.com

GENERAL ELECTION RESULT

		%
Blunt, C. (Con)*	26,688	53.4
Kulka, J. (Lib Dem)	13,097	26.2
Hull, R. (Lab)	5,672	11.4
Fox, J. (UKIP)	2,089	4.2
Brown, K. (BNP)	1,345	2.7
Essex, J. (Green)	1,087	2.2
Majority	13,591	27.19
Electorate	71,604	
Turnout	49,978	69.80

**Member of last parliament*

CONSTITUENCY SNAPSHOT

Conservatives have represented this constituency since 1945; the current incumbent, Crispin Blunt, is a former army officer. He was first elected in 1997 with a 7,741 majority. In 2001 he went on to increase his majority to 8,025 votes, and again in 2005 to 10,988.

Blunt held the seat with 26,688 votes giving the Conservatives a majority of 13,591 at the 2010 general election.

The seat gained the Preston ward from Epsom and Ewell.

Reigate has excellent transport links to London, Brighton and the south coast. The M25 and M23 cross the borough and Gatwick airport is on the doorstep; good rail links make commuting to London easy.

Reigate is situated at the foot of Colley Hill and Reigate Hill on the North Downs in Surrey. It is a market town, with a long and distinguished history, once used as a stopover for travellers on the Pilgrims Way. Pleasant countryside, and a number of pretty rural villages surround the town itself.

The main employers in the area are Legal and General, Fidelity, Watson Wyatt, First National Finance, and the office headquarters of Pfizer.

Nicholas Boles

Grantham and Stamford

Boundary changes

Tel: 020 7219 3000
E-mail: nick.boles.mp@parliament.uk
Website: www.nickboles.com

Conservative

Date of birth: 2 November 1965

Education: Winchester College; Magdalen College, Oxford (BA politics, philosophy and economics 1987); John F Kennedy School of Government, Harvard University (MPP master of public policy 1989); Single

Non-political career: Longwall Holdings Ltd: Chief executive 1995-2000, Chairman 2000-; Director, Policy Exchange 2002-07; Chief of staff to Boris Johnson as London Mayor 2008; Westminster City Council: Councillor 1998-2002, Chair, Housing Committee 1999-2001

Political career: Contested Hove 2005 general election. Member for Grantham and Stamford since 6 May 2010 general election

Political interests: Education, local government, foreign affairs

Other organisations: Century; *Publications:* Blue tomorrow (Politicos 2001)

Recreations: Sailing, skiing, running, playing the piano

Nicholas Boles MP, House of Commons, London SW1A 0AA
Tel: 020 7219 3000 E-mail: nick.boles.mp@parliament.uk
Constituency: c/o Conservative Office, North Street, Bourne, Lincolnshire PE10 9AJ Tel: 01778 421498 Fax: 01778 394443
Website: www.nickboles.com

GENERAL ELECTION RESULT

		%
Boles, N. (Con)	26,552	50.3
Bisnauthsing, H. (Lib Dem)	11,726	22.2
Bartlett, M. (Lab)	9,503	18.0
Robinson, C. (BNP)	2,485	4.7
Wells, A. (UKIP)	1,604	3.0
Horn, M. (Lincs Ind)	929	1.8
Majority	14,826	28.08
Electorate	78,000	
Turnout	52,799	67.69

CONSTITUENCY SNAPSHOT

The constituency was created in 1997, taking more than half its electors from the old Stamford and Spalding seat; the rest were from Grantham. Notional figures for Grantham and Stamford gave Quentin Davies a large majority. However, a swing of 13 per cent reduced his majority to 2,692. But the Conservatives vote recovered and Davies was re-elected in 2005 with a 7,445 majority.

In June 2007 Quentin Davies defected to the Labour Party. Nicholas Boles held the seat in 2010 for the Tories with a majority of 14,826.

Boundary changes moved Barrowby and Peascliffe wards and part-wards Ermine and Witham Valley to Sleaford and Hykeham, while part-ward Truesdale is now entirely in the seat.

A largely rural seat in the south-west corner of Lincolnshire, Grantham and Stamford is made up of territory that has always elected Tory MPs with large majorities.

The two eponymous towns mark very nearly the northern and southern extremities of the constituency.

Stamford is a beautiful Georgian stone town, whose centre is a conservation area, while Grantham is a typical 19th-century East Midlands manufacturing town. It manufactures products from tractors to shoes, with Wordsworth Holdings, makers of earth-moving equipment, one of the major employers. Food processing is another important industry.

Peter Bone

Wellingborough ***(returning MP)***

Boundary changes

Tel: 020 7219 8496
E-mail: bonep@parliament.uk

Conservative

Date of birth: 19 October 1952; Son of late William and Marjorie Phyliss Bone

Education: Stewards Comprehensive School, Harlow, Essex; Westcliff-on-Sea Grammar School, Essex; Married Jeanette Sweeney 1981 (2 sons 1 daughter)

Non-political career: Financial director Essex Electronics and Precision Engineering Group 1977-83; Chief executive High Tech Electronics Company 1983-90; Managing director: Palm Travel (West) Ltd 1990-, AJWB Travel Ltd; Councillor, Southend-on-Sea Borough Council 1977-86; Former Member Southern Airport Management Committee

Political career: Contested Islwyn 1992, Pudsey 1997 and Wellingborough 2001 general elections. Member for Wellingborough 2005-10, for Wellingborough (revised boundary) since 6 May 2010 general election; *Select Committees:* Member: Joint Committee on Statutory Instruments and Commons Committee on Statutory Instruments 2005-, Trade and Industry 2005-07, Health 2007-10; Contested Mid and West Wales 1994 European Parliament election; Deputy chair Southend West Conservative Association 1977-84; Press secretary to Paul Channon MP 1982-84; Member National Union Executive Committee 1993-96; Founder member All Wales Conservative Policy Group (Think Tank); Member Executive 1922 Committee 2007-

Other organisations: Wellingborough Golf Club; *Publications:* Contributor Telegraph, The Times, Daily Express, Western Mail; Numerous TV appearances and radio interviews

Recreations: Running marathons for charity, cricket

Peter Bone MP, House of Commons, London SW1A 0AA
Tel: 020 7219 8496 Fax: 020 7219 0301
E-mail: bonep@parliament.uk
Constituency: 21 High Street, Wellingborough, Northamptonshire NN8 4JZ Tel: 01933 279343

GENERAL ELECTION RESULT

		%
Bone, P. (Con)*	24,918	48.2
Buckland, J. (Lab)	13,131	25.4
Barron, K. (Lib Dem)	8,848	17.1
Haynes, A. (UKIP)	1,636	3.2
Walker, R. (BNP)	1,596	3.1
Spencer, T. (England)	530	1.0
Hornett, J. (Green)	480	0.9
Crofts, P. (TUSC)	249	0.5
Donaldson, G. (Ind)	240	0.5
Lavin, M. (Ind)	33	0.1
Majority	11,787	22.82
Electorate	76,857	
Turnout	51,661	67.22

**Member of last parliament*

CONSTITUENCY SNAPSHOT

A Conservative seat since 1974, Wellingborough was won by Labour with a majority of just 187 in 1997. They held the seat four years later with a far stronger majority of 2,355 over the Tories.

However, in 2005 a 2.9 per cent swing to the Conservatives returned current Tory MP Peter Bone to Parliament with a small 687 majority.

Bone increased his majority to 11,787 at the 2010 general election. There was a 10.8 per cent swing from Labour.

Boundary changes were minimal.

Essentially made up of the three Northamptonshire towns of Wellingborough, Rushden and Higham Ferrers, the constituency of Wellingborough has prospered in recent years with an improvement to road and rail links, and has diversified from traditional industries.

Although just over one-fifth of constituents work in the manufacturing industry, the industrial base has expanded into more diverse light and service industries, such as distribution, with development such as the growth of the Park Farm estate.

Farming is also important in the rural parts of the seat, while good rail links to London also serve a healthy population of commuters.

Peter Bottomley

Worthing West (returning MP)

Boundary changes

Tel: 020 7219 5060
E-mail: bottomleyp@parliament.uk
Website: www.peterbottomley.org.uk

Conservative

Date of birth: 20 July 1944; Son of Sir James Bottomley, KCMG, HM Diplomatic Service, and Barbara Bottomley, social worker

Education: Comprehensive School, Washington DC; Westminster School; Trinity College, Cambridge (BA economics 1966, MA); Married Virginia Garnett (later MP as Virginia Bottomley, now Baroness Bottomley of Nettlestone) 1967 (1 son 2 daughters)

Non-political career: Industrial sales, industrial relations, industrial economics; Former member, TGWU

Political career: Contested Greenwich, Woolwich West February and October 1974 general elections. Member for Greenwich, Woolwich West 1975 by-election to 1983, for Eltham 1983-97, for Worthing West 1997-2010, for Worthing West (revised boundary) since 6 May 2010 general election; PPS: to Cranley Onslow as Minister of State, Foreign and Commonwealth Office 1982-83, to Norman Fowler as Secretary of State for Health and Social Security 1983-84; Parliamentary Under-Secretary of State: Department of Employment 1984-86, Department of Transport (Minister for Roads and Traffic) 1986-89, Northern Ireland Office (Agriculture, Environment) 1989-90; PPS to Peter Brooke as Secretary of State for Northern Ireland 1990; *Select Committees:* Member: Standards and Privileges 1997-2002, Unopposed Bills (Panel) 1997-2010, Constitutional Affairs 2003-05, Ecclesiastical Committee; President, Conservative Trade Unionists 1978-80

Political interests: Southern Africa, El Salvador, USA

Other organisations: Trustee, Christian Aid 1978-84; Chair: Family Forum 1980-82, Church of England Children's Society 1982-84; Member, Council of NACRO 1997-2003; RIIA; OSCE Parliamentary Assembly; NATO Parliamentary Assembly; Fellow, Industry and Parliament Trust; Trustee, Dr Busby's Trustees (Willen) Main Charity; Gold Medal, Institute of the Motor Industry 1988; Former Fellow, Institute of Personnel Management; Fellow, Institute of Road Safety Officers; Court Member, Drapers' Company; Former Parliamentary swimming and occasional dinghy sailing champion

Recreations: Children, canoeing

Peter Bottomley MP, House of Commons, London SW1A 0AA
Tel: 020 7219 5060 Fax: 020 7219 1212
E-mail: bottomleyp@parliament.uk
Constituency: None publicised Website: www.peterbottomley.org.uk

GENERAL ELECTION RESULT

		%
Bottomley, P. (Con)*	25,416	51.7
Thorpe, H. (Lib Dem)	13,687	27.9
Ross, I. (Lab)	5,800	11.8
Wallace, J. (UKIP)	2,924	6.0
Aherne, D. (Green)	996	2.0
Dearsley, S. (Christian)	300	0.6
Majority	11,729	23.88
Electorate	75,945	
Turnout	49,123	64.68

**Member of last parliament*

CONSTITUENCY SNAPSHOT

Worthing West was created from the old seat of Worthing in 1997. In 1997 Worthing's previous MP, Sir Terrence Higgins, stood down, and Conservative Peter Bottomley replaced him here.

Bottomley held on with a reduced majority of 7,713. In the 2001 general election Bottomley's share of the vote rose by 1.3 per cent. His majority increased by 342 votes to 9,379 in 2005.

In 2010 Bottomley held the seat for the Conservatives with a safe 11,729 majority.

The seat gained the part-wards of Central and Salvington from East Worthing and Shoreham.

Worthing, a coastal town in West Sussex, is a bustling modern commercial centre with a population of around 100,000. Worthing West contains most of the town as well as Goring-by-Sea, and the coastal villages of Ferring, East Preston, Kingston, and Rustington.

In addition to the retired population, Worthing has an active working population and numerous companies are based in the area. The majority of jobs are in the service sector, and local government is a major employer.

Tourism creates plentiful employment in the hotel and retail sector, while manufacturing is also important.

Karen Bradley

Staffordshire Moorlands

Boundary changes

Tel: 020 7219 3000
E-mail: karen.bradley.mp@parliament.uk
Website: www.karenbradley.co.uk

Conservative

Date of birth: 12 March 1970

Education: Buxton Girls School, Buxton; Imperial College, London (BSc mathematics 1991); Married Neil Austen Bradley 2001 (2 sons)

Non-political career: Student accountant then manager, Deloittes 1991-98; Senior manager, KPMG 1998-2004; Self-employed economic and fiscal adviser 2004-; Senior manager, KPMG 2007-

Political career: Contested Manchester Withington 2005 general election. Member for Staffordshire Moorlands since 6 May 2010 general election

Political interests: Economy, rural affairs, home affairs, childcare

Recreations: Reading

Karen Bradley MP, House of Commons, London SW1A 0AA
Tel: 020 7219 3000 E-mail: karen.bradley.mp@parliament.uk
Constituency: Staffordshire Moorlands Conservatives, Churchill House, 30 Russell Street, Leek, Staffordshire ST13 5JF
Tel: 01538 382393 Fax: 01538 382383
Website: www.karenbradley.co.uk

GENERAL ELECTION RESULT

		%
Bradley, K. (Con)	19,793	45.2
Atkins, C. (Lab)*	13,104	29.9
Jebb, H. (Lib Dem)	7,338	16.8
Povey, S. (UKIP)	3,580	8.2
Majority	6,689	15.27
Electorate	62,071	
Turnout	43,815	70.59

**Member of last parliament*

CONSTITUENCY SNAPSHOT

Following the Second World War this seat was held by both Labour and the Tories for 25 and 27 years respectively. Harold Davies held the seat for Labour from 1945 until his defeat in 1970 by Sir David Knox.

In 1997 Sir David Knox retired and the Labour candidate, Charlotte Atkins, won with a 10,049-vote majority. Her majority fell a further 3,400 votes in 2005 to just 2,438.

In 2010 Karen Bradley defeated Atkins to take the seat for the Conservatives with a 6,689 majority following a 5.7 per cent swing.

Boundary changes moved Butt Lane, Kidsgrove, Ravenscliffe and Talke into Stoke-on-Trent North. Alton and Churnet wards were transferred from Stone, while Bagnall and Stanley, and Brown Edge and Endon joined the seat from Stoke-on-Trent North.

This is Staffordshire's northernmost constituency, containing the town of Leek and Peak District countryside as well as the ex-mining communities of Biddulph and Kidsgrove.

Leek was traditionally a working-class, textiles-based market town, but it now also provides a home to a growing number of commuters.

The Britannia Building Society is based in the town and is the largest employer with 1,800 workers. Leek United Building Society, another mutual, is also based in the town. Using its proximity to the National Park the area is developing a tourist sector.

The economy in Staffordshire Moorlands is very mixed with the numbers employed in agriculture, mining and quarrying

Rt Hon **Ben Bradshaw**

Exeter (returning MP)

Boundary changes

Tel: 020 7219 6597
E-mail: bradshawb@parliament.uk
Website: www.benbradshaw.co.uk

Date of birth: 30 August 1960; Son of late Canon Peter Bradshaw and late Daphne Bradshaw, teacher

Education: Thorpe St Andrew School, Norwich; Sussex University (BA German 1982); Freiburg University, Germany; Civil partner Neal Thomas Dalgleish 2006

Non-political career: BBC 1986-97: Reporter and presenter 1986-97, Berlin correspondent during fall of Berlin Wall 1989-91, Reporter *World At One* and *World This Weekend*, Radio 4 1991-97; Member, NUJ, GMB, USDAW

Political career: Member for Exeter 1997-2010, for Exeter (revised boundary) since 6 May 2010 general election; Introduced Pesticides Act (Private Member's Bill) 1998; PPS to John Denham as Minister of State, Department of Health 2000-01; Parliamentary Under-Secretary of State, Foreign and Commonwealth Office 2001-02; Parliamentary Secretary, Privy Council Office 2002-03; Department for Environment, Food and Rural Affairs 2003-07: Parliamentary Under-Secretary of State 2003-06, Minister of State (MoS) 2006-07; MoS for Health Services, Department of Health 2007-09; Minister for the South West 2007-09; Secretary of State for Culture, Media and Sport 2009-10; Shadow Secretary of State for Culture, Olympics, Media and Sport 2010-; *Select Committees:* Member: European Scrutiny 1998-2001; Labour Movement for Europe, Member: Labour Campaign for Electoral Reform, SERA, Christian Socialist Movement

Political interests: Foreign affairs, environment, transport, modernisation of Parliament; Europe – particularly Germany and Italy, USA

Other organisations: PC 2009; Argos Consumer Journalist of the Year 1989; Anglo-German Foundation Journalist of the Year 1990; Sony News Reporter Award 1993; Norfolk County Scholar Honorary fellowship Humboldt University, Berlin; Whipton Labour, Exeter; *Publications:* Numerous for the BBC on domestic and foreign affairs

Recreations: Cycling, walking, cooking, music

Rt Hon Ben Bradshaw MP, House of Commons, London SW1A 0AA
Tel: 020 7219 6597 Fax: 020 7219 0950
E-mail: bradshawb@parliament.uk
Constituency: Labour HQ, 26B Clifton Hill, Exeter, Devon EX1 2DJ
Tel: 01392 275004 Fax: 01392 435523
Website: www.benbradshaw.co.uk

GENERAL ELECTION RESULT

		%
Bradshaw, B. (Lab)*	19,942	38.2
Foster, H. (Con)	17,221	33.0
Oakes, G. (Lib Dem)	10,581	20.3
Crawford, K. (UKIP)	1,930	3.7
Gale, C. (Lib)	1,108	2.1
Black, P. (Green)	792	1.5
Farmer, R. (BNP)	673	1.3
Majority	2,721	5.21
Electorate	77,157	
Turnout	52,247	67.72

**Member of last parliament*

CONSTITUENCY SNAPSHOT

Since the Second World War Exeter had been predominately a Conservative seat. However, the present Labour incumbent, Ben Bradshaw, has been here since 1997. Labour then increased its share of the vote and the size of its majority by a couple of percentage points in the 2001 general election, but in 2005 Labour's vote dropped by 8.7 per cent. However, Ben Bradshaw was still re-elected with a majority of 7,665.

One of only four Labour seats in the South West, former Ben Bradshaw's majority was reduced to 2,721 following a 6 per cent swing in 2010.

The seat lost two wards, St Loyes and Topsham, to East Devon.

Exeter is Devon's prosperous county town and a university city.

Exeter displays many of the same economic and social characteristics of other small cities such as Chester, Worcester and York with a bustling commercial centre, a distinguished university and a vibrant social life.

The compact city centre has a large number of town houses and flats. Beyond there are numerous suburban semis and Victorian housing.

Graham Brady

Altrincham and Sale West (returning MP)

Boundary changes

Tel: 020 7219 4604
E-mail: bradyg@parliament.uk
Website: www.grahambradymp.co.uk

Conservative

Date of birth: 20 May 1967; Son of John Brady, accountant, and Maureen Brady, neé Birch, medical secretary

Education: Altrincham Grammar School; Durham University (BA law 1989); Married Victoria Lowther 1992 (1 son 1 daughter)

Non-political career: Shandwick PLC 1989-90; Assistant director of publications, Centre for Policy Studies 1990-92; Public affairs director, The Waterfront Partnership 1992-97; Independent Governor and member Audit Committee, Manchester Metropolitan University 2008

Political career: Member for Altrincham and Sale West 1997-2010, for Altrincham and Sale West (revised boundary) since 6 May 2010 general election; PPS to Michael Ancram as Conservative Party Chairman 1999-2000; Opposition Whip 2000; Opposition Spokesperson for: Employment 2000-01, Schools 2001-03; PPS to Michael Howard as Leader of the Opposition 2003-04; Shadow Minister for Europe 2004-07; *Select Committees:* Member: Education and Employment 1997-2001, Education and Employment (Employment Sub-Committee) 1997-2001, Office of the Deputy Prime Minister 2004-05, Office of the Deputy Prime Minister (Urban Affairs Sub-Committee) 2004-05, Treasury 2007-10, Reform of the House of Commons 2009-10, Chairmen's Panel 2009-10; Chair Durham University Conservative Association 1987-88; National Union Executive Committee 1988; Chair Northern Area Conservative Collegiate Forum 1987-89; Vice-chair East Berkshire Conservative Association 1993-95; 1922 Committee: Member Executive 1998-2000, 2007-10, Chair 2010-

Political interests: Education, health, Europe; Commonwealth, Far East, British Overseas Territories

Other organisations: Vice-Patron Friends of Rosie (research into children's cancer); Vice-President Altrincham Chamber of Trade Commerce and Industry 1997-; Patron Family Contact Line; *Publications:* Towards an Employees' Charter – and Away From Collective Bargaining (Centre for Policy Studies 1991)

Recreations: Family, gardening, reading

Graham Brady MP, House of Commons, London SW1A 0AA
Tel: 020 7219 4604 Fax: 020 7219 1649
E-mail: bradyg@parliament.uk
Constituency: Altrincham and Sale West Conservative Association, Thatcher House, Delahays Farm, Green Lane, Timperley, Cheshire WA15 8QW Tel: 0161-904 8828 Fax: 0161-904 8868
Website: www.grahambradymp.co.uk

GENERAL ELECTION RESULT

		%
Brady, G. (Con)*	24,176	49.0
Brophy, J. (Lib Dem)	12,581	25.5
Ross, T. (Lab)	11,073	22.4
Bullman, K. (UKIP)	1,563	3.2
Majority	11,595	23.47
Electorate	71,254	
Turnout	49,393	69.32

**Member of last parliament*

CONSTITUENCY SNAPSHOT

The Tories have held Altrincham and Sale West throughout the post-Second World War period, mostly with sizeable majorities.

Fergus Montgomery was MP from 1972. In 1997 Graham Brady took the mantle of parliamentary candidate and in the face of the Labour's national victory, held this seat by a majority of 1,505. He built his majority up by the 2001 general election to 2,941. Graham Brady's majority increased by over 4,000 votes in 2005.

In 2010 Brady held the seat in 2010 with a majority of 11,595.

Boundary changes were minimal.

Situated to the south of Manchester and to the north of Tatton, Altrincham and Sale West is, in the main, a residential constituency. Altrincham itself is very much a town of character in its own right, and its history as a market centre stretches back to the thirteenth century.

As with the entire Greater Manchester conurbation the transport links are excellent and bring wealth and prosperity as the more well-heeled of the city's workers seek solace in the smaller towns outside the city centre. The numbers of managerial, white collar and professional workers is well above the national average.

The building, gradual improvement, and advancement of the MetroLink light rail system that has provided a new link between Trafford and Manchester city centre have helped the area economically.

Tom Brake

Carshalton and Wallington ***(returning MP)***

Boundary changes

Tel: 020 7219 0924
E-mail: braket@parliament.uk
Website: www.tombrake.co.uk

Date of birth: 6 May 1962; Son of Michael and Judy Brake

Education: Lycee International, St Germain-en-Laye, France; Imperial College, London (BSc physics 1983); Married Candida Goulden 1998 (1 daughter 1 son)

Non-political career: Principal consultant (IT), Cap Gemini 1983-97; Councillor: London Borough of Hackney 1988-90, London Borough of Sutton 1994-98

Political career: Contested Carshalton and Wallington 1992 general election. Member for Carshalton and Wallington 1997-2010, for Carshalton and Wallington (revised boundary) since 6 May 2010 general election; Liberal Democrat: Spokesperson for: Environment, Transport in London and Air Transport 1997-99, Environment, Transport, the Regions, Social Justice and London Transport 1999-2001, Whip 2000-04, Spokesperson for: Transport, Local Government and the Regions 2001-02, Transport 2002-03, Shadow Secretary of State for: International Development 2003-05, Transport 2005-06, Shadow Minister for: Communities and Local Government 2006-07, London and the Olympics 2007-10, Home Office 2008-10; *Select Committees:* Member: Environment, Transport and Regional Affairs 1997-2001, Environment, Transport and Regional Affairs (Environment Sub-Committee) 1997-2001, Environment, Transport and Regional Affairs (Transport Sub-Committee) 1999-2000, Accommodation and Works 2001-03, Transport 2002-03, Home Affairs 2008-10

Political interests: Environment, transport, sport, international development, home affairs; France, Portugal, Russia, Australia

Other organisations: Collingwood Athletic Club

Recreations: Sport, film, eating

Tom Brake MP, House of Commons, London SW1A 0AA
Tel: 020 7219 0924 E-mail: braket@parliament.uk
Constituency: Kennedy House, 5 Nightingale Road, Carshalton, Surrey SM5 2DN Tel: 020 8255 8155 Fax: 020 8395 4453
Website: www.tombrake.co.uk

GENERAL ELECTION RESULT

		%
Brake, T. (Lib Dem)*	22,180	48.3
Andrew, K. (Con)	16,920	36.9
Khan, S. (Lab)	4,015	8.7
Day, F. (UKIP)	1,348	2.9
Lewis, C. (BNP)	1,100	2.4
Dow, G. (Green)	355	0.8
Majority	5,260	11.46
Electorate	66,520	
Turnout	45,918	69.03

**Member of last parliament*

CONSTITUENCY SNAPSHOT

In 1997 an 11.8 per cent swing to the Liberal Democrat candidate Tom Brake was enough to remove the Conservative incumbent, Nigel Forman, who had been MP for 21 years. In 2001 the Liberal Democrats more than doubled their majority to 4,547.

However, in 2005 there was a 4.4 per cent swing to the Conservatives, which allowed them to close in on Brake, who was returned with a 1,068 majority. Brake increased a shaky majority of 1,068 to a healthier 5,260.

There were minor boundary changes: the six wards that straddled the seat and Sutton and Cheam have been realigned: Carshalton Central, St Helier, and the Wrythe wards are now entirely within Carshalton and Wallington; while Belmont, Sutton Central, and Sutton South wards are completely contained in Sutton and Cheam.

Carshalton and Wallington is a socially mixed constituency consisting on the one hand of leafy suburbs, such as those around Carshalton Beeches, and on the other of working class estates in places such as Wrythe and Beddington.

Many of the seat's large number of skilled non-manual workers either commute in to central London or make the much shorter trip to nearby Croydon.

Angie Bray

Ealing Central and Acton

New constituency

Tel: 020 7219 7055
E-mail: angie.bray.mp@parliament.uk
Website: www.angiebray.co.uk

Conservative

Date of birth: 13 October 1953; Daughter of late Benedict Bray and Patricia Bray

Education: Downe, House, Newbury, Berkshire; St Andrews University (MA medieval history 1975); London College of Printing (radio journalism); Partner Nigel Hugh-Smith

Non-political career: Radio presenter British Forces Broadcasting 1979-80; Radio presenter/producer/reporter/editor LBC 1980-88; Researcher *Right Talk*, Channel 4 political programme 1988; Head of broadcasting unit Conservative Central Office 1989-91; Press secretary to Conservative Party chairman 1991-92; Public affairs consultant 1992-2000; Member, National Union of Journalists (NUJ) 1979-88; Greater London Assembly: Member 2000-08, Member, Notting Hill Carnival Review Group 2000-08, Deputy Chair, Culture, Sport and Tourism Committee 2004-06, Leader, Conservative group 2006-07, Spokesperson for: Congestion Charging, Notting Hill Carnival, Culture, Sport and Tourism; Governor, Berrymead Junior School

Political career: Contested East Ham 1997 general election. Member for Ealing Central and Acton since 6 May 2010 general election; Kensington and Chelsea Conservative Political Forum: Chair 1999-2000, President 2000-03; Vice-President, Hammersmith and Fulham Conservative Association 2000-

Political interests: London issues, transport, NHS; Italy, Spain, USA

Other organisations: Freedom of City of London; Conservative Friends of Israel; Conservative Arab Network; Conservative Friends of Poland; Ealing Lawn Tennis Club

Recreations: History, music, travel, tennis, my dogs, cinema

Angie Bray MP, House of Commons, London SW1A 0AA
Tel: 020 7219 7055 E-mail: angie.bray.mp@parliament.uk
Constituency: 39 Broughton Road, London W13 8QW
Tel: 020 8810 0579 Website: www.angiebray.co.uk

GENERAL ELECTION RESULT

		%
Bray, A. (Con)	17,944	38.0
Mahfouz, B. (Lab)	14,228	30.1
Ball, J. (Lib Dem)	13,041	27.6
Carter, J. (UKIP)	765	1.6
Edwards, S. (Green)	737	1.6
Fernandes, S. (Christian)	295	0.6
Akaki, S. (Ind EACPS)	190	0.4
Majority	3,716	7.87
Electorate	63,489	
Turnout	47,200	74.34

CONSTITUENCY SNAPSHOT

This new seat is a successor to Ealing, Acton and Shepherd's Bush. It will also inherit the eastern-most areas of the Ealing Southall constituency.

The original Acton seat had been mainly in Labour hands since 1945 apart from the a Conservative win in 1959, and a brief interlude, 1968 to 1970, when the future Tory Cabinet Minister Kenneth Baker won it in a by-election. Conservative Angie Bray took this three-way Tory-Labour-Lib Dem marginal with 38 per cent of the vote and a majority of 3,716.

However, the addition of some of the parts of Ealing in 1974 was just enough to swing it to the Conservatives, and brought about the election of another future Minister, Sir George Young.

Clive Soley, Labour MP for Hammersmith since 1979, had followed a minority of his electorate into the new seat and won in 1997 with a majority of 15,650. He retired in 2005 and was succeeded by Andy Slaughter, whose majority was almost half his predecessor's, at 5,520.

The new seat is an area wide-ranging in its social and ethnic diversity. The proximity of Heathrow Airport has a huge influence on transport and the environment in West London. It also provides employment for many constituents.

Ealing Studios, standard bearer for the British film industry, is also based here.

Julian Brazier

Canterbury (returning MP)

Boundary changes

Tel: 020 7219 5178
E-mail: brazierj@parliament.uk
Website: www.julianbrazier.co.uk

Conservative

Date of birth: 24 July 1953; Son of Lieutenant Colonel Peter Hendy Brazier, retired, and Patricia Audrey Helen, neé Stubbs

Education: Wellington College, Berkshire; Brasenose College, Oxford (Scholarship BA mathematics and philosophy 1975, MA); London Business School; Married Katherine Elizabeth Blagden 1984 (3 sons)

Non-political career: TA officer 1972-82, 1989-92; Charter Consolidated Ltd 1975-84: economic research 1975-77, corporate finance 1977-81, Secretary executive committee of Board 1981-84; Management consultant H B Maynard International 1984-87

Political career: Contested Berwick-upon-Tweed 1983 general election. Member for Canterbury 1987-2010, for Canterbury (revised boundary) since 6 May 2010 general election; PPS to Gillian Shephard as: Minister of State, HM Treasury 1990-92, Secretary of State for Employment 1992-93; Opposition Whip 2001-02; Shadow Minister for: Work and Pensions 2002-03, Home Affairs 2003, Foreign Affairs 2003-05, Transport (aviation and shipping) 2005-10; *Select Committees:* Member: Defence 1997-2001; President Conservative Family Campaign 1995-2001; Vice-chair Conservative Party Listening to Churches Programme 2000-03; Member Cornerstone Group 2005-

Political interests: Defence, foreign affairs, economics, law and order, families, countryside; Middle East, South Africa, USA, Australia, New Zealand, Russia, Lebanon

Other organisations: President Canterbury Sea Cadets 2009-; Territorial Decoration 1993; Highland Park/*The Spectator* Backbencher of the Year (jointly) 1996; Kent and Canterbury; East Kent and Canterbury Conservatives Club; *Publications:* Co-author Not Fit to Fight: The Cultural Subversion of the Armed Forces in Britain and America (Social Affairs Unit, 1999); Ten pamphlets on defence, social and economic issues (with Bow Group, Centre for Policy Studies and Conservative 2000)

Recreations: Cross-country running, science, philosophy

Julian Brazier TD MP, House of Commons, London SW1A 0AA
Tel: 020 7219 5178 Fax: 020 7219 0643
E-mail: brazierj@parliament.uk
Constituency: 54 The Strand, Walmer, Deal, Kent CT14 7DP
Tel: 01304 379669 Website: www.julianbrazier.co.uk

GENERAL ELECTION RESULT

		%
Brazier, J. (Con)*	22,050	44.8
Voizey, G. (Lib Dem)	16,002	32.5
Samuel, J. (Lab)	7,940	16.1
Farmer, H. (UKIP)	1,907	3.9
Meaden, G. (Green)	1,137	2.3
Belsey, A. (MRP)	173	0.4
Majority	6,048	12.29
Electorate	76,808	
Turnout	49,209	64.07

**Member of last parliament*

CONSTITUENCY SNAPSHOT

From five-figure Conservative majorities in the 1970s, 1980s and early 1990s the Tory vote fell away in 1997 leaving the incumbent MP Julian Brazier with a majority of 3,964. In 2001 his majority fell further to 2,069.

In 2005 there was a swing away from Labour that benefited both the Liberal Democrats and Conservatives and ensured Brazier a much healthier majority of 7,471.

Brazier was re-elected in 2010 with 22,050 votes giving him a majority of 6,048.

Boundary changes were minimal, with the seat losing the Marshside ward to North Thanet.

The constituency of Canterbury is best known for its cathedral city, but it also includes a number of surrounding villages, and the seaside town of Whitstable (famous for its oysters) on the North Kent coastline.

There is a large concentration of higher education facilities and a correspondingly high percentage of students, attending the University of Kent, Christ Church University College, Kent Institute of Art and Design and Canterbury College. The large education sector also contributes many jobs to the economy.

This is a relatively prosperous constituency with one of the largest and most diverse economies in Kent. There is a strong light engineering and manufacturing base at the major business parks in Whitstable and nearby Herne Bay (just outside the constituency).

Kevin Brennan

Cardiff West (returning MP)

Boundary changes

Tel: 020 7219 8156
E-mail: brennank@parliament.uk
Website: www.kevinbrennan.co.uk

Date of birth: 16 October 1959; Son of late Michael John Brennan, steelworker and Beryl Marie, née Evans, school cook/cleaner

Education: St Alban's RC Comprehensive, Pontypool; Pembroke College, Oxford (BA philosophy, politics and economics 1982) (President Oxford Union 1982); University College of Wales, Cardiff (PGCE history 1985); Glamorgan University (MSc education management 1992); Married Amy Lynn Wack, poetry editor, 1988 (1 daughter)

Non-political career: News editor, volunteer organiser Cwmbran Community Press 1982-84; Head of economics and business studies Radyr Comprehensive School 1985-94; Research officer to Rhodri Morgan MP 1995-99; Special adviser to Rhodri Morgan as First Minister National Assembly for Wales 2000-01; NUT 1984-94; TGWU/Unite 1995-; Musicians union 2003-08; Councillor Cardiff City Council: Chair: Finance Committee 1993-96, Economic Scrutiny Committee 1999-2001

Political career: Member for Cardiff West 2001-10, for Cardiff West (revised boundary) since 6 May 2010 general election; PPS to Alan Milburn as Chancellor of the Duchy of Lancaster 2004-05; Assistant Government Whip 2005-06; Government Whip 2006-07; Parliamentary Under-Secretary of State, Department for Children, Schools and Families 2007-08; Parliamentary Secretary, Cabinet Office 2008-09; Minister of State (Further Education, Skills, Apprenticeships and Consumer Affairs), Departments for Business, Innovation and Skills and Children, Schools and Families 2009-10; *Select Committees:* Member: Public Administration 2001-05; Member: Fabian Society, Bevan Foundation; Chair Cardiff West Constituency Labour Party 1998-2000; Member Labour Campaign Electoral Reform

Political interests: Economy, constitutional affairs, creative industries; Ireland, USA

Other organisations: Chair Yes for Wales Cardiff 1997; Member parliamentary rock band 'MP4'

Recreations: Rugby, golf, reading, cricket, music

Kevin Brennan MP, House of Commons, London SW1A 0AA
Tel: 020 7219 8156 E-mail: brennank@parliament.uk
Constituency: c/o Transport House, 1 Cathedral Road,
Cardiff CF11 9SD Tel: 029 2022 3207 Fax: 029 2023 0422
Website: www.kevinbrennan.co.uk

GENERAL ELECTION RESULT

		%
Brennan, K. (Lab)*	16,893	41.3
Jones-Evans, A. (Con)	12,143	29.7
Hitchinson, R. (Lib Dem)	7,186	17.6
Islam, M. (PIC)	2,868	7.0
Henessey, M. (UKIP)	1,117	2.7
Griffiths, J. (Green)	750	1.8
Majority	4,750	11.60
Electorate	62,787	
Turnout	40,957	65.23

**Member of last parliament*

CONSTITUENCY SNAPSHOT

Former Speaker George Thomas held the seat for Labour between 1945 and 1983. In 1983 the Conservatives' Stefan Terlezski won the seat but this was the only occasion Labour has lost here since 1929.

Stefan Terlezski's 1,774 majority was overturned in 1987, when Rhodri Morgan regained the seat for Labour. Morgan increased his majority in 1992 and further still in 1997 to 15,628. Morgan vacated the Westminster seat in 2001 to focus on his role as Wales' First Minister.

Kevin Brennan succeeded Morgan as MP in 2001. In the 2005 general election Brennan's majority remained a solid 8,167. Kevin Brennan was returned with a reduced majority of 4,750 in 2010.

Boundary changes bring the remainder of Creigiau/St Fagans and the Pentyrch ward into the constituency from Pontypridd.

A residential constituency including the inner city wards of Riverside and Canton, the middle-class Radyr and St Fagans and the large council estates in Ely and Caerau on the city's south western edge.

The M4 is the commercial artery of the area, running along the seat's northern border.

The £50 million project to create a new home for Cardiff City Football Club was completed in 2009. Cardiff Blues rugby union team also play at the new stadium which is the centrepiece of a large-scale development project in Leckwith which also includes a retail park, new homes and a new athletics stadium.

Andrew Bridgen

North West Leicestershire

No boundary changes

Tel: 020 7219 3000
E-mail: andrew.bridgen.mp@parliament.uk
Website: www.andrewbridgen.com

Date of birth: 28 October 1964

Education: Pingle School, Swadlincote; Nottingham University (BSc biological sciences 1986); CPC road haulage operations 1991; Married Jacqueline Cremin 2000 (2 sons)

Non-political career: Royal Marine officer training; Managing director, AB Produce plc (market gardening business) 1988-; Business member, East Midlands Regional Assembly 1999-2000

Political career: Member for North West Leicestershire since 6 May 2010 general election; North West Leicestershire Conservative Association

Political interests: Business and enterprise, civil liberties, law and order, armed forces

Other organisations: Regional committee member: Business for Sterling, The 'no' campaign; Ivanhoe Club, Ashby; Burton Rugby Club

Recreations: Military history, skiing, fishing, driving, reading, country pursuits

Andrew Bridgen MP, House of Commons, London SW1A 0AA
Tel: 020 7219 3000 E-mail: andrew.bridgen.mp@parliament.uk
Constituency: North West Leicestershire Conservative Association, Enterprise House, Repton Road, Westminster Industrial Estate, Measham, Derbyshire DE12 7DT Tel: 01530 514625
Website: www.andrewbridgen.com

GENERAL ELECTION RESULT

		%	+/-
Bridgen, A. (Con)	23,147	44.6	8.7
Willmott, R. (Lab)	15,636	30.1	-15.2
Reynolds, P. (Lib Dem)	8,639	16.6	4.6
Meller, I. (BNP)	3,396	6.5	3.4
Green, M. (UKIP)	1,134	2.2	-1.1
Majority	7,511	14.46	
Electorate	71,219		
Turnout	51,952	72.95	

CONSTITUENCY SNAPSHOT

In 1997 Labour's David Taylor achieved a swing of 13.5 per cent, giving him a majority of 13,219. This swing to Labour was helped by the de-selection of the former Conservative MP David Ashby who had held the seat since its creation in 1983.

In 2001 Labour's majority fell to 8,157, and in 2005 it was halved to 4,477. In 2010 Andrew Bridgen took the seat for the Conservatives with a 7,511 majority.

The constituency of North West Leicestershire covers the area of the old Leicestershire coalfields. It includes Ashby de la Zouch and Castle Donnington. Coalville is the biggest town.

There is a fairly even split between manual and non-manual workers in the constituency. It is very much a post-mining constituency which is learning to replace the pits with other industry.

The main sources of employment are small to medium-sized businesses including manufacturing, retail and distribution. The largest source of employment in North West Leicestershire is the expanding East Midlands Airport, closely followed by DHL in the north of the constituency.

Steve Brine

Winchester

Boundary changes

Tel: 020 7219 3000
E-mail: steve.brine.mp@parliament.uk
Website: www.stevebrine.com

Conservative

Date of birth: 28 January 1974

Education: Bohunt Comprehensive School; Highway College, Portsmouth; Liverpool University (BA history 2006) (Student Union President); Married Susie (1 daughter)

Non-political career: Journalist, BBC Radio; Journalist, WGN Radio, Chicago USA; Former director, Azalea Group (public relations and marketing firm)

Political career: Member for Winchester since 6 May 2010 general election

Political interests: NHS, media, planning and development; Italy, USA

Other organisations: Liphook Golf Club, Hampshire

Recreations: Football, skiing, tennis, golf, live music

Steve Brine MP, House of Commons, London SW1A 0AA
Tel: 020 7219 3000 E-mail: steve.brine.mp@parliament.uk
Constituency: The Coach House, Worthy Park, Abbots Worthy, Winchester, Hampshire SO21 1AN Tel: 01962 791110
Website: www.stevebrine.com

GENERAL ELECTION RESULT

		%
Brine, S. (Con)	27,155	48.5
Tod, M. (Lib Dem)	24,107	43.1
Davies, P. (Lab)	3,051	5.5
Penn-Bull, J. (UKIP)	1,139	2.0
Lancaster, M. (England)	503	0.9
Majority	3,048	5.45
Electorate	73,806	
Turnout	55,955	75.81

CONSTITUENCY SNAPSHOT

Previously a Conservative seat, the general election of 1997 elected Liberal Democrat candidate Mark Oaten by two votes. The Conservatives won a legal challenge to have the vote recontested, and a 'by-election' was held in November 1997. Mark Oaten won a majority of 21,556.

By 2001 Oaten retained a respectable majority of 9,634 over the Tories. In 2005 Oaten's majority fell slightly to 7,576.

In January 2006 Oaten announced his candidacy to succeed Charles Kennedy as party leader. Days later he had withdrawn his bid. He decided not to contest Winchester at the general election.

The Liberal Democrats were defeated in 2010 with a 9.1 per cent swing to the Conservative candidate, Steve Brine, who secured a 3,048 majority.

The seat gained three wards and a part-ward from Romsey, a part-ward from Eastleigh, and loses 11 wards to the new Meon Valley seat.

On the edge of the South Downs, Winchester is England's ancient capital. Its many museums, galleries and shops make it key Hampshire tourist attraction, and the famous private school, Winchester College, adds to its historical and elite status.

Winchester's socio-economic profile is that of a well-heeled and well-educated community. A third of families have very high incomes and the schools are among the best in the region.

Many of Winchester's residents commute daily into London and locally hi-tech companies such IBM, who have their headquarters in the area, have become large employers.

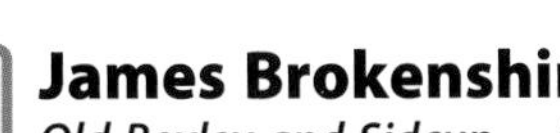

James Brokenshire

Old Bexley and Sidcup ***(returning MP)***

Boundary changes

Tel: 020 7219 8400
E-mail: brokenshirej@parliament.uk
Website: www.jamesbrokenshire.com

Conservative

Date of birth: 8 January 1968; Son of Joan and Peter Brokenshire

Education: Davenant Foundation Grammar School; Cambridge Centre for Sixth Form Studies; Exeter University (LLB 1990); Married Cathrine Anne Mamelok 1999 (2 daughters 1 son)

Non-political career: Trainee, solicitor, partner Jones Day Gouldens Solicitors 1991-2005

Political career: Member for Hornchurch May 2005-10, for Old Bexley and Sidcup since 6 May 2010 general election; Shadow Minister for Home Affairs 2006-10; Parliamentary Under-Secretary of State (Minister for Crime Prevention), Home Office 2010-; *Select Committees:* Member Constitutional Affairs 2005-06

Political interests: Health, housing and regeneration, law and order; Botswana

Recreations: Community radio, watching cricket, hill walking

James Brokenshire MP, House of Commons, London SW1A 0AA
Tel: 020 7219 8400 Fax: 020 7219 2043
E-mail: brokenshirej@parliament.uk
Constituency: Old Bexley and Sidcup Conservative Association, 19 Station Road, Sidcup, Kent DA15 7EB Tel: 020 8300 3471
Website: www.jamesbrokenshire.com

GENERAL ELECTION RESULT

		%
Brokenshire, J. (Con)*	24,625	54.1
Everitt, R. (Lab)	8,768	19.3
Borrowman, D. (Lib Dem)	6,996	15.4
Brooks, J. (BNP)	2,132	4.7
Coburn, D. (UKIP)	1,532	3.4
Cheeseman, E. (England)	520	1.1
Hemming-Clarke, J. (Ind)	393	0.9
Rooks, J. (Green)	371	0.8
Dynamite, N. (Loony)	155	0.3
Majority	15,857	34.86
Electorate	65,665	
Turnout	45,492	69.28

**Member of last parliament*

CONSTITUENCY SNAPSHOT

Elected Leader of the Conservative Party in 1965, Ted Heath lost the 1966 general election and his own majority was halved to the lowest of his career, just 2,333. Nevertheless, he won the next election in 1970 and became Prime Minister.

In the 1979 general election there was a swing back to the Conservatives and Heath gained almost 60 per cent of the vote. The following three general elections provided similar levels of support.

In 1997 Labour reduced Heath's majority to 3,569. After 14 terms of office, Heath retired in 2001 and was replaced by Derek Conway. He almost tripled his majority in 2005, which was 9,920. Ted Heath's old seat continues to be a Conservative stronghold despite the Conway controversy. James Brokenshire has increased the party's majority to 15,857.

The seat lost part of Danson ward to Bexleyheath and Crayford.

With owner-occupation accounting for 85 per cent of households, the highest proportion in London, this is a particularly suburban constituency.

Manufacturing is slightly higher than many constituencies in London because of the seat's proximity to the Thames Gateway area and North Kent's more industrial economic base.

A proposal to solve London's waste crisis by building an electricity-generating incinerator facility on the banks of the Thames in nearby Belvedere has caused local controversy but has been given the go-ahead.

Annette Brooke

Mid Dorset and North Poole *(returning MP)*

Boundary changes

Tel: 020 7219 8193
E-mail: brookea@parliament.uk
Website: www.annettebrooke.org.uk

Date of birth: 7 June 1947; Daughter of Ernest Henry Kelley, bookbinder, and Edna Mabel Kelley

Education: Romford Technical College; London School of Economics (BSc Econ 1968); Hughes Hall, Cambridge (Cert Ed 1969); Married Mike Brooke 1969 (2 daughters)

Non-political career: Open University 1971-91: Counsellor, Tutor: social sciences, economics 1969-85; Various college posts: Reading, Aylesbury, Poole, Bournemouth; Head of economics Talbot Heath School Bournemouth 1984-94; Partner Broadstone Minerals 1988; Owner Gemini shop Poole 1994-; Councillor Poole Borough Council 1986-2003: Chair: Planning 1991-96, Education 1996-2000, Sheriff 1996-97, Mayor 1997-98

Political career: Member for Mid Dorset and Poole North 2001-10, for Mid Dorset and North Poole (revised boundary) since 6 May 2010 general election; Liberal Democrat: Whip 2001-03, Spokesperson for: Home Affairs 2001-04, Children 2004-10, Shadow Minister for: Education 2005-06, Families 2006-10, Young People 2007, Schools 2008-10; *Select Committees:* Member: Public Administration 2001-05, Procedure 2005-06, Public Accounts 2006-08, Children, Schools and Families 2007-10

Political interests: Children and young people, home affairs, microfinance; Ghana, Kenya

Other organisations: Patron Julia's House Children's Hospice 2001-

Recreations: Gym, reading, shopping with daughters

Annette Brooke MP, House of Commons, London SW1A 0AA
Tel: 020 7219 8193 Fax: 020 7219 1898
E-mail: brookea@parliament.uk
Constituency: Broadstone Liberal Hall, 14 York Road, Broadstone, Dorset BH18 8ET Tel: 01202 693555 Fax: 01202 658420
Website: www.annettebrooke.org.uk

GENERAL ELECTION RESULT

		%
Brooke, A. (Lib Dem)*	21,100	45.1
King, N. (Con)	20,831	44.5
Brown, D. (Lab)	2,748	5.9
Evans, D. (UKIP)	2,109	4.5
Majority	269	0.57
Electorate	72,647	
Turnout	46,788	64.40

**Member of last parliament*

CONSTITUENCY SNAPSHOT

Created in 1997, the seat was formed from wards previously in North Dorset, Bournemouth West, South Dorset and Poole.

The Conservative notional majority of 6,540 was greatly reduced as Conservative Christopher Fraser secured the seat with a reduced majority of 1.4 per cent. The Liberal Democrats' Annette Brooke defeated Fraser to win the seat with a majority of 681. In 2005 voters returned her with an increased majority of 5,482. Brooke's majority fell to just 269 in 2010.

Boundary changes brought the wards of Wimborne Minster and Colehill East, and Colehill West, entirely within the seat's boundaries, whilst Alderney and Creekmoor part-wards move into Bournemouth West and Poole respectively.

On the border between town and country, Mid Dorset and Poole North is primarily a residential constituency, and more affluent than the centre of Poole. Chemical, pharmaceutical, electronic and engineering industries are the notable employers in the area.

Tourism is also important to the local economy, with many visitors drawn to the seaside and the many yacht clubs based in Poole Harbour. Canford Heath is a Site of Special Scientific Interest and part of the Dorset Heathlands Special Protection Area. To the north of Poole and in Wareham there are several industrial estates and there is some agriculture based around Bere Regis.

Rt Hon **Gordon Brown**

Kirkcaldy and Cowdenbeath ***(returning MP)***

No boundary changes

Tel: 020 7219 2968

Date of birth: 20 February 1951; Son of late Rev. Dr John Brown and late Jessie Brown, née Souter

Education: Kirkcaldy High School; Edinburgh University (MA 1972, PhD 1982); Married Sarah Macaulay 2000 (1 daughter deceased 2 sons)

Non-political career: Edinburgh University: Rector 1972-75, Temporary lecturer 1975-76; Lecturer in politics, Glasgow College of Technology 1976-80; Journalist, then editor, Scottish Television current affairs department 1980-83; Member, TGWU

Political career: Member for Dunfermline East 1983-2005, for Kirkcaldy and Cowdenbeath since 5 May 2005 general election; Opposition Spokesperson for: Trade and Industry 1985-87, Shadow Chief Secretary to the Treasury 1987-89; Opposition Spokesman for Trade and Industry 1989-92; Shadow Chancellor of the Exchequer 1992-97; Chancellor of the Exchequer 1997-2007; Prime Minister, First Lord of the Treasury and Minister for the Civil Service June 2007-10; Member, Scottish Executive Labour Party 1977-83; Chairman, Labour Party in Scotland 1983-84; Former Member, Labour Party National Executive Committee; Head, General Election Campaign (Strategy) 1999-2001; Leader Labour Party 2007-10

Political interests: Economic policy, employment, health, social security, Scotland

Other organisations: Governor, European Investment Bank 1997-2007; Commonwealth Parliamentary Association (UK Branch): Joint Hon Treasurer (ex-officio) 1997-99, Former Joint Hon Secretary, Vice-President 2007-10; PC 1996; *The Spectator*/Highland Park Parliamentarian of the Year 1997; Channel 4 and *The House* Magazine Speechmaker of the Year 1999; Channel 4 Politician of the Year 2000, 2001; *GQ* Politician of the Year 2005; *Publications:* Co-editor Values, Visions and Voices: An Anthology of Socialism; Co-author John Smith: Life and Soul of the Party; Maxton; Where There is Greed; Speeches 1997-2006; Courage: Eight Portraits (2007); Britain's Everyday Heroes (2007)

Recreations: Tennis, football, reading, writing

Rt Hon Gordon Brown MP, House of Commons, London SW1A 0AA
Tel: 020 7219 2968 Fax: 020 7219 5734
Constituency: 318-324 High Street, Cowdenbeath, Fife KY4 9QS
Tel: 01383 611702 Fax: 01383 611703
E-mail: kirkcaldyandcowdenbeathclp@yahoo.co.uk

GENERAL ELECTION RESULT

		%	+/-
Brown, G. (Lab)*	29,559	64.5	6.5
Chapman, D. (SNP)	6,550	14.3	-0.2
Mainland, J. (Lib Dem)	4,269	9.3	-3.7
Paterson, L. (Con)	4,258	9.3	-1.0
Adams, P. (UKIP)	760	1.7	0.4
Archibald, S. (Ind)	184	0.4	
MacLaren of MacLaren, D. (Ind)	165	0.4	
Jackson, D. (Land Power)	57	0.1	
Majority	23,009	50.24	
Electorate	73,665		
Turnout	45,802	62.18	

**Member of last parliament*

CONSTITUENCY SNAPSHOT

Harry Gourlay served as Labour MP from 1959 until his retirement in 1987. Lewis Moonie was returned in 1987 and held this seat for Labour with impressive majorities until retiring in 2005.

In 2005 the southern Fife constituencies were redrawn. The vast majority of Kirkcaldy voters found themselves in the new Kirkcaldy and Cowdenbeath division, where Lewis Moonie made way for Gordon Brown, whose Dunfermline East seat was abolished. Gordon Brown was returned with a majority of 18,216.

Former Prime Minister Gordon Brown held the seat with an absolute majority of 23,009 and a 64.5 per cent vote-share.

This Fife constituency has a long coastline along the Firth of Forth but tourism comes a poor second to large-scale industry, despite the decline of coalmining and linoleum manufacture.

Coastal Kirkcaldy, nicknamed the 'Lang Toun', occupies a long arc on the north of the Firth. It's Fife's largest town and grew to prosperity through the Victorian boom in the textile, linoleum and coal industries. The home of Raith Rovers Football Club, the town of Kirkcaldy is also the birthplace of the economist Adam Smith.

Cowdenbeath grew as a mining town in the late 19th century. Most industry is now located on three industrial estates around the town.

Lyn Brown

West Ham (returning MP)

Boundary changes

Tel: 020 7219 6999
E-mail: brownl@parliament.uk
Website: www.lynbrown.org.uk

Date of birth: 13 April 1960; Daughter of Joseph and Iris Brown

Education: Plashet Comprehensive School; Whitelands College, Roehampton (London University BA English and religious studies 1982); Married John Cullen 2008

Non-political career: Residential social worker, London Borough of Ealing Council 1984-85; Newham Voluntary Agencies, Newham 1985-87; London Borough of Waltham Forest Council 1988-2005; Unison; London Borough of Newham: Councillor 1988-2005, Chair, Direct Services Organisation 1989-90, Chair, Leisure 1992-2002, Cabinet Member for Culture and Community 2002-05; Founder Member and Chair, London Library Development Agency 1999-2006; Chair: Cultural Services Executive, Local Government Association 2000-03, Culture and Tourism Panel, Association of London Government 2002-05; Member: London Regional Sports Board -2007, London Arts Board -2007, Museums, Libraries and Archives Council, London -2007: Judge, Golden Dagger Award 2005-07

Political career: Contested Wanstead and Woodford general election 1992. Member for West Ham 2005-10, for West Ham (revised boundary) since 6 May 2010 general election; PPS: to Phil Woolas as Minister of State, Department for Communities and Local Government 2006-07, to John Denham as Secretary of State for Innovations, Universities and Skills 2007-09; Assistant Government Whip 2009-10; *Select Committees:* Member: ODPM/Communities and Local Government 2005-07; Member: Co-operative Party, Fabian Society

Political interests: Poverty, housing, libraries, local government, sexual and reproductive health, foreign affairs; Africa, Assyria, Bangladesh, China, India, Pakistan

Recreations: Walking, reading, relaxing with friends

Lyn Brown MP, House of Commons, London SW1A 0AA
Tel: 020 7219 6999 Fax: 020 7219 0864
E-mail: brownl@parliament.uk
Constituency: None publicised Tel: 020 8470 3463
Website: www.lynbrown.org.uk

GENERAL ELECTION RESULT

		%
Brown, L. (Lab)*	29,422	62.7
Morris, V. (Con)	6,888	14.7
Pierce, M. (Lib Dem)	5,392	11.5
Gain, S. (CPA)	1,327	2.8
Malik, K. (Ind)	1,245	2.7
Davidson, M. (NF)	1,089	2.3
Gandy, K. (UKIP)	766	1.6
Lithgow, J. (Green)	645	1.4
Agbogun-Toko, G. (Ind)	177	0.4
Majority	22,534	47.99
Electorate	85,313	
Turnout	46,951	55.03

**Member of last parliament*

CONSTITUENCY SNAPSHOT

Since 1950 Labour MPs have generally enjoyed absolute majorities in this constituency. Tony Banks achieved a majority of just under 7,000 at his first election in 1983 and by his retirement in 2005 he had an absolute majority of 15,645.

His successor Lyn Brown won the seat in 2005 with a reduced majority of 9,801. Like East Ham, this is one of Labour's safest seats. Brown increased her vote-share to over 60 per cent with a 22,534 majority.

The seat has gained Custom House ward from Poplar and Canning Town and East Ham and the part wards of Canning Town North and Canning Town South from Poplar and Canning Town.

West Ham is typical of an East London constituency, but is undergoing a great amount of redevelopment due to the Olympics and Thames Gateway projects.

West Ham is an area of significant ethnic diversity.

The site of the 2012 Olympic Games will bring jobs, regeneration and investment to the area and is hoped will leave a legacy to benefit the local community.

Transport in the area will be greatly improved with the new international rail station at Stratford becoming a stop on the Eurostar route. The station is due to open in 2010, when Stratford regional station is connected to the new Dockland Light Railway extension. The planned Crossrail service will serve Stratford and Custom House stations in the constituency from 2017.

Rt Hon **Nick Brown**

Newcastle upon Tyne East ***(returning MP)***

New constituency

Tel: 020 7219 6814
E-mail: nickbrownmp@parliament.uk
Website: www.nickbrownmp.com

Date of birth: 13 June 1950

Education: Tunbridge Wells Technical High School; Manchester University (BA 1971)

Non-political career: Proctor and Gamble advertising department; Legal adviser for northern region of GMBATU 1978-83; Councillor, Newcastle upon Tyne City Council 1980-83

Political career: Member for Newcastle upon Tyne East 1983-97, for Newcastle upon Tyne East and Wallsend 1997-2010, for Newcastle upon Tyne East since 6 May 2010 general election; Opposition Frontbench Spokesperson for: Legal Affairs 1985-92, Treasury and Economic Affairs 1988-94; Deputy to Margaret Beckett as Shadow Leader of the Commons 1992-94; Opposition Spokesperson for Health 1994-95; Opposition Deputy Chief Whip 1995-97; Government Chief Whip 1997-98; Minister of Agriculture, Fisheries and Food 1998-2001; Minister of State for Work, Department of Work and Pensions 2001-03; Deputy Government Chief Whip 2007-08; Minister for the North East 2007-10; Government Chief Whip 2008-10; Shadow Parliamentary Secretary to the Treasury and Opposition Chief Whip 2010-; *Select Committees:* Member: Broadcasting 1994-95, Selection 1996-97, 2007-08, Administration 2007-09

Political interests: Australia, China, Japan, New Zealand, USA

Other organisations: PC 1997; Freeman, Newcastle 2001

Rt Hon Nick Brown MP, House of Commons, London SW1A 0AA
Tel: 020 7219 6814 Fax: 020 7219 5941
E-mail: nickbrownmp@parliament.uk
Constituency: 1 Mosley Street, Newcastle upon Tyne NE1 1YE
Tel: 0191-261 1408 Fax: 0191-261 1409
Website: www.nickbrownmp.com

GENERAL ELECTION RESULT

		%
Brown, N. (Lab)*	17,043	45.0
Taylor, W. (Lib Dem)	12,590	33.3
Llewellyn, D. (Con)	6,068	16.0
Spence, A. (BNP)	1,342	3.6
Gray, A. (Green)	620	1.6
Levy, M. (Comm GB)	177	0.5
Majority	4,453	11.77
Electorate	64,487	
Turnout	37,840	58.68

**Member of last parliament*

CONSTITUENCY SNAPSHOT

The constituency was created out of wards previously part of the Newcastle upon Tyne Central and Newcastle upon Tyne East and Wallsend constituencies. It includes the areas of Jesmond, Heaton, Byker and Walker.

Newcastle upon Tyne Central has been in Labour hands since 1987. In 1997 Jim Cousins took over 59 per cent of the vote with a 16,480 majority. In 2001 his majority had slipped to 11,605 as the Liberal Democrats moved into second place. In 2005 Labour's majority was reduced to 3,982.

Nick Brown has represented Newcastle upon Tyne East and Wallsend Labour since 1997. His 24,000 majority fell to 14,223 in 2001 as the Lib Dems overtook the Tories for second place. Brown's majority almost halved in 2005 to 7,565. Brown held on to his revised seat with a relatively small majority of 4,453.

Geographically the seat does not include any of the true city centre and is primarily made up of large residential areas.

The great shipbuilding industry of the Tyne, once the mainstay of the economy, is now essentially non-existent. The Swan Hunter shipyard had provided the last link to the shipping business, and closed in July 2006.

Russell Brown

Dumfries and Galloway ***(returning MP)***

No boundary changes

Tel: 020 7219 4429
E-mail: brownr@parliament.uk
Website: www.russellbrownmp.com

Date of birth: 17 September 1951; Son of late Howard Russell Brown and late Muriel Brown

Education: Annan Academy, Dumfriesshire; Married Christine Calvert 1973 (2 daughters)

Non-political career: Variety of posts including quality inspection and production supervisor ICI 1974-97; Member TGWU 1974-: Branch secretary and Chair 1979-85; Councillor: Dumfries and Galloway Regional Council 1986-96, Annandale and Eskdale District Council 1988-96, Dumfries and Galloway Unitary Council 1995-97

Political career: Member for Dumfries 1997-2005, for Dumfries and Galloway since 5 May 2005 general election; PPS: to Leaders of the House of Lords: Lord Williams of Mostyn 2002-03, Baroness Amos 2003-05, Alistair Darling 2005-06, Douglas Alexander 2006-07, to Lord Drayson as Minister of State, Ministry of Defence and Department for Business, Enterprise and Regulatory Reform 2007, to Secretaries of State for Scotland: Des Browne 2007-08, Jim Murphy 2008-10, to Gareth Thomas as Minister of State, Department for International Development 2009-10; *Select Committees:* Member: European Legislation 1997-98, European Scrutiny 1998-99, Scottish Affairs 1999-2001, Regulatory Reform 1999-05, Standards and Privileges 2001-03, Joint Committee on Consolidation, Etc, Bills 2001-10, Joint Committee on Conventions 2006

Political interests: Employment, welfare state, health and safety, energy policy; European Union

Other organisations: Chair Local Community Education Project 1991-97; Fellow Industry and Parliament Trust 2004

Recreations: Sport (especially football)

Russell Brown MP, House of Commons, London SW1A 0AA
Tel: 020 7219 4429 Fax: 020 7219 0922
E-mail: brownr@parliament.uk
Constituency: 13 Hanover Street, Stranraer,
Dumfries and Galloway DG9 7SB Tel: 01776 705254
Fax: 01776 703006, 5 Friars Vennel, Dumfries DG1 2RQ
Tel: 01387 247902 Fax: 01387 247903
Website: www.russellbrownmp.com

GENERAL ELECTION RESULT

		%	+/-
Brown, R. (Lab)*	23,950	45.9	4.8
Duncan, P. (Con)	16,501	31.6	-3.7
Wood, A. (SNP)	6,419	12.3	0.2
Brodie, R. (Lib Dem)	4,608	8.8	0.5
Wright, B. (UKIP)	695	1.3	
Majority	7,449	14.28	
Electorate	74,581		
Turnout	52,173	69.95	

**Member of last parliament*

CONSTITUENCY SNAPSHOT

Galloway has changed hands a number of times since October 1974 when the SNP candidate George Thompson won it from the Tories. Ian Lang took the seat back for the Conservatives in 1979, comfortably retaining it in 1983, when the seat was renamed Galloway and Upper Nithsdale. In 1997 the SNP's Alasdair Morgan defeated Lang. In 2001, Peter Duncan became the only Scottish Conservative MP by a margin of 74 votes.

Boundary changes in 2005 combined the Galloway area of the Galloway and Upper Nithsdale seat with 14 wards from Dumfries to create the new Dumfries and Galloway seat. Labour's Russell Brown, who had been MP for Dumfries, defeated Peter Duncan with a majority of 2,922. A key Tory target, Russell Brown held the seat in 2010 with an increased majority of 7,449.

Situated in south west Scotland, this is the sixth largest seat in the United Kingdom by area, covering over 1,500 square miles. The geographical bulk of the seat is very rural, and the constituency contains the highest proportion of people employed in farming, fishing and forestry in the UK.

The main urban centre of the seat is Dumfries which is the regional centre for public and private services. Stranraer is a major ferry terminal, and the constituency's biggest private employer. The Solway Firth is the site of the first offshore wind farm in Scotland.

Jeremy Browne

Taunton Deane (returning MP)

New constituency

Tel: 020 7219 2354
E-mail: brownej@parliament.uk
Website: www.tauntonlibdems.org.uk/biography.php

Date of birth: 17 May 1970; Son of Sir Nicholas Walker Browne and Diane Browne

Education: Bedales School, Petersfield; Nottingham University (BA politics 1992); Married Charlotte Callen 2004 (divorced)

Non-political career: Dewe Rogerson Ltd 1994-96; Liberal Democrat director of press and broadcasting 1997-2000; Edelman Communications Worldwide 2000-02; Associate Director ReputationInc 2003-04

Political career: Contested Enfield Southgate 1997 general election. Member for Taunton 2005-10, for Taunton Deane since 6 May 2010 general election; Liberal Democrat: Shadow Minister for Foreign and Commonwealth Office 2005-07, Whip 2006-07, Shadow Minister for Home Affairs 2007, Shadow Chief Secretary to the Treasury 2007-10; Minister of State, Foreign and Commonwealth Office 2010-; *Select Committees:* Member: Home Affairs 2005-08

Political interests: Economy, policing, armed forces, Parkinson's disease, pensions

Jeremy Browne MP, House of Commons, London SW1A 0AA
Tel: 020 7219 2354 E-mail: brownej@parliament.uk
Constituency: Liberal Democrat Office, Masons House, Magdalene Street, Taunton, Somerset TA1 1SG Tel: 01823 337874
Website: www.tauntonlibdems.org.uk/biography.php

GENERAL ELECTION RESULT

		%
Browne, J. (Lib Dem)*	28,531	49.1
Formosa, M. (Con)	24,538	42.2
Jevon, M. (Lab)	2,967	5.1
McIntyre, T. (UKIP)	2,114	3.6
Majority	3,993	6.87
Electorate	82,537	
Turnout	58,150	70.45

**Member of last parliament*

CONSTITUENCY SNAPSHOT

The Conservatives held Taunton for most of the 20th century. However, their vote had been in decline since 1979 and in 1997 they lost the seat to the Liberal Democrat candidate Jackie Ballard. This setback was temporarily reversed in 2001 when Adrian Flook won the seat back for the Tories with a majority of 235.

In 2005 the Liberal Democrats once again regained control of Taunton from the Tories. Jeremy Browne managed to increase the share of the vote by 2 per cent, giving him a slim majority of 573. Jeremy Browne won re-election in this new seat in 2010 with a majority of 3,993 over the Conservatives.

The new seat of Taunton Deane is only marginally different from the old Taunton seat: three wards and two part-wards from West Somerset District are now in Bridgwater and West Somerset.

Taunton Deane is a predominantly rural constituency with one or two large market towns.

Taunton is seen as the gateway to the South West, with both the M5 and main-line rail services passing through the constituency. This accessibility has enabled the town itself to become a major commercial and administrative centre, with both Somerset County Council and Taunton Deane Council's main offices based here.

Fiona Bruce

Congleton

No boundary changes

Tel: 020 7219 3000
E-mail: fiona.bruce.mp@parliament.uk
Website: www.fionabruce.co.uk

Conservative

Education: Qualified solicitor 1981; Married with children

Non-political career: Partner, Fiona Bruce & Co LLP; Warrington Borough Council: Councillor 2003-, Executive Member for Finance; School governor

Political career: Contested Warrington South 2005 general election. Member for Congleton since 6 May 2010 general election

Political interests: Tanzania

Other organisations: Member, National Committee of Lawyers' Christian Fellowship; Overall winner, Women into Business Award 2003; *Publications:* Co-author, There is such a thing as society (Politicos 2002)

Fiona Bruce MP, House of Commons, London SW1A 0AA
Tel: 020 7219 3000 E-mail: fiona.bruce.mp@parliament.uk
Constituency: Congleton Conservative Association, Conservative Office, Churchyardside, Nantwich, Cheshire CW5 5DE
Tel: 01270 625144 Website: www.fionabruce.co.uk

GENERAL ELECTION RESULT

		%	+/-
Bruce, F. (Con)	23,250	45.8	0.6
Hirst, P. (Lib Dem)	16,187	31.9	5.1
Bryant, D. (Lab)	8,747	17.2	-10.4
Slaughter, L. (UKIP)	2,147	4.2	
Edwards, P. (Ind)	276	0.5	
Rothwell, P. (Ind)	94	0.2	
Parton, A. (Ind)	79	0.2	
Majority	7,063	13.91	
Electorate	73,692		
Turnout	50,780	68.91	

CONSTITUENCY SNAPSHOT

This seat has been held by Conservative Ann Winterton since its creation in 1983.

Ann Winterton was re-elected with an increased majority of 8,246 in 2005.

Winterton retired and in 2010 the Conservative candidate, Fiona Bruce held the seat with a majority of 7,063.

The seat of Congleton comprises a collection of small affluent villages and towns, of which Congleton is the largest. Situated south of Tatton and north east of Crewe, it is part of the Cheshire commuter belt serving the metropolitan areas to the north.

Good transport links, including mainline rail links and the M6 motorway, make it a natural settlement for commuters.

The majority of the workforce is employed in non-manual work, and concentrations of managers and professionals are well above the regional average. All schools in Congleton are comprehensives.

The manufacturing sector is quite healthy, and includes the remnants of the textile industries, around which the towns grew. An important area of economic activity for the constituency is the production of car airbags. Congleton is also home to a large part of the UK sand industry, with several quarries dotting the area. The world's largest movable radio telescope is also in Congleton, at Jodrell Bank.

Rt Hon **Malcolm Bruce**

Gordon (returning MP)

No boundary changes

Tel: 020 7219 6233
E-mail: hernandeza@parliament.uk
Website: www.malcolmbruce.org.uk

Date of birth: 17 November 1944; Son of David Stewart Bruce, agricultural merchant and hotelier, and Kathleen Elmslie Bruce

Education: Wrekin College, Shropshire; St Andrews University (MA economics and political science 1966); Strathclyde University (MSc marketing 1971); CPE and Inns of Court School of Law 1995; Married Veronica Jane Wilson 1969 (divorced 1992) (1 son 1 daughter); married Rosemary Elizabeth Vetterlein 1998 (2 daughters 1 son)

Non-political career: Trainee journalist, *Liverpool Post* 1966-67; Boots section buyer 1968-69; Research and information officer, NE Scotland Development Authority 1971-75; Director, Noroil Publishing House (UK) Ltd. 1975-81; Joint editor/publisher, Aberdeen Petroleum Publishing 1981-84; Member, NUJ

Political career: Contested Angus North and Mearns October 1974, Aberdeenshire West 1979 general elections. Member for Gordon 1983-97, Gordon (revised boundary) 1997-2005, for Gordon (revised boundary) since 5 May 2005 general election; Liberal Spokesperson for Energy 1985-87; Scottish Liberal Spokesperson for Education 1986-87; Alliance Spokesperson for Employment 1987; Liberal Spokesperson for Trade and Industry 1987-88; SLD Spokesperson for Natural Resources (energy and conservation) 1988-89; Liberal Democrat Spokesperson for: The Environment and Natural Resources 1989-90, Scottish Affairs 1990-92, Trade and Industry 1992-94, The Treasury 1994-99; Chair, Liberal Democrat Parliamentary Party 1999-2001; Liberal Democrat Shadow Secretary of State for: Environment, Food and Rural Affairs 2001-02, Trade and Industry 2003-05; *Select Committees:* Member: Scottish Affairs 1990-92, Trade and Industry 1992-94, Treasury 1997-99, Standards and Privileges 1999-2001; Chair: International Development 2005-10; Member: Liaison 2005-10, Quadripartite (Committees on Strategic Export Controls)/Arms Export Controls 2006-10, Joint Committee on National Security Strategy 2010; Leader Scottish: Social and Liberal Democrats 1988-89, Liberal Democrats 1989-92; President Scottish Liberal Democrats 2000-

Political interests: Energy, gas industry, oil industry, industrial policy, trade policy, deaf children, Scottish home rule and federalism; USA, Canada, South Africa, Zimbabwe, Eastern Europe, the Balkans, Hungary, Czech Republic, Baltic States, Scandinavia

Other organisations: Vice-President, National Deaf Children's Society, President, Grampian Branch; Vice-President, Combined Heat and Power Association; Rector, Dundee University 1986-89; Member, UK Delegation Parliamentary Assembly of the Council of Europe/Western European Union 2000-05; Trustee Royal National Institute for the Deaf; PC 2006

Recreations: Golf, cycling, walking, theatre and music

Rt Hon Malcolm Bruce MP, House of Commons, London SW1A 0AA Tel: 020 7219 6233 Fax: 020 7219 2334
E-mail: hernandeza@parliament.uk
Constituency: 67 High Street, Inverurie, Aberdeenshire AB51 3QT
Tel: 01467 623413 Fax: 01467 624994
Website: www.malcolmbruce.org.uk

GENERAL ELECTION RESULT

		%	+/-
Bruce, M. (Lib Dem)*	17,575	36.0	-8.9
Thomson, R. (SNP)	10,827	22.2	6.3
Crockett, B. (Lab)	9,811	20.1	-0.1
Thomson, R. (Con)	9,111	18.7	1.1
Edwards, S. (Green)	752	1.5	
Jones, E. (BNP)	699	1.4	
Majority	6,748	13.83	
Electorate	73,420		
Turnout	48,775	66.43	

**Member of last parliament*

CONSTITUENCY SNAPSHOT

In the 1983 general election Malcolm Bruce gained Gordon for the SDP/Liberal Alliance, defeating Conservative James Cran. Bruce held the seat easily in 1987, but suffered a massive backlash in 1992 when his majority was cut to just 274.

With the fall of the Tory vote in Scotland in 1997 Bruce's majority grew to nearly 7,000. He increased his vote even further in 2001.The 2005 boundary review moved Donmouth voters to Aberdeen North and brought wards around the Bridge of Don and Dyce into Gordon. The Liberal Democrat majority at Westminster was boosted by the changes and Malcolm Bruce won with a 11,020 majority. Bruce's majority in 2010 was reduced but still decent at 6,748.

In the 1980s Gordon was the most rapidly expanding constituency in Scotland, as oil-rich Aberdeen attracted workers to its growing commuter belt. Towns such as Ellon and Inverurie, to the north of the city, grew out of all recognition.

Forestry, agriculture and food processing including whisky distilleries are important industries. Other industries include paper at Inverurie and engineering supplies for the oil and gas industries.

Keith is a market town which grew up around the textile industry, though it is now dependent on whisky and agriculture.

Chris Bryant

Rhondda (returning MP)

No boundary changes

Tel: 020 7219 8315
E-mail: bryantc@parliament.uk
Website: www.chris-bryant.co.uk

Date of birth: 11 January 1962; Son of Rees Bryant and Anne Gracie, née Goodwin

Education: Cheltenham College; Mansfield College, Oxford (BA English 1983, MA); Ripon College, Cuddesdon (MA CertTheol 1986); Civil partner Jared Cranney 2010

Non-political career: Church of England: Ordained Deacon 1986, Priest 1987; Curate All Saints High Wycombe 1986-89; Diocesan youth chaplain Diocese of Peterborough 1989-91; Agent Holborn and St Pancras Labour Party 1991-93; Local government development officer Labour Party 1993-94; London manager Common Purpose 1994-96; Freelance author 1996-98; Head European Affairs BBC 1998-2000; GMB 1991-94; MSF 1994-; London Borough of Hackney: Councillor 1993-98, Chief whip 1994-95

Political career: Contested Wycombe 1997 general election. Member for Rhondda since 7 June 2001 general election; PPS: to Lord Falconer of Thoroton as Lord Chancellor 2005-06, to Harriet Harman as Leader of the House of Commons 2007-08; Deputy Leader of the House of Commons 2008-09; Parliamentary Under-Secretary of State, Foreign and Commonwealth Office 2009-10; *Select Committees:* Member: Culture, Media and Sport 2001-05, Joint Committee on House of Lords Reform 2002-10, Public Accounts 2007, Modernisation of the House of Commons 2007-10; Chair Christian Socialist Movement 1993-98; Labour Movement for Europe: Chair 2002-07, Vice-chair 2007-

Political interests: Wales, European affairs, broadcasting, information economy; Spain, Latin America

Other organisations: Associate National Youth Theatre of Great Britain; Ferndale RFC; *Publications:* Reclaiming The Ground (Hodder and Stoughton, 1993); John Smith: An Appreciation (Hodder and Stoughton, 1994); Possible Dreams (Hodder and Stoughton, 1995); Stafford Cripps: The First Modern Chancellor (Hodder and Stoughton, 1997); Glenda Jackson: The Biography (HarperCollins, 1999)

Recreations: Swimming, theatre

Chris Bryant MP, House of Commons, London SW1A 0AA
Tel: 020 7219 8315 Fax: 020 7219 1792
E-mail: bryantc@parliament.uk
Constituency: 5 Cemetery Rd, Porth, Rhondda,
Mid Glamorgan CF39 0LG Tel: 01443 687697 Fax: 01443 686405
Website: www.chris-bryant.co.uk

GENERAL ELECTION RESULT

		%	+/-
Bryant, C. (Lab)*	17,183	55.3	-12.5
Davies, G. (PIC)	5,630	18.1	2.3
Wasley, P. (Lib Dem)	3,309	10.7	0.2
Howe, P. (Ind)	2,599	8.4	
Henderson, J. (Con)	1,993	6.4	0.9
John, T. (UKIP)	358	1.2	
Majority	11,553	37.18	
Electorate	51,554		
Turnout	31,072	60.27	

**Member of last parliament*

CONSTITUENCY SNAPSHOT

Since the seat was re-created in 1974 after previously being abolished, Labour has always returned an MP in this seat. Trevor Alec Jones preceded Allan Rogers who was the MP from 1983 until 2001. In 1987 he polled his largest majority: 30,754.

Chris Bryant was first elected in 2001 with a majority of 16,047 on. A very minor swing towards Bryant in 2005 gave him a majority of 16,242. Despite a 7.5 per cent swing to Plaid Cymru Chris Bryant was re-elected with a 11,553 majority.

Situated in the South Wales valleys to the north west of Cardiff, Rhondda incorporates towns such as Porth, Tonypandy and Treorchy.

The name Rhondda conjures up an image of coal-mining and village communities. The last of the coal from deep mining was brought to the surface at Maerdy Colliery in - 1986. Smaller privately owned drift mines still exist, and there have been significant projects to reclaim the land from the old mines and bring new industry and investment to the valley.

Transport links have been improved with the opening of the Porth relief road.

Karen Buck

***Westminster North** (returning MP)*

New constituency

Tel: 020 7219 3533
E-mail: buckk@parliament.uk
Website: www.karenbuck.org.uk

Labour

Date of birth: 30 August 1958

Education: Chelmsford High School; London School of Economics (BSc Econ, MSc Econ, MA social policy and administration); Married Barrie Taylor (1 son)

Non-political career: Research and development worker, Outset (charity specialising in employment for disabled people) 1979-83; London Borough of Hackney: specialist officer developing services/employment for disabled people 1983-86, public health officer 1986-87; Member, TGWU; Councillor Westminster City Council 1990-97

Political career: Member for Regent's Park and Kensington North 1997-2010, for Westminster North since 6 May 2010 general election; Parliamentary Under-Secretary of State, Department for Transport 2005-06; Parliamentary assistant to Tony McNulty as Minister for London 2008-10; *Select Committees:* Member: Social Security 1997-2001, Selection 1999-2001, Work and Pensions 2001-05, Home Affairs 2006-09, Home Affairs Sub-Committee 2008-09, Children, Schools and Families 2009-10; Chair: London 2009-10; Labour Party Policy Directorate (Health) 1987-92; Labour Party Campaign Strategy Co-ordinator 1992-99

Political interests: Housing, urban regeneration, health care, welfare, children

Recreations: Music: rock, soul, jazz, opera

Karen Buck MP, House of Commons, London SW1A 0AA
Tel: 020 7219 3533 Fax: 020 7219 3664
E-mail: buckk@parliament.uk
Constituency: The Labour Party, 4(G) Shirland Mews,
London W9 3DY Tel: 020 8968 7999 Fax: 020 8960 0150
Website: www.karenbuck.org.uk

GENERAL ELECTION RESULT

		%
Buck, K. (Lab)*	17,377	43.9
Cash, J. (Con)	15,251	38.5
Blackburn, M. (Lib Dem)	5,513	13.9
Smith, T. (Green)	478	1.2
Curry, S. (BNP)	334	0.8
Badzak, J. (UKIP)	315	0.8
Bahaijoub, A. (Ind)	101	0.3
Roseman, E. (England)	99	0.3
Fajardo, G. (Christian)	98	0.3
Dharamsey, A. (Ind)	32	0.1
Majority	2,126	5.37
Electorate	66,739	
Turnout	39,598	59.33

**Member of last parliament*

CONSTITUENCY SNAPSHOT

In 1992 the four seats within the Boroughs of Kensington, Chelsea and Westminster were all Conservative held. Since 1997 there have been three seats and Regent's Park and North Kensington has been Labour since Karen Buck was elected in 1997 with a majority of almost 15,000.

Her majority has since declined and was 6,131 in 2005. Despite a candidate with close links to David Cameron, the Tories failed to pick up this seat in 2010. Labour's Karen Buck won by 2,126 votes

This new constituency is largely composed of the old Regent's Park and Kensington North seat, with part of the Bayswater ward from the Cities of London and Westminster.

In the east of the constituency is St John's Wood, one of the most affluent areas in London. The areas north of Notting Hill Gate on either side of Ladbroke Grove, beyond the relatively small number of expensive houses and flats, are mostly made up of housing estates.

Most people work in central London and the economy is heavily dependent on the West End and the City.

In matters of education, a very high proportion of wealthy parents send their children to private schools, and there is a high cross-constituency flow during the school run. There are relatively few comprehensive schools and a high proportion of church schools.

Robert Buckland

South Swindon

Boundary changes

Tel: 020 7219 3000
E-mail: robert.buckland.mp@parliament.uk
Website: www.robertbuckland.co.uk

Conservative

Date of birth: 22 September 1968; Younger son of Roger and Barbara Buckland

Education: St Michael's School, Bryn, Llanelli; Hatfield College, Durham (BA law 1990); Inns of Court School of Law 1991; Married Sian Caroline Pugh Reed 1997 (twin son and daughter)

Non-political career: Called to the Bar 1991; Barrister, Wales and Chester circuit 1992-: Iscoed Chambers, Swansea -1999, 30 Park Place, Cardiff 1999-2007, Apex Chambers 2007-09, Recorder of Crown Court 2009-; Councillor, Dyfed County Council 1993-96

Political career: Contested Islwyn 1995 by-election, Preseli Pembrokeshire 1997 and South Swindon 2005 general elections. Member for South Swindon since 6 May 2010 general election; Conservative Party: Constituency chairman: Llanelli 1993-96; Swansea West 1999-2000; Board Member, Tory Reform Group 2000-03; Member: Conservative Group for Europe 2002-, Conservative Foreign Affairs Forum 2006-

Political interests: Criminal justice, constitutional affairs, foreign affairs, education

Other organisations: Member, European Movement 2000-; Member: Carlton, Llanelli Conservative, Swindon Conservative; Glamorgan County Cricket Club; Crawshays Welsh RFC

Recreations: Music, wine, family, church architecture, watching rugby, football and cricket

Robert Buckland MP, House of Commons, London SW1A 0AA
Tel: 020 7219 3000 E-mail: robert.buckland.mp@parliament.uk
Constituency: South Swindon Conservatives, Unit 17, Dorcan Business Village, Murdock Road, Swindon, Wiltshire SN3 5HY
Tel: 01793 522123 Fax: 01793 523940
Website: www.robertbuckland.co.uk

GENERAL ELECTION RESULT

		%
Buckland, R. (Con)	19,687	41.8
Snelgrove, A. (Lab)*	16,143	34.3
Hooton, D. (Lib Dem)	8,305	17.6
Tingey, R. (UKIP)	2,029	4.3
Miles, J. (Green)	619	1.3
Kirk, A. (Christian)	176	0.4
Evans, K. (Ind)	160	0.3
Majority	3,544	7.52
Electorate	72,622	
Turnout	47,119	64.88

**Member of last parliament*

CONSTITUENCY SNAPSHOT

With its industrial heritage, South Swindon has a history as a Labour seat, holding the seat almost continuously from 1945 to 1983 (Conservative's Christopher Ward briefly held the seat between 1969 and 1970), when it was won by the Conservatives. The Conservatives held the seat until 1997 increasing their majority at each election.

This all changed in 1997 when Julia Drown gained the seat for Labour. In 2005 Drown retired and the Labour majority was reduced here as Anne Snelgrove was elected with a majority of only 1,353. Conservative Robert Buckland defeated Anne Snelgrove by 3,544 votes to take the seat.

Boundary changes for the election were minimal.

While Swindon itself is an industrial town, South Swindon constituency also includes a number of outlying rural areas.

The railway and its associated industries were once the major employers in the town, but other industries, particularly hi-tech manufacturing, have taken their place.

Companies such as Intel, Zurich Financial Services, Motorola, Honda and the Nationwide Building Society are all based in Swindon.

Richard Burden

Birmingham, Northfield ***(returning MP)***

Boundary changes

Tel: 020 7219 2318
E-mail: burdenr@parliament.uk
Website: www.richardburden.com

Date of birth: 1 September 1954; Son of late Kenneth Rodney Burden, engineer, and Pauline Burden, secretary

Education: Wallasey Technical Grammar School; Bramhall Comprehensive School, Stockport; St John's College of Further Education, Manchester; York University (BA politics 1978); Warwick University (MA industrial relations 1979); Married Jane Slowey 2001 (1 stepson 2 stepdaughters)

Non-political career: President, York University Students' Union 1976-77; NALGO: Branch organiser North Yorkshire 1979-81, West Midlands District Officer 1981-92; Member TGWU 1979-; Sponsored by TGWU 1989-96

Political career: Contested Meriden 1987 general election. Member for Birmingham Northfield 1992-2010, for Birmingham, Northfield (revised boundary) since 6 May 2010; PPS to Jeffrey Rooker: as Minister of State and Deputy Minister, Ministry of Agriculture, Fisheries and Food 1997-99, as Minister of State, Department of Social Security 1999-2001; Adviser on motor sports to Richard Caborn, as Minister of State for Sport 2002-07; *Select Committees:* Member: Trade and Industry 2001-05, International Development 2005-10, Quadripartite (Committees on Strategic Export Controls)/Arms Export Controls 2006-10; Chair: West Midlands 2009-10; Founder member Bedale Labour Party 1980; Executive member Labour Middle East Council, Vice-Chair 1994-95; Member Co-operative Party; Chair Labour Campaign for Electoral Reform 1996-98, Vice-Chair 1998-; Member Fabian Society

Political interests: Industrial policy – especially motor and motorsport industries, poverty, health, constitution, electoral reform, regeneration, regional government, international development, community empowerment; Middle East, Europe

Other organisations: Co-chair Parliamentary Advisory Council on Transport Safety (PACTS) 1995-98; Founded Joint Action for Water Services (Jaws) 1985 to oppose water privatisation, Secretary 1985-90; Fellow Industry and Parliament Trust 1999; Kingshurst Labour, Austin Sports and Social, Austin Branch British Legion; 750 Motor, Historic Sports Car Club; *Publications:* Tap Dancing – Water, The Environment and Privatisation, 1988

Recreations: Cinema, motor racing, travel, food

Richard Burden MP, House of Commons, London SW1A 0AA
Tel: 020 7219 2318 Fax: 020 7219 2170
E-mail: burdenr@parliament.uk
Constituency: No constituency office published Tel: 0121-475 9295
Fax: 0121-476 2400 Website: www.richardburden.com

GENERAL ELECTION RESULT

		%
Burden, R. (Lab)*	16,841	40.3
Huxtable, K. (Con)	14,059	33.6
Dixon, M. (Lib Dem)	6,550	15.7
Orton, L. (BNP)	2,290	5.5
Borthwick, J. (UKIP)	1,363	3.3
Pearce, S. (Green)	406	1.0
Rodgers, D. (Common Good)	305	0.7
Majority	2,782	6.65
Electorate	71,338	
Turnout	41,814	58.61

**Member of last parliament*

CONSTITUENCY SNAPSHOT

Up until 1979 the constituency saw a succession of Labour victories, but in that year Jocelyn Cadbury took the seat for the Conservatives. After Cadbury's death in 1982, John Spellar won the by-election for Labour. He held the seat for just one year before being beaten by Conservative Roger King in 1983. King held the seat for nine years but in 1992 was defeated by Labour's Richard Burden.

Burden consolidated his lead in 1997 and 2001 and was returned with a safe majority of 6,454 in 2005. In 2010 Burden was re-elected with a majority of 2,782 following a swing of 6.6 per cent to the Conservatives.

The seat gained parts of Northfield and Weoley wards from Birmingham Selly Oak, and Kings Norton from both the Selly Oak and Hall Green divisions. Bourneville and Bartley Green part-wards were lost to Selly Oak and Edgbaston respectively.

Birmingham Northfield is located to the south of the city.

Traditionally the seat's lifeblood was car manufacturing, specifically the Rover plant at Longbridge. The closure hit the employment of the constituents for those directly employed at the plant and those working in associated industries. Regeneration thus remains a priority.

The South Birmingham Primary Care Trust, which is responsible for providing much of the medical care in the area.

Aidan Burley

Cannock Chase

Boundary changes

Tel: 020 7219 3000
E-mail: aidan.burley.mp@parliament.uk
Website: www.aidanburleymp.org

Conservative

Date of birth: 22 January 1979; Son of Lois and Geoff Burley

Education: King Edward VI School, Edgbaston; West House School, Birmingham; St John's College, Oxford (BA theology)

Non-political career: Management consultant: Accenture, Hedra/Mouchel; Assistant to David Willetts MP 2001; Political researcher to Philip Hammond MP 2002; Special adviser (police reform taskforce) to Nick Herbert MP 2007; Councillor, London Borough of Hammersmith and Fulham Council 2006-10; Governor, St Thomas of Canterbury Primary School, Fulham 2006-07

Political career: Member for Cannock Chase since 6 May 2010 general election; Member, Conservative Party 1997-; Vice-chair, Oxford University Conservative Association 1999-2000

Political interests: Police reform, social mobility, welfare; New Zealand, USA

Other organisations: Royal Automobile Club, Pall Mall; Rugeley Rugby Club

Recreations: Rugby, tennis, football

Aidan Burley MP, House of Commons, London SW1A 0AA
Tel: 020 7219 3000 E-mail: aidan.burley.mp@parliament.uk
Constituency: c/o Cannock Chase Conservative Association, 90 High Green, Cannock WS11 1BE Website: www.aidanburleymp.org

GENERAL ELECTION RESULT

		%
Burley, A. (Con)	18,271	40.1
Woodward, S. (Lab)	15,076	33.1
Hunt, J. (Lib Dem)	7,732	17.0
McKenzie, M. (UKIP)	2,168	4.8
Majorowicz, T. (BNP)	1,580	3.5
Turville, R. (Ind)	380	0.8
Walters, M. (Ind)	93	0.2
Majority	3,195	7.01
Electorate	74,509	
Turnout	45,559	61.15

CONSTITUENCY SNAPSHOT

From 1945 until 1970 the mining communities made up the vast majority of the seat's population and Cannock returned Labour's Jennie Lee (wife of Aneurin Bevan) to the Commons. In 1970, however, Patrick Cormack won for Cannock the Conservatives, reflecting the boundary changes that added commuter villages to the seat. When many of these communities were transferred out of the constituency in 1974 Labour regained the seat until further changes in 1983. This enabled Tory candidate Gerald Howarth to Cannock and Burntwood.

Labour's Tony Wright won the seat back for Labour in 1992. In 1997 the renamed Cannock Chase helped Wright to secure a 14,478 majority. He was re-elected in 2005 with a majority of 9,227.

Wright retired at the 2010 general election and the Labour candidate was unable to hold the seat following a 14 per cent swing to the Conservative candidate Aidan Burley.

Boundary changes at the election will make the seat completely coterminous with the District of Cannock Chase.

Situated in southern Staffordshire, Cannock Chase is comprised of the towns of Cannock and Rugely and surrounding small villages.

Cannock Chase itself is an area of rural beauty that boasts an Iron Age hill fort and an ancient hunting forest. 1,214 hectares of the chase are conserved as one of Britain's largest country parks and it attracts a huge number of visitors annually.

International companies such as Finning, Glynwed Pipe systems and JCB Hydrapower have found a home in Cannock Chase.

Rt Hon **Andy Burnham**

Leigh (returning MP)

Boundary changes

Tel: 020 7219 8250
E-mail: burnhama@parliament.uk
Website: www.andyburnham.org

Labour

Date of birth: 7 January 1970; Son of Kenneth Roy Burnham, telecommunications engineer, and Eileen Mary Burnham, née Murray

Education: St Aelred's RC High School, Merseyside; Fitzwilliam College, Cambridge (BA English 1991, MA); Married Marie-France van Heel 2000 (1 son 2 daughters)

Non-political career: Researcher to Tessa Jowell MP 1994-97; Parliamentary officer NHS Confederation 1997; Administrator Football Task Force 1997-98; Special adviser to Chris Smith as Secretary of State for Culture, Media, and Sport 1998-2001; TGWU 1995-; Unison 2000-; Chair Supporters Direct 2002-05

Political career: Member for Leigh 2001-10, for Leigh (revised boundary) since 6 May 2010 general election; PPS: to David Blunkett as Home Secretary 2003-04, to Ruth Kelly as Secretary of State for Education and Skills 2004-05; Parliamentary Under-Secretary of State, Home Office 2005-06; Minister of State, Department of Health (Delivery and Reform) 2006-07; Chief Secretary to the Treasury 2007-08; Secretary of State for: Culture, Media and Sport 2008-09, Health 2009-10; Shadow Secretary of State for Health 2010-; *Select Committees:* Member: Health 2001-03; Member Co-operative Party

Political interests: Health, sport, media, education, crime

Other organisations: PC 2007; Lowton Labour Club; *Publications:* Football in the Digital Age (Mainstream Publishing) 1999; Supporters Direct – the changing face of the football business (Frank Cass) 2000

Recreations: Football, cricket, rugby league, (Leigh RLFC, Everton FC)

Rt Hon Andy Burnham MP, House of Commons, London SW1A 0AA Tel: 020 7219 8250 Fax: 020 7219 4381
E-mail: burnhama@parliament.uk
Constituency: 10 Market Street, Leigh, Lancashire WN7 1DS
Tel: 01942 682353 Fax: 01942 682354
Website: www.andyburnham.org

GENERAL ELECTION RESULT

		%
Burnham, A. (Lab)*	24,295	51.3
Awan, S. (Con)	9,284	19.6
Blackburn, C. (Lib Dem)	8,049	17.0
Chadwick, G. (BNP)	2,724	5.8
Lavelle, M. (UKIP)	1,535	3.2
Bradbury, N. (Ind)	988	2.1
Dainty, T. (Ind)	320	0.7
Hessell, R. (Christian)	137	0.3
Majority	15,011	31.71
Electorate	76,350	
Turnout	47,332	61.99

**Member of last parliament*

CONSTITUENCY SNAPSHOT

Leigh has returned a Labour MP in every contest since 1922. In 2001 Andy Burnham succeeded Lawrence Cunliffe, who had stepped down after holding the seat since 1979.

Andy Burnham increased his majority by almost 1,000 votes in 2005 to 17,272. Burnham held the seat in 2010 with a reduced majority of 15,011.

Boundary changes exchanged part-wards between the seat and neighbouring Makerfield, while losing part-wards to Bolton West and Wigan.

Leigh is on the old Lancashire coalfield, nestled between Manchester and Liverpool and is made up of the eponymous town and several smaller working-class communities. Light industry, in the form of printing and electronics, has replaced the declining mining and textile industries, and Leigh is a vibrant retail centre today.

Leigh bears all the hallmarks of a solid, stable, working-class community, with a high proportion of manual workers.

The National Coalfields Programme has invested £19.4 million in the site of the former Bickershaw Colliery for regeneration and there is also a regeneration project under way at the picturesque Pennington Country Park, right in the heart of the seat.

Conor Burns

Bournemouth West

Boundary changes

Tel: 020 7219 3000
E-mail: conor.burns.mp@parliament.uk
Website: www.localconservatives.com

Conservative

Date of birth: 24 September 1972

Education: St Columba's College, St Albans; Southampton University (BA modern history and politics with philosophy 1994); Single

Non-political career: Director, Policy Research Centre for Business Ltd 1997; Company secretary, DeHavilland Global Knowledge Distribution plc 1998; Sales director, insurance company; Associate director, PLMR 2009-; Southampton City Council: Councillor 1999-2002, Housing and urban regeneration spokesperson 1999, Education and employment spokesperson 1999

Political career: Contested Eastleigh 2001 and 2005 general elections. Member for Bournemouth West since 6 May 2010 general election; Chair, Southampton University Conservative Association 1992

Political interests: Mental health, foreign affairs; Northern Ireland

Other organisations: Board member, Spitfire Tribute Foundation

Recreations: Swimming, snooker

Conor Burns MP, House of Commons, London SW1A 0AA
Tel: 020 7219 3000 E-mail: conor.burns.mp@parliament.uk
Constituency: Bournemouth West Conservatives, 135 Hankinson Road, Bournemouth BH9 1HR Tel: 01202 776607
Website: www.localconservatives.com

GENERAL ELECTION RESULT

		%
Burns, C. (Con)	18,808	45.2
Murray, A. (Lib Dem)	13,225	31.8
Carr-Brown, S. (Lab)	6,171	14.8
Glover, P. (UKIP)	2,999	7.2
Taylor, H. (Ind)	456	1.1
Majority	5,583	13.40
Electorate	71,753	
Turnout	41,659	58.06

CONSTITUENCY SNAPSHOT

A Tory seat for as long as it has existed, for just short of 30 years Bournemouth West was represented by Sir John Eden. Sir John Butterfill replaced Sir John on his retirement in 1983. He was returned with a 4,031 majority in 2005. Butterfill retired in 2010 and his successor Conor Burns won a 5,583 majority.

Boundary changes moved part-wards Winton East, Alderney and Branksome East into the seat from Bournemouth East, while Eastcliff and Springbourne, Moordown, and Queen's Park part-wards moved from this seat to Bournemouth East.

Bournemouth blossomed in the 19th century as a result of the Victorian love of the seaside, and is sufficiently large to warrant its division into two constituencies. Bournemouth West, which is home to much of the town's tourist trade is, like its twin seat to the East.

Bournemouth is a fast growing and prosperous town. The backbone of the local economy remains tourism. Visitors enjoy Bournemouth's miles of beaches and traditional seaside attractions, but increasingly people are also drawn to the area for its bars and clubs.

Simon Burns

Chelmsford (returning MP)

New constituency

Tel: 020 7219 6811
E-mail: burnss@parliament.uk
Website: www.simonburnsmp.com

Conservative

Date of birth: 6 September 1952; Son of late Major B. S. Burns MC and Mrs Anthony Nash

Education: Christ the King School, Accra, Ghana; Stamford School, Lincolnshire; Worcester College, Oxford (BA history 1975); Married Emma Clifford 1982 (divorced) (1 son 1 daughter)

Non-political career: Assistant to Sally Oppenheim MP 1975-81; Director and company secretary, What to Buy for Business Ltd 1981-83; Conference organiser, Institute of Directors 1983-87

Political career: Contested Alyn and Deeside 1983 general election. Member for Chelmsford 1987-97, for Chelmsford West 1997-2010, for Chelmsford since 6 May 2010 general election; PPS: to Timothy Eggar as Minister of State at: Departments of Employment 1989-90, Education and Science 1990-92, Trade and Industry 1992-93, to Gillian Shephard as Minister of Agriculture, Fisheries and Food 1993-94; Assistant Government Whip 1994-95; Government Whip 1995-96; Parliamentary Under-Secretary of State, Department of Health 1996-97; Opposition Spokesperson for: Social Security 1997-1998, Environment, Transport and the Regions (Planning, Housing and Construction) 1998-99, Health 2001-05; Shadow Minister for: Health and Education 2001-04, Health 2004-05; Opposition Whip 2005-10; Minister of State for Health, Department of Health 2010-; *Select Committees:* Member: Health 1999-05, Public Accounts 2000-01, Armed Forces Bill 2005-06, Administration 2006-09, Selection 2007-08; 1922 Committee: Executive Member 1999, Treasurer 1999-2001

Political interests: Health; USA

Other organisations: Honorary PhD Anglia University

Recreations: Photography, American politics, reading

Simon Burns MP, House of Commons, London SW1A 0AA
Tel: 020 7219 6811 Fax: 020 7219 1035
E-mail: burnss@parliament.uk
Constituency: Chelmsford Conservative Association, 88 Rectoru Lane, Chelmsford, Essex CM1 1RF Tel: 01245 352875
Website: www.simonburnsmp.com

GENERAL ELECTION RESULT

		%
Burns, S. (Con)*	25,207	46.2
Robinson, S. (Lib Dem)	20,097	36.8
Dixon, P. (Lab)	5,980	11.0
Wedon, K. (UKIP)	1,527	2.8
Bateman, M. (BNP)	899	1.7
Thomson, A. (Green)	476	0.9
Breed, C. (England)	254	0.5
Sherman, B. (Beer)	153	0.3
Majority	5,110	9.36
Electorate	77,529	
Turnout	54,593	70.42

**Member of last parliament*

CONSTITUENCY SNAPSHOT

Between 1945 and 1950 Chelmsford was held by Labour MP Ernest Millington, but since then it has been held by the Conservatives. Sir Hubert Ashton held the seat from 1950 to 1964, followed by the high-profile Norman St John-Stevas from 1964 to 1987. Simon Burns was first elected in 1987 with a majority of 7,761.

Burns's majority was cut in 1997, the year the Chelmsford West seat was created, on a 7.2 per cent swing to the Lib Dems. He was re-elected in 2005 with a 9,620 majority. The Conservatives retained the seat with Burn's majority falling to 5,110 votes at the 2010 general election.

The majority of the new constituency is from the abolished West Chelmsford seat with three wards from the former Maldon and East Chelmsford seat.

Chelmsford is a prosperous retail, administrative and manufacturing centre. It is the county town of Essex and the home of the county cricket team and Anglia Ruskin University. The council has developed an ambitious town centre area action plan for further development.

The majority of employment in the area is in the service industry, with a significant manufacturing and financial services element.

David Burrowes

Enfield Southgate (returning MP)

Boundary changes

Tel: 020 7219 8144
E-mail: burrowesd@parliament.uk
Website: www.davidburrowes.com

Conservative

Date of birth: 12 June 1969; Son of Mary, née Walpole, and John Burrowes

Education: Highgate School, London; Exeter University (LLB 1991); Married Janet Rosemary Coekin 1996 (4 sons 2 daughters)

Non-political career: Shepherd Harris and Co, Enfield: Solicitor 1995-2005, Consultant 2005-; London Borough of Enfield: Councillor 1994-2006, Cabinet member for Voluntary and Community Development 2002-04

Political career: Contested Edmonton 2001 general election. Member for Enfield Southgate 2005-10, for Enfield Southgate (revised boundary) since 6 May 2010 general election; Shadow Minister for Justice 2007-10; *Select Committees:* Member: Public Administration 2005-10, Armed Forces Bill 2005-06, Joint Committee on the Draft Legal Services Bill 2006, Joint Committee on the Draft Human Tissue and Embryos Bill 2007; Co-founder and trustee, Conservative Christian Fellowship 1990; Vice-chair, Exeter University Conservatives 1990-95; President and chair, Conservative Christian Fellowship 1990-95; Member, Enfield Southgate Conservative Association Executive 1995-98; Member Conservative Human Rights Commission 2005-; Deputy chair Conservative Social Justice Review's Addictions Working Party 2005-07; Chair of Trustees, Conservative Christian Fellowship 2006-

Political interests: Criminal justice system, family policy, drugs and alcohol policy and voluntary sector, umbilical cord blood banking, treatment and research; Cyprus, Israel

Other organisations: Patron: Nightingale Community Hospice Trust, Street Pastors, Ascension Trust, Faith Action Magazine; *Publications:* Co-author Moral Basis of Conservatism (1995); Such a Thing as Society: Maggie's Children and Volunteering. Policy Exchange (2006); Contributor to chapters on Addictions in 'Breakdown Britain' and 'Breakthrough Britain' (Conservative Social Justice Review 2007)

Recreations: Cricket, football, cycling

David Burrowes MP, House of Commons, London SW1A 0AA
Tel: 020 7219 8144 Fax: 020 7219 5289
E-mail: burrowesd@parliament.uk
Constituency: 1C Chaseville Parade, Chaseville Park Road, Winchmore Hill, London N21 1PG Tel: 020 8360 0234 Fax: 020 8364 2766
Website: www.davidburrowes.com

GENERAL ELECTION RESULT

		%
Burrowes, D. (Con)*	21,928	49.4
Charalambous, B. (Lab)	14,302	32.3
Khan, J. (Lib Dem)	6,124	13.8
Krakowiak, P. (Green)	632	1.4
Brock, R. (UKIP)	505	1.1
Mukhopadhyay, A. (Ind)	391	0.9
Billoo, S. (Respect)	174	0.4
Weald, B. (England)	173	0.4
Malakounides, M. (Ind)	88	0.2
Sturgess, J. (Better Britain)	35	0.1
Majority	7,626	17.19
Electorate	64,138	
Turnout	44,352	69.15

**Member of last parliament*

CONSTITUENCY SNAPSHOT

Enfield Southgate had been a Conservative seat since 1950 until 1997 when Michael Portillo was defeated by Labour's Stephen Twigg by 1,433 votes. Mr Portillo had represented the seat since winning it in a 1984 by-election.

In 2001 Twigg increased his majority to 5,546. However, David Burrowes took the constituency back for the Conservatives in the 2005. Burrowes increased his majority to 7,626 in 2010.

The seat gained Grange ward and Bowes and Palmers Green wards are now entirely within the seats boundaries, having previously been shared with Edmonton.

Local transport services are under pressure and further investment is needed. The area is served by WAGN trains and the Piccadilly Line on the underground. The North Circular Road (A406) has been the subject of controversial expansion proposals.

Despite heavy criticism in recent years Chase Farm Hospital has improved and extra investment in the NHS has led to new developments, for example, the refurbishment of its accident and emergency department.

The North Middlesex Hospital accident and emergency department has also been refurbished.

Paul Burstow

Sutton and Cheam (returning MP)

Boundary changes

Tel: 020 7219 1196
E-mail: burstowp@parliament.uk
Website: www.paulburstow.org.uk

Date of birth: 13 May 1962; Son of Brian Burstow, tailor, and Sheila Burstow

Education: Glastonbury High School For Boys; Carshalton College of Further Education (business studies); South Bank Polytechnic (BA business studies); Married Mary Kemm 1995 (1 son 2 daughters)

Non-political career: Buyer Allied Shoe Repairs 1985-86; Salesman Kall Kwick Printers, Chiswick 1986-87; Organisation of Social Democrat/Liberal Democrat Councillors: Organising secretary 1987-89, Campaigns officer 1992-96, Political secretary 1996-97; London Borough of Sutton: Councillor 1986-2002, Chair, Environment Services 1988-96, Deputy Leader 1994-99

Political career: Contested Sutton and Cheam 1992 general election. Member for Sutton and Cheam 1997-2010, for Sutton and Cheam (revised boundary) since 6 May 2010 general election; Liberal Democrat: Spokesperson for: Disabled People 1997-98, Social Services and Community Care 1997-99, Local Government 1997-99, Older People 1999-2003, Shadow Secretary of State for Health 2003-05, Spokesperson for London 2005-06, Chief Whip 2006-10; Minister of State for Care Services, Department of Health 2010-; *Select Committees:* Member: Health 2003-04, 2005-06, Finance and Services 2006-10, Modernisation of the House of Commons 2006-07, Public Accounts 2008-10; Former Member: SDP/Liberal Alliance, London Regional Liberal Democrat Executive; Member, Federal Policy Committee 1988-90

Political interests: Environment, disability, community safety, ageing

Other organisations: National Liberal

Recreations: Cooking, reading, cycling, walking, keeping fit

Paul Burstow MP, House of Commons, London SW1A 0AA
Tel: 020 7219 1196 Fax: 020 7219 0974
E-mail: burstowp@parliament.uk
Constituency: 234 Gander Green Lane, Cheam, Surrey SM3 9QF
Tel: 020 8288 6550 Fax: 020 8288 6553
Website: www.paulburstow.org.uk

GENERAL ELECTION RESULT

		%
Burstow, P. (Lib Dem)*	22,156	45.7
Stroud, P. (Con)	20,548	42.4
Allen, K. (Lab)	3,376	7.0
Clarke, J. (BNP)	1,014	2.1
Pickles, D. (UKIP)	950	2.0
Hickson, P. (Green)	246	0.5
Dodds, J. (England)	106	0.2
Connolly, M. (CPA)	52	0.1
Cullip, M. (Libertarian)	41	0.1
Hammond, B. (Ind Fed UK)	19	0.0
Majority	1,608	3.31
Electorate	66,658	
Turnout	48,508	72.77

**Member of last parliament*

CONSTITUENCY SNAPSHOT

For 50 of the 52 years from 1945 to 1997 Sutton and Cheam was represented by only Tory MPs. The Liberal Graham Tope captured the seat at a by-election in 1972, but Tory Sir Neil Macfarlane won at the 1974 general election. He remained MP here for 18 years, retiring in 1992 and replaced by Lady Olga Maitland. Her tenure was not to equal that of her predecessor: she lost in 1997 with a swing of 13 per cent to the Lib Dems' Paul Burstow.

Burstow held his seat in 2005 with a majority of 2,846. He was re-elected in 2010 with a 1,608 vote lead despite a strong challenge from Conservative Phillipa Stroud.

Boundary changes are minor.

The areas of Sutton and Cheam are at the south-west boundary of Greater London, nestling on the edge of the North Downs not far from Epsom.

This is a prosperous constituency, though Cheam to the south of the constituency is more affluent than Sutton.

Sutton's close proximity to central London, the M25 orbital motorway, and Gatwick Airport has attracted a number of major employers to the area. Among the biggest are Reed Business Publishing, Canon, the Crown Agents, Securicor, and Sainsbury's.

Alistair Burt

North East Bedfordshire (returning MP)

Boundary changes

Tel: 020 7219 8132
E-mail: burta@parliament.uk
Website: www.alistair-burt.co.uk

Conservative

Date of birth: 25 May 1955; Son of James Hendrie Burt and Mina Christie Burt

Education: Bury Grammar School, Lancashire; St John's College, Oxford (BA jurisprudence 1977); Married Eve Alexandra Twite 1983 (1 son 1 daughter)

Non-political career: Solicitor private practice 1980-98; Executive search consultant Whitehead Mann GKR 1997-2001; Councillor London Borough of Haringey 1982-84

Political career: Member for Bury North 1983-97. Contested Bury North 1997 general election. Member for North East Bedfordshire 2001-10, for North East Bedfordshire (revised boundary) since 6 May 2010 general election; PPS to Kenneth Baker as Secretary of State for the Environment, for Education and Science and Chancellor of the Duchy of Lancaster 1985-90; Department of Social Security: Parliamentary Under-Secretary of State 1992-95, Minister of State 1992-97: and Minister for Disabled People 1995-97; Opposition Spokesperson for Education and Skills 2001-02; PPS to Leaders of the Opposition: Iain Duncan Smith 2002-03, Michael Howard 2003-05; Shadow Minister for Communities and Local Government 2005-08; Opposition Assistant Chief Whip 2008-10; Parliamentary Under-Secretary of State, Foreign and Commonwealth Office 2010-; *Select Committees:* Member: International Development 2001, Procedure 2001-02, International Development 2002-03, Office of the Deputy Prime Minister 2002, Selection 2008-10, Administration 2009-10; Vice-President Tory Reform Group 1985-88; Chair Bow Group industry committee 1987-92; Deputy chairman Conservative Party 2007-: local government 2007-08, development 2008-

Political interests: Church affairs, trade and industry, Third World, foreign affairs, agriculture, rural affairs, disability, sport, poverty, social affairs

Other organisations: Secretary Parliamentary Christian Fellowship 1985-97; Patron Habitat for Humanity UK 1997-; Vice-president Headway Bedford 2000-; Chair Christians in Parliament 2002-06; Chair Enterprise Forum 1998-2001; Fellow Industry and Parliament Trust 2006; Solicitors Part 2 1980

Recreations: Football, modern art, walking, outdoor leisure

Alistair Burt MP, House of Commons, London SW1A 0AA
Tel: 020 7219 8132 Fax: 020 7219 1740
E-mail: burta@parliament.uk
Constituency: Biggleswade Conservative Club, St Andrews Street, Biggleswade, Bedfordshire SG18 8BA Tel: 01767 313 385
Fax: 01767 316 697 Website: www.alistair-burt.co.uk

GENERAL ELECTION RESULT

		%
Burt, A. (Con)*	30,989	55.8
Pitt, M. (Lib Dem)	12,047	21.7
Brown, E. (Lab)	8,957	16.1
Capell, B. (UKIP)	2,294	4.1
Seeby, I. (BNP)	1,265	2.3
Majority	18,942	34.10
Electorate	78,060	
Turnout	55,552	71.17

**Member of last parliament*

CONSTITUENCY SNAPSHOT

The Conservative Sir Nicholas Lyell QC was elected to this seat in 1997 with an 11.6 per cent majority. Sir Nicholas retired in 2001 and his successor, Alistair Burt, held the seat for the Conservatives with an increased majority of 8,577.

In 2005 Burt polled the same percentage of the vote as in 2001. However, with support for Labour falling, the Conservative majority was increased to 12,257. Burt's majority rose to 18,942 at the 2010 general election.

The seat gained the part-ward of Langford and Henlow Village from Mid Bedfordshire, but lost the part-wards of Goldington, Kingsbrook to Bedford; and Houghton, Haynes, Southill and Old Warden to Mid Bedfordshire.

North East Bedfordshire is a popular area with wealthy London and Bedford commuters. The historic towns of Biggleswade and Sandy are the largest population centres.

Employment prospects in the area have been helped by the excellent transport links and the development of new industrial and technology parks in the area. The location is superb for research and development purposes, situated as it is with London, Cambridge and Oxford all within short commuter distances.

The Jordan's flour milling, cereal and crunchy bar company is based in Biggleswade and is a large source of employment for the town.

Lorely Burt

Solihull (returning MP)

Boundary changes

Tel: 020 7219 8269
E-mail: burtl@parliament.uk
Website: www.lorelyburt.org.uk

Date of birth: 10 September 1954; Daughter of Hazel June, née Abbiss, and Raymond Claude Baker

Education: High Arcal Grammar School, Dudley; University College of Wales, Swansea (BSc Econ economics 1975); Open University (MBA 1997); Married Richard Burt 1992 (1 daughter from previous marriage, 1 stepson)

Non-political career: Assistant governor Pucklechurch Remand Centre and HMP Holloway 1975-78; Personnel and training posts Beecham, Eurostar, Forte and Mercers 1978-84; Managing director Kudos Leisure Ltd training company 1984-97; Director: Ace Creative Enterprises Ltd marketing company 1994-99, Mansion House Group 1999-2002; Self-employed estate planning consultant 2002-05; Councillor Dudley Metropolitan Borough Council 1998-2003

Political career: Contested Dudley South 2001 general election. Member for Solihull 2005-10, for Solihull (revised boundary) since 6 May 2010 general election; Liberal Democrat: Whip 2005-06, Shadow Minister for: Northern Ireland 2005-06, Small Business, Women and Equality 2006-07, Business, Enterprise and Regulatory Reform 2007-09, Business, Innovation and Skills 2009-10; *Select Committees:* Member: Treasury 2005-06, Regulatory Reform 2006-10; Contested West Midlands 2004 European Parliament election; Member Liberal Democrat: Federal Policy Committee 2002-03, West Midlands regional executive 2002-; Chair Liberal Democrat Parliamentary Party 2007-

Political interests: Industry, workplace culture, equality, planning, women in prison

Other organisations: FInstSMM 1998

Recreations: Theatre, cinema, socializing, food

Lorely Burt MP, House of Commons, London SW1A 0AA
Tel: 020 7219 8269 Fax: 020 7219 5199 E-mail: burtl@parliament.uk
Constituency: 81 Warwick Road, Solihull, West Midlands B92 7HP
Tel: 0121-706 9593 Fax: 0121-706 9365
Website: www.lorelyburt.org.uk

GENERAL ELECTION RESULT

		%
Burt, L. (Lib Dem)*	23,635	42.9
Throup, M. (Con)	23,460	42.6
Merrill, S. (Lab)	4,891	8.9
Terry, A. (BNP)	1,624	3.0
Ison, J. (UKIP)	1,200	2.2
Watts, N. (SMRA)	319	0.6
Majority	175	0.32
Electorate	77,863	
Turnout	55,129	70.80

**Member of last parliament*

CONSTITUENCY SNAPSHOT

Throughout the 1980s and early 1990s Tory John Taylor's share of the vote never dropped below 60 per cent. Although his share plummeted by over 16 per cent in 1997, neither Labour nor the Lib Dems came close to unseating him.

In 2001 Taylor's margin remained virtually unchanged. However, in 2005 the Lib Dem's Lorely Burt took the seat with a 10 per cent swing and a very narrow 279 majority. Burt won Solihull in 2010 despite it being notionally a Conservative seat. However, she won by the narrowest of margins, just 175 votes.

Boundary changes were minimal: four part-wards were exchanged between the seat and Meriden.

Solihull, on the south-eastern fringes of Birmingham, is one of the most desirable residential areas of the West Midlands conurbation. St Alphege and Shirley South in particular are exemplars of middle-class suburbia.

Manufacturing has until very recently been a very important staple and Land-Rover's Lode Lane plant was based here.

Public administration, education and health are now dominant employment sectors.

Dan Byles

North Warwickshire

Boundary changes

Tel: 020 7219 7179
E-mail: dan.byles.mp@parliament.uk
Website: www.danbyles.co.uk/conservatives

Conservative

Date of birth: 24 June 1974

Education: Warwick School; Leeds University (economics and management studies 1996) Nottingham Trent University (MA creative writing); Married Prashanthi Katangoor Reddy 2007

Non-political career: Medical support officer (left with major rank), Royal Army Medical Corps 1996-2005; Freelance defence consultant 2005-

Political career: Member for North Warwickshire since 6 May 2010 general election; Vice-chair, Knighton Branch, South Leicester Conservatives

Political interests: Defence, economic policy, energy security

Other organisations: Fellow, Royal Geographical Society; Guinness World Record Holder, rowed across the Atlantic Ocean in 101 days in 23-foot rowing boat

Dan Byles MP, House of Commons, London SW1A 0AA
Tel: 020 7219 7179 E-mail: dan.byles.mp@parliament.uk
Constituency: North Warwickshire Conservative Association, Albert Buildings, 2 Castle Mews, Rugby CV21 2XL Tel: 07970 937599
Website: www.danbyles.co.uk/conservatives

GENERAL ELECTION RESULT

		%
Byles, D. (Con)	18,993	40.2
O'Brien, M. (Lab)*	18,939	40.1
Martin, S. (Lib Dem)	5,481	11.6
Holmes, J. (BNP)	2,106	4.5
Fowler, S. (UKIP)	1,335	2.8
Lane, D. (England)	411	0.9
Majority	54	0.11
Electorate	70,143	
Turnout	47,265	67.38

**Member of last parliament*

CONSTITUENCY SNAPSHOT

The seat was created in 1983 from parts of the Meriden and Nuneaton constituencies. Mike O'Brien took the seat for Labour in 1992, from the Tories' Francis Maude with a majority 1,453.

O'Brien's majority increased tenfold in 1997 to 14,767. A 2.8 per cent swing to the Conservatives in 2005 left O'Brien with a 7,553 majority. In 2010 O'Brien was defeated following a 7.7 per cent swing to the Conservative candidate, Dan Byles who was elected with a majority of 54.

The seat gained part of the Bede and Slough Ward from the Nuneaton constituency. It also loses the wards of Arley, Whitacare and Hartshill.

North Warwickshire lies to the east of Birmingham and north of Coventry. It comprises a collection of post-industrial villages and the town of Bedworth.

Historically, there was a large coal mining industry, but this has almost petered out. The district is relatively remote from the rest of Warwickshire, as the county is almost split in two by the West Midlands.

North Warwickshire still has the mines and canal networks that dominated its economy during the industrial revolution; it still retains an economy based on manufacturing and production industries.

As elsewhere in the Midlands, the production and construction industries are strong.

Rt Hon **Liam Byrne**

Birmingham, Hodge Hill ***(returning MP)***

Boundary changes

Tel: 020 7219 6953
E-mail: byrnel@parliament.uk
Website: www.liambyrne.co.uk

Date of birth: 2 October 1970

Education: Burnt Mill Comprehensive, Harlow, Essex; Manchester University (BA politics and modern history); Harvard Business School, USA (Fulbright Scholar MBA); Married Sarah 1998 (2 sons 1 daughter)

Non-political career: Andersen Consulting 1993-96; Leader of Labour Party's Office 1996-97; N M Rothschild 1997-99; Co-founder eGS Group Ltd 2000-04; Member National Council NUS; Member Amicus

Political career: Member for Birmingham Hodge Hill 15 July 2004 by-election to 2010, for Birmingham, Hodge Hill (revised boundary) since 6 May 2010 general election; Parliamentary Under-Secretary of State, Department of Health (Care Services) 2005-06; Minister of State, Home Office 2006-08 (Policing, Security and Community Safety 2006, Citizenship, Immigration and Nationality 2006-07, Borders and Immigration 2007-08); Minister for the West Midlands 2007-08; Minister of State, HM Treasury 2008; Minister for the Cabinet Office; Chancellor of the Duchy of Lancaster (attending Cabinet) 2008-09; Chair Council of Regional Ministers 2008-10; Chief Secretary to the Treasury 2009-10; Shadow Chief Secretary to the Treasury 2010-; *Select Committees:* Member: European Scrutiny 2005-10, European Standing B 2005-06; Adviser 1997 general election campaign; Member: Christian Socialist Movement, Fabian Society

Political interests: Anti-social behaviour, drugs, social policy, welfare reform, youth policy; Kashmir

Other organisations: Fellow, Social Market Foundation; PC 2008; *Publications:* Local Government transformed (1996); Information Age Government (1997); Cities of Enterprise, New Strategies for Full Employment (2002); A Chance to Serve? (Progress 2002); Britain in 2020 (2003); The Fate We're In (Progress 2003); Reinventing Government Again (2004); The Left's Agenda for Science (2004); Why Labour Won: Lessons from 2005 (Fabian Society 2005); Powered by Politics: Reforming Parties from the Inside (2005); Power to the People, Next Steps for New Labour (Progress); From Free Movement to Fair Movement: The Immigration Debate in the UK (in Rethinking Immigration and Integration: A New Centre-Left Agenda) (Policy Network 2007); From Choice to Control: Empowering Public Services (in Public Matters: The Renewal of the Public Realm) (2007); A Common Place (Fabian Society 2007)

Recreations: Running, music, family

Rt Hon Liam Byrne MP, House of Commons, London SW1A 0AA
Tel: 020 7219 6953 Fax: 020 7219 1431
E-mail: byrnel@parliament.uk
Constituency: Tel: 0121-789 7287 Fax: 0121-789 9824
Website: www.liambyrne.co.uk

GENERAL ELECTION RESULT

		%
Byrne, L. (Lab)*	22,077	52.0
Khan, T. (Lib Dem)	11,775	27.8
Parekh, S. (Con)	4,936	11.6
Lumby, R. (BNP)	2,333	5.5
Rafiq, W. (UKIP)	714	1.7
Johnson, P. (SDP)	637	1.5
Majority	10,302	24.28
Electorate	75,040	
Turnout	42,427	56.54

**Member of last parliament*

CONSTITUENCY SNAPSHOT

Labour has won this seat at every general election since 1950 when it was formed from part of Yardley. Prominent Labour politician Roy Jenkins was the first MP of Stechford, as it was then known, and he held the constituency for 27 years.

Jenkins' departure in January 1977 to become European Commission President prompted a by-election in which control briefly passed to the Conservative. Terry Davis won the constituency back for Labour in 1979 and held the seat until his retirement in 2005.

In 2010 Liam Byrne held the seat for Labour with a majority of 10,302.

Bordesley Green, spanning the south section of the seat to the west of Birmingham Yardley, has been brought fully inside this seat, as has Washwood Heath. Losses are few: part of Stechford and Yardley North went to Birmingham Yardley, though this did constitute a sizeable area to the south west of the constituency.

Hodge Hill consists of a wedge-shaped portion of Birmingham fanning out from Saltley towards the eastern suburbs.

This is one of the most deprived seats in the country. The Washwood Heath ward contains a large Asian community whereas the Hodge Hill and Shard End wards are overwhelmingly white and local authority housing is more common.

Rt Hon Dr **Vincent Cable**

Twickenham (returning MP)

No boundary changes

Tel: 020 7219 1106
E-mail: cablev@parliament.uk
Website: www.vincentcable.org.uk

Date of birth: 9 May 1943; Son of late Leonard Cable and Edith Cable

Education: Nunthorpe Grammar School, York; Fitzwilliam College, Cambridge (President of Union) (BA natural science and economics 1966); Glasgow University (PhD international economics 1973); Married Dr Olympia Rebelo (died 2001) (2 sons 1 daughter); married Rachel Wenban Smith 2004

Non-political career: Finance officer, Kenya Treasury 1966-68; Economics lecturer, Glasgow University 1968-74; Diplomatic Service 1974-76; Deputy director Overseas Development Institute 1976-83; Special Adviser to John Smith as Secretary of State for Trade 1979; Special Adviser to Sir Sonny Ramphal as Commonwealth Secretary-General 1983-90; Adviser to World Commission on Environment and Development (Brundtland Commission) 1985-87; Group planning Shell 1990-93; Head economics programme Chatham House 1993-95; Chief economist Shell International 1995-97; Visiting fellow, Nuffield College, Oxford and London School of Economics (Centre for Global Governance); Special professor of economics, Nottingham University 1999; Research fellow, international economics, Royal Institute of International Affairs; Councillor (Labour), Glasgow City Council 1971-74

Political career: Contested Glasgow Hillhead (Labour) 1970, York (SDP/Alliance) 1983 and 1987, Twickenham (Liberal Democrat) 1992 general elections. Member for Twickenham since 1 May 1997 general election; Liberal Democrat: Spokesperson for the Treasury (EMU and The City) 1997-99, Principal Spokesperson for Trade and Industry 1999-2003, Shadow Chancellor of the Exchequer 2003-10; Secretary of State for Business, Innovation and Skills; President of the Board of Trade 2010-; *Select Committees:* Member: Treasury (Treasury Sub-Committee) 1998-99, Treasury 1998-99; Liberal Democrat Party: Deputy Leader 2006-10, Acting Leader 2007

Political interests: Economic policy, development, policing, energy, environment; India, Russia, China, Nigeria, Kenya

Other organisations: PC 2010; *House Magazine* Opposition Politician of the Year 2008; *Public Affairs News* Politician of the Year 2008; CAB Parliamentarian of the Year 2008; Channel 4 Political Impact Award 2009; Channel 4 Opposition Politician 2009; *The Oldie* 'I Told You So' Award 2009; British Legion Club, Twickenham; *Publications:* Wide variety of books and pamphlets including: Protectionism and Industrial Decline (1983), The New Giants: China and India (Chatham House 1994), The World's New Fissures; The Politics of Identity (Demos 1995), Globalisation and Global Governance, (Chatham House 1999), Multiple Identities, (Demos 2005), Public Services: Reform with a Purpose, (Centre for Reform 2005); The Storm (Atlantic 2009)

Recreations: Ballroom and Latin dancing, classical music, riding, walking

Rt Hon Dr Vincent Cable MP, House of Commons, London SW1A 0AA Tel: 020 7219 1106 Fax: 020 7219 1191
E-mail: cablev@parliament.uk
Constituency: 2a Lion Road, Twickenham, Middlesex TW1 4JQ
Tel: 020 8892 0215 Fax: 020 8892 0218
Website: www.vincentcable.org.uk

GENERAL ELECTION RESULT

		%	+/-
Cable, V. (Lib Dem)*	32,483	54.4	2.8
Thomas, D. (Con)	20,343	34.1	1.7
Tomlinson, B. (Lab)	4,583	7.7	-3.7
Gilbert, B. (UKIP)	868	1.5	
Roest, S. (Green)	674	1.1	-1.7
Hurst, C. (BNP)	654	1.1	
Cole, H. (CURE)	76	0.1	
Armstrong, P. (Magna Carta)	40	0.1	
Majority	12,140	20.33	
Electorate	79,861		
Turnout	59,721	74.78	

**Member of last parliament*

CONSTITUENCY SNAPSHOT

Twickenham had been a long-standing Conservative seat, returning members between 1945 to 1997. In 1992 the Liberal Democrats made headway in the parliamentary constituency, reducing Toby Jessel's margin to 10.2 per cent.

In the 1997 general election the Liberal Democrats won on a swing just short of 9 per cent that delivered the seat to Vincent Cable with a majority of 4,281. In 2001 Cable was re-elected with a majority of 7,655. In 2005 Cable was again returned as MP on a turnout of over 71 per cent. Cable has made this a safe seat for his party, winning by 12,140 votes in 2010.

A leafy, largely residential constituency on the banks of the Thames in south west London, Twickenham is perhaps best known as the home of English rugby.

Twickenham's rugby stadium holds some 82,000 people. It also doubles as a music venue.

The constituency also includes the communities of Teddington and Hampton, including Hampton Court Palace.

Twickenham lies directly below the flight paths both to and from Heathrow Airport.

Alun Cairns

Vale of Glamorgan

Boundary changes

Tel: 020 7219 3000
E-mail: alun.cairns.mp@parliament.uk
Website: www.aluncairns.com

Conservative

Date of birth: 30 July 1970; Son of Hugh Cairns, retired, and Margaret Cairns

Education: Ysgol Gyfun Ddwyieithog Ystalyfera; University of Wales (MBA 2001); Married Emma Elizabeth Turner 1996 (1 son)

Non-political career: Board Member, Reserve and Cadet Forces in Wales; Lloyd's Bank Group 1989-99: Business development consultant 1992-98, Field manager 1998-99

Political career: Contested Gower 1997 and Vale of Glamorgan 2005 general elections. Member for Vale of Glamorgan since 6 May 2010 general election; Contested Bridgend constituency 1999 and 2003 National Assembly for Wales elections. AM for South Wales West region since 6 May 1999: Welsh Conservative: Spokesperson for: Economic Development 1999-2000, Economic Development and Europe 2000-03, Economic Development and Transport 2003-07; Shadow Minister for: Education and Lifelong Learning 2007-08, Local Government 2008-09, Heritage 2009-; Spokesperson for the Economy 2009-; Shadow Chief Whip and Business Manager 2009-; Member, Swansea West Conservative Association 1987-; Deputy Chairperson, Welsh Young Conservatives 1995-96; Chaired one of William Hague's Policy Advisory Groups 1996-97; Conservative Economic Spokesperson in Wales 1997-98; South Wales West Regional Policy Co-ordinator 1998-99; Conservative Economic Development Spokesperson 1999-

Political interests: Economy, trade and industry, Welsh language, SEN; South East Asia

Recreations: Running, computing, skiing, gardening, shooting, squash

Alun Cairns MP, House of Commons, London SW1A 0AA
Tel: 020 7219 3000 E-mail: alun.cairns.mp@parliament.uk
Constituency: 5 Lias Road, Porthcawl CF36 3AH Tel: 01656 773060
Website: www.aluncairns.com

GENERAL ELECTION RESULT

		%
Cairns, A. (Con)	20,341	41.8
Davies, A. (Lab)	16,034	33.0
Parrott, E. (Lib Dem)	7,403	15.2
Johnson, I. (PlC)	2,667	5.5
Mahoney, K. (UKIP)	1,529	3.1
Thomas, R. (Green)	457	0.9
Harrold, J. (Christian)	236	0.5
Majority	4,307	8.85
Electorate	70,262	
Turnout	48,667	69.27

CONSTITUENCY SNAPSHOT

In 1983 Sir Raymond Gower was the Conservative MP for the region. Labour's John Smith took control at the by-election in 1989 caused by Gower's death, only to lose it again to Tory Walter Sweeney in 1992. Labour won five years later in 1997 when John Smith won the seat back with a 10,532 majority.

In 2001 the Conservatives clawed their way back to within 5,000 votes and in 2005 they further reduced the Labour majority to 1,808. Alun Cairns won the seat for the Tories with a 6.1 per cent swing.

Boundary changes have added St Bride's Major and part of the Llandow/Ewenny wards that were in Bridgend. The Sully electoral division has moved into Cardiff South and Penarth.

Based around the town of Barry, many of the residential areas in Vale of Glamorgan are home to Cardiff's wealthier commuters. Barry port continues to be important to the local economy, with tourism and agriculture being other key sectors.

Transport infrastructure is good. The M4 runs along the northern boundary. A new defence training academy will be created at St Athan, creating 5,000 jobs and an estimated £60 million annual boost for the local economy. It is due to have its first intake in 2012 and will be fully operational by 2017.

David Cairns

Inverclyde (returning MP)

No boundary changes

Tel: 020 7219 8242
E-mail: cairnsd@parliament.uk
Website: www.davidcairns.com

Labour

Date of birth: 7 August 1966; Son of John Cairns and late Theresa Cairns

Education: Notre Dame High School, Greenock; Gregorian University, Rome; Franciscan Study Centre, Canterbury; Single

Non-political career: Priest 1991-94; Director Christian Socialist Movement 1994-97; Research assistant to Siobhan McDonagh MP 1997-2001; Community Union; London Borough of Merton: Councillor 1998-2002, Chief whip 1999-2001

Political career: Member for Greenock and Inverclyde 2001-05, for Inverclyde since 5 May 2005 general election; PPS to Malcolm Wicks as Minister of State, Department for Work and Pensions 2003-05; Parliamentary Under-Secretary of State: Scotland Office 2005-07, Northern Ireland Office 2006-07; Minister of State, Scotland Office 2007-08; *Select Committees:* Member: Joint Committee on Consolidation of Bills Etc 2001-05; Member: Fabian Society, Christian Socialist Movement

Political interests: Defence, employment, welfare, small businesses; Israel, Italy, USA

Other organisations: Amnesty International; Fellow Industry and Parliament Trust

Recreations: Travel, watching football, visiting extended family

David Cairns MP, House of Commons, London SW1A 0AA
Tel: 020 7219 8242 Fax: 020 7219 1772
E-mail: cairnsd@parliament.uk
Constituency: The Parliamentary Office, 20 Union Street, Greenock, Renfrewshire PA16 8JL Tel: 01475 791820 Fax: 01475 791821
Website: www.davidcairns.com

GENERAL ELECTION RESULT

		%	+/-
Cairns, D. (Lab)*	20,993	56.0	5.4
Nelson, I. (SNP)	6,577	17.5	-2.0
Hutton, S. (Lib Dem)	5,007	13.4	-3.6
Wilson, D. (Con)	4,502	12.0	1.8
Campbell, P. (UKIP)	433	1.2	
Majority	14,416	38.43	
Electorate	59,209		
Turnout	37,512	63.36	

**Member of last parliament*

CONSTITUENCY SNAPSHOT

Dr Norman Godman served as the Labour MP here from 1983 until his retirement in 2001.

Before the 1997 election the seat was altered and renamed Greenock and Inverclyde, losing Port Glasgow to West Renfrewshire. In return Greenock gained most of the remainder of the Inverclyde area. In 2001 David Cairns replaced Godman as Labour MP with a 9,890 majority.

The seat was renamed Inverclyde in 2005 as boundaries were altered to be identical to those of Inverclyde council. At the election Cairns was returned with a 11,259 majority. David Cairns was returned in 2010 with a 14,426 majority and 56 per cent of the vote.

This seat on the banks of the Clyde is mainly rural and coastal though the population is concentrated in Greenock and Port Glasgow. These grew up on the shipbuilding industry and both have suffered from the decline of manufacturing and the loss of dockyard jobs. The last remaining yard in the seat is Fergusons' Lower Clyde shipyard at Port Glasgow.

In recent years some diversification has taken place and computer and electronics firms are the major new employers. Smaller towns include Gourock, a dowdy seaside resort, and Wemyss Bay, a little port which has a ferry link with Bute.

Inverclyde suffers from many of the issues familiar with areas that have suffered from a decline in heavy industry, including comparatively low incomes and poor health.

Rt Hon **David Cameron**

Witney (returning MP)

Boundary changes

E-mail: contact via https://email.number10.gov.uk/

Date of birth: 9 October 1966; Son of Ian Donald Cameron and Mary Fleur Cameron, née Mount

Education: Eton College; Brasenose College, Oxford (BA philosophy, politics, economics 1988); Married Smantha Sheffield 1996 (2 sons, 1 deceased, 1 daughter)

Non-political career: Conservative Research Department 1988-92: Head of political section, Member Prime Minister's Question Time briefing team; Special adviser to: Norman Lamont as Chancellor of the Exchequer 1992-93, Michael Howard as Home Secretary 1993-94; Director of corporate affairs Carlton Communications plc 1994-2001

Political career: Contested Stafford 1997 general election. Member for Witney 2001-10, for Witney (revised boundary) since 6 May 2010 general election; Shadow Minister for: Privy Council Office 2003, Local and Devolved Government Affairs 2004; Member Shadow Cabinet 2004-10; Shadow Secretary of State for Education and Skills 2005; Leader of the Opposition 2005-10; Prime Minister, First Lord of the Treasury and Minister for the Civil Service 2010-; *Select Committees:* Member: Home Affairs 2001-04, Modernisation of the House of Commons 2003; Deputy Chairman Conservative Party 2003; Head of Policy Co-ordination Conservative Party 2004; Leader Conservative Party 2005-

Other organisations: Patron: Carterton Educational Trust, St Mary's Church Preservation Trust, Mulberry Bush School Standlake, Trips, Outings and Activities for the Learning, Disabled (T.O.A.D), Bampton Classical Opera, Victoria History of Oxfordshire Trust, KIDS; Vice-president National Society for Epilepsy; Epilepsy Research Foundation; Vice-President, Commonwealth Parliamentary Association (UK Branch) 2005-; PC 2005; Hansard Society Opening Up Politics Award 2007

Recreations: Tennis, cooking

Rt Hon David Cameron MP, 10 Downing Street, London SW1A 2AA
Fax: 020 7925 0918 Website: www.whitneyconservatives.com

GENERAL ELECTION RESULT

		%
Cameron, D. (Con)*	33,973	58.8
Barnes, D. (Lib Dem)	11,233	19.4
Goldberg, J. (Lab)	7,511	13.0
MacDonald, S. (Green)	2,385	4.1
Tolstoy-Miloslavsky, N. (UKIP)	2,001	3.5
Hope, A. (Loony)	234	0.4
Wesson, P. (Ind)	166	0.3
Cook, J. (Ind)	151	0.3
Bex, C. (Wessex Reg)	62	0.1
Barschak, A. (Ind)	53	0.1
Majority	22,740	39.36
Electorate	78,766	
Turnout	57,769	73.34

**Member of last parliament*

CONSTITUENCY SNAPSHOT

The seat today known as Witney was established in 1974 and has been represented by a Conservative ever since: Douglas Hurd represented the seat for 23 years until he retired in 1997. He was succeeded by Shaun Woodward, who defected to Labour in 1999. Witney Conservative Association demanded that he resign, but he refused and stayed in the seat until 2001, when the Labour Party transferred him to the safe St Helens South.

The local party selected David Cameron, who was returned with a 7,973 majority in 2001. He almost doubled his 2005 majority, which was 14,156.

Cameron was returned with a majority of 22,740 at the 2010 general election.

The seat lost the part-ward of Kirtlington to Henley, and Yarnton, Gosford and Water Eaton part-ward to Oxford West and Abingdon.

This Oxfordshire constituency west of Oxford covers the town of Witney itself, Eynsham, Chipping Norton, RAF Brize Norton, Carterton, Burford, Charlbury and Woodstock.

Witney is an old industrial town with a steadily growing population and was once most famous for its blanket factories. They have been replaced by a number of new factories and industrial estates.

The constituency also contains part of the Cotswolds and Blenheim Palace: tourism is therefore an important factor in sustaining the local economy.

INVITATION TO JOIN US IN THE PURSUIT OF HUMAN DIGNITY, LIBERTY AND DEVELOPMENT

WWW.LI.COM

LEGATUM INSTITUTE, 11 CHARLES STREET, MAYFAIR, LONDON W1J 5DW, UK
TELEPHONE: +44 207 148 5400, FACSIMILE: +44 207 148 5401

Alan Campbell

Tynemouth (returning MP)

Boundary changes

Tel: 020 7219 6619
E-mail: campbellal@parliament.uk
Website: www.alancampbellmp.co.uk

Date of birth: 8 July 1957; Son of Albert Campbell and Marian, neé Hewitt

Education: Blackfyne Secondary School, Consett; Lancaster University (BA politics 1978); Leeds University (PGCE 1979); Newcastle Polytechnic (MA history 1984); Married Jayne Lamont 1991 (1 son 1 daughter)

Non-political career: Whitley Bay High School 1980-89; Hirst High School, Ashington, Northumberland: Teacher 1989-97, Head of sixth form, Head of department

Political career: Member for Tynemouth 1997-2010, for Tynemouth (revised boundary) since 6 May 2010 general election; PPS: to Lord Macdonald of Tradeston as Minister for the Cabinet Office and Chancellor of the Duchy of Lancaster 2001-03, to Adam Ingram as Minister of State, Ministry of Defence 2003-05; Assistant Government Whip 2005-06; Government Whip 2006-08; Parliamentary Under-Secretary of State (Crime Reduction), Home Office 2008-10; *Select Committees:* Member: Public Accounts 1997-2001, Armed Forces Bill 2005-06, Selection 2006-08

Political interests: Education, constitutional reform, shipbuilding and offshore industries; Falkland Islands

Recreations: Family

Alan Campbell MP, House of Commons, London SW1A 0AA
Tel: 020 7219 6619 Fax: 020 7219 3006
E-mail: campbellal@parliament.uk
Constituency: 99 Howard Street, North Shields,
Tyne and Wear NE30 1NA Tel: 0191-257 1927 Fax: 0191-257 6537
Website: www.alancampbellmp.co.uk

GENERAL ELECTION RESULT

		%
Campbell, A. (Lab)*	23,860	45.3
Morton, W. (Con)	18,121	34.4
Appleby, J. (Lib Dem)	7,845	14.9
Brooke, D. (BNP)	1,404	2.7
Payne, N. (UKIP)	900	1.7
Erskine, J. (Green)	538	1.0
Majority	5,739	10.90
Electorate	75,680	
Turnout	52,668	69.59

**Member of last parliament*

CONSTITUENCY SNAPSHOT

Traditionally, Tyneside had been the only seat in Tyne and Wear to be Conservative. Dame Irene Ward was the longest-serving incumbent of this seat, representing the area from 1950 to 1974. The seat was only lost by the Tories in 1997, when Alan Campbell for Labour took over from Neville Trotter with a 11,273 majority.

Campbell's majority has fallen at each subsequent election and was 4,143 in 2005. Alan Campbell won again in 2010 with an improved 5,739 majority.

Boundary changes have resulted in the ward of Riverside being lost to North Tyneside and Chirton, Collingwood, Monkseaton South, St Mary's and Valley all now entirely within the seat's boundaries after previously being shared with North Tyneside.

Tynemouth has a long coastline at the south eastern tip of the old Northumberland county.

The seat's main economy has traditionally been shipbuilding. This area was one of the principal production areas of Victorian Britain. Alongside the ship builders, marine engineering and fishing were the main industries.

These have all declined and have been replaced by employment within the service industries and public sector, the majority of the seat's employment now deriving from this area. The developing tourist industry in the area is also becoming a source of new jobs.

Gregory Campbell

East Londonderry (returning MP)

Boundary changes

Tel: 020 7219 8495
E-mail: campbellg@parliament.uk

Date of birth: 15 February 1953; Son of James Campbell and Martha Joyce (née Robinson)

Education: Londonderry Technical College; Magee College (Extra-Mural Certificate political studies 1982); Married Frances Patterson 1979 (1 son 3 daughters)

Non-political career: Civil servant 1972-82, 1986-94; Self-employed (set up publishing company) 1994-99; Councillor, Londonderry City Council 1981-

Political career: Contested Foyle 1983, 1987, 1992 and East Londonderry 1997 general elections. Member for East Londonderry 2001-10, for East Londonderry (revised boundary) since 6 May 2010 general election; DUP Spokesperson for: Defence 2005-07, Culture, Media and Sport 2005-, Work and Pensions 2007-09, Transport 2009, Work and Pensions 2009-; *Select Committees:* Member: Transport, Local Government and the Regions 2001-02, Transport, Local Government and the Regions (Transport Sub-Committee) 2001-02, Transport 2002-04, Northern Ireland Affairs 2004-09; Member: Northern Ireland Assembly 1982-86, Northern Ireland Forum for Political Dialogue 1996-98; MLA for East Londonderry 1998-: Minister: for Regional Development 2000-01, of Culture, Arts and Leisure 2008-09; DUP: Security Spokeman 1994; Treasurer; Senior Party Officer

Political interests: Economic development, tourism, employment, enterprise, trade and industry; *Publications:* Discrimination: The Truth (1987); Discrimination: Where Now? (1993); Ulster's Verdict on the Joint Declaration (1994); Working Toward 2000 (1998)

Recreations: Football, music, reading

Gregory Campbell MP, House of Commons, London SW1A 0AA
Tel: 020 7219 8495 Fax: 020 7219 1953
E-mail: campbellg@parliament.uk
Constituency: 25 Bushmills Road, Coleraine,
Co Londonderry BT52 2BP Tel: 028 7032 7327 Fax: 028 7032 7328

GENERAL ELECTION RESULT

		%
Campbell, G. (DUP)*	12,097	34.6
Ó'Hoisín, C. (Sinn Féin)	6,742	19.3
McAuley, L. (UCUNF)	6,218	17.8
Conway, T. (SDLP)	5,399	15.5
Ross, W. (TUV)	2,572	7.4
Fitzpatrick, B. (All)	1,922	5.5
Majority	5,355	15.32
Electorate	63,220	
Turnout	34,950	55.28

**Member of last parliament*

CONSTITUENCY SNAPSHOT

The seat has always been held by a unionist and the DUP gained the seat from the UUP in 2001.

The seat was held by Willie Ross, a member of the UUP and strong opponent of the Belfast Agreement, from 1974 until 2001 when there was a 6.5 per cent swing from the UUP to the DUP's Gregory Campbell.

In 2005's general election Campbell increased his majority to 7,727. The seat was held by the DUP in 2010, however, Campbell's majority decreased to 5,355 following a 4.1 per cent swing to Sinn Féin.

The constituency gained Banagher and Claudy wards from Foyle.

Despite its name, the constituency includes no part of the city of Londonderry, but is named after the county of the same name.

This mainly rural and Protestant constituency lies in the north-western part of Northern Ireland. The main town is Coleraine, where the main campus of the University of Ulster is based. The university is an important employer and overall driver of the seat's economy. Coleraine itself is a popular shopping centre and is one of the most affluent pockets of the North West.

The constituency includes the beautiful Roe valley and the seaside resorts of Portrush and Portstewart making this an attractive spot for tourists. Both tourism and business have been boosted by the recent introduction of a ferry service between Magilligan point in the constituency and the Donegal fishing village of Greencastle.

Rt Hon Sir **Menzies Campbell**

North East Fife ***(returning MP)***

No boundary changes

Tel: 020 7219 4446
E-mail: campbellm@parliament.uk
Website: www.mingcampbell.org.uk

Date of birth: 22 May 1941; Son of late George and Elizabeth Campbell

Education: Hillhead High School, Glasgow; Glasgow University (MA arts 1962, LLB law 1965); Stanford University, California (post graduate studies in international law 1966-67); Married Elspeth Mary Urquhart 1970

Non-political career: Called to the Bar (Scotland) 1968; QC (Scotland) 1982; Competed: 1964 (Tokyo) Olympics, 1966 Commonwealth Games (Jamaica); UK Athletics Team Captain 1965-66; UK 100 metres record holder 1967-74; Chair, Royal Lyceum Theatre Company, Edinburgh 1984-87

Political career: Contested Greenock and Port Glasgow February and October 1974, East Fife 1979, North East Fife 1983 general elections. Member for North East Fife 1987-2005, for North East Fife (revised boundary) since 5 May 2005 general election; Liberal Spokesperson for Arts, Broadcasting and Sport 1987-88; SLD Spokesperson for Defence, Sport 1988-89; Liberal Democrat: Spokesperson for: Scotland (Legal Affairs, Lord Advocate) 1987-99, Defence and Disarmament, Sport 1989-94, Foreign Affairs and Defence, Sport 1994-97, Foreign Affairs (Defence and Europe) 1997-99, Principal Spokesperson for Defence and Foreign Affairs 1999-2001, Shadow Secretary of State for Foreign and Commonwealth Affairs 2001-06; Leader Liberal Democrat Party 2006-07; *Select Committees:* Member: Trade and Industry 1990-92, Defence 1992-97, 1997-99, Foreign Affairs 2008-10; Chair Scottish Liberal Party 1975-77; Member Liberal Democrat Peel Group 2001-; Deputy Leader Liberal Democrat Party 2003-06; Leader Liberal Democrat Party 2006-07

Political interests: Defence, foreign affairs, legal affairs, sport, arts; Middle East, North America

Other organisations: Member: Board of the British Council 1998-2002, Council of the Air League 1999-2006; Member: North Atlantic Assembly 1989-, UK Delegation, Parliamentary Assembly of OSCE 1992-97, 1999-; Chancellor St Andrews University 2006-; CBE 1987; PC 1999; Kt 2004; Highland Park/*The Spectator* Member to Watch 1996; Channel 4 Opposition Politician of the Year 2004; *House Magazine* Opposition Politician of the Year 2004; Herald Diageo Westminster Politician of the Year 2004; *Oldie Magazine* Politician of the Year 2005; Political Studies Association Parliamentarian of the Year 2005; Three honorary doctorates from Scottish universities; Reform

Recreations: All sports, theatre, music

Rt Hon Sir Menzies Campbell CBE QC MP, House of Commons, London SW1A 0AA Tel: 020 7219 4446 Fax: 020 7219 0559
E-mail: campbellm@parliament.uk
Constituency: North East Fife Liberal Democrats, 16 Millgate, Cupar, Fife KY15 5EG Tel: 01334 656361 Fax: 01334 654045
Website: www.mingcampbell.org.uk

GENERAL ELECTION RESULT

		%	+/-
Campbell, M. (Lib Dem)*	17,763	44.3	-7.7
Briggs, M. (Con)	8,715	21.8	2.3
Hood, M. (Lab)	6,869	17.2	4.4
Campbell, R. (SNP)	5,685	14.2	3.8
Scott-Hayward, M. (UKIP)	1,032	2.6	1.2
Majority	9,048	22.58	
Electorate	62,969		
Turnout	40,064	63.62	

**Member of last parliament*

CONSTITUENCY SNAPSHOT

The most famous incumbent of the East Fife seat was Liberal Prime Minster Herbert Asquith, who held the then Fife East seat from 1886 until his defeat in 1918. In the inter-and post-war years the seat was held by the Conservatives. In 1987 Menzies Campbell won North East Fife (renamed in 1983) at his third attempt. He has increased his percentage majority in each successive general election.

Boundary changes in 2005 brought in the 3,500 voters of the Leven East ward from Central Fife. Campbell was re-elected with a majority of 12,571. Former Liberal Democrat leader Menzies Campbell held the seat with a 9,048 majority in 2010.

This constituency is rather more prosperous than its Fife neighbours, bearing few traces of heavy industry and is instead characterised by coastline and countryside.

The main town is St Andrews, the home of golf and the location of one of Scotland's ancient universities.

North East Fife has acres of rich farmland and a number of small fishing villages and those working in agriculture represent twice the Scottish average, however, the service industry now employs more people than any other.

Other attractions include Falkland, a former royal palace, and Scotland's Secret Bunker, the former nuclear command centre for Scotland.

RAF Leuchars, home to the Eurofighter Typhoon jet, is of huge importance to the local economy. It was confirmed in May 2008 that a minimum of two squadrons will remain at Leuchars until at least 2040, securing the base's long-term future.

Ronnie Campbell

Blyth Valley (returning MP)

No boundary changes

Tel: 020 7219 4216
E-mail: campbellr@parliament.uk

Date of birth: 14 August 1943; Son of Ronnie and Edna Campbell

Education: Ridley High School, Blyth; Married Deirdre McHale 1967 (5 sons including twins 1 daughter)

Non-political career: Miner 1958-86; NUM Lodge Chairman, Bates Colliery, Blyth 1982-86; NUM Sponsored MP; Councillor: Blyth Borough Council 1969-74, Blyth Valley Council 1974-88

Political career: Member for Blyth Valley since 11 June 1987 general election; *Select Committees:* Member: Public Administration 1997-2001, Catering 2001-05, Health 2005-07

Political interests: China, USA, Far East, Africa

Other organisations: Patron: ME Association, Spartans Supporters Club

Recreations: Furniture restoration, stamp collecting, antiques

Ronnie Campbell MP, House of Commons, London SW1A 0AA
Tel: 020 7219 4216 Fax: 020 7219 4358
E-mail: campbellr@parliament.uk
Constituency: 42 Renwick Road, Blyth, Northumberland NE24 2LQ
Tel: 01670 363050 Fax: 01670 355192

GENERAL ELECTION RESULT

		%	+/-
Campbell, R. (Lab)*	17,156	44.5	-10.0
Reid, J. (Lib Dem)	10,488	27.2	-3.7
Flux, B. (Con)	6,412	16.6	2.8
Fairbairn, S. (BNP)	1,699	4.4	
Condon, J. (UKIP)	1,665	4.3	
Elliott, B. (Ind)	819	2.1	
White, A. (England)	327	0.9	
Majority	6,668	17.29	
Electorate	64,263		
Turnout	38,566	60.01	

**Member of last parliament*

CONSTITUENCY SNAPSHOT

In the February 1974 general election Labour deselected the independently-minded MP Eddie Milne, who then ran as an Independent. He defeated the official Labour candidate, only to lose to John Ryman by narrow margins in the October 1974 and 1979 general elections.

In 1987 Ryman was replaced as Labour candidate and MP by Ronnie Campbell, though the SDP lost by a slim 853 votes. In the aftermath of the SDP's break-up, Labour's position has been strengthened considerably. By 1997 Mr Campbell had a majority of nearly 18,000. In 2001 this majority was cut by 5,548 votes to 12,188. Campbell's majority was cut once again in 2005 to 8,527. Campbell was re-elected with a 6,668 majority in 2010.

Blyth Valley lies on the east coast in Northumberland. It is immediately south of Wansbeck, east of Hexham, and to the north of North Tyneside and Tynemouth. The area was historically associated with coal mining, but the closure of the Bates Colliery in 1986 prompted alternative economic development in the constituency.

About £1 million from the Lottery fund was earmarked for the regeneration of historic buildings in Blyth in 2007. Furthermore, a major £3 million redevelopment of the town's Market Place began early in 2008.

Alistair Carmichael

Orkney and Shetland (returning MP)

No boundary changes

Tel: 020 7219 8181
E-mail: carmichaela@parliament.uk
Website: www.alistaircarmichael.org.uk

Date of birth: 15 July 1965; Son of Alexander Calder Carmichael, farmer and Mina, née McKay

Education: Islay High School, Argyll; Aberdeen University (LLB Scots law 1992, Dip LP 1993); Married Kathryn Jane Eastham 1987 (2 sons)

Non-political career: Hotel manager 1984-89; Procurator fiscal depute Procurator Fiscal Service 1993-96; Solicitor private practice 1996-2001

Political career: Contested Paisley South 1987 general election. Member for Orkney and Shetland since 7 June 2001 general election; Scottish Liberal Democrat Spokesperson on the Energy Review 2001-02; Liberal Democrat: Deputy Spokesperson for: Northern Ireland 2002-05, Home Affairs 2004-06, Shadow Secretary of State for: Transport 2006-07, Northern Ireland and Scotland 2007-08, 2008-10; Deputy Chief Whip (Comptroller of HM Household) 2010-; *Select Committees:* Member: Scottish Affairs 2001-05, 2008-10 International Development 2001-02, Public Accounts 2005-06, Joint Committee on Consolidation, Etc, Bills 2008-10, Members' Allowances 2009-10; Member Liberal Democrat Federal Policy Committee 2004-

Political interests: Transport, agriculture, fishing industry, criminal justice, energy; Burma, Palestine/Israel, Uzbekistan

Other organisations: Amnesty International; Elder Church of Scotland 1995-; Director, Solicitors Will Aid (Scotland) Ltd

Recreations: Amateur dramatics, music

Alistair Carmichael MP, House of Commons, London SW1A 0AA
Tel: 020 7219 8181 Fax: 020 7219 1787
E-mail: carmichaela@parliament.uk
Constituency: Orkney: 31 Broad Street, Kirkwall, Orkney KW15 1DH
Tel: 01856 876541 Fax: 01856 876162, Shetland: 171 Commercial Street, Lerwick, Shetland ZE1 0HX Tel: 01595 690044
Fax: 01595 690055 Website: www.alistaircarmichael.org.uk

GENERAL ELECTION RESULT

		%	+/-
Carmichael, A. (Lib Dem)*	11,989	62.0	10.6
Cooper, M. (Lab)	2,061	10.7	-3.5
Mowat, J. (SNP)	2,042	10.6	0.3
Nairn, F. (Con)	2,032	10.5	-2.8
Smith, R. (UKIP)	1,222	6.3	3.9
Majority	9,928	51.32	
Electorate	33,085		
Turnout	19,346	58.47	

**Member of last parliament*

CONSTITUENCY SNAPSHOT

From February 1950 until his retirement in 1983 Jo Grimmond, the Liberal Party leader from 1956 to 1967, held the seat. His successor Jim Wallace steadily increased his majority from around 4,000 in 1983 to nearly 7,000 in 1997.

Wallace stood down in 2001 and was replaced by Alistair Carmichael, however, Wallace's huge 1997 majority was cut in half. Carmichael was returned with a 6,627 majority in 2005 which represents a huge 37 per cent margin. Alistair Carmichael won almost 60 per cent of the vote and an absolute majority in 2010.

The Orkney Islands are seven miles from the Scottish mainland while the Shetland Islands are nearer to Norway than to England.

Agriculture and fishing remain extremely important to both island groups despite their decline. Since the early 1970s they have been cushioned from this by the jobs created from the exploration of oil in the North Sea, especially at the substantial oil terminal facilities at Sullom Voe and at Flotta.

Tourism is of growing importance. Attractions include the pre-historic village of Skara Brae and the evocative Ring of Bogar standing stones and henge in Orkney, while Shetland boasts Jarlshof Prehistoric and Norse Settlement.

In recent years Orkney has become a centre for research into renewable energy. It is home to the International Centre for Island Technology as well as the European Marine Energy Centre.

Neil Carmichael

Stroud

Boundary changes

Tel: 020 7219 3000
E-mail: neil.carmichael.mp@parliament.uk
Website: www.neilcarmichael.co.uk

Conservative

Date of birth: 1961

Education: St Peter's School, York; Nottingham University (BA politics 1982); Married Laurence (1 son twin daughters)

Non-political career: Farmer 1982-; Public affairs consultant, Strategic Impact 2002-; Councillor, Northumberland County Council 1989-93

Political career: Contested Leeds East 1992 and Stroud 2001 and 2005 general elections. Member for Stroud since 6 May 2010 general election

Political interests: International affairs, European Union, education, rural affairs, public services; EU, especially Poland; Middle East

Other organisations: Member: Foreign Affairs Forum, Royal Institute of International Affairs, Chatham House

Recreations: Travel, golf, motor racing, environment

Neil Carmichael MP, House of Commons, London SW1A 0AA
Tel: 020 7219 3000 E-mail: neil.carmichael.mp@parliament.uk
Constituency: Southview House, Parkend, Paganhill, Stroud, Gloucestershire GL5 4BB Tel: 01453 757990
Website: www.neilcarmichael.co.uk

GENERAL ELECTION RESULT

		%
Carmichael, N. (Con)	23,679	40.8
Drew, D. (Lab/Co-op)*	22,380	38.6
Andrewartha, D. (Lib Dem)	8,955	15.5
Whiteside, M. (Green)	1,542	2.7
Parker, S. (UKIP)	1,301	2.2
Lomas, A. (Ind)	116	0.2
Majority	1,299	2.24
Electorate	78,305	
Turnout	57,973	74.03

**Member of last parliament*

CONSTITUENCY SNAPSHOT

A Conservative seat in the decades following the second world war, Stroud fell to Labour in 1997. MP David Drew held the seat in the 2001 general election, with his lead over the Conservatives increasing to 5,039. However, in 2005 his majority over the Conservatives was cut to 350. This key marginal seat only required a 2 per cent swing for Conservative Neil Carmichael to defeat Labour's David Drew by 1,299 votes.

Boundary changes moved Minchinhampton and part-ward Wotton-under-Edge to The Cotswolds.

Stroud lies to the south of Gloucester. Much of the constituency is truly rural in character. It is only through the sparsely populated belt across the middle of the constituency that one will see a scattered handful of urbanised villages including Caincross, Cam, and Rodborough. The major market towns include Stroud itself, Dursley in the south of the constituency, and the smaller towns of Berkeley, Stonehouse and Nailsworth.

In the past the primary industry in the Stroud was the wool trade. There are a large number of small- to medium-size manufacturing and engineering firms, including Lister Petters, Delphi and Renishaws.

Dairy farming is a major occupation in the constituency with a large dairy processing plant in Stonehouse where milk for products such as Yoplait and Frijj are prepared.

Douglas Carswell

Clacton (returning MP)

New constituency

Tel: 020 7219 8397
Website: www.douglascarswell.com

Conservative

Date of birth: 3 May 1971; Son of Wilson Carswell OBE FRCS and Margaret, née Clark

Education: Charterhouse, Godalming, Surrey; University of East Anglia (BA history 1993); King's College, London (MA British imperial history 1994); Married Clementine 2007 (1 daughter)

Non-political career: Corporate affairs manager, satellite television broadcaster, Italy 1997-99; Chief project officer INVESCO Asset Management 1999-2003

Political career: Contested Sedgefield 2001 general election. Member for Harwich 2005-10, for Clacton since 6 May 2010 general election; *Select Committees:* Member: Joint Committee on Human Rights 2005-08, Children, Schools and Families and predecessor 2006-08, 2009-10, Public Accounts 2009-10; Press officer Conservative Central Office 1997; Policy Unit Conservative Party 2004-05; Co-founder, Direct Democracy Group

Political interests: Crime and policing, immigration, Britain's independence, education, NHS reform, local government finance reform, decentralisation, direct democracy and localism

Other organisations: Clacton Conservative; *Publications:* Author of ten published books and pamphlets, including: Direct Democracy (2002); Paying for Localism (2004); Direct Democracy: an agenda for a new model party (2005); The Localist Papers (2007); The Plan: 12 months to renew Britain (2008); Written for *Financial Times*, *Mail on Sunday*, *Daily Mail* and *Daily Telegraph*

Recreations: Gardening, riding, swimming, running

Douglas Carswell MP, House of Commons, London SW1A 0AA
Tel: 020 7219 8397
Constituency: 84 Station Road, Clacton-on-Sea, Essex CO15 1SP
Tel: 01255 423112 E-mail: douglas@douglascarswell.com
Website: www.douglascarswell.com

GENERAL ELECTION RESULT

		%
Carswell, D. (Con)*	22,867	53.0
Henderson, I. (Lab)	10,799	25.0
Green, M. (Lib Dem)	5,577	12.9
Taylor, J. (BNP)	1,975	4.6
Allen, T. (Tendring)	1,078	2.5
Southall, C. (Green)	535	1.2
Humphrey, C. (Ind)	292	0.7
Majority	12,068	27.99
Electorate	67,194	
Turnout	43,123	64.18

**Member of last parliament*

CONSTITUENCY SNAPSHOT

This new constituency takes in the now abolished Harwich seat in the main, but without the town of Harwich. The maritime seat includes the town of the same name.

From 1945 to 1997 the old seat of Harwich returned three MPs: Sir Stanley Holmes (Liberal), Sir Julian Ridsdale (Liberal/Conservative) and Iain Sproat (Conservative), all of whom regularly took over 50 per cent of the vote.

In 1997 Ivan Henderson won the seat for Labour by 1,216 votes. In 2001 he increased his majority to 2,596. However, in 2005 Conservative candidate Douglas Carswell won with a majority of just under 1,000. Carswell increased his majority at the 2010 general election to 12,068.

This constituency occupies the easternmost coastal segment of north Essex, but excludes the port of Harwich to the north. Seaside resorts are strung down the coastline. There is a rural hinterland to the west, but the bulk of the seat is coastal.

Unemployment is a significant issue in the area, exacerbated by the very seasonal nature of the local economy. Much will depend on the success of Project Tendring, which is attempting to promote not only economic development, but physical, social and environmental transformation.

William Cash

Stone (returning MP)

Boundary changes

Tel: 020 7219 6330
E-mail: mcconaloguej@parliament.uk
Website: www.epolitix.com/Bill-Cash

Conservative

Date of birth: 10 May 1940; Son of Paul Cash, MC (killed in action, 1944) and Moyra Roberts, née Morrison

Education: Stonyhurst College, Clitheroe, Lancashire; Lincoln College, Oxford (MA history); Married Bridget Mary Lee 1965 (2 sons 1 daughter)

Non-political career: Solicitor 1967-: Solicitor, William Cash & Company 1979-

Political career: Member for Stafford 1984-97, for Stone 1997-2010, for Stone (revised boundary) since 6 May 2010 general election; Shadow Attorney General 2001-03; *Select Committees:* Member: European Scrutiny 1998-2010, Joint Committee on Consolidation, Etc, Bills 2005-10; Chair, Friends of Bruges Group in the House of Commons 1989-

Political interests: European Union, trade and industry, media, small businesses, heritage, debt relief; East Africa, Europe

Other organisations: Vice-President, Conservative Small Business Bureau 1986-2000; Founder and Chair, European Foundation 1993-; Beefsteak, Carlton, Vincent's (Oxford); *Publications:* Against a Federal Europe (1991); Europe – The Crunch (1992); AEA – The Associated European Area (2000)

Recreations: Local history, cricket, jazz

William Cash MP, House of Commons, London SW1A 0AA
Tel: 020 7219 6330 Fax: 020 7219 3935
E-mail: mcconaloguej@parliament.uk
Constituency: 50 High Street, Stone, Staffordshire ST15 8AU
Tel: 01785 811000 Fax: 01785 811000 Website: www.epolitix.com/Bill-Cash

GENERAL ELECTION RESULT

		%
Cash, W. (Con)*	23,890	50.6
Tinker, C. (Lib Dem)	10,598	22.4
Lewis, J. (Lab)	9,770	20.7
Illsley, A. (UKIP)	2,481	5.3
Hoppe, D. (Green)	490	1.0
Majority	13,292	28.14
Electorate	66,979	
Turnout	47,229	70.51

**Member of last parliament*

CONSTITUENCY SNAPSHOT

Tory Bill Cash was MP for Stafford from 1984 to 1997. Stone was formed out of the three formerly Conservative constituencies of Stafford, Mid Staffordshire and Staffordshire Moorlands. Stafford and Staffordshire Moorlands became Labour seats in 1997.

Stone was given a notional Conservative majority of 15,000, but in fact Cash won by just 3,818 votes in 1997. Since then Cash's majority has grown - to 13,292 in 2010 - but the number of Conservative votes has fallen (23,890 in 2010 compared to 24,859 in 1997).

Boundary changes have moved the two north-east wards of Alton and Churnet to Staffordshire Moorlands, while the south-east wards of Seighford and Haywood and Hixon are now entirely within Stafford's boundaries. In addition, Chartley and Church Eaton wards are now completely within the seat, having previously been shared with Stafford.

Stone is a vast, mainly rural, constituency sprawling between Stoke to the north and Stafford to the south and stretching west to east almost across the entire width of Staffordshire.

The seat contains three medium-sized market towns, Cheadle, Eccleshall, and its namesake Stone, though the seat lacks a major urban centre.

The seat contains a population that tends to be slightly older than average, with a significant number of constituents in the 40 to 65 age bracket.

Employment includes managerial and professional occupations. Many local people commute to big companies in nearby towns and cities such as Stoke and Stafford.

Martin Caton

Gower (returning MP)

Boundary changes

Tel: 020 7219 5111
E-mail: catonm@parliament.uk
Website: www.martin-caton.co.uk

Date of birth: 15 June 1951; Son of William John Caton and Pauline Joan Caton, retired shopkeepers

Education: Newport (Essex) Grammar School; Norfolk School of Agriculture (National Certificate in Agriculture 1971); Aberystwyth College of Further Education (Higher National Certificate in Applied Biology 1980); Married Bethan Evans 1996 (2 step daughters)

Non-political career: Agriculture research, Welsh Plant Breeding Station, Aberystwyth 1972-84; Political researcher to David Morris MEP 1984-97; Member, GMB; Former Section Treasurer/Membership Secretary, IPCS; Councillor: Mumbles Community Council 1986-90, Swansea City Council 1988-95, City and County of Swansea 1995-97

Political career: Member for Gower 1997-2010, for Gower (revised boundary) since 6 May 2010 general election; *Select Committees:* Member: Welsh Affairs 1997-2005, Joint Committee on Consolidation, Etc, Bills 2001-10, Chairmen's Panel 2003-10, Environmental Audit 2005-10; Member: Socialist Environmental Resources Association, Socialist Health Association

Political interests: Environment, planning, education, European Union

Other organisations: Member, CND Cymru

Recreations: Reading, walking, theatre, thinking about gardening

Martin Caton MP, House of Commons, London SW1A 0AA
Tel: 020 7219 5111 E-mail: catonm@parliament.uk
Constituency: 9 Pontardulais Road, Gorseinon, Swansea,
West Glamorgan SA4 4FE Tel: 01792 892100 Fax: 01792 892375
Website: www.martin-caton.co.uk

GENERAL ELECTION RESULT

		%
Caton, M. (Lab)*	16,016	38.4
Davies, B. (Con)	13,333	32.0
Day, M. (Lib Dem)	7,947	19.1
Price, D. (PIC)	2,760	6.6
Jones, A. (SOTBTH)	963	2.3
Triggs, G. (UKIP)	652	1.6
Majority	2,683	6.44
Electorate	61,696	
Turnout	41,671	67.54

**Member of last parliament*

CONSTITUENCY SNAPSHOT

This constituency has been represented by Labour MPs for decades.

In 1997 new MP Martin Caton increased the Labour share of the vote to just below 54 per cent, but it fell in 2001, thanks to small gains by both the Conservatives and Plaid Cymru. In 2005 it was the Lib Dems' turn to make ground and Caton's vote fell again. But Caton's majority was large enough to absorb the small swing against him and he retained the seat with a majority of 6,703. Caton's majority was reduced to just 2,683 in 2010.

Boundary changes here are negligible. The seat gained the small part of Clydach ward that was previously in Neath.

This seat includes not only the scenic holiday area of the Gower peninsula, with its attractive seaside villages and many sandy beaches, but also the inland industrial area of the Lliw valley.

The Gower peninsula was the first area in the UK to be designated as an Area of Outstanding Beauty in 1956.

The Lliw valley has a history of steel manufacture and anthracite mining. It now makes use of its position on the M4 corridor to attract new businesses.

There are pockets of wealth in the Gower, particularly in the affluent Swansea suburb of Mumbles where the owner-occupancy rates are very high. As is common in coastal areas, this is a demographically older than average constituency.

Jenny Chapman

Darlington

Boundary changes

Tel: 020 7219 3000
E-mail: jenny.chapman.mp@parliament.uk
Website: www.jennychapman.co.uk

Date of birth: 25 September 1973

Education: Hummersknott School, Darlington; Brunel University (BSc psychology 1996); Durham University (MA medieval archaeology 2004); Married Tony Chapman 2002 (2 sons)

Non-political career: Member, GMB; Darlington Council: Councillor 2007-, Cabinet Member for Children and Young People; Governor, Branksome School; Member: North East Strategic Partnership for Asylum and Refugee Support, Darlington Partnership Board

Political career: Member for Darlington since 6 May 2010 general election

Political interests: Children, families, employment, transport, economy

Other organisations: Member, National Trust; Trustee: Darlington Rape Crisis Centre, Arthur Wharton Foundation

Jenny Chapman MP, House of Commons, London SW1A 0AA
Tel: 020 7219 3000 E-mail: jenny.chapman.mp@parliament.uk
Constituency: 3-5 Bakehouse Hill, Darlington, Co Durham DL1 5QA
Tel: 01325 488390 Website: www.jennychapman.co.uk

GENERAL ELECTION RESULT

		%
Chapman, J. (Lab)	16,891	39.4
Legard, E. (Con)	13,503	31.5
Barker, M. (Lib Dem)	10,046	23.4
Foster, A. (BNP)	1,262	2.9
Bull, C. (UKIP)	1,194	2.8
Majority	3,388	7.90
Electorate	69,352	
Turnout	42,896	61.85

CONSTITUENCY SNAPSHOT

Labour held Darlington between 1945 and 1951 and the Conservatives then represented it until 1964 when it returned to Labour in 1983. Michael Fallon won it in 1983 for the Conservatives, but lost to Alan Milburn in 1992, who has remained the MP for Darlington until 2010.

Mr Milburn gained his seat that year with a margin of just over 5 per cent, but increased his lead in 1997, with a swing of over 14 per cent. Labour's majority fell to 10,384 in 2001 and increased by 20 votes in 2005. Following Alan Milburn's retirement and a 9 per cent swing to the Tories, new Labour MP Jenny Chapman has a majority of just 3,388.

Darlington gained the whole of the Faverdale and Harrowgate Hill wards from Sedgefield, having previously been shared between the seats.

Darlington, an industrial and market town on Durham's southern border, is the largest town in County Durham. Known historically as a railway town, the closure of the rail works was followed by decline in other heavy industries, notably iron and steel. The economy is focused on the technology and telecommunications industries.

Major employers in the area include Fujitsu, Samsung, and the blue-chip companies Cleveland Bridge and AMEC Construction.

Rehman Chishti

Gillingham and Rainham

New constituency

Tel: 020 7219 7075
E-mail: rehman.chishti.mp@parliament.uk
Website: www.rehmanchishti.com

Conservative

Date of birth: 4 October 1978

Education: Fort Luton High School for Boys; Chatham Grammar School for Girls; University of Wales, Aberystwyth (law 2000); Inns of Court School of Law (Bar Vocational Course: Post-graduate Diploma law 2001)

Non-political career: Special adviser to Benazir Bhutto 1999-2007; Called to the Bar, Lincoln's Inn 2001; Barrister, Goldsmith Chambers, London 2003-09; Special adviser to Francis Maude MP as Chair of Conservative Party 2006-07; Medway Council: Councillor 2003-, Cabinet member for Community Safety and Enforcement 2007-10; Governor, Chatham Grammar School for Girls

Political career: Contested (Lab) Horsham 2005 general election. Member for Gillingham and Rainham since 6 May 2010 general election; Diversity adviser to Francis Maude MP 2006-; Deputy chair (political), Gillingham and Rainham Conservative Association 2007

Political interests: Law and order, criminal justice system, foreign affairs, NHS

Recreations: Cricket, running, reading, squash, tennis

Rehman Chishti MP, House of Commons, London SW1A 0AA
Tel: 020 7219 7075 E-mail: rehman.chishti.mp@parliament.uk
Constituency: Gillingham and Rainham Conservatives, Burden House, 200 Canterbury Street, Gillingham, Kent ME7 5XG
Tel: 01634 853344 Website: www.rehmanchishti.com

GENERAL ELECTION RESULT

		%
Chishti, R. (Con)	21,624	46.2
Clark, P. (Lab)*	12,944	27.7
Stamp, A. (Lib Dem)	8,484	18.1
Oakley, R. (UKIP)	1,515	3.2
Ravenscroft, B. (BNP)	1,149	2.5
Lacey, D. (England)	464	1.0
Marchant, T. (Green)	356	0.8
Bryan, G. (Ind)	141	0.3
Meegan, G. (Medway)	109	0.2
Majority	8,680	18.55
Electorate	70,865	
Turnout	46,786	66.02

**Member of last parliament*

CONSTITUENCY SNAPSHOT

This new seat is formed from a large part of the old Gillingham seat, with a part-ward each from Medway and Chatham and Aylesford.

Gillingham was formed in 1918 and had only returned a Labour MP once before the coming of New Labour. The election in 1997 saw a swing against the Conservatives and Tory James Couchman's majority of 16,638 was wiped out as Labour's Paul Clark was returned with a majority of 1,980. This improved slightly in 2,272, but in 2005 his lead fell to just 254.

Clark was defeated in the 2010 general election with a 9.3 per cent swing to the Conservative candidate, Rehman Chishti.

The constituency is dominated by the town of Gillingham and the surrounding smaller towns, including Rainham, and is densely populated and largely residential. The estuary location attracted the Royal Naval Dockyard to the area in the seventeenth century, where it remained until its closure in 1984.

Major new employers include Delphi Systems and RHM Frozen Foods. The increasingly significant financial sector includes offices of Lloyds TSB, Halifax, Abbey and NatWest.

The Chatham Maritime University Campus is predominantly within this constituency at Pembroke in the former Royal Naval base. The importance of regeneration in the area is indicated by the fact that the South East England Development Agency has offices here.

Christopher Chope

Christchurch (returning MP)

Boundary changes

Tel: 020 7219 5808
E-mail: chopec@parliament.uk

Date of birth: 19 May 1947; Son of late Judge Robert Chope and of Pamela Chope, née Durell

Education: St Andrew's School, Eastbourne; Marlborough College; St Andrew's University (LLB 1970); Married Christine Mary Hutchinson 1987 (1 son 1 daughter)

Non-political career: Barrister, Inner Temple 1972; Consultant, Ernst and Young 1992-98; London Borough Wandsworth Council: Councillor 1974-83, Council Leader 1979-83; Member: Health and Safety Commission 1992-97, Local Government Commission for England 1994-95

Political career: Member for Southampton Itchen 1983-92, for Christchurch 1997-2010, for Christchurch (revised boundary) since 6 May 2010 general election; PPS to Peter Brooke as Minister of State, HM Treasury 1986; Parliamentary Under-Secretary of State: Department of the Environment 1986-90, Department of Transport (Minister for Roads and Traffic) 1990-92; Opposition Spokesperson for: the Environment, Transport and the Regions 1997-98, Trade and Industry 1998-99, the Treasury 2001-02; Shadow Minister for: Transport 2002-03, Environment and Transport 2003-05; *Select Committees:* Member: Trade and Industry 1999-2002, Chairmen's Panel 2005-10, Procedure 2005-10, Administration 2006-10; Member Executive Committee Society of Conservative Lawyers 1983-86; Vice-chair Conservative Party 1997-98; 1922 Committee: Member Executive 2001-05, 2005-06, Secretary 2006-10, Vice-chair 2010-

Other organisations: Member Parliamentary Delegation to Council of Europe; Fellow Industry and Parliament Trust 2001; OBE 1982

Christopher Chope OBE MP, House of Commons, London SW1A 0AA Tel: 020 7219 5808 Fax: 020 7219 6938
E-mail: chopec@parliament.uk
Constituency: 18a Bargates, Christchurch, Dorset BH23 1QL
Tel: 01202 474949 Fax: 01202 475548
Website: www.christchurchconservatives.com

GENERAL ELECTION RESULT

		%
Chope, C. (Con)*	27,888	56.4
Hurll, M. (Lib Dem)	12,478	25.3
Deeks, R. (Lab)	4,849	9.8
Williams, D. (UKIP)	4,201	8.5
Majority	15,410	31.18
Electorate	68,861	
Turnout	49,416	71.76

**Member of last parliament*

CONSTITUENCY SNAPSHOT

At the time of the 1992 general election, sitting MP Robert Adley held the seat with a majority of 23,000. However, at the by-election held one year later following his death, Liberal Democrat Diana Maddock won the seat on a 35 per cent swing, winning a majority of over 16,000.

Diana Maddock failed to hold on in Christchurch in 1997 by just over 2,000 votes, losing to Conservative Christopher Chope. Christopher Chope was returned in 2005 with a majority of 15,559. Chope was re-elected in 2010 with a majority of 15,410.

Boundary changes moved Three Cross and Potterne, Newtown, Verwood Stephen's Castle wards and Verwood Dewlands part-ward to North Dorset, while Longham, Parley and Stapehill will move entirely within this seat.

Christchurch is situated to the east and north east of Bournemouth on the Dorset coast.

Over a third of the population is of pensionable age. The knock-on effect of a low number of people engaged in active employment.

The constituency covers much more than the town of Christchurch itself and also includes Bournemouth Airport. The airport has assisted in bringing in much industry to the area including VT Aerospace, AIM Aviation, and FR Aviation.

James Clappison

Hertsmere (returning MP)

No boundary changes

Tel: 020 7219 5027
E-mail: clappisonj@parliament.uk
Website: www.jamesclappison.co.uk

Conservative

Date of birth: 14 September 1956; Son of late Leonard Clappison, farmer, and Dorothy Clappison

Education: St Peter's School, York; The Queen's College, Oxford (BA philosophy, politics and economics 1978); Gray's Inn, London; Married Helen Margherita Carter 1984 (1 son 3 daughters)

Non-political career: Barrister 1981-

Political career: Contested Barnsley East 1987 general election, Bootle May and November 1990 by-elections. Member for Hertsmere since 9 April 1992 general election; PPS to Baroness Blatch as Minister of State: Department for Education 1992-94, Home Office 1994-95; Parliamentary Under-Secretary of State, Department of the Environment 1995-97; Opposition Spokesperson for: Home Affairs (Crime, Immigration and Asylums) 1997-99, Education and Employment 1999-2000; Shadow: Financial Secretary, HM Treasury 2000-01, Minister for: Work 2001-02, the Treasury 2002, Work and Pensions 2007-10; *Select Committees:* Member: Health 1992-94, Home Affairs 2002-10, Constitutional Affairs 2003-05, European Scrutiny 2007-10; Contested Yorkshire South 1989 European Parliament election

Political interests: Home affairs, economic policy, health, education; Israel

Other organisations: United Oxford and Cambridge University, Carlton

Recreations: Bridge, walking

James Clappison MP, House of Commons, London SW1A 0AA
Tel: 020 7219 5027 Fax: 020 7219 0514
E-mail: clappisonj@parliament.uk
Constituency: 104 High Street, London Colney,
Hertfordshire AL2 1QL Tel: 01727 828221 Fax: 01727 828404
Website: www.jamesclappison.co.uk

GENERAL ELECTION RESULT

		%	+/-
Clappison, J. (Con)*	26,476	56.0	3.0
Russell, S. (Lab)	8,871	18.8	-8.3
Rowlands, A. (Lib Dem)	8,210	17.4	-0.9
Rutter, D. (UKIP)	1,712	3.6	
Seabrook, D. (BNP)	1,397	3.0	
Krishna-Das, A. (Green)	604	1.3	
Majority	17,605	37.24	
Electorate	73,062		
Turnout	47,270	64.70	

**Member of last parliament*

CONSTITUENCY SNAPSHOT

The Conservative vote fell in 1997 as their share of the vote dropped by 13.5 per cent, reducing James Clappison's majority from 18,966 to 3,075. In 2001 the constituency recorded a swing back to the Conservatives of almost twice the national average, raising the majority to almost 5,000.

In 2005 the voters of Hertsmere returned James Clappison with a majority of more than 11,000. The seat was held by Clappison in 2010 with an increased majority of 17,605.

Hertsmere is in the south of Hertfordshire, just north of London and is typical commuter terrain. The major settlements are Elstree, Radlett, Borehamwood, Bushey and Potters Bar.

Hertsmere is well served by the A1(M), M1 and M25, as well as train links to King's Cross and Euston, and as a result, is home to the headquarters of the O2 mobile phone company, Cardif Pinnacle Insurance, Adecco Alfred Marks and Pizza Hut.

However, the constituency is not dependent on administrative and managerial work. Grunwick Processing Laboratories (Bonus Print) and part of the National Blood Transfusion Service, for example, are based here. The Elstree Film Studios, as well as Millennium and Hillside Studios are also to be found within the constituency.

Rt Hon **Greg Clark**

Tunbridge Wells (returning MP)

Boundary changes

Tel: 020 7219 6977
E-mail: gregclarkmp@parliament.uk
Website: www.gregclark.org

Date of birth: 28 August 1967; Son of John and Patricia Clark

Education: St Peter's Comprehensive, South Bank, Middlesbrough; Magdalene College, Cambridge (BA economics 1989, MA); London School of Economics (PhD 1992); Married Helen Fillingham 1999 (2 daughters 1 son)

Non-political career: Consultant, Boston Consulting Group 1991-94; Teaching and research, LSE and Open University Business School 1994-96; Commercial Policy BBC: Chief Adviser 1997-99, Controller 1999-2001; Special adviser to Ian Lang as Secretary of State for Trade and Industry 1996-97; Director of Policy Conservative Party 2001-05; Councillor Westminster City Council 2002-05

Political career: Member for Tunbridge Wells 2005-10, for Tunbridge Wells (revised boundary) since 6 May 2010 general election; Shadow Minister for: Charities, Voluntary Bodies and Social Enterprise 2006-07, Cabinet Office 2007-08; Shadow Secretary of State for Energy and Climate Change 2008-10; Minister of State for Decentralisation, Department for Communities and Local Government 2010-; *Select Committees:* Member: Public Accounts 2005-07

Political interests: Economics, poverty, welfare reform, transport, health, housing development, energy and climate change

Other organisations: PC 2010

Rt Hon Greg Clark MP, House of Commons, London SW1A 0AA
Tel: 020 7219 6977 Fax: 020 7219 5245
E-mail: gregclarkmp@parliament.uk
Constituency: Tunbridge Wells Conservative Association, 84 London Road, Tunbridge Wells, Kent TN1 1EA Tel: 01892 522581
Fax: 01892 522582 Website: www.gregclark.org

GENERAL ELECTION RESULT

		%
Clark, G. (Con)*	28,302	56.2
Hallas, D. (Lib Dem)	12,726	25.3
Heather, G. (Lab)	5,448	10.8
Webb, V. (UKIP)	2,054	4.1
Dawe, H. (Green)	914	1.8
McBride, A. (BNP)	704	1.4
Bradbury, F. (Ind)	172	0.3
Majority	15,576	30.95
Electorate	72,042	
Turnout	50,320	69.85

**Member of last parliament*

CONSTITUENCY SNAPSHOT

A Conservative stronghold, the seat's MP from 1974 to 1997 was former cabinet minister Sir Patrick Mayhew. In his last four elections his majority always exceeded 15,000.

He was replaced on his retirement by Archie Norman. At the 1997 general election, following boundary changes, the Tory majority slipped to 7,506 but increased to 9,730 in 2001.

After Norman stood down in 2005, Greg Clark was elected with a majority of 9,988. Clark held the seat with 28,302 votes giving him a majority of 15,576 at the 2010 general election.

The seat gained Hawkhurst and Sandhurst ward from Maidstone and the Weald.

The town of Tunbridge Wells was founded in 1606 and became a popular spa resort throughout the 18th and 19th centuries.

Apart from the outlying communities of Sherwood, Southborough and Pembury, the town is surrounded by an agricultural hinterland and the unspoilt beauty of the Weald with its many attractive villages centred on the small town of Paddock Wood.

Royal Tunbridge Wells attracts tourists to its architecturally and historically important buildings and its shops, especially in the historic Georgian colonnade known as the Pantiles. Outside the town itself the countryside is predominantly apple and hop country.

The proportion of the workforce in professional, managerial or technical jobs, and several thousand commute into London or the surrounding towns to work.

Katy Clark

North Ayrshire and Arran ***(returning MP)***

No boundary changes

Tel: 020 7219 4113
E-mail: clarkk@parliament.uk
Website: www.katyclarkmp.org.uk

Date of birth: 3 July 1967; Daughter of Dr Norman and Esther Ruth Clark

Education: Kyle Academy, Ayr; Aberdeen University (LLB 1990); Edinburgh University (Diploma of Legal Practice 1991); 1 daughter

Non-political career: Qualified solicitor – Scotland, England and Wales; Head of membership legal services, UNISON; TGWU, GMB, NUS (Scotland) Women's officer; Member Executive Scottish Council for Civil Liberties 1995-98

Political career: Contested Galloway and Upper Nithsdale 1997 general election. Member for North Ayrshire and Arran since 5 May 2005 general election; *Select Committees:* Member: Scottish Affairs 2005-10, Procedure 2005-10, Crossrail Bill 2006-07, European Scrutiny 2006-10, Joint Committee on the Draft Human Tissue and Embryos Bill 2007; Chair, Aberdeen University Labour club 1988; Secretary, Labour Civil Liberties Group

Political interests: Policy development, equality, human rights

Katy Clark MP, House of Commons, London SW1A 0AA
Tel: 020 7219 4113 Fax: 020 7219 4002
E-mail: clarkk@parliament.uk
Constituency: 53 Main Street, Kilbirnie, Ayrshire KA25 7BX
Tel: 01505 684127 Fax: 01505 684349
Website: www.katyclarkmp.org.uk

GENERAL ELECTION RESULT

		%	+/-
Clark, K. (Lab)*	21,860	47.4	3.6
Gibson, P. (SNP)	11,965	26.0	8.0
Lardner, P. (Con)	7,212	15.6	-2.7
Cole-Hamilton, G. (Lib Dem)	4,630	10.0	-6.4
McDaid, L. (SLP)	449	1.0	0.3
Majority	9,895	21.46	
Electorate	66,110		
Turnout	46,116	69.76	

**Member of last parliament*

CONSTITUENCY SNAPSHOT

Boundary changes in 1983 detached Bute from the Ayrshire North and Bute division, adding a swathe of the Garnock valley to form Cunninghame North. Ayrshire North and Bute had been regularly won by the Conservatives and although the sitting MP John Corrie retained the seat in 1983, in 1987 he was unseated by Labour's Brian Wilson. Wilson slightly increased his majority in 1992, and then quadrupled it in 1997.

After the 2005 boundary changes the North Ayrshire and Arran seat contained the whole of Cunninghame North and five wards from Cunninghame South. The Conservatives benefited from a notional 2.7 per cent swing against Labour, but Brian Wilson's successor Katy Clark was nevertheless returned with a majority of 11,296. Katy Clarke's majority fell to 9,895 in 2010 despite increasing her vote-share.

North Ayrshire and Arran stretches along a long strip of east coast mainland and includes the Isle of Arran. Largs, Fairlie and West Kilbride - wealthy commuting areas to the north - contrast with the southern industrial belt which runs from Ardrossan to Kilwinning.

The Garnock valley pits have closed and the seat contains the ex-mining and steel industry towns of Dalry, Beith and Kilburnie. Textiles are also in decline and the main local industries now are agriculture and tourism, with the latter centred on the Arran and the seaside resort of Largs.

A £50 million regeneration scheme at Ardrossan harbour has been completed. A new ferry terminal was completed in 2006, along with waterfront properties.

Rt Hon **Kenneth Clarke**

Rushcliffe (returning MP)

Boundary changes

Tel: 020 7219 4528
E-mail: clarkek@parliament.uk

Conservative

Date of birth: 2 July 1940; Son of late Kenneth, watchmaker and jeweller, and Doris Clarke

Education: Nottingham High School; Gonville and Caius College, Cambridge (BA law 1962, LLB 1963) (President, Cambridge Union 1963); Married Gillian Mary Edwards 1964 (1 son 1 daughter)

Non-political career: Called to the Bar 1963; Member, Midland Circuit, practising from Birmingham; QC 1980; Deputy Chair, British American Tobacco 1998-; Director: Independent News and Media (UK), Independent News and Media plc; Member Advisory Board Centaurus Capital

Political career: Contested Mansfield Notts 1964 and 1966 general elections. Member for Rushcliffe 1970-2010, for Rushcliffe (revised boundary) since 6 May 2010 general election; PPS to Sir Geoffrey Howe as Solicitor General 1971-72; Assistant Government Whip 1972-74; Government Whip 1973-74; Opposition Spokesperson for: Social Services 1974-76, Industry 1976-79; Parliamentary Secretary, Ministry of Transport 1979-80; Parliamentary Under-Secretary of State, Department of Transport 1980-82; Minister for Health 1982-85; Paymaster General and Employment Minister 1985-87; Chancellor, Duchy of Lancaster and Minister of Trade and Industry 1987-88; Secretary of State for: Health 1988-90, Education and Science 1990-92; Home Secretary 1992-93, Chancellor of the Exchequer 1993-97; Shadow Secretary of State for Business, Enterprise and Regulatory Reform/Innovation and Skills 2009-10; Lord Chancellor and Secretary of State for Justice 2010-; *Select Committees:* Member: Joint Committee on House of Lords Reform 2003-10; Joint Committee on Tax Law Rewrite Bills: Member 2005-09, Chair 2007-09; Chair: Cambridge University Conservative Association 1961, Federation Conservative Students 1963-65; Contested Conservative Party leadership, 1997, 2001 and 2005; Chair Democracy Task Force 2005-

Political interests: Economic policy, National Health Service

Other organisations: PC 1984; Three honorary law doctorates; Honorary Fellow, Gonville and Caius College, Cambridge; Bencher, Grays Inn; Liveryman, The Clockmakers Company; Garrick

Recreations: Birdwatching, football, cricket, jazz, Formula 1 motor racing

Rt Hon Kenneth Clarke QC MP, House of Commons, London SW1A 0AA Tel: 020 7219 4528 Fax: 020 7219 4841
E-mail: clarkek@parliament.uk
Constituency: Rushcliffe House, 17/19 Rectory Road, West Bridgford, Nottingham NG2 6BE Tel: 0115-981 7224 Fax: 0115-981 7273
Website: www.rushcliffeconservatives.com

GENERAL ELECTION RESULT

		%
Clarke, K. (Con)*	27,470	51.2
Khan, K. (Lib Dem)	11,659	21.7
Clayworth, A. (Lab)	11,128	20.7
Faithfull, M. (UKIP)	2,179	4.1
Mallender, R. (Green)	1,251	2.3
Majority	15,811	29.45
Electorate	72,955	
Turnout	53,687	73.59

**Member of last parliament*

CONSTITUENCY SNAPSHOT

When Ken Clarke became MP for Rushcliffe in 1970, his defeated opponent was Labour's Antony Gardner, who had been the Member for four years.

In 1997, despite the loss of similar, nearby constituencies Broxtowe and Gedling to Labour, Clarke held the seat with a reduced majority of 5,055. Clarke built on this lead in 2001 and 2005, with majorities of 7,357 and 12,974 respectively.

Clarke increased his majority in 2010 to 15,811 despite a 0.6 per cent swing to the Lib Dems.

Boundary changes moved Bingham East, Bingham West, Cranmer, Oak and Thoroton wards to Newark.

Rushcliffe is an affluent, leafy seat in the suburbs of south and east Nottingham. The seat consists mostly of the town of West Bridgford, along with smaller villages such as Radcliffe-on-Trent and East Leake.

West Bridgford apart, where the bulk of Rushcliffe's population is based, this seat is predominantly rural. Much of the electorate commute into the city of Nottingham to work.

Major employers in the area include Nottinghamshire County Council, Nottingham Forest Football Club and the Trent Bridge test cricket ground, all of which are based in the constituency.

Rt Hon **Tom Clarke**

Coatbridge, Chryston and Bellshill ***(returning MP)***

No boundary changes

Tel: 020 7219 6997
E-mail: clarket@parliament.uk
Website: www.tomclarke.org.uk

Date of birth: 10 January 1941; Son of late James Clarke

Education: Columba High School, Coatbridge; Scottish College of Commerce

Non-political career: Assistant director, Scottish Council for Educational Technology (Scottish Film Council) 1966-82; Member, GMB; Councillor: Coatbridge Town Council 1964-74, Monklands District Council 1974-82; Provost of Monklands 1974-82; JP 1972; President, Convention of Scottish Local Authorities 1978-80

Political career: Member for Coatbridge and Airdrie 1982 by-election to 1983, for Monklands West 1983-97, for Coatbridge and Chryston 1997-2005, for Coatbridge, Chryston and Bellshill since 5 May 2005 general election; Author and Sponsor Disabled Persons (Services, Representation and Consultation) Act 1986; Shadow Minister for UK Personal Social Services 1987-92; Shadow Secretary of State for: Scotland 1992-93, International Development 1993-94; Shadow Cabinet Minister for Disabled People's Rights 1995-97; Minister of State (Film and Tourism), Department of National Heritage/for Culture, Media and Sport 1997-98; *Select Committees:* Member: Administration 2008-10

Political interests: Film industry, foreign affairs, disability rights, civil service, local and regional government, international development; Africa, Central America, Asia, Eastern Europe, Gulf States, Indonesia, Peru, Philippines, South Africa, USA

Other organisations: Labour Member PAD Group to Iran, sponsored by Archbishop of Canterbury 1989; Led CPA delegations to Australia 2000; Observer Peruvian election 2001; Led IPU Rwanda 2002; Led IPU Bahrain and Kuwait 2005; Fellow, Industry and Parliament Trust; CBE 1980; PC 1997; Coatbridge Municipal Golf; *Publications:* Director of award winning amateur film Give us a Goal (1972); Joint chair, film review A Bigger Picture (1998)

Recreations: Films, walking, reading

Rt Hon Tom Clarke CBE MP, House of Commons, London SW1A 0AA Tel: 020 7219 6997 Fax: 020 7219 6094
E-mail: clarket@parliament.uk
Constituency: Municipal Buildings, Kildonan Street, Coatbridge, North Lanarkshire ML5 3LF Tel: 01236 600800 Fax: 01236 600808
Website: www.tomclarke.org.uk

GENERAL ELECTION RESULT

		%	+/-
Clarke, T. (Lab)*	27,728	66.6	2.3
McGlinchey, F. (SNP)	7,014	16.9	3.3
Elder, K. (Lib Dem)	3,519	8.5	-3.5
Houston, F. (Con)	3,374	8.1	0.9
Majority	20,714	49.75	
Electorate	70,067		
Turnout	41,635	59.42	

**Member of last parliament*

CONSTITUENCY SNAPSHOT

Labour's Tom Clarke won the Coatbridge and Airdrie seat at a by-election following the previous Labour MP James Dempsey's death in 1982. Dempsey had held the seat since 1959.

In 1983 Coatbridge and Airdrie was split between Monklands East and Monklands West. Clarke went with Coatbridge to the western division, which he held in 1987 and 1992.

The seat was renamed Coatbridge and Chryston in 1997, which Clarke retained in both 1997 and 2001.

In 2005 the Boundary Commission trimmed the seat's northern border, while adding Bellshill from Hamilton North and Bellshill, giving the seat its new name of Coatbridge, Chryston and Bellshill. Clarke won with a majority of 19,519. This super safe Labour seat continues to deliver huge majorities for Tom Clarke - 20,714 this year.

Situated on the western side of the Central Scotland belt between Glasgow and Edinburgh the seat centres on the town of Coatbridge.

Coatbridge was once an iron and coal town. The coal ran out in the early 20th century and the ironworks were all closed by the 1960s.

This seat suffers from economic problems which are typical of the decline of mining and heavy industry and their effects of depopulation and economic uncertainty. Many constituents still work in manufacturing jobs, though numbers are still decreasing. Strathclyde Business Park provides local employment and investment and Kwik Fit Insurance Services is a major employer.

Rt Hon **Nick Clegg**

Sheffield Hallam (returning MP)

Boundary changes

Tel: 020 7219 5090
E-mail: cleggn@parliament.uk
Website: www.nickclegg.org.uk

Date of birth: 7 January 1967; Son of Hermance Eulalie Van Den Wall Bake and Nicholas Peter Clegg

Education: Westminster School; Cambridge University (BA social anthropology 1989, MA); political philosophy, Minnesota University, USA (Cambridge – Minnesota Fellowship Award 1990); College of Europe, Bruges, Belgium (diploma European affairs 1992); Married Miriam Gonzalez Durantez 2000 (3 sons)

Non-political career: Trainee journalist *Nation Magazine*, New York 1990; Political consultant GJW Government Relations 1992-93; European Commission: official 1994-96, Adviser to European Commission Vice-president Sir Leon Brittan 1996-99; Part-time lecturer Sheffield University, Guest lecturer, Cambridge University 2004/05. Columnist for *Guardian Unlimited* 2003-06

Political career: Member for Sheffield Hallam since 5 May 2005 general election; Liberal Democrat: Spokesperson for Foreign and Commonwealth Office 2005-06, Shadow Home Secretary 2006-07, Leader 2007-; Deputy Prime Minister, Lord President of the Council (with special responsibility for political and constitutional reform) 2010-; *Select Committees:* Member Joint Committees on: Consolidation, Etc, Bills 2005-08, Tax Law Rewrite Bills 2005-08; MEP for East Midlands 1999-2004

Political interests: Trade and industry, education, globalisation, constitutional reform, Europe

Other organisations: PC 2008; *Financial Times* David Thomas prize 1993

Recreations: Literature, tennis, spending time with his children, the outdoors, skiing and mountaineering

Rt Hon Nick Clegg MP, House of Commons, London SW1A 0AA
Tel: 020 7219 5090 Fax: 020 7219 4483
E-mail: cleggn@parliament.uk
Constituency: 85 Nethergreen Road, Sheffield,
South Yorkshire S11 7EH Tel: 0114-230 9002 Fax: 0114-230 9614
Website: www.nickclegg.org.uk

GENERAL ELECTION RESULT

		%
Clegg, N. (Lib Dem)*	27,324	53.4
Bates, N. (Con)	12,040	23.6
Scott, J. (Lab)	8,228	16.1
James, N. (UKIP)	1,195	2.3
Barnard, S. (Green)	919	1.8
Wildgoose, D. (England)	586	1.2
Fitzpatrick, M. (Ind)	429	0.8
Green, R. (Christian)	250	0.5
Adshead, M. (Loony)	164	0.3
Majority	15,284	29.89
Electorate	69,378	
Turnout	51,135	73.70

**Member of last parliament*

CONSTITUENCY SNAPSHOT

The seat was Conservative for most of the 20th century; for 28 years until 1987 the MP was John Osborn. Osborn's successor Irvine Patnick still had a sizable majority, which suffered only a slight reduction to 6,741 in 1992.

In 1997 the Lib Dem share of the vote increased by more than 20 per cent and Patnick was defeated with a 18.6 per cent swing. The Liberal Democrat victor was Richard Allan, who increased his majority to 9,347. Allan retired in 2005 and was succeeded by Nick Clegg who retained most of that majority.

Clegg retained the seat for the Lib Dems with a strong 15,284 majority.

Boundary changes swapped a number of part-wards between the seat and the other Sheffield divisions.

This is South Yorkshire's south-western seat. It stretches from the western edge of Sheffield city centre into the rural Peak District.

The leafy, hilly areas to the west of the city were where the captains of Sheffield's steel and engineering industries made their homes. And unlike in many cities, the middle classes stayed within its boundaries.

It is a wealthy constituency, with a high percentage of professionally-qualified people and a high percentage of non-manual workers. In sharp contrast to other Sheffield seats, unemployment tends to be lower than average.

Geoffrey Clifton-Brown

The Cotswolds (returning MP)

Boundary changes

Tel: 020 7219 5147
E-mail: cliftonbrowng@parliament.uk
Website: www.cliftonbrown.co.uk

Conservative

Date of birth: 23 March 1953; Son of Robert and the late Elizabeth Clifton-Brown

Education: Eton College; Royal Agricultural College, Cirencester (ARICS); Married Alexandra Peto-Shepherd 1979 (divorced 2003) (1 son 1 daughter)

Non-political career: Graduate estate surveyor, Property Services Agency, Dorchester 1975; Investment surveyor, Jones Lang Wootton 1975-79; Managing director, own farming business in Norfolk 1979-

Political career: Member for Cirencester and Tewkesbury 1992-97, for Cotswold 1997-2010, for The Cotswolds since 6 May 2010 general election; PPS to Douglas Hogg as Minister of Agriculture, Fisheries and Food 1995-97; Opposition Whip 1999-2001; Opposition Spokesperson for: Environment, Food and Rural Affairs 2001, Transport, Local Government and the Regions 2001-02; Shadow Minister for: Local Government 2002-03, Local and Devolved Government 2003-04; Opposition Whip 2004-05; Assistant Chief Whip 2005; Shadow Minister for: Foreign Affairs 2005-07, Trade 2007, International Development 2007-10, Trade 2009-10; *Select Committees:* Member: Public Accounts 1997-99, Broadcasting 2000-01, Administration 2001-10, Selection 2005-06, Finance and Services 2005-10; Chair, North Norfolk Constituency Association 1986-91

Political interests: Economy, taxation, foreign affairs, environment, agriculture; Brazil, China, Venezuela, India, Mexico

Other organisations: Vice-chair: Charities Property Association 1993-2002, Small Business Bureau 1995-, Euro Atlantic Group 1995-; Fellow Industry and Parliament Trust 1996; Armed Forces Parliamentary Fellowship 1997; Fellow, Royal Institute of Chartered Surveyors (FRICS) 2002; Liveryman, Worshipful Company of Farmers; Freeman, City of London; Carlton, Farmers'; *Publications:* Privatisation of the State Pension – Secure Funded Provision for all (Bow Group, 1996)

Recreations: Fishing, other rural pursuits

Geoffrey Clifton-Brown MP, House of Commons, London SW1A 0AA Tel: 020 7219 5147 Fax: 020 7219 2550
E-mail: cliftonbrowng@parliament.uk
Constituency: Unit 1143, Regent Court, Gloucester Business Park, Hucclecote, Gloucestershire GL3 4AD Tel: 01452 371630
Fax: 0845 009 0109 Website: www.cliftonbrown.co.uk

GENERAL ELECTION RESULT

		%
Clifton-Brown, G. (Con)*	29,075	53.0
Collins, M. (Lib Dem)	16,211	29.6
Dempsey, M. (Lab)	5,886	10.7
Blake, A. (UKIP)	2,292	4.2
Lister, K. (Green)	940	1.7
Steel, A. (Ind)	428	0.8
Majority	12,864	23.46
Electorate	76,728	
Turnout	54,832	71.46

**Member of last parliament*

CONSTITUENCY SNAPSHOT

Before 1997 what is now The Cotswolds was part of the much larger Cirencester and Tewkesbury constituency. The seat has a solid Conservative history. Nicholas Ridley retired after 33 years in 1992 and was replaced by Geoffrey Clifton-Brown, who has represented the new Cotswolds seat since its inception. He won by 11,983 in 2001 and 9,892 votes in 2005. Clifton-Brown was re-elected with a 12,864 majority in 2010.

Boundary changes added Minchinhampton and part-ward Wotton-under-Edge from Stroud.

This seat is nestled in the heart of the gentle Cotswold hills on the edge of Gloucestershire. It is a largely rural seat, and is popular with tourists. Significant towns within the seat include Cirencester, the district seat and largest town, as well as Lechdale, Chipping Campden, Stow-on-the-Wold, and Tetbury.

Tourists, flock to the dozens of market towns constructed of beautiful Cotswold stone. In fact the constituency has the highest number of listed buildings in the UK. Tourism has replaced agriculture as the principal economic activity in the region.

Agriculture remains an important industry in the Cotswolds, and Cirencester is the site of one of the best agricultural colleges in the country, the Royal Agricultural College.

Rt Hon **Ann Clwyd**

Cynon Valley (returning MP)

Boundary changes

Tel: 020 7219 6609
E-mail: clwyda@parliament.uk

Date of birth: 21 March 1937; Daughter of Gwilym and Elizabeth Lewis

Education: Holywell Grammar School; The Queen's School, Chester; University College of Wales, Bangor; Married Owen Roberts 1963

Non-political career: Journalist, *Guardian*; Broadcaster, BBC; Member: NUJ, TGWU

Political career: Contested Denbigh 1970 and Gloucester October 1974 general elections. Member for Cynon Valley 3 May 1984 by-election to 2010, for Cynon Valley (revised boundary) since 6 May 2010 general election; Shadow Minister of Education and Women's Rights 1987-88; Shadow Secretary of State for: International Development 1989-92, Wales 1992, National Heritage 1992-93; Opposition Spokesperson for: Employment 1993-94, Foreign Affairs 1994-95; Assistant to John Prescott as Deputy Leader of Labour Party 1994-95; *Select Committees:* Member: International Development 1997-2005; European Parliament: MEP for Mid and West Wales 1979-84; Member Labour Party National Executive Committee 1983-84; Chair Tribune Group 1986-87

Political interests: Human rights, international development, animal welfare; Cambodia, Iran, Iraq, Russia, East Timor, Turkey, Vietnam

Other organisations: Member, Arts Council 1975-79; Vice-chair, Welsh Arts Council 1975-79; Royal Commission on NHS 1976-79; Inter-Parliamentary Union: Executive committee member, British Group, Chair 2004-07; Special Envoy to Prime Minister on Human Rights in Iraq 2003-; White Robe Gorsedd Member of Royal National Eisteddfod of Wales; PC 2004; BBC/*House Magazine* Backbencher of the Year 2003; *Spectator* Backbencher of the Year; Channel 4 Campaigning Politician of the Year 2003-04; HTV Communicator of the Year 2005; Hon. Fellow: North East Wales Institute of Higher Education 1996, University of Wales, Bangor 2004; Hon. LLD, University of Wales, Carmarthen 2006

Recreations: Walking, boating

Rt Hon Ann Clwyd MP, House of Commons, London SW1A 0AA
Tel: 020 7219 6609 Fax: 020 7219 5943
E-mail: clwyda@parliament.uk
Constituency: 6 Dean Court, Dean Street, Aberdare,
Mid Glamorgan CF44 7BN Tel: 01685 871394 Fax: 01685 883006

GENERAL ELECTION RESULT

		%
Clwyd, A. (Lab)*	15,681	52.5
Davies, D. (PlC)	6,064	20.3
Thacker, L. (Lib Dem)	4,120	13.8
Ash, J. (Con)	3,010	10.1
Hughes, F. (UKIP)	1,001	3.4
Majority	9,617	32.19
Electorate	50,656	
Turnout	29,876	58.98

**Member of last parliament*

CONSTITUENCY SNAPSHOT

Since its creation in 1983, Labour candidates have won every contest here. The first MP was Ioan Evans who had been MP for the predecessor Aberdare seat since 1974. Aberdare had been held by the Labour Party since 1922.

Evans died in 1984 and the by-election was won by Labour's Ann Clwyd. Clwyd won all general elections contested since then by huge margins and her 2005 majority was 13,259 over Plaid Cymru. Clwyd was re-elected in 2010 with a 9,617 majority.

Cilfynydd and Glyncoch electoral divisions were moved from Potypridd to Cynon Valley.

This seat was previously known as Aberdare, and encompasses the town of that name. It is a former mining area and was home to the last deep mine in Wales, the worker-owned Tower colliery.

The mines and most of the heavy industry that once formed the backbone of the economy in South Wales have now gone, replaced by new industries housed on industrial estates throughout the constituency.

As one of the key old mining districts this is a seat with a large number of sufferers from industrial diseases.

Vernon Coaker

Gedling (returning MP)

Boundary changes

Tel: 020 7219 6627
E-mail: coakerv@parliament.uk
Website: www.vernon-coaker-mp.co.uk

Date of birth: 17 June 1953; Son of Edwin Coaker

Education: Drayton Manor Grammar School, London; Warwick University (BA politics 1974); Trent Polytechnic (PGCE 1976); Married Jacqueline Heaton 1978 (1 son 1 daughter)

Non-political career: Humanities teaching in Nottinghamshire: Manvers School 1976-82, Arnold Hill School 1982-89, Bramcote Park School 1989-95, Big Wood School 1995-97; Member: NUT, UNITE; Councillor, Rushcliffe Borough Council 1983-97

Political career: Contested Gedling 1987 and 1992 general elections. Member for Gedling 1997-2010, for Gedling (revised boundary) since 6 May 2010 general election; PPS: to Stephen Timms: as Minister of State, Department of Social Security 1999, as Financial Secretary, HM Treasury 1999-2001, as Minister of State for Schools and Learners, Department for Education and Skills 2001-02, as Minister of State, Department of Trade and Industry 2002, to Estelle Morris as Secretary of State for Education and Skills 2002, to Tessa Jowell as Secretary of State for Culture, Media and Sport 2002-03; Assistant Government Whip 2003-05; Government Whip 2005-06; Home Office: Parliamentary Under-Secretary of State (Crime Reduction) 2006-08, Minister of State (Policing, Crime and Security) 2008-09; Minister of State, Department of Children, Schools and Families 2009-10; *Select Committees:* Member: Social Security 1998-99, European Standing Committee B 1998

Political interests: Environment, education, welfare reform, foreign policy, sport; France, Kosovo, Macedonia, Angola

Recreations: Sport, walking

Vernon Coaker MP, House of Commons, London SW1A 0AA
Tel: 020 7219 6627 E-mail: coakerv@parliament.uk
Constituency: 2A Parkyn Road, Daybrook, Nottingham NG5 6BG
Tel: 0115-920 4224 Fax: 0115-920 4500
Website: www.vernon-coaker-mp.co.uk

GENERAL ELECTION RESULT

		%
Coaker, V. (Lab)*	19,821	41.1
Laughton, B. (Con)	17,962	37.3
Bateman, J. (Lib Dem)	7,350	15.3
Adcock, S. (BNP)	1,598	3.3
Marshall, D. (UKIP)	1,459	3.0
Majority	1,859	3.86
Electorate	70,590	
Turnout	48,190	68.27

**Member of last parliament*

CONSTITUENCY SNAPSHOT

Created in 1983 to replace the Carlton constituency, Gedling and its predecessor had, until the mid-1990s, been considered Tory territory. From 1966 to 1987 the seat was held by RAF veteran Sir Phillip Holland, at which point it was passed on to Andrew Mitchell following Holland's retirement. Mitchell maintained the large majority that Sir Phillip had built, with a lead of well over 10,000 at the 1992 election.

In 1997 Labour's Vernon Coaker took the seat with a majority of nearly 4,000. He increased his lead to 5,598 in 2001, but it fell to 3,811 four years later. Coaker held the seat in 2010 with a reduced majority of 1,859.

Boundary changes were minimal.

A relatively affluent constituency to the north and east of Nottingham, Gedling has seen major changes in its economic focus over the last 20 years. Gedling colliery was a major employer until its closure in 1991. Similarly, the traditional textile industry (particularly lace) that Nottingham was once famous is in decline.

The service industry has stepped in to replace many of the jobs lost through the decline of manufacturing and coal mining, with distribution centres and supermarkets established in the area. Boots, based in the nearby Broxtowe seat, is another major employer.

Ann Coffey

Stockport (returning MP)

Boundary changes

Tel: 020 7219 4546
E-mail: coffeya@parliament.uk
Website: www.anncoffeymp.com

Date of birth: 31 August 1946; Daughter of late John Brown, MBE, Flight-Lieutenant, RAF, and of Marie Brown, nurse

Education: Nairn Academy; Bodmin and Bushey Grammar Schools; Polytechnic of South Bank, London (BSc sociology 1967); Walsall College of Education (Postgraduate Certificate in Education 1971); Manchester University (MSc psychiatric social work 1977); Married 1973 (divorced 1989) (1 daughter); married Peter Saraga 1998

Non-political career: Trainee social worker, Walsall Social Services 1971-72; Social worker: Birmingham 1972-73, Gwynedd 1973-74, Wolverhampton 1974-75, Stockport 1977-82, Cheshire 1982-88; Team leader, fostering, Oldham Social Services 1988-92; Member, USDAW; Stockport Metropolitan Borough Council: Councillor 1984-92, Leader Labour Group 1988-92; Member, District Health Authority 1986-90

Political career: Contested Cheadle 1987 general election. Member for Stockport 1992-2010, for Stockport (revised boundary) since 6 May 2010 general election; Opposition Whip 1995-96; Opposition Spokeswoman on Health 1996-97; Joint PPS to Tony Blair as Prime Minister 1997-98; PPS to Alistair Darling as Secretary of State for: Social Security/Work and Pensions 1998-2002, Transport 2002-06, Trade and Industry 2006-07, Chancellor of the Exchequer 2007-10; *Select Committees:* Member: Trade and Industry 1993-95, Modernisation of the House of Commons 2000-10

Political interests: Children, health, education, community development

Other organisations: Fellow Industry and Parliament Trust 1994

Recreations: Photography, drawing, cinema, swimming, reading

Ann Coffey MP, House of Commons, London SW1A 0AA
Tel: 020 7219 4546 Fax: 020 7219 0770
E-mail: coffeya@parliament.uk
Constituency: 207a Bramhall Lane, Stockport, Cheshire SK2 6JA
Tel: 0161-483 2600 Fax: 0161-483 1070
Website: www.anncoffeymp.com

GENERAL ELECTION RESULT

		%
Coffey, A. (Lab)*	16,697	42.7
Holland, S. (Con)	9,913	25.3
Bodsworth, S. (Lib Dem)	9,778	25.0
Warner, D. (BNP)	1,201	3.1
Kelly, M. (UKIP)	862	2.2
Barber, P. (Green)	677	1.7
Majority	6,784	17.34
Electorate	63,525	
Turnout	39,128	61.59

**Member of last parliament*

CONSTITUENCY SNAPSHOT

The Stockport seat was created in 1983, and in 1992 Labour won it on a 13 per cent swing. A large majority of this new support for the Labour candidate, Ann Coffey, came from former SDP supporters. The Conservative share of the vote has fallen in every election here since 1983.

The 1997 election resulted in Stockport's biggest majority in living memory. However, in 2005 Coffey received 2,600 fewer votes than in 2001, which mainly went to the Liberal Democrats, reducing her majority to 9,000.

Coffey was re-elected with a smaller majority of 6,784 at the 2010 general election.

The seat gained three part-wards from Denton and Reddish and a part-ward from both Hazel Grove and Cheadle. It lost two part-wards to Hazel Grove and a part-ward to Denton and Reddish.

Part of Greater Manchester, Stockport has its own identity as a historic market town, with a strong sense of community. This is very much an urban seat, with no country dwellers among its electorate.

The seat is predominantly residential and residents have good transport connections to Manchester by road, rail and the bus network.

Stockport's historic covered market hall has received significant investment and there are exciting plans for the regeneration of the Hillgate area.

Dr **Therese Coffey**

Suffolk Coastal

Boundary changes

Tel: 020 7219 3000
E-mail: therese.coffey.mp@parliament.uk
Website: www.theresecoffey.com

Conservative

Date of birth: 18 November 1971; Daughter of late Tom Coffey and Sally Coffey

Education: St Mary's College, Crosby; St Edward's College, Liverpool; University College, London (BSc 1993; PhD chemistry 1997)

Non-political career: Chartered management accountant, Mars UK Ltd 1997-2007; Finance director, Mars Drinks UK 2007-09; Property finance manager, BBC 2009-; Councillor, Whitchurch Town Council 1999-2003

Political career: Contested Wrexham 2005 general election. Member for Suffolk Coastal since 6 May 2010 general election; Contested South East 2004 and 2009 European Parliament elections; Member, Conservative Party 1988-; National deputy chair, Conservative Students 1993-94; Chair, North West Hampshire Conservatives 2006-09; Deputy regional chair, South East 2009; Member, Conservative Way Forward

Political interests: Rural affairs, enterprise, trade and industry, innovation, defence, international development, animal welfare; Commonwealth, EU

Other organisations: Member: Bow Group, CAMRA

Dr Therese Coffey MP, House of Commons, London SW1A 0AA
Tel: 020 7219 3000 E-mail: therese.coffey.mp@parliament.uk
Constituency: c/o Suffolk Coastal Conservative Association, National Hall, Sun Lane, Woodbridge, Suffolk IP12 1EG Tel: 01394 380001
Website: www.theresecoffey.com

GENERAL ELECTION RESULT

		%
Coffey, T. (Con)	25,475	46.4
Cooper, D. (Lib Dem)	16,347	29.8
Leeder, A. (Lab)	8,812	16.1
Bush, S. (UKIP)	3,156	5.8
Fulcher, R. (Green)	1,103	2.0
Majority	9,128	16.63
Electorate	76,687	
Turnout	54,893	71.58

CONSTITUENCY SNAPSHOT

John Selwyn Gummer, who had previously held the Eye seat (under a previous boundary change) in 1979, was elected as MP for Suffolk Coastal with 58 per cent of the vote in the 1983 general election. Gummer's position held firm in the 1987 and 1992 elections.

At the 1997 general election John Gummer had his majority cut from a notional 16,700 to just 3,254. Gummer's majority has recovered and was 9,685 in 2005. Gummer retired in 2010 and Therese Coffey held the seat for the Conservatives with a 9,128 majority.

Boundary changes were minimal.

Suffolk Coastal covers almost the whole of Suffolk's sea frontage, apart from the area around Lowestoft, which is in Waveney.

The area's economy is largely divided between tourism and industry. Felixstowe, the biggest container port in the UK, is the area's largest employer.

There are sizeable industrial developments in Felixstowe, Woodbridge and Leiston as well as the Sizewell nuclear power plant. Adnams has a nationally renowned brewery in Southwold.

Damian Collins

Folkestone and Hythe

Boundary changes

Tel: 020 7219 3000
E-mail: damian.collins.mp@parliament.uk
Website: www.damiancollins.com

Date of birth: 4 February 1974

Education: St Mary's High School, Herefordshire; Belmont Abbey School, Herefordshire; St Benet's Hall, Oxford (BA modern history 1996); Married Sarah Richardson 2004 (1 daughter)

Non-political career: Desk officer, Conservative Party Research Department 1996-98; Press officer, Conservative Party Press Office 1998-99; Account director, M&C Saatchi 1999-2005; Managing Director, Influence Communications Ltd 2005-08; Senior counsel, Lexington Communications 2008-

Political career: Contested Northampton North 2005 general election. Member for Folkestone and Hythe since 6 May 2010 general election; President, Oxford University Conservative Association 1995

Political interests: Enterprise, economy, regeneration, social mobility, local food, creative industries, international relations

Other organisations: Political officer, Bow Group 2003-04; *Publications:* Conservative Revival (Politicos 2006); The New Blue (Social Market Foundation 2008)

Recreations: Sport (football, cricket, rugby union)

Damian Collins MP, House of Commons, London SW1A 0AA
Tel: 020 7219 3000 E-mail: damian.collins.mp@parliament.uk
Constituency: 4 West Cliff Gardens, Folkstone, Kent CT20 1SP
Tel: 01303 253524 Website: www.damiancollins.com

GENERAL ELECTION RESULT

		%
Collins, D. (Con)	26,109	49.5
Beaumont, L. (Lib Dem)	15,987	30.3
Worsley, D. (Lab)	5,719	10.8
McKenna, F. (UKIP)	2,439	4.6
Williams, H. (BNP)	1,662	3.2
Kemp, P. (Green)	637	1.2
Plumstead, D. (Ind)	247	0.5
Majority	10,122	19.17
Electorate	78,003	
Turnout	52,800	67.69

CONSTITUENCY SNAPSHOT

Conservative for much of the last century, the constituency had been represented by former Conservative party leader Michael Howard from 1983 until his retirement in 2010.

Howard's majority halved over at the 1987 and 1992 general elections. Despite a large swing against him in 1997, he held on with a majority of 6,332, which was further reduced to 5,907 in 2001. In 2005 Howard's majority increased to 11,680.

In 2010 the seat was held for the Conservatives by Damian with a 10,122 majority.

The seat gained the Saxon ward from Ashford.

This Kentish coastal constituency features the medieval Cinque ports of Hythe and Romney, the town of Folkestone, a scattering of pretty villages and fertile areas such as Romney Marsh and the scenic Elham Valley further inland.

The relative distance from London together with the presence of cross-channel traffic results in a social profile largely in line with national averages.

Small businesses are the dominant employers. Tourism plays a part too in the southernmost part of the 'Garden of England'. Folkestone is also the home of several insurance firms, some of which used to be involved in the shipping trade but have since diversified into other fields.

Folkestone is home of the Eurotunnel terminal so it remains an important departure and arrival point for cross-channel traffic.

Oliver Colvile

Plymouth, Sutton and Devonport

New constituency

Tel: 020 7219 3000
E-mail: oliver.colvile.mp@parliament.uk

Conservative

Date of birth: 26 August 1959

Education: Stowe School, Buckingham; Single

Non-political career: Director, small public relations company 1993-95; Account director, Rowland Sallingbury Casey 1993, 1995-96; Proprietor, Oliver Colvile & Associates 1996-10; Director, Policy Communications 2005-; National Society of Conservative Agents 1981-93; Chair, London branch Conservative Agents 1986-87; Editor, National Society of Conservative Agents' Journal 1992-93; Governor, St Andrew's Primary School

Political career: Contested Plymouth Sutton 2001 and 2005 general elections. Member for Plymouth, Sutton and Devonport since 6 May 2010 general election; Agent, Conservative Party 1981-93; Vice and deputy chair, Battersea Conservative Association 1997-99; Chair, Shaftesbury branch Battersea Conservative Association 1997-2000

Political interests: Malawi, South Africa, Zimbabwe

Other organisations: Conservative Foreign Affairs Forum; Director, Enterprise Forum; Stonehouse Lawn Tennis Club; Surrey County Cricket Club; Plymouth Albion Rugby Club; Royal Western Yacht Club

Recreations: Cricket, rugby, horse racing

Oliver Colvile MP, House of Commons, London SW1A 0AA
Tel: 020 7219 3000 E-mail: oliver.colvile.mp@parliament.uk
Constituency: Plymouth Sutton and Devonport Conservative Party, The Studio, 3 Belmont Place, Plymouth PL3 4DN Tel: 01752 293995
Website: www.plymouthsuttonconservatives.com

GENERAL ELECTION RESULT

		%
Colvile, O. (Con)	15,050	34.3
Gilroy, L. (Lab/Co-op)*	13,901	31.7
Evans, J. (Lib Dem)	10,829	24.7
Leigh, A. (UKIP)	2,854	6.5
Brown, A. (Green)	904	2.1
Gerrish, B. (Ind)	233	0.5
Hawkins, R. (SLP)	123	0.3
Majority	1,149	2.62
Electorate	71,035	
Turnout	43,894	61.79

**Member of last parliament*

CONSTITUENCY SNAPSHOT

Plymouth, Sutton and Devonport is very similar to the old Plymouth Sutton constituency. The wards of Stoke and Devonport, which previously straddled both seats, are now entirely in this seat; while Ham ward, which was also shared between the two seats, is now in the Moor View division.

Plymouth Sutton was held by the Conservative Alan Clark between 1974 and 1992. However, the seat was significantly altered in 1997, and sitting MP Gary Streeter decided to contest Devon South West. Labour's Linda Gilroy gained the seat in 1997, polling over half the votes cast, she was re-elected in 2005 with a 4,109 majority. This new constituency is notionally a Conservative gain as Oliver Colville won a 1,149 majority over Labour.

Taking in the Devon towns of Sutton and Devonport this maritime seat occupies the southern part of the city of Plymouth, including the naval dockyards. Historically one of the most important naval bases in Britain, Devonport remains the largest naval base in Western Europe.

The local economy is largely dominated by the naval base with electronics, engineering and boat building, defence and public administration having primary roles.

The city was largely destroyed during the Second World War and the old harbour area and fish market around the Hoe are the most important of the remaining few historic areas. The city centre is currently being redeveloped as part of the Plymouth 2020 project.

Michael Connarty

Linlithgow and East Falkirk ***(returning MP)***

No boundary changes

Tel: 020 7219 5071
E-mail: connartym@parliament.uk
Website: www.mconnartymp.com

Date of birth: 3 September 1947; Son of late Patrick and Elizabeth Connarty

Education: St Patrick's High School, Coatbridge; Stirling University (BA economics 1972); Glasgow University/Jordanhill College of Education (DCE 1975); Married Margaret Doran 1969 (1 son 1 daughter)

Non-political career: Stirling University: President Student Association 1970-71, Hon President (Rector) 1983-84; Teacher economics and modern studies (secondary and special needs) 1975-92; Chair, Stirling Economic Development Co. 1987-90; Member: Unite, EIS: Central Region President 1983-84, National Council EIS 1984-85; Stirling District Council: Councillor 1977-90, Council leader 1980-90; JP 1977-90

Political career: Contested Stirling 1983 and 1987 general elections. Member for Falkirk East 1992-2005, for Linithgow and East Falkirk since 5 May 2005 general election; PPS to Tom Clarke, as Minister of State, Department for Culture, Media and Sport 1997-98; *Select Committees:* Member: Information 1997-2001; European Scrutiny: Member 1998-2010, Chair 2006-10; Member: Liaison 2006-10; Member, Labour Party Scottish Executive Committee 1981-82, 1983-92; Chair, LP Scottish Local Government Committee 1988-90; Vice-Chair, COSLA Labour Group 1988-90; Chair, Stirlingshire Co-operative Party 1990-92

Political interests: Economy and enterprise, international development, European Union, industry, skills and training, youth affairs, crime, drug abuse, small businesses; Middle East, Latin America, Australia, USA

Other organisations: Member, Socialist Education Association 1978-; Vice-chair, Scottish Medical Aid for Palestinians 1988-95; Chair, Board of Scottish National Jazz Orchestra 2006-; Board Member, Parliamentary Office of Science and Technology (POST) 1997-; Life Member: International Parliamentary Union 1992-, Commonwealth Parliamentary Association 1992-; British American Parliamentary Group 1992-; Fellow Industry and Parliament Trust 1994

Recreations: Family, jazz and classical music, reading, walking

Michael Connarty MP, House of Commons, London SW1A 0AA
Tel: 020 7219 5071 Fax: 020 7219 2541
E-mail: connartym@parliament.uk
Constituency: 62 Hopetown Street, Bathgate, West Lothian EH48 4PD
Tel: 01506 676711 Fax: 01506 676722, Room 8, 5 Kerse Road, Grangemouth, Stirlingshire FK3 8HQ Tel: 01324 474832
Fax: 01324 666811 Website: www.mconnartymp.com

GENERAL ELECTION RESULT

		%	+/-
Connarty, M. (Lab)*	25,634	49.8	2.2
Smith, T. (SNP)	13,081	25.4	1.9
Glenn, S. (Lib Dem)	6,589	12.8	-2.5
Stephenson, A. (Con)	6,146	12.0	0.1
Majority	12,553	24.40	
Electorate	80,907		
Turnout	51,450	63.59	

**Member of last parliament*

CONSTITUENCY SNAPSHOT

Labour has won the Linlithgow seat (West Lothian from 1950 until 1983) in every election since the Second World War. For most of those years the MP was Tam Dalyell, who held West Lothian from 1962 until his retirement in 2005.

In 2005 Linlithgow lost Blackburn and Fauldhouse to an enlarged Livingston, but gained more than half the old Falkirk East seat. Linlithgow and East Falkirk was notionally safer for Labour and Michael Connarty (who came with the Falkirk East wards) won convincingly with a 11,202 majority. Connarty has increased his majority to 12,553 in 2010.

Situated in the central industrial belt, the constituency spreads from Grangemouth and Bo'ness down the south bank of the Forth to the ancient burgh of Linlithgow.

The seat is characterised by slag heaps left over from the era of shale-mining around the villages of Armadale, Blackburn and Whitburn, and the larger town of Bathgate.

Traditional industries like textiles have declined. Industry is now concentrated in Bo'Ness and Grangemouth, which house electronic and communications companies.

Linlithgow was the birthplace of Mary Queen of Scots and that connection, as well as its palace, makes it a popular tourist destination.

Grangemouth has both a modern container port and a vast petro-chemical and chemical works. BP's oil refinery is a key economic driver of the area.

Rosie Cooper

West Lancashire (returning MP)

No boundary changes

Tel: 020 7219 5690
E-mail: cooperre@parliament.uk
Website: www.rosiecooper.net

Labour

Date of birth: 5 September 1950; Daughter of William and Rose Cooper

Education: Bellerive Convent Grammar School; Liverpool University; single

Non-political career: Concept Design Partnership & W Cooper Limited 1973-80; The Littlewoods Organisation 1980-2001: merchandiser 1980-92, PR manager 1994-95; group corporate communications manager 1995-2000, seconded as project manager for government task force on equal pay 1999-2001; USDAW; Liverpool City Councillor 1973-2000: Lord Mayor 1992-93, Labour housing spokesperson 1999-2000; Member and vice-chair Liverpool Health Authority 1994-96

Political career: Contested Knowsley North 1986 by-election and 1987 general election, Liverpool Broadgreen 1992 general election. Member for West Lancashire since 5 May 2005 general election; PPS: to Lord Rooker as Minister of State, Department for Environment, Food and Rural Affairs 2006-07, to Ben Bradshaw: as Minister of State, Department for Health 2007-09, as Secretary of State for Culture, Media and Sport 2009-10; *Select Committees:* Member: European Scrutiny 2005-06, Northern Ireland Affairs 2005-10, Justice 2007-08, North West 2009-10, Justice 2010; Contested North West region 2004 European Parliament election

Political interests: Health, disability equality, housing; Northern Ireland

Other organisations: Director Merseyside Centre for Deaf People 1973-2004; Chair Liverpool Women's Hospital 1996-2005; Board member Cosmopolitan Housing Association

Recreations: Theatre, music, cinema, community affairs

Rosie Cooper MP, House of Commons, London SW1A 0AA
Tel: 020 7219 5690 Fax: 020 7219 5278
E-mail: cooperre@parliament.uk
Constituency: 127 Burscough Street, Ormskirk, Lancashire L39 2EP
Tel: 01695 570094 Fax: 01695 570094 Website: www.rosiecooper.net

GENERAL ELECTION RESULT

		%	+/-
Cooper, R. (Lab)*	21,883	45.1	-2.7
Owens, A. (Con)	17,540	36.2	2.4
Gibson, J. (Lib Dem)	6,573	13.6	-0.4
Noone, D. (UKIP)	1,775	3.7	1.7
Cranie, P. (Green)	485	1.0	
Braid, D. (Clause 28)	217	0.5	
Majority	4,343	8.96	
Electorate	75,975		
Turnout	48,473	63.80	

**Member of last parliament*

CONSTITUENCY SNAPSHOT

West Lancashire was created in 1983. Before that it was called Ormskirk and was held by Harold Wilson, the Labour Prime Minister.

However, the Conservative Kevin Hind won in 1983. He kept the seat until 1992 when it fell to Labour's Colin Pickthall with a 2,077 majority, which increased to over 17,000 by 1997. He retired in 2005 and was replaced by Rosie Cooper who retained the seat for Labour with a 6,084 majority.

In 2010 Cooper was re-elected with a majority of 4,343.

West Lancashire is, despite its name, in the very south west corner of the county. Its two main towns are Ormskirk and Skelmersdale. Ormskirk is an old historic market town and is home to Edge Hill University.

The influx of students to the area has had an impact on the town, bringing a new vitality. Skelmersdale was designated a new town in 1961, and on its creation was populated by mass emigration from Liverpool.

The constituency has a strong service sector, particularly in the public health and education sector.

One of the major current campaigns locally is to gain funding for an Ormskirk by-pass.

Rt Hon **Yvette Cooper**

Normanton, Pontefract and Castleford ***(returning MP)***

New constituency

Tel: 020 7219 5080
E-mail: coopery@parliament.uk
Website: www.yvettecooper.com

Date of birth: 20 March 1969; Daughter of Tony and June Cooper

Education: Eggars Comprehensive; Balliol College, Oxford (BA philosophy, politics and economics 1990); Harvard University (Kennedy Scholar 1991); London School of Economics (MSc economics 1995); Married Ed Balls (now MP) 1998 (2 daughters 1 son)

Non-political career: Economic researcher for John Smith MP 1990-92; Domestic policy specialist, Bill Clinton presidential campaign 1992; Policy adviser to Labour Treasury teams 1992-94; Economic columnist/Leader writer, *The Independent* 1995-97; Member, TGWU, GMB

Political career: Member for Pontefract and Castleford 1997-2010, for Normanton, Pontefract and Castleford since 6 May 2010 general election; Parliamentary Under-Secretary of State, Department of Health (Public Health) 1999-2002; Parliamentary Secretary, Lord Chancellor's Department 2002-03; Office of the Deputy Prime Minister/Department for Communities and Local Government 2003-08: Parliamentary Under-Secretary of State 2003-05, Minister of State (Minister for Housing and Planning) 2005-07, Minister for Housing (attending cabinet) 2007-08; Chief Secretary to the Treasury 2008-09; Secretary of State for Work and Pensions 2009-10; Shadow Secretary of State for Work and Pensions 2010-; Shadow Minister for Women and Equalities 2010-; *Select Committees:* Member: Education and Employment 1997-99, Education and Employment (Employment Sub-Committee) 1997-99

Political interests: Unemployment, coal industry, poverty, equal opportunities; USA

Other organisations: PC 2007

Rt Hon Yvette Cooper MP, House of Commons, London SW1A 0AA
Tel: 020 7219 5080 Fax: 020 7219 0912
E-mail: coopery@parliament.uk
Constituency: 1 York Street, Castleford, West Yorkshire WF10 1JS
Tel: 01977 553388 Fax: 01977 559753
Website: www.yvettecooper.com

GENERAL ELECTION RESULT

		%
Cooper, Y. (Lab)*	22,293	48.2
Pickles, N. (Con)	11,314	24.5
Rush, C. (Lib Dem)	7,585	16.4
Thewlis-Hardy, G. (BNP)	3,864	8.4
Allen, G. (Ind)	1,183	2.6
Majority	10,979	23.74
Electorate	82,239	
Turnout	46,239	56.23

**Member of last parliament*

CONSTITUENCY SNAPSHOT

This new constituency on the eastern outcrop of West Yorkshire consists of parts of the abolished Normanton and Pontefract and Castleford seats. Pontefract and Castleford was dominated in the twentieth century by Labour, electing a succession of local miners. Normanton was formerly within a separate constituency of the same name. It was held by Cooper's husband, Ed Balls in 2005 and had been in Labour hands for over a century when abolished.

Last in this line of former miners was Geoffrey Lofthouse, who won the nomination for the by-election of 1978. He stood down in 1997 and made way for Yvette Cooper. She won a 15,246 majority in 2005.

In 2010 Cooper won the new seat for Labour with a strong 10,979 majority despite a 12.5 per cent swing to the Tories.

Pontefract is the best known and more historic of the three towns in the title, but Castleford is the largest. Together with the third, Normanton, they form an area based on coal and criss-crossed by motorways.

The traditional coal mining industry has now vanished but one remaining pit, Kellingley Colliery, keeps the industry alive. The major employers nowadays are the great power stations at Ferrybridge, in the constituency, and Drax and Eggborough, just outside. Knottingley has always been rather different, with a history of shipbuilding, glass-making, lime-burning and pottery among its industries.

Jeremy Corbyn

Islington North (returning MP)

No boundary changes

Tel: 020 7219 3545
E-mail: corbynj@parliament.uk
Website: www.epolitix.com/Jeremy-Corbyn

Labour

Date of birth: 26 May 1949; Son of David Benjamin and Naomi Loveday Jocelyn Corbyn

Education: Adams Grammar School, Newport, Shropshire; (3 sons)

Non-political career: Full-time organiser, National Union of Public Employees 1975-83; Also worked for Tailor and Garment workers and AUEW; NUPE sponsored MP; Member, RMT Parliamentary Campaigning Group 2002-; Councillor, Haringey Borough Council 1974-84: Chair: Community Development 1975-78, Public Works 1978-79, Planning 1980-81

Political career: Member for Islington North since 9 June 1983 general election; *Select Committees:* Member: Social Security 1991-97, London 2009-10

Political interests: People of Islington, defence, welfare state, NHS, campaigning for socialism in the community and against racism, anti-imperialism and internationalism, transport safety, environment, Irish affairs, liberation Islington Local Agenda 21

Recreations: Running, railways

Jeremy Corbyn MP, House of Commons, London SW1A 0AA
Tel: 020 7219 3545 Fax: 020 7219 2328
E-mail: corbynj@parliament.uk
Constituency: 86 Durham Road, London N7 7DU Tel: 020 7561 7488
Website: www.epolitix.com/Jeremy-Corbyn

GENERAL ELECTION RESULT

		%	+/-
Corbyn, J. (Lab)*	24,276	54.5	3.6
Jamieson-Ball, R. (Lib Dem)	11,875	26.7	-3.1
Berrill-Cox, A. (Con)	6,339	14.2	2.4
Dixon, E. (Green)	1,348	3.0	-4.0
Lennon, D. (UKIP)	716	1.6	
Majority	12,401	27.83	
Electorate	68,120		
Turnout	44,554	65.41	

**Member of last parliament*

CONSTITUENCY SNAPSHOT

The Borough of Islington had three constituencies until 1983 when Islington Central was abolished and only North and South remained. Michael O'Halloran, the then MP for Islington North, along with John Grant who lost his Central seat in the changes, had both moved to the SDP by the time of the general election. They both then competed for the northern seat, with Grant running as the official SDP candidate. The competing elements of the SDP resulted in Labour's Jeremy Corbyn winning the seat, which he has held ever since.

In the 1997 Corbyn polled almost 70 per cent of the vote giving him a 19,955 majority. However, by 2005 it had fallen to 6,716. Corbyn increased his majority to 12,401 and received just under 55 per cent of the vote in 2010.

Islington North spans from Hillrise ward in the north to Mildmay and Highbury in the south. Arsenal's football stadium, The Emirates, falls within its borders and geographically it is the smallest seat in the UK.

The constituency's close proximity to Upper Street in Islington South makes it attractive to young professionals, many of whom live around the Holloway Road.

There is a large student population, with the University of North London campus of the Metropolitan University situated close to Holloway Road.

Geoffrey Cox

***Torridge and West Devon** (returning MP)*

Boundary changes

Tel: 020 7219 4719
E-mail: coxg@parliament.uk
Website: www.geoffreycox.co.uk

Conservative

Date of birth: 30 April 1960; Son of Michael and Diane Cox

Education: King's College, Taunton; Downing College, Cambridge (BA English and law 1981); Married Patricia Margaret Jean Macdonald 1985 (1 daughter 2 sons)

Non-political career: Barrister, Thomas More Chambers 1982-2001; Standing counsel to Mauritius 1996-2000; Queen's Counsel 2003; Member NFU

Political career: Contested Torridge and West Devon 2001 general election. Member for Torridge and West Devon 2005-10, for Torridge and West Devon (revised boundary) since 6 May 2010 general election; *Select Committees:* Member: Environment, Food and Rural Affairs 2006-10

Political interests: Agriculture, education, defence, legal and constitutional issues; Mauritius

Recreations: Reading, walking dogs, swimming, countryside

Geoffrey Cox MP, House of Commons, London SW1A 0AA
Tel: 020 7219 4719 Fax: 020 7219 4307 E-mail: coxg@parliament.uk
Constituency: 2 Bridge Chambers, Lower Bridge Street, Bideford, Devon EX39 2BU Tel: 01237 459001 Fax: 01237 459003
Website: www.geoffreycox.co.uk

GENERAL ELECTION RESULT

		%
Cox, G. (Con)*	25,230	45.7
Symons, A. (Lib Dem)	22,273	40.3
Julian, R. (UKIP)	3,021	5.5
Jones, D. (Lab)	2,917	5.3
Simmons, C. (Green)	1,050	1.9
Baker, N. (BNP)	766	1.4
Majority	2,957	5.35
Electorate	76,574	
Turnout	55,257	72.16

**Member of last parliament*

CONSTITUENCY SNAPSHOT

This seat had been predominantly Conservative since the Second World War until the defection of Emma Nicholson, the sitting Tory MP, to the Liberal Democrats in 1995. In 1997 John Burnett took over from Nicholson and retained the seat for the Liberal Democrats.

At the 2001 election Burnett hung onto Torridge and West Devon, albeit with a reduced majority of under 1,200. Burnett retired in 2005 and Conservative Geoffrey Cox won with a 3,236 majority. Geoffrey Cox won a majority of 2,957 for the revised seat in 2010.

The seat lost a number of eastern wards, including Oakhampton East and West, to the new Central Devon seat. The seat gained Buckland Monachorum and part-ward Walkham from South West Devon.

There are very few places in the UK that are as rural as Torridge and West Devon. This is currently the largest seat in the county and includes the town of Tavistock as well as large parts of Dartmoor National Park.

There is a significant agricultural industry here, with the highest percentage of people involved in farming in the whole of the South West.

The age profile here is similar to many South West constituencies, with large numbers of older and retired people.

Stephen Crabb

Preseli Pembrokeshire ***(returning MP)***

Boundary changes

Tel: 020 7219 6518
E-mail: crabbs@parliament.uk
Website: www.stephencrabb.com

Conservative

Date of birth: 20 January 1973

Education: Tasker Milward VC School, Haverfordwest; Bristol University (BSc politics 1995); London Business School (MBA 2004); Married Béatrice Alice Claude Odile Monnier 1996 (1 son 1 daughter)

Non-political career: Research assistant to Andrew Rowe MP 1995-96; Parliamentary affairs officer National Council for Voluntary Youth Services 1996-98; Policy and campaign manager London Chamber of Commerce 1998-2002; Self-employed marketing consultant 2002-05

Political career: Contested Preseli Pembrokeshire 2001 general election. Member for Preseli Pembrokeshire 2005-10, for Preseli Pembrokeshire (revised boundary) since 6 May 2010 general election; Opposition Whip 2009-10; Assistant Government Whip 2010-; *Select Committees:* Member: Welsh Affairs 2005-07, International Development 2007-09, Treasury 2008-09; Chair: North Southwark and Bermondsey Conservative Association 1998-2000, Conservative Party Human Rights Commission 2007-

Political interests: Energy, trade, human rights, young people; France, USA, India, Middle East

Other organisations: Patron Haverfordwest Mencap 2005-; Balfour, Haverfordwest , Haverfordwest century AFC

Recreations: Rugby, long distance running, cooking, family

Stephen Crabb MP, House of Commons, London SW1A 0AA
Tel: 020 7219 6518 Fax: 020 7219 8409
E-mail: crabbs@parliament.uk
Constituency: 20 Upper Market Street, Haverfordwest, Pembrokeshire SA61 1QA Tel: 01437 763527
Website: www.stephencrabb.com

GENERAL ELECTION RESULT

		%
Crabb, S. (Con)*	16,944	42.8
Rees, M. (Lab)	12,339	31.2
Tregoning, N. (Lib Dem)	5,759	14.5
Jones-Davies, H. (PlC)	3,654	9.2
Lawson, R. (UKIP)	906	2.3
Majority	4,605	11.63
Electorate	57,419	
Turnout	39,602	68.97

**Member of last parliament*

CONSTITUENCY SNAPSHOT

Jackie Lawrence won the seat for Labour in 1997 with a 8,736 majority. Preseli Pembrokeshire was created that year when Pembrokeshire was split in two.

In 2001 the seat registered a swing of 6.6 per cent to the Conservatives, well above their average performance in Wales. Jackie Lawrence stood down in 2005 and the Conservative candidate Stephen Crabb won the seat by 607 votes. Crabb increased his majority to 4,605 in 2010.

Boundary changes have been minimal.

Pembrokeshire forms the south-western peninsula of Wales. The county covers 1,600 square kms, a third of which form the Pembrokeshire Coast National Park, one of three national parks in the country along with Snowdonia and the Brecon Beacons.

The main towns in the constituency are Fishguard, Haverfordwest and Milford Haven, as well as the little cathedral city of St David's famous for being the smallest city in the United Kingdom. Milford Haven is extremely important, especially for the power industry.

Pembrokeshire's peripheral situation is hindered by being poorly served by road and rail links.

David Crausby

***Bolton North East** (returning MP)*

Boundary changes

Tel: 020 7219 4092
E-mail: crausbyd@parliament.uk
Website: www.epolitix.com/david-crausby

Date of birth: 17 June 1946; Son of late Thomas Crausby, factory worker/club steward, and of Kathleen Crausby, cotton worker

Education: Derby Grammar School, Bury; Bury Technical College; Married Enid Noon 1965 (2 sons)

Non-political career: Shop steward/works convenor, AEEU 1968-97; Full-time works convenor 1978-97; Chair Amicus (AEEU) Group 2001-; Councillor, Bury Council 1979-92, Chair of Housing 1985-92

Political career: Contested Bury North 1987 and Bolton North East 1992 general elections. Member for Bolton North East 1997-2010, for Bolton North East (revised boundary) since 6 May 2010 general election; *Select Committees:* Member: Administration 1997-2001, Social Security 1999-2001, Defence 2001-10, Quadripartite (Committees on Strategic Export Controls)/Arms Export Controls 2006-10; Chair: North West 2009-10

Political interests: Industrial relations, pensions, housing, defence

Other organisations: Political secretary National Union of Labour Clubs

Recreations: Football, cinema, walking

David Crausby MP, House of Commons, London SW1A 0AA
Tel: 020 7219 4092 Fax: 020 7219 3713
E-mail: crausbyd@parliament.uk
Constituency: 580 Blackburn Road, Astley Bridge, Bolton, Lancashire BL1 7AL Tel: 01204 303340 Fax: 01204 304401
Website: www.epolitix.com/david-crausby

GENERAL ELECTION RESULT

		%
Crausby, D. (Lab)*	19,870	46.0
Dunleavy, D. (Con)	15,786	36.5
Ankers, P. (Lib Dem)	5,624	13.0
Johnson, N. (UKIP)	1,815	4.2
Armston, N. (You)	182	0.4
Majority	4,084	9.45
Electorate	67,281	
Turnout	43,227	64.25

**Member of last parliament*

CONSTITUENCY SNAPSHOT

Bolton North East, formerly Bolton East, was a national weathervane seat from 1950 to 1979. In 1979 Labour MP David Young held on despite the first Thatcher victory; however, he lost the seat to the Tories in 1983 and the seat remained blue until 1997.

In 1997 Labour's David Crausby won the seat at his third attempt, with a majority of 12,669. Crausby's majority halved to 4,103 in 2005. Crausby held the seat in 2010 with a majority of 4,084.

The seat gained two part-wards from Bolton South East and one from Bolton West in exchange for a part-ward to each of those seats.

Bolton is an industrial town in the north-west quadrant of Greater Manchester. To the west lies Wigan, and Darwen is situated immediately to the north. Bolton North East contains roughly half the town's urban area, along with several suburban wards that are home to affluent private housing estates.

In the northern and eastern extremes of the seat the land is more rural in character.

Around a quarter of the workforce is employed in manufacturing dominated by building products, engineering, paper and printing.

Mary Creagh

Wakefield (returning MP)

Boundary changes

Tel: 020 7219 6984
E-mail: creaghm@parliament.uk
Website: www.marycreagh.co.uk

Date of birth: 2 December 1967; Daughter of Thomas and Elizabeth Creagh

Education: Bishop Ullathorne RC Comprehensive, Coventry; Pembroke College, Oxford (BA modern languages (French/Italian) 1990); London School of Economics (MSc European studies 1997); Married Adrian Pulham 2001 (1 son 1 daughter)

Non-political career: Stagiare Socialist group, European Parliament 1990; Assistant Stephen Hughes MEP 1991; Press officer: European Youth Forum 1991-95, London Enterprise Agency 1995-97; Lecturer in entrepreneurship Cranfield School of Management 1997-2005; GMB: Member 1991-95, 2003-, Chair Brussels branch 1992-95; Member UNISON 2004-; London Borough of Islington: Councillor 1998-2005, Leader Labour group 2000-04

Political career: Member for Wakefield 2005-10, for Wakefield (revised boundary) since 6 May 2010 general election; PPS: to Ministers of State, Department of Health: Andy Burnham 2006-07, Lord Warner 2006, to Andy Burnham: as Chief Secretary to the Treasury 2007-08, as Secretary of State for Culture, Media and Sport 2008-09; Assistant Government Whip 2009-10; *Select Committees:* Member: Joint Committee on Human Rights 2005-07, Finance and Services 2007-10, Yorkshire and the Humber 2009; Member: Co-operative Party 1995-, Fabians 1995-

Political interests: Europe, employment, social policy, disability issues, Irish community, human rights, children's issues; Rwanda, Democratic Republic of Congo

Other organisations: Member: European Movement 1995-, Amnesty International 1997-

Recreations: Family, yoga, cycling, swimming, food

Mary Creagh MP, House of Commons, London SW1A 0AA
Tel: 020 7219 6984 Fax: 020 7219 4257
E-mail: creaghm@parliament.uk
Constituency: 20-22 Cheapside, Wakefield, West Yorkshire WF1 2TF
Tel: 01924 204319 Fax: 01924 299723
Website: www.marycreagh.co.uk

GENERAL ELECTION RESULT

		%
Creagh, M. (Lab)*	17,454	39.3
Story, A. (Con)	15,841	35.6
Smith, D. (Lib Dem)	7,256	16.3
Senior, I. (BNP)	2,581	5.8
Hawkins, M. (Green)	873	2.0
Harrop, M. (Ind)	439	1.0
Majority	1,613	3.63
Electorate	70,834	
Turnout	44,444	62.74

**Member of last parliament*

CONSTITUENCY SNAPSHOT

Labour has never lost Wakefield since the 1930s, but have come close on occasions. In 1997 a swing of 10.6 per cent to Labour gave David Hinchliffe a majority of 14,604 to return to the seat he had represented since 1987.

In 2005 David Hinchliffe retired. His replacement, Mary Creagh, retained a majority of 5,154. Creagh was re-elected with a majority of 1,613 at the 2010 general election.

The seat lost all wards from the boroughs of Kirklees and Wakefield, while gaining Osset and Horbury and South wards from Normanton as well as three part-wards that were shared between them.

This constituency takes in most of the city of Wakefield and a number of smaller villages out to the south west of the city in southern West Yorkshire.

While the mines have gone, engineering still continues, but the economy is now far more diverse, with distribution and retail trades, telecommunications companies and an industrial estate. Many commute to work in Leeds and Sheffield, with new housing appearing as a result. There is some farming in the rural wards, but the biggest employers are now the local authority and the health service.

One of the largest regeneration schemes is the Wakefield Waterfront Project. The development provides new retail and industrial units alongside the Hepworth Gallery.

Dr **Stella Creasy**

Walthamstow

Boundary changes

Tel: 020 7219 3000
E-mail: stella.creasy.mp@parliament.uk
Website: www.workingforwalthamstow.org.uk

Labour/Co-operative

Date of birth: 1977

Education: Sixth form college, Colchester; Cambridge University (psychology); London School of Economics (PhD psychology)

Non-political career: Former researcher to Douglas Alexander MP, Charles Clarke MP and Ross Cranston MP; Former deputy director, Involve; Head of public affairs, Scout Association; Member, Unite; Waltham Forest Council: Former councillor, Former Deputy Mayor, Former Mayor

Political career: Member for Walthamstow since 6 May 2010 general election; Member: SERA, Labour Women's Network

Other organisations: Fabian Society

Dr Stella Creasy MP, House of Commons, London SW1A 0AA
Tel: 020 7219 3000 E-mail: stella.creasy.mp@parliament.uk
Constituency: Walthamstow Labour Party, 23 Orford Road, Walthamstow, London E17 9NL Tel: 020 8520 6586
Website: www.workingforwalthamstow.org.uk

GENERAL ELECTION RESULT

		%
Creasy, S. (Lab/Co-op)	21,252	51.8
Ahmed, F. (Lib Dem)	11,774	28.7
Hemsted, A. (Con)	5,734	14.0
Chisholm-Benli, J. (UKIP)	823	2.0
Perrett, D. (Green)	767	1.9
Taaffe, N. (TUSC)	279	0.7
Mall, A. (Christian)	248	0.6
Warburton, P. (Ind)	117	0.3
Majority	9,478	23.12
Electorate	64,625	
Turnout	40,994	63.43

CONSTITUENCY SNAPSHOT

Before 1974 Walthamstow was divided into two divisions: East and West. The latter formerly held by Labour Prime Minister Clement Attlee.

Labour's Eric Deakins won the amalgamated seat in both the 1974 elections having formerly been the member for the western division. He remained MP for Walthamstow until 1987 when Hugo Summerson won the seat for the Tories.

Labour's by Neil Gerrard defeated the Tories with a swing of 5.5 per cent. In 1997 Gerrard benefited from a swing just short of 18 per cent giving him a majority of 17,000. Labour's Stella Creasy was elected as the new MP for this seat, with a majority of 9,478 and 52 per cent of the vote.

Gerrard's majority almost halved in 2005 to 7,993.

The seat gained Higham Hill part-ward from Chingford and Woodford Green.

This seat in north-east London is a culturally and ethnically diverse place. Walthamstow market is the longest daily street market in Europe.

The south-west corner of the constituency touches the Lea Valley area, which is targeted for massive regeneration and development for the 2012 Olympic Games. The proposed Olympic park should bring jobs and investment to the borough of Waltham Forest.

Mike Crockart

Edinburgh West

No boundary changes

Tel: 020 7219 3000
E-mail: mike.crockart.mp@parliament.uk

Education: Perth High School; Edinburgh University (BSc social services 1987); Married (2 sons)

Non-political career: Police constable, Lothians and Borders Police 1990-98; Standard Life Assurance: Systems developer 1998-2005, Lead business service developer 2006-07, IT project manager 2007-

Political career: Contested Edinburgh North and Leith 2005 general election. Member for Edinburgh West since 6 May 2010 general election; Contested Edinburgh North and Leith constituency 2007 Scottish Parliament election; Convener, Edinburgh West Liberal Democrats 2009-

Recreations: Photography, classical music

Mike Crockart MP, House of Commons, London SW1A 0AA
Tel: 020 7219 3000 E-mail: mike.crockart.mp@parliament.uk
Constituency: 120 Clifton Road, West Clifton, Steading, Livingston EH53 0PN Tel: 0131-333 2623
Website: www.edinburghwestlibdems.org.uk

GENERAL ELECTION RESULT

		%	+/-
Crockart, M. (Lib Dem)	16,684	35.9	-13.5
Day, C. (Lab)	12,881	27.7	9.1
Geddes, S. (Con)	10,767	23.2	3.7
Cleland, S. (SNP)	6,115	13.2	4.1
Majority	3,803	8.19	
Electorate	65,161		
Turnout	46,447	71.28	

CONSTITUENCY SNAPSHOT

Lord James Douglas-Hamilton became Tory MP for Edinburgh West in October 1974. In 1983 he was just 498 votes away from losing to the Liberal/SDLP alliance and in 1987 his majority, though increased, was 1,234. In 1992 he managed a win by 879 votes.

After contesting the seat since 1970 Donald Gorrie triumphed over Lord James in 1997 with a majority of 7,253. In the 2001 general election John Barrett succeeded Donald Gorrie.

The 2005 enlargement of Edinburgh West confirmed the Liberal Democrats' hold. Parts of Pilton and Craigleith were lost to Edinburgh North and Leith but Murrayfield and Stenhouse were gained from the disbanded Edinburgh Central. The Liberal Democrats achieved a majority of 13,600. Mike Crockart was elected for the Lib Dems in 2010 following John Barrett's retirement with a 93,803 majority.

The western Edinburgh division includes Edinburgh Airport as well as South Queensferry and Edinburgh suburbs including Cramond.

Notable landmarks include the southern ends of the Forth road and rail bridges and Murrayfield, Scotland's national rugby stadium. South Gyle, a major business and shopping centre, is located in this constituency.

Transport Initiatives Edinburgh will begin work on Edinburgh's new tram system in June 2008. The first phase of the development will be a 22-stop tram route starting from Newhaven, going through Princes Street, and then going through the constituency with stops at the Gyle Shopping Centre and Gogarburn, before terminating at Edinburgh Airport.

Tracey Crouch

Chatham and Aylesford

Boundary changes

Tel: 020 7219 3000
E-mail: tracey.crouch.mp@parliament.uk
Website: www.traceycrouch.org

Conservative

Date of birth: 24 July 1975

Education: Hull University (BA law and politics 1996)

Non-political career: Researcher to Rt Hon Michael Howard MP 1996-98; Public affairs manager, Harcourt 1998-2000; Senior public affairs manager, Westminster Strategy 2000-03; Chief of staff to: Damian Green MP 2003, Rt Hon David Davis MP 2003-05; Norwich Union/Aviva 2005-: Senior political adviser 2005-07, Head of public affairs 2007-

Political career: Member for Chatham and Aylesford since 6 May 2010 general election

Political interests: Home affairs, education, sport, economic affairs

Other organisations: FA coaching level 1 2006

Recreations: Sport, music, reading

Tracey Crouch MP, House of Commons, London SW1A 0AA
Tel: 020 7219 3000 E-mail: tracey.crouch.mp@parliament.uk
Constituency: 200 Canterbury Street, Gillingham, Kent ME7 5XG
Tel: 01634 853322 Website: www.traceycrouch.org

GENERAL ELECTION RESULT

		%
Crouch, T. (Con)	20,230	46.2
Shaw, J. (Lab)*	14,161	32.3
McClintock, J. (Lib Dem)	5,832	13.3
McCarthy-Stewart, C. (BNP)	1,365	3.1
Newton, S. (UKIP)	1,314	3.0
Varnham, S. (England)	400	0.9
Arthur, D. (Green)	396	0.9
Smith, M. (Christian)	109	0.3
Majority	6,069	13.85
Electorate	71,122	
Turnout	43,807	61.59

**Member of last parliament*

CONSTITUENCY SNAPSHOT

Chatham and Aylesford was created in 1997 and Conservative Andrew Rowe, whose previous seat of Mid Kent covered most of the area of the new seat, moved to Faversham and Mid Kent.

This was fortuitous for him as Labour's Jonathan Shaw, overturned the 13,000 notional Tory majority with one of 2,790. He held the seat with an increased majority of 4,340 in 2001 but this fell to 2,332 in 2005.

Labour was defeated in the 2010 general election with a 11.1 per cent swing to Conservative Tracey Crouch, who secured a 6,069 majority.

The seat gained one part-ward each from Medway and Gillingham, and lost one part-ward each to Gilligham and Rainham and Rochester and Strood.

Chatham has a long historical connection with the Royal Navy. Aylesford is a fairly small town in the south of the constituency with its surrounding commuter villages and towns.

Chatham used to be heavily dependent on the naval dockyard which had existed there since Tudor times but its closure in 1984 impacted employment in the constituency. Now just outside the constituency, the docks are being regenerated into residential, commercial and leisure facilities.

Employment in the constituency is more diverse since the docks were closed. Paper, packaging and cement production are major industries and Aylesford's location and travel links has made it a major distribution centre. A high speed rail-link into St Pancras opened in 2009.

Jon Cruddas

Dagenham and Rainham ***(returning MP)***

New constituency

Tel: 020 7219 8161
E-mail: cruddasj@parliament.uk
Website: www.joncruddas.org.uk

Date of birth: 7 April 1962; Son of John, sailor, and Pat, housewife, Cruddas

Education: Oaklands RC Comprehensive, Portsmouth; Warwick University 1981-88 (BSc economics, MA industrial relations, PhD industrial and business studies); University of Wisconsin, USA Visiting fellow 1987-88; Married Anna Mary Healy 1992 (1 son)

Non-political career: Policy officer Labour Party Policy Directorate 1989-94; Chief assistant to General Secretary Labour Party 1994-97; Deputy political secretary Prime Minister's political office Downing Street 1997-2001; TGWU 1989-2001: Branch secretary 1992-94

Political career: Member for Dagenham 2001-10, for Dagenham and Rainham since 6 May 2010 general election; *Select Committees:* Member: Public Accounts 2003-05

Political interests: Labour law, industrial economy, economic regeneration

Other organisations: Dagenham Working Men's, Dagenham Royal Naval Association; White Hart Dagenham Angling Society

Recreations: Golf, angling

Jon Cruddas MP, House of Commons, London SW1A 0AA
Tel: 020 7219 8161 Fax: 020 7219 1756
E-mail: cruddasj@parliament.uk
Constituency: 10 Royal Parade, Church Street, Dagenham, Essex RM10 9XB Tel: 020 8984 7854
Website: www.joncruddas.org.uk

GENERAL ELECTION RESULT

		%
Cruddas, J. (Lab)*	17,813	40.3
Jones, S. (Con)	15,183	34.3
Bourke, J. (Lib Dem)	3,806	8.6
Litwin, C. (UKIP)	1,569	3.6
Kennedy, G. (Ind)	308	0.7
Watson, P. (Christian)	305	0.7
Rosaman, D. (Green)	296	0.7
Majority	2,630	5.95
Electorate	69,764	
Turnout	44,232	63.40

**Member of last parliament*

CONSTITUENCY SNAPSHOT

The new constituency comprises the wards of Chadwell Heath, Eastbrook, Heath, River, Village and Whalebone from Dagenham, and the wards of Elm Park, Rainham and Wennington and South Hornchurch from Hornchurch.

Dagenham has been a Labour seat for the whole of the post-second world war period. Jon Cruddas was first elected in 2001 with a 8,693 majority. He held the seat in 2005 although his majority fell slightly. Hornchurch had switched between Labour and the Tories since 1945. Labour's John Cryer held the seat between 1997 and 2005 when he lost to the Conservative James Brokenshire. Leading Labour left-winger Jon Cruddas faced a 5 per cent swing to the Tories, but hung on with a majority of 2,630.

Dagenham's economic history is intertwined with the history of the massive Ford motor works; however, the company stopped full car production in Dagenham in 2002. There is a relatively small industrial area around Rainham, home to Tilda Rice and Rainham Steel.

As part of the Thames Gateway Regeneration projects the area will benefit from redevelopment and improved transport links. The seat will be served by the new East London Transit bus service which comes into operation between 2010 and 2013, as well as the proposed extension to the Docklands Light Railway to Dagenham Docks.

John Cryer

Leyton and Wanstead

Boundary changes

Tel: 020 7219 7100
E-mail: john.cryer.mp@parliament.uk
Website: www.johncryer.co.uk

Date of birth: 11 April 1964; Son of late Bob Cryer, MP and of Ann Cryer, MP (qv)

Education: Oakbank School, Keighley; Hatfield Polytechnic (BA literature and history 1985); London College of Printing (Postgraduate Certificate Print Journalism 1988); Married Narinder Bains 1994 (2 sons 1 daughter)

Non-political career: Journalist: *Tribune* 1992-96, *Morning Star* 1989-92; Freelance journalist: *Labour Briefing* (editor), *Guardian, GPMU Journal, T&G Record*; Lloyd's of London Publications; Political officer: ASLEF 2005-06, Unite 2006-; Member: TGWU 1986-, NUJ 1988-, UCATT 1997-

Political career: Member for Hornchurch 1997-2005, for Leyton and Wanstead since 6 May 2010 general election; *Select Committees:* Member: Deregulation and Regulatory Reform 1997-2002; Member, Executive of Labour Euro Safeguards Committee; Press officer, Defend Clause Four Campaign 1995; Member, Co-operative Party; Secretary, Labour Against the Euro

Political interests: Employment, social security, education, further education, European Union, health, economic policy, industry, coal industry, transport; Australia, India, USA

Other organisations: Member: CND, Amnesty International, Transport on Water, Tibet Support Group, Keighley and Worth Valley Railway, RAF Hornchurch Association; Patron, St Francis Hospice; Member, Hornchurch Historical Society; Member: House of Commons Cricket Club, House of Commons Rugby Club, House of Commons Boxing Club; *Publications:* Co-author with Ann Cryer, Boldness be my Friend: Remembering Bob Cryer MP, 1996; Many articles mainly in political publications

Recreations: Swimming, reading, sport, old cars, cinema

John Cryer MP, House of Commons, London SW1A 0AA
Tel: 020 7219 7100 E-mail: john.cryer.mp@parliament.uk
Constituency: Tel: 07966 589833 Website: www.johncryer.co.uk

GENERAL ELECTION RESULT

		%
Cryer, J. (Lab)	17,511	43.6
Qureshi, F. (Lib Dem)	11,095	27.6
Northover, E. (Con)	8,928	22.2
Wood, G. (UKIP)	1,080	2.7
Gunstock, A. (Green)	562	1.4
Clift, J. (BNP)	561	1.4
Bhatti, S. (Christian)	342	0.9
Levin, M. (Ind Fed UK)	80	0.2
Majority	6,416	15.98
Electorate	63,541	
Turnout	40,159	63.20

CONSTITUENCY SNAPSHOT

Leyton and Wanstead was created in 1997, combining Leyton with parts of Wanstead and Woodford. Leyton had traditionally returned Labour MPs to Parliament. Bryan Magee was MP between 1974 and 1983 before being taken over by Harry Cohen. He became MP for Leyton and Wanstead in 1997.

In contrast, Wanstead and Woodford, the other ancestor of this constituency, was Conservative until it was abolished in 1997. Cohen's 2005 majority was a much-reduced, but still safe, 6,857. New MP John Cryer held the seat for Labour with a majority of 6,416 and 43.6 per cent of the vote.

The seat gained Snaresbrook and Wanstead partwards from Ilford North.

Leyton and Wanstead straddles the boroughs of Waltham Forest and Redbridge, though it takes the majority of its area from Waltham Forest. Within the constituency Leyton is a working-class area with inner-city traits, while Wanstead and Snaresbrook are more suburban.

The main sources of employment are in the public sector such as healthcare and the local authorities. The development of nearby Stratford as a transport hub for local, national and international services created jobs.

The south-west corner of the constituency touches the Lea Valley area, which is targeted for massive regeneration and development as part of the London 2012 Olympic Games plan.

Alex Cunningham

Stockton North

Boundary changes

Tel: 020 7219 3000
E-mail: alex.cunningham.mp@parliament.uk
Website: www.stockton-north.com

Labour

Date of birth: 1 May 1955

Education: Branksome Comprehensive, Darlington; Queen Elizabeth Sixth Form; Darlington College of Technology (Certificate journalism 1976); Married Evaline 1977 (2 sons)

Non-political career: Journalist: *Darlington and Stockton Times* 1974-76, *The Mail*, Hartlepool 1976-77, Radio Tees 1977-97, Radio Clyde 1979, *Evening Gazette* 1979-84; Public relations officer, British Gas 1984-89; Transco: Communications adviser 1995-2000; Head of communications 2000-02; Managing director, Tees Valley Communicators 2002-; National Union of Journalists: Member 1974-80, Father of Chapel 1977-79; Member, National Union of Public Employees/Unison 1980-; Cleveland County Council: Councillor 1984-97, Vice-chair Education Committee 1984-99, Chair, Standing Advisory Council for Religious Education 1984-99; Councillor, Stockton Borough Council 1999-; Council member, Museums, Libraries and Archives Council

Political career: Member for Stockton North since 6 May 2010 general election; Stockton North CLP: Press Officer 1984-, Chair, vice-chair, secretary 1985-95; Member, Co-operative Party 1986-

Political interests: Children's services, education, health, leisure, culture

Other organisations: Member: Arts Council England North East, Socialist Education Association 1984-

Recreations: Sport, reading, travel

Alex Cunningham MP, House of Commons, London SW1A 0AA
Tel: 020 7219 3000 E-mail: alex.cunningham.mp@parliament.uk
Constituency: 10 Lapwing Lane, Norton, Stockton on Tees TS20 1LT
Tel: 01642 551251 Website: www.stockton-north.com

GENERAL ELECTION RESULT

		%
Cunningham, A. (Lab)	16,923	42.9
Galletley, I. (Con)	10,247	25.9
Latham, P. (Lib Dem)	6,342	16.1
Macpherson, J. (BNP)	1,724	4.4
Cook, F. (Ind)*	1,577	4.0
Parkin, G. (UKIP)	1,556	3.9
Saul, I. (England)	1,129	2.9
Majority	6,676	16.90
Electorate	67,363	
Turnout	39,498	58.63

**Member of last parliament*

CONSTITUENCY SNAPSHOT

Stockton North has been a Labour seat since 1945. The last Conservative to sit in this seat was former Prime Minister Harold Macmillan, who was MP from 1924 to 1945, with the exception of a two-year break.

Although Labour's majority dropped from 21,357 in 1997 to 14,647 in 2001, the party's vote-share stayed more or less the same. MP Frank Cook's majority fell again in 2005, to 12,437. Frank Cook's de-selection as the Labour candidate and independent campaign didn't stop Alex Cunningham taking the seat with a 6,676 majority.

Boundary changes moved part-ward Bishopsgarth and Elm Tree to Stockton South whilst part-wards Newtown, Stockton Town centre, and Western Parishes became fully incorporated within this seat.

Stockton North is a mixture of urban and rural wards. The seat includes the north of Stockton town and Billingham, once home to the ICI chemicals plant.

Stockton North can be said to be dominated both physically, and to some extent economically, by the plant, one of the largest employers in the area. The plant is now owned by firms such as Tharp and Tioxide.

Stockton is a working-class region, with over half the population involved in manual occupations. Nearly one-fifth of the working population is involved in manufacturing industry, and Teesside Airport, which is within this seat, is also a major provider of local jobs.

James Cunningham

Coventry South (returning MP)

Boundary changes

Tel: 020 7219 6362
E-mail: sastrej@parliament.uk
Website: www.epolitix.com/Jim-Cunningham

Labour

Date of birth: 4 February 1941; Son of Adam and Elizabeth Cunningham

Education: Columba High School, Coatbridge; Tillycoultry College, Ruskin Courses (Labour movement, industrial law); Married Marion Douglas Podmore 1985 (1 son 1 daughter 1 stepson 1 stepdaughter)

Non-political career: Engineer Rolls-Royce 1965-88; MSF shop steward 1968-88; Coventry City Council: Councillor 1972-92, Leader of the Council 1988-92

Political career: Member for Coventry South East 1992-97, for Coventry South 1997-2010, for Coventry South (revised boundary) since 6 May 2010 general election; PPS to Mike O'Brien: as Solicitor General 2005-07, as Minister of State: Department for Work and Pensions 2007-08, Department of Energy and Climate Change 2008-09, Department of Health 2009-10; *Select Committees:* Member: Home Affairs 1993-97, Trade and Industry 1997-2001, Chairmen's Panel 1998-2001, Constitutional Affairs 2003-05, Office of the Deputy Prime Minister 2005, Procedure 2005-06; Chair Coventry South East CLP 1977-79

Political interests: Economic policy, European Union, industrial relations, NHS; USA, Eastern Europe, Russia

Recreations: Walking, reading, historical buildings

James Cunningham MP, House of Commons, London SW1A 0AA
Tel: 020 7219 6362 Fax: 020 7219 4907
E-mail: sastrej@parliament.uk
Constituency: Rooms 9-11 Palmer House, Palmer Lane, Burges, Coventry, Warwickshire CV1 1HL Tel: 024 7655 3159
Fax: 024 7655 3159 Website: www.epolitix.com/Jim-Cunningham

GENERAL ELECTION RESULT

		%
Cunningham, J. (Lab)*	19,197	41.8
Foster, K. (Con)	15,352	33.4
Patton, B. (Lib Dem)	8,278	18.0
Taylor, M. (UKIP)	1,767	3.9
Griffiths, J. (TUSC)	691	1.5
Gray, S. (Green)	639	1.4
Majority	3,845	8.37
Electorate	73,652	
Turnout	45,924	62.35

**Member of last parliament*

CONSTITUENCY SNAPSHOT

Coventry South was created from Coventry South West and South East in 1997. The boundary changes signalled the end of the Conservative presence in Coventry. Coventry South West had contained most of the city's middle-class voters and was the party's seat in the city between 1979 and 1997.

James Cunningham won comfortably for Labour in 1997. In the 2005 general election Coventry South followed the pattern across the West Midlands, with Cunningham retaining his seat on a slightly reduced majority. Cunningham was re-elected with a majority of 3,845 in 2010 giving Labour a 41.8 per cent share of the vote.

Boundary changes moved parts of Earlsdon and Westwood formerly in Coventry North West and parts of Binley and Willenhall and St Michael's previously in Coventry North East inside Coventry South's boundaries. The inclusion of all of Binley and Willenhall extends Coventry South's north-western boundary.

Coventry South covers a mixture of working- and middle-class residential areas. Wainbody and Earlsdon contain some of the most affluent areas in Coventry and include desirable suburban family houses, the King Henry VIII School and Warwick University. However, the constituency also covers traditionally working-class areas such as Binley and Willenhall.

Large numbers of constituents work in education and manufacturing, although the dented and declining motor industry has affected jobs here.

Tony Cunningham

Workington (returning MP)

Boundary changes

Tel: 020 7219 8344
E-mail: cunninghamt@parliament.uk

Date of birth: 16 September 1952; Son of late Daniel Cunningham, docker, and Bessie, neé Lister

Education: Workington Grammar School; Liverpool University (BA history and politics 1975); Didsbury College (PGCE 1976); TESL; Married Anne Margaret Gilmore 1984 (1 daughter 1 son 1 stepdaughter 1 stepson)

Non-political career: Teacher: Alsager Comprehensive School 1976-80, Mikunguni Trade School, Zanzibar 1980-82, Netherhall School, Maryport 1983-94; Chief executive Human Rights NGO 1999-2000; NUT 1976-94: Local secretary 1985-94; AEEU 1993-; Allerdale Borough Council: Councillor 1987-94, Leader 1992-94

Political career: Member for Workington 2001-10, for Workington (revised boundary) since 6 May 2010 general election; PPS to Elliot Morley as Minister of State, Department for Environment, Food and Rural Affairs 2003-05; Assistant Government Whip 2005-08; Government Whip 2008-10; *Select Committees:* Member: European Scrutiny 2001-04, Catering 2001-05, Selection 2006-10; European Parliament: MEP for Cumbria and North Lancashire 1994-99. Contested North West Region 1999 election

Political interests: Third World, education, tourism, sport, small businesses; Sub-Saharan Africa

Other organisations: Patron: Mines Advisory Group 1994-, VSO 1994-; Station Road Working Men's, John Street

Recreations: Sport, running, reading, Workington RFC

Tony Cunningham MP, House of Commons, London SW1A 0AA
Tel: 020 7219 8344 Fax: 020 7219 1947
E-mail: cunninghamt@parliament.uk
Constituency: Moss Bay House, 40 Peart Road, Derwent Howe, Workington, Cumbria CA14 3YT Tel: 01900 65815
Fax: 01900 68348

GENERAL ELECTION RESULT

		%
Cunningham, T. (Lab)*	17,865	45.5
Pattinson, J. (Con)	13,290	33.9
Collins, S. (Lib Dem)	5,318	13.6
Wingfield, M. (BNP)	1,496	3.8
Lee, S. (UKIP)	876	2.2
Logan, R. (England)	414	1.1
Majority	4,575	11.65
Electorate	59,607	
Turnout	39,259	65.86

**Member of last parliament*

CONSTITUENCY SNAPSHOT

Labour has won every general election here since 1918. However, in the 1976 by-election the Conservative candidate Richard Page was elected to office. The seat was reclaimed in 1979 by Labour's Dale Campbell-Savours, who held the seat until 2001, handing it to Tony Cunningham upon his retirement.

Campbell-Savours built up his majority to over 19,000 in 1997, a sizable increase on the 9,600 obtained in 1992. Cunningham received less support in 2001 and still less in 2005, winning a 6,895 majority. Cunningham was re-elected in 2010 with a smaller majority of 4,575.

The seat gained two wards and a part-ward from Penrith and the Border, and loses the wards of Crummock, Dalton, Derwent Valley and Keswick to Copeland.

Much of this seat is made up of the Lake District's National Park and the glorious surrounding countryside including Workington itself.

The decline in coalmining and steelworks has led to a demand for opportunities for new employment. Workington has attracted new industries such as footwear, plastics, electronics and fibre manufacturing.

Despite the rural nature of the area only a small percentage of people work in agriculture, with most of the countryside used for commercial purposes. The natural beauty of the area attracts millions of visitors every year, giving many of the population work in the service industry supporting tourism.

Margaret Curran

Glasgow East

No boundary changes

Tel: 020 7219 3000
E-mail: margaret.curran.mp@parliament.uk
Website: www.margaretcurranmsp.co.uk

Date of birth: 24 November 1958; Daughter of late James Curran, labourer, and late Rose Curran, cleaner

Education: Our Lady and St Francis, Glasgow; Glasgow University (MA history and economic history 1981); Dundee College (Post-graduate Certificate community education 1982); Married Robert Murray (2 sons)

Non-political career: Social work department, Strathclyde Regional Council: Welfare rights officer 1982-83, Community worker 1983-87, Senior community worker 1987-89; Lecturer in community education, Strathclyde University 1989-99; Member, Transport and General Workers' Union (TGWU)

Political career: Contested Glasgow East by-election 24 July 2008. Member for Glasgow East since 6 May 2010 general election; MSP for Glasgow Baillieston constituency since 6 May 1999: Scottish Labour: Deputy Whip 1999-2000; Deputy Minister for Social Justice 2000-02; Minister for: Social Justice 2002-03, Communities 2003-04, Parliamentary Business 2004-07; Shadow Cabinet Secretary: for Justice 2007, for Health and Wellbeing 2007-08, without Portfolio with special responsibility for Policy Development 2008-09; Former chair, Scottish Organisation of Labour Students; Election agent to Mohammad Sarwar 1997 general election; Member, Scottish Labour Women's Caucus

Political interests: Social inclusion, community empowerment, women's issues, neighbourhood regeneration housing; Ireland, Scotland, USA

Other organisations: Member, Amnesty International; *Publications:* Book references in community education journals

Recreations: Films, books, country music, theatre

Margaret Curran MP, House of Commons, London SW1A 0AA
Tel: 020 7219 3000 E-mail: margaret.curran.mp@parliament.uk
Constituency: Westwood Business Centre, 69 Aberdalgie Road, Glasgow G34 9HJ Tel: 0141-771 4844 Fax: 0141-771 4877
Website: www.margaretcurranmsp.co.uk

GENERAL ELECTION RESULT

		%	+/-
Curran, M. (Lab)	19,797	61.6	1.0
Mason, J. (SNP)*	7,957	24.7	7.8
Ward, K. (Lib Dem)	1,617	5.0	-6.8
Khan, H. (Con)	1,453	4.5	-2.4
Finnie, J. (BNP)	677	2.1	
Curran, F. (SSP)	454	1.4	-2.1
Thackeray, A. (UKIP)	209	0.7	
Majority	11,840	36.81	
Electorate	61,516		
Turnout	32,164	52.29	

**Member of last parliament*

CONSTITUENCY SNAPSHOT

Until 1997 most of this seat was known as Glasgow Provan. Jimmy Wray became the seat's Labour MP in 1987 and achieved a majority of nearly 15,000 in 1997 for the new seat of Glasgow Baillieston. In 2001 Jimmy Wray's majority fell to under 10,000.

Glasgow Baillieston was one of the least changed of the old constituencies in the 2005 boundary review, surviving intact as Glasgow East. The seat gained the Shettleston, Tollcross Park, Braidfauld, and Parkhead wards from the Shettleston division.

In 2005 Jimmy Wray retired and David Marshall, MP for the old Shettleston, took the seat for Labour with a 13,507 majority. Marshall stepped down as MP in June 2008. In the subsequent by-election, the SNP's John Mason won the seat by 365 votes. Mason couldn't hold on to the seat at the general election as MSP Margaret Curran won for Labour with a 3,934 majority.

Glasgow East is a largely working class residential seat and contains the vast and notorious Easterhouse council estate. It does however have some more upmarket housing areas such as the smart detached homes around Mount Vernon

Celtic Park will host the opening ceremony of the 2014 Commonwealth Games and the seat will also host the cycling events. A second swimming pool is to be built in Tollcross.

Nic Dakin

Scunthorpe

Boundary changes

Tel: 020 7219 3000
E-mail: nick.dakin.mp@parliament.uk
Website: www.nicdakin.com

Married Audrey (3 children)

Non-political career: John Leggott College: Vice-principal, Principal; North Lincolnshire Council: Councillor, Council Leader

Political career: Member for Scunthorpe since 6 May 2010 general election

Recreations: Scunthorpe United F.C

Nic Dakin MP, House of Commons, London SW1A 0AA
Tel: 020 7219 3000 E-mail: nick.dakin.mp@parliament.uk
Constituency: c/o Labour Party, Kinsley Labour Club, Cole Street, Scunthorpe, North Lincolnshire DN15 6QS Tel: 07825 632025
Website: www.nicdakin.com

GENERAL ELECTION RESULT

		%
Dakin, N. (Lab)	14,640	39.5
Johnson, C. (Con)	12,091	32.7
Poole, N. (Lib Dem)	6,774	18.3
Collins, J. (UKIP)	1,686	4.6
Ward, D. (BNP)	1,447	3.9
Hurst, N. (Green)	396	1.1
Majority	2,549	6.88
Electorate	63,089	
Turnout	37,034	58.70

CONSTITUENCY SNAPSHOT

Scunthorpe was created in 1997, mainly from the Glanford and Scunthorpe seat which had been won by Labour's Elliot Morley in 1987.

Morley's majority in 1987 was just 512. He expanded his lead in 1992 to more than 8,000. Morley's first election in the revised Scunthorpe seat left him with a 14,173 majority. This has shrunk in the two general elections since but Labour's lead remained 8,963 in 2005.

In 2010 Nic Dakin held the seat for Labour with a 39.5 per cent share of the vote.

Boundary changes were minimal.

The constituency encompasses the famous Lincolnshire steel town itself and a large expanse of rural North Lincolnshire to the south and east.

Scunthorpe is a town founded on the steel industry in the mid-19th century using local ironstone, and its fortunes have risen and fallen with the industry.

There has been a substantial decline since the 1980. Other industries have moved in to fill the gaps, including food, electronics and chemicals companies. Lloyds Banking Group has a large call centre here. Despite this, unemployment is high.

Simon Danczuk

Rochdale

Boundary changes

Tel: 020 7219 3000
E-mail: simon.danczuk.mp@parliament.uk
Website: www.simondanczuk.com

Labour

Date of birth: 24 October 1966

Education: Gawthorpe Comprehensive School, Padiham; Lancaster University (economics and sociology 1991); Married (1 son 1 daughter)

Non-political career: Production worker, Main Gas, Padiham 1982-86; Labourer, ICI Factory, Darwen 1986-88; Barman, ICI Sports and Social Club, Darwen 1988-91; Research assistant, Sociology Department, Lancaster University 1991-93; Research officer, Bolton Bury Training and Enterprise Council 1993-95; Research consultant, Opinion Research Co-operation International 1995-97; Research co-ordinator, Big Issue in the North Trust 1997-98; Media and public relations officer, Big Issue in the North 1998-99; Managing director, Vision Twentyone 1999-; Member: AEU 1982-86, GMB 1987-; Councillor, Blackburn with Darwen Council 1993-2001

Political career: Member for Rochdale since 6 May 2010 general election; Secretary, Rossendale and Darwen Labour Party 1991-93; Member, North West Labour Party Regional Board 1993-2007

Political interests: Social and economic regeneration, environment, housing; Middle East, Palestine

Other organisations: Executive committee member, Labour Friends of Palestine and the Middle East; Member, Royal Society of Arts 2009-; Rochdale Labour Club; Milnrow Cricket Club

Simon Danczuk MP, House of Commons, London SW1A 0AA
Tel: 020 7219 3000 E-mail: simon.danczuk.mp@parliament.uk
Constituency: Rochdale Labour, 89-91 Oldham Road,
Rochdale OL16 5QR Tel: 01706 750135
Website: www.simondanczuk.com

GENERAL ELECTION RESULT

		%
Danczuk, S. (Lab)	16,699	36.4
Rowen, P. (Lib Dem)*	15,810	34.4
Dean, M. (Con)	8,305	18.1
Jackson, C. (NF)	2,236	4.9
Denby, C. (UKIP)	1,999	4.4
Salim, M. (IZB)	545	1.2
Whitehead, J. (Ind)	313	0.7
Majority	889	1.94
Electorate	78,952	
Turnout	45,907	58.15

**Member of last parliament*

CONSTITUENCY SNAPSHOT

Rochdale has been held by all three major parties since 1945. The 1951 Conservative victory brought about a period of seven years when a Tory MP represented the town. Labour then held the seat for a 14-year period, before the Liberal Cyril Smith was elected in 1972. Smith held Rochdale for 20 years before retiring in 1992.

Liz Lynne held the seat for the Liberal Democrats in 1992 with a majority of 1,839. Labour's candidate Lorna Fitzsimons ousted Lynne with a 4.8 per cent swing in 1997.

Lib Dem Paul Rowen defeated Fitzsimons at the 2005 election with a 7.7 per cent swing, and a majority of 444. Simon Danczuk took Rochdale back for Labour in 2010 by the narrowest of margins, just 889 votes.

The seat gained four part-wards from Oldham and Saddleworth, and one part-ward from Heywood and Middleton. It lost two part-wards to Heywood and Middleton.

The birthplace of the co-operative movement, Rochdale is a manufacturing centre where engineering and textiles are the most important industries.

The constituency consists of the industrial town of Rochdale as well as the attractive, Pennine-hugging town of Littleborough and its environs.

Rochdale will benefit from the extension of the Metrolink tram system, due to come into operation in 2011.

Rt Hon **Alistair Darling**

Edinburgh South West (returning MP)

No boundary changes

Tel: 020 7219 4584
E-mail: darlinga@parliament.uk
Website: www.alistairdarlingmp.org.uk

Date of birth: 28 November 1953

Education: Loretto School; Aberdeen University (LLB 1976); Married Margaret McQueen Vaughan 1986 (1 son 1 daughter)

Non-political career: Solicitor 1978-82; Advocate 1984-; Lothian Regional Council: Councillor 1982-87, Chair, Lothian Region Transport Committee 1986-87

Political career: Member for Edinburgh Central 1987-2005, for Edinburgh South West since 5 May 2005 general election; Opposition Spokesperson for: Home Affairs 1988-92, Treasury, Economic Affairs and the City 1992-96; Sponsored Solicitors (Scotland) Act 1988 (Private Member's Bill); Shadow Chief Secretary to the Treasury 1996-97; Chief Secretary to the Treasury 1997-98; Secretary of State for: Social Security/Work and Pensions 1998-2002, Transport 2002-06, Scotland 2003-06, Trade and Industry 2006-07; Chancellor of the Exchequer 2007-10; Shadow Chancellor of the Exchequer 2010-; Member, Labour Party's Economic Commission 1994-97

Political interests: Transport, education, health, economic policy, constitution

Other organisations: Governor European Investment Bank 2007-10; PC 1997

Rt Hon Alistair Darling MP, House of Commons, London SW1A 0AA Tel: 020 7219 4584 E-mail: darlinga@parliament.uk
Constituency: 22A Rutland Square, Edinburgh EH1 2BB
Tel: 0131-476 2552 Fax: 0131-656 0368
Website: www.alistairdarlingmp.org.uk

GENERAL ELECTION RESULT

		%	+/-
Darling, A. (Lab)*	19,473	42.8	3.1
Rust, J. (Con)	11,026	24.3	1.0
McKay, T. (Lib Dem)	8,194	18.0	-3.0
Stewart, K. (SNP)	5,530	12.2	1.6
Cooney, C. (Green)	872	1.9	-1.5
Fox, C. (SSP)	319	0.7	-0.6
Bellamy, C. (Comm League)	48	0.1	
Majority	8,447	18.58	
Electorate	66,359		
Turnout	45,462	68.51	

**Member of last parliament*

CONSTITUENCY SNAPSHOT

Malcolm Rifkind lost his 23-year tenure of Edinburgh Pentlands in 1997, on the night the Conservatives lost all their Scottish seats. Dr Lynda Clark took Pentlands for Labour. In 2001 Rifkind cut Clark's majority in half.

The seat was enlarged and renamed Edinburgh South West in 2005. The seat retained the boundaries of Edinburgh Pentlands, except in the north east, where it gained the city wards Balerno and Baberton, but lost Fairmilehead, South Morningside, North Morningside/Grange and Merchiston to Edinburgh South. At the general election Lynda Clark stepped aside for Alistair Darling, whose Edinburgh Central seat was abolished. He held the seat on a slightly reduced majority of 7,242. Alistair Darling has a respectable majority of 8,447 in this seat with an improved vote-share on 2005.

Set against the backdrop of the Pentland hills, this constituency contains a mixture of city, suburban and rural areas. There are middle-class residential areas such as Colinton and Balerno, as well as the affluent new housing developments along the A70 road south to Lanark.

The seat contains Napier University and Heart of Midlothian Football Club is based at Tynecastle Stadium in Gorgie.Transport Initiatives Edinburgh is working on Edinburgh's new tram system. The first phase of the development will be a 22-stop tram route starting from Newhaven, going through Princes Street, into the constituency with stops at Haymarket and Murrayfield, before terminating at Edinburgh Airport.

Edward Davey

Kingston and Surbiton ***(returning MP)***

Boundary changes

Tel: 020 7219 3512
E-mail: daveye@parliament.uk
Website: www.edwarddavey.co.uk

Date of birth: 25 December 1965; Son of late John George Davey, solicitor, and of late Nina Joan Davey (neé Stanbrook), teacher

Education: Nottingham High School; Jesus College, Oxford (BA philosophy, politics and economics 1988); Birkbeck College, London (MSc economics 1993); Married Emily Gasson 2005 (1 son)

Non-political career: Senior economics adviser to Liberal Democrat MPs 1989-93; Management consultant, Omega Partners 1993-97; Director, Omega Partners Postal 1996-97

Political career: Member for Kingston and Surbiton 1997-2010, for Kingston and Surbiton (revised boundary) since 6 May 2010 general election; Liberal Democrat: London Whip 1997-2000, Spokesperson for: the Treasury (Public Spending and Taxation) 1997-99, Economy 1999-2001, London 2000-03, Shadow Chief Secretary to the Treasury 2001-02, Spokesperson for Office of the Deputy Prime Minister 2002-05, Shadow Secretary of State for: Education and Skills 2005-06, Trade and Industry 2006, Chief of Staff to Sir Menzies Campbell as Leader of the Liberal Democrats 2006-07; Shadow Secretary of State for Foreign and Commonwealth Affairs 2007-10; Parliamentary Under-Secretary of State (Minister for Employment Relations, Consumer and Postal Affairs), Department for Business, Innovation and Skills 2010-; *Select Committees:* Member: Procedure 1997-2000, Treasury 1999-2001, Treasury (Treasury Sub-Committee) 1999-2001; Chair, Costing Group (costing all policies for manifesto) 1992 and 1997 general elections; Member, Federal Policy Committee 1994-95; Liberal Democrat Policy Group (Economics, Tax and Benefits and Transport); Member, Association of Liberal Democrat Councillors; Chair Campaigns and Communications Committee 2006-

Political interests: Taxation, economics, internet, employment, environment, modernisation of Parliament; Latin America

Other organisations: Patron: Jigsaw, Kingston Special Needs Project; Goodwill Ambassador for Children of Peace; Trustee, Kidsout; Royal Humane Society Honourable Testimonial; Chief Constable London Transport Police Commendation 1994; Royal Humane Society 1994; Member National Liberal Club, Surbiton; *Publications:* Making MPs Work for our Money: Reforming Budget Scrutiny (Centre for Reform), 2000

Recreations: Music, walking, swimming

Edward Davey MP, House of Commons, London SW1A 0AA
Tel: 020 7219 3512 Fax: 020 7219 0250
E-mail: daveye@parliament.uk
Constituency: Liberal Democrats, 21 Berrylands Road, Surbiton, Surrey KT5 8QX Tel: 020 8288 0161 Fax: 020 8288 1090
Website: www.edwarddavey.co.uk

GENERAL ELECTION RESULT

		%
Davey, E. (Lib Dem)*	28,428	49.8
Whately, H. (Con)	20,868	36.5
Freedman, M. (Lab)	5,337	9.3
Greensted, J. (UKIP)	1,450	2.5
Walker, C. (Green)	555	1.0
Drummer, M. (Loony)	247	0.4
May, T. (Christian)	226	0.4
Majority	7,560	13.24
Electorate	81,116	
Turnout	57,111	70.41

**Member of last parliament*

CONSTITUENCY SNAPSHOT

A Conservative seat, Richard Tracey held Surbiton from 1983 to 1992 and Norman Lamont held Kingston until 1997, when Liberal Democrat Edward Davey won by just 56 votes.

In 2001 Davey secured a 15,676 majority, but it almost halved in 2005 to 8,966. One of several Liberal Democrat constituencies in south west London, Ed Davey held the seat with a majority of 7,560.

Beverley ward is now entirely within the seats boundaries having previously been shared with Richmond Park.

Kingston and Surbiton's expanses of semi-detached family homes are mainly inhabited by high-earning, upper-middle-class residents.

The constituency is largely residential although Kingston's town centre attracts shoppers from a wider area.

The A3 passes through the constituency, providing good links with the M25. South West Trains take about half an hour to get to central London. The closest Tube stations are a bus journey away in either Richmond or Wimbledon.

Wayne David

Caerphilly ***(returning MP)***

Boundary changes

Tel: 020 7219 8152
E-mail: davidw@parliament.uk
Website: www.waynedavid.labour.co.uk

Date of birth: 1 July 1957; Son of David Haydn David, teacher, and Edna Amelia, née Jones, housewife

Education: Cynffig Comprehensive School, Kenfig Hill, Mid Glamorgan; University College, Cardiff (BA history and Welsh history 1979); University College, Swansea (economic history research 1979-82); University College, Cardiff (PGCE FE 1983); Married Catherine Thomas 1991 (divorced 2007)

Non-political career: History teacher Brynteg Comprehensive School 1983-85; Tutor organiser Workers' Educational Association South Wales District 1985-89; Policy adviser youth policy Wales Youth Agency 1999-2001; Member: MSF 1983-2004, AEEU 1998-2004, AMICUS 2004-07, UNITY 2007-; Cefn Cribwr Community Council: Councillor 1985-91, Chair 1986-87

Political career: Member for Caerphilly 2001-10, for Caerphilly (revised boundary) since 6 May 2010 general election; Team PPS, Ministry of Defence 2005; PPS to Adam Ingram as Minister of State, Ministry of Defence 2005-06; Assistant Government Whip 2007-08; Parliamentary Under-Secretary of State, Wales Office 2008-10; *Select Committees:* Member: European Scrutiny 2001-07, Standards and Privileges 2004-05, Joint Committee on Conventions 2006, Welsh Affairs 2007; European Parliment: MEP for South Wales 1989-94, for South Wales Central 1994-99: Vice-president Socialist Group 1994-98, Leader European Parliamentary Labour Party 1994-98; Contested Rhondda 1999 National Assembly for Wales election; Ex-officio Member of Labour Party NEC 1994-98

Political interests: European affairs, economy, education; Poland, Bulgaria, Belgium

Other organisations: President: Aber Valley Male Voice Choir 2001-; Council for Wales of Voluntary Youth Services 2002-; Caerphilly Local History Society 2006-; Vice-president Cardiff UN Association 1989-; Fellow Cardiff University 1995; Bargoed Labour Club; *Publications:* Contributor: The Future of Europe, Problems and Issues for the 21st Century (1996); Remaining True (biography of Ness Edwards MP) (2006)

Recreations: Music, playing the oboe

Wayne David MP, House of Commons, London SW1A 0AA
Tel: 020 7219 8152 Fax: 020 7219 1751
E-mail: davidw@parliament.uk
Constituency: Community Council Offices, Newport Road, Bedwas, Caerphilly, Mid Glamorgan CF83 8YB Tel: 029 2088 1061
Fax: 029 2088 1954 Website: www.waynedavid.labour.co.uk

GENERAL ELECTION RESULT

		%
David, W. (Lab)*	17,377	44.9
Caulfield, M. (Con)	6,622	17.1
Whittle, L. (PIC)	6,460	16.7
David, K. (Lib Dem)	5,688	14.7
Reid, L. (BNP)	1,635	4.2
Jenkins, T. (UKIP)	910	2.4
Majority	10,755	27.80
Electorate	62,134	
Turnout	38,692	62.27

**Member of last parliament*

CONSTITUENCY SNAPSHOT

Caerphilly has been won by Labour at every election since its creation after the First World War. The only brief period when Labour did not hold the seat was due to the SDP defection of Ednyfed Hudson Davies in 1981. He stood down in 1983.

Between 1983 and 2001 this seat was held at Westminster by Ron Davies who led the successful devolution campaign.

The former leader of the Labour group in the European Parliament, Wayne David, succeeded him in Caerphilly in 2001. Mr David retained the seat with a 14,425 majority in 2010.

In 2005 there was a small swing back to Labour from Plaid Cymru and David won a majority of 15,359. David was re-elected in 2010 with a 10,755 majority.

Boundary changes moved Aberbargoed and Maesycwmmer into Islwyn.

This constituency covers the lower half of the Rhymney Valley and includes areas of upland and rural countryside. It is named after its main town which is dominated by Caerphilly Castle.

Many of the small towns and villages dotted along the valley owe their existence to the former mines and iron works.

The old industries have gone to be replaced by light industry.

The southern part of the seat has become commuter belt for a growing Cardiff. The parts of the constituency closest to Cardiff are enjoying an economic upturn but there remain serious socio-economic problems in the older industrial northern end of the division.

Ian Davidson

Glasgow South West ***(returning MP)***

No boundary changes

Tel: 020 7219 3610
E-mail: iandavidsonmp@parliament.uk
Website: www.epolitix.com/ian-davidson

Labour/Co-operative

Date of birth: 8 September 1950; Son of Graham Davidson and Elizabeth Crowe

Education: Jedburgh Grammar School; Galashiels Academy; Edinburgh University (MA); Jordanhill College; Married Morag Christine Ann Mackinnon 1978 (1 son 1 daughter)

Non-political career: Sabbatical Chair National Association of Labour Students 1973-74; Researcher for Janey Buchan, MEP 1978-85; Project manager Community Service Volunteers 1985-92; Member ASTMS, MSF, AMICUS, UNITE; Strathclyde Regional Council: Councillor 1978-92, Chair, Education Committee 1986-92

Political career: Member for Glasgow Govan 1992-97, for Glasgow Pollok 1997-2005, for Glasgow South West since 5 May 2005 general election; *Select Committees:* Member: Selection 1997-99, Public Accounts 1997-2010, Scottish Affairs 2005-10; Member Co-operative Party; Secretary: Tribune Group, Trade Union Group of Labour MPs 1998-2002; Chair Co-operative Parliamentary Group 1998-99; Founder and Chair Labour Against the Euro 2002-; Chair Scottish Regional Group of Labour MPs 2003-04

Political interests: Local and regional government, international development, local economic development, defence, co-operative movement, trade and industry, trade unions, shipbuilding, Europe, poverty, euro (against); Africa, Europe, Commonwealth, USA, Japan, British Overseas Territories

Recreations: Family, sport, distance running, swimming, rugby

Ian Davidson MP, House of Commons, London SW1A 0AA
Tel: 020 7219 3610 Fax: 020 7219 2238
E-mail: iandavidsonmp@parliament.uk
Constituency: 3 Kilmuir Drive, Glasgow G46 8BW Tel: 0141-621 2216
Fax: 0141-621 2154 Website: www.epolitix.com/ian-davidson

GENERAL ELECTION RESULT

		%	+/-
Davidson, I. (Lab/Co-op)*	19,863	62.5	2.4
Stephens, C. (SNP)	5,192	16.3	1.0
Nelson, I. (Lib Dem)	2,870	9.0	-2.6
Forrest, M. (Con)	2,084	6.6	0.8
Sheridan, T. (TUSC)	931	2.9	
Orr, D. (BNP)	841	2.7	
Majority	14,671	46.16	
Electorate	58,182		
Turnout	31,781	54.62	

**Member of last parliament*

CONSTITUENCY SNAPSHOT

Glasgow South West was created in the 2005 boundary changes and is largely the old Pollok seat. Ian Davidson became that seat's MP in 1997.

The 2005 boundary changes which brought Govan, Ibrox and Mosspark into the Glasgow South West seat did not alter its political character. At the general election Davidson was the only Glaswegian MP to improve on his notional majority from 2001 as he was returned with a majority of 44.8 per cent. Ian Davidson retained the seat in 2010 with a 14,671 majority and 62 per cent of the vote.

The decline of shipbuilding hit the northern part of this Clydeside seat very hard, though Govan is home to one of Glasgow's two remaining shipyards, which is crucially dependent on Royal Navy and Ministry of Defence contracts.

The Clydeside areas of Ibrox and Govan are the constituency's most deprived. There are some better estates towards the old pit village at Nitshill.

The area is marked by post-war social housing and industrial decline, although one of the country's first ever industrial estates at Hillingdon is still going strong.

David Davies

Monmouth (returning MP)

No boundary changes

Tel: 020 7219 8360
E-mail: daviesd@parliament.uk
Website: www.david-daviesmp.co.uk

Conservative

Date of birth: 27 July 1970; Son of Peter and Kathleen Davies

Education: Bassaleg Comprehensive, Newport; Married Aliz Harnisfoger 2003 (1 daughter 1 son)

Non-political career: British Steel Corporation 1988-89; Youth hostel manager, USA; Casual work in Australia 1989-91; Manager, Burrow Heath Ltd (forwarder and tea importers) 1991-99

Political career: Contested Bridgend 1997 general election. Member for Monmouth since 5 May 2005 general election; *Select Committees:* Member: Welsh Affairs 2005-10, Home Affairs 2007-10, Home Affairs Sub-Committee 2008-09; National Assembly for Wales: AM for Monmouth constituency 1999-2007: Deputy Leader/Business Secretary, Welsh Conservative Party 1999; Chief Whip, Welsh Conservative Party 1999-2001; Organiser for anti-Assembly 'No' Campaign 1997; Campaign manager for Rod Richards as leader of Welsh Conservative Party 1998

Political interests: Home affairs, including prisons and sentencing, defence, homeland security; Australia, France, Hungary, Germany, Iran, Israel

Other organisations: President NSPCC (south east Wales branch); Special Constable British Transport Police 2007-; Oriental (London); Chepstow Conservative; Abergavenny Conservative; Usk Conservative; Monmouth Conservative

Recreations: Surfing, history, languages

David Davies MP, House of Commons, London SW1A 0AA
Tel: 020 7219 8360 Fax: 020 7219 2806
E-mail: daviesd@parliament.uk
Constituency: The Grange, 16 Maryport Street, Usk, Monmouthshire NP15 1AB Tel: 01291 672817 Fax: 01291 672737
Website: www.david-daviesmp.co.uk

GENERAL ELECTION RESULT

		%	+/-
Davies, D. (Con)*	22,466	48.3	1.5
Sandison, H. (Lab)	12,041	25.9	-11.0
Blakebrough, M. (Lib Dem)	9,026	19.4	6.6
Clark, J. (PIC)	1,273	2.7	0.6
Rowe, D. (UKIP)	1,126	2.4	1.2
Millson, S. (Green)	587	1.3	
Majority	10,425	22.41	
Electorate	62,768		
Turnout	46,519	74.11	

**Member of last parliament*

CONSTITUENCY SNAPSHOT

The seat has changed between labour and Conservatives since 1966.

A by-election in 1991 saw Labour's Huw Edwards hold the seat until the general election in 1992 when he was then defeated by Conservative Roger Evans. Huw Edwards regained the seat in 1997 and 2001. He then lost the seat for the Labour party in 2005 to Conservative David Davies.

His 5.4 per cent swing gained him a 4,527 majority. It was the first general election seat won in Wales by the Conservatives since the 1992 election. Davies increased the Tory majority to 10,425 in 2010.

This is a largely rural constituency in east Wales bordering England. Its main population centre is Monmouth itself. The other main towns are Abergavenny and Usk.

There are many commuters who head over the improved Severn links from its southern areas to jobs in Bristol. Many other commuters head to Newport.

The area supports a rural economy with farming and a developing tourist industry providing local jobs.

Geraint Davies

Swansea West

No boundary changes

Tel: 020 7219 3000
E-mail: geraint.davies.mp@parliament.uk
Website: www.geraintdavies.org.uk

Labour/Co-operative

Date of birth: 3 May 1960; Son of David Thomas Morgan Davies, civil servant, and of Betty Ferrer Davies

Education: Llanishen Comprehensive, Cardiff; JCR President, Jesus College, Oxford (BA philosophy, politics and economics 1982); Married Dr Vanessa Fry 1991 (3 daughters)

Non-political career: Sales and Marketing Trainee; Group Product Manager, Unilever 1982-88; Marketing Manager, Colgate Palmolive Ltd 1988-89; Managing Partner, Pure Crete 1989-97; Chair, Flood Risk Management Wales, Environment Agency 2005-; Member, GMB; Councillor, Croydon Council 1986-97: Chair, Housing Committee 1994-96, Council Leader 1996-97; Governor, Dylan Thomas Community School

Political career: Contested Croydon South 1987 and Croydon Central 1992 general elections. Member for Croydon Central 1997-2005, for Swansea West since 6 May 2010 general election; Team PPS, Department for Constitutional Affairs 2003-05; *Select Committees:* Member: Public Accounts 1997-2003; Chair, Labour Finance and Industry Group 1998-2005; Member Co-operative Party

Political interests: Treasury, trade and industry, housing, children's issues, transport, environment, human rights, equality; Crete, Wales

Other organisations: Royal Humane Society Award for saving a man's life; Ruskin House, Croydon

Recreations: Family, singing

Geraint Davies MP, House of Commons, London SW1A 0AA
E-mail: geraint.davies.mp@parliament.uk
Constituency: 31 High Street, Swansea SA1 1LG Tel: 07552 835929
Website: www.geraintdavies.org.uk

GENERAL ELECTION RESULT

		%	+/-
Davies, G. (Lab/Co-op)	12,335	34.7	-7.1
May, P. (Lib Dem)	11,831	33.2	
Kinzett, R. (Con)	7,407	20.8	4.9
Roberts, H. (PlC)	1,437	4.0	-2.4
Bateman, A. (SOTBTH)	910	2.6	
Jenkins, T. (UKIP)	716	2.0	0.2
Ross, K. (Green)	404	1.1	-1.1
McCloy, I. (Ind)	374	1.1	
Williams, R. (TUSC)	179	0.5	
Majority	504	1.42	
Electorate	61,334		
Turnout	35,593	58.03	

CONSTITUENCY SNAPSHOT

Apart from a brief Conservative interlude from 1959-64, this has been a Labour seat since the Second World War. Alan Williams won it back for Labour in 1964 and has won every general election contest since. He became Father of the House after the 2005 general election and will stand down in 2010.

After a long period where Alan Williams enjoyed large majorities the seat has become less secure for Labour. At the 2005 general election the Liberal Democrats achieved a 9.6 per cent swing to reduce Williams' majority to 4,269. The Lib Dems came close to taking this normally safe Labour seat in 2010 but Geraint Davies won the election by just 504 votes.

The City and County of Swansea is a mixture of dramatic coastlines, areas of outstanding natural beauty, commerce and industrial activity.

The area is well served by the fast rail link to London, the M4 motorway and sea links to Ireland. The city has been described as the gateway to west Wales and occupies a strategic position in the historical, political and economic development of Wales.

This western division includes much of the centre of Wales' second city, including Swansea University and the developing Maritime Quarter on the west bank of the Tawe. The seat also contains some of the city's more prosperous suburbs.

Glyn Davies

Montgomeryshire

Boundary changes

Tel: 020 7219 3000
E-mail: glyn.davies.mp@parliament.uk
Website: glyndaviesam.blogspot.com

Conservative

Date of birth: 16 February 1944

Education: Llanfair Caerinian High School; University College of Wales, Aberyswyth (diploma international law and relations 1995); Married (4 children)

Non-political career: Principal, T E Davies & Son (livestock farmers) 1976-; Member: National Farmers' Union, Farmers Union of Wales; Montgomeryshire District Council: Councillor 1979-89, Chair 1985-89, Chair, Planning Committee 1982-87, Chair, Finance Committee 1987-89; Development Board for Rural Wales: Member 1986-, Chair 1989-94; Member: Welsh Development Agency 1989-94, Welsh Tourist Board 1989-94

Political career: Contested Montgomeryshire 1997 general election. Member for Montgomeryshire since 6 May 2010 general election; Contested Montgomeryshire constituency 1999 and 2003 National Assembly for Wales elections; AM for Mid and West Wales region 1999-2007: Conservative spokesperson for: Agriculture and the Rural Economy 1999, Finance 1999-2001, Culture, Media, Sport and the Welsh Language 2001-03, Local Government, Environment and Planning 2003-05, Finance, Rural Affairs, Environment and Planning/Finance 2005-06

Other organisations: Member: RSPB, National Trust, Montgomeryshire Wildlife Trust, Wildfowl and Wetlands Trust, CLA; President, Campaign for the Protection of Rural Wales 2007; Development Board for Rural Wales: Member 1986-, Chair 1989-94; Member: Welsh Development Agency 1989-94, Welsh Tourist Board 1989-94

Recreations: Sport and fitness, countryside issues, family, house and garden

Glyn Davies MP, House of Commons, London SW1A 0AA
Tel: 020 7219 3000 E-mail: glyn.davies.mp@parliament.uk
Constituency: Montgomeryshire Conservatives, 20 High Street, Welshpool, Powys SY21 7JP Tel: 01938 552315
Website: glyndaviesam.blogspot.com

GENERAL ELECTION RESULT

		%
Davies, G. (Con)	13,976	41.3
Öpik, L. (Lib Dem)*	12,792	37.8
Fychan, H. (PIC)	2,802	8.3
Colbourne, N. (Lab)	2,407	7.1
Rowlands, D. (UKIP)	1,128	3.3
Ellis, M. (NF)	384	1.1
Lawson, B. (Ind)	324	1.0
Majority	1,184	3.50
Electorate	48,730	
Turnout	33,813	69.39

**Member of last parliament*

CONSTITUENCY SNAPSHOT

Delwyn Williams took this previously Liberal seat in 1979 for the Tories and lost it again in 1983. It is a mark on the otherwise unblemished Liberal history here epitomised by the long serving parliamentarians including Clement Davies, Emlyn Hooson and more recently Alex Carlile, until Lembit Öpik's election in 1997.

In the 2005 general election there was a 7 per cent swing to the Liberal Democrats, giving Öpik a lead of 7,173. Lembit Opik was a surprise loser on election night when the Tories' Glyn Davies captured the seat with a 13.2 per cent swing.

Boundary changes have moved the Llanrhaedr-ym-Mochnant/Llanslin electoral division into the seat from Clwyd South.

This is a rural constituency covering the north of Powys. The main towns include Machynlleth, Llanidloes, Montgomery, Newtown and Welshpool.

Newtown is known as the birthplace of Robert Owen, and his former home is a museum.

The constituency's main income comes from the agricultural sector, light industry and a significant tourist trade.

The population is older than average and this is exacerbated by a number of retirees moving into the area.

Philip Davies

Shipley (returning MP)

Boundary changes

Tel: 020 7219 8264
E-mail: daviesp@parliament.uk
Website: www.philipdavies.me.uk

Conservative

Date of birth: 5 January 1972; Son of Peter Davies and Marlyn Lifsey

Education: Old Swinford Hospital School, Stourbridge; Huddersfield University (BA historical and political studies 1993); Married Deborah Gail Hemsley 1994 (2 sons)

Non-political career: Asda Stores: Management training scheme 1995-97, Deputy customer services manager 1997, Customer relations manager 1997-98, Call centre manager 1998-99, Customer service project manager 2000-04, Senior marketing manager 2004-05

Political career: Contested Colne Valley 2001 general election. Member for Shipley 2005-10, for Shipley (revised boundary) since 6 May 2010 general election; *Select Committees:* Member: Culture, Media and Sport 2006-10, Modernisation of the House 2007-10; Member Executive 1922 Committee 2006-

Political interests: Law and order, Europe, education

Recreations: Horseracing, cricket

Philip Davies MP, House of Commons, London SW1A 0AA
Tel: 020 7219 8264 Fax: 020 7219 0667
E-mail: daviesp@parliament.uk
Constituency: Shipley Conservatives Association, 76 Otley Road, Shipley, West Yorkshire BD18 3SA Tel: 01274 592248
Website: www.philipdavies.me.uk

GENERAL ELECTION RESULT

		%
Davies, P. (Con)*	24,002	48.6
Hinchcliffe, S. (Lab)	14,058	28.4
Harris, J. (Lib Dem)	9,890	20.0
Warnes, K. (Green)	1,477	3.0
Majority	9,944	20.12
Electorate	67,689	
Turnout	49,427	73.02

**Member of last parliament*

CONSTITUENCY SNAPSHOT

The seat was held by Labour until 1950, but then fell to Geoffrey Hirst, a Tory who spent the last years of his tenure as an Independent.

Marcus Fox took over for the Tories in 1970 and held the seat for 27 years. In 1992 his majority was more than 12,000. In 1997 Labour's Chris Leslie managed to gain a swing of nearly 14 per cent and was returned with a majority of nearly 3,000.

In 2005 Tory Philip Davies defeated Leslie with a majority of just 422. Davies increased this majority in 2010 with 9,944.

Boundary changes realigned the Bradford seats with city council wards, moving a series of part-wards between the seats.

This West Yorkshire seat covers the small towns on the north-western fringe of Bradford: Shipley and Baildon. It also includes the rural areas between Bradford and Keighley as well as the small market town of Bingley.

Shipley, Baildon and Bingley are typical West Riding towns favoured by the middle classes. Successful industrialists used to move up the valleys away from the grime of their own mills.

There are still the remnants of the textile industry, though it has been hit hard. Other industries include light engineering and some farming, but the constituency is largely residential with a high level of owner-occupancy.

Rt Hon **David Davis**

Haltemprice and Howden ***(returning MP)***

Boundary changes

Tel: 020 7219 5900
E-mail: davisd@parliament.uk

Conservative

Date of birth: 23 December 1948; Son of late Ronald and Elizabeth Davis

Education: Bec Grammar School; Warwick University (BSc molecular science, computing science 1971); London Business School (MSc business studies 1973); Harvard Business School (AMP 1985); Married Doreen Cook 1973 (1 son 2 daughters)

Non-political career: Joined Tate & Lyle 1974; Finance director, Manbré & Garton 1976-80; Managing director, Tate & Lyle Transport 1980-82; President, Redpath-Labatt joint venture 1982-84; Strategic planning director, Tate & Lyle 1984-87; Non-Executive director, Tate & Lyle 1987-90

Political career: Member for Boothferry 1987-97, for Haltemprice and Howden from 1997 to 18 June 2008, 11 July 2008 by-election to 2010, for Haltemprice and Howden (revised boundary) since 6 May 2010 general election; PPS to Francis Maude as Financial Secretary to Treasury 1988-90; Assistant Government Whip 1990-93; Parliamentary Secretary, Office of Public Service and Science 1993-94; Minister of State, Foreign and Commonwealth Office 1994-97; Member, Public Accounts Commission 1997-2001; Shadow: Deputy Prime Minister with responsibility for the Cabinet Office 2002-03, Secretary of State for Home, Constitutional and Legal Affairs 2003-04, Home Secretary 2003-08; *Select Committees:* Chair: Public Accounts 1997-2001; Member: Liaison 1998-2001; Contested Conservative Party leadership 2001; Party Chairman 2001-02; Member Conservative Policy Board 2001-; Contested Conservative Party leadership 2005

Political interests: Health, law and order, industry, agriculture

Other organisations: PC 1997; *Publications:* How to Turn Round a Company (1988); The BBC Viewer's Guide to Parliament (1989)

Recreations: Mountaineering, flying light aircraft, writing

Rt Hon David Davis MP, House of Commons, London SW1A 0AA
Tel: 020 7219 5900 Fax: 020 7219 1961
E-mail: davisd@parliament.uk
Constituency: Spaldington Court, Spaldington, Howden,
East Yorkshire DN14 7NG Tel: 01430 430365 Fax: 01430 430253

GENERAL ELECTION RESULT

		%
Davis, D. (Con)*	24,486	50.2
Neal, J. (Lib Dem)	12,884	26.4
Marten, D. (Lab)	7,630	15.7
Cornell, J. (BNP)	1,583	3.3
Robinson, J. (England)	1,485	3.1
Oakes, S. (Green)	669	1.4
Majority	11,602	23.81
Electorate	70,403	
Turnout	48,737	69.23

**Member of last parliament*

CONSTITUENCY SNAPSHOT

This seat was created in 1997 from parts of David Davis' Boothferry seat and most of the equally Conservative seat of Beverley, albeit without the town itself.

Notional 1992 results gave the Tories a 17,000 majority to defend in Haltemprice and Howden. But in 1997 the Conservative vote fell by 15 per cent. Davis increased his majority to 5,116 in 2005.

David Davis resigned his seat in June 2008 over the issue of 42-day detention for terrorist suspects. The by-election was held on 10 July with Davis standing against a record 25 candidates. Neither Labour nor Lib Dems contested the by-election. Davis was returned with a 15,355 majority. At the 2010 general election Davis was re-elected with a 11,602 majority.

Boundary changes resulted in a couple of villages being traded with Beverley and Holderness.

This is a part suburban, part rural East Yorkshire constituency. It stretches from the western edge of Hull along the A63/M62 past a large number of small towns to Howden.

Haltemprice, from a defunct 14th century priory, describes the smart northern and western suburbs of Hull. Most of the seat's population is in these areas which include Cottingham, Kirk Ella and Willerby.

The biggest single local employer is BAE Systems military aircraft factory at Brough on the Humber.

Nick de Bois

Enfield North

Boundary changes

Tel: 020 7219 3000
E-mail: nick.debois.mp@parliament.uk
Website: www.nickdebois.com

Conservative

Date of birth: 23 February 1959; Son of late WG Col John de Bois and late Paula de Bois

Education: Culford School, Bury St Edmunds; Cambridge College of Arts and Technology (HND business studies 1981); Married Vanessa Gillian Coleman 1982 (divorced) (1 son 3 daughters)

Non-political career: Public relations manager, Advertising Standards Authority 1982-84; Various roles, now managing director, Rapier Design Group 1984-

Political career: Contested Stalybridge and Hyde 1997 and Enfield North 2001 and 2005 general elections. Member for Enfield North since 6 May 2010 general election; Member, Conservative Party 1992-; Deputy Chair, Huntington Conservative Association 1992-97

Political interests: Crime, trade and industry, healthcare, foreign affairs; USA, Asia, Pacific

Recreations: Travel, children's story writing, keen rugby fan and gym enthusiast

Nick de Bois MP, House of Commons, London SW1A 0AA
Tel: 020 7219 3000 E-mail: nick.debois.mp@parliament.uk
Constituency: Enfield North Conservatives, 276 Baker Street, Enfield, Middlesex EN1 3LD Tel: 020 8363 0653
Website: www.nickdebois.com

GENERAL ELECTION RESULT

		%
de Bois, N. (Con)	18,804	42.3
Ryan, J. (Lab)*	17,112	38.5
Smith, P. (Lib Dem)	5,403	12.2
Avery, T. (BNP)	1,228	2.8
Jones, M. (UKIP)	938	2.1
Linton, B. (Green)	489	1.1
Williams, A. (Christian)	161	0.4
Weald, R. (England)	131	0.3
Athow, A. (WRP)	96	0.2
Daniels, G. (Ind)	91	0.2
Majority	1,692	3.81
Electorate	66,258	
Turnout	44,453	67.09

**Member of last parliament*

CONSTITUENCY SNAPSHOT

The Conservatives took the seat in 1979, when Tim Eggar won the constituency from Labour's Bryan Davies, and held on to it for four terms. In the 1992 general election Eggar won a majority of over 9,000.

Conservative fortunes changed in the 1997 general election when Labour's Joan Ryan won with a majority of 6,822. Her majority fell by two-thirds in 2001, and by a further third to 1,920 in 2005. Conservative Nick du Bois gained this competitive seat from Joan Ryan in 2010 with a majority of 1,692.

The seat lost Ponders End ward to Edmonton, and gained Southbury part-ward in return. In addition, Highlands part-ward was gained from Enfield Southgate in exchange for Grange part-ward.

Enfield North is the northernmost constituency in London, with industrial and urban centres giving way to more rural green belt areas in the north of the region. It includes large Turkish, Bangladeshi, Cypriot and Italian communities.

This seat is partly industrial, mainly in the area east of the Cambridge Road. In contrast it also adjoins the green belt with the open countryside of Enfield Chase bordering Hertfordshire.

Engineering, chemicals, printing and food processing are the main industries.

Expansion of the busy North Circular Road (A406), various traffic-calming schemes and improvement of Enfield rail stations and train services are local transport issues.

Rt Hon **John Denham**

Southampton Itchen (returning MP)

Boundary changes

Tel: 020 7219 4515
E-mail: denhamj@parliament.uk
Website: www.johndenham.org.uk

Labour

Date of birth: 15 July 1953; Son of Edward and Beryl Denham

Education: Woodroffe Comprehensive School, Lyme Regis; Southampton University (BSc chemistry 1974); President Student's Union 1976-77; Married Ruth Eleanore Dixon 1979 (divorced) (1 son 1 daughter); Partner, Sue Littlemore (1 son)

Non-political career: Advice worker, Energy Advice Agency, Durham 1977-78; Transport campaigner, Friends of the Earth 1978-79; Head of youth affairs, British Youth Council 1979-83; Campaigner, War on Want 1984-88; Consultant to various voluntary organisations 1988-92; Member AMICUS (MSF); Hampshire County Council: Councillor 1981-89; Southampton City Council: Councillor 1989-92, Chair Housing Committee 1990-92

Political career: Contested Southampton Itchen 1983 and 1987 general elections. Member for Southampton Itchen 1992-2010, for Southampton Itchen (revised boundary) since 6 May 2010 general election; Opposition Spokesperson for Social Security 1995-97; Department of Social Security: Parliamentary Under-Secretary of State 1997-98, Minister of State 1998-99; Minister of State: Department of Health 1999-2001, Home Office 2001-03; Secretary of State for: Innovation, Universities and Skills 2007-09, Communities and Local Government 2009-10; Shadow Secretary of State for Communities and Local Government 2010-; *Select Committees:* Chair: Home Affairs 2003-07; Member: Liaison 2003-07, Liaison (Liaison Sub-Committee) 2003-07

Other organisations: Fellow Industry and Parliament Trust 1996; PC 2000

Recreations: Cooking, walking, music, football, rugby, cricket

Rt Hon John Denham MP, House of Commons, London SW1A 0AA
Tel: 020 7219 4515 E-mail: denhamj@parliament.uk
Constituency: 20-22 Southampton Street, Southampton,
Hampshire SO15 2ED Tel: 023 8033 9807 Fax: 023 8033 9907
Website: www.johndenham.org.uk

GENERAL ELECTION RESULT

		%
Denham, J. (Lab)*	16,326	36.8
Smith, R. (Con)	16,134	36.3
Goodall, D. (Lib Dem)	9,256	20.8
Kebbell, A. (UKIP)	1,928	4.3
Spottiswoode, J. (Green)	600	1.4
Cutter, T. (TUSC)	168	0.4
Majority	192	0.43
Electorate	74,532	
Turnout	44,412	59.59

**Member of last parliament*

CONSTITUENCY SNAPSHOT

This longstanding Labour seat was represented from 1955 to 1970 by Horace King, who became the first Labour Speaker of the House of Commons in 1965. Labour continued to represent this seat until the Conservatives took control in 1983.

In the 1992 general election Labour's John Denham took the seat from the Tories with a majority of 551. He increased his majority in 1997 general election and there was little change in 2001. In 2005 Denham was returned again with a majority of 9,302. The seat was held by Denham in 2010 with a tiny majority of 192.

The seat lost two part-wards to Southampton Test (Bevois and Freemantle), and one part-ward (Swaythling) to the new seat of Romsey and Southampton North.

The Southampton constituencies are named after the two rivers flowing through the city, and Itchen is the city's eastern side. It contains the city centre, most of the docks, marina and exclusive Ocean Village quarter, as well as inner-city council estates.

Southampton's airport has also made the city a popular departure point for regional travellers to Europe.

The constituency includes the impoverished Thornhill area in the east of the city. It was given £49 million to spend over a ten-year period, culminating in 2010, to regenerate health and education, enhance the living environment, and reduce crime and unemployment.

Gloria De Piero

Ashfield

Boundary changes

Tel: 020 7219 3000
E-mail: gloria.depiero.mp@parliament.uk
Website: www.gloria4mp.org.uk

Non-political career: Political correspondent, GMTV -2010

Political career: Member for Ashfield since 6 May 2010 general election

Gloria De Piero MP, House of Commons, London SW1A 0AA
Tel: 020 7219 3000 E-mail: gloria.depiero.mp@parliament.uk
Constituency: Ashfield Labour Party, PO Box 9536, Kirkby-in-Ashfield, Nottingham NG17 8WB Tel: 07961 676552
Website: www.gloria4mp.org.uk

GENERAL ELECTION RESULT

		%
De Piero, G. (Lab)	16,239	33.7
Zadrozny, J. (Lib Dem)	16,047	33.3
Hickton, G. (Con)	10,698	22.2
Holmes, E. (BNP)	2,781	5.8
Ellis, T. (England)	1,102	2.3
Coleman, T. (UKIP)	933	1.9
Smith, E. (Ind)	396	0.8
Majority	192	0.40
Electorate	77,379	
Turnout	48,196	62.29

CONSTITUENCY SNAPSHOT

Ashfield has only once elected a member who was not a Labour candidate that was at the 1977 by-election when Conservative Tim Smith wiped out a 23,000 majority. It was to be a brief interlude, however, as Frank Haynes won it back for Labour in 1979.

Geoff Hoon was first elected in 1992 with a majority of nearly treble the previous election. In 1997 Hoon increased his majority to a massive 22,728. Labour's majority has fallen since and was 10,213 in 2005. Hoon retired in 2010 and Gloria De Piero held the seat for Labour on a reduced majority of 192.

Boundary changes were minor.

Traditionally a coal-mining area before the collapse of the industry in the 1980s and 90s, Ashfield contains the towns of Kirkby, Sutton and Eastwood, as well as large swathes of farmland and rural areas.

It remains a largely working-class constituency, with manufacturers such as Boots and L'Oreal stepping in to replace the mines as major employers in the area.

The flagship development is Sherwood Park near Junction 27 of the M1, an Enterprise Zone business park which employs 4,000 people. Boots, among other major companies, has a presence there.

Caroline Dinenage

Gosport

No boundary changes

Tel: 020 7219 3000
E-mail: caroline.dinenage.mp@parliament.uk
Website: www.caroline4gosport.co.uk

Conservative

Date of birth: 28 October 1971; Daughter of Fred Dinenage, tv presenter

Education: Wykjeham House, Fareham; Oaklands RC Comprehensive, Waterlooville; University of Wales, Swansea (BA English and politics); Married Carlos (2 sons)

Non-political career: Director, Recognition Express; Councillor, Winchester District Council 1998-2003

Political career: Contested Portsmouth South 2005 general election. Member for Gosport since 6 May 2010 general election

Political interests: Defence (particularly supporting service families), small businesses, franchising

Other organisations: Cowdray Park Polo Club

Recreations: Portsmouth F.C, netball, skiing

Caroline Dinenage MP, House of Commons, London SW1A 0AA
Tel: 020 7219 3000 E-mail: caroline.dinenage.mp@parliament.uk
Constituency: 167 Stoke Road, Gosport, Hampshire PO12 1SE
Tel: 023 9252 2121 Website: www.caroline4gosport.co.uk

GENERAL ELECTION RESULT

		%	+/-
Dinenage, C. (Con)	24,300	51.8	7.1
Hylands, R. (Lib Dem)	9,887	21.1	4.5
Giles, G. (Lab)	7,944	16.9	-14.5
Rice, A. (UKIP)	1,496	3.2	-1.0
Bennett, B. (BNP)	1,004	2.1	
Shaw, B. (England)	622	1.3	
Smith, C. (Green)	573	1.2	-1.7
Smith, D. (Ind)	493	1.1	
Read, C. (Ind)	331	0.7	
Hart, B. (Ind)	289	0.6	
Majority	14,413	30.71	
Electorate	72,720		
Turnout	46,939	64.55	

CONSTITUENCY SNAPSHOT

Peter Viggers held the seat from its 1974 creation until 2010. His old five-figure majorities have decreased to four figures and he achieved a lead of 5,730 in 2005.

Viggers retired in 2010 and Caroline Dinenage retained the seat for the Tories with a majority of 14,413.

Gosport is a maritime seat. The peninsula faces Portsmouth to the east across the harbour and the Isle of Wight to the west across the Solent. The Portsmouth Naval Base has employed Gosport's residents for hundreds of years, and strong economic ties to the armed services remain.

The town is a major port and there are ship- and yacht-building facilities as well as various light industries.

The distribution of the labour force is heavily skewed towards managerial and skilled manual labour, and the workforce is particularly strong in mechanical, electrical, instrument engineering and high technology skills.

Jonathan Djanogly

Huntingdon (returning MP)

Boundary changes

Tel: 020 7219 2367
E-mail: djanoglyj@parliament.uk
Website: www.jonathandjanogly.com

Conservative

Date of birth: 3 June 1965; Son of Sir Harry Djanogly CBE and Carol Djanogly

Education: University College School, London; Oxford Polytechnic (BA law and politics 1987); Guildford College of Law (law finals 1988) ICAEW (corporate finance qualification); Married Rebecca Jane Silk 1991 (1 son 1 daughter)

Non-political career: Partner: SJ Berwin LLP Solicitors 1988-, Mail order retail business 1994-2002; Councillor Westminster City Council 1994-2001: Chairman: Traffic Committee 1995-96, Contracts 1996-97, Social Services Committee 1998-99, Environment Committee 1999-2000

Political career: Contested Oxford East 1997 general election. Member for Huntingdon 2001-10, for Huntingdon (revised boundary) since 6 May 2010 general election; Shadow: Minister for Home, Constitutional and Legal Affairs 2004-05, Solicitor General 2005-10, Minister for Trade and Industry/Business, Enterprise and Regulatory Reform/Business, Innovation and Skills 2005-10 (Corporate Governance 2006-09, Business 2009-10); Parliamentary Under-Secretary of State, Ministry of Justice 2010-; *Select Committees:* Member: Trade and Industry 2001-05, Joint Committee on Statutory Instruments 2001-02; Chairman Oxford Polytechnic Conservative Association 1986-87; Vice-chairman Westminster North Conservative Association 1993-94

Political interests: Small businesses, trade, environment, rural affairs, transport, planning

Recreations: Sport, arts, theatre, reading histories and biographies, Britain's countryside and heritage

Jonathan Djanogly MP, House of Commons, London SW1A 0AA
Tel: 020 7219 2367 Fax: 020 7219 0476
E-mail: djanoglyj@parliament.uk
Constituency: 8 Stukeley Road, Huntingdon,
Cambridgeshire PE29 6XG Tel: 01480 437840 Fax: 01480 453012
Website: www.jonathandjanogly.com

GENERAL ELECTION RESULT

		%
Djanogly, J. (Con)*	26,516	48.9
Land, M. (Lib Dem)	15,697	28.9
Cox, A. (Lab)	5,982	11.0
Curtis, I. (UKIP)	3,258	6.0
Salt, J. (Ind)	1,432	2.6
Clare, J. (Green)	652	1.2
Jug, L. (Loony)	548	1.0
Holliman, C. (Animal)	181	0.3
Majority	10,819	19.94
Electorate	83,557	
Turnout	54,266	64.94

**Member of last parliament*

CONSTITUENCY SNAPSHOT

For the majority of the duration of his tenure former prime minister John Major secured over 60 per cent of the vote, apart from in 1997, when his vote declined to 55 per cent, a majority of 18,000.

In 2001 Major retired and Jonathan Djanogly retained the seat for the Tories, although they dropped, fractionally, below 50 per cent of the vote for the first time in over two decades. At the 2005 election the Tory vote climbed back over 50 per cent and Jonathan Djanogly was re-elected with a majority of almost 13,000. Djanogly held the seat by 10,819 votes in 2010 .

Boundary changes slightly reduced the size of the constituency as three part-wards were moved to North West Cambridgeshire.

Huntingdon is a rural and affluent community, with excellent transport links to both London and Cambridge. Aided by the excellent transport links in the constituency, including the A1(M), a number of companies have recently relocated their headquarters to Huntingdon.

The manufacturing industry accounts for a high percentage of industry in the constituency.

Huntingdon Life Sciences is the largest private sector employer, and also vital to the economy. Undertaking product development and safety testing for the pharmaceutical, chemical and biotechnological industries, HLS has been the target of animal rights protestors.

Jim Dobbin

Heywood and Middleton ***(returning MP)***

Boundary changes

Tel: 020 7219 4530
E-mail: dobbinj@parliament.uk

Labour/Co-operative

Date of birth: 26 May 1941; Son of William Dobbin, miner, and Catherine Dobbin, neé McCabe, mill worker

Education: St Columba's RC High, Cowdenbeath; St Andrew's RC High, Kirkcaldy; Napier College, Edinburgh (BSc bacteriology, virology 1970); Married Pat Russell 1964 (2 sons 2 daughters)

Non-political career: Microbiologist, NHS 1966-94; Member, UNITE; Rochdale Metropolitan Borough Council: Councillor 1983-92, 1994-97, Chairman of Housing 1986-90, Leader of Labour Group 1994-96, Leader of Council 1996-97

Political career: Contested Bury North 1992 general election. Member for Heywood and Middleton 1997-2010, for Heywood and Middleton (revised boundary) since 6 May 2010 general election; *Select Committees:* Member: European Scrutiny 1998-2010, Joint Committee on Consolidation, Etc, Bills 2001-10, Communities and Local Government 2007-09; Chair, Rochdale District Labour Party 1980-81: Executive Member, Rochdale Constituency Labour Party 1986-87

Political interests: Local and regional government, health, housing, transport, small businesses, life issues, involuntary tranquiliser addiction; America (North and South), Spain, Africa

Other organisations: Fellow Industry and Parliament Trust 2001; Knight of St Gregory (Papal Order) 2008; (Fellow of Institute of Medical Lab Sciences) FIMLS

Recreations: Walking, football

Jim Dobbin MP, House of Commons, London SW1A 0AA
Tel: 020 7219 4530 Fax: 020 7219 2696
E-mail: dobbinj@parliament.uk
Constituency: 45 York Street, Heywood, Lancashire OL10 4NN
Tel: 01706 361135 Fax: 01706 625703

GENERAL ELECTION RESULT

		%
Dobbin, J. (Lab/Co-op)*	18,499	40.1
Holly, M. (Con)	12,528	27.2
Hobhouse, W. (Lib Dem)	10,474	22.7
Greenwood, P. (BNP)	3,239	7.0
Cecil, V. (UKIP)	1,215	2.6
Lee, C. (Ind)	170	0.4
Majority	5,971	12.95
Electorate	80,171	
Turnout	46,125	57.53

**Member of last parliament*

CONSTITUENCY SNAPSHOT

Middleton was previously half of the Middleton and Prestwich seat, the home of Jim Callaghan (not the late Prime Minister) from 1974. In 1983 Middleton separated from Prestwick (which became part of Bury South), and joined with Heywood, previously linked to Royton (which went to Oldham West). Mr Callaghan continued to hold the new seat until 1997 when Jim Dobbin took over. Dobbin secured five-figures majorities in all his electoral victories until 2010. His majority fell only marginally in 2005 to 11,083.

In 2010 Dobbin was re-elected with a much-reduced majority of 5,971.

The seat gained the part-wards of Bamford and Norden wards from Rochdale, in exchange for the Spotland and Falinge part-ward.

Situated between Manchester and Rochdale, this is effectively the second Rochdale seat. Once heavily reliant on textiles, the area has now undergone industrial diversification.

The Middleton Arndale centre has had substantial improvement work done to its gardens in an attempt to deal with concerns about its appearance but trade is in constant decline as people travel to shop in Manchester's city centre. Rochdale Metropolitan Borough Council has been using European funding to help maintain the regeneration of the area.

Rt Hon **Frank Dobson**

Holborn and St Pancras (returning MP)

Boundary changes

Tel: 020 7219 4452
E-mail: patelm@parliament.uk
Website: frankdobson.co.uk

Date of birth: 15 March 1940; Son of late James William Dobson, railwayman, and Irene Dobson

Education: Archbishop Holgate's Grammar School, York; London School of Economics (BSc(Econ) 1962); Married Dr Janet Mary Alker 1967 (1 daughter 2 sons)

Non-political career: Worked at HQ of: CEGB 1962-70, Electricity Council 1970-75; Assistant Secretary, Office of Local Ombudsman 1975-79; RMT; Camden Borough Council: Councillor 1971-76, Leader 1973-75; Member Court University of York 2001-; Governor Royal Veterinary College 2002-; Member London School of Hygiene and Tropical Medicine 2008-

Political career: Member for Holborn and St Pancras 1979-2010, for Holborn and St Pancras (revised boundary) since 6 May 2010 general election; Opposition Spokesperson for Education 1981-83; Shadow Health Minister 1983-87; Shadow Leader, House of Commons and Campaigns Co-ordinator 1987-89; Shadow: Secretary of State for: Energy 1989-92, Employment 1992-93, Transport 1993-94, Minister for London 1993-97, Secretary of State for Environment 1994-97; Secretary of State for Health 1997-99; *Select Committees:* Member: Administration 2005-08

Political interests: Central London, transport, energy, redistribution of wealth, government reform; South Africa, Bangladesh

Other organisations: Chair, Network South Africa 2004; PC 1997; Covent Garden Community Centre

Recreations: Walking, theatre, watching cricket and football

Rt Hon Frank Dobson MP, House of Commons, London SW1A 0AA
Tel: 020 7219 4452 Fax: 020 7219 6956
E-mail: patelm@parliament.uk Website: frankdobson.co.uk

GENERAL ELECTION RESULT

		%
Dobson, F. (Lab)*	25,198	46.1
Shaw, J. (Lib Dem)	15,256	27.9
Lee, G. (Con)	11,134	20.4
Bennett, N. (Green)	1,480	2.7
Carlyle, R. (BNP)	779	1.4
Spencer, M. (UKIP)	587	1.1
Chapman, J. (Ind)	96	0.2
Susperregi, M. (England)	75	0.1
Meek, I. (Ind)	44	0.1
Majority	9,942	18.19
Electorate	86,863	
Turnout	54,649	62.91

**Member of last parliament*

CONSTITUENCY SNAPSHOT

Represented by Labour's Frank Dobson since its creation in 1983, this seat is culturally and socially diverse. It has remained loyal to Dobson, who has maintained a healthy majority which peaked in 1997, when he took 65 per cent of the vote.

Dobson's defeat in the London mayoral elections in 2000 led to a small drop in the Labour vote in 2001. In 2005 Dobson's majority more than halved in 2005 to 4,787. Former Health Secretary and London Mayoral candidate Frank Dobson held this seat for Labour with a 9,942 majority.

The seat gained four part-wards from Hampstead and Highgate.

This constituency includes a mixture of residential, commercial and institutional land in the northern segment of central London, including the tourist centres of Covent Garden and Camden Town, Regent's Park and the celebrity haven of Primrose Hill, as well as Bloomsbury, where University College London is based.

In the northern part are the residential areas of Kentish Town and Gospel Oak.

The rail terminal for Eurostar moved to St Pancras International in 2007, bringing trains from France and Belgium to the constituency. The seat is served by almost all Underground lines and is also home to Euston and King's Cross stations.

Thomas Docherty

Dunfermline and West Fife

No boundary changes

Tel: 020 7219 3000
E-mail: thomas.docherty.mp@parliament.uk

Education: Studying at Open University (history degree); Married Katie (1 son)

Non-political career: Research Assistant to Scott Barrie MSP 2001; Public Affairs Officer, BNFL; Network Rail; Account director, communications consultancy

Political career: Contested Tayside North 2001 general election. Member for Dunfermline and West Fife since 6 May 2010 general election; Contested South of Scotland region 2003 Scottish Parliament election; Chair, Dunfermline and West Fife Labour Party

Recreations: Dunfermline Athletic F.C

Thomas Docherty MP, House of Commons, London SW1A 0AA
Tel: 020 7219 3000 E-mail: thomas.docherty.mp@parliament.uk
Constituency: 74 Eardley Crescent, Dunfermline, Fife KY11 8NE
Tel: 01383 739424 Website: www.dunfermlinelabour.org.uk

GENERAL ELECTION RESULT

		%	+/-
Docherty, T. (Lab)	22,639	46.3	-1.1
Rennie, W. (Lib Dem)*	17,169	35.1	14.9
McCall, J. (SNP)	5,201	10.6	-8.3
Hacking, B. (Con)	3,305	6.8	-3.6
Inglis, O. (UKIP)	633	1.3	-0.2
Majority	5,470	11.18	
Electorate	73,769		
Turnout	48,947	66.35	

**Member of last parliament*

CONSTITUENCY SNAPSHOT

Richard Douglas represented the Labour seat of Dunfermline from 1979, through boundary changes in 1983 when the seat was renamed Dunfermline West, until he defected to the SNP in 1990 before returning in 1992. His successor was Labour's Rachel Squire.

In 2005 the seat was enlarged to take in the Inverkeithing wards from Dunfermline East. Rachel Squire won Dunfermline and West Fife with a majority of 11,562 over the Liberal Democrats.

Rachel Squire died in January 2006 and in the by-election Willie Rennie, the Liberal Democrat candidate took the seat with a swing of more than 16 per cent. Rennie was unable to hold the seat at the general election. Labour's Thomas Docherty was elected with a 5,740 majority.

For over 500 years Dunfermline was Scotland's capital. Its abbey became the burial place of Scottish kings and queens, including Robert the Bruce. Tourism, however, supplies a limited number of jobs. One such attraction is the Deep-Sea World Aquarium in North Queensferry.

The area's most visible landmarks are the Forth bridges. A five-year project to build a new bridge across the Forth just to the west of the current crossing is due to start in 2011

The traditional industry in Dunfermline was textiles, but this declined in the post-war period. The old mines in West Fife have largely been replaced by electronics and computers firms. The majority of employment opportunities are now in service sectors.

Rt Hon **Nigel Dodds**

Belfast North ***(returning MP)***

Boundary changes

Tel: 020 7219 8419
E-mail: doddsn@parliament.uk
Website: www.nigeldodds.co.uk

Date of birth: 20 August 1958; Son of late Joseph Alexander Dodds, civil servant, and Doreen Dodds, née McMahon

Education: Portora Royal School, Enniskillen; St John's College, Cambridge (BA law 1980); Queen's University, Belfast Institute of Professional Legal Studies (Cert PLS 1981); Married Diane Harris (later MLA as Diane Dodds, now MEP) 1985 (2 sons 1 daughter)

Non-political career: Barrister 1981-83; European Parliament Secretariat (non-attached members) 1984-96; Member of Senate, Queen's University, Belfast 1985-93; Belfast City Council: Councillor 1985-2010, Lord Mayor Belfast 1988-89, 1991-92, Vice-President Association of Local Authorities of Northern Ireland 1989-90

Political career: Contested Antrim East 1992 general election. Member for Belfast North 2001-10, for Belfast North (revised boundary) since 6 May 2010 general election; DUP Chief Whip 2001-; DUP Spokesperson for: Treasury 2005-07, Work and Pensions 2005-07, Business of the House 2005-, Justice 2007-, Business, Enterprise and Regulatory Reform 2007-; *Select Committees:* Member: Members' Allowances 2009-10, Joint Committee on Statutory Instruments and Commons Committee on Statutory Instruments 2009-10; Member Northern Ireland Forum for Political Dialogue 1996-98; MLA for Belfast North 1998-: Minister of: Social Development 1999-2000, 2001-02, Enterprise, Trade and Investment 2007-08, Finance and Personnel 2008-09; Secretary DUP 1992-2008; Member, Northern Ireland Forum for Political Dialogue 1996-98; Deputy Leader, DUP 2008-

Political interests: European affairs, constitution, social policy; France, USA

Other organisations: OBE 1997; PC 2010

Rt Hon Nigel Dodds OBE MP, House of Commons, London SW1A 0AA Tel: 020 7219 8419 Fax: 020 7219 2347
E-mail: doddsn@parliament.uk
Constituency: 39 Shore Road, Belfast BT15 3QB Tel: 028 9077 4774
Fax: 028 9077 7685 Website: www.nigeldodds.co.uk

GENERAL ELECTION RESULT

		%
Dodds, N. (DUP)*	14,812	40.0
Kelly, G. (Sinn Féin)	12,588	34.0
Maginness, A. (SDLP)	4,544	12.3
Cobain, F. (UCUNF)	2,837	7.7
Webb, B. (All)	1,809	4.9
McAuley, M. (Ind)	403	1.1
Majority	2,224	6.01
Electorate	65,504	
Turnout	36,993	56.47

**Member of last parliament*

CONSTITUENCY SNAPSHOT

The constituency has always been held by a unionist of one party or another. Cecil Walker was the Ulster Unionist MP from 1983 until 2001 when he was defeated by Nigel Dodds of the DUP. Dodds went on to increase his percentage majority in 2005, though his numerical majority of 5,188 was down by 1,200.

Dodds held onto the seat with a majority of 2,224 in 2010 closely followed by Sinn Féin's Gerry Kelly.

The seat was enlarged for the 2010 election to include some suburban Newtownabbey wards from East Antrim and South Antrim.

The constituency takes in the northern end of the city of Belfast. It sits on Belfast Lough and includes the magnificent Belfast Castle.

The seat has a Protestant majority but has a substantial Catholic minority. The constituency's Ardoyne area has been the site of many sectarian flashpoints.

The constituency is highly socially mixed. The areas around Belfast Castle include tree-lined avenues and large houses.

Pat Doherty

West Tyrone (returning MP)

No boundary changes

Tel: 020 7219 8159
E-mail: dohertyp@parliament.uk

Date of birth: 18 July 1945

Education: St Joseph's College, Lochwinnoch; Married (2 sons 3 daughters)

Non-political career: Site engineer 1975

Political career: Contested West Tyrone 1997 general election. Member for West Tyrone since 7 June 2001 general election; Contested Donegal North East 1989 Dáil general election, 1996 by-election and 1997 general election, Connaught/Ulster 1989 and 1994 European Parliament elections. Leader of delegation to Dublin Forum for Peace and Reconciliation 1994-96, Member Castle Buildings talks team 1997-98; MLA for West Tyrone 1998-: Sinn Féin Spokesperson for Agriculture; Member, Assembly Commission 2009-; Sinn Féin: Activist 1970-84; Elections Director 1984-85; National organiser 1985-88; Vice-president 1988-2009; Leader, delegation to Dublin Forum for Peace and Reconciliation 1994-96, Member, Castle Buildings talks team 1997-98

Political interests: Irish national self-determination

Other organisations: Founder member Local Credit Union 1992

Recreations: Walking, reading, building stone walls

Pat Doherty MP, House of Commons, London SW1A 0AA
Tel: 020 7219 8159 E-mail: dohertyp@parliament.uk
Constituency: 1A Melvin Road, Strabane, Co Tyrone BT82 9AE
Tel: 028 7188 6464 Fax: 028 7188 0120
Website: www.westtyronesinnfein.com

GENERAL ELECTION RESULT

		%	+/-
Doherty, P. (Sinn Féin)*	18,050	48.4	10.0
Buchanan, T. (DUP)	7,365	19.8	2.2
Hussey, R. (UCUNF)	5,281	14.2	
Byrne, J. (SDLP)	5,212	14.0	5.0
Bower, M. (All)	859	2.3	
McClean, C. (Ind)	508	1.4	
Majority	10,685	28.67	
Electorate	61,148		
Turnout	37,275	60.96	

**Member of last parliament*

CONSTITUENCY SNAPSHOT

At the first general election for the new West Tyrone constituency in 1997 the nationalist electorate was split between Sinn Féin and the SDLP, allowing Ulster Unionist William Thompson to take the seat with a small majority.

A coalescence of nationalists behind Sinn Féin's Pat Doherty enabled him to claim the seat ahead of both Thompson and his SDLP rival Brid Rodgers in the 2001 general election.

The 2005 general election was notable for the principle challenge to Pat Doherty coming from Dr Kieran Deeney, campaigning for the retention of hospital services in Omagh. Doherty was able to hold the seat with a majority of 5,005. Doherty doubled his majority to 10,685 in 2010.

The constituency has one of the largest Catholic populations in Northern Ireland. Roughly mid-way between Belfast and Derry, it is a mainly rural seat. It covers two district council areas centred on its major towns, Strabane and Omagh.

Omagh is a major administrative and service area. Agriculture is an important employer, along with associated processing industries. There is also some manufacturing including textiles production.

Rt Hon **Jeffrey Donaldson**

***Lagan Valley** (returning MP)*

Boundary changes

Tel: 020 7219 3407
E-mail: donaldsonjm@parliament.uk
Website: www.jeffreydonaldson.org

Date of birth: 7 December 1962; Son of James and Sarah Anne Donaldson

Education: Kilkeel High School; Castlereagh College (Diploma electrical engineering 1982); Married Eleanor Cousins 1987 (2 daughters)

Non-political career: Ulster Defence Regiment 1980-85; Agent to Enoch Powell MP 1983-84; Personal assistant to Sir James Molyneaux MP 1984-85; Partner, financial services and estate agency business 1986-96; Former Member, AEEU; Alderman Lisburn City Council 2005-; Member Northern Ireland Policing Board 2007-08

Political career: Member for Lagan Valley 1997-2010, for Lagan Valley (revised boundary) since 6 May 2010 general election (UUP May 1997 to January 2004, DUP since January 2004); Ulster Unionist Spokesperson for: Trade and Industry 1997-2000, Environment, Transport and the Regions 2000-01, Treasury 2001-02, Transport, Local Government and the Regions 2001-02, Work and Pensions 2001-03, Defence 2002-03, Trade and Industry 2002-03; DUP Spokesperson for: Education 2004-05, Defence 2004-05, 2007-, Transport 2005-07, International Development 2005-07, Home Office 2007-, Transport 2009-; *Select Committees:* Member: Northern Ireland Affairs 1997-2000, Environment, Transport and Regional Affairs 2000-01, Environment, Transport and Regional Affairs (Transport Sub-Committee) 2000-01, Regulatory Reform 2001-05, Joint Committee on Statutory Instruments 2001-06, Transport 2004-07, 2009-10; Member, Northern Ireland Assembly 1985-86; Member: Northern Ireland Forum 1996-98, Northern Ireland Assembly: MLA for Lagan Valley 2003-; Junior Minister, Office of the First Minister and Deputy First Minister 2008-09; Ulster Unionist Council: Honorary Secretary 1988-2000, Vice-president 2000-03; Resigned from UUP 15 January 2004. Party Officer, Democratic Unionist Party 2004-

Political interests: Christian values, constitution, transport, defence, international development; Belarus, Ethiopia, Israel, Northern Ireland, South Africa, USA

Other organisations: Member: Presbyterian Church, Loyal Orange Order, Constitutional Monarchy Association, Regimental Association of the Ulster Defence Regiment; Trustee, Royal Ulster Rifles Association; PC 2007

Recreations: Hill-walking, reading, local history, church

Rt Hon Jeffrey Donaldson MP, House of Commons, London SW1A 0AA Tel: 020 7219 3407 Fax: 020 7219 0696
E-mail: donaldsonjm@parliament.uk
Constituency: The Old Town Hall, 29 Castle Street, Lisburn, Co Antrim BT27 4DH Tel: 028 9266 8001 Fax: 028 9267 1845
Website: www.jeffreydonaldson.org

GENERAL ELECTION RESULT

		%
Donaldson, J. (DUP)*	18,199	49.8
Trimble, D. (UCUNF)	7,713	21.1
Lunn, T. (All)	4,174	11.4
Harbinson, K. (TUV)	3,154	8.6
Heading, B. (SDLP)	1,835	5.0
Butler, P. (Sinn Féin)	1,465	4.0
Majority	10,486	28.70
Electorate	65,257	
Turnout	36,540	55.99

**Member of last parliament*

CONSTITUENCY SNAPSHOT

Lagan Valley has consistently returned high-profile MPs to Westminster. The seat was represented by the UUP leader Jim Molyneux from 1983 to 1997, when Enoch Powell's former assistant Jeffrey Donaldson won the seat.

Running as a DUP candidate for the first time in 2005 Donaldson polled 54.7 per cent of the vote for a majority of 14,117. Donaldson retained the seat in 2010 with 18,199 votes; however, there was a 3.3 per cent swing to the Ulster Conservatives and Unionists.

Lagan Valley lost the Glenavy ward to South Antrim, and Dunmurry to West Belfast in the boundary review.

This prosperous area lies to the south-west of Belfast and contains most of Lisburn and a small part of Banbridge district councils.

The core of the constituency is Lisburn, a busy retail centre, which was granted city status in 2002. Lisburn has a strong industrial and commercial base. Investment and development has helped maintain Lisburn's strong economic growth: it has the highest rate of inward investment in Northern Ireland outside Belfast.

The Lagan Valley seat as a whole has low unemployment relative to the rest of the province.

Tourist attractions include Hillsborough Castle and the Lagan Valley itself is designated an Area of Outstanding Natural Beauty.

Brian Donohoe

Central Ayrshire ***(returning MP)***

No boundary changes

Tel: 020 7219 6230
E-mail: donohoeb@parliament.uk
Website: www.briandonohoemp.co.uk

Date of birth: 10 September 1948; Son of late George and Catherine Donohoe

Education: Irvine Royal Academy; Kilmarnock Technical College (National certificate in engineering 1972); Married Christine Pawson 1973 (2 sons)

Non-political career: Apprentice engineer Ailsa Shipyard 1965-70; Draughtsman/engineer Hunterston Nuclear Power Station 1970-77; Draughtsman ICI Organics Division 1977-81; NALGO District Officer 1981-92; Convenor, Political and Education Committee TASS 1969-81; Secretary, Irvine Trades Council 1973-82; Member, TGWU Parliamentary Campaigning Group 1992-; Chair: Cunninghame Industrial Development Committee 1975-85, North Ayrshire and Arran Local Health Council 1977-79

Political career: Member for Cunninghame South 1992-2005, for Central Ayrshire since 5 May 2005 general election; PPS to Lord Adonis at Department for Transport 2008-10: as Minister of State 2008-09, as Secretary of State 2009-10; *Select Committees:* Member: Environment, Transport and Regional Affairs 1997-2001, Environment, Transport and Regional Affairs (Environment Sub-Committee) 1997-2001, Environment, Transport and Regional Affairs (Transport Sub-Committee) 1997-2001, Transport, Local Government and the Regions 2001-02, Transport, Local Government and the Regions (Transport Sub-Committee) 2001-02, Transport 2002-05, Administration 2005-10; Treasurer, Cunninghame South Constituency Labour Party 1983-91

Political interests: Health, local and regional government, transport, small businesses; Singapore, Indonesia, Malaysia, USA, Taiwan

Other organisations: Board Member Thrive 2003-; Fellow Industry and Parliament Trust 1995, 2001

Recreations: Gardening

Brian Donohoe MP, House of Commons, London SW1A 0AA
Tel: 020 7219 6230 Fax: 020 7219 5388
E-mail: donohoeb@parliament.uk
Constituency: 17 Townhead, Irvine, Strathclyde, Ayrshire KA12 0BL
Tel: 01294 276844 Fax: 01294 313463
Website: www.briandonohoemp.co.uk

GENERAL ELECTION RESULT

		%	+/-
Donohoe, B. (Lab)*	20,950	47.7	1.4
Golden, M. (Con)	8,943	20.4	-1.7
Mullen, J. (SNP)	8,364	19.1	7.5
Chamberlain, A. (Lib Dem)	5,236	11.9	-4.1
McDaid, J. (SLP)	422	1.0	-0.1
Majority	12,007	27.34	
Electorate	68,352		
Turnout	43,915	64.25	

**Member of last parliament*

CONSTITUENCY SNAPSHOT

Central Ayrshire was created in 2005. The new constituency comprises 49 per cent of Ayr's electorate, including Prestwick and Troon; 47 per cent from Cunninghame South, centring around the Irvine wards; and Annbank, Mossblown and St Quivox from Carrick, Cumnock and Doon Valley.

Ayr had been a Conservative seat until 1997 when Sandra Osborne took it for Labour and held it in 2001. Cunninghame South had always been a Labour seat, and had been held by Brian Donohoe since 1992.

Brian Donohoe became the seat's MP in 2005 with a majority of 10,423 over the Conservatives. Donohoe held the seat for Labour in 2010 with an increased majority of 12,007.

Starting just north of Ayr itself, Central Ayrshire sweeps up the west coast through the pleasant resorts of Prestwick and Troon, incorporating Prestwick Airport and a series of seaside towns. Its largest population centre is Irvine in the north, which was designated a New Town in 1966, despite having been a Royal Burgh since the 14th century.

Traditional industries in the area include farming and paper production. Tourism is also important.

Irvine Bay Regeneration Company is working on a variety of projects extending from Ardrossan to Irvine in the decade to 2016. Projects which have either been completed or are in planning stages include new golf courses, the regeneration of the coastal towns, and redevelopment of the harbour.

Frank Doran

Aberdeen North ***(returning MP)***

No boundary changes

Tel: 020 7219 3481
E-mail: doranf@parliament.uk
Website: www.frankdoran.org.uk

Date of birth: 13 April 1949; Son of Francis Anthony and Betty Hedges Doran

Education: Ainslie Park Secondary School; Leith Academy; Dundee University (LLB 1975); Married Patricia Ann Govan 1967 (divorced) (2 sons); partner Joan Ruddock MP

Non-political career: Solicitor 1977-88; Member, GMB 1983-

Political career: Member for Aberdeen South 1987-92, for Aberdeen Central 1997-2005, for Aberdeen North since 5 May 2005 general election; Opposition Spokesperson for Energy 1988-92; PPS to Ian McCartney as Minister of State: Department of Trade and Industry 1997-99, Cabinet Office 1999-2001; *Select Committees:* Member: Culture, Media and Sport 2001-05, Finance and Services 2005-10; Chair: Administration 2005-10; Member: Liaison 2005-10; Contested North-East Scotland 1984 European Parliament election; Secretary: GMB Westminster Parliamentary Group 2001-, Trade Union Group of Labour MPs 2001-

Political interests: Energy, childcare, families, mental health, employment

Other organisations: Founder Member, Scottish Legal Action Group 1974; Chair, Dundee Association for Mental Health 1979-82; Fellow Industry and Parliament Trust 1990; Aberdeen Trades Council

Recreations: Cinema, art, football, sport

Frank Doran MP, House of Commons, London SW1A 0AA
Tel: 020 7219 3481 Fax: 020 7219 0682
E-mail: doranf@parliament.uk
Constituency: 69 Dee Street, Aberdeen AB11 6EE Tel: 01224 252715
Fax: 01224 252716 Website: www.frankdoran.org.uk

GENERAL ELECTION RESULT

		%	+/-
Doran, F. (Lab)*	16,746	44.4	2.0
Strathdee, J. (SNP)	8,385	22.2	
Chapman, K. (Lib Dem)	7,001	18.6	-5.3
Whyte, S. (Con)	4,666	12.4	3.0
Jones, R. (BNP)	635	1.7	
Robertson, E. (SSP)	268	0.7	-1.2
Majority	8,361	22.18	
Electorate	64,808		
Turnout	37,701	58.17	

**Member of last parliament*

CONSTITUENCY SNAPSHOT

Aberdeen North has been substantially redrawn twice in the past two decades but it has continually sent Labour representatives to Westminster. Bob Hughes held the seat from 1970 to 1997. Malcolm Savidge was MP from 1997 until 2005 when the Scottish boundaries were redrawn to reduce the number of Scottish MPs. Frank Doran, who had been MP for Aberdeen Central, which formed a large part of the redrawn Aberdeen North, was selected for this seat and held the seat from the Lib Dems in second place. Doran held the seat with a solid majority of 8,361 and 44.4 per cent of the vote to the SNP's 22.2 per cent.

The seat is largely urban and working-class estates such as Seaton, Linksfield, Balgownie and Tillydrone dominate. The oil industry has not brought the comfortable white-collar prosperity to the northern division of Aberdeen. The occupational distribution is skewed towards manual jobs, many in oil and related industries.

The seat includes the Aberdeen Royal Infirmary medical complex, which is the size of a small town.

Other landmarks include Aberdeen University and Pittodrie Stadium, home ground of Aberdeen F.C.

Rt Hon **Stephen Dorrell**

Charnwood (returning MP)

Boundary changes

Tel: 020 7219 4472
E-mail: dorrells@parliament.uk
Website: www.stephendorrell.org.uk

Date of birth: 25 March 1952; Son of late Philip Dorrell, company director

Education: Uppingham School, Rutland; Brasenose College, Oxford (BA law 1973); Married Penelope Anne Taylor 1980 (3 sons 1 daughter)

Non-political career: Director, family industrial clothing firm 1975-87, 1997-

Political career: Contested Kingston-upon-Hull East October 1974 general election. Member for Loughborough 1979-97, for Charnwood 1997-2010, for Charnwood (revised boundary) since 6 May 2010 general election; PPS to Peter Walker as Secretary of State for Energy 1983-87; Assistant Government Whip 1987-88; Government Whip 1988-90; Parliamentary Under-Secretary of State, Department of Health 1990-92; Financial Secretary, HM Treasury 1992-94; Secretary of State for: National Heritage 1994-1995, Health 1995-97; Member Shadow Cabinet 1997-98: Shadow Secretary of State for Education and Employment 1997-98; *Select Committees:* Honorary Member: Public Accounts 1992-94, Member: Joint Committee on Consolidation, Etc, Bills 2005-10

Political interests: Economics, foreign affairs

Other organisations: Chairman, Millennium Commission 1994-95; PC 1994

Recreations: Reading, walking

Rt Hon Stephen Dorrell MP, House of Commons, London SW1A 0AA Tel: 020 7219 4472 Fax: 020 7219 5838
E-mail: dorrells@parliament.uk
Website: www.stephendorrell.org.uk

GENERAL ELECTION RESULT

		%
Dorrell, S. (Con)*	26,560	49.6
Webber-Jones, R. (Lib Dem)	11,531	21.5
Goodyer, E. (Lab)	10,536	19.7
Duffy, C. (BNP)	3,116	5.8
Storier, M. (UKIP)	1,799	3.4
Majority	15,029	28.07
Electorate	74,473	
Turnout	53,542	71.89

**Member of last parliament*

CONSTITUENCY SNAPSHOT

Charnwood was created in 1997 out of a number of middle-class suburbs on the outskirts of Leicester. The notional majority that Conservative Stephen Dorrell (MP for Loughbrough 1979-97) took to the poll in the 1997 general election was over 22,000. In the event the former Health Secretary won the seat with a majority of 5,900. In 2001 he increased his majority to 7,739 despite a 12.5 per cent fall in turnout. This majority was increased by just under 1,000 votes in 2005.

Dorrell held the seat in 2010 with a majority of 15,029.

Boundary changes were minor, several part-wards moved to both the Bosworth and Loughborough seats.

Situated on the north-eastern outskirts of Leicester, the seat contains a number of middle-class suburbs as well as the rural parts of Charnwood Forest, after which the seat was named.

The massive AstraZeneca site near Loughborough is the second largest employer in the Charnwood area with around 1,000 staff.

The site is an important centre for chemical research and keeps the division at the forefront of chemical science. Loughborough University is another key employer in the area.

Nadine Dorries

Mid Bedfordshire (returning MP)

Boundary changes

Tel: 020 7219 4239
E-mail: dorriesn@parliament.uk
Website: www.dorries.org.uk

Conservative

Date of birth: 21 May 1957; Daughter of Sylvia and George Bargery

Education: Halewood Grange Comprehensive, Liverpool; Warrington District School of Nursing; Married Paul Dorries 1984 (divorced) (3 daughters)

Non-political career: Former nurse; Businesswoman; Director, BUPA; Adviser to Oliver Letwin MP 2002-05

Political career: Contested Hazel Grove 2001 general election (as Nadine Bargery). Member for Mid Bedfordshire 2005-10, for Mid Bedfordshire (revised boundary) since 6 May 2010 general election; *Select Committees:* Member: Education and Skills 2005-06, Science and Technology 2007, Innovation, Universities[, Science] and Skills/Science and Technology 2007-10, Energy and Climate Change 2009-10

Political interests: Law and order, social structure, health, rural affairs; Zambia, South Africa

Recreations: Family, friends, walking, reading, dogs

Nadine Dorries MP, House of Commons, London SW1A 0AA
Tel: 020 7219 4239 Fax: 020 7219 6428
E-mail: dorriesn@parliament.uk
Constituency: Mid-Bedfordshire Conservative Association, St Michaels Close, High Street, Shefford, Bedfordshire SG17 5DD
Tel: 01462 811992 Fax: 01462 811010 Website: www.dorries.org.uk

GENERAL ELECTION RESULT

		%
Dorries, N. (Con)*	28,815	52.5
Jack, L. (Lib Dem)	13,663	24.9
Reeves, D. (Lab)	8,108	14.8
Hall, B. (UKIP)	2,826	5.2
Bailey, M. (Green)	773	1.4
Cooper, J. (England)	712	1.3
Majority	15,152	27.60
Electorate	76,023	
Turnout	54,897	72.21

**Member of last parliament*

CONSTITUENCY SNAPSHOT

This seat has been continuously held by the Conservative party since 1945. Tory Jonathan Sayeed won Mid Bedfordshire in 1997 with a majority reduced to 13.5 per cent.

In 2005 Sayeed was replaced by Nadine Dorries who won Mid Bedfordshire with a majority of 11,355. Dorries held the seat in 2010 with a 15,152 majority.

The seat lost its part of Kempston South ward to Bedford, and the part-ward of Langford and Henlow Village to North East Bedfordshire. The seat gained Wilshamstead from Bedford, and Houghton, Haynes, Southill and Old Warden part-ward from North East Bedfordshire.

Mid Bedfordshire is situated to the east of Milton Keynes, and its north meets with the county town seat of Bedford. It contains the three small towns of Flitwick, Ampthill and Shefford and includes the tourist attractions of Woburn Abbey, and its safari park.

The constituency as a whole is well served by transport links. There are, therefore, high levels of commuting to larger employment centres within the county and beyond.

Local jobs are in agriculture, market gardening, tourism and education, with some light industry and retail employment in Ampthill.

Cranfield University in the north has an international reputation for research and for its aeronautical engineering, science and MBA degrees.

Jim Dowd

Lewisham West and Penge *(returning MP)*

New constituency

Tel: 020 7219 4617
E-mail: dowdj@parliament.uk
Website: www.jimdowd.org.uk

Date of birth: 5 March 1951; Son of late James and Elfriede Dowd

Education: Sedgehill Comprehensive School, London; London Nautical School; Single

Non-political career: Apprentice telephone engineer, GPO (now BT) 1967-72; Station manager, Heron Petrol Stations Ltd. 1972-73; Telecommunications engineer, Plessey Company 1973-92; Member: POEU 1967-72, UNITE (MSF) 1973-, GMB; London Borough of Lewisham: Councillor 1974-94, Deputy Leader 1984-86, Mayor 1992; Member, Lewisham and North Southwark District Health Authority

Political career: Contested Beckenham 1983 and Lewisham West 1987 general elections. Member for Lewisham West 1992-2010, for Lewisham West and Penge since 6 May 2010 general election; Opposition Whip for London 1993-95; Opposition Spokesperson for Northern Ireland 1995-97; Government Whip 1997-2001; *Select Committees:* Member: Health 2001-10

Political interests: NHS, transport, economic policy, industrial policy, environment, housing, animal welfare, human rights, education

Other organisations: Member several animal welfare organisations; Fellow Industry and Parliament Trust 1996; Bromley Labour Club

Recreations: Music, reading, theatre, Cornwall

Jim Dowd MP, House of Commons, London SW1A 0AA
Tel: 020 7219 4617 Fax: 020 7219 2686
E-mail: dowdj@parliament.uk
Constituency: 43 Sunderland Road, Forest Hill, London SE23 2PS
Tel: 020 8699 2001 Fax: 020 8699 2001
Website: www.jimdowd.org.uk

GENERAL ELECTION RESULT

		%
Dowd, J. (Lab)*	18,501	41.1
Feakes, A. (Lib Dem)	12,673	28.1
Phillips, C. (Con)	11,489	25.5
Staveley, P. (UKIP)	1,117	2.5
Phoenix, R. (Green)	931	2.1
Hammond, S. (CPA)	317	0.7
Majority	5,828	12.94
Electorate	69,022	
Turnout	45,028	65.24

**Member of last parliament*

CONSTITUENCY SNAPSHOT

Lewisham West has switched its party affiliation seven times since 1945. However, it has returned a Conservative member only twice since 1971: in 1983 and 1987.

After contesting the seat unsuccessfully in 1987, Labour's Jim Dowd was successful in 1992 gaining it from the Conservative John Maples. Dowd consolidated this success with a sizable swing in 1997 and his 2005 majority was a very safe 9,932. This new seat was won by Labour's Jim Dowd with a respectable majority of 5,828 with the Liberal Democrats in second place.

Lewisham West and Penge is in south London, created from Lewisham West seat and three wards from Beckenham: Crystal Palace, Penge and Cator and Clock House.

A large proportion work in the public sector, particularly education and health. There are very few sites for new social housing, so refurbishment of old buildings is more common.

The Horniman museum, a Victorian tea trader's collection of anthropological and ethnological artefacts, is a rare visitor's attraction here. There are no underground services but there is an expanding bus network and overland trains run to London Bridge.

The East London Line extension due to open in 2010, will improve access between inner London communities, its southern extension connecting New Cross Gate with West Croydon mainline station.

Gemma Doyle

West Dunbartonshire

No boundary changes

Tel: 020 7219 3000
E-mail: gemma.doyle.mp@parliament.uk
Website: www.gemmadoyle.org.uk

Labour/Co-operative

Education: Glasgow University

Non-political career: Institute of Mechanical Engineers; Conference manager; Political adviser to Scottish Labour MPs' group

Political career: Member for West Dunbartonshire since 6 May 2010 general election

Political interests: Employment, public services, the elderly

Gemma Doyle MP, House of Commons, London SW1A 0AA
Tel: 020 7219 3000 E-mail: gemma.doyle.mp@parliament.uk
Website: www.gemmadoyle.org.uk

GENERAL ELECTION RESULT

		%	+/-
Doyle, G. (Lab/Co-op)	25,905	61.3	9.5
McCormick, G. (SNP)	8,497	20.1	-1.6
Watt, H. (Lib Dem)	3,434	8.1	
McIntyre, M. (Con)	3,242	7.7	1.2
Sorbie, M. (UKIP)	683	1.6	0.8
McGavigan, K. (SLP)	505	1.2	
Majority	17,408	41.19	
Electorate	66,085		
Turnout	42,266	63.96	

CONSTITUENCY SNAPSHOT

The current seat is most similar to the pre-1983 seat of West Dunbartonshire, which after the Second World War continually returned Labour Members.

John McFall represented Dumbarton until 2005, and although Dumbarton was not always quite as secure as other Clydeside constituencies, McFall polled more than 50 per cent of the vote in 1997 and 2001.

West Dunbartonshire was made up of just over half of Dumbarton, and the remainder from the Clydebank side of the old Clydebank and Milngavie seat.

In 2005 John McFall won with a 12,553 majority. A very safe Labour seat represented by influential backbencher John McFall until the election. Gemma Doyle took over with a 17,408 majority.

The seat combines the western, less affluent parts of the old Clydebank and Milngavie (centred on Clydebank) with the West Dunbartonshire wards of Dumbarton (including the town).

Attempts have been made to diversify the Clydebank industrial base, with some success, thanks largely to the town having one of Scotland's first enterprise zones. Tourism is increasing and in 2002 Loch Lomond and Trossachs became Scotland's first National Park.

Industrial sites at Clydebank Riverside and Dumbarton Waterfront are being regenerated and the seat is home to Allied Distillers in Dumbarton as well as the Auchentoshan distillery.

Jackie Doyle-Price

Thurrock

Boundary changes

Tel: 020 7219 3000
E-mail: jackie.doyleprice.mp@parliament.uk
Website: www.winwithjackie.com

Conservative

Date of birth: 5 August 1969

Education: Notre Dame RC, Sheffield; Durham University (economics and politics 1991); Partner John

Non-political career: Administrative officer, South Yorkshire Police 1992; Parliamentary officer, City of London Corporation 1993-2000; Assistant private secretary to the Rt Hon the Lord Mayor of the City of London 2000-05; Associate, Financial Services Authority 2005

Political career: Contested Sheffield Hillsborough 2005 general election. Member for Thurrock since 6 May 2010 general election; Treasurer, National Association of Conservative Graduates 1994-1997; Chair, Lewisham Deptford Constituency Association 1997-99

Political interests: Welfare, foreign affairs, vocational education

Recreations: Theatre, reading, film, watching soaps

Jackie Doyle-Price MP, House of Commons, London SW1A 0AA
Tel: 020 7219 3000 E-mail: jackie.doyleprice.mp@parliament.uk
Constituency: Thurrock Conservatives, Titan Works, Hogg Lane, Grays, Essex RM17 5DU Tel: 01268 583307
Website: www.winwithjackie.com

GENERAL ELECTION RESULT

		%
Doyle-Price, J. (Con)	16,869	36.8
Morris, C. (Lab)	16,777	36.6
Davis, C. (Lib Dem)	4,901	10.7
Colgate, E. (BNP)	3,618	7.9
Broad, C. (UKIP)	3,390	7.4
Araba, A. (Christian)	267	0.6
Majority	92	0.20
Electorate	92,390	
Turnout	45,822	49.60

CONSTITUENCY SNAPSHOT

Labour had held Thurrock since the Second World War, but their majority had fallen by the 1980s. Oonagh Macdonald, who had represented Thurrock for Labour between 1976 and 1987, saw her majority reduced to just 1,722 in 1983.

In 1987 the Conservatives' Tim Janman won the seat with a majority of 690. In 1992 Andrew Mackinlay restored the seat to Labour and was re-elected in 1997 with a 17,256 vote majority. Mackinlay's majority has reduced at each election since and was 6,375 in 2005.

Labour was defeated at the 2010 general election with Jackie Doyle-Price securing a small majority of 92 for the Tories.

Boundary changes were minimal.

The constituency of Thurrock, which borders Greater London, includes the towns of Grays, Tilbury and Purfleet and covers 18 miles of the north bank of the river Thames.

An area historically known for its quarrying and heavy industry, it is now better known for retail services and as a distribution centre. The riverside is still an important industrial area, with manufacturing and port activities along the Thames.

The port of Tilbury and the Lakeside Shopping Centre are the area's largest employers. Tilbury is a major cruise ship terminal, and Tilbury and Purfleet handle millions of tonnes of freight annually.

Richard Drax

South Dorset

No boundary changes

Tel: 020 7219 3000
E-mail: richard.drax.mp@parliament.uk
Website: richarddrax.com

Conservative

Date of birth: 29 January 1958

Education: Harrow School; Royal Agricultural College, Cirencester (Diploma of Membership rural land management 1990); Westminster Press (Diploma journalism 1995); Divorced (2 daughters 2 sons)

Non-political career: Officer, Coldstream Guards 1978-87; Journalist: *Yorkshire Evening Press* 1991-96, *TyneTees*, *Calendar*, *Daily Telegraph* 1996-97; Journalist/Reporter, *BBC South Today*, *BBC Solent* 1997-2006

Political career: Member for South Dorset since 6 May 2010 general election

Political interests: Defence

Recreations: Sailing, golf, skiing

Richard Drax MP, House of Commons, London SW1A 0AA
Tel: 020 7219 3000 E-mail: richard.drax.mp@parliament.uk
Constituency: c/o South Dorset Conservative Association, Building C51, Winfrith Technology Centre, Winfrith, Dorchester DT2 8DH
Tel: 01305 851900 Fax: 01308 851900 Website: richarddrax.com

GENERAL ELECTION RESULT

		%	+/-
Drax, R. (Con)	22,667	45.1	7.2
Knight, J. (Lab)*	15,224	30.3	-11.3
Kayes, R. (Lib Dem)	9,557	19.0	3.3
Hobson, M. (UKIP)	2,034	4.0	0.8
Heatley, B. (Green)	595	1.2	
Kirkwood, A. (GMVY)	233	0.5	
Majority	7,443	14.79	
Electorate	73,838		
Turnout	50,310	68.14	

**Member of last parliament*

CONSTITUENCY SNAPSHOT

South Dorset had long been a Tory seat. In the Thatcher and Major years the Conservatives enjoyed large majorities here.

In 1997, however, Labour made inroads and MP Ian Bruce retained his seat narrowly after his majority was reduced from over 12,600 to just 77.

Labour's Jim Knight was successful in 2001, giving him a majority of 153, over twice the margin his predecessor had received. He was able to increase his majority in 2005 to 1,812 lead. Jim Knight was defeated in 2010 by Conservative Richard Drax with a 7,443 majority.

South Dorset is centred primarily on the seaside resort of Weymouth, including the outcrop of Portland to the south, and stretching east along the south coast to the Isle of Purbeck and the small resort town of Swanage.

There is some farming in South Dorset and also some light industry, including the Wytch Farm offshore oil field and the Portland stone and Purbeck marble quarries. The defence industry and tourism are the biggest employers, and Bovington army camp is based in the seat.

South Dorset has a revered coastline, and the constituency is home to several points of interest, including the Bovington tank museum, Lawrence of Arabia's home at Cloud's Hill, Corfe Castle and many features associated with the novels of Thomas Hardy.

Jack Dromey

Birmingham, Erdington

Boundary changes

Tel: 020 7219 3000
E-mail: jack.dromey.mp@parliament.uk

Date of birth: 29 September 1948

Education: Cardinal Vaughan Grammar School; Married Harriet Harman (now MP) 1982 (2 sons 1 daughter)

Non-political career: Chair for 15 years, Joint Industrial Council, Ministry of Defence; Secretary: South East Regional Council, TUC, Brent Trades Council 1976-78; Transport and General Workers' Union 1978-2003: Has served at all levels of the union from district officer to national organiser, Deputy general secretary 2003-08; Deputy general secretary, Unite 2008-; Founder member, Greater London Enterprise Board

Political career: Member for Birmingham, Erdington since 6 May 2010 general election; Treasurer, Labour Party 2004-

Political interests: Workers' rights (including equalities and the Vulnerable Workers' Agenda), manufacturing, housing, transport, international development (including supply chain ethical trading)

Other organisations: Global Organising Alliance; Former executive council member and chair, National Council for Civil Liberties

Recreations: Music, gym, walking, family

Jack Dromey MP, House of Commons, London SW1A 0AA
Tel: 020 7219 3000 E-mail: jack.dromey.mp@parliament.uk

GENERAL ELECTION RESULT

		%
Dromey, J. (Lab)	14,869	41.8
Alden, R. (Con)	11,592	32.6
Holtom, A. (Lib Dem)	5,742	16.2
McHugh, K. (BNP)	1,815	5.1
Foy, M. (UKIP)	842	2.4
Tomkins, T. (Ind)	240	0.7
Williams, T. (NF)	229	0.6
Gray, T. (Christian)	217	0.6
Majority	3,277	9.22
Electorate	66,405	
Turnout	35,546	53.53

CONSTITUENCY SNAPSHOT

This constituency was formed from Birmingham Aston and Sutton Coldfield in 1974 and has been Labour's ever since. Robin Corbett inherited the seat from Julius Silverman in 1983 with a majority of just 231 votes. By 1997 he had transformed this majority into 12,657 votes.

Siôn Simon, who replaced Corbett in 2001, was re-elected in 2005 with a 9,575 majority. Simon stood down in 2010 and was replaced by Jack Dromey who held the seat for Labour with a 3,277 majority despite a 10.4 per cent swing to the Tories.

Boundary changes have moved Erdington, Kingstanding and Tyburn wards fully within this seat giving the constituency marginally extended northern borders.

This seat is a working-class constituency to the north-east of Birmingham.

The local economy was hard hit by the closure of the MG Rover plant in April 2005. A large proportion of the workforce is engaged in manual employment and the professional and managerial sectors are under-represented.

Recent health sector boosts for Birmingham Erdington have included the regeneration and creation of community and health facilities at The Sanctuary, Eden Court Medical Practice as part of the massive 1993-2005 Castle Vale estate Housing Action Trust regeneration project.

James Duddridge

Rochford and Southend East (returning MP)

Boundary changes

Tel: 020 7219 4830
E-mail: duddridgej@parliament.uk
Website: www.jamesduddridge.com

Conservative

Date of birth: 26 August 1971; Son of Philip and Jenny Duddridge

Education: Crestwood School, Eastleigh, Hampshire; Huddersfield New College; Wells Blue School; Essex University (BA government 1993); Married Kathryn (Katy) Brigid Thompson 2004 (2 sons)

Non-political career: Research assistant to Bernard Jenkin MP 1991-93; Retail and merchant banking, Barclays Bank 1993-2002: Barclays Bank of Swaziland 1995-96, Barclays Bank Head Office 1996, Sales director, Banque Belgolaise, Ivory Coast 1997-98, National sales manager, Barclays 1998-2001. Service Delivery Director, Barclays Bank Botswana 2001-02; Account director and consultant, YouGov 2000-05; Director, Okavango Ltd 2002-05

Political career: Contested Rother Valley 2001 general election. Member for Rochford and Southend East 2005-10, for Rochford and Southend East (revised boundary) since 6 May 2010 general election; Opposition Whip 2008-10; Government Whip 2010-; *Select Committees:* Member: Environment, Food and Rural Affairs 2005-10, International Development 2006-08, Strategic Export Controls (Quadripartite Committee)/Arms Export Controls 2007-08; Chair, Wells Young Conservatives 1989-91; Campaigns department, Conservative Central Office 1989-91; Chair, Essex University Conservative Students 1990-91; General election campaign manager to Stephen Shakespeare 1997; Executive Committee member Conservative Way Forward 2000-01; Adviser, Lady Miller Postal Services Bill 1999; Member Bow Group 1999-

Political interests: African politics, pensions; Southern African countries

Other organisations: Student representative, Huddersfield Police Forum 1987-88; Speaker for Westminster Foundation for Democracy 2003-04; Member executive committee British Group Inter-Parliamentary Union (IPU) 2005-

Recreations: Running, cycling, Southampton FC, Southend United FC

James Duddridge MP, House of Commons, London SW1A 0AA
Tel: 020 7219 4830 Fax: 020 7219 3888
E-mail: duddridgej@parliament.uk
Constituency: Suite 1, Strand House, 742 Southchurch Road, Southend on Sea, Essex SS1 2PS Tel: 01702 616135
Fax: 01702 619071 Website: www.jamesduddridge.com

GENERAL ELECTION RESULT

		%
Duddridge, J. (Con)*	19,509	46.9
Bonavia, K. (Lab)	8,459	20.3
Longley, G. (Lib Dem)	8,084	19.4
Moyies, J. (UKIP)	2,405	5.8
Strobridge, G. (BNP)	1,856	4.5
Vaughan, A. (Green)	707	1.7
Chytry, A. (Ind)	611	1.5
Majority	11,050	26.54
Electorate	71,080	
Turnout	41,631	58.57

**Member of last parliament*

CONSTITUENCY SNAPSHOT

A year after losing his seat in Glasgow, Tory Sir Teddy Taylor bounced back with a win in a by-election at Southend East in 1979, replacing former MP Sir Stephen McAdden.

Throughout the 1980s and early 1990s, Sir Teddy received majorities in the tens of thousands. In 1997 Sir Teddy's majority was cut from 13,111 to just 4,225. He retired in 2005.

James Duddridge held the seat for the Tories with a 5,490 majority. At the 2010 general election the Conservatives majority doubled to 11,050.

Boundary changes were minor, with the loss of only two part-wards to neighbouring seats.

This constituency combines part of the residential district of Rochford with the eastern part of the Essex seaside resort of Southend-on-Sea, including the town centre.

It includes Rochford itself and Great Wakering, along with the sparsely populated coastal marshland area between the river Roach and the mouth of the Thames.

There are excellent rail connections to London and Southend has its own airport. Many residents commute to London for work but the main employers in the area are Customs and Excise, the leisure industry and Keymed, a company producing medical and industrial equipment.

Michael Dugher

Barnsley East

New constituency

Tel: 020 7219 3000
E-mail: michael.dugher.mp@parliament.uk
Website: www.michaeldugher.co.uk

Date of birth: 26 April 1975

Education: Nottingham University; Married Joanna (2 daughters)

Non-political career: Head of policy, Amalgamated Engineering and Electrical Union (AEEU); Special Adviser to: Stephen Byers MP as Secretary of State for Transport, Local Government and the Regions (subsequently Department for Transport) 2001-02, Geoffrey Hoon MP as: Secretary of State for Defence 2003-05, Lord Privy Seal and Leader of the House of Commons 2005-06; UK director, political relations, EDS 2006-07 Special Adviser to Geoffrey Hoon MP as Chief Whip 2007-08; Political Adviser on political press issues to Gordon Brown as the Prime Minister 2009-10

Political career: Contested Skipton and Ripon 2001 general election. Member for Barnsley East since 6 May 2010 general election

Recreations: History, music, watching football

Michael Dugher MP, House of Commons, London SW1A 0AA
Tel: 020 7219 3000 E-mail: michael.dugher.mp@parliament.uk
Website: www.michaeldugher.co.uk

GENERAL ELECTION RESULT

		%
Dugher, M. (Lab)	18,059	47.1
Brown, J. (Lib Dem)	6,969	18.2
Hockney, J. (Con)	6,329	16.5
Porter, C. (BNP)	3,301	8.6
Watson, T. (UKIP)	1,731	4.5
Hogan, K. (Ind)	712	1.9
Devoy, E. (Ind)	684	1.8
Capstick, K. (SLP)	601	1.6
Majority	11,090	28.89
Electorate	68,435	
Turnout	38,386	56.09

CONSTITUENCY SNAPSHOT

When originally created in 1983, Barnsley East was a Labour seat dominated by the National Union of Mineworkers. Former miner Terry Patchett was MP from 1983 until his death in 1996. Jeff Ennis won the by-election for Labour.

Barnsley East made way for Barnsley East and Mexborough in 1997. In 2001 the Lib Dems pushed the Tories into third place. Despite a further 4.4 per cent swing to the Lib Dems in 2005, Labour's majority remained a large 14,125.

In 2010 Michael Dugher held the seat for Labour with a 11,090 majority.

South Yorkshire's constituencies were redrawn extensively and the new seat of Barnsley East contains wards from all three of the town's divisions. The majority of the wards are from Barnsley East and Mexborough but without the Doncaster Borough wards seats. The new seat extends southward to include wards from the old Barnsley West and Penistone constituency while Cudworth returns from Barnsley Central.

Surrounding Barnsley's eastern outskirts, this constituency is a series of small towns built for the coal industry.

The most famous name is Grimethorpe, with its famous colliery band, which starred in the film 'Brassed Off'.

While only a few miners remain in the area, the other old industries: engineering and glassmaking are still important.

Rt Hon **Alan Duncan**

Rutland and Melton ***(returning MP)***

Boundary changes

Tel: 020 7219 5204
E-mail: duncana@parliament.uk
Website: www.alanduncan.org.uk

Conservative

Date of birth: 31 March 1957; Son of late Wing-Commander James Duncan, OBE, and Anne, née Carter

Education: Merchant Taylors' School, Northwood; St John's College, Oxford (BA philosophy, politics and economics 1979) (President, Oxford Union 1979); Harvard University (Kennedy Scholar 1981-82); Civil partner James Dunseath 2008

Non-political career: Graduate trainee, Shell International Petroleum 1979-81; Marc Rich & Co 1981-88; Oil trader and adviser to governments and companies on oil supply, shipping and refining 1989-92; Visiting Fellow, St Antony's College, Oxford 2002-03

Political career: Contested Barnsley West and Penistone 1987 general election. Member for Rutland and Melton 1992-2010, for Rutland and Melton (revised boundary) since 6 May 2010 general election; PPS to Dr Brian Mawhinney: as Minister of State, Department of Health 1993-94, as Chairman Conservative Party 1995-97; Parliamentary Political Secretary to William Hague as Leader of the Conservative Party 1997-98; Opposition Spokesperson for: Health 1998-99, Trade and Industry 1999-2001, Foreign and Commonwealth Affairs 2001-03; Shadow: Secretary of State for: Constitutional Affairs 2003-04, International Development 2004-05, Transport 2005, Trade and Industry/Business, Enterprise and Regulatory Reform 2005-09, Leader of the House of Commons 2009; Member House of Commons Commission 2009; Shadow Minister for Prisons 2009-10; Minister of State, Department for International Development 2010-; *Select Committees:* Member: Social Security 1992-95; Vice-Chairman Conservative Party 1997-98

Political interests: International trade, international economics, social security, Middle East

Other organisations: PC 2010; Liveryman, Merchant Taylors' Company; Freeman, City of London; Beefsteak; *Publications:* Co-author: (CPC pamphlet) Bearing the Standard: Themes for a Fourth Term (1991), Who Benefits? Reinventing Social Security, An End to Illusions (1993), Saturn's Children: How the State Devours Liberty, Prosperity and Virtue (1995); Beware Blair (1997)

Recreations: Shooting, skiing

Rt Hon Alan Duncan MP, House of Commons, London SW1A 0AA
Tel: 020 7219 5204 Fax: 020 7219 2529
E-mail: duncana@parliament.uk
Constituency: 33 High Street, Melton Mowbray, Leicestershire LE13 0TR Tel: 01664 411211
Website: www.alanduncan.org.uk

GENERAL ELECTION RESULT

		%
Duncan, A. (Con)*	28,228	51.1
Hudson, G. (Lib Dem)	14,228	25.8
Morgan, J. (Lab)	7,893	14.3
Baker, P. (UKIP)	2,526	4.6
Addison, K. (BNP)	1,757	3.2
Higgins, L. (Ind)	588	1.1
Majority	14,000	25.35
Electorate	77,185	
Turnout	55,220	71.54

**Member of last parliament*

CONSTITUENCY SNAPSHOT

Until 1997 Conservatives were consistently achieving around 60 per cent of the vote here. Alan Duncan was first elected in 1992. His majority fell by 16,699 votes in 1997 to 8,836. There have been swings back in the Tories' favour in 2001 and 2005 and Duncan's 2005 majority was a much healthier 12,930.

In 2010 Duncan held the seat with an increased 14,000 majority despite a 3.7 per swing to the Lib Dems.

Boundary changes were minimal.

Lying just south of Nottingham, Rutland and Melton is one of the most rural constituencies in the country. It consists of the county unitary authority of Rutland, with the small market towns of Oakham and Uppingham. The largest town in the seat is Melton Mowbray.

This rural constituency is relatively wealthy, with a larger than average number of high-income families and very few pockets of extreme poverty.

The largest employers are all retail, including Pedigree Masterfoods in Melton Mowbray and Samworth Brothers Foods Group. The other main occupations are, predictably, agriculture and small businesses dependent on hunting, such as farriers.

It is also a strong commuting region, with many people travelling to the main surrounding towns of Leicester and Peterborough.

Rt Hon **Iain Duncan Smith**

Chingford and Woodford Green ***(returning MP)***

Boundary changes

Tel: 020 7219 2664/1210
E-mail: alambridesl@parliament.uk
Website: www.iainduncansmith.org

Date of birth: 9 April 1954; Son of late Group Captain W. G. G. Duncan Smith, DSO, DFC, and Pamela, neé Summers

Education: HMS Conway (Cadet School); Universita per Stranieri, Perugia, Italy; RMA Sandhurst; Dunchurch College of Management; Married Hon. Elizabeth Wynne Fremantle 1982 (2 sons 2 daughters)

Non-political career: Commissioned, Scots Guards 1975-81; Active service in: Northern Ireland 1976, Rhodesia/Zimbabwe 1979-80; ADC to Major-General Sir John Acland, KCB, CBE, Commander of Commonwealth Monitoring Force in Zimbabwe 1979-81; GEC Marconi 1981-88; Director: Bellwinch Property 1988-89, Publishing Director Jane's Information Group 1989-92

Political career: Contested Bradford West 1987 general election. Member for Chingford 1992-97, for Chingford and Woodford Green 1997-2010, for Chingford and Woodford Green (revised boundary) since 6 May 2010 general election; Member, Shadow Cabinet 1997-2003; Shadow Secretary of State for: Social Security 1997-99, Defence 1999-2001; Leader of the Opposition 2001-03; Secretary of State for Work and Pensions 2010-; *Select Committees:* Member: Health 1993-95, Administration 1993-97, Standards and Privileges 1995-97; Vice-chair, Fulham Conservative Association 1991; Chair, Conservative Policy Board 2001-03; Leader, Conservative Party 2001-03

Political interests: Finance, small businesses, transport, defence, environment, social policy

Other organisations: Founder and chairman Centre for Social Justice 2004-; Trustee: Haven House Childrens Hospice, Whitefields School Community Trust; PC 2001; Freeman, City of London 1993; *Publications:* Co-author Who Benefits? Reinventing Social Security; Game, Set and Match? (Maastricht); Facing the Future (Defence and Foreign and Commonwealth Affairs); 1994 and Beyond; A Response to Chancellor Kohl; A Race against time, Europe's growing vulnerablity to missile attack (2002); The Devil's Tune (Robson Books 2003)

Recreations: Cricket, rugby, tennis, sport in general, painting, theatre, family, shooting, fishing

Rt Hon Iain Duncan Smith MP, House of Commons, London SW1A 0AA Tel: 020 7219 2664/1210 Fax: 020 7219 4867
E-mail: alambridesl@parliament.uk
Constituency: 20A Station Road, Chingford, London E4 7BE
Tel: 020 8524 4344 Fax: 020 8523 9697
Website: www.iainduncansmith.org

GENERAL ELECTION RESULT

		%
Duncan Smith, I. (Con)*	22,743	52.8
Arakelian, C. (Lab)	9,780	22.7
Seeff, G. (Lib Dem)	7,242	16.8
Leppert, J. (BNP)	1,288	3.0
Jones, N. (UKIP)	1,133	2.6
Craig, L. (Green)	650	1.5
Above, N. (Ind)	202	0.5
White, B. (Ind)	68	0.2
Majority	12,963	30.07
Electorate	64,831	
Turnout	43,106	66.49

**Member of last parliament*

CONSTITUENCY SNAPSHOT

The former seat of Norman Tebbit, Chingford is now held by former Conservative leader Iain Duncan Smith. The Woodford part of the seat has a Conservative tradition and was the last seat represented by Winston Churchill until his retirement in 1964.

Iain Duncan Smith was first elected in 1992 with a majority of 14,938. As with many other parts of outer London, the swing to Labour in 1997 was above even the high national average. A lower turnout in 2001 further reduced Duncan Smith's majority. This was reversed in 2005, when he doubled his majority to 10,641. Iain Duncan-Smith had no difficulty in holding on to this safe Conservative seat, winning a 12,963 majority.

Boundary changes were minimal. As well as large swathes of inter-war semi-detached housing, the seat also contains parts of Epping Forest and several other green areas.

On the fringe of Essex, this north-east London seat is fairly typical suburbia.

There have been worries over the future of Whipps Cross Hospital; a local campaign aims to keep it a fully-funded and functioning general hospital.

Philip Dunne

Ludlow (returning MP)

No boundary changes

Tel: 020 7219 2388
E-mail: dunnep@parliament.uk
Website: www.philipdunne.com

Conservative

Date of birth: 14 August 1958; Son of Sir Thomas Dunne and Henrietta, née Crawley

Education: Eton College; Keble College, Oxford (BA philosophy, politics and economics 1980, MA); Married Domenica Margaret Anne Fraser 1989 (2 sons 2 daughters)

Non-political career: Graduate trainee to senior manager S G Warburg & Co Ltd 1980-88; Director of corporate development James Gulliver Associates 1988-90; Partner Phoenix Securities and successor 1991-2001; Managing Director Donaldson, Lufkin and Jenette 1997-2001; Ottakar's plc: Co-founder director (non exec) 1987-2006, Chairman (non exec) 1998-2006; Chairman (non exec) Baronsmead VCT 4 plc 2001-; Director Ruffer Investment Management Limited and Ruffer LLP 2002-09 (non executive 2005-09); Partner Gatley Farms 1987-; NFU 1987-; South Shropshire District Council: Councillor 2001-07, Conservative group leader 2003-05; Governor, Westminster Foundation for Democracy 2008-

Political career: Member for Ludlow since 5 May 2005 general election; Opposition Whip 2008-10; Assistant Government Whip 2010-; *Select Committees:* Member: Work and Pensions 2005-06, Public Accounts 2006-09; Treasury 2007-08; Deputy chairman International Office and Conservatives Abroad 2008-

Political interests: Agriculture, business (especially small business), economy, financial services, health, international affairs, local government; Hong Kong, Middle East, USA

Other organisations: Non-executive director Juvenile Diabetes Research Foundation 1999-2006, Country Land and Business Association; Whites; Church Stretton Golf Club; Kington Golf Club

Recreations: Country sports, skiing, travel

Philip Dunne MP, House of Commons, London SW1A 0AA
Tel: 020 7219 2388 Fax: 020 7219 0788
E-mail: dunnep@parliament.uk
Constituency: Ludlow Constituency Conservative Association, 54 Broad Street, Ludlow, Shropshire SY8 1GP Tel: 01584 872187
Fax: 01584 876345 Website: www.philipdunne.com

GENERAL ELECTION RESULT

		%	+/-
Dunne, P. (Con)*	25,720	52.8	7.9
Kidd, H. (Lib Dem)	15,971	32.8	-7.8
Hunt, A. (Lab)	3,272	6.7	-3.9
Gill, C. (UKIP)	2,127	4.4	2.7
Evans, C. (BNP)	1,016	2.1	
Morrish, J. (Green)	447	0.9	-0.9
Powell, A. (Loony)	179	0.4	
Majority	9,749	20.01	
Electorate	66,631		
Turnout	48,732	73.14	

**Member of last parliament*

CONSTITUENCY SNAPSHOT

Before 2001 the last time a non-Tory represented Ludlow was in the 19th century, so Matthew Green's victory for the Lib Dems here in 2001 caused a sensation. He was elected with a 1,630 majority.

However, Philip Dunne won the seat back for the Tories in 2005 with a 4.1 per cent swing. In 2010 the Tories retained the seat securing a 7.8 per cent swing from the Lib Dems. Dunne's majority was 9,749.

The seat is predominantly rural. Much of this south Shropshire countryside is made up of uplands and is designated as an Area of Outstanding Natural Beauty and around four-fifths of it is used for agricultural purposes.

The seat's largest town is Ludlow, dominated by its medieval castle. In addition to tourism the manufacture of agricultural machinery and clothing are linchpins of the economy. The seat's other substantial town is Bridgnorth. Situated to the east of the constituency, it is more exposed to the influence of the West Midlands conurbation, but is similar to Ludlow in appearance and culture.

The relative affluence of the seat is not entirely local - it also reflects the presence of a substantial number of commuters to the urban sprawl of Birmingham.

Mark Durkan

Foyle (returning MP)

Boundary changes

Tel: 020 7219 5096
E-mail: durkanm@parliament.uk

Social Democratic and Labour Party

Date of birth: 26 June 1960; Son of late Brendan Durkan, police officer, and late Isobel Durkan

Education: St Columb's College, Derry; Queen's University, Belfast (politics); Ulster University (public policy management); Married Jackie Green 1993 (1 daughter)

Non-political career: Deputy President, Union of Students in Ireland 1982-84; Parliamentary Assistant to John Hume MP 1984-98; Councillor, Derry City Council 1993-2000; Member: Northern Ireland Housing Council 1993-95, Western Health and Social Services Council 1993-2000

Political career: Member for Foyle 2005-10, for Foyle (revised boundary) since 6 May 2010 general election; SDLP Spokesperson for: Finance, International Development, Foreign Affairs, Home Affairs and Justice; Member: Forum for Peace and Reconciliation (Dublin) 1994-96, Northern Ireland Forum for Political Dialogue 1996-98; Northern Ireland Assembly: MLA for Foyle since 25 June 1998: Minister of Finance and Personnel 1999-2001, Deputy First Minister 2001-02; Member Preparation for Government Committee 2006-07; Chair, SDLP 1990-95; Member: SDLP Talks Team: Brooke/Mayhew Talks 1991-92, Castle Buildings Talks 1996-98, Leader, SDLP 2001-10

Mark Durkan MP, House of Commons, London SW1A 0AA
Tel: 020 7219 5096 Fax: 020 7219 2694
E-mail: durkanm@parliament.uk
Constituency: Second Floor, 23 Bishop Street, Derry,
Co Derry BT48 6PR Tel: 028 7136 0700 Fax: 028 7136 0808
Website: www.markdurkan.net

GENERAL ELECTION RESULT

		%
Durkan, M. (SDLP)*	16,922	44.7
Anderson, M. (Sinn Féin)	12,098	31.9
Devenney, M. (DUP)	4,489	11.9
McCann, E. (Ind)	2,936	7.8
Harding, D. (UCUNF)	1,221	3.2
McGrellis, K. (All)	223	0.6
Majority	4,824	12.73
Electorate	65,843	
Turnout	37,889	57.54

**Member of last parliament*

CONSTITUENCY SNAPSHOT

The seat was held under the name Londonderry by the Ulster Unionists until 1983. In 1983 civil rights leader and SDLP founder John Hume took the recast Foyle seat, and proceeded to dominate the electoral scene for next two decades. He stood down in 2005, opening a vacancy for his successor as party leader, Mark Durkan who was elected with a 5,957 majority.

Durkan held the seat in 2010 with a 4,824 majority despite a 0.2 per cent swing to Sinn Féin.

Two rural wards, Banagher and Claudy, were lost to East Londonderry as a result of population growth in the city areas.

This constituency centres on Derry, Northern Ireland's second city.

The seat has three major educational institutions including the University of Ulster campus at Magee. Derry is the principal retail centre in the north west of Ireland. Foyle has the second highest proportion of Catholics in Northern Ireland.

Derry traditionally had a strong manufacturing base centred on textiles and clothing. Growth in service sector employment reflects the city's increasingly important role as the main commercial and administrative centre for the region. In recent years there has been huge investment in the seat with new hotels, theatre, port and airport, museums and galleries and shopping facilities.

Tourism benefits from the calming of the political situation. The city has one of the best examples of city walls in Europe. Its walls were never breached, despite several sieges.

Angela Eagle

Wallasey (returning MP)

Boundary changes

Tel: 020 7219 4074
E-mail: eaglea@parliament.uk
Website: www.angelaeaglemp.co.uk

Labour

Date of birth: 17 February 1961; Daughter of André Eagle, print-worker, and late Shirley Eagle, dressmaker and student

Education: Formby High School; St John's College, Oxford (BA philosophy, politics and economics 1983); Civil partnership Maria Exall 2008

Non-political career: COHSE 1984-92: first as a researcher, then as National Press Officer; Member: COHSE, NUJ, UNISON

Political career: Member for Wallasey 1992-2010, for Wallasey (revised boundary) since 6 May 2010 general election; Opposition Whip 1996-97; Parliamentary Under-Secretary of State: Department of the Environment, Transport and the Regions (Minister for Green Issues and Regeneration) 1997-98, Department of Social Security 1998-2001, Home Office 2001-02; Exchequer Secretary, HM Treasury 2007-09; Minister of State (Minister for Pensions and the Ageing Society), Department for Work and Pensions 2009-10; *Select Committees:* Member: Public Accounts 1995-97, 2002-03, 2007-09, Treasury 2003-07, Treasury (Treasury Sub-Committee) 2003-10; Active at branch, women's section, general committee levels in Crosby Constituency 1978-80; Chairman: Oxford University Fabian Club 1980-83, National Conference of Labour Women 1991; Vice-chair PLP 2005-; Member Labour Party NEC 2005-

Political interests: Economic policy, NHS, politics of sport

Other organisations: Member, British Film Institute; *Publications:* Columnist and regular contributor to Tribune

Recreations: Chess, cricket, cinema

Angela Eagle MP, House of Commons, London SW1A 0AA
Tel: 020 7219 4074; 020 7219 5057 Fax: 020 7219 2654
E-mail: eaglea@parliament.uk
Constituency: 6 Manor Road, Liscard, Wallasey, Merseyside CH45 4JB
Tel: 0151-637 1979 Fax: 0151-638 5861
Website: www.angelaeaglemp.co.uk

GENERAL ELECTION RESULT

		%
Eagle, A. (Lab)*	21,578	51.8
Fraser, L. (Con)	13,071	31.4
Pitt, S. (Lib Dem)	5,639	13.5
Snowden, D. (UKIP)	1,205	2.9
Mwaba, E. (Ind)	107	0.3
Majority	8,507	20.42
Electorate	65,915	
Turnout	41,654	63.19

**Member of last parliament*

CONSTITUENCY SNAPSHOT

In the Labour years of 1945 and 1966 Ernest Marples held the seat for the Conservatives.

During the 1980s and 1990s there was a move away from the Conservative Party in Merseyside, and Labour gained its first Member for Wallasey in the form of Angela Eagle in 1992, with a majority of over 3,800.

In 1997 Eagle's majority swelled to nearly 20,000. However, it fell in both subsequent general elections and was 9,109 in 2005. Eagle held the seat in 2010 with 21,578 votes giving her a majority of 8,507.

The seat gained Moreton West and Saughall Massie part-ward from Wirral West and Seacombe part-ward from Birkenhead, while losing Hoylake and Meols part-ward to Wirral West.

The constituency of Wallasey is across the Mersey from Liverpool, on the northern tip of the Wirral peninsula. It encompasses residential areas, derelict docklands, council estates and the seaside resort of New Brighton.

As in other constituencies on the Wirral, there were deep concerns over attempts by Mersey Travel to raise tolls on traffic passing through the tunnel underneath the Mersey, which connects the Wirral peninsula with Liverpool.

Attempts to regenerate the area are important in New Brighton. The scheme includes a leisure centre, cinema, bars and cafés, shops, executive apartments and a complete refurbishment of the Floral Pavilion.

Maria Eagle

Garston and Halewood ***(returning MP)***

New constituency

Tel: 020 7219 4019
E-mail: eaglem@parliament.uk

Date of birth: 17 February 1961; Daughter of André Eagle, print-worker, and late Shirley Eagle, dressmaker and student

Education: Formby High School; Pembroke College, Oxford (BA philosophy, politics and economics 1983); College of Law, London (Common Professional Exam, Law Society Finals 1990)

Non-political career: Voluntary sector 1983-90; Articles of clerkship, Brian Thompson & Partners, Liverpool 1990-92; Goldsmith Williams, Liverpool 1992-95; Senior Solicitor, Steven Irving & Co, Liverpool 1994-97; Member GMB

Political career: Contested Crosby 1992 general election. Member for Liverpool Garston 1997-2010, for Garston and Halewood since 6 May 2010 general election; PPS to John Hutton as Minister of State, Department of Health 1999-2001; Parliamentary Under-Secretary of State: Department for Work and Pensions (Minister for Disabled People) 2001-05, Department for Education and Skills 2005-06 (Minister for Children and Families 2005-06, for Young People 2006), Northern Ireland Office 2006-07; Ministry of Justice 2007-10: Parliamentary Under-Secretary of State 2007-09, Minister of State 2009-10; Government Equalities Office 2008-10: Parliamentary Under-Secretary of State 2008-09, Minister of State (Deputy Minister for Women and Equality) 2009-10; *Select Committees:* Member: Public Accounts 1997-99; Campaigns organiser, Press officer, Merseyside West Euro Constituency Labour Party 1983-84; Constituency Labour Party secretary, Press officer, political education officer 1983-85; Campaigns organiser Crosby 1993-96

Political interests: Transport, housing, employment; Australia, Nicaragua, USA

Other organisations: Played cricket for Lancashire as a Junior; Played chess for England and Lancashire; Fellow Industry and Parliament Trust 2001; *Publications:* Co-author High Time or High Tide for Labour Women

Recreations: Cinema, chess, cricket

Maria Eagle MP, House of Commons, London SW1A 0AA
Tel: 020 7219 4019 Fax: 020 7219 1157
E-mail: eaglem@parliament.uk
Constituency: Unit House, Speke Boulevard, Liverpool, Merseyside L24 9HZ Tel: 0151-448 1167 Fax: 0151-448 0976

GENERAL ELECTION RESULT

		%
Eagle, M. (Lab)*	25,493	59.5
Keaveney, P. (Lib Dem)	8,616	20.1
Downey, R. (Con)	6,908	16.1
Hammond, T. (UKIP)	1,540	3.6
Raby, D. (Respect)	268	0.6
Majority	16,877	39.41
Electorate	71,312	
Turnout	42,825	60.05

**Member of last parliament*

CONSTITUENCY SNAPSHOT

Liverpool Garston was once a barometer swing seat: it went with the national results in both 1974 elections, and even as late as the 1979 general election, when Tory Malcolm Thornton was returned and served until 1983, when Labour's Eddie Loyden took over and represented the seat for 14 years.

Following Loyden's retirement in 1997, Maria Eagle held the seat for Labour with a majority of 18,000. Eagle was re-elected in 2005 with a reduced majority of 7,193 following a swing to the Liberal Democrats.

In 2010 Eagle won Garston and Halewood with a majority of 16,877.

This new seat comprises three wards from the Knowsley South, four wards and a part-ward from the Liverpool Garston seat and a part-ward from Liverpool Wavertree.

This new seat to the south of Liverpool seat combines some of the most well-heeled residential areas in the city, including Allerton and Woolton, as well as large council estates such as Speke.

Garston includes some of the dockland that was devastated by the recession and the downturn in the shipping industry in the early part of the 1980s.

The economy of the area has been improved by the expansion of the John Lennon airport.

Jonathan Edwards

Carmarthen East and Dinefwr

Boundary changes

Tel: 020 7219 3000
E-mail: jonathan.edwards.mp@parliament.uk
Website: www.jonathanedwards.org.uk

Date of birth: 26 April 1976

Education: Ysgol Gymraeg Rhydaman; Ysgol Gyfun Maes yr Yrfa; University of Wales, Aberystwyth (history and politics); Post-graduate Degree (international history)

Non-political career: Chief of staff to Rhodri Glyn Thomas AM and Adam Price MP; National Campaigns Directorate, Plaid Cymru 2005-07; Citizens Advice Cymru 2007-; Councillor, Carmarthen Town Council; Sheriff of Carmarthen Town

Political career: Member for Carmarthen East and Dinefwr since 6 May 2010 general election; Plaid Cymru Spokesperson for: Business, Innovation and Skills 2010-, Communities and Local Government 2010-, Culture, Olympics, Media and Sport 2010-, Transport 2010-, Treasury 2010-

Political interests: Social justice, foreign affairs

Other organisations: Penygroes cricket team

Recreations: Cricket, Swansea City F.C

Jonathan Edwards MP, House of Commons, London SW1A 0AA
Tel: 020 7219 3000 E-mail: jonathan.edwards.mp@parliament.uk
Constituency: 37 Wind Street, Ammanford,
Carmarthenshire SA18 3DN Tel: 01269 597677
Website: www.jonathanedwards.org.uk

GENERAL ELECTION RESULT

		%
Edwards, J. (PlC)	13,546	35.6
Gwyther, C. (Lab)	10,065	26.5
Morgan, A. (Con)	8,506	22.4
Powell, B. (Lib Dem)	4,609	12.1
Atkinson, J. (UKIP)	1,285	3.4
Majority	3,481	9.16
Electorate	52,385	
Turnout	38,011	72.56

CONSTITUENCY SNAPSHOT

In its previous form, as Carmarthen, the seat was the scene of Plaid Cymru's first-ever Westminster election victory in 1966, when it was won by Gwynfor Evans. It was then lost in 1970 to Labour's Gwynoro Jones, who retained it by only three votes in a controversial election in February 1974. Evans regained it in the second general election that year, only to lose it again in 1979. Between 1979 and 2001 it was held for Labour by Roger Thomas (1979 to 1987) and then Alan Williams.

In 2001 Adam Price won the seat for Plaid Cymru. He increased his majority to 6,718 in 2005. Adam Price stood down in 2010. Jonathan Edwards held the seat for Plaid Cymru with a 3,481 majority.

Boundary changes were very minor, only moving the part of the Cynwyl Elfed ward that was in this seat into Carmarthen West and South Pembrokeshire.

Covering a large rural area to the east of Carmarthen, this seat also contains part of the Amman Valley, an old anthracite coalfield.

The economy has historically been based on manual labour. Farming and mining were the traditional mainstays.

Llanarthne is home to the National Botanic Gardens of Wales. The seat has one of the largest percentages of Welsh speakers.

Clive Efford

Eltham (returning MP)

Boundary changes

Tel: 020 7219 4057
E-mail: effordc@parliament.uk
Website: www.cliveefford.org.uk

Date of birth: 10 July 1958; Son of Stanley Efford, retired civil servant and Mary Agnes Elizabeth Christina Efford, neé Caldwell

Education: Walworth Comprehensive School; Southwark Further Education College; Married Gillian Vallins 1981 (3 daughters)

Non-political career: Youth and community worker assistant to warden, Pembroke College Mission 1976; Partner family-owned jewellery and watch repair business 1981-85; Taxi driver 1987-97; Member, T&GWU: Member Passenger Transport Committee of T&G; represented T&G on London Taxi Board; London Borough of Greenwich: Councillor: 1986-98, Chair: Social Services 1989-90, Health and Environment 1992-96, Secretary Labour Group 1986-87; Chief Whip Labour Group 1990-92; Chair Eltham area planning and transport committee 1992-97

Political career: Contested Eltham 1992 general election. Member for Eltham 1997-2010, for Eltham (revised boundary) since 6 May 2010 general election; Presented two bills in Parliament on energy efficiency and energy conservation; Assistant to Tony McNulty as Minister for London 2008-10; PPS: to Margaret Beckett as Minister of State, Department for Communities and Local Government 2008-09, to John Healey as Minister of State, Department for Communities and Local Government 2009; *Select Committees:* Member: Procedure 1997-2001, Standing Orders 1999-2000, Transport 2002-09, London 2009-10; Member Labour Friends of India

Political interests: Welfare state, health, transport, education, environment, local and regional government, energy conservation, energy efficiency, energy from waste, waste management, recycling, social housing

Other organisations: Plumstead Co-op Club; CIU Club; Woolwich Catholic Club

Recreations: Football (FA Preliminary Coachers Club)

Clive Efford MP, House of Commons, London SW1A 0AA
Tel: 020 7219 4057 E-mail: effordc@parliament.uk
Constituency: 132 Westmount Road, Eltham, London SE9 1UT
Tel: 020 8850 5744 Fax: 020 8294 2166
Website: www.cliveefford.org.uk

GENERAL ELECTION RESULT

		%
Efford, C. (Lab)*	17,416	41.5
Gold, D. (Con)	15,753	37.5
Toole, S. (Lib Dem)	5,299	12.6
Woods, R. (BNP)	1,745	4.2
Adams, R. (UKIP)	1,011	2.4
Hayles, A. (Green)	419	1.0
Tibby, M. (England)	217	0.5
Graham, A. (Ind)	104	0.3
Majority	1,663	3.96
Electorate	62,590	
Turnout	41,964	67.05

**Member of last parliament*

CONSTITUENCY SNAPSHOT

Eltham has changed hands between Labour and the Conservatives a number of times since the Second World War. Peter Bottomley held the seat for over two decades between 1975 and 1997.

Mr Bottomley won by a margin of 1,666 in 1992, with Labour increasing their vote at the expense of the Liberal Democrats. Bottomley moved to Worthing West just before the 1997 election. Eltham fell to Labour's Clive Efford. His majority of over 10,182 fell to just under 7,000 in 2001.

A further swing away from Labour cut Efford's majority to 3,276 in 2005. A small swing to the Tories didn't stop Clive Efford holding this marginal seat with a majority of 1,663.

The seat gained four part-wards from Greenwich and Woolwich and lost two part-wards in return. Plumstead part-ward moved to Erith and Thamesmead.

This south east London constituency in the southern part of Greenwich borough sits between the more inner-city Lewisham and Greenwich constituencies and the suburbia of Bromley.

The constituency is not served by the London underground and the Jubilee Line reached neighbouring Greenwich and Woolwich only in 1999. The A20 and the A2 cut through the constituency.

Eltham has secured significant regeneration funding from the public and private sector to total £67 million over seven years until 2007.

Julie Elliott

Sunderland Central

New constituency

Tel: 020 2719 7500
E-mail: julie.elliott.mp@parliament.uk
Website: www.julie4sunderland.com

Date of birth: 1963

Education: Whitburn Junior School; Seaham Northlea Comprehensive; Newcastle Polytechnic (Degree government and public policy)

Non-political career: Regional officer, National Asthma Campaign 1998-99; Political officer, GMB 1999-; Secretary and treasurer, Northern Trade Union Liaison Organisation; Governor and chair, Whitburn Comprehensive School

Political career: Member for Sunderland Central since 6 May 2010 general election; Member, Labour Party 1984-; Agent, Tynemouth 1997 general election; Vice-chair, Labour North Board

Political interests: Employment and skills, regeneration, health inequalities, education

Recreations: Swimming, walking, baking, Rugby Union

Julie Elliott MP, House of Commons, London SW1A 0AA
Tel: 020 2719 7500 E-mail: julie.elliott.mp@parliament.uk
Constituency: Julie Elliott's Campaign Centre, Lynas House, Frederick Street, Sunderland SR1 1NA Tel: 0191-514 5222
Website: www.julie4sunderland.com

GENERAL ELECTION RESULT

		%
Elliott, J. (Lab)	19,495	45.9
Martin, L. (Con)	12,770	30.1
Dixon, P. (Lib Dem)	7,191	16.9
McCaffrey, J. (BNP)	1,913	4.5
Featonby-Warren, P. (UKIP)	1,094	2.6
Majority	6,725	15.76
Electorate	74,485	
Turnout	42,682	57.30

CONSTITUENCY SNAPSHOT

This new seat has been created out of parts of the old Sunderland seats, and includes the centre of the city and the suburbs of Ryhope, Fullwell, Southwick, Hendon and the tourist resort of Roker.

This industrial base of the North East has maintained its strong support for the Labour Party. Bill Etherington was first elected in 1987 and won a 9,995 majority in 2005. This new seat is classic Labour territory and despite a 5 per cent swing to the Tories Julie Elliott won with a comfortable 6,725 majority.

South of the River Wear, Sunderland is the southern sister of Newcastle upon Tyne and rivalry has existed for years, especially over the local football teams.

Sunderland's economy was for years focused on coalmining and shipbuilding, but these industries and others have disappeared from the city, along with the jobs that the locals relied on.

As a response to this decline, millions of pounds have been invested in the city's regeneration since the late 1980s. The site of the last coal mine, Wearmouth Colliery, is now occupied by the Stadium of Light, the home of Sunderland AFC.

Nissan built a factory in the city in 1986 which provides thousands of jobs and still operates today. The city has seen many new residential and commercial developments, and the service industries have plugged some of the jobs gap.

Michael Ellis

Northampton North

Boundary changes

Tel: 020 7219 3000
E-mail: michael.ellis.mp@parliament.uk
Website: www.michaelellis.co.uk

Date of birth: 1967

Education: LLB 1993; Inns of Court School of Law (bar vocational course)

Non-political career: Called to the Bar, Middle Temple 1993; Barrister, Clarendon Chambers, Northampton; Councillor, Northamptonshire County Council 1997

Political career: Member for Northampton North since 6 May 2010 general election

Recreations: Gym, theatre

Michael Ellis MP, House of Commons, London SW1A 0AA
Tel: 020 7219 3000 E-mail: michael.ellis.mp@parliament.uk
Constituency: 78 St George's Avenue, Northampton NN2 6JF
Tel: 01604 717188 Fax: 01604 716508
Website: www.michaelellis.co.uk

GENERAL ELECTION RESULT

		%
Ellis, M. (Con)	13,735	34.1
Keeble, S. (Lab)*	11,799	29.3
Simpson, A. (Lib Dem)	11,250	27.9
Beasley, R. (BNP)	1,316	3.3
MacArthur, J. (UKIP)	1,238	3.1
Lochmuller, T. (Green)	443	1.1
Fitzpatrick, E. (Ind)	334	0.8
Webb, T. (Christian)	98	0.2
Mildren, M. (Ind)	58	0.1
Majority	1,936	4.81
Electorate	64,230	
Turnout	40,271	62.70

**Member of last parliament*

CONSTITUENCY SNAPSHOT

This was a Conservative seat with healthy majorities, but in 1997 Labour's Sally Keeble won the seat with a 10,000 majority, a swing of 13 per cent to Labour.

Sally Keeble was re-elected in 2001 with a 7,893 margin over the Conservatives. In 2005, with a 4.8 per cent swing to the Conservatives, Keeble's majority was halved to just under 4,000.

In 2010 Keeble lost the seat to the Conservative Candidate, Michael Ellis. Ellis secured a majority of 1,936.

The seat lost its part-wards of Ecton Brook, Old Duston, Weston, St James, and the whole of Spencer ward to Northampton South. In return, the seat gained the rest of its Abingdon ward from Northampton South.

A large section of the constituency lies in the 1968 new-town development of Northampton, which sprawls north-east towards Wellingborough, north of the river Nene. It is a socially mixed, entirely urban seat comprising residential suburbs.

Since the decline of Britain's boot and shoe industry, Northampton has become a major distribution centre and something of a centre for financial services. The Weston Favell credit union is here as well as part of the headquarters of the Nationwide Building Society.

Jane Ellison

Battersea

Boundary changes

Tel: 020 7219 3000
E-mail: jane.ellison.mp@parliament.uk
Website: www.janeellison.net

Date of birth: 1964

Education: Oxford University (BA politics, philosophy and economics); Partner John

Non-political career: John Lewis Partnership, London: Manager, customer direct marketing, Senior manager, customer magazine, *Source*; Former Councillor, London Borough of Barnet Council; Governer, Honeywell Junior and Infants School, Battersea

Political career: Contested Pendle 2005 general election. Member for Battersea since 6 May 2010 general election; Member, Conservative Party 1983-

Political interests: Social exclusion, public transport, public services

Other organisations: Member, Battersea Society; Friend of Battersea Park

Recreations: Walking, singing in choir

Jane Ellison MP, House of Commons, London SW1A 0AA
Tel: 020 7219 3000 E-mail: jane.ellison.mp@parliament.uk
Constituency: c/o Wandsworth Conservatives, 3 Summerstown, London SW17 0QB Tel: 020 8944 0378
Website: www.janeellison.net

GENERAL ELECTION RESULT

		%
Ellison, J. (Con)	23,103	47.4
Linton, M. (Lab)*	17,126	35.1
Moran, L. (Lib Dem)	7,176	14.7
Evans, G. (Green)	559	1.2
MacDonald, C. (UKIP)	505	1.0
Salmon, H. (Ind)	168	0.3
Fox, T. (Ind)	155	0.3
Majority	5,977	12.25
Electorate	74,300	
Turnout	48,792	65.67

**Member of last parliament*

CONSTITUENCY SNAPSHOT

Battersea was created in 1983 with the merger of Battersea North and Battersea South. From 1935 until its abolition, the southern division elected an unbroken string of Labour MPs. The old northern was held by Labour from 1946 until 1983. Labour at first held the unified constituency too, but in 1987 a swing of 4.6 per cent to the Conservatives gave John Bowis the seat.

Battersea elected Martin Linton for Labour in 1997 with a 10.2 per cent swing. There was a further increase in Labour support in 2001, however, a swing to the Conservatives in 2005 gave Linton a majority of just 163. Jane Ellison took this key marginal seat for the Conservatives with a 6.5 per cent swing, winning a healthy 5,977 majority.

Boundary changes were minimal, with the seat gaining the part of Fairfield ward that was in Putney, while losing Wandsworth Common ward to Tooting.

Thanks to the influx of commuters, Battersea's social and demographic profile has changed considerably over the last quarter century. By 2001 the number of skilled manual workers was less than half the national average.

Striking as it is to those long familiar with the area, the gentrification of Battersea is sometimes overstated. Owner-occupancy may be higher than in the past but it is still low compared with the national average.

Despite its nationwide fame, Battersea power station has not been redeveloped since being decommissioned in 1983 - numerous plans having fallen through.

Louise Ellman

Liverpool Riverside (returning MP)

Boundary changes

Tel: 020 7219 5210
E-mail: ellmanl@parliament.uk
Website: www.louiseellman.co.uk

Labour/Co-operative

Date of birth: 14 November 1945; Daughter of late Harold and Anne Rosenberg

Education: Manchester High School for Girls; Hull University (BA sociology 1967); York University (MPhil social administration 1972); Married Geoffrey Ellman 1967 (1 son 1 daughter)

Non-political career: Open University tutor/further education lecturer; Member, TGWU; Councillor Lancashire County Council 1970-97: Leader of Council 1981-97; Councillor, West Lancashire District Council 1974-87; Vice-Chair, Lancashire Enterprises 1982-97; Founder Chair, Northwest Regional Association 1991-93

Political career: Member for Liverpool Riverside 1997-2010, for Liverpool Riverside (revised boundary) since 6 May 2010 general election; *Select Committees:* Member: Environment, Transport and Regional Affairs 1997-2001, Environment, Transport and Regional Affairs (Environment Sub-Committee) 1997-2001, Transport, Local Government and the Regions 2001-02, Transport, Local Government and the Regions (Transport Sub-Committee) 2001-02, Transport, Local Government and the Regions (Urban Affairs Sub-Committee) 2001-02, Transport 2002-10: Chair 2008-10; Member: Liaison 2008-10, Liaison (National Policy Statements Sub-committee) 2009-10; Member, Co-op Party; Vice-chair Labour Friends of Israel

Political interests: Regional government, local government, transport, public services, arts; Middle East

Other organisations: Chair Jewish Labour Movement 2004

Louise Ellman MP, House of Commons, London SW1A 0AA
Tel: 020 7219 5210 Fax: 020 7219 2592
E-mail: ellmanl@parliament.uk
Constituency: 515 The Cotton Exchange Building, Old Hall Street, Liverpool, Merseyside L3 9LQ Tel: 0151-236 2969
Fax: 0151-236 4301 Website: www.louiseellman.co.uk

GENERAL ELECTION RESULT

		%
Ellman, L. (Lab/Co-op)*	22,998	59.3
Marbrow, R. (Lib Dem)	8,825	22.7
Wu, K. (Con)	4,243	10.9
Crone, T. (Green)	1,355	3.5
Stafford, P. (BNP)	706	1.8
Gaskell, P. (UKIP)	674	1.7
Majority	14,173	36.53
Electorate	74,539	
Turnout	38,801	52.05

**Member of last parliament*

CONSTITUENCY SNAPSHOT

Labour has maintained is position within the seat for a number of decades. Even in the 1980s Robert Parry secured majorities around the 20,000 mark.

In 1997 Louise Ellman, replaced Robert Parry. In 2001 her majority fell to 13,950. Despite an 11 per cent swing to the Liberal Democrats Ellman held Riverside with a 10,214 majority. Ellman was re-elected in 2010 with a majority of 14,173.

The seat gained two part-wards from Liverpool Wavertree, and a part-ward each from Liverpool Garston and Liverpool Walton. It lost one part-ward to both Liverpool Wavertree and Liverpool Walton.

The seat includes the city centre with its cathedrals and universities, and, as its name suggests, the waterfront stretching from the working port to the north through the decayed old Dockland and to the more pleasant redeveloped Albert Dock and Festival Gardens. The seat was the site of the Toxteth riots in 1981.

Lime Street station is undergoing a £15 million renovation, which will be completed in 2013. The regeneration of the Kings waterfront has provided a new sports arena, and a conference and exhibition centre venue, and there are also ambitious plans to reconnect the city with the Mersey through a cruise liner port and a reworking of the Liverpool-Leeds canal.

Tobias Ellwood

Bournemouth East (returning MP)

Boundary changes

Tel: 020 7219 4349
E-mail: ellwoodt@parliament.uk
Website: www.tobiasellwood.com

Conservative

Date of birth: 12 August 1966; Son of Peter and Dr Caroline Ellwood

Education: Vienna International School, Austria; Loughborough University of Technology (BA design and technology 1990); City University Business School (MBA 1998); Married Hannah Ryan 2005

Non-political career: Army officer, Royal Green Jackets 1991-96; Researcher to Tom King MP 1996-97; Senior business development manager: London Stock Exchange 1998-2002, Allen and Overy 2002-04; Councillor, Dacorum Borough Council 1999-2003

Political career: Contested Worsley 2001 general election. Member for Bournemouth East 2005-10, for Bournemouth East (revised boundary) since 6 May 2010 general election; Opposition Whip 2005-07; Shadow Minister for Culture, Media and Sport 2007-10; *Select Committees:* Member: Environmental Audit 2005-06; Treasurer, Bow Group 2000; Chair, Conservative Insight 2000; Branch chair, South West Hertfordshire Conservative Association 1998-2003

Political interests: Defence, education, environment, tourism; Afghanistan, Gibraltar, Indonesia, Middle East, USA

Other organisations: CBI London Council 2000; *Publications:* Introduction to the Conservative Party

Recreations: Volleyball, windsurfing, saxophone, theatre

Tobias Ellwood MP, House of Commons, London SW1A 0AA
Tel: 020 7219 4349 Fax: 020 7219 0946
E-mail: ellwoodt@parliament.uk
Constituency: Boscombe Conservative Club, Haviland Road West, Boscombe, Bournemouth, Dorset BH1 4JW Tel: 01202 397047
Fax: 01202 397047 Website: www.tobiasellwood.com

GENERAL ELECTION RESULT

		%
Ellwood, T. (Con)*	21,320	48.4
Northover, L. (Lib Dem)	13,592	30.9
Stokes, D. (Lab)	5,836	13.3
Hughes, D. (UKIP)	3,027	6.9
Humphrey, S. (Ind)	249	0.6
Majority	7,728	17.55
Electorate	71,125	
Turnout	44,024	61.90

**Member of last parliament*

CONSTITUENCY SNAPSHOT

This seat has been Conservative since its creation, with David Atkinson returnng large majorities since before 1979, although this was greatly reduced in 1997 in an election where the Conservatives lost over 14 per cent of their vote.

In 2001 Atkinson's majority was further reduced to 3,434. David Atkinson stood down in 2005 and Tobias Ellwood increased the Conservative majority by 1,800 votes. Tobias Ellwood won this safe Tory seat with a 7,728 and just shy of a 50 per cent vote share.

Boundary changes moved Winton East part-ward to Bournemouth West, while part-wards Eastcliff and Springbourne, Moordown, and Queen's Park moved into the constituency.

The Dorset constituency of Bournemouth East, which includes the communities of Boscombe, Southbourne and Throop, is traversed by the river Stour which spills into Christchurch Bay on the constituency's boundary.

Bournemouth is a fast growing and prosperous town. The backbone of the local economy remains tourism. Visitors enjoy Bournemouth's miles of beaches and traditional seaside attractions, but increasingly people are also drawn to the area for its pubs and clubs.

Employment in Bournemouth is predominantly in the services sector. Financial services account for 10 per cent of industry, while education, health and social work account for 20 per cent of employment.

Charlie Elphicke

Dover

Boundary changes

Tel: 020 7219 3000
E-mail: charlie.elphicke.mp@parliament.uk
Website: www.elphicke.com

Conservative

Date of birth: 14 March 1971

Education: Felsted School, Essex; Nottingham University (LLB 1993); Inns of Court School of Law (Bar Finals 1994); Married Natalie Ross Pears 1996 (1 son 1 daughter)

Non-political career: Formerly ran printing business; Called to the Bar, Middle Temple 1994; Solicitor: Supreme Court of England and Wales, Cameron, McKenna and Wilde Sapte 1996-2001; Partner: Reed Smith 2001-05, Mayer Brown 2006, Hunton & Williams Solicitors; Councillor, London Borough of Lambeth Council 1994-98

Political career: Contested St Albans 2001 general election. Member for Dover since 6 May 2010 general election; Chair, Dulwich and West Norwood Conservatives 1999-2000

Political interests: Poverty alleviation, wealth creation, transport

Other organisations: Research fellow, Centre for Policy Studies

Recreations: Sailing, walking by the sea, spending time with family

Charlie Elphicke MP, House of Commons, London SW1A 0AA
Tel: 020 7219 3000 E-mail: charlie.elphicke.mp@parliament.uk
Constituency: c/o Dover and Deal Conservative Association, 54 The Strand, Walmer, Deal, Kent CT14 7DP Tel: 01304 379669
Website: www.elphicke.com

GENERAL ELECTION RESULT

		%
Elphicke, C. (Con)	22,174	44.0
Prosser, G. (Lab)*	16,900	33.5
Brigden, J. (Lib Dem)	7,962	15.8
Matcham, V. (UKIP)	1,747	3.5
Whiting, D. (BNP)	1,104	2.2
Walters, M. (England)	216	0.4
Clark, D. (CPA)	200	0.4
Lee-Delisle, G. (Ind)	82	0.2
Majority	5,274	10.47
Electorate	71,832	
Turnout	50,385	70.14

**Member of last parliament*

CONSTITUENCY SNAPSHOT

Between 1945 and 1970 the constituency switched between Labour and Conservative in line with the government of the day. But from 1970 the Conservatives held the seat for the next 27 years, represented by Peter Rees until 1987 and then David Shaw until 1997. Mr Shaw's majority was cut to 833 at the 1992 election.

The seat was won by Labour's Gwyn Prosser in 1997 with a 11,739 majority. Prosser held the seat in 2001, with a reduced majority of 5,199. In 2005 the Labour and Tory vote held steady and Prosser won a satisfactory majority of 4,941.

Gwyn Prosser was defeated in the 2010 general election with a 10.4 per cent swing to the Conservative candidate, Charlie Elphicke.

Boundary changes were minimal.

Dover is a town rich in heritage and dominated by the famous white cliffs and the ferry port, along with some very attractive surrounding countryside. The working-class town of Dover and many towns that were based around the old Kent coalfields sit alongside rather more genteel seaside spots and numerous affluent villages.

Some 10,000 jobs are provided by the historic Port of Dover, the busiest passenger ferry port in the world, which handles almost 2 million lorries and over 15 million passengers a year. Tourism, packaging, chemical instruments, agriculture and engineering are also important employment sectors.

Natascha Engel

North East Derbyshire ***(returning MP)***

Boundary changes

Tel: 020 7219 4709
E-mail: engeln@parliament.uk
Website: www.nataschaengelmp.org.uk

Labour

Date of birth: 9 April 1967; Daughter of Christina Sheehan and Achaz Engel

Education: Kent College, Canterbury, Kent; King's School, Canterbury, Kent; King's College, London (BA German and Portuguese 1990); Westminster University (MA technical and specialist translation 1992); Married David Salisbury Jones 2001 (3 sons)

Non-political career: Journalist *Dover Express* 1990; English and German teacher, Spain 1990-92; Teletext subtitler for ITV and Channel 5 1993-96; Organiser Trade Union Congress Organising Academy 1996-97; Trade Union liaison officer Labour Party 1997-2001; Programme director Smith Institute 2001-02; Ballot co-ordinator Trade Union Political Fund 2002-03; Member: GMB/VCATT

Political career: Member for North East Derbyshire 2005-10, for North East Derbyshire (revised boundary) since 6 May 2010 general election; PPS: to Peter Hain as Secretary of State for Work and Pensions 2007-08, to Liam Byrne as Minister for the Cabinet Office and Chancellor of the Duchy of Lancaster 2008-09, to John Denham as Secretary of State for Communities and Local Government 2009; *Select Committees:* Member: Work and Pensions 2005-07, Reform of the House of Commons 2009-10; Labour Party: National trade union policy co-ordinator 1998-2000, National trade union general election co-ordinator 2000-01

Political interests: Youth, welfare rights, regeneration, pensions, sexual health; Germany, Spain, USA

Other organisations: Fabian Society, Amnesty International; *Publications:* Several pamphlets including: Shop Stewards' Pocket Policy Guide, Trade Union Links with the Labour Party, Rights Won By Unions, Age of Regions, Learning to Organise

Recreations: Sports

Natascha Engel MP, House of Commons, London SW1A 0AA
Tel: 020 7219 4709 Fax: 020 7219 0209
E-mail: engeln@parliament.uk
Constituency: 62 Market Street, Eckington, Derbyshire S21 4JH
Tel: 01246 439018 Fax: 01246 439024
Website: www.nataschaengelmp.org.uk

GENERAL ELECTION RESULT

		%
Engel, N. (Lab)*	17,948	38.2
Merriman, H. (Con)	15,503	33.0
Bull, R. (Lib Dem)	10,947	23.3
Bush, J. (UKIP)	2,636	5.6
Majority	2,445	5.20
Electorate	71,422	
Turnout	47,034	65.85

**Member of last parliament*

CONSTITUENCY SNAPSHOT

In the 1950s and 1960s the Labour MPs were miners and were elected with sizable majorities. But by February 1974 their margin had fallen to 14 per cent and by 1983 Labour's majority was reduced to just over 2,000.

But then the trend reversed and Harry Barnes increased his margin in 1987. In 1997 there was a swing of 12 per cent to Labour and Harry Barnes was re-elected with a large 18,321 majority. Harry Barnes retired in 2005 and was replaced by Natascha Engel who was able to keep Labour's majority in five figures.

Engel secured a much-reduced 2,445 majority following a swing of 8.6 per cent to the Tories at the 2010 general election.

A small number of wards were lost to Bolsover and Chesterfield.

An oddly shaped constituency, North East Derbyshire surrounds Chesterfield on three sides. The constituency stretches from the heavily industrialised at the south east of Sheffield to other former mining areas around Clay Cross, but it also includes rural and residential areas on the fringes of the Peak District National Park. Dronfield, the seat's largest town, is now largely a dormitory suburb for Sheffield.

Bill Esterson

Sefton Central

New constituency

Tel: 020 7219 3000
E-mail: bill.esterson.mp@parliament.uk
Website: www.billesterson.org.uk

Labour

Date of birth: 27 October 1966; Son of Derek and Joyce Esterson

Education: Rochester Mathematical School; Leeds University (BSc maths and philosophy 1990); Married Caroline (1 son 1 daughter)

Non-political career: Director, training consultancy; Unite; Medway Council: Councillor 1995-, Labour Spokesperson for Children's Services

Political career: Member for Sefton Central since 6 May 2010 general election

Political interests: Children's service

Other organisations: Trustee, Chatham Maritime Trust

Recreations: Playing hockey and cricket

Bill Esterson MP, House of Commons, London SW1A 0AA
Tel: 020 7219 3000 E-mail: bill.esterson.mp@parliament.uk
Constituency: 31 Liverpool Road North, Maghull, Merseyside L31 2HB Tel: 07976 628730
Website: www.billesterson.org.uk

GENERAL ELECTION RESULT

		%
Esterson, B. (Lab)	20,307	41.9
Jones, D. (Con)	16,445	33.9
Clein, R. (Lib Dem)	9,656	19.9
Harper, P. (UKIP)	2,055	4.2
Majority	3,862	7.97
Electorate	67,512	
Turnout	48,463	71.78

CONSTITUENCY SNAPSHOT

This new seat combines wards from Crosby and Knowsley North and Sefton East.

Until 1997 Crosby had all the hallmarks of a safe Tory seat: middle-class, owner-occupied, and containing some of Liverpool's most affluent suburbs. The Conservatives' post second world-war reign had been punctuated only once by Shirley Williams' by-election victory for the SDP in 1981. Claire Curtis-Thomas held Crosby for Labour from 1987 until it was abolished in 2010. Curtis-Thomas retired in 2010.

Knowsley North and Sefton East was a Labour seat from its creation in 1983. George Howarth represented the seat from 1986 and had a 16,269 majority in 2005.

Labour's Bill Esterson was elected for the new seat with a majority of 3,862.

This new Merseyside seat connects the majority of the old Knowsley North and Sefton East Seat with areas from neighbouring Crosby. This creates a socially mixed seat, as the constituency comprises two very separate entities.

Major employers in the constituency include Kodak and the News International operations.

George Eustice

Camborne and Redruth

New constituency

Tel: 020 7219 3000
E-mail: george.eustice.mp@parliament.uk
Website: www.georgeeustice.co.uk

Conservative

Education: Truro Cathedral School; Truro School; Cornwall College, Poole

Non-political career: Trevaskis Fruit Farm; Conservative Party: Campaign director, anti-Euro 'No Campaign'; Head of press, 2005 general election; Press Secretary to Conservative Leader David Cameron 2005-07; External relations co-ordinator, Conservative HQ 2008-09; Associate director, Portland PR 2009-

Political career: Member for Camborne and Redruth since 6 May 2010 general election; Contested South West region (UKIP) 1999 European Parliament election; Member, UKIP 1998-99; Conservative Party: Campaign director, anti-Euro 'No Campaign'; Head of press, 2005 general election; Press Secretary to Conservative Leader David Cameron 2005-07; External relations co-ordinator, Conservative HQ 2008-

George Eustice MP, House of Commons, London SW1A 0AA
Tel: 020 7219 3000 E-mail: george.eustice.mp@parliament.uk
Constituency: Camborne and Redruth Conservative Club, Tehidy Road, Camborne, Cornwall TR14 8TB
Website: www.georgeeustice.co.uk

GENERAL ELECTION RESULT

		%
Eustice, G. (Con)	15,969	37.6
Goldsworthy, J. (Lib Dem)*	15,903	37.4
Robinson, J. (Lab)	6,945	16.3
Elliott, D. (UKIP)	2,152	5.1
Jenkin, L. (Meb Ker)	775	1.8
McPhee, E. (Green)	581	1.4
Hawkins, R. (SLP)	168	0.4
Majority	66	0.16
Electorate	63,968	
Turnout	42,493	66.43

**Member of last parliament*

CONSTITUENCY SNAPSHOT

The Liberal Democrats have a stronghold in Cornwall but this seat has been claimed by both the Tories and Labour in equal measure. It was the constituency of former Olympic athlete and Conservative Sebastian Coe in 1992 for one parliament, until Labour's Candy Atherton won in 1997.

Atherton was re-elected in 2001, however, in 2005 a 10.4 per cent swing for the Liberal Democrats allowed them to leap from third to first, their candidate Julia Goldsworthy winning with a 1,886 majority. Goldsworthy lost as the seat swung back to the Conservatives, with George Eustice winning a miniscule majority of 66.

Camborne and Redruth was created out of the majority of Falmouth and Camborne (with the exception of the Falmouth wards), and the northern four wards from St Ives. In addition Mount Hawke ward from the west of Truro and St Austell.

Camborne was once one of the richest mining areas in the world, whilst Redruth was the commercial capital of the mining industry. Since its decline much of Cornwall's poverty has been concentrated in this seat. However, it is hoped that the local economy might benefit from tin-mining.

Although there is great deal of rural land here, much of it uninhabited, the population density in this constituency is one of the highest in the South West, with Camborne, Redruth, and Poole making the largest conurbation in Cornwall.

Christopher Evans

Islwyn

Boundary changes

Tel: 020 7219 3000
E-mail: chris.evans.mp@parliament.uk

Labour/Co-operative

Education: Porth County Comprehensive; Pontypridd College; Trinity College, Carmarthen (history)

Non-political career: Book maker; Official, Union of Finance Staff 2004; Parliamentary researcher to Don Touhig MP; Member, Unite

Political career: Contested Cheltenham 2005 general election. Member for Islwyn since 6 May 2010 general election; Member, Co-operative Party

Other organisations: Member, Fabian Society

Recreations: Watching sports, running, reading

Christopher Evans MP, House of Commons, London SW1A 0AA
Tel: 020 7219 3000 E-mail: chris.evans.mp@parliament.uk

GENERAL ELECTION RESULT

		%
Evans, C. (Lab/Co-op)	17,069	49.2
Thomas, D. (Con)	4,854	14.0
Lewis, S. (PlC)	4,518	13.0
Ali, A. (Lib Dem)	3,597	10.4
Rees, D. (Ind)	1,495	4.3
Voisey, J. (BNP)	1,320	3.8
Crew, J. (UKIP)	936	2.7
Taylor, P. (Ind)	901	2.6
Majority	12,215	35.21
Electorate	54,826	
Turnout	34,690	63.27

CONSTITUENCY SNAPSHOT

Islwyn and its predecessor seat Bedwellty have been won by Labour at every general election since the latter was created in 1918. Neil Kinnock first won Bedwellty in 1970 and he held the seat, which became Islwyn in 1983, until he resigned the seat to become a European Commissioner. Labour's Don Touhig won the February 1995 by-election with a majority of 13,097. In 2005 Touhig achieved a majority of 15,740 . Don Touhig retired in 2010 and was succeeded by Christopher Evans who won with a 12,215 majority.

Islwyn has been enlarged. The new voters come from the Aberbargoed and Maesycwmmer electoral divisions which were transferred from Caerphilly.

Set in the Western valley of Gwent and part of Caerphilly, this constituency, which is named after a Welsh language poet of the 19th century, includes Blackwood, Newbridge and Risca.

Islwyn is a former mining district, with the Oakdale mine the last to close in 1989, and has since attracted new light industry, which has become a mainstay of the economy. It has Wales' largest proportion of its workforce in manufacturing sectors.

The re-opening of the Ebbw Valley Line reconnects Newbridge and Risca with the national rail network which could presage these valleys towns becoming commuter areas for Cardiff.

Graham Evans

Weaver Vale

Boundary changes

Tel: 020 7219 3000
E-mail: graham.evans.mp@parliament.uk

Date of birth: 10 November 1963

Education: Poynton County High; Manchester Metropolitan University (BA business studies 2000); Postgraduate Diploma marketing management; Married Cheryl 1995 (1 daughter 2 sons)

Non-political career: BAe Systems; Sun Chemical; Hewlett Packard; UK managing director, Italian manufacturing company; Macclesfield Borough Council: Councillor 2000-, Chair, Community Development Committee

Political career: Contested Worsley 2005 general election. Member for Weaver Vale since 6 May 2010 general election; North West Area Officer, Conservative Party

Political interests: Education, health, trade, Ministry of Defence

Other organisations: Member, Countryside Alliance

Recreations: Football, running, British history

Graham Evans MP, House of Commons, London SW1A 0AA
Tel: 020 7219 3000 E-mail: graham.evans.mp@parliament.uk
Constituency: Weaver Vale Conservatives, Vale House Business Centre, Aston Lane North, Runcorn WA7 3PA Tel: 01928 790547
Website: www.weavervaleconservatives.com; www.cllrgrahamevans.com

GENERAL ELECTION RESULT

		%
Evans, G. (Con)	16,953	38.5
Stockton, J. (Lab)	15,962	36.3
Hampson, P. (Lib Dem)	8,196	18.6
Marsh, C. (BNP)	1,063	2.4
Remfry, P. (UKIP)	1,018	2.3
Thorp, H. (Green)	338	0.8
Cooksley, M. (Ind)	270	0.6
Reynolds, T. (Ind)	133	0.3
Charlton, W. (Ind)	57	0.1
Majority	991	2.25
Electorate	66,538	
Turnout	43,990	66.11

CONSTITUENCY SNAPSHOT

The seat was created in 1997 from parts of four existing seats: Eddisbury, Tatton, Warrington South, and Halton. Mike Hall won the seat in that year by over 10,000 votes.

The 2001 general election produced relatively little change, other than a larger-than-average fall in turnout. In 2005 Hall was elected with less than 50 per cent of the vote for the first time, but with a majority of 6,855.

Hall retired before the 2010 general election. The Conservatives took the seat with Graham Evans securing a small majority of 991.

The seat gained the part-wards of Hartford and Whitegate and Leftwich and Kingsmead from Eddisbury, and lost the part-wards of Castlefields, Halton Brook and Mersey to Halton and Rudheath and South Witton to Tatton.

The Cheshire constituency of Weaver Vale has a varied landscape. Centred on industrial Northwich, the seat takes in rural Helsby, popular with hill-walkers, and affluent commuter towns such as Hartford.

Salt-mining is the major industry here, and the presence of salt led to the establishment of the huge ICI works at Winnington.

The development of Northwich originated from its wealth gained from the salt works.

Jonathan Evans

Cardiff North

No boundary changes

Tel: 020 7219 3000
E-mail: jonathan.evans.mp@parliament.uk
Website: www.jonathanevans.co.uk

Conservative

Date of birth: 2 June 1950; Son of David and Harriet Evans

Education: Lewis School, Pengram; Howardian High School, Cardiff; Law Society's College of Law, Guildford and London; Married Margaret Thomas 1975 (2 daughters 1 son)

Non-political career: Leo Abse and Cohen solicitors: Trainee 1968-73, Solicitor 1973-87, Managing partner 1987-92; Insurance director, Eversheds law firm 1997-99

Political career: Contested Ebbow Vale February and October 1974, Wolverhampton North East 1979 and Brecon and Radnor 1987 general elections. Member for Brecon and Radnor 1992-97, for Cardiff North since 6 May 2010 general election; Parliamentary Private Secretary to Michael Mates as Minister of State for Northern Ireland 1992-94; Minister for Corporate and Consumer Affairs, Department of Trade and Industry 1994-95; Parliamentary Secretary, Lord Chancellor's Department, 1995-96; Under Secretary of State for Wales 1996-97; MEP for Wales 1999-2009: Conservative EP Leader 2001-09; Member: Japan Delegation 1999-2004, Economic and Monetary Affairs Committee 1999-2009; Chair: United States Delegation 2004-09; Member: Conference of Delegation Chairmen 2004-09; Chair, Cardiff Central Young Conservatives 1968; Vice-chair, Wales Conservative Political Centre 1974-76; Member, Conservative Working Party on Devolution in Wales 1975; Chair, Welsh Conservative Parliamentary Candidates 1985-90; Conservative spokesperson for Wales 1997-98

Political interests: Housing, family law, agriculture, rural affairs, economic and monetary affairs, trade and industry

Other organisations: Fellow, Royal Society of Arts 1995

Recreations: Watching rugby, music, family, reading

Jonathan Evans MP, House of Commons, London SW1A 0AA
Tel: 020 7219 3000 E-mail: jonathan.evans.mp@parliament.uk
Constituency: c/o Welsh Consevatives, 4 Penlline Road, Whitchurch, Cardiff CF14 2XS Tel: 029 2061 6031 Fax: 029 2061 3539
Website: www.jonathanevans.co.uk

GENERAL ELECTION RESULT

		%	+/-
Evans, J. (Con)	17,860	37.5	1.1
Morgan, J. (Lab)*	17,666	37.1	-1.9
Dixon, J. (Lib Dem)	8,724	18.3	-0.4
Rhys, L. (PIC)	1,588	3.3	-0.9
Gwyn, L. (UKIP)	1,130	2.4	1.2
Von Ruhland, C. (Green)	362	0.8	
Thomson, D. (WCP)	300	0.6	
Majority	194	0.41	
Electorate	65,553		
Turnout	47,630	72.66	

**Member of last parliament*

CONSTITUENCY SNAPSHOT

The constituency was created in 1983 from the old Cardiff North West seat, which included part of Barry. Tory Gwilym Jones was the first winner in the seat and continued to represent it until 1997.

In 1992 Labour established themselves as credible challengers to the Tories by squeezing the third-placed Lib Dem vote. In 1997 Julie Morgan overturned the small Tory majority and transformed it into one for Labour of 8,126 votes.

In 2005 the Conservatives achieved a 5.9 per cent swing to cut Julie Morgan's majority to just 1,146. Tory Jonathan Evans managed to win this key target seat in 2010 with a tiny 194 majority from Labour's Julie Morgan.

The northern Cardiff division includes the most attractive suburbs surrounding the Welsh capital. These include Lisvane, Llandaff and Whitchurch.

Arguably the most prosperous place in Wales, the seat has very high levels of home ownership and a large number of those homes are large detached houses. There are also former council estates at former council estates in Llandaff North and Gabalfa.

Major employers include the Inland Revenue, Companies House and the University Hospital of Wales.

Nigel Evans

***Ribble Valley* (returning MP)**

Boundary changes

Tel: 020 7219 6939
E-mail: evansn@parliament.uk
Website: www.nigelmp.com

Conservative

Date of birth: 10 November 1957; Son of late Albert Evans, and Betty Evans

Education: Dynevor School; University College of Wales, Swansea (BA politics 1979); Single

Non-political career: Management family retail newsagent and convenience store 1979-90; West Glamorgan County Council: Councillor 1985-91, Deputy Leader, Conservative Group 1990-91

Political career: Contested Swansea West 1987 general election and Pontypridd 1989 and Ribble Valley 1991 by-elections. Member for Ribble Valley 1992-2010, for Ribble Valley (revised boundary) since 6 May 2010 general election; PPS : to David Hunt: as Secretary of State for Employment 1993-94, as Chancellor of the Duchy of Lancaster 1994-95, to Tony Baldry as Minister of State, Ministry of Agriculture, Fisheries and Food 1995-96, to William Hague as Secretary of State for Wales 1996-97; Opposition Spokesperson for: Scotland and Wales 1997-99, Wales 1999-2001; Shadow Secretary of State for Wales 2001-03; *Select Committees:* Member: Welsh Affairs 2003-05, Trade and Industry 2003-05, Culture, Media and Sport 2005-09, International Development 2009-10, Chairmen's Panel 2009-10; Chair Conservative Welsh Parliamentary Candidates Policy Group 1990; President Conservative North West Parliamentary Candidates Group 1991; Secretary North West Conservative MPs 1992-97; Vice-chair: Conservative Party (Wales) 1999-2001, Conservative Party (Conservatives Abroad) 2004-05

Political interests: Education, small businesses, US elections, local and regional government, defence, agriculture, international politics, European affairs, telecommunications, space; Australia, Bahrain, Caribbean, Egypt, Europe, Far East, Gibraltar, USA

Other organisations: Has worked on three US presidential elections in New York, Florida and California; British Inter-Parliamentary Union: Treasurer 2005-08, Vice-chair 2008-10; Member executive Commonwealth Parliamentary Association 2005-; Member: Council of Europe 2006, Western European Union 2006-; UK chair Technological and Aerospace committee; Hon Treasurer, Commonwealth Parliamentary Association (UK Branch) 2010-; Fellow Industry and Parliament Trust 1998; Carlton, countryclubuk.com

Recreations: Tennis, swimming, running, theatre, cinema, arts

Nigel Evans MP, House of Commons, London SW1A 0AA
Tel: 020 7219 6939 Fax: 020 7219 2568
E-mail: evansn@parliament.uk
Constituency: 9 Railway View, Clitheroe, Lancashire BB7 2HA
Tel: 01200 425939 Fax: 01200 422904 Website: www.nigelmp.com

GENERAL ELECTION RESULT

		%
Evans, N. (Con)*	26,298	50.3
Foster, P. (Lab)	11,529	22.1
Knox, A. (Lib Dem)	10,732	20.5
Rush, S. (UKIP)	3,496	6.7
Johnson, T. (Ind)	232	0.4
Majority	14,769	28.25
Electorate	78,068	
Turnout	52,287	66.98

**Member of last parliament*

CONSTITUENCY SNAPSHOT

Ribble Valley has been Tory since its inception in 1983, when it was won by David Waddington until he stepped down in 1991. This led to a by-election and a Liberal Democrat victory. Michael Carr won with a majority of over 4,000, but could not consolidate this success and Nigel Evans re-took the seat for the Conservatives at the 1992 general election.

Since 1992 Evans has maintained a sizable majority. He has consistently polled over 50 per cent of the vote. In 2010 Evans was re-elected with a comfortable majority of 14,769.

The seat gained a number of wards from Preston and South Ribble, while losing others to Preston and Wyre and Preston North.

This is a mainly residential area, but there is a growing tourist industry as farmers diversify to cope with the decline of agriculture. Growth in tourism will depend on better transport links to the area.

The Ribble Valley has historically low employment and as elsewhere in Lancashire, a higher percentage of jobs in the manufacturing sector than the national average. The local economy is kept vibrant by major companies based in Clitheroe, such as Tarmac, Castle Cement and Ultraframe.

David Evennett

Bexleyheath and Crayford ***(returning MP)***

Boundary changes

Tel: 020 7219 8403
E-mail: evennettd@parliament.uk
Website: www.davidevennett.org.uk

Conservative

Date of birth: 3 June 1949; Son of late Norman Thomas Evennett and Irene, née Turner

Education: Buckhurst Hill County High School for Boys; London School of Economics (BSc Econ economics 1971, MSc Econ politics 1972); Married Marilyn Smith 1975 (2 sons)

Non-political career: Schoolmaster Ilford County High School 1972-74; Marine insurance broker Lloyds 1974-81; Member Lloyds 1976-92; Director Lloyds Underwriting Agency 1982-91; Commercial liaison manager Bexley College 1997-2001; Consultant J&H Marsh and McLennan (UK) then Marsh (UK) Ltd 1998-2000; Freelance lecturer 2001-05; Councillor London Borough of Redbridge 1974-78

Political career: Contested Hackney South and Shoreditch 1979 general election. Member for Erith and Crayford 1983-97. Contested Bexleyheath and Crayford 1997 and 2001 general elections. Member for Bexleyheath and Crayford since 5 May 2005 general election; PPS: to Baroness Blatch as Minister of State for Education 1992-93, to John Redwood as Secretary of State for Wales 1993-95, to Baroness Blatch and David Maclean as Ministers of State, Home Office 1995-96, to Gillian Shephard as Secretary of State for Education and Employment 1996-1997; Opposition Whip 2005-09; Shadow Minister for: Innovations, Universities and Skills 2009, Universities and Skills 2009-10; *Select Committees:* Member: Education and Skills 2005-06

Political interests: Education, economy, transport, London; Australia, Austria, Canada, Italy, New Zealand, Sweden, USA

Other organisations: Bexleyheath Conservative Club

Recreations: Travel, reading, cinema, family

David Evennett MP, House of Commons, London SW1A 0AA
Tel: 020 7219 8403 Fax: 020 7219 2163
E-mail: evennettd@parliament.uk
Constituency: Bexleyheath and Crayford Conservative Association, 17 Church Road, Bexleyheath, Kent DA7 4DD Tel: 020 8303 4695
Fax: 020 8303 1497 Website: www.davidevennett.org.uk

GENERAL ELECTION RESULT

		%
Evennett, D. (Con)*	21,794	50.5
Dawber, H. (Lab)	11,450	26.5
Scott, K. (Lib Dem)	5,502	12.7
James, S. (BNP)	2,042	4.7
Dunford, J. (UKIP)	1,557	3.6
Griffiths, J. (England)	466	1.1
Ross, A. (Green)	371	0.9
Majority	10,344	23.95
Electorate	64,985	
Turnout	43,182	66.45

**Member of last parliament*

CONSTITUENCY SNAPSHOT

This seat was created before the 1997 election from parts of Conservative Bexleyheath and the Labour-Tory marginal of Erith and Crayford. In 1997 Nigel Beard won with a victory for Labour, winning 45.5 per cent of the vote and taking a 3,415 majority over Tory David Evennett.

The Tories looked as if they might recover the seat in 2001 but Nigel Beard defied expectations again, returning the seat with a majority of 1,472. However, the Tories won the seat in 2005 with a 6.4 per cent swing, giving David Evennett a 4,551 majority. Evennett increased the Tory majority to 10,344 in 2010.

Boundary changes have been minimal.

Local industries have declined in the area since the 1980s and this is now a mainly residential, suburban part of London's commuter belt. Vickers, Fraser and Chalmers were all major engineering companies in the area that have closed down.

It is hoped that the development of the Thames Gateway will provide new housing, jobs and transport infrastructure and the Crossrail route from Heathrow Airport will pass through central London through Greenwich and the constituency to Dartford and the Channel Tunnel Rail Link.

Michael Fabricant

Lichfield (returning MP)

Boundary changes

Tel: 020 7219 5022
E-mail: fabricantm@parliament.uk
Website: www.michael.fabricant.mp.co.uk

Conservative

Date of birth: 12 June 1950; Son of late Isaac Nathan Fabricant, and of Helena Fabricant, neé Freed

Education: Brighton, Hove and Sussex Grammar School, Brighton; Loughborough University (BSc economics and law 1973); Sussex University (MSc systems and econometrics 1974); Oxford University/London University/University of Southern California, Los Angeles, USA (PhD econometrics and economic forecasting 1975-78); Single

Non-political career: Economist and founder director, leading broadcast and communications group, manufacturing and commissioning electronics equipment to radio stations to 48 countries 1980-91; Adviser, Home Office on broadcasting matters; Staff, then freelance radio broadcaster and journalist 1968-80; Adviser to foreign governments on establishment and management of radio stations, including Russian Federation 1980-91; Has lived and worked extensively in Europe, Africa, the Far East, former Soviet Union, and USA; Member: Council of the Institution of Electrical Engineers 1996-2000, Senate of the Engineering Council 1996-2002; Director Engineering and Technology Board 2002-06

Political career: Contested South Shields 1987 general election. Member for Mid-Staffordshire 1992-97, for Lichfield 1997-2010, for Lichfield (revised boundary) since 6 May 2010 general election; Presented Bills to strengthen economic and political ties between UK, USA, Canada, Australia and New Zealand; Promoted legislation to encourage flying of Union Flag and to force Government to undertake and publish regular financial cost-benefit analyses of Britain's membership of European Union; PPS to Michael Jack as Financial Secretary to the Treasury 1996-97; Shadow Minister for: Trade and Industry 2003, Economic Affairs 2003-05; Opposition Whip 2005-10; Government Whip 2010-; *Select Committees:* Member: Culture, Media and Sport 1997-99, Home Affairs 1999-2001, Catering 1999-2001, Liaison 2001-03; Chair: Information 2001-03; Member: Finance and Services 2001-04, Culture, Media and Sport 2001-05, Administration 2009-10; Chair Brighton Pavilion Conservative Association 1985-88; Member Conservative Way Forward; Associate Member European Research Group; Member Conservative Against a Federal Europe; Member 1922 Committee Executive 2001-03; Chair Conservative Friends of America 2007-

Political interests: Broadcasting and media, business, defence, engineering, enterprise, exports, foreign affairs, heritage, industry, inland waterways, international aid and development, international trade, internet, manufacturing, police and security issues, science and technology, technology, telecommunications, trade and industry, Wales; USA, Australia, Eastern Europe, Middle East

Other organisations: Member: Inter-Parliamentary Union, Commonwealth Parliamentary Association; CEng; FIET; FRSA; Rottingdean (Sussex)

Recreations: Reading, music, fell-walking, skiing and listening to the Omnibus Edition of The Archers

Michael Fabricant MP, House of Commons, London SW1A 0AA
Tel: 020 7219 5022 E-mail: fabricantm@parliament.uk
Constituency: 28a Tamworth Street, Lichfield, Staffordshire WS13 6JJ
Tel: 01543 417868 Website: www.michael.fabricant.mp.co.uk

GENERAL ELECTION RESULT

		%
Fabricant, M. (Con)*	28,048	54.4
Jackson, I. (Lib Dem)	10,365	20.1
Hyden, S. (Lab)	10,230	19.8
Maunder, K. (UKIP)	2,920	5.7
Majority	17,683	34.29
Electorate	72,586	
Turnout	51,563	71.04

**Member of last parliament*

CONSTITUENCY SNAPSHOT

In 1992 Michael Fabricant was responsible for defeating the Labour MP Sylvia Heal from Mid Staffordshire after she had won the by-election with a 21 per cent swing in 1990.

When Mid Staffordshire was dismembered in 1997, Fabricant won Lichfield with only 238 votes. In 2001 Fabricant secured a 4,426-vote majority. He added a further 3,000 to his majority in 2005 and increased it once again in 2010 to 17,683.

There were minor changes to Lichfield's boundaries. The seat gained Needwood from Burton, as well as the part of Yoxall that was also in Burton's boundaries.

Lichfield is an affluent seat situated in south-east Staffordshire includes the cathedral city from which the constituency takes its name, the town of Burntwood, and surrounding Staffordshire villages.

The largest urban area is the city of Lichfield, a historic market town made famous by its cathedral. There are many Birmingham and West Midlands commuters here and there was a great deal of residential expansion during the 1980s and 1990s.

In total, a fifth of constituents are managers or senior officials, while there are fewer working in elementary occupations than the national average.

Michael Fallon

Sevenoaks (returning MP)

Boundary changes

Tel: 020 7219 6482
E-mail: fallonm@parliament.uk
Website: www.michaelfallonmp.org.uk

Conservative

Date of birth: 14 May 1952; Son of late Martin Fallon, OBE, FRICS, and Hazel Fallon

Education: Epsom College, Surrey; St Andrews University (MA classics and ancient history 1974); Married Wendy Elisabeth Payne 1986 (2 sons)

Non-political career: European Educational Research Trust 1974-75; Conservative Research Department 1975-79 (seconded to Opposition Whips Office, House of Lords 1975-77, EEC Desk Officer 1977-79); Secretary, Lord Home's Committee on Future of the House of Lords 1977-78; Joint Managing Director, European Consultants Ltd 1979-81; Assistant to Baroness Elles MEP 1979-83; Director, Quality Care Homes plc 1992-97; Chief Executive, Quality Care Developments Ltd 1996-97; Director: Just Learning Ltd 1996-, Bannatyne Fitness Ltd 1999-2000, Just Learning Holdings 2001-, Just Learning Development Ltd 2001-, Careshare Ltd, 2003-, Collins Stewart Tullet Plc, 2004-06 Tullett Prebon Plc 2006-, Attendo AB 2008-

Political career: Contested Darlington March 1983 by-election. Member for Darlington 1983-92, for Sevenoaks 1997-2010, for Sevenoaks (revised boundary) since 6 May 2010 general election; PPS to Cecil Parkinson as Secretary of State for Energy 1987-88; Assistant Government Whip 1988-90; Government Whip May-July 1990; Parliamentary Under-Secretary of State, Department of Education and Science 1990-92; Opposition Frontbench Spokesperson for: Trade and Industry June-December 1997, the Treasury December 1997-98; *Select Committees:* Member: Treasury 1999-2010, Treasury (Treasury Sub-Committee) 1999-2001; Chair: Treasury (Treasury Sub-Committee) 2001-10; Member Executive 1922 Committee 2005-07

Political interests: Constitution, public sector, education, Treasury

Other organisations: Non-executive director International Care and Relief 1998-2003; Board member Centre for Policy Studies 2009-; Member: Higher Education Funding Council 1992-97, Deregulation Task Force 1994-97, Advisory Council, Social Market Foundation 1994-2000; Academy; *Publications:* Brighter Schools (Social Market Foundation, 1993); Putting Social Mobility Back Into Britain (NTB, 2007)

Recreations: Skiing, opera, visiting classical sites

Michael Fallon MP, House of Commons, London SW1A 0AA
Tel: 020 7219 6482 Fax: 020 7219 6791
E-mail: fallonm@parliament.uk
Constituency: Bank House, 13 Vestry Road, Sevenoaks, Kent TN14 5EL Tel: 01732 452261 Fax: 01732 465839
Website: www.michaelfallonmp.org.uk

GENERAL ELECTION RESULT

		%
Fallon, M. (Con)*	28,076	56.8
Bullion, A. (Lib Dem)	10,561	21.4
Siddorn, G. (Lab)	6,541	13.2
Heath, C. (UKIP)	1,782	3.6
Golding, P. (BNP)	1,384	2.8
Uncles, L. (England)	806	1.6
Ellis, M. (Ind)	258	0.5
Majority	17,515	35.45
Electorate	69,591	
Turnout	49,408	71.00

**Member of last parliament*

CONSTITUENCY SNAPSHOT

This seat has had continuous Conservative representation since it came into existence, except for a short Liberal interlude in 1923-24. In 1997 new candidate Michael Fallon retained the seat for the party with a majority of 10,461.

He retained the seat in 2001 with a majority of 10,154. By 2005 Fallon achieved more than 50 per cent of the votes cast and an increased majority of 12,970.

In 2010 Fallon held the seat with a strong 17,515 majority.

The seat gained the part-wards of Farningham, Horton Kirby and South Darenth, and Fawkham and West Kingsdown from Dartford, in exchange for the part-ward of Hartley and Hodsoll Street.

The main centres of population here are Sevenoaks itself, Swanley, Westerham, Dunton Green and New Ash Green.

The scenery is picturesque English countryside and it is home to many country houses, small towns and traditional Kent villages with great historical associations.

Sevenoaks has fast become commuter country, with direct rail services to London Bridge, Cannon Street, Blackfriars and Charing Cross.

It has one of the highest proportions of professional workers in the country. There is some light industry, and an element of farming, but the majority of inhabitants are owner-occupying middle-class commuters.

Paul Farrelly

Newcastle-under-Lyme ***(returning MP)***

No boundary changes

Tel: 020 7219 8262
E-mail: farrellyp@parliament.uk
Website: www.paulfarrelly.com

Date of birth: 2 March 1962; Son of late Thomas Farrelly and Anne, née King

Education: Wolstanton County Grammar School; Marshlands Comprehensive, Newcastle-Under-Lyme; St Edmund Hall, Oxford (BA philosophy, politics and economics 1984); Married Victoria Jane Perry 1998 (1 son 2 daughters)

Non-political career: Manager corporate finance division Barclays De Zoete Wedd Ltd 1984-90; Reuters Ltd 1990-95: Correspondent, News editor; Deputy city and business editor *Independent on Sunday* 1995-97; City editor *The Observer* 1997-2001; NUJ; Unite; Unity

Political career: Contested Chesham and Amersham 1997 general election. Member for Newcastle-under-Lyme since 7 June 2001 general election; *Select Committees:* Member: Joint Committee on Consolidation, Etc, Bills 2001-10, European Standing Committee B 2003-05, Science and Technology 2003-05, Unopposed Bills (Panel) 2004-10, Culture, Media and Sport 2005-10; Member, Co-operative Party; Vice-chair Hornsey and Wood Green CLP 1994-95; Newcastle-under-Lyme CLP 1998-2006: Campaign co-ordinator and organiser, Political education officer; Member Socialist Education Association; Member Labour Party Irish Society

Political interests: Education, health, employment, trade and industry, regeneration, investment, European affairs, pensions, crime; Germany, Italy, France, Japan, Russia, Ireland, Norway, Australia, New Zealand, China

Other organisations: Member: Amnesty International, Greenpeace; Trentham RUFC, Finchley RFC, Commons and Lords RFC, Commons and Lords FC

Recreations: Rugby, football, writing, biography, history, architecture

Paul Farrelly MP, House of Commons, London SW1A 0AA
Tel: 020 7219 8262 Fax: 020 7219 1986
E-mail: farrellyp@parliament.uk
Constituency: Waterloo Buildings, Dunkirk, Newcastle-under-Lyme, Staffordshire ST5 2SW Tel: 01782 715033 Fax: 01782 613174
Website: www.paulfarrelly.com

GENERAL ELECTION RESULT

		%	+/-
Farrelly, P. (Lab)*	16,393	38.0	-7.0
Jenrick, R. (Con)	14,841	34.4	9.6
Jones, N. (Lib Dem)	8,466	19.6	0.9
Nixon, D. (UKIP)	3,491	8.1	4.5
Majority	1,552	3.59	
Electorate	69,433		
Turnout	43,191	62.21	

**Member of last parliament*

CONSTITUENCY SNAPSHOT

Newcastle-under-Lyme has one of the longest records of continuous Labour representation in the country. It first returned the party in 1919 when the sitting MP, Josiah Wedgwood, of the famous local pottery dynasty, defected from the Liberals. Newcastle-under-Lyme has remained Labour ever since. Paul Farrelly replaced Llin Golding in 2001 and has held the seat since.

Farrelly held the seat for Labour in 2010 with a 1,552 majority despite a 8.4 per cent swing to the Conservatives.

Virtually equidistant between Birmingham and Manchester, Newcastle-under-Lyme is sandwiched between scenic north Shropshire and south Cheshire to the west and runs almost seamlessly into sprawling Stoke-on-Trent to the east.

The seat encompasses considerable variety. In the east it extends into the industrial Potteries and to ex-coal mining communities such as Silverdale and Chesterton, while in the west it reaches into Keele University as well as rural villages like Madeley.

The pottery industry still has a presence here, alongside other local industries such as textiles and bakeries. In recent years 'the Potteries' has become an expanding centre of business parks and warehouses with a number of national and international distribution companies setting up bases in the borough.

Tim Farron

Westmorland and Lonsdale ***(returning MP)***

Boundary changes

Tel: 020 7219 8498
E-mail: farront@parliament.uk
Website: www.timfarron.co.uk

Date of birth: 27 May 1970; Son of Chris Farron and late Susan Farron, née Trenchard

Education: Lostock Hall High School, Preston, Lancashire; Runshaw Tertiary College, Leyland; Newcastle University (BA politics 1991); Married Rosie Alison Cantley 2000 (2 daughters 2 sons)

Non-political career: Lancaster University: Adult education officer 1992-96, Student support officer 1996-98, Faculty administrator 1998-2002; Head of faculty administration St Martin's College, (Ambleside, Lancaster, Carlisle) 2002-05; Association of University Teachers 1995-; Councillor: Lancashire County Council 1993-2000, South Ribble Borough Council 1995-99, South Lakeland District Council 2004-08

Political career: Contested North West Durham 1992, South Ribble 1997 and Westmorland and Lonsdale 2001 general elections. Member for Westmorland and Lonsdale 2005-10, for Westmorland and Lonsdale (revised boundary) since 6 May 2010 general election; Liberal Democrat: Spokesperson for Youth Affairs 2005-06; PPS to Sir Menzies Campbell as Leader of the Liberal Democrats 2006-07; Shadow Minister for: Home Affairs 2007, Countryside 2007-08; Shadow Secretary of State for Environment, Food and Rural Affairs 2008-10; *Select Committees:* Member: Education and Skills 2005-06, Environmental Audit 2006-07; Contested North West England 1999 European Parliament election

Political interests: Education, rural affairs, youth work, health, crime and policing, social care

Other organisations: Amnesty International 1993-; President, Kendal and South Westmorland Liberal Club; Lib Dem Christian Forum; Cumbria Wildlife; Lakes Line User Group

Recreations: Fell–walking, running, cycling, football, watching Blackburn Rovers, music

Tim Farron MP, House of Commons, London SW1A 0AA
Tel: 020 7219 8498 Fax: 020 7219 2810
E-mail: farront@parliament.uk
Constituency: Acland House, Yard 2, Stricklandgate, Kendal, Cumbria LA9 4ND Tel: 01539 723403 Fax: 01539 740800
Website: www.timfarron.co.uk

GENERAL ELECTION RESULT

		%
Farron, T. (Lib Dem)*	30,896	60.0
McKeever, G. (Con)	18,632	36.2
Todd, J. (Lab)	1,158	2.3
Mander, J. (UKIP)	801	1.6
Majority	12,264	23.82
Electorate	67,881	
Turnout	51,487	75.85

**Member of last parliament*

CONSTITUENCY SNAPSHOT

This seat had a tradition of long-term Conservative incumbents from 1945 up to Tim Collins, who took the seat in 1997, before losing to Liberal Democrat Tim Farron in 2005.

Tim Collins actually only polled 184 fewer votes in the election, but the Liberal Democrats gained over 3,200, giving Tim Farron a majority of just 267.

Farron was re-elected with a 60 per cent share of the vote in 2010, securing a majority of 12,264.

The seat lost the Broughton ward and the part-ward of Crake Valley to Barrow and Furness.

Situated in the heart of the Lake District, Westmorland and Lonsdale boasts spectacular scenery and unsurprisingly, tourism is the main industry. Centred around the towns of Kendal and Windermere, the seat also includes parts of both the Lake District National Park and the Yorkshire Dales National Park.

Agriculture, particularly sheep farming, has traditionally been a key employer in this rural constituency, although more constituents are now employed in tourism.

There is also some light industry to be found, especially in Kendal, home to textiles and the famous mint cake. Visitor numbers are boosted by literary connections to Wordsworth, Coleridge, and Beatrix Potter.

Lynne Featherstone

Hornsey and Wood Green (returning MP)

No boundary changes

Tel: 020 7219 8401
E-mail: featherstonel@parliament.uk
Website: www.lynnefeatherstone.org

Date of birth: 20 December 1951; Daughter of late Joseph Woolf and Gladys Ryness

Education: South Hampstead High School, London; Oxford Polytechnic (Diploma communications and design 1974); Married Stephen Featherstone 1982 (divorced 2002) (2 daughters)

Non-political career: Graphic designer, London and Australia 1974-77; Freelance designer 1977-80; Managing director, Inhouse Outhouse Design 1980-87; Strategic design consultant 1987-97; Director Ryness Electrical Supplies Ltd 1991-2002; Councillor, Haringey Council 1998-2006: Leader of Opposition 1998-2003; Member Greater London Assembly 2000-05: Chair Assembly Committee on Transport 2003-05; Member Metropolitan Police Authority 2000-05

Political career: Contested Hornsey and Wood Green 1997 and 2001 general elections. Member for Hornsey and Wood Green since 5 May 2005 general election; Liberal Democrat: Spokesperson for: Home Affairs 2005-06, London 2006-07, Shadow: Secretary of State for International Development 2006-07, Minister for Youth and Equalities 2008-10; Parliamentary Under-Secretary of State (Minister for Equalities), Home Office and Government Equalities Office 2010-; *Select Committees:* Member: Environmental Audit 2005-06

Political interests: Transport, policing

Other organisations: *Daily Mail* 'unsung hero' 2002; *Publications:* Marketing and Communications Techniques for Architects (Longman 1992)

Recreations: Writing poetry, film

Lynne Featherstone MP, House of Commons, London SW1A 0AA
Tel: 020 7219 8401 Fax: 020 7219 0008
E-mail: featherstonel@parliament.uk
Constituency: 100 Uplands Road, London N8 9BR Tel: 020 8340 5459
Fax: 020 8340 5459 Website: www.lynnefeatherstone.org

GENERAL ELECTION RESULT

		%	+/-
Featherstone, L. (Lib Dem)*	25,595	46.5	3.3
Jennings, K. (Lab)	18,720	34.0	-4.2
Merrin, R. (Con)	9,174	16.7	4.0
McAskie, P. (Green)	1,261	2.3	-2.7
De Roche, S. (Ind)	201	0.4	
Kapur, R. (Ind)	91	0.2	
Majority	6,875	12.49	
Electorate	79,916		
Turnout	55,042	68.87	

**Member of last parliament*

CONSTITUENCY SNAPSHOT

After the Second World War, Hornsey and Wood Green was a Conservative seat. Sir David Gammans held it until 1957 when he was succeeded by his wife. In 1966 Lady Gammans retired and was replaced by Sir Hugh Rossi who occupied the seat for 26 years. However, when he retired in 1992 Labour's Barbara Roche won the seat with a 9 per cent majority.

In the 1997 Roche extended her majority to 20,499, but it was halved in 2001. Liberal Democrat Lynne Featherstone took the seat in 2005 with a 14.6 per cent swing. Featherstone retained the seat in 2010 with an increased majority of 6,875.

Hornsey and Wood Green is in the western part of the borough of Haringey and covers Muswell Hill and the steep hills of Wood Green. The majority of the population work in central London and commute using public transport.

The local economy is dominated by retailing and services and also has one of the strongest manufacturing sectors in London.

Within the constituency is the famous Alexandra Palace, which offers views over the rest of London.

Rt Hon **Frank Field**

Birkenhead (returning MP)

Boundary changes

Tel: 020 7219 5193
E-mail: fieldf@parliament.uk
Website: www.frankfield.co.uk

Labour

Date of birth: 16 July 1942; Son of late Walter Field

Education: St Clement Danes Grammar School, London; Hull University (BSc economics 1963)

Non-political career: Teacher in further education 1964-69; Director: Child Poverty Action Group 1969-79, Low Pay Unit 1974-80; Non-executive director Medicash 2003-; Councillor, Hounslow Borough Council 1964-68

Political career: Contested Buckinghamshire South 1966 general election. Member for Birkenhead 1979-2010, for Birkenhead (revised boundary) since 6 May 2010 general election; Opposition Spokesperson for Education 1980-81; Minister of State, Department of Social Security (Welfare Reform) 1997-98; *Select Committees:* Chair: Social Security 1990-97; Member: Public Accounts 2002-05, Ecclesiastical Committee

Political interests: Poverty and income redistribution, church affairs; Poland

Other organisations: Chair Churches Conservation Trust 2001-07; Cathedral Fabrics Commission for England; PC 1997; Three honorary doctorates; Two honorary fellowships; *Publications:* Publications on low pay, poverty and social issues since 1971; Neighbours From Hell, 2003

Rt Hon Frank Field MP, House of Commons, London SW1A 0AA
Tel: 020 7219 5193 Fax: 020 7219 0601
E-mail: fieldf@parliament.uk
Constituency: Tel: 0800 028 0293 Website: www.frankfield.co.uk

GENERAL ELECTION RESULT

		%
Field, F. (Lab)*	22,082	62.2
Gilbert, A. (Con)	6,887	19.4
Kelly, S. (Lib Dem)	6,554	18.5
Majority	15,195	42.78
Electorate	62,773	
Turnout	35,523	56.59

**Member of last parliament*

CONSTITUENCY SNAPSHOT

Mirroring the Labour stronghold across the Mersey, this seat, bordering inner-city Liverpool is very safe Labour territory. Frank Field has served here since 1979 and won over 70 per cent of the vote in both 1997 and 2001.

Frank Field was returned with a 12,934 majority in 2005. In 2010 Field was re-elected with a 15,195 majority despite a swing of 2.7 per cent to the Conservatives.

The seat gained two part-wards from Wirral South and one from Wirral West, while losing two part-ward to Wirral South and another to Wallasey.

Birkenhead is situated on the east bank of the Mersey facing Liverpool city centre, which is just a one-mile drive away through the road and rail tunnels under the river.

Birkenhead has been the largest conurbation on the Wirral peninsula since its sudden development, prompted by shipyard prosperity, in the Victorian era. After a period of decline, most of the docks have been redeveloped and the shipyard is now a major repair facility.

Mark Field

Cities of London and Westminster ***(returning MP)***

Boundary changes

Tel: 020 7219 8160
E-mail: fieldm@parliament.uk
Website: www.markfieldmp.com

Conservative

Date of birth: 6 October 1964; Son of late Major Peter Charles Field and Ulrike Field, neé Peipe

Education: Reading School; St Edmund Hall, Oxford (BA law 1987, MA) (JCR President); College of Law, Chester (solicitors' finals 1988); Married Michèle Louise Acton 1994 (divorced 2006); married Victoria Margaret Elphicke 2007 (1 son)

Non-political career: Trainee solicitor 1988-90; Solicitor Freshfields 1990-92; Employment consultant 1992-94; Director and co-owner Kellyfield Consulting 1994-2001; Member advisory board London School of Commerce 2005-; Councillor Royal London Borough of Kensington and Chelsea 1994-2002

Political career: Contested Enfield North 1997 general election. Member for Cities of London and Westminster 2001-10, for Cities of London and Westminster (revised boundary) since 6 May 2010 general election; Opposition Whip 2003-04; Shadow: Minister for London 2003-05, Financial Secretary to the Treasury 2005, Minister for Culture 2005-06; *Select Committees:* Member: Constitutional Affairs 2003-04, Procedure 2008-10; Association/Ward Officer Kensington and Chelsea and Islington North Associations 1989-99

Political interests: Economy, small businesses, international development, foreign affairs, employment, education; USA, Germany, India, China

Other organisations: Freeman Merchant Taylors Livery Company; Freeman City of London; City of London Club (honorary) Carlton (honorary); *Publications:* Contributing Chapter to A Blue Tomorrow (Politicos 2001) and various articles for national newspapers on financial services, pensions and civil liberties issues

Recreations: Football, cricket, popular/rock music, walking in London, history of London

Mark Field MP, House of Commons, London SW1A 0AA
Tel: 020 7219 8160 Fax: 020 7219 1980
E-mail: fieldm@parliament.uk
Constituency: 90 Ebury Street, London SW1W 9QD
Tel: 020 7730 8181 Fax: 020 7730 4520
Website: www.markfieldmp.com

GENERAL ELECTION RESULT

		%
Field, M. (Con)*	19,264	52.2
Rowntree, D. (Lab)	8,188	22.2
Smith, N. (Lib Dem)	7,574	20.5
Chase, D. (Green)	778	2.1
Weston, P. (UKIP)	664	1.8
Roseman, F. (England)	191	0.5
Delderfield, D. (Ind)	98	0.3
Nunn, J. (Pirate)	90	0.2
Mad, C. (Ind)	84	0.2
Majority	11,076	29.99
Electorate	66,489	
Turnout	36,931	55.54

**Member of last parliament*

CONSTITUENCY SNAPSHOT

The City of London was joined with the City of Westminster in 1948 to form one constituency. Mark Field was elected for the first time in 2001, having replaced Peter Brooke, who had been the MP since 1977.

Field was re-elected in 2005 with an increased majority of 8,095. Field achieved a majority of 11,076 over his Labour opponent Dave Rowntree - the drummer from Blur.

Bryanston and Dorset Square ward is now entirely within the seat's boundaries, having previously been shared with Regent's Park and Kensington North seat. Lancaster Gate and Bayswater wards were moved to Westminster North.

The Cities of London and Westminster seat contains the two historical centres of London: the City of London is one of the world's leading international financial centres, while Westminster contains the Houses of Parliament and Whitehall, the political heart of the country.

The constituency is home to some of the wealthiest residents in the country at exclusive addresses in Mayfair, Belgravia and Knightsbridge.

The bulk of the population is found in Westminster, with only 6,000 or so residents in the City of London, where companies outnumber residents. Unsurprisingly, tourism is a major employer.

Jim Fitzpatrick

Poplar and Limehouse ***(returning MP)***

New constituency

Tel: 020 7219 5085
E-mail: fitzpatrickj@parliament.uk
Website: www.jimfitzpatrickmp.co.uk

Labour

Date of birth: 4 April 1952; Son of James and Jean, née Stones, Fitzpatrick

Education: Holyrood Senior Secondary, Glasgow; Married Jane Lowe 1980 (divorced) (1 son 1 daughter); Married Dr Sheila Hunter 2003

Non-political career: Trainee, Tytrak Ltd, Glasgow 1970-73; Driver, Mintex Ltd, London 1973-74; Firefighter, London Fire Brigade 1974-97; Member National Executive Council, Fire Brigades Union

Political career: Member for Poplar and Canning Town 1997-2010, for Poplar and Limehouse since 6 May 2010 general election; PPS to Alan Milburn as Secretary of State for Health 1999-2001; Assistant Government Whip 2001-03; Government Whip 2003-05; Parliamentary Under-Secretary of State: Office of the Deputy Prime Minister 2005-06, Department of Trade and Industry (Employment Relations, Postal Services, London) 2006-07, Department for Transport 2007-09; Minister of State, Department for Environment, Food and Rural Affairs (Minister for Food, Farming and the Environment) 2009-10; *Select Committees:* Member: Selection 2003-05; Chair Barking Constituency Labour Party 1989-90; Member, London Labour Executive 1988-2000; Chair Greater London Labour Party 1991-2000

Political interests: Poverty, regeneration, racism, fire, animal welfare; Bangladesh

Other organisations: Patron: SS Robin. Richard House Trust Daneford Trust; Fire Brigade Long Service and Good Conduct Medal (20 years) 1994; Hon President Millwall Rugby Football Club; Parliamentary football team

Recreations: Reading, TV/film, West Ham United FC

Jim Fitzpatrick MP, House of Commons, London SW1A 0AA
Tel: 020 7219 5085; 020 7219 6215 Fax: 020 7219 2776
E-mail: fitzpatrickj@parliament.uk
Constituency: No constituency office publicised Tel: 020 7536 0562
Fax: 020 7536 0572 Website: www.jimfitzpatrickmp.co.uk

GENERAL ELECTION RESULT

		%
Fitzpatrick, J. (Lab)*	18,679	40.0
Archer, T. (Con)	12,649	27.1
Galloway, G. (Respect)*	8,160	17.5
Fryer, J. (Lib Dem)	5,209	11.2
Lochner, W. (UKIP)	565	1.2
Osborne, A. (England)	470	1.0
Smith, C. (Green)	449	1.0
Mahmud, K. (Ind)	293	0.6
Hoque, M. (Ind)	167	0.4
Thornton, J. (Ind)	59	0.1
Majority	6,030	12.91
Electorate	74,956	
Turnout	46,700	62.30

**Member of last parliament*

CONSTITUENCY SNAPSHOT

Poplar and Canning Town was created in the 1995 boundary review from parts of Bow and Poplar, represented by Labour's Mildred Gordon from 1987 to 1997 and Newham South, represented by Nigel Spearing, also for Labour, from 1974 to 1997. Jim Fitzpatrick took the amalgamated seat in 1997. He held the seat with a reduced majority in 2005. Despite George Galloway's efforts, this seat remained Labour. Former minister Jim Fitzpatrick scored a 6,030 majority with the Tories second.

Poplar and Canning Town encompasses most of the old Poplar and Canning Town seat, with some partial gains from Bethnal Green and Bow. The Newham wards of the old Poplar and Canning Town have been spilt between the constituencies of East Ham and West Ham.

Poplar and Limehouse is East London heartland, a multi-racial area.

The relocation in the 1980s of many print media companies to Wapping brought some employment into the area. The development of the Docklands has also led to an increase in the number of people working in the financial, media and service industries.

The constituency has been home to the famous Billingsgate fish market since 1983. Transport links are good, with the Jubilee and the Docklands Light Railway serving the area.

Robert Flello

Stoke-on-Trent South ***(returning MP)***

Boundary changes

Tel: 020 7219 6744
E-mail: flellor@parliament.uk
Website: www.robertflello.co.uk

Date of birth: 14 January 1966; Son of Valerie, née Hughes, and Alfred Douglas Flello

Education: King's Norton Boys' School; University of Wales, Bangor (BSc chemistry 1987); Married Teresa Gifoli 1990 (divorced) (1 daughter 1 stepson)

Non-political career: Executive officer Inland Revenue 1987-89; Tax consultant Price Waterhouse 1989-94; Manager Arthur Andersen 1994-2000; Director Platts Flello Ltd 2000-03; Chief executive officer Malachi Community Trust 2003-04; Member: Unite, Unity, USDAW; Councillor Birmingham City Council 2002-04

Political career: Member for Stoke-on-Trent South 2005-10, for Stoke-on-Trent South (revised boundary) since 6 May 2010 general election; PPS: to Lord Falconer of Thoroton as Lord Chancellor 2006-07, to Hazel Blears: as Minister without Portfolio 2007, as Secretary of State for Communities and Local Government 2007-09, to Bob Ainsworth as Secretary of State for Defence 2009-10; *Select Committees:* Member: Science and Technology 2005-07

Political interests: Employment, home affairs, Treasury matters, transport, defence; Italy, Cyprus, Norway

Recreations: Running, motorbike riding, reading especially ancient history, cooking, visiting castles, exploring historical sites particularly Roman and Greek

Robert Flello MP, House of Commons, London SW1A 0AA
Tel: 020 7219 6744 Fax: 020 7219 5400
E-mail: flellor@parliament.uk
Constituency: Travers Court, City Road, Penton, Stoke-on-Trent, Staffordshire ST4 2PY Tel: 01782 844810
Website: www.robertflello.co.uk

GENERAL ELECTION RESULT

		%
Flello, R. (Lab)*	15,446	38.8
Rushton, J. (Con)	11,316	28.4
Ali, Z. (Lib Dem)	6,323	15.9
Coleman, M. (BNP)	3,762	9.4
Barlow, M. (UKIP)	1,363	3.4
Follows, T. (SIG)	1,208	3.0
Breeze, M. (Ind)	434	1.1
Majority	4,130	10.36
Electorate	68,031	
Turnout	39,852	58.58

**Member of last parliament*

CONSTITUENCY SNAPSHOT

Like the city's other two constituencies, Stoke-on-Trent South has returned Labour MPs since well before 1945. Jack Ashley represented the seat between 1966 and 1992, and before him Ellis Smith. In 1992 Ashley retired.

In 1997 Labour secured 62 per cent of the vote. With a change of MP from George Stevenson to Rob Flello in 2005 Labour's majority fell to 8,681. Flello held the seat in 2010 with a reduced majority of 4,130.

Boundary changes were minor.

Stoke's southern constituency covers the pottery towns of Longton and Fenton, in addition to the neighbouring areas of Blurton, Weston Coyney and Trentham.

Longton and Fenton comprise two of the Potteries' six towns and until the 19th century were dominated by coal-mining and iron works, but subsequently became a major centre for the production of bone china, which remains important.

The constituency is heavily working-class like the rest of Stoke. The seat also contains some more affluent, middle-class suburbs. The constituency's economy is still dominated by manufacturing.

Rt Hon **Caroline Flint**

Don Valley (returning MP)

Boundary changes

Tel: 020 7219 4407
E-mail: flintc@parliament.uk
Website: www.carolineflint.co.uk

Date of birth: 20 September 1961; Daughter of late Wendy Flint, neé Beasley, clerical/shop employee

Education: Twickenham Girls School; Richmond Tertiary College; University of East Anglia (BA American history/literature and film studies); Divorced; married Phil Cole 2001 (1 son 1 daughter 1 stepson)

Non-political career: Management trainee Greater London Council/Inner London Education Authority 1984-85; Policy officer ILEA 1985-87; Head, Women's Unit, National Union of Students 1988-89; Lambeth Council 1989-93: Equal opportunities officer 1989-91, Welfare and staff development officer 1991-93; Senior researcher/Political officer, GMB Trade Union 1994-97; Former shop steward: NALGO at GLC/ILEA, GMB at Lambeth Council

Political career: Member for Don Valley 1997-2010, for Don Valley (revised boundary) since 6 May 2010 general election; Joint PPS to Ministers of State, Foreign and Commonwealth Office 1999-2001; PPS: to Peter Hain as Minister of State: Department of Trade and Industry 2001, Foreign and Commonwealth Office 2001-02, to John Reid: as Minister without Portfolio and Party Chair 2002-03, as Leader of the House of Commons and President of the Council 2003; Parliamentary Under-Secretary of State (PUSS), Home Office 2003-05; Department of Health 2005-07: PUSS (Public Health) 2005-06, Minister of State (MoS) (Public Health) 2006-07; MoS, Department for Work and Pensions (Minister for Employment and Welfare Reform) 2007-08; Minister for Yorkshire and the Humber 2007-08; Minister for Housing and Planning (attending Cabinet), Department for Communities and Local Government 2008; Minister of State, Foreign and Commonwealth Office (Europe) 2008-09; *Select Committees:* Member: Education and Employment 1997-99, Education and Employment (Education Sub-Committee) 1997-99, Administration 2001-05, Modernisation of the House of Commons 2003; National Women's Officer, Labour Students 1983-85; Executive Member, Labour Co-ordinating Committee 1984-85; Chair, Brentford and Isleworth Constituency Labour Party 1991-95; Branch Chair, Branch Secretary and GC Delegate; Facilitator, Labour National Policy Forums 1994-97; Associate Editor, *Renewal* 1995-2000; Member: Fabian Society, Trade Union Group of Labour MPs, Progress

Political interests: Employment, education and training, childcare, welfare to work, family friendly employment, crime, anti-social behaviour, House of Commons modernisation, education

Other organisations: Chair Working For Childcare 1991-95; Board member: Sure Start Denaby Main Partnership 2000-03, Doncaster Early Years Development and Childcare Partnership 2001-03; President, Denaby Utd FC 2001-02; Member, GMB Group of MPs; Labour Party adviser to Police Federation of England and Wales 1999; Member: Inter-Parliamentary Union 1997-, British American Parliamentary Group 1997-; PC 2008

Recreations: Cinema, family and friends

Rt Hon Caroline Flint MP, House of Commons, London SW1A 0AA
Tel: 020 7219 4407 Fax: 020 7219 1277
E-mail: flintc@parliament.uk
Constituency: Meteor House, First Avenue, Auckley, Doncaster, South Yorkshire DN9 3GA Tel: 01302 623330 Fax: 01302 775099
Website: www.carolineflint.co.uk

GENERAL ELECTION RESULT

		%
Flint, C. (Lab)*	16,472	37.9
Stephens, M. (Con)	12,877	29.7
Simpson, E. (Lib Dem)	7,422	17.1
Toseland, E. (BNP)	2,112	4.9
Shaw, W. (UKIP)	1,904	4.4
Aston, B. (England)	1,756	4.0
Williams, M. (Ind)	887	2.0
Majority	3,595	8.28
Electorate	73,214	
Turnout	43,430	59.32

**Member of last parliament*

CONSTITUENCY SNAPSHOT

Before 1983 this seat ringed Doncaster entirely, creating a large area of mining villages. Only in 1983, after boundary changes, did the Labour vote fall below 50 per cent, but their vote recovered and in 1992 Martin Redmond had a majority of more than 13,500. Martin Redmond died just before the 1997 election.

Caroline Flint became the seat's first woman MP. She won 58 per cent of the vote and a majority of nearly 15,000. Both the Lib Dems and the Conservatives recovered slightly in 2001, and in 2005 there was another swing to the Tories. However, Flint was still left with a 8,598 majority. In 2010 Flint retained the seat with 16,472 votes giving Labour a majority of 3,595.

The seat lost Sprotbrough part-ward to Doncaster North while the wards of Thorne and Conisbrough and Denaby are now fully in the seat.

This seat encircles the South Yorkshire town of Doncaster to the south and east. A former mining area, its last pit, at Rossington, closed in 2007.

Nowadays the biggest employers are the local authority, the prison service, the NHS and a number of call-centre operators. Polypipe, which makes specialist plastic tubing, has its headquarters here.

The former RAF Finningley site has been transformed into Robin Hood Airport Doncaster-Sheffield, creating many jobs.

Paul Flynn

Newport West ***(returning MP)***

No boundary changes

Tel: 020 7219 3478
E-mail: flynnp@parliament.uk
Website: www.paulflynnmp.co.uk

Date of birth: 9 February 1935; Son of late James and late Kathleen Flynn

Education: St Illtyd's College, Cardiff; University College of Wales, Cardiff; Married 2nd Samantha Cumpstone 1985 (1 stepson 1 stepdaughter and 1 son and 1 daughter (deceased) from previous marriage)

Non-political career: Chemist steel industry 1962-83; Broadcaster Gwent Community Radio 1983-84; Research officer for Llewellyn Smith as Labour MEP for South Wales 1984-87; Councillor: Newport Council 1972-81, Gwent County Council 1974-83

Political career: Contested Denbigh October 1974 general election. Member for Newport West since 11 June 1987 general election; Opposition Spokesman on: Health and Social Security 1988-89, Social Security 1989-90; *Select Committees:* Member: Welsh Affairs 1997-98, Environmental Audit 2003-05, Public Administration 2005-10

Political interests: Health, medicinal and illegal drugs, social security, pensions, animal welfare, devolution, Welsh affairs, constitutional reform, modernisation of Parliament; Baltic States, Eastern Europe, Hungary, Romania, Israel

Other organisations: Board Member, Parliamentary Office of Science and Technology (POST) 1997-; Member UK Delegation to Council of Europe and Western European Union 1997-; Campaign for Freedom of Information Award 1991; Highland Park/*The Spectator* Backbencher of the Year (jointly) 1996; *New Statesman* Best Website of an Elected Representative 2000-; BCS MP Website Awards for Design 2008; *Publications:* Commons Knowledge. How to be a Backbencher (1997); Baglu Mlaen (Staggering Forward) (1998); Dragons Led by Poodles (1999)

Recreations: Local history, photography

Paul Flynn MP, House of Commons, London SW1A 0AA
Tel: 020 7219 3478 Fax: 020 7219 2433
E-mail: flynnp@parliament.uk
Constituency: Tel: 01633 262348 Fax: 01633 760532
Website: www.paulflynnmp.co.uk

GENERAL ELECTION RESULT

		%	+/-
Flynn, P. (Lab)*	16,389	41.3	-3.5
Williams, M. (Con)	12,845	32.3	2.9
German, V. (Lib Dem)	6,587	16.6	-1.3
Windsor, T. (BNP)	1,183	3.0	
Moelwyn Hughes, H. (UKIP)	1,144	2.9	0.5
Rees, J. (PIC)	1,122	2.8	-0.8
Bartolotti, P. (Green)	450	1.1	-0.4
Majority	3,544	8.92	
Electorate	54,437		
Turnout	39,720	72.97	

**Member of last parliament*

CONSTITUENCY SNAPSHOT

The Conservatives won the inaugural parliamentary contest in Newport West in 1983 when Mark Robinson won the seat. It was Paul Flynn who took this seat back for Labour from the Conservatives in 1987. He increased his majority in 1992 and 1997.

But the electoral tide has begun to turn - the 2001 and 2005 general elections recorded shifts of votes of around 5 per cent away to the Conservatives and Flynn's majority fell from 14,357 in 1997 to 5,458 in 2005. Paul Flynn held on in 2010 with a majority of 3,544.

The western division of Wales' newest city has enjoyed more inward investment and is generally better-off than its neighbouring Newport seat.

The constituency takes in the main shopping centre of the city and the docklands area. It also takes in countryside and villages that wrap round the west and north of the city.

The economy is based on steel, aluminium and high-tech firms. The expansion of the service sector, in particular the hospitality industry, has helped to transform the economy.

Civil Service restructuring has benefited the area. The National Statistics Office and the Prison Service's shared service centre are located here.

Newport hosts the Ryder Cup golf tournament in 2010.

Don Foster

Bath (returning MP)

Boundary changes

Tel: 020 7219 4805
E-mail: fosterd@parliament.uk
Website: www.donfoster.co.uk

Date of birth: 31 March 1947; Son of late John Anthony Foster, vicar and late Iris Edith Foster, neé Ellison

Education: Lancaster Royal Grammar School; Keele University (BSc physics and psychology 1969, CEd 1969); Bath University (MEd 1981); Married Victoria Jane Dorcas Pettegree 1968 (1 son 1 daughter)

Non-political career: Science teacher Sevenoaks School, Kent 1969-75; Science project director Resources for Learning Development Unit, Avon LEA 1975-80; Education lecturer Bristol University 1980-89; Management consultant Pannell Kerr Forster 1989-92; Councillor Avon County Council 1981-89; Executive Association of County Councils 1985-89; Joint Hon. President British Youth Council 1992-99

Political career: Contested (Liberal/Alliance) Bristol East 1987 general election. Member for Bath 1992-2010, for Bath (revised boundary) since 6 May 2010 general election; Liberal Democrat: Spokesperson for: Education 1992-95, Education and Employment 1995-97; Principal Spokesperson for: Environment, Transport, the Regions and Social Justice 1999-2001, Transport, Local Government and the Regions 2001-02, Shadow Secretary of State for: Transport 2002-03, Culture, Media and Sport 2003-10, Shadow Minister for the Olympics 2007-10; *Select Committees:* Member: Education and Employment 1996-99, Education and Employment (Education Sub-Committee) 1997-99; President Liberal Democrat Youth and Students 1993-95

Political interests: Education, local and regional government, transport, culture, media, sport and tourism; Africa, Israel

Other organisations: National Campaign for Nursery Education: Vice-chair 1993-99, President 1999-2001; President, British Association for Early Childhood Education 1998-2002; Vice-chair British Association for Central and Eastern Europe 1994-97; Trustee, Open School and Education Extra 1993-99; Honorary Fellow, Bath College of High Education 1995; CPhys; MInstP; National Liberal; *Publications:* Resource-based Learning in Science (1979); Science With Gas (1981); Co-author: Aspects of Science (1984), Reading About Science (1984), Nuffield Science (1986); Teaching Science 11-13 (1987); From the Three Rs to the Three Cs (2003); Numerous educational and political articles and pamphlets

Recreations: Classical music, travel, sport

Don Foster MP, House of Commons, London SW1A 0AA
Tel: 020 7219 4805 Fax: 020 7219 2695
E-mail: fosterd@parliament.uk
Constituency: 31 James Street West, Bath, Somerset BA1 2BT
Tel: 01225 338973 Fax: 01225 463630 Website: www.donfoster.co.uk

GENERAL ELECTION RESULT

		%
Foster, D. (Lib Dem)*	26,651	56.6
Richter, F. (Con)	14,768	31.4
Ajderian, H. (Lab)	3,251	6.9
Lucas, E. (Green)	1,120	2.4
Warrender, E. (UKIP)	890	1.9
Hewett, S. (Christian)	250	0.5
A.N., O. (Ind)	69	0.2
Geddis, S. (Ind)	56	0.1
Craig, R. (ATSP)	31	0.1
Majority	11,883	25.24
Electorate	65,603	
Turnout	47,086	71.77

**Member of last parliament*

CONSTITUENCY SNAPSHOT

From 1945 to 1992 Bath was a Conservative seat. In 1979 Chris Patten became MP. However, Patten was defeated by Liberal Democrat Don Foster by 3,768 votes in 1992.

Despite the appendage of rural areas when the seat's boundaries were changed in 1995, the Lib Dems strengthened their position. In 1997 and 2001 they increased their majority. However, in 2005 this trend was reversed and the Liberal Democrat majority over the Tories was more than halved to 4,638. Foster was re-elected with an increased 11,883 majority in 2010.

The seat lost Bathavon North and part of Bathavon South to North East Somerset.

With the withering of the engineering base so central to the constituency following the Second World War, the local economy is now heavily dependent on tourism. The entire city has been designated a World Heritage Site, and, with several well-known attractions including Bath Abbey and the Royal Crescent, the area attracts over three million visitors a year.

Alongside tourism, the local economy is also supported by the presence of two universities: Bath University and Bath Spa University.

Bath has a disproportionate population of wealthy young singles, reinforcing the notion that it is a fashionable place to live.

Yvonne Fovargue

Makerfield

Boundary changes

Tel: 020 7219 3000
E-mail: yvonne.fovargue.mp@parliament.uk
Website: www.yvonnefovargue.com

Date of birth: 29 November 1956; Daughter of late Kenneth Gibbon and Irene Gibbon, retired

Education: Sale Girls Grammar School; Leeds University (BA English 1978); Manchester City College (PGCE English and religious studies 1979); NVQ strategic management level 5 2003; Married Paul Kenny 2009 (1 daughter)

Non-political career: Housing department, Manchester City Council: Housing information manager 1979-82, Estate manager 1982-86; Newton le Willows Citizens Advice Bureau/St Helen's District Citizens Advice Bureau: Manager 1986-92, Chief executive 1992-2010; Member 1979-: NALGO, NUPE ASTMS, Amicus, Unite; Councillor, Warrington Borough Council 2004-10

Political career: Member for Makerfield since 6 May 2010 general election; Vice-chair, Warrington South CLP 2008-10

Political interests: Third sector, consumer credit and debt, employment law

Other organisations: Member, Mensa

Recreations: Reading, theatre, music

Yvonne Fovargue MP, House of Commons, London SW1A 0AA
Tel: 020 7219 3000 E-mail: yvonne.fovargue.mp@parliament.uk
Constituency: c/o Unite The Union, 100 Hallgate, Wigan WN1 1HP
Tel: 01942 244337 Website: www.yvonnefovargue.com

GENERAL ELECTION RESULT

		%
Fovargue, Y. (Lab)	20,700	47.3
Ali, I. (Con)	8,210	18.8
Crowther, D. (Lib Dem)	7,082	16.2
Brierley, R. (Ind)	3,424	7.8
Haslam, K. (BNP)	3,229	7.4
Mather, J. (Ind)	1,126	2.6
Majority	12,490	28.53
Electorate	73,641	
Turnout	43,771	59.44

CONSTITUENCY SNAPSHOT

Makerfield was created in 1983 and is a Labour-voting seat. In 1997 Ian McCartney won a majority of 58 per cent. In 2001 McCartney's majority fell slightly, but was still 17,750. In that year McCartney's percentage majority was exactly the same as the turnout: 50.92 per cent. Despite polling almost 1,400 fewer votes in 2005, Ian McCartney increased his majority to 18,149.

McCartney stood down in 2010 and Yvonne Fovargue held the seat for Labour with a majority of 12,490.

Boundary changes moved the historic heart of the constituency, Ince-in-Makerfield, into neighbouring Wigan, while the seat has gained wards from Leigh.

Makerfield lies on the strip of land between Liverpool and Manchester. The largest town in the seat is Ashton-in-Makerfield, which sits amid small working-class towns and villages spread across the Lancashire coalfield.

The seat is something of a demographic anomaly with virtually no members of ethnic minorities, the number of one-parent families is well below the national average and the percentage of manual workers is disproportionately high.

Rt Hon Dr **Liam Fox**

North Somerset ***(returning MP)***

New constituency

Tel: 020 7219 4198
E-mail: douglasi@parliament.uk
Website: www.liamfoxmp.co.uk

Conservative

Date of birth: 22 September 1961; Son of William Fox, teacher, and Catherine Fox

Education: St Bride's High School, East Kilbride; Glasgow University (MB, ChB 1983, MROGP 1989); Married Jesme Baird 2005

Non-political career: General practitioner, Beaconsfield, Buckinghamshire and Nailsea, North Somerset; Divisional surgeon, St John's Ambulance, Buckinghamshire

Political career: Contested Roxburgh and Berwickshire 1987 general election. Member for Woodspring 1992-2010, for North Somerset since 6 May 2010 general election; PPS to Michael Howard as Home Secretary 1993-94; Assistant Government Whip 1994-95; Government Whip 1995-96; Parliamentary Under-Secretary of State, Foreign and Commonwealth Office 1996-97; Opposition Spokesperson for: Constitutional Affairs, Scotland and Wales 1997-99; Member Shadow Cabinet 1998-: Shadow: Secretary of State for Health 1999-2003, Foreign Secretary 2005, Secretary of State for Defence 2005-10; Secretary of State for Defence 2010-; *Select Committees:* Member: Scottish Affairs 1992-93; Chair, West of Scotland Young Conservatives 1983; National Vice-Chair, Scottish Young Conservatives 1983-84; Secretary, West Country Conservative Members' Committee 1992-93; Co-chair Conservative Party 2003-05; Contested Conservative Party leadership 2005

Political interests: Health, economic policy, foreign affairs; USA

Other organisations: Member, Central Committee, Families for Defence 1987-89; President, Glasgow University Club 1982-83; Guest of US State Department, involving study of drug abuse problems in USA, and Republican Party campaigning techniques 1985; PC 2010; World Debating Competition, Toronto (Individual speaking prize) 1982; Best Speaker's Trophy, Glasgow University 1983; *Publications:* Making Unionism Positive (1988)

Recreations: Tennis, swimming, cinema, theatre

Rt Hon Dr Liam Fox MP, House of Commons, London SW1A 0AA
Tel: 020 7219 4198 Fax: 020 7219 3968
E-mail: douglasi@parliament.uk
Constituency: 71 High Street, Nailsea, North Somerset BS48 1AW
Tel: 01275 790090 Fax: 01275 790091
Website: www.liamfoxmp.co.uk

GENERAL ELECTION RESULT

		%
Fox, L. (Con)*	28,549	49.3
Mathew, B. (Lib Dem)	20,687	35.7
Parry-Hearn, S. (Lab)	6,448	11.1
Taylor, S. (UKIP)	2,257	3.9
Majority	7,862	13.57
Electorate	77,304	
Turnout	57,941	74.95

**Member of last parliament*

CONSTITUENCY SNAPSHOT

The new seat of North Somerset was created from the whole of Woodspring with the addition of the part of Wrington ward that was in Weston-Super-Mare.

Woodspring was created in 1983 and has been represented by only two MPs, both of them Conservatives.

Sir Paul Dean, the sitting MP for North Somerset contested the new constituency, four-fifths of which had been drawn from his old one. He represented Woodspring with very large majorities until he retired in 1992.

Sir Paul's replacement was Dr Liam Fox who was re-elected in 2005 with a reduced majority of 6,016. Fox won a comfortable majority of 7,862 in this new seat in 2010.

Situated on the west coast between Bristol and Weston-Super-Mare, North Somerset is home to many commuters working in the two urban centres.

The largest town, Clevedon, is primarily a residential town for commuters from Bristol, but attracts a significant number of tourists as well.

To the north, Portishead has a more industrial history. Its coal-operated power station closed in 1980, and the docks are now the site of a major redevelopment which should double the size of the town in coming years.

Another commuter town is Nailsea, a former coal-mining town which became famous for its glass in the eighteenth and nineteenth centuries.

Dr **Hywel Francis**

Aberavon (returning MP)

No boundary changes

Tel: 020 7219 8121
E-mail: francish@parliament.uk
Website: www.hywelfrancis.co.uk

Date of birth: 6 June 1946; Son of David Francis, miners' union official and Catherine Francis, housewife

Education: Whitchurch Grammar School, Cardiff; University College of Wales, Swansea (BA history 1968, PhD 1978); Married Mair Georgina Price 1968 (1 daughter 2 sons (1 deceased))

Non-political career: Organisation department assistant TUC 1971-72; University College of Wales, Swansea 1972-99: Senior research assistant 1972-74, Department of Adult Continuing Education: Tutor and lecturer 1974-86, Director 1987-99, Professor 1992-99; Special adviser to Paul Murphy as Secretary of State for Wales 1999-2000; Fellow National Centre for Public Policy University of Wales, Swansea 2000-01; Member: AUT 1974-2001, ISTC Community 2000-

Political career: Member for Aberavon since 7 June 2001 general election; Sponsored Carers (Equal Opportunities) Act 2004; *Select Committees:* Welsh Affairs: Member 2001-10, Chair 2005-10; Member: European Standing Committee B 2003-05, Liaison 2005-10, Liaison (National Policy Statements Sub-committee) 2009-10; National Assembly for Wales: contested South Wales West 1999 election; Member: Socialist Education Association 1999-, Co-operative Party 1999-

Political interests: Carers' rights, disability rights, citizenship, European affairs, lifelong learning, steel, coal; France, India, Italy, Ireland, Cuba, South Africa, China, Venezuela

Other organisations: Honorary Parliamentary Patron National Institute for Adult Continuing Education 2005-; Member Down's Syndrome Association; Trustee, Bevan Foundation 2001-; Vice-president, Carers UK; President: Côr Meibion Aberafan, Port Talbot Town Cricket Club, Welsh Miners' Museum, Seven Sisters RFC; Honorary Life Member SNAC; Vice-president Aberavon RFC; Vice-president, Friends of Cyprus; Founder and trustee Bevan Foundation Think-Tank 2000-; Trustee Paul Robeson Wales Trust 2001-; Member Gorsedd of National Eisteddfod 1986; Emeritus Professor, Swansea University; Fellow Royal Society of the Arts (FRSA) 1988; Aberavon RFC, Briton Ferry Steel Cricket Club, Port Talbot Cricket Club; *Publications:* Co-author The Fed: A history of the South Wales miners in the Twentieth Century (Lawrence and Wishart, 1980, 1998; Miners against Fascism (Lawrence and Wishart, 1984, 2004); Co-editor Communities and their Universities (Lawrence and Wishart, 1996); Wales: A learning country (Welsh Centre for Lifelong Learning, 1999); History on Our Side: Wales and the 1984-85 Miners' Strike (2009)

Recreations: Walking, cycling, swimming, cinema, reading, writing

Dr Hywel Francis MP, House of Commons, London SW1A 0AA
Tel: 020 7219 8121 E-mail: francish@parliament.uk
Constituency: Eagle House, 2 Talbot Road, Port Talbot,
West Glamorgan SA13 1DH Tel: 01639 897660 Fax: 01639 891725
Website: www.hywelfrancis.co.uk

GENERAL ELECTION RESULT

		%	+/-
Francis, H. (Lab)*	16,073	51.9	-8.0
Davies, K. (Lib Dem)	5,034	16.3	2.6
Jones, C. (Con)	4,411	14.3	4.1
Nicholls-Jones, P. (PIC)	2,198	7.1	-4.6
Edwards, K. (BNP)	1,276	4.1	
Tutton, A. (Ind)	919	3.0	
Beany, C. (NMB)	558	1.8	
Callan, J. (UKIP)	489	1.6	
Majority	11,039	35.66	
Electorate	50,789		
Turnout	30,958	60.95	

**Member of last parliament*

CONSTITUENCY SNAPSHOT

Ramsay Macdonald, the first Labour Prime Minister, held the seat between 1922 and 1929. His successor MPs in the seat have all been Labour representatives.

In 1997 sitting Labour MP Sir John Morris achieved 71.3 per cent of the vote. He retired in 2001 making Dr Hywel Francis the seat's first new MP for over 40 years.

Francis's majority marginally declined in 2005, but was still a very safe 13,937. Francis was re-elected in 2010 with a slightly reduced majority of 11,039.

The constituency is dominated by the town of Port Talbot. The constituency is bordered by the Bristol Channel to the south and is situated just to the east of Swansea Bay.

This is a firmly industrial constituency. The dramatic towers of the steel works dominate the skyline. Steel remains a major source of employment. However, industrial decline has led to high unemployment rates here.

Aberavon is still dealing with the consequences of its industrial past. There are efforts in place to improve the local environment to attract visitors and make the area a better place to live.

Rt Hon **Mark Francois**

Rayleigh and Wickford ***(returning MP)***

New constituency

Tel: 020 7219 8287
E-mail: mark.francois.mp@parliament.uk
Website: www.markfrancoismp.com

Conservative

Date of birth: 14 August 1965; Son of Reginald Charles Francois, engineer, and Anna Maria Francois, née Carloni, cook

Education: St Nicholas Comprehensive School, Basildon; Bristol University (BA history 1986); King's College, London (MA war studies 1987); Married Karen Thomas 2000 (divorced 2006)

Non-political career: TA 1983-89, commissioned 1985; Management trainee Lloyds Bank 1987; Market Access International Public Affairs Consultancy 1988-95: Consultant, Director; Public affairs consultant Francois Associates 1996-2001; Councillor Basildon District Council 1991-95

Political career: Contested Brent East 1997 general election. Member for Rayleigh 2001-10, for Rayleigh and Wickford since 6 May 2010 general election; Opposition Whip 2002-04; Shadow: Economic Secretary 2004-05, Paymaster General 2005-07, Minister for Europe 2007-10; Government Whip (Vice-Chamberlain of HM Household) 2010-; *Select Committees:* Member: Environmental Audit 2001-05, European Standing Committee A 2002-05

Political interests: Defence, local and regional government, housing, environment

Other organisations: President: Friends of Rayleigh and Rochford CAB 2001-, Friends of Holy Trinity Church, Rayleigh 2002-, Rayleigh Division, St John Ambulance 2002-; Patron, Rayleigh Branch of Royal British Legion 2002-; Member, Royal United Services Institute for Defence Studies 1991-; PC 2010; Carlton, Rayleigh Conservative

Recreations: Reading, sports, military history, travel

Rt Hon Mark Francois MP, House of Commons, London SW1A 0AA
Tel: 020 7219 8287 Fax: 020 7219 1858
E-mail: mark.francois.mp@parliament.uk
Constituency: 25 Bellingham Lane, Rayleigh, Essex SS6 7ED
Tel: 01268 742044 Fax: 01268 741833
Website: www.markfrancoismp.com

GENERAL ELECTION RESULT

		%
Francois, M. (Con)*	30,257	57.8
Gaszczak, S. (Lib Dem)	7,919	15.1
Le-Surf, M. (Lab)	7,577	14.5
Hayter, J. (England)	2,219	4.2
Callaghan, T. (UKIP)	2,211	4.2
Evennett, A. (BNP)	2,160	4.1
Majority	22,338	42.68
Electorate	75,905	
Turnout	52,343	68.96

**Member of last parliament*

CONSTITUENCY SNAPSHOT

This new Essex constituency is based on most of the former Rayleigh seat, with the exception of South Woodham, Rettendon and Runwell, which now form part of the new Maldon seat. Wickford has been added from the former Billericay seat, and is one of the main centres of population, along with Rayleigh and Hockley.

In Rayleigh Michael Clark ended an 18-year parliamentary career when he retired in 2001, and Mark Francois took over the reins, elected with a majority of 8,290. Comparatively the Conservatives were at an historic low, but he still had a majority of just under 20 per cent. In 2005 Rayleigh voted along more traditional lines, as support for Labour fell and Francois was returned to Parliament with a huge majority of 14,726.

Billericay, from which the town of Wickford was a part has been Conservative since its reconstitution in 1983, and the Billericay MP John Baron had a very comfortable majority of 11,206 in 2005.

Francois won the new seat with a majority of 22,338 at the 2010 general election.

Before the Second World War the constituency was largely rural, known for its attractive villages and picturesque riverside views. Rapid population growth since has led to much of the land being developed, although there are still many quiet, attractive riverside areas along the Crouch.

George Freeman

Mid Norfolk

Boundary changes

Tel: 020 7219 7239
E-mail: george.freeman.mp@parliament.uk
Website: www.georgefreeman.co.uk

Conservative

Date of birth: 12 July 1967; Son of Arthur Freeman, National Hunt jockey and trainer, and Joanna Philipson

Education: Radley College, Oxford; Girton College, Cambridge (BA geography 1989); Married Eleanor Holmes (1 son 1 daughter)

Non-political career: Parliamentary officer, National Farmers Union 1990-92; Founder, The Local Identity Agency 1992-97; Director, Early Stage Ventures, Merlin Ventures 1997-2001; Chief executive officer, Amedis Pharmaceuticals 2001-03; Director, 4D Biomedical 2003-; Adviser to Norwich Research Park Venture Fund; Non-executive director, Elsoms Seeds Ltd; Governor, Aerington Primary School 1995-96; Board member, Greater Cambridge Partnership 2005-10

Political career: Contested Stevenage 2005 general election. Member for Mid Norfolk since 6 May 2010 general election

Political interests: Constitution, crime, civil society, localism, rural economy, infrastructure funding, universities and innovation, biotechnology, bioethics, healthcare reform; France, USA

Other organisations: Founding secretary, Rural Economy Group 1994; Trustee, Cambridge Union Society 2005-09; Norfolk Club; Rob Roy Boat Club

Recreations: Sailing, horseracing, hill walking, rowing

George Freeman MP, House of Commons, London SW1A 0AA
Tel: 020 7219 7239 E-mail: george.freeman.mp@parliament.uk
Constituency: Currently being set up.
Website: www.georgefreeman.co.uk

GENERAL ELECTION RESULT

		%
Freeman, G. (Con)	25,123	49.5
Newman, D. (Lib Dem)	11,267	22.2
Hughes, E. (Lab)	8,857	17.5
Coke, R. (UKIP)	2,800	5.5
Birt, T. (Green)	1,457	2.9
Kelly, C. (BNP)	1,261	2.5
Majority	13,856	27.29
Electorate	74,260	
Turnout	50,765	68.36

CONSTITUENCY SNAPSHOT

Richard Ryder took Mid Norfolk for the Conservatives in 1983. He retired in 1997 and new Conservative candidate, Keith Simpson, scraped a majority of just 1,336 after a swing to Labour of 13 per cent. His majority recovered and was 7,560 in 2005.

George Freeman held the seat for the Tories with a majority of 13,856 in 2010.

Boundary changes were extensive. The seat gained 16 wards from South and South West Norfolk. The new wards are mainly rural villages and market towns such as Watton, Buckenham and Northfields. Mid Norfolk lost the main towns of Aylsham and Acle. These were important market towns connected with food production and food processing, a major source of income for the area.

The economy of Mid Norfolk will also be affected by the loss of tourism benefits which were concentrated in the east of the constituency around Coltishall, Wroxham and wards in the Norfolk Broads which were lost to Broadland.

This predominantly rural seat takes in a large area north of Norwich. The seat stretches across the heart of the county from Dereham, with its agricultural processing, light manufacturing and retail, to Wicklewood.

The area has a high number of commuters, many of whom work in Norwich.

Mike Freer

Finchley and Golders Green

Boundary changes

Tel: 020 7219 7071
E-mail: mike.freer.mp@parliament.uk
Website: www.finchleyconservatives.com

Non-political career: Retail catering industry; Retail gaming industry; Relationship director, Barclays Bank plc; Self-employed consultant; London Borough of Barnet Council: Councillor 1990-94, 2001-, Council Leader; Non-executive director, London Development Agency

Political career: Contested Harrow West 2005 general election. Member for Finchley and Golders Green since 6 May 2010 general election; Conservative Friends of Cyprus; Conservative Friends of Israel; Friend of British-Asian Conservative Link

Other organisations: Non-executive Director, St Matthews Housing Association; Member, Friends of Windsor Open Space; Chair, Barnet Multi-faith Forum

Recreations: Cycling, reading

Mike Freer MP, House of Commons, London SW1A 0AA
Tel: 020 7219 7071 E-mail: mike.freer.mp@parliament.uk
Constituency: Finchley and Golders Green Conservatives, 212 Ballards Lane, Finchley, London N3 2LX Tel: 020 8445 4292
Website: www.finchleyconservatives.com

GENERAL ELECTION RESULT

		%
Freer, M. (Con)	21,688	46.0
Moore, A. (Lab)	15,879	33.7
Edge, L. (Lib Dem)	8,036	17.0
Cummins, S. (UKIP)	817	1.7
Lyven, D. (Green)	737	1.6
Majority	5,809	12.32
Electorate	77,198	
Turnout	47,157	61.09

CONSTITUENCY SNAPSHOT

Margaret Thatcher was MP for this seat from 1959 until 1992 when she passed it on to Hartley Booth. In 1997 Labour's Rudi Vis beat the Conservative John Marshall. He went on to hold the seat in 2001, slightly increasing his vote-share. However, he lost around 3,000 votes in 2005 ending up with a majority of 741. This seat was a key Tory target and a 5.8 per cent swing from Labour gave Conservative Mike Freer a 5,809 majority.

The constituency lost one part-ward to Chipping Barnet and another to Hendon. It gained part of Woodhouse ward from Chipping Barnet and the parts of Finchley Church End, Garden Suburb and Golders Green wards that were in Hendon.

Leafy Hampstead Garden Suburb is very affluent, while pockets around N10, East Finchley and Childs Hill are relatively deprived.

The seat has one of the fastest-growing populations in the country, a trend which is expected to continue due to development and regeneration.

There are plans for a £4,000 million scheme to regenerate the areas of Cricklewood, Brent Cross and West Hendon which include the creation of a new town centre, 7,500 homes, retail and leisure space, a new main line railway station, major improvements to public transport provision and a range of community facilities.

Lorraine Fullbrook

South Ribble

Boundary changes

Tel: 020 7219 3000
E-mail: lorraine.fullbrook.mp@parliament.uk
Website: www.telllorraine.com

Conservative

Date of birth: 1959; Married to Mark

Non-political career: Former press and media adviser; Consultant 2000-; Hart District Council: Councillor 2002-04, Leader 2003-04

Political career: Contested South Ribble 2005 general election. Member for South Ribble since 6 May 2010 general election

Political interests: Law and order, economy, immigration, EU

Recreations: Reading, collecting advertising memorabilia, travel

Lorraine Fullbrook MP, House of Commons, London SW1A 0AA
Tel: 020 7219 3000 E-mail: lorraine.fullbrook.mp@parliament.uk
Constituency: South Ribble Conservative Association, Unit 6, Enterprise House, Meadowcroft, Pope Lane, Whitestake, Preston PR4 4BA Website: www.telllorraine.com

GENERAL ELECTION RESULT

		%
Fullbrook, L. (Con)	23,396	45.5
Borrow, D. (Lab)*	17,842	34.7
Fisher, P. (Lib Dem)	7,271	14.1
Duxbury, D. (UKIP)	1,895	3.7
Gauci, R. (BNP)	1,054	2.1
Majority	5,554	10.79
Electorate	75,822	
Turnout	51,458	67.87

**Member of last parliament*

CONSTITUENCY SNAPSHOT

The first Member for this constituency was the Conservative Sir Robert Atkins in 1983. Previously the Member for Preston North, he then moved to this seat.

In the 1997 general election, characteristically for Lancashire, a Labour candidate defeated the incumbent Conservative. In South Ribble it was David Borrow who was the winner with a majority of 5,084. However, this majority has slowly been reduced by the Conservatives and was 2,184 in 2005.

Borrow was defeated in 2010 with a swing of 8.1 per cent to the Conservative candidate, Lorraine Fullbrook.

The seat gained two wards from Chorley and lost the wards of Farington East and Farington West and the part-wards of Bamber Bridge West, Lostock Hall and Tardy Gate to Ribble Valley.

South Ribble lies in south and south west of Lancashire, covering the districts of Chorley, South Ribble and West Lancashire. Leyland, famed for the bus and truck manufacturer, is the largest town in the district with a population of 40,000.

The famous Leyland trucks are a vital employer in the area. The company has become a global business in recent years and is now owned by the American firm PACCAR.

Richard Fuller

Bedford

Boundary changes

Tel: 020 7219 3000
E-mail: richard.fuller.mp@parliament.uk
Website: www.richardfuller.org.uk

Education: Bedford Modern School; Oxford University (BA); Harvard Business School (MBA)

Non-political career: Partner: Management consultancy, Technology venture capital business

Political career: Contested Bedford 2005 general election. Member for Bedford since 6 May 2010 general election; Chair, Oxford University Conservative Association 1983; National chair, Young Conservatives 1985-87

Richard Fuller MP, House of Commons, London SW1A 0AA
Tel: 020 7219 3000 E-mail: richard.fuller.mp@parliament.uk
Constituency: Bedford and Kempston Conservative Association, Unit 1, Hassett House, Hassett Street, Bedford MK40 1HA
Tel: 01234 351412 Website: www.richardfuller.org.uk

GENERAL ELECTION RESULT

		%
Fuller, R. (Con)	17,546	38.9
Hall, P. (Lab)*	16,193	35.9
Vann, H. (Lib Dem)	8,957	19.9
Adkin, M. (UKIP)	1,136	2.5
Dewick, W. (BNP)	757	1.7
Foley, B. (Green)	393	0.9
Bhandari, S. (Ind)	120	0.3
Majority	1,353	3.00
Electorate	68,491	
Turnout	45,102	65.85

**Member of last parliament*

CONSTITUENCY SNAPSHOT

The Conservatives lost this seat, held for them by Trevor Skeet since 1970, in 1997. Labour needed a swing of only 5 per cent to win; the swing to Labour was in fact 13 per cent, giving Patrick Hall the seat with a majority of over 8,000.

Hall's majority fell in subsequent elections and was 3,383 in 2005. Labour was defeated in the 2010 general election with a 5.5 per cent swing to the Conservative candidate, Richard Fuller.

The seat lost its part-ward of Wilshamstead to Mid Bedfordshire, while gaining two part-wards, Kingsbrook and Goldington, from North-East Bedfordshire, and part-ward Kempston South from Mid-Bedfordshire.

Bedford is an industrialised market town that continues to grow. It lies 50 miles north of London and today the seat is in one of the most cosmopolitan areas outside of the capital. Almost 50 separate ethnic groups are represented in the Borough of Bedford that gives the seat its name.

The area retains its high levels of manufacturing, which is the highest in the South East outside London. The constituency has a wide range of employment opportunities, for instance in brewing and light industry.

There are excellent transport links by rail and road, making it a major commuter area for London.

Roger Gale

North Thanet (returning MP)

Boundary changes

Tel: 020 7219 4087
E-mail: galerj@parliament.uk
Website: www.rogergale.co.uk

Conservative

Date of birth: 20 August 1943; Son of Richard Byrne Gale, solicitor, and Phyllis Mary, neé Rowell

Education: Thomas Hardye School, Dorchester; Guildhall School of Music and Drama (LGSM&D 1963); Married Wendy Bowman 1964 (divorced 1967); married Susan Linda Sampson 1971 (divorced 1980) (1 daughter); married Susan Gabrielle Marks 1980 (2 sons)

Non-political career: Freelance broadcaster 1963-; Programme director, Radio Scotland 1965; Personal assistant to general manager, Universal Films 1971-72; Freelance reporter, BBC Radio London 1972-73; Producer: Radio 1 *Newsbeat*, BBC Radio 4 *Today* 1973-76; Director, BBC Children's Television 1976-79; Senior producer, Children's Television, Thames TV; Editor, Teenage Unit; Producer special projects, Thames TV 1979-83; Member: NUJ -2005, Equity, BECTU -2005

Political career: Contested Birmingham Northfield 1982 by-election. Member for North Thanet 1983-2010, for North Thanet (revised boundary) since 6 May 2010 general election; PPS to Ministers of State for the Armed Forces: Archibald Hamilton 1992-93, Jeremy Hanley 1993-94; *Select Committees:* Member: Home Affairs 1990-92, Broadcasting 1997-05, Chairmen's Panel 1997-2010, Procedure 2007-10; President Conservative Animal Welfare; Vice-Chairman, Holborn and St Pancras Conservative Association 1971-72; Vice-Chairman Conservative Party 2001-03

Political interests: Education, animal welfare, media, broadcasting, tourism, leisure industry, licensed trade; Cyprus, Cuba, Tunisia, Mongolia, Africa (Southern and Western)

Other organisations: Vice-President, St John (Herne Bay); President, Herne Bay Air Cadets; Hon. Member, British Veterinary Association, Lord's Taverners; Delegate, Council of Europe 1987-89; Delegate, Western European Union 1987-89; International Election Observer, Mongolia, South Africa, Mozambique, Ghana, The Gambia, Kenya, Macedonia; Fellow, Industry and Parliament Trust; Chairman, Try Angle Awards Foundation; Patron, Animals Worldwide; RSPCA Richard Martin Award for Outstanding Contribution to Animal Welfare; LGSM&D; Freeman, City of London; Farmer's; Royal College of Defence Studies; Royal Temple Yacht Club; Kent County Cricket; Kent County Cricket, Royal Temple Yacht

Recreations: Swimming, sailing

Roger Gale MP, House of Commons, London SW1A 0AA
Tel: 020 7219 4087 Fax: 020 7219 6828
E-mail: galerj@parliament.uk
Constituency: The Old Forge, 215a Canterbury Road, Birchington, Kent CT7 9AH Tel: 01843 848588 Fax: 01843 844856
Website: www.rogergale.co.uk

GENERAL ELECTION RESULT

		%
Gale, R. (Con)*	22,826	52.7
Britton, M. (Lab)	9,298	21.5
Murphy, L. (Lib Dem)	8,400	19.4
Parker, R. (UKIP)	2,819	6.5
Majority	13,528	31.21
Electorate	69,432	
Turnout	43,343	62.43

**Member of last parliament*

CONSTITUENCY SNAPSHOT

Conservative MP Roger Gale has represented the seat since 1983, when his unsuccessful opponent was a young Cherie Booth. When her husband was elected Prime Minister in 1997 Mr Gale won with a majority of 2,766 votes. However, this was a fall from his majority of 18,210 in 1992.

Gale more than doubled his lead in 2001 to 6,650. Although his share of the vote dropped slightly in 2005, his majority actually increased to 7,634. The seat was held by Gale with a 13,528 majority in 2010.

The seat lost the Cliftonville East and West wards to South Thanet, while gaining Marshside ward from Canterbury as well as the part-ward of Thanet Villages from South Thanet.

North Thanet consists of a 13-mile long coastal strip in northern Kent that contains the resorts of Birchington and Margate, along with Herne Bay. Tourism is important to the local economy, as is agriculture inland, and a certain amount of light industry in the larger towns.

Thanet as a whole is particularly well situated for companies with European interests, making it an ideal base for manufacturing for export or import, distribution and logistics or company headquarters.

The Queen Elizabeth the Queen Mother Hospital in Margate is one of the region's flagship acute hospitals.

Mike Gapes

Ilford South (returning MP)

No boundary changes

Tel: 020 7219 6485
E-mail: gapesm@parliament.uk
Website: www.mikegapes.org.uk

Labour/Co-operative

Date of birth: 4 September 1952; Son of Frank Gapes, retired postal worker, and Emily Gapes, retired office worker

Education: Buckhurst Hill County High School; Fitzwilliam College, Cambridge (MA economics 1975); Middlesex Polytechnic, Enfield (Diploma industrial relations 1976); Married Frances Smith 1992 (divorced 2004) (1 daughter 2 stepdaughters)

Non-political career: Voluntary Service Overseas (VSO) teacher, Swaziland 1971-72; Secretary, Cambridge Students' Union 1973-74; Chair National Organisation of Labour Students 1976-77; National student organiser, Labour Party 1977-80; Research officer, Labour Party International Department 1980-88; Senior international officer, Labour Party 1988-92; Member, TGWU

Political career: Contested Ilford North 1983 general election. Member for Ilford South since 9 April 1992; PPS to: Paul Murphy as Minister of State, Northern Ireland Office 1997-99, Lord Rooker as Minister of State, Home Office 2001-02; *Select Committees:* Member: Foreign Affairs 1992-97, Defence 1999-2001, 2003-05, Liaison 2005-10; Chair: Foreign Affairs 2005-10; Member: Quadripartite (Committees on Strategic Export Controls)/Arms Export Controls 2006-10, Joint Committee on National Security Strategy 2010; Member: Labour National Policy Forum and Joint Policy Committee 1996-2005, Labour Friends of Israel 1997-, Labour Friends of India 1999-; Chair Co-op Party, Parliamentary Group 2000-01; Trade union liaison officer, London Group of Labour MPs 2001-05; Member Labour Middle East Council 2001-

Political interests: Defence, international affairs, European Union, economic policy, education, mental health

Other organisations: President, Redbridge United Chinese Association 1992-; Vice-President, Redbridge Chamber of Commerce 1992-; Member, Redbridge Racial Equality Council 1992-; Council Member Voluntary Service Overseas 1997-; Trustee Parkside Community Association 1999-; Vice-President, Valentines Park Conservationists 2000-; Chair, Westminster Foundation for Democracy 2002-05; Vice-President Council of European National Youth Committees 1977-79; Council Member Royal Institute of International Affairs 1996-99; Member: NATO Parliamentary Assembly 2002-05, OSCE Parliamentary Assembly 2005-; Fellow Industry and Parliament Trust 2005; Vice-President, Ilford Football Club; West Ham United Supporters' Club

Recreations: Watching football at West Ham, blues and jazz music

Mike Gapes MP, House of Commons, London SW1A 0AA
Tel: 020 7219 6485 Fax: 020 7219 0978
E-mail: gapesm@parliament.uk
Constituency: No constituency office publicised
Website: www.mikegapes.org.uk

GENERAL ELECTION RESULT

		%	+/-
Gapes, M. (Lab/Co-op)*	25,311	49.4	0.8
Boutle, T. (Con)	14,014	27.4	0.2
Al-Samerai, A. (Lib Dem)	8,679	17.0	-3.5
Chowdhry, W. (Green)	1,319	2.6	
Murray, T. (UKIP)	1,132	2.2	0.6
Jestico, J. (SKGH)	746	1.5	
Majority	11,297	22.06	
Electorate	75,246		
Turnout	51,201	68.04	

**Member of last parliament*

CONSTITUENCY SNAPSHOT

The balance of power has shifted between Labour and the Conservatives 11 times since the Second World War.

Neil Thorne won it for the Tories in 1979 and held it until in 1992 when the Labour candidate Mike Gapes gained it with a majority of just 402. He was returned in 1997 with a majority of 14,200.

Gapes retained Ilford South in 2005 although his majority had fallen to 9,228. Gapes achieved a majority of 11,297 in 2010 with a slight increase in his vote-share.

This constituency in north-east London encompasses most of Ilford. A major shopping and commercial centre, it is also the administrative centre of the London Borough of Redbridge. BT and the King George hospital are also major employers.

A high number of constituents travel to work by public transport. Crossrail will increase transport provision, and Ilford railway station will be a stop on the new service, due to become operational by 2017. Ilford South will also be served by the East London Transit, a new bus service which will operate between Ilford and Dagenham Docks and will open in phases from 2010 to 2013.

Barry Gardiner

Brent North (returning MP)

Boundary changes

Tel: 020 7219 4046
E-mail: gardinerb@parliament.uk
Website: www.barrygardiner.com

Date of birth: 10 March 1957; Son of late John Flannegan Gardiner, general manager, Kelvin Hall, and of late Sylvia Strachan, doctor

Education: Haileybury College, Hertford; St Andrews University (MA philosophy 1983); Harvard University (J. F. Kennedy Scholarship 1983-84); Cambridge University (research 1984-87); Married Caroline Smith 1979 (3 sons 1 daughter)

Non-political career: Partner, Mediterranean Average Adjusting Co 1987-97; Occasional lecturer, Academy of National Economy, Moscow 1992-96; Member: MSF, GMB; Cambridge City Council: Councillor 1988-94, Chair of Finance, Mayor 1992-93

Political career: Member for Brent North 1997-2010, for Brent North (revised boundary) since 6 May 2010 general election; PPS to Beverley Hughes as Minister of State, Home Office 2002-04; Parliamentary Under-Secretary of State: Northern Ireland Office 2004-05, Department of Trade and Industry 2005-06, Department for Environment, Food and Rural Affairs (Biodiversity, Landscape and Rural Affairs) 2006-07; Prime Minister's Special Envoy for Forestry 2007-08; PPS to Lord Mandelson as Secretary of State for Business, Enterprise and Regulatory Reform/Business, Innovation and Skills 2009-10; *Select Committees:* Member: Procedure 1997-2001, Broadcasting 1998-2001, Public Accounts 1999-2002, Joint Committee on Consolidation of Bills Etc 2001-10; Member, Labour Finance and Industry Group; Chair Labour Friends of India 1999-2002, 2008-09

Political interests: Economic policy, trade and industry, education, foreign affairs, environment; India, Sri Lanka, Russia, Georgia, China

Other organisations: ACII; Member, Shipwrights' Company; Freeman, City of London; Royal Overseas League; *Publications:* Various articles on shipping and maritime affairs; Articles on political philosophy in *Philosophical Quarterly*

Recreations: Walking, music, reading philosophy, bird-watching

Barry Gardiner MP, House of Commons, London SW1A 0AA
Tel: 020 7219 4046 Fax: 020 7219 2495
E-mail: gardinerb@parliament.uk
Website: www.barrygardiner.com

GENERAL ELECTION RESULT

		%
Gardiner, B. (Lab)*	24,514	46.9
Patel, H. (Con)	16,486	31.5
Allie, J. (Lib Dem)	8,879	17.0
Malik, A. (Ind)	734	1.4
Francis, M. (Green)	725	1.4
Webb, S. (UKIP)	380	0.7
Vamadeva, J. (Brent North Ind)	333	0.6
Tailor, A. (England)	247	0.5
Majority	8,028	15.35
Electorate	83,896	
Turnout	52,298	62.34

**Member of last parliament*

CONSTITUENCY SNAPSHOT

In the 1997 and 2001 general elections Labour increased its vote by the largest percentage in the country. Before Barry Gardiner won the seat for Labour in 1997, it was the home of veteran Tory MP Sir Rhodes Boyson, having been represented by the Conservatives since its creation in 1974.

Barry Gardiner was re-elected with a much-reduced majority of 5,641. Despite a swing to the Conservatives, Barry Gardiner held the seat for Labour with a majority of 8,028.

The seat lost part of Tokyngton and Welsh Harp wards to Brent Central following the boundary changes, taking in culturally and economically diverse areas from Alperton, Barnhill, Sudbury and Wembley Central from Brent South.

Stretching from Wembley Stadium, through Harrow on the Hill in the west to Fryent Country Park in the east, much of the seat is made up of the inter-world war suburban semis immortalised by John Betjeman as Metroland, areas such as Sudbury, North Wembley, Kenton, Kingsbury and Queensbury.

There is little council housing and a relatively large private rental sector, with the proportion of owner-occupiers well above the London average.

Wembley stadium is over the boundary in Brent Central, but Brent North will still benefit from investment in the area, new jobs and transport links.

Edward Garnier

***Harborough** (returning MP)*

Boundary changes

Tel: 020 7219 6524
E-mail: garniere@parliament.uk
Website: www.edwardgarnier.co.uk

Conservative

Date of birth: 26 October 1952; Son of late Colonel William d'Arcy Garnier, and Hon. Mrs Garnier

Education: Wellington College, Berkshire; Jesus College, Oxford (BA modern history 1974, MA); College of Law, London; Married Anna Caroline Mellows 1982 (2 sons 1 daughter)

Non-political career: Barrister; Called to the Bar, Middle Temple 1976; QC 1995; Assistant Recorder 1998; Recorder 2000; Bencher, Middle Temple 2001

Political career: Contested Hemsworth 1987 general election. Member for Harborough 1992-2010, for Harborough (revised boundary) since 6 May 2010 general election; PPS to: Alastair Goodlad and David Davis as Ministers of State, Foreign and Commonwealth Office 1994-95, Sir Nicholas Lyell as Attorney-General and Sir Derek Spencer as Solicitor-General 1995-97, Roger Freeman as Chancellor of the Duchy of Lancaster 1996-97; Shadow: Minister, Lord Chancellor's Department 1997-99, Attorney General 1999-2001, Minister for: Home Affairs 2005-07, Justice 2007-09, Attorney General 2009-10; Solicitor General 2010-; *Select Committees:* Member: Home Affairs 1992-95; Treasurer Macleod Group of Conservative MPs 1995-97; Member Executive 1922 Committee 2002-05; Chair, Executive Committee Society of Conservative Lawyers 2003-

Political interests: Agriculture, defence, foreign affairs, education, constitutional affairs

Other organisations: Foreign Affairs Forum: Secretary 1988-92, Vice-chair 1992-; Visiting Parliamentary Fellow, St Antony's College, Oxford 1996-97; Director, Great Britain-China Centre 1998-; White's, Pratt's, Vincent's (Oxford); *Publications:* Co-author Bearing the Standard: Themes for a Fourth Term (1991); Facing the Future (1993); Contributor to Halsbury's Laws of England (4th edition 1985)

Recreations: Shooting, cricket, tennis, skiing, opera, biographical research

Edward Garnier QC MP, House of Commons, London SW1A 0AA
Tel: 020 7219 6524 Fax: 020 7219 6735
E-mail: garniere@parliament.uk
Constituency: 24 Nelson Street, Market Harborough, Leicestershire LE16 9AY Tel: 01858 464146 Fax: 01858 410013
Website: www.edwardgarnier.co.uk

GENERAL ELECTION RESULT

		%
Garnier, E. (Con)*	26,894	49.0
Haq, Z. (Lib Dem)	17,017	31.0
McKeever, K. (Lab)	6,981	12.7
Dickens, G. (BNP)	1,715	3.1
King, M. (UKIP)	1,462	2.7
Ball, D. (England)	568	1.0
Stephenson, J. (Ind)	228	0.4
Majority	9,877	18.00
Electorate	77,917	
Turnout	54,865	70.41

**Member of last parliament*

CONSTITUENCY SNAPSHOT

The constituency is a long-time Conservative stronghold. For more than three decades Sir John Farr regularly gained well over half the vote. He was succeeded in 1992 by Edward Garnier QC.

A swing away from the Conservatives in 1997 still left Garnier with a 6,524 majority. His majority fell to 5,252 in 2001 and fell once more in 2005 to 3,892. Garnier retained the seat in 2010 with a 9,877 majority.

Boundary changes were minimal.

The constituency is predominantly rural and is home to a clutch of historic villages and country houses. The undisputed hub is Market Harborough, which is currently expanding rapidly and thriving economically.

The seat also encompasses the south-eastern suburbs of Leicester, giving it a more varied profile. Oadby is conspicuously middle class while Wigston, a former railway town, is more mixed and relatively less prosperous.

Traditional employment sources of textiles and farming are in steep decline and the area is now populated mainly by commuters to Leicester, Northampton and London, owing to the excellent transport links.

Mark Garnier

Wyre Forest

Boundary changes

Tel: 020 7219 3000
E-mail: mark.garnier.mp@parliament.uk
Website: www.markgarnier.co.uk

Conservative

Date of birth: 26 February 1963; Son of late Peter Garnier, motoring writer, and Patricia Garnier (née Dowden), journalist

Education: Charterhouse, Godalming, Surrey; Married Caroline Louise Joyce 2001 (2 sons 1 daughter)

Non-political career: Manager, Swiss Bank Corporation 1982-89; Managing director, South China Securities (UK) Ltd 1989-95; Executive director, Daiwa Europe Ltd 1995-96; Executive, L.C.F Edmond de Rothschild Securities 1996-97; Executive director, Bear Stearns 1998; Self-employed Hedge Fund adviser 1999-2005; Partner, CGR Capital LLP 2006-; Councillor Forest of Dean District Council 2003-07

Political career: Contested Wyre Forest 2005 general election. Member for Wyre Forest since 6 May 2010 general election; Deputy chairman (membership) Forest of Dean Conservative Association 2003-04

Political interests: Health issues, rural interests, transport, economic issues

Other organisations: Court assistant, Worshipful Company of Coachmakers and Coach Harness Makers of London; Freeman of the City of London; Royal Automobile Club; Carlton Club; North London Rifle Club; De Havilland Owners Club

Recreations: Historic aviation, historic motorsport, full-bore target rifle, shooting, fishing, photography, writing, skiing

Mark Garnier MP, House of Commons, London SW1A 0AA
Tel: 020 7219 3000 E-mail: mark.garnier.mp@parliament.uk
Constituency: Wyre Forest Conservatives, Margaret Thatcher House, 35 Mill Street, Kidderminster, Worcestershire DY11 6XB
Tel: 01562 823820 Fax: 01562 862231
Website: www.markgarnier.co.uk

GENERAL ELECTION RESULT

		%
Garnier, M. (Con)	18,793	36.9
Taylor, R. (Ind KHHC)*	16,150	31.7
Knowles, N. (Lab)	7,298	14.3
Farmer, N. (Lib Dem)	6,040	11.9
Wrench, M. (UKIP)	1,498	2.9
Howells, G. (BNP)	1,120	2.2
Majority	2,643	5.19
Electorate	76,711	
Turnout	50,899	66.35

**Member of last parliament*

CONSTITUENCY SNAPSHOT

The seat was held by Tory Anthony Coombs from the 1950s. In 1997, however, Labour's David Lock unseated Coombs with a 18 per cent swing.

This seat witnessed one of the few notable events of the 2001 general election. Retired rheumatologist consultant Dr Richard Taylor contested the seat as an independent fighting to preserve Kidderminster Hospital's services. His campaign was given added support by the withdrawal of the local Lib Dem candidate. Dr Taylor's won the seat with a 17,630 majority and he entered the Commons as its only independent member.

In 2005 Dr Taylor held on to the seat, with a much-reduced majority of 5,250 after a 14 per cent swing to the Conservatives. In 2010 Tory Mark Garnier defeated Taylor by 2,643 votes after the Lib Dems contested the seat.

At the election boundary changes have made the seat coterminous with Wyre Forest District Council.

Wyre Forest is a mixture of urban and rural areas in Worcestershire. It comprises the three towns of Kidderminster, Stourport and Bewdley and takes its name from the Forest of Wyre at the western side of the constituency.

Kidderminster is a medium-sized industrial town, famous for manufacturing carpets, which still plays an important part in the local economy with a number of industrial parks and trading centres.

Stourport is more picturesque and is reliant on tourism for its income. However, much of the seat is made up of small rural villages.

David Gauke

South West Hertfordshire ***(returning MP)***

Boundary changes

Tel: 020 7219 4459
E-mail: gauked@parliament.uk
Website: www.davidgauke.com

Date of birth: 8 October 1971; Son of Jim Gauke and Susan Hall

Education: Northgate High School, Ipswich; St Edmund Hall, Oxford (BA law 1993); College of Law, Chester (legal practice course 1995); Married Rachel Rank 2000 (3 sons)

Non-political career: Parliamentary research assistant to Barry Legg MP 1993-94; Trainee solicitor and solicitor, Richards Butler 1995-99; Solicitor, Macfarlanes 1999-2005

Political career: Contested Brent East 2001 general election. Member for South West Hertfordshire 2005-10, for South West Hertfordshire (revised boundary) since 6 May 2010 general election; Shadow Exchequer Secretary to the Treasury 2007-10; Exchequer Secretary, HM Treasury 2010-; *Select Committees:* Member: Procedure 2005-07, Treasury 2006-07, Joint Committee on Tax Law Rewrite Bills 2009; Deputy chair, Brent East Conservative Association 1998-2000; Member: Conservative Friends of Israel 2000-; Centre for Policy Studies 2003-

Political interests: Financial services, education, Europe

Other organisations: Rickmansworth Conservative Club; Tring Conservative Club

Recreations: Football, cricket, country walks

David Gauke MP, House of Commons, London SW1A 0AA
Tel: 020 7219 4459 Fax: 020 7219 4759
E-mail: gauked@parliament.uk
Constituency: South West Hertfordshire Conservative Association, Scots Bridge House, Scots Hill, Rickmansworth, Hertfordshire WD3 3BB Tel: 01923 771781 Fax: 01923 779471
Website: www.davidgauke.com

GENERAL ELECTION RESULT

		%
Gauke, D. (Con)*	30,773	54.2
Townsend, C. (Lib Dem)	15,853	27.9
Mann, H. (Lab)	6,526	11.5
Benson, M. (UKIP)	1,450	2.6
Gates, D. (BNP)	1,302	2.3
Hannaway, J. (Ind)	846	1.5
Majority	14,920	26.29
Electorate	78,248	
Turnout	56,750	72.53

**Member of last parliament*

CONSTITUENCY SNAPSHOT

This seat has been in Conservative hands since the 1950s. Current MP David Gauke was easily able to increase the Conservative majority in 2005 to 8,473 with a 47 per cent share of the vote.

The Conservatives' share of the vote grew to 54.2 per cent at the 2010 general election.

Boundary changes were minimal.

Possibly one of the most bizarrely shaped constituencies in the UK, South West Hertfordshire is approximately 22 miles long, and at its widest point, four miles wide. It follows the contours of the Grand Union Canal, stretching from Tring to Moor Park. It is largely rural, and comprised mainly of small towns and villages.

The main northern town, Berkhamsted, is largely residential although it is also home to Roussel Uclaf, a major pharmaceutical company and an important employer in the area. Camelot, the National Lottery organisers, are also based in the seat.

The south of the constituency is served by the Metropolitan Underground line to central London, as well as the A41 in the north, and M25 in the south, and the area is natural commuter territory. The towns of Rickmansworth, Chorleywood and Croxley Green are prime examples of the dormitory towns that dominate this predominantly middle-class constituency.

Andrew George

St Ives (returning MP)

Boundary changes

Tel: 020 7219 4588
E-mail: davistw@parliament.uk
Website: www.andrewgeorge.org.uk

Date of birth: 2 December 1958; Son of Reginald Hugh George, horticulturist, and Diana May, née Petherick, teacher and musician

Education: Helston Grammar School; Helston School; Sussex University (BA cultural and community studies 1980); University College, Oxford (MSc agricultural economics 1981); Married Jill Elizabeth Marshall 1987 (1 son 1 daughter)

Non-political career: Charity worker for various rural community development bodies, Nottinghamshire 1981-85, Cornwall 1986-97; Deputy director Cornwall Rural Community Council 1994-97

Political career: Contested St Ives 1992 general election. Member for St Ives 1997-2010, for St Ives (revised boundary) since 6 May 2010 general election; Liberal Democrat Shadow Minister for: Fisheries 1997-2005; Disabilities 1999-2001; PPS to Charles Kennedy as Leader of the Liberal Democrat Party 2001-02; Liberal Democrat Shadow: Minister for Food and Rural Affairs 2002-05, Secretary of State for International Development 2005-06; *Select Committees:* Member: Agriculture 1997-2000, Communities and Local Government 2007-10

Political interests: International development, Cornwall, economic development, housing, fishing industry, agriculture, social exclusion, devolution, small nations, racism, domestic violence, immigration, environment, minority groups, health services and health professions, global TB; All small nations, Africa, Canada, Sri Lanka, Yemen

Other organisations: Commons and Lords Cricket Club, Commons and Lords Rugby Club, Commons Football Team, Leedstown Cricket Club; *Publications:* Cornwall at the Crossroads (1989); A View from the Bottom Left-hand Corner (Patten Press, 2002)

Recreations: Cricket, football, rugby, tennis, swimming, writing, walking, Cornish culture, cycling, gardening, drawing, singing

Andrew George MP, House of Commons, London SW1A 0AA
Tel: 020 7219 4588 Fax: 020 7219 5572
E-mail: davistw@parliament.uk
Constituency: Trewella, 18 Mennaye Road, Penzance,
Cornwall TR18 4NG Tel: 01736 360020 Fax: 01736 332866
Website: www.andrewgeorge.org.uk

GENERAL ELECTION RESULT

		%
George, A. (Lib Dem)*	19,619	42.7
Thomas, D. (Con)	17,900	39.0
Latimer, P. (Lab)	3,751	8.2
Faulkner, M. (UKIP)	2,560	5.6
Andrewes, T. (Green)	1,308	2.9
Rogers, J. (Corn Dem)	396	0.9
Reed, S. (Meb Ker)	387	0.8
Majority	1,719	3.74
Electorate	66,930	
Turnout	45,921	68.61

**Member of last parliament*

CONSTITUENCY SNAPSHOT

A Conservative seat since the 1930s, though with an earlier Liberal tradition, St Ives fell to the Liberal Democrats in 1997.

In 1997 the Liberal Democrat Andrew George took the seat on his second attempt with a swing of more than 8 per cent and a majority of 7,170. His majority increased in 2005 to 11,609. A 10.4 per cent swing to the Conservatives in 2010 almost decimated Liberal Democrat Andrew George's majority, now just 1,719.

Boundary changes moved Wendron, Gwinear, Gwithian and Hayle East, Hayle North, and Hayle South wards to the new Camborne and Redruth seat.

The most south-westerly constituency in the country stretches from Land's End northwards to Godrevy Head north of the seaside town from which it takes its name. The seat also includes the Isles of Scilly. But the largest town is Penzance, the commercial centre of West Cornwall.

The region has a rich cultural history, which combined with the climate, a wild and beautiful landscape, dotted with antiquities, generates millions of pounds for the tourist industry.

St Ives itself, with its wide sandy beaches, has hosted a famous artistic community since the opening of Tate St Ives in 1993, helping to draw in thousands of visitors per year. There is a thriving construction industry and fishing and agriculture are also important.

Nick Gibb

***Bognor Regis and Littlehampton** (returning MP)*

Boundary changes

Tel: 020 7219 6374
E-mail: gibbn@parliament.uk

Conservative

Date of birth: 3 September 1960; Son of late John McLean Gibb, civil engineer, and Eileen Mavern Gibb, schoolteacher

Education: Maidstone Boys' Grammar School, Kent; Roundhay School, Leeds; Thornes House School, Wakefield; Durham University (BA law 1981); Single

Non-political career: Chartered accountant, specialising in taxation, KPMG, London 1984-97

Political career: Contested Stoke-on-Trent Central 1992 general election and Rotherham 1994 by-election. Member for Bognor Regis and Littlehampton 1997-2010, for Bognor Regis and Littlehampton (revised boundary) since 6 May 2010 general election; Opposition Spokesperson for: the Treasury December 1998-99, Trade and Industry 1999-2001, Transport, Local Government and the Regions 2001; Shadow Minister for: Education and for Young People 2005, Schools 2005-10; Minister of State for Schools, Department for Education 2010-; *Select Committees:* Member: Social Security 1997-98, Treasury 1998, Treasury (Treasury Sub-Committee) 1998, Public Accounts 2001-03, Education and Skills 2003-05

Political interests: Economics, taxation, education, social security; USA, Israel

Other organisations: Fellow, Institute of Chartered Accountants in England and Wales (FCA)

Recreations: Long-distance running, skiing

Nick Gibb MP, House of Commons, London SW1A 0AA
Tel: 020 7219 6374 Fax: 020 7219 1395
E-mail: gibbn@parliament.uk
Constituency: 2 Flansham Business Centre, Hoe Lane, Bognor Regis, West Sussex PO22 8NH Tel: 01243 587016

GENERAL ELECTION RESULT

		%
Gibb, N. (Con)*	24,087	51.4
McDougall, S. (Lib Dem)	11,024	23.5
Jones, M. (Lab)	6,508	13.9
Denny, D. (UKIP)	3,036	6.5
Moffat, A. (BNP)	1,890	4.0
Briggs, M. (Ind)	235	0.5
Majority	13,063	27.88
Electorate	70,812	
Turnout	46,852	66.16

**Member of last parliament*

CONSTITUENCY SNAPSHOT

Bognor Regis and Littlehampton was created from most of the pre-1997 Arundel seat, which had been represented by the Conservative Sir Michael Marshall since 1974. In 1997 he stepped aside in favour of the current incumbent, Nick Gibb.

Compared with the old Arundel seat, the Conservative vote fell by 13 per cent in Bognor Regis and Littlehampton in 1997 alongside a similar gain for Labour. In 2001 Gibb retained a majority of 5,643. His majority grew to almost 7,822 in 2005.

The Conservatives retained the seat with 24,087 votes in 2010 giving Gibb a majority of 13,063.

The seat gained the part-wards of Felpham East and Yapton from Arundel and South Downs.

The seat covers a coastal strip of West Sussex where the South Downs fall away to the English Channel. The urban areas of Littlehampton and Bognor Regis are on either side of the river Arun.

Bognor Regis is recorded as having the highest annual hours of sunshine in the United Kingdom, and so unsurprisingly has many retirees and holiday resorts are based around Pagham Harbour and Aldwick. The Butlins Family Entertainment Resort is large employer.

The number of small and medium-sized enterprises in the Arun District is above the national average, and they employ the majority of constituents. Light industry can be found in Littlehampton.

Stephen Gilbert

St Austell and Newquay

New constituency

Tel: 020 7219 3000
E-mail: stephen.gilbert.mp@parliament.uk
Website: www.stephengilbert.org.uk

Date of birth: 6 November 1976

Education: Fowey Community School, Cornwall; St Austell College; Aberystwyth University (BScEcon international politics 1998); London School of Economics (MScEcon international relations 2000)

Non-political career: Parliamentary assistant to Lembit Öpik MP 1998; Research and media assistant to Robin Teverson MEP 1998-99; Account executive, PPS 2000-02; Public affairs manager, IMA 2002-04; Public affairs manager, Fidelity Investments 2004-05; Account manager, Deborah Clark Associates 2005-07; Councillor: Restormel Borough Council 1998-2002, London Borough of Haringey Council 2002-06

Political career: Member for St Austell and Newquay since 6 May 2010 general election; Member, Liberal Democrats 1992-

Political interests: Communities, affordable housing, environment, civil liberties

Other organisations: St Austell Rugby Club

Recreations: Cinema, gym, travel

Stephen Gilbert MP, House of Commons, London SW1A 0AA
Tel: 020 7219 3000 E-mail: stephen.gilbert.mp@parliament.uk
Constituency: c/o St Austell and Newquay Lib Dems, 10 South Street, St Austell, Cornwall PL25 5BN Tel: 01726 63443
Website: www.stephengilbert.org.uk

GENERAL ELECTION RESULT

		%
Gilbert, S. (Lib Dem)	20,189	42.7
Righton, C. (Con)	18,877	40.0
Jameson, L. (Lab)	3,386	7.2
Cole, D. (Meb Ker)	2,007	4.3
Medway, C. (UKIP)	1,757	3.7
Fitton, J. (BNP)	1,022	2.2
Majority	1,312	2.78
Electorate	76,346	
Turnout	47,238	61.87

CONSTITUENCY SNAPSHOT

The new seat is mainly comprised of wards from Truro and St Austell, combined with wards from the south west of North Cornwall and two south-west wards from South East Cornwall.

Truro and St Austell had a mixed parliamentary history over the last 60 years. This was a Tory seat until 1974, when it fell to the Liberals, who have held onto it ever since. Matthew Taylor first won the seat in 1987 at the tender age of 24.

In 2001 Taylor won a majority of over 8,000. It was a similar story in 2005 when Matthew Taylor was elected for the fifth time with a 7,403 majority. This new seat elected Liberal Democrat Stephen Gilbert in 2010, although his majority is just 1,312 following a notional 4.8 per cent swing to the Tories.

St Austell and Newquay stretches from the south east to the north coast of Cornwall and takes in a huge rural heartland in between the big touristic towns of St Austell and Newquay.

Once well known for its clay-mining St Austell's china clay industry now employs around 3,000 people. However, the industry still commands a higher annual output than ever before.

Tourism is now the biggest industry in the seat, with the Eden Project and the popular surfing town of Newquay both major attractions.

Michelle Gildernew

Fermanagh and South Tyrone ***(returning MP)***

No boundary changes

Tel: 020 7219 8162
E-mail: gildernewm@parliament.uk

Date of birth: 28 March 1970

Education: St Catherine's College, Armagh; University of Ulster, Coleraine; Married Jimmy (2 sons 1 daughter)

Political career: Member for Fermanagh and South Tyrone since 7 June 2001 general election; MLA for Fermanagh and South Tyrone 1998-; Former Sinn Féin Spokesperson for Social Development; Member, Preparation for Government Committee 2006-07; Minister of Agriculture and Rural Development 2007-; Sinn Féin: Member, Inter-Party talks team; Press officer 1997; Head of London office 1997-98

Political interests: Housing, rural affairs, education

Other organisations: Aghaloo GFC

Michelle Gildernew MP, House of Commons, London SW1A 0AA
Tel: 020 7219 8162 Fax: 020 7219 6107
E-mail: gildernewm@parliament.uk
Constituency: Thomas Clarke House, 60 Irish Street, Dungannon, Co Tyrone BT70 1QD Tel: 028 8772 2776

GENERAL ELECTION RESULT

		%	+/-
Gildernew, M. (Sinn Féin)*	21,304	45.5	7.8
Connor, R. (Ind)	21,300	45.5	
McKinney, F. (SDLP)	3,574	7.6	-7.0
Kamble, V. (All)	437	0.9	
Stevenson, J. (Ind)	188	0.4	
Majority	4	0.01	
Electorate	67,908		
Turnout	46,803	68.92	

**Member of last parliament*

CONSTITUENCY SNAPSHOT

The seat was taken by Sinn Féin's Michelle Gildernew in 2001 after the retirement of Ken Maginnis, a moderate Ulster Unionist who had held the seat for 18 years. Before this the seat had a colourful electoral history, having returned nationalist publican Frank Maguire until his death during 1981's IRA hunger strikes. In the subsequent by-election, starving Maze prisoner Bobby Sands dramatically took the seat, and after his death he was briefly succeeded by his electoral agent, Owen Carron.

Gildernew was returned with a 4,582 majority in 2005. She just managed to retain this seat in 2010 after scraping a majority of only four votes; the unionists had put forward a joint candidate, the Independent Rodney Connor.

This sprawling rural border seat is in the south-west of Northern Ireland.

The area's natural beauty belies the fact that it witnessed some of the ugliest violence of the Troubles.

The constituency has a significant manufacturing sector as well as having the largest number of agricultural workers in Northern Ireland. The tourism sector also makes a significant contribution to the local economy.

Rt Hon **Cheryl Gillan**

Chesham and Amersham ***(returning MP)***

Boundary changes

Tel: 020 7219 5146
E-mail: gillanc@parliament.uk
Website: www.cherylgillan.co.uk

Conservative

Date of birth: 21 April 1952; Daughter of late Adam Mitchell Gillan, company director, and late Mona Gillan

Education: Cheltenham Ladies' College; College of Law; Chartered Institute of Marketing; Married John Coates Leeming 1985

Non-political career: International Management Group 1977-84; Director, British Film Year 1984-86; Senior marketing consultant, Ernst and Young 1986-91; Marketing director, Kidsons Impey 1991-93; Consultant PKF 1999-2005

Political career: Member for Chesham and Amersham 1992-2010, for Chesham and Amersham (revised boundary) since 6 May 2010 general election; PPS to Viscount Cranborne as Leader of the House of Lords and Lord Privy Seal 1994-95; Parliamentary Under-Secretary of State, Department of Education and Employment 1995-97; Shadow Minister for: Trade and Industry 1997-98, Foreign and Commonwealth Affairs 1998-2001, International Development 1998-2001; Opposition Whip 2001-03; Shadow: Minister for Home Affairs 2003-05, Secretary of State for Wales 2005-10; Secretary of State for Wales 2010-; *Select Committees:* Member: Science and Technology 1992-95, Procedure 1994-95, Public Accounts 2003-04; Contested Greater Manchester Central 1989 European Parliament election; Chairman, Bow Group 1987-88

Political interests: Industry, space, international affairs, defence, education, employment; Former Soviet Union, Europe, Hungary, Poland, USA, Japan, Pacific Rim, China, Commonwealth

Other organisations: Member Executive Committee, Commonwealth Parliamentary Association (CPA) UK Branch 1998-: UK Representative British Islands and Mediterranean region 1999-2004, international treasurer 2004-06; Member, NATO Parliamentary Assembly 2003-05; PC 2010; FCIM; Member, Worshipful Company of Marketors; Freeman, City of London; RAC

Recreations: Golf, music, gardening

Rt Hon Cheryl Gillan MP, House of Commons, London SW1A 0AA
Tel: 020 7219 5146 Fax: 020 7219 2762
E-mail: gillanc@parliament.uk
Constituency: 7A Hill Avenue, Amersham, Buckinghamshire HP6 5BD
Tel: 01494 721577 Fax: 01494 722107
Website: www.cherylgillan.co.uk

GENERAL ELECTION RESULT

		%
Gillan, C. (Con)*	31,658	60.4
Starkey, T. (Lib Dem)	14,948	28.5
Gajadharsingh, A. (Lab)	2,942	5.6
Stevens, A. (UKIP)	2,129	4.1
Wilkins, N. (Green)	767	1.5
Majority	16,710	31.86
Electorate	70,333	
Turnout	52,444	74.57

**Member of last parliament*

CONSTITUENCY SNAPSHOT

A conservative stronghold, their vote dropped by 13 per cent in 1997, however, Cheryl Gillan still polled more than half of the vote.

In 2001 there was virtually no swing at all, and the drop in Gillan's majority of 2,000 was almost entirely due to a 9 per cent fall in turnout.

In 2005 turnout was up, which helped the Conservatives restore their majority to 13,798. Gillan held the seat in 2010 with a majority of 16,710.

The seat gained Great Missenden ward and the two part-wards of Ballinger, South Heath and Chartridge, and Prestwood and Heath End from Aylesbury, while losing both Hazlemere North and Hazlemere South wards to Wycombe.

Nearly half the workforce is in professional, managerial or technical jobs, the fifth-highest percentage outside London. While a majority of constituents commute, the constituency's most important employer is GE Healthcare Technologies, and the headquarters of Amersham Health International and its diagnostic imaging business.

The seat's attractions include the beautiful Chiltern countryside and the relative ease of commuting to London. The Chiltern Railway provides one of the few reliable rail services in the country. Education is also good education as Buckinghamshire's selective schools get some of the best results in the country.

Sheila Gilmore

Edinburgh East

No boundary changes

Tel: 020 7219 3000
E-mail: sheila.gilmore.mp@parliament.uk
Website: www.edinburgheast.net

Labour

Education: Law

Non-political career: Teacher; Lawyer, solicitor's firm, Edinburgh; Consultant (unpaid), Gilmore Lewis Solicitors; Councillor, Edinburgh City Council 1991-2007

Political career: Member for Edinburgh East since 6 May 2010 general election; Contested Edinburgh Pentlands constituency 2007 Scottish Parliament election; Election agent to Nigel Griffiths MP

Political interests: Minimum wage, local bus services, the elderly

Other organisations: Director: EDI, Craigmiller Joint Venture Company, South Edinburgh Partnership, Capital City Homes; Member, Spokes

Sheila Gilmore MP, House of Commons, London SW1A 0AA
Tel: 020 7219 3000 E-mail: sheila.gilmore.mp@parliament.uk
Constituency: 78 Buccleuch Street, Edinburgh EH8 9NH
Tel: 0131-667 8538 Website: www.edinburgheast.net

GENERAL ELECTION RESULT

		%	+/-
Gilmore, S. (Lab)	17,314	43.4	3.5
Kerevan, G. (SNP)	8,133	20.4	3.4
Hope, B. (Lib Dem)	7,751	19.4	-4.9
Donald, M. (Con)	4,358	10.9	0.6
Harper, R. (Green)	2,035	5.1	-0.6
Clark, G. (TUSC)	274	0.7	
Majority	9,181	23.03	
Electorate	60,941		
Turnout	39,865	65.42	

CONSTITUENCY SNAPSHOT

Gavin Strang held Edinburgh East and Musselburgh for Labour in 1970. In the 1983 boundary review Edinburgh East lost Musselburgh to East Lothian, but the 1995 boundary changes returned Musselburgh to this seat. In the Labour victory of 1997 Strang increased his majority to 14,500 and the SNP pushed the Conservatives into third place.

In 2001 Westminster Strang maintained his lead over the nationalists. Boundary changes in 2005 once again removed Musselburgh and added four wards from Edinburgh Central, as well as Prestonfields from Edinburgh South. Strang achieved a majority of over 6,000 with the Liberal Democrats taking second place. Strang retired in 2010 and Sheila Gilmore held the seat for Labour with a 9,181 majority.

This seat includes landmarks such as Edinburgh Castle, Arthur's Seat, the Palace of Holyrood House, as well as the architecturally acclaimed Scottish Parliament.

Naturally for such a historic seat, tourism is a vital part of the local economy. Edinburgh Castle is Scotland's most popular admission-charging attraction. The National Gallery of Scotland is the country's second most-visited free attraction.

Edinburgh is getting a new tram system. The system, copying successful schemes in Manchester and Croydon, will be the first trams in Edinburgh since 1956. The first phase of the development is a 22-stop route starting in the constituency from Newhaven, going up Leith Walk, stopping at Waverley station and going along Princes Street, travelling west through the city before terminating at Edinburgh Airport.

Patricia Glass

North West Durham

Boundary changes

Tel: 020 7219 3000
E-mail: pat.glass.mp@parliament.uk
Website: www.pat-glass.org.uk

Married Bob (2 children)

Non-political career: Local education authorities; Government adviser on education; Councillor, Lanchester Parish Council

Political career: Member for North West Durham since 6 May 2010 general election

Political interests: Education

Patricia Glass MP, House of Commons, London SW1A 0AA
Tel: 020 7219 3000 E-mail: pat.glass.mp@parliament.uk
Constituency: North West Durham Labour Party Campaign, 13 Trafalgar Street, Consett, Co Durham DH8 0AP Tel: 01388 764959
Website: www.pat-glass.org.uk

GENERAL ELECTION RESULT

		%
Glass, P. (Lab)	18,539	42.3
Temple, O. (Lib Dem)	10,927	24.9
Tempest, M. (Con)	8,766	20.0
Stelling, W. (Ind)	2,472	5.6
Stewart, M. (BNP)	1,852	4.2
McDonald, A. (UKIP)	1,259	2.9
Majority	7,612	17.37
Electorate	70,618	
Turnout	43,815	62.05

CONSTITUENCY SNAPSHOT

The area has elected Labour MPs since its coalmining days, though most of the seams were exhausted even before Ernie Armstrong became MP in 1964. He served for 23 years until 1987 he was succeeded by his daughter Hilary.

In 1997 a swing of 11.4 per cent gave Labour a majority of nearly 25,000. Hilary Armstrong was re-elected in 2005 with a majority of 13,443. An 8.3 per cent swing to the Liberal Democrats gave new MP Pat Glass a much reduced majority of 7,612 in 2010.

The seat lost Bishop Auckland Town part-ward to Bishop Auckland and Tanfield part-ward to North Durham.

North West Durham is a large, sparsely populated constituency. The landscape outside Consett has a stark beauty, and the Wear Valley and surrounding moors are increasingly attractive to tourists. The economy of this region was built solely on coal and steel but following its decline, new industries such as engineering have developed.

Hill farming, food production and processing are important. International Cuisine at Consett is the biggest single private employer with a workforce of around 500, along with Derwent Valley Foods. HMH Engineering, a number of small steel castings companies, and AS&T, an aerospace company, all contribute to the local economy.

John Glen

Salisbury

Boundary changes

Tel: 020 7219 3000
E-mail: john.glen.mp@parliament.uk
Website: www.johnglenmp.com

Conservative

Date of birth: 1 April 1974; Son of Philip Glen, nursery man, and Thalia Glen, hairdresser

Education: King Edward's School, Bath; Mansfield College, Oxford (BA modern history 1996, MA) (Student Union President); Judge Institute, Cambridge (MBA 2003); Married Emma O'Brien 2008 (1 stepson 1 stepdaughter)

Non-political career: Parliamentary researcher to Michael Bates MP and Gary Streeter MP 1996-97; Strategy consultant, Andersen Consulting 1997-2004: Head of political section, Office of William Hague MP as Leader of the Opposition (on secondment) 2000-01; Conservative Party: Deputy director, Conservative Research Department 2004-05, Director, Conservative Research Department 2005-06; Senior adviser to global head of strategy, Accenture 2006-10; Director, Walton Bates 2007-; JP, Westminster 2006-

Political career: Contested Plymouth Devonport 2001 general election. Member for Salisbury since 6 May 2010 general election

Political interests: Policy development, youth issues, armed forces, foreign affairs, education, health

Other organisations: Board member, Centre for Policy Studies 2009-; Chippenham Constitutional Club; National Club

Recreations: Church, family, eating out, friends

John Glen MP, House of Commons, London SW1A 0AA
Tel: 020 7219 3000 E-mail: john.glen.mp@parliament.uk
Constituency: The Morrison Hall, 12 Brown Street, Salisbury, Wiltshire SP1 1HE Tel: 01722 323050 Fax: 01722 333345
Website: www.johnglenmp.com

GENERAL ELECTION RESULT

		%
Glen, J. (Con)	23,859	49.2
Radford, N. (Lib Dem)	17,893	36.9
Gann, T. (Lab)	3,690	7.6
Howard, F. (UKIP)	1,392	2.9
Witheridge, S. (BNP)	765	1.6
Startin, N. (Green)	506	1.0
Arthur, K. (Ind)	257	0.5
Holme, J. (Ind)	119	0.3
Majority	5,966	12.31
Electorate	67,429	
Turnout	48,481	71.90

CONSTITUENCY SNAPSHOT

The seat has been in Conservative hands since 1945. Between 1983 and 1992 their share of the vote never dropped below 50 per cent. Even in 1997 Robert Key was returned with a majority of over 6,000.

The Conservatives' share of the vote increased by almost 4 per cent in 2001, and the Conservative position was strengthened in 2005 after Key was returned with a 11,142 majority. A Liberal Democrat surge halved the Conservative majority to 5,966 but their new candidate John Glen still won with just under 50 per cent of the vote.

Salibsury lost Bulford and Durringotn wards to Devizes; and Donhead, Fonthill and Nadder, Tisbury and Fovant and Knoyle part-ward to South West Wiltshire.

The Wiltshire seat of Salisbury takes in the city of the same name and the surrounding rural villages. The two most famous aspects of the seat are Stonehenge and Salisbury Cathedral.

The seat has strong military links, and large parts of the constituency are marked as danger areas on maps due to their use in military training exercises.

While the Ministry of Defence is the largest single employer, other public sector agencies also provide employment.

Salisbury has excellent rail links to London, Exeter, Bristol and many south coast resorts. However, commuting is not particularly common. This is because the local economy is especially strong and diverse.

Mary Glindon

North Tyneside

Boundary changes

Tel: 020 7219 3000
E-mail: mary.glindon.mp@parliament.uk
Website: www.northtynesidelabour.co.uk

Labour

Date of birth: 13 January 1957; Daughter of Margaret and Cecil Mulgrove

Education: Sacred Heart Grammar School, Fenham, Newcastle upon Tyne; Newcastle upon Tyne Polytechnic (BSc sociology 1979); Married Raymond Glindon 2000 (1 daughter 1 stepson 1 stepdaughter)

Non-political career: Clerical officer, civil service 1980-85; Administrator, local government 1987-88; Administrator/community development/manager, Centre for Unemployment 1988-2004; Administrator, NHS call centre 2005; Trainee dispenser, NHS 2005-06; Travel sales adviser, call centre 2006; Sales assistant, department store 2006-08; Administration officer, Department for Work and Pensions and Child Maintenance and Enforcement Commission 2008-10; Member: North Tyneside Trades Union Council, GMB; Councillor, North Tyneside Council 1995-; Deputy Mayor 1998-99, Mayor 1999-2000; School governor, two primary schools

Political career: Member for North Tyneside since 6 May 2010 general election; Member, Labour Party 1990-

Other organisations: Founding member and treasurer, Battle Hill Community Development Project 1983-; Member: Victor Mann Trust, Kettlewell Education Trust

Mary Glindon MP, House of Commons, London SW1A 0AA
Tel: 020 7219 3000 E-mail: mary.glindon.mp@parliament.uk
Constituency: 7 Palmersville, Forest Hall,
Newcastle upon Tyne NE12 9HN Tel: 0191-268 9111
Website: www.northtynesidelabour.co.uk

GENERAL ELECTION RESULT

		%
Glindon, M. (Lab)	23,505	50.7
Ord, D. (Lib Dem)	10,621	22.9
Mohindra, G. (Con)	8,514	18.4
Burrows, J. (BNP)	1,860	4.0
Blake, C. (UKIP)	1,306	2.8
Batten, B. (NF)	599	1.3
Majority	12,884	27.76
Electorate	77,690	
Turnout	46,405	59.73

CONSTITUENCY SNAPSHOT

North Tyneside was created in 1997 out of Wallsend and was held by Stephen Byers until his retirement in 2010

Wallsend was a Labour seat in 1945 with sizable majorities in every post-war general election. Ted Garrett served the seat from 1964 to 1992 when he retired and was replaced by Stephen Byers. Byers managed to maintain a high level of support after his election in 1992, winning over 30,000 votes. The Wallsend constituency was abolished in 1997 and was mostly absorbed by the new seat of Newcastle upon Tyne and Wallsend. Stephen Byers retired in 2010 and his replacement Mary Glindon won easily with a majority of 12,884.

The seat now contains the Wallsend area previously in the abolished Newcastle upon Tyne East and Wallsend.

North Tyneside lies on the north bank of the river Tyne, east of Newcastle.

A former mining community the seat is mainly residential, covering the town of Longbenton and the sprawling council estate of the Killingsworth Township.

North Tyneside has many of the traits of a traditional Labour heartland. The seat has a solidly white working-class population, with less than 1 per cent from an ethnic minority. Although the seat is based around mining villages, the mining industry declined heavily in the 1980s.

Roger Godsiff

Birmingham, Hall Green ***(returning MP)***

Boundary changes

Tel: 020 7219 5191
E-mail: godsiffr@parliament.uk
Website: www.epolitix.com/roger-godsiff

Date of birth: 28 June 1946; Son of late George Godsiff, chargehand/fitter, and Gladys Godsiff

Education: Catford Comprehensive School, London; Married Julia Brenda Morris 1977 (1 son 1 daughter)

Non-political career: Banking 1965-70; Political officer APEX 1970-88; Senior research officer GMB 1988-91; Member of and sponsored by GMB; London Borough of Lewisham: Councillor 1971-90, Mayor 1977

Political career: Contested Birmingham Yardley 1983 general election. Member for Birmingham Small Heath 1992-97, for Birmingham Sparkbrook and Small Heath 1997-2010, for Birmingham, Hall Green since 6 May 2010 general election; Member, Co-operative Party

Political interests: European Union, foreign affairs, sport, recreation, immigration; America, Asia, Indian sub-continent, Middle East

Other organisations: Member, Executive Committee, IPU 1999; Fellow Industry and Parliament Trust 1994; Chairman Charlton Athletic Community Trust 2002-; Member, Charlton Athletic Supporters Club

Recreations: Sport in general, particularly football

Roger Godsiff MP, House of Commons, London SW1A 0AA
Tel: 020 7219 5191 Fax: 020 7219 2221
E-mail: godsiffr@parliament.uk
Constituency: 62 Horse Shoes Lane, Sheldon, Birmingham B26 3HY
Tel: 0121-603 2299 Fax: 0121-603 2299 Website: www.epolitix.com/roger-godsiff

GENERAL ELECTION RESULT

		%
Godsiff, R. (Lab)*	16,039	32.9
Yaqoob, S. (Respect)	12,240	25.1
Evans, J. (Lib Dem)	11,988	24.6
Barker, J. (Con)	7,320	15.0
Blumenthal, A. (UKIP)	950	2.0
Gardner, A. (Ind)	190	0.4
Majority	3,799	7.80
Electorate	76,580	
Turnout	48,727	63.63

**Member of last parliament*

CONSTITUENCY SNAPSHOT

Created in 1950, Birmingham Hall Green experienced forty-seven years of uninterrupted Conservative control. In 1997 with the highest swing in Birmingham, Labour's Stephen McCabe won a majority of 8,420 votes. He held the seat until 2010 when he moved to Birmingham Selly Oak following boundary changes.

In 2010 Roger Godsiff held the seat for Labour with a majority of 3,799 despite a 11.7 per cent swing to Respect.

There are four wards in this much-changed seat: Hall Green; Moseley and Kings Heath; Sparkbrook; and Springfield. Moseley and Kings Heath is an entirely new arrival, taken in part from Sparkbrook and Small Heath and in part from Selly Oak. Sparkbrook is also all-new, being formed from territory from Sparkbrook and Small Heath, Selly Oak and Edgbaston. Finally, new arrival Springfield has been formed from segments previously in Selly Oak and Sparkbrook and Small Heath. Two wards were lost: Billesley and Brandwood, large wards south of the new seat, went to Selly Oak.

Birmingham Hall Green was a moderately well-to-do seat before the recent changes. The Hall Green ward, which borders on affluent Solihull and is retained under the new constituency configuration, has lower than average levels of deprivation for the region. However, the gain of the Sparkbrook and Small Heath wards can be expected to alter Hall Green's profile significantly. These two inner-city wards have higher unemployment and correspondingly higher levels of deprivation.

Rt Hon **Paul Goggins**

Wythenshawe and Sale East ***(returning MP)***

No boundary changes

Tel: 020 7219 5865
E-mail: gogginsp@parliament.uk
Website: www.paulgoggins.org

Labour

Date of birth: 16 June 1953; Son of John Goggins and late Rita Goggins

Education: St Bede's College, Manchester; Ushaw College, Durham 1971-73; Birmingham Polytechnic (Certificate residential care of children and young people 1976); Manchester Polytechnic (Certificate of Qualification in Social Work 1982); Married Wyn Bartley 1977 (2 sons 1 daughter)

Non-political career: Child care worker, Liverpool Catholic Social Services 1974-75; Officer-in-charge, local authority children's home, Wigan 1976-84; Project director, NCH Action For Children, Salford 1984-89; National director, Church Action On Poverty 1989-97; Member TGWU; Councillor, Salford City Council 1990-98

Political career: Member for Wythenshawe and Sale East since 1 May 1997 general election; PPS: to John Denham as Minister of State: Department of Social Security 1998-99, Department of Health 1999-2000; to David Blunkett: as Secretary of State for Education and Employment 2000-01, as Home Secretary 2001-03; Parliamentary Under-Secretary of State: Home Office 2003-06, Northern Ireland Office (NIO) 2006-07; Minister of State, NIO 2007-10; *Select Committees:* Member: Social Security 1997-98

Political interests: Poverty, unemployment, housing, transport, global poverty, democratic renewal, community regeneration

Other organisations: Patron Trafford Crossroads 1997-; Hon. President Wythenshawe Mobile 1997-; Member CAFOD Board 2000-03; Former Trustee Russian European Trust 2001-03; PC 2009

Recreations: Watching Manchester City football team, walking, singing

Rt Hon Paul Goggins MP, House of Commons, London SW1A 0AA
Tel: 020 7219 5865 Fax: 020 7219 1268
E-mail: gogginsp@parliament.uk
Constituency: 2/19 Alderman Downward House, Wythenshawe, Manchester M22 5RF Tel: 0161-499 7900 Fax: 0161-499 7911
Website: www.paulgoggins.org

GENERAL ELECTION RESULT

		%	+/-
Goggins, P. (Lab)*	17,987	44.1	-8.0
Clowes, J. (Con)	10,412	25.6	3.3
Eakins, M. (Lib Dem)	9,107	22.4	0.9
Todd, B. (BNP)	1,572	3.9	
Cassidy, C. (UKIP)	1,405	3.5	0.4
Worthington, L. (TUSC)	268	0.7	
Majority	7,575	18.59	
Electorate	79,923		
Turnout	40,751	50.99	

**Member of last parliament*

CONSTITUENCY SNAPSHOT

The seat was held for the Conservatives by Eveline Hill for 14 years until 1964 when Alf Morris, who became a prominent campaigner for the disabled, gained the seat for Labour. Labour has regularly polled over 50 per cent of the vote.

Morris retired in 1997 after 33 years as MP and was replaced by Paul Goggins, who has represented the seat ever since. Goggins was re-elected with a majority of 10,827 in 2005 and held the seat again in 2010 by 7,575 votes.

Wythenshawe and Sale East is a constituency whose two parts are quite different. Wythenshawe, an overspill estate from the City of Manchester, is working-class, while the eastern part of the seat includes Sale, a comfortable middle class part of Cheshire from which many commute into Manchester.

The growth of Manchester Airport and the success of housing and social regeneration have brought new opportunities to the local area.

The government is currently consulting on the expansion of air traffic to meet rising demand at Manchester Airport, part of which is in the constituency.

Zac Goldsmith

Richmond Park

Boundary changes

Tel: 020 7219 3000
E-mail: zac.goldsmith.mp@parliament.uk
Website: www.zacgoldsmith.com

Date of birth: 20 January 1975; Son of Sir James Goldsmith and Lady Annabel Vane-Tempest-Stewart

Education: Eton College; Married Sheherazade Ventura-Bentley 1999 (separated) (1 son 2 daughters)

Non-political career: Redefining Progress, San Francisco, USA 1994-95; International Society for Ecology and Culture 1995-97; Editor, *Ecologist* 1997-2007

Political career: Member for Richmond Park since 6 May 2010 general election; Deputy chairman, Quality of Life Policy Group, Conservative Party 2005-

Political interests: Anti-social behaviour, the environment

Other organisations: Beacon Prize for Young Philanthropist of the Year 2003; International Environmental Leadership, Global Green Award 2004; Richmond Green Champion 2010; *Publications:* Author, The Constant Economy (Atlantic Books 2009)

Zac Goldsmith MP, House of Commons, London SW1A 0AA
Tel: 020 7219 3000 E-mail: zac.goldsmith.mp@parliament.uk
Constituency: 372 Upper Richmond Road West, London SW14 7JU
Tel: 020 8878 7866 Fax: 020 8939 0331
Website: www.zacgoldsmith.com

GENERAL ELECTION RESULT

		%
Goldsmith, Z. (Con)	29,461	49.7
Kramer, S. (Lib Dem)*	25,370	42.8
Tunnicliffe, E. (Lab)	2,979	5.0
Dul, P. (UKIP)	669	1.1
Page, J. (Green)	572	1.0
May, S. (CPA)	133	0.2
Hill, C. (Ind)	84	0.1
Majority	4,091	6.90
Electorate	77,060	
Turnout	59,268	76.91

**Member of last parliament*

CONSTITUENCY SNAPSHOT

The current constituency is the product of boundary reviews after the 1979 and 1992 general elections. Before 1997 there was the Richmond and Barnes constituency. Lib Dem Jenny Tonge won the seat from Tory Jeremy Hanley in 1997.

Tonge's majority in 2001 was just under 5,000 and she stood down in 2005. Her successor Susan Kramer won by 3,701 votes. A hard-fought campaign saw Tory environmentalist Zac Goldsmith take the seat from Liberal Democrat Susan Kramer on a 7 per cent swing.

Boundary changes were minor: part of Beverley ward was lost to Kingston and Surbiton.

This constituency includes all of Richmond Park, as well as Kew Gardens and Old Deer Park. Richmond Park covers around 2,500 acres and is the largest green space in London, enclosed as a hunting park by Charles I in 1637.

Herds of deer still roam the park and it is designated a site of special scientific interest by English Nature.

Richmond has the some of the highest property prices of any London local authority.

Richmond is on the Heathrow Airport flight path.

Helen Goodman

Bishop Auckland (returning MP)

Boundary changes

Tel: 020 7219 4346
E-mail: goodmanh@parliament.uk
Website: www.helengoodman.co.uk

Labour

Date of birth: 2 January 1958; Daughter of Alan and Hanne Goodman

Education: Lady Manners School, Bakewell; Somerville College, Oxford (BA philosophy, politics and economics 1979); Married Charles Seaford 1988 (2 children)

Non-political career: Research assistant to Phillip Whitehead MP 1979-80; Civil servant HM Treasury, ending as Head of Strategy Unit 1980-97; Adviser Czechoslovak Prime Minister's Office 1990-91; Director of Commission on Future of Multi Ethnic Britain 1998; Head of strategy Children's Society 1998-2002; Chief executive National Association of Toy and Leisure Libraries 2002-05; FDA branch secretary HM Treasury 1986-88; GMB

Political career: Member for Bishop Auckland 2005-10, for Bishop Auckland (revised boundary) since 6 May 2010 general election; PPS to Harriet Harman as Minister of State, Ministry of Justice 2007; Parliamentary Secretary, Office of the Leader of the House of Commons 2007-08; Assistant Government Whip 2008-09; Parliamentary Under-Secretary of State, Department for Work and Pensions 2009-10; *Select Committees:* Member: Public Accounts 2005-07, Joint Committee on the Draft Climate Change Bill 2007; Chair Camden Co-operative Party 1997-98; Member National Policy Forum 2005-07

Political interests: Economics, environment, children, international development, human rights; Denmark, Czech Republic

Recreations: Cooking, family

Helen Goodman MP, House of Commons, London SW1A 0AA
Tel: 020 7219 4346 Fax: 020 7219 0444
E-mail: goodmanh@parliament.uk
Constituency: 1 Cockton Hill Road, Bishop Auckland,
Co Durham DL14 6EN Tel: 01388 603075 Fax: 01388 603075
Website: www.helengoodman.co.uk

GENERAL ELECTION RESULT

		%
Goodman, H. (Lab)*	16,023	39.0
Harrison, B. (Con)	10,805	26.3
Wilkes, M. (Lib Dem)	9,189	22.3
Walker, A. (BNP)	2,036	5.0
Zair, S. (LLPBPP)	1,964	4.8
Brothers, D. (UKIP)	1,119	2.7
Majority	5,218	12.68
Electorate	68,370	
Turnout	41,136	60.17

**Member of last parliament*

CONSTITUENCY SNAPSHOT

Bishop Auckland has been a Labour seat since 1935. Bishop Auckland had a Labour majority of less than 7,000 in 1979. In 1983, Derek Foster's majority dropped to 4,306 after a strong showing by the Liberal Alliance.

Labour gradually advanced before 1992, but in 1997 a swing of 15.5 per cent gave Labour nearly two-thirds of the vote and a 20,000 majority. In 2001 the Conservatives recovered with a swing of nearly 5 per cent.

Helen Goodman succeeded Derek Foster in 2005 with a majority of 10,047. This seat has been solidly Labour for years but a 7.2 per cent swing to the Conservatives halved Helen Goodman's majority to 5,218 in 2010.

Minor boundary changes added the part of the Bishop Auckland Town ward that was previously in North West Durham.

Bishop Auckland stretches from former Durham coalfield towns in the east to the Pennines in the west, combining highly industrialised areas with historic towns and open countryside.

The east of the constituency, dominated by the coalfield and the largely working-class towns of Bishop Auckland, Shildon and Spennymoor. The main industry in the rural areas is farming; mainly sheep on the higher land and mixed in the low-lying areas around Barnard Castle. Agriculture is in decline, with many farms diversifying to take advantage of growing tourism.

Robert Goodwill

Scarborough and Whitby ***(returning MP)***

No boundary changes

Tel: 020 7219 8268
E-mail: goodwillr@parliament.uk
Website: www.robertgoodwill.co.uk

Conservative

Date of birth: 31 December 1956; Son of Robert William and Joan Goodwill

Education: Bootham School, York; Newcastle University (BSc agriculture 1979); Married Maureen Short 1987 (2 sons 1 daughter)

Non-political career: Farmer 1979-; Member, then branch chairman National Farmers Union

Political career: Contested Redcar 1992 and North West Leicestershire 1997 general elections. Member for Scarborough and Whitby since 5 May 2005 general election; Opposition Whip 2006-07; Shadow Minister for Transport 2007-10; Assistant Government Whip 2010-; *Select Committees:* Member: Transport 2005-06; European Parliament: Contested Cleveland and Richmond 1994, Yorkshire (south) 1998 elections, MEP for Yorkshire and the Humber 1999-2004: Deputy Conservative leader 2003-04

Political interests: Agriculture, fisheries, environment, transport; Ukraine, Moldova, Belarus

Other organisations: Patron, National Traction Engine Trust; Farmers

Recreations: Steam ploughing, travel

Robert Goodwill MP, House of Commons, London SW1A 0AA
Tel: 020 7219 8268 Fax: 020 7219 8108
E-mail: goodwillr@parliament.uk
Constituency: 21 Huntriss Row, Scarborough,
North Yorkshire YO11 2ED Tel: 01723 365656 Fax: 01723 362577
Website: www.robertgoodwill.co.uk

GENERAL ELECTION RESULT

		%	+/-
Goodwill, R. (Con)*	21,108	42.8	1.9
David, A. (Lab)	12,978	26.3	-12.0
Exley-Moore, T. (Lib Dem)	11,093	22.5	6.6
James, M. (UKIP)	1,484	3.0	1.0
Scott, T. (BNP)	1,445	2.9	
Cluer, D. (Green)	734	1.5	-1.1
Popple, P. (Ind)	329	0.7	
Boddington, J. (Green Soc)	111	0.2	
Majority	8,130	16.50	
Electorate	75,443		
Turnout	49,282	65.32	

**Member of last parliament*

CONSTITUENCY SNAPSHOT

Until 1997 Scarborough had only known Conservative representation since 1918. Sir Michael Shaw, MP from 1966, regularly polled more than half the total vote until retiring in 1992 when he was replaced by fellow Tory John Sykes.

The swing against Sykes in the 1997 general election was almost 15 per cent and Labour's Lawrie Quinn emerged victorious. Sykes tried to make a comeback in 2001 and the Tory vote recovered slightly, but the overall swing to the Tories was less than 1 per cent, with Quinn retaining the seat.

The Conservatives' Robert Goodwill won the seat in 2005 with a 5.1 per cent swing, giving him a majority of 1,245. In 2010 Goodwill increased his majority to a strong 8,130.

This North Yorkshire constituency covers both the seaside towns in its name as well as many small villages inland.

Scarborough is the biggest holiday resort on the Yorkshire coast. Whitby is known for its jet production, fishing fleet and as an inspiration for Bram Stoker's Dracula.

Outside the resorts, most of the rest of the constituency is in the North York Moors. Apart from tourism, there is also light engineering and food processing including McCain frozen food.

Rt Hon **Michael Gove**

Surrey Heath (returning MP)

No boundary changes

Tel: 020 7219 6804
E-mail: govem@parliament.uk
Website: www.michaelgove.com

Date of birth: 26 August 1967; Son of Ernest and Christine Gove

Education: Robert Gordon's College, Aberdeen; Lady Margaret Hall, Oxford (BA English 1988); Married Sarah Rosemary Vine 2001 (1 daughter 1 son)

Non-political career: Reporter *Aberdeen Press and Journal* 1989; Researcher/reporter Scottish Television 1990-91; Reporter BBC News and Current Affairs 1991-96; *The Times*: writer and editor 1996-2005, writer 2005-; National Union of Journalists 1989-

Political career: Member for Surrey Heath since 5 May 2005 general election; Shadow: Minister for Housing 2005-07, Secretary of State for Children, Schools and Families 2007-10; Secretary of State for Education 2010-; *Select Committees:* Member: European Scrutiny 2005-07

Political interests: Education, crime, terrorism

Other organisations: Chair, Policy Exchange 2003-05; PC 2010; *Publications:* Michael Portillo – The Future of the Right (Fourth Estate 1995); The Price of Peace (CPS 2000); Celsius 7/7 (Weidenfeld-Nicolson 2005)

Rt Hon Michael Gove MP, House of Commons, London SW1A 0AA
Tel: 020 7219 6804 Fax: 020 7219 4829
E-mail: govem@parliament.uk
Constituency: Curzon House, Church Road, Windlesham, Surrey GU20 6BH Tel: 01276 472468 Fax: 01276 451602
Website: www.michaelgove.com

GENERAL ELECTION RESULT

		%	+/-
Gove, M. (Con)*	31,326	57.6	6.4
Hilliar, A. (Lib Dem)	14,037	25.8	-2.9
Willey, M. (Lab)	5,552	10.2	-6.4
Stroud, M. (UKIP)	3,432	6.3	
Majority	17,289	31.81	
Electorate	77,690		
Turnout	54,347	69.95	

**Member of last parliament*

CONSTITUENCY SNAPSHOT

The old constituency Surrey North West had the distinction of recording the largest majority in the country in the 1992 general election: 28,394 for the late Sir Michael Grylls, who had represented the seat since 1974. Sir Michael retired in 1997, and his successor was Nick Hawkins, who exchanged Blackpool South for Surrey Heath. He was returned with a majority of 16,287, the second largest Conservative majority in the UK, behind only John Major's Huntingdon.

His majority fell to 10,819 in 2001 and he was deselected in April 2004, the first Conservative MP to suffer this fate since 1997. In July that year the local association selected Michael Gove, who was duly elected in 2005 with a 10,845 majority.

In 2010 Gove retained the seat for the Conservatives with a strong 17,289 majority.

This largely suburban constituency on the western edge of Surrey comprises small and medium-sized urban areas, military training land and open countryside and is home to many well-off London commuters.

There is a strong military presence in the area. Camberley is home to the Royal Military Academy and the Staff College.

Most industrial and commercial activity is concentrated around Camberley and Frimley. S C Johnson has its British base in Frimley Green and is a major employer.

Richard Graham

Gloucester

Boundary changes

Tel: 020 7219 3000
E-mail: richard.graham.mp@parliament.uk
Website: www.richardgraham.org

Conservative

Date of birth: 4 April 1958

Education: Christ Church College, Oxford (history 1979); Certificate investment management (IMC); Married Anthea 1989 (1 daughter 2 sons)

Non-political career: Airline manager, Cathay Pacific Airways and John Swire & Sons 1980-86; Diplomat, HM Diplomatic Service 1986-92: First secretary, Nairobi High Commission, First secretary, Peking Embassy, Trade Commissioner, China, HM Consul, Macau; Investment manager 1992-2009: Director, Baring Asset Management, Director, Greater China Fund Inc 1994-2004, Head of Institutional and International Business, Baring Asset Management; Cotswold District Council: Councillor 2003-07, Chair, Overview and Scrutiny Committee

Political career: Member for Gloucester since 6 May 2010 general election; Contested South West England 2004 European Parliament election

Other organisations: Chair, British Chamber of Commerce, Shanghai; Vice-chair, Board of Airline Representatives in the Philipines; Former member, Executive Council, China-Britain Business Council; Member: Pensions Group, International Financial Services Ltd, London, RAF Assocation; Gloucester City Winget Cricket Club; Marylebone Cricket Club

Recreations: Cricket, squash

Richard Graham MP, House of Commons, London SW1A 0AA
Tel: 020 7219 3000 E-mail: richard.graham.mp@parliament.uk
Constituency: Gloucester Conservatives, Unit 1143, Regent Court, Gloucester Business Park, Hucclecote, Gloucester GL3 4AD
Tel: 01452 371630 Fax: 01452 371640
Website: www.richardgraham.org

GENERAL ELECTION RESULT

		%
Graham, R. (Con)	20,267	39.9
Dhanda, P. (Lab)*	17,847	35.2
Hilton, J. (Lib Dem)	9,767	19.2
Smith, M. (UKIP)	1,808	3.6
Platt, A. (England)	564	1.1
Meloy, B. (Green)	511	1.0
Majority	2,420	4.77
Electorate	79,322	
Turnout	50,764	64.00

**Member of last parliament*

CONSTITUENCY SNAPSHOT

In the decades immediately following the Second World War Gloucester was held by Labour. Gradually, however, the city moved towards the Conservatives, who took the seat in 1970 and held it until 1997.

In that year Labour's Tess Kingham was able to take the seat with a majority of 8,259. Tess Kingham retired in 2001. Her successor Parmjit Dhanda maintained a Labour hold with a 2005 majority of 4,271. Conservative Richard Graham defeated Dhanda on an 8.9 per cent swing in 2010. He won a 2,420 majority.

Boundary changes were minor, moving the Longlevens ward to Tewkesbury.

The county seat of Gloucester is more diverse than Cheltenham, the county's other major town. This historic city is home to such landmarks as Gloucester Cathedral and Britain's most inland port.

The local economy maintains a healthy mix of service sector and manufacturing activities. There are several large employers within the financial services sector, most notably the Cheltenham and Gloucester mortgage company. Birds Eye Wall's operates one of the world's largest ice cream factories in the city.

Tourism is a significant industry dependent on visitors to Gloucester. The top attraction in the town is the Gloucester Docks area, which is to be the focal point of urban regeneration scheme.

Helen Grant

Maidstone and The Weald

Boundary changes

Tel: 020 7219 3000
E-mail: helen.grant.mp@parliament.uk
Website: www.helengrant.org

Conservative

Date of birth: 28 September 1961; Daughter of Dr Gladys Spedding and Dr Julius Okwboye, both retired

Education: St Aidans Comprehensive School, Carlisle; Trinity Comprehensive School, Carlisle; Hull University (LLB 1982); College of Law, Guildford (Solicitors Finals 1984); Married Simon Grant 1991 (2 sons)

Non-political career: Articled clerk, Cartmell Mawson & Maine, Carlisle 1985-87; Assistant solicitor, Hempsons, London 1987-88; Fayers & Co, London: Associate solicitor 1988-92, Equity partner 1992-94; Maternity sabattical 1994-95; Consultant solicitor, T G Baynes & Co, Kent 1995-96; Senior partner/owner, Grants Solicitors LLP 1996-; Non-executive director, Croydon NHS Primary Care Trust 2005-07

Political career: Member for Maidstone and The Weald since 6 May 2010 general election; Member, Labour Party 2004-05; Conservative Party: Member 2006-, Deputy Chair, diversity group, Croydon Central and Croydon South Conservative Federation 2006-08, Special adviser to Oliver Letwin MP as Chair of Party Policy Review 2006-, Member, Social Mobility Task Force 2007-08

Political interests: Justice, business and enterprise, crime, law and order, women, children and families, social mobility; Chagos Islands/Diego Garcia

Other organisations: Member, Bow Group; Centre for Social Justice: Member, Family Division Policy Group 2006-, Member, Family Law Reform Commission 2007-; Carlton Club; Kingswood Lawn Tennis Club; *Publications:* State of the Nation/Fractured Families (Centre for Social Justice 2006); Breakthrough Britain (Centre for Social Justice 2007); Every Family Matters (Centre for Social Justice 2009)

Recreations: Tennis, movies, family life, sporting events

Helen Grant MP, House of Commons, London SW1A 0AA
Tel: 020 7219 3000 E-mail: helen.grant.mp@parliament.uk
Constituency: Maidstone and The Weald Conservative Association, 3 Albion Place, Maidstone, Kent ME14 5DY Tel: 01622 752463
Fax: 01622 764427 Website: www.helengrant.org

GENERAL ELECTION RESULT

		%
Grant, H. (Con)	23,491	48.0
Carroll, P. (Lib Dem)	17,602	36.0
Seeruthun, R. (Lab/Co-op)	4,769	9.8
Kendall, G. (UKIP)	1,637	3.4
Jeffery, S. (Green)	655	1.3
Butler, G. (NF)	643	1.3
Simmonds, H. (Christian)	131	0.3
Majority	5,889	12.04
Electorate	71,041	
Turnout	48,928	68.87

CONSTITUENCY SNAPSHOT

Nineteenth-century Tory Benjamin Disraeli was an MP for this area for a time, and the seat and its predecessors have supported a long line of Conservative Members. Ann Widdecombe was first elected in 1987 and restored the majority to five figures. Widdecombe increased her majority to more than 16,000 in 1992 and despite boundary changes she still achieved a majority of 9,603 in 1997.

In 2001 her majority grew to 10,318 and in 2005 a further swing enabled her to increase it to 14,856. Widdecombe retired in 2010 and Helen Grant retained the seat for the Conservatives with a 5,889 majority.

The seat gained part of the East ward from Faversham and Mid Kent, in exchange for Boughton, Monchelsea and Chart Sutton wards and part of Park Wood ward. It lost Hawkhurst and Sandhurst wards to Tunbridge Wells.

This seat is home to commuters and light industry in Maidstone, and more agricultural pursuits on the Weald. Maidstone is a prosperous county town.

The Fremlin Walk retail development, which opened in 2005, gave Maidstone the second largest shopping centre in Kent after from Bluewater. The M2 and M20 serve the needs of commuters to London.

The rest of the constituency is rural, with lush countryside, pretty villages and small towns. Apple and other fruit-growing are important.

James Gray

North Wiltshire (returning MP)

Boundary changes

Tel: 020 7219 6237
E-mail: jamesgraymp@parliament.uk
Website: www.jamesgray.org

Conservative

Date of birth: 7 November 1954; Son of late Very Revd John R. Gray, Moderator of General Assembly of Church of Scotland, and Dr Sheila Gray

Education: Glasgow High School; Glasgow University (MA history 1975); Christ Church, Oxford (history thesis 1975-77); Married Sarah Ann Beale 1980 (divorced) (2 sons 1 daughter); married Mrs Philippa Mayo 2009

Non-political career: Honourable Artillery Company (TA) 1978-84; Member, HAC Court of Assistants 2002-07; Management trainee, P & O 1977-78; Anderson Hughes & Co Ltd (Shipbrokers) 1978-84; Member, Baltic Exchange 1978-91, Pro Bono Member 1997-; Managing director, GNI Freight Futures Ltd, Senior Manager, GNI Ltd (Futures Brokers) 1984-1992; Director: Baltic Futures Exchange 1989-91; Special Adviser to Secretaries of State for Environment: Michael Howard 1992-93, John Gummer 1993-95; Director Westminster Strategy 1995-96; Union of Country Sports Workers

Political career: Contested Ross, Cromarty and Skye 1992 general election. Member for North Wiltshire 1997-2010, for North Wiltshire (revised boundary) since 6 May 2010 general election; Opposition Whip 2000-01; Opposition Spokesman for Defence 2001-02; Shadow Minister for: Environment, Food and Rural Affairs 2002-03, Environment and Transport 2003-05; Shadow Secretary of State for Scotland May 2005; *Select Committees:* Member: Environment, Transport and Regional Affairs (Transport Sub-Committee) 1997-2001, Environment, Transport and Regional Affairs 1997-2000, Environment, Transport and Regional Affairs (Environment Sub-Committee) 1997-2001, Broadcasting 2001-03, Regulatory Reform 2005-10, Environment, Food and Rural Affairs 2007-10; Deputy Chairman, Wandsworth Tooting Conservative Association 1994-96

Political interests: Countryside, agriculture, defence, environment, foreign affairs; America, China, Mongolia, Sri Lanka, Nepal

Other organisations: Vice-President, HAC Saddle Club;President: Chippenham Multiple Sclerosis Society, Association of British Riding Schools; Vice-chairman, Charitable Properties Association; Consultant, British Horse Industry Confederation 1995-2001; Member: Armed Forces Parliamentary Scheme (Army) 1998, Post Graduate Scheme 2000, Royal College of Defence Studies 2003; Parliamentary delegate to Council of Europe and Western European Union 2007-; Member, Honourable Artillery Company; Freeman, City of London 1978; President, Chippenham Constitutional 2000-; Wootton Bassett Conservative; Pratt's; Member, Avon Vale Foxhounds; *Publications:* Financial Risk Management in the Shipping Industry (1985); Futures and Options for Shipping (1987) (Lloyds of London Book Prize winner); Shipping Futures (1990); Crown v Parliament: Who decides on Going to War (2003)

Recreations: Riding horses, heritage and local history

James Gray MP, House of Commons, London SW1A 0AA
Tel: 020 7219 6237 Fax: 020 7219 1163
E-mail: jamesgraymp@parliament.uk
Constituency: North Wilts Conservative Association, Unit 15, Forest Gate, Pewsham, Chippenham, Wiltshire SN15 3RS
Tel: 01249 652851 Fax: 01249 448582 Website: www.jamesgray.org

GENERAL ELECTION RESULT

		%
Gray, J. (Con)*	25,114	51.6
Evemy, M. (Lib Dem)	17,631	36.2
Hughes, J. (Lab)	3,239	6.7
Bennett, C. (UKIP)	1,908	3.9
Chamberlain, P. (Green)	599	1.2
Allnatt, P. (Ind)	208	0.4
Majority	7,483	15.37
Electorate	66,313	
Turnout	48,699	73.44

**Member of last parliament*

CONSTITUENCY SNAPSHOT

This seat has been in Conservative hands continuously since 1924. In 1992 the Tories achieved a majority of just under 15,000 votes, but by 1997 their majority had fallen to under 3,500 as MP James Gray was first elected.

The Conservatives recovered at the 2001 elections, and 2005 presented a similar picture, as James Gray increased his majority over the Liberal Democrats to 5,303. Gray won re-election with over 50 per cent of the votes and a majority of 7,483 in 2010.

North Wiltshire was altered considerably following the recent review. The seat gained nine wards from Devizes, centred on the town of Calne, while the largest town of Chippenham was given its own seat.

The Cotswolds reaches into the western and northern ends of the constituency. It is bordered in the east by the Marlborough Downs and Swindon.

North Wiltshire has a significant manufacturing industry, especially in the food and engineering sectors. However, these sources of employment are focused almost exclusively on Malmesbury. In the more rural areas the economy has been badly hit by the closure of military bases and the decline of agriculture.

The natural beauty of the area has attracted many commuters in recent years.

Rt Hon **Chris Grayling**

Epsom and Ewell ***(returning MP)***

Boundary changes

Tel: 020 7219 8194
E-mail: graylingc@parliament.uk
Website: www.chrisgrayling.net

Conservative

Date of birth: 1 April 1962; Son of John and Elizabeth Grayling

Education: Royal Grammar School, High Wycombe; Sidney Sussex College, Cambridge (BA history 1984); Married Susan Clare Dillistone 1987 (1 son 1 daughter)

Non-political career: BBC News: Trainee 1985-86, Producer 1986-88; Programme editor *Business Daily* Channel 4 1988-91; Business development manager BBC Select 1991-93; Director: Charterhouse Prods Ltd 1993, Workhouse Ltd 1993-95, SSVC Group 1995-97; Change consultant and European marketing director Burson Marsteller 1997-2001; Councillor London Borough of Merton 1998-2002

Political career: Contested Warrington South 1997 general election. Member for Epsom and Ewell 2001-10, for Epsom and Ewell (revised boundary) since 6 May 2010 general election; Opposition Whip 2002; Shadow Spokesperson for Health 2002-03; Shadow Minister for: Public Services, Health and Education 2003-04, Higher Education 2004-05, Health 2005; Shadow Leader of the House of Commons 2005: Ex-officio member House of Commons' Commission 2005; Shadow: Secretary of State for: Transport 2005-07, Work and Pensions 2007-09, Home Secretary 2009-10; Minister of State, Department for Work and Pensions 2010-; *Select Committees:* Member: Transport, Local Government and the Regions 2001-02, Transport, Local Government and the Regions (Transport Sub-Committee) 2001-02, Transport, Local Government and the Regions (Urban Affairs Sub-Committee) 2001-02, Transport 2002, Modernisation of the House of Commons 2005-06

Political interests: Transport, welfare reform, pensions, home affairs

Other organisations: Member Corporation of Merton College 1999-2001; Chair Epsom Victim Support 2001-07; PC 2010; *Publications:* The Bridgwater Heritage (1983); A Land Fit for Heroes (1985); Co-author Just Another Star? (1987)

Recreations: Golf, cricket, football

Rt Hon Chris Grayling MP, House of Commons, London SW1A 0AA
Tel: 020 7219 8194 Fax: 020 7219 1763
E-mail: graylingc@parliament.uk
Constituency: 212 Barnett Wood Lane, Ashtead, Surrey KT21 2DB
Tel: 01372 271036 Fax: 01372 270906
Website: www.chrisgrayling.net

GENERAL ELECTION RESULT

		%
Grayling, C. (Con)*	30,868	56.2
Lees, J. (Lib Dem)	14,734	26.8
Montgomery, C. (Lab)	6,538	11.9
Wallace, E. (UKIP)	2,549	4.6
Ticher, P. (RRG)	266	0.5
Majority	16,134	29.36
Electorate	78,104	
Turnout	54,955	70.36

**Member of last parliament*

CONSTITUENCY SNAPSHOT

Post-Second World War electoral representation of this constituency is uniformly Conservative. Long tenures held by members are crowned by knighthoods: Sir Archibald Southby, Sir Peter Rawlinson and Sir Archie Hamilton.

In 1997 Sir Archie's 1992 majority of 22,060 was halved to 11,525. Following Sir Archie's retirement Chris Grayling was selected. In 2001 he gained back some of the lost ground and in 2005 he won a 16,447 majority.

In 2010 Grayling retained the seat for the Conservatives with a strong 16,134 majority.

The seat gained three part-wards from Mole Valley, in exchange for one part-ward; and lost the Preston ward to Reigate.

A part of Surrey very much within the commuter belt, Epsom and Ewell runs from Worcester Park in the north to Ashtead in the south.

As much of the area is contained by the M25 there is little open countryside, as towns such as Epsom, Ewell, Ashtead and Stoneleigh merge into one another.

Over half the workforce is employed in professional, managerial or technical occupations.

Though many of the working population commute, there are a fair number of corporations based in the constituency, and Toyota and Esso UK are headquartered in nearby Burgh Heath and Leatherhead respectively. The British engineering consultancy W S Atkins is based in Epsom itself.

Tom Greatrex

Rutherglen and Hamilton West

No boundary changes

Tel: 020 7219 3000
E-mail: tom.greatrex.mp@parliament.uk

Labour/Co-operative

Date of birth: 30 September 1974

Education: Judd School, Tonbridge; London School of Economics (BSc economics, government and law 1996); Married Laura 2003 (twin daughters)

Non-political career: Researcher, Opposition Whips Office 1996-97; Special adviser to Nick Brown MP: as Chief Whip 1997-98, as Minister of Agriculture, Fisheries and Food 1998-99; Regional officer, GMB 1999-2004; Head of policy and public affairs, East Dunbartonshire Council 2004-06; Corporate affairs director, NHS 24 2006-07; Special adviser to Secretaries of State for Scotland: Douglas Alexander MP 2007, Des Browne MP 2007-08, Jim Murphy MP 2008-10; Member, GMB

Political career: Member for Rutherglen and Hamilton West since 6 May 2010 general election

Political interests: Manufacturing, economic policy, energy policy, constitution; India, Portugal, Brazil

Recreations: Fulham F.C, cinema

Tom Greatrex MP, House of Commons, London SW1A 0AA
Tel: 020 7219 3000 E-mail: tom.greatrex.mp@parliament.uk
Constituency: Unit 11, Strathclyde Business Centre, 416 Hamilton Road, Cambuslang, Lanarkshire G72 7XR

GENERAL ELECTION RESULT

		%	+/-
Greatrex, T. (Lab/Co-op)	28,566	60.8	5.3
Horne, G. (SNP)	7,564	16.1	2.2
Robertson, I. (Lib Dem)	5,636	12.0	-6.3
Macaskill, M. (Con)	4,540	9.7	1.3
Murdoch, J. (UKIP)	675	1.4	0.4
Majority	21,002	44.70	
Electorate	76,408		
Turnout	46,981	61.49	

CONSTITUENCY SNAPSHOT

Labour's Gregor Mackenzie captured the seat from the Conservatives at the 1964 by-election following the death of Tory Richard Brooman-White.

Mackenzie retired in 1987 and handed the seat to Tommy McAvoy. Boundary changes in 2005 moved most of Rutherglen out of the Glasgow parliamentary constituencies and the South Lanarkshire wards joined the Hamilton South seat to form Rutherglen and Hamilton West. Tommy McAvoy survived a swing of 5.4 per cent Liberal Democrats and returning to Westminster with a 16,112 majority. Labour's Tom Greatrex inherited a very safe seat from Tommy McAvoy in 2010 winning over 60 per cent of the vote and a 21,002 majority.

The constituency contains two towns which are part of the outskirts of Glasgow: Rutherglen, the oldest burgh in Scotland; and Cambuslang, once known as Scotland's largest village because no council or provost represented its population of 17,000.

Many constituents work in Hamilton, where there are numerous industrial and business parks, providing employment in light industry and service industries with blue-chip technologies in the Hamilton International Technology Park. Big employers in the area include South Lanarkshire Council, Philips Lighting and Scottish Gas.

Damian Green

Ashford (returning MP)

Boundary changes

Tel: 020 7219 3518
E-mail: greend@parliament.uk
Website: www.damian4ashford.org.uk

Conservative

Date of birth: 17 January 1956; Son of Howard and late Audrey Green

Education: Reading School; Balliol College, Oxford (BA philosophy, politics and economics 1977, MA); President, Oxford Union 1977; Married Alicia Collinson 1988 (2 daughters)

Non-political career: Financial journalist, BBC Radio 1978-82; Business producer, Channel 4 News 1982-84; News editor, business news, *The Times* 1984-85; Business editor, Channel 4 News, 1985-87; Programme presenter and city editor, *Business Daily* 1987-92; Special Adviser, Prime Minister's Policy Unit 1992-94; Self-employed public affairs consultant 1995-97

Political career: Contested Brent East 1992 general election. Member for Ashford 1997-2010, for Ashford (revised boundary) since 6 May 2010 general election; Opposition Spokesperson for: Education and Employment 1998-99, Environment 1999-2001; Shadow Secretary of State for: Education and Skills 2001-03, Transport 2003-04; Shadow Minister for Immigration 2005-10; Minister of State for Immigration, Home Office 2010-; *Select Committees:* Member: Culture, Media and Sport 1997-98, Procedure 1997-98, Home Affairs 2004-05, Treasury 2005-06; Vice-President, Tory Reform Group 1997-; Chair Conservative Parliamentary Mainstream Group 2003-; Member Executive 1922 Committee 2004-05

Political interests: Economic policy, foreign affairs, media, education, employment, rural affairs; France, Italy, Moldova, Georgia

Other organisations: Member, SPUC; *Publications:* ITN Budget Fact Book (1984, 85, 86); A Better BBC (1990); The Cross-Media Revolution (1995); Communities in the Countryside (1996); Regulating the Media in the Digital Age (1997); 21st Century Conservatism (1998); The Four Failures of the New Deal (1999); Better Learning (2002); More than Markets (2003); Co-author Controlling Economic Migration (2006)

Recreations: Football, cricket, opera, cinema

Damian Green MP, House of Commons, London SW1A 0AA
Tel: 020 7219 3518 Fax: 020 7219 0904
E-mail: greend@parliament.uk
Constituency: c/o Hardy House, The Street, Bethersden, Ashford, Kent TN26 3AG Tel: 01233 820454 Fax: 01233 820111
Website: www.damian4ashford.org.uk

GENERAL ELECTION RESULT

		%
Green, D. (Con)*	29,878	54.1
Took, C. (Lib Dem)	12,581	22.8
Clark, C. (Lab)	9,204	16.7
Elenor, J. (UKIP)	2,508	4.5
Campkin, S. (Green)	1,014	1.8
Majority	17,297	31.34
Electorate	81,269	
Turnout	55,185	67.90

**Member of last parliament*

CONSTITUENCY SNAPSHOT

Ashford was represented by Tory MP Bill Deedes then Sir Keith Speed until 1997 when the current MP, Damian Green, took over.

Green won a 13,298 vote lead over Labour in 2005, with the Liberal Democrats in third place. The seat was held by Green in 2010 with a 17,297 majority.

The seat lost Saxon Shore ward to Folkestone and Hythe.

Set in the 'Garden of England', Ashford is a picturesque constituency with a relatively large rural population scattered across its villages and market towns.

Once a quiet market town and focal point for the farming community, Ashford's location and excellent transport links have helped it to emerge rapidly.

Situated in the Channel Tunnel corridor, Ashford is served by the M20, the port of Dover just 20 miles away, and the Channel Tunnel at Folkestone.

Ashford enjoys the benefits of a varied commercial base: high-tech companies, chemical and biotechnology industries, major European frozen food manufacturers, and national call-centres all operate here.

The main business types in Ashford are the distribution, hotel and restaurant sector, and the finance and insurance sector.

Kate Green

Stretford and Urmston

Boundary changes

Tel: 020 7219 3000
E-mail: kate.green.mp@parliament.uk
Website: www.kategreen.org

Date of birth: 2 May 1960

Education: Currie High School; Edinburgh University (LLB 1982); Divorced

Non-political career: Various roles, Barclays Bank 1982-97; Whitehall and Industry Group (on secondment), Home Office 1997-99; Director, National Council for One Parent Families 2000-04; Chief executive, Child Poverty Action Group 2004-09; Member: Unite 2000-, GMB 2009-; Magistrate, City of London 1993-2007; Member, National Employment Panel 2001-07; Chair, London Child Poverty Commission 2006-09

Political career: Contested Cities of London and Westminster 1997 general election. Member for Stretford and Urmston since 6 May 2010 general election; Member, Labour Party 1990-; Chair and branch secretary

Political interests: Children and families, employment, exclusion, poverty

Other organisations: Trustee: The Avenues Youth Project 1998-2003, End Child Poverty 2000-09, Family and Parenting Institute 2000-07, Institute for Fiscal Studies 2006-09; Member, Fawcett Society 2006-, Fabian Society 2009-; OBE 2005

Kate Green MP, House of Commons, London SW1A 0AA
Tel: 020 7219 3000 E-mail: kate.green.mp@parliament.uk
Constituency: Stretford and Urmston Labour Party, The Morris Hall, 9 Atkinson Road, Urmston, Manchester M41 9AD Tel: 0161-748 8580
Website: www.kategreen.org

GENERAL ELECTION RESULT

		%
Green, K. (Lab)	21,821	48.6
Williams, A. (Con)	12,886	28.7
Cooke, S. (Lib Dem)	7,601	16.9
Owen, D. (UKIP)	1,508	3.4
Westbrook, M. (Green)	916	2.0
Jacob, S. (Christian)	178	0.4
Majority	8,935	19.90
Electorate	70,091	
Turnout	44,910	64.07

CONSTITUENCY SNAPSHOT

This is a relatively new constituency, first contested in 1997 and created from Stretford and Davyhulme. The former was inclined to the Labour Party, and the latter to the Conservatives, having been represented by Winston Churchill, the grandson of the wartime leader.

In 1997 a swing of nearly 10 per cent to Labour gave their candidate Beverley Hughes the seat. There was a further 2.5 per cent swing in 2001, but Hughes' majority was reduced to 7,851 in 2005.

Hughes retired in 2010 and Kate Green held the seat for Labour with a 48.6 per cent vote-share.

Boundary changes were minimal. Bucklow-St Martins ward, which the seat previously shared with Altrincham and Sale West, is now entirely within the seat's boundaries.

A south-west suburb of Manchester, Stretford and Urmston is industrial as well as residential in character. The divisions in the constituency are exemplified by its being both the home of the more working-class game of football at Manchester United, and the more genteel pursuit of cricket at Lancashire county cricket club, both of which have grounds in the constituency.

Stretford and Urmston is also the location for the Trafford centre, a retail shopping centre and regional sports complex. There is also a business park in Carrington, which consists mainly of companies in the chemical industry.

Justine Greening

Putney (returning MP)

Boundary changes

Tel: 020 7219 8300
E-mail: greeningj@parliament.uk
Website: www.justinegreening.co.uk

Conservative

Date of birth: 30 April 1969

Education: Oakwood Comprehensive School, Rotherham, Yorkshire; Thomas Rotherham College, Rotherham; Southampton University (BSc business economics and accounting 1990); London Business School (MBA 2000); Single

Non-political career: Audit assistant, PriceWaterhouse 1991-94; Audit assistant manager, Revisuisse PriceWaterhouse 1995-96; Finance manager, SmithKline Beecham, 1996-2001; Business strategy manager, GlaxoSmithKline, 2001-02; Sales and marketing finance manager, Centrica 2002-05; Councillor Epping Town Council 1998-2002

Political career: Contested Ealing, Acton and Shepherd's Bush 2001 general election. Member for Putney 2005-10, for Putney (revised boundary) since 6 May 2010 general election; Shadow Minister for: the Treasury 2007-09, Communities and Local Government 2009-10; Economic Secretary, HM Treasury 2010-; *Select Committees:* Member: Work and Pensions 2005-07; The Bow Group: Member 1998-, Political officer 1999-2000; Vice-chair (Youth) Conservative Party 2005-

Political interests: Vocational education, youth crime, environment; *Publications:* 'A Wholly Healthy Britain' in A Blue Tomorrow (2000)

Recreations: Swimming, cycling

Justine Greening MP, House of Commons, London SW1A 0AA
Tel: 020 7219 8300 Fax: 020 7219 5000
E-mail: greeningj@parliament.uk
Constituency: 3 Summerstown, London SW17 0BQ
Tel: 020 8946 4557 Fax: 020 8944 6839
Website: www.justinegreening.co.uk

GENERAL ELECTION RESULT

		%
Greening, J. (Con)*	21,223	52.0
King, S. (Lab)	11,170	27.4
Sandbach, J. (Lib Dem)	6,907	16.9
Mackenzie, B. (Green)	591	1.5
Darby, P. (BNP)	459	1.1
Wareham, H. (UKIP)	435	1.1
Majority	10,053	24.65
Electorate	63,370	
Turnout	40,785	64.36

**Member of last parliament*

CONSTITUENCY SNAPSHOT

Putney was Tory during the 1950s. Between 1964 and 1979, however, the seat was held by Labour's Hugh Jenkins. In 1979 Putney voted in Tory MP David Mellor.

Between 1979 and 1997 the Tories regularly polled around 50 per cent of the vote. In 1997, Putney's electorate voted in favour of New Labour candidate Tony Coleman.

In 2005, Tory candidate Justine Greening won the seat from Labour with a 6.5 per cent swing. Conservative rising star Justine Greening achieved a massive increase in her majority from 1,766 to 10,053 on a 9.9 per cent swing away from Labour.

Boundary changes have been minor. Fairfield was shared between Putney and Battersea; with the boundary changes the ward is now entirely within the latter's boundaries.

Bordered by Richmond Park to the west, Wimbledon to the south, and Tooting to the east, Putney is on the cusp between inner and outer London.

It is also the birthplace of English democracy, Putney Church being the place where Cromwell and the Levellers met to debate England's constitution after the Civil War.

Its proximity to central London and position to other prosperous areas of south-west London like Fulham has contributed to Putney becoming very desirable.

Putney is under the flight path for Heathrow Airport.

Lilian Greenwood

Nottingham South

Boundary changes

Tel: 020 7219 3000
E-mail: lilian.greenwood.mp@parliament.uk
Website: liliangreenwood.blogspot.com

Date of birth: 26 March 1966; Daughter of Harry Greenwood, lecturer, and Patricia Greenwood, typist

Education: Canon Slade, Bolton; St Catharine's College, Cambridge (BA economics and social and political science 1987); Southbank University, London (MSc sociology and social policy 1991); Married Ravi Subramanian 2008 (3 daughters)

Non-political career: Research officer: Local Authority Conditions of Service Advisory Board (LACSAB) 1988-89, Civil and Public Services Association (CPSA) 1989-92; Trade union organiser, currently regional head of campaigns and policy, Unison 1992-; Branch equality officer: NALGO 1988-89, GMB 1989-92

Political career: Member for Nottingham South since 6 May 2010 general election; Member, Co-operative Party

Political interests: Employment rights, pensions

Other organisations: Member: Fabian Society, Compass 2007-; Holme Pierrepont Running Club

Recreations: Running, walking, cinema, reading

Lilian Greenwood MP, House of Commons, London SW1A 0AA
Tel: 020 7219 3000 E-mail: lilian.greenwood.mp@parliament.uk
Constituency: Nottingham Labour, Unit 13A, John Folman Business Centre, Nottingham NG3 4NB Tel: 0115-924 5406
Website: liliangreenwood.blogspot.com

GENERAL ELECTION RESULT

		%
Greenwood, L. (Lab)	15,209	37.3
Holland, R. (Con)	13,437	32.9
Sutton, T. (Lib Dem)	9,406	23.1
Woodward, T. (BNP)	1,140	2.8
Browne, K. (UKIP)	967	2.4
Butcher, M. (Green)	630	1.5
Majority	1,772	4.34
Electorate	67,441	
Turnout	40,789	60.48

CONSTITUENCY SNAPSHOT

Labour has held the seat since 1992, before that, constituents had elected the Conservative Martin Brandon-Bravo since its 1983 creation.

Labour's Alan Simpson won the seat in 1992 with a majority of 3,181. He increased this to 13,364 in 1997, and although his vote has declined since, his lead was at 7,486 in 2005. Alan Simpson retired in 2010 and Lilian Greenwood held the seat for Labour with a 1,772 majority.

Boundary changes moved Basford part-ward to Nottingham North and St Ann's and Arboretum part-wards to Nottingham East. Leen Valley ward is now entirely within the seat having previously been shared between the three city seats. In addition the part of Bridge Ward that was in Nottingham East moved in the division.

Nottingham South is perhaps the most socially and economically mixed constituency in the county. The city seat ranges from the council estates of Clifton, to the vast student population of Lenton, to the prospering and constantly changing city centre. The south-western Wollanton wards are some of the wealthiest in the region, with high numbers of the professional and managerial class.

Raleigh, the cycle manufacturer, was the major employer in the area until its closure some ten years ago. The old site now hosts student accommodation. The Boots factory in the nearby Broxtowe constituency employs a number of Nottingham South residents.

Rt Hon **Dominic Grieve**

Beaconsfield (returning MP)

Boundary changes

Tel: 020 7219 6220
E-mail: grieved@parliament.uk
Website: www.dominicgrieve.org.uk

Conservative

Date of birth: 24 May 1956; Son of late W. P. Grieve, MP 1964-83, and of late Evelyn, neé Mijouain

Education: Westminster School; Magdalen College, Oxford (BA modern history, 1978, MA 1989); Central London Polytechnic (Diploma in law 1980); Married Caroline Hutton 1990 (2 sons and 1 son deceased)

Non-political career: Territorial Army 1981-83; Councillor, London Borough of Hammersmith and Fulham 1982-86

Political career: Contested Norwood 1987 general election. Member for Beaconsfield 1997-2010, for Beaconsfield (revised boundary) since 6 May 2010 general election; Opposition Spokesperson for: Constitutional Affairs and Scotland 1999-2001, Home Office 2001-03; Shadow: Attorney General 2003-09, Home Secretary 2008-09, Secretary of State for Justice 2009-10; Attorney General 2010-; *Select Committees:* Member: Joint Committee on Statutory Instruments 1997-2001, Environmental Audit 1997-2001; President, Oxford University Conservative Association 1977; Society of Conservative Lawyers: Chair Research Committee 1992-95, Chair Finance and General Purposes 2006-

Political interests: Law and order, environment, defence, foreign affairs, European Union, constitution; France, Luxembourg

Other organisations: Vice-chair/director, Hammersmith and Fulham MIND 1986-89; Lay visitor to police stations 1990-96; Member Council of: Franco-British Society, Luxembourg Society; Member, London Diocesan Synod of Church of England 1994-2000; Member John Muir Trust; PC 2010; *House Magazine* Opposition Politician of the Year 2006 *Spectator* Politician of the Year 2006; Channel 4 Politicians' politician of the year 2007; Carlton

Recreations: Mountaineering, skiing, scuba diving, fell-walking, architecture and art

Rt Hon Dominic Grieve MP, House of Commons, London SW1A 0AA Tel: 020 7219 6220 Fax: 020 7219 4803
E-mail: grieved@parliament.uk
Constituency: Disraeli House, 12 Aylesbury End, Beaconsfield, Buckinghamshire HP9 1LW Tel: 01494 673745 Fax: 01494 670428
Website: www.dominicgrieve.org.uk

GENERAL ELECTION RESULT

		%
Grieve, D. (Con)*	32,053	61.1
Edwards, J. (Lib Dem)	10,271	19.6
Miles, J. (Lab)	6,135	11.7
Gray-Fisk, D. (UKIP)	2,597	5.0
Bailey, J. (Green)	768	1.5
Cowen, A. (Expense)	475	0.9
Baron, Q. (Ind)	191	0.4
Majority	21,782	41.50
Electorate	74,982	
Turnout	52,490	70.00

**Member of last parliament*

CONSTITUENCY SNAPSHOT

Beaconsfield is one of the safest Conservative seats in the country. Despite the Tory vote falling below 50 per cent in 1997 for the first time, MP Dominic Grieve still won with a majority of 13,987. In 2005 this majority increased to 15,253.

The Conservatives retained the seat with 32,053 votes giving Grieve a majority of 21,782 in 2010.

The seat lost the Tylers Green and Loudwater ward to Wycombe, but gained the big Tory strongholds of Marlow North and West, and Marlow South East from Wycombe.

Set in Buckinghamshire, Beaconsfield is one of the richest corners of the Home Counties. It is an affluent middle-class constituency and home to the aristocratic house of Cliveden and Pinewood Studios.

There is a large pharmaceutical industry here and a large number of IT businesses. Nearby Heathrow, though not in the constituency, provides employment for many constituents.

The proximity of Beaconsfield to London makes it popular with city commuters, and many find work in neighbouring Slough with its large manufacturing industry.

Schools in Beaconsfield are very good and many people are attracted to the area for the quality of its education, particularly its grammar schools.

Nia Griffith

Llanelli (returning MP)

No boundary changes

Tel: 020 7219 6102
E-mail: griffithn@parliament.uk
Website: www.niagriffith.org.uk

Labour

Date of birth: 4 December 1956; Daughter of Prof T Gwynfor Griffith, professor of Italian, and member of Gorsedd of Bards and Dr Rhiannon Griffith, née Howell, medical doctor

Education: Newland High School, Hull; Somerville College, Oxford (BA modern languages 1979); University College of North Wales, Bangor (PGCE 1980); Married Richard Leggett 1982 (divorced) (no children)

Non-political career: Language teacher 1980-92, 1997-2005; Education adviser 1992-97, Estyn schools inspector 1992-97; Head of modern languages Morriston Comprehensive School, Swansea 1997-2005; Chair Carmarthenshire Youth Project 1998-2005; NUT; USDAW; Carmarthen Town Council: councillor 1987-99: sheriff 1997, deputy mayor 1998

Political career: Member for Llanelli since 5 May 2005 general election; PPS: at Department for Environment, Food and Rural Affairs 2007-08, to Harriet Harman as Minister for Women and Equality 2008-10; *Select Committees:* Member: European Scrutiny 2005-07, Welsh Affairs 2005-10, Joint Committee on Human Rights 2006-07, Joint Committee on the Draft Climate Change Bill 2007; Secretary Carmarthenshire County Labour Party 1994-99, 2004-05; Chair Carmarthen West and South Pembrokeshire Constituency Labour Party 1999-2000

Political interests: Environment, Europe, community issues, cycle paths, industry, energy, equalities; France, Italy, Spain

Other organisations: Member, Amnesty International; *Publications:* Co-author Ciao BK3 Italian textbook (Nelson, 1990); 100 ideas for teaching languages (Continuum press, 2005)

Recreations: Arts, European cinema, music, cycling

Nia Griffith MP, House of Commons, London SW1A 0AA
Tel: 020 7219 6102 Fax: 020 7219 4560
E-mail: griffithn@parliament.uk
Constituency: 6 Queen Victoria Road, Llanelli, Dyfed SA15 2TL
Tel: 01554 756374 Fax: 01554 741183
Website: www.niagriffith.org.uk

GENERAL ELECTION RESULT

		%	+/-
Griffith, N. (Lab)*	15,916	42.5	-4.4
Davies, M. (PIC)	11,215	29.9	3.5
Salmon, C. (Con)	5,381	14.4	0.7
Edwards, M. (Lib Dem)	3,902	10.4	-2.4
Marshall, A. (UKIP)	1,047	2.8	
Majority	4,701	12.55	
Electorate	55,637		
Turnout	37,461	67.33	

**Member of last parliament*

CONSTITUENCY SNAPSHOT

Llanelli has been held by a Labour MP since 1922. Denzil Davies was MP from 1970 until 2005 and, for the most part, enjoyed sizable majorities.

Davies retired in 2005 and Labour selected the former deputy mayor of Carmarthen, Nia Griffith, to contest the seat. At the election Griffith increased the Labour majority with a swing of 1.4 per cent from Plaid Cymru giving her a majority of 7,234. Nia Griffiths won a reduced 4,701 majority in the face of a 4 per cent swing to Plaid in 2010.

Llanelli is the largest town in Carmarthenshire, situated in the industrial south-east of the county.

Traditionally Llanelli's main industries were steel and tinplate, giving it the nickname 'Tresosban' (saucepan town) and the rugby anthem 'sosban fach'.

With the decline of Llanelli's traditional industries, the economy has diversified, and industrial estates have been built to meet the demands of new pharmaceutical, chemical, and manufacturing companies.

On the western side of the constituency Burry Port, which was developed for the export of coal, and Kidwelly, once the largest centre for tinplate manufacture, have become part of a growing tourism and leisure industry.

Andrew Griffiths

Burton

Boundary changes

Tel: 020 7219 3000
E-mail: andrew.griffiths.mp@parliament.uk
Website: www.voteandrew.co.uk

Date of birth: 19 October 1970

Education: High Arcal School, Sedgley, Dudley; Single

Non-political career: Family engineering business; Manager, Halifax Plc; Chief of staff to Jonathan Evans MEP 1999; Farming adviser to Neil Parish MEP -2004; Chief of staff to: Rt Hon Theresa May MP 2004-06, Hugo Swire MP 2006-07, Eric Pickles MP 2007-10; Former school governor

Political career: Contested Dudley North 2001 general election. Member for Burton since 6 May 2010 general election; Contested West Midlands 2004 European Parliament election

Political interests: Farming, rural affairs

Recreations: Sport, architecture, music

Andrew Griffiths MP, House of Commons, London SW1A 0AA
Tel: 020 7219 3000 E-mail: andrew.griffiths.mp@parliament.uk
Constituency: Gothard House, 9 St Paul's Square, Burton-upon-Trent, Staffordshire DE14 2EF Tel: 01283 568894
Website: www.voteandrew.co.uk

GENERAL ELECTION RESULT

		%
Griffiths, A. (Con)	22,188	44.5
Smeeth, R. (Lab)	15,884	31.9
Rodgers, M. (Lib Dem)	7,891	15.8
Hewitt, A. (BNP)	2,409	4.8
Lancaster, P. (UKIP)	1,451	2.9
Majority	6,304	12.65
Electorate	74,874	
Turnout	49,823	66.54

CONSTITUENCY SNAPSHOT

Labour won in 1945, lost by just 277 votes in 1966 and took the seat in 1997. Sir Ivan Lawrence held the seat for the Tories from 1974 to 1997. In 1983 he won with a majority of 11,647. Janet Dean won the seat for Labour in 1997 with a majority of 6,330. In the 2001 and 2005 general elections the Conservative share fell further, leaving Dean with 1,421 majority for her third term.

Labour was defeated at the 2010 general election with a 8.7 per swing of the vote to the Conservative candidate, Andrew Griffiths.

Boundary changes were minimal.

Situated along the eastern edge of Staffordshire, Burton comprises the towns of Burton upon Trent and Uttoxeter and a considerable amount of the surrounding countryside.

Burton is a predominantly working-class seat that straddles the urban-rural divide. Many rural areas like Stretton and Stapenhill are marked by substantial prosperity.

The local economy has a high proportion of manual work. Burton itself has strong associations with the brewing industry, the town having five brewers, and is also home to the production of Marmite. Meanwhile, the nearby village of Rocester is the base of JCB, who are a major local employer.

Ben Gummer

Ipswich

Boundary changes

Tel: 020 7219 3000
E-mail: ben.gummer.mp@parliament.uk
Website: www.bengummer.com

Conservative

Date of birth: 19 February 1978; Son of John Gummer, MP, and Penelope Gummer, née Gardner

Education: Peterhouse College, Cambridge (BA history 2000, MA); Single

Non-political career: Businessman and writer

Political career: Member for Ipswich since 6 May 2010 general election

Political interests: Education, prison reform

Ben Gummer MP, House of Commons, London SW1A 0AA
Tel: 020 7219 3000 E-mail: ben.gummer.mp@parliament.uk
Constituency: Ipswich Conservatives, Middle Barn, Longlands Place, Wenham Road, Washbrook, Ipswich, Suffolk IP8 3EZ
Tel: 0845 634 9197 Fax: 0845 634 9198
Website: www.bengummer.com

GENERAL ELECTION RESULT

		%
Gummer, B. (Con)	18,371	39.1
Mole, C. (Lab)*	16,292	34.7
Dyson, M. (Lib Dem)	8,556	18.2
Streatfield, C. (UKIP)	1,365	2.9
Boater, D. (BNP)	1,270	2.7
Glover, T. (Green)	775	1.7
Christofi, K. (Christian)	149	0.3
Turtill, P. (Ind)	93	0.2
Wainman, S. (Ind)	70	0.2
Majority	2,079	4.43
Electorate	78,371	
Turnout	46,941	59.90

**Member of last parliament*

CONSTITUENCY SNAPSHOT

Tory Ernle Money was elected in 1970. He was re-elected in February 1974, but lost in October 1974 to the Labour's Ken Weetch by 1,733 votes.

In 1987 Weetch lost his seat, but his successor, Tory MP Michael Irvine, lasted only a single term, losing by 335 votes in 1992 to Labour's Jamie Cann. Cann was re-elected in 1997 and 2001 with just over half the vote. He died in the autumn of 2001.

Chris Mole won the by-election with a majority of 4,087 votes. In 2005 Mole increased his majority to 5,332. Mole was defeated in 2010 on a 8.1 per cent swing to the Conservative candidate, Ben Gummer.

The seat lost the part-ward of Whittonand to North Ipswich and gained three part-wards from Central Suffolk and North Ipswich.

Situated on the river Orwell, the constituency of Ipswich takes in the urban area of Suffolk's county town and the majority of its suburbs. Ipswich is a large regional town with a burgeoning high-tech industry sector.

Ipswich is also the bureaucratic hub of East Anglia. Major employers include HM Revenue and Customs, the Environment Agency and Axa Insurance.

The Ip-City Centre provides conference rooms and office space; located near the town centre and station, this major business park development has already attracted Hewlett Packard and NTL.

Andrew Gwynne

***Denton and Reddish** (returning MP)*

Boundary changes

Tel: 020 7219 4708
E-mail: gwynnea@parliament.uk
Website: www.andrewgwynne.co.uk

Date of birth: 4 June 1974; Son of Richard John Gwynne and Margaret Elisabeth Gwynne née Ridgway

Education: Egerton Park Community High School, Denton; North East Wales Institute of Higher Education, Wrexham (HND business and finance 1995); Salford University (BA politics and contemporary history 1998); Married Allison Louise Dennis 2003 (2 sons 1 daughter)

Non-political career: Assistant to European Declarative System (EDS) programme manager ICL 1990-92; National Computing Centre, Y2K team 1999-2000; Researcher for Andrew Bennett MP 2000-05; European co-ordinator Arlene McCarthy MEP 2000-01; Unite (formerly AEEU and Amicus) 2000-; Tameside MBC: Councillor 1996-2008, Chair Denton and Audenshaw district assembly 1998-2001, Chair resources and community services scrutiny panel 2003-04

Political career: Member for Denton and Reddish 2005-10, for Denton and Reddish (revised boundary) since 6 May 2010 general election; PPS: to Baroness Scotland of Asthal as Minister of State, Home Office 2005-07, to Jacqui Smith as Home Secretary 2007-09, to Ed Balls as Secretary of State for Children, Schools and Families 2009-10; *Select Committees:* Member: Procedure 2005-10, Court of Referees 2007-10; Chair: Denton and Reddish Constituency Labour Party 1998-2004, Labour Friends of Israel 2007-

Political interests: Education and skills, regeneration, local government, environment; India, China, USA, Israel/Palestinian Authority, Latin America, Commonwealth

Other organisations: Denton Labour Club

Recreations: Reading, computing, history, family

Andrew Gwynne MP, House of Commons, London SW1A 0AA
Tel: 020 7219 4708 Fax: 020 7219 4548
E-mail: gwynnea@parliament.uk
Constituency: Town Hall, Market Street, Denton,
Greater Manchester M34 2AP Tel: 0161-320 1504
Fax: 0161-320 1503 Website: www.andrewgwynne.co.uk

GENERAL ELECTION RESULT

		%
Gwynne, A. (Lab)*	19,191	51.0
Searle, J. (Con)	9,360	24.9
Broadhurst, S. (Lib Dem)	6,727	17.9
Robinson, W. (UKIP)	2,060	5.5
Dennis, J. (Ind)	297	0.8
Majority	9,831	26.12
Electorate	64,765	
Turnout	37,635	58.11

**Member of last parliament*

CONSTITUENCY SNAPSHOT

In 1983 the seat was constructed from parts of Stockport North, Brinnington, and Gorton.

Having doubled his 1992 majority to over 20,000 in 1997 the Labour MP Andrew Bennett began his fifth term as representative in 2001 with a majority shorn of 5,000 votes.

Bennett stood down in 2005 after 22 years; his successor Andrew Gwynne held the seat for Labour on a reduced, but still impressive, majority of 13,498.

Gwynne was re-elected in 2010 with a majority of 9,831 there was a 6.2 per cent swing to the Tories.

The seat gains the part-ward of Reddish South from Stockport and the part-ward of Audenshaw from Ashton under Lyne, while losing seven part-wards to Ashton under Lyne, Stalybridge and Hyde and Stockport.

Denton and Reddish is on the outskirts of Manchester, lending it proximity to the city's airport and industry on one side, and the Pennine moors on the other.

There is a high proportion of skilled manual workers, large swathes of terraced houses in Reddish, Denton and Dukinfield, but also Houldsworth Mill, a large 18th century building recently renovated to provide stylish office and residential space.

Despite its industrial heritage, the division is firmly lodged within Stockport's green belt. The picturesque Reddish Vale country park (part of the Tame Valley) follows the river right through the constituency.

Sam Gyimah

East Surrey

No boundary changes

Tel: 020 7219 3000
E-mail: sam.gyimah.mp@parliament.uk
Website: www.samgyimah.com

Date of birth: 10 August 1976

Education: Achimota Secondary School, Ghana; Freman College, Hertfordshire; Somerville College, Oxford (BA politics, philosophy and economics 1999) (Union President 1997)

Non-political career: Investment banker, Goldman Sachs 1999-2003; Chair, Career Ability Ltd 2003-06; Director, workology.com 2006-; Former school governor, London

Political career: Member for East Surrey since 6 May 2010 general election

Political interests: Protecting the green belt and local environment, local services

Other organisations: Former board member, Nacro; Chair, Bow Group 2007; Member, development board, Somerville College, Oxford; Entrepreneur of the Future, CBI 2005

Recreations: Skiing, Arsenal F.C, running, cooking

Sam Gyimah MP, House of Commons, London SW1A 0AA
Tel: 020 7219 3000 E-mail: sam.gyimah.mp@parliament.uk
Constituency: c/o East Surrey Conservative Association, 2 Hoskins Road, Oxted, Surrey RH8 9HT Website: www.samgyimah.com

GENERAL ELECTION RESULT

		%	+/-
Gyimah, S. (Con)	31,007	56.8	0.9
Lee, D. (Lib Dem)	14,133	25.9	2.2
Rodda, M. (Lab)	4,925	9.0	-5.7
Windsor, H. (UKIP)	3,770	6.9	2.5
Hogbin, M. (Loony)	422	0.8	
Pratt, S. (Ind)	383	0.7	
Majority	16,874	30.88	
Electorate	76,855		
Turnout	54,640	71.09	

CONSTITUENCY SNAPSHOT

This seat in all its various incarnations since 1918 has only elected a Conservative MP. In 1997 Peter Ainsworth retained this seat with a majority of 15,093, the third largest Conservative majority.

Mr Ainsworth succeeded the former Chancellor and Foreign Secretary Sir Geoffrey Howe in 1992. Ainsworth's majority fell slightly in 2001, but increased it to 15,921 in 2005.

Peter Ainsworth retired in 2010 and Sam Gyimah retained the seat for the Conservatives with a strong 16,874 majority.

This constituency covers the eastern section of Surrey, bordering Kent, and includes the small towns of Caterham, Horley and Warlingham.

For what is essentially a London commuter seat East Surrey has a charmingly pastoral nature. Development has been limited to narrow valleys and established upland settlements by the North Downs, and much of the area is covered with wooded hillsides and rolling arable land. Unsurprisingly, house prices are among the highest in the country.

The largest single employer is Gatwick Airport and its related businesses. Gatwick lies just over the south-west boundary of the constituency.

Although there is some traditional industry in Oxted, the other sources of employment are for the most part small businesses in the financial, technical and retail sectors, with a smattering of manufacturing.

Rt Hon **William Hague**

Richmond (Yorkshire) ***(returning MP)***

Boundary changes

Tel: 020 7219 4611
E-mail: haguew@parliament.uk
Website: www.williamhague.org.uk

Conservative

Date of birth: 26 March 1961; Son of Nigel and Stella Hague

Education: Wath-upon-Dearne Comprehensive School, Yorkshire; Magdalen College, Oxford (BA philosophy, politics and economics 1982) (President, Oxford Union 1981); INSEAD Business School, France 1985-86; Married Ffion Jenkins 1997

Non-political career: Shell UK 1982-83; McKinsey and Company 1983-88; Political adviser to Sir Geoffrey Howe as Chancellor of the Exchequer and Leon Brittan as Chief Secretary to the Treasury 1983; Political and economic adviser JCB 2001-; Non-executive director AES Engineering 2001-; Member Political Council of Terra Firma Capital Partners 2001-; Non-executive director AMT Sybex

Political career: Contested Wentworth 1987 general election. Member for Richmond (Yorkshire) 23 February 1989 by-election to 2010, for Richmond (Yorkshire) (revised boundary) since 6 May 2010 general election; PPS to Norman Lamont as Chancellor of the Exchequer 1990-93; Department of Social Security: Joint Parliamentary Under-Secretary of State 1993-94, Minister of State for Social Security and Disabled People 1994-95; Secretary of State for Wales 1995-97; Leader of the Opposition 1997-2001; Shadow Foreign Secretary and Senior Member of the Shadow Cabinet 2005-10; First Secretary of State, Secretary of State for Foreign and Commonwealth Affairs (Foreign Secretary) 2010-; *Select Committees:* Member: Joint Committee on House of Lords Reform 2003-10; President Oxford University Conservative Association 1981; Leader Conservative Party June 1997-2001

Political interests: Agriculture, economic policy

Other organisations: International Democrat Union, Global Alliance of Conservative, Christian Democrat and like-minded parties: Chair 1999-2002, Deputy Chair 2002-05, Assistant chair 2005-; Vice-President, Commonwealth Parliamentary Association (UK Branch) 2010-; PC 1995; *The Spectator*/Highland Park Parliamentarian of the Year 1998; National Book Awards History Book of the Year for biography of Pitt the Younger 2005; Threadneedle/*Spectator* Speech of the Year 2007; Beefsteak, Carlton, Buck's, Pratt's, Budokwai, Mark's; *Publications:* Speaking with Conviction (Conservative Policy Forum 1998); I will Give you Back your Country (Conservative Policy Forum 2000); Biography of William Pitt the Younger (2004); Biography of William Wilberforce (2007)

Recreations: Walking, sailing, cross country, skiing, judo

Rt Hon William Hague MP, House of Commons, London SW1A 0AA
Tel: 020 7219 4611 Fax: 020 7219 1890
E-mail: haguew@parliament.uk
Constituency: c/o 67 High Street, Northallerton,
North Yorkshire DL7 8EG Tel: 01609 779093 Fax: 01609 778172
Website: www.williamhague.org.uk

GENERAL ELECTION RESULT

		%
Hague, W. (Con)*	33,541	62.8
Meredith, L. (Lib Dem)	10,205	19.1
Driver, E. (Lab)	8,150	15.3
Rowe, L. (Green)	1,516	2.8
Majority	23,336	43.69
Electorate	79,478	
Turnout	53,412	67.20

**Member of last parliament*

CONSTITUENCY SNAPSHOT

Conservative majorities here have been consistently in five figures since the Second World War, with the exception of the 1989 by-election (caused by Leon Brittain's appointment as European Commissioner). William Hague, defending a majority of nearly 20,000, held the seat by 2,634 votes. In the four general elections since, Hague has re-established the lead for the Conservatives and his 2005 majority was 17,807. Hague increased his majority in 2010 to 23,336.

Richmond was enlarged with the addition of four Hambleton wards from Vale of York.

This is farming country, from the hill farming of Swaledale and Wensleydale, to the lusher areas further east and upland sheep country on the North York Moors.

A third of the population are country dwellers and tourism is a major industry. The constituency includes the northern part of the Yorkshire Dales national park, which draws more than eight million visitors a year, as well as attractions like Richmond itself, Middleham Castle, Catterick racecourse and Aysgarth Falls. There are no big towns, the largest being the North Riding's county town, Northallerton, and Richmond itself.

The biggest settlement is in fact Catterick Garrison, which together with RAF Leeming provides a big military presence in the area. Otherwise, the area is highly desirable for prosperous commuters to the big centres of Teesside.

Rt Hon **Peter Hain**

Neath (returning MP)

Boundary changes

Tel: 020 7219 3925
E-mail: hainp@parliament.uk
Website: www.peterhain.org

Labour

Date of birth: 16 February 1950; Son of Walter and Adelaine Hain

Education: Pretoria Boys High School, South Africa; Emanuel School, Wandsworth, London; Queen Mary College, London University (BSc economics and political science 1973); Sussex University (MPhil political science 1976); Married Patricia Western 1975 (divorced 2002) (2 sons); married Elizabeth Haywood 2003

Non-political career: Head of research, Union of Communication Workers 1976-91; Member, GMB

Political career: Contested Putney 1983 and 1987 general elections. Member for Neath 4 April 1991 by-election to 2010, for Neath (revised boundary) since 6 May 2010 general election; Opposition Whip 1995-96; Opposition Spokesperson for Employment 1996-97; Parliamentary Under-Secretary of State, Welsh Office 1997-99; Minister of State: Foreign and Commonwealth Office 1999-2001, Department of Trade and Industry (Energy and Competitiveness) 2001, Foreign and Commonwealth Office (Europe) 2001-02; Government representative European Union Convention 2002-03; Secretary of State for Wales 2002-08; Leader of the House of Commons and Lord Privy Seal 2003-05; Secretary of State for: Northern Ireland 2005-07, Work and Pensions 2007-08, Wales 2009-10; Shadow Secretary of State for Wales 2010-; *Select Committees:* Chair: Modernisation of the House of Commons 2003-05; Leader, Young Liberals 1971-73; Member Labour Party 1977-

Political interests: Social justice, democratic renewal, including Lords reform, electoral reform and devolution, environmental policy, including renewable energy, foreign affairs; Southern Africa

Other organisations: Director *Tribune* Newspaper 1991-97; Former Member Anti-Apartheid Movement; Chair 'Stop the Seventy Tour' (which disrupted the South African rugby tour, and stopped the South African cricket tour to Britain) 1969-70; Founder *Anti-Nazi League* 1977; PC 2001; *am.pm* Welsh Politician of the Year 2006; BBC Welsh MP of the Year 2007; Royal British Legion, Resolven, Resolven Rugby Club; Resolven Rugby, Ynysygerwn Cricket; *Publications:* 15 books including Ayes to the Left: A future for socialism (1995)

Recreations: Rugby, soccer, cricket, motor racing, rock and folk music

Rt Hon Peter Hain MP, House of Commons, London SW1A 0AA
Tel: 020 7219 3925 Fax: 020 7219 3816
E-mail: hainp@parliament.uk
Constituency: 39 Windsor Road, Neath, West Glamorgan SA11 1NB
Tel: 01639 630152 Fax: 01639 641196 Website: www.peterhain.org

GENERAL ELECTION RESULT

		%
Hain, P. (Lab)*	17,172	46.3
Llywelyn, A. (PlC)	7,397	19.9
Little, F. (Lib Dem)	5,535	14.9
Owens, E. (Con)	4,847	13.1
Green, M. (BNP)	1,342	3.6
Bevan, J. (UKIP)	829	2.2
Majority	9,775	26.33
Electorate	57,186	
Turnout	37,122	64.91

**Member of last parliament*

CONSTITUENCY SNAPSHOT

This seat has been represented by long-serving Labour MPs. Donald Coleman was the MP from 1964 until his death in 1991. In the by-election of that year Peter Hain continued the Labour tradition.

The big gains here since 1997 have been made by Plaid Cymru. There was a swing to them of nearly 12 per cent in 2001, and a further swing of 3.4 per cent in 2005. However, Peter Hain's majority is still a safe 12,710. Hain brushed off a 4.6 per cent swing to Plaid Cymru in 2010 to hold this seat for Labour with a majority of 9,775.

The seat loses a part of Clydach to the Gower.

This West Glamorgan constituency is centred on the town of Neath, although there is a significant population in Dulais and in the Upper Swansea and Neath valleys.

Traditional industry included copper smelting, steelworks and coal mining. The area has suffered from the decline in the heavy industry that provided such a large part of the local economy. Light industry has been encouraged. The skills base shows why average wages here tend to be lower than the national average.

Regeneration plans in Neath are some of the most ambitious town-centre renovation projects in the country. A rugby ball-shaped museum, library and heritage centre has been unveiled as the centrepiece of the town centre development.

Robert Halfon

Harlow

Boundary changes

Tel: 020 7219 3000
E-mail: robert.halfon.mp@parliament.uk
Website: www.roberthalfon.com

Date of birth: 22 March 1969; Son of Clement and Jenny Halfon

Education: Highgate School, London; Exeter University (BA politics 1991; MA Russian and East European politics 1992); Single

Non-political career: Parliamentary Researcher to a number of Conservative MPs including Harold Elliston MP and Michael Fabricant MP 1992-94; Head of Research, Market Access Ltd 1994-98; Policy Analyst, APCO UK 1998-2000; Political director, Renewing One Nation, Conservative Central Office 2000-01; Chief of staff to Oliver Letwin MP 2001-05; Political director, Conservative Friends of Israel 2005-; Councillor, Roydon Parish Council

Political career: Contested Harlow 2001 and 2005 general elections. Member for Harlow since 6 May 2010 general election; Chair: Western Area Conservative Students 1987-90, Exeter University Conservative Association 1989-90; Deputy Chair, Vauxhall Conservative Association 1998-2000; Member, Conservative Way Forward

Political interests: Education, conservation/green belt, literacy, social action, information technology, terrorism, housing, community cohesion; Israel, Russia, USA

Other organisations: Fellow, Royal Society of Arts; Member, Co-operative Society; Member, Advisory Board, Centre for Social Justice; National Conservative Excellence Award for Social Action 2008; United and Cecil Club, Carlton Club, Harlow British Legion, Great Parndon Community Association, Maypole Social Club, East India Club, Royal Overseas League; *Publications:* Retreat or Reform, Institute for European Defence and Strategic Studies, 1994; Corporate Irresponsibility, Social Affairs Unit, 1998; Capitalist Must Fight Back *Wall Street Journal*, 1998

Recreations: Watching football, season ticket holder Chelsea FC, countryside, books

Robert Halfon MP, House of Commons, London SW1A 0AA
Tel: 020 7219 3000 E-mail: robert.halfon.mp@parliament.uk
Constituency: Harlow Conservatives, Latton Bush Centre, Southern Way, Harlow, Essex CM18 7BL Tel: 01279 429251
Fax: 01279 429251 Website: www.roberthalfon.com

GENERAL ELECTION RESULT

		%
Halfon, R. (Con)	19,691	44.9
Rammell, B. (Lab)*	14,766	33.7
White, D. (Lib Dem)	5,990	13.7
Butler, E. (BNP)	1,739	4.0
Croft, J. (UKIP)	1,591	3.6
Adeeko, O. (Christian)	101	0.2
Majority	4,925	11.22
Electorate	67,439	
Turnout	43,878	65.06

**Member of last parliament*

CONSTITUENCY SNAPSHOT

Conservative Jerry Hayes held Harlow for 14 years, from 1983 to 1997. But in 1997 Bill Rammell was elected on an 11.3 per cent swing to Labour.

Rammell's majority of 10,514 was halved in 2001, and in 2005 it took three recounts before a declaration could be made. Rammell returned to Parliament for a third term with a majority of under 100; support for Labour fell by 6.4 per cent while the Conservative vote increased by the same figure.

Labour was defeated in the 2010 general election with a 5.9 per cent swing to the Conservative candidate, Robert Halfon.

Boundary changes were minor.

Harlow is a west Essex constituency, bordering Hertfordshire. Previously predominantly rural, in 1946 it became one of several new towns created by Attlee's Labour government, and now supports an urban population of just under 80,000.

Although mainly urban, Harlow contains a significant area of greenbelt land, and villages such as Roydon and Sheering.

There are some important large employers, such as Nortel, GlaxoSmithKline and Merck Sharp and Dohme but a growing number of small businesses.

Duncan Hames

Chippenham

New constituency

Tel: 020 7219 7240
E-mail: duncan.hames.mp@parliament.uk
Website: www.duncanhames.org.uk

Date of birth: 16 June 1977

Education: Watford Boys' Grammar School; New College, Oxford (BA philosophy, politics and economics 1998)

Non-political career: Recruitment, Northwich Park Hospital 1995; Business consultant, Deloitte Consulting 1998-2004; Director, Chippenham Consultants Limited 2005-; Governor, Westwood with Ilford School 2002-06; Councillor, West Wiltshire District Council 2003-07; South West England Regional Development Agency: Board member 2003-09, Chair, Audit Committee 2008-; Board Member, Culture South West 2006-08; Governor, George Ward School 2006-

Political career: Contested Tottenham 2000 by-election and Watford 2001 and Westbury 2005 general elections. Member for Chippenham since 6 May 2010 general election; Vice-president, Liberal Democrat Youth and Students 2000-02; Member, Federal Finance and Administration Committee 2001

Duncan Hames MP, House of Commons, London SW1A 0AA
Tel: 020 7219 7240 E-mail: duncan.hames.mp@parliament.uk
Constituency: 17 St Marys Place, Chippenham SN15 1EN
Tel: 01249 652602 Fax: 08707 622665
Website: www.duncanhames.org.uk

GENERAL ELECTION RESULT

		%
Hames, D. (Lib Dem)	23,970	45.8
Emmanuel-Jones, W. (Con)	21,500	41.1
Lovell, G. (Lab)	3,620	6.9
Reid, J. (UKIP)	1,718	3.3
Simpkins, M. (BNP)	641	1.2
Fletcher, S. (Green)	446	0.9
Maguire, J. (England)	307	0.6
Sexton, R. (Christian)	118	0.2
Majority	2,470	4.72
Electorate	72,105	
Turnout	52,320	72.56

CONSTITUENCY SNAPSHOT

Chippenham is a new seat, created primarily from North Wiltshire also includes wards from Devizes and Westbury.

The three seats from which this constituency has been formed have all returned a Tory MP continuously for at least the last 50 years. Liberal Democrat Duncan Hames won this new seat in 2010 with a 2,470 vote lead.

The seat is based around the town of Chippenham, which is the largest town in rural North Wiltshire, lying between the Marlborough Downs to the East, the Cotswolds to the North and West, and Salisbury Plain to the South.

The seat comprises three other main towns: Bradford on Avon; Corsham; and Melksham. Chippenham was historically a market town based at a crossing of the River Avon, although it has now developed into a commuter town.

Several large businesses have been based in the region. The Invensys factory undertakes railway signalling contracts for Network Rail. There are a number of other industrial sites around the town, Bumpers Farm being the largest.

Chippenham's population has grown rapidly in recent years. This expansion can be attributed to the development of large housing estates (indeed, entirely new suburbs) such as the vast Cepen Park district to the west of the town, and the Pewsham development to the east.

David Hamilton

Midlothian (returning MP)

No boundary changes

Tel: 020 7219 8257
E-mail: hamiltonda@parliament.uk
Website: www.davidhamiltonmp.co.uk

Labour

Date of birth: 24 October 1950; Son of David Hamilton and Agnes Gardner

Education: Dalkeith High School; Married Jean Trench Macrae 1969 (2 daughters)

Non-political career: Miner National Coal Board 1965-84; Unemployed 1984-87; Employment training scheme supervisor Midlothian Council 1987-89; Placement and training officer Craigmillar Festival Society 1989-92; Chief executive Craigmillar Opportunities Trust 1992-2000; NUM 1965-87, 2001-: Delegate 1976-87, Joint union chair 1981-87; TGWU 1987-2000; Councillor, Midlothian Council 1995-2001: Convenor Strategic Services Committee 1995-2001; Convention of Scottish Local Authorities (COSLA): Chair Economic Development, Planning and Transport Committee 1997-99; Chair Midlothian Innovation Technology Trust 2002-

Political career: Member for Midlothian 2001-05, for Midlothian (revised boundary) since 5 May 2005 general election; PPS to Ed Miliband as Secretary of State for Energy and Climate Change 2008-10; *Select Committees:* Member: Broadcasting 2001-05, Procedure 2001-05, Scottish Affairs 2003-05, 2007-08, Work and Pensions 2003-05, European Scrutiny 2005-07, Defence 2005-10

Political interests: Defence, energy, biotechnology; Cyprus, EU, Gibraltar, USA

Other organisations: Chair: Midlothian Innovation Technology Trust 2002-, Gullane Miners' Home 2004-09; Dalkeith Miners Welfare; Honorary President Midlothian Artists

Recreations: Films, theatre, grandchildren

David Hamilton MP, House of Commons, London SW1A 0AA
Tel: 020 7219 8257 Fax: 020 7219 2532
E-mail: hamiltonda@parliament.uk
Constituency: PO Box 11, 95 High Street, Dalkeith,
Midlothian EH22 1HL Tel: 0131-654 1585 Fax: 0131-654 1586
Website: www.davidhamiltonmp.co.uk

GENERAL ELECTION RESULT

		%	+/-
Hamilton, D. (Lab)*	18,449	47.0	1.6
Beattie, C. (SNP)	8,100	20.6	3.7
Laird, R. (Lib Dem)	6,711	17.1	-9.1
Callander, J. (Con)	4,661	11.9	2.5
Baxter, I. (Green)	595	1.5	
Norrie, G. (UKIP)	364	0.9	
McCleery, G. (Ind)	196	0.5	
Duncan, W. (Solidarity)	166	0.4	
Majority	10,349	26.37	
Electorate	61,387		
Turnout	39,242	63.93	

**Member of last parliament*

CONSTITUENCY SNAPSHOT

Liberal William Ewart Gladstone is Midlothian's most famous former MP, but in more recent times a series of former coal miners have represented the constituency for Labour.

Midlothian lost Penicuik to Tweeddale, Ettrick and Lauderdale in 1997. Eric Clarke held the redrawn seat in the general election with a 9,870 majority.

In 2001 Eric Clarke's successor David Hamilton became the fifth successive former miner to hold the seat for Labour 1945 and held the seat with a 9,014 majority. In the boundary review of 2005 Penicuik was moved back into the constituency from Tweeddale, Ettrick and Lauderdale. David Hamilton held on to the seat with a slightly reduced majority of 7,265. Hamilton held the seat in 2010 with 47 per cent of the vote.

This is a commuter-belt constituency south of the city of Edinburgh. Its main towns are Dalkeith and Penicuik

Formerly a mining and textiles area, the old industries have closed and been replaced with hi-tech industries such as bio-technology. The economic importance of Edinburgh means local unemployment is low and the area is growing. The first major council house development in Scotland for 20 years is in Dalkeith.

In 2006 MSPs gave their backing to the restoration of the railway line from Edinburgh to the Borders and it is hoped that the local economy will be boosted by an influx of Edinburgh commuters; new affordable housing is being built to accommodate them.

Fabian Hamilton

Leeds North East ***(returning MP)***

Boundary changes

Tel: 020 7219 3493
E-mail: hamiltonf@parliament.uk
Website: www.leedsne.co.uk

Date of birth: 12 April 1955; Son of late Mario Uziell-Hamilton, solicitor, and late Adrianne Uziell-Hamilton (Her Honour Judge Uziell-Hamilton)

Education: Brentwood School, Brentwood, Essex; York University (BA social sciences 1977); Married Rosemary Ratcliffe 1980 (1 son 2 daughters)

Non-political career: Taxi driver 1978-79; graphic designer 1979-94; consultant and dealer, Apple Macintosh computer systems 1994-97; Member: SLADE 1978-82, NGA 1982-91, GPMU 1991-2005, Amicus 2005-07, UNITE 2007-; Councillor, Leeds City Council 1987-98: Chair: Race Equality Committee 1988-94, Economic Development Committee 1994-96, Education Committee 1996-97

Political career: Contested Leeds North East 1992 general election. Member for Leeds North East 1997-2010, for Leeds North East (revised boundary) since 6 May 2010 general election; *Select Committees:* Member: Administration 1997-2001, Foreign Affairs 2001-10, Quadripartite (Committees on Strategic Export Controls)/Arms Export Controls 2006-10; Member: Co-op Party 1981-, Fabian Society 1990-; Vice-chair Labour Friends of Israel Executive 1997-

Political interests: Education, transport, small businesses, anti-racism, international development, alternative fuels, foreign affairs, holocaust education, prison health, hospices and palliative care; Middle East, Europe, Southern Africa, Caribbean and Indian sub-continent, Cyprus, Kashmir, Turkey, Iran, Tibet, Japan, Korea, Russia, Iceland

Other organisations: Member Jewish Labour Movement; Governor Northern School of Contemporary Dance; Trustee, Heart Research UK

Recreations: Film, opera, cycling, computers, photography

Fabian Hamilton MP, House of Commons, London SW1A 0AA
Tel: 020 7219 3493 Fax: 020 7219 5540
E-mail: hamiltonf@parliament.uk
Constituency: 335 Roundhay Road, Leeds LS8 4HT
Tel: 0113-249 6600 Fax: 0113-235 9866 Website: www.leedsne.co.uk

GENERAL ELECTION RESULT

		%
Hamilton, F. (Lab)*	20,287	42.7
Lobley, M. (Con)	15,742	33.1
Choudhry, A. (Lib Dem)	9,310	19.6
Hendon, W. (UKIP)	842	1.8
Redmond, T. (BNP)	758	1.6
Foote, C. (Green Soc)	596	1.3
Majority	4,545	9.56
Electorate	67,899	
Turnout	47,535	70.01

**Member of last parliament*

CONSTITUENCY SNAPSHOT

Sir Keith Joseph was the Tory MP from 1956-87, but his majorities fell towards the end of his tenure. Even so, in 1987 the new Conservative candidate Timothy Kirkhope inherited a margin of more than 17 per cent.

In 1992 Kirkhope's majority was halved. Labour's Fabian Hamilton leapt into second place ahead of the Lib Dems. Hamilton achieved a swing of nearly 12 per cent in 1997, and captured the seat with a majority of 6,959.

Hamilton's majority increased in 2001 but there was a 2.6 per cent swing back to the Conservatives in 2005 and the Labour majority was cut to 5,262. In 2010 Hamilton was re-elected with a 4,545 majority.

The seat lost part of rural Harewood to Elmet and Rothwell, while gaining part-wards from Leeds Central and Leeds North West.

This residential constituency ranges from inner-city Chapeltown to Roundhay, the affluent suburbs of Moortown to the Yorkshire countryside around Eccup.

The suburban semi rules in Leeds North East. The proportion of residents who are owner-occupiers is the highest of the four Leeds city centre seats.

There is little industry within the constituency itself, the biggest local employers being Chapel Allerton Hospital and the Moor Allerton Centre on the northern ring road. Although nearly all the jobs are in service industries, many people work in the burgeoning financial and educational institutions in the city.

Rt Hon **Philip Hammond**

Runnymede and Weybridge ***(returning MP)***

No boundary changes

Tel: 020 7219 4055
E-mail: hammondp@parliament.uk

Date of birth: 4 December 1955; Son of Bernard Lawrence Hammond, civil engineer and local government officer

Education: Shenfield School, Brentwood, Essex; University College, Oxford (MA politics, philosophy and economics 1977); Married Susan Carolyn Williams-Walker 1991 (2 daughters 1 son)

Non-political career: Assistant to Chair then marketing manager Speywood Laboratories Ltd 1977-81; Director Speywood Medical Ltd 1981-83; Established and ran medical equipment manufacturing and distribution companies 1983-94; Director Castlemead Ltd 1984-; Director various medical equipment manufacturing companies 1983-96; Partner CMA Consultants 1993-95; Director Castlemead Homes Ltd 1994-2004; Consultant to Government of Malawi 1995-97; Director Consort Resources Ltd 1999-2003

Political career: Contested Newham North East 1994 by-election. Member for Runnymede and Weybridge since 1 May 1997 general election; Opposition Spokesperson for: Health and Social Services 1998-2001, Trade and Industry 2001-02; Shadow: Minister for Local and Devolved Government Affairs 2002-05, Chief Secretary to the Treasury 2005, Secretary of State for Work and Pensions 2005-07, Chief Secretary to the Treasury 2007-10; Secretary of State for Transport 2010-; *Select Committees:* Member: Unopposed Bills (Panel) 1997-2004, Environment, Transport and Regional Affairs 1998, Environment, Transport and Regional Affairs (Transport Sub-Committee) 1998, Trade and Industry 2002; Chair East Lewisham Conservative Association 1989-96; Member Greater London Area Executive Council 1989-96

Political interests: Economic policy, international trade, European Union, defence, social security, transport, housing and planning, energy, health; Latin America, Germany, Italy, Southern and Eastern Africa

Other organisations: PC 2010; Carlton

Recreations: Travel, cinema, walking

Rt Hon Philip Hammond MP, House of Commons, London SW1A 0AA Tel: 020 7219 4055 Fax: 020 7219 5851
E-mail: hammondp@parliament.uk
Constituency: Runnymede, Spelthorne and Weybridge, Conservative Association, 55 Cherry Orchard, Staines, Middlesex TW18 2DQ
Tel: 01784 453544 Fax: 01784 466109
Website: www.runnymedeweybridgeconservatives.com

GENERAL ELECTION RESULT

		%	+/-
Hammond, P. (Con)*	26,915	55.9	4.7
Falconer, A. (Lib Dem)	10,406	21.6	3.8
Greenwood, P. (Lab)	6,446	13.4	-9.6
Micklethwait, T. (UKIP)	3,146	6.5	2.6
Gould, J. (Green)	696	1.5	-1.3
Sammons, D. (Ind)	541	1.1	
Majority	16,509	34.29	
Electorate	72,566		
Turnout	48,150	66.35	

**Member of last parliament*

CONSTITUENCY SNAPSHOT

A Conservative MP has represented this seat, in its various guises, since World War Two. Philip Hammond inherited the seat from Sir Geoffrey Pattie in 1997.

From Sir Geoffrey's five-figure majorities in the 1970s and 80s, Mr Hammond's 1997 majority was a reduced 9,875 votes. The general election of 2001 was almost a re-run of 1997, with virtually the same results recorded by the three parties.

In 2005 Hammond achieved a five-figure lead of 12,349. He held the seat in 2010 with a 16,509 majority.

Lying in the affluent commuter belt west of London, Runneymede and Weybridge seat is part suburban and part rural. The borough of Runnymede is named after the historic meadows near the River Thames where King John signed the Magna Carta in 1215.

There is hardly any industry in the constituency, and most of the seat's workforce is in professional, managerial or associate technical and professional positions.

The borough is also becoming a major location for knowledge-based sectors, including information technology, telecommunications and advanced business services. As a result the area has undergone a surge in high quality office development over the last few years.

The area is close to Heathrow (which provides a significant number of local jobs) with direct access to the M3 and M25 motorways.

Stephen Hammond

Wimbledon (returning MP)

Boundary changes

Tel: 020 7219 3401
E-mail: hammonds@parliament.uk
Website: www.stephenhammondmp.co.uk

Date of birth: 4 February 1962; Son of Bryan Norman Walter and Janice Eve Hammond

Education: King Edward VI School, Southampton; Richard Hale School, Hertford; Queen Mary College, London University (BSc econ 1982); Married Sally Patricia Brodie 1991 (1 daughter)

Non-political career: Trainee analyst, Reed Stenhouse Investment Services 1983-85; Fund manager, Canada Life 1987-88; Stockbroker, UBS Philips and Drew 1987-91; Director UK equities, Dresdner Kleinwort Benson Securities 1991-98; Director Pan European research, Commerzbank Securities 1998-2001; Merton Borough Council: Councillor 2002-06, Environment spokesman 2002-04; Deputy group leader 2004-06

Political career: Contested North Warwickshire 1997 and Wimbledon 2001 general elections. Member for Wimbledon since 5 May 2005 general election; Shadow Minister for Transport 2005-10; *Select Committees:* Member: Regulatory Reform 2005-08; Chair, Stevenage Conservatives 1991-94; Member, Eastern Area Executive 1992-94; Chairman Wimbledon 2001-03

Political interests: Health, financial affairs, transport, foreign affairs; EU, especially Portugal, India, China, USA, Sri Lanka

Other organisations: Various Wimbledon and Merton bodies

Recreations: Reading, sport, relaxing with family, cooking

Stephen Hammond MP, House of Commons, London SW1A 0AA
Tel: 020 7219 3401 Fax: 020 7219 0462
E-mail: hammonds@parliament.uk
Constituency: Wimbledon Conservative Association, c/o 1 Summerstown, London SW17 0BQ Tel: 020 8944 2905
Website: www.stephenhammondmp.co.uk

GENERAL ELECTION RESULT

		%
Hammond, S. (Con)*	23,257	49.1
Sheehan, S. (Lib Dem)	11,849	25.0
Judge, A. (Lab)	10,550	22.3
McAleer, M. (UKIP)	914	1.9
Thacker, R. (Green)	590	1.2
Martin, D. (Christian)	235	0.5
Majority	11,408	24.07
Electorate	65,723	
Turnout	47,395	72.11

**Member of last parliament*

CONSTITUENCY SNAPSHOT

From 1950 the seat was held by the Tories for 47 years. In 1997, however, on a swing of 18 per cent the Labour candidate Roger Casale was elected with a majority of 2,990.

The Conservatives regained Wimbledon in 2005 on a 7.2 per cent swing. Stephen Hammond now holds the seat with a 2,301 majority. Despite voting Labour in 1997 and 2001, Wimbledon has since become a solid Tory seat, with Stephen Hammond winning 49 per cent of the vote.

Boundary changes were minimal.

Wimbledon in south-west London is best known for its world-famous tennis courts and is an affluent and suburban constituency. It is spacious and suburban, with ample shopping, convenient transport links to both Central London and outer London and Surrey, and spacious parklands.

Close to Gatwick, and Heathrow, and with good rail, tube, and tram links, Wimbledon is a good location for business. The number of constituents employed in professional occupations is above average, as is the number in managerial and technical positions.

Wimbledon is to benefit from the development of the Nelson Community Hospital, which will ease the burden on the area's hospitals and play a role in regenerating the area.

Matt Hancock

West Suffolk

Boundary changes

Tel: 020 7219 3000
E-mail: matthew.hancock.mp@parliament.uk
Website: www.matthewhancock.co.uk

Date of birth: 2 October 1978

Education: Farndon County Primary School; King's School, Chester; Exeter College, Oxford (BA politics, philosophy and economics 1999); Christ College, Cambridge (Master's economics 2003); Married Martha 2006 (1 son 1 daughter)

Non-political career: Border Business Systems, Farndon; Economist, Bank of England 2000-05; Chief of staff to George Osborne MP 2005-10

Political career: Member for West Suffolk since 6 May 2010 general election; Member, Conservative Party 1999-

Political interests: Rural affairs

Recreations: Walking, cooking

Matt Hancock MP, House of Commons, London SW1A 0AA
Tel: 020 7219 3000 E-mail: matthew.hancock.mp@parliament.uk
Constituency: West Suffolk Conservatives, 4a Exeter Road, New Market, Suffolk CB8 8LT Tel: 01638 565945
Fax: 01638 662279 Website: www.matthewhancock.co.uk

GENERAL ELECTION RESULT

		%
Hancock, M. (Con)	24,312	50.6
Brooks-Gordon, B. (Lib Dem)	11,262	23.4
Ahmed, O. (Lab)	7,089	14.7
Smith, I. (UKIP)	3,085	6.4
Johns, R. (BNP)	1,428	3.0
Appleby, A. (Ind)	540	1.1
Young, C. (CPA)	373	0.8
Majority	13,050	27.14
Electorate	74,413	
Turnout	48,089	64.62

CONSTITUENCY SNAPSHOT

Richard Spring was elected the Tory MP for Bury St Edmunds in 1992. When the Boundary Commission relocated that seat, moving it towards the coast to take in the area east of the eponymous town, Spring was nominated for West Suffolk. In 1997 he won the seat by a majority of 1,867.

In 2001 Spring extended his majority to 4,295. In 2005 he was re-elected with a 20 per cent majority (8,909) and the support of almost half the electorate.

Matthew Hancock held the seat for the Conservatives in 2010 with a majority of 13,050.

The seat lost two part-wards and gained two from the constituency of Bury St Edmunds, in addition to losing one part-ward to South Suffolk.

Composed of prosperous provincial towns and rural communities, the constituency encompasses the market town of Brandon to the military community of Lakenheath.

Local industry is reliant on manufacturing, primarily the refinement of agricultural products.

The market town of Haverhill has meat processing plants and there is also an abundance of light manufacturing works. The leisure industry accounts for a significant proportion of the region's employment.

The largest US Air Force base in England, RAF Lakenheath, employs a substantial proportion of the West Suffolk population as well.

Mike Hancock

Portsmouth South (returning MP)

Boundary changes

Tel: 020 7219 1102
E-mail: hancockm@parliament.uk
Website: www.mikehancock.co.uk

Date of birth: 9 April 1946; Son of Thomas William Hancock and Margaret Eva, neé Cole

Education: Copnor and Portsea School, Hampshire; Married Jacqueline Elliott 1967 (1 son 1 daughter)

Non-political career: Director, BBC Daytime; District Officer for Hampshire, Isle of Wight and Channel Islands Mencap 1989-97; Councillor Portsmouth City Council 1971-: Leader Liberal Democrat Group 1989-97; Councillor Hampshire County Council 1973-97: Leader of Opposition 1977-81, 1989-93, Leader 1993-97; Vice-chairman Portsmouth Docks 1992-2002

Political career: Contested Portsmouth South (SDP) 1983 and (SDP/Alliance) 1987 general elections. Member (SDP) for Portsmouth South 1984-87. Member for Portsmouth South 1997-2010, for Portsmouth South (revised boundary) since 6 May 2010 general election; Liberal Democrat Spokesperson for: Foreign Affairs, Defence and Europe (Defence) 1997-99-; Environment, Transport, the Regions and Social Justice (Planning) 2000-01; *Select Committees:* Member: Public Administration 1997-99, Defence 1999-2010, Chairmen's Panel 2000-10; Contested Wight and Hampshire South European Parliamentary election 1994; Member: Labour Party 1968-81, Social Democrat Party 1981-87, Liberal Democrat Party 1987-

Political interests: European affairs, defence, sport; Russia, Romania, Moldova, Ukraine

Other organisations: Chairman Southern Branch, NSPCC 1989-92; Chair Liberal Group Council of Europe; Leader Liberal Group Western European Union; NATO Parliamentary Assembly; Trustee, Royal Marine Museum; CBE 1992; *Publications:* Council of Europe Report on International Abduction of children by one of the parents, 2002

Recreations: Supporter Portsmouth Football Club

Mike Hancock CBE MP, House of Commons, London SW1A 0AA
Tel: 020 7219 1102 Fax: 020 7219 2496
E-mail: hancockm@parliament.uk
Constituency: 1A Albert Road, Southsea, Hampshire PO5 2SE
Tel: 02392 861055 Fax: 02392 830530
Website: www.mikehancock.co.uk

GENERAL ELECTION RESULT

		%
Hancock, M. (Lib Dem)*	18,921	45.9
Drummond, F. (Con)	13,721	33.3
Ferrett, J. (Lab)	5,640	13.7
Martin, C. (UKIP)	876	2.1
Crompton, G. (BNP)	873	2.1
Dawes, T. (Green)	716	1.7
DuCane, I. (England)	400	1.0
Cummings, L. (JACP)	117	0.3
Majority	5,200	12.60
Electorate	70,242	
Turnout	41,264	58.75

**Member of last parliament*

CONSTITUENCY SNAPSHOT

Conservative Sir Ralph Bonner Pink represented the seat from 1966 until his death in 1984. The subsequent by-election saw SDP candidate Mike Hancock win the seat with a majority of 1,341.

Hancock then lost the seat to the Conservative David Martin by just 205 votes in 1987. In 1997 Hancock won the seat back, now as a Liberal Democrat, defeating Martin with a majority of 4,327. He was re-elected in 2001 with an improved 6,094-vote lead and again in 2005 with a smaller majority of 3,362.

Hannock held the seat with a 5,200 majority at the 2010 general election.

Boundary changes were minimal.

This Hampshire constituency covers the densely populated area of central Portsmouth, the smart and gentrified area of Old Portsmouth with the historic dockyard and the resort of Southsea.

The modern naval dockyard is a major employer, with large numbers of people also working in private-sector defence industries such as Lockheed Martin, Marconi-GEC, and BAe Systems.

The expanding and highly successful council-owned continental ferry port employs around 2,000 people directly, and is responsible for a significant number of jobs through suppliers and servicing industries.

The regeneration of Portsmouth Harbour has transformed the waterfront. The centrepiece, the Millennium Spinnaker Tower has proved to be a popular attraction.

Greg Hands

Chelsea and Fulham ***(returning MP)***

New constituency

Tel: 020 7219 5448
E-mail: handsg@parliament.uk
Website: www.greghands.com

Conservative

Date of birth: 14 November 1965; Son of Edward and Mavis Hands

Education: Dr Challoner's Grammar School, Amersham; Robinson College, Cambridge (BA modern history 1989); Married Irina Hundt 2005 (1 daughter 1 son)

Non-political career: Banker 1989-97; Hammersmith and Fulham Borough Council: Councillor 1998-2006: Leader Conservative group 1999-2003; Prison visitor HMP Wormwood Scrubs 2002-04

Political career: Member for Hammersmith and Fulham 2005-10, for Chelsea and Fulham since 6 May 2010 general election; Shadow Minister for the Treasury 2009-10; *Select Committees:* Member: ODPM/Communities and Local Government 2006-08, European Scrutiny 2007-10, Communities and Local Government 2009-10

Political interests: Finance, foreign affairs, housing, local government; Central and Eastern Europe, Germany, Ireland, North Korea, Russia and ex-USSR

Other organisations: Trustee: Brunswick Club for Young People 2003-, FRODO Romanian Orphans Charity 2008-

Recreations: Playing and watching football, local history, British, German and Soviet history, photography

Greg Hands MP, House of Commons, London SW1A 0AA
Tel: 020 7219 5448 Fax: 020 7219 6801
E-mail: handsg@parliament.uk
Constituency: 4 Greyhound Road, London W6 8NX
Tel: 020 7835 5446 Fax: 020 7385 1711
Website: www.greghands.com

GENERAL ELECTION RESULT

		%
Hands, G. (Con)*	24,093	60.5
Hilton, A. (Lab)	7,371	18.5
Hazell, D. (Lib Dem)	6,473	16.2
Stephenson, J. (Green)	671	1.7
Gittos, T. (UKIP)	478	1.2
McDonald, B. (BNP)	388	1.0
Courtenay, R. (NICCF)	196	0.5
Roseman, G. (England)	169	0.4
Spickernell, G. (BEP)	17	0.0
Majority	16,722	41.96
Electorate	66,295	
Turnout	39,856	60.12

**Member of last parliament*

CONSTITUENCY SNAPSHOT

The new seat of Chelsea and Fulham is made up of six wards from the old Hammersmith and Fulham seat and five wards from the old Kensington and Chelsea seat.

Kensington and Chelsea is one of the strongest Conservative seats in the country, returning Alan Clarke, Michael Portillo and Malcolm Rifkind to Parliament. Rifkind was elected in 2005 with a 12,418 majority.

Labour's Michael Stewart served in Hammersmith and Fulham for 24 years until 1979, when the seat fell to the Conservatives' Martin Stevens. Stevens died in 1986 and Labour's Nick Raynsford won the by-election only to lose to Matthew Carrington in 1987. Labour's Iain Coleman won in 1997 and held the seat until retiring in 2005. The Tories took the seat in 2005 as Greg Hands secured a 5,029 majority. As the name suggests, this constituency is solidly Conservative. Greg Hands won over 60 per cent of the vote and a 16,722 majority in 2010.

Much of Chelsea is a desirable area to live, popular with wealthy expatriates. Fulham was a working-class area for the first half of the twentieth century, but is now an expensive part of London.

The new Imperial Wharf railway station opened in 2009 on the London Overground network. The £7 million project, towards the south of constituency, has taken place alongside redevelopment of a former industrial site, which has been developed into a luxury apartment complex.

Rt Hon **David Hanson**

Delyn (returning MP)

No boundary changes

Tel: 020 7219 5064
E-mail: hansond@parliament.uk
Website: www.davidhanson.org.uk

Labour

Date of birth: 5 July 1957; Son of late Brian Hanson, fork lift driver and of Glenda Hanson, wages clerk

Education: Verdin Comprehensive School, Winsford, Cheshire; Hull University (BA drama 1978, Certificate of Education 1980); Married Margaret Mitchell 1986 (2 sons 2 daughters)

Non-political career: Vice-president Hull University Students' Union 1978-79; Trainee Co-operative Union 1980-81; Manager Plymouth Co-operative 1981-82; Various posts with Spastics Society 1982-89; Director Re-Solv (Society for the Prevention of Solvent Abuse) 1989-92; T&G, USDAW; Vale Royal Borough Council 1983-91: Councillor 1983-91, Labour Leader, Leader of Council 1989-91; Councillor Northwich Town Council 1987-91

Political career: Contested Eddisbury 1983 and Delyn 1987 general elections. Member for Delyn since 9 April 1992 general election; PPS to Alastair Darling as Chief Secretary to the Treasury 1997-98; Assistant Government Whip 1998-99; Parliamentary Under-Secretary of State, Wales Office 1999-2001; PPS to Tony Blair as Prime Minister 2001-05; Minister of State: Northern Ireland Office 2005-07, Ministry of Justice 2007-09, Home Office 2009-10; *Select Committees:* Member: Welsh Affairs 1992-95; Contested Cheshire West 1984 European Parliament election; Member, Leadership Campaign Team 1994-97

Political interests: Foreign affairs, heritage, local and regional government, solvent abuse; South Africa, Cyprus

Other organisations: Fellow Industry and Parliament Trust 1998; PC 2007

Recreations: Football, cinema, family

Rt Hon David Hanson MP, House of Commons, London SW1A 0AA
Tel: 020 7219 5064 Fax: 020 7219 2671
E-mail: hansond@parliament.uk
Constituency: 64 Chester Street, Flint, Flintshire CH6 5DH
Tel: 01352 763159 Fax: 01352 730140
Website: www.davidhanson.org.uk

GENERAL ELECTION RESULT

		%	+/-
Hanson, D. (Lab)*	15,083	40.8	-4.8
Sandbach, A. (Con)	12,811	34.6	8.5
Brereton, B. (Lib Dem)	5,747	15.5	-2.3
Ryder, P. (PIC)	1,844	5.0	-2.4
Matthys, J. (BNP)	844	2.3	
Haigh, A. (UKIP)	655	1.8	0.2
Majority	2,272	6.14	
Electorate	53,470		
Turnout	36,984	69.17	

**Member of last parliament*

CONSTITUENCY SNAPSHOT

Delyn, created in 1983, was won by the Conservative Keith Raffan, following in the footsteps of previous Tory MPs, Nigel Birch and Sir Anthony Meyer, who between them had represented the area since 1950.

Raffan's 1983 majority was just under 6,000, but was cut to just 1,200 in 1987.

In 1992 Labour won Delyn as David Hanson was elected with a majority of 2,039. In 1997 he extended his majority. There were small decreases in the Labour vote share in 2001 and 2005, but Hanson retained a sizeable majority of 6,644 in 2005. David Hanson's majority slumped to 2,272 in 2010.

This north-east Wales seat covers Holywell, Flint, and the market town Mold, as well as a number of smaller villages set among the Clwydian hills.

The constituency is divided between the Deeside conurbation and the rural hinterland of Clwyd. The former is the more industrial, while the latter is more agricultural, and with a greater number of Welsh speakers.

While the colliery at Point of Ayr has closed, the major gas terminal still dominates what remains an industrial landscape.

A number of constituents commute to work in nearby Chester or other parts of north-west England.

Flintshire is one of the more affluent areas of Wales. It has higher than average wage levels and lower unemployment.

Rt Hon **Harriet Harman**

Camberwell and Peckham (returning MP)

Boundary changes

Tel: 020 7219 4218
E-mail: harmanh@parliament.uk
Website: www.harrietharman.org

Labour

Date of birth: 30 July 1950; Daughter of late John Bishop Harman, and of Anna Harman

Education: St Paul's Girls' School; York University (BA politics 1978); Married Jack Dromey 1982 (2 sons 1 daughter)

Non-political career: Legal officer, National Council for Civil Liberties 1978-82; Queen's Counsel 2001; Member, Unite (TGWU sector)

Political career: Member for Peckham 1982-1997, for Camberwell and Peckham 1997-2010, for Camberwell and Peckham (revised boundary) since 6 May 2010 general election; Member, Public Accounts Commission; Shadow Minister, Social Services 1984, 1985-87; Spokesperson for Health 1987-92; Shadow Chief Secretary to the Treasury 1992-94; Shadow Secretary of State for: Employment 1994-95, Health 1995-96; Social Security 1996-97; Secretary of State for Social Security and Minister for Women 1997-98; Solicitor General 2001-05; Minister of State, Department for Constitutional Affairs/Ministry of Justice 2005-07; Leader of the House of Commons and Lord Privy Seal 2007-10; Ex-officio member House of Commons Commission 2007-10; Minister for Women and Equality 2007-10; Member, Speaker's Committee for the Independent Parliamentary Standards Authority 2009-; Acting Leader of the Opposition 2010-; *Select Committees:* Chair Modernisation of the House of Commons 2007-10; Member, Labour Party National Executive Committee 1993-98; Deputy Leader Labour Party 2007-; Chair Labour Party 2007-; Acting Leader Labour Party 2010-

Political interests: Women, social services, provision for under-fives, law, domestic violence, civil liberties

Other organisations: Chair Childcare Commission 1999-; PC 1997

Rt Hon Harriet Harman QC MP, House of Commons, London SW1A 0AA Tel: 020 7219 4218 Fax: 020 7219 4877
E-mail: harmanh@parliament.uk
Website: www.harrietharman.org

GENERAL ELECTION RESULT

		%
Harman, H. (Lab)*	27,619	59.2
Blango, C. (Lib Dem)	10,432	22.4
Stranack, A. (Con)	6,080	13.0
Jones, J. (Green)	1,361	2.9
Robby Munilla, Y. (England)	435	0.9
Ogunleye, J. (WRP)	211	0.5
Sharkey, M. (SLP)	184	0.4
Francis, D. (Ind)	93	0.2
Robbins, S. (Ind)	87	0.2
Knox, P. (Ind)	82	0.2
Mountford, J. (AWL)	75	0.2
Majority	17,187	36.84
Electorate	78,618	
Turnout	46,659	59.35

**Member of last parliament*

CONSTITUENCY SNAPSHOT

Represented by Labour since 1945, the party's Harriet Harman has held Camberwell and Peckham since her election in 1983. Labour's deputy leader Harriet Harman held on with an increased majority of 17,187. A 3 per cent swing to the Lib Dems did nothing to threaten this safe seat.

Camberwell and Peckham was enlarged, Faraday, Liversey, Peckham Rye and The Lane wards are now entirely within the seats boundaries. South Camberwell ward has also been added from Dulwich and West Norwood.

The seat is one of the most ethnically diverse areas of London, with large Afro-Caribbean and African populations in Peckham in particular.

The area is socially as well as ethnically diverse. Despite its reputation as an inner-city constituency, parts of Camberwell, such as Grove Lane, contain fine Georgian houses and areas such as Nunhead, further to the east, have experienced considerable regeneration in recent times.

The massive King's College and Maudsley Hospitals are largely based within the seat and are major employers.

The East London tube line extension through Peckham Rye will improve transport access in the area and efforts continue to regenerate the area.

Mark Harper

Forest of Dean ***(returning MP)***

No boundary changes

Tel: 020 7219 5056
E-mail: harperm@parliament.uk
Website: www.markharper.org

Conservative

Date of birth: 26 February 1970; Son of James and Jane Harper

Education: Headlands School, Swindon, Wiltshire Swindon College; Brasenose College, Oxford (BA philosophy, politics and economics 1991); Married Margaret Whelan 1999

Non-political career: Auditor, KPMG 1991-95; Intel Corporation (UK) Ltd: Senior finance analyst 1995-97, Finance manager 1997-2000, Operations manager 2000-02; Own accountancy practice 2002-06

Political career: Contested Forest of Dean 2001 general election. Member for Forest of Dean since 5 May 2005 general election; Shadow Minister for: Defence 2005-07, Work and Pensions (Disabled People) 2007-10; Parliamentary Secretary, Cabinet Office 2010-; *Select Committees:* Member: Administration 2005-06, Work and Pensions 2009; South Swindon Conservative Association: Treasurer 1993-98, Deputy chair 1998

Political interests: Education, special needs education, law and order, health, defence; USA, Israel

Recreations: Walking the dogs, travel, cinema

Mark Harper MP, House of Commons, London SW1A 0AA
Tel: 020 7219 5056 Fax: 020 7219 0937
E-mail: harperm@parliament.uk
Constituency: 53 High Street, Cinderford, Gloucestershire GL14 2SU
Tel: 01594 823482 Fax: 01594 823623
Website: www.markharper.org

GENERAL ELECTION RESULT

		%	+/-
Harper, M. (Con)*	22,853	46.9	6.2
Hogan, B. (Lab)	11,789	24.2	-12.3
Coleman, C. (Lib Dem)	10,676	21.9	4.8
Congdon, T. (UKIP)	2,522	5.2	2.8
Greenwood, J. (Green)	923	1.9	-0.2
Majority	11,064	22.69	
Electorate	68,419		
Turnout	48,763	71.27	

**Member of last parliament*

CONSTITUENCY SNAPSHOT

The coal mining which typified local industry in the Forest of Dean rendered it a Labour seat throughout most of the twentieth century. In fact, Labour held the seat almost continuously between 1918 and 1979.

The Labour vote in the Forest was eroded throughout the post-Second World War era, resulting a victory for the Conservative candidate Paul Marland in 1979.

Marland was re-elected in 1983 and 1987, but following boundary changes, the seat was won by Labour in 1997. However, Conservative candidate Mark Harper won the seat with a majority of 2,049. Harper increased his majority to 11,064 in 2010.

This constituency is the second largest in Gloucestershire, and is sparsely populated, but renowned for its picturesque scenery. The forest, its namesake, lies west of the river Severn, and is a National Forest Park.

For decades the economy in the Forest of Dean was driven by quarrying and mining. Some quarrying continues, but the last colliery closed in 1965.

The Forest is sharply differentiated from surrounding constituencies in Gloucestershire, where the economy is more reliant on IT and on the financial services, aerospace and engineering sectors. GlaxoSmithKline is the largest employer in the constituency.

Richard Harrington

Watford

Boundary changes

Tel: 020 7219 3000
E-mail: richard.harrington.mp@parliament.uk
Website: www.richardforwatford.com

Conservative

Date of birth: 4 November 1957

Education: Leeds Grammar School; Keble College, Oxford (law and jurisprudence 1979); Married Jessie 1983 (2 sons)

Non-political career: Assistant to managing director, Waitrose; Founder, now non-executive director, Harvington Properties 1983-; Managing director, then chairman, holiday resort company 1990-2000; Governor, University College School, Hampstead 2000-

Political career: Member for Watford since 6 May 2010 general election; Treasurer, Watford Conservative Party 2007-

Other organisations: Chair, executive board, Conservative Friends of Israel; Oriental club

Recreations: Cinema, watching football

Richard Harrington MP, House of Commons, London SW1A 0AA
Tel: 020 7219 3000 E-mail: richard.harrington.mp@parliament.uk
Constituency: 137 The Parade, High Street, Watford, Hertfordshire WD17 1NA Tel: 01923 296790
Website: www.richardforwatford.com

GENERAL ELECTION RESULT

		%
Harrington, R. (Con)	19,291	34.9
Brinton, S. (Lib Dem)	17,866	32.4
Ward, C. (Lab)*	14,750	26.7
Emerson, A. (BNP)	1,217	2.2
Eardley, G. (UKIP)	1,199	2.2
Brandon, I. (Green)	885	1.6
Majority	1,425	2.58
Electorate	80,798	
Turnout	55,208	68.33

**Member of last parliament*

CONSTITUENCY SNAPSHOT

At the 1997 general election, a swing of 12 per cent to Labour gained them the seat held by the Conservatives' Tristan Garel-Jones, MP since 1979. The victor Claire Ward maintained her majority in the general election of 2001 returning by a 5,555-vote margin.

However, in 2005 a 13 per cent swing to the Lib Dems brought the Party within 1,148 of winning. In 2010 Ward was defeated and Labour was returned in third place. The Conservative candidate, Richard Harrington secured a majority of 1,425.

Boundary changes were minimal. The seat lost its part of the Bedmond and Primrose Hill ward to St Albans.

Watford is largely an urban seat in the south-west corner of Hertfordshire, but it also includes the suburbs of Abbots Langley, Leavesden, Carpenders Park and Oxhey Hall. Over the years Watford's traditional industries of engineering, brewing and printing have declined. Of the three, only printing is still a substantial employer.

Traditional industries have been replaced by a booming service sector. The local authority is now the biggest employer locally, but an increasing number of large companies are establishing headquarters in the area.

Rebecca Harris

Castle Point

No boundary changes

Tel: 020 7219 3000
E-mail: rebecca.harris.mp@parliament.uk

Date of birth: 22 December 1967; Daughter of Philip and Louise Harris

Education: London School of Economics (BSc government); Married Frank Skelton 1999 (1 son)

Non-political career: Marketing director, Philimore and Co (publisher) 1997-2007; Campaign officer, Conservative Research Department; Special adviser to Tim Yeo MP 2003-; Chichester District Council: Councillor 1999-2003, Deputy chair, scrutiny committee 1999-2003

Political career: Member for Castle Point since 6 May 2010 general election; Campaign co-ordinator, Conservative Campaign HQ 2000-01; North West London area officer, Conservative Party 2007-08

Political interests: Small business, education and skills, planning

Other organisations: Hadleigh Conservative Club; Canvey Island Conservative Club; Benfleet Conservative Club

Recreations: Gardening, walking

Rebecca Harris MP, House of Commons, London SW1A 0AA
Tel: 020 7219 3000 E-mail: rebecca.harris.mp@parliament.uk
Constituency: c/o Castle Point Conservatives, Bernard Braine House, 8 Green Road, Benfleet, Essex SS7 5JT Tel: 01268 792992
Fax: 01268 792992 Website: www.castlepointconservatives.com

GENERAL ELECTION RESULT

		%	+/-
Harris, R. (Con)	19,806	44.0	-3.2
Spink, B. (Ind)*	12,174	27.0	
Ware-Lane, J. (Lab)	6,609	14.7	-15.0
D'Cruz, B. (Lib Dem)	4,232	9.4	-0.7
Howell, P. (BNP)	2,205	4.9	
Majority	7,632	16.95	
Electorate	67,284		
Turnout	45,026	66.92	

**Member of last parliament*

CONSTITUENCY SNAPSHOT

Castle Point, and its predecessor South East Essex, was represented by the Conservative Sir Bernard Braine for 37 years until his retirement in 1992. His successor Bob Spink secured a majority of over 16,800.

In 1997, however, Castle Point was witness to one of the biggest swings against a sitting MP, with a 17 per cent swing to Labour that allowed Christine Butler into parliament with a majority of 1,143.

Spink reclaimed the seat for the Tories in 2001 with a majority of 985. He increased the Tory majority to 8,201 in 2005 before resigning the Tory Whip in 2008 to sit as an independent. Rebecca Harris held the seat for the Conservatives with a 7,632 majority at the 2010 general election.

Situated on the coastline of south-east Essex on the Thames estuary, this seat takes its name from two of the most prominent landmarks in the constituency, Hadleigh Castle and Canvey Point.

Outside the four main settlements the metropolitan green belt covers around 85 per cent of the seat.

Castle Point is a largely residential constituency from which many commute to work. It has a high level of home ownership.

The borough's industrial estates require significant investment and the 2007-21 Sustainable Community Strategy targets specific industrial estates for regeneration.

Tom Harris

Glasgow South (returning MP)

No boundary changes

Tel: 020 7219 8237
E-mail: tomharrismp@parliament.uk
Website: www.tomharrismp.com

Date of birth: 20 February 1964; Son of Tom Harris, lorry/taxi driver, and Rita Harris, née Ralston, office clerk

Education: Garnock Academy, Kilbirnie, Ayrshire; Napier College, Edinburgh (HND journalism 1986); Married Carolyn Moffat 1998 (3 sons, 1 from previous marriage)

Non-political career: Trainee reporter *East Kilbride News* 1986-88; Reporter *Paisley Daily Express* 1988-90; Press officer: Scottish Labour Party 1990-92, Strathclyde Regional Council 1993-96; Senior media officer Glasgow City Council 1996; Public relations manager East Ayrshire Council 1996-98; Chief public relations and marketing officer Strathclyde Passenger Transport Executive 1998-2001; NUJ 1984-97; UNISON 1997-2004; AMICUS 2004-

Political career: Member for Glasgow Cathcart 2001-05, for Glasgow South since 5 May 2005 general election; PPS: to John Spellar as Minister of State, Northern Ireland Office 2003-05, to Patricia Hewitt as Secretary of State for Health 2005-06; Parliamentary Under-Secretary of State, Department for Transport 2006-08; *Select Committees:* Member: Science and Technology 2001-04; Member, Labour Friends of Israel

Political interests: Welfare reform, economy, foreign affairs, immigration and asylum, transport; USA, Israel, Iraq, Northern Ireland

Recreations: Astronomy, cinema, hillwalking

Tom Harris MP, House of Commons, London SW1A 0AA
Tel: 020 7219 8237 Fax: 020 7219 1769
E-mail: tomharrismp@parliament.uk
Constituency: c/o Queens Park Football Club, Somerville Drive, Mount Florida, Glasgow G42 9BA Tel: 0141-649 9780
Fax: 0141-636 9349 Website: www.tomharrismp.com

GENERAL ELECTION RESULT

		%	+/-
Harris, T. (Lab)*	20,736	51.7	4.6
Fleming, M. (SNP)	8,078	20.2	7.5
Mustapha, S. (Lib Dem)	4,739	11.8	-7.2
Rankin, D. (Con)	4,592	11.5	-1.1
Campbell, M. (Green)	961	2.4	-2.0
Coyle, M. (BNP)	637	1.6	
Smith, B. (Solidarity)	351	0.9	
Majority	12,658	31.57	
Electorate	65,029		
Turnout	40,094	61.66	

**Member of last parliament*

CONSTITUENCY SNAPSHOT

In 1979 Labour's John Maxton took the seat with a majority of 1,600. Tom Harris inherited Glasgow South in 2001 and increased his predecessor's percentage majority.

The seat was redrawn in 2005 and Glasgow South now contains the whole of the Cathcart division Maxwell Park, Langside and Pollokshaws from Glasgow Govan, and half of King's Park which was formerly in Glasgow Rutherglen. At the general election Harris held the seat with a 28 per cent majority over the Liberal Democrats. Tom Harris won another large majority of 12,658 with over 50 per cent of the vote.

This constituency contain a large proportion of Glasgow's city parks, particularly the Pollok County Park which is home to the internationally-renowned Burrell Collection and its custom-built museum.

Hampden Park, the national football stadium is here, surrounded by some of the constituency's leafier residential areas. Glasgow was awarded the 2014 Commonwealth Games in November 2007 and Hampden Park will host the closing ceremony as well as all track and field events.

It contains the estate of Castlemilk, once the largest council house estate in Europe, and a strong contrast to the more prosperous residential areas of Cathcart south of the Clyde.

Simon Hart

Carmarthen West and South Pembrokeshire

Boundary changes

Tel: 020 7219 3000
E-mail: simon.hart.mp@parliament.uk
Website: www.simon-hart.com

Conservative

Date of birth: 15 August 1963

Education: Radley College, Oxfordshire; Royal Agriculture College, Cirencester (Diploma rural estate management 1984); Married Abigail Holland 1998 (1 son 1 daughter)

Non-political career: Territorial Army; Chartered surveyor, Knight, Frank & Rutley 1986-88; Associated to sole principal, Llewellyn Humphreys 1988-98; Associate land agent, Balfour, Burd & Benson 1998-99; Countryside Alliance 1999-: Campaigns director 1999-2003, Chief executive 2003-; Governor, Tavernspite CP School

Political career: Member for Carmarthen West and South Pembrokeshire since 6 May 2010 general election

Political interests: Rural affairs, small business

Other organisations: Member, Liberty; Farmers Club; Cresselly Cricket Club

Recreations: Crickets, all aspects of country sports

Simon Hart MP, House of Commons, London SW1A 0AA
Tel: 020 7219 3000 E-mail: simon.hart.mp@parliament.uk
Constituency: Town Moor, Moorfield Road, Narberth, Pembrokeshire SA67 7AG Tel: 01834 860102
Website: www.simon-hart.com

GENERAL ELECTION RESULT

		%
Hart, S. (Con)	16,649	41.1
Ainger, N. (Lab)*	13,226	32.7
Gossage, J. (Lib Dem)	4,890	12.1
Dixon, J. (PIC)	4,232	10.5
Clarke, R. (UKIP)	1,146	2.8
Langen, H. (Ind)	364	0.9
Majority	3,423	8.45
Electorate	57,519	
Turnout	40,507	70.42

**Member of last parliament*

CONSTITUENCY SNAPSHOT

Labour's Nick Ainger was first elected in 1992 to serve as the MP for Pembroke. With the creation in 1997 of the new constituency, Carmarthen West and South Pembrokeshire, he became the MP for this revised seat, with a majority of 9,621. In the partial Tory recovery in Wales at the 2005 general election they reduced Nick Ainger's majority to 1,910. The Tories' Simon Hart defeated Nick Ainger to win a 3,423 majority in this key target seat.

Minor changes brought the remainder of the Cynwyl Elfed electoral division into this seat from Carnarthen East and Dinefwr, while the small part of Maenclochog that was in this seat moved to Preseli Pembrokeshire.

As well as most of Carmarthen, this seat contains part of Pembrokeshire Coast National Park; coastal resorts such as Tenby and towns Pembroke and Pembroke Dock.

With coastal towns and countryside, it is a natural retirement area and there are a large number of pensioners.

Poet Dylan Thomas lived in Laugharne in the years leading up to his death. Welsh language culture is important as the number of Welsh speakers in the constituency is higher than average with almost a third of the population being able to speak Welsh.

Nick Harvey

North Devon ***(returning MP)***

Boundary changes

Tel: 020 7219 6232
E-mail: yorkec@parliament.uk
Website: www.nickharveymp.com

Date of birth: 3 August 1961; Son of Frederick Harvey, civil servant, and Christine Harvey, teacher

Education: Queen's College, Taunton; Middlesex Polytechnic (BA business studies 1983); Married Kate Fox 2003 (1 daughter 1 son)

Non-political career: President Middlesex Polytechnic Students' Union 1981-82; Communications and marketing executive: Profile PR Ltd 1984-86, Dewe Rogerson Ltd 1986-91; Communications Consultant 1991-; Former member NUJ

Political career: Contested Enfield Southgate (Liberal/Alliance) 1987 general election. Member for North Devon 1992-2010, for North Devon (revised boundary) since 6 May 2010 general election; Liberal Democrat Spokesperson for: Transport 1992-94, Trade and Industry 1994-97, Constitution (English Regions) 1997-99; Principal Spokesperson for: Health 1999-2001, Culture, Media and Sport 2001-03; Member and Spokesperson House of Commons Commission 2005-; Liberal Democrat Shadow Secretary of State for Defence 2006-10; Member, Speaker's Committee for the Independent Parliamentary Standards Authority 2009-; Minister of State for the Armed Forces 2010-; *Select Committees:* Member: Trade and Industry 1994-95, European Scrutiny 2004-05, Home Affairs 2005-06, Standards and Privileges 2005-10; National vice-chair Union of Liberal Students 1981-82; Chair: Candidates Committee 1993-98, Campaigns and Communications 1994-99

Political interests: Economics, European Union

Other organisations: Vice-President, Federation of Economic Development Authorities (FEDA) 2000-; UK member: Council of Europe 2005-07, Western European Union 2005-07; Honorary Doctorate, Middlesex University 2000

Recreations: Travel, football, walking, music

Nick Harvey MP, House of Commons, London SW1A 0AA
Tel: 020 7219 6232 Fax: 020 7219 2683
E-mail: yorkec@parliament.uk
Constituency: The Castle Centre, Barnstaple, Devon EX31 1DR
Tel: 01271 328631 Fax: 01271 345664
Website: www.nickharveymp.com

GENERAL ELECTION RESULT

		%
Harvey, N. (Lib Dem)*	24,305	47.4
Milton, P. (Con)	18,484	36.0
Crowther, S. (UKIP)	3,720	7.3
Cann, M. (Lab)	2,671	5.2
Knight, L. (Green)	697	1.4
Marshall, G. (BNP)	614	1.2
Cann, R. (Ind)	588	1.2
Vidler, N. (England)	146	0.3
Sables, G. (Comm GB)	96	0.2
Majority	5,821	11.34
Electorate	74,508	
Turnout	51,321	68.88

**Member of last parliament*

CONSTITUENCY SNAPSHOT

Since the Second World War, the seat has been split fairly evenly between the Liberals and the Tories. North Devon has been held by the present incumbent, Lib Dem MP Nick Harvey, since 1992. The Liberal Jeremy Thorpe held the seat for 20 years between 1959 and 1979 with all years before and after having been Tory.

The Liberal Democrats held this seat in the 2001 general election with a reduced majority of 2,984. In 2005 Nick Harvey was able to increasing his majority to 4,972. Harvey increased his majority slightly in 2010 to 5,821.

Taw, and Taw Vale wards Sandford and Creedy partward moved to the new Central Devon constituency.

The constituency has a thriving tourist industry in the coastal towns such as Ilfracombe, Woolacombe and Braunton, but further inland towns such as Barnstaple and South Molton are dependent on light manufacturing and the retail sector.

Transport is a major issue here. Problems range from the inadequacies of the national rail network to the road congestion in tourist resorts. There is no direct rail access, only infrequent buses, giving the area a sense of extreme remoteness.

Rt Hon Sir **Alan Haselhurst**

Saffron Walden (returning MP)

Boundary changes

Tel: 020 7219 5214
E-mail: haselhursta@parliament.uk
Website: www.siralanhaselhurst.net

Conservative

Date of birth: 23 June 1937; Son of late John Haselhurst and Alice, née Barraclough

Education: King Edward VI School, Birmingham; Cheltenham College; Oriel College, Oxford; Married Angela Margaret Bailey 1977 (2 sons 1 daughter)

Non-political career: Secretary, Treasurer, Librarian, Oxford Union Society 1959-60; Executive chemicals and plastics industry 1960-70; Public affairs consultant 1974-97

Political career: Member for Middleton and Prestwich 1970-February 1974, for Saffron Walden 7 July 1977 by-election to 2010, for Saffron Walden (revised boundary) since 6 May 2010 general election; PPS to Mark Carlisle as Secretary of State, Education and Science 1979-81; Chairman Ways and Means and Deputy Speaker 1997-; *Select Committees:* Ex officio chair: Chairmen's Panel 1997-2010; Ex officio member: Court of Referees 1997-2010, Standing Orders 1998-2010, Unopposed Bills (Panel) 2000-10; Member: Finance and Services 2008-10; President, Oxford University Conservative Association 1958; National Chair, Young Conservative Movement 1966-68; Deputy Chair, Conservative Group for Europe 1982-85

Political interests: Education, aerospace, aviation, youth affairs, European Union, agriculture, community development; USA, South Africa, Australia

Other organisations: Chair, Commonwealth Youth Exchange Council 1978-81; Fellow Industry and Parliament Trust 1982; Chair of Trustees, Community Projects Foundation 1986-97; Knighted 1995; PC 1999; MCC; Essex County Cricket Club, Executive Committee Member 1996-; *Publications:* Occasionally Cricket (Queen Anne Press, 1999); Eventually Cricket (Queen Anne Press, 2001); Incidentally Cricket (Queen Anne Press, 2003); Accidentally Cricket (Professional and Higher Partnership, 2009)

Recreations: Hi-fi, watching cricket, gardening

Rt Hon Sir Alan Haselhurst MP, House of Commons, London SW1A 0AA Tel: 020 7219 5214 Fax: 020 7219 5600
E-mail: haselhursta@parliament.uk
Constituency: The Old Armoury, Saffron Walden, Essex CB10 1JN
Tel: 01799 506349 Fax: 01799 506047
Website: www.siralanhaselhurst.net

GENERAL ELECTION RESULT

		%
Haselhurst, A. (Con)*	30,155	55.4
Wilcock, P. (Lib Dem)	14,913	27.4
Light, B. (Lab)	5,288	9.7
Lord, R. (UKIP)	2,288	4.2
Mitchell, C. (BNP)	1,050	1.9
Hossain, R. (Green)	735	1.4
Majority	15,242	28.00
Electorate	76,035	
Turnout	54,429	71.58

**Member of last parliament*

CONSTITUENCY SNAPSHOT

This constituency is Conservative territory and one of the few areas where they still command five-figure majorities. Sir Alan Haselhurst has been the MP since 1977.

In the four general elections between 1979 and 1992 Sir Alan polled over 50 per cent of the vote, and increased his majority in the last two to 17,424 votes.

In 2005 the Conservative share of the vote was back to an overall majority over all the other parties at 51 per cent and a majority of 13,008 over the Liberal Democrats. Haselhurst was re-elected in 2010 with a 3.4 per cent swing from the Lib Dems.

The seat gained four wards from West Chelmsford while losing ten wards or part-wards to Braintree.

The constituency of Saffron Walden in Essex is extremely rural and agricultural. The only towns are small, including Saffron Walden itself, plus Great Dunmow, Stansted Mountfitchet and Thaxted.

Saffron Walden is a well-preserved medieval market town. Agriculture and tourism are important industries, but with some jobs in manufacturing and services Stansted airport is the largest employer.

The constituency has important transport links. The M11 motorway runs from north to south at its western end, almost parallel with the mainline railway. The A120 runs from west to east.

Dai Havard

Merthyr Tydfil and Rhymney ***(returning MP)***

Boundary changes

Tel: 020 7219 8255
E-mail: havardd@parliament.uk
Website: www.epolitix.com/Dai-Havard

Date of birth: 7 February 1950; Son of late Eileen, shop worker, and Ted Havard, miner

Education: Secondary modern school, Treharris; Grammar Technical, Quakers Yard, Edwardsville; Comprehensive school, Afon Taf; St Peter's College, Birmingham (Certificate in Education); Warwick University (MA industrial relations); Married Julia Watts 1986 (separated)

Non-political career: MSF full time officer: Studies tutor 1971-75, Researcher 1975-79, Education 1975-82, Official 1989-, Delegation leader: Wales Labour Party, Conferences; Wales secretary; AMICUS

Political career: Member for Merthyr Tydfil and Rhymney 2001-10, for Merthyr Tydfil and Rhymney (revised boundary) since 6 May 2010 general election; *Select Committees:* Member: European Standing Committee C, Regulatory Reform 2001-05, Defence 2003-10; Wales Labour Party Joint Policy Committee

Political interests: Education, lifelong learning, health, cancer and blood, industrial relations and working conditions; *Publications:* Contributor to academic publications on trade union and economic development

Recreations: Hillwalking, horse riding, birdwatching, Commons and Lords Rugby team

Dai Havard MP, House of Commons, London SW1A 0AA
Tel: 020 7219 8255 Fax: 020 7219 1449
E-mail: havardd@parliament.uk
Constituency: Unit 4, Triangle Business Park, Pentrebach, Merthyr Tydfil, Mid Glamorgan CF48 4TQ Tel: 01685 379247
Fax: 01685 387563 Website: www.epolitix.com/Dai-Havard

GENERAL ELECTION RESULT

		%
Havard, D. (Lab)*	14,007	43.7
Kitcher, A. (Lib Dem)	9,951	31.0
Hill, M. (Con)	2,412	7.5
Tovey, C. (Ind)	1,845	5.8
Jones, G. (PIC)	1,621	5.1
Barnes, R. (BNP)	1,173	3.7
Brown, A. (UKIP)	872	2.7
Cowdell, A. (SLP)	195	0.6
Majority	4,056	12.64
Electorate	54,715	
Turnout	32,076	58.62

*Member of last parliament

CONSTITUENCY SNAPSHOT

This seat and its predecessors have a long Labour history, going back to the election of Keir Hardie in 1900.

The boundaries were revised in 1983 and created Merthyr Tydfil and Rhymney, largely from the old Merthyr Tydfil seat. Ted Rowlands represented the new seat from its creation until he retired in 2001. Dai Havard replaced Rowlands and won with a majority of 14,923.

In 2005 Havard's majority was reduced slightly to 13,934. Havard was returned with a 4,056-vote lead in 2010 following a 16.9 per cent swing to the Liberal Democrats.

Boundary changes to the seat are minimal. Sirhowy ward was split between Merthyr Tydfil and Rhymney and Blaenau Gwent, but the part within this seat was small and had no voters. The ward is now entirely within Blaenau Gwent.

The constituency boundaries run south from the Brecon Beacons national park through the Taff valley and takes in parts of the Rhymney Valley in South Wales.

Merthyr was one of the birthplaces of the industrial revolution. Its iron works was once the world's largest and it had a steam railway before Stockton and Darlington.

Merthyr itself has shrunk significantly since its 19th century heyday.

There has been some success in replacing job following the closure of the mining and heavy industry but the area's biggest employer, the Hoover factory closed in 2009.

John Hayes

South Holland and The Deepings ***(returning MP)***

Boundary changes

Tel: 020 7219 1389
E-mail: hayesj@parliament.uk

Date of birth: 23 June 1958; Son of late Henry John and Lily Hayes

Education: Colfe's Grammar School, London; Nottingham University (BA politics 1980, PGCE history/English 1982); Married Susan Hopewell 1997 (2 sons)

Non-political career: Data Base Ltd IT company 1983-99: Director 1986-97, Non-executive director 1997-99; Associate professor American University in London; Councillor, Nottinghamshire County Council 1985-98

Political career: Contested Derbyshire North East 1987 and 1992 general elections. Member for South Holland and The Deepings 1997-2010, for South Holland and The Deepings (revised boundary) since 6 May 2010 general election; Shadow Minister for Schools 2000-01; Opposition Pairing Whip 2001-02; Shadow Minister for: Agriculture, Fisheries and Food 2002-03, Local and Devolved Government (Housing and Planning) 2003-05, Transport 2005, Vocational Education 2005-09, Lifelong Learning, Further and Higher Education 2009, Universities and Skills 2009-10; Minister of State for Further Education, Skills and Lifelong Learning, Department for Business, Innovation and Skills 2010-; *Select Committees:* Member: Agriculture 1997-99, Education and Employment 1998-99, Education and Employment 1999-2000, Education and Employment (Education Sub-Committee) 1999-2000, Selection 2001-02, Administration 2001-02; Former chair Young Conservatives; Vice-chair Conservatives Against Federal Europe; Vice-chair Conservative Party 1999-2000; Member 1992 Group; Joint chair Cornerstone Group 2004-

Political interests: Education, elections and campaigning, political ideas and philosophy, local government, agriculture, commerce and industry, welfare of the elderly and disabled, disability; England, Italy, Spain, USA

Other organisations: Countryside Member NFU; Countryside Alliance, SPUC; Patron, Headway Cambridgeshire; Carlton, Spalding; *Publications:* Representing Rural Britain – Blair's Bogus Claim (Conservative Policy Forum 2000); Answer the Question: Prime Ministerial Accountability and the Rule of Parliament (Politica 2000); Tony B. Liar (Conservative Party 2001); The Right to Own: Conservative Action on Housing (Conservative Party 2004); The Right Homes in the Right Places (Conservative Party 2005); Being Conservative: A Cornerstone of Policies to Revive Tory Britain (Cornerstone Group 2005); Towards a Virtuous Circle of Learning (NIACE 2006); Towards a Gold Standard for Craft, Guaranteeing Professional Apprenticeships (Centre for Policy Studies 2007); From Social Engineering to Social Aspiration: Strategies to Broaden Access to Higher Education (UALL/Birkbeck 2008)

Recreations: The arts (particularly English painting, poetry and prose), good food and wine, many sports (including darts), studying history, gardening, making jam, antiques, architecture and aesthetics

John Hayes MP, House of Commons, London SW1A 0AA
Tel: 020 7219 1389 Fax: 020 7219 2273
E-mail: hayesj@parliament.uk
Constituency: 20 Station Street, Spalding, Lincolnshire PE11 1EB
Tel: 01775 711534 Fax: 01775 713905

GENERAL ELECTION RESULT

		%
Hayes, J. (Con)*	29,639	59.1
Conroy, J. (Lib Dem)	7,759	15.5
Gould, G. (Lab)	7,024	14.0
Fairman, R. (UKIP)	3,246	6.5
Harban, R. (BNP)	1,796	3.6
Baxter, A. (Green)	724	1.4
Majority	21,880	43.60
Electorate	76,243	
Turnout	50,188	65.83

**Member of last parliament*

CONSTITUENCY SNAPSHOT

The seat was created in 1997 from some of the most rural parts of two strongly Conservative seats, Stamford and Spalding and Holland-with-Boston. The notional Conservative majority for John Hayes in the new seat was nearly 17,000, but a drop in turnout and an 8.5 per cent swing to Labour reduced it to 7,991.

Haye's majority has since recovered and was a safe 15,780 in 2005. In 2010 Hayes held the seat with an increased majority of 21,880.

Boundary changes were minimal.

This flat, largely fenland constituency is the twelfth most rural in Great Britain. Nearly an eighth of the working population are engaged in agriculture and horticulture, the third highest figure in England. The other main industries are agriculturally related: food-processing and road haulage.

The main town, Spalding is the centre of a major region of flower and vegetable growth. Many vegetables are sold to large companies, with little being available for sale locally.

At the western end of the constituency the communities of Market Deeping, West Deeping, and Deeping St James in the South Kesteven district have been growing fast, now surrounded by new housing, and home to many people who commute to work in Peterborough.

Oliver Heald

North East Hertfordshire ***(returning MP)***

Boundary changes

Tel: 020 7219 6354
E-mail: healdo@parliament.uk
Website: www.oliverhealdmp.com

Date of birth: 15 December 1954; Son of late J A Heald, chartered engineer and Joyce, neé Pemberton, teacher

Education: Reading School; Pembroke College, Cambridge (MA law 1976); Married Christine Whittle 1979 (1 son 2 daughters)

Non-political career: Barrister, Middle Temple 1977-; Member, Committee on Standards in Public Life 2008-

Political career: Contested Southwark and Bermondsey 1987 general election. Member for North Hertfordshire 1992-97, for North East Hertfordshire 1997-2010, for North East Hertfordshire (revised boundary) since 6 May 2010 general election; PPS: to Sir Peter Lloyd as Minister of State, Home Office 1994, to William Waldegrave as Minister of Agriculture, Fisheries and Food 1994-95; Sponsored Private Member's Bill: Insurance Companies (Reserves) Act 1995; Parliamentary Under-Secretary of State, Department of Social Security 1995-97; Opposition Whip 1997-2000; Opposition Spokesperson for: Home Affairs 2000-01, Health 2001-02; Shadow: Minister for Work and Pensions 2002-03, Leader of the House 2003-05; Member House of Commons' Commission 2003-05; Shadow: Secretary of State for Constitutional Affairs 2004-07, Chancellor of the Duchy of Lancaster 2005-07; *Select Committees:* Member: Administration 1998-2000, Modernisation of the House of Commons 2003-05, Work and Pensions 2007-10, Selection 2009-10; Chair North Hertfordshire Conservative Association 1984-86; Southwark and Bermondsey Conservative Association: President 1993-98, Patron 1998-

Political interests: Industrial relations, environment, law and order, pensions; *Publications:* Co-author Auditing the New Deal: What Figures for the Future (Politeia, 2004)

Recreations: Sport, family

Oliver Heald MP, House of Commons, London SW1A 0AA
Tel: 020 7219 6354 Fax: 020 7219 4478
E-mail: healdo@parliament.uk
Constituency: No constituency office publicised Tel: 01763 247640
Fax: 01763 247640 Website: www.oliverhealdmp.com

GENERAL ELECTION RESULT

		%
Heald, O. (Con)*	26,995	53.5
Annand, H. (Lib Dem)	11,801	23.4
Kirkman, D. (Lab)	8,291	16.4
Smyth, A. (UKIP)	2,075	4.1
Bland, R. (Green)	875	1.7
Campbell, R. (Ind)	209	0.4
Ralph, D. (YRDPL)	143	0.3
Reichardt, P. (Ind)	36	0.1
Majority	15,194	30.13
Electorate	72,200	
Turnout	50,425	69.84

**Member of last parliament*

CONSTITUENCY SNAPSHOT

In 1997 Tory Oliver Heald's vote-share fell by 10 per cent, and a majority of over 14,000 was cut to just over 3,000.

In 2005 there was a return to voting normality in North East Hertfordshire with the Conservatives winning again with a majority approaching five figures. Support for Oliver Heald increased by 3.2 per cent, while the Labour vote fell away. In 2010 the seat was held by Heald with a 15,194 majority.

The seat lost its part of the Graveley and Wymondley ward to Hitchin and Harpenden. It gained the rest of Hertford Rural South ward from Hertford and Stortford; Walkern from Stevenage; and Letchworth Wilbury from Hitchin and Harpenden.

The constituency contains Letchworth, the first Garden City and, less famously, Baldock, Royston and Puckeridge.

The constituency is a mixture of small- to medium-sized research-based technology companies, light engineering and agriculture. The largest employer is Johnson Matthey, the precious metals and autocatalyst group.

Agriculture is primarily arable, although there are sheep breeders to the south of the constituency, as well as some dairy and pig farming.

Rt Hon **John Healey**

Wentworth and Dearne ***(returning MP)***

New constituency

Tel: 020 7219 6359
E-mail: healeyj@parliament.uk
Website: www.johnhealeymp.co.uk

Date of birth: 13 February 1960; Son of Aidan Healey, prison service, and Jean Healey, teacher

Education: Lady Lumley's Comprehensive School, Pickering; St Peter's School, York; Christ's College, Cambridge (Scholar; BA 1982); Married Jackie Bate 1993 (1 son)

Non-political career: Journalist/deputy editor *House Magazine* 1983-84; Disability campaigner for three national charities 1984-90; Tutor Open University Business School 1989-92; Campaigns manager Issue Communications 1990-92; Head of communications MSF Union 1992-94; Campaigns and communications director TUC 1994-97; Member, GMB

Political career: Contested Ryedale 1992 general election. Member for Wentworth 1997-2010, for Wentworth and Dearne since 6 May 2010 general election; PPS to Gordon Brown as Chancellor of the Exchequer 1999-2001; Parliamentary Under-Secretary of State, Department for Education and Skills (Adult Skills) 2001-02; HM Treasury 2002-07: Economic Secretary 2002-05, Financial Secretary 2005-07; Minister of State, Department for Communities and Local Government 2007-10: Minister for Local Government 2007-09, Minister for Housing (attending Cabinet) 2009-10; Shadow Minister for Housing 2010-; *Select Committees:* Member: Education and Employment 1997-99, Education and Employment (Employment Sub-Committee) 1997-99, Public Accounts 2005-07, Joint Committee on Tax Law Rewrite Bills 2005-09

Political interests: Employment, trade unions, economic regeneration, industrial relations, disability, local and regional government

Other organisations: Member Speaker's Committee on the Electoral Commission -2009; PC 2008

Recreations: Family

Rt Hon John Healey MP, House of Commons, London SW1A 0AA
Tel: 020 7219 6359 Fax: 020 7219 2451
E-mail: healeyj@parliament.uk
Constituency: 79 High Street, Wath upon Dearne, Rotherham, South Yorkshire S63 7QB Tel: 01709 875943 Fax: 01709 874207
Website: www.johnhealeymp.co.uk

GENERAL ELECTION RESULT

		%
Healey, J. (Lab)*	21,316	50.6
Donelan, M. (Con)	7,396	17.6
Love, N. (Lib Dem)	6,787	16.1
Wilkinson, J. (UKIP)	3,418	8.1
Baldwin, G. (BNP)	3,189	7.6
Majority	13,920	33.06
Electorate	72,586	
Turnout	42,106	58.01

**Member of last parliament*

CONSTITUENCY SNAPSHOT

The new seat of Wentworth and Dearne extends beyond the Borough of Rotherham into the east of Barnsley, including the Dearne wards from Barnsley East and Mexborough, the wards of Rawmarsh and Silverwood.

Wentworth constituency was created in 1983 combining Dearne Valley and Rother Valley. Its first MP Peter Hardy was the former Member for Rother Valley. In 1987 Hardy's majority topped the 20,000 mark, and went even higher in 1992.

Hardy retired in 1997 and John Healey secured the Labour candidacy and won a majority of nearly 24,000. Small swings to the Tories in 2001 and 2005 reduced his majority to a still very large 15,056.

Healey won the new seat in 2010 with a majority of 13,920.

The seat mainly consists of small town mining communities in the South Yorkshire valleys.The area's economy was affected by the pit closures in the 1980s and 1990s. It was the impending closure of Cortonwood colliery near Brampton which helped spark off the miners' strike of 1984/85.Many people still work in manufacturing. The new growth industries are customer services or call-centres based in the Dearne Valley Enterprise Zone.

Regeneration projects have included a large business park on the site of the former Manvers colliery and the Dearne Valley Parkway.

David Heath

Somerton and Frome *(returning MP)*

Boundary changes

Tel: 020 7219 6245
E-mail: heathd@parliament.uk
Website: www.davidheath.co.uk

Date of birth: 16 March 1954; Son of Eric and Pamela Heath

Education: Millfield School, Street; St John's College, Oxford (MA physiological sciences 1976); City University, London (ophthalmic optics 1979); Married Caroline Netherton 1987 (1 son 1 daughter)

Non-political career: Qualified optician in practice 1979-85; Parliamentary consultant Worldwide Fund for Nature 1990-91; Consultant to various NGOs/charities; Member Audit Commission 1994-97; Somerset County Council: Councillor 1985-97, Council Leader 1985-89; Chairman, Avon and Somerset Police Authority 1993-96

Political career: Contested Somerton and Frome 1992 general election. Member for Somerton and Frome 1997-2010, for Somerton and Frome (revised boundary) since 6 May 2010 general election; Liberal Democrat: Spokesperson for: Foreign Affairs 1997-99, Agriculture, Rural Affairs and Fisheries 1999-2001, Work and Pensions 2001-02, Science 2001-03, Lord Chancellor's Department/Department for Constitutional Affairs 2002-06, Home Office 2002-05, Science 2004, Shadow Leader of the House 2005-07, Spokesperson for Cabinet Office 2006-07, Shadow: Secretary of State for Justice and Lord Chancellor 2007-08, Leader of the House of Commons 2009-10; Parliamentary Secretary (Deputy Leader of the House of Commons) 2010-; *Select Committees:* Member: Foreign Affairs 1997-99, Foreign Affairs 1997-98, Standards and Privileges 2001-05, Science and Technology 2001-03, Modernisation of the House of Commons 2005-06, Court of Referees 2007-10, Justice 2008-10; Member: Liberal Party National Executive 1988-89, Liberal Democrats Federal Executive 1990-92, 1993-95; Chair Liberal Democrat Commission on Privacy 2008-

Political interests: Education, local and regional government, rural affairs, environment, home affairs, constitutional affairs; Balkans, Europe, France, USA

Other organisations: Member, Witham Friary Friendly Society; Vice-chair: Association of County Councils 1994-97, Committee of Local Police Authorities 1993-97; Member Academic Council of Wilton Park 2002-; Member: Council of Local Authorities and Regions of Europe 1993-97, Parliamentary Assembly of the Organisation for Security and Co-operation in Europe (OSCE) 1997-; CBE 1989; FADO; Hon Fellow College of Optometrists; National Liberal

Recreations: Cricket, rugby football, until recently pig breeding

David Heath CBE MP, House of Commons, London SW1A 0AA
Tel: 020 7219 6245 Fax: 020 7219 5939
E-mail: heathd@parliament.uk
Constituency: 14 Catherine Hill, Frome, Somerset BA11 1BZ
Tel: 01373 473618 Fax: 01373 455152
Website: www.davidheath.co.uk

GENERAL ELECTION RESULT

		%
Heath, D. (Lib Dem)*	28,793	47.5
Rees-Mogg, A. (Con)	26,976	44.5
Oakensen, D. (Lab)	2,675	4.4
Harding, B. (UKIP)	1,932	3.2
Warry, N. (Ind)	236	0.4
Majority	1,817	3.00
Electorate	81,548	
Turnout	60,612	74.33

**Member of last parliament*

CONSTITUENCY SNAPSHOT

The seat was created in 1983, but its precursor was a strong Conservative seat and in 1983 Somerton and Frome elected a Conservative MP with a majority of over 9,000. However, after that the Conservatives came under pressure from the Liberal Democrats. The party's David Heath took the seat in 1997 with a majority of just 130. Heath's 2005 majority had increased but was just 812 votes. Heath increased his lead to a still marginal 1,817 in 2010.

Boundary changes moved two part-wards into the seat from both Yeovil and Wells in return fro losing one part-ward to each of them.

Somerton and Frome is one of the largest rural constituencies in England, covering almost 900 square miles. It borders Wiltshire to the east, Bath and north-east Somerset to the north and Dorset to the south.

The constituency is a predominantly agricultural one, although the countryside does provide opportunities for tourism. Frome is the major industrial centre, and is home to a number of agricultural processing industries, such as cheese and milk production.

The Royal Naval Air Station, Yeovilton, is also situated in the constituency. A large multi-role air base, it is home to the Royal Navy Sea Harriers, Support Helicopter Force and Commando Helicopter Force and is a significant local employer.

Christopher Heaton-Harris

Daventry

Boundary changes

Tel: 020 7219 3000
Website: www.heatonharris.org.uk

Conservative

Date of birth: 28 November 1967

Education: Tiffin Grammar School for Boys, Kingston-upon-Thames, Surrey; Wolverhampton Polytechnic; Married Jayne Yvonne Carlow 1990 (2 daughters)

Non-political career: Various positions, What 4 Ltd (wholesale fresh produce company) 1989-99; Fleishman-Hillard 2009-10

Political career: Contested Leicester South 1997 general election and 2004 by-election. Member for Daventry since 6 May 2010 general election; MEP for East Midlands 1999-2009: Founder member, Campaign for Parliamentary Reform 2001; Chief Whip, EP Conservatives 2001-04; Member: Budgetary Control Committee 1999-2004, Delegation for relations with the NATO Parliamentary Assembly 2002-09, Central America Delegation 2004-09; Internal Market and Consumer Protection Committee 2004-07, 2008-09, Culture and Education Committee 2007-09

Political interests: Economic policy, campaign strategy, defence, education, youth policy

Recreations: Football referee, sport

Christopher Heaton-Harris MP, House of Commons, London SW1A 0AA Tel: 020 7219 3000
Constituency: Boswell House, 9 Prospect Court, Blisworth, Northamptonshire NN7 3DG Tel: 01604 859721 Fax: 01604 859329
E-mail: chris@heatonharris.com Website: www.heatonharris.org.uk

GENERAL ELECTION RESULT

		%
Heaton-Harris, C. (Con)	29,252	56.5
McGlynn, C. (Lib Dem)	10,064	19.4
Corazzo, P. (Lab)	8,168	15.8
Broomfield, J. (UKIP)	2,333	4.5
Bennett-Spencer, A. (England)	1,187	2.3
Whiffen, S. (Green)	770	1.5
Majority	19,188	37.06
Electorate	71,451	
Turnout	51,774	72.46

CONSTITUENCY SNAPSHOT

Daventry has a long Conservative history. Tim Boswell was first elected in 1987. He suffered a huge drop in his majority in 1997 but it recovered by over 2,000 votes in 2001 to 9,649.

In 2005 the Tories pushed further into the lead with a majority of 14,686. Boswell retired in 2010 and Chris Heaton-Harris held the seat for the Conservatives with a 19,188 majority.

The seat lost nineteen wards and five of its southern part-wards to South Northamptonshire. The seat now spreads further north-east, with seven wards and two part-ward gained from Kettering, two part-wards from Northampton South, and two wards from Wellingborough.

The seat comprises elegant villages, only a handful of towns and large tracts of rural heartland. The town of Daventry has expanded rapidly over the past decade or so, building on its well-placed location between Northampton and Rugby and its good transport links to London.

The seat enjoys a strong and extremely varied employment base, with agriculture and rural industries, leisure and tourism, warehousing and distribution and light engineering all employing a sizeable proportion of the working population.

John Hemming

Birmingham, Yardley ***(returning MP)***

Boundary changes

Tel: 020 7219 4345
E-mail: hemmingj@parliament.uk
Website: john.hemming.name

Date of birth: 16 March 1960; Son of Melvin John and Doreen Hemming

Education: King Edward's School, Birmingham; Magdalen College, Oxford (BA atomic, nuclear and theoretical physics 1981, MA); Married Christine Margaret Richards 1981 (2 daughters 1 son); partner Emily Cox (1 daughter)

Non-political career: Founder and senior partner, John Hemming and Company 1983; Founder: Marketnet 1994, Music Mercia International 1997; Member, Musicians' Union 1997; Birmingham City Council: Councillor 1990-, Deputy leader 2004-05, Liberal Democrat Group leader 2004-

Political career: Contested Birmingham Hall Green 1983, Birmingham Small Heath 1987, Birmingham Yardley 1992, 1997 and 2001 general elections. Member for Birmingham Yardley 2005-10, for Birmingham, Yardley (revised boundary) since 6 May 2010 general election; *Select Committees:* Member: Regulatory Reform 2005-10, Procedure 2006-10, Joint Committee on the Draft Legal Services Bill 2006, Modernisation of the House of Commons 2008-10

Political interests: Energy, family policy, law and order, health

Recreations: Jazz piano

John Hemming MP, House of Commons, London SW1A 0AA
Tel: 020 7219 4345 Fax: 020 7219 0152
E-mail: hemmingj@parliament.uk
Constituency: 1772 Coventry Road, Birmingham B26 1PB
Tel: 0121-722 3417 Fax: 0121-722 3437
Website: john.hemming.name

GENERAL ELECTION RESULT

		%
Hemming, J. (Lib Dem)*	16,162	39.6
Kelly, L. (Lab)	13,160	32.2
Jenkins, M. (Con)	7,836	19.2
Lumby, T. (BNP)	2,153	5.3
Duffen, G. (UKIP)	1,190	2.9
Morris, P. (NF)	349	0.9
Majority	3,002	7.35
Electorate	72,321	
Turnout	40,850	56.48

**Member of last parliament*

CONSTITUENCY SNAPSHOT

Yardley was traditionally a Conservative/Labour marginal for most of the post-war period. Labour's Estelle Morris beat David Bevan in 1992 by 162 votes. In 1997 Morris extended her majority by over 5,000 votes. However, by 2001 the contest was firmly between the Liberal Democrats and Labour. Morris retained her seat, albeit with a reduced majority.

Estelle Morris retired in 2005 general election and John Hemming won the seat for the Lib Dems with a majority of 2,672. Hemming was re-elected in 2010 securing a majority of 3,002.

The seat has gained part-wards from Birmingham Sparkbrook and Small Heath (Acocks Green and South Yardley) and Birmingham Hodge Hill (Stechford and Yardley North).

Suburban Birmingham Yardley is free from the inner-city characteristics found in many of Birmingham's other constituencies.

There is a preponderance of manual labour and few white-collar jobs. The constituency's largest area of employment is public administration, education and health. Manufacturing and construction are also important.

Gordon Henderson

Sittingbourne and Sheppey

Boundary changes

Tel: 020 7219 3000
E-mail: gordon.henderson.mp@parliament.uk

Conservative

Date of birth: 27 January 1948

Education: Fort Luton; Rochester Mathematical School; Married Louise Crowder 1994 (1 son 2 daughters)

Non-political career: Manager, Woolworths 1964-79; Self-employed restaurateur 1979-83; Senior contracts officer, GEC Marconi Avionics 1983-93; Operations manager, Beams UK 1993-2007; Management consultant 2008-; Deputy leader Conservative Group, Swale Borough Council 1986-90, 1991-95; Member, Kent Police Authority 1989-93; Councillor, Kent County Council 1989-93

Political career: Contested Luton South 2001 and Sittingbourne and Sheppey 2005 general elections. Member for Sittingbourne and Sheppey since 6 May 2010 general election; Member, Conservative Party

Political interests: Law and order, education, constitutional affairs; Southern Africa, India

Other organisations: Director, Swale Community Action Project; Sheerness Conservative Club

Recreations: Reading, writing, football

Gordon Henderson MP, House of Commons, London SW1A 0AA
Tel: 020 7219 3000 E-mail: gordon.henderson.mp@parliament.uk
Constituency: Halfway Conservative Hall, 14-16 Minster Road, Sheppey, Kent ME12 3JH Tel: 01795 665251
Website: www.sittingbournesheppeyconservatives.com

GENERAL ELECTION RESULT

		%
Henderson, G. (Con)	24,313	50.1
Harrison, A. (Lab)	11,930	24.6
Nevols, K. (Lib Dem)	7,934	16.3
Davison, I. (UKIP)	2,610	5.4
Tames, L. (BNP)	1,305	2.7
Young, M. (Loony)	319	0.7
Cassidy, D. (Ind)	158	0.3
Majority	12,383	25.49
Electorate	75,354	
Turnout	48,578	64.47

CONSTITUENCY SNAPSHOT

Created in 1997 Sittingbourne and Sheppey was won by Labour's Derek Wyatt from his Conservative opponent, Sir Roger Moate, overturning a majority of 16,351 votes to win by 1,929 votes.

In 2001 Wyatt increased his majority to 3,509 votes. The Tories almost regained the seat in 2005 when a swing back to them reduced Wyatt's majority to just 79.

Labour was defeated in the 2010 general election with a 12.7 per cent swing going to the Conservative candidate, Gordon Henderson.

The seat gained the Teynham and Lynsted part-ward that was previously in Faversham and Mid Kent.

At the point on the north Kent coast where the Thames estuary meets the North Sea, Sittingbourne is an expanding country town, while the marshy Isle of Sheppey is a flat area cut off geographically from the Kent mainland by the river Swale.

Local companies operate across a wide range of industries, from pharmaceuticals to more traditional paper and construction products. The healthcare and pharmaceutical sectors are represented not only by manufacturing operations, but also by a cluster of research-led companies that have grown up around Kent Science Park.

There is a great deal of construction work going on in the constituency, with the Thames Gateway Project a major source of funds for regeneration and development.

Mark Hendrick

Preston (returning MP)

Boundary changes

Tel: 020 7219 4791
E-mail: hendrickm@parliament.uk
Website: www.prestonmp.co.uk

Labour/Co-operative

Date of birth: 2 November 1958; Son of Brian Francis Hendrick, timber worker, and Jennifer, née Chapman, clerk/typist

Education: Salford Grammar School; Liverpool Polytechnic (BSc electrical and electronic engineering 1982); Manchester University (MSc computer science 1985, CertEd 1992); Volkshochschule, Hanau, Germany ('Zertifikat Deutsch als Fremdsprache'); Married Yu Yannan 2008

Non-political career: Student engineer Ministry of Defence 1979; Werk student AEG Telefunken 1981; Science and Engineering Research Council 1982-84, 1985-88; Lecturer in electronics and software design, Stockport college 1990-94; Member GMB; Councillor Salford City Council 1987-95; Representative Salford City Council as an alternate director Manchester Airport plc 1987-94

Political career: Member for Preston 23 November 2000 by-election to 2010, for Preston (revised boundary) since 6 May 2010 general election; PPS: to Margaret Beckett: as Secretary of State for Environment, Food and Rural Affairs 2003-06, as Foreign Secretary 2006-07, to Jack Straw as Lord Chancellor and Secretary of State for Justice 2007-08, to Ivan Lewis as Minister of State, Foreign and Commonwealth Office 2009-10; *Select Committees:* Member: European Scrutiny 2001-04, International Development 2009-10; European Parliament: MEP for Lancashire Central 1994-99; Chair Eccles constituency Labour party 1990-94; Member, Preston and District Co-operative Party 1994-; Chair Labour/Co-operative Parliamentary Group 2005-06

Political interests: Foreign affairs, defence, European affairs, economic and industrial affairs, international development; USA, Japan, Germany, Poland, Hungary, China

Other organisations: CEng; Chartered Electrical Engineer; Deepdale Labour; Penwortham Sports and Social; *Publications:* The euro and Co-operative Enterprise: Co-operating with the euro, Co-operative Press Ltd 1998; Changing States: A Labour Agenda for Europe, Mandarin Paperbacks 1996

Recreations: Football, boxing, chess, travel, foreign languages

Mark Hendrick MP, House of Commons, London SW1A 0AA
Tel: 020 7219 4791 Fax: 020 7219 5220
E-mail: hendrickm@parliament.uk
Constituency: PTMC, Marsh Lane, Preston, Lancashire PR1 8UQ
Tel: 01772 883575 Fax: 01772 887188
Website: www.prestonmp.co.uk

GENERAL ELECTION RESULT

		%
Hendrick, M. (Lab/Co-op)*	15,668	48.2
Jewell, M. (Lib Dem)	7,935	24.4
Warner-O'Neill, N. (Con)	7,060	21.7
Muirhead, R. (UKIP)	1,462	4.5
Ambroze, G. (Christian)	272	0.8
Tayya, K. (Ind)	108	0.3
Majority	7,733	23.79
Electorate	62,460	
Turnout	32,505	52.04

**Member of last parliament*

CONSTITUENCY SNAPSHOT

Preston has been a Labour seat since its creation in 1983 when it was won by Stan Thorne. Mark Hendrick took over the seat for Labour in a 2000 by-election caused by the death of Audrey Wise.

Hendrick won a slightly reduced majority of 9,047 in 2005, which fell to 7,733 in 2010.

The seat gained Ingol ward, while losing one part-ward to Wyre and Preston North and four part-wards and three wards to Ribble Valley.

Preston is an old cotton town at the heart of the county of Lancashire, on the river Ribble. Preston was granted city status in 2002 to celebrate the Golden Jubilee.

There are excellent transport links: the West Coast mainline serves Preston as do the M6, the M61 and the M65. These links are crucial for Preston to revitalise the local economy.

BAE Systems one of the largest employers. The service industry is dominant in Preston with over a quarter of jobs in public administration.

Charles Hendry

Wealden (returning MP)

Boundary changes

Tel: 020 7219 8333
E-mail: hendryc@parliament.uk
Website: www.charleshendry.com

Conservative

Date of birth: 6 May 1959; Son of late Charles W R Hendry and Margaret Anne Hendry

Education: Rugby School; Edinburgh University (BCom business studies 1981); Married Sallie Moores, née Smith 1995 (2 sons 1 stepson 1 stepdaughter)

Non-political career: Account director Ogilvy and Mather PR 1982-88; Special adviser: to John Moore as Secretary of State for Social Services 1988, to Antony Newton as: Minister of Trade and Industry 1988-89, Secretary of State for Social Security 1989-90; Burson-Marsteller: Senior counsellor public affairs 1990-92, Associate director public relations; Agenda Group: Chief executive 1999-01, Non-executive chair 2001- 04; Director, Incredi Bull Ideas 2003-04

Political career: Contested Clackmannan 1983 and Mansfield 1987 general elections. Member for High Peak 1992-1997. Contested High Peak 1997 general election. Member for Wealden 2001-10, for Wealden (revised boundary) since 6 May 2010 general election; PPS: to William Hague and Lord Mackay of Ardbrecknish as Ministers of State, Department of Social Security 1994-95, to Gillian Shephard as Secretary of State for Education and Employment 1995; Opposition Whip 2001-02; Shadow Minister for: Young People 2002-05, Higher Education 2005, Trade and Industry/Business, Enterprise and Regulatory Reform 2005-08 (Energy, Science and Technology 2006-07, Energy, Industry and Postal Affairs 2007-08), Energy 2008-10; Minister of State, Department for Energy and Climate Change 2010-; *Select Committees:* Member: Procedure 1992-95, European Standing Committee B 1992-95, Northern Ireland Affairs 1994-97, Culture, Media and Sport 2003-04, Energy and Climate Change 2009-10; President Edinburgh University Conservative Association 1979-80; Vice-chair: Scottish Federation of Conservative Students 1980-81, Battersea Conservative Association 1981-83; Vice-chair Conservative Party 1995-97; Chief of staff Leader of Opposition 1997; Head of Business liaison, Conservative Party 1997-99; Deputy Chairman, Conservative Party 2003-05

Political interests: Trade and industry, youth policy, training, urban regeneration, social affairs, housing, homelessness, rural affairs, agriculture; USA, Europe, Southern Africa, Russia

Other organisations: President British Youth Council 1992-97; Development board member Tusk Force 1992-98; Patron The Big Issue Foundation 1995-; Joint Honorary President, British Youth Council 1992-97; Trustee: Drive for Youth 1989-98, UK Youth Parliament 2002-: co-chair 2006-

Recreations: Tennis, skiing, family, opera, rugby, travel

Charles Hendry MP, House of Commons, London SW1A 0AA
Tel: 020 7219 8333 Fax: 020 7219 1977
E-mail: hendryc@parliament.uk
Constituency: Wealden Conservative Association, The Granary, Bales Green Farm, Arlington, East Sussex BN27 6SH Tel: 01323 489289
Fax: 01323 484847 Website: www.charleshendry.com

GENERAL ELECTION RESULT

		%
Hendry, C. (Con)*	31,090	56.6
Bowers, C. (Lib Dem)	13,911	25.3
Blackmore, L. (Lab)	5,266	9.6
Docker, D. (UKIP)	3,319	6.0
Jonas, D. (Green)	1,383	2.5
Majority	17,179	31.25
Electorate	76,537	
Turnout	54,969	71.82

**Member of last parliament*

CONSTITUENCY SNAPSHOT

This Conservative seat elected Evelyn Emmet in 1955, then one of a minority of female MPs. Geoffery Johnson Smith held Wealden from 1965 to 2001, with vote shares of over 60 per cent from the 1980s until 1997. In 1997 he still polled 50 per cent of the vote and was returned with a 14,204 majority.

Johnson Smith retired in 2001 and Charles Hendry, previously MP for High Peak, retained the seat in 2001 and 2005. Hendry was re-elected in 2010 with a 17,179 majority.

Chiddingly and East Hoathly, and Hellingly wards, previously shared with Lewes, were moved entirely within the seat. Wealden lost the wards of Heathfield North and Central, and Cross in Hand/Five Ashes as well as part of Heathfield East to Bexhill and Battle.

Wealden covers a very broad area of East Sussex, much of it within the High Weald Area of Outstanding Natural Beauty, a patchwork of well-wooded ridges and valleys in the South Downs.

There is no main town as such, but a collection of small towns such as Uckfield, Wadhurst, Crowborough, Hailsham and Forest Row, alongside many villages and extensive woodland.

Agriculture is integral to the local economy and countryside issues are very important. The natural beauty of the area attracts many tourists.

Stephen Hepburn

Jarrow (returning MP)

Boundary changes

Tel: 020 7219 4134
E-mail: hepburns@parliament.uk
Website: www.epolitix.com/Stephen-Hepburn

Date of birth: 6 December 1959; Son of Peter and Margaret Hepburn

Education: Springfield Comprehensive, Jarrow; Newcastle University (BA politics); Single

Non-political career: Labourer, South Tyneside Metropolitan Borough Council; Research assistant to Don Dixon MP; Member, UCATT; South Tyneside Council: Councillor 1985-, Chair Finance Committee 1989-90, Deputy Leader 1990-97

Political career: Member for Jarrow 1997-2010, for Jarrow (revised boundary) since 6 May 2010 general election; *Select Committees:* Member: Administration 1997-2001, Defence 1999-2001, Accommodation and Works 2003-05, Northern Ireland Affairs 2004-10, Administration 2009-10

Political interests: Small businesses

Other organisations: Neon CIU, Jarrow, Iona Catholic Club, Hebburn; President, Jarrow FC, Patron, Jarrow Roofing FC

Recreations: Football

Stephen Hepburn MP, House of Commons, London SW1A 0AA
Tel: 020 7219 4134 E-mail: hepburns@parliament.uk
Constituency: 136/137 Tedco Business Centre, Viking Industrial Estate, Jarrow, Tyne and Wear NE32 3DT Tel: 0191-420 0648
Fax: 0191-489 7531 Website: www.epolitix.com/Stephen-Hepburn

GENERAL ELECTION RESULT

		%
Hepburn, S. (Lab)*	20,910	53.9
Milburn, J. (Con)	8,002	20.6
Appleby, T. (Lib Dem)	7,163	18.5
Swaddle, A. (BNP)	2,709	7.0
Majority	12,908	33.28
Electorate	64,350	
Turnout	38,784	60.27

**Member of last parliament*

CONSTITUENCY SNAPSHOT

Labour MPs have consistently polled large majorities here. In 2001 Stephen Hepburn received over 66 per cent of the vote, giving him an absolute majority of 17,595. Stephen Hepburn's majority fell by over 3,500 in 2005 to 13,904, yet this still represented a margin of 41 per cent.

Boundary changes moved the wards of Pelaw and Heworth (previously part of Gateshead East and Washington West), Bede (previously part of South Shields) Cleadon and East Boldon (previously part of South Shields) entirely within the seat. Hepburn defied a swing to the Tories to win a 12,908 majority in 2010.

The south Tyneside constituency of Jarrow will forever be linked with the Jarrow March of October 1936, a protest against the extreme poverty being experienced at the time in the North East.

Traditional industries in the area such as coal mining and shipbuilding have almost vanished and new light industry has been encouraged.

Currently manufacturing remains the industry employing the most constituents, closely followed by wholesale, retail and trade.

Rt Hon **Nick Herbert**

Arundel and South Downs ***(returning MP)***

Boundary changes

Tel: 020 7219 4080
E-mail: herbertn@parliament.uk
Website: www.nickherbert.com

Date of birth: 7 April 1963; Son of Michael and Judy Le Q Herbert

Education: Haileybury, Hertford; Magdalene College, Cambridge (BA law and land economy 1985); Civil partner Jason Eades 2008

Non-political career: British Field Sports Society 1990-96: Director of political affairs 1992-96 (co-founder Countryside Movement); Chief executive Business for Sterling 1998-2000 (founder of the 'No' Campaign); Director, Reform 2002-05

Political career: Contested Berwick-upon-Tweed 1997 general election. Member for Arundel and South Downs 2005-10, for Arundel and South Downs (revised boundary) since 6 May 2010 general election; Shadow: Minister for Police Reform 2005-07, Secretary of State for: Justice 2007-09, Environment, Food and Rural Affairs 2009-10; Minister of State for Police, Home Office and Ministry of Justice 2010-; *Select Committees:* Member: Home Affairs 2005-06

Political interests: Rural affairs, public services, the economy

Other organisations: PC 2010

Recreations: Watching cricket, racing, country sports, cinema, theatre, opera

Rt Hon Nick Herbert MP, House of Commons, London SW1A 0AA
Tel: 020 7219 4080 Fax: 020 7219 1295
E-mail: herbertn@parliament.uk
Constituency: Arundel and South Downs Conservative Association, The Old Town Hall, 38 High Street, Arundel, West Sussex BN44 3YE
Tel: 01903 816880 Fax: 01903 810348
Website: www.nickherbert.com

GENERAL ELECTION RESULT

		%
Herbert, N. (Con)*	32,333	57.8
Deedman, D. (Lib Dem)	15,642	27.9
Lunnon, T. (Lab)	4,835	8.6
Bower, S. (UKIP)	3,172	5.7
Majority	16,691	29.81
Electorate	77,564	
Turnout	55,982	72.18

**Member of last parliament*

CONSTITUENCY SNAPSHOT

Formed in 1997, Arundel and South Downs is one of two seats created from the old Arundel constituency represented by Tory Sir Michael Marshall.

Tory Howard Flight had represented the constituency since its creation until he was deselected shortly before the 2005 general election. He had received a majority of 13,704 in 2001.

After Flight was removed he gave his backing to his replacement, Nick Herbert, who was elected with a 11,309 majority. Herbert's vote-share increased to 57.8 per cent at the 2010 general election and he was returned with a 16,691 majority.

The seat gained part-wards from Horsham, Chichester and Mid Sussex, and lost part-wards to Bognor Regis and Littlehampton, Horsham and Mid Sussex.

This is a quiet, predominantly rural constituency stretching across the north of the South Downs. Arundel, the only major inland town is the ancestral home of the Dukes of Norfolk and has its own Roman Catholic cathedral.

Gatwick Airport is a major employer.

Agriculture and forestry are key employment markets; likewise the leisure and tourism industry is important in this historic and picturesque constituency. The South Downs are a significant attraction.

By-passes are needed at Arundel and Worthing to relieve major bottlenecks on the A27, the primary south coast trunk road.

Lady **Sylvia Hermon**

North Down (returning MP)

No boundary changes

Tel: 020 7219 8491
E-mail: hermons@parliament.uk
Website: www.sylviahermon.org

Independent

Date of birth: 11 August 1955; Daughter of Robert and Mary Paisley

Education: Dungannon High School for Girls; Aberstwyth University, Wales (BA law 1977); Chester College of Law (Part II Solicitors' Qualifying Examinations 1978); Married Sir John Hermon OBE QPM 1988 (died 2008) (2 sons)

Non-political career: Lecturer European, international and constitutional law Queen's University, Belfast 1978-88

Political career: Member for North Down since 7 June 2001 general election (UUP 2001 to March 2010, Independent since March 2010); UUP Spokesperson for: Home Affairs 2001-05, Trade and Industry 2001-02, Youth and Women's Issues 2001-05, Culture, Media and Sport 2002-05; *Select Committees:* Member: Northern Ireland Affairs 2005-10; Author and committee member addressing Patten Report, also of Criminal Justice Review 2000; Ulster Unionist Executive 1999; Constituency chair North Down Unionist Constituency Association 2001-03; Resigned from the UUP March 2010, now sits as an Independent

Political interests: Policing, human rights, European affairs, health, education; Republic of Ireland, India, Russia

Other organisations: Member Speaker's Committee on the Electoral Commission; *Publications:* A Guide to EEC Law in Northern Ireland, (SLS Legal Publications (NI) 1986)

Recreations: Fitness training, swimming, ornithology

Lady Hermon MP, House of Commons, London SW1A 0AA
Tel: 020 7219 8491 Fax: 020 7219 1969
E-mail: hermons@parliament.uk
Constituency: 17a Hamilton Road, Bangor, Co Down BT20 4LF
Tel: 028 9127 5858 Fax: 028 9127 5747
Website: www.sylviahermon.org

GENERAL ELECTION RESULT

		%	+/-
Hermon, S. (Ind)*	21,181	63.3	
Parsley, I. (UCUNF)	6,817	20.4	
Farry, S. (All)	1,876	5.6	-2.0
Kilpatrick, M. (TUV)	1,634	4.9	
Agnew, S. (Green)	1,043	3.1	
Logan, L. (SDLP)	680	2.0	-1.1
Parker, V. (Sinn Féin)	250	0.8	0.1
Majority	14,364	42.90	
Electorate	60,698		
Turnout	33,481	55.16	

**Member of last parliament*

CONSTITUENCY SNAPSHOT

James Kilfedder, a former Speaker of the Stormont Assembly, a Conservative and then independent Unionist, held the seat from 1970 until his death in 1995.

The seat was then taken by the leader of the anti-Good Friday Agreement United Kingdom Unionist Party, Bob McCartney QC, who held it until defeated at the 2001 general election by Ulster Unionist Sylvia Hermon.

In 2005 Hermon held here with a 4,944 majority becoming the only DUP and she became the only Ulster Unionist MP of the 2005 Parliament. Hermon held the seat as an independent in 2010, after leaving the UUP in March that year, with a 14,364 majority.

This beautiful coastal constituency is on the Ards Peninsula bordering the southern shores of Belfast Lough, on the east of Northern Ireland.

It is a predominantly Protestant, middle class and suburban dormitory area. It is the least deprived part of Northern Ireland.

The major service areas in the constituency are the wholesale and retail trade, health and social work and light manufacturing.

Tourism is important and the area contains some notable attractions. The Ulster Folk and Transport Museum near Helen's Bay is the second most popular museum/visitor centre in Northern Ireland (after the Giant's Causeway).

David Heyes

Ashton under Lyne (returning MP)

Boundary changes

Tel: 020 7219 8129
E-mail: heyesd@parliament.uk
Website: davidheyes.com

Labour

Date of birth: 2 April 1946; Son of Harold Heyes, police officer and Lilian Heyes, neé Crowe

Education: Blackley Technical High School, Manchester; Open University (BA social sciences 1987); Married Judith Egerton-Gallagher 1968 (1 son 1 daughter)

Non-political career: Local government officer: Manchester City Council 1962-74, Greater Manchester Council 1974-86, Oldham Metropolitan Borough Council 1987-90; Self-employed computer graphics 1990-95; Deputy district manager Manchester Citizens Advice Bureau service 1995-2001; Member UNISON (formerly NALGO) 1962-; Oldham Metropolitan Borough Council: Councillor 1992-2004: Labour Group Secretary 1993-2000, Chair Personnel Committee 1994-2000

Political career: Member for Ashton under Lyne since 7 June 2001 general election; *Select Committees:* Member: Public Administration 2001-10

Political interests: Social exclusion, health, education, work and pensions, local and regional government

Other organisations: Development worker Voluntary Action Manchester 1993-95

David Heyes MP, House of Commons, London SW1A 0AA
Tel: 020 7219 8129 Fax: 020 7219 1738
E-mail: heyesd@parliament.uk
Constituency: St Michael's Court, St Michael's Square, Stamford Street, Ashton-Under-Lyne, Lancashire OL6 6XN
Tel: 0161-331 9307 Fax: 0161-330 9420 Website: davidheyes.com

GENERAL ELECTION RESULT

		%
Heyes, D. (Lab)*	18,604	48.4
Kennedy, S. (Con)	9,510	24.8
Larkin, P. (Lib Dem)	5,703	14.8
Lomas, D. (BNP)	2,929	7.6
McManus, A. (UKIP)	1,686	4.4
Majority	9,094	23.66
Electorate	67,564	
Turnout	38,432	56.88

**Member of last parliament*

CONSTITUENCY SNAPSHOT

Labour has held Ashton under Lyne continuously since 1935.

In 2001 the seat experienced a small swing away from Labour, though not enough to prevent the retiring MP Robert Sheldon from passing the seat to party colleague David Heyes. The majority was down 7,000 from 1997.

Heyes held on to his five-figure majority in 2005. A 2.8 per cent swing to the Conservatives made no significant dent in his 13,952 majority.

In 2010 Heyes held the seat with a reduced majority of 9,094. There was a 7.3 per cent swing to the Conservatives.

Boundary changes have resulted in of Droylsden East and St Peter's part-wards coming in from neighbouring Denton and Reddish and part-wards being lost to Oldham West and Royton, Denton and Reddish and Stalybridge and Hyde.

Situated to the east of Manchester Central and to the south of the two Oldham constituencies, Ashton under Lyne is a post-industrial, urban constituency comprising a chain of built-up valley communities.

It has a strong industrial heritage in textiles and coal-mining, and as a market town. Most of the workers here are still in manual trades. Textile mills and engineering have given way to a wide range of modern industries, including computer technology.

Ashton Moss Retail Park is expanding its office accommodation, attracting businesses and the public sector relocating from central Manchester.

Meg Hillier

Hackney South and Shoreditch *(returning MP)*

Boundary changes

Tel: 020 7219 5325
E-mail: meghilliermp@parliament.uk
Website: www.meghillier.com

Labour/Co-operative

Date of birth: 14 February 1969

Education: Portsmouth High School; St Hilda's College, Oxford (BA philosophy, politics and economics 1990); City University, London (diploma in newspaper journalism 1991); Married Joe Simpson 1997 (1 son 1 daughter)

Non-political career: Reporter *South Yorkshire Times* 1991; Petty officer P&O European Ferries 1992; PR officer Newlon Housing Group 1993; *Housing Today*: Reporter 1994-95, Features editor 1995-98; Freelance journalist 1998-2000; TGWU; London Borough of Islington: Councillor 1994-2002, Chair Neighbourhood Services Committee 1995-97, Mayor 1998-99; London Assembly member for North East London 2000-04; Board member, Transport for London 2004-05

Political career: Member for Hackney South and Shoreditch 2005-10, for Hackney South and Shoreditch (revised boundary) since 6 May 2010 general election; PPS to Ruth Kelly as Secretary of State for Communities and Local Government 2006-07; Parliamentary Under-Secretary of State (Identity), Home Office 2007-10; *Select Committees:* Member: Northern Ireland Affairs 2005-06

Political interests: Nigeria, Ghana, Turkey, West and East Africa

Other organisations: Member: Co-operative Party, Fabian Society; Trustee War Memorials Trust 2001-

Meg Hillier MP, House of Commons, London SW1A 0AA
Tel: 020 7219 5325 Fax: 020 7219 8768
E-mail: meghilliermp@parliament.uk
Website: www.meghillier.com

GENERAL ELECTION RESULT

		%
Hillier, M. (Lab/Co-op)*	23,888	55.7
Raval, D. (Lib Dem)	9,600	22.4
Nayyar, S. (Con)	5,800	13.5
Lane, P. (Green)	1,493	3.5
King, M. (UKIP)	651	1.5
Rae, B. (Lib)	539	1.3
Williams, J. (Christian)	434	1.0
Davies, P. (Comm League)	110	0.3
De La Haye, D. (Ind)	95	0.2
Tuckett, J. (Ind)	26	0.1
Spinks, M. (Ind)	20	0.1
Majority	14,288	33.34
Electorate	72,816	
Turnout	42,858	58.86

**Member of last parliament*

CONSTITUENCY SNAPSHOT

Labour have dominated the seat since the post-war period, regularly polling above 60 per cent. Ron Brown held the seat throughout the 1970s and early 1980s, but defected to the SDP in 1981. Labour regained the seat in 1983 and the party has held it ever since.

Meg Hiller succeeded Brian Sedgemore in 2005 with a majority of 10,204. Hillier increased her share of the vote to over 55 per cent with a 14,288 majority.

Hackney South and Shoreditch gained one-part ward from Hackney North and Stoke Newington and lost two part-wards in return.

Hackney South and Shoreditch extends from the southern part of Hackney, up to its northern tip at Dalston, and down to Victoria Park and Shoreditch in the south.

Shoreditch High Street tube station opened in April 2010, at the northern end of the East London Line, with the link extending to Highbury and Islington in 2011, as part of the Overground line.

Shoreditch is now known for its trendy shops and bars, while also boasting a vibrant music and arts scene.

The Olympic Park, which will house the media and broadcast centre for journalists reporting on the Games, will be based in Hackney Wick. The facilities will be transformed into a new employment hub for East London after the games.

Julie Hilling

Bolton West

Boundary changes

Labour

Tel: 020 7219 3000
E-mail: julie.hilling.mp@parliament.uk
Website: www.juliehilling.org.uk

Non-political career: National President, Community and Youth Workers Union; Senior regional organiser, Transport Salaried Staffs' Association

Political career: Member for Bolton West since 6 May 2010 general election; Vice-chair, Bolton West Constituency Labour Party

Julie Hilling MP, House of Commons, London SW1A 0AA
Tel: 020 7219 3000 E-mail: julie.hilling.mp@parliament.uk
Constituency: 108 Market Street, West Houghton, Bolton BL5 3AZ
Tel: 01942 812463 Website: www.juliehilling.org.uk

GENERAL ELECTION RESULT

		%
Hilling, J. (Lab)	18,327	38.5
Williams, S. (Con)	18,235	38.3
Pearcey, J. (Lib Dem)	8,177	17.2
Lamb, H. (UKIP)	1,901	4.0
Mann, R. (Green)	545	1.2
Jones, J. (Ind)	254	0.5
Bagnall, D. (You)	137	0.3
Majority	92	0.19
Electorate	71,250	
Turnout	47,576	66.77

CONSTITUENCY SNAPSHOT

In the elections of the 1980s the Conservative Tom Sackville was the MP and he held it at the 1992 election with a majority of only 1,079. In 1997 the seat fell to Labour's Ruth Kelly with a majority of 7,072.

At the 2005 general election Ruth Kelly's majority fell by almost two-thirds to 2,064. In 2010 Julie Hilling replaced Kelly and held the seat for Labour with a small majority of 92.

Boundary changes moved Halliwell, Hulton and Rumworth wards to the neighbouring Bolton seats. Atherton ward moved into the seat, having previously been shared between Leigh and Worsley.

Despite being home to Bolton Wanderers Football Club, Bolton West includes little territory actually situated within the town of Bolton. Instead, it covers the suburban and rural land between Bolton and Wigan, and is home to commuters and the majority of those in non-manual professions; hardly any of Bolton's industry is found in this seat.

While many residents commute to Manchester the local economy is growing and the seat has attracted a great deal of inward investment. The Middlebrook development includes the impressive Reebok stadium, home of Bolton Wanderers FC, the Bolton Arena, a sports academy that hosted several racket sports events during the 2002 Commonwealth Games, as well as a retail park.

Damian Hinds

East Hampshire

Boundary changes

Tel: 020 7219 3000
E-mail: damian.hinds.mp@parliament.uk
Website: www.damianhinds.info

Date of birth: 27 November 1969

Education: St Ambrose Grammar, Altrincham; Trinity College, Oxford (BA philosophy, poiltics and economics 1992, MA) (Oxford Union President); Married Jacqui Morel 2007

Non-political career: Research analyst, Mercer Management Consulting 1992-95; Various marketing and commercial management roles, Holiday Inn/Bass plc 1995-2003; Strategy director, Greene King Plc 2003-05; Freelance adviser to the hotel trade 2003-05, 2007-

Political career: Contested Stretford and Urmston 2005 general election. Member for East Hampshire since 6 May 2010 general election

Political interests: Inner city renewal, education, welfare, crime reduction, housing

Other organisations: Chair, policy development group, Bow Group 2001-02; *Publications:* Co-author, Power to the People (Bow Group 1998); Editor, The Ideas Book 2000 (Bow Group 1999): Co-editor, Go Zones: Policies for the Places Politics Forgot (Bow Group 2004)

Recreations: Music

Damian Hinds MP, House of Commons, London SW1A 0AA
Tel: 020 7219 3000 E-mail: damian.hinds.mp@parliament.uk
Constituency: 14a Butts Road, Alton, Hampshire GU34 1ND
Tel: 01420 84122 Website: www.damianhinds.info

GENERAL ELECTION RESULT

		%
Hinds, D. (Con)	29,137	56.8
Carew, A. (Lib Dem)	15,640	30.5
Edbrooke, J. (Lab)	4,043	7.9
McGuinness, H. (UKIP)	1,477	2.9
Williams, M. (England)	710	1.4
Jerrard, D. (JACP)	310	0.6
Majority	13,497	26.30
Electorate	72,250	
Turnout	51,317	71.03

CONSTITUENCY SNAPSHOT

Michael Mates held the seat and its predecessors from 1974 until his retirement in 2010. From the second largest Conservative majority in the country in 1992 (29,165), Mr Mates' majority fell to 5,509 in 2005.

Michael Mates retired in 2010 and Damian Hinds retained the seat for the Conservatives with 29,137 votes giving him a strong majority of 13,497.

Boundary changes in the constituency were significant following the creation of Meon Valley seat. This seat gained 11 wards and one part-ward from North East Hampshire, and lost nine wards and one part-ward to Meon Valley.

This constituency contains some beautiful countryside along with the historic towns of Alton and Petersfield. Over 70 per cent of the land in this constituency is rural, but there remains a relatively strong manufacturing industry.

Many of the residents commute to London or the surrounding larger towns such as Winchester, and there is ample local employment in the constituency's main towns of Alton and Petersfield.

Mark Hoban

Fareham (returning MP)

No boundary changes

Tel: 020 7219 8191
E-mail: hobanm@parliament.uk
Website: www.markhoban.com

Conservative

Date of birth: 31 March 1964; Son of Tom Hoban, general manager, and Maureen, neé Orchard

Education: St Leonards RC Comprehensive School, Durham; London School of Economics (BSc Econ 1985); Married Fiona Jane Barrett 1994

Non-political career: Pricewaterhouse Coopers 1985-2001: Chartered accountant, Manager 1990-92, Senior manager 1992-2001

Political career: Contested South Shields 1997 general election. Member for Fareham since 7 June 2001 general election; Opposition Whip 2002-03; Shadow Minister for: Public Services, Health and Education 2003-04, Education 2004-05, Treasury 2005-10; Financial Secretary, HM Treasury 2010-; *Select Committees:* Member: Science and Technology 2001-03, European Standing Committee A 2001-05; General election campaign manager 1987, 1992; Political vice-chair Southampton Itchen Conservative Association 1991-93

Political interests: Economy, trade and industry, education, health

Other organisations: Honorary Vice-President, Society of Maritime Industries; Associate of Institute of Chartered Accountants of England and Wales 1988; Liveryman Fruiterers' Company 2003-; Freeman, City of London 2003

Recreations: Cooking, reading, travel, entertaining

Mark Hoban MP, House of Commons, London SW1A 0AA
Tel: 020 7219 8191 Fax: 020 7219 1709
E-mail: hobanm@parliament.uk
Constituency: 14 East Street, Fareham, Hampshire PO16 0BN
Tel: 01329 233573 Fax: 01329 234197
Website: www.markhoban.com

GENERAL ELECTION RESULT

		%	+/-
Hoban, M. (Con)*	30,037	55.3	5.7
Bentley, A. (Lib Dem)	12,945	23.8	2.2
Carr, J. (Lab)	7,719	14.2	-11.4
Richards, S. (UKIP)	2,235	4.1	1.2
Doggett, P. (Green)	791	1.5	
Jenkins, J. (England)	618	1.1	
Majority	17,092	31.45	
Electorate	75,878		
Turnout	54,345	71.62	

**Member of last parliament*

CONSTITUENCY SNAPSHOT

Since becoming a separate constituency in 1974 Fareham has returned only Tory MPs. Sir Peter Lloyd served as the MP between 1979 and 2001. In 1997 Labour made a big advance to second place and almost doubled their vote.

There was virtually no swing in 2001, when Mark Hoban succeeded Lloyd as MP. Labour slipped back in 2005 allowing the Conservatives to re-establish a five-figure majority of 11,702.

Hoban held the seat in 2010 with a 17,092 majority and there was a 1.7 per cent swing of the vote in his favour.

Situated between Southampton and Portsmouth, Fareham is predominantly suburban. With the Solent and river Hamble to the west, the constituency is famous for yachting (the mouth of the river is protected from the elements by the Isle of Wight). Portsmouth Harbour marks the eastern edge of the constituency.

Fareham has strong connections with the Navy, and this still contributes to the local economy.

A fairly high proportion of residents are employed in the manufacturing industry, mainly in the defence, aviation, and maritime sectors.

The main economic activity in Fareham is now retail. Fareham has also become a popular choice for the location of business call-centres, attracted no doubt by good communications and transport: the M27 runs through the north of the constituency, allowing for easy access to Southampton and Portsmouth.

Who's who in the payments industry?

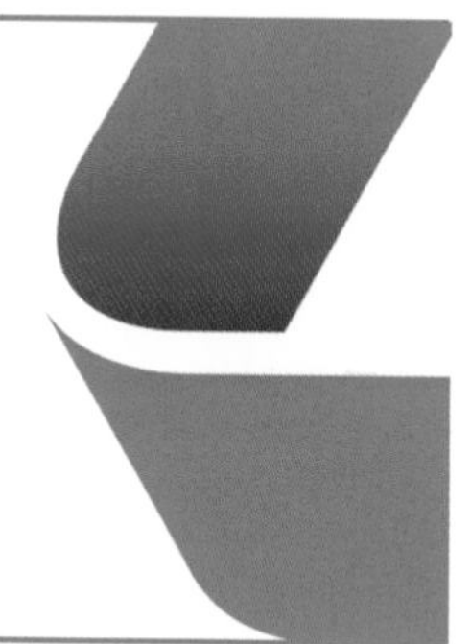

The payments industry has different players and separate industry groups. These include:

- Bacs (bacs.co.uk);
- CHAPS Sterling Scheme (chapsco.co.uk);
- Cheque and Credit Clearing Company (chequeandcredit.co.uk);
- Dedicated Cheque and Plastic Crime Unit (DCPCU) (dcpcu.org.uk);
- Faster Payments Scheme (chapsco.co.uk);
- Financial Fraud Action UK (financialfraudaction.org.uk);
- Payments Council (paymentscouncil.org.uk);
- SWIFT UK (swift.com); and
- The UK Cards Association (theukcardsassociation.org.uk).

We provide people, facilities and expertise to this range of companies and brands, which are recognised externally and have individual responsibilities.

We have managed the development and launches of major innovations in payments, such as chip and PIN and Faster Payments, but we also make sure that money continues to move around the economy smoothly every day of the year.

If you have any questions about the work of the different parts of the payments industry, or require some specific information or statistics on payment methods, plastic cards or fraud prevention, then please get in contact.

Sandra Quinn, director of communications
Tel: 020 3217 8234
Email: sandra.quinn@ukpayments.org.uk

Rosalind Beaumont, public affairs manager
Tel: 020 3217 8280
Email: rosalind.beaumont@ukpayments.org.uk

Rt Hon **Margaret Hodge**

Barking ***(returning MP)***

Boundary changes

Tel: 020 7219 6666
E-mail: hodgem@parliament.uk
Website: www.epolitix.com/Margaret-Hodge

Date of birth: 8 September 1944; Daughter of Hans and Lisbeth Oppenheimer

Education: Bromley High School; Oxford High School; London School of Economics (BSc economics 1966); Married Andrew Watson 1968 (divorced 1978) (1 son 1 daughter); married Henry Hodge (later Mr Justice Hodge, he died 2009) 1978 (2 daughters)

Non-political career: Teaching and market research 1966-73; Senior consultant Price Waterhouse 1992-94; Member TGWU; Councillor London Borough of Islington 1973-94: Chair Housing Committee 1975-79, Leader 1982-92

Political career: Member for Barking 1994-2010, for Barking (revised boundary) since 6 May 2010 general election; Parliamentary Under-Secretary of State, Department for Education and Employment (Employment and Equal Opportunities) 1998-2001; Minister of State: Department for Education and Skills 2001-05: (Lifelong Learning and Higher Education 2001-03, Lifelong Learning, Further and Higher Education 2003, Children, Young People and Families 2003-05), Department for Work and Pensions (Employment and Welfare Reform) 2005-06, Department of Trade and Industry (Industry and the Regions) 2006-07, Department for Culture, Media and Sport 2007-08, 2009-10 (Culture, Creative Industries and Tourism 2007-08, Culture and Tourism 2009-10); *Select Committees:* Member: Education and Employment 1996-97, Deregulation 1996-97, Liaison 1997-98 Chair: Education and Employment (Education Sub-Committee) 1997-98 Chair (Education): Education and Employment 1997-98 Joint Chair: Education and Employment 1997-98 Chair (Education): Education and Employment (Education Sub-Committee) 1997-98, Member: Education and Employment (Employment Sub-Committee) 1997-98; Member, Labour Party Local Government Committee 1983-92; Chair: London Group of Labour MPs 1995-98, Fabians 1997-98

Political interests: Education, local and regional government, housing, inner cities, democratic reform, London government

Other organisations: Member Home Office Advisory Committee on Race Relations 1988-92; Director: University College, Middlesex Hospitals; Governor London School of Economics 1990-2001; Chair, Association of London Authorities 1984-92; Vice-Chair, AMA 1991-92; Fellow Industry and Parliament Trust 1996; MBE 1978; PC 2003; Hon. Fellow University of North London; Hon. DCL City 1993; *Publications:* Quality, Equality and Democracy; Beyond the Town Hall; Fabian pamphlet on London Government, Not Just the Flower Show; Numerous articles

Recreations: Family, opera, piano, travel, cooking

Rt Hon Margaret Hodge MBE MP, House of Commons, London SW1A 0AA Tel: 020 7219 6666 E-mail: hodgem@parliament.uk
Constituency: 102 North Street, Barking, Essex IG11 8LA
Tel: 020 8594 1333 Fax: 020 8594 1131 Website: www.epolitix.com/Margaret-Hodge

GENERAL ELECTION RESULT

		%
Hodge, M. (Lab)*	24,628	54.3
Marcus, S. (Con)	8,073	17.8
Griffin, N. (BNP)	6,620	14.6
Carman, D. (Lib Dem)	3,719	8.2
Maloney, F. (UKIP)	1,300	2.9
Hargreaves, G. (Christian)	482	1.1
Forbes, J. (Green)	317	0.7
Dowling, C. (Loony)	82	0.2
Darwood, T. (Ind)	77	0.2
Sijuwola, D. (Restoration)	45	0.1
Majority	16,555	36.51
Electorate	73,864	
Turnout	45,343	61.39

**Member of last parliament*

CONSTITUENCY SNAPSHOT

Barking has been a Labour seat since 1945. Jo Richardson became the Member for Barking in 1974, doubling her majority to 6,268 in 1992. Margaret Hodge, who was elected in the 1994 by-election following Richardson's death, gained a majority of 15,896.

Hodge held on to her seat in 2005, but her vote was 13 per cent down on 2001. The fragility of support for both Labour and the Conservatives was demonstrated by the gain in support for the BNP, who with 16.9 per cent of the vote out-polled the Liberal Democrats for third place. In 2010 Hodge fought off a campaign against BNP leader Nick Griffin and was returned with an increased majority of 16,555.

Barking has gained Albion and Valence wards from Dagenham seat as part of the Boundary Commission review.

Barking is characterised by a largely homogenous white working-class culture. Only the west of the constituency approaches the multiculturalism found in inner East London.

As part of the Thames Gateway, Barking is one of the areas identified for London's planned expansion in housing. The new housing development known as Barking Riverside is situated close to Barking town centre. The project will progress over the next 25 years.

Crossrail will help to improve links to central London, with a new tunnel crossing central London connecting it with rail services in East London. Services are expected to start in 2017.

Sharon Hodgson

Washington and Sunderland West ***(returning MP)***

New constituency

Tel: 020 7219 5160
E-mail: hodgsons@parliament.uk
Website: www.sharonhodgson.org

Date of birth: 1 April 1966; Daughter of Joan Cohen, née Wilson

Education: Heathfield Senior High School, Gateshead; Newcastle College (HEFC English 1997); TUC, National Education Centre (Open college network diploma in labour party organising 2000); Married Alan Hodgson 1990 (1 son 1 daughter)

Non-political career: Payroll/account clerk, Tyneside Safety Glass, Team Valley Trading Estate, Gateshead 1982-88; Northern Rock Building Society, Gosforth 1988-92; Payroll administrator, Burgess Microswitch, Team Valley Trading Estate, Gateshead 1992-94; Charity administrator, The Total Learning Challenge (educational charity), Newcastle 1998-99; Regional organiser, Labour North 1999-2000; Constituency organiser Mitcham and Morden CLP 2000-02; Labour link co-ordinator, London, Unison 2002-05; Member: GMB 1999-2007; Unite 2007-, CWU

Political career: Member for Gateshead East and Washington West 2005-10, for Washington and Sunderland West since 6 May 2010 general election; PPS: to Liam Byrne as Minister of State, Home Office 2006-07, to Bob Ainsworth as Minister of State, Ministry of Defence 2007-08, to Dawn Primarolo as Minister of State, Department of Health 2008-09; Assistant Government Whip 2009-10; *Select Committees:* Member: Regulatory Reform 2005-10, European Scrutiny 2006, Court of Referees 2007-10, Children, Schools and Families 2007-10, North East 2009-10, Ecclesiastical Committee; Women's officer, Tyne Bridge CLP 1998-2000; Constituency secretary Mitcham and Morden CLP 2002-05; Member: Fabian Society 2004-, Christian Socialist Movement 2005-

Political interests: Anti-social behaviour, regional regeneration (especially North East), education, employment and jobs, health (especially cancer), social inclusion, child care, transport, child poverty, trade justice/fair trade, welfare, school nutrition, affordable energy efficiency, special educational needs

Recreations: Reading, cinema, cooking, shopping, travel, family

Sharon Hodgson MP, House of Commons, London SW1A 0AA
Tel: 020 7219 5160 Fax: 020 7219 4493
E-mail: hodgsons@parliament.uk
Constituency: Vermont House, Concord, Washington,
Tyne and Wear NE37 2SQ Tel: 0191-417 2000 Fax: 020 7219 4493
Website: www.sharonhodgson.org

GENERAL ELECTION RESULT

		%
Hodgson, S. (Lab)*	19,615	52.3
Cuthbert, I. (Con)	8,157	21.7
Andras, P. (Lib Dem)	6,382	17.0
McDonald, I. (BNP)	1,913	5.1
Hudson, L. (UKIP)	1,267	3.4
Majority	11,458	30.69
Electorate	68,910	
Turnout	37,334	54.18

**Member of last parliament*

CONSTITUENCY SNAPSHOT

This area has been Labour for decades. This new seat has been formed from sections of the two Sunderland seats and the Washington divisions, and as its name suggests, takes in the western suburbs of the city of Sunderland and all the post-war new town of Washington. The town is not entirely new and contains Washington Old Hall, home of the ancestors of George Washington, the first President of the United States.

Despite a large 11.6 per cent notional swing to the Conservatives, Labour's Sharon Hodgson won this new seat with a majority of 11,458.

Historically, Washington and Sunderland were heavily involved in the coal industry and many of the old communities of Washington grew up around the pits. This provided historical links between two urban areas.

Washington was also involved in the chemical industry and the Washington Chemical Works was a major employer in the 19th century. This later became the Cape/Newalls Works producing insulation. The Pattinson Town area of Washington grew up around the chemical works, and is now known as the Pattinson industrial estate and Teal Farm housing estate.

Currently, Washington's main industries include textiles, electronics, car assembly, chemicals and electrical goods. The Nissan plant which falls within the new constituency is the major employer.

Kate Hoey

Vauxhall (returning MP)

Boundary changes

Tel: 020 7219 5989
E-mail: hoeyk@parliament.uk

Date of birth: 21 June 1946; Daughter of Thomas and Letitia Hoey

Education: Belfast Royal Academy; Ulster College of Physical Education (Diploma teaching 1964); City of London College, London (BSc economics 1968); Single

Non-political career: Lecturer Southwark College 1972-76; Senior lecturer Kingsway College 1976-85; Educational adviser to Arsenal Football Club 1985-89; Member, GMB; Councillor: Hackney Borough Council 1978-82, Southwark Borough Council 1988-89;

Political career: Contested Dulwich 1983 and 1987 general elections. Member for Vauxhall 15 June 1989 by-election to 2010, for Vauxhall (revised boundary) since 6 May 2010; Opposition Spokesperson for Citizen's Charter and Women 1992-93; PPS to Frank Field as Minister of State, Department of Social Security 1997-98; Parliamentary Under-Secretary of State: Home Office (Metropolitan Police, European Union, Judicial Co-operation) 1998-99, Department for Culture, Media and Sport (Minister for Sport) 1999-2001; *Select Committees:* Member: Broadcasting 1991-97, Social Security 1994-97, Science and Technology 2004-05, Northern Ireland Affairs 2007-10

Political interests: Sport, foreign affairs, housing, countryside; Angola, Bosnia, Oman, Tibet, Zimbabwe

Other organisations: Chair Countryside Alliance 2005-; Hon Vice-President: Surrey County Cricket Club, British Wheelchair Basketball Association; President Clay Pigeon Shooting Association; Hon President British Pistol Club; Trustee Outward Bound Trust; *The Spectator*/Highland Park Debater of the Year Award 1998; University of Ulster Distinguished Graduate 2000; *Publications:* Occasional articles on sport in the press

Kate Hoey MP, House of Commons, London SW1A 0AA
Tel: 020 7219 5989 Fax: 020 7219 5985
E-mail: hoeyk@parliament.uk

GENERAL ELECTION RESULT

		%
Hoey, K. (Lab)*	21,498	49.8
Pidgeon, C. (Lib Dem)	10,847	25.1
Chambers, G. (Con)	9,301	21.5
Healy, J. (Green)	708	1.6
Navarro, J. (England)	289	0.7
Martin, L. (Christian)	200	0.5
Lambert, D. (Socialist)	143	0.3
Drinkall, J. (AWP)	109	0.3
Kapetanos, J. (Animal)	96	0.2
Majority	10,651	24.66
Electorate	74,811	
Turnout	43,191	57.73

**Member of last parliament*

CONSTITUENCY SNAPSHOT

Since 1983 when Vauxhall came into being in its present form it has known only Labour MPs. Until 1989 it was represented by Stuart Holland, and ever since by Kate Hoey. Hoey has consistently won majorities of over 50 per cent. Former minister and now an adviser to the London Mayor, Kate Hoey retained this safe Labour seat with 50 per cent of the vote.

At the next election the seat loses parts of the wards of Coldharbour and Herne Hill to Dulwich and West Norwood.

Just across the Thames from the House of Commons, Vauxhall is an inner-city constituency at the north end of the London Borough of Lambeth.

It includes some areas of Clapham and Brixton and is home to some famous London landmarks: the London Eye; the Oval cricket ground; Lambeth Palace; the National Theatre; and the South Bank Arts Centre.

Healthcare in Vauxhall is relatively well catered for, thanks to the local Guy's and St Thomas's NHS Trust. Lambeth LEA caters for a highly diverse population with around 150 languages being spoken.

George Hollingbery

Meon Valley

New constituency

Tel: 020 7219 3000
E-mail: george.hollingbery.mp@parliament.uk
Website: www.georgehollingbery.com

Conservative

Date of birth: 12 October 1963

Education: Radley College; Lady Margaret Hall, Oxford (BA human sciences 1985); The Wharton School, Pennsylvania (MBA 1991); Married to Janette Marie White (1 son 2 daughters)

Non-political career: Stockbroker, Robert Fleming Securities 1985-89; Non-executive director and shareholder, Lister Bestcare Ltd 1991-95; Director and founder, Pet Depot Ltd 1994-99; Chairman and founder, Companion Care Veterinary Group 1998-2001; Winchester City Council: Councillor 1999-, Deputy leader of Conservative group, Council Deputy Leader 2006-08

Political career: Contested Winchester 2005 general election. Member for Meon Valley since 6 May 2010 general election; Deputy chairman, Winchester Conservative Association 1999-2001; Chairman, Winchester campaign team 2001 general election

Political interests: Finance, countryside issues, entrepreneurship, education

Recreations: Field sports, modern garden design, modern crafts

George Hollingbery MP, House of Commons, London SW1A 0AA
Tel: 020 7219 3000 E-mail: george.hollingbery.mp@parliament.uk
Constituency: The Coach House, Worthy Park, Winchester, Hampshire SO21 1AN Tel: 0845 634 6166
Website: www.georgehollingbery.com

GENERAL ELECTION RESULT

		%
Hollingbery, G. (Con)	28,818	56.2
Leffman, L. (Lib Dem)	16,693	32.6
Linsley, H. (Lab)	3,266	6.4
Harris, S. (UKIP)	1,490	2.9
Harris, P. (England)	582	1.1
Coats, S. (Animal)	255	0.5
Quar, G. (Ind)	134	0.3
Majority	12,125	23.66
Electorate	70,488	
Turnout	51,238	72.69

CONSTITUENCY SNAPSHOT

This new seat is made up from large parts of East Hampshire and Winchester, and a part-ward from Havant.

Winchester was a safe Tory seat for almost 50 years when it was won by the Lib Dems' Mark Oaten in 1997. Oaten held the seat with a 7,476 majority in 2005 and retired in 2010.

East Hampshire is a safe Conservative seat. Michael Mates held the seat (and its predecessors) from 1974 until returning in 2010.

In 2010 George Hollingbery won the new seat for the Conservatives with a strong 12,125 majority.

The seat has a substantial urban population including the towns of Waterlooville and Horndean. Meon Valley covers some beautiful countryside in southern England.

Agriculture is a big industry in the more rural areas of the constituency and watercress production is widespread in this and neighbouring constituencies.

Small businesses account for a good slice of employment, for example the Wickham Vineyard which provides English wine to the House of Commons. The Portsmouth's Naval Dockyard is important for the region and the constituency as it provides or supports a large number of jobs.

Philip Hollobone

Kettering (returning MP)

Boundary changes

Tel: 020 7219 8373
E-mail: hollobonep@parliament.uk

Date of birth: 7 November 1964; Son of Thomas and Patricia Hollobone

Education: Dulwich College, London; Lady Margaret Hall, Oxford (BA modern history and economics 1987, MA); Married Donna Anne Cooksey 2001 (1 son 1 daughter)

Non-political career: Soldier and paratrooper, Territorial Army 1984-93; Industry research analyst, various 1987-2003; Councillor: London Borough of Bromley 1990-94, Kettering Borough Council 2003-

Political career: Contested Lewisham East 1997 and Kettering 2001 general elections. Member for Kettering 2005-2010, for Kettering (boundary changes) since 6 May 2010 general election; *Select Committees:* Member: Crossrail Bill 2006-07, Transport 2006-10; Chairman Bromley and Chislehurst Conservative Association 1999; Deputy chairman Kettering Constituency Conservative Association 2002-

Philip Hollobone MP, House of Commons, London SW1A 0AA
Tel: 020 7219 8373 Fax: 020 7219 8802
E-mail: hollobonep@parliament.uk
Constituency: Tel: 01536 414715

GENERAL ELECTION RESULT

		%
Hollobone, P. (Con)*	23,247	49.1
Sawford, P. (Lab)	14,153	29.9
Nelson, C. (Lib Dem)	7,498	15.8
Skinner, C. (BNP)	1,366	2.9
Hilling, D. (England)	952	2.0
Bishop, D. (Bus-Pass)	112	0.2
Majority	9,094	19.21
Electorate	68,837	
Turnout	47,328	68.75

**Member of last parliament*

CONSTITUENCY SNAPSHOT

Kettering had been a Conservative seat for 14 years when Labour's Philip Sawford produced a swing of 11 per cent, giving him a majority of 189 in 1997.

In 2001 the Tories needed a tiny swing to win the seat, yet Sawford achieved one in his favour trebling his majority. However, the Conservatives managed to take the seat in 2005 and Philip Hollobone was elected with a 3,301 majority.

Hollobone held the seat in 2010 with a majority of 9,094.

The seat lost Boughton and Pitsford, Brixworth, Clipston, Moulton, Spratton, Walgrave, Welford, and its part-wards of West Haddon and Guilsborough, and Yelvercroft to Daventry.

This Northamptonshire seat is made up of three semi-industrial towns: Burton Latimer, Desborough and Rothwell. It also includes numerous villages around the Welland Valley.

The seat contains the headquarters of Weetabix and Pegasus (accounting software). By far the biggest employer in the area is the Kettering General Hospital.

The area is connected to the national road network by the A14, and this has increased employment prospects in the area.

Adam Holloway

Gravesham ***(returning MP)***

No boundary changes

Tel: 020 7219 8402
E-mail: hollowaya@parliament.uk
Website: www.adamholloway.co.uk

Conservative

Date of birth: 29 July 1965; Son of Revd Roger Holloway OBE and Anne, née Alsopp

Education: Cranleigh School, Surrey; Magdalene College, Cambridge (MA theology and social and political science 1987) Imperial College, London (MBA business 1998) Royal Military Academy Sandhurst (Commission 1987); Single

Non-political career: Commissioned, Grenadier Guards 1987-92; Presenter: World in Action, Granada TV 1992-93; Senior reporter: ITN 1993-97, *Tonight with Trevor McDonald* 2000-01, *Sunday Times*/ITN/Sky News, Iraq War 2003

Political career: Member for Gravesham since 5 May 2005 general election; *Select Committees:* Member: Defence 2006-10, Arms Export Controls 2009-10

Political interests: Defence, crime

Other organisations: Trustee: Christian Aid 1997-2001, Map Action 2002-; Gravesend Conservative Club; Northfleet Conservative Club

Adam Holloway MP, House of Commons, London SW1A 0AA
Tel: 020 7219 8402 Fax: 020 7219 2871
E-mail: hollowaya@parliament.uk
Constituency: Tel: 01474 332097 Website: www.adamholloway.co.uk

GENERAL ELECTION RESULT

		%	+/-
Holloway, A. (Con)*	22,956	48.5	5.0
Smith, K. (Lab)	13,644	28.8	-13.2
Arrowsmith, A. (Lib Dem)	6,293	13.3	2.6
Clark, G. (UKIP)	2,265	4.8	2.9
Uncles, S. (England)	1,005	2.1	0.7
Crawford, R. (Green)	675	1.4	
Dartnell, A. (Ind)	465	1.0	
Majority	9,312	19.69	
Electorate	70,195		
Turnout	47,303	67.39	

**Member of last parliament*

CONSTITUENCY SNAPSHOT

In 1997 Labour's national success was reflected here, when Chris Pond gained the seat for them with a majority of 5,779. This decreased to a 4,862 in 2001.

In 2005 Adam Holloway, a former Grenadier Guards officer and television reporter, gained the seat back for the Conservatives with a majority of just 654.

The seat was held by Holloway with a 9,312 majority at the 2010 general election.

Situated on the south bank of the industrially developed Thames estuary, Gravesham is centred on the north Kent towns of Gravesend and Northfleet. However, numerous picturesque villages lie in the south of the seat.

Residents are comfortably off, and around four-fifths work in the service sector, which has gradually replaced traditional industries. Gravesend today is a busy commercial town and serves a large area as a shopping centre.

There is a relatively high proportion of ethnic minority residents in the constituency, mostly Sikhs.

The constituency falls within the Kent Thameside area, one of the two principal growth areas within the Thames Gateway project which aims to provide 120,000 more homes and 180,000 jobs in the region by 2016.

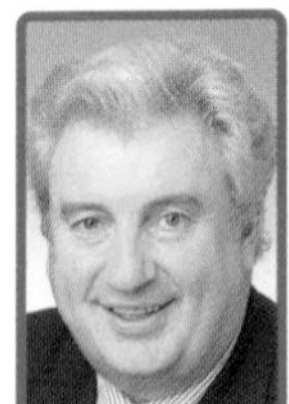

Jim Hood

Lanark and Hamilton East ***(returning MP)***

No boundary changes

Tel: 020 7219 4585
E-mail: hoodj@parliament.uk
Website: www.jimhoodmp.org.uk

Date of birth: 16 May 1948; Son of late William, miner, and Bridget Hood

Education: Lesmahagow Higher Grade School, Coatbridge College; Nottingham University/WEA (economics, industrial relations and communication); Married Marion Stewart McCleary 1967 (1 son 1 daughter)

Non-political career: Mining engineer 1964-87; Member, NUM 1964-: Official 1973-87, Leader of Nottinghamshire striking miners in 1984-85 national miners' strike; Member AEEU/Amicus/UNITE 1996-; Councillor, Newark and Sherwood District Council 1979-87

Political career: Member for Clydesdale 1987-2005, for Lanark and Hamilton East since 5 May 2005 general election; *Select Committees:* Member: Liaison 1992-2006, Defence 1997-2001, Chairmen's Panel 1997-10; European Scrutiny: Member 1998-2007, Chair 1998-2006

Political interests: NHS, home affairs, agriculture, environment, energy, housing, education, alcohol abuse and under-age drinking, European Union, defence

Other organisations: Member UK Delegation to the NATO Parliamentary Assembly 2005-; Member Parliamentary Assembly to: Council of Europe 2008-, Western European Union 2008-; Fellow, Industry and Parliament Trust; Armed Forces Parliamentary Scheme

Recreations: Gardening, reading, writing

Jim Hood MP, House of Commons, London SW1A 0AA
Tel: 020 7219 4585 Fax: 020 7219 5872
E-mail: hoodj@parliament.uk
Constituency: c/o Council Offices, South Vennel, Lanark ML11 7JT
Tel: 01555 673177 Fax: 01555 673188
Website: www.jimhoodmp.org.uk

GENERAL ELECTION RESULT

		%	+/-
Hood, J. (Lab)*	23,258	50.0	4.0
Adamson, C. (SNP)	9,780	21.0	3.3
McGavigan, C. (Con)	6,891	14.8	2.0
Herbison, D. (Lib Dem)	5,249	11.3	-7.3
McFarlane, D. (Ind)	670	1.4	0.5
Sale, R. (UKIP)	616	1.3	0.3
Majority	13,478	28.95	
Electorate	74,773		
Turnout	46,554	62.26	

**Member of last parliament*

CONSTITUENCY SNAPSHOT

Jimmy Hood was first elected for Labour in 1987 increasing his majority to a high of 13,809 in 1997.

2005 boundary changes created the new Lanark and Hamilton East constituency. Several southern Clyde Valley wards were lost; as were Stonehouse and Lesmahagow. Uddingston and Bothwell to the north were added; as well as the populous eastern wards of Hamilton.

Jimmy Hood won the new seat with a majority just under 12,000. Labour's Jim Hood maintained his solid lead with 50 per cent of the vote and a 13,478 majority in 2010.

This constituency forms a narrow urban strip running south-west from the Glasgow suburbs, along the northernmost boundary of the South Lanarkshire council area.

In 878 AD the first meeting of the Scots Parliament was held in Lanark.

New Lanark was founded in 1785 as a model industrial community. The whole of Hamilton, Lanark and their environs boomed and declined with cotton and coal but by the 1930s Hamilton was declared a distressed area as the factories and mills closed all over the Clyde Valley. However, the area's proximity to Glasgow transformed it into a commuter base for professionals and public administrators.

Light engineering survives in the towns of Lanark, Biggar, Larkhall and Stonehouse, and the extraction of sand and gravel still takes place around Carstairs and Lanark. Coal and cotton survive mainly as heritage sites: New Lanark is now a major tourist attraction and a world heritage site.

Kelvin Hopkins

Luton North (returning MP)

Boundary changes

Tel: 020 7219 6670
E-mail: hopkinsk@parliament.uk
Website: www.epolitix.com/Kelvin-Hopkins

Date of birth: 22 August 1941; Son of late Professor Harold Horace Hopkins, FRS, physicist and mathematician, and Joan Avery Frost, medical secretary

Education: Queen Elizabeth's Grammar School, High Barnet; Nottingham University (BA politics, economics and mathematics with statistics); Married Patricia Langley 1965 (1 son 1 daughter)

Non-political career: TUC Economic Department 1969-70, 1973-77; Policy and research officer, NALGO/UNISON 1977-94; Member, GMB; Delegate, Luton Trades Union Council; Councillor, Luton Borough 1972-76

Political career: Contested Luton North 1983 general election. Member for Luton North 1997-2010, for Luton North (revised boundary) since 6 May 2010 general election; Adviser on Yachting to Richard Caborn, as Minister of State for Sport 2002-07; *Select Committees:* Member: European Standing Committee B 1998-, Broadcasting 1999-2001, Public Administration 2002-10, Crossrail Bill 2006-07, European Scrutiny 2007-10; Vice-Chair, Central Region Labour Party 1995-96

Political interests: Economic policy, employment, transport, arts; France, Sweden

Other organisations: Chair of Governors, Luton College of Higher Education 1985-89; Member Mary Seacole House, Luton; Hon. Vice-President, UK Carrom Federation; Fellow Industry and Parliament Trust 2000; Hon. Fellow, Luton University 1993; Luton Socialist, Lansdowne (Luton); Luton Town Football Club, UK Carrom Federation; *Publications:* Various NALGO publications

Recreations: Music, photography, sailing on the Norfolk Broads

Kelvin Hopkins MP, House of Commons, London SW1A 0AA
Tel: 020 7219 6670 Fax: 020 7219 0957
E-mail: hopkinsk@parliament.uk
Constituency: 3 Union Street, Luton, Bedfordshire LU1 3AN
Tel: 01582 488208 Fax: 01582 480990 Website: www.epolitix.com/Kelvin-Hopkins

GENERAL ELECTION RESULT

		%
Hopkins, K. (Lab)*	21,192	49.3
Brier, J. (Con)	13,672	31.8
Martins, R. (Lib Dem)	4,784	11.1
Brown, C. (UKIP)	1,564	3.6
Rose, S. (BNP)	1,316	3.1
Hall, S. (Green)	490	1.1
Majority	7,520	17.48
Electorate	65,062	
Turnout	43,018	66.12

**Member of last parliament*

CONSTITUENCY SNAPSHOT

Luton North was a Conservative seat until 1997, when MP Kelvin Hopkins won it for Labour with a majority of 9,626. The Tory vote fell away further in 2001, increasing the Labour majority to 9,977.

In 2005 support for Labour dropped by 8 per cent and Hopkins' winning margin fell below 6,500.

Labour held the seat in 2010 with a swing of 0.5 per cent from the Conservatives. Hopkins majority increased to 7,520.

Boundary changes were minimal.

This Bedfordshire constituency has become very much an urban, residential seat, having lost its former rural fringe to Mid Bedfordshire in 1995, and some of Luton's town area to Luton South with the recent boundary changes.

This constituency has less industry than its neighbour, Luton South, but includes the area's most up-market residential housing. It excludes the town centre but does include the Luton and Dunstable Hospital and the main campus of Barnfield College of Further Education within its boundaries. Service industries are the growth areas providing most of the employment opportunities today.

The local economy is aided by excellent transport and communication links. The M1 runs across the west of the seat and the Thameslink rail service runs commuters directly into London.

Kris Hopkins

Keighley

Boundary changes

Tel: 020 7219 3000
E-mail: kris.hopkins.mp@parliament.uk
Website: www.krishopkins.co.uk

Date of birth: 1963

Education: Leeds University (Degree communications and cultural studies); Married Kersten (1 daughter)

Non-political career: Duke of Wellington's Regiment; Part-time media and communications lecturer; Bradford council: Councillor 1998-, Deputy leader 2004-06, Council leader 2006-; Conservative group leader 2006-; Chair: Bradford Vision, Humber Regional Housing Board

Political career: Contested Leeds West 2001 and Halifax 2005 general elections. Member for Keighley since 6 May 2010 general election

Recreations: Walking, running, photography

Kris Hopkins MP, House of Commons, London SW1A 0AA
Tel: 020 7219 3000 E-mail: kris.hopkins.mp@parliament.uk
Constituency: Keighley and Ilkley Conservative Association, Churchill House, North Street, Keighley, West Yorkshire BD21 3AF
Tel: 01535 210108 Website: www.krishopkins.co.uk

GENERAL ELECTION RESULT

		%
Hopkins, K. (Con)	20,003	41.9
Thomas, J. (Lab)	17,063	35.8
Fekri, N. (Lib Dem)	7,059	14.8
Brons, A. (BNP)	1,962	4.1
Latham, P. (UKIP)	1,470	3.1
Smith, S. (NF)	135	0.3
Majority	2,940	6.16
Electorate	65,893	
Turnout	47,692	72.38

CONSTITUENCY SNAPSHOT

Conservative Joan Hall took the seat from Labour in 1970, but Labour's Bob Cryer won it in 1974. He held out against the Tory advance in 1979 by just 78 votes but was defeated in 1983, as Tory Gary Waller took the seat with a majority of over 5,000. He went on to hold the seat for 14 years.

In 1997, Bob Cryer's widow Ann secured a majority of 7,132, on a 10 per cent swing for Labour.

In 2001 a small swing to the Conservatives reduced Cryer's majority to 4,005. In 2005 there was a small swing back to Labour and Cryer's majority rose to 4,852. The Conservatives seized the seat from Labour in 2010, with Kris Hopkins securing a 2,940 majority.

The only boundary change here was a ward swap on Ilkley Moor.

Industry has traditionally been a mixture of textiles and engineering. Both have declined, and the biggest single employer is the Airedale General Hospital, which serves a wide area, including parts of east Lancashire.

The Bronte village of Haworth and the picturesque Worth Valley are both here. Ilkley is a popular town as a base for exploring the Yorkshire Dales.

Martin Horwood

Cheltenham ***(returning MP)***

Boundary changes

Tel: 020 7219 4784
E-mail: horwoodm@parliament.uk
Website: www.martinhorwood.net

Date of birth: 12 October 1962; Son of Don and Nina Horwood, née Edge

Education: Cheltenham College; The Queen's College, Oxford (BA modern history 1984); Married Dr Shona Arora 1995 (1 daughter 1 son)

Non-political career: Account executive Ted Bates Advertising 1985-86; Director of development British Humanist Association 1986-88; Creative co-ordinator Help the Aged 1988-90; Donor marketing manager Oxfam 1990-95; Director of communications and fundraising Oxfam (India) 1995-96; Director of fundraising Alzheimer's Society 1996-2001; Senior consultant then head of consultancy Target Direct Marketing 2001-05; TGWU 1990-95; MSF/Amicus/Unite 1996-; Councillor Vale of White Horse District Council 1991-95

Political career: Contested Oxford East 1992 and Cities of London and Westminster 2001 general elections. Member for Cheltenham 2005-10, for Cheltenham (revised boundary) since 6 May 2010 general election; Liberal Democrat Shadow Minister for: Home Affairs 2005-06, Environment 2006-10, Climate Change 2009-10; *Select Committees:* Member: ODPM/Communities and Local Government 2005-07, Environmental Audit 2007-10; President Oxford Student Liberal Society 1983; Chair Union of Liberal Students 1984-85; Chair Liberal Information Network (LINk) 1987-90

Political interests: Voluntary sector, sustainable development, environment; India, Tibet

Other organisations: Member: Campaign to Protect Rural England 2006-, Cheltenham Civic Society 2007-; United Nations Association 2008-

Recreations: Cycling, drawing, astronomy, geneaology

Martin Horwood MP, House of Commons, London SW1A 0AA
Tel: 020 7219 4784 Fax: 020 7219 1185
E-mail: horwoodm@parliament.uk
Constituency: 16 Hewlett Road, Cheltenham,
Gloucestershire GL52 6AA Tel: 01242 224889 Fax: 01242 256658
Website: www.martinhorwood.net

GENERAL ELECTION RESULT

		%
Horwood, M. (Lib Dem)*	26,659	50.5
Coote, M. (Con)	21,739	41.2
Green, J. (Lab)	2,703	5.1
Bowman, P. (UKIP)	1,192	2.3
Hanks, K. (Loony)	493	0.9
Majority	4,920	9.32
Electorate	78,998	
Turnout	52,786	66.82

**Member of last parliament*

CONSTITUENCY SNAPSHOT

For most of the post-Second World War period the Conservatives received strong support here. However, in 1992 the Liberal Democrats won the seat with a swing of nearly 6 per cent, electing Nigel Jones.

Jones consolidated the Lib Dem position over the next three elections, before ill-health forced him to stand down in 2005. Martin Horwood was elected for the party albeit with a reduced majority of 2,303. Number six on the Conservative target list, but Horwood won re-election with an increased 4,920 majority.

Boundary changes were minor and relate to six wards that were shared between Cheltenham and Tewkesbury. Leckhampton, Oakley, Up Hatherley, and Warden Hill are now completely in Cheltenham's boundaries; while Prestbury and Swindon village wards have moved in their entirety to Tewkesbury.

As Britain's largest inland spa town, Cheltenham is a popular attraction for tourists and visitors. It has a charming ambience, characterised by the elegant Victorian and Regency buildings which house a large proportion of its inhabitants.

The largest employer in the constituency is the Government Communications Headquarters (GCHQ). The presence of GCHQ has arguably had a considerable impact on the character of Cheltenham's population.

Cheltenham has a vibrant cultural and entertainment scene, including an international music festival second only to that of Edinburgh.

Stewart Hosie

Dundee East (returning MP)

No boundary changes

Tel: 020 7219 8164
E-mail: hosies@parliament.uk
Website: www.stewarthosie.com

SNP
Scottish National Party

Date of birth: 3 January 1963; Son of R A Hosie, architectural ironmonger, and E A Hosie, bookkeeper

Education: Carnoustie High School; Bell Street Tech (HD computer studies 1981); Dundee College of Technology 1981; Married Shona Robison (later MSP) 1997 (1 daughter)

Non-political career: Group IS manager MIH 1988-93; Systems analyst various organisations 1993-96; Year 2000/EMU project manager Stakis Plc/Hilton 1996-2000; Various project management posts 2000-05; MSF 1992

Political career: Contested Kirkcaldy 1992 and 1997 general elections. Member for Dundee East since 5 May 2005 general election; SNP Spokesperson for: Treasury 2005-, Women 2005-07, Home Affairs 2005-07, Economy 2005-07; SNP: Deputy leader parliamentary group 2007-; Chief Whip 2007-; Contested Kirkcaldy constituency 1999 Scottish Parliament election; SNP youth convener 1986-89; SNP national secretary 1999-2003; Organisation convener 2003-05

Political interests: Economic development, job creation

Other organisations: Endorsed by the Save the Scottish Regiments Campaign

Recreations: Football, hill-walking, rugby

Stewart Hosie MP, House of Commons, London SW1A 0AA
Tel: 020 7219 8164 Fax: 020 7219 6716
E-mail: hosies@parliament.uk
Constituency: SNP Parliamentary Offices, 8 Old Glamis Road, Dundee DD3 8HP Tel: 01382 623200 Fax: 01382 903205
Website: www.stewarthosie.com

GENERAL ELECTION RESULT

		%	+/-
Hosie, S. (SNP)*	15,350	37.8	0.7
Murray, K. (Lab)	13,529	33.4	-2.8
Bustin, C. (Con)	6,177	15.2	2.5
Sneddon, C. (Lib Dem)	4,285	10.6	-0.8
Baird, S. (Green)	542	1.3	
Arthur, M. (UKIP)	431	1.1	0.3
Gorrie, A. (SSP)	254	0.6	-0.7
Majority	1,821	4.49	
Electorate	65,471		
Turnout	40,568	61.96	

**Member of last parliament*

CONSTITUENCY SNAPSHOT

From 1950 Dundee East returned Labour Members for more than two decades. However, the SNP's Gordon Wilson held the seat from 1974 to 1987. Labour's John McAllion increased his majority from 1,000 in 1987 to just under 10,000 in 1997.

McAllion stood down in 2001 and Iain Luke held the seat for Labour with a majority of nearly 4,500.

Boundary changes for the 2005 election reduced Luke's notional majority and a 1.1 per cent swing to the SNP's Stewart Hosie was enough to unseat him. He increased his majority to 1,821 in 2010.

Dundee East has a more industrial character than its sister seat to the west, fanning out from the docklands through mixed residential areas as far as the town of Carnoustie and the affluent suburb of Monifieth in the north-west.

The seat incorporates the prosperous middle class enclaves of Balgillo, Barnhill and Broughty Ferry. It also contains older tenement districts and some large council estates such as Douglas and Whitfield.

DC Thomson owns a hefty proportion of the Scottish national and regional press including the Courier and the Sunday Post and is a major employer in the east of the city.

Carnoustie is famous for being one of the hosts of the Open Championship.

Rt Hon **George Howarth**

Knowsley ***(returning MP)***

New constituency

Tel: 020 7219 6902
E-mail: howarthg@parliament.uk
Website: www.georgehowarth.org.uk

Date of birth: 29 June 1949; Son of late George Howarth and of Eleanor Howarth

Education: Schools in Huyton; Liverpool Polytechnic (BA social sciences 1977); Married Julie Rodgers 1977 (2 sons 1 daughter)

Non-political career: Engineering apprentice 1966-70; Engineer 1970-75; Teacher 1977-82; Co-operative Development Services 1980-82; Chief executive Wales Co-operative Centre 1982-86; UNITE; Councillor Huyton Urban District Council 1971-75; Knowsley Borough Council: Councillor 1975-86, Deputy Leader 1982-83

Political career: Member Knowsley North 13 November 1986 by-election to 1997, for Knowsley North and Sefton East 1997-2010, for Knowsley since 6 May 2010 general electionn; Opposition Spokesperson for: the Environment 1989-92, Environmental Protection 1993-94, Home Affairs 1994-97; Parliamentary Under-Secretary of State: Home Office 1997-99, Northern Ireland Office 1999-2001; Member, Intelligence and Security Committee; *Select Committees:* Member: Public Accounts 2002-03, Modernisation of the House of Commons 2005-10; Chair Armed Forces Bill 2005-06; Member: Joint Committee on Conventions 2006, Chairmen's Panel 2009-10; Chair, Knowsley South Labour Party 1981-85; Secretary, Knowsley Borough District Labour Party 1977-80; Member, North West Region Executive, Labour Party 1981-84

Political interests: Housing, environment, crime, disorder; Middle East, South Africa

Other organisations: PC 2005

Recreations: Coarse fishing, family, reading

Rt Hon George Howarth MP, House of Commons, London SW1A 0AA Tel: 020 7219 6902 Fax: 020 7219 0495
E-mail: howarthg@parliament.uk
Constituency: Lathom House, North Mersey Business Centre, Woodward Road, Kirkby, Merseyside L33 7UY Tel: 0151-546 9918 Fax: 0151-546 9918 Website: www.georgehowarth.org.uk

GENERAL ELECTION RESULT

		%
Howarth, G. (Lab)*	31,650	70.9
Clucas, F. (Lib Dem)	5,960	13.4
Dunne, D. (Con)	4,004	9.0
Greenhalgh, S. (BNP)	1,895	4.2
Rundle, A. (UKIP)	1,145	2.6
Majority	25,690	57.53
Electorate	79,561	
Turnout	44,654	56.13

**Member of last parliament*

CONSTITUENCY SNAPSHOT

The new seat of Knowsley combines wards from Knowsley North and Sefton East with others from Knowsley South.

Knowsley North and Sefton East had been in Labour's hands since its creation in 1983, and Knowsley South (Huyton at the time) was Harold Wilson's seat for 40 years. George Howarth represented the northern division for Labour from 1986, while Edward O'Hara was the member of Knowsley South since 1990 until retiring in 2010.

Although George Howarth's majority fell in 2005, he still polled over 63 per cent of the vote, and his majority was 16,269. Howarth won the new seat in 2010 with a majority of 25,690 giving Labour 70.9 per cent vote-share.

Situated to the east of Liverpool and centred around the town of Knowsley, the seat also includes the towns of Kirkby and Huyton-with-Roby.

The constituency retains much of the characteristics of the rest of the Merseyside seats by having a very low ethnic minority population, comprising just over 1 per cent of the population.

Plans to relocate Everton Football club to Kirby from the centre of Liverpool are ongoing.

Gerald Howarth

Aldershot (returning MP)

Boundary changes

Tel: 020 7219 5650
E-mail: geraldhowarth@parliament.uk
Website: www.geraldhowarth.com

Conservative

Date of birth: 12 September 1947; Son of Mary and late James Howarth, retired company director

Education: Bloxham School, Banbury; Southampton University (BA English 1969); Married Elizabeth Squibb 1973 (1 daughter 2 sons)

Non-political career: Commissioned RAFVR 1968; Assistant manager, loan syndication Bank of America International Ltd 1971-77; European Arab Bank 1977-81: Manager and personal assistant to group managing director 1979, Manager, loan syndications 1980; Loan syndication manager responsible for arranging project and other loans in Africa, Middle East and South America, Standard Chartered Bank plc 1981-83; Joint managing director, Taskforce Communications 1993-95; Member, National Union of Seamen 1966; Councillor London Borough of Hounslow 1982-83

Political career: Member for Cannock and Burntwood 1983-92, for Aldershot 1997-2010, for Aldershot (revised boundary) since 6 May 2010 general election; PPS: to Michael Spicer: as Parliamentary Under-Secretary of State, Department of Energy 1987-90, as Minister of State, Department of the Environment 1990; to Sir George Young as Minister of State, Department of the Environment 1990-91, to Margaret Thatcher, MP 1991-92; Shadow Minister for Defence 2002-10; Parliamentary Under-Secretary of State, Ministry of Defence 2010-; *Select Committees:* Member: Home Affairs 1997-2001, Defence 2001-03, Armed Forces Bill 2005-06; Member Greater London Area CPC Advisory Committee; Vice-chair City Conservative Forum 1981-84; Founder Member, No Turning Back Group; Executive Member 1922 Committee 2000-02; Chair 92 Group of Conservative MPs 2001-

Political interests: Aerospace, aviation, defence, media, privatisation; Chile, Germany, Pakistan, Russia, South Africa

Other organisations: General Secretary, Society for Individual Freedom 1969-71; Director, Freedom Under Law 1973-77; President, Air Display Association Europe 2002-; Council member Air League 2005 -; Fellow, Industry and Parliament Trust, Trustee, Vulcan to the Sky 2006-; Britannia Airways Parliamentary Pilot of the Year 1988; Freeman Guild of Air Pilots and Air Navigators; Aldershot Conservative, Liveryman; *Publications:* Co-author No Turning Back (1985), and further publications by the Group

Recreations: Flying, tennis, DIY, family

Gerald Howarth MP, House of Commons, London SW1A 0AA
Tel: 020 7219 5650 Fax: 020 7219 1198
E-mail: geraldhowarth@parliament.uk
Constituency: Conservative Club (not for correspondence), Victoria Road, Aldershot, Hampshire GU11 1JX Tel: 01252 323637
Fax: 01252 323637 Website: www.geraldhowarth.com

GENERAL ELECTION RESULT

		%
Howarth, G. (Con)*	21,203	46.7
Collett, A. (Lib Dem)	15,617	34.4
Slater, J. (Lab)	5,489	12.1
Snare, R. (UKIP)	2,041	4.5
Cowd, G. (EIP)	803	1.8
Brimicombe, J. (Christian)	231	0.5
Majority	5,586	12.31
Electorate	71,469	
Turnout	45,384	63.50

**Member of last parliament*

CONSTITUENCY SNAPSHOT

Gerald Howarth took over from the late Sir Julian Critchley in 1997. In 1992 the Tories polled over 58 per cent of the vote but in 1997 they dropped to 42 per cent. In 2001 and 2005 little changed.

In 2010 Gerald Howarth retained the seat for the Conservatives with a 5,586 majority giving the Tories a 46.7 per cent share of the vote.

The seat gained part of Blackwater ward from North East Hampshire in exchange for part of Fleet North, part of Hartley Wintney, and all of Yateley East, Yateley North and Yateley West.

Located in North East Hampshire and close to the border with Surrey, Aldershot is perhaps best known as the traditional home of the British Army.

The constituency also encompasses the town of Farnborough, famous for its biennial international air show.

The constituency is largely urban but has substantial areas of open countryside and although it is a very affluent seat for UK as a whole.

Farnborough is generally regarded as the birthplace of British flight and also supports a large number of the constituency's jobs as the home of the aeronautical research and development industry. A number of defence companies such as BAE Systems and Qinetiq are based there, and Nokia has its global research and development base in the town.

John Howell

Henley (returning MP)

Boundary changes

Tel: 020 7219 4828
E-mail: howelljm@parliament.uk
Website: www.johnhowellmp.com

Conservative

Date of birth: 27 July 1955; Son of Alexander and Gladys Howell

Education: Battersea Grammar School, London; Edinburgh University (MA archaeology 1978); St John's College, Oxford (DPhil prehistoric archaeology 1981); Married Alison Parker 1987 (1 son 2 daughters)

Non-political career: Ernst & Young 1987-96; Business presenter BBC World Service Television 1996-97; Director: Fifth World Productions Ltd 1996-2003, Media Presentation Consultants Ltd 2005-; Councillor, Oxfordshire County Council 2004-09: Cabinet member for Change Management 2005-08

Political career: Member for Henley 26 June 2008 by-election to 2010, for Henley (revised boundary) since 6 May 2010 general election; *Select Committees:* Member: Work and Pensions 2009-10

Political interests: Rural issues, social policy, local government, foreign affairs; Central and Eastern Europe, South Asia

Other organisations: OBE 2000; *Publications:* Neolithic Northern France (1983); Understanding Eastern Europe: the context of change (1994)

Recreations: Music, theatre

John Howell OBE MP, House of Commons, London SW1A 0AA
Tel: 020 7219 4828; 020 7219 6676 Fax: 020 7219 2606
E-mail: howelljm@parliament.uk
Constituency: PO Box 84, Watlington, Oxfordshire OX49 5XD
Tel: 01491 613072 Website: www.johnhowellmp.com

GENERAL ELECTION RESULT

		%
Howell, J. (Con)*	30,054	56.2
Crick, A. (Lib Dem)	13,466	25.2
McKenzie, R. (Lab)	5,835	10.9
Hughes, L. (UKIP)	1,817	3.4
Stevenson, M. (Green)	1,328	2.5
Bews, J. (BNP)	1,020	1.9
Majority	16,588	30.99
Electorate	75,005	
Turnout	53,520	71.36

**Member of last parliament*

CONSTITUENCY SNAPSHOT

This constituency has been in Conservative hands since 1945. Until 1997 the Conservative share of the vote barely dropped below 60 per cent. Michael Heseltine held the seat from 1974 until 2001. In 2001 Boris Johnson was elected with a majority of 8,458.

In 2008 Johnson was elected Mayor of London, and resigned as an MP in early June. He was replaced by John Howell who predictably held the seat for the Tories, with an increased majority of 10, 116.

The Conservatives retained the seat in 2010 with 30,054 votes giving Howell a majority of 16,588.

The seat gained Otmoor and Kirtlington wards.

Henley-on-Thames is in the south of this Oxfordshire seat and Thame is in the north, with other towns including Goring, Wheatley and Great Milton inbetween, set in lush countryside along the most beautiful stretches of the River Thames.

The constituency has become something of a dormitory for commuters to both London and Reading, and is easily accessible by both the M40, in the north east of the constituency, and the M4, just south of the constituency.

It combines a large farming community with a strong professional sector, and is home to Invesco Perpetual.

Tourism is another important industry, with the annual rowing regatta attracting visitors and rowers from around the world. Henley is a very affluent constituency, one of the richest in the United Kingdom.

Hon **Lindsay Hoyle**

Chorley (returning MP)

Boundary changes

Tel: 020 7219 3515
E-mail: wilsonp@parliament.uk
Website: www.lindsayhoyle.com

Date of birth: 10 June 1957; Son of Baron Hoyle (qv) and late Pauline Hoyle

Education: Lords College, Bolton; Horwich FE; Bolton TIC (City & Guilds Construction); Married Lynda Fowler (divorced 1982); married Catherine Swindley (2 daughters)

Non-political career: Company director; Shop steward; Member, AMICUS (MSF); Co-Chair of the Unite Parliamentary Group; Councillor: Adlington Town Council 1980-98, Chorley Borough Council 1980-98: Chair Economic Development, Deputy Leader 1994-97; Mayor of Chorley 1997-98

Political career: Member for Chorley 1997-2010, for Chorley (revised boundary) since 6 May 2010 general election; Parliamentary assistant to Beverley Hughes as Minister for the North West 2008-10; *Select Committees:* Member: Catering 1997-05, Trade and Industry/Business, Enterprise and Regulatory Reform/Business and Enterprise/Business, Innovation and Skills 1998-2010, European Scrutiny 2005-10, Quadripartite (Committees on Strategic Export Controls) 2006-07

Political interests: Trade and industry, sport, defence, small businesses, agriculture; British Overseas Territories, Falkland Islands, Gibraltar

Other organisations: Armed Forces Parliamentary Scheme (Royal Marines) 1998-; Member, Cuerdon Valley Trust; Member: Adlington Cricket Club, Chorley Cricket Club

Recreations: Cricket, Rugby League

Hon Lindsay Hoyle MP, House of Commons, London SW1A 0AA
Tel: 020 7219 3515 Fax: 020 7219 3831
E-mail: wilsonp@parliament.uk
Constituency: 35-39 Market Street, Chorley, Lancashire PR7 2SW
Tel: 01257 271555 Fax: 01257 277462
Website: www.lindsayhoyle.com

GENERAL ELECTION RESULT

		%
Hoyle, L. (Lab)*	21,515	43.2
Cullens, A. (Con)	18,922	38.0
Fenn, S. (Lib Dem)	6,957	14.0
Hogan, N. (UKIP)	2,021	4.1
Curtis, C. (Ind)	359	0.7
Majority	2,593	5.21
Electorate	70,950	
Turnout	49,774	70.15

**Member of last parliament*

CONSTITUENCY SNAPSHOT

Post-war Chorley was a Labour seat, until Constance Monks won it for the Conservatives in the 1970 election. The seat then became a national weathervane, falling to whichever party formed the government.

Since 1997 Lindsey Hoyle has held this seat for Labour. He was re-elected with a 7,625 majority in 2005. Labour retained the seat in 2010 giving Hoyle a majority of 2,593.

The seat lost the wards of Eccleston and Mawdesley and Lostock to South Ribble.

Chorley is a market town in southern Lancashire. The town's wealth came principally from the cotton industry and as late as the 1970s its skyline was dominated by chimneys. These have since disappeared as Chorley, like many other Lancashire towns, has had to adapt to the modern industrial era.

The town has adapted well to the modern economy, successfully building a strong service sector and has a higher proportion than the national average of people working in that sector.

Chorley and many of its surrounding villages act as satellite communities for the larger neighbouring towns of Bolton and Preston.

Simon Hughes

Bermondsey and Old Southwark ***(returning MP)***

New constituency

Tel: 020 7219 6256
E-mail: simon@simonhughes.org.uk
Website: www.simonhughes.org.uk

Date of birth: 17 May 1951; Son of late James Henry Hughes and of Sylvia, née Ward

Education: Llandaff Cathedral School, Cardiff; Christ College, Brecon; Selwyn College, Cambridge (BA law 1973, MA); Inns of Court School of Law; College of Europe, Bruges (Certificate in Higher European Studies 1975); Single

Non-political career: Barrister Called to the Bar, Inner Temple 1974; In practice 1978-

Political career: Member (Liberal 1983-88, Liberal Democrat since 1988) for Southwark and Bermondsey February 1983 by-election to 1997, for North Southwark and Bermondsey 1997-2010, for Bermondsey and Old Southwalk since 6 May 2010 general election; Liberal Spokesperson for the Environment 1983-88; Liberal Democrat: Spokesperson for: Health 1988, London 1988-97, Deputy Chief Whip 1989-99; Spokesperson for: Education, Science and Training 1988-92, Church of England 1988-97, Environment and Natural Resources 1992-94, Urban Affairs and Young People 1994-97, Health 1995-99, Home and Legal Affairs 1999-2003, London 2003-04; Shadow: Office of the Deputy Prime Minister 2005, Attorney General 2005-07, Secretary of State for Constitutional Affairs/Justice 2006-07, Leader of the House of Commons 2007-09, Secretary of State for Energy and Climate Change 2009-10; *Select Committees:* Member: Accommodation and Works 1992-97, Joint Committee on Conventions 2006, Modernisation of the House of Commons 2007-10, Ecclesiastical Committee; Chair, Liberal Party's Home Affairs Panel 1977-83; President, National League of Young Liberals 1986-92, Vice-President, Liberal Democrat Youth and Students 1983-86, President 1992-; Vice-Chair, Southwark and Bermondsey Liberal Association 1981-83; President Liberal Democrats 2004-08; Contested Liberal Democrat leadership 1999, 2006

Political interests: Human rights, civil liberties, youth affairs, social affairs, housing, environment; Commonwealth, southern Africa, west Africa, latin America, eastern Europe, Cyprus, South Africa

Other organisations: London mayoral candidate 2004; Trainee, EEC Brussels 1976; Trainee and member Secretariat, Directorate and Commission on Human Rights, Council of Europe, Strasbourg 1976-77; Chair, Thames Festival Trust; Honorary Fellow, South Bank University; Redriff (Rotherhithe); *Publications:* Co-author Human Rights in Western Europe – The Next 30 Years (1981); The Prosecutorial Process in England and Wales (1981); Across the Divide – Liberal Values for Defence and Disarmament (1986); Pathways to Power (1992); Who Goes Where – Asylum: Opportunity not Crisis (2002); Co-author Beyond Blair (2006)

Recreations: Music, theatre, history, sport (Millwall football club, Glamorgan county cricket club and Wales rugby football union), the countryside and open air

Simon Hughes MP, House of Commons, London SW1A 0AA
Tel: 020 7219 6256 Fax: 020 7219 6567
E-mail: simon@simonhughes.org.uk
Constituency: 4 Market Place, London SE16 3UQ Tel: 020 7232 2557
Website: www.simonhughes.org.uk

GENERAL ELECTION RESULT

		%
Hughes, S. (Lib Dem)*	21,590	48.4
Shawcross, V. (Lab)	13,060	29.3
Morrison, L. (Con)	7,638	17.1
Tyler, S. (BNP)	1,370	3.1
Chance, T. (Green)	718	1.6
Kirkby, A. (Ind)	155	0.4
Freeman, S. (Ind)	120	0.3
Majority	8,530	19.10
Electorate	77,623	
Turnout	44,651	57.52

**Member of last parliament*

CONSTITUENCY SNAPSHOT

Between 1950 and 1979 North Southwark and Bermondsey was held by Labour's Bob Mellish.

After Mellish's resignation in 1982 the subsequent by-election produced the largest post-Second World War by-election swing of 44.2 per cent. The Liberal Simon Hughes was elected and has held the seat ever since. He was returned with a majority in 2005. The revised seat remains one of the Liberal Democrats' safest urban seats and Simon Hughes was re-elected with a 8,530 majority.

Unlike the majority of new constituencies formed from the boundary review, Bermondsey and old Southwark's boundaries are almost identical to that of North Southwark and Bermondsey. Only two southern part-wards, Faraday and Liversey, are not in the new seat; both are now in Camberwell and Peckham.

The constituency is one of the poorest constituencies in London. Stretching from Limehouse Reach past Surrey and Rotherhithe docks to London Bridge station and on to Waterloo Bridge it is, however, also home to some of London's great cultural landmarks: the Globe Theatre, Southwark Cathedral, the Tate Modern art gallery and the new Greater London Assembly building.

Part of the regeneration of the constituency along the South Bank includes the creation of the so-called London Bridge Quarter. At its centre will be The Shard, which will be the tallest building in the United Kingdom when completed in 2012.

Rt Hon **Chris Huhne**

Eastleigh (returning MP)

Boundary changes

Tel: 020 7219 4997
Website: www.chrishuhne.org.uk

Date of birth: 2 July 1954; Son of Peter Huhne and Ann, née Gladstone Murray

Education: Westminster School; Sorbonne, Paris (Certificate French language and civilisation 1972); Magdalen College, Oxford (BA philosophy, politics and economics 1975, MA); Married Vicky Pryce née Coumouzis 1984 (1 daughter 2 sons 2 stepdaughters)

Non-political career: Freelance journalist, India 1975-76; Trainee *Liverpool Daily Post* and *Liverpool Echo* 1976-77; Brussels correspondent *The Economist* 1977-80; *The Guardian*: leader writer 1980-84, economics editor and columnist 1984-90; Economics and assistant editor *Independent on Sunday* 1990-91; Business and city editor *Independent* and *Independent on Sunday* 1991-94; Managing director and founder Sovereign Ratings IBCA Ltd 1994-97; Managing director and chief economist Fitch IBCA Ltd 1997-99; Vice-chair sovereign and international finance Fitch Ratings Ltd 1999-2003; Member National Union of Journalists

Political career: Contested Reading East 1983, Oxford West and Abingdon 1987 general elections. Member for Eastleigh 2005-10, for Eastleigh (revised boundary) since 6 May 2010 general election; Liberal Democrat Shadow: Chief Secretary to the Treasury 2005-06, Secretary of State for Environment, Food and Rural Affairs 2006-07, Home Secretary 2007-10, Secretary of State for Justice and Lord Chancellor 2008-09; Secretary of State for Energy and Climate Change 2010-; MEP for South East 1999-2005: Deputy leader EP Liberal Democrat Group, Economic spokesman, ELDR group; Chair Press and Broadcasting Policy Panel 1994-95; Economic adviser 1997 general election; Member Economic Policy Commission 1998; Advisory board member Centre for Reform 1998-; Joint chair Policy Panel on Global Stability, Security and Sustainability 1999-2000; Chair Expert Commission of Britain's adoption of the Euro 1999-2000; Commission on Public Services 2001-02; Contested Liberal Democrat leadership 2006 and 2007

Political interests: European single currency, economics, third world debt and development, Europe, electoral reform, financial services; Hong Kong, China and ASEAN countries

Other organisations: Director Electoral Reform (Ballot Services) Ltd 1988-95; Council member: Britain in Europe 1999-2005, Consumers' Association 2001-04; PC 2010; Wincott Junior Financial Journalist of the Year 1981; Financial Journalist of the Year 1990; *Publications:* Co-author Debt and Danger: The World Financial Crisis (1985); Real World Economics: Essays on Imperfect Markets and Fallible Governments (1990-91); The Ecu Report: the Single European Currency (1991); Co-author Both Sides of the Coin: the Case for the Euro and European Monetary Union (1999)

Recreations: family, football, cinema, history

Rt Hon Chris Huhne MP, House of Commons, London SW1A 0AA
Tel: 020 7219 4997 Fax: 020 7219 02141
Constituency: Eastleigh Liberal Democrats, 109A Leigh Road, Eastleigh, Hampshire SO50 9DR Tel: 023 8062 0007
Fax: 023 8061 8245 E-mail: chris@chrishuhne.org.uk
Website: www.chrishuhne.org.uk

GENERAL ELECTION RESULT

		%
Huhne, C. (Lib Dem)*	24,966	46.5
Hutchings, M. (Con)	21,102	39.3
Barraclough, L. (Lab)	5,153	9.6
Finch, R. (UKIP)	1,933	3.6
Pewsey, T. (England)	249	0.5
Stone, D. (Ind)	154	0.3
Low, K. (NLP)	93	0.2
Majority	3,864	7.20
Electorate	77,435	
Turnout	53,650	69.28

**Member of last parliament*

CONSTITUENCY SNAPSHOT

Eastleigh was created in 1955 and represented by the Conservatives until the incumbent, Stephen Milligan, died in 1994. In the resulting by-election the Conservative majority of 17,702 became a Liberal Democrat lead of 9,239 for David Chidgey.

In 1997 Chidgey was able to hold on to the seat, and was re-elected in 2001 with an improved share of the vote. Chidgey stood down in 2005 and the party selected Chris Huhne to replace him. He retained by the seat by 568 votes.

Huhne retained the seat in 2010 with a majority of 3,864.

The sole boundary change here was the loss of the Chandler's Ford West part-ward to Winchester.

Eastleigh is an old industrial Hampshire town. It has a working-class base and many of its residents commute into neighbouring Southampton.

Historically, it was home to a rail works and a Pirelli factory, but most of the old industry is gone or going. The constituency is also home to numerous wealthy villages along the Solent and river Itchen.

As a satellite of Southampton, Eastleigh has few facilities of its own and relies on the services provided by its larger neighbour.

Rt Hon **Jeremy Hunt**

South West Surrey ***(returning MP)***

Boundary changes

Tel: 020 7219 6813
E-mail: huntj@parliament.uk
Website: www.localconservatives.org

Conservative

Date of birth: 1 November 1966; Son of Nick and Meriel Hunt

Education: Charterhouse, Surrey; Magdalen College, Oxford (BA philosophy, politics and economics 1988, MA); Married Lucia Guo 2009

Non-political career: Management consultant Outram Cullinan and Co 1988-89 English teacher Japan 1990-91 Founder/Managing Director Hotcourses Ltd 1991-2005

Political career: Member for South West Surrey 2005-10, for South West Surrey (revised boundary) since 6 May 2010 general election; Shadow: Minister for Disabled People 2005-07, Secretary of State for Culture, Media and Sport 2007-10; Secretary of State for Culture, Olympics, Media and Sport 2010-; *Select Committees:* Member: International Development 2005-06

Political interests: Education, international development; Japan, Africa

Other organisations: PC 2010

Recreations: Latin music and dance

Rt Hon Jeremy Hunt MP, House of Commons, London SW1A 0AA
Tel: 020 7219 6813 E-mail: huntj@parliament.uk
Constituency: SW Surrey Conservative Association, 2 Royal Parade, Tilford Road, Hindhead, Surrey GU26 6TD Tel: 01428 604520
Fax: 01428 607498 Website: www.localconservatives.org

GENERAL ELECTION RESULT

		%
Hunt, J. (Con)*	33,605	58.7
Simpson, M. (Lib Dem)	17,287	30.2
Mollet, R. (Lab)	3,419	6.0
Meekins, R. (UKIP)	1,486	2.6
Allan, C. (Green)	690	1.2
Hamilton, H. (BNP)	644	1.1
Leighton, L. (Pirate)	94	0.2
Price, A. (Ind)	34	0.1
Majority	16,318	28.50
Electorate	77,980	
Turnout	57,259	73.43

**Member of last parliament*

CONSTITUENCY SNAPSHOT

Formerly held by Virginia Bottomley, South West Surrey and its predecessor has elected only Conservative MPs since World War Two. The Conservative majority fell in 1997 from 14,975 to 2,694, and then down to just 861 in 2001.

Mrs Bottomley stood down in 2005 and the Tories selected local man Jeremy Hunt as her replacement, who won the seat and restored the majority to 5,711.

Hunt retained the seat with 33,605 votes giving him a majority of 16,318 at the 2010 general election.

The seat gained the part-ward of Bramley, Busbridge and Hascombe from Guildford, in exchange for the part-ward of Alford, Cranleigh Rural and Ellens Green.

Lying on the Sussex and Hampshire borders, South West Surrey combines open countryside and residential areas. The main towns are Farnham, Godalming and Haslemere, set in woodland and fields; local landmarks include the Devil's Punchbowl and Frensham Ponds.

Farnham is the largest town and has a population of around 37,000 and is a historic and architecturally important old market town with a conservation area covering the town centre.

Historically, the main industries in the area were paper, leather, wool and cloth. However, it is now a base for commuters to London. Key employment sectors are finance services, distribution, hospitality, public administration, education and health.

Tristram Hunt

Stoke-on-Trent Central

Boundary changes

Tel: 020 7219 3000
E-mail: tristram.hunt.mp@parliament.uk

Date of birth: 31 May 1974; Son of Julian Hunt (now Lord Hunt of Chesterton) and Marylla Shephard

Education: University College School; Trinity College, Cambridge (BA history 1995); Chicago University (Post-graduate Fellowship); Cambridge University (PhD Victorian civic pride 2000); Married Juliet Thornback (2004) (1 son)

Non-political career: Senior researcher, Labour Party election campaign 1997; Special adviser, Department of Trade and Industry 1998-2001; Research fellow, Institute for Public Policy Research 2001; Associate fellow, Centre for History and Economics, King's College, Cambridge 2001-02; History lecturer, Queen Mary University, London 2003-

Political career: Member for Stoke-on-Trent Central since 6 May 2010 general election

Other organisations: Trustee, Heritage Lottery Fund; Fellow, Royal Historical Society; *Publications:* Numerous publications in academic journals; Author: Building Jerusalem: The Rise and Fall of the Victorian City (Weidenfeld and Nicolson 2004), The Frock-Coated Communist: The Revolutionary Life of Friedrich Engels (Penguin 2009)

Tristram Hunt MP, House of Commons, London SW1A 0AA
Tel: 020 7219 3000 E-mail: tristram.hunt.mp@parliament.uk

GENERAL ELECTION RESULT

		%
Hunt, T. (Lab)	12,605	38.8
Redfern, J. (Lib Dem)	7,039	21.7
Bhatti, N. (Con)	6,833	21.0
Darby, S. (BNP)	2,502	7.7
Lovatt, C. (UKIP)	1,402	4.3
Breeze, P. (Ind)	959	3.0
Elsby, G. (Ind)	399	1.2
Ward, B. (Ind)	303	0.9
Walker, A. (Ind)	295	0.9
Wright, M. (TUSC)	133	0.4
Majority	5,566	17.14
Electorate	60,995	
Turnout	32,470	53.23

CONSTITUENCY SNAPSHOT

The central constituency has given its MP the largest victories over the past couple of decades. In 1983 Labour's Mark Fisher, an old Etonian and son of a Conservative MP, returned a majority of 8,250 votes and nearly 50 percent of the vote.

Fisher's majority was almost 20,000 in 1997. Since the 2001 and 2005 general elections the Labour majority has fallen to under 10,000. Mark Fisher retired in 2010 and Tristram Hunt was elected and held the seat for Labour with a majority of 5,566.

Minor boundary changes see little in the way of change to the constituency.

The city of Stoke-on-Trent is an amalgamation of six towns that was created in 1910 with the federation of the boroughs of Hanley, Burslem, Longton and Stoke, together with the districts of Tunstall and Fenton. These are often referred to collectively as the Potteries.

These days the town is the administrative centre of the city and is celebrated as the home of famous pottery manufacturers Spode, Biltons and Portmeirion.

Hanley boasts a large shopping centre and also contains the city's cultural quarter, which consists of two refurbished theatres, the Royal and the Regent, along with the concert venue the Victoria Hall.

Mark Hunter

Cheadle (returning MP)

Boundary changes

Tel: 020 7219 3889
E-mail: hunterm@parliament.uk
Website: www.markhunter.org.uk

Date of birth: 25 July 1957; Son of Arthur Brian and Betty Elizabeth Mary Hunter

Education: Audenshaw Grammar School, Manchester; Married Lesley Graham 1997 (1 daughter 1 son)

Non-political career: Advertising manager: Associated Newspapers, Guardian Media Group; Councillor Tameside Metropolitan Borough Council (MBC) 1980-89; Stockport MBC: Councillor 1996-06, Chair Education Committee 1997-2001, Deputy Leader 2001-02, Leader 2002-05

Political career: Contested Stockport 2001 general election. Member for Cheadle 14 July 2005 by-election to 2010, for Cheadle (revised boundary) since 6 May 2010 general election; Liberal Democrat Shadow Minister for: Office of the Deputy Prime Minister 2005-06, Home Affairs 2006-07, Foreign and Commonwealth Office 2007; PPS to Nick Clegg as Leader of the Liberal Democrats 2007-10; Liberal Democrat Shadow Minister for Transport 2008-10; Assistant Government Whip 2010-; *Select Committees:* Member: Trade and Industry/Business, Enterprise and Regulatory Reform/Business and Enterprise 2005-08, Quadripartite (Committees on Strategic Export Controls)/Arms Export Controls 2007-08

Political interests: Local government, human rights, international affairs

Recreations: Football, reading, theatre, good restaurants

Mark Hunter MP, House of Commons, London SW1A 0AA
Tel: 020 7219 3889 Fax: 020 7219 0813
E-mail: hunterm@parliament.uk
Constituency: Hillson House, 3 Gill Bent Road, Cheadle Hulme, Cheadle, Stockport, Cheshire SK8 7LE Tel: 0161-486 1359
Fax: 0161-486 9005 Website: www.markhunter.org.uk

GENERAL ELECTION RESULT

		%
Hunter, M. (Lib Dem)*	24,717	47.1
Jeffreys, B. (Con)	21,445	40.8
Miller, M. (Lab)	4,920	9.4
Moore, T. (UKIP)	1,430	2.7
Majority	3,272	6.23
Electorate	72,458	
Turnout	52,512	72.47

**Member of last parliament*

CONSTITUENCY SNAPSHOT

Cheadle first came to national attention in 1966 when Liberal Dr Michael Winstanley won the seat from the Tories, though on very different boundaries. Tom Normanton regained the seat for the Conservatives in 1970. Stephen Day, the sitting Tory MP since 1987, held off a strong Liberal Democrat challenge in 1997 by 3,000 votes.

Liberal Democrat Patsy Calton defeated Mr Day at her third attempt in 2001, with a majority of 33, the smallest in the country.

Despite not being able to campaign due to illness, Patsy Calton increased her 2005 majority to 4,020. Patsy Calton died shortly after the election. Day stood again for the Conservatives at the by-election against Lib Dem Mark Hunter. Hunter won a majority of 3,657.

Hunter held the seat in 2010 with a slightly reduced majority of 3,272.

Boundary changes were minimal.

Cheadle is an attractive and affluent commuter area to the south of Stockport, including the exclusive suburbs of Cheadle Hulme and Bramhall. The seat contains several top-performing schools, including the independent Cheadle Hulme School.

It has among the highest proportion of professional and managerial workers north of Watford, the highest proportion of owner-occupiers and the highest proportion of detached housing of any seat in the North of England.

Manchester Airport, two miles away, is another major contributor to the local economy.

Dr **Julian Huppert**

Cambridge

Boundary changes

Tel: 020 7219 3000
E-mail: julian.huppert.mp@parliament.uk
Website: www.julianhuppert.org.uk

Date of birth: 21 July 1978; Son of Prof Felicia Huppert, professor of psychology, and Prof Herbert Huppert FRS, professor of theoretical geophysics

Education: Perse School, Cambridge; Trinity College, Cambridge (BA MSci natural sciences 2000, MA); Cambridge University (PhD biological chemistry 2005); Partner Dr Caroline Wright

Non-political career: Team member, review of Bulgarian education policy, Organisation for Economic Co-operation and Development (OECD) 2000; Business analyst, Monis Software Ltd 2000-01; Director and chief executive officer, Cambridge Laboratory Innovations 2003-05; Postdoctoral researcher, Trinity College, Cambridge: Wellcome Trust Sanger Institute 2005-07, Unilever Centre for Molecular Science Informatics, Cambridge University 2007-08; Academic fellow (Research Councils UK), Computational Biology, Cambridge University 2007-; Fellow and director of studies, Clare College, Cambridge 2009-; Cambridgeshire County Council: Councillor 2001-09, Leader, Liberal Democrat group 2004-07

Political career: Contested Huntingdon 2005 general election. Member for Cambridge since 6 May 2010 general election

Political interests: Science, internationalism, human rights, DNA database, civil liberties, education, transport, evidence-based policy, UN and foreign affairs, wellbeing, environment, climate change

Other organisations: Chair, Friends of Stourbridge Common; Liberty: Member, National Council Member 2009-; Member: Electoral Reform Society, CTC, Dignity in Dying, British Humanist Association; *Publications:* Numerous publications in peer-reviewed scientific journals

Recreations: Cycling, music, climbing, walking

Dr Julian Huppert MP, House of Commons, London SW1A 0AA
Tel: 020 7219 3000 E-mail: julian.huppert.mp@parliament.uk
Constituency: Cambridge Liberal Democrats, 16 Signet Court, Cambridge CB5 8LA Tel: 01223 313765
Website: www.julianhuppert.org.uk

GENERAL ELECTION RESULT

		%
Huppert, J. (Lib Dem)	19,621	39.1
Hillman, N. (Con)	12,829	25.6
Zeichner, D. (Lab)	12,174	24.3
Juniper, T. (Green)	3,804	7.6
Burkinshaw, P. (UKIP)	1,195	2.4
Booth, M. (TUSC)	362	0.7
Old, H. (Ind)	145	0.3
Majority	6,792	13.55
Electorate	77,081	
Turnout	50,130	65.04

CONSTITUENCY SNAPSHOT

Anne Campbell made history in 1997 when she became the first Labour MP to retain Cambridge, which she had won from the Conservatives in 1992. A majority of under 600 rose to over 14,000 in 1997. However, in 2001, her majority fell to just under 9,000.

In 2005 the Liberal Democrats' candidate David Howarth increased the party's vote-share by 18.9 per cent, overtaking Labour to take the seat with a 4,339 majority. In 2010 Julian Huppert retained the seat for the Lib Dems with a 6,792 majority.

Boundary changes moved the wards of Cherry Hinton, Coleridge and Trumpington entirely into the seat, which is likely to make the constituency more 'town' and less 'gown'. Both Coleridge and Cherry Hinton are suburban in character, with large estates of inter-war semi-detached housing. Trumpington, in the south of the city, is leafier with some upmarket properties and desirable schools.

Cambridge is world-famous as being home to one of the most prestigious universities in England. The university dominates the city in every way, although the high-technology sector rose to prominence in the late twentieth century in the form of 'Silicon Fen'.

There is also some commercial and administrative employment within Cambridge, as the town acts as the administrative centre of the region. Additionally there is employment and income from tourism.

Nick Hurd

Ruislip, Northwood and Pinner ***(returning MP)***

New constituency

Tel: 020 7219 6648
E-mail: hurdn@parliament.uk
Website: www.nickhurd.com

Conservative

Date of birth: 13 May 1962; Son of Baron Hurd of Westwell (qv) and Tatiana, née Eyre

Education: Eton College; Exeter College, Oxford (BA classics 1984); Married Kim Richards 1988 (separated 2008) (2 sons 2 daughters)

Non-political career: Investment manager Morgan Grenfell 1985-90; Corporate finance executive Crown Communications 1990-92; Managing director Passport Magazine Directories 1992-94; Flemings Bank (Brazil-based) 1995-99; Founder Small Business Network 2002; Director Band-X Ltd 2001-06; Chief of staff to Tim Yeo MP 2003-05; Non-Executive Director Sancroft Ltd 2008-; Governor Coteford Junior School

Political career: Member for Ruislip Northwood 2005-10, for Ruislip, Northwood and Pinner since 6 May 2010 general election; Opposition Whip 2007-08; Sponsored Sustainable Communities Act 2007; Shadow Minister for Charities[, Social Enterprise and Volunteering] 2008-10; Parliamentary Secretary (Minister for Civil Society), Cabinet Office 2010-; *Select Committees:* Member: Environmental Audit 2005-10, Joint Committee on the Draft Climate Change Bill 2007

Political interests: Environment, community, penal reform, health; Brazil, China

Other organisations: Member Vote No to the EU Constitution Campaign; Trustee Greenhouse Schools Project

Recreations: Sport, music

Nick Hurd MP, House of Commons, London SW1A 0AA
Tel: 020 7219 6648 Fax: 020 7219 4854
E-mail: hurdn@parliament.uk
Constituency: Ruislip-Northwood Conservative Association, 20b High Street, Northwood, Middlesex HA6 1BN Tel: 01923 822876 Fax: 01923 841514 Website: www.nickhurd.com

GENERAL ELECTION RESULT

		%
Hurd, N. (Con)*	28,866	57.5
MacDonald, A. (Lab)	9,806	19.5
Papworth, T. (Lib Dem)	8,345	16.6
Pontey, J. (UKIP)	1,351	2.7
Edward, I. (NF)	899	1.8
Lee, G. (Green)	740	1.5
Akhtar, R. (Christian)	198	0.4
Majority	19,060	37.96
Electorate	70,873	
Turnout	50,205	70.84

**Member of last parliament*

CONSTITUENCY SNAPSHOT

The Conservatives have represented this seat continuously since the mid-20th century. John Wilkinson was elected in 1979, winning over 60 per cent of the vote, until 1997. Nick Hurd, son of former Foreign Secretary Douglas Hurd, succeeded Wilkinson in 2005 with a majority of almost 9,000. In 2010 Hurd won easily with almost 58 per cent of the vote and a huge 19,060 majority.

Ruislip, Northwood and Pinner was formed from Hatch End, Pinner, Pinner South from Harrow West; Eastcote and East Ruislip, Harefield, Northwood and Northwood Hills from Ruislip Northwoood; and West Ruislip and Ickenham from Uxbridge.

An affluent suburban constituency, Ruislip, Northwood and Pinner is situated on the north-western peripheries of the capital and has more in common with adjoining South West Hertfordshire than the urban areas to the south and east.

Surrounded by golf courses, the constituency contains private estates and other clusters of exclusivity, but the norm is suburban town houses and semis.

There is no major industry in the area and the biggest local employer outside the public sector, Express Dairies is now located in the new constituency of Uxbridge and South Ruislip. The majority of constituents commute to work in finance, commerce or retail in the West End or City.

Eric Illsley

Barnsley Central ***(returning MP)***

Boundary changes

Tel: 020 7219 1543
E-mail: illsleye@parliament.uk
Website: www.ericillsley.co.uk

Independent

Date of birth: 9 April 1955; Son of John and Maud Illsley

Education: Barnsley Holgate Grammar School; Leeds University (LLB 1977); Married Dawn Webb 1978 (2 daughters)

Non-political career: Yorkshire Area NUM: Compensation officer 1978-81, Assistant head of general department 1981-84, Head of general department and chief administration officer 1984-87; Member, AMICUS

Political career: Member for Barnsley Central 1987-2010, for Barnsley Central (revised boundary) since 6 May 2010 general election (Labour 1987-2010, Independent since May 2010); Opposition Whip 1991-94; Opposition Spokesperson for: Health 1994-95, Local Government 1995, Northern Ireland 1995-97; *Select Committees:* Member: Procedure 1991-2010, Foreign Affairs 1997-2010, Chairmen's Panel 2000-10; Chair: Yorkshire and the Humber 2009-10; Secretary, Barnsley Constituency Labour Party 1981-83, Treasurer 1980-81; Secretary and election agent, Yorkshire South European Labour Party 1984-86; Member, Mining Group of MPs 1987-97; Hon. Treasurer, Yorkshire Regional Group of Labour MP 1997-2010; Labour Whip withdrawn May 2010

Political interests: Trade unions, mining, energy, social security, glass industry; Australia, France

Other organisations: Patron, Barnsley Alzheimer's Disease Society; Member, Executive Committee: Inter-Parliamentary Union 1997-, Commonwealth Parliamentary Association (CPA) UK Branch 1997-; Fellow Industry and Parliament Trust 1992

Recreations: Golf

Eric Illsley MP, House of Commons, London SW1A 0AA
Tel: 020 7219 1543 Fax: 020 7219 4863
E-mail: illsleye@parliament.uk
Constituency: 18 Regent Street, Barnsley, South Yorkshire S70 2HG
Tel: 01226 730692 Fax: 01226 779429 Website: www.ericillsley.co.uk

GENERAL ELECTION RESULT

		%
Illsley, E. (Lab)*	17,487	47.3
Wiggin, C. (Lib Dem)	6,394	1.7
Tempest, P. (Con)	6,388	1.7
Sutton, I. (BNP)	3,307	0.9
Silver, D. (UKIP)	1,727	0.5
Wood, D. (Ind)	732	0.2
Devoy, T. (Ind)	610	0.2
Robinson, T. (SLP)	356	0.1
Majority	11,093	29.98
Electorate	65,543	
Turnout	37,001	56.45

**Member of last parliament*

CONSTITUENCY SNAPSHOT

Former miner Roy Mason was MP for Barnsley for 30 years from 1953 and then for the renamed and redrawn Barnsley Central for another four. When he retired in 1987 he was replaced by the senior NUM official Eric Illsley. Illsley's share of the vote has consistently been above 60 per cent. His majority was a very comfortable 12,732 in 2005.

At the 2010 general election Illsley secured a majority of 11,093.

Barnsley Central gained four part-wards that were shared with Barnsley West and Penistone in addition to its Darton East ward.

This South Yorkshire constituency of is the smallest of the three Barnsley divisions, in both area and population. As the name implies, it includes the centre of the town as well as former pit villages to the east.

The town has a strong coalmining history. It has been latterly the national headquarters of the National Union of Mineworkers.

The seat once had a dozen pits within its borders. The last one closed in the early 1990s, leaving a deep hole in the economy.

The town's other traditional industries survive, including glassmaking and textiles. But the biggest single employer is the local council.

Huw Irranca-Davies

Ogmore (returning MP)

Boundary changes

Tel: 020 7219 4027
E-mail: irrancadaviesh@parliament.uk
Website: www.huwirranca-davies.org.uk

Date of birth: 22 January 1963; Son of Gethin Davies and Teresa Davies, née Griffiths

Education: Gowerton Comprehensive School; Crewe and Alsager College of Higher Education (BA combined studies 1986); Swansea Institute of Higher Education (MSc European leisure resort management 1996); Married Joanna Irranca 1990 (3 sons)

Non-political career: Leisure facility management 1986-96: Lliw Valley Borough Council, Community Leisure Management Ltd, London Borough of Southwark, Cardiff Institute of Higher Education, Swansea College; Senior lecturer and course director, business faculty, Swansea Institute of Higher Education 1996-2002; Member, UCATT

Political career: Contested Brecon and Radnorshire 2001 general election. Member for Ogmore 14 February 2002 by-election-2010, for Ogmore (revised boundary) since 6 May 2010 general election; PPS: to Jane Kennedy as Minister of State: Northern Ireland Office 2003-04, Department for Work and Pensions 2004-05, to Tessa Jowell as Secretary of State for Culture, Media and Sport 2005-06; Assistant Government Whip 2006-07; Parliamentary Under-Secretary of State: Wales Office 2007-08, Department for Environment, Food and Rural Affairs 2008-10 (Minister for the Natural and Marine Environment 2008-10, for Wildlife and Rural Affairs 2008-09); *Select Committees:* Member: Joint Committee on Statutory Instruments 2002-04, Procedure 2002-05; Vice-president, Neath Constituency Labour Party 2001-02; Secretary, Ystalyfera branch 1999-2002

Political interests: Social justice, community regeneration, devolution, international development, European Union; Middle East, Northern Ireland

Other organisations: Member, Bevan Foundation; Trustee and director, Charitable Trust (community regeneration); Chair, Ogmore Valley Male Voice Choir; President, Maesteg Celtic Cricket Club

Recreations: Hill-walking, cycling, most sport, family

Huw Irranca-Davies MP, House of Commons, London SW1A 0AA
Tel: 020 7219 4027 Fax: 020 7219 0134
E-mail: irrancadaviesh@parliament.uk
Constituency: Unit 2, 112-113 Commercial Street, Maesteg, Mid Glamorgan CF34 9DL Tel: 01656 737777 Fax: 01656 737788
Website: www.huwirranca-davies.org.uk

GENERAL ELECTION RESULT

		%
Irranca-Davies, H. (Lab)*	18,644	53.8
Moore, E. (Con)	5,398	15.6
Radford, J. (Lib Dem)	5,260	15.2
Clark, D. (PIC)	3,326	9.6
Thomas, K. (BNP)	1,242	3.6
Passey, C. (UKIP)	780	2.3
Majority	13,246	38.23
Electorate	55,527	
Turnout	34,650	62.40

**Member of last parliament*

CONSTITUENCY SNAPSHOT

Held by Labour ever since its creation in 1918, this is a former mining seat. Sir Ray Powell was the Labour MP from the 1979 general election until his death in 2001.

In the by-election Huw Irranca-Davies, retained the seat. In the 2005 general election Irranca-Davies' majority climbed to 13,703. Irranca-Davies retained this very safe Labour seat with a 13,246 majority despite a 4.3 per cent swing to the Conservatives.

Boundary changes have moved Cowbridge into Vale of Glamorgan, and Aberkenfig and Cefn Cribwr have been added to the seat from Bridgend.

This is a typical former mining valley seat, named after Ogmore Vale and Ogmore Forest and embracing two valleys between Maesteg and Pontypridd.

The largest town is Maesteg. This was once a metal-working town but it now primarily a dormitory town.

Employment is varied and mainly based along the M4 corridor in the major industrial parks. Businesses range from telecommunications and assembly work to call-centres.

The Dragon International Film Studio complex is based at Llanilid, between Pencoed and Llanharan.

Glenda Jackson

Hampstead and Kilburn ***(returning MP)***

New constituency

Tel: 020 7219 4008
E-mail: jacksong@parliament.uk
Website: www.glenda-jackson.co.uk

Labour

Date of birth: 9 May 1936; Daughter of Harry and Joan Jackson

Education: West Kirby County Grammar School for Girls; RADA; Married Roy Hodges 1958 (divorced 1976) (1 son)

Non-political career: Actress: Plays include: *The Idiot* 1962, *Love's Labour's Lost, Hamlet* 1965, *Three Sisters* 1967, *Hedda Gabler* 1975; Films include: *Women in Love, Mary, Queen of Scots, A Touch of Class*; Television includes *Elizabeth R* 1971; Member, Royal Shakespeare Company 1963-67, 1979-80; Member, Greater London Assembly advisory cabinet for homelessness 2000-04

Political career: Member for Hampstead and Highgate 1992-2010, for Hamstead and Kilburn since 6 May 2010 general election; Opposition Spokeswoman on Transport 1996-97; Parliamentary Under-Secretary of State, Department of the Environment, Transport and the Regions 1997-99; Resigned in July 1999 reshuffle

Political interests: Overseas aid and development, housing, environment

Other organisations: Member: Anti-Apartheid Movement, Amnesty International, Has campaigned for: Oxfam, Shelter, Friends of the Earth; President, The National Toy Libraries Association; CBE 1978; Best film actress awards: Variety Clubs of Great Britain 1971, 1975, 1978, NY Film critics 1971, Oscar 1971, 1974

Recreations: Cooking, gardening, reading Jane Austen

Glenda Jackson CBE MP, House of Commons, London SW1A 0AA
Tel: 020 7219 4008 Fax: 020 7219 2112
E-mail: jacksong@parliament.uk
Website: www.glenda-jackson.co.uk

GENERAL ELECTION RESULT

		%
Jackson, G. (Lab)*	17,332	32.8
Philp, C. (Con)	17,290	32.7
Fordham, E. (Lib Dem)	16,491	31.2
Campbell, B. (Green)	759	1.4
Nielsen, M. (UKIP)	408	0.8
Moore, V. (BNP)	328	0.6
Omond, T. (Tamsin)	123	0.2
Alcantara, G. (Ind)	91	0.2
Majority	42	0.08
Electorate	79,713	
Turnout	52,822	66.27

**Member of last parliament*

CONSTITUENCY SNAPSHOT

Hampstead and Kilburn is a cross-borough seat taking most of the wards from Hampstead and Highgate as well as two from Brent East and Queens Park ward, which was previously shared between Brent East and South.

Glenda Jackson turned to politics and took the Hampstead and Highgate seat from the Conservatives in 1992, who had held it since 1974. Jackson beat Conservative candidate Oliver Letwin with a 5 per cent margin in 1992. By 1997 Ms Jackson increased her majority to over 13,000.

Glenda Jackson held onto the seat in the 2001 and 2005 general elections but her majority had fallen to 3,729. The tightest London seat in 2010, Labour's Glenda Jackson won by just 42 votes over the Conservatives.

This affluent constituency has long been associated with millionaires, mansions and money. These can be found around Hampstead, but there are more socially mixed and deprived areas around Kilburn.

There is a large Afro-Caribbean and Irish community in Brondesbury Park, Kilburn and Queen's Park. Hampstead and Kilburn enjoys extremely good public services, with schools in high demand and many specialist health clinics at the Royal Free Hospital.

In 2006 Swiss Cottage underwent an £85 million redevelopment project, bringing together a leisure centre, library, a park and housing.

Stewart Jackson

Peterborough ***(returning MP)***

Boundary changes

Tel: 020 7219 8286
E-mail: jacksonsj@parliament.uk
Website: www.stewartjackson.org.uk

Conservative

Date of birth: 31 January 1965; Son of Sylvia Alice Theresa and Raymond Thomas Jackson

Education: London Nautical School, Southwark, London Chatham House Grammar School, Ramsgate, Kent; Royal Holloway College, London University (BA economics and public administration 1988); Thames Valley University (MA human resource management 2001); Married Sarah O'Grady 1999 (1 daughter)

Non-political career: Business banking manager Lloyds Bank plc 1993-96; Retail branch manager Lloyds TSB Group 1996-98; Business services manager Aztec training and enterprise council for SW London 1998-2000; Business adviser – human resources Business Link for London 2000-05; Member, Lloyds TSB Group Union 1989-98; Councillor London Borough of Ealing 1990-98

Political career: Contested Brent South 1997 and Peterborough 2001 general elections. Member for Peterborough 2005-10, for Peterborough (revised boundary) since 6 May 2010 general election; Opposition Whip 2007-08; Shadow Minister for Communities and Local Government 2008-10; *Select Committees:* Member: Regulatory Reform 2005-10, Health 2006-07; Deputy chair Ealing North Conservative Association 1998-2000

Political interests: Housing, planning, environment, home affairs, regeneration; USA, Pakistan, Kashmir

Other organisations: Good Neighbours Scheme, Peterborough Salvation Army 2005-; Board of Trustees, London City YMCA 1993-98; Carlton Club; Peterborough Conservative

Recreations: Reading, travel, theatre, cinema

Stewart Jackson MP, House of Commons, London SW1A 0AA
Tel: 020 7219 8286; 020 7219 5046 Fax: 020 7219 5169
E-mail: jacksonsj@parliament.uk
Constituency: Peterborough Conservative Association, 193 Dogsthorpe Road, Peterborough, Cambridgeshire PE1 3AT
Tel: 01733 343190 Fax: 01733 343150
Website: www.stewartjackson.org.uk

GENERAL ELECTION RESULT

		%
Jackson, S. (Con)*	18,133	40.4
Murphy, E. (Lab)	13,272	29.5
Sandford, N. (Lib Dem)	8,816	19.6
Fox, F. (UKIP)	3,007	6.7
King, R. (England)	770	1.7
Radic, F. (Green)	523	1.2
Swallow, J. (Ind)	406	0.9
Majority	4,861	10.82
Electorate	70,316	
Turnout	44,927	63.89

**Member of last parliament*

CONSTITUENCY SNAPSHOT

Peterborough was predominantly a Conservative seat from 1950 to 1997, with Labour holding it for just one Parliament in the late 1970s. There were major boundary changes in 1997, when a third of the constituents were moved into Cambridgeshire North West. The then sitting MP, Brian Mawhinney, chose to fight the new seat, and, thus, in 1997, Helen Brinton stood and took Peterborough for Labour with over 50 per cent of the vote (She later became Helen Clark). She failed to build on this success, though, and in 2005 Stewart Jackson took the seat for the Tories with a majority of 2,740.

Jackson held the seat with a majority of 4,861 at the 2010 general election.

Wards north-east of the city (Eye and Thorney and Newborough) were added to the constituency from Cambridgeshire North West and Cambridgeshire North East.

Peterborough lies halfway between the East Anglian coast and the Midlands. Its good road and rail links have turned it into a major distribution centre. The East Coast Mainline provides travel to London in 50 minutes and, as a result, Peterborough has developed into something of a commuter town.

Peterborough is home to light industry, agricultural markets and a small but growing commercial centre. The cathedral is something of a tourist draw.

Margot James

Stourbridge

Boundary changes

Tel: 020 7219 3000
E-mail: margot.james.mp@parliament.uk
Website: www.margotjames.com

Conservative

Education: Millfield School, Somerset; London School of Economics (BSc economics and government); Partner Jay

Non-political career: Maurice James Industries; Former researcher to Sir Anthony Durant MP; Former press officer, Conservative Central Office; Co-founder and Director, Shire Health 1986-99; Ogilvy & Mather: Head of European healthcare, Regional president, pharmaceutical division 2005-; Non-executive director, Parkside NHS Trust 1998-2003; Councillor, Kensington and Chelsea Borough Council 2006-08

Political career: Contested Holborn and St Pancras 2005 general election. Member for Stourbridge since 6 May 2010 general election; Chair, London School of Economics Conservative Association; Vice-chair for women's issues, Conservative Party 2005-

Other organisations: Communicator of the Year 1997

Recreations: Cooking, theatre, travel, opera, walking the dog

Margot James MP, House of Commons, London SW1A 0AA
Tel: 020 7219 3000 E-mail: margot.james.mp@parliament.uk
Constituency: Stourbridge Conservative Association, Church Chambers, Halesowen B63 3BB Tel: 01384 226053
Website: www.margotjames.com

GENERAL ELECTION RESULT

		%
James, M. (Con)	20,153	42.7
Waltho, L. (Lab)*	14,989	31.7
Bramall, C. (Lib Dem)	7,733	16.4
Westrop, M. (UKIP)	2,103	4.5
Weale, R. (BNP)	1,696	3.6
Duckworth, W. (Green)	394	0.8
Nicholas, A. (Ind)	166	0.4
Majority	5,164	10.93
Electorate	69,637	
Turnout	47,234	67.83

**Member of last parliament*

CONSTITUENCY SNAPSHOT

Halesowen and Stourbridge was a Tory seat from 1974 until 1997, although before that period it changed hands several times. Sir John Stokes held the seat for the party from 1974 until his retirement in 1992.

Stokes was replaced by Tory Warren Hawksley with a margin of victory of over 10 per cent. However, in 1997 Hawksley lost to Labour's Debra Shipley.

Shipley represented Stourbridge for one parliament. Labour's Lynda Waltho held the seat by 407 votes in 2005. Waltho was defeated at the 2010 general election by the Conservative candidate, Margot James. James secured a majority of 5,164.

Amblecote, Quarry Bank and Dudley Wood, and Cradley and Foxcote wards all now fall completely within this seat after gaining the parts that were in Halesowen and Rowley Regis and Dudley South respectively. One part-ward was lost to each of these seats.

Lying on the edge of rural Worcestershire, Stourbridge has increasingly become a commuter town for those working in nearby West Midlands' towns and cities. It retains much of its small-town appeal.

Glass has historically been the main industry in the town with a large plant in Amblecote, but recent scaling down has been felt within the constituency.

Siân James

Swansea East (returning MP)

No boundary changes

Tel: 020 7219 6954
E-mail: sianjamesmp@parliament.uk
Website: www.sianjamesmp.co.uk

Labour

Date of birth: 24 June 1959; Daughter of Melbourne and Martha Griffiths

Education: Cefn Saeson Comprehensive School; University of Wales, Swansea (BA Welsh 1989); Married Martin James 1976 (1 son 1 daughter)

Non-political career: Field officer National Federation of Young Farmers' Clubs 1990-91; Save the Children 1991-94; Deputy public affairs manager National Trust 1994-98; Communications manager Securicor 1998-99; Lobbyist Association of Train Operating Companies 1999-2003; Director, Welsh Women's Aid 2003-2005; Neath Town Councillor 2004-

Political career: Member for Swansea East since 5 May 2005 general election; PPS to Gareth Thomas as Minister of State, Departments for Business, Enterprise and Regulatory Reform and for International Development 2008-09; *Select Committees:* Member: Welsh Affairs 2005-10, Procedure 2005-10, Crossrail Bill 2006-07, Constitutional Affairs/Justice 2006-10

Political interests: Social exclusion, public transport, work and pensions, Welsh affairs, children's issues, domestic abuse; Slovakia, Portugal, Cuba, Burma

Recreations: Reading, antiques, model railways, dolls houses

Siân James MP, House of Commons, London SW1A 0AA
Tel: 020 7219 6954 Fax: 020 7219 0958
E-mail: sianjamesmp@parliament.uk
Constituency: 485 Llangyfelach Road, Brynhyfryd, Swansea SA5 9EA
Tel: 01792 455089 Fax: 01792 643496
Website: www.sianjamesmp.co.uk

GENERAL ELECTION RESULT

		%	+/-
James, S. (Lab)*	16,819	51.5	-5.1
Speht, R. (Lib Dem)	5,981	18.3	-1.8
Holliday, C. (Con)	4,823	14.8	4.7
Jones, D. (PIC)	2,181	6.7	-0.2
Bennett, C. (SOTBTH)	1,715	5.3	
Rogers, D. (UKIP)	839	2.6	0.4
Young, T. (Green)	318	1.0	-0.6
Majority	10,838	33.17	
Electorate	51,554		
Turnout	32,676	63.38	

**Member of last parliament*

CONSTITUENCY SNAPSHOT

Held by the Labour party since 1922, the seat was represented between October 1974 and 2005 by Donald Anderson who had established the third biggest Labour majority by 1997.

Anderson stood down in 2005 and was replaced by Siân James. She suffered a decline in support but the 9.3 per cent swing to the Lib Dems, who climbed to second place, still left her with a majority of 11,249. James was re-elected in 2010 with a 10,838 majority and over 50 per cent of the vote.

The eastern Swansea seat covers the industrial parts of the city including the port.

Like many areas which grew and thrived on traditional manufacturing industries like coal and steel, Swansea has been affected by major economic changes.

The Driver and Vehicle Licensing Agency (DVLA), and the Morriston Hospital, which has specialist cardiac and burns units, are situated here.

Cathy Jamieson

Kilmarnock and Loudoun

No boundary changes

Tel: 020 7219 3000
E-mail: cathy.jamieson.mp@parliament.uk
Website: www.cathyjamiesonmsp.co.uk

Labour/Co-operative

Date of birth: 3 November 1956; Daughter of Robert Jamieson, retired motor mechanic, and Mary Jamieson, retired office administrator

Education: James Hamilton Academy, Kilmarnock; Glasgow School of Art (BA Hons fine art 1979); Goldsmith's College, London (Post-graduate Higher Diploma art 1980); Glasgow University (CQSW 1983); Glasgow Caledonian University (Certificate management 1996); Married Ian Sharpe 1976 (1 son)

Non-political career: Strathclyde Regional Council: Trainee social worker 1980-81; Social worker 1983-86; Community intermediate treatment worker 1986-88; Senior intermediate treatment worker 1988-92; Principal officer, Who Cares? Scotland 1992-99; Transport and General Workers' Union (TGWU)/Unite: Member, Chair, Unite Group of Labour MSPs

Political career: Member for Kilmarnock and Loudoun since 6 May 2010; MSP for Carrick, Cumnock and Doon Valley constituency since 6 May 1999: Scottish Labour: Minister for: Education and Young People 2001-03, Justice 2003-07; Member, Scottish Parliamentary Bureau 2007-08; Shadow Minister for Parliamentary Business 2007; Acting Shadow First Minister 2007, 2008; Shadow Cabinet Secretary for: Health and Wellbeing 2008-09, Housing and Regeneration 2009; Various positions at local branch and constituency level 1980-99 including: Chair, Cunninghame South Constituency Labour Party; Vice-chair, South of Scotland Euro Constituency Labour Party; Election agent for Alex Smith MEP 1994; Member, Labour's: Scottish Executive 1996-99, 2000-08, National Executive 1998; Vice-chair, Scottish Co-operative Party 1998-99; Labour Party in the Scottish Parliament: Deputy Leader 2000-08, Interim Leader 2007, 2008; Contested Scottish Labour Leader in the Scottish Parliament election 2008

Political interests: Co-operative movement, voluntary sector, social economy, workers' rights, anti-poverty, children, criminal justice; Western Sahara

Other organisations: Trustee, Barony A Frame; *Publications:* Various publications in professional/political journals and magazines

Recreations: Kilmarnock FC, art, photography, Ayrshire history

Cathy Jamieson MP, House of Commons, London SW1A 0AA
Tel: 020 7219 3000 E-mail: cathy.jamieson.mp@parliament.uk
Constituency: Block 1, Cumnock Community College, Caponacre Industrial Estate, Cumnock KA18 1SH Tel: 0845 458 1800
Fax: 0845 458 1801 Website: www.cathyjamiesonmsp.co.uk

GENERAL ELECTION RESULT

		%	+/-
Jamieson, C. (Lab/Co-op)	24,460	52.5	5.4
Leslie, G. (SNP)	12,082	26.0	-1.7
McAlpine, J. (Con)	6,592	14.2	2.9
Tombs, S. (Lib Dem)	3,419	7.3	-3.8
Majority	12,378	26.59	
Electorate	74,131		
Turnout	46,553	62.80	

CONSTITUENCY SNAPSHOT

Willie Ross held the Kilmarnock seat for Labour from 1946 until his retirement in 1979. Labour's William McKelvey then held Kilmarnock and Loudoun (Kilmarnock until 1983) until a stroke forced him to retire in 1997.

Des Browne increased Labour's majority to 7,256 in 1997, and increased to over 10,000 in 2001.

Before the 2005 election, Kilmarnock and Loudoun was enlarged by 10,000 voters from Mauchline, Auchinleck, Catrine and Muirkirk from Carrick, Cumnock and Doon Valley. Browne achieved a majority of 8,703 at the redrawn seat. MSP Cathy Jamieson replaced Des Browne in 2010 winning this seat with a 12,378 majority.

This constituency is based in and around Kilmarnock in Ayrshire, stretching to the south and east towards the outskirts of Cumnock.

Kilmarnock, lying to the south west of Glasgow, is by far the largest town in this industrial constituency and is home to a number of engineering plants. It is famed as the home of Johnny Walker Whisky, one of the most famous exports in Scotland. The distillery has been Kilmarnock's largest single private employer. However, owner Diageo has announced the closure of the Kilmarnock plant in 2011.

Scotland's first private prison is HMP Kilmarnock, located in Hurlford to the east of the town.

Sajid Javid

Bromsgrove

No boundary changes

Tel: 020 7219 7027
E-mail: sajid.javid.mp@parliament.uk
Website: www.sajidjavid.com

Conservative

Date of birth: 5 December 1969

Education: Exeter University (economics and politics); Married Laura (4 children)

Non-political career: Former vice-president, Chase Manhattan Bank; Former managing director, Deutsche Bank; Former board member, Deutsche International (Asia) Ltd; Businessman; Former governor, Normand Croft Community School

Political career: Member for Bromsgrove since 6 May 2010 general election

Political interests: Civil liberties, free enterprise, education, foreign affairs

Recreations: Gym, running, hiking, cricket

Sajid Javid MP, House of Commons, London SW1A 0AA
Tel: 020 7219 7027 E-mail: sajid.javid.mp@parliament.uk
Constituency: Bromsgrove Conservative Association, 37 Worcester Road, Bromsgrove, Worcestershire B61 7DN Tel: 01527 872135
Website: www.sajidjavid.com

GENERAL ELECTION RESULT

		%	+/-
Javid, S. (Con)	22,558	43.7	-8.2
Burden, S. (Lab)	11,250	21.8	-8.0
Ling, P. (Lib Dem)	10,124	19.6	4.6
Morson, S. (UKIP)	2,950	5.7	1.7
Kriss, A. (Brom Ind Con)	2,182	4.2	
Wainwright, E. (BNP)	1,923	3.7	
France, M. (Ind)	336	0.7	
Wheatley, K. (Ind)	307	0.6	
Majority	11,308	21.90	
Electorate	73,086		
Turnout	51,630	70.64	

CONSTITUENCY SNAPSHOT

Bromsgrove has spent the vast majority of its existence in Conservative hands, with their majority as high as 17,000 votes in the 1980s. In 1997 Julie Kirkbride took over from the sitting Tory Roy Thomason. In 2005 Kirkbride successfully defended her seat and her majority increased to 10,080.

Kirkbride stood down in 2010 and Sajid Javid held the seat for the Conservatives with a 11,308 majority.

Situated in the north-east corner of Worcestershire and to the south-west of Birmingham, this seat is made up of the town of Bromsgrove, satellite villages, and Birmingham dormitory suburbs.

The services sector accounts for the majority of employment and there is a higher than average proportion of skilled non-manual workers.

Farming plays a role in the economy and most of the seat is still classified as green belt. Notable companies in the constituency include Britannic Assurance, GKN, and Bayer UK Ltd. The proportion of people in managerial and professional occupations is above both the West Midlands and national averages.

Bernard Jenkin

Harwich and North Essex ***(returning MP)***

New constituency

Tel: 020 7219 4029
E-mail: jenkinbc@parliament.uk
Website: www.bernardjenkinmp.com

Conservative

Date of birth: 9 April 1959; Son of Rt Hon. Baron Jenkin of Roding (qv)

Education: Highgate School, London; William Ellis School, London; Corpus Christi College, Cambridge (BA English literature 1982) (President, Cambridge Union Society 1982); Married Anne Strutt 1988 (2 sons)

Non-political career: Ford Motor Co Ltd 1983-86; Venture Capital manager, 3i plc 1986-88; Manager, Legal and General Ventures Ltd 1989-92; Adviser, Legal and General Group plc 1992-95

Political career: Contested Glasgow Central 1987 general election. Member for North Colchester 1992-97, for North Essex 1997-2010, for Harwich and North Essex since 6 May 2010 general election; PPS to Michael Forsyth as Secretary of State for Scotland 1995-97; Opposition Spokesperson for: Constitutional Affairs, Scotland and Wales 1997-98, Environment, Transport and the Regions (Roads and Environment) 1998; Shadow Minister for Transport 1998-2001; Member, Shadow Cabinet 1999-2003; Shadow Secretary of State for: Defence 2001-03, The Regions 2003-05; Shadow Minister for Energy 2005; *Select Committees:* Member: European Standing Committee B 1992-97, Social Security 1993-97, Defence 2006-10, Arms Export Controls 2008-10; Deputy Chairman (Candidates) Conservative Party 2005-06

Political interests: Economic policy, trade, European Union, defence, foreign affairs; USA, New Zealand, Singapore, Chile, France, Germany, Iraq, Pakistan, Afghanistan, India, Russia, Georgia

Other organisations: Governor, Central Foundation Girls' School ILEA 1985-89; Governor, London Goodenough Trust for Overseas Graduates 1992-2001; Member Council of St Paul's Cathedral 2006-; Colchester Conservative Constitutional Club; *Publications:* Maastricht: Game Set and Match? (1993); Who Benefits: Reinventing Social Security (1993); A Conservative Europe: 1994 and beyond (1994); Fairer Business Rates (1996); A Defence Policy for the UK: Matching Commitments and Resources (2007)

Recreations: Sailing, music (especially opera), fishing, family, DIY

Bernard Jenkin MP, House of Commons, London SW1A 0AA
Tel: 020 7219 4029 Fax: 020 7219 5963
E-mail: jenkinbc@parliament.uk
Constituency: North Essex Conservative Association, Unit C2, East Gores Farm, Salmons Lane, Coggeshall, Colchester, Essex CO6 1RZ
Tel: 01376 564292 Fax: 01376 564812
Website: www.bernardjenkinmp.com

GENERAL ELECTION RESULT

		%
Jenkin, B. (Con)*	23,001	46.9
Raven, J. (Lib Dem)	11,554	23.6
Barrenger, D. (Lab)	9,774	20.0
Anselmi, S. (UKIP)	2,527	5.2
Robey, S. (BNP)	1,065	2.2
Fox, C. (Green)	909	1.9
Thompson Bates, P. (Ind)	170	0.4
Majority	11,447	23.36
Electorate	70,743	
Turnout	49,000	69.26

**Member of last parliament*

CONSTITUENCY SNAPSHOT

The new seat includes most of the old North Essex constituency, except the area to the south west of Colchester. It also includes Harwich, but not the other Essex coastal towns to the south and their hinterland, which have gone to the new Clacton seat.

North Essex, and its predecessor North Colchester, has been solid Tory territory. Bernard Jenkin was first elected to the seat in 1992 and in 2005 was re-elected with a 10,903 majority.

The Harwich seat was also traditionally Conservative. From 1945 to 1997 its three MPs all regularly took over 50 per cent of the vote. In 1997 Labour's Ivan Henderson won by 1,216 votes. He retained the seat in 2001. However, in 2005 support for Labour fell and the Conservative candidate, Douglas Carswell, took the seat with a majority of just under 1,000.

The Conservatives won the seat in 2010, giving Bernard Jenkin a majority of 11,447.

The new seat is very mixed, with the town and international port of Harwich in the east, but the rest of the seat much more rural.

This contrast is reflected in the economic and social background. Employment in Harwich is dominated by port-related industries, with important international freight and ferry services. The parts of the seat from the old North Essex constituency are more white-collar, with many travelling to work in Colchester.

Rt Hon **Alan Johnson**

Kingston upon Hull West and Hessle ***(returning MP)***

Boundary changes

Tel: 020 7219 5227
E-mail: johnsona@parliament.uk
Website: www.alanjohnson.org

Date of birth: 17 May 1950; Son of late Stephen Arthur and Lillian May Johnson

Education: Sloane Grammar School, Chelsea; Married Judith Cox 1968 (divorced) (1 son 2 daughters); married Laura Jane Patient 1991 (1 son)

Non-political career: Postman 1968-87; Local officer Slough UCW 1974-81; Union of Communication Workers: Branch official 1976, Executive Council 1981-87, National officer 1987-93, General Secretary 1993-95; Member General Council, TUC 1993-95; Executive Member Postal, Telegraph and Telephone International 1993-97; Director Unity Bank Trust plc 1993-97; Joint General Secretary Communication Workers Union 1995-97; Member, CWU

Political career: Member for Hull West and Hessle 1997-2010, for Kingston upon Hull West and Hessle since 6 May 2010 general election; PPS to Dawn Primarolo at HM Treasury: as Financial Secretary 1997-99, as Paymaster General 1999; Department of Trade and Industry 1999-2003: Parliamentary Under-Secretary of State (Competitiveness) 1999-2001, Minister of State 2001-03: (Employment Relations and Regions 2001-02, Employment Relations, Industry and the Regions 2002-03); Minister of State, Department for Education and Skills (Lifelong Learning, Further and Higher Education) 2003-04; Secretary of State for: Work and Pensions 2004-05, Trade and Industry 2005-06, Education and Skills 2006-07, Health 2007-09; Secretary of State for the Home Office (Home Secretary) 2009-10; Shadow Secretary of State for the Home Office (Home Secretary) 2010-; *Select Committees:* Member: Trade and Industry 1997-98; Member: Southern Regional Executive of Labour Party 1981-87, Member Labour Party National Executive Committee 1995-97, Labour Campaign for Electoral Reform

Political interests: Education, electoral reform, employment, Post Office

Other organisations: Member World Executive, Postal, Telegraph and Telephone International (PTTI) 1993-97; PC 2003

Recreations: Tennis, cooking, reading, radio, music, football

Rt Hon Alan Johnson MP, House of Commons, London SW1A 0AA
Tel: 020 7219 5227 Fax: 020 7219 5856
E-mail: johnsona@parliament.uk
Constituency: Goodwin Resource Centre, Icehouse Road, Hull, Humberside HU3 2HQ Tel: 01482 219211 Fax: 01482 219211
Website: www.alanjohnson.org

GENERAL ELECTION RESULT

		%
Johnson, A. (Lab)*	13,378	42.5
Ross, M. (Lib Dem)	7,638	24.2
Shores, G. (Con)	6,361	20.2
Horden, K. (UKIP)	1,688	5.4
Scott, E. (BNP)	1,416	4.5
Mawer, P. (England)	876	2.8
Gibson, K. (TUSC)	150	0.5
Majority	5,740	18.22
Electorate	69,017	
Turnout	31,507	45.65

**Member of last parliament*

CONSTITUENCY SNAPSHOT

Since 1955 Hull West has returned Labour Members. Stuart Randall, MP from 1983, polled over 50 per cent of the vote in the contests that followed.

In 1997 Stuart Randall stood down and entered the House of Lords. The new candidate was Alan Johnson, then leader of the Communication Workers' Union. In the election he increased the Labour majority to over 15,500. Small swings and falling turnout have cut his majority slightly since. He won by 9,450 votes over the Liberal Democrats in 2005.

In 2010 the seat was held by Johnson with a 5,740 majority.

The Hull seats have been redrawn so that the constituency boundaries coincide with the local government wards. As a result, this seat lost a small part of Avenue ward to Hull North.

This seat includes a large part of the city centre and stretches just outside the city limits to the northern end of the Humber Bridge.

More than half the workforce is made up of manual workers, with a high proportion of the unskilled and semi-skilled.

Main employers include Kingston Communications, the former council-owned telecommunications company. The constituency is home to Hull City football club and Hull FC rugby league side.

Diana Johnson

Kingston upon Hull North ***(returning MP)***

Boundary changes

Tel: 020 7219 5647
E-mail: johnsond@parliament.uk
Website: www.dianajohnson.co.uk

Labour

Date of birth: 25 July 1966; Daughter of late Eric and Ruth Johnson

Education: Sir John Deane's Sixth Form College, Cheshire; Northwich County Grammar School for Girls, Cheshire; Queen Mary College, London University (LLB 1989); Council for Legal Education (law finals 1991)

Non-political career: Volunteer/locum lawyer Tower Hamlets Law Centre 1991-94; Employment, immigration and education lawyer North Lewisham Law Centre 1995-99; Employment lawyer Paddington Law Centre 1999-2002; National Officer FDA Trade Union 2002-03; Member: TGWU UNISON; London Borough of Tower Hamlets: Councillor 1994-2002, Chair: social services 1997-2000, social services and health scrutiny panel 2000-02; Legal visiting member of Mental Health Act Commission 1995-98; Member Greater London Assembly 2003-04; Member Metropolitan Police Authority 2003-04; Non-executive director Newham Healthcare Trust 1998-2001; Non-executive director Tower Hamlets PCT 2001-05

Political career: Contested Brentwood and Ongar 2001 general election. Member for Hull North 2005-10, for Kingston upon Hull North since 6 May 2010 general election; PPS to Stephen Timms: as Minister of State, Department for Work and Pensions 2005-06, as Chief Secretary to the Treasury 2006-07; Assistant Government Whip 2007-09; Parliamentary Under-Secretary of State for Schools, Department for Children, Schools and Families 2009-10; *Select Committees:* Member: Public Accounts 2005; Member: Co-operative Party, Labour Women's Network, Fabian Society

Political interests: Employment rights, health, education, animal welfare, policing

Other organisations: Member: Fawcett Society, Amnesty International

Recreations: Cinema, dog walking, theatre, Hull City FC

Diana Johnson MP, House of Commons, London SW1A 0AA
Tel: 020 7219 5647 Fax: 020 7219 0959
E-mail: johnsond@parliament.uk
Constituency: Unit 8, Hull Business Centre, Guildhall Road, Hull, Humberside HU1 1HJ Tel: 01482 319135/6 Fax: 01482 319137
Website: www.dianajohnson.co.uk

GENERAL ELECTION RESULT

		%
Johnson, D. (Lab)*	13,044	39.2
Healy, D. (Lib Dem)	12,403	37.3
Aitken, V. (Con)	4,365	13.1
Mainprize, J. (BNP)	1,443	4.3
Barlow, P. (UKIP)	1,358	4.1
Deane, M. (Green)	478	1.4
Cassidy, M. (England)	200	0.6
Majority	641	1.93
Electorate	64,082	
Turnout	33,291	51.95

**Member of last parliament*

CONSTITUENCY SNAPSHOT

This was the location of a by-election in 1966, when Kevin McNamara defended a Labour majority of just 1,000 against the Conservative Toby Jessel. He held the seat with a majority of 5,351.

Since then the area has stuck firmly with Labour. McNamara's seat became Kingston-upon-Hull Central from 1974 until 1983 when the Hull North seat was redrawn.

Conservatives' support has been falling steadily and in 2001 they dropped to third place behind the Lib Dems. Kevin McNamara retired in 2005 and Diana Johnson retained the seat for Labour with a majority of 7,351. Labour retained the seat in 2010 with 13,044 votes giving Johnson a small majority of 641.

The Hull seats have been redrawn so that their boundaries coincide with the local government wards. This seat lost parts of Sutton and Holderness wards to Hull East and gained a part of Avenue from Hull West and Hessle and part of Bransholme West from Hull East.

This is a largely working-class East Yorkshire seat taking in the northern Hull districts with some leafy areas around the university.

The university is one of the main employers, along with the public sector. This constituency has a growing student population.

The Sutton Field industrial estate houses many small businesses from computers to bakeries and there is a retail park attached to the modern Kingswood estate.

Gareth Johnson

Dartford

Boundary changes

Tel: 020 7219 3000
E-mail: gareth.johnson.mp@parliament.uk

Date of birth: 12 October 1969; Son of Alan Johnson, retired milkman, and Ruth Johnson

Education: Dartford Grammar School; University of the West of England (Post-graduate Diploma law); College of Law (legal practice course 1995); Married Wendy Morris 1997 (1 son 1 daughter)

Non-political career: Legal adviser, Magistrates Court Service 1988-98; Solicitor, Gary Jacobs Mehta & Co 1997-2002; Assistant solicitor, then solicitor, Thomas Boyd Whyte 2002-; London Borough of Bexley Council: Councillor 1998-2002, Cabinet Member for Policy and Resources 1998-2002; Board of Governors, Dartford Grammar Girls School

Political career: Contested Lewisham West 2001 and Dartford 2005 general elections. Member for Dartford since 6 May 2010 general election

Political interests: Home affairs, environment

Other organisations: Dartford Conservative Club

Recreations: Cricket, rugby

Gareth Johnson MP, House of Commons, London SW1A 0AA
Tel: 020 7219 3000 E-mail: gareth.johnson.mp@parliament.uk
Constituency: Dartford Conservatives, First Floor, Westgate House, Spital Street, Dartford, Kent DA1 2EH Tel: 01322 220704
Fax: 01322 220704 Website: www.dartfordconservatives.com

GENERAL ELECTION RESULT

		%
Johnson, G. (Con)	24,428	48.8
Adams, J. (Lab)	13,800	27.6
Willis, J. (Lib Dem)	7,361	14.7
Rogers, G. (England)	2,178	4.4
Palmer, R. (UKIP)	1,842	3.7
Tindame, S. (Ind)	264	0.5
Crockford, J. (FDP)	207	0.4
Majority	10,628	21.22
Electorate	76,271	
Turnout	50,080	65.66

CONSTITUENCY SNAPSHOT

Dartford was created in 1955 and since 1964 it has elected its MP from the current governing party.

Having been a Conservative seat during the Thatcher and Major years, the seat went Labour at the 1997 general election. Dr Howard Stoate won a majority of 4,328. His majorities fell in subsequent elections and were 3,306 and 706 in 2001 and 2005 respectively.

The Conservatives seized the seat from Labour in 2010, with Gareth Johnson securing a 10,628 majority.

The seat gained the part-ward of Hartley and Hodsoll Street from Sevenoaks, in exchange for two part-wards to Stevenage.

Home to the Dartford tunnels and bridge as well as the M25, Dartford is just inside Kent, on the outskirts of south-east London. It combines urban areas including Dartford itself and more rural areas.

The key to Dartford's current economic success is its location. The new Channel Tunnel rail-link passes through the constituency at the Ebbsfleet international station.

The constituency has a traditional industrial base in engineering and pharmaceuticals, and has been subject to a large amount of redevelopment over recent years. It is home to the Bluewater shopping centre and a large private finance initiative-funded hospital in the Darenth Valley in the south of the constituency.

Jo Johnson

Orpington

Boundary changes

Tel: 020 7219 3000
E-mail: jo.johnson.mp@parliament.uk
Website: www.jo-johnson.com

Date of birth: 1971; Son of Stanley Johnson and Charlotte Johnson, née Fawcett

Education: European School, Uccle, Brussels; Hall School, Hampstead; Eton College; Balliol College, Oxford (BA modern history); INSEAD (MBA 2000); Married Amelia Gentleman (2 children)

Non-political career: Corporate financial, Deutsche Bank; *Financial Times* 1997-: Lex column 1997, Paris correspondent 2001-04, Bureau chief, South Asia 2005-08, Head of Lex 2008-, Associate editor

Political career: Member for Orpington since 6 May 2010 general election

Political interests: Business, finance; France, India; *Publications:* Co-author, The Man Who Tried To Buy The World (2003)

Jo Johnson MP, House of Commons, London SW1A 0AA
Tel: 020 7219 3000 E-mail: jo.johnson.mp@parliament.uk
Constituency: Orpington Conservative Association, 6 Sevenoaks Road, Orpington, Kent BR6 9JJ Tel: 01689 820347
Website: www.jo-johnson.com

GENERAL ELECTION RESULT

		%
Johnson, J. (Con)	29,200	59.7
McBride, D. (Lib Dem)	12,000	24.5
Morgan, S. (Lab)	4,400	9.0
Greenhough, M. (UKIP)	1,360	2.8
Galloway, T. (Green)	511	1.0
Snape, C. (England)	199	0.4
Majority	17,200	35.17
Electorate	67,732	
Turnout	48,911	72.21

CONSTITUENCY SNAPSHOT

Liberal Eric Lubbock defeated the Conservatives at the 1962 by-election. He went on to hold Orpington in the next two general elections but since 1970 the seat has been Conservative. John Horam became MP in 1992.

In 1997, the Tories' notional majority of 18,000 was cut to under than 3,000. In 2005 Orpington was a Lib Dem target, requiring a swing of just 0.3 per cent; but Horam held on with an increased majority on a high turnout. Boris Johnson's brother Jo held this seat for the Conservatives, following John Horam's retirement, with a 12 per cent swing away from the Liberal Democrats and a 17,200 majority.

The seat lost Cray Valley West to Bromley and Chislehurst and Bromley Common and Keston part-ward to Beckenham.

Orpington is a leafy, primarily suburban constituency on the London-Kent borders and there is more open space than elsewhere in the city.

The constituency includes very prosperous wards such as Chelsfield and Farnborough. Cray Valley East is significantly less prosperous, however.

Many constituents commute to work in central London. Others are employed in the Cray Valley commercial and industrial area or at Biggin Hill Airport.

Andrew Jones

Harrogate and Knaresborough

Boundary changes

Tel: 020 7219 3000
E-mail: andrew.jones.mp@parliament.uk

Conservative

Date of birth: 28 November 1963

Education: Bradford Grammar School; Leeds University (BA English 1985)

Non-political career: Marketing manager: Gary Places plc 1989-96, Kingfisher plc 1985-88, 1996-98; Marketing Store; Account director, M&C Saatchi 1998-2000; Sales and marketing director, Bettys and Taylors of Harrogate; Harrogate Borough Council: Councillor 2003-, Cabinet Member, Resources 2006-

Political career: Contested Harrogate and Knaresborough 2001 general election. Member for Harrogate and Knaresborough since 6 May 2010 general election; Member, Conservative Party 1987-

Political interests: Renewable energy, recycling

Other organisations: Chair, Bow Group 1998-99; Member, Yorkshire County Cricket Club

Recreations: Cricket, squash, walking, theatre, music

Andrew Jones MP, House of Commons, London SW1A 0AA
Tel: 020 7219 3000 E-mail: andrew.jones.mp@parliament.uk
Constituency: Harrogate and Knaresborough Conservatives, 57 East Parade, Harrogate, North Yorkshire HG1 5LQ Tel: 01423 542630
Fax: 01423 541445
Website: www.harrogateknaresboroughconservatives.com

GENERAL ELECTION RESULT

		%
Jones, A. (Con)	24,305	45.7
Kelley, C. (Lib Dem)	23,266	43.8
McNerney, K. (Lab)	3,413	6.4
Gill, S. (BNP)	1,094	2.1
Majority	1,039	1.96
Electorate	75,269	
Turnout	53,134	70.59

CONSTITUENCY SNAPSHOT

In 1997 Harrogate had been represented by a Conservative MP for as long as anyone could remember, and for nearly a quarter of a century by Robert Banks. Boundary changes had removed 12,000 rural voters but even this gave the Conservatives a 9000-vote notional majority in the redrawn and renamed Harrogate and Knaresborough. Banks retired and the Tory nomination was won by former Chancellor Norman Lamont.

However, the Liberal Democrat Phil Willis won with a majority of over 6,000. Willis increased his majority in 2001, and in 2005 increased it further to 10,429.

The Conservatives seized the seat from the Lib Dems in 2010 with Andrew Jones securing a 1,039 majority.

A large rural area was added to the seats from the old Skipton and Ripon and Vale of York constituencies to the north and east of Harrogate.

Harrogate is a Victorian spa town, famed as the home of Betty's tearooms and Yorkshire Tea. It hosts the annual Great Yorkshire Show and has become known as a conference centre.

Knaresborough is a much smaller market town to the east. It is known for Mother Shipton's Well and its castle.

This is one of the most affluent parts of Yorkshire, benefiting from its own successful economy and from the growth of Leeds, for which it acts as an executive dormitory. The number of managerial and skilled non-manual workers is well above average.

David Jones

Clwyd West (returning MP)

Boundary changes

Tel: 020 7219 8070
E-mail: jonesdi@parliament.uk
Website: www.davidjonesmp.com

Conservative

Date of birth: 22 March 1952; Son of late Bryn Jones and Elspeth née Savage-Williams

Education: Ruabon Grammar School, Wrexham; University College London (LLB law 1973); Chester College of Law; Married Sara Eluned Tudor 1982 (2 sons)

Non-political career: Senior partner David Jones & Company, Llandudno 1985-2005;

Political career: Contested Conwy 1997 and City of Chester 2001 general elections. Member for Clwyd West 2005-10, for Clwyd West (revised boundary) since 6 May 2010 general election; Shadow Minister for Wales 2006-10; Parliamentary Under-Secretary of State, Wales Office 2010-; *Select Committees:* Member: Welsh Affairs 2005-10; National Assembly for Wales: contested 1999 election; AM for North Wales 2002-03; Chair, Conwy Conservative Association 1998-99

Political interests: Law and order, constitution, Welsh affairs, countryside; Middle East

Recreations: Travel

David Jones MP, House of Commons, London SW1A 0AA
Tel: 020 7219 8070 Fax: 020 7219 0142
E-mail: jonesdi@parliament.uk
Constituency: 3 Llewelyn Road, Colwyn Bay, Clwyd LL29 7AP
Tel: 01492 530505 Fax: 01492 534157
Website: www.davidjonesmp.com

GENERAL ELECTION RESULT

		%
Jones, D. (Con)*	15,833	41.5
Hutton, D. (Lab)	9,414	24.7
Gruffydd, L. (PlC)	5,864	15.4
Jones, M. (Lib Dem)	5,801	15.2
Nicholson, W. (UKIP)	864	2.3
Griffiths, D. (WCP)	239	0.6
Blakesley, J. (Ind)	96	0.3
Majority	6,419	16.84
Electorate	57,913	
Turnout	38,111	65.81

**Member of last parliament*

CONSTITUENCY SNAPSHOT

Clwyd West was created for the 1997 general election and is made up mainly of the former Conservative Clwyd North West seat. The first winner was Labour's Gareth Thomas.

The Tories narrowed the gap in 2001, and David Jones captured the seat for the party in 2005 with a majority of just 133. Jones increased his majority to 6,419 in 2010 with an 8.4 per cent swing from Labour.

Clwyd West was slightly enlarged with the addition of small parts of three electoral divisions which were previously split between this seat and Clwyd South.

This constituency lies in the centre of North Wales. Its short coastline reaches from Colwyn Bay to Kinmel Bay and is home to most of the voting population of the seat. The division stretches inland to take in the town of Ruthin and parts of rural Denbighshire and Conwy.

It is a largely rural constituency. Agriculture is a major industry and the Welsh Language is widely spoken.

Colwyn Bay is the largest town in the constituency and the second largest in North Wales. Tourism is a key revenue earner for the constituency and the region is rich in both cultural and natural heritage, benefiting from its coastal position and rural backdrop.

It is also a popular retirement area. The seat has the highest percentage of elderly people in Wales.

Graham Jones

Hyndburn

Boundary changes

Tel: 020 7219 3000
E-mail: graham.jones.mp@parliament.uk
Website: hhgrahamjones.blogspot.com

Labour

Non-political career: Hyndburn Borough Council: Councillor, Leader, Labour group; Councillor, Lancashire County Council; Board member: Barnfield and Hyndburn Ltd, Globe Enterprises Ltd, Hyndburn Homes Repairs Ltd, Hyndburn Homes Industrial and Provident Society Ltd

Political career: Member for Hyndburn since 6 May 2010 general election

Graham Jones MP, House of Commons, London SW1A 0AA
Tel: 020 7219 3000 E-mail: graham.jones.mp@parliament.uk
Website: hhgrahamjones.blogspot.com

GENERAL ELECTION RESULT

		%
Jones, G. (Lab)	17,531	41.1
Buckley, K. (Con)	14,441	33.8
Rankine, A. (Lib Dem)	5,033	11.8
Shapcott, D. (BNP)	2,137	5.0
Barker, G. (UKIP)	1,481	3.5
Logan, K. (CPA)	795	1.9
Gormley, K. (Green)	463	1.1
Reid, C. (England)	413	1.0
Hall, C. (Ind)	378	0.9
Majority	3,090	7.24
Electorate	67,221	
Turnout	42,672	63.48

CONSTITUENCY SNAPSHOT

The seat dates from 1983 when it replaced the Accrington seat which covered most of the same area. Before 1983 this was a Labour seat but was won by the Conservatives that year. However, the majority was slender with only 21 votes between the top two candidates. Ken Hargreaves, the victorious Conservative, held the seat until 1992 when Greg Pope regained it for Labour.

In 1997 Pope's majority was 11,000 but has fallen since and was 5,587 in 2005. Pope retired in 2001 and Graham Jones held the seat for Labour in 2010 with a majority of 3,090.

The seat gained Greenfield part-ward from Rossendale and Darwen.

Hyndburn covers the region in Lancashire between Blackburn and Burnley, including the small towns of Great Harwood, Accrington and Oswaldtwistle. The seat also borders Rossendale to the south.

The seat's best-known town is Accrington, with its football club, Accrington Stanley.

The constituency played a critical role in the industrial advancements of the eighteenth century. In 1764 James Harvey of Oswaldtwistle invented the spinning jenny, and eight years later in 1772 James Hacking invented the carding machine in Huncoat.

There is still a strong manufacturing base here, as still commonly in Lancashire, but the constituency struggles to adapt to the changing nature of the British economy.

Helen Jones

Warrington North ***(returning MP)***

Boundary changes

Tel: 020 7219 4048
E-mail: jonesh@parliament.uk
Website: www.epolitix.com/helen-jones

Date of birth: 24 December 1954; Daughter of late Robert Edward Jones and of Mary Scanlan

Education: Ursuline Convent, Chester; University College, London (BA English); Chester College; Liverpool University (MEd); Manchester Metropolitan University; Married Michael Vobe 1988 (1 son)

Non-political career: English teacher; Development officer MIND; Justice and peace officer Liverpool Archdiocese; Solicitor; MSF Labour Party Liaison Officer, North West Coast Region; Councillor, Chester City Council 1984-91

Political career: Contested Shropshire North 1983 and Ellesmere Port and Neston 1987 general elections. Member for Warrington North 1997-2010, for Warrington North (revised boundary) since 6 May 2010 general election; PPS to Dawn Primarolo as Minister of State, Department of Health 2007-08; Assistant Government Whip 2008-09; Government Whip 2009-10; *Select Committees:* Member: Catering 1997-98, Public Administration 1998-2000, Standing Orders 1999-2000, Education and Employment 1999-2001, Education and Employment (Education Sub-Committee) 1999-2001, Unopposed Bills (Panel) 1999-2010, Standing Orders 2001-10, Education and Skills 2003-07, Administration 2005-07, Selection 2009-10; Contested Lancashire Central 1984 European Parliament election

Political interests: Education, health; Wales, Africa, Uganda, England, Scotland, Ireland, Italy, Finland, Norway

Recreations: Gardening, reading, cooking

Helen Jones MP, House of Commons, London SW1A 0AA
Tel: 020 7219 4048 E-mail: jonesh@parliament.uk
Constituency: Gilbert Wakefield House, 67 Bewsey Street, Warrington, Cheshire WA2 7JQ Tel: 01925 232480
Fax: 01925 232239 Website: www.epolitix.com/helen-jones

GENERAL ELECTION RESULT

		%
Jones, H. (Lab)*	20,135	45.5
Campbell, P. (Con)	13,364	30.2
Eccles, D. (Lib Dem)	9,196	20.8
Scott, A. (Ind)	1,516	3.4
Majority	6,771	15.32
Electorate	71,601	
Turnout	44,211	61.75

**Member of last parliament*

CONSTITUENCY SNAPSHOT

The Labour Party has held this seat for decades, and has rarely faced serious opposition.

In the 1983 general election, the year this seat was created, Labour won, as it has done so at every election since then, including 1997, when current incumbent Helen Jones was elected. She was re-elected with a 12,204 majority in 2005. Jones held the seat in 2010 with a reduced majority of 6,771.

The seat gained Fairfield and Howley part-ward from Warrington South, in exchange for the part-wards of Bewsey and Whitecross and Whittle Hall; they had previously been shared between the two divisions.

This north Cheshire constituency contains the inner-city core of the industrial town just north of the Mersey.

There are a surprising number of high-income families in Warrington North, making up around one in five of the population, but they are outnumbered by low-rise council tenants, who make up nearly a quarter of the population, double that of Warrington South.

Regeneration of the Wire Works development on Winwick Road will transform the north side of the town centre with the construction of retail outlets, bars, apartments and a multi-screen cinema.

Kevan Jones

North Durham (returning MP)

Boundary changes

Tel: 020 7219 8219
E-mail: kevanjonesmp@parliament.uk
Website: www.kevanjonesmp.org.uk

Date of birth: 25 April 1964

Education: Portland Comprehensive, Worksop, Nottinghamshire; Newcastle upon Tyne Polytechnic (BA government and public policy 1985); University of Southern Maine, USA

Non-political career: Parliamentary assistant to Nick Brown MP 1985-89; Regional organiser GMB Union 1992-99; GMB: Political officer 1989-2001, Senior organiser 1999-2001; Newcastle City Council: Councillor 1990-2001, Chair Public Health 1993-97, Chief Whip 1994-2000, Chair Development and Transport 1997-2001

Political career: Member for North Durham 2001-10, for North Durham (revised boundary) since 6 May 2010 general election; Parliamentary Under-Secretary of State (Minister for Veterans), Ministry of Defence 2008-10; *Select Committees:* Member: Defence 2001-09, Administration 2005-09, Armed Forces Bill 2005-06; Northern Region Labour Party: Chair 1998-2000, Vice-chair 2000-

Political interests: Regeneration, transport, employment, regional policy, local and regional government, defence; Afghanistan, Iraq, Poland, United Arab Emirates, USA

Other organisations: Patron Chester Le Street Mind 2001-; Member European Cities Environment Committee 1994-99; Sacriston Workingmens Club

Recreations: Golf

Kevan Jones MP, House of Commons, London SW1A 0AA
Tel: 020 7219 8219 Fax: 020 7219 1759
E-mail: kevanjonesmp@parliament.uk
Constituency: Fulforth Centre, Sacriston, Co Durham DH7 6JT
Tel: 0191-371 8834 Fax: 0191-371 8834
Website: www.kevanjonesmp.org.uk

GENERAL ELECTION RESULT

		%
Jones, K. (Lab)*	20,698	50.5
Skelton, D. (Con)	8,622	21.1
Lindley, I. (Lib Dem)	8,617	21.0
Molloy, P. (BNP)	1,686	4.1
Reid, B. (UKIP)	1,344	3.3
Majority	12,076	29.48
Electorate	67,548	
Turnout	40,967	60.65

**Member of last parliament*

CONSTITUENCY SNAPSHOT

This is a seat with one of the longest histories of continuous Labour representation. The current seat is similar to the old seat of Chester-le-Street, which was taken in the election of 1906, and never lost. Giles Radice became MP in 1973, and remained in the seat for 28 years. Kevan Jones succeeded him in 2001.

Kevan Jones was re-elected in 2005, with a majority of 16,781 after polling 64 per cent of the vote. Despite a 9.1 per cent swing to the Conservatives, Kevan Jones held the seat with a majority of 12,076.

Minor boundary changes moved Tanfield ward entirely within the seat's boundaries.

A largely rural area, North Durham stretches from the village of Bournmoor, situated on the outskirts of the old market town of Chester-le-Street in the east, to Stanley in the west.

This compact seat borders North West Durham to the west, Tyne and Wear to the north and east, and the Durham City constituency to the south, and is as such a commuter constituency.

Much employment within the constituency is in the education and the local government sector. Despite the expanses of countryside between pit villages, there is little agricultural activity, but there is tourism, with the famous open air museum at Beamish a popular attraction.

Marcus Jones

Nuneaton

Boundary changes

Tel: 020 7219 3000
E-mail: marcus.jones.mp@parliament.uk
Website: www.marcus-jones.co.uk

Conservative

Date of birth: 5 April 1974; Son of Brian Jones, signwriter, and Jean Jones, legal cashier

Education: St Thomas More School, Nuneaton; King Edward VI College; Married Suzanne 2004 (1 son)

Non-political career: Conveyancing manager, Tustain Jones & Co, Solicitors 1999-2009; Nuneaton and Bedworth Borough Council: Councillor 2005-, Leader, Conservative group 2006-09, Council Leader 2008-09

Political career: Member for Nuneaton since 6 May 2010 general election

Recreations: Family, watching Coventry City FC, angling

Marcus Jones MP, House of Commons, London SW1A 0AA
Tel: 020 7219 3000 E-mail: marcus.jones.mp@parliament.uk
Constituency: Nuneaton Conservative Party Offices, Albert Buildings, 2 Castle Mews, Rugby CV21 2XL Website: www.marcus-jones.co.uk

GENERAL ELECTION RESULT

		%
Jones, M. (Con)	18,536	41.5
Innes, J. (Lab)	16,467	36.9
Jebb, C. (Lib Dem)	6,846	15.3
Findley, M. (BNP)	2,797	6.3
Majority	2,069	4.63
Electorate	67,837	
Turnout	44,646	65.81

CONSTITUENCY SNAPSHOT

The seat returned Labour candidates without interruption from 1935 to 1983. In 1983 it went to the Conservatives' Lewis Stevens.

The Conservatives held the seat for two terms, and in 1992 Labour's Bill Olner took the seat back. In the 1997 general election the swing against the Tories resulted in a fall of over 12 per cent in their share of the vote. Labour's incumbent Bill Olner, returned to the Commons with a majority of 13,540 votes.

In the 2005 general election Olner's majority fell by more than two-thirds to just 2,281 votes. Bill Olner retired in 2010 and Marcus Jones took the seat for the Conservatives with a majority of 2,069.

Boundary changes have been minimal.

Nuneaton in the north-east of Warwickshire stretches round the eastern side of Coventry.

The town of Nuneaton forms the constituency's centre. On the edge of the Warwickshire coalfield, it grew rapidly following the industrial revolution and further developed with the growth of manufacturing in Coventry and Birmingham.

The constituency has some light engineering works and is also popular with warehousing and distribution companies because of its proximity to the M6. The workforce is professional and of more routine occupation than the national average.

Susan Elan Jones

Clwyd South

Boundary changes

Tel: 020 7219 3000
E-mail: susan.jones.mp@parliament.uk

Date of birth: 1 June 1968; Daughter of Richard Jones, retired steelworks costs clerk, and Eirlys Jones, retired medical secretary

Education: Grango Comprehensive School, Rhosllannerchrugog; Ruabon School Sixth Form; Bristol University (BA English 1989); Cardiff University (MA applied English language studies 1992)

Non-political career: English teacher: Tomakomai English School, Japan 1990-91, Atsuma Board of Education, Japan 1992-94; Corporate development fundraiser, Muscular Dystrophy Campaign 1995-96; Fundraiser, USPG 1997-2002; Director, Caris Haringey 2002-05; Fundraising executive, Housing Justice 2005-; Member, Unite 1996-; London Borough of Southwark Council: Councillor 2006-09, Deputy opposition leader 2007-09

Political career: Contested Surrey Heath 1997 general election. Member for Clwyd South since 6 May 2010 general election; Chair, Bristol University Labour Club 1986-87; Member: National Committee, Labour Students 1989-90, Labour Campaign for Electoral Reform 1996-

Other organisations: Member, Christian Socialist Movement 2006-

Recreations: Classical music

Susan Elan Jones MP, House of Commons, London SW1A 0AA
Tel: 020 7219 3000 E-mail: susan.jones.mp@parliament.uk
Constituency: Currently being set up.

GENERAL ELECTION RESULT

		%
Jones, S. (Lab)	13,311	38.4
Bell, J. (Con)	10,477	30.2
Roberts, B. (Lib Dem)	5,965	17.2
Ryder, J. (PIC)	3,009	8.7
Hynes, S. (BNP)	1,100	3.2
Powell, N. (UKIP)	819	2.4
Majority	2,834	8.17
Electorate	53,748	
Turnout	34,681	64.53

CONSTITUENCY SNAPSHOT

Clwyd South was created for the 1997 general election from parts of Clwyd South West and Wrexham. In 1983 the Clwyd South West seat fell to the Conservatives, largely due to the Labour MP for Wrexham Tom Ellis defecting to the SDP-Liberal Alliance and standing in the Clwyd South West seat.

Labour regained the seat in 1987 through Martyn Jones. He increased his majority at the two subsequent elections and in 1997, in the new Clwyd South seat, this majority jumped from 10 per cent to 35 per cent. It fell slightly in the 2001 election and a further swing to the Tories in 2005 reduced the Labour majority to 6,348. New MP Susan Jones was elected with a 2,843 majority after a 5.8 per cent swing to the Tories.

The seat has lost the parts of four wards that were previously within its boundaries to Clwyd West and Vale of Clwyd. The Llanrhaedr-ym-Mochnant/Llanslin electoral division has been moved to Montgomeryshire.

This constituency is in North Wales on the border with England and incorporates the Wrexham council areas to the south and west of the town itself as well as parts of rural Denbighshire.Employment is varied. Agriculture is a major employer in the rural areas. There is still an above average sized manufacturing base, though the traditional coal and steel industries have closed.

In 2009 the Pontcysyllte Aqueduct was listed as a UNESCO World Heritage Site.

Rt Hon **Tessa Jowell**

Dulwich and West Norwood ***(returning MP)***

Boundary changes

Tel: 020 7219 3409
E-mail: jowellt@parliament.uk

Date of birth: 17 September 1947; Daughter of Dr. Kenneth Palmer and Rosemary Palmer, radiographer

Education: St Margaret's School, Aberdeen; Aberdeen (MA); Edinburgh University; Goldsmith's College, London University; Married Roger Jowell 1970 (divorced 1977); married David Mills 1979 (1 son 1 daughter 3 stepchildren)

Non-political career: Child care officer, London Borough of Lambeth 1969-71; Psychiatric social worker, Maudsley Hospital 1972-74; Assistant director, MIND 1974-86; Director: Community care special action project, Birmingham 1987-90, Joseph Rowntree Foundation, Community Care Programme 1990-92; Senior visiting research fellow: Policy Studies Institute 1987-90, King's Fund Institute 1990-92; Member: TGWU, Amicus; Councillor, London Borough of Camden 1971-86; Vice-chair, then chair, Social Services Committee of Association of Metropolitan Authorities 1978-86; Mental Health Act Commission 1985-90; Chair Millennium Commission

Political career: Contested Ilford North 1978 by-election and 1979 general election. Member for Dulwich 1992-97, for Dulwich and West Norwood 1997-2010, for Dulwich and West Norwood (revised boundary) since 6 May 2010 general election; Opposition Whip 1994-95; Opposition Spokesperson for: Women 1995-96, Health 1994-95, 1996-97; Minister of State: Department of Health (Minister for Public Health) 1997-99, Department for Education and Employment (Minister for Employment, Welfare to Work and Equal Opportunities) 1999-2001; Minister for Women 1999-2001; Department for Culture, Media and Sport: Secretary of State 2001-07: Minister for: Women 2005-06, the Olympics 2005-07, the Olympics and London; Paymaster General (also attending Cabinet, reporting to Prime Minister, based in Cabinet Office) 2007-08, the Olympics; Paymaster General 2008-10; Minister for the Cabinet Office 2009-10; Minister for London 2009-10; Shadow Minister for the Cabinet Office 2010-; Shadow Minister for the Olympics and for London 2010-; *Select Committees:* Member: Social Security1992, Health 1992-94

Political interests: Young people, political engagement; Italy, India, China

Other organisations: Governor, National Institute for Social Work 1985-97; Member Central Council for Training and Education in Social Work 1983-89; Trustee Amelia Ward Prize Fund; PC 1998; Visiting Fellow, Nuffield College, Oxford 1993-2003; *Publications:* Various articles on social policy

Recreations: Family, reading, walking

Rt Hon Tessa Jowell MP, House of Commons, London SW1A 0AA
Tel: 020 7219 3409 Fax: 020 7219 2702
E-mail: jowellt@parliament.uk
Constituency: No constituency office publicised

GENERAL ELECTION RESULT

		%
Jowell, T. (Lab)*	22,461	46.6
Mitchell, J. (Lib Dem)	13,096	27.2
Adegoke, K. (Con)	10,684	22.2
Collins, S. (Green)	1,266	2.6
Jones, E. (UKIP)	707	1.5
Majority	9,365	19.42
Electorate	72,817	
Turnout	48,214	66.21

**Member of last parliament*

CONSTITUENCY SNAPSHOT

Dulwich and West Norwood was created in from the old constituencies of Dulwich and Norwood in 1997, and straddles parts of the boroughs of Lambeth and Southwark.

The Tories won in Dulwich in 1987, however, five years later Tessa Jowell won the seat for Labour. She registered 61 per cent share of the vote in 1997. Jowell's 2001 majority of 12,310 fell by 3,503 votes in 2005. She maintained a healthy Labour lead in this seat with 46.6 per cent of the vote and a 9,365 majority.

Cold Harbour and Herne Hill wards are now entirely within the seat, having previously been shared between Streatham, Vauxhall and the constituency. The part of Thurlow Park ward was also moved here. Two part-wards and South Camberwell ward moved to Camberwell and Peckham.

The South Circular Road traverses the constituency from east to west. It is a diverse constituency and includes the affluent area around Dulwich Village.

There is also much council housing in Gipsy Hill and across the constituency. There is a large ethnic population.

Around three-fifths of school pupils come from ethnic communities, in a borough which has the largest Afro-Caribbean and the third-largest African population in the UK.

Eric Joyce

Falkirk ***(returning MP)***

No boundary changes

Tel: 020 7219 6210
E-mail: ericjoycemp@parliament.uk
Website: www.epolitix.com/Eric-Joyce

Date of birth: 13 October 1960; Son of late Leslie Robert Joyce and Sheila McKay, née Christie

Education: Perth Academy; Stirling University (BA religious studies 1986); Royal Military Academy, Sandhurst 1987; Bath University (MA education 1994); Keele University (MBA education 1995); Married Rosemary Jones 1991 (twin daughters)

Non-political career: Private, Black Watch Regiment 1978-81; Officer 1987-99; Commission for Racial Equality 1999-2000; Member UNISON

Political career: Member for Falkirk West 21 December 2000 by-election to 2005, for Falkirk since 5 May 2005 general election; PPS: to Mike O'Brien as Minister of State: Foreign and Commonwealth Office 2003-04, Department of Trade and Industry 2004-05, to Margaret Hodge as Minister of State: Department for Work and Pensions 2005-06, Department of Trade and Industry 2006; to John Hutton as Secretary of State for: Work and Pensions 2006-07, Business, Enterprise and Regulatory Reform 2007-08, Defence 2008-09, to Bob Ainsworth as Secretary of State for Defence 2009; *Select Committees:* Member: Scottish Affairs 2001-03, Procedure 2001-05; Executive Member, Fabian Society 1998-

Political interests: Foreign affairs, international development (especially education issues), defence, trade and industry (especially oil and gas, GM crops), higher education, asylum and immigration; Argentina, Turkey, USA, China, Democratic Republic of Congo

Other organisations: Fellow Industry and Parliament Trust 2004; Camelon Labour Club; *Publications:* Arms and the Man – Renewing the Armed Services (Fabian Society, 1997); Now's the Hour: New Thinking for Holyrood (Fabian Society, 1999)

Recreations: Climbing, judo, most sports

Eric Joyce MP, House of Commons, London SW1A 0AA
Tel: 020 7219 6210 Fax: 020 7219 2090
E-mail: ericjoycemp@parliament.uk
Constituency: The Studio, Burnfoot Lane, Falkirk, Stirlingshire FK1 5BH Tel: 01324 638919 Fax: 01324 679449
Website: www.epolitix.com/Eric-Joyce

GENERAL ELECTION RESULT

		%	+/-
Joyce, E. (Lab)*	23,207	45.7	-5.0
McNally, J. (SNP)	15,364	30.3	8.9
Mackie, K. (Con)	5,698	11.2	1.3
Leach, K. (Lib Dem)	5,225	10.3	-5.7
Goldie, B. (UKIP)	1,283	2.5	
Majority	7,843	15.45	
Electorate	81,869		
Turnout	50,777	62.02	

**Member of last parliament*

CONSTITUENCY SNAPSHOT

Dennis Canavan became MP for West Stirlingshire in October 1974. He held the seat until 1997, though the seat was renamed Falkirk West in 1983.

After his election to the Scottish Parliament Canavan rarely attended the House of Commons and in November 2000 he resigned his seat. In the resulting by-election Labour's Eric Joyce won by 705 votes from the SNP. Joyce was able to extend his majority at the 2001 general election.

In 2005 six wards were added from Falkirk East. Eric Joyce's majority was 13,475. He was re-elected with a 7,843 majority.

Set in Scotland's old industrial heartland, the seat takes in the town of Falkirk and stretches west to include Denny, Stenhousemuir and Banknock.

The economy relied heavily on manufacturing, with distilling and engineering the main industries. Most heavy industry has gone, the last distillery closed and more people are now employed in the service sector than in manufacturing.

There is growing tourism, stimulated by the spectacular Falkirk Wheel, at the intersection of the Forth and Clyde and Union canals. Its rotating boatlift (the world's first) has won awards for industrial innovation.

Rt Hon Sir **Gerald Kaufman**

Manchester Gorton ***(returning MP)***

Boundary changes

Tel: 020 7219 5145
E-mail: kaufmang@parliament.uk

Date of birth: 21 June 1930; Son of Louis and Jane Kaufman

Education: Leeds Grammar School; The Queen's College, Oxford (MA philosophy, politics and economics 1953)

Non-political career: Assistant general secretary Fabian Society 1954-55; Political staff *Daily Mirror* 1955-64; Political correspondent *New Statesman* 1964-65; Parliamentary press liaison officer, Labour Party 1965-70; Member: GMB, NUJ; Member: Royal Commission on Lords Reform 1999-2000, Speaker's Committee on the Electoral Commission

Political career: Contested Bromley 1955 and Gillingham 1959 general elections. Member for Ardwick 1970-1983, for Manchester Gorton 1983-2010, for Manchester Gorton (revised boundary) since 6 May 2010 general election; Parliamentary Under-Secretary of State for the Environment 1974-75; Department of Industry 1975-79: Parliamentary Under-Secretary 1975, Minister of State 1975-79; Opposition Frontbench Spokesperson for the Environment 1979-80; Shadow: Environment Secretary 1980-83, Home Secretary 1983-87, Foreign Secretary 1987-92; *Select Committees:* Member: Liaison 1992-05; Chair: Culture, Media and Sport 1997-05; Member: Labour Party National Executive 1991-92, Fabian Society

Other organisations: PC 1978; Hilal-i-Pakistan 1999; Kt 2004; President: Gorton and District Sunday Football League; *Publications:* Co-author, How to Live Under Labour (1964); Editor, The Left (1966); To Build the Promised Land (1973); How to Be a Minister (1980, 1997); Editor, Renewal (1983); My Life in the Silver Screen (1985); Inside the Promised Land (1986); Meet Me In St Louis (1994)

Recreations: Cinema, theatre, opera, concerts, travel

Rt Hon Sir Gerald Kaufman MP, House of Commons, London SW1A 0AA Tel: 020 7219 5145 Fax: 020 7219 6825
E-mail: kaufmang@parliament.uk
Constituency: Tel: 0161-248 0073 Fax: 0161-248 0073

GENERAL ELECTION RESULT

		%
Kaufman, G. (Lab)*	19,211	50.1
Afzal, Q. (Lib Dem)	12,508	32.6
Healy, C. (Con)	4,224	11.0
Hall, J. (Green)	1,048	2.7
Zulfikar, M. (Respect)	507	1.3
Reissmann, K. (TUSC)	337	0.9
Harrison, P. (Christian)	254	0.7
Dobson, T. (Pirate)	236	0.6
Majority	6,703	17.49
Electorate	75,933	
Turnout	38,325	50.47

**Member of last parliament*

CONSTITUENCY SNAPSHOT

Since Labour won the seat in 1906 they have only failed to win here in 1931. Gerald Kaufman has held this seat and its predecessor in parliament since 1970 when he became the member for Ardwick, which was reconstituted as Manchester Gorton in 1983.

Before the 2005 election Kaufman had a majority of 11,304, but his majority almost halved to at 5,808. in 2010 Kaufman increased his majority to 6,703.

Boundary changes moved part-wards to Manchester Central and Manchester Withington, while the wards of Whalley Range, Gorton North, and Fallowfield, which were previously shared with Manchester Central, are now completely within the seat's boundaries.

Situated to the south and east of the city centre, Manchester Gorton takes in Fallowfield and Rusholme in the west and Levenshulme in the east.

The seat is mostly residential with around half the population owner-occupiers. The Asian community here makes up almost a fifth of the population.

Rusholme is famously home to the neon-lit strip known as the Curry (or Golden) mile, full of Indian restaurants and Asian jewellers.

The 2002 Commonwealth Games delivered a considerable boost to the local economy. The Commonwealth Village itself was based in the seat at Owens Park, Fallowfield.

Daniel Kawczynski

Shrewsbury and Atcham ***(returning MP)***

No boundary changes

Tel: 020 7219 6249
E-mail: kawczynskid@parliament.uk
Website: www.daniel4shrewsbury.co.uk

Conservative

Date of birth: 24 January 1972; Son of Leonard and Halina Kawczynski

Education: St George's College, Weybridge; Stirling University (BA business studies with French 1994); Married Kate Lumb 2000 (1 daughter)

Non-political career: Sales account manager telecommunications, BT, Cable & Wireless, Xerox, 1994-04; Owner/joint manager, equestrian centre and livery stables

Political career: Contested Ealing Southall 2001 general election. Member for Shrewsbury and Atcham since 5 May 2005 general election; *Select Committees:* Member: Environment, Food and Rural Affairs 2005-07, Justice 2007-09, International Development 2008-10; Chairman Stirling University Conservative Association 1991-93

Political interests: Agriculture, foreign affairs; Poland, Saudi Arabia

Other organisations: Hon. President Shrewsbury Parkinson's Society

Recreations: Golf, vegetable and fruit growing

Daniel Kawczynski MP, House of Commons, London SW1A 0AA
Tel: 020 7219 6249 Fax: 020 7219 1047
E-mail: kawczynskid@parliament.uk
Constituency: Unit 1, Benbow Business Park, Harlescott Lane, Shrewsbury, Shropshire SY1 3FA Tel: 01743 466477
Fax: 01743 465774 Website: www.daniel4shrewsbury.co.uk

GENERAL ELECTION RESULT

		%	+/-
Kawczynski, D. (Con)*	23,313	44.0	6.4
West, C. (Lib Dem)	15,369	29.0	6.2
Tandy, J. (Lab/Co-op)	10,915	20.6	-13.4
Lewis, P. (UKIP)	1,627	3.1	0.4
Whittall, J. (BNP)	1,168	2.2	
Whittaker, A. (Green)	565	1.1	-1.2
Gollings, J. (Impact)	88	0.2	
Majority	7,944	14.98	
Electorate	75,438		
Turnout	53,045	70.32	

**Member of last parliament*

CONSTITUENCY SNAPSHOT

In 1997 Labour's Paul Marsden became the seat's first non-Conservative Member after overturning Derek Conway's 10,965 majority on a 11.4 per cent swing. He was re-elected in 2001 and in December that year he defected to the Lib Dems. Marsden returned to Labour in 2005 but did not contest the seat at the general election. Labour lost the seat to the Conservatives in 2005. Daniel Kawczynski won a 1,808 majority.

Kawczynski was re-elected in 2010 with a majority of 7,944 giving the Conservatives a 43.9 per cent share of the vote.

The seat consists of the county town of Shrewsbury and a substantial chunk of surrounding Shropshire countryside.

Nestled in a great loop of the river Severn, Shrewsbury is a medieval town with a wealth of 15th century black-and-white Tudor houses and narrow cobbled streets. However, the town also has a few wards in the top quarter of the most deprived in England, including Castlefields and Ditherington.

The services sector, manufacturing, tourism, and agriculture are all important to the economy here. In addition the borough council, the county council and the health authority are based in Shrewsbury and provide a great deal of employment.

Barbara Keeley

Worsley and Eccles South ***(returning MP)***

New constituency

Tel: 020 7219 8025
E-mail: keeleyb@parliament.uk
Website: www.barbarakeeley.co.uk

Date of birth: 26 March 1952; Daughter of Edward and Joan Keeley

Education: Mount St Mary's College, Leeds; Salford University (BSc politics and contemporary history 1994); Married Colin Huggett 1985

Non-political career: IBM UK Limited: Systems programmer 1983, Field systems engineer 1983-87, Field systems engineering manager 1987-89; Consultant and adviser in community regeneration 1989-94, 1995-2001; Area manager Business in the Community North West 1994-95; Consultant Princess Royal Trust for Carers 2001-05; Research on policy issues related to primary health care for Princess Royal Trust 2003-05; GMB; Councillor Trafford Borough 1995-2004: Vice-chair social services 1995-97, Council Cabinet Member 1997-99, 2000-04; Director Trafford's pathfinder Children's Trust 2002-04

Political career: Member for Worsley 2005-10, for Worsley and Eccles South since 6 May 2010 general election; PPS: to Jim Murphy: as Parliamentary Secretary, Cabinet Office 2006, as Minister of State, Department for Work and Pensions 2006-07, to Harriet Harman as Minister for Women 2007-08; Assistant Government Whip 2008-09; Deputy Leader of the House of Commons 2009-10; *Select Committees:* Member: Constitutional Affairs 2005-06, Finance and Services 2006-10

Political interests: Health and social care, carers, urban and community regeneration, gender and equality; European Union, Israel/Middle East, Tibet

Other organisations: Member: Amnesty International, Fabian Society; *Publications:* Co-author Carers Speak Out, 2002, Primary Carers, 2003

Recreations: Jogging, swimming, live music

Barbara Keeley MP, House of Commons, London SW1A 0AA
Tel: 020 7219 8025 Fax: 020 7219 3847
E-mail: keeleyb@parliament.uk
Constituency: First Floor, 37 Manchester Road, Walkden, Greater Manchester M28 3NS Tel: 0161-799 4159
Fax: 0161-799 5829 Website: www.barbarakeeley.co.uk

GENERAL ELECTION RESULT

		%
Keeley, B. (Lab)*	17,892	42.9
Lindley, I. (Con)	13,555	32.5
Gadsden, R. (Lib Dem)	6,883	16.5
Townsend, A. (UKIP)	2,037	4.9
Whitelegg, P. (England)	1,334	3.2
Majority	4,337	10.40
Electorate	72,473	
Turnout	41,701	57.54

**Member of last parliament*

CONSTITUENCY SNAPSHOT

The new seat is comprised of the eastern half of the Worsley seat and the southern half of Eccles. Worsley and Eccles South is now entirely within the City of Salford, all Wigan Borough wards that were previously in Worsley having moved to Leigh or Bolton West.

Labour held Worsley since its creation in 1983. Terry Lewis retired at the 2005 general election after representing Worsley for 18 years. At the election the Labour candidate, Barbara Keeley replaced him with a majority of 9,368.

Ian Stewart won the Eccles seat in 1997, after Joan Lestor, the MP here since 1987, stood down. As part of Labour's 1997 highpoint Mr Stewart delivered a majority of 21,916. Ian Stewart retired in 2010.

Barbara Keeley won the new seat for Labour in 2010 with a majority of 4,337.

This is a socially mixed seat, encompassing some of the most sought-after residential areas in Greater Manchester and some more deprived areas. Worsley town is renowned for its pastoral beauty, and its canal is lined with timbered buildings dating from the 19th century whereas Eccles is suburban and industrial.

Most of this area is not rich but neither is most of it very deprived. Worsley and Boothstown wards are very comfortable communities in the main.

Alan Keen

Feltham and Heston ***(returning MP)***

Boundary changes

Tel: 020 7219 2819
E-mail: alankeenmp@parliament.uk
Website: www.alankeen.com

Labour/Co-operative

Date of birth: 25 November 1937; Son of late Jack and Gladys Keen

Education: St William Turner's School, Redcar, Cleveland; Married Ann Fox 1980 (now MP as Ann Keen) (2 sons 1 daughter)

Non-political career: Part-time tactical scout (assessing opposition tactics) Middlesbrough FC 1967-85; Miscellaneous positions in private industry and commerce, mainly in the fire protection industry 1963-92; Member, GMB; Councillor, London Borough of Hounslow 1986-90

Political career: Member for Feltham and Heston 1992-2010, for Feltham and Heston (revised boundary) since 6 May 2010 general election; *Select Committees:* Member: Education 1995-96, Deregulation 1995-96, Culture, Media and Sport 1997-10; Member Co-operative Party 1992-; Secretary, Labour First Past the Post Group 1997-

Political interests: Commerce, industry, foreign affairs, development, democracy, defence, sport, culture

Recreations: Playing and listening to music, Association football, athletics, cricket, jazz enthusiast

Alan Keen MP, House of Commons, London SW1A 0AA
Tel: 020 7219 2819 Fax: 020 7219 0985
E-mail: alankeenmp@parliament.uk
Constituency: Labour Party Office, Manor Place, Feltham, Middlesex TW14 9BT Tel: 020 8890 4489 Fax: 020 8893 2606
Website: www.alankeen.com

GENERAL ELECTION RESULT

		%
Keen, A. (Lab/Co-op)*	21,174	43.6
Bowen, M. (Con)	16,516	34.0
Wilson, M. (Lib Dem)	6,669	13.7
Donnelly, J. (BNP)	1,714	3.5
Shadbolt, J. (UKIP)	992	2.0
Anstis, E. (Green)	530	1.1
Tripathi, D. (Ind)	505	1.0
Khaira, A. (Ind)	180	0.4
Williams, R. (Ind)	168	0.4
Linley, M. (WRP)	78	0.2
Majority	4,658	9.60
Electorate	81,058	
Turnout	48,526	59.87

**Member of last parliament*

CONSTITUENCY SNAPSHOT

Labour held the seat through the 1960s and 1970s, latterly under the stewardship of Russell Kerr. Kerr's majority was reduced in the early 1980s and the Conservatives secured a narrow victory in 1983.

In 1992 Labour candidate Alan Keen managed to win the seat by a small margin. However, in 1997 he was elected with a huge 15,273 majority and it only suffered a small decline in 2001, but in 2005 Keen's majority was halved to 6,820. His wife lost her seat following the expenses scandal, but Labour's Alan Keen managed to cling on with a decent majority of 4,658.

Feltham and Heston gained three wards that were previously shared with Brentford and Isleworth.

A largely seat close to Heathrow, Feltham and Heston is a mix of quiet suburban neighbourhoods with patches of industrial estates.

Feltham's local economy benefited from a large regeneration project in 2006 with the construction of The Centre, a £100 million development that encompasses 800 apartments, 50 retail units, a hotel, a library and a medical centre.

Heathrow Airport is the mainstay of the local economy. The seat is also home to a large youth offenders' institute.

Chris Kelly

Dudley South

Boundary changes

Tel: 020 7219 3000

Conservative

Date of birth: 1978

Education: Wolverhampton Grammar School; Oxford Brookes University (BA history and politics 1999); Tanaka Business School, Imperial College London (MBA 2003)

Non-political career: Oxford University Officer Training Corp 1996-1998; Keltruck Ltd, West Bromwich 1999-2002: Marketing Executive 1999-2000, Marketing Manager 2000-02; Parliamentary assistant to Michael Howard MP 2004-05; Keltruck Ltd, West Bromwich 2004-: Non-executive Director 2004-05, Marketing Director 2006-

Political career: Member for Dudley South since 6 May 2010 general election; Member, Conservative Party 1996-; Deputy chair (finance), Black Country Conservatives 2006-

Other organisations: Executive officer, International Young Democrat Union 2004-05

Recreations: Sport, travel

Chris Kelly MP, House of Commons, London SW1A 0AA
Tel: 020 7219 3000
Constituency: Dudley Conservative Federation, Church Chambers, 26 High Street, Halesowen B63 3BB Tel: 0121-550 1445
E-mail: office@dudleysouthconservatives.com; chris@dudleysouthconservatives.com
Website: www.dudleysouthconservatives.com; www.tellchris.com

GENERAL ELECTION RESULT

		%
Kelly, C. (Con)	16,450	43.1
Harris, R. (Lab)	12,594	33.0
Bramall, J. (Lib Dem)	5,989	15.7
Rowe, P. (UKIP)	3,132	8.2
Majority	3,856	10.10
Electorate	60,572	
Turnout	38,165	63.01

CONSTITUENCY SNAPSHOT

The old Dudley West, and before that Brierley Hill, had swung between the Conservatives and Labour reflecting national trends. John Blackburn won for the Conservatives in 1979; by 1992 he had secured a majority of over 10,000. When Blackburn died in 1994 the subsequent by-election saw Labour's Ian Pearson win with a 29 per cent swing and a majority of over 20,000.

In 2001, however, Labour's majority was cut by half and fell further in 2005 to 4,244. The Conservative candidate, Chris Kelly took the seat from Labour in 2010 with a majority of 3,856.

Parts of Brookmoor and Pensnett and Netherton, Woodside and St Andrews were transferred from Dudley North while Stourbridge has surrendered its segment of Brierley Hill. The seat lost Quarry Bank and Dudley Wood to Stourbridge.

Dudley South is a working-class residential seat mixing older industrial communities such as Brierley Hill and Pensnett with more modern and affluent developments like Kingswinford and Wordsley.

The seat still contains the bulk of Dudley's declining glass quarter. Besides manufacturing, wholesale and retail trades account for a high proportion of jobs. Expansion in the retail and services sectors has been assisted by the construction of the Merry Hill shopping centre in Brierley Hill.

Liz Kendall

Leicester West

Boundary changes

Tel: 020 7219 3000
E-mail: liz.kendall.mp@parliament.uk
Website: www.lizkendall.org

Date of birth: 1971

Education: Cambridge University (history)

Non-political career: Special Adviser to Harriet Harman MP as Secretary of State for Social Security and Minister for Women 1997-98; Research fellow, King's Fund; Associate director, health, social care and children's early years, Institute for Public Policy Research; Director, Maternity Alliance; Special Adviser to Patricia Hewitt MP as Secretary of State for: Trade and Industry and Minister for Women and Equality 2004-05, Health 2005-07; Director, Ambulance Service Network; Member, Unite

Political career: Member for Leicester West since 6 May 2010 general election; Member: Labour Party 1992-, Co-operative Party

Political interests: Employment, care for the elderly

Other organisations: Member, Fabian Society

Liz Kendall MP, House of Commons, London SW1A 0AA
Tel: 020 7219 3000 E-mail: liz.kendall.mp@parliament.uk
Constituency: c/o Labour Party Office, 5 Frog Island, Leicester LE3 5AG Tel: 0116-253 7374 Website: www.lizkendall.org

GENERAL ELECTION RESULT

		%
Kendall, L. (Lab)	13,745	38.4
Harvey, C. (Con)	9,728	27.2
Coley, P. (Lib Dem)	8,107	22.6
Reynolds, G. (BNP)	2,158	6.0
Ingall, S. (UKIP)	883	2.5
Forse, G. (Green)	639	1.8
Huggins, S. (Ind)	181	0.5
Score, S. (TUSC)	157	0.4
Dyer, S. (Pirate)	113	0.3
Bowley, D. (Ind)	108	0.3
Majority	4,017	11.21
Electorate	64,900	
Turnout	35,819	55.19

CONSTITUENCY SNAPSHOT

The seat has been Labour's since the 1920s. It was represented by Greville Janner for 25 years and before that by his father, Barnett. In 1997 Labour's Patricia Hewitt achieved a majority of 12,864. There were small swings to the Conservatives in 2001 and 2005 but Ms Hewitt was returned with a majority of 9,070 in 2005.

Hewitt retired in 2010 and Elizabeth Kendall retained the seat for Labour with a majority of 4,017.

As with the other two Leicester seats, boundary changes were minimal and relate only to three wards that had straddled the seat with the two others in the city. Abbey and Latimer wards were shared by the east and west divisions; Abbey is now completely in East, while Latimer has moved to West. Likewise Castle ward has moved entirely within Leicester South's boundaries.

The textile industry has traditionally been a major employer in Leicester. Over one fifth of the constituency work in manufacturing industries. The majority of the constituency work in unskilled occupations, and only small numbers work in managerial, professional and technical jobs.

The constituency differs from Leicester East and Leicester South by being by far the most working class of the three seats, and also having the highest proportion of council housing on large estates like North Braunstone and Mowmacre.

Rt Hon **Charles Kennedy**

Ross, Skye and Lochaber ***(returning MP)***

No boundary changes

Tel: 020 7219 0356
E-mail: kennedyc@parliament.uk
Website: www.charleskennedy.org.uk

Date of birth: 25 November 1959; Son of Ian Kennedy, crofter, and Mary MacVarish MacEachen

Education: Lochaber High School, Fort William; Glasgow University (MA politics, philosophy and English 1982); Indiana University (1982-83); Married Sarah Gurling 2002 (1 son)

Non-political career: President, Glasgow University Union 1980-81; Winner, British Observer Mace Debating Tournament 1982; Journalist with BBC Highland, at Inverness 1982; Rector Glasgow University 2008-

Political career: Member for Ross, Cromarty and Skye 1983-97, for Ross, Skye and Inverness West 1997-2005, for Ross, Skye and Lochaber since 5 May 2005 general election; Alliance Spokesman for Social Security 1987; SDP Spokesman for: Scotland and Social Security 1987-88, Trade and Industry 1988-89; Liberal Democrat Spokesman for: Health 1989-92, European Union Affairs 1992-97, Agriculture, Fisheries, Food and Rural Affairs 1997-99; Leader, Liberal Democrat Party 1999-2006; *Select Committees:* Member: Standards and Privileges 1997-99; Chair: Glasgow University Social Democratic Club 1979-80, SDP Scotland 1986-88; President Liberal Democrat Party 1990-94; Former Member Liberal Democrat: Federal Executive Committee, Policy Committee; Leader 1999-2006

Political interests: Scotland, social policy, broadcasting, European Union

Other organisations: Member, Scottish Crofters Foundation; Vice-President Liberal International 2006-; President, European Movement 2008-; PC 1999; *The Spectator*: Member to Watch 1989, Politician of the Year 2004; Doctorate Glasgow University 2001; National Liberal; *Publications:* The Future of Politics, 2000; Associate editor The House Magazine 2006-

Recreations: Reading, writing, music, swimming, golf, journalism, broadcasting

Rt Hon Charles Kennedy MP, House of Commons, London SW1A 0AA Tel: 020 7219 0356 Fax: 020 7219 4881
E-mail: kennedyc@parliament.uk
Constituency: 5 MacGregor's Court, Dingwall, Ross and Cromarty IV15 9HS Tel: 01349 862152 Fax: 01349 866829
Website: www.charleskennedy.org.uk

GENERAL ELECTION RESULT

		%	+/-
Kennedy, C. (Lib Dem)*	18,335	52.6	-6.0
McKendrick, J. (Lab)	5,265	15.1	0.2
Stephen, A. (SNP)	5,263	15.1	5.5
Cameron, D. (Con)	4,260	12.2	2.2
Scott, E. (Green)	777	2.2	-1.1
Anderson, P. (UKIP)	659	1.9	0.4
Campbell, R. (Ind)	279	0.8	
Majority	13,070	37.52	
Electorate	51,836		
Turnout	34,838	67.21	

**Member of last parliament*

CONSTITUENCY SNAPSHOT

In 1964 Alasdair Mackenzie won what was then Ross and Cromarty for the Liberals. In 1970 Hamish Gray gained the seat for the Conservatives. The 1983 boundary changes added the island of Skye and in that year Charles Kennedy, a 23 year-old Glasgow University graduate, defeated Gray, becoming the youngest MP and the only SDP MP who had not defected from Labour.

1995 boundary changes replaced parts of Easter Ross with western Inverness. Kennedy held the seat and by 2001 he had tripled his 1997 majority to nearly 13,000.

The most recent boundary review stripped the Inverness wards from Kennedy's seat, adding Lochaber instead. Kennedy increased his majority over Labour to 14,219. He won with a slightly-reduced 13,070 majority in 2010.

This is the UK's largest constituency, covering two million acres of Highlands and Islands. Tourism is already a major industry, assisted by the stark and spectacular scenery which includes Ben Nevis and the Mallaig to Fort William railway (which has attracted even more attention since featuring in the Harry Potter films).

Inland, numerous lochs combine with villages such as Kinlochleven and the historic Glencoe.

Many residents are self-employed crofters living in tiny coastal farming communities, two-thirds of the population are owner occupiers and the seat has twice as many workers employed in agriculture than the national average. The area is noted for salmon and whisky (it is home to three distilleries).

Rt Hon **Sadiq Khan**

Tooting (returning MP)

Boundary changes

Tel: 020 7219 6967
E-mail: sadiqkhanmp@parliament.uk
Website: www.sadiqkhan.org.uk

Labour

Date of birth: 8 October 1970; Son of late Amanullah Ahmed Khan and of Sehrun Nisa Khan

Education: Ernest Bevin Secondary Comprehensive, London; University of North London (LLB 1992); College of Law, Guildford (Law Society finals 1993); Married Saadiya Ahmad 1994 (2 daughters)

Non-political career: Christian Fisher Solicitors: Trainee solicitor 1993-95, Solicitor 1995-98, Partner 1998-2000; Equity partner Christian Fisher Khan Solicitors 2000-02; Equity partner and co-founder Christian Khan Solicitors 2002-04; Visiting lecturer University of North London and London Metropolitan University 1998-2004; Member: GMB, UNISON, CWU group of Labour MPs; Wandsworth Borough Council: Councillor 1994-2006, Deputy leader Labour group 1996-2001

Political career: Member for Tooting 2005-10, for Tooting (revised boundary) since 6 May 2010 general election; PPS to Jack Straw as Leader of the House of Commons 2007; Assistant Government Whip 2007-08; Parliamentary Under-Secretary of State, Department for Communities and Local Government 2008-09; Minister of State, Department for Transport (attending cabinet) 2009-10; Shadow Secretary of State for Transport 2010-; *Select Committees:* Member: Public Accounts 2005-07

Political interests: Social justice, crime, international affairs, public services

Other organisations: Founder: Human Rights Lawyers Association Chair: Liberty 2001-04, Legal affairs committee, Muslim Council of Britain 2004-05; Vice chair: Legal Action Group 1999-2004, Law Society 1993-, Fabian Society, Executive Committee 2006-, Friends of the Earth; Patron Progress 2005-; Honorary Alderman London Borough of Wandsworth; PC 2009; Windsor Fellowship 1992; Esso Law Bursary 1992; Society of Black Lawyers Bursary 1992; Sweet & Maxwell Law Prize 1993; Spectator Newcomer of Year 2005; *Publications:* Challenging Racism (Lawrence and Wishart 2003); Police Misconduct: Legal Remedies (Legal Action Group 2005); Articles in various publications on legal matters and policing

Recreations: Playing and watching sports, cinema, family, friends, local community

Rt Hon Sadiq Khan MP, House of Commons, London SW1A 0AA
Tel: 020 7219 6967 Fax: 020 7219 6477
E-mail: sadiqkhanmp@parliament.uk
Constituency: Tooting Labour Party, 58 Trinity Road,
London SW17 7RH Tel: 020 8682 2897 Fax: 020 8682 3416
Website: www.sadiqkhan.org.uk

GENERAL ELECTION RESULT

		%
Khan, S. (Lab)*	22,038	43.5
Clarke, M. (Con)	19,514	38.5
Butt, N. (Lib Dem)	7,509	14.8
McDonald, S. (UKIP)	624	1.2
Vickery, R. (Green)	609	1.2
John-Richards, S. (Ind)	190	0.4
Paul, S. (Christian)	171	0.3
Majority	2,524	4.98
Electorate	73,836	
Turnout	50,655	68.60

**Member of last parliament*

CONSTITUENCY SNAPSHOT

Labour's Tom Cox represented the seat from its creation in 1974 until 2005. Cox's majority narrowed in 1979 to 10 per cent, and in 1983 and 1987 the gap was closed even further. His majority of 5,045 in 1979 was reduced to 1,441 in 1987.

Labour's majority increased in 1992 when Cox was returned by a 4,107-vote margin. In 1997 a swing of over 12 per cent gave Labour a 32 per cent majority and in 2001, with a reduction in Labour's lead, Mr Cox retained a five-figure majority.

In 2005 Labour's vote-share fell by 11 per cent, however, Cox's successor, Sadiq Khan, was still returned with a majority of 5,381. The seat that would herald a Conservative majority government eventually stayed Labour, with Sadiq Khan achieving a 2,524 majority.

Boundary changes here are minor: Wandsworth Common ward is now entirely within Tooting's boundaries, having previously been shared with Battersea.

Tooting is one of three seats within the south London Borough of Wandsworth, along with Battersea to the north and Putney to the north east.

The major local hospital, St George's is within the constituency.

The seat is home to Tooting Bec Lido, the largest outdoor freshwater swimming pool in England and thrives today as a major attraction in the area.

Simon Kirby

Brighton Kemptown

Boundary changes

Tel: 020 7219 3000
E-mail: simon.kirby.mp@parliament.uk

Date of birth: 22 December 1964

Education: Hastings Grammar School; Open University (BSc mathematical modelling 1995); Married Elizabeth 1992 (2 daughters 4 sons)

Non-political career: Managing director, C-Side Ltd 1993-2001; Councillor: East Sussex County Council 1992-93, 2005-09, Brighton Borough Council 1995-97, Brighton and Hove City Council 1996-99, Mid Sussex District Council 1999-2001

Political career: Member for Brighton Kemptown since 6 May 2010 general election; Vice-chair, Bexhill and Battle Conservatives 2005-06

Political interests: Business

Other organisations: Carlton Club

Recreations: Brighton and Hove Albion Football Club

Simon Kirby MP, House of Commons, London SW1A 0AA
Tel: 020 7219 3000 E-mail: simon.kirby.mp@parliament.uk
Constituency: Brighton Conservatives, Ground Floor Office, 370 South Coast Road, Telscombe Cliffs, East Sussex BN10 7ES
Tel: 01273 587319 Fax: 01273 589178
Website: www.brightonandhoveconservatives.com

GENERAL ELECTION RESULT

		%
Kirby, S. (Con)	16,217	38.0
Burgess, S. (Lab/Co-op)	14,889	34.9
Williams, J. (Lib Dem)	7,691	18.0
Duncan, B. (Green)	2,330	5.5
Chamberlain-Webber, J. (UKIP)	1,384	3.2
Hill, D. (TUSC)	194	0.5
Majority	1,328	3.11
Electorate	66,017	
Turnout	42,705	64.69

CONSTITUENCY SNAPSHOT

With only a brief interruption from 1964 to 1970, the constituency had continuous Conservative representation from 1950 until Sir Andrew Bowden suffered a swing of almost 14 per cent in 1997 that resulted in former Labour councillor Dr Desmond Turner's election with a majority of 3,534.

Turner's majority increased by almost 1,500 votes in 2001 but fell to just 2,737 in 2005.

Labour was defeated in the 2010 general election with a 4 per cent swing of the vote to the Conservative candidate Simon Kirby, who secured 16,217 votes.

Boundary changes transferred the wards of Hanover and Elm Grove to Brighton Pavilion, while shifting Moulsecoomb and Bevendean and Queen's Park into the constituency.

The Kemptown division stretches from the council estates of Whitehawk and Moulsecoomb to the small town of Peacehaven, some six miles from Brighton's city centre.

Brighton and Hove has over recent years grown to be a successful business location, and has topped the key British Enterprises survey of places to do business.

It is also a popular leisure destination, and the tourism industry remains a significant part of the local economy. The constituency boasts the UK's largest marina and a popular summer racecourse.

Rt Hon **Greg Knight**

East Yorkshire ***(returning MP)***

Boundary changes

Tel: 020 7219 8417
E-mail: sothcottt@parliament.uk
Website: www.gregknight.com

Conservative

Date of birth: 4 April 1949; Son of Albert George Knight, company director, and Isabel, née Bell

Education: Alderman Newton's Grammar School, Leicester; College of Law, London; College of Law, Guildford (solicitor 1973)

Non-political career: Solicitor 1973-89, 1997-; Business consultant 1997-2001; Councillor: Leicester City Council 1976-79, Leicestershire County Council 1977-83

Political career: Member for Derby North 1983-97. Contested Derby North 1997 general election. Member for Yorkshire East 2001-10, for East Yorkshire (revised boundary) since 6 May 2010 general election; PPS to David Mellor as Minister of State: Foreign and Commonwealth Office 1987-88, Department of Health 1988-89; Assistant Government Whip 1989-90; Government Whip 1990-93; Government Deputy Chief Whip 1993-96; Minister of State Department of Trade and Industry 1996-97; Deputy Shadow Leader of the House 2002-03; Shadow Minister for: Culture, Media and Sport 2003, Environment and Transport 2003-05, Transport 2005; *Select Committees:* Member: Broadcasting 1993-96, Finance and Services 1993-96, Modernisation of the House of Commons 2001-03, 2005-10, Procedure: Member 2005-10, Chair 2005-10; Member: Liaison 2006-10, Administration 2006-10, Standards and Privileges 2009-10, Reform of the House of Commons 2009-10; Chair Leicester and Leicestershire Young Conservatives 1972-73; Vice-chair Conservative Parliamentary Candidates Association 1997-2001

Political interests: Consumer issues, information technology, music, arts, home affairs; USA, Spain

Other organisations: Executive Committee Member, British-American Parliamentary Group 2001-; PC 1995; Bridlington Conservative; *Publications:* Co-author Westminster Words (1988); Honourable Insults (1990); Parliamentary Sauce (1993); Right Honourable Insults (1998); Naughty Graffiti (2005)

Recreations: Classic and vintage cars, music

Rt Hon Greg Knight MP, House of Commons, London SW1A 0AA
Tel: 020 7219 8417 E-mail: sothcottt@parliament.uk
Constituency: 18 Exchange Street, Driffield, East Yorkshire YO25 6LJ
Tel: 01377 232757 Website: www.gregknight.com

GENERAL ELECTION RESULT

		%
Knight, G. (Con)*	24,328	47.5
Adamson, R. (Lib Dem)	10,842	21.2
Rounding, P. (Lab)	10,401	20.3
Daniels, C. (UKIP)	2,142	4.2
Pudsey, G. (BNP)	1,865	3.6
Allerston, R. (SDP)	914	1.8
Jackson, M. (Green)	762	1.5
Majority	13,486	26.31
Electorate	80,342	
Turnout	51,254	63.79

**Member of last parliament*

CONSTITUENCY SNAPSHOT

Before the 1997 election, much of the old Bridlington seat was redrawn to correspond with the Borough of East Yorkshire, itself now subsumed into the East Riding unitary authority.

In 1997 Tory John Townend, who had been MP for Bridlington, had a notional majority of more than 12,000 to defend, an 8.7 per cent swing to Labour cut the margin to little more than a quarter of that.

Townend retired in 2001 and was replaced by Greg Knight. In both 2001 and 2005 Knight achieved swings in his favour and his 2005 majority was 6,283. The seat was held by Knight in 2010 with a 13,486 majority.

Rural Beverley was transferred to Beverley and Holderness in exchange for voters from the eastern Wolds.

This constituency covers the northern parts of the East Riding of Yorkshire. Its main town is Bridlington, a shellfish port and minor conference centre as well as a holiday resort with a large number of camp sites.

Combining countryside and coast, this out of the way corner of Yorkshire is traditionally dependent on farming, fishing and tourism.

The west of the constituency, with the towns of Pocklington, Market Weighton and Stamford Bridge, is a popular area for commuters to Hull and York.

Dr **Kwasi Kwarteng**

Spelthorne

No boundary changes

Tel: 020 7219 3000
E-mail: kwasi.kwarteng.mp@parliament.uk
Website: www.kwart2010.com

Date of birth: 26 May 1975; Son of Alfred Kwasi Kwarteng, economist, and Charlotte Kwarteng, barrister

Education: Eton College; Trinity College, Cambridge (BA classics and history 1996, MA; PhD British history 2000); Kennedy Scholar, Harvard University, USA 1997; Birkbeck College, London (Post-graduate Certificate economics 2000); Certificate investment management 2005; Single

Non-political career: Financial analyst: Investment banking 2000-04, Fund management 2004-06; Freelance journalist and author 2006-

Political career: Contested Brent East 2005 general election. Member for Spelthorne since 6 May 2010 general election

Political interests: Economy and finance, energy, education; Middle East, Russia

Other organisations: Chair, Bow Group 2006-06; *Publications:* Author, Ghosts of Empire (Bloomsbury, due to be published 2011)

Recreations: Music, foreign languages, travel

Dr Kwasi Kwarteng MP, House of Commons, London SW1A 0AA
Tel: 020 7219 3000 E-mail: kwasi.kwarteng.mp@parliament.uk
Constituency: Spelthorne Conservative Association, 55 Cherry Orchard, Staines, Middlesex TW18 2SQ Tel: 07743 842768
Website: www.kwart2010.com

GENERAL ELECTION RESULT

		%	+/-
Kwarteng, K. (Con)	22,261	47.1	-3.2
Chapman, M. (Lib Dem)	12,242	25.9	8.9
Tyler-Moore, A. (Lab)	7,789	16.5	-10.7
Browne, C. (UKIP)	4,009	8.5	3.9
Swinglehurst, I. (Ind)	314	0.7	
Littlewood, R. (Best)	244	0.5	
Couchman, P. (TUSC)	176	0.4	
Gore, J. (CIP)	167	0.4	
Leon-Smith, G. (Ind)	102	0.2	
Majority	10,019	21.18	
Electorate	70,479		
Turnout	47,304	67.12	

CONSTITUENCY SNAPSHOT

Conservative David Wilshire first won the seat in 1987, increasing an already sizable majority of 13,506 to 20,050. However, in 1997 the Tory majority collapsed to 3,473.

The 2001 general election brought little change and Wilshire's majority dropped slightly to 3,262. In 2005 Mr Wilshire was re-elected again with a healthy majority of 9,936.

David Wilshire retired in 2010 and Kwasi Kwarteng held the seat for the Conservatives with a majority of 10,019.

Just south of Heathrow airport and north of the Thames, Spelthorne is a built-up area with fewer open green spaces, private roads and woodlands than other seats in Surrey.

Most of the land surrounding the urban areas of Spelthorne is designated as greenbelt, and there are a large number of reservoirs which helps to keep it distinct from London, and the area is still quite affluent.

The major centres of population are Ashford, Shepperton, Stanwell, Sunbury and Staines, which has a major shopping centre providing retail jobs.

Communications and the financial sector also account for a large number of jobs. Heathrow, one of the busiest airports in the world, is a huge employer.

Eleanor Laing

Epping Forest (returning MP)

Boundary changes

Tel: 020 7219 2086
E-mail: lainge@parliament.uk
Website: www.eleanorlaing.com

Conservative

Date of birth: 1 February 1958; Daughter of late Matthew Pritchard and Betty, née McFarlane

Education: St Columba's School, Kilmacolm, Renfrewshire; Edinburgh University (BA 1982, LLB) (First woman President of Union); Married Alan Laing 1983 (divorced 2003) (1 son)

Non-political career: Practised law in Edinburgh, City of London and industry 1983-89; Special Adviser to John MacGregor: as Secretary of State for Education 1989-90, as Leader of the House of Commons 1990-92, as Secretary of State for Transport 1992-94

Political career: Contested Paisley North 1987 general election. Member for Epping Forest 1997-2010, for Epping Forest (revised boundary) since 6 May 2010 general election; Opposition Whip 1999-2000; Opposition Spokesperson for: Constitutional Affairs and Scotland 2000-01, Education and Skills 2001-03; Shadow Minister for: Children 2003, Women 2004-07; Shadow Secretary of State for Scotland 2005; Shadow Minister for: Women and Equality 2005-07, Justice 2007-10; *Select Committees:* Member: Education and Employment 1997-98, Education and Employment (Employment Sub-Committee) 1997-98, Environment, Transport and Regional Affairs 1998-99, Environment, Transport and Regional Affairs (Transport Sub-Committee) 1998-99, Office of the Deputy Prime Minister 2004-05, Office of the Deputy Prime Minister (Urban Affairs Sub-Committee) 2004-05

Political interests: Education, transport, economic policy, constitution, devolution; Australia, Gibraltar, New Zealand, Uganda, USA

Recreations: Theatre, music, golf

Eleanor Laing MP, House of Commons, London SW1A 0AA
Tel: 020 7219 2086 Fax: 020 7219 0980
E-mail: lainge@parliament.uk
Constituency: Thatcher House, 4 Meadow Road, Loughton, Essex IG10 4HX Tel: 020 8508 6608 Fax: 020 8508 8099
Website: www.eleanorlaing.com

GENERAL ELECTION RESULT

		%
Laing, E. (Con)*	25,148	54.0
Haigh, A. (Lib Dem)	10,017	21.5
Curtis, K. (Lab)	6,641	14.3
Richardson, P. (BNP)	1,982	4.3
Smith, A. (UKIP)	1,852	4.0
Pepper, S. (Green)	659	1.4
Sawyer, K. (England)	285	0.6
Majority	15,131	32.48
Electorate	72,198	
Turnout	46,584	64.52

**Member of last parliament*

CONSTITUENCY SNAPSHOT

From 1955 until his death in 1988 veteran Tory Sir John Biggs-Davison represented Epping Forest. In the by-election and the 1992 general election Steven Norris consolidated the gains made by his predecessor. Norris stood down in 1997 and Eleanor Laing was selected to contest the seat for the Tories. Despite a 13.6 per cent swing to Labour she was elected with a majority of 5,252.

She doubled her majority in 2001 and in 2005 she produced an even more comprehensive victory, winning a majority of 14,358. In 2010 Laing held the seat for the Conservatives with a strong 15,131 majority.

Boundary changes were minimal.

Stretching from the edge of Greater London into the rural tranquillity of Epping Forest, this constituency centres on the commuter towns of Loughton, Chigwell and Waltham Abbey, along with a scattering of rural towns and villages to the north.

Population is concentrated in areas where there are good transport links to London, and apart from the towns and larger villages the district lies entirely within the metropolitan green belt.

Managerial, professional and associate professional and technical staff comprises approximately half of the working population.

Norman Lamb

North Norfolk (returning MP)

Boundary changes

Tel: 020 7219 0542
E-mail: lambn@parliament.uk
Website: www.normanlamb.org.uk

Date of birth: 16 September 1957; Son of late Hubert Horace Lamb, professor of climatology and Beatrice Moira Lamb, neé Milligan, nurse

Education: George Abbot School, Guildford, Surrey; Wymondham College, Wymondham, Norfolk; Leicester University (LLB 1980); Qualified as solicitor 1984; Married Mary Elizabeth Green 1984 (2 sons)

Non-political career: Norwich City Council: Trainee solicitor 1982-84, Senior assistant solicitor 1984-85; Steele and Company Norfolk: Solicitor 1986-87; Partner Steele and Company Norfolk 1987-2001; Consultant 2001-06; Norwich City Council: Councillor 1987-91, Group leader 1989-91

Political career: Contested North Norfolk 1992 and 1997 general elections. Member for North Norfolk 2001-10, for North Norfolk (revised boundary) since 6 May 2010 general election; Liberal Democrat Spokesperson for: International Development 2001-02, the Treasury 2002-05, Shadow Secretary of State for Trade and Industry 2005-06; Chief of Staff to Sir Menzies Campbell as Leader of the Liberal Democrats 2006; Liberal Democrat Shadow Secretary of State for Health 2006-10; Chief Parliamentary and Political Adviser to the Deputy Prime Minister 2010-; Assistant Whip 2010-; *Select Committees:* Member: Treasury 2003-05, Treasury (Treasury Sub-Committee) 2003-10; Chair Tottenham Liberals 1980-81; Norwich South Liberals 1985-87

Political interests: Health, employment, social affairs, constitution, environment, international development; United States, South Africa

Other organisations: Norwich City Football Club; *Publications:* Remedies in the Employment Tribunal, Sweet and Maxwell 1998

Recreations: Walking, football

Norman Lamb MP, House of Commons, London SW1A 0AA
Tel: 020 7219 0542 Fax: 020 7219 1963
E-mail: lambn@parliament.uk
Constituency: Guyton House, 5 Vicarage Street, North Walsham, Norfolk NR28 9DQ Tel: 01692 403752 Fax: 01692 500818
Website: www.normanlamb.org.uk

GENERAL ELECTION RESULT

		%
Lamb, N. (Lib Dem)*	27,554	55.5
Ivory, T. (Con)	15,928	32.1
Harris, P. (Lab)	2,896	5.8
Baker, M. (UKIP)	2,680	5.4
Boswell, A. (Green)	508	1.0
Mann, S. (Ind)	95	0.2
Majority	11,626	23.41
Electorate	67,841	
Turnout	49,661	73.20

**Member of last parliament*

CONSTITUENCY SNAPSHOT

Before the 2001 general election Norfolk had not had a Liberal MP since 1929. From 1970 to 1997 Ralph Howell held the seat for the Conservatives. The general election of 1997 maintained the Conservatives in the seat with David Prior, but with a majority of only 1,294.

Norman Lamb became the Liberal Democrat MP for North Norfolk in 2001 after defeating Mr Prior by 483 votes. He returned in 2005 with a 10,606 majority. Lamb held the seat in 2010 with a majority of 11,626.

The seat lost six of its southerly wards to the new constituency of Broadland.

North Norfolk stretches along the majority of the Norfolk coastline taking in the large seaside towns of Sheringham and Cromer. Nearly 20 per cent of the population lives outside these main settlements in numerous rural villages.

The area has a narrow economic structure which is dependent on seasonal tourism, agriculture, hunting and forestry fishing, along with local service provision.

The North Norfolk Railway serves the constituency well, linking the inland with the seaside resorts on the 10½-mile trip. This tourist trip boosts the local economy in summer.

Rt Hon **David Lammy**

Tottenham (returning MP)

No boundary changes

Tel: 020 7219 0899
E-mail: lammyd@parliament.uk
Website: www.davidlammy.co.uk

Date of birth: 19 July 1972; Son of Rosalind Lammy, council officer

Education: The King's School, Peterborough; School of Oriental and African Studies, London University (LLB 1993); Harvard Law School, USA (LLM 1997); Married Nicola Green 2005 (2 children)

Non-political career: Barrister, 3 Serjeants Inn, Philip Naughton QC 1994-96; Attorney, Howard Rice Nemerovsky Canada Falk & Rabkin 1997-98; Barrister, D J Freeman 1998-2000; Member Amicus branch of Unite; Member: Greater London Assembly 2000, Archbishops' Council 1999-2002

Political career: Member for Tottenham since 22 June 2000 by-election; PPS to Estelle Morris as Secretary of State for Education and Skills 2001-02; Parliamentary Under-Secretary of State: Department of Health 2002-03, Department for Constitutional Affairs 2003-05, Department for Culture, Media and Sport 2005-07, Department for Innovation, Universities and Skills (DIUS) (Skills) 2007-08; Minister of State (Higher Education and Intellectual Property) DIUS/Department for Business, Innovation and Skills 2008-10; *Select Committees:* Member: Public Administration 2001, Procedure 2001; Member: Fabian Society, Society of Labour Lawyers, Christian Socialist Movement

Political interests: Health, Treasury (regeneration), arts and culture, education, international development; USA, Caribbean, Latin America, Africa

Other organisations: ActionAid: Trustee 2000-06, Honorary Ambassador 2006-; Honorary Doctorate of Law, University of East London 2004; PC 2008; Home House; The Honourable Society of Lincoln's Inn; *Publications:* Leading Together, 2002

Recreations: Film, live music, Spurs FC

Rt Hon David Lammy MP, House of Commons, London SW1A 0AA
Tel: 020 7219 0899 Fax: 020 7219 0357
E-mail: lammyd@parliament.uk
Website: www.davidlammy.co.uk

GENERAL ELECTION RESULT

		%	+/-
Lammy, D. (Lab)*	24,128	59.3	1.6
Schmitz, D. (Lib Dem)	7,197	17.7	1.0
Sullivan, S. (Con)	6,064	14.9	1.5
Sutton, J. (TUSC)	1,057	2.6	
Gray, A. (Green)	980	2.4	-2.2
McKenzie, W. (UKIP)	466	1.2	
Watson, N. (Ind)	265	0.7	
Kadara, A. (Christian)	262	0.6	
Thompson, S. (Ind)	143	0.4	
Carr, E. (Ind)	124	0.3	
Majority	16,931	41.61	
Electorate	69,933		
Turnout	40,687	58.18	

**Member of last parliament*

CONSTITUENCY SNAPSHOT

Since the 1950s Tottenham has been a Labour seat. Norman Atkinson unseated the Labour defector Alan Brown in 1964, and served until his death in 1987. Bernie Grant won the 1987 general election contest and increased his majority in both 1992 and 1997, polling 70 per cent of the vote on the latter occasion. He died in 2000.

Current MP David Lammy became Tottenham's MP at the 2000 by-election. Lammy has a majority of over 13,000 with 57.9 per cent of the vote. Lammy held the seat with almost 60 per cent of the vote and an increased majority of 16,931.

Tottenham falls within the London borough of Haringey in North London, stretching from Seven Sisters in the south to White Hart Lane and Northumberland Park in the north.

Industry contributes a great deal to Tottenham's economic output. The strong industrial presence is built around engineering and confectionery firms, while high-tech industry is also doing well, particularly at the Lea Valley Technopark.

Two higher education establishments are also based in the constituency: the University of Middlesex and the College of North East London.

Large Cypriot, Turkish and Irish communities live here, as well as people of West African and Caribbean origin.

Mark Lancaster

Milton Keynes North ***(returning MP)***

New constituency

Tel: 020 7219 8414
E-mail: lancasterm@parliament.uk
Website: lancaster4mk.com

Conservative

Date of birth: 12 May 1970; Son of Revd Ron Lancaster MBE and Kath Lancaster

Education: Kimbolton School, Huntingdon; Buckingham University (BSc business studies 1991, PhD 2007); Exeter University (MBA 1994); Married Katherine Elizabeth Reader 1995 (separated)

Non-political career: Officer Royal Engineers 1988-90; Major Royal Engineers (TA) 1990-; Director, Kimbolton Fireworks Ltd 1990-2005; Councillor Huntingdon District Council 1995-99: Chair Leisure committee 1996-99; Vice-chair British Fireworks Association 1999-2006; Parliamentary Adviser Royal Society of Chemistry

Political career: Contested Nuneaton 2001 general election. Member for Milton Keynes North East 2005-10, for Milton Keynes North since 6 May 2010 general election; Opposition Whip 2006-07; Shadow Minister for International Development 2007-10; *Select Committees:* Member: Office of the Deputy Prime Minister 2005-06, Defence 2006, Communities and Local Government 2008-09, International Development 2009-10

Political interests: Defence, international development, commerce; China, India, Nepal, USA

Other organisations: Vice-chairman MKSNAP 2004-; Patron Willen Hospice 2006-; Territorial Decoration (TD) 2002; Member, Worshipful Company of Fanmakers; United and Cecil Club; Army & Navy; *Publications:* Contributor, Fireworks Principles and Practice (Chemical Publishing 1999)

Recreations: Cricket, football, collecting classic British motorcycles

Mark Lancaster MP, House of Commons, London SW1A 0AA
Tel: 020 7219 8414 Fax: 020 7219 6685
E-mail: lancasterm@parliament.uk
Constituency: 13a High Street, Newport Pagnell, Buckinghamshire MK16 8AR Tel: 01908 615757 Fax: 01908 618433
Website: lancaster4mk.com

GENERAL ELECTION RESULT

		%
Lancaster, M. (Con)*	23,419	43.5
Pakes, A. (Lab/Co-op)	14,458	26.8
Hope, J. (Lib Dem)	11,894	22.1
Phillips, M. (UKIP)	1,772	3.3
Hamilton, R. (BNP)	1,154	2.1
Francis, A. (Green)	733	1.4
Lennon, J. (CPA)	206	0.4
Fensome, M. (Loony)	157	0.3
Vyas, A. (Ind)	95	0.2
Majority	8,961	16.63
Electorate	85,841	
Turnout	53,888	62.78

**Member of last parliament*

CONSTITUENCY SNAPSHOT

In 1997 Brian White took Milton Keynes North East for Labour by 240 votes. In 2001 there was a 1.8 per cent swing towards Labour, which took White's majority to just over 1,800.

In 2005 the Labour majority was overturned by the Conservatives on a 3.6 per cent swing. The Tories fielded a new candidate, Mark Lancaster, who achieved a small 1,665 majority. Mark Lancaster won the new seat in 2010 with a 8,961 majority.

Milton Keynes North is essentially the previous Milton Keynes North East. However, the new seat now includes all of Campbell Park, Middleton and Wolverton wards, which were previously shared with Milton Keynes South West.

This Buckinghamshire seat comprises new town areas of Milton Keynes, along Newport Pagnell, Olney and Woburn Sands.

One of the largest employers in Milton Keynes is the Open University, based in the South constituency. The national headquarters of Abbey National, Amazon's distribution centre and BT's training centre are also here.

Milton Keynes had the country's first multiplex cinema, the first NHS Direct centre, and even has a ski slope with real snow. Cars and motor-racing are important, with the Silverstone racing circuit nearby.

The constituency has a considerable rural area, with numerous villages and arable and dairy farming.

Rt Hon **Andrew Lansley**

South Cambridgeshire ***(returning MP)***

Boundary changes

Tel: 020 7219 2538
E-mail: lansleya@parliament.uk
Website: www.andrewlansley.co.uk

Conservative

Date of birth: 11 December 1956; Son of Thomas Lansley, OBE, and Irene Lansley

Education: Brentwood School; Exeter University (BA politics 1979) (President, Guild of Students 1977-78); Married Marilyn Biggs 1985 (divorced 2001) (3 daughters); married Sally Low 2001 (1 daughter 1 son)

Non-political career: Department of [Trade and] Industry 1979-87: Private secretary to Norman Tebbit as Secretary of State for Trade and Industry 1984-85; Principal private secretary to Norman Tebbit as Chancellor of the Duchy of Lancaster 1985-87; British Chambers of Commerce 1987-90: Policy director 1987-89, Deputy director-general 1989-90; Director Conservative Research Department 1990-95; Director Public Policy Unit 1995-97; Vice-President, Local Government Association

Political career: Member for South Cambridgeshire 1997-2010, for South Cambridgeshire (revised boundary) since 6 May 2010 general election; Member Shadow Cabinet 1999-2001: Shadow: Minister for the Cabinet Office and Policy Renewal 1999-2001; Chancellor of the Duchy of Lancaster 1999-2001; Member Shadow Cabinet 2003-: Shadow Secretary of State for Health 2003-10; Secretary of State for Health 2010-; *Select Committees:* Member: Health 1997-98, Trade and Industry 2001-04; Vice-chairman Conservative Party (with responsibility for policy renewal) 1998-99

Political interests: Trade and industry, economic policy, small businesses, health, local and regional government, police, film industry; USA, Japan, Egypt, Israel, France, Germany, South Africa

Other organisations: Patron: ASPIRE (Spinal injury), STRADA (Stroke and Action for Dysphasic Adults, Cambridge), Headway (Acquired Brain injury); Member, National Union Executive Committee 1990-95; CBE 1996; PC 2010; *Publications:* A Private Route (1988); Co-author Conservatives and the Constitution (1997); Do the right thing – Why Conservatives must achieve greater fairness and diversity in candidate selection (2002); Extending the Reach (2003)

Recreations: Spending time with my children, films, biography, history, cricket

Rt Hon Andrew Lansley CBE MP, House of Commons, London SW1A 0AA Tel: 020 7219 2538 Fax: 020 7219 6835
E-mail: lansleya@parliament.uk
Constituency: 153 St Neots Road, Hardwick, Cambridge CB3 7QJ
Tel: 01954 212707 Fax: 01954 211625
Website: www.andrewlansley.co.uk

GENERAL ELECTION RESULT

		%
Lansley, A. (Con)*	27,995	47.4
Kindersley, S. (Lib Dem)	20,157	34.1
Sadiq, T. (Lab)	6,024	10.2
Page, R. (Ind)	1,968	3.3
Davies-Green, H. (UKIP)	1,873	3.2
Saggers, S. (Green)	1,039	1.8
Majority	7,838	13.27
Electorate	78,995	
Turnout	59,056	74.76

Member of last parliament

CONSTITUENCY SNAPSHOT

Boundary changes in 1983 created the new constituency of South West Cambridgeshire. Conservative Sir Anthony Grant represented the seat for the 14 years it existed under that name, increasing his vote-share to nearly 60 per cent in 1992.

In 1997 there were major boundary changes as the constituency moved eastwards. Renamed South Cambridgeshire, it was won by the Tories' Andrew Lansley. He was re-elected in 2005 with an 8,000 majority. The Conservatives retained the seat with 27,995 votes in 2010 giving Lansley a majority of 7,838.

Boundary changes moved the Cambridge suburbs of Trumpington, Cherry Hinton and Coleridge into Cambridge city. At the same time Cottenham and the Abingtons part-wards were fully incorporated into the seat.

The seat extends from the southern suburbs of Cambridge city towards Hinxton and Melbourn with their high-technology and biotech industry clusters. The seat is oddly shaped and sparsely populated, with most residents clustered in the south-east.

South Cambridgeshire has been at the centre of the so-called Cambridge Phenomenon: the profusion of science parks which are major sites for intensive research and development.

Manufacturing is also important in the constituency, much of it clustered around Bar Hill with its proximity to the A14 and M11 to London. In the more rural areas of the constituency, cattle farming is also important, as are grass crops.

Pauline Latham

Mid Derbyshire

New constituency

Tel: 020 7219 3000
E-mail: pauline.latham.mp@parliament.uk
Website: www.paulinelatham.co.uk

Date of birth: 4 February 1948

Education: Bramcote Hill Technical Grammar School; Married Derek Latham 1968 (1 daughter 2 sons)

Non-political career: Proprieter, Humble plc 1976-87; Director, Michael St Development 1982-; Former school governor; Councillor: Derbyshire County Council 1987-2002, Derby City Council 1992-96, 1998-; Mayor of Derby 2007-08

Political career: Contested Broxtowe 2001 general election. Member for Mid Derbyshire since 6 May 2010 general election; Contested East Midlands 1999 and 2004 European Parliament elections

Political interests: Education, international development

Other organisations: OBE 1992

Pauline Latham OBE MP, House of Commons, London SW1A 0AA
Tel: 020 7219 3000 E-mail: pauline.latham.mp@parliament.uk
Constituency: Mid Derbyshire Conservative Association, 26 Chapel Street, Spondon, Derby DE21 7JP Tel: 01332 834295
Website: www.paulinelatham.co.uk

GENERAL ELECTION RESULT

		%
Latham, P. (Con)	22,877	48.3
Dhindsa, H. (Lab)	11,585	24.5
McIntosh, S. (Lib Dem)	9,711	20.5
Allsebrook, L. (BNP)	1,698	3.6
Kay, T. (UKIP)	1,252	2.6
Seerius, R. (Loony)	219	0.5
Majority	11,292	23.85
Electorate	66,297	
Turnout	47,342	71.41

CONSTITUENCY SNAPSHOT

This is a new constituency, formed from the Belper and Duffield area of the old West Derbyshire seat, plus northern and eastern suburbs of Derby, mostly from Derby North, and smaller areas from Amber Valley and Erewash.

West Derbyshire had been represented by Conservative MPs since 1950. Patrick McLoughlin first won it in a by-election in 1986 by 100 votes, following the departure of Matthew Parris to become a journalist. However he started to build a much larger majority at the 1987 general election and his majority in 2005 was a comfortable 10,753.

Pauline Latham held the seat for the Conservatives with a 5.7 per cent swing of the vote from Labour.

This is mainly a suburban area serving Derby, including the large new developments of Oakwood and Allestree. Allestree has seen most of its growth in the last 40 years, and Oakwood is Derby's largest and newest suburb, and still under pressure to accommodate more housing. To the north the constituency extends through Duffield up to the town of Belper, which is also home to many Derby commuters.

It is a largely prosperous area. The University of Derby lies within this constituency and provides significant employment opportunities and the Derbyshire Building Society is based in Duffield.

Ian Lavery

Wansbeck

No boundary changes

Tel: 020 7219 3000
Website: www.ianlavery.co.uk

Labour

Education: New College, Durham (HNC mining engineering); Married Hilary (2 sons)

Non-political career: Miner, National Coal Board: Lynemouth Colliery 1980, Ellington Colliery 1980-92; National Union of Mine Workers: General Secretary, Northumberland Area 1992-2002, President 2002-; National Union of Mineworkers: Member 1980-, Representative, Ellington Colliery 1986-92; Former councillor, Wansbeck District Council

Political career: Member for Wansbeck since 6 May 2010 general election; Member, Ashington Town branch, Labour Party; Executive committee member, Wansbeck CLP

Political interests: Local regeneration, employment, energy, climate change, poverty, internationalism

Other organisations: Chair: Ashington Community Football Club, Hirst Welfare Centre, Ashington Group – The Pitmen Painters, Northumberland Miners P&B Fund; Trustee: Northumberland Aged Miners Homes Association, North East Area Miners Trust, Woodhorn Museum, North East CISWO Trust

Ian Lavery MP, House of Commons, London SW1A 0AA
Tel: 020 7219 3000
Constituency: Wansbeck Constituency Labour Party, 94 Station Road, Ashington, Northumberland NE63 8RN Tel: 01670 523100
E-mail: contact@ianlavery.co.uk Website: www.ianlavery.co.uk

GENERAL ELECTION RESULT

		%	+/-
Lavery, I. (Lab)	17,548	45.9	-9.0
Reed, S. (Lib Dem)	10,517	27.5	1.2
Storey, C. (Con)	6,714	17.5	2.7
Finlay, S. (BNP)	1,418	3.7	
Stokoe, L. (UKIP)	974	2.5	
Best, N. (Green)	601	1.6	-1.8
Reid, M. (Ind)	359	0.9	
Flynn, M. (Christian)	142	0.4	
Majority	7,031	18.37	
Electorate	63,045		
Turnout	38,273	60.71	

CONSTITUENCY SNAPSHOT

The connection between miners and politicians has traditionally been strong in this seat. Labour has received loyal and strong support since 1945.

When Denis Murphy succeeded Jack Thompson in 1997, he was the only former miner in the 183-strong 1997 intake, having worked in the Ashington-Ellington pit.

Murphy's share of the vote dropped in 2001 by almost 10,000 votes. Although Murphy suffered a swing of 3.1 per cent against him at the 2005 election, it was only half of that experienced across the North East. His majority was 10,581. Ian Lavery took over from Denis Murphy in this safe Labour seat and delivered a reduced, but solid, majority of 7,031.

Formerly known as Morpeth, the name derives from the market and commuting town, which makes up only a small percentage of the overall population. The seat was renamed Wansbeck, after the river which runs through it, in 1983.

Wansbeck constituency is a mixture of social groups from the middle-class commuter town of Morpeth to the former mining communities of Ashington, Bedlington, Newbiggin and Pegswood. The last remaining pit in the North East at Ellington, employing 340 people, closed in January 2005.

Manual labour has been replaced as the prominent provider of jobs by service sector work in Wansbeck including public administration, education and health.

Rt Hon **David Laws**

Yeovil (returning MP)

Boundary changes

Tel: 020 7219 8413
E-mail: lawsd@parliament.uk
Website: www.yeovil-libdems.org.uk

Date of birth: 30 November 1965; Son of DA Laws and Mrs MT Davies

Education: St George's College, Weybridge, Surrey; King's College, Cambridge (BA economics 1987); Single

Non-political career: Vice-president, JP Morgan and Company 1987-92; Barclays de Zoete Wedd Ltd 1992-94: Managing director, Head US Dollar and Sterling treasuries 1992-94

Political career: Contested Folkestone and Hythe 1997 general election. Member for Yeovil 2001-10, for Yeovil (revised boundary) since 6 May 2010 general election; Liberal Democrat: Spokesman for Defence 2001-02, Shadow: Chief Secretary to the Treasury 2002-05, Secretary of State for: Work and Pensions 2005-07, Children, Schools and Families 2007-10; Chief Secretary to the Treasury 2010; *Select Committees:* Member: Treasury 2001-03, Treasury (Treasury Sub-Committee) 2001-03; Liberal Democrat Parliamentary Party: Economics adviser 1994-97, Director of Policy and Research 1997-99

Political interests: Economy, education, pensions, public service reform; Egypt, Ethiopia, France, Jordan

Other organisations: PC 2010; Winner 1984 Observer Mace National Schools Debating Competition

Recreations: Running, reading, desert regions

Rt Hon David Laws MP, House of Commons, London SW1A 0AA
Tel: 020 7219 8413 Fax: 020 7219 8188
E-mail: lawsd@parliament.uk
Constituency: 5 Church Street, Yeovil, Somerset BA20 1HB
Tel: 01935 425 025 Fax: 01935 433 652
Website: www.yeovil-libdems.org.uk

GENERAL ELECTION RESULT

		%
Laws, D. (Lib Dem)*	31,843	55.7
Davis, K. (Con)	18,807	32.9
Skevington, L. (Lab)	2,991	5.2
Pearson, N. (UKIP)	2,357	4.1
Baehr, R. (BNP)	1,162	2.0
Majority	13,036	22.81
Electorate	82,314	
Turnout	57,160	69.44

**Member of last parliament*

CONSTITUENCY SNAPSHOT

Yeovil was represented by the Conservatives from 1918 until 1983, when voters switched to the Alliance, and a Conservative majority of almost 9,000 was converted to a majority of almost 3,500 for Paddy Ashdown.

In 1997 Ashdown had a majority of over 11,000. However, in 2001 Ashdown stepped down, and his successor, David Laws, had a reduced majority of 3,928. In 2005 David Laws increased his majority to 8,562. Laws won re-election with an increased majority of 13,036 in 2010.

Boundary changes moved Blackmoor Vale and Camelot part-wards entirely within Somerton and Frome, while Ivelchester ward becomes fully contained within this seat.

The Somerset constituency of Yeovil covers much more territory than merely the town after which it is named, taking in Chard, Crewkerne, Ilminster, as well as many picturesque villages.

The economic core of the constituency is the thriving market town of Yeovil. Indeed, Yeovil's reputation as a centre of the aircraft and defence industries has lived on into the 21st century, despite attempts at diversification and the creation of numerous industrial estates. AgustaWestland Helicopters is the biggest employer. The town also boasts strong industrial and commercial sectors, as well as light industry and hi-tech engineering.

Mark Lazarowicz

Edinburgh North and Leith *(returning MP)*

No boundary changes

Tel: 020 7219 8222
E-mail: lazarowiczm@parliament.uk
Website: www.marklazarowicz.org.uk

Labour/Co-operative

Date of birth: 8 August 1953; Son of Jerzy Witold Lazarowicz and Ivy Lazarowicz, neé Eacott

Education: St Benedicts School, London; St Andrews University (MA moral philosophy and medieval history 1976); Edinburgh University (LLB 1992); Diploma Legal Practice 1993; Married Caroline Elizabeth Johnston 1993 (1 daughter 3 sons)

Non-political career: Organiser Scottish Education and Action for Development 1978-80; General secretary British Youth Council Scotland 1980-82; Organiser Scottish Education and Action for Development 1982-86; Advocate 1996-; TGWU 1978-; City of Edinburgh District Council: Councillor 1980-96, Leader of Council 1986-93; Councillor City of Edinburgh Council 1999-2001

Political career: Contested Edinburgh Pentlands 1987 and 1992 general elections. Member for Edinburgh North and Leith 2001-05, for Edinburgh North and Leith (revised boundary) since 5 May 2005 general election; PPS to David Cairns as Minister of State, Scotland Office 2007-08; Prime Minister's Special Representative on Carbon Trading 2008-; *Select Committees:* Member: Scottish Affairs 2001-03, Regulatory Reform 2002-05, Environment, Food and Rural Affairs 2002-05, Modernisation of the House of Commons 2005-10, Environmental Audit 2007-10, Joint Committee on the Draft Climate Change Bill 2007; Vice-convener Scottish Parliament Cross-Party Tackling Debt Group 2007-; Member Co-operative Party; Chair Scottish Labour Party 1989-90; Member: Socialist Environment and Resources Association (SERA), SERA Parliamentary Group; Chair Co-operative Party Parliamentary Group 2008-09

Political interests: Environment, transport, consumer issues, co-operative issues, constitution, finance, economy, small businesses; *Publications:* Co-author The Scottish Parliament: An Introduction (T and T Clark, 1st edition 1999, 2nd edition 2000, 3rd edition 2004); Various articles, papers and pamphlets on political and legal issues

Recreations: Jogging, walking, cycling

Mark Lazarowicz MP, House of Commons, London SW1A 0AA
Tel: 020 7219 8222 Fax: 020 7219 1761
E-mail: lazarowiczm@parliament.uk
Constituency: 5 Croall Place, Edinburgh EH7 4LT Tel: 0131-557 0577
Fax: 0131-557 5759 Website: www.marklazarowicz.org.uk

GENERAL ELECTION RESULT

		%	+/-
Lazarowicz, M. (Lab/Co-op)*	17,740	37.5	3.3
Lang, K. (Lib Dem)	16,016	33.8	4.7
McGill, I. (Con)	7,079	15.0	-3.7
Cashley, C. (SNP)	4,568	9.7	-0.5
Joester, K. (Green)	1,062	2.2	-3.6
Hein, J. (Lib)	389	0.8	
Black, W. (TUSC)	233	0.5	
Jacobsen, D. (SLP)	141	0.3	
Macintyre, C. (Ind)	128	0.3	
Majority	1,724	3.64	
Electorate	69,204		
Turnout	47,356	68.43	

**Member of last parliament*

CONSTITUENCY SNAPSHOT

In 1979 Ron Brown was elected as Labour MP for Edinburgh Leith. In April 1988 Brown was suspended from the Commons and later de-selected as the Labour candidate. Labour's Malcolm Chisholm won the seat.

In 1997 Malcolm Chisholm's majority increased to 10,978. He stood down from Westminster in 2001 to concentrate on the Scottish Parliament and Mark Lazarowicz maintained Chisholm's percentage majority. The Liberal Democrats have gradually chipped away at Labour's majority here but Mark Lazarowicz held on with a 1,724 vote lead.

In 2005 the seat gained Dean from Edinburgh Central and Craigleith and the rest of Pilton from Edinburgh West. Lazarowicz was returned with a reduced majority of 2,153.

This constituency incorporates the port of Leith as well as the northern suburbs of Edinburgh. The redeveloped docklands and the northern new town areas have become more elegant as Edinburgh as a whole has prospered. Trendy cafés and restaurants line the quayside, and numerous warehouses have been converted into expensive flats.

The Royal Yacht Britannia is now permanently moored in Leith Harbour.

The northern Edinburgh division, once teeming with manual labourers, is increasingly home to managerial and professional workers.

Transport Initiatives Edinburgh are working on Edinburgh's new tram system. The first phase of the development will be a 22-stop tram route starting in the constituency from Newhaven, going up Leith Walk, through Princes Street travelling west through the city and terminating at Edinburgh Airport.

Andrea Leadsom

South Northamptonshire

New constituency

Tel: 020 7219 3000
E-mail: andrea.leadsom.mp@parliament.uk
Website: www.andrealeadsom.com

Date of birth: 13 May 1963

Education: Tonbridge Girls Grammar; Warwick University (political science 1984); Married Ben Leadsom 1993 (1 daughter 2 sons)

Non-political career: Various roles, B2W 1987-91; Financial institutions director, Barclays Bank 1991-97; Managing director, De Putron (funds managment) 1997-99; Head of corporate governance, Invesco Perpetual 1999-; Councillor, South Oxfordshire District Council 2003-07

Political career: Contested Knowsley South 2005 general election. Member for South Northamptonshire since 6 May 2010 general election

Political interests: Economy, early years development

Andrea Leadsom MP, House of Commons, London SW1A 0AA
Tel: 020 7219 3000 E-mail: andrea.leadsom.mp@parliament.uk
Constituency: Boswell House, 9 Prospect Court, Courteenhall Road, Blisworth, Northampton NN7 3DG Tel: 01604 859721; 07834 843507 Fax: 01604 859329 Website: www.andrealeadsom.com

GENERAL ELECTION RESULT

		%
Leadsom, A. (Con)	33,081	55.2
Collins, S. (Lib Dem)	12,603	21.0
May, M. (Lab)	10,380	17.3
Mahoney, B. (UKIP)	2,406	4.0
Tappy, T. (England)	735	1.2
Rock, M. (Green)	685	1.1
Majority	20,478	34.19
Electorate	82,032	
Turnout	59,890	73.01

CONSTITUENCY SNAPSHOT

South Northamptonshire is a predominantly rural new constituency, created out of wards previously in Daventry and Northampton South.

Daventry has a long Conservative history, and since 1997 there has been a steady fall in support for Labour. In 2005 the Tories pushed further into the lead as Tim Boswell, MP from 1987, was re-elected with an increased majority of 14,686.

Northampton South in 2005 has traditionally been a Conservative seat, although it was held by Labour between 1997 and 2005.

In 2010 Andrea Leadsom won the new seat for the Conservatives with a majority of 20,478.

Geographically the seat reaches up to the south of Northampton, but does not include any significant portion of the town itself. However, it does benefit from its proximity to the county town, and also Milton Keynes, both of which provide employment opportunities within easy commuting distance. It includes the towns of Brackley, and Towcester, and several villages, the largest being Middleton Cheney, Roade and Silverstone.

About half a mile to the south of Silverstone village is the Silverstone motor racing circuit. The racing industry also provides a significant amount of employment in the immediate area.

The seat straddles the M1 and A5, and has easy access to and from London.

Jessica Lee

Erewash

Boundary changes

Tel: 020 7219 3000
E-mail: jessica.lee.mp@parliament.uk
Website: www.jessicaforerewash.com

Conservative

Date of birth: 1976

Education: Royal Holloway, University of London (history and politics); Law

Non-political career: Called to the Bar 2000

Political career: Contested Camberwell and Peckham 2005 general election. Member for Erewash since 6 May 2010 general election; Member, Conservative Party 1991-

Recreations: Cooking, reading, theatre

Jessica Lee MP, House of Commons, London SW1A 0AA
Tel: 020 7219 3000 E-mail: jessica.lee.mp@parliament.uk
Constituency: Erewash Conservative Association, The New Media Centre, New Tythe Street, Long Eaton, Derbyshire NG10 2DL
Tel: 0115-946 1333 Website: www.jessicaforerewash.com

GENERAL ELECTION RESULT

		%
Lee, J. (Con)	18,805	39.5
Pidgeon, C. (Lab)	16,304	34.2
Garnett, M. (Lib Dem)	8,343	17.5
Bailey, M. (BNP)	2,337	4.9
Sutton, J. (UKIP)	855	1.8
Fletcher, L. (Green)	534	1.1
Wilkins, L. (Ind)	464	1.0
Majority	2,501	5.25
Electorate	69,654	
Turnout	47,642	68.40

CONSTITUENCY SNAPSHOT

Labour and the Conservatives had alternating success here in the decades following the Second World War when the seat was known as South East Derbyshire. Erewash was created in 1970, when Peter Rost took the seat for the Conservatives. He retired in 1992. Angela Knight won the seat for the Party fairly comfortably in 1992, before Liz Blackman took the seat with a 9,135 majority in Labour's 1997 victory.

Support for both Labour and the Conservatives fell in 2005 and Blackman was returned to Westminster with a 7,084 majority. Blackman was defeated in 2010 with Jessica Lee securing a majority of 2,501 for the Conservatives.

Boundary changes moved two wards in the west of the constituency into the new Mid Derbyshire constituency.

The constituency of Erewash lies between Nottingham and Derby, bounded by the Trent, Derwent and Erewash rivers and split down the middle by the M1.

The seat's name derives from the river that marks its boundary with Nottinghamshire. Population is concentrated in market towns along the eastern edge of the constituency, with open country and many villages to the west.

The local economy was traditionally dominated by lace-making, coal mining, iron working and the textile industry. The mines have long since closed, and the manufacturing base has diversified and continues to be the dominant source of employment.

Phillip Lee

Bracknell

Boundary changes

Tel: 020 7219 3000
E-mail: phillip.lee.mp@parliament.uk
Website: www.phillip-lee.com

Date of birth: 28 September 1970

Education: Sir William Borlase's Grammar School, Marlow; King's College, London (BSc human biology 1993); Keble College, Oxford (MSc biological anthropology 1994); St Mary's Hospital Medical School, Imperial College, London (MBBS 1999); Single

Non-political career: St Mary's Hospital, London; Wexham Park Hospital, Slough; Stoke Mandeville Hospital, Aylesbury; GP, Thames Valley; Councillor, Beaconsfield Town Council 2001-02

Political career: Contested Blaenau Gwent 2005 general election. Member for Bracknell since 6 May 2010 general election; Beaconsfield Conservative Association: Member 1992-2009, Deputy chair (membership and finance) 2005-07, Deputy chair (political) 2007-08; Member, Maidenhead Conservative Association 2009; Executive member Conservative Friends of Bangladesh

Political interests: Science, energy security policy; Bangladesh, Middle East

Other organisations: Old Grumblers Cricket Club; Marlow Waterski Club

Recreations: Skiing, football, rugby union

Phillip Lee MP, House of Commons, London SW1A 0AA
Tel: 020 7219 3000 E-mail: phillip.lee.mp@parliament.uk
Constituency: Bracknell Conservative Association, 10 Milbanke Court, Milbanke Way, Western Road, Bracknell, Berkshire RG12 1RP
Tel: 01344 868286 Website: www.phillip-lee.com

GENERAL ELECTION RESULT

		%
Lee, P. (Con)	27,327	52.4
Earwicker, R. (Lib Dem)	11,623	22.3
Piasecki, J. (Lab)	8,755	16.8
Barter, M. (UKIP)	2,297	4.4
Burke, M. (BNP)	1,253	2.4
Young, D. (Green)	825	1.6
Haycocks, D. (Scrap)	60	0.1
Majority	15,704	30.12
Electorate	76,885	
Turnout	52,140	67.82

CONSTITUENCY SNAPSHOT

Bracknell, and its predecessor East Berkshire, was served by Andrew MacKay from 1983 until returning in 2010. He won East Berkshire in 1983 and a majority of 16,099, which this had increased to 28,680 in 1992. The national Labour victory in 1997 reduced it to 10,387.

In 2005 MacKay more than doubled his majority to 12,036. In 2010 Phillip Lee retained the seat for the Conservatives with a strong 15,704 majority.

The wards of Crown Wood and Harmans Water are now entirely within the constituency. Binfield and Warfield, Warfield Harvest Ride wards and Winkfield and Cranbourne part-ward were moved to Windsor.

Bracknell is situated in the M4 corridor in the southern corner of Berkshire. The constituency is home to several affluent villages and a number of fine mansions set in striking estates.

Institutions of note in the area include the Royal Military Academy at Sandhurst.

With its proximity to the M4, good rail links, and nearby Heathrow airport, Bracknell

is home to numerous hi-tech industries and houses the European headquarters of over 20 international companies ranging from Dell, Hewlett Packard and Siemens, to BMW and pharmaceutical giant, Boehringer Ingelheim.

John Leech

Manchester Withington ***(returning MP)***

Boundary changes

Tel: 020 7219 8353
E-mail: leechj@parliament.uk
Website: www.john-leech.co.uk

Date of birth: 11 April 1971; Son of Rev. John and Jean Leech

Education: Manchester Grammar School; Loretto College, Edinburgh; Brunel University (BSc history and politics 1994); Partner Catherine Kilday

Non-political career: Assistant restaurant manager McDonald's 1995-97; Customer relations RAC Ltd 1998-2005; Councillor Manchester City Council 1998-2008: Deputy leader Liberal Democrats Group 2003-05

Political career: Member for Manchester Withington 2005-10, for Manchester Withington (revised boundary) since 6 May 2010 general election; Liberal Democrat Shadow Minister for Transport 2006-10; *Select Committees:* Member: Transport 2005-10

Political interests: Housing, planning, transport

Recreations: Amateur dramatics, football

John Leech MP, House of Commons, London SW1A 0AA
Tel: 020 7219 8353 Fax: 020 7219 0442
E-mail: leechj@parliament.uk
Constituency: 8 Gawsworth Avenue, East Didsbury, Manchester M20 5NF Tel: 0161-434 3334 Fax: 0161-434 3206
Website: www.john-leech.co.uk

GENERAL ELECTION RESULT

		%
Leech, J. (Lib Dem)*	20,110	44.6
Powell, L. (Lab)	18,260	40.5
Green, C. (Con)	5,005	11.1
Candeland, B. (Green)	798	1.8
Gutfreund-Walmsley, B. (UKIP)	698	1.6
Zalzala, Y. (Ind)	147	0.3
Farmer, M. (Ind)	57	0.1
Majority	1,850	4.10
Electorate	74,371	
Turnout	45,075	60.61

**Member of last parliament*

CONSTITUENCY SNAPSHOT

When Fred Silvester lost Withington in 1987 to the Labour's Keith Bradley, the Tories lost their last remaining seat in Manchester, a seat they had held since 1931. In 2001 Labour retained won a 11,524 majority and the Liberal Democrats pushed the Tories into third place.

At the 2005 general election, Keith Bradley lost his seat after 18 years to his Liberal Democrat opponent John Leech by 667 votes. This was the first time that the Liberal Democrats had held a seat in Manchester since the decline of the old Liberal Party in the 1930s. Leech was re-elected in 2010 with a majority of 1,850.

The seat gained Chorlton part-ward from Manchester Central and Old Moat and Withington part-wards from Manchester Gorton.

This mainly residential seat to the south of Manchester city centre includes the areas of Didsbury, Withington and Chorlton.

The number of owner-occupiers is low, those renting privately are well above the national average; this is mainly attributable to the students and young professionals who now live here.

The division has good transport links, and Chorlton will be added to the Metrolink tram system in 2011.

Jeremy Lefroy

Stafford

Boundary changes

Tel: 020 7219 3000
E-mail: jeremy.lefroy.mp@parliament.uk
Website: www.jeremylefroy.info

Conservative

Date of birth: 30 May 1959

Education: Highgate School, London; King's College, Cambridge (BA classics 1980); Married Janet Elizabeth Mackay 1985 (1 son 1 daughter)

Non-political career: Foreman, Ford Motor Company 1980-81; Trainee accountant, Arthur Andersen 1981-84; Finance manager/director, Cowan de Groot plc 1984-86; Finance manager, EDM Schluter Ltd 1986-88; General manager/managing director, African Coffee Company Ltd, Tanzania 1989-2000; Director and part-owner, African Speciality Products Ltd 2000-; ASTMS 2000-01; Newcastle-under-Lyme Borough Council: Councillor 2003-07, Shadow finance and resources spokesman 2004-06, Cabinet member for finance and resources 2006-07

Political career: Contested Newcastle-under-Lyme 2005 general election. Member for Stafford since 6 May 2010 general election; Contested West Midlands 2004 European Parliament election; Treasurer, Newcastle-under-Lyme Conservative Association 2003-06

Political interests: Sustainable development and enterprise, urban regeneration, environment; Kenya, Peru, Switzerland, Tanzania, Uganda

Other organisations: Member, Conservative Christian Fellowship 2002-; Director, Tanzania Coffee Board 1997-99; Chairman, Tanzania Coffee Association 1997-99

Recreations: Playing and writing music, hill-walking, sport

Jeremy Lefroy MP, House of Commons, London SW1A 0AA
Tel: 020 7219 3000 E-mail: jeremy.lefroy.mp@parliament.uk
Constituency: Stafford Conservative Association, Castle Street, Stafford ST16 2ED Tel: 01785 252273 Fax: 01785 259462
Website: www.jeremylefroy.info

GENERAL ELECTION RESULT

		%
Lefroy, J. (Con)	22,047	43.9
Kidney, D. (Lab)*	16,587	33.0
Stamp, B. (Lib Dem)	8,211	16.3
Goode, R. (UKIP)	1,727	3.4
Hynd, R. (BNP)	1,103	2.2
Shone, M. (Green)	564	1.1
Majority	5,460	10.87
Electorate	70,587	
Turnout	50,239	71.17

**Member of last parliament*

CONSTITUENCY SNAPSHOT

Before 1997 the seat was known as Stafford and Stone and was solid territory for the Conservatives. Bill cash held the seat with a much reduced 3,980 majority at the 1984 by-election caused by Hugh Fraser's death. Cash went on to consolidate his majority.

After the boundaries were redrawn in 1997 Bill Cash decided to contest Stone. The Conservative candidate, a young David Cameron, had a tough fight and lost to Labour's David Kidney by 4,314 votes. Kidney was re-elected in 2005 with a 2,121 majority.

The Conservatives took the seat from Kidney in 2010 with Jeremy Lefroy securing a majority of 5,460.

Boundary changes exchanged two rural and village wards each way with the Stone constituency.

This constituency is situated to the north of the West Midlands conurbation in central Staffordshire. It consists of the county town of Stafford, and a ring of surrounding countryside.

This is a mixed, semi-rural constituency. Stafford is an ancient town ringed by a new road system.

Stafford's economic development historically came from its status as a railway town but it is now the commercial and administrative centre for the county and economic activity is more varied. The services sector is the biggest employer.

Edward Leigh

Gainsborough (returning MP)

Boundary changes

Tel: 020 7219 6480
E-mail: leighe@parliament.uk
Website: www.edwardleigh.net

Date of birth: 20 July 1950; Son of late Sir Neville Leigh, former Clerk to the Privy Council

Education: Oratory School, Reading, Berkshire; French Lycee, London; Durham University (BA history 1972) (President of Union); Married Mary Goodman 1984 (3 sons 3 daughters)

Non-political career: Member Conservative Research Department 1973-75; Principal correspondence sercretary to Margaret Thatcher as Leader of the Opposition 1976-77; Barrister, Inner Temple 1977-; Councillor: Richmond Borough Council 1974-78, GLC 1977-81; Chair National Council for Civil Defence 1979-83; Director Coalition For Peace Through Security 1981-83

Political career: Contested Teesside, Middlesbrough October 1974 general election. Member for Gainsborough and Horncastle 1983-97, for Gainsborough 1997-2010, for Gainsborough (revised boundary) since 6 May 2010 general election; Member Public Accounts Commission; PPS to John Patten as Minister of State, Home Office 1990; Parliamentary Under-Secretary of State, Department of Trade and Industry 1990-93; *Select Committees:* Member: Social Security 1997-2000; Public Accounts: Member 2000-01, Chair 2001-10; Member: Liaison 2001-10; Member governing council Conservative Christian Fellowship; Chair Cornerstone Group 2004-

Political interests: Defence, foreign affairs, agriculture, families

Other organisations: Veteran Member, Honourable Artillery Company; Fellow Industry and Parliament Trust 1983; Knight of Honour and Devotion Sovereign Military Order of Malta; Fellow Institute of Arbitrators 1999-; *Publications:* Right Thinking (1982); Onwards from Bruges (1989); Choice and Responsibility – The Enabling State (1990)

Recreations: Walking, reading

Edward Leigh MP, House of Commons, London SW1A 0AA
Tel: 020 7219 6480 Fax: 020 7219 4883
E-mail: leighe@parliament.uk
Constituency: 23 Queen Street, Market Rasen, Lincolnshire LN8 3EN
Tel: 01673 844501 Fax: 01673 849003
Website: www.edwardleigh.net

GENERAL ELECTION RESULT

		%
Leigh, E. (Con)*	24,266	49.3
O'Connor, P. (Lib Dem)	13,707	27.8
McMahon, J. (Lab)	7,701	15.6
Pearson, S. (UKIP)	2,065	4.2
Porter, M. (BNP)	1,512	3.1
Majority	10,559	21.44
Electorate	72,144	
Turnout	49,251	68.27

**Member of last parliament*

CONSTITUENCY SNAPSHOT

The seat has remained Conservative since the Liberal MP Sir Richard Winfrey lost in 1924. Sir Marcus Kimball was secure as MP from 1956 to 1983. In 1983 the seat was renamed Gainsborough and Horncastle and the Liberal/Alliance candidate mounted a strong challenge with nearly 41 per cent of the vote, but Sir Marcus's successor Edward Leigh still had more than half the vote.

Boundary changes in 1997 moved the town of Horncastle out of the constituency and Leigh's majority was halved to under 7,000. In 2001 and 2005 the Conservatives consolidated their vote and Edward Leigh was returned with majorities of over 8,000. In 2010 Edward Leigh retained the seat for the Conservatives with a majority of 10,559.

Boundary changes moved the wards of Binbrook, Ludford, and Roughton entirely within the Louth and Horncastle constituency.

A largely rural constituency, Gainsborough stretches across north-west Lincolnshire from the town of Gainsborough on the Trent, eastwards beyond Market Rasen and south to the edge of Lincoln.

Gainsborough is the seat's only industrial centre and the most working-class area with a variety of small industries.

The constituency is predominantly flat agricultural land and also includes part of the Lincolnshire Wolds. The public sector and service industries are major employers, and many people commute to Scunthorpe, Sheffield and Grimsby.

Charlotte Leslie

Bristol North West

Boundary changes

Tel: 020 7219 3000
E-mail: charlotte.leslie.mp@parliament.uk
Website: www.charlotteleslie.com

Conservative

Date of birth: 1978

Education: Balliol College, Oxford (BA classics 2001)

Non-political career: BBC television; Former education adviser, The Young Foundation; Former adviser to David Willetts MP; Editor, *Crossbow*; Public affairs officer, National Autistic Society; Education associate, Portland PR 2009

Political career: Member for Bristol North West since 6 May 2010 general election; Policy adviser, Public Services Policy Review Report, Conservative Party

Political interests: Education

Other organisations: Council member, Bow Group; *Publications:* More Good School Places (Policy Exchange 2005); The Invisible Children (Bow Group 2007); SEN – The Truth About Inclusion (Bow Group 2008)

Recreations: Surfing, writing, drawing, swimming, boxing training

Charlotte Leslie MP, House of Commons, London SW1A 0AA
Tel: 020 7219 3000 E-mail: charlotte.leslie.mp@parliament.uk
Constituency: 5 Westfield Park, Bristol BS6 6LT Tel: 0117-973 6812
Fax: 0117-923 8153 Website: www.charlotteleslie.com

GENERAL ELECTION RESULT

		%
Leslie, C. (Con)	19,115	38.0
Harrod, P. (Lib Dem)	15,841	31.5
Townend, S. (Lab)	13,059	25.9
Upton, R. (UKIP)	1,175	2.3
Carr, R. (England)	635	1.3
Dunn, A. (Green)	511	1.0
Majority	3,274	6.50
Electorate	73,469	
Turnout	50,336	68.51

CONSTITUENCY SNAPSHOT

Since 1950 Bristol North West has been an electoral weathervane seat: its member represents the governing party in each general election.

From 1979 to 1997 the seat was in Conservative hands, until Doug Naysmith was handed a Labour majority of almost 21 per cent. He was re-elected with a 8,962 majority in 2005.

Conservative Charlotte Leslie won a 3,274 majority in 2010 in this previously Labour seat and pushed them into third place behind the Lib Dems.

The seat lost all its South Gloucestershire wards to the new seat of Filton and Bradley Stoke, whilst it gains Stoke-Bishop, Henleaze, Westbury-upon-Trym and the remaining parts of Horfield, Lockleaze and Kingsweston wards, all of which are currently part of Bristol West.

Bristol has been a maritime city for centuries but its docks are no longer in the centre of town. The Bristol Port Company's docks are situated in the west end of the constituency at Avonmouth and its workforce is more highly skilled and better paid than in the past.

Southmead Hospital is also a large employer in the area.

Chris Leslie

Nottingham East

Boundary changes

Labour/Co-operative

Tel: 020 7219 3000
E-mail: chris.leslie@parliament.uk

Date of birth: 28 June 1972; Son of Michael and Dania Leslie

Education: Bingley Grammar School; Leeds University (BA politics and parliamentary studies 1994; MA industrial and labour studies 1996); Married Nicola (1 daughter)

Non-political career: Office administrator 1994-96; Political research assistant 1996-97; Director, New Local Government Network 2005-; Member: TGWU, GMB; Councillor, Bradford City Council 1994-98

Political career: Member for Shipley 1997-2005, for Nottingham East since 6 May 2010 general election; PPS to Lord Falconer as Minister of State, Cabinet Office 1998-2001; Parliamentary Secretary, Cabinet Office 2001-02; Parliamentary Under-Secretary of State for: Local Government and the Regions, Office of the Deputy Prime Minister 2002-03, Department for Constitutional Affairs 2003-05; *Select Committees:* Member: Public Accounts 1997-98

Political interests: Industrial policy, economic policy, environment, local and regional government

Other organisations: Trustee, Consumer Credit Counselling Service

Recreations: Travel, tennis, cinema, art

Chris Leslie MP, House of Commons, London SW1A 0AA
Tel: 020 7219 3000 E-mail: chris.leslie@parliament.uk
Constituency: c/o Unison, Vivien Avenue, Sherwood, Nottingham NG5 1AF Tel: 0115-847 5472

GENERAL ELECTION RESULT

		%
Leslie, C. (Lab/Co-op)	15,022	45.4
Boote, S. (Lib Dem)	8,053	24.3
Lamont, E. (Con)	7,846	23.7
Wolfe, P. (UKIP)	1,138	3.4
Hoare, B. (Green)	928	2.8
Sardar, P. (Christian)	125	0.4
Majority	6,969	21.05
Electorate	58,707	
Turnout	33,112	56.40

CONSTITUENCY SNAPSHOT

The Labour Party lost to the Conservatives here in 1983 and 1987. However, John Heppell won the seat back for the party in 1992 with a comfortable majority of 7,680. He extended his lead to 15,419 in 1997. Heppell's majority was, however, cut in 2001 and 2005 to 10,320 and 6,939 respectively.

The Liberal Democrats appear to have taken advantage of the slipping Conservative vote by edging their way into second place in the seat. In 2010 Christopher Leslie held the seat for Labour with a majority of 6,969.

Boundary changes added the parts of the inner-city wards of Arboretum and St Ann's that were in Nottingham South, while losing parts of the Basford and Bestwood wards to Nottingham North, and parts of Bridge and the Leen Valley to Nottingham South.

Nottingham East contains many of the city's poorest areas. However, the more affluent wards of Mapperley and Sherwood are also in the constituency.

As with other parts of Nottingham employment has been hit by the loss of textiles jobs in the city. Boots, based on the other side of the city, is a major employer.

There is relatively little industry in the seat itself, and the area has traditionally been a densely populated residential part of town.

Rt Hon **Oliver Letwin**

West Dorset (returning MP)

No boundary changes

Tel: 020 7219 0826
E-mail: letwino@parliament.uk

Date of birth: 19 May 1956; Son of Professor William Letwin and late Dr Shirley Robin Letwin

Education: Eton College; Trinity College, Cambridge (BA history 1978, MA, PhD philosophy 1982); London Business School; Married Isabel Grace Davidson 1984 (1 son 1 daughter)

Non-political career: Visiting fellow (Procter Fellow), Princeton University, USA 1980-81; Research fellow, Darwin College, Cambridge 1981-82; Special adviser to Sir Keith Joseph as Secretary of State for Education 1982-83; Special adviser, Prime Minister's Policy Unit 1983-86; N. M. Rothschild & Son, Merchant Bank: Manager 1986, Assistant Director 1987, Director 1991-2003, Managing Director 2003, Non-Executive Director 2005-

Political career: Contested Hackney North 1987 and Hampstead and Highgate 1992 general elections. Member for West Dorset since 1 May 1997 general election; Opposition Spokesperson for Constitutional Affairs, Scotland and Wales 1998-99; Shadow: Financial Secretary 1999-2000, Chief Secretary to the Treasury 2000-01, Home Secretary 2001-03, Secretary of State for Economic Affairs and Shadow Chancellor of the Exchequer 2003-05, Secretary of State for Environment, Food and Rural Affairs 2005; Minister of State, Cabinet Office 2010-; *Select Committees:* Member: Deregulation 1998-99, European Standing Committee B 1998; Member, Conservative Disability Group; Chairman: Conservative Policy Review 2005-, Conservative Research Department 2005-

Political interests: Economics, employment, education; Eastern Europe, Africa

Other organisations: Patron, Joseph Weld Hospice; PC 2002; Fellow, Royal Society of Arts; *Publications:* Ethics, Emotion and the Unity of the Self (1985); Aims of Schooling (1986); Privatising the World (1989); Drift to Union (1989); The Purpose of Politics (1999); Plus articles and reviews in learned and popular journals

Recreations: Skiing, sailing, tennis, reading, writing books

Rt Hon Oliver Letwin MP, House of Commons, London SW1A 0AA
Tel: 020 7219 0826 Fax: 020 7219 4405
E-mail: letwino@parliament.uk
Constituency: Chapel House, Dorchester Road, Maiden Newton, Dorset DT2 0BG Tel: 01300 321188 Fax: 01300 321233

GENERAL ELECTION RESULT

		%	+/-
Letwin, O. (Con)*	27,287	47.6	1.2
Farrant, S. (Lib Dem)	23,364	40.8	-1.1
Bick, S. (Lab)	3,815	6.7	-1.1
Chisholm, O. (UKIP)	2,196	3.8	1.8
Greene, S. (Green)	675	1.2	-0.6
Majority	3,923	6.84	
Electorate	76,869		
Turnout	57,337	74.59	

**Member of last parliament*

CONSTITUENCY SNAPSHOT

The Conservatives have held this seat since 1945, with current incumbent Oliver Letwin presiding over the seat since 1997. Letwin's 1997 margin of victory of 1,840 votes was lower than the 8,011 majority that his predecessor had held five years earlier.

In 2001, however, the Liberal Democrats made gains exactly matching the percentage of votes lost by Labour, and Letwin's majority was further reduced as a result, to just over 1,400. In 2005 Oliver Letwin was returned with an increased majority of 2,461. Oliver Letwin held this seat despite a strong Liberal Democrat vote, taking a 3,923 lead in 2010.

The main town in the rural constituency of West Dorset is Dorchester. Other towns in the constituency include Cerne Abbas, Maiden Newton, North Chideock, Beaminster, Puddletown, and the seaside resort of Lyme Regis.

West Dorset is an economically buoyant constituency. Demand for land to build industrial estates on is outstripping supply.

There is a large amount of farming in this rural constituency, and jobs are also to be found in tourism. Thomas Hardy's old House at Max Gate, and both Sherborne and Maiden Castles attract visitors, while Lyme Regis is an increasingly popular seaside resort.

Brandon Lewis

Great Yarmouth

No boundary changes

Tel: 020 7219 3000
E-mail: brandon.lewis.mp@parliament.uk
Website: www.tellbrandonlewis.com

Conservative

Date of birth: 20 June 1971

Education: Forest School, Chigwell; Buckingham University (BSc economics; LLB law); King's College, London (LLM commercial law); Inns of Court, School of Law (Bar Vocational Course); Married Justine Yolanda Rappolt (1 son 1 daughter)

Non-political career: Director, Woodlands Schools Ltd 2001-; Brentwood Borough Council: Councillor 1998-2009, Leader 2004-09

Political career: Contested Sherwood 2001 general election. Member for Great Yarmouth since 6 May 2010 general election

Other organisations: Carlton Club

Recreations: Reading, theatre, running, cycling, swimming, golf, fly fishing

Brandon Lewis MP, House of Commons, London SW1A 0AA
Tel: 020 7219 3000 E-mail: brandon.lewis.mp@parliament.uk
Constituency: Suite 20, Yarmouth Business Park, Suffolk Road, Great Yarmouth, Norfolk NR31 0ER Tel: 01493 650505
Fax: 0845 094 4202 Website: www.tellbrandonlewis.com

GENERAL ELECTION RESULT

		%	+/-
Lewis, B. (Con)	18,571	43.1	5.0
Wright, A. (Lab)*	14,295	33.2	-12.3
Partridge, S. (Lib Dem)	6,188	14.4	3.3
Baugh, A. (UKIP)	2,066	4.8	0.6
Tann, B. (BNP)	1,421	3.3	
Biggart, L. (Green)	416	1.0	
McMahon-Morris, M. (LTT)	100	0.2	
Majority	4,276	9.93	
Electorate	70,315		
Turnout	43,057	61.23	

**Member of last parliament*

CONSTITUENCY SNAPSHOT

The support from the rural and coastal villages granted the Conservative MP Anthony Fell a total of 28 years in office between 1951 and 1983.

In 1983 his Conservative successor Michael Cartiss was elected with a majority of 11,200, a quarter of the vote. Cartiss's majority fell over the years, but it was not until Labour's national victory in 1997, with a swing of 13.9 per cent, that the Tories lost. The Labour MP Anthony David Wright has lost ground to the Tories since his win in 1997, when he polled 53 per cent of the vote. His 1997 majority was more than halved in 2005.

Tony Wright was defeated in the 2010 general election with a 8.7 per cent swing to the Conservative candidate, Brandon Lewis.

A seaside town, which has had continual unemployment problems, Great Yarmouth has politically been polarised between the urban area of Yarmouth and the villages of the constituency's rural element.

Half the constituents in the Great Yarmouth area live in the urban Yarmouth and Gorleston areas with the rest in the agricultural areas between Winterton and Hopton.

These economic indicators are exacerbated by the seasonal nature of employment in the key sectors of the local economy - agriculture, tourism and the exploitation of offshore gas supplies.

Ivan Lewis

Bury South ***(returning MP)***

Boundary changes

Tel: 020 7219 6404
E-mail: lewisi@parliament.uk
Website: www.ivanlewis.org.uk

Date of birth: 4 March 1967; Son of Joe and late Gloria Lewis

Education: William Hulme Grammar School; Stand College; Bury Further Education College; Married Juliette Fox 1990 (divorced) (2 sons)

Non-political career: Co-ordinator, Contact Community Care Group 1986-89; Community care manager, Jewish Social Services 1989-92; Chief executive, Manchester Jewish Federation 1992-97; Member UNITE; Councillor, Bury Metropolitan Borough Council 1990-98

Political career: Member for Bury South 1997-2010, for Bury South (revised boundary) since 6 May 2010 general election; PPS to Stephen Byers as Secretary of State for Trade and Industry 1999-2001; Parliamentary Under-Secretary of State, Department for Education and Skills 2001-05: (for Young People and Learning 2001-02, for Adult Learning and Skills 2002, for Young People and Adult Skills 2002-03, for Skills and Vocational Education 2003-05); Economic Secretary, HM Treasury 2005-06; Parliamentary Under-Secretary of State: Department of Health (Care Services) 2006-08, Department for International Development 2008-09; Minister of State, Foreign and Commonwealth Office 2009-10; *Select Committees:* Member: Deregulation 1997-99, Health 1999; Chair, Bury South Labour Party 1991-96; Vice-chair, Labour Friends of Israel 1997-2001

Political interests: Health, crime, education; Israel, USA

Other organisations: Chair, Bury MENCAP 1989-92; Founder Member, Co-ordinator and Chair, Contact Community Care Group 1986-92; Trustee, Holocaust Educational Trust

Recreations: Manchester City FC

Ivan Lewis MP, House of Commons, London SW1A 0AA
Tel: 020 7219 6404 E-mail: lewisi@parliament.uk
Constituency: 381 Bury New Road, Prestwich, Manchester M25 1AV
Tel: 0161-773 5500 Fax: 0161-773 7959
Website: www.ivanlewis.org.uk

GENERAL ELECTION RESULT

		%
Lewis, I. (Lab)*	19,508	40.4
Wiseman, M. (Con)	16,216	33.6
D'Albert, V. (Lib Dem)	8,796	18.2
Purdy, J. (BNP)	1,743	3.6
Chadwick, P. (UKIP)	1,017	2.1
Morris, V. (England)	494	1.0
Heron, G. (Green)	493	1.0
Majority	3,292	6.82
Electorate	73,544	
Turnout	48,267	65.63

**Member of last parliament*

CONSTITUENCY SNAPSHOT

After the creation of this second Bury seat in 1983, Bury South contained the bulk of the old Middleton and Prestwich constituency, and the Radcliffe part of the old Bury and Radcliffe division.

In 1997 Tory David Sumberg's majority was overturned to secure a 12,381 majority for Labour's Ivan Lewis. A further collapse in the Tory vote in Bury South in 2001 increased Lewis's majority, but it fell to 8,912 in 2005.

Lewis held the seat in 2010 with a majority of 3,292 following a 8 per cent swing to the Conservatives.

Boundary changes were minimal. Unsworth and Church wards straddled the two divisions: the former ward is now entirely within the South's boundaries, while the latter is in Bury North.

Bury South does not have much to do with the town of Bury, but is instead centred on the working-class town of Radcliffe. It also includes Manchester's affluent northern suburbs, such as Prestwich.

Bury South is more urban in character than Bury North. There is not a great deal of social housing and there are few council estates in the constituency.

There have been attempts at economic diversification and the area has a burgeoning reputation as a tourist centre: the East Lancashire Railway, the Fusiliers Museum and the 500-acre Prestwich Forest Park are notable attractions.

Dr **Julian Lewis**

New Forest East (returning MP)

Boundary changes

Tel: 020 7219 4179
E-mail: lewisj@parliament.uk
Website: www.julianlewis.net

Conservative

Date of birth: 26 September 1951; Son of late Samuel Lewis and late Hilda Lewis

Education: Dynevor Grammar School, Swansea; Balliol College, Oxford (BA philosophy and politics 1977); St Antony's College, Oxford (DPhil strategic studies 1981, MA); Doctoral research (strategic studies) 1975-77, 1978-81

Non-political career: Seaman, HM Royal Naval Reserve 1979-82; Secretary Campaign for Representative Democracy 1977-78; Research director and director, Coalition for Peace Through Security 1981-85; Director, Policy Research Associates 1985-; Deputy director, Conservative Research Department 1990-96

Political career: Contested Swansea West 1983 general election. Member for New Forest East 1997-2010, for New Forest East (revised boundary) since 6 May 2010 general election; Opposition Whip 2001-02; Shadow Minister for: Defence 2002-04, the Cabinet Office 2004-05, Defence 2005-10; *Select Committees:* Member: Welsh Affairs 1998-2001, Defence 2000-01; Treasurer Oxford University Conservative Association 1971; Secretary Oxford Union 1972; Executive member 1922 Committee 2001

Political interests: Defence, security, foreign affairs, European affairs; Western Europe, Central and Eastern Europe, Russia

Other organisations: Joint organiser of campaign against militant infiltration of the Labour Party 1977-78; Athenaeum, Hon president Totton Conservative; *Publications:* Changing Direction: British Military Planning for Post-War Strategic Defence 1942-1947 (1988, 2003, 2008); Who's Left? An Index of Labour MPs and Left-Wing Causes 1985-1992 (1992); Labour's CND Cover-Up (1992); The Liberal Democrats: The Character of Their Politics (1993); What's Liberal? Liberal Democrat Quotations and Facts (1996)

Recreations: History, fiction, films, music, photography

Dr Julian Lewis MP, House of Commons, London SW1A 0AA
Tel: 020 7219 4179 E-mail: lewisj@parliament.uk
Constituency: 3 The Parade, Southampton Road, Cadnam, Hampshire SO40 2NG Tel: 023 8081 4817
Website: www.julianlewis.net

GENERAL ELECTION RESULT

		%
Lewis, J. (Con)*	26,443	52.9
Scriven, T. (Lib Dem)	15,136	30.3
Sopowski, P. (Lab)	4,915	9.8
Day, P. (UKIP)	2,518	5.0
Golden, B. (Green)	1,024	2.1
Majority	11,307	22.60
Electorate	72,858	
Turnout	50,036	68.68

**Member of last parliament*

CONSTITUENCY SNAPSHOT

The post-Second World War history of the seat is dominated by the Conservatives. But the party's lead began to fall through the late 1980s and 1990s. By 1997, the Conservative vote in the seat was around 20 per cent below what it had been two decades before.

Dr Julian Lewis has held the seat since 1997. His majority in 2005 was 6,551. Lewis held the seat in 2010 with a 3.2 per cent swing in his favour and a 11,307 majority.

The seat gained the part-ward of Boldre and Sway from New Forest West.

Encompassing a broad swathe of the famous Hampshire woodland and heath, known for its wild ponies, as well as significant shipping and petrochemical industries, New Forest East is a diverse constituency.

The affluent villages of the forest and a clutch of wealthy seaside settlements provide the seat's middle-class base, but these are offset by the economic presence of the shipping and related industries.

The electorate is concentrated in the east of the seat, principally in the towns of Totton, Marchwood, Hythe and Dibden. The Fawley oil is the single largest employer in the area, with thousands more employed in engineering, transport and manufacturing. The western half of the seat, by contrast, is green, attractive and affluent.

Ian Liddell-Grainger

Bridgwater and West Somerset ***(returning MP)***

New constituency

Tel: 020 7219 8149
E-mail: liddelli@parliament.uk
Website: www.liddellgrainger.org.uk

Conservative

Date of birth: 23 February 1959; Son of late David Liddell-Grainger, farmer, and Ann Grainger

Education: Millfield School, Somerset; South of Scotland Agricultural College, Edinburgh (National Certificate of Agriculture 1978); Married Jill Nesbitt 1985 (1 son 2 daughters)

Non-political career: Major Fusiliers TA; Family farm Berwickshire 1980-85; Managing director property management and development companies group 1985-2000; Councillor: Tynedale District Council 1989-95, Northern Area Council 1992-95

Political career: Contested Torridge and Devon West 1997 general election. Member for Bridgwater 2001-10, for Bridgwater and West Somerset since 6 May 2010 general election; *Select Committees:* Member: Public Administration 2001-10, Scottish Affairs 2002-05, Environment, Food and Rural Affairs 2003-05, Crossrail Bill 2006-07, Environmental Audit 2007-10; Contested Tyne and Wear 1994 European Parliament election; Member Conservative agricultural forum 1992-97; President Tyne Bridge Conservative Association 1993-96

Political interests: Business, economy, defence, rural affairs, farming, taxation, education; USA, Vietnam, Africa especially South Africa, Hong Kong, Singapore, Switzerland

Other organisations: Member IPU, CPA

Recreations: Walking, travel, skiing, family, gardening

Ian Liddell-Grainger MP, House of Commons, London SW1A 0AA
Tel: 020 7219 8149 E-mail: liddelli@parliament.uk
Constituency: 16 Northgate, Bridgwater, Somerset TA6 3EU
Tel: 01278 458383 Fax: 01278 433613
Website: www.liddellgrainger.org.uk

GENERAL ELECTION RESULT

		%
Liddell-Grainger, I. (Con)*	24,675	45.3
Butt Philip, T. (Lib Dem)	15,426	28.3
Pearce, K. (Lab)	9,332	17.1
Hollings, P. (UKIP)	2,604	4.8
Treanor, D. (BNP)	1,282	2.4
Graham, C. (Green)	859	1.6
Cudlipp, B. (Ind)	315	0.6
Majority	9,249	16.97
Electorate	76,560	
Turnout	54,493	71.18

**Member of last parliament*

CONSTITUENCY SNAPSHOT

The new seat of Bridgwater and West Somerset includes all the wards from the old Bridgwater seat with the addition of the old Taunton seat.

Bridgwater has been in Tory hands since the 1950s. Although support had fallen since a peak in the 1970s, the seat is still relatively safe for the party.

Ian Liddell-Granger was first elected in 2001 and was re-elected in 2005 with a 8,469 majority. Liddell-Grainger won this new seat in 2010 with a majority of 9,249.

Taking its name from the small industrial town and port of Bridgwater, this seat stretches along north-west Somerset to the Devon border, taking in the Quantock Hills, part of Exmoor, the beautiful cliffs around Porlock, and the resort town of Minehead.

The major employment sectors in the constituency are retailing, manufacturing, health, and social services. In addition tourism is important to the local economy, as is agriculture. Visitors are attracted to the region not just by the natural beauty of the area, but also by the famous Bridgwater Carnival. Former fishing villages have transformed themselves into tourist villages.

David Lidington

Aylesbury (returning MP)

Boundary changes

Tel: 020 7219 3432
E-mail: davidlidingtonmp@parliament.uk
Website: www.davidlidington.co.uk

Conservative

Date of birth: 30 June 1956; Son of Roy and Rosa Lidington

Education: Haberdashers' Aske's School, Hertfordshire; Sidney Sussex College, Cambridge (MA history, PhD); Married Helen Parry 1989 (4 sons)

Non-political career: British Petroleum 1983-86; Rio Tinto Zinc 1986-87; Special Adviser to Douglas Hurd: as Home Secretary 1987-89, as Foreign Secretary 1989-90; Senior consultant, Public Policy Unit 1991-92

Political career: Contested Vauxhall 1987 general election. Member for Aylesbury since 9 April 1992 general election; PPS: to Michael Howard as Home Secretary 1994-97, to William Hague as Leader of the Opposition 1997-99; Opposition Spokesperson for Home Affairs 1999-2001; Shadow: Financial Secretary 2001-02, Minister for Agriculture and the Fisheries 2002, Secretary of State for: Environment, Food and Rural Affairs 2002-03, Northern Ireland 2003-07, Minister for Foreign and Commonwealth Affairs 2007-10; Minister of State, Foreign and Commonwealth Office 2010-; *Select Committees:* Member: Education 1992-96; Chair International Office and Conservatives Abroad

Political interests: Europe, Hong Kong

Other organisations: Aylesbury Conservative

Recreations: History, choral singing, reading

David Lidington MP, House of Commons, London SW1A 0AA
Tel: 020 7219 3432 Fax: 020 7219 6438
E-mail: davidlidingtonmp@parliament.uk
Constituency: 100 Walton Street, Aylesbury,
Buckinghamshire HP21 7QP Tel: 01296 482102 Fax: 01296 398481
Website: www.davidlidington.co.uk

GENERAL ELECTION RESULT

		%
Lidington, D. (Con)*	27,736	52.2
Lambert, S. (Lib Dem)	15,118	28.4
White, K. (Lab)	6,695	12.6
Adams, C. (UKIP)	3,613	6.8
Majority	12,618	23.73
Electorate	77,934	
Turnout	53,162	68.21

**Member of last parliament*

CONSTITUENCY SNAPSHOT

In 1997 the Conservative current Tory MP David Lidington's vote dropped below 50 per cent for the first time since 1979, but David Lidington (MP since 1992) still retained a majority of 8,419.

Labour made small gains again in 2001, but Lidington increased his majority to 10,009. In 2005 Lidington was re-elected with a 11,065 majority.

The seat was retained by Lidington in 2010 with a 12,618 majority following a 2.1 per cent swing from the Liberal Democrats.

The seat lost Great Missenden, Prestwood and Heath End and part of the Ballinger, South Heath and Chartridge ward to Chesham and Amersham. It also lost Icknield and The Risboroughs to Buckingham, and part of Hambleden Valley to Wycombe. Aston Clinton, Cold harbour, Elmhurst and Watermead, Greater Hughenden, and Quarrendon wards are now entirely within the seat, having previously been shared with Buckingham or Wycombe.

As well as the urban centre of Aylesbury, this relatively rural seat in Buckinghamshire includes small outlying towns and villages such as Aston Clinton, Stokenchurch and Wendover. The Prime Minister's country residence at Chequers is also here.

The public sector is a significant source of employment: Stoke Mandeville Hospital is the largest employer and the headquarters of both the Buckinghamshire County Council and Aylesbury Vale District Councils are in Aylesbury.

Rt Hon **Peter Lilley**

Hitchin and Harpenden ***(returning MP)***

Boundary changes

Tel: 020 7219 4577
E-mail: lilleyp@parliament.uk
Website: www.peterlilley.co.uk

Conservative

Date of birth: 23 August 1943; Son of Arnold and Lillian (née Elliott) Lilley

Education: Dulwich College, London; Clare College, Cambridge (BA natural sciences and economic sciences 1965); Married Gail Ansell 1979

Non-political career: Economic adviser in developing countries 1966-72; Investment adviser on North Sea oil and other energy industries 1972-84; Partner, W Greenwell & Co 1979-86; Director: Great Western Resources Ltd 1985-87, Greenwell Montague Stockbrokers 1986-87 (head, oil investment department); JP Morgan Claverhouse Investment Trust 1997-2008, Idox Plc 2002- Melchior Japan Investment Trust 2006- Tethys Petroleum Ltd 2006-; Member, School of Management Advisory Board, Southampton University 2002-

Political career: Contested Haringey, Tottenham October 1974 general election. Member for St Albans 1983-97, for Hitchin and Harpenden 1997-2010, for Hitchin and Harpenden (revised boundary) since 6 May 2010 general election; Joint PPS: to Lord Bellwin as Minister of State and William Waldegrave as Parliamentary Under-Secretary of State, Department of Environment 1984, to Nigel Lawson, as Chancellor of the Exchequer 1984-87; Economic Secretary to the Treasury 1987-89; Financial Secretary to the Treasury 1989-90; Secretary of State for: Trade and Industry 1990-92, Social Security 1992-97; Member, Shadow Cabinet and Shadow Chancellor of the Exchequer 1997-98; Deputy Leader of the Opposition (with overall responsibility for development of party policy) 1998-99; Chair Bow Group 1973-75; Consultant director, Conservative Research Department 1979-83; Contested Leadership of the Conservative Party June 1997; Chair Globalisation and Global Poverty Policy Group 2006-

Political interests: Economic policy, European Union, education, race relations; France

Other organisations: Trustee, Parliamentary Contributory Pension Fund; Chairman, House of Commons Members Fund; PC 1990; Carlton, Beefsteak; *Publications:* You Sincerely Want to Win? – Defeating Terrorism in Ulster (1972); Lessons for Power (1974); Co-author Delusions of Income Policy (1977); Contributor End of the Keynesian Era (1980); Thatcherism, the Next Generation (1989); The Mais Lecture Benefits and Costs: Securing the Future of the Social Security (1993); Patient Power (Demos, 2000); Common Sense on Cannabis (Social Market Foundation, 2001); Taking Liberties (Adam Smith Institute, 2002); Save Our Pensions (Social Market Foundation, 2003); Identity Crisis (Bow Group, 2004); Too Much of a Good Thing (Centre for Policy Studies, 2005); Tony Duke of York (Bow Group, 2006); In It Together – Report of Commission on Global Poverty (Conservative Party, 2007); Paying for Success (Policy Exchange, 2008)

Recreations: Mending ancient walls

Rt Hon Peter Lilley MP, House of Commons, London SW1A 0AA
Tel: 020 7219 4577 Fax: 020 7219 3840
E-mail: lilleyp@parliament.uk
Constituency: Riverside House, 1 Place Farm, Wheathampstead, Hertfordshire AL4 8SB Tel: 01582 834344 Fax: 01582 834884
Website: www.peterlilley.co.uk

GENERAL ELECTION RESULT

		%
Lilley, P. (Con)*	29,869	54.6
Quinton, N. (Lib Dem)	14,598	26.7
de Botton, O. (Lab)	7,413	13.6
Wilkinson, G. (UKIP)	1,663	3.0
Wise, R. (Green)	807	1.5
Henderson, M. (Ind)	109	0.2
Byron, S. (CURE)	108	0.2
Hannah, E. (YRDPL)	90	0.2
Rigby, P. (Ind)	50	0.1
Majority	15,271	27.91
Electorate	73,851	
Turnout	54,707	74.08

**Member of last parliament*

CONSTITUENCY SNAPSHOT

The seat was created in 1997 and in that year the Conservatives' Peter Lilley polled just under 46 per cent of the vote to win the seat by over 6,500 votes. At the 2001 election he increased his share of the vote but his majority dropped marginally.

The Conservatives increased their majority to just under 11,400 in 2005, polling a little below 50 per cent of the vote. In 2010 Lilley held the seat with a strong 15,271 majority.

The seat gained the part-wards of Graveley and Wymondley from North East Hertfordshire, and Sandridge from St Albans, while losing the part-wards of Letchworth Wilbury to North East Hertfordshire, and Marshalswick North to St Albans.

This Hertfordshire constituency is made up of the towns of Hitchin and Harpenden, and from the many surrounding villages. Harpenden is close to the M1 and Hitchin is close to the A1, both benefitting economically from these good transport links.

Many of the inhabitants of Harpenden commute into London, although some employment can also be found in the adjoining towns of Stevenage, Letchworth and Luton. Hitchin is the more socially diverse of the two towns and, with its old market town roots, is the more self-sufficient and self-contained of the two.

Stephen Lloyd

Eastbourne

Boundary changes

Tel: 020 7219 3000
E-mail: stephen.lloyd.mp@parliament.uk

Date of birth: 15 June 1957; Son of John Lloyd, retired shipping director, and late Nuala Lloyd, nurse

Education: St George's College, Weybridge; Married Patricia 1993 (divorced 2001)

Non-political career: Commodity broker, Cominco UK Ltd 1977-80; Actor 1981-82; Proprietor, Radio Production Company 1983-90; Membership and campaigns manager, Hearing Concern 1990-92; Freelance campaigns and buiness development co-ordinator, various leading charities 1992-98; Business development director and head of diversity services, Grass Roots Group plc 1998-2005; Freelance business development consultant, including Grass Roots Group, Federation of Small Business 2005-

Political career: Contested Beaconsfield 2001 and Eastbourne 2005 general elections. Member for Eastbourne since 6 May 2010 general election; Maidenhead Liberal Democrats: Chair 1999-2002, Press officer 1999-2002; Membership secretary, Chilterns region 1999-2002

Political interests: Crime prevention and victim support, small business, fairness in equality issues, the environment, international development

Other organisations: Electoral Reform Society; Liberal Democrat Business Forum; Greenpeace; Amnesty International; Fellow, Royal Society of Arts; *Publications:* Age of Opportunity (Liberal Democrats) 2000 Challenge of Disability (Grass Roots Group) 1998

Recreations: Reading, classic movies, eating out

Stephen Lloyd MP, House of Commons, London SW1A 0AA
Tel: 020 7219 3000 E-mail: stephen.lloyd.mp@parliament.uk
Constituency: 100 Seaside Road, Eastbourne, East Sussex BN21 3PF
Tel: 01323 733030 Website: www.eastbournelibdems.co.uk

GENERAL ELECTION RESULT

		%
Lloyd, S. (Lib Dem)	24,658	47.3
Waterson, N. (Con)*	21,223	40.7
Brinson, D. (Lab)	2,497	4.8
Shing, S. (Ind)	1,327	2.6
Needham, R. (UKIP)	1,305	2.5
Poulter, C. (BNP)	939	1.8
Baldry, M. (Ind)	101	0.2
Gell, K. (Ind)	74	0.1
Majority	3,435	6.59
Electorate	77,840	
Turnout	52,124	66.96

**Member of last parliament*

CONSTITUENCY SNAPSHOT

The Conservatives had held this seat for 72 years, until the sitting MP, Ian Gow, was killed outside his constituency home by an IRA car bomb in July 1990. The Liberal Democrats won the subsequent by-election. They lost the seat at the general election when Nigel Waterson regained it for the Tories.

In 2005 Waterson was returned with a reduced majority of 1,124. Waterson was defeated in the 2010 general election with a 4 per cent swing to the Liberal Democrat candidate, Stephen Lloyd, who secured a 3,435 majority.

Boundary changes moved Willingdon ward completely within the seat's boundaries from Lewes, in exchange for East Dean ward.

The elegant seafront of this resort belies what is one of the fastest-growing towns in the region. Also taking in villages such as Wannock, Friston and East Dean, the constituency of Eastbourne includes the spectacular headland of Beachy Head.

The traditionally quiet and refined nature of Eastbourne attracts a significant number of retirees.

Numerous small to medium-sized firms are based in the district and Eastbourne has benefited from growth in the economy. Service industries constitute the largest sector, employing over 32,000 people in the area.

The conference industry continues to thrive here, and in recent years the market for language tuition has grown exceptionally fast. An estimated 40,000 language students visit the town annually.

Tony Lloyd

Manchester Central (returning MP)

Boundary changes

Tel: 020 7219 6626
E-mail: lloydt@parliament.uk
Website: www.tonylloydmp.co.uk

Date of birth: 25 February 1950; Son of late Sydney Lloyd, lithographic printer and Ciceley Lloyd, administrative officer

Education: Stretford Grammar School; Nottingham University (BSc maths); Manchester Business School (diploma in business administration); Married Judith Ann Tear 1974 (1 son 3 daughters)

Non-political career: Business administration lecturer Salford university; GMB; Councillor, Trafford District Council 1979-84

Political career: Member for Stretford 1983-97, for Manchester Central 1997-2010, for Manchester Central (revised boundary) since 6 May 2010 general election; Opposition Spokesperson for: Transport 1988-89, Employment 1988-92, 1993-94, Education 1992-94, The Environment and London 1994-95, Foreign and Commonwealth Affairs 1995-97; Minister of State, Foreign and Commonwealth Office 1997-99; *Select Committees:* Member: North West 2009-10

Political interests: Civil liberties, disarmament, community relations, employment and industrial policy, human rights, overseas aid and development

Other organisations: Leader UK Delegation to Parliamentary Assembly of: Council of Europe/Western European Union 2000-07, OSCE 2005-

Tony Lloyd MP, House of Commons, London SW1A 0AA
Tel: 020 7219 6626 Fax: 020 7219 2585
E-mail: lloydt@parliament.uk
Constituency: Tel: 0161-232 0872 Fax: 0161-232 1865
Website: www.tonylloydmp.co.uk

GENERAL ELECTION RESULT

		%
Lloyd, T. (Lab)*	21,059	52.7
Ramsbottom, M. (Lib Dem)	10,620	26.6
Rahuja, S. (Con)	4,704	11.8
Trebilcock, T. (BNP)	1,636	4.1
O'Donovan, G. (Green)	915	2.3
Weatherill, N. (UKIP)	607	1.5
Sinclair, R. (SLP)	153	0.4
Cartwright, J. (Ind)	120	0.3
Leff, J. (WRP)	59	0.2
Skelton, R. (SEP)	54	0.1
Majority	10,439	26.15
Electorate	90,110	
Turnout	39,927	44.31

**Member of last parliament*

CONSTITUENCY SNAPSHOT

The seat was created in 1974 and has always been held by Labour. However, Labour's vote-share has been declining since 2001. Nevertheless Tony Lloyd, who has been MP here since 1997 since moving from the Stretford seat, won a 9,776 majority in 2005.

Lloyd was re-elected in 2010 with 21,059 votes giving him a majority of 10,439.

The seat gained the Ardwick and Moss Side part-wards from Manchester Gorton and a ward and a part-ward from Manchester Blackley. It lost a part-ward to both Blackley and Broughton and Manchester Withington and three part-wards to Manchester Gorton.

This seat includes the commercial, retail and business core of the city. The seat includes Manchester University, Boddington's brewery, Granada television studios and Chinatown, as well as many newly developed city-centre apartment buildings.

The seat has a diverse ethnic makeup and is home to large Indian, Pakistani and West Indian communities together with an African community, mainly from west Africa, but also in recent years from Somalia.

The city itself is a centre of banking and has a major manufacturing base that employs nearly 300,000 people in the area.

Elfyn Llwyd

Dwyfor Meirionnydd ***(returning MP)***

New constituency

Tel: 020 7219 3555
E-mail: llwyde@parliament.uk
Website: www.elfynllwyd.plaidcymru.org

Date of birth: 26 September 1951; Son of late Huw Meirion and Hefina Hughes

Education: Dyffryn Conwy School; Llanrwst Grammar School; University College of Wales, Aberystwyth (LLB law 1974); College of Law, Chester (Solicitor 1977); Married Eleri, née Llwyd 1974 (1 son 1 daughter)

Non-political career: Solicitor 1977-97; President, Gwynedd Law Society 1990-91; Barrister, Gray's Inn 1997-; Member Select Committee on Standards and Privileges 2005-; Council member, University of Wales, Aberystwyth 1992; Member, Parliamentary Panel UNICEF 1993-; Council member National Library of Wales

Political career: Member for Meirionnydd Nant Conwy 1992-2010, for Dwyfor Meirionnydd since 6 May 2010 general election; Plaid Cymru: Spokesperson for: Transport 1992-94, Trade and Industry 1992-94; Parliamentary Whip 1995-2001, Parliamentary Spokesperson for: Northern Ireland 1997-99, Housing 1997-2005, Local Government 1997-2006, Tourism 1997-2005, Home Affairs 1999-; Leader, Plaid Cymru Parliamentary Party 1999-; Plaid Cymru Spokesperson for: Defence 2001-06, Foreign and Commonwealth Affairs 2004-, Constitutional Affairs 2005-06, Environment, Food and Rural Affairs 2005-; Group Whip 2005-; Plaid Cymru Spokesperson for: Business, Enterprise and Regulatory Reform 2006-09, Justice 2007-, Defence 2009-, Energy and Climate Change 2009-10, Cabinet Office 2009-10, Constitution 2010-; *Select Committees:* Member: Welsh Affairs 1992-97, Welsh Affairs 1998-2001, Standards and Privileges 2005-10, Reform of the House of Commons 2009-10; Member, Plaid Cymru Policy Cabinet 1994-, Parliamentary Leader 1997-

Political interests: Civil liberties, agriculture, tourism, home affairs; Spain, Scotland, USA, Wales, Greece

Other organisations: Parliamentary Friend, NSPCC Wales 1994; Patron Abbeyfield Wales 1994; Hon member, Gorsedd of Bards 1998; Member British Irish Parliamentary Body; Chair, Dolgellau Hatchery Trust; President: Estimaner Angling Association, Betws-y-Coed Football Club, Llanuwchllyn Football Club, Bala Rugby Club; Vice-President, Dolgellau Old Grammarians' Rugby Club

Recreations: Pigeon breeding, choral singing, rugby, fishing, cycling

Elfyn Llwyd MP, House of Commons, London SW1A 0AA
Tel: 020 7219 3555 Fax: 020 7219 2633
E-mail: llwyde@parliament.uk
Constituency: Angorfa, Heol Meurig, Dolgellau, Gwynedd LL40 1LN
Tel: 01341 422661 Fax: 01341 423990
Website: www.elfynllwyd.plaidcymru.org

GENERAL ELECTION RESULT

		%
Llwyd, E. (PlC)*	12,814	44.3
Baynes, S. (Con)	6,447	22.3
Humphreys, A. (Lab)	4,021	13.9
Churchman, S. (Lib Dem)	3,538	12.2
Hughes, L. (Ind)	1,310	4.5
Wykes, F. (UKIP)	776	2.7
Majority	6,367	22.03
Electorate	45,354	
Turnout	28,906	63.73

**Member of last parliament*

CONSTITUENCY SNAPSHOT

Meirionnydd and the Llyn peninsular are combined as the new constituency of Dwyfor Meirionydd. Meirionnydd had been a Liberal seat from 1945 until 1966, when Labour won it. Plaid Cymru's Dafydd Elis-Thomas took the seat in February 1974 and held it in revised forms as Meirionnydd from 1974-83 and Meirionnydd Nant Conwy from 1983-92. Elfyn Llwyd held the seat in 1992 for Plaid Cymru and has enjoyed solid majorities since. The Llyn peninsular was formerly part of the Caernarfon constituency, also held by Plaid Cymru at every general election between February 1974 and 2005. Llwyd won this new seat in 2010 with 44.3 per cent of the vote and a 6,367 majority.

Meirionnydd Nant Conwy had the smallest number of constituents of any seat in England and Wales in 2005, just 32,000. The electorate of the new seat is still small at around 49,000, but is much nearer the UK average.

This seat is in many ways the spiritual home of Welsh nationalism and the Welsh language.

The principal towns are Pwllheli and Porthmadog. However, the seat is largely rural. It takes in a large part of the Snowdonia National Park, Snowdon itself is on the northern border with the new Arfon constituency.

The traditional heavy industry of slate mining is largely a thing of the past. Tourism and hill farming are the main activities. The Llyn peninsular is a popular holiday destination.

Naomi Long

Belfast East

Boundary changes

Tel: 020 7219 3000
E-mail: naomi.long.mp@parliament.uk

Alliance

Date of birth: 13 December 1971; Daughter of Olive Emily Johnston and James Dobbin Johnston

Education: Mersey Street Primary; Bloomfield Collegiate; Queen's University, Belfast (MEng civil engineering 1994); Married Michael Long 1995

Non-political career: Graduate engineer, Parkman (NI) Ltd 1994-96; Queens University, Belfast 1996-99; Mulholland and Doherty Consulting Engineers 1999-2000; Belfast City Council: Councillor 2001-, Alliance Group Leader, Member: Policy and Resources Committee, Development Committee, Town Planning Committee, Belfast District Policing Partnership Board, East Belfast Community Education Centre Management Committee, Lord Mayor of Belfast 2009-

Political career: Member for Belfast East since 6 May 2010 general election; MLA for Belfast East since 26 November 2003: Member, Preparation for Government Committee 2006; Alliance Spokesperson for Office of First Minister and Deputy First Minister 2007-; Alliance Party: Member 1994-, Deputy Leader; Spokesperson for Regional Development 2007-

Naomi Long MP, House of Commons, London SW1A 0AA
Tel: 020 7219 3000 E-mail: naomi.long.mp@parliament.uk
Constituency: 56 Upper Newtownards Road, Belfast BT4 3EL
Tel: 028 9047 2004 Fax: 028 9065 6408

GENERAL ELECTION RESULT

		%
Long, N. (All)	12,839	37.2
Robinson, P. (DUP)*	11,306	32.8
Ringland, T. (UCUNF)	7,305	21.2
Vance, D. (TUV)	1,856	5.4
Donnelly, N. (Sinn Féin)	817	2.4
Muldoon, M. (SDLP)	365	1.1
Majority	1,533	4.45
Electorate	59,007	
Turnout	34,488	58.45

**Member of last parliament*

CONSTITUENCY SNAPSHOT

This was the seat of DUP leader and Northern Ireland's First Minister Peter Robinson. Robinson had held the seat since 1979. In 2005 Robinson's majority was reduced to 5,877 and he was defeated in 2010 with a 22.9 per cent swing to Naomi Long of the Alliance Party.

Boundary changes have added five wards from Strangford while losing two to South Belfast.

Belfast East contains Stormont, with its statue of the Unionist leader Edward Carson dominating the driveway to the Assembly buildings. The seat is predictably the most overwhelmingly Protestant, with fewer than 10 per cent of residents identifying themselves as Catholic. This is the smallest proportion of Catholics in Northern Ireland.

With government buildings, the Harland and Wolff shipyard, an aircraft factory and the city airport within the constituency, unemployment is usually lower than in other parts of Belfast.

The Shorts aerospace plant is of vital importance to the constituency as a whole.

The seat is socially mixed, combining some wards with the highest income levels in Northern Ireland with some with some wards suffering serious deprivation.After decades of decline in the docklands, a massive redevelopment in the area now known as the Titanic quarter is under way around the centrepiece of The Odyssey, a new sports and entertainment centre. Future plans include a blue-chip technology district, high-tech research and an expansion of the modern residential blocks.

Jack Lopresti

Filton and Bradley Stoke

New constituency

Tel: 020 7219 3000
E-mail: jack.lopresti.mp@parliament.uk
Website: www.jacklopresti.com

Conservative

Date of birth: 1969; Married Lucy (2 sons 1 daughter)

Non-political career: Gunner, 266 Battery, Royal Artillery; Served with 29 Commando Regiment RA in Helmand Province, Afghanistan autumn 2008; Estate agent 1998-2001; Independent mortgage broker 2001-05; Regional development manager, Treasurer's Department, Conservative Party 2005-07; Councillor, Bristol City Council 1999-2007

Political career: Contested Bristol East 2001 general election. Member for Filton and Bradley Stoke since 6 May 2010 general election; Contested South West region 2004 European Parliament election

Other organisations: Member: International Churchill Society, General George Patton Historical Society

Recreations: Running half-marathons

Jack Lopresti MP, House of Commons, London SW1A 0AA
Tel: 020 7219 3000 E-mail: jack.lopresti.mp@parliament.uk
Constituency: 5 Westfield Park, Bristol BS6 6LT Tel: 0117-973 6812
Website: www.jacklopresti.com

GENERAL ELECTION RESULT

		%
Lopresti, J. (Con)	19,686	40.8
Boulton, I. (Lab)	12,772	26.4
Tyzack, P. (Lib Dem)	12,197	25.3
Knight, J. (UKIP)	1,506	3.1
Scott, D. (BNP)	1,328	2.8
Lucas, J. (Green)	441	0.9
Johnson, R. (Christian)	199	0.4
None-of-the-Above Vote, Z. (Ind)	172	0.4
Majority	6,914	14.31
Electorate	69,003	
Turnout	48,301	70.00

CONSTITUENCY SNAPSHOT

This new South Gloucestershire seat, Filton and Bradley Stoke, is largely made up of the eastern most Bristol North West seat, whose extent is now limited to the City of Bristol Unitary Authority. The seat also includes four wards from the west of the now defunct Northavon seat, and three wards from the centre-north of Kingswood.

As Bristol North West, eight MPs had represented the seat since 1950 and the pattern of alternation corresponded exactly with that of the victorious party in each general election. Tory Jack Lopresti won the new constituency in 2010 with a 6,914 majority on a notional 6.4 per cent swing from Labour.

Filton is a centre for the aviation industry. Parts for the Airbus A380 are manufactured at the company's Filton plant. Other aerospace companies in Filton include BAE Systems, Rolls-Royce and MBDA factories. In 2003 Concorde returned to Filton to be kept there permanently as the centrepiece of a projected air museum. Other companies in the seat include, Viridor, Hewlett Packard and the Royal Mail.

Cribbs Causeway, just north of Filton airfield, is the largest shopping centre in South West England. The constituency also includes the villages of Almondsbury and Severn Beach to the West.

Jonathan Lord

Woking

No boundary changes

Tel: 020 7219 3000
E-mail: jonathan.lord.mp@parliament.uk

Conservative

Education: Shrewsbury School; Merton College, Oxford (history); Married Caroline (1 son 1 daughter)

Non-political career: Director, Saatchi and Saatchi -2000; International campaigns manager, Hewlitt-Packard; Marketing consultant; Westminster City Council: Councillor 1994-2002, Council Deputy Leader; Councillor, Surrey County Council 2009-

Political career: Contested Oldham West and Royton 1997 general election. Member for Woking since 6 May 2010 general election; President, Oxford University Conservative Association 1983; Campaign manager to Anne Milton MP 2005 general election; Chair, Guildford Conservative Association

Recreations: Cricket, theatre, walking

Jonathan Lord MP, House of Commons, London SW1A 0AA
Tel: 020 7219 3000 E-mail: jonathan.lord.mp@parliament.uk
Constituency: Woking Conservatives, Churchill House, Chobham Road, Woking, Surrey GU21 4AA Tel: 01483 773384
Fax: 01483 770060 Website: www.wokingconservatives.org.uk

GENERAL ELECTION RESULT

		%	+/-
Lord, J. (Con)	26,551	50.3	3.0
Sharpley, R. (Lib Dem)	19,744	37.4	4.5
Miller, T. (Lab)	4,246	8.0	-8.2
Burberry, R. (UKIP)	1,997	3.8	0.9
Roxburgh, J. (TPP)	204	0.4	
Temple, R. (MCCP)	44	0.1	
Majority	6,807	12.90	
Electorate	73,838		
Turnout	52,786	71.49	

CONSTITUENCY SNAPSHOT

This seat has only ever elected Tory MPs and Humfrey Malins was selected to contest the seat in 1997. He had previously represented Croydon North West from 1983, but to Labour in 1992. In 1997 he was tested by the presence of an 'Official Conservative Candidate', who appeared above him on the ballot slip and managed to obtain 3,933 votes. Combined with a swing to the Liberal Democrats, Malins' majority was reduced to just 5,678. This represented a drop of over 12,000 from the notional 1992 majority.

In 2001 Malins' majority was 6,759, but fell to 6,612 in 2005. He retired in 2010 and Jonathan Lord held the seat for the Conservatives with a 6,807 majority.

Woking is the largest town in Surrey and has become a retail and service centre for the stockbroker belt. Extensive office development took place in the town centre in the 1980s attracting industry based on new technologies.

The town has expanded in recent years in both population and business facilities which has led to redevelopment of the town's facilities, including the Ambassadors complex.

The majority of employers based in the constituency are local small- and medium-sized businesses, but large firms such as Cap Gemini, Ernst and Young and British American Tobacco have also relocated to the area.

Tim Loughton

East Worthing and Shoreham ***(returning MP)***

Boundary changes

Tel: 020 7219 4471
E-mail: loughtont@parliament.uk
Website: www.timloughton.com

Conservative

Date of birth: 30 May 1962; Son of Reverend Michael Loughton and Pamela Dorothy Loughton

Education: The Priory School, Lewes, Sussex; Warwick University (BA classical civilisation 1983); Clare College, Cambridge (Research Mesopotamian archaeology 1983-84); Married Elizabeth Juliet MacLauchlan 1992 (1 son 2 daughters)

Non-political career: Fund manager Montagu Loebl Stanley/Flemings London 1984-, Director 1992-2000; General election PA to Tim Eggar MP 1987; Formerly BIFU

Political career: Contested Sheffield Brightside 1992 general election. Member for East Worthing and Shoreham 1997-2010, for East Worthing and Shoreham (revised boundary) since 6 May 2010 general election; Opposition Spokesperson for: Regeneration, Poverty, Regions, Housing 2000-01, Health 2001-03; Shadow Minister for: Health 2003-07, Children 2003-10; Parliamentary Under-Secretary of State, Department for Education 2010-; *Select Committees:* Member: Environmental Audit 1997-2001, European Standing committee C 1999-2001; Chair Lewes Young Conservatives 1978; Vice-chair: Sussex Young Conservatives 1979, Lewes Constituency Conservative Association 1979, South East Area Young Conservatives 1980; Secretary Warwick University Conservative Association 1981-82; Member Bow Group 1985-92; Vice-chair Battersea Conservative Association 1990-91; Member London Area Conservative Executive Committee 1993-96; Life Vice-President Sheffield Brightside Constituency Association 1993-; Deputy Chair Battersea Constituency Conservative Association 1994-96; Executive Committee Member, Selsdon Group 1994-2003; Member Carlton Club Political Committee 1994-2004; Chair Conservative Disability Group 1998-2006

Political interests: Finance, foreign affairs, home affairs, education (special needs), environmental taxation, environment and housing, disability, animal welfare, health, children's issues; Latin America, Middle East, Indian sub-continent

Other organisations: Member, Patron, President, Vice-president numerous Worthing and West Sussex organisations; Member: Royal Institute International Affairs, CPA, IPU; MSi(Dip); Patron, Worthing Hockey

Recreations: Skiing, tennis, hockey, wine, archaeology, classics

Tim Loughton MP, House of Commons, London SW1A 0AA
Tel: 020 7219 4471 Fax: 020 7219 0461
E-mail: loughtont@parliament.uk
Constituency: Haverfield House, 4 Union Place, Worthing,
West Sussex BN11 1LG Tel: 01903 235168 Fax: 01903 219755
Website: www.timloughton.com

GENERAL ELECTION RESULT

		%
Loughton, T. (Con)*	23,458	48.5
Doyle, J. (Lib Dem)	12,353	25.5
Benn, E. (Lab)	8,087	16.7
Glennon, M. (UKIP)	2,984	6.2
Board, S. (Green)	1,126	2.3
Maltby, C. (England)	389	0.8
Majority	11,105	22.95
Electorate	74,001	
Turnout	48,397	65.40

**Member of last parliament*

CONSTITUENCY SNAPSHOT

East Worthing and Shoreham was created in 1997 from the old Shoreham and Worthing seats.

At the general election the Conservative majority fell in both new seats by almost 5,000, with Labour enjoying a corresponding rise, but Tory Tim Loughton was still elected with a majority of 5,000.

Loughton's majority increased to 6,139 in 2001 and was extended further in 2005 to 8,183. In 2010 Loughton held the seat, increasing his majority to 11,105.

The seat lost two part-wards to Worthing West.

The seat is an eclectic mix, containing residential parts of East Worthing, industrial Shoreham-by-Sea, and smaller outlying communities.

The constituency has an above average concentration of elderly residents, who make up almost a quarter of the population.

There is a good deal of light industry in the area, and Shoreham is the premier Sussex port, serving a hinterland of over 400,000 people. In addition, many people are employed by the local authority, tourism and the service sector. Shoreham has the oldest commercial airfield in the UK, used by flying schools, private pilots and the Sussex Police air support unit.

The constituency is adjoined by the South Downs, an area awarded National Park status in 2010, which will affect council planning rights.

Andy Love

Edmonton (returning MP)

Boundary changes

Tel: 020 7219 6377
E-mail: lovea@parliament.uk
Website: www.andylovemp.com

Labour/Co-operative

Date of birth: 21 March 1949; Son of late James Love and Olive Love

Education: Greenock High School; Strathclyde University (BSc physics 1973); Association of Chartered Institute of Secretaries 1996; Married Ruth Rosenthal 1983

Non-political career: Parliamentary Officer Co-operative Party 1993-97; Member (branch chairman 1980-83) TGWU/Unite; National Executive Member, NACO 1989-92; Councillor London Borough of Haringey 1980-86

Political career: Contested Edmonton 1992 general election. Member for Edmonton 1997-2010, for Edmonton (revised boundary) since 6 May 2010 general election; PPS: to Jacqui Smith as Minister of State: Department of Health 2001-03, Department of Trade and Industry 2003-05, to John Healey as Minister of State, Department for Communities and Local Government 2008-09; *Select Committees:* Member: Public Accounts 1997-2001, Regulatory Reform 1999-05, Treasury 2005-10; Chair: Hornsey and Wood Green Labour Party 1987-89, Policy Committee Greater London Labour Party 1992-94, Co-operative Parliamentary Group 1999-2001

Political interests: Housing, regeneration, mutuality, small businesses; Cyprus, Sri Lanka, Lebanon, Mexico

Other organisations: Vice-chair North London FE College 1987-90; Vice-patron: Heal Cancer Charity, Helen Rollason Cancer Appeal 1999-; Patron Nightingale Hospice Trust 2001-; Trustee Industrial Common Ownership Fund (ICOF) 1996-; Fellow Industry and Parliament Trust 2004; FCIS, FRSA; Royal Society of Arts; Muswell Hill Golf Club

Recreations: History, opera, cinema, golf

Andy Love MP, House of Commons, London SW1A 0AA
Tel: 020 7219 6377 Fax: 020 7219 6623
E-mail: lovea@parliament.uk
Constituency: Broad House, 205 Fore Street, Edmonton, London N18 2TZ Tel: 020 8803 0574 Fax: 020 8807 1673
Website: www.andylovemp.com

GENERAL ELECTION RESULT

		%
Love, A. (Lab/Co-op)*	21,665	53.7
Charalambous, A. (Con)	12,052	29.9
Kilbane-Dawe, I. (Lib Dem)	4,252	10.5
Freshwater, R. (UKIP)	1,036	2.6
Johnson, J. (Green)	516	1.3
Basarik, E. (Reform 2000)	379	0.9
Morrison, C. (Christian)	350	0.9
McLean, D. (Ind)	127	0.3
Majority	9,613	23.81
Electorate	63,902	
Turnout	40,377	63.19

**Member of last parliament*

CONSTITUENCY SNAPSHOT

Labour held the Edmonton seat for almost four decades between 1945 and 1983. In 1983 the seat fell to the Conservatives with the election of Ian Twinn. In 1997 the seat was retaken for Labour by Andy Love with a majority of over 14,000 votes.

Since then there have been small swings towards the Conservatives but Love was re-elected with a 8,075 majority in 2005. No change here for Labour's Andy Love. He retained this seat with a slight increase in his vote-share and a 9,613 majority.

The constituency gained Ponders End ward from Enfield North as well as the part-wards of Bush Hill Park and Upper Edmonton from Enfield Southgate. It lost three part-wards to Enfield Southgate and one part-ward to Enfield North.

Edmonton is in north London, above Tottenham, with Chingford and Woodford Green to the east, and Enfield to the north and west.

Cypriots, both Greek and Turkish, are a sizeable local community. A substantial number of people are of Bangladeshi, Afro-Caribbean and African origin.

There are no London Underground stations in the constituency, but there are two railway lines to Liverpool Street in the City. The deteriorating service, run by rail firm WAGN, and overcrowding are issues of concern.

Dr **Caroline Lucas**

Brighton Pavilion

Boundary changes

Tel: 020 7219 7025
E-mail: caroline.lucas.mp@parliament.uk
Website: www.carolineforpavilion.org

Green Party

Date of birth: 9 December 1960

Education: Malvern Girls' College; Exeter University: English literature (BA 1983), English and women's studies (PhD 1989); Kansas University, United States (scholarship 1983-84); Journalism (diploma 1987); Married Richard Savage 1991

Non-political career: Oxfam: Press officer 1989-91, Communications officer, Asia desk 1991-94, Policy adviser on trade and environment 1994-97, Team leader, Trade and investment, Policy department 1998-99; Policy adviser on trade and investment, Department for International Development 1997-98; Author; Councillor, Oxfordshire County Council 1993-97

Political career: Contested Oxford East 1992 general election. Member for Brighton Pavillion since 6 May 2010 general election; MEP for South East 1999-2010: Intergroup on the Welfare and Conservation of Animals: Vice-president 2004-09, President 2009-10; Green Party: National press officer 1987-89, Co-chair, party council 1989-90, Member, regional council 1997-99, Leader 2008-

Political interests: Trade, gender, food safety, animal welfare, development aid, poverty, environment; Palestine, Burma, Tibet

Other organisations: Vice-president: Stop the War Coalition, RSPCA; Member, national council, Campaign for Nuclear Disarmament; Michael Kay Award for animal welfare (2006); Michael Kay Award for services to European animal welfare (RSPCA 2006); *Observer* Ethical Politican of the Year (2007); *Publications:* Co-author: Writing for Women (Oxford University Press 1989); Reforming World Trade (Oxfam 1996); Co-author: With Ruth Mayne: Global Trade and the Rise of New Social Issues (Routledge 1999), Watchful in Seattle: WTO Threats to Public Services, Food and the Environment (1999); With Mike Woodin: The Euro or a Sustainable Future for Britain (2000), Green Alternatives to Globalisation: A Manifesto (Pluto 2004); With Colin Hines: From Seattle to Nice: Challenging the Free Trade Agenda at the Heart of Enlargement (2000), Stopping the Great Food Swap: Relocalising Europe's Food Supply (2001)

Recreations: Gardening, country walks

Dr Caroline Lucas MP, House of Commons, London SW1A 0AA
Tel: 020 7219 7025 E-mail: caroline.lucas.mp@parliament.uk
Website: www.carolineforpavilion.org

GENERAL ELECTION RESULT

		%
Lucas, C. (Green)	16,238	31.3
Platts, N. (Lab)	14,986	28.9
Vere, C. (Con)	12,275	23.7
Millam, B. (Lib Dem)	7,159	13.8
Carter, N. (UKIP)	948	1.8
Fyvie, I. (SLP)	148	0.3
Kara, S. (CURE)	61	0.1
Atreides, L. (Ind)	19	0.0
Majority	1,252	2.42
Electorate	74,004	
Turnout	51,834	70.04

CONSTITUENCY SNAPSHOT

Once a traditional Tory seaside town, dwindling Conservative majorities and boundary changes favourable to Labour made this seat a target in 1997. David Lepper won the seat for Labour with a 16 per cent swing. His majority of 13,181 was reduced by some margin in 2001, and almost halved to 5,030 in 2005.

In 2010 Caroline Lucas was returned as the first Green Party MP to be elected to the House of Commons with a 1,252 majority.

Boundary changes moved part of Hanover and Elm Grove into the constituency from Brighton Kemptown, in exchange for Queen's Park and Moulsecoombe and Bevendean part-wards. Brunswick, Adelaide and Golsmid part-wards move entirely within Hove's boundaries.

The constituency takes in much of visitor-orientated town centre, and stretches inland as far as the base of the South Downs at Patcham and Falmer.

Its two universities mean that the constituency houses a significant student vote. Brighton Pavilion is a more affluent constituency than the neighbouring seat of Brighton Kemptown, and has, on average, a younger population than its neighbour.

Brighton and Hove has over recent years grown to be a major centre for financial services, new media, and business services. Tourism is important locally, and Brighton plays host to an impressively eclectic combination of traditional and modern British culture.

Ian Lucas

Wrexham (returning MP)

No boundary changes

Tel: 020 7219 8346
E-mail: lucasi@parliament.uk
Website: www.ianlucas.co.uk

Labour

Date of birth: 18 September 1960; Son of Colin Lucas, process engineer and Alice Lucas, cleaner

Education: Greenwell Comprehensive School, Gateshead; Royal Grammar School, Newcastle upon Tyne; New College, Oxford (BA jurisprudence 1982); College of Law, Christleton law (Solicitor's Final Exam 1983); Married Norah Anne Sudd 1986 (1 daughter 1 son)

Non-political career: Russell-Cooke Potter and Chapman Solicitors: Articled clerk, assistant solicitor 1983-86; Solicitor's Admission 1985; Assistant Solicitor: Percy Hughes and Roberts 1986-87, Lees Moore and Price 1987-89, Roberts Moore Nicholas Jones 1989-92, DR Crawford 1992-97; Principal Crawford Lucas 1997-2000; Partner Stevens Lucas, Oswestry 2000-01; AMICUS/MSF 1996-

Political career: Contested Shropshire North 1997 general election. Member for Wrexham since 7 June 2001 general election; PPS: to Bill Rammell as Minister of State, Department for Education and Skills 2005-06, to Liam Byrne as Minister of State, Home Office 2007-08; Assistant Government Whip 2008-09; Parliamentary Under-Secretary of State, Department for Business, Innovation and Skills 2009-10; *Select Committees:* Member: Environmental Audit 2001-03, Procedure 2001-02, Transport 2003-05, Public Accounts 2007; Chair Wrexham Labour Party 1992-93; Vice-chair North Shropshire Labour Party 1993-2000; Society of Labour Lawyers 1996-; Fabian Society 2000-

Political interests: Economy, European affairs, health, education, environment, manufacturing; Germany, Japan, USA, Lesotho

Other organisations: Chair Committee member Homeless in Oswestry Action Project 1993-2000; Patron Dynamic Wrexham (for children with disabilities) 2001-; Fellow Industry and Parliament Trust 2005

Recreations: History, film, football, cricket, painting

Ian Lucas MP, House of Commons, London SW1A 0AA
Tel: 020 7219 8346 Fax: 020 7219 1948
E-mail: lucasi@parliament.uk
Constituency: Vernon House, 41 Rhosddu Road, Wrexham, Clwyd LL11 2NS Tel: 01978 355743 Fax: 01978 310051
Website: www.ianlucas.co.uk

GENERAL ELECTION RESULT

		%	+/-
Lucas, I. (Lab)*	12,161	36.9	-8.8
Rippeth, T. (Lib Dem)	8,503	25.8	2.4
Hughes, G. (Con)	8,375	25.4	5.6
Jones, A. (PlC)	2,029	6.2	0.5
Roberts, M. (BNP)	1,134	3.4	0.4
Humberstone, J. (UKIP)	774	2.4	
Majority	3,658	11.09	
Electorate	50,872		
Turnout	32,976	64.82	

**Member of last parliament*

CONSTITUENCY SNAPSHOT

Labour's Dr John Marek was the MP for the constituency from 1983 but retired from Westminster in 2001.

Ian Lucas held the seat for Labour at the 2001 general election with a majority of 9,188, which was only down by just over 2,500 from 1997. The Labour majority was reduced again in 2005, however, Lucas's 6,819 majority still represented a 22 per cent margin. Lucas won a relatively low majority of 3,658 in this usually safe seat due to a strong challenge from the Liberal Democrats in 2010.

Wrexham is the largest town in North Wales, situated close to the English border.

Wrexham has fared better than many similar communities in successfully diversifying its economy in the wake of the collapse of the steel and coal industries.

This is still a major manufacturing centre. Sharp, JCB and Tetrapak are among the large companies with a presence in the Wrexham area.

The large brownfield site at Eagles Meadow has undergone a £95 million redevelopment of Wrexham town centre.

Peter Luff

Mid Worcestershire (returning MP)

Boundary changes

E-mail: luffpj@parliament.uk
Website: www.peterluff.org.uk

Conservative

Date of birth: 18 February 1955; Son of late Thomas Luff, master printer, and late Joyce Luff

Education: Windsor Grammar School; Corpus Christi College, Cambridge (BA economics 1976, MA); Married Julia Jenks 1982 (1 son 1 daughter)

Non-political career: Research assistant to Peter Walker MP 1977-80; Head of private office to Edward Heath MP 1980-82; Company secretary, family stationery business, Luff & Sons Ltd to 1987; Account director, director and managing director, Good Relations Public Affairs Ltd 1982-87; Special Adviser to Lord Young of Graffham as Secretary of State for Trade and Industry 1987-89; Senior consultant, Lowe Bell Communications 1989-90; Assistant managing director, Good Relations Ltd 1990-92

Political career: Contested Holborn and St Pancras 1987 general election. Member for Worcester 1992-97, for Mid Worcestershire 1997-2010, for Mid Worcestershire (revised boundary) since 6 May 2010 general electionion; PPS: to Tim Eggar as Minister of State, Department of Trade and Industry 1993-96, to Lord Mackay of Clashfern as Lord Chancellor 1996-97, to Ann Widdecombe as Minister for Prisons, Home Office 1996-97; Opposition Whip 2000-05; Assistant Chief Whip 2002-05; Parliamentary Under-Secretary of State, Ministry of Defence 2010-; *Select Committees:* Member: Welsh Affairs 1992-97, Consolidation Etc Joint Bills Committee 1995-97, Liaison 1997-2000; Chair: Agriculture 1997-2000; Member: Information 2001-05, Selection 2002-05, Administration 2002-06; Chair: Trade and Industry/Business, Enterprise and Regulatory Reform/Business and Enterprise/Business, Innovation and Skills 2005-10; Member: Liaison 2005-10, Quadripartite (Committees on Strategic Export Controls)/Arms Export Controls 2006-09, Liaison (National Policy Statements Sub-committee) 2009-10, Liaison Sub-Committee 2010, Joint Committee on National Security Strategy 2010; Chair, Conservative Parliamentary Friends of India 2001-05; Member Executive 1922 Committee 2005-

Political interests: Railways, trade and industry, rural affairs, performing arts, international development; China, Falkland Islands, Hong Kong, India, Israel, Mongolia

Other organisations: Patron: Conservative Students 1995-98, Worcestershire ME Support Group; Vice-President: Severn Valley Railway 1997-, Evesham Rowing Club 1997-, Droitwich Canals Trust 1997-; Worcester Birmingham Canal Society 2001-; Chairman, Worcester Cathedral Council 2002-08; Member: Joseph Rowntree Inquiry into Planning for Housing 1992-94, Armed Forces Parliamentary Scheme (Royal Navy) 1996, 2002; Hon Fellow, Chartered Institute of Public Relations; Worcestershire County Cricket; *Publications:* Supporting Excellence – Funding Dance and Drama Students (Bow Group, 1995)

Recreations: Steam railways, theatre, photography, shooting, diving

Peter Luff MP, House of Commons, London SW1A 0AA
E-mail: luffpj@parliament.uk
Constituency: No constituency office publicised Tel: 01905 763952
Website: www.peterluff.org.uk

GENERAL ELECTION RESULT

		%
Luff, P. (Con)*	27,770	54.5
Rowley, M. (Lib Dem)	11,906	23.4
Lunn, R. (Lab)	7,613	15.0
White, J. (UKIP)	3,049	6.0
Matthews, G. (Green)	593	1.2
Majority	15,864	31.15
Electorate	72,171	
Turnout	50,931	70.57

**Member of last parliament*

CONSTITUENCY SNAPSHOT

Previously the constituency had been split between the Mid Worcestershire, Worcester and South Worcestershire seats. In 1997 the seat was contested by the previous MP for Worcester, Peter Luff, who took 47 per cent of the vote, giving him a majority of just under 9,500.

In the 2001 general election the Conservatives strengthened their position on a reduced turnout, breaching the 50 per cent mark. This pattern was repeated in 2005 producing a 2 per cent swing to the Tories. Luff retained the seat with a majority of 15,864 at the 2010 general election.

Recent boundary changes have had only a minor effect to this constituency.

Mid Worcestershire is a picturesque constituency that stretches from the edge of Kidderminster through Droitwich, which is also the major town, through Evesham to Broadway on the edge of the Cotswolds.

The M5 enables both Droitwich and Evesham to act as commuter villages for the West Midlands conurbation, although both also have light industry.

Industrial estates and distribution hubs are expanding. The other major economic forces are tourism, fruit growing and market gardening and horticultural processing and distribution.

Karen Lumley

Redditch

Boundary changes

Tel: 020 7219 3000
E-mail: karen.lumley.mp@parliament.uk
Website: www.tellkaren.com

Conservative

Date of birth: 28 March 1964

Education: Rugby High School for Girls; East Warwickshire College of Further Education (business studies); Married Richard Gareth Lumley 1984 (1 son 1 daughter)

Non-political career: Trainee accountant, Ford Motor Company 1982-84; Assistant accountant, John Bull Group 1984-85; Company secretary, RKL Geological Services Ltd 1989-; Group leader, Wrexham Borough Council 1991-96; Councillor: Clwyd County Council 1993-96, Redditch Borough Council 2001-03; Chair, Vaynor First School, Redditch

Political career: Contested Delyn 1997 and Redditch 2001 and 2005 general elections. Member for Redditch since 6 May 2010 general election; Contested Delyn constituency 1999 National Assembly for Wales election; Deputy chair: Welsh Young Conservatives 1986-87, Welsh Conservative Party 1999-2000

Political interests: Education, health, foreign affairs; Bosnia, Serbia, Montenegro

Recreations: Cooking, knitting, reading

Karen Lumley MP, House of Commons, London SW1A 0AA
Tel: 020 7219 3000 E-mail: karen.lumley.mp@parliament.uk
Constituency: Redditch Conservatives, 37 Worcester Road, Bromsgrove, Worcestershire B61 7DN Tel: 01527 579348
Website: www.tellkaren.com

GENERAL ELECTION RESULT

		%
Lumley, K. (Con)	19,138	43.5
Smith, J. (Lab)*	13,317	30.3
Lane, N. (Lib Dem)	7,750	17.6
Davis, A. (UKIP)	1,497	3.4
Ingram, A. (BNP)	1,394	3.2
White, K. (Green)	393	0.9
Schittone, V. (England)	255	0.6
Beverley, S. (Christian)	101	0.2
Swansborough, P. (Ind)	100	0.2
Fletcher, D. (Nobody)	73	0.2
Majority	5,821	13.22
Electorate	68,550	
Turnout	44,018	64.21

**Member of last parliament*

CONSTITUENCY SNAPSHOT

Redditch was created in 1997; before this it had made up the bulk of Mid Worcestershire, and before that had been included in Bromsgrove and Redditch.

Jacqui Smith took the new seat with a majority of 6,125. Smith retained her seat on a reduced majority of 2,484 votes in 2001.

There was no swing in 2005 and Smith's majority rose slightly to 2,716. In 2010 Smith was defeated. Karen Lumley took the seat for the Conservatives with a majority of 5,821.

Boundary changes were minimal: Inkberrow Ward, which was previously shared between Redditch and Mid Worcestershire, is now completely within the seat's boundaries.

The Redditch constituency sits eight miles south of Birmingham in the north east of Worcestershire and comprises the new town of Redditch and a small amount of surrounding rural countryside.

Redditch was designated a new town in 1964 as part of an effort to deal with the West Midlands' rapidly expanding population.

The seat has a long history of needle-making and houses the National Needle Museum. It is still home to light industry, including needle and fish hook making alongside the headquarters of Halfords.

The town's excellent transport connections have also made it into a dormitory town for Birmingham.

Steve McCabe

Birmingham, Selly Oak ***(returning MP)***

Boundary changes

Tel: 020 7219 3509
E-mail: mccabes@parliament.uk
Website: www.stevemccabe-mp.org.uk

Date of birth: 4 August 1955; Son of James and Margaret McCabe

Education: Port Glasgow, Senior Secondary; Moray House College, Edinburgh (Diploma in Social Studies 1977, Certificate Qualification Social Work 1977); Bradford University (MA social work 1986); Married Lorraine Lea Clendon 1991 (divorced) (1 son 1 daughter)

Non-political career: Social work with young offenders 1977-85; Lecturer in social work NE Worcestershire College 1989-91; Part-time researcher British Association of Social Workers 1989-91; Part-time child protection social worker 1989-91; Central Council for Education in Social Work 1991-97; Member: MSF, UNITE; Shop steward, NALGO 1978-82; Birmingham City Council: Councillor 1990-98, Chair, Transportation Committee 1993-96

Political career: Member for Birmingham Hall Green 1997-2010, for Birmingham, Selly Oak since 6 May 2010 general election; PPS to Charles Clarke: as Secretary of State for Education and Skills 2003-04, as Home Secretary 2004-05; Assistant Government Whip 2006-07; Government Whip 2007-10; *Select Committees:* Member: Deregulation 1997-99, Northern Ireland Affairs 1998-2003, Joint Committee on House of Lords Reform 2003-10, Home Affairs 2005-06

Political interests: Community care, transport, economic issues, police and security issues

Other organisations: Local Cricket Club

Recreations: Reading, football, hill walking

Steve McCabe MP, House of Commons, London SW1A 0AA
Tel: 020 7219 3509 Fax: 020 7219 0367
E-mail: mccabes@parliament.uk
Constituency: No constituency office publicised Tel: 0121-443 3878
Fax: 0121-441 4779 Website: www.stevemccabe-mp.org.uk

GENERAL ELECTION RESULT

		%
McCabe, S. (Lab)*	17,950	38.6
Dawkins, N. (Con)	14,468	31.1
Radcliffe, D. (Lib Dem)	10,371	22.3
Orton, L. (BNP)	1,820	3.9
Burgess, J. (UKIP)	1,131	2.4
Burn, J. (Green)	664	1.4
Leeds, S. (Christian)	159	0.3
Majority	3,482	7.48
Electorate	74,805	
Turnout	46,563	62.25

**Member of last parliament*

CONSTITUENCY SNAPSHOT

From its creation in 1955 until October 1974 the seat was in the hands of Tory MP Harold Gurden. Tom Litterrick won for Labour in 1974. Anthony Beaumont-Dark took the seat back for the Tories in 1979 and held on to it for three terms.

When Lynne Jones won the seat for Labour in 1992 her hold on the seat was no less tenuous than her predecessor's, with a majority of just 2,060. But in 1997 on a 12 per cent swing she won the largest majority in the seat's history.

Jones successfully defended her seat in 2005 before retiring in 2010. Steve McCabe moved from the Hall Green division in to hold the seat for Labour with a majority of 3,482.

Birmingham Selly Oak, though retaining its name, was substantially altered in the boundary review that reduced the city's constituencies from ten to nine. Only two part-wards that existed in the seat's previous incarnation remain. These are a part of Bournville ward and a part of Selly Oak ward. Completely new additions are the wards of Billesley and Brandwood, swapped for Sparkbrook and Springfield with Birmingham Hall Green.

The Selly Oak and Bournville wards resemble the leafy suburbs of neighbouring Edgbaston, but extensive council estate development in the King's Norton ward helped change the seat's character.

Bournville houses many white-collar residents who commute to the city or the university.

Michael McCann

East Kilbride, Strathaven and Lesmahagow

No boundary changes

Tel: 020 7219 3000
E-mail: michael.mccann.mp@parliament.uk

Date of birth: 2 January 1964; Son of Charles and Bridget McCann

Education: St Brides High School; St Andrews High School; Married Tracy 1989 (1 son 1 daughter)

Non-political career: Civil servant, Overseas Development Administration/Department for International Development 1982-92; Scottish officer, Civil and Public Services Association 1992-98; Deputy Scottish secretary, Public and Commercial Services Union 1998-2008; Senior parliamentary researcher to Adam Ingram MP; Elected member, Civil and Public Services Association 1982-92; Member, GMB 1992-; South Lanarkshire Council: Councillor 1999-, Council Deputy Leader 2007-

Political career: Member for East Kilbride, Strathaven and Lesmahagow since 6 May 2010 general election; Member, Labour Party 1987-; Secretary, East Kilbride, Strathaven and Lesmahagow CLP 2004-

Political interests: Energy policy, international aid, economics; Africa, Europe, USA

Recreations: Golf, music

Michael McCann MP, House of Commons, London SW1A 0AA
Tel: 020 7219 3000 E-mail: michael.mccann.mp@parliament.uk
Constituency: c/o South Lanarkshire Council, Beckford Street, Hamilton, Lanarkshire ML3 0AA Tel: 01698 454945

GENERAL ELECTION RESULT

		%	+/-
McCann, M. (Lab)	26,241	51.5	2.8
McKenna, J. (SNP)	11,738	23.0	5.2
Simpson, G. (Con)	6,613	13.0	3.0
Loughton, J. (Lib Dem)	5,052	9.9	-6.6
Robb, K. (Green)	1,003	2.0	-1.3
Houston, J. (Ind)	299	0.6	0.3
Majority	14,503	28.47	
Electorate	76,534		
Turnout	50,946	66.57	

CONSTITUENCY SNAPSHOT

Nearly three decades after East Kilbride was designated a New Town, the resulting population growth forced the creation of a new parliamentary constituency centred on the town and its hinterland in 1974.

Adam Ingram inherited the seat in 1987. His majority reached a peak of 17,384 in 1997.

The seat was redrawn and renamed East Kilbride, Strathaven and Lesmahagow in 2005, incorporating three wards from the old Clydesdale seat. Adam Ingram won the new seat with a majority of 14,723 over the SNP. Labour's Michael McCann had no difficulty holding on to this safe seat for his party, taking a 14,503 majority and over 50 per cent of the vote.

Most constituents are found in East Kilbride to the north of the constituency. The seat stretches south to take in large parts of rural South Lanarkshire.

East Kilbride is one of the more successful new towns. It has grown from a sleepy village of 2,500 to a large town of 75,000. The town is characterised by low unemployment and a highly skilled workforce.

A high proportion of the seat's workforce is employed in manufacturing, with a host of engineering, printing and textile companies surviving alongside new high-tech firms.

Strathaven is a small market town with a ruined castle. It grew as a textiles town in the 18th and 19th centuries. Lesmahagow is a small town which grew around a 12th century priory.

Kerry McCarthy

Bristol East (returning MP)

Boundary changes

Tel: 020 7219 4510
E-mail: mccarthyk@parliament.uk
Website: www.kerrymccarthymp.org

Date of birth: 26 March 1965; Daughter of Oliver Haughney and Sheila Rix

Education: Denbigh High School, Luton; Luton Sixth Form College; Liverpool University (BA Russian, politics and linguistics 1986); Law Society (CPE and final solicitors examinations 1992); Single

Non-political career: Legal assistant South Bedfordshire Magistrates Court 1986-88; Litigation assistant Neves Solicitors, Luton 1988-89; Trainee solicitor Wilde Sapte 1992-94; Legal manager Abbey National Treasury Services 1994-96; Senior counsel, debt markets Merrill Lynch Europe Plc 1996-99; Lawyer The Labour Party 2001; Regional director Britain in Europe campaign 2002-04; Head of public policy The Waterfront Partnership 2004-05; TGWU 1994-2007; Unite 2007-; Luton Borough Council: Councillor 1995-96, 1999-2003, Chair of housing and cabinet member 1999-01; Director of London Luton Airport 1999-2003

Political career: Member for Bristol East 2005-10, for Bristol East (revised boundary) since 6 May 2010 general election; PPS: to Rosie Winterton as Minister of State, Department of Health 2007, to Douglas Alexander as Secretary of State for International Development 2007-09; Assistant Government Whip 2009-10; *Select Committees:* Member: Treasury 2005-07, South West 2009-10; Chair Luton North Constituency Labour Party (CLP) 1994-96; Secretary Luton North CLP 1996-99; National policy forum 1998-2005; Economic policy commission 1998-2005

Political interests: Economic policy, international trade/aid, crime and justice, community cohesion, transport; Russia, Middle East, Somalia

Other organisations: Member: Howard League for Penal Reform, Labour Animal Welfare Society; St George Labour

Recreations: Travel, scuba diving, F1 motor racing

Kerry McCarthy MP, House of Commons, London SW1A 0AA
Tel: 020 7219 4510 Fax: 020 7219 8105
E-mail: mccarthyk@parliament.uk
Constituency: 326A Church Road, St George, Bristol,
Gloucestershire BS5 8AJ Tel: 0117-939 9901 Fax: 0117-939 9902
Website: www.kerrymccarthymp.org

GENERAL ELECTION RESULT

		%
McCarthy, K. (Lab)*	16,471	36.6
Shafi, A. (Con)	12,749	28.3
Popham, M. (Lib Dem)	10,993	24.4
Jenkins, B. (BNP)	1,960	4.4
Collins, P. (UKIP)	1,510	3.4
Vowles, G. (Green)	803	1.8
Wright, S. (England)	347	0.8
Lynch, R. (TUSC)	184	0.4
Majority	3,722	8.27
Electorate	69,448	
Turnout	45,017	64.82

**Member of last parliament*

CONSTITUENCY SNAPSHOT

In the immediate post-Second World War years the old constituency of Bristol South East, from which half of Bristol East was drawn in 1983, was largely supportive of Labour. Tony Benn represented Bristol South East from 1950 until 1983.

Jonathan Sayeed took the new seat for the Conservatives in 1983 and held it until 1992. The seat has stayed with Labour ever since and Kerry McCarthy was elected with a majority of 8,621 in 2005.

Despite a 4.5 per cent swing to the Conservatives, McCarthy held on with a reduced 3,722 majority

The seat has gained two wards from Kingswood, lost two to Bristol West and lost a part-ward to Bristol South.

Brislington West is similar in character to the slightly more affluent northern regions of the Bristol South constituency, comprising terraced Victorian houses occupied by skilled workers or professionals.

Bristol East is more sparsely populated than Bristol South, with large amounts of open space and a marked dependence on car travel.

Many workers in Bristol East are employed to the east of the constituency in the electronics and aerospace operations based just outside the city.

Jason McCartney

Colne Valley

Boundary changes

Tel: 020 7219 3000
E-mail: jason.mccartney.mp@parliament.uk
Website: www.jasonmccartney.com

Conservative

Date of birth: 29 January 1968

Education: Lancaster Royal Grammar School; RAF College, Cranwell (officer training 1988); Leeds Trinity (Post-graduate Diploma broadcast journalism 1997); Married Sally 2002 (2 daughters)

Non-political career: Officer, Royal Air Force 1988-97; Journalist, BBC Radio 1997-98; Broadcast journalist, ITV Yorkshire 1998-2007; Senior lecturer, broadcast journalism, Leeds Trinity 2007-08; Television broadcast consultant, Maypole Media 2007-; Senior lecturer, journalism, Leeds Metropolitan University 2008-; National Union of Journalists: Member 1998-, Father of Chapel, ITV Yorkshire 2005-07

Political career: Member for Colne Valley since 6 May 2010 general election

Political interests: Military, crime, broadcasting, sport, pensions

Other organisations: RAF club; Huddersfield Town Supporters' Trust; Yorkshire County Cricket Club; Huddersfield Town Supporters' Trust

Recreations: Cricket, tennis, Huddersfield Town FC, steam trains, museums with my daughters

Jason McCartney MP, House of Commons, London SW1A 0AA
Tel: 020 7219 3000 E-mail: jason.mccartney.mp@parliament.uk
Constituency: Colne Valley Conservatives, Spring Villa, 16 Church Lane, Brighouse HD6 1AT Tel: 01484 717959 Fax: 01484 712933
Website: www.jasonmccartney.com

GENERAL ELECTION RESULT

		%
McCartney, J. (Con)	20,440	37.0
Turner, N. (Lib Dem)	15,603	28.2
Abrahams, D. (Lab)	14,589	26.4
Fowler, B. (BNP)	1,893	3.4
Roberts, M. (UKIP)	1,163	2.1
Ball, C. (Green)	867	1.6
Grunsell, J. (TUSC)	741	1.3
Majority	4,837	8.75
Electorate	80,062	
Turnout	55,296	69.07

CONSTITUENCY SNAPSHOT

For much of the 1960s and 1970s Colne Valley was fought over by Labour and the Liberals. In 1987 the Conservatives' Graham Riddick won the seat pushing Labour into third place. In 1992 Riddick increased his majority to more than 7,000 and Labour moved back into second place.

In 1995 Riddick was embroiled in the cash-for-questions scandal and lost in 1997 on a swing of more than 10 per cent, as Labour's Kali Mountford secured victory. Mountford's majority was cut to 1,501 in 2005.

Labour was defeated in the 2010 general election with a 6.5 per cent swing going to the Conservative candidate, Jason McCartney.

Boundary changes were minimal, exchanging four part-wards with Huddersfield.

Situated in West Yorkshire but bordering Lancashire, Derbyshire and South Yorkshire, this seat has stretches of open countryside as well as a number of small towns and villages including Holmfirth and Marsden.

The area was once a centre of the West Riding wool industry. The industry is in decline, but there are still some employed in textiles and allied trades.

The constituency has a high level of owner-occupancy and a higher than average proportion of professional and managerial workers.

The biggest single employer in the constituency is the NHS, with St Luke's and Holmfirth hospitals and Huddersfield Royal Infirmary all in the area.

Karl McCartney

Lincoln

Boundary changes

Tel: 020 7219 3000
E-mail: karl.mccartney.mp@parliament.uk

Conservative

Date of birth: 25 October 1968

Education: Birkenhead School for Boys; Newton High School; Willink School, Burghfield; St David's University College (BA geography 1991) (Student Union President 1991-92); Kingston University Business School (MBA 1998); Married Cordelia Emma Julia Pyne 1999 (1 son)

Non-political career: Hasbro UK 1992-93; Agent and researcher, Conservative Central Office 1993-96; Corporate affairs, Corporation of London 1996-2001; Director, MLS Ltd (Consultancy) 2000-; Public relations manager, Norton Rose 2001; London Communications Agency 2002-03; Campaign director, Sir Keith Park Memorial Campaign 2007-; Wrotham Parish Council 1999-2004; Magistrate 1999-; Upper Witham Internal Drainage Board 2007-; Witham Third District Internal Drainage Board 2008-

Political career: Contested Lincoln 2005 general election. Member for Lincoln since 6 May 2010 general election

Political interests: Small business, education, sport, transport, crime and the judiciary; The Commonwealth, Italy, New Zealand, Northern Ireland, Scotland, Wales

Other organisations: Trustee: Friends of Wrotham St Georges 1999-, Lincoln Racecourse Trust 2008-; Freedom of the City of London 1999; Westminster Wanderers, Football Club; Westminster Lobbyists XV; The Fighting Pilgrims, Rugby Club; Conservative Party Agents XI Cricket Club

Recreations: Football, rugby, cricket, snowboarding, croquet, golf, hill walking, classic cars

Karl McCartney MP, House of Commons, London SW1A 0AA
Tel: 020 7219 3000 E-mail: karl.mccartney.mp@parliament.uk
Constituency: c/o Lincoln Conservatives, 1a Farrier Road, Lincoln LN6 3RU Tel: 01522 687261; 07970 039767
Fax: 01522 687261 Website: www.lincolnconservatives.co.uk

GENERAL ELECTION RESULT

		%
McCartney, K. (Con)	17,163	37.5
Merron, G. (Lab)*	16,105	35.2
Shore, R. (Lib Dem)	9,256	20.2
West, R. (BNP)	1,367	3.0
Smith, N. (UKIP)	1,004	2.2
Coleman, E. (England)	604	1.3
Walker, G. (Ind)	222	0.5
Majority	1,058	2.31
Electorate	73,540	
Turnout	45,721	62.17

**Member of last parliament*

CONSTITUENCY SNAPSHOT

The seat has swung in the post-war period from Labour to the Conservatives and back again. After 18 years of Tory representation Labour took the seat back in 1997, when Gillian Merron won with a majority of more than 11,000. There was a tiny swing back to the Tories in 2001, and again in 2005. After the 2005 general election, Merron was left with a 4,614 majority.

Merron was defeated in 2010 with a 5.9 per cent swing to the Conservative candidate, Karl McCartney.

Boundary changes moved part-ward Heighington and Washingborough to Sleaford and North Hykeham, while Skellingthorpe and part-ward Bracebridge Heath and Waddington move into the seat from Sleaford.

Around its ancient cathedral and castle, Lincoln was a historically industrial city, but the economy is now based mainly on public administration, commerce, arable farming, and tourism.

Many of Lincoln's industrial giants have long ceased production in the city, leaving large empty industrial warehouse-like buildings. More recently, these buildings have become multi-occupant units, with the likes of Lincs FM radio station taking up space. Like many other cities in Britain, Lincoln has developed a growing IT economy.

Transport and distribution are important in a city which is the focus of a large agricultural region.

Dr **Gregg McClymont**

Cumbernauld, Kilsyth and Kirkintilloch East

No boundary changes

Tel: 020 7219 3000
E-mail: gregg.mcclymont.mp@parliament.uk
Website: www.greggmcclymont.com

Education: Cumbernauld High School; Glasgow University (MA history 1997); Pennsylvania University, USA (MA history); Oxford University (PhD)

Non-political career: Former speech-writer for John Reid MP; Lecturer, Keble College, Oxford; Fellow and history lecturer, St Hugh's College, Oxford 2007-

Political career: Member for Cumbernauld, Kilsyth and Kirkintilloch East since 6 May 2010 general election

Dr Gregg McClymont MP, House of Commons, London SW1A 0AA
Tel: 020 7219 3000 E-mail: gregg.mcclymont.mp@parliament.uk
Constituency: 30 Park Way, Kildrum, Cumbernauld G67 2BU
Website: www.greggmcclymont.com

GENERAL ELECTION RESULT

		%	+/-
McClymont, G. (Lab)	23,549	57.2	6.2
Hepburn, J. (SNP)	9,794	23.8	1.9
Ackland, R. (Lib Dem)	3,924	9.5	-5.1
Fraser, S. (Con)	3,407	8.3	1.4
O'Neill, W. (SSP)	476	1.2	-1.7
Majority	13,755	33.43	
Electorate	64,037		
Turnout	41,150	64.26	

CONSTITUENCY SNAPSHOT

Labour's Norman Hogg won Dunbartonshire East from the Conservatives in 1979. Hogg held the seat in 1983 when it was altered and renamed Cumbernauld and Kilsyth. His replacement Rosemary McKenna held the seat for Labour in 1997.

In 2005 Cumbernauld and Kilsyth kept its 14 North Lanarkshire wards and gained 17,000 electors from the old Strathkelvin and Bearsden constituency. Despite a swing to the SNP, Rosemary McKenna was returned with a majority of 11,562. Rosemary McKenna retired in 2010 and Gregg McClymont took the mantle with a majority of 13,755.

Bisected by the main road between Glasgow and Stirling and the Forth and Clyde Canal, this seat straddles the border between North Lanarkshire and East Dunbartonshire. Its population is concentrated in the east, especially in Cumbernauld.

Cumbernauld was developed as a New Town as part of the Clyde Valley Regional Plan, whose strategy was to disperse people from the crowded centre of Glasgow.

Cumbernauld is home to A.G. Barr, the maker of Irn-Bru. There is a large HM Revenue and Customs office and a number of call centres.

Parts of the Antonine Wall can be seen as it runs between Kilsyth and Kirkintilloch. The wall marked the most northerly boundary of the Roman Empire.

The A80 through Cumbernauld is being upgraded to motorway, improving the town's links to Glasgow and Stirling.

Dr **William McCrea**

South Antrim (returning MP)

Boundary changes

Tel: 020 7219 8525
E-mail: mccreaw@parliament.uk

Date of birth: 6 August 1948; Son of late Robert Thomas McCrea, farmer, and late Sarah McCrea

Education: Cookstown Grammar School; Marietta Bible College, Ohio, USA (doctorate of divinity 1989); Theological College of Free Presbyterian Church of Ulster; Married Anne McKnight 1971 (2 sons 3 daughters)

Non-political career: Civil servant, Northern Ireland Department of Health and Social Services 1966-82; Director, Daybreak Recording Company 1981-; Board of Governors Magherafelt High School; Magherafelt District Council: Councillor 1973-, Chairman 1977-81, 2002-03

Political career: Member for Mid Ulster 1983 to 17 December 1985 (resigned seat in protest against Anglo-Irish Agreement), 23 January 1986 by-election to 1997, for South Antrim 21 September 2000 by-election to 2001, for South Antrim 2005-10, for South Antrim (revised boundary) since 6 May 2010 general election; Member, Public Accounts Commission; DUP Spokesperson for Environment, Food and Rural Affairs 2005-, Local Government 2009-; DUP Shadow Leader of the House 2009-; *Select Committees:* Member Chairmen's Panel 2006-10; Northern Ireland Assembly: Member 1982-86; Member, Northern Ireland Forum for Political Dialogue 1996-98; MLA for Mid Ulster 1998-: DUP Spokesperson for the Environment 1998; Deputy Whip DUP Assembly Group; Member, Preparation for Government Committee 2006-07; Vice-Chairman, DUP Central Executive Committee 1998-; Member, DUP Environmental Policy Group 1998-; Chairman, DUP Group on Review of Public Administration, Northern Ireland 2006-

Political interests: Agriculture, health, elderly issues, environment, special needs education, planning; USA

Other organisations: Member: Woodland Trust, The Loyal Orange Order, Royal Black Institution and Apprentice Boys of Derry; Gospel recording artist; *Publications:* In His Pathway – The Story of the Reverend William McCrea (1980)

Recreations: Gospel music, horse riding

Dr William McCrea MP, House of Commons, London SW1A 0AA
Tel: 020 7219 8525 Fax: 020 7219 2347
E-mail: mccreaw@parliament.uk
Constituency: 5-7 School Street, The Square, Ballyclare,
Co Antrim BT39 9BE Tel: 028 9334 2727 Fax: 028 9334 2707

GENERAL ELECTION RESULT

		%
McCrea, W. (DUP)*	11,536	33.9
Empey, R. (UCUNF)	10,353	30.4
McLaughlin, M. (Sinn Féin)	4,729	13.9
Byrne, M. (SDLP)	2,955	8.7
Lawther, A. (All)	2,607	7.7
Lucas, M. (TUV)	1,829	5.4
Majority	1,183	3.48
Electorate	63,054	
Turnout	34,009	53.94

**Member of last parliament*

CONSTITUENCY SNAPSHOT

Clifford Forsythe held the seat for the Ulster Unionist Party from 1983 until his death in 2000. In the resulting by-election David Burnside was narrowly defeated at the hands of the former DUP MP for Mid Ulster Reverend William McCrea.

Burnside managed to take the seat back for his party by a very narrow margin at the 2001 general election. But, in keeping with electoral developments across Northern Ireland, McCrea re-took the seat for the DUP in 2005 with a majority of 3,448. The DUP retained the seat in 2010, McCrea was re-elected with a 1,183 majority.

This seat lost five mostly-suburban Newtonabbey wards from the Glengormley area to North Belfast.

This large rural seat lies at the heart of Ulster to the north of Belfast. It stretches from the river Bann and Lough Neagh in the west to the edge of Belfast. The main towns are Antrim on the banks of Lough Neagh and Ballyclare to the east.

South Antrim has good transport links. Belfast international airport is located at Aldergrove in the constituency. The airport is a major employer, with connected service industries.

This is a largely Protestant and Unionist seat, with Catholics forming just over a quarter of the population.

There is a major eel fishing site at Toome and most of the eels that are eaten in Europe come from this constituency.

Siobhain McDonagh

***Mitcham and Morden** (returning MP)*

Boundary changes

Tel: 020 7219 4678
E-mail: mcdonaghs@parliament.uk
Website: www.siobhainmcdonagh.org.uk

Date of birth: 20 February 1960; Daughter of Breda, née Doogue, psychiatric nurse and Cumin McDonagh, building labourer

Education: Holy Cross Convent, New Malden; Essex University (BA government 1981); Single, no children

Non-political career: Clerical officer, DHSS 1981-83; Housing Benefits assistant 1983-84; Receptionist, Homeless Persons Unit, London Borough of Wandsworth 1984-86; Housing adviser 1986-88; Development co-ordinator, Battersea Church Housing Trust 1988-97; Member, GMB; Councillor London Borough of Merton 1982-1997: Chair Housing Committee 1990-95

Political career: Contested Mitcham and Morden 1987 and 1992 general elections. Member for Mitcham and Morden 1997-2010, for Mitcham and Morden (revised boundary) since 6 May 2010 general election; PPS to John Reid: as Secretary of State for Defence 2005-06, as Home Secretary 2006-07; Assistant Government Whip 2007-08; *Select Committees:* Member: Social Security 1997-98, Health 2000-05, Unopposed Bills (Panel) 2004-10, London 2009-10

Political interests: Health, housing, quality of life, welfare reform

Other organisations: Member: South Mitcham Community Centre, Colliers Wood Community Centre, Grenfell Housing Association, Merton MIND; Vice-President QUIT (smoking cessation charity); Trustee Mitcham Garden Village

Recreations: Travel, friends, music

Siobhain McDonagh MP, House of Commons, London SW1A 0AA
Tel: 020 7219 4678 Fax: 020 7219 0986
E-mail: mcdonaghs@parliament.uk
Constituency: 1 Crown Road, Morden, Surrey SM4 5DD
Tel: 020 8542 4835 Fax: 020 8544 0377
Website: www.siobhainmcdonagh.org.uk

GENERAL ELECTION RESULT

		%
McDonagh, S. (Lab)*	24,722	56.5
Hampton, M. (Con)	11,056	25.2
Coman, L. (Lib Dem)	5,202	11.9
Martin, T. (BNP)	1,386	3.2
Mills, A. (UKIP)	857	2.0
Roy, S. (Green)	381	0.9
Alagaratnam, R. (Ind)	155	0.4
Redgrave, E. (Ind)	38	0.1
Majority	13,666	31.20
Electorate	65,939	
Turnout	43,797	66.42

**Member of last parliament*

CONSTITUENCY SNAPSHOT

Bruce Douglas-Mann represented Mitcham and Morden for Labour from its creation in 1974, and held it for the party in 1979. Then in 1981, just weeks after being reselected by his constituency party, he defected to the SDP. Mann submitted himself for re-election, but lost to the Conservative Angela Rumbold by 4,000 votes.

Labour's vote-share increased at each subsequent election and in 1997 Siobhain McDonagh finally unseated Rumbold on her third attempt.

Labour's vote-share fell by 4 per cent in 2005 but they won more votes than all the others put together, with McDonagh winning a 12,560 majority. She achieved a majority of 13,666 in 2010.

Boundary changes were minimal and related only to the seven wards that straddled the seat with Wimbledon. Colliers Wood, Lavender Fields, and St Helier wards are now completely within the seat's boundaries, while the other four wards have moved to Wimbledon.

This south-west London seat comprises areas such as Colliers Wood which are very much part of London, as well as areas around Mitcham Common which identify more with Surrey.

With so many commuters transport into London is always going to be a big issue here. A new Tramlink extension is planned, linking Mitcham to Tooting and the London Underground.

Dr **Alasdair McDonnell**

Belfast South ***(returning MP)***

Boundary changes

Tel: 020 7219 8528
E-mail: mcdonnella@parliament.uk
Website: www.alasdairmcdonnell.com

Social Democratic and Labour Party

Date of birth: 1 September 1949; Son of late Charles McDonnell and late Margaret (née McIlhatton)

Education: St McNissis College, Garron Tower, Co Antrim; University College Dublin Medical School (MB, BCh, BAO 1974); Married Olivia Nugent 1998 (2 daughters 2 sons)

Non-political career: Junior hospital doctor, Belfast 1975-79; Full-time GP 1979-99; Part-time GP 1999-2009; Member, BMA; Councillor, Belfast City Council 1977-81, 1985-2001: Deputy Mayor of Belfast 1995-96

Political career: Contested North Antrim 1970, Belfast South 1979 general election, 1982 by-election, 1983, 1987, 1992, 1997 and 2001 general elections. Member for Belfast South 2001-05, for Belfast South (revised boundary) since 6 May 2010 general election; SDLP Spokesperson for: Employment and Learning 2005-07, Economic Development 2005-07, Education 2005-08, Health 2005-, Enterprise, Trade and Investment 2007-08, Europe 2008-, Enterprise and Regulatory Reform 2008-09, Innovation and Universities 2008-09, Northern Ireland Affairs 2008-, Business, Innovation and Skills 2009-; *Select Committees:* Member: Northern Ireland Affairs 2005-10; Member Northern Ireland Forum for Political Dialogue 1996; Northern Ireland Assembly: MLA for Belfast South 1998-; Member, Preparation for Government Committee 2006-07; SDLP Spokesperson for Enterprise, Trade and Investment 2007-; Deputy Leader, SDLP 2004-10

Political interests: Urban renewal, economic reconstruction, job creation, information technology, biotechnology; Atlantic Canada, France, Germany, Netherlands, Serbia and Balkans, USA

Dr Alasdair McDonnell MP, House of Commons, London SW1A 0AA Tel: 020 7219 8528 Fax: 020 7219 2832
E-mail: mcdonnella@parliament.uk
Constituency: 120A Ormeau Road, Belfast BT7 2EB
Tel: 028 9024 2474 Fax: 028 9043 9935
Website: www.alasdairmcdonnell.com

GENERAL ELECTION RESULT

		%
McDonnell, A. (SDLP)*	14,026	41.0
Spratt, J. (DUP)	8,100	23.7
Bradshaw, P. (UCUNF)	5,910	17.3
Lo, A. (All)	5,114	15.0
McGibbon, A. (Green)	1,036	3.0
Majority	5,926	17.33
Electorate	59,524	
Turnout	34,186	57.43

**Member of last parliament*

CONSTITUENCY SNAPSHOT

Reverend Robert Bradford held the seat, first for Vanguard, then as an Ulster Unionist, from February 1974 until his assassination in November 1981. Reverend Martin Smyth, a long-standing leader of the Orange Order, won the resulting by-election and held the seat for the Ulster Unionist Party until 2005.

The rival unionist parties failed to agree an electoral pact after Smyth's retirement in 2005 and the subsequently split unionist vote allowed the SDLP's Alasdair McDonnell to become the seat's first nationalist representative with a majority over the DUP of 1,235. The seat was retained by McDonnell with a 8.4 per cent swing to the party in 2010.

South Belfast gained four wards: Hillfoot and Wynchurch from East Belfast, and Carryduff East and Carryduff West from Strangford.

Belfast South consists of the southern quarter of the Belfast City Council area parts of Castlereagh. As well as being home to Queen's University and its large student population, this affluent constituency is also home to many of Belfast's most historic landmarks: City Hall, the Europa Hotel, the opera house and the famous Victorian Crown Bar.

The biggest employers are Queen's University Belfast, the City Hospital and numerous call-centres.

Tourism is a growing sector as visitor numbers rise following a decline in sectarian violence. The Botanic Gardens are the most visited site in Northern Ireland after the Giant's Causeway.

John McDonnell

Hayes and Harlington (returning MP)

Boundary changes

Tel: 020 7219 6908
E-mail: mcdonnellj@parliament.uk
Website: www.john-mcdonnell.net

Date of birth: 8 September 1951; Son of late Robert and Elsie McDonnell

Education: Great Yarmouth Grammar School, Burnley Technical College; Brunel University (BSc government and politics); Birkbeck College, London University (MSc politics and sociology); Married Marilyn Cooper 1971 (divorced 1987) (2 daughters); married Cynthia Pinto 1995 (1 son)

Non-political career: Shopfloor production worker 1968-73; Assistant head, social insurance department, National Union of Mineworkers 1977-78; Researcher, TUC 1978-82; Head of policy unit, London Borough of Camden 1985-87; Chief Executive: Association of London Authorities 1987-95, Association of London Government 1995-97; Former Shop Steward, UNISON; Co-ordinator, RMT Parliamentary Group 2002-; Chair: Bakers and Allied Workers Union Parliamentary Group, PCS Parliamentary Group; Member: Justice Trade Unions Group, ASLEF Parliamentary Group; Secretary: FBU Group, NUJ Group, Justice Unions Group; Councillor GLC 1981-86: Chair Finance Committee 1982-85, Deputy Leader 1984-85

Political career: Contested Hayes and Harlington 1992 general election. Member for Hayes and Harlington 1997-2010, for Hayes and Harlington (revised boundary) since 6 May 2010 general election; *Select Committees:* Member: Deregulation and Regulatory Reform 1999-2002, Unopposed Bills (Panel) 1999-2004; Member Labour Party: Committee on Ireland, CND; Chair: Labour Representation Committee, Socialist Campaign Group of MPs; Member UNISON Group; Chair: RMT Group, PCS Group; Secretary: FBU Group, Justice Trade Unionist Group, NUJ Group

Political interests: Economics, local and regional government, Irish affairs, environment, aviation, public administration; Gambia, Iran, Ireland, Kenya, Lango, Nulo Mountains, Punjab, Somalia, Tanzania

Other organisations: Chair Friends of Lake Farm Country Park; Member: Hayes Irish Society, Hayes and Harlington History Society, Hayes and Harlington Community Development Forum, Hayes and Harlington Canal Society; Member, Friends of Ireland – Coalition in support of Belfast Agreement; Chair: Britain and Ireland Human Rights Centre, Hands Off Venezuela Group, Hands Off People of Iran; Treasurer Liberation; Member, London Wildlife Trust; Hayes and Harlington Workingmen's; Hillingdon Outdoor Activities Centre; Wayfarer Sailing Association; Vice-president, Hayes Football Club; Patron, Hayes Cricket Club; *Publications:* Editor, Labour Herald; Another World is Possible: a manifesto for 21st century socialism

Recreations: Sailing, football refereeing, cycling, gardening, theatre, cinema

John McDonnell MP, House of Commons, London SW1A 0AA
Tel: 020 7219 6908 E-mail: mcdonnellj@parliament.uk
Constituency: Pump Lane, Hayes, Middlesex UB3 3NB
Tel: 020 8569 0010 Fax: 020 8569 0109
Website: www.john-mcdonnell.net

GENERAL ELECTION RESULT

		%
McDonnell, J. (Lab)*	23,377	54.8
Seaman-Digby, S. (Con)	12,553	29.4
Khalsa, S. (Lib Dem)	3,726	8.7
Forster, C. (BNP)	1,520	3.6
Cripps, A. (NF)	566	1.3
Dixon, C. (England)	464	1.1
Lee, J. (Green)	348	0.8
Shahzad, A. (Christian)	83	0.2
Majority	10,824	25.39
Electorate	70,233	
Turnout	42,637	60.71

**Member of last parliament*

CONSTITUENCY SNAPSHOT

This seat has generally been loyal to the Labour Party since 1945. However, Neville Sanderson, elected in 1971, left the party when he joined the SDP in 1981.

In 1983 the Conservative Terry Dicks emerged victorious and held the seat until 1997 when he retired and the seat was won by Labour's John McDonnell by more than 14,000 votes. McDonnell increased his percentage majority, on a smaller share of the vote in 2001. There was a 4 per cent swing to the Conservatives in 2005 but he still achieved a majority of 19,009. McDonnell saw no real change in his vote and held the seat with a majority of 10,824.

The constituency will gained three part wards - Botwell, Heathrow Villages and West Drayton - that were previously shared with Uxbridge.

This is a suburban constituency at the western extreme of the Greater London area. Criss-crossed by motorways and home to industrial land-use, Hayes and Harlington is ethnically diverse, and covers a large geographical area, including most of Heathrow Airport.

Its proximity to Heathrow ensures excellent transport links, situated as it is on the M25, the M4 and A4, and numerous other major thoroughfares.

Heathrow Airport is a major employer for residents of the constituency.

Rt Hon **Pat McFadden**

Wolverhampton South East ***(returning MP)***

Boundary changes

Tel: 020 7219 4036
E-mail: mcfaddenp@parliament.uk
Website: www.patmcfadden.com

Date of birth: 26 March 1965; Son of James and Annie McFadden

Education: Holyrood Secondary School, Glasgow; Edinburgh University (MA politics 1988); Single

Non-political career: Adviser to Donald Dewar MP, Scottish Affairs spokesperson 1988-93; Speechwriter and policy adviser to John Smith MP as Labour Party leader 1993; Policy adviser to Tony Blair MP as Labour Party leader and political secretary to him as Prime Minister 1994-2005; Member: TGWU, Community Union

Political career: Member for Wolverhampton South East 2005-10, for Wolverhampton South East (revised boundary) since 6 May 2010 general election; Parliamentary Secretary, Cabinet Office 2006-07; Minister of State (Employment Relations and Postal Affairs 2007-09), Department for Business, Enterprise and Regulatory Reform/Business, Innovation and Skills 2007-10 (attending Cabinet 2009-10); Shadow Secretary of State for Business, Innovation and Skills 2010-

Other organisations: PC 2008

Recreations: Reading and sport

Rt Hon Pat McFadden MP, House of Commons, London SW1A 0AA
Tel: 020 7219 4036 Fax: 020 7219 5665
E-mail: mcfaddenp@parliament.uk
Constituency: Crescent House, Broad Street, Bilston,
West Midlands WV14 0BZ Tel: 01902 405762 Fax: 01902 402381
Website: www.patmcfadden.com

GENERAL ELECTION RESULT

		%
McFadden, P. (Lab)*	16,505	47.7
Wood, K. (Con)	9,912	28.6
Whitehouse, R. (Lib Dem)	5,207	15.0
Fanthom, G. (UKIP)	2,675	7.7
Handa, S. (Ind)	338	1.0
Majority	6,593	19.03
Electorate	60,450	
Turnout	34,637	57.30

**Member of last parliament*

CONSTITUENCY SNAPSHOT

Unlike both the Wolverhampton South West and North East seats which were Conservative in the 1980s and 1990s, Wolverhampton South East, once known as Bilston, was Labour over those years. Dennis Turner increased his majority to 10,240 in 1992, and 15,182 in 1997.

Turner retired in 2005 and Labour's candidate, Pat McFadden, was able to secure the seat with a 10,495 majority. McFadden retained the seat in 2010 with a reduced majority of 6,593.

The seat gained Coseley East ward from Dudley North and East Park and Ettingshall part-wards from Wolverhampton South West.

Situated north of Dudley, Wolverhampton South East is a long-standing Labour seat. Manufacturing was the traditional industry here, but has been in decline now for some years.

The area covered by this seat has been made a health action zone, with funding channelled into local innovation projects and voluntary organisations.

Alison McGovern

Wirral South

Boundary changes

Tel: 020 7219 3000
E-mail: alison.mcgovern.mp@parliament.uk
Website: www.alisonmcgovern.org.uk

Date of birth: 1980; Daughter of Mike McGovern, British Rail telecoms engineer, and Ann McGovern, nurse

Education: Wirral Grammar School; University College, London (BA philosophy); Married Ashwin Kumar

Non-political career: Researcher, House of Commons 2002-06; Public affairs manager: Network Rail 2006-08, The Art Fund 2008-09, Creativity, Culture and Education 2009; London Borough of Southwark Council: Councillor 2006-, Deputy Leader, Labour group

Political career: Member for Wirral South since 6 May 2010 general election

Political interests: Employment, education and skills, local regeneration

Other organisations: Trustee, London Gallery

Alison McGovern MP, House of Commons, London SW1A 0AA
Tel: 020 7219 3000 E-mail: alison.mcgovern.mp@parliament.uk
Constituency: 38 Bebington Road, Wirral, Merseyside CH62 5BH
Tel: 0151-644 7990 Website: www.alisonmcgovern.org.uk

GENERAL ELECTION RESULT

		%
McGovern, A. (Lab)	16,276	40.8
Clarke, J. (Con)	15,745	39.5
Saddler, J. (Lib Dem)	6,611	16.6
Scott, D. (UKIP)	1,274	3.2
Majority	531	1.33
Electorate	56,099	
Turnout	39,906	71.13

CONSTITUENCY SNAPSHOT

The seat was formed from parts of Wirral and Bebington and Ellesmere Port in 1983. Barry Porter held it for the Conservative Party from its creation until his death in 1996. At the by-election in February 1997 there was a swing to Labour, whose candidate Ben Chapman won the seat.

Chapman polled 2,000 fewer votes in 2005 but retained the seat with a 3,724 majority. Ben Chapman retired in 2010 and Alison McGovern held the seat for Labour with a majority of 531.

The seat gained the part-wards of Bebington and Bromborough from Birkenhead, in exchange for the part-wards of Prenton and Rock Ferry. It also lost the part-wards of Pensby and Thingwall and West Kirkby and Thurstaton to Wirral West.

The Wirral has long been home to the more affluent sections of Merseyside society, containing the more comfortable suburbs of Liverpool and Birkenhead. Wirral South also contains a substantial element of the peninsula's petrochemical industry.

The issues here that most concern voters are public services. Many of the middle-class voters in this constituency commute to work in Liverpool through the Mersey Tunnel, which connects the Wirral peninsula with the rest of Merseyside.

Jim McGovern

Dundee West (returning MP)

No boundary changes

Tel: 020 7219 4938
E-mail: mcgovernj@parliament.uk
Website: www.jimmcgovern.co.uk

Date of birth: 17 November 1956; Son of Thomas and Alice McGovern

Education: Lawside Roman Catholic Academy, Dundee; Telford College, Edinburgh (City and Guilds Glazing Craft) (1976); Married Norma Ward 1991 (1 son 1 daughter)

Non-political career: Glazier: Lindsay and Scott 1973-87, Dundee District Council 1987-97; GMB official 1997-2005; GMB; Councillor Tayside Regional Council 1994-96

Political career: Member for Dundee West since 5 May 2005 general election; PPS to Pat McFadden as Minister of State, Department for Business, Enterprise and Regulatory Reform 2007-08; *Select Committees:* Member: Scottish Affairs 2005-07, 2008-10

Political interests: Employment rights; Cuba, Ireland, Poland, Spain

Recreations: Reading, gym, watching football

Jim McGovern MP, House of Commons, London SW1A 0AA
Tel: 020 7219 4938 Fax: 020 7219 4812
E-mail: mcgovernj@parliament.uk
Constituency: 7 West Wynd (off Perth Road), Dundee DD1 4JQ
Tel: 01382 322100 Fax: 01382 322696
Website: www.jimmcgovern.co.uk

GENERAL ELECTION RESULT

		%	+/-
McGovern, J. (Lab)*	17,994	48.5	4.0
Barrie, J. (SNP)	10,716	28.9	-1.1
Barnett, J. (Lib Dem)	4,233	11.4	-3.0
Stewart, C. (Con)	3,461	9.3	1.0
McBride, A. (Ind)	365	1.0	
McFarlane, J. (TUSC)	357	1.0	
Majority	7,278	19.60	
Electorate	63,013		
Turnout	37,126	58.92	

**Member of last parliament*

CONSTITUENCY SNAPSHOT

The Western Dundee seat has returned a Labour Member at every election since the Second World War. From 1979 to 2005 Ernie Ross had a majority peaking at almost 12,000 in 1997. This fell in 2001 to 7,000.

The two Dundee seats were extended north beyond the city boundaries into Angus in 2005. Ernie Ross's successor Jim McGovern won for Labour with a majority of 5,379. A key SNP target, Jim McGovern increased his majority to 7,278 in 2010.

Dundee was once known for 'jute, jam and journalism': now the jute mills are long closed and Dundee is marketed as the 'city of discovery' in an attempt to increase tourism. The area remains a hive of industry, with food processing and publishing still important and new high-tech firms establishing themselves.

More than half the population live in council or ex-council estates and the skyline is crowded with tower blocks. The cityscape is changing as high rises are demolished under the council's regeneration scheme and the large-scale development of private sector homes continues. Residents are still by and large staunchly working-class, but there are some more middle-class areas around Dundee Law park.

The city centre, both universities and the airport are in this seat. The seat also contains both Dundee and Dundee United football clubs.

Dundee's most famous former MP was Winston Churchill, who held one of the city's seats (which were then fought jointly) from 1918 until 1922.

Martin McGuinness

Mid Ulster (returning MP)

No boundary changes

Tel: 020 7219 8157

Sinn Féin

Date of birth: 23 May 1950

Education: Christian Brothers' Technical College; Married Bernie 1974 (2 sons 2 daughters)

Non-political career: Sinn Féin: Chief negotiator mid 1980s-, Representative to Dublin Forum for Peace and Reconciliation 1994-95

Political career: Contested Foyle 1983, 1987 and 1992 general elections. Member for Mid Ulster since 1 May 1997 general election; Member, Northern Ireland Assembly 1982; Chief Negotiator, Sinn Féin, Castle Buildings Talks 1997-98; MLA for Mid Ulster 1998-: Minister for Education, Northern Ireland Assembly 1999-2002 (suspension); Member, Preparation for Government Committee 2006-07; Deputy First Minister 2007-; Member, Sinn Féin 1970-

Political interests: South Africa

Recreations: Cooking, walking, reading, fly-fishing

Martin McGuinness MP, House of Commons, London SW1A 0AA
Tel: 020 7219 8157
Constituency: 26 Burn Road, Cookstown, Co Tyrone BT80 8DN
Tel: 028 8676 5850 Fax: 028 8676 6734
E-mail: sinnfeincookstown@yahoo.com

GENERAL ELECTION RESULT

		%	+/-
McGuinness, M. (Sinn Féin)*	21,239	52.0	4.9
McCrea, I. (DUP)	5,876	14.4	-8.9
Quinn, T. (SDLP)	5,826	14.3	-3.0
Overend, S. (UCUNF)	4,509	11.0	
Millar, W. (TUV)	2,995	7.3	
Butler, I. (All)	397	1.0	
Majority	15,363	37.62	
Electorate	64,594		
Turnout	40,842	63.23	

**Member of last parliament*

CONSTITUENCY SNAPSHOT

Despite the nationalist majority in Mid Ulster, the seat was held by unionists for most of its history. William McCrea of the DUP gained the seat in 1983 and held it until 1997 when the nationalist vote, increased by boundary changes for that election, swung behind the high-profile figure of Martin McGuinness.

McGuinness quickly built up his electoral base, extending his majority in 2001 and 2005. In the 2010 general election McGuiness' majority was 15,363 giving him a 52 per cent share of the vote.

This rural constituency lies between the Sperrin Mountains in the west and Lough Neagh in the east. It covers part of Dungannon and all of Cookstown and Magherafelt district councils. Its key towns are Cookstown, Magherafelt and Coalisland. However, the vast majority of the electorate is found in numerous villages.

The local economy is largely agricultural. Brick-making takes place near Coalisland and there are several sand and gravel quarries.

Tourism centres on Lough Neagh, the largest freshwater lake in the British Isles. It is particularly marketed as a venue for angling trips.

Rt Hon **Anne McGuire**

Stirling (returning MP)

No boundary changes

Tel: 020 7219 5829
E-mail: mcguirea@parliament.uk
Website: www.annemcguiremp.org.uk

Date of birth: 26 May 1949; Daughter of late Albert Long, railway signalman, and late Agnes Long, shop worker

Education: Our Lady of St Francis Secondary School, Glasgow; Glasgow University (MA politics with history 1971); Notre Dame College of Education (Diploma in Secondary Education 1975); Married Len McGuire 1972 (1 son 1 daughter)

Non-political career: Supply teacher history/modern studies 1982-84; Development worker/senior manager Community Service Volunteers 1984-93; Depute Director Scottish Council for Voluntary Organisations 1993-97; National Executive, GMB 1987-91; Councillor, Strathclyde Regional Council 1980-82

Political career: Member for Stirling 1997-2005, for Stirling (revised boundary) since 5 May 2005 general election; PPS to Donald Dewar as Secretary of State for Scotland December 1997-98; Assistant Government Whip 1998-2001; Government Whip 2001-02; Parliamentary Under-Secretary of State: Scotland Office 2002-05, Department for Work and Pensions (Minister for Disabled People) 2005-08; Member: Labour Party Scottish Executive 1984-97; Chair Labour Party Scotland 1992-93

Political interests: European Union, rural development, urban regeneration; USA, Germany, China

Other organisations: PC 2008

Recreations: Reading, walking, watching football

Rt Hon Anne McGuire MP, House of Commons, London SW1A 0AA
Tel: 020 7219 5829 Fax: 020 7219 2503
E-mail: mcguirea@parliament.uk
Constituency: 22 Viewfield Street, Stirling FK8 1UA
Tel: 01786 446515 Fax: 01786 446513
Website: www.annemcguiremp.org.uk

GENERAL ELECTION RESULT

		%	+/-
McGuire, A. (Lab)*	19,558	41.8	5.8
Dalrymple, B. (Con)	11,204	23.9	-1.1
Lindsay, A. (SNP)	8,091	17.3	4.7
Reed, G. (Lib Dem)	6,797	14.5	-6.2
Ruskell, M. (Green)	746	1.6	-1.4
Henke, P. (UKIP)	395	0.8	0.4
Majority	8,354	17.85	
Electorate	66,080		
Turnout	46,791	70.81	

**Member of last parliament*

CONSTITUENCY SNAPSHOT

Labour's held Stirling and Falkirk and the renamed Stirling, Falkirk and Grangemouth for the whole of the post-war period.

Michael Forsyth won a redrawn Stirling for the Conservatives in 1983. However, in 1997 Labour's Anne McGuire achieved a swing of 7.7 per cent giving her an impressive majority of 6,411.

In 2005 Stirling's boundaries were enlarged slightly to include the remainder of Stirling council area. McGuire retained her seat but her majority was reduced to 4,767. Anne McGuire held the seat in 2010 with an increased majority of 8,354.

The seat is centred on the ancient Scottish burgh with its hilltop castle and includes historic sites Bannockburn and Stirling Bridge. In March 2002 Stirling achieved city status. With good transport connections to the major cities of Glasgow and Edinburgh, Stirling is home to a large number of commuters. It is a relatively prosperous area with a substantial financial services sector.

The electorate is concentrated in the city but the seat extends to Loch Lomond, the Trossachs (including Loch Katrine), Killin and Loch Tay: some 800 square miles of countryside. Tourism is of growing importance to the area and the Loch Lomond and The Trossachs region became Scotland's first National Park in 2000.

Anne McIntosh

***Thirsk and Malton** (returning MP)*

New constituency

Tel: 020 7219 3541
E-mail: mcintosha@parliament.uk
Website: www.epolitix.com/webminster/Anne-McIntosh

Conservative

Date of birth: 20 September 1954; Daughter of Dr Alastair McIntosh, medical practitioner, and Grethe-Lise McIntosh

Education: Harrogate Ladies' College; Edinburgh University (LLB 1977); Århus University, Denmark (European law 1978); Married John Harvey 1992

Non-political career: Trainee, EEC Competition Directorate, Brussels 1978; Legal adviser, Didier & Associates, Brussels 1979-80; Apprentice, Scottish Bar, Edinburgh 1980-82; Admitted to Faculty of Advocates 1982; Advocate, practising with European Community Law Office, Brussels 1982-83; Adviser, European Democratic Group, principally on Transport, Youth Education, Culture, Tourism, Relations with Scandinavia, Austria and Yugoslavia 1983-89

Political career: Contested Workington 1987 general election. Member for Vale of York 1997-2010, for Thirsk and Malton since 6 May 2010 general election; Opposition Spokesperson for Culture, Media and Sport 2001-02; Shadow Minister for: Transport 2002-03, Environment and Transport 2003-05, Foreign Affairs 2005, Work and Pensions 2005-06, Children, Young People and Families 2006-07, Environment, Food and Rural Affairs 2007-10; *Select Committees:* Member: Environment, Transport and Regional Affairs 1999-2001, Environment, Transport and Regional Affairs (Transport Sub-Committee) 1999-2001, European Standing Committee C 1999-2001, European Scrutiny 2000-03, Transport, Local Government and the Regions (Transport Sub-Committee) 2001-02, Transport, Local Government and the Regions (Urban Affairs Sub-Committee) 2001-02, Transport, Local Government and the Regions 2001-02, Transport 2003-05, Environment, Food and Rural Affairs 2007-10; European Parliament: MEP for Essex North East 1989-94, and for Essex North and Suffolk South 1994-99: European People's Party Bureau Member 1994-97; Executive member 1922 Committee 2000-01

Political interests: Transport, tourism, legal affairs, animal welfare; Central and Eastern Europe, Scandinavia

Other organisations: President Yorkshire First – Enterprise in Yorkshire; Member: Yorkshire Agricultural Society, Anglo-Danish Society; Vice-President National Eye Research (Yorkshire) Advisory Board; Patron Thirsk Museum Society; Co-Chair, European Transport Safety Council 1994-99; President, Anglia Enterprise in Europe 1989-99; Fellow Industry and Parliament Trust 1995; Graduate Armed Forces Parliamentary Scheme, Royal Navy 2000; Honorary Doctorate of Laws Anglia Polytechnic University 1997; Yorkshire Agricultural Society; Royal Over-seas League; Royal Automobile Club

Recreations: Swimming, reading, cinema

Anne McIntosh MP, House of Commons, London SW1A 0AA
Tel: 020 7219 3541 Fax: 020 7219 0972
E-mail: mcintosha@parliament.uk
Constituency: Thirsk and Malton Conservative Association, 109 Town Street, Old Malton, North Yorkshire YO17 7HD Tel: 01845 523835
Website: www.epolitix.com/webminster/Anne-McIntosh

GENERAL ELECTION RESULT

		%
McIntosh, A. (Con)*	20,167	52.8
Keal, H. (Lib Dem)	8,886	23.3
Roberts, J. (Lab)	5,169	13.5
Horton, T. (UKIP)	2,502	6.6
Clark, J. (Lib)	1,418	3.7
Majority	11,281	29.52
Electorate	76,231	
Turnout	38,215	50.13

**Member of last parliament*

CONSTITUENCY SNAPSHOT

The new seat covers the entire Ryedale district as well as the Hambleton council areas formerly in the Vale of York.

This seat is largely a combination Vale of York and Ryedale. The Vale of York seat was created in 1997 when Tory Anne McIntosh won the seat with a majority of nearly 10,000. In 2001 and 2005 McIntosh further pulled away and in 2005 she registered a 13,712 majority.

Ryedale briefly departed from the Tory fold in 1986, when a Liberal won the seat at a by-election. However, John Greenway won the seat back for the Tories at the general election a year later. A Lib Dem challenge in 1997 failed to unseat him and by 2005 Greenway's majority was 10,469.

Anne McIntosh was elected for this new seat in 2010 at a deferred election caused by the death of the UKIP candidate prior to the general election. Her majority is 11,281.

Agriculture and its associated industries are the predominant features of the Thirsk area, covering the rich, mainly flat farmland to the north of York. There is some light engineering.

The rolling acres and charming villages of North Yorkshire belie the fact that manufacturing is the areas biggest source of employment.

Tourism and leisure is the area's second biggest employer. Flamingo Land at Kirkby Misperton alone attracts a million visitors a year, and other attractions include Castle Howard and Filey seaside resort.

Ann McKechin

Glasgow North (returning MP)

No boundary changes

Tel: 020 7219 8239
E-mail: mckechina@parliament.uk
Website: www.annmckechinmp.net

Labour

Date of birth: 22 April 1961; Daughter of late William McKechin and of Anne, neé Coyle

Education: Sacred Heart High School, Paisley; Paisley Grammar School; Strathclyde University (LLB Scots law 1981); Single

Non-political career: Solicitor 1983-; Pacitti Jones Solicitors, Glasgow 1986-2000: Solicitor, Partner 1990-2000; TGWU/Unite

Political career: Member for Glasgow Maryhill 2001-05, for Glasgow North since 5 May 2005 general election; PPS to Jacqui Smith as Minister of State: Department of Trade and Industry 2005, Department for Education and Skills 2005; Parliamentary Under-Secretary of State, Scotland Office 2008-10; *Select Committees:* Member: Scottish Affairs 2001-05, Standing Orders 2001-10, Information 2001-05, International Development 2005-09; Contested West of Scotland region 1999 Scottish Parliament election; Glasgow Kelvin Labour Party: Constituency secretary 1995-98, Women's officer 2000-01; Manifesto Group Chair for International Development Policy 2007-08; Member Co-operative Party

Political interests: International development, economics, small businesses; Rwanda, Africa

Other organisations: World Development Movement 1998-2004: Scottish representative 1998-2001, Council member 1999-2004; Member Management Board, Mercycorps Scotland 2003-08; Member Steering Committee WTO Parliamentary Conference 2003-06; Member Delegation to NATO Parliamentary Assembly 2005-08; Member Management Board World Development Trust 2004-08; Fellow Industry and Parliament Trust 2005

Recreations: Dancing, films, art history

Ann McKechin MP, House of Commons, London SW1A 0AA
Tel: 020 7219 8239 Fax: 020 7219 1770
E-mail: mckechina@parliament.uk
Constituency: 154 Raeberry Street, Glasgow G20 6EA
Tel: 0141-946 1300 Fax: 0141-946 1412
Website: www.annmckechinmp.net

GENERAL ELECTION RESULT

		%	+/-
McKechin, A. (Lab)*	13,181	44.5	5.3
Gordon, K. (Lib Dem)	9,283	31.4	4.0
Grady, P. (SNP)	3,530	11.9	-1.0
Boyle, E. (Con)	2,089	7.1	-1.7
Bartos, M. (Green)	947	3.2	-4.4
Main, T. (BNP)	296	1.0	
McCormack, A. (TUSC)	287	1.0	
Majority	3,898	13.16	
Electorate	51,416		
Turnout	29,613	57.59	

**Member of last parliament*

CONSTITUENCY SNAPSHOT

Jim Craigen represented predecessor seat Maryhill from 1974 to 1987 and was succeeded on his retirement by Maria Fyfe who by 1997 had increased Labour's vote-share to nearly 65 per cent.

Ann McKechin kept Labour's share of the vote above 60 per cent in the 2001 general election.

Glasgow seats were substantiall redrawn in 2005. Glasgow North was made up of most of the Maryhill division, a third of Kelvin and a small part of the old Anniesland seat. Ann McKechin's majority was reduced to 3,338. McKechin's majority was reduced to 3,898 by the Liberal Democrats.

This constituency ranges from the wealthy and bohemian West End to the genteel Victorian terraces of Kelvinside and the working-class areas of Maryhill and Summerston. It extends north out of the city past the course of the Antonine Wall.

Features include the Forth and Clyde Canal, Partick Thistle Football Club, and Glasgow University. The University is the second oldest in Scotland, is consistently ranked among the best in the UK, and boasts some of the finest buildings in the city.

Large employers include the Western Infirmary, based in the West End.

Transport in the constituency received a boost with the opening of the Kelvindale Station and the extension to the northern suburban railway line between Maryhill and Anniesland.

Catherine McKinnell

Newcastle upon Tyne North

Boundary changes

Tel: 020 7219 3000
E-mail: catherine.mckinnell.mp@parliament.uk
Website: www.catherinemckinnell.co.uk

Labour

Education: Sacred Heart Comprehensive School, Fenham; Edinburgh University (politics and history 2000); Married Rhys (2 children)

Non-political career: Employment solicitor, Newcastle

Political career: Member for Newcastle upon Tyne North since 6 May 2010 general election

Catherine McKinnell MP, House of Commons, London SW1A 0AA
Tel: 020 7219 3000 E-mail: catherine.mckinnell.mp@parliament.uk
Constituency: 1 Lily Terrace, Westerhope,
Newcastle upon Tyne NE5 2LP Tel: 07885 761749
Website: www.catherinemckinnell.co.uk

GENERAL ELECTION RESULT

		%
McKinnell, C. (Lab)	17,950	40.9
Beadle, R. (Lib Dem)	14,536	33.1
Parkinson, S. (Con)	7,966	18.1
Gibson, T. (BNP)	1,890	4.3
Proud, I. (UKIP)	1,285	2.9
Heyman, A. (Green)	319	0.7
Majority	3,414	7.77
Electorate	67,110	
Turnout	43,946	65.48

CONSTITUENCY SNAPSHOT

In 1997 Labour's Doug Henderson, Member since 1987, captured over 62 per cent of the vote.

In the third biggest swing in the North East in 2005, at 11.2 per cent, the Liberal Democrats received 4,777 more votes than in 2001. Nevertheless Doug Henderson had a margin of 7,023. Doug Henderson retired in 2010. Catherine McKinnell was returned for Labour but the majority fell to 3,414 in the face of a Liberal Democrat advance.

The seat lost its part-wards of Benwell and Scotswood, Fenham, Kenton, and West Gosforth to Newcastle-upon-Tyne Central. It gained Castle, Denton, East Gosforth, Fawdon, and Woolsington wards, which were previously shared with Newcastle upon Tyne Central.

Very little of the seat is composed of built-up districts, instead open countryside, villages and small towns north of the city covers most of the area, encompassing rural, industrial and residential areas.

Though the shipbuilding industry has been in major decline, the constituency is home to many companies that feed into this industry, and some constituents are employed by shipyards in nearby areas or by subcontractors in the constituency.

Newcastle airport, which falls within the constituency boundaries, is a major employer, as are the Sanofi-Winthrop medical laboratory, British Bakers, and Nestlé Rowntree. The seat is also home to Newcastle racecourse.

Mary Macleod

Brentford and Isleworth

Boundary changes

Tel: 020 7219 3000
E-mail: mary.macleod.mp@parliament.uk
Website: www.marymacleod.com

Conservative

Education: Glasgow University

Non-political career: Management consultant, Andersen Consulting; Policy adviser, HM The Queen's private office, Buckingham Palace 1998-99; Managing director, MCG 2002-; Policy adviser to David Willetts MP; School governor

Political career: Contested Ross, Skye and Inverness West 1997 general election. Member for Brentford and Isleworth since 6 May 2010 general election; Member, Conservative Party 1992-; Chair, Conservative Candidates Association

Recreations: Sport, music, art, reading, clay pigeon shooting

Mary Macleod MP, House of Commons, London SW1A 0AA
Tel: 020 7219 3000 E-mail: mary.macleod.mp@parliament.uk
Constituency: Brentford and Isleworth Conservatives, 433 Chiswick High Road, London W4 4AU Tel: 020 8994 1406
Fax: 020 8994 7203 Website: www.marymacleod.com

GENERAL ELECTION RESULT

		%
Macleod, M. (Con)	20,022	37.2
Keen, A. (Lab)*	18,064	33.6
Dakers, A. (Lib Dem)	12,718	23.7
Hargreaves, J. (UKIP)	863	1.6
Hunt, J. (Green)	787	1.5
Winnett, P. (BNP)	704	1.3
Cunningham, D. (England)	230	0.4
Bhatti, A. (Christian)	210	0.4
Pillai, E. (CPA)	99	0.2
Vanneck-Surplice, T. (Ind)	68	0.1
Majority	1,958	3.64
Electorate	83,546	
Turnout	53,765	64.35

**Member of last parliament*

CONSTITUENCY SNAPSHOT

This seat was created in 1974 by the merger of areas of Heston, Isleworth, Brentford and Chiswick and was held by the Tories until 1997.

Brentford and Isleworth was one of several seats in London that Labour won for the first time in 1997. Ann Keen won a majority of 14,424 on a swing of 14 per cent.

Keen held the seat in 2001 and again in 2005, although there was a 6.8 per cent swing from Labour to the Conservatives on the latter occasion. The expenses scandal cost Labour's Ann Keen this seat. Mary MacLeod won a 1,958 majority for the Tories on a 6 per cent swing.

Minor boundary changes moved the wards of Heston Central, Heston East and Hounslow West completely within Feltham and Heston's boundaries.

The constituency contains a diverse mix of communities along the north side of the Thames as it winds through outer west London. Unlike many seats in London, the area nearest to the centre of the city, Chiswick, is the most attractive residential area, while the outer areas, such as Hounslow, have a more inner-city character.

A number of multinationals have established offices along the 'Golden Mile' of the M4 such as GlaxoSmithKline, British Sky Broadcasting and Cable and Wireless.

Heathrow Airport, just to the west of the seat, is also a major employer.

Rt Hon **Patrick McLoughlin**

***Derbyshire Dales** (returning MP)*

New constituency

Tel: 020 7219 3511
E-mail: patrick.mcloughlin.mp@parliament.uk
Website: www.epolitix.com/Patrick-McLoughlin

Conservative

Date of birth: 30 November 1957; Son of Patrick Alphonsos McLoughlin

Education: Cardinal Griffin Comprehensive School, Cannock; Staffordshire College of Agriculture; Married Lynne Patricia Newman 1984 (1 son 1 daughter)

Non-political career: Agricultural worker 1974-79; Various positions with National Coal Board 1979-86; Councillor: Cannock Chase District Council 1980-87, Staffordshire County Council 1981-87

Political career: Contested Wolverhampton South East 1983 general election. Member for West Derbyshire 8 May 1986 by-election to 2010, for Derbyshire Dales since 6 May 2010 general election; PPS: to Angela Rumbold as Minister of State, Department of Education 1987-88, to Lord Young of Graffham as Secretary of State for Trade and Industry 1988-89; Parliamentary Under-Secretary of State, Department of Transport (Minister for Aviation and Shipping) 1989-92; Joint Parliamentary Under-Secretary of State, Department of Employment 1992-93; Parliamentary Under-Secretary of State, Department of Trade and Industry (Trade and Technology) 1993-94; Assistant Government Whip 1995-96; Government Whip 1996-97; Opposition: Pairing Whip 1997-98, Deputy Chief Whip 1998-2005, Chief Whip 2005-10; Parliamentary Secretary to the Treasury 2010-; Chief Whip 2010-; *Select Committees:* Member: Broadcasting 1994-95, Selection 1997-2001, Finance and Services 1998-2005, Accommodation and Works 2001-05, Modernisation of the House of Commons 2004-05, Selection 2005, Administration 2005; National Vice-Chair, Young Conservatives 1982-84

Political interests: Agriculture, education

Other organisations: PC 2005

Rt Hon Patrick McLoughlin MP, House of Commons, London SW1A 0AA Tel: 020 7219 3511
E-mail: patrick.mcloughlin.mp@parliament.uk
Website: www.epolitix.com/Patrick-McLoughlin

GENERAL ELECTION RESULT

		%
McLoughlin, P. (Con)*	24,378	52.1
Naitta, J. (Lib Dem)	10,512	22.5
Swindell, C. (Lab)	9,061	19.4
Guiver, I. (UKIP)	1,779	3.8
Stockell, J. (Green)	772	1.7
Delves, N. (Loony)	228	0.5
Y'Mech, A. (Humanity)	50	0.1
Majority	13,866	29.64
Electorate	63,367	
Turnout	46,780	73.82

**Member of last parliament*

CONSTITUENCY SNAPSHOT

This new constituency covers the most rural part of Derbyshire and is largely based on the former West Derbyshire seat, with the exception of Belper and Duffield, which are now in Mid Derbyshire.

The seat has been Conservative since 1950. Matthew Parris, first elected in 1979, resigned in 1986. By then the Conservative majority was more than 15,000 but at the by-election his successor Patrick McLoughlin won by only 100 votes.

He restored the majority to five figures in 1987, and by 1992 it had topped 18,000. But Labour's national victory in 1997 reduced the Conservative majority to 4,885. The Conservatives rallied somewhat in 2001, and in 2005 a 3.2 per cent swing in their favour brought McLoughlin's majority back into five figures. McLoughlin won the new seat for the Tories in 2010 with a majority of 13,866.

The seat is largely rural with four small market towns - Ashbourne, Bakewell, Matlock and Wirksworth - and over 100 villages.

This is a prosperous area. Traditional industries such as quarrying and agriculture are still strong, but declining, and being partly replaced by growth in tourism related services and farm diversification enterprises.

The area is a prime tourist destination and has an above average number of people employed in tourism related industries.

Angus MacNeil

Na h-Eileanan An Iar** **(returning MP)

No boundary changes

Tel: 020 7219 8476
E-mail: macneila@parliament.uk

SNP

Scottish National Party

Date of birth: 21 July 1970; Son of Iain MacNeil, postman and crofter, and late Clare MacNeil, district nurse

Education: Castlebay Secondary School, Isle of Barra; Nicolson Institute, Stornoway, Isle of Lewis; Strathclyde University (BEng civil engineering 1992); Jordanhill College (PGCE primary teaching and bilingualism 1996); Married Jane Douglas 1998 (3 daughters)

Non-political career: Civil engineer Lilley Construction Ltd, Edinburgh 1992-93; Radio reporter BBC, Inverness 1993-95; Primary teacher Salen Primary School, Mull 1996-98; Gaelic development officer Lochaber 1998-99; Education lecturer part-time Inverness College 1999-

Political career: Contested Inverness East, Nairn and Lochaber 2001 general election. Member for Na h-Eileanan An Iar since 5 May 2005 general election; SNP Spokesperson for: Transport 2005-, Environment 2005-07, Food and Rural Affairs 2005-, Fishing 2005-, Tourism 2005-, Work and Pensions 2007-08, Scotland Office 2008-; *Select Committees:* Member: Scottish Affairs 2005-09; Convener Lochaber branch SNP 1999

Political interests: Economics of Small States; Norway, Iceland, Faroe Islands

Recreations: Football, sailing, fishing

Angus MacNeil MP, House of Commons, London SW1A 0AA
Tel: 020 7219 8476 Fax: 020 7219 6111
E-mail: macneila@parliament.uk
Constituency: 31 Bayhead Street, Stornoway, Isle of Lewis, Outer Hebrides HS1 2DU Tel: 01851 702272 Fax: 01851 701767

GENERAL ELECTION RESULT

		%	+/-
MacNeil, A. (SNP)*	6,723	45.7	0.8
MacSween, D. (Lab)	4,838	32.9	-1.6
Murray, M. (Ind)	1,412	9.6	
Davis, J. (Lib Dem)	1,097	7.5	-0.5
Norquay, S. (Con)	647	4.4	
Majority	1,885	12.81	
Electorate	22,266		
Turnout	14,717	66.10	

**Member of last parliament*

CONSTITUENCY SNAPSHOT

Since the Second World War this seat has been held for long periods by both Labour and the SNP.

From 1935 to 1970 Malcolm Macmillan represented the islands for Labour. He lost the seat to Donald Stewart, the only SNP member elected in 1970. On Stewart's retirement in 1987 the SNP vote collapsed, resulting in the election of Labour's Calum MacDonald.

The SNP halved MacDonald's majority in 2001 and a 9.3 per cent swing to the SNP helped Angus MacNeil take the seat. MacNeil held on to this marginal SNP-Labour seat with an increased 1,885 majority.

The constituency, called by the Gaelic name for the Western Isles, stretches 130 spectacular miles from the Butt of Lewis in the north to Barra Head in the south. Lewis is the largest island, but the seat also includes Harris, North and South Uist, and Benbecula.

Two thirds of the population speaks Gaelic and many northern communities are devoutly Presbyterian.

The number of small crofters helps to explain the relatively high proportion of owner-occupiers. Depopulation, particularly emigration among the 18-29 age group, remains the major issue in the islands, caused by the shortage of employment opportunities.

Traditional industries such as fishing, whisky, farming and Harris tweed are all in decline. Small island schools and hospitals in remote areas will increasingly come under threat of closure.

Stephen McPartland

Stevenage

Boundary changes

Tel: 020 7219 3000
E-mail: stephen.mcpartland.mp@parliament.uk
Website: www.stephenmcpartland.co.uk

Conservative

Date of birth: 9 August 1976

Education: Liverpool College; Liverpool University (BA history 1997); Liverpool John Moores University (MSc technology management 1998); Married Emma

Non-political career: Agent, North East Hertfordshire Conservative Association 2001-10; Membership director, British American Business (American Chamber of Commerce) 2008-10

Political career: Member for Stevenage since 6 May 2010 general election

Political interests: Healthcare (particularly cancer treatment and respiratory diseases), education, satellite technology, international trade, policing, addiction treatment, urban regeneration, government procurement of IT projects; China, India, USA

Recreations: Reading, keeping fit, cinema

Stephen McPartland MP, House of Commons, London SW1A 0AA
Tel: 020 7219 3000 E-mail: stephen.mcpartland.mp@parliament.uk
Constituency: Stevenage Conservatives, 32-33 Beverley Road, Stevenage, Hertfordshire SG1 4PR Tel: 01438 361150
Website: www.stephenmcpartland.co.uk

GENERAL ELECTION RESULT

		%
McPartland, S. (Con)	18,491	41.4
Taylor, S. (Lab)	14,913	33.4
Davies, J. (Lib Dem)	7,432	16.6
Mason, M. (UKIP)	2,004	4.5
Green, M. (BNP)	1,007	2.3
Vickers, C. (England)	366	0.8
Phillips, S. (NCDMV)	327	0.7
Cox, D. (Ind)	80	0.2
Ralph, A. (YRDPL)	31	0.1
Majority	3,578	8.01
Electorate	68,937	
Turnout	44,651	64.77

CONSTITUENCY SNAPSHOT

Labour's Barbara Follett won the Stevenage seat in 1997 with 55.3 per cent of the vote: enough to give her a majority of 11,582. Conservative support fell away, as their MP since 1983 Tim Wood polled only 32.8 per cent of the vote.

In 2005 the Conservative Party enjoyed a 6.9 per cent swing in their favour, and Labour's majority was reduced to 3,139. Labour was defeated with a 8 per cent swing going to the Conservative candidate, Stephen McPartland.

Boundary changes were minimal.

This Hertfordshire constituency is based around the town of Stevenage, which was Britain's first post-Second World War new town, with some notable examples of modern architecture.

Companies in the constituency include ICL, Glaxo Wellcome, Du Pont and the Dynamics Division of British Aerospace, although the latter has cut the number of jobs in the past decade. Financial and business services comprise the largest share of total business in Stevenage.

Wholesale and retail trade and repair of motor vehicles are the largest category of employment, accounting for a fifth of economic activity.

The town has good transport links: it is situated on the main railway line going north from St Pancras, and on the A1(M).

Rt Hon Dr **Denis MacShane**

Rotherham (returning MP)

Boundary changes

Tel: 020 7219 4060
E-mail: macshaned@parliament.uk
Website: www.epolitix.com/denis-macshane

Date of birth: 21 May 1948

Education: Merton College, Oxford (MA modern history); Birkbeck College, London (PhD international economics); Partner Carol Barnes (1 daughter deceased); married Nathalie Pham 1987 (divorced 2003) (1 son 3 daughters)

Non-political career: BBC producer 1969-77; Policy director International Metal Workers' Federation 1980-92; President National Union of Journalists 1978-79 Director European Policy Institute 1992-94; Member: Community Life, National Union of Journalists

Political career: Contested Solihull October 1974 general election. Member for Rotherham 5 May 1994 by-election to 2010, for Rotherham (revised boundary) since 6 May 2010 general election; Foreign and Commonwealth Office 1997-2005: PPS: to Joyce Quin, Derek Fatchett and Tony Lloyd as Ministers of State 1997-99, to Geoff Hoon as Minister of State 1999, Joint PPS to the Ministers of State 1999-2001, Parliamentary Under-Secretary of State 2001-02, Minister of State 2002-05; *Select Committees:* Member: Deregulation 1996-97; Chair Fabian Society 2001-02

Political interests: International economics, European Union, manufacturing; Europe, East and South East Asia

Other organisations: Member: Council Royal Institute of International Affairs, Council of Europe and NATO Parliamentary Assemblies 2005-; Fellow Industry and Parliament Trust 1999; PC 2005; Honorary Fellow, Birkbeck College, London University; *Publications:* Several books on international politics, Edward Heath (biography 2006); Globalising Hatred: The New Antisemitism (2008)

Recreations: Family, walking

Rt Hon Dr Denis MacShane MP, House of Commons, London SW1A 0AA Tel: 020 7219 4060 Fax: 020 7219 6888
E-mail: macshaned@parliament.uk
Constituency: 4 Hall Grove, Rotherham, South Yorkshire S60 2BS
Tel: 01709 837577 Fax: 01709 835622 Website: www.epolitix.com/denis-macshane

GENERAL ELECTION RESULT

		%
MacShane, D. (Lab)*	16,741	44.6
Whiteley, J. (Con)	6,279	16.7
Taylor, R. (Lib Dem)	5,994	16.0
Guest, M. (BNP)	3,906	10.4
Thirlwall, P. (Ind)	2,366	6.3
Vines, C. (UKIP)	2,220	5.9
Majority	10,462	27.89
Electorate	63,565	
Turnout	37,506	59.00

**Member of last parliament*

CONSTITUENCY SNAPSHOT

The closest Labour came to losing the seat since 1945 was at the 1976 by-election, but Stan Crowther still held it by 4,500 votes.

When he retired in 1992 he was replaced by Jimmy Boyce, who died less than two years later. Denis MacShane retained the seat for Labour at the by-election with a 6,954 majority.

In 1997 MacShane's majority grew to more than 21,000, but it fell in 2001 and 2005. There was a bigger swing away from Labour in 2005, but this time it favoured the Lib Dems. Nevertheless, Denis MacShane was returned with a 35 per cent majority. In 2010 MacShane was re-elected with a majority of 10,462.

The seats boundaries were realigned with local government wards. Rotherham gained part of Brinsworth and Catcliffe in exchange for part of Sitwell from Rother Valley, while the seat also gained parts of Rotherham East and Valley from Wentworth with part-wards of Rawmarsh and Silverwood going to its replacement, Wentworth and Dearne.

This urban constituency contains the old coal and steel town of Rotherham as well as its suburbs to the north-west: Greasbrough and Thorpe Hesley.

The decline of its heavy industries led to high unemployment, much of it long-term.

Most new jobs come from call-centres and retail outlets as well as in firms on the industrial estates close to the M1 which forms the constituency's western boundary. More and more people travel to work outside the constituency, especially to Sheffield.

Fiona Mactaggart

Slough (returning MP)

Boundary changes

Tel: 020 7219 3416
E-mail: mactaggartf@parliament.uk
Website: www.fionamactaggart.org.uk

Date of birth: 12 September 1953; Daughter of late Sir Ian Mactaggart and late Rosemary Belhaven

Education: Cheltenham Ladies College; London University: King's College (BA English 1975), Goldsmiths' College (Postgraduate Certificate teaching 1987), Institute of Education (MA 1993)

Non-political career: Vice-president, National Secretary, National Union of Students 1978-81; Press and public relations officer National Council for Voluntary Organisations 1981; General secretary Joint Council for the Welfare of Immigrants 1982-86; Primary school teacher 1987-92; Public relations officer, private property company 1992; Lecturer in primary education Institute of Education 1992-97; Member: TGWU 1982-86, NUJ, ASTMS 1981 NUT 1987-92, AUT 1992-97, GMB 1997-; London Borough of Wandsworth: Councillor 1986-90, Leader Labour Group 1988-90

Political career: Member for Slough 1997-2010, for Slough (revised boundary) since 6 May 2010 general election; PPS to Chris Smith as Secretary of State for Culture, Media and Sport December 1997-2001; Parliamentary Under-Secretary of State, Home Office 2003-06: (Race Equality, Community Policy and Civil Renewal 2003-05, Offender Management and Criminal Justice 2005-06); *Select Committees:* Member: Public Administration 1997-98, Education and Skills/Children, Schools and Families 2006-10, Joint Committee on Human Rights 2009-10; Member: Fabian Society, National Policy Forum

Political interests: Human rights, civil liberties, home affairs, education, arts

Other organisations: Chair, Liberty 1994-96, Editorial Board, Renewal; Chair, Commonweal Housing 2007-

Recreations: Walking, talking, reading, the arts, watching television

Fiona Mactaggart MP, House of Commons, London SW1A 0AA
Tel: 020 7219 3416 Fax: 020 7219 0989
E-mail: mactaggartf@parliament.uk
Constituency: 29 Church Street, Slough, Berkshire SL1 1PL
Tel: 01753 518161 Fax: 01753 550293
Website: www.fionamactaggart.org.uk

GENERAL ELECTION RESULT

		%
Mactaggart, F. (Lab)*	21,884	45.8
Coad, D. (Con)	16,361	34.3
Tucker, C. (Lib Dem)	6,943	14.5
Mason-Apps, P. (UKIP)	1,517	3.2
Kennet, M. (Green)	542	1.1
Chaudhary, S. (Christian)	495	1.0
Majority	5,523	11.57
Electorate	77,068	
Turnout	47,742	61.95

**Member of last parliament*

CONSTITUENCY SNAPSHOT

John Watts was Conservative MP for Slough from 1983 to 1997. In 1983 Watts was elected with a majority of 3,106 over Labour. In 1987 Watts increased his majority to 4,090.

In 1992 Watts' majority fell, with Labour coming within 514 votes of victory. Fiona Mactaggart took the seat in 1997 for Labour, with a 13,071 majority, on the back of a 13.8 per cent swing. In 2005 Mactaggart secured victory with a majority of 7,851.

Mactaggart held the seat for Labour with a 5,523 majority at the 2010 general election.

Slough gained the part-wards of Foxborough, Kederminster and Upton from Windsor.

Slough is in Britain's very own 'silicon valley', but struggles to shake off its unenviable reputation for concrete housing estates and office blocks.

The Slough Trading Estate provides 20,000 jobs in over 400 businesses. Heavy industry has been replaced by modern offices, including those of Nintendo, Black and Decker and online retailer Amazon.com.

Slough is well integrated into the UK transport and communications network: it is situated between the M4, M40 and the M25 and there is an excellent rail link into central London. Slough will be a stop on Crossrail, the new trans-London rail link due to come into service in 2017.

Esther McVey

Wirral West

Boundary changes

Tel: 020 7219 3000
E-mail: esther.mcvey.mp@parliament.uk
Website: www.esthermcvey.com

Date of birth: 24 October 1967; Daughter of James and Barbara McVey

Education: Belvedere School, Liverpool; Queen Mary and Westfield, London (LLB 1990); City University, London (Post-graduate Course radio journalism 1991); John Moore's University, Liverpool (MSc corporate governance 2009, winner North of England Excellence Award)

Non-political career: Director, JG McVey & Co Ltd 2000-06; Managing director, Making It (UK) Ltd 2002-10; Founder, Winning Women 2003-10

Political career: Contested Wirral West 2005 general election. Member for Wirral West since 6 May 2010 general election

Political interests: Law and order and sentencing, transport, education, city regeneration

Other organisations: Board member: Madeleine McCann Fund 2007-08, North West Women's Enterprise Forum 2008-10

Recreations: Theatre, cinema, walking

Esther McVey MP, House of Commons, London SW1A 0AA
Tel: 020 7219 3000 E-mail: esther.mcvey.mp@parliament.uk
Constituency: Wirral West Conservative Association, 24 Meols Drive, Hoylake, Wirral CH47 4AN Tel: 0151-632 1052
Website: www.esthermcvey.com

GENERAL ELECTION RESULT

		%
McVey, E. (Con)	16,726	42.5
Davies, P. (Lab)	14,290	36.3
Reisdorf, P. (Lib Dem)	6,630	16.8
Griffiths, P. (UKIP)	899	2.3
Kirwan, D. (Ind)	506	1.3
James, D. (CSP)	321	0.8
Majority	2,436	6.19
Electorate	55,050	
Turnout	39,372	71.52

CONSTITUENCY SNAPSHOT

The early incumbents of the Wirral seat were long-serving Conservatives. Selwyn Lloyd, who was both Foreign Secretary and Speaker during his long parliamentary career, held the seat for 31 years from 1945. The cabinet minister David Hunt had served in the seat since 1976 when he defeated in 1997 by Stephen Hesford who took the seat on a swing to Labour.

Hesford extended his majority on a reduced turnout in 2001, but was re-elected in 2005 only after a recount. His majority was 1,097.

Stephen Hesford retired in 2010 and Esther McVey won the seat for the Conservatives with a majority of 2,436.

The seat gained two part-wards from Wirral South and one from Wallasey, while losing two part-wards to Birkenhead and two to Wirral West.

On the far side of the Wirral peninsula in north west England, Wirral West is the wealthiest and most rural of the four constituencies on the peninsula, and therefore popular with commuters.

Despite its name, it is in fact situated on the north-western corner of the peninsula facing the Irish Sea and the banks of the river Dee.

Khalid Mahmood

Birmingham, Perry Barr (returning MP)

Boundary changes

Tel: 020 7219 8141
E-mail: mahmoodk@parliament.uk

Date of birth: 13 July 1961

Non-political career: Former engineer; AEEU; Former adviser Danish International Trade Union; Birmingham City Council 1990-93: Councillor, Chair Race Relations

Political career: Member for Birmingham Perry Barr 2001-10, for Birmingham, Perry Bar (revised boundary) since 6 May 2010 general election; PPS to Tony McNulty as Minister of State: Department for Transport 2004-05, Home Office 2005-06; *Select Committees:* Member: Broadcasting 2001-05, Home Affairs 2009-10; Local Constituency Labour Party: Secretary, Vice-chair; Member: Socialist Health Association, Socialist Education Association; Labour Finance and Industry Group: National member, Midlands branch executive member

Political interests: Community relations, British industry, international trade, terrorism

Other organisations: Adviser President of Olympic Council Asia; Member governing body: Neighbourhood forum, South Birmingham CHC

Khalid Mahmood MP, House of Commons, London SW1A 0AA
Tel: 020 7219 8141 Fax: 020 7219 1745
E-mail: mahmoodk@parliament.uk
Constituency: Unit 22, Paper Mill End, Birmingham B44 8NH
Tel: 0121-356 8264/8 Fax: 0121-356 8278

GENERAL ELECTION RESULT

		%
Mahmood, K. (Lab)*	21,142	50.3
Hamilton, K. (Lib Dem)	9,234	22.0
Norton, W. (Con)	8,960	21.3
Ward, M. (UKIP)	1,675	4.0
Tyrrell, J. (SLP)	527	1.3
Hey-Smith, D. (Christian)	507	1.2
Majority	11,908	28.32
Electorate	71,304	
Turnout	42,045	58.97

**Member of last parliament*

CONSTITUENCY SNAPSHOT

Labour's Jeff Rooker won this seat in 1974, and with subsequent boundary changes, he increased his majority to 18,957 in 1997.

Rooker retired in 2001 election and was replaced by Khalid Mahmood. Mahmood was re-elected in 2005 with a 7,948 majority and held the seat in 2010 with a majority of 11,908, giving Labour a 50.3 per cent share of the vote.

Redrawn constituency boundaries sees the seat gain parts of Oscott and Lozells and East Handsworth wards, to bring them fully within the constituency, but surrendered parts of Aston - taking a section out of its bottom right-hand corner - and Kingstanding to Ladywood.

Birmingham Perry Barr is a seat of two distinct parts to the north west of the city: overall the constituency is characterised by leafy suburbs, especially in Oscott and Perry Bar, but the Handsworth wards have inner-city features and pockets of council development.

The main areas of employment are manufacturing and public administration, education and health. By far the largest local employer is Birmingham City University is based in the constituency.

Shabana Mahmood

Birmingham, Ladywood

Boundary changes

Tel: 020 7219 3000
E-mail: shabana.mahmood.mp@parliament.uk
Website: www.shabanamahmood.co.uk

Daughter of Mahmood Ahmed

Education: Lincoln College, Oxford (law)

Non-political career: Former barrister, Berrymans Lace Mawer

Political career: Member for Birmingham, Ladywood since 6 May 2010 general election

Shabana Mahmood MP, House of Commons, London SW1A 0AA
Tel: 020 7219 3000 E-mail: shabana.mahmood.mp@parliament.uk
Constituency: Ladywood Labour, FREEPOST, Birmingham B29 4BR
Tel: 07772 129543 Website: www.shabanamahmood.co.uk

GENERAL ELECTION RESULT

		%
Mahmood, S. (Lab)	19,950	55.7
Khan, A. (Lib Dem)	9,845	27.5
Ghani, N. (Con)	4,277	11.9
Booth, C. (UKIP)	902	2.5
Beck, P. (Green)	859	2.4
Majority	10,105	28.20
Electorate	73,646	
Turnout	35,833	48.66

CONSTITUENCY SNAPSHOT

Its physical contours have changed but Birmingham Ladywood is an old name: Neville Chamberlain defeated Oswald Mosely here in the 1920s. Labour has held the seat since 1929 apart from a brief interlude from 1969 to 1970 when Wallace Lawler won it for the Liberals at a by-election. Clare Short replaced John Sever here in 1983 when he was deselected before the general election.

Clare Short resigned the Labour whip in 2006, sitting as independent, before standing down in 2010. Shabana Mahmood was elected for Labour with a majority of 10,105.

Boundary changes moved part of Aston from Birmingham Perry Barr, a piece of Ladywood from Birmingham Edgbaston, and a part of Nechells from the now defunct Birmingham Sparkbrook and Small Heath. The seat ceded several part-wards to its neighbours, and the former Ladywood borders have been chiselled away from all directions: Washwood Heath to the south-east, Perry Barr to the north and Lozells and East Handsworth to the north-west.

Covering almost all of Birmingham city centre, Ladywood is an inner-city seat.

Ladywood is the most central ward, covering most of the city centre. The Aston and Nechells wards north and north-east of the city centre comprise mainly post-Second World War housing and have a large Muslim community. Birmingham Ladywood has one of the lowest proportions of professional and managerial workers in the country.

Anne Main

St Albans (returning MP)

Boundary changes

Tel: 020 7219 8270
E-mail: maina@parliament.uk
Website: www.annemain.com

Conservative

Date of birth: 17 May 1957; Daughter of Rita and late George Wiseman

Education: Bishop of Llandaff Secondary School, Cardiff; University College of Wales, Swansea (BA English 1978); Sheffield University (PGCE 1979); Married Stephen Tonks 1978 (died 1991) (1 son 2 daughters); married Andrew Jonathan Main 1995 (1 son)

Non-political career: Teaching and family 1979-80; Home-maker 1980-90; Carer for terminally ill husband 1990-91; Single parent and supply teacher 1991-95; NUT 1979-80; Councillor South Buckinghamshire District Council 2001-05

Political career: Member for St Albans 2005-10, for St Albans (revised boundary) since 6 May 2010 general election; *Select Committees:* Member: ODPM/Communities and Local Government 2005-10, Energy and Climate Change 2009-10; Deputy branch chairman, Beaconsfield 2002-05; Chair and founder Conservative Friends of Bangladesh

Political interests: Environment, education, health; Bangladesh

Other organisations: St Albans Civic Society 2003-; Fellow Industry and Parliament Trust 2007; Conservative Women's Club; St Albans Conservative; Beaconsfield Conservative

Recreations: Dog walking, art, reading, food and wine, exploring France

Anne Main MP, House of Commons, London SW1A 0AA
Tel: 020 7219 8270 Fax: 020 7219 3058
E-mail: maina@parliament.uk
Constituency: 104 High Street, London Colney, St Albans, Hertfordshire AL2 1QL Tel: 01727 825100 Fax: 01727 828404
Website: www.annemain.com

GENERAL ELECTION RESULT

		%
Main, A. (Con)*	21,533	40.8
Walkington, S. (Lib Dem)	19,228	36.4
Mills, R. (Lab)	9,288	17.6
Stocker, J. (UKIP)	2,028	3.8
Easton, J. (Green)	758	1.4
Majority	2,305	4.36
Electorate	70,058	
Turnout	52,835	75.42

**Member of last parliament*

CONSTITUENCY SNAPSHOT

In 1997, having previously performed poorly at the polls, Labour won in St Albans, with a sizable 14.7 per cent swing, giving their candidate Kerry Pollard a majority of 4,459.

Mr Pollard slightly increased his majority in 2001, however, he could not hold on in 2005. Ann Main won the seat for the Conservatives with a 6.6 per cent swing, giving her a 1,361 majority.

In 2010 Main was re-elected with a 2,305 majority.

The seat lost its part of the Sandridge ward to Hitchin and Harpenden. It gained the rest of Marshalswick North ward from Hitchin and Harpenden; and Bedmond and Primrose Hill from Watford.

This Hertfordshire constituency contains the cathedral city of St Albans to the north, and the towns of London Colney and Bricket Wood to the south. It is home to many commuters into London.

Two motorways dissect the constituency, the M25 and M1. These communication links have enabled the city and surrounding towns to diversify from traditional businesses, such as printing and musical instrument manufacture, into electronics and service industries.

John Mann

Bassetlaw (returning MP)

Boundary changes

Tel: 020 7219 8345
E-mail: mannj@parliament.uk
Website: www.johnmannmp.com

Date of birth: 10 January 1960; Son of James Mann and Brenda Cleavin

Education: Bradford Grammar School; Manchester University (BA Econ 1982); ITD Diploma 1992; Married Joanna White 1986 (2 daughters 1 son)

Non-political career: Head research and education AEU 1988-90; National training officer TUC 1990-95; Liaison officer National Trade Union and Labour Party 1995-2000; Director Abraxas Communications Ltd 1998-2002; AEEU 1985-; Councillor London Borough of Lambeth 1986-90

Political career: Member for Bassetlaw 2001-10, for Bassetlaw (revised boundary) since 6 May 2010 general election; PPS: to Richard Caborn as Minister for Sport 2005-07, to Tessa Jowell as Minister for: the Olympics and London 2007-08, the Olympics 2008, the Olympics; Paymaster General 2009; *Select Committees:* Member: Information 2001-05, Treasury 2003-05, 2009-10, Treasury (Treasury Sub-Committee) 2003-10, Unopposed Bills (Panel) 2004-10; Contested East Midlands 1999 European Parliament election

Political interests: Small businesses, training, economic regeneration, sport, drugs

Other organisations: Fellow Industry and Parliament Trust 2003; MIPD; IPD, YHA, Manton Miners; *Publications:* Labour and Youth: The Missing Generation (Fabian Society 1985); The Real Deal (Fabian Society 2006)

Recreations: Football, cricket, fellwalking and mountaineering

John Mann MP, House of Commons, London SW1A 0AA
Tel: 020 7219 8345 Fax: 020 7219 5965
E-mail: mannj@parliament.uk
Constituency: 68a Carlton Road, Worksop, Nottinghamshire S80 1PH
Tel: 01909 506 200 Fax: 01909 532447
Website: www.johnmannmp.com

GENERAL ELECTION RESULT

		%
Mann, J. (Lab)*	25,018	50.5
Girling, K. (Con)	16,803	33.9
Dobbie, D. (Lib Dem)	5,570	11.2
Hamilton, A. (UKIP)	1,779	3.6
Whitehurst, G. (Ind)	407	0.8
Majority	8,215	16.57
Electorate	76,542	
Turnout	49,577	64.77

**Member of last parliament*

CONSTITUENCY SNAPSHOT

Since 1935 constituents have elected just three different MPs in the area, all of them representatives of the Labour Party. First World War veteran Captain Fred Bellenger served as Member from 1935 until his death in 1968.

Despite winning the by-election by just 740 votes Bellenger's successor, Joe Ashton, represented Bassetlaw until 2001. After his final election in 1997 his majority was over 17,000.

Labour's position under current MP John Mann has fallen. In 2005 Mann's majority was 10,837 and in 2010 it fell further to 8,215.

Boundary changes were substantial, with the town of Retford moving to the constituency from Newark.

The most northerly constituency in Nottinghamshire, Bassetlaw shares much in common with its near neighbours in South Yorkshire. Both areas were until the early 1990s heavily reliant on the coal mining industry.

The largest employment sector is food manufacture. The largest and best known is Premier Foods in Worksop, producer of brands such as Batchelors and Oxo. Wilkinson also owns a huge distribution centre south of the town.

While still relatively small, there is a growing tourism industry based around the remaining parts of Sherwood Forest.

Gordon Marsden

Blackpool South (returning MP)

Boundary changes

Tel: 020 7219 1262
E-mail: gordonmarsdenmp@parliament.uk
Website: www.gordonmarsden.co.uk

Labour

Date of birth: 28 November 1953; Son of late George Henry and Joyce Marsden

Education: Stockport Grammar School; New College, Oxford (MA history 1976); London University (PhD research in combined historical studies 1976-80); Harvard University (Kennedy Scholarship) 1978-79

Non-political career: Open University tutor/associate lecturer, arts faculty 1977-97; Public relations consultant 1980-85; Chief public affairs adviser to English Heritage 1984-85; Editor: *History Today* 1985-97, *New Socialist* 1989-90; Member, GMB; Member, Association of British Editors; Judge, Ford Conservation Awards UK 1990-97; Board Member, Institute of Historical Research 1996-; President, British Resorts and Destinations Association 1998-, Member, National Skills Commission 2006-

Political career: Contested Blackpool South 1992. Member for Blackpool South 1997-2010, for Blackpool South (revised boundary) since 6 May 2010 general election; PPS: to Lord Irvine of Lairg as Lord Chancellor 2001-03, to Tessa Jowell as Secretary of State for Culture, Media and Sport 2003-05, to Michael Wills as Minister of State, Ministry of Justice 2007, to John Denham as Secretary of State for Communities and Local Government 2009-10; *Select Committees:* Member: Deregulation 1997-99, Education and Employment 1998-2001, Education and Employment (Education Sub-Committee) 1998-2001, Education and Skills 2005-07, Innovation, Universities[, Science] and Skills/Science and Technology 2007-10, Ecclesiastical Committee; Member Fabian Society 1975-: Chairman Young Fabians 1980-81, Chair Research and and Public Committee 2000-01; Chair Seaside and Coastal Towns Manifesto Group 2007-

Political interests: Heritage, education, international affairs, social affairs, disability, human rights; USA, Russia, North Africa, Caribbean, Eastern Europe

Other organisations: President, Blackpool Disability Services 2000-; Trustee, Dartmouth Street Trust; Board: History Today Trust, Gareth Butler Trust; Gibbs Prize in History 1975; Kennedy Scholar, Harvard 1978-79; Parliamentary Fellow St Antony's College, Oxford 2003; Centenary Fellowship Historical Association 2006; *Publications:* Editor, Victorian Values 1990, 1998; Contributor to The History Debate (1990); Low Cost Socialism (1997); Contributor The English Question (Fabian Society 2000); International History of Censorship (2001)

Recreations: Theatre, early music and medieval culture, swimming, heritage sites, architecture

Gordon Marsden MP, House of Commons, London SW1A 0AA
Tel: 020 7219 1262 Fax: 020 7219 5859
E-mail: gordonmarsdenmp@parliament.uk
Constituency: 304 Highfield Road, Blackpool, Lancashire FY4 3JX
Tel: 01253 344143 Fax: 01253 344940
Website: www.gordonmarsden.co.uk

GENERAL ELECTION RESULT

		%
Marsden, G. (Lab)*	14,449	41.1
Bell, R. (Con)	12,597	35.8
Holt, D. (Lib Dem)	5,082	14.4
Goodwin, R. (BNP)	1,482	4.2
Howitt, H. (UKIP)	1,352	3.8
Tun, S. (Integrity)	230	0.7
Majority	1,852	5.26
Electorate	63,025	
Turnout	35,192	55.84

**Member of last parliament*

CONSTITUENCY SNAPSHOT

This seat was for many years a Conservative one. However, the seat moved to Labour in 1997. The MP elected was Gordon Marsden, who has held the seat ever since. His majority decreased by over 3,000 in 2001, but remained fairly constant in 2005.

Marsden was re-elected in 2010 with a 1,852 majority giving Labour a 41 per cent vote-share.

The seat gained the part-ward of Brunswick from Blackpool North and Fleetwood, and lost the wards of Layton and Park to Blackpool North and Cleveleys.

Blackpool is a traditional seaside holiday resort in the North West of England and its southern constituency includes the town's main tourist attractions: piers, tower, pleasure beach and also Blackpool Airport.

The tourist industry has always played a major part in this area. The success of the seaside resort is essential for the local economy. Although it has declined since its heyday, Blackpool has adapted well and now caters for many weekend holidaymakers on short breaks on England's coastline rather than longer-term visitors, as previously. It has many hotels that help make Blackpool the most visited seaside resort in the Britain.

Rt Hon **Francis Maude**

Horsham (returning MP)

Boundary changes

Tel: 020 7219 2494
E-mail: francis.maude.mp@parliament.uk
Website: www.francismaude.com

Date of birth: 4 July 1953; Son of late Baron Maude of Stratford-upon-Avon, PC (Life Peer), author and journalist, and late Lady Maude

Education: Abingdon School; Corpus Christi, Cambridge (MA history 1976) (Hulse Prize and Avory Studentship); College of Law (Forster Boulton Prize and Inner Temple Law Scholarship 1977); Married Christina Jane Hadfield 1984 (2 sons 3 daughters)

Non-political career: Called to Bar, Inner Temple 1977; Practising barrister 1977-85; Head of global privatisation, Salomon Bros International 1992-93; Managing Director, global privatisation, Morgan Stanley & Co Ltd 1993-97; Chairman, Deregulation Task Force 1993-97; Non-executive Director: Benfield Group plc 1999-, Deputy chair 2003-08, Businesses for Sale Company plc 2000-02; Chairman: Prestbury Holdings PLC 2002-09, Jubilee Investment Trust plc 2003-07, The Mission Marketing Group 2006-; Councillor, Westminster City Council 1978-84

Political career: Member for North Warwickshire 1983-92, for Horsham 1997-2010, for Horsham (revised boundary) since 6 May 2010 general election; PPS to Peter Morrison as Minister of State for Employment 1984; Government Whip 1985-87; Parliamentary Under-Secretary of State, Department of Trade and Industry 1987-89; Minister of State, Foreign and Commonwealth Office 1989-90; Financial Secretary to the Treasury 1990-92; Member, Shadow Cabinet 1997-2001: Shadow Secretary of State: for National Heritage 1997, for Culture, Media and Sport 1997-98; Shadow: Chancellor of the Exchequer 1998-2000, Secretary of State for Foreign and Commonwealth Affairs 2000-01, Minister for the Cabinet Office and Shadow Chancellor of the Duchy of Lancaster 2007-10; Minister for the Cabinet Office; Paymaster General 2010-; *Select Committees:* Member: Public Accounts 1990-92; Member Executive 1922 Committee 1997; Chairman: Conservatives for Change (CChange) 2002-, Conservative Party 2005-07

Other organisations: Chairman, Governors of Abingdon School 1994-2003; PC 1992

Recreations: Skiing, reading, opera

Rt Hon Francis Maude MP, House of Commons, London SW1A 0AA
Tel: 020 7219 2494 Fax: 020 7219 2990
E-mail: francis.maude.mp@parliament.uk
Constituency: Gough House, Madeira Avenue, Horsham,
West Sussex RH12 1RL Tel: 01403 242000 Fax: 01403 210600
Website: www.francismaude.com

GENERAL ELECTION RESULT

		%
Maude, F. (Con)*	29,447	52.7
Newman, G. (Lib Dem)	17,987	32.2
Skudder, A. (Lab)	4,189	7.5
Aldridge, H. (UKIP)	2,839	5.1
Fitter, N. (Green)	570	1.0
Lyon, S. (Christian)	469	0.8
Duggan, J. (TPP)	253	0.5
Kissach, D. (Ind)	87	0.2
Majority	11,460	20.52
Electorate	76,835	
Turnout	55,841	72.68

**Member of last parliament*

CONSTITUENCY SNAPSHOT

Since the Second World War this seat has been firmly Conservative. Their support has declined since 1997 when Francis Maude was elected with a majority of 15,000. Subsequently his majority has continued to fall, down to 13,666 in 2001 and 12,627 in 2005.

Maude held the seat in 2010 with a 11,460 majority.

The seat gained part of the Billinghurst and Shipley ward from Arundel and South Downs and part of Ardingly and Balcombe from Mid Sussex. The seat lost a number of wards to Arundel and South Downs, Chichester and Mid Sussex.

As well as the town of Horsham, this constituency also includes a number of small villages, including Warnham, the birthplace of the poet Shelley.

The constituency is well served by transport links, with the M23 and Gatwick Airport within easy reach. While Horsham does serve as a commuter town for Brighton and London, it also has a substantial number of local office workers.

The centre of the iron-smelting industry in Tudor times, Horsham has little industry today. Major local employers include Royal Sun Alliance and the headquarters of the RSPCA.

Rt Hon **Theresa May**

Maidenhead (returning MP)

Boundary changes

Tel: 020 7219 5206
E-mail: mayt@parliament.uk
Website: www.tmay.co.uk

Conservative

Date of birth: 1 October 1956; Daughter of late Rev Hubert and Zaidee Brasier

Education: Wheatley Park Comprehensive School, Holton, Oxfordshire; St Hugh's College, Oxford (BA geography 1977, MA); Married Philip John May 1980

Non-political career: Association for Payment Clearing Services 1985-97: Various posts latterly senior adviser, international affairs; Councillor, London Borough of Merton 1986-94

Political career: Contested North-West Durham 1992 general election and Barking 1994 by-election. Member for Maidenhead 1997-2010, for Maidenhead (revised boundary) since 6 May 2010 general election; Opposition Spokeswoman for Education and Employment (schools, disabled people and women) 1998-99; Member Shadow Cabinet 1999-: Spokeswoman for Women's Issues 1999-2001, Shadow Secretary of State for: Education and Employment 1999-2001, Transport, Local Government and the Regions 2001-02, Transport 2002, Environment and Transport 2003-04, the Family 2004-05, Culture, Media and Sport 2005; Shadow Leader of the House of Commons 2005-09; Member House of Commons Commission 2006-09; Shadow: Minister for Women 2007-, Secretary of State for Work and Pensions 2009-10; Secretary of State for the Home Office (Home Secretary) 2010-; Minister for Women and Equalities 2010-; *Select Committees:* Member: Education and Employment 1997-98, Education and Employment (Education Sub-Committee) 1997-99, Modernisation of the House of Commons 2006-10; Chair: Conservative Disability Group 1997-98, Conservative Party 2002-03

Political interests: Education, disability, local government

Other organisations: Patron: National Rheumatoid Arthritis Society, Electric Eels, Mission Direct; Fellow, Royal Geographical Society; Trustee, Maidenhead Civic Society; PC 2003; Maidenhead Conservative

Recreations: Walking, cooking

Rt Hon Theresa May MP, House of Commons, London SW1A 0AA
Tel: 020 7219 5206 Fax: 020 7219 1145 E-mail: mayt@parliament.uk
Constituency: Maidenhead Conservative Association, 2 Castle End Farm, Ruscombe, Berkshire RG10 9XQ Tel: 0118-934 5433
Website: www.tmay.co.uk

GENERAL ELECTION RESULT

		%
May, T. (Con)*	31,937	59.5
Hill, T. (Lib Dem)	15,168	28.2
McDonald, P. (Lab)	3,795	7.1
Wight, K. (UKIP)	1,243	2.3
Rait, T. (BNP)	825	1.5
Forbes, P. (Green)	482	0.9
Prior, P. (FR)	270	0.5
Majority	16,769	31.22
Electorate	72,844	
Turnout	53,720	73.75

**Member of last parliament*

CONSTITUENCY SNAPSHOT

The Conservatives had kept a consistent vote of almost 60 per cent in the former seat of Windsor and Maidenhead until 1992 when their vote-share fell.

In 1997 the seat's Michael Trend, decided to contest Windsor, leaving the way open for Theresa May to take over Maidenhead. May held the seat comfortably in 1997 and was re-elected with a 6,231 majority in 2005.

May was re-elected in 2010 with a 16,769 majority following a 7.8 per cent swing in her favour.

The ward of Bray joined the constituency from Windsor, while the Loddon ward was lost to Reading East.

One of the most prosperous constituencies in the country, Maidenhead boasts thriving industries and pretty Thames-side villages.

The town of Maidenhead boasts old family firms as well as the European headquarters of several multinationals such as Hitachi and Nortel Networks, attracted by its good transport links and proximity to Heathrow Airport and the M4 motorway.

Apart from the town, much of the constituency is bounded by the Thames and many attractive villages.

Paul Maynard

Blackpool North and Cleveleys

New constituency

Tel: 020 7219 3000
E-mail: paul.maynard.mp@parliament.uk
Website: www.paulmaynard.co.uk

Conservative

Date of birth: 16 December 1975

Education: St Ambrose College; University College, Oxford (BA modern history 1997)

Non-political career: Researcher, Hodgart Temporal 1997-99; Health policy officer, Conservative Party 1999-2002; Head of home affairs, Conservative Research Department 2001-02; Senior researcher, Reform 2003; Special adviser to Dr Liam Fox MP, Conservative Party Co-chairman 2003-

Political career: Contested Twickenham 2005 general election. Member for Blackpool North and Cleveleys since 6 May 2010 general election; Vice-chair, Weaver Vale Conservative Association 1997-99

Political interests: Education, social policy; Australia, Germany

Paul Maynard MP, House of Commons, London SW1A 0AA
Tel: 020 7219 3000 E-mail: paul.maynard.mp@parliament.uk
Constituency: 70 Redbank Road, Bispham, Blackpool FY2 9HY
Tel: 01253 590545 Website: www.paulmaynard.co.uk

GENERAL ELECTION RESULT

		%
Maynard, P. (Con)	16,964	41.8
Martin, P. (Lab)	14,814	36.5
Greene, B. (Lib Dem)	5,400	13.3
Hopwood, R. (UKIP)	1,659	4.1
Clayton, J. (BNP)	1,556	3.8
Davies, T. (Loony)	198	0.5
Majority	2,150	5.30
Electorate	65,888	
Turnout	40,591	61.61

CONSTITUENCY SNAPSHOT

There are very few differences between the new Blackpool North and Cleveleys and the abolished Blackpool North and Fleetwood: Layton and Park wards were added from Blackpool South, as was the part of Victoria ward that was in Lancaster and Wyre; in addition Brunswick and Staina part-wards are now entirely within Blackpool South and Wyre and Preston North respectively.

Blackpool North and Fleetwood was Conservative from 1945 to 1997 before Labour secured victory. The beneficiary for Labour then was Joan Humble, who took the seat with a majority of 8,946. In 2001 her majority fell to 5,721. Election results differed only very slightly in 2005 and Humble was returned with a 5,062 majority.

Humble retired and the seat was taken by the Conservative candidate, Paul Maynard who secured a majority of 2,150 in 2010.

This new Lancashire seat takes in mainly suburban areas to the north of Blackpool with the majority of the tourist sites situated in Blackpool South.

Although Blackpool North and Cleveleys does not have the major tourist attractions within its boundary, it does benefit from visitors. In particular, the hotel and restaurant sector does especially well. There is also a very strong public administration sector in the area.

The Maritime and Coastguard Agency is a well-valued organisation among the local residents.

Rt Hon **Michael Meacher**

Oldham West and Royton (returning MP)

Boundary changes

Tel: 020 7219 4532
E-mail: meacherm@parliament.uk
Website: www.epolitix.com/Michael-Meacher

Date of birth: 4 November 1939; Son of late George H. Meacher and Dorris, née Foxell

Education: Berkhamsted School, Hertfordshire; New College, Oxford (BA Greats 1962); London School of Economics (social administration Diploma 1963); Married Molly Christine Reid 1962 (divorced 1987, later Baroness Meacher) (2 sons 2 daughters); married Lucianne Sawyer, neé Craven 1988

Non-political career: Secretary, Danilo Dolci Trust 1964; Sembal research fellow in social gerontology, Essex University 1965-66; Lecturer in social administration: York University 1966-69, London School of Economics 1970; Visiting professor to Department of Sociology, Surrey University 1980-86; Member, UNISON

Political career: Contested Colchester 1966 general election and Oldham West 1968 by-election. Member for Oldham West 1970-97, for Oldham West and Royton 1997-2010, for Oldham West and Royton (revised boundary) since 6 May 2010 general election; Parliamentary Under-Secretary of State: Department of Industry 1974-75, Department of Health and Social Security 1975-76, Department of Trade 1976-79; Member Shadow Cabinet 1983-97: Principal Opposition Frontbench Spokesperson for: Health and Social Security 1983-87, Employment 1987-89, Social Security 1989-92, Overseas Development and Co-operation 1992-93, Citizen's Charter and Science 1993-94, Transport 1994-95, Education and Employment 1995-96, Environmental Protection 1996-97; Minister of State: Department of the Environment, Transport and the Regions (Environment) 1997-2001, Department for Environment, Food and Rural Affairs 2001-03 (Environment 2001-02, Environment and Agri-Environment 2002-03); *Select Committees:* Member: Environmental Audit 1997-2003; Contested Deputy Leadership, Labour Party 1983; Member, Labour Party National Executive Committee 1983-89; Contested Leadership, Labour Party 2007

Political interests: Economics and social policy, redistribution of income and wealth, industrial democracy, civil liberties, housing, democracy and accountability

Other organisations: First Base (housing charity for young people); Fellow Industry and Parliament Trust 1989; PC 1997; *Publications:* The Care of Old People (Fabian Society, 1969); Taken For A Ride: Special Residential Homes for the Elderly Mentally Infirm: A Study of Separatism in Social Policy (1972); Socialism with a Human Face – the Political Economy in the 1980s (1982); Diffusing Power – The key to Socialist Revival (1992); Numerous articles and pamphlets on social and economic policy

Recreations: Sport, music, reading, photography (camcorder)

Rt Hon Michael Meacher MP, House of Commons, London SW1A 0AA Tel: 020 7219 4532; 020 7219 6461 Fax: 020 7219 5945
E-mail: meacherm@parliament.uk
Constituency: 11 Church Lane, Oldham,
Greater Manchester OL1 3AN Tel: 0161-626 5779
Fax: 0161-626 8572 Website: www.epolitix.com/Michael-Meacher

GENERAL ELECTION RESULT

		%
Meacher, M. (Lab)*	19,503	45.5
Ghafoor, K. (Con)	10,151	23.7
Alcock, M. (Lib Dem)	8,193	19.1
Joines, D. (BNP)	3,049	7.1
Roberts, H. (UKIP)	1,387	3.2
Miah, S. (Respect)	627	1.5
Majority	9,352	21.79
Electorate	72,651	
Turnout	42,910	59.06

**Member of last parliament*

CONSTITUENCY SNAPSHOT

Unlike its eclectic neighbour to the east, Oldham West and Royton has been Labour since the creation of Oldham West in 1950. Michael Meacher has represented the constituency since 1970.

In the 1997 general election Meacher achieved a majority of 16,201. At the 2005 general election, turnout in the seat decreased to 53 per cent, and Michael Meacher's majority fell by 3,000 votes to 10,454. Meacher was re-elected in 2010 with a majority of 9,352.

Boundary changes swapped some part-wards with the neighbouring seats of Oldham East and Saddleworth and Ashton-under-Lyne.

Oldham West and Royton is situated to the north and east of the Manchester city seats. It contains the majority of the old industrial town of Oldham, the smaller town of Royton and the town of Chadderton.

Tommyfield Market is the former political meeting-place at the heart of Oldham and is home to a large outdoor permanent market that gives the town centre, despite its size, a Lancashire market town feel.

Tourism to the area has been given a boost by the reopening of the local canal network.

Oldham will benefit from an extension to the Metrolink tram system from 2011, connecting it to central Manchester.

Alan Meale

Mansfield (returning MP)

Boundary changes

Tel: 020 7219 4159
E-mail: mealea@parliament.uk
Website: www.alanmeale.co.uk

Date of birth: 31 July 1949; Son of late Albert Henry Meale, and of Elizabeth Meale

Education: St Joseph's Roman Catholic School, Bishop Auckland, Co. Durham; Durham University; Ruskin College, Oxford; Sheffield Hallam University; Married Diana Gilhespy 1983 (1 son 1 daughter)

Non-political career: Author and editor; Development officer; Researcher for MPs Barbara Castle, Tony Benn, Dennis Skinner, Albert Booth; Parliamentary and political adviser to Michael Meacher as Spokesperson for Health and Social Security 1984-87; National employment development officer, NACRO 1977-80; Assistant to Ray Buckton, General Secretary of ASLEF 1979-84; Governor Portland Training College 1988-

Political career: Member for Mansfield 1987-2010, for Mansfield (revised boundary) since 6 May 2010 general election; Opposition Whip 1992-94; PPS to John Prescott: as Deputy Leader of the Labour Party 1994-97, as Deputy Prime Minister and Secretary of State for the Environment, Transport and the Regions 1997-98; Parliamentary Under-Secretary of State, Department of the Environment, Transport and the Regions 1998-99; Adviser to Richard Caborn, as Minister of State for Sport 2002-05; *Select Committees:* Member: Home Affairs 1990-92, Court of Referees 1999-2001; Chair Crossrail Bill 2006-07; Member, Co-operative Party

Political interests: Home affairs, European affairs, transport, health, social security, drug abuse, human rights, environment, poverty, sport, unemployment, media, music; Cyprus, Europe, Ireland

Other organisations: Member, War Pensions Board 1989-97; Parliamentary Representative, SSAFA 1990-94; Commonwealth War Graves Commissioner 2003-; Former Executive Member: Commonwealth Parliamentary Association (CPA), Inter-Parliamentary Union (IPU); Member, UK Delegation Parliamentary Assembly of the Council of Europe (CoE)/Western European Union 2000-; CoE President CTTs Environment, Agriculture, Local and Regional Democracy: First Vice-President 2001-08, President 2008-; Chairman CoE Sustainable Development 2002-04; Chair CPA Cyprus Group (British Section) 2007-; Representative Kyoto Protocol; Industry and Parliament Trust: Fellow 1970, Postgraduate Fellow 1993; Honorary Senatorship of Louisiana (USA); Freeman, State of Louisiana, USA; Freeman, City of: Mansfield, Ohio, USA; Morphou, Cyprus

Recreations: Environment, reading, writing, arts, politics, sports, Mansfield Football Club, Cyprus

Alan Meale MP, House of Commons, London SW1A 0AA
Tel: 020 7219 4159 E-mail: mealea@parliament.uk
Website: www.alanmeale.co.uk

GENERAL ELECTION RESULT

		%
Meale, A. (Lab)*	18,753	38.8
Critchlow, T. (Con)	12,741	26.3
Wyatt, M. (Lib Dem)	7,469	15.4
Camilleri, P. (Ind)	4,339	9.0
Hamilton, D. (UKIP)	2,985	6.2
Hill, R. (BNP)	2,108	4.4
Majority	6,012	12.42
Electorate	80,069	
Turnout	48,395	60.44

**Member of last parliament*

CONSTITUENCY SNAPSHOT

Mansfield has much in common with its near neighbour Ashfield's political outlook. Constituents have elected a Labour member since the 1920s. In the 1987 election Labour's Alan Meale won the seat of just 56 votes. Meale was able to build a comfortable majority throughout the 1990s, with nearly 12,000 in 1992 and over 20,000 in 1997. In 2001 Labour's lead was almost halved to 11,038, although in 2005 Meale was one of the few Labour MPs to increase his majority, building to 11,365.

Meale held the seat for Labour in 2010 with a reduced majority of 6,012.

The constituency gained Birklands and Meden wards from Bassetlaw.

Mansfield has diversified both economically and socially since the collapse of the mining industry in the area. The major employers are now the local council and the large Sherwood Forest Hospital Trust, along with a number of smaller textile, distribution and light engineering companies.

While still a largely working-class town, Mansfield has nonetheless experienced an influx of the middle classes in the last ten years, many of whom commute to South Yorkshire and Nottingham to work.

Ian Mearns

Gateshead

New constituency

Tel: 020 7219 3000
E-mail: ian.mearns.mp@parliament.uk

Date of birth: 1957

Education: St Mary's Technical School, Newcastle; Partner Anne

Non-political career: Northern Gas 1974; Gateshead Council: Councillor 1983-; Former Cabinet Member for: Lifelong Learning, Jobs and Employment; Council Deputy Leader 2002-; Council representative, Local Government Association; Member: Association of North East Councils, North East Regional Authority; Chair of governors: Kelvin Grove Primary School, Gateshead, Thomas Hepburn Community Comprehensive, Felling

Political career: Member for Gateshead since 6 May 2010 general election

Other organisations: Patron, Redheugh Boys Club

Ian Mearns MP, House of Commons, London SW1A 0AA
Tel: 020 7219 3000 E-mail: ian.mearns.mp@parliament.uk
Constituency: Gateshead Labour Party Campaign Office, 292-96 High Street, Gateshead NE8 1EL Tel: 0191-477 0651

GENERAL ELECTION RESULT

		%
Mearns, I. (Lab)	20,712	54.1
Hindle, F. (Lib Dem)	8,163	21.3
Anderson, H. (Con)	5,716	14.9
Scott, K. (BNP)	1,787	4.7
Tennant, J. (UKIP)	1,103	2.9
Redfern, A. (Green)	379	1.0
Brunskill, E. (TUSC)	266	0.7
Walton, D. (Christian)	131	0.3
Majority	12,549	32.80
Electorate	66,492	
Turnout	38,257	57.54

CONSTITUENCY SNAPSHOT

The new Gateshead seat incorporates a similar number of wards from the constituencies of Tyne Bridge and Gateshead East and Washington West.

In Gateshead East and Washington West Sharon Hodgson's Labour majority fell at the 2005 general election to 13,407, after a 7.3 per cent swing to the Liberal Democrats, Labour having received a 72 per cent share of the vote in 1997.

The constituency MP for Tynebridge, David Clelland, has occupied the seat since 1985, winning 61 per cent of the vote in 2005 with a majority of 10,400. Like Gateshead East and Washington West, there was a swing to the Liberal Democrats in 2005. Labour's Ian Mearns won the new seat with a majority of 12,549 despite a notional 4 per cent swing to the Lib Dems.

The seat is a re-establishment of a constituency that existed between 1832 and 1950, essentially made up of Gateshead Town centre, giving the seat an urban character.

Together with its fellow urban conurbation, Newcastle, Gateshead is a former industrial town that forms the core of Tyneside. There is currently a rebranding exercise attempting to transform the two into a single visitor destination ingeniously titled 'NewcastleGateshead'.

The principal businesses and major companies for the wider Gateshead area include BAE Systems, Komatsu, International Coatings and Myson Radiators. The nearby Metro Centre also provides plentiful employment for the people of Gateshead.

Mark Menzies

Fylde

Boundary changes

Tel: 020 7219 3000
E-mail: mark.menzies.mp@parliament.uk
Website: www.markmenzies.org.uk

Conservative

Date of birth: 1971

Education: Kiel School, Dumbarton; Glasgow University (MA economic history 1994)

Non-political career: Candidate trainee, Marks & Spencer 1994-95; Asda supermarkets 1995-2008; Marketing consultant, Morrisons supermarkets 2008-09

Political career: Contested Glasgow Govan 2001 and Selby 2005 general elections. Member for Fylde since 6 May 2010 general election; Member, Conservative Party 1987-

Political interests: Public services, bureaucracy, transport, NHS dentistry, energy, economics

Other organisations: Social innovation marketing award, IGD/Unilever 2007

Mark Menzies MP, House of Commons, London SW1A 0AA
Tel: 020 7219 3000 E-mail: mark.menzies.mp@parliament.uk
Constituency: Fylde Conservative Association, Bradshaw Lane, Greenhalgh, Lancashire PR4 3JA Tel: 01772 671533
Website: www.markmenzies.org.uk

GENERAL ELECTION RESULT

		%
Menzies, M. (Con)	22,826	52.3
Winlow, B. (Lib Dem)	9,641	22.1
Robinson, L. (Lab)	8,624	19.7
Bleeker, M. (UKIP)	1,945	4.5
Mitchell, P. (Green)	654	1.5
Majority	13,185	30.18
Electorate	65,917	
Turnout	43,690	66.28

CONSTITUENCY SNAPSHOT

The Conservatives have returned members here ever since the seat was created in 1945, with Sir Edward Gardner serving for the shortest period, 17 years. Michael Jack, was first elected in 1983 and was re-elected with a 12,459 majority in 2005.

Michael Jack retired in 2010 Mark Menzies held the seat for the Conservatives with a majority of 13,185.

The seat lost Preston Rural East, Preston Rural North and Great Eccleston part-wards to Wyre and Preston North and Ingol part-ward to Preston.

The constituency of Fylde is based on a coastal plain in West Lancashire. It lies on the north bank of the river Ribble and stretches up towards Morecambe Bay. Its most well-known town is Lytham St Annes, a popular retirement destination, but is also home to market towns Kirkham and Wesham.

Fylde is one of the more affluent constituencies in Lancashire.

There is a strong manufacturing base which provides jobs for about a quarter of the working population of Fylde. The influx of older wealthy people brings in extra money to the local economy.

The future of the Springfields nuclear site is an important issue in Fylde. The site is currently bidding to build a new reactor and if successful this would boost the local economy with many extra jobs created.

Patrick Mercer

Newark (returning MP)

Boundary changes

Tel: 020 7219 8477
E-mail: millicanh@parliament.uk
Website: www.patrickmercer.org.uk

Conservative

Date of birth: 26 June 1956; Son of late Eric Mercer, Bishop of Exeter, and Rosemary, née Denby

Education: King's School, Chester; Exeter College, Oxford (MA modern history 1980); Royal Military Academy, Sandhurst (commission 1975); Staff College (psc 1988); Married Catriona Jane Beaton, publisher, 1990 (1 son)

Non-political career: Regular Army officer, Worcestershire and Sherwood Foresters Regiment 1974-98: Head of strategy, Army Training and Recruiting Agency 1997-98, Commanding battalion in Bosnia, Canada, Tidworth, Operational service in the Balkans and Ulster; Reporter, BBC Radio 4 *Today* Programme 1999; Freelance journalist 2000-01; Member, King's College London mission to East Timor 2000

Political career: Member for Newark 2001-10, for Newark (revised boundary) since 6 May 2010 general election; Shadow Minister for Homeland Security 2003-07; *Select Committees:* Member: Defence 2001-03, Home Affairs 2007-10; Chair: Home Affairs Sub-Committee 2008-09

Political interests: Agriculture, prisons, defence, Northern Ireland, home affairs; Ukraine, Russia, Israel, Serbia, Bosnia

Other organisations: Honorary Colonel, Nottinghamshire Army Cadet Force; President, Newark Patriotic Fund; MBE 1993; OBE 1997; Mentioned in Despatches 1982, Gallantry commendation 1991; Newark Working Men's, Newark Conservative; *Publications:* Give Them a Volley and Charge (Spellmount, 1997); Inkermann: The Soldier's Battle (Osprey, 1997); To Do and Die (Harper Collins, 2009)

Recreations: Painting, walking, bird-watching, history, country sports

Patrick Mercer OBE MP, House of Commons, London SW1A 0AA
Tel: 020 7219 8477 Fax: 020 7219 1961
E-mail: millicanh@parliament.uk
Constituency: Newark and Retford Conservative Association, Belvedere, London Road, Newark, Nottinghamshire NG24 1TN
Tel: 01636 612837 Fax: 01636 612837
Website: www.patrickmercer.org.uk

GENERAL ELECTION RESULT

		%
Mercer, P. (Con)*	27,590	53.9
Campbell, I. (Lab)	11,438	22.3
Jenkins, P. (Lib Dem)	10,246	20.0
Irvine, T. (UKIP)	1,954	3.8
Majority	16,152	31.53
Electorate	71,785	
Turnout	51,228	71.36

**Member of last parliament*

CONSTITUENCY SNAPSHOT

Before 1979's Tory victory Labour had held the seat since 1950. Tory MP Richard Alexander's majority rose from over 5,000 in 1979 to more than 14,000 in 1983. He went on to hold the seat until 1997.

In 1997 Fiona Jones secured a lead of 3,016 for Labour, overturning a Conservative one of 8,229. In 2001 the Conservatives, Patrick Mercer won the seat back, with a comfortable majority of 4,073. He increased his majority to 6,464 in 2005.

In 2010 Mercer held the seat with a strong majority of 16,152 giving the Conservatives a 53.9 per cent vote-share.

Newark lost the Retford ward to Bassetlaw, while gaining the predominantly rural area surrounding the north of Bingham from Rushcliffe.

Perhaps most famous for having William Gladstone as its MP, Newark has more in common with rural Lincolnshire, which it borders, than the rest of Nottinghamshire.

The town of Newark-on-Trent is one of the oldest in the Midlands, and retains a charm that has led to an increasingly affluent population. The town is now a popular commuter area for those working in Nottingham. Surrounding villages are more mixed.

The largest single employer is NSK, a bearings manufacturer. Local fruit farms, and those over the county border in Lincolnshire, have attracted significant numbers of foreign workers to the area.

Steve Metcalfe

South Basildon and East Thurrock

New constituency

Tel: 020 7219 3000
Website: www.vote4metcalfe.com

Date of birth: 9 January 1966

Education: Loughton School; Married Angela Claire Giblett 1988 (1 son 1 daughter)

Non-political career: Driver, Metloc Printers 1984-85; Order clerk, Burrup Mathison, London 1985-86; Metloc Printers Ltd (family business): Sales executive 1986-87, Studio manager 1987-92, Director 1992-; Epping Forest District Council: Customer service e-government and ICT 2003-06, Customer service including waste management portfolio holder 2006-

Political career: Contested Ilford South 2005 general election. Member for South Basildon and East Thurrock since 6 May 2010 general election; Deputy chairman, Essex Area Conservatives 2002-06

Political interests: Economy, small business, foreign policy, waste management, environment

Other organisations: Member: Conservative Friends of Israel 2006-, Conservative Christian Fellowship 2006-; Founder, Wasters Wine Society; United and Cecil Club; Woodford Rugby Club

Recreations: Theatre, wine tasting, travel

Steve Metcalfe MP, House of Commons, London SW1A 0AA
Tel: 020 7219 3000
Constituency: South Basildon and East Thurrock Conservatives, St Clere's Hall Farm Golf Club, St Clere's Hall, London Road, Stanford-Le-Hope, Essex SS17 0LX Tel: 01375 642397
Fax: 01375 642397 E-mail: stephen@vote4metcalfe.com
Website: www.vote4metcalfe.com

GENERAL ELECTION RESULT

		%
Metcalfe, S. (Con)	19,624	43.9
Smith, A. (Lab/Co-op)*	13,852	31.0
Williams, G. (Lib Dem)	5,977	13.4
Smith, K. (UKIP)	2,639	5.9
Roberts, C. (BNP)	2,518	5.6
X, N. (Ind)	125	0.3
Majority	5,772	12.90
Electorate	71,815	
Turnout	44,735	62.29

**Member of last parliament*

CONSTITUENCY SNAPSHOT

The three constituencies which have contributed to this new seat were represented by two Labour MPs (Basildon and Thurrock), and a Conservative (Billericay) until 2010.

However, the seat is predominantly made up of wards from Basildon. Since its creation in 1974 Basildon has been a constituency that has reflected the political colour of the Government of the day: from Labour's Eric Moonman who held the seat from 1974 to 1979, through the Conservatives Harvey Proctor (1979 to 1983) and David Amess (1983 to 1997), to the Labour incumbent Angela Evans Smith. Smith's majority was a reduced 3,142 in 2005.

Smith lost the new seat with a 7.5 per cent swing to the Conservative candidate, Stephen Metcalfe.

Although this Essex seat covers much of the same area of East Thurrock that was contained within the old Basildon seat, it includes only the southern suburbs of Basildon, plus Pitsea, which was formerly in the Billericay constituency.

Stanford le Hope is the major town. There is some farmland in the north, but the southern area is dominated by commercial and industrial activity on the northern bank of the Thames.

There is a concentrated area of commercial and industrial activity along the North Thames riverside, which includes the Coryton oil refinery area and the former Shell Haven refinery site, now being redeveloped.

Rt Hon **Alun Michael**

Cardiff South and Penarth ***(returning MP)***

Boundary changes

Tel: 020 7219 5980
E-mail: alunmichaelmp@parliament.uk
Website: www.alunmichael.com

Labour/Co-operative

Date of birth: 22 August 1943; Son of late Leslie Michael and of Elizabeth Michael

Education: Colwyn Bay Grammar School; Keele University (BA literature and philosophy 1966); Married Mary Crawley 1966 (2 sons 3 daughters)

Non-political career: Journalist, *South Wales Echo* 1966-72; Youth Worker, Cardiff City Council 1972-74; Youth and Community Worker, South Glamorgan CC 1974-87; Branch Secretary, National Union of Journalists 1967-70; Member CYWU 1971-86; General Secretary, Welsh Association of FE and Youth Service Officers 1973-75; Member: TGWU 1974-86, GMB 1986-; JP, Cardiff 1972-; Chair, Cardiff Juvenile Bench 1986-87; Councillor Cardiff City Council 1973-89

Political career: Member for Cardiff South and Penarth 1987-2010, for Cardiff South and Penarth (revised boundary) since 6 May 2010 general election; Opposition Whip 1987-88; Opposition Spokesperson for: Welsh Affairs 1988-92, Home Affairs 1992-97; The Voluntary Sector 1994-97; Minister of State, Home Office (Minister for Criminal Policy also responsible for Police and the Voluntary Sector) 1997-98; Secretary of State for Wales 1998-99; Minister of State: Department for Environment, Food and Rural Affairs 2001-05: (Rural Affairs 2001-02, Rural Affairs and Urban Quality of Life 2002-03, Rural Affairs and Local Environmental Quality 2003-05), Department of Trade and Industry 2005-06; *Select Committees:* Member: Welsh Affairs 2007-10, Justice 2007-10; National Assembly for Wales: AM for Mid and West Wales region 1999-2000: First Secretary 1999-2000; Chair, Co-operative Group of MPs 1990-92; Member: National Executive, Co-operative Party (representing Wales), Christian Socialist Movement, Labour Friends of Israel

Political interests: Local and regional government, housing, youth work, juvenile justice, voluntary sector, community development, economic development, co-operative development, political ideas and philosophy; Germany, South Africa, Israel, Canada, Somalia, USA, Japan

Other organisations: National Vice-president Youth Hostels Association 1990-2001; Member of Board Crime Concern 1993-97; Member Committee on Standards in Public Life 2006-; Member: Commonwealth Parliamentary Association (CPA) (delegation to South Africa and Canada), Inter-Parliamentary Association (IPA); Fellow Industry and Parliament Trust 2007; PC 1998; Penarth Labour, Grange Stars (Cardiff), Earlswood (Cardiff); Penarth and Dinas Runners; *Publications:* Contributor: Restoring Faith in Politics (1966), Challenges to a Challenging Faith (1995); Editor: Tough on Crime and Tough on the Causes of Crime (1997), Building the Future Together (1997)

Recreations: Long-distance walking, running, reading, opera, music

Rt Hon Alun Michael JP MP, House of Commons, London SW1A 0AA Tel: 020 7219 5980 Fax: 020 7219 5930
E-mail: alunmichaelmp@parliament.uk
Constituency: PO Box 453, Cardiff CF11 9YN Tel: 029 2022 3533
Fax: 029 2022 9947 Website: www.alunmichael.com

GENERAL ELECTION RESULT

		%
Michael, A. (Lab/Co-op)*	17,262	38.9
Hoare, S. (Con)	12,553	28.3
Hannigan, D. (Lib Dem)	9,875	22.3
Aslam, F. (PIC)	1,851	4.2
Ziegler, S. (UKIP)	1,145	2.6
Burke, G. (Ind)	648	1.5
Townsend, M. (Green)	554	1.3
Bate, C. (Christian)	285	0.6
Griffiths, R. (Comm)	196	0.4
Majority	4,709	10.61
Electorate	73,704	
Turnout	44,369	60.20

**Member of last parliament*

CONSTITUENCY SNAPSHOT

The southern Cardiff seat has been held by Labour since 1945. Former Prime Minister James Callaghan was MP here from 1945 to 1987 when it was called Cardiff South. He was followed by Alun Michael, who in addition to being an MP was an Assembly Member between 1999 and 2000. He was First Secretary of the National Assembly until he resigned in February 2000.

An increase in the Lib Dem vote in the 2005 general election, meant that Michael's majority was reduced to 9,237. Michaels held on in 2010 with a 4,710 lead.

Boundary changes have added the Sully ward in Vale of Glamorgan to the seat.

Straddling Cardiff Bay, this seat includes the area around the National Assembly for Wales and the pretty Victorian seaside resort of Penarth in Vale of Glamorgan.

The regeneration of south Cardiff has led to an influx of largely young, middle-class residents. Many of these have moved into new upmarket accommodation around Cardiff Bay.

The Cardiff wards are still notably poorer than those in Vale of Glamorgan. The beautiful Vale of Glamorgan provides a real change of scenery from the city and Penarth's tourism potential will be increased by the continuing growth of the Cardiff economy. The Vale offers plenty of activities and caters for a diverse cross-section of tastes and interests.

Rt Hon **David Miliband**

South Shields (returning MP)

Boundary changes

Tel: 020 7219 8320
E-mail: milibandd@parliament.uk
Website: www.davidmiliband.info

Date of birth: 15 July 1965; Son of Ralph Miliband and Marion, née Kozak

Education: Haverstock Comprehensive School; Corpus Christi College, Oxford (BA philosophy, politics and economics 1987); Massachusetts Institute of Technology (MSc political science 1989); Married Louise Shackelton 1998 (2 adopted sons)

Non-political career: Parliamentary officer National Council for Voluntary Organisations 1987-88; Research fellow Institute for Public Policy Research 1989-94; Secretary Commission on Social Justice 1992-94; Head of Policy Office, Leader of the Opposition 1994-97; Head of Prime Minister's Policy Unit 1997-2001; TGWU 1989-; Secretary Social Justice Commission

Political career: Member for South Shields since 7 June 2001 general election; Minister of State, Department for Education and Skills (School Standards) 2002-04; Minister for the Cabinet Office 2004-05; Minister of Communities and Local Government, Office of the Deputy Prime Minister 2005-06; Secretary of State for: Environment, Food and Rural Affairs 2006-07, Foreign and Commonwealth Affairs (Foreign Secretary) 2007-10; Shadow Secretary of State for Foreign and Commonwealth Affairs (Foreign Secretary) 2010-; President SERA 2007-

Political interests: Education, employment, foreign affairs

Other organisations: Founder Centre for European Reform; Vice-President, Commonwealth Parliamentary Association (UK Branch) 2007-10; PC 2005; Whiteleas Social, Cleadon Social; President, South Shields Football Club; *Publications:* Editor Reinventing the Left, Polity Press (1994); Co-editor Paying for Inequality (Rivers Oram Press 1994)

Rt Hon David Miliband MP, House of Commons, London SW1A 0AA Tel: 020 7219 8320 E-mail: milibandd@parliament.uk
Constituency: South Shields Constituency Labour Party, Ede House, 143 Westoe Road, South Shields, Tyne and Wear NE33 3PD
Tel: 0191-456 8910 Fax: 0191-456 5842
Website: www.davidmiliband.info

GENERAL ELECTION RESULT

		%
Miliband, D. (Lab)*	18,995	52.0
Allen, K. (Con)	7,886	21.6
Psallidas, S. (Lib Dem)	5,189	14.2
Watson, D. (BNP)	2,382	6.5
Ford, S. (Green)	762	2.1
Kaikavoosi, S. (Ind)	729	2.0
Thompson, V. (Ind)	316	0.9
Navabi, S. (Ind)	168	0.5
Majority	11,109	30.42
Electorate	63,294	
Turnout	36,518	57.70

**Member of last parliament*

CONSTITUENCY SNAPSHOT

This constituency has been Labour since 1935. A swing of 2.8 percent towards the Liberal Democrats meant that the results from the 2005 election differed only marginally from 2001. David Miliband (MP since 2001) was re-elected with a slightly reduced majority of 12,312. Miliband held on easily to his safe seat with a majority of 11,109.

Boundary changes moved Biddick and All Saints, Simonside and Rekendyke, and Whitburn and Marsden wards all completely within the constituency, rather than shared with Jarrow, as previously. Bede and Cleadon and East Bolden wards were lost to Jarrow.

The seaside town of South Shields, north of Jarrow, has problems associated with the decline of traditional local industries. All the coal mines have closed, and ships are no longer built here, but the Tyne is still busy with ship repairs and offshore oil platforms. Employment is heavily oriented towards manufacturing.

However, as heavy industry has declined, South Shields has turned to other sectors, especially the service sector, which now predominates. Light engineering and electronic companies have also replaced some of the heavy industry.

Rt Hon **Ed Miliband**

Doncaster North (returning MP)

Boundary changes

Tel: 020 7219 4778
E-mail: milibande@parliament.uk
Website: www.edmilibandmp.com

Date of birth: 24 December 1969; Son of Ralph Miliband and Marion, née Kozak

Education: Corpus Christi College, Oxford (BA philosophy, politics and economics); London School of Economics (MSc Econ); Partner Justine Thornton (1 son)

Non-political career: Television journalist; Speechwriter and researcher to: Harriet Harman MP 1993, Gordon Brown as Shadow Chancellor of the Exchequer 1994-97; HM Treasury: Special adviser to Gordon Brown as Chancellor of the Exchequer 1997-2002, Chairman Council of Economic Advisers 2004-05; Lecturer in government Harvard University 2002-04; TGWU/USDAW

Political career: Member for Doncaster North 2005-10, for Doncaster North (revised boundary) since 6 May 2010 general election; Parliamentary Secretary, Cabinet Office 2006-07; Minister for the Cabinet Office; Chancellor of the Duchy of Lancaster 2007-08; Secretary of State for Energy and Climate Change 2008-10; Shadow Secretary of State for Energy and Climate Change 2010-

Other organisations: PC 2007

Rt Hon Ed Miliband MP, House of Commons, London SW1A 0AA
Tel: 020 7219 4778 E-mail: milibande@parliament.uk
Constituency: Hutton Business Centre, Bridge Works, Bentley, Doncaster, South Yorkshire DN5 9QP Tel: 01302 875462
Fax: 01302 876097 Website: www.edmilibandmp.com

GENERAL ELECTION RESULT

		%
Miliband, E. (Lab)*	19,637	47.3
Brodie, S. (Con)	8,728	21.0
Sanderson, E. (Lib Dem)	6,174	14.9
Chambers, P. (BNP)	2,818	6.8
Crawshaw, W. (England)	2,148	5.2
Andrews, L. (UKIP)	1,797	4.3
Rawcliffe, B. (TUSC)	181	0.4
Majority	10,909	26.30
Electorate	72,381	
Turnout	41,483	57.31

**Member of last parliament*

CONSTITUENCY SNAPSHOT

Formed in 1983, this was a seat dominated by coalmining and the National Union of Mineworkers. The Labour majority has never fallen below five figures, even in Labour's 1983 nadir Michael Welsh was returned with a majority of 12,711.

Welsh held the seat until retiring in 1992, when he was succeeded by former miner Kevin Hughes. In 1997 Hughes had a majority of nearly 22,000.

Illness forced Hughes to retire in 2005 and new Labour candidate Ed Miliband won the seat with a 12,656 majority. In 2010 Miliband was re-elected with a reduced majority of 10,909.

The constituency was extended to the south-west to include the ward of Mexborough (from the old Barnsley East and Mexborough seat) and the entire ward of Sprotbrough.

This constituency is on the eastern edge of the old Yorkshire coalfield to the north of Doncaster itself. There is also a large number of villages and small towns including Adwick le Street and Bentley.

This is traditionally one of the most working-class seats in the country. It has a large proportion of manual workers. Manufacturing decline has led to high unemployment.

The rural areas of the constituency support a large number of small and medium-sized farms.

Owner-occupancy has increased substantially in the constituency, but a large number of households are classified as being in financial hardship.

Andrew Miller

Ellesmere Port and Neston ***(returning MP)***

Boundary changes

Tel: 020 7219 3580
E-mail: millera@parliament.uk
Website: www.andrew-miller-mp.co.uk

Labour

Date of birth: 23 March 1949; Son of late Ernest and Daphne Miller

Education: Hayling Island Secondary School; Highbury Technical College; London School of Economics (Diploma industrial relations 1977); Married Frances Ewan Keeble 1975 (2 sons 1 daughter)

Non-political career: Technician Portsmouth Polytechnic (analyst in geology) 1967-76; Regional official MSF (formerly ASTMS) 1977-92; Member MSF 1968-

Political career: Member for Ellesmere Port and Neston 1992-2010, for Ellesmere Port and Neston (revised boundary) since 6 May 2010 general election; PPS to Ministers, Department of Trade and Industry 2001-05; *Select Committees:* Member: Science and Technology 1992-97, Information 1992-2001, Joint Committee on Human Rights 2001; Chair: Regulatory Reform 2005-10; Member: Liaison 2005-10, Joint Committee on Conventions 2006; Member NW Regional Executive Committee 1984-92; President Computing for Labour 1993-; Chair: Leadership Campaign Team 1997-98, North West Group of Labour MPs 1997-98; Member Scientists for Labour 1997-

Political interests: Industry, economic policy, science and technology, communications and information technology, pensions; China, Europe, Hungary, Malta, USA

Other organisations: Patron: Road Peace, Chester Childbirth Trust, Parents Against Drug Abuse; Member, First Steps Team working with the Foreign Office to promote relations with EU and prospective EU member states with specific responsibility for Hungary and Malta 2001-; Fellow Industry and Parliament Trust 1995; Officers' Cross of the Order of Merit (Hungary) 2004; Vice-President: Alvanley Cricket Club, Chester and Ellesmere Port Athletics Club

Recreations: Walking, photography, tennis, cricket

Andrew Miller MP, House of Commons, London SW1A 0AA
Tel: 020 7219 3580 Fax: 020 7219 3796
E-mail: millera@parliament.uk
Constituency: Whitby Hall Lodge, Stanney Lane, Ellesmere Port, Cheshire CH65 6QY Tel: 0151-357 3019 Fax: 0151-356 8226
Website: www.andrew-miller-mp.co.uk

GENERAL ELECTION RESULT

		%
Miller, A. (Lab)*	19,750	44.7
Penketh, S. (Con)	15,419	34.9
Aspinall, D. (Lib Dem)	6,663	15.1
Crocker, H. (UKIP)	1,619	3.7
Starkey, J. (Ind)	782	1.8
Majority	4,331	9.79
Electorate	63,097	
Turnout	44,233	70.10

**Member of last parliament*

CONSTITUENCY SNAPSHOT

Conservative Michael Woodcock held the then new seat from 1983 until 1992, when Andrew Miller won it for Labour.

Since 1997 Andrew Miller's share of the vote has fallen at each election, while the Conservative's has risen, albeit marginally. Miller's majority was 6,486 in 2005. Miller was re-elected in 2010 with a reduced majority of 4,331.

The seat gained Elton part-ward from the City of Chester, and lost Barrow part-ward to Eddisbury.

Squeezed between the marshy estuary of the Dee and Mersey, the seat is socially, but also physically, polarised: industrial landscapes contrast with beautiful countryside and tourist spots.

Next to the Mersey is the Stanlow oil refinery complex. The petrochemicals industry employs around 1,000 workers, a tenth of its 1980s workforce, but technological improvements have increased productivity to record levels: it is now the most complex of its type in Europe. There is a power station at Ince as well as docks, paper works, oil depots, sewage works, fertiliser factories and other, smaller concerns.

The most significant economic development in the last decade has been the opening of the Cheshire Oaks Designer Outlet Village. It has been expanded to include a deep-sea leisure centre and an IMAX cinema.

Maria Miller

Basingstoke (returning MP)

Boundary changes

Tel: 020 7219 5749
E-mail: foxlc@parliament.uk
Website: www.mariamiller.co.uk

Conservative

Date of birth: 26 March 1964; Daughter of John and June Lewis

Education: Brynteg Comprehensive, Bridgend; London School of Economics (BSc economics 1985); Married Iain George Miller 1990 (1 daughter 2 sons)

Non-political career: Advertising executive, Grey Advertising Ltd 1985-90; Marketing manager, Texaco 1990-94; Company director: Grey Advertising Ltd 1995-99, The Rowland Company/PR21 1999-2003

Political career: Contested Wolverhampton North East 2001 general election. Member for Basingstoke 2005-10, for Basingstoke (revised boundary) since 6 May 2010 general election; Shadow Minister for: Education 2005-06, Family Welfare, including Child Support Agency 2006-07, Families 2007-10; Parliamentary Under-Secretary of State, Department for Work and Pensions 2010-; *Select Committees:* Member: Trade and Industry 2005-06, Children, Schools and Families 2007; President Wolverhampton North East Conservative Association 2001-07; Chairman Wimbledon Conservative Association 2002-03

Political interests: Housing, education, media; Canada

Maria Miller MP, House of Commons, London SW1A 0AA
Tel: 020 7219 5749 Fax: 020 7219 5722 E-mail: foxlc@parliament.uk
Constituency: The Mount, Bounty Road, Basingstoke,
Hampshire RG21 3DD Tel: 01256 322207
Website: www.mariamiller.co.uk

GENERAL ELECTION RESULT

		%
Miller, M. (Con)*	25,590	50.5
Shaw, J. (Lib Dem)	12,414	24.5
Pepperell, F. (Lab)	10,327	20.4
Howell, S. (UKIP)	2,076	4.1
Saul, S. (BCM)	247	0.5
Majority	13,176	26.01
Electorate	75,470	
Turnout	50,654	67.12

**Member of last parliament*

CONSTITUENCY SNAPSHOT

Andrew Hunter held this seat for the Conservatives from 1983 until 2005. When Mr Hunter was elected in 1983 he presided over a majority of 12,450. This increased in 1987 and 1992, but in 1997 it fell to 2,397. This was further reduced in 2001 when it dropped to 880.

However, in 2005, new MP Maria Miller won a 4,680 majority. The seat was retained by Miller with a 13,176 majority following a 4.6 per cent swing in her favour.

The seat gained three part-wards from North West Hampshire in exchange for three wards and a part-ward to North East Hampshire.

Situated in the M3 corridor in North Hampshire, Basingstoke has become an increasingly urban constituency as hi-tech industries, office developments, and London commuters have made it their home.

Basingstoke is an economically thriving constituency due to rapid development in recent decades.

Electronics, micro-computing, and security printing industries are based here, many firms have offices in the town, and the AA has its headquarters here. Central and local Government are also major employers.

The town's proximity to the M3 and its good rail links to central London and neighbouring large towns like Reading such as Reading make it a commuter favourite.

Nigel Mills

Amber Valley

Boundary changes

Tel: 020 7219 3000
E-mail: nigel.mills.mp@parliament.uk
Website: www.ambervalleyconservatives.com

Education: Newcastle University (classics)

Non-political career: Former accountant, PriceWaterhouseCoopers; Amber Valley Borough Council: Councillor 2004-08, Chair, scrutiny committee; Councillor, Heanor and Loscoe Town Council 2007-

Political career: Member for Amber Valley since 6 May 2010 general election; Deputy chair, Amber Valley Conservative Association

Political interests: Employment, crime, anti-social behaviour, education

Recreations: Sport

Nigel Mills MP, House of Commons, London SW1A 0AA
Tel: 020 7219 3000 E-mail: nigel.mills.mp@parliament.uk
Constituency: 232 Cromford Road, Langley Mill,
Nottingham NG16 4HB Tel: 01629 57205 Fax: 01629 580943
Website: www.ambervalleyconservatives.com

GENERAL ELECTION RESULT

		%
Mills, N. (Con)	17,746	38.6
Mallaber, J. (Lab)*	17,210	37.5
Snowdon, T. (Lib Dem)	6,636	14.4
Clarke, M. (BNP)	3,195	7.0
Ransome, S. (UKIP)	906	2.0
'Thing, S. (Loony)	265	0.6
Majority	536	1.17
Electorate	70,171	
Turnout	45,958	65.49

**Member of last parliament*

CONSTITUENCY SNAPSHOT

The seat was created in 1983, carved out of the former constituencies of Ilkeston and Belper. Ilkeston had been dominated by Labour since the Second World War, with Ray Fletcher holding the seat for more than 20 years until the 1980s. It passed to the Conservatives in 1983. Phillip Oppenheim retained the seat for the next 14 years.

Judy Mallaber took the seat for Labour in the 1997 general election with a majority of 11,613. In 2005 her majority was down to 5,275. Mallaber was defeated in 2010 with a 6.9 per cent swing to the Conservative candidate, Nigel Mills.

The constituency lost three of the more rural wards: one to Derbyshire Dales and two to Mid Derbyshire.

Amber Valley is one of the most populated non-city districts in the East Midlands and is the most populated district in Derbyshire apart from the city of Derby. The constituency's three main towns are Alfreton, Heanor and Ripley.

Chocolate giant Thorntons now calls this constituency home, as do Denby Pottery and Bowmer and Kirkland, the construction and engineering company. There are also stretches of appealing rural land, and the local farming industry continues to endure despite long-term economic decline. An increasing range of jobs are supported by tourism.

Anne Milton

Guildford (returning MP)

Boundary changes

Tel: 020 7219 8392
E-mail: miltona@parliament.uk
Website: www.annemilton.co.uk

Date of birth: 3 November 1955

Education: Haywards Heath Grammar School, Sussex; St Bartholomew's Hospital, London (RGN 1977); Polytechnic of the South Bank, London (Diploma district nursing 1982); Married Dr Graham Henderson (3 sons 1 daughter)

Non-political career: St Bartholomew's Hospital, London: Staff nurse 1977-78, Research nurse 1978-81; District nursing sister, City and Hackney Health Authority (HA) 1981-83; Nursing sister St Thomas Hospital 1983-85; Medical adviser to: East London and City HA 1985-2000, Social housing providers 1994-2004; Councillor Reigate Borough 1999-2004: Conservative group leader 2001-03

Political career: Member for Guildford 2005-10, for Guildford (revised boundary) since 6 May 2010 general election; Shadow Minister for: Tourism 2006-07, Health 2007-10; Parliamentary Under-Secretary of State (Public Health), Department of Health 2010-; *Select Committees:* Member: Health 2005-06

Political interests: Environment, health and social care, voluntary sector

Recreations: Gardening, reading, family

Anne Milton MP, House of Commons, London SW1A 0AA
Tel: 020 7219 8392 Fax: 020 7219 5239
E-mail: miltona@parliament.uk
Constituency: 17a Home Farm, Loseley Park, Guildford, Surrey GU3 1HS Tel: 01483 300330 Fax: 01483 300321
Website: www.annemilton.co.uk

GENERAL ELECTION RESULT

		%
Milton, A. (Con)*	29,618	53.3
Doughty, S. (Lib Dem)	21,836	39.3
Shand, T. (Lab)	2,812	5.1
Manzoor, M. (UKIP)	1,021	1.8
Morris, J. (TPP)	280	0.5
Majority	7,782	14.00
Electorate	77,082	
Turnout	55,567	72.09

**Member of last parliament*

CONSTITUENCY SNAPSHOT

Guildford had been Conservative since 1906. That changed when Liberal Democrat Sue Doughty defeated the sitting member Nick St Aubyn in 2001. She overturned a Tory majority of 5,000 to win by 538 votes.

In 2005 the seat flipped back to the Conservatives. Anne Milton's majority was even smaller at 347. The seat was held by Milton in 2010 with an increased majority of 7,782.

Guildford swapped one part-ward with South West Surrey under boundary changes.

Guildford boasts an abundance of medieval architecture and the borough contains some exceptionally beautiful countryside.

London is only 30 miles to the north, and Heathrow and Gatwick are each about 40 minutes away. It has a thriving local economy and supports Surrey University, which, combined with its research park, is a key economic player and the largest employer in the seat.

Small- and medium-sized service companies thrive, and the town has a particularly high complement of accountants and solicitors.

More jobs are provided by the growing cluster of new technology businesses. The largest companies include Avaya, BOC Ltd, Vision Engineering, Kobe Steel and the Smith Group. Guildford is also the location for the administrative headquarters of a number of world-class companies including Colgate-Palmolive, Standard Life Healthcare, Legal & General and Cornhill Insurance.

Rt Hon **Andrew Mitchell**

Sutton Coldfield (returning MP)

Boundary changes

Tel: 020 7219 8516
E-mail: andrewmitchellmp@parliament.uk
Website: www.andrew-mitchell-mp.co.uk

Conservative

Date of birth: 23 March 1956; Son of Sir David Mitchell, vintner and politician, and Pam Mitchell

Education: Rugby School; Jesus College, Cambridge (MA history 1978); President of the Union 1978; Married Sharon Denise Bennet 1985 (2 daughters)

Non-political career: UN Peacekeeping Forces Cyprus: 1st Royal Tank Regiment (SSLC); International and corporate finance Lazard Brothers and Company Ltd 1979-87; Lazard Brothers: Consultant 1987-92, Director 1997-; Director: Miller Insurance Group 1997-2001, Financial Dynamics Holdings 1997-2002; Senior strategy adviser: Boots 1997-2000, Andersen Consulting/Accenture 1997-; Director Commer Group 1998-2002; Supervisory board member The Foundation 1999-

Political career: Contested Sunderland South 1983 general election. Member for Gedling 1987-97. Contested Gedling 1997 general election. Member for Sutton Coldfield 2001-10, for Sutton Coldfield (revised boundary) since 6 May 2010 general election; PPS: to William Waldegrave as Minister of State, Foreign and Commonwealth Office 1988-90, to John Wakeham as Secretary of State for Energy 1990-92; Assistant Government Whip 1992-93; Government Whip 1993-95; Parliamentary Under-Secretary of State, Department of Social Security 1995-97; Shadow Minister for: Economic Affairs 2003-04, Home Affairs 2004-05; Shadow Secretary of State for International Development 2005-10; Secretary of State for International Development 2010-; *Select Committees:* Member: Work and Pensions 2001-03, Modernisation of the House of Commons 2002-04; Chair Cambridge University Conservative Association 1977; Secretary One Nation Group of Conservative MPs 1989-92, 2005-; Vice-chair Conservative Party (candidates) 1992-93

Political interests: International development, health, defence, economy; USA, Africa, Far East

Other organisations: English Speaking Union Council International Debate Council 1998-; Council of management GAP 1999-2006; Vice-chairman Alexandra Rose Charity 1999-; Council SOS SAHEL 1992-; PC 2010; Liveryman, Vintner's Company; Carlton, Chair Coningsby 1984-85

Recreations: Music, windsurfing, skiing, walking

Rt Hon Andrew Mitchell MP, House of Commons, London SW1A 0AA Tel: 020 7219 8516 Fax: 020 7219 1981
E-mail: andrewmitchellmp@parliament.uk
Constituency: Sutton Coldfield Conservative Association, 36 High Street, Sutton Coldfield, West Midlands B72 1UP Tel: 0121-354 2229 Fax: 0121-321 1762 Website: www.andrew-mitchell-mp.co.uk

GENERAL ELECTION RESULT

		%
Mitchell, A. (Con)*	27,303	54.0
Pocock, R. (Lab)	10,298	20.4
Brighton, R. (Lib Dem)	9,117	18.0
Grierson, R. (BNP)	1,749	3.5
Siddall-Jones, E. (UKIP)	1,587	3.1
Rooney, J. (Green)	535	1.1
Majority	17,005	33.61
Electorate	74,489	
Turnout	50,589	67.91

**Member of last parliament*

CONSTITUENCY SNAPSHOT

Sutton Coldfield has consistently returned a Conservative MP with considerable majorities since its creation in 1945. The seat was home to former cabinet minister Sir Norman Fowler from 1974 until he stood down in 2001, and then passed to Andrew Mitchell.

Tory majorities here have, however, been generally falling since 1979. The seat fell from the Tories' third safest in 1997 to number 27 in 2001. In 2005 Andrew Mitchell was returned with a 12,283 majority. Mitchell increased his majority in 2010 to 17,005.

Boundary changes have been minimal.

Sutton Coldfield is a largely middle-class, leafy suburban area on the outskirts of Birmingham.

Large proportions of inhabitants are commuters and work outside the constituency in neighbouring Birmingham.

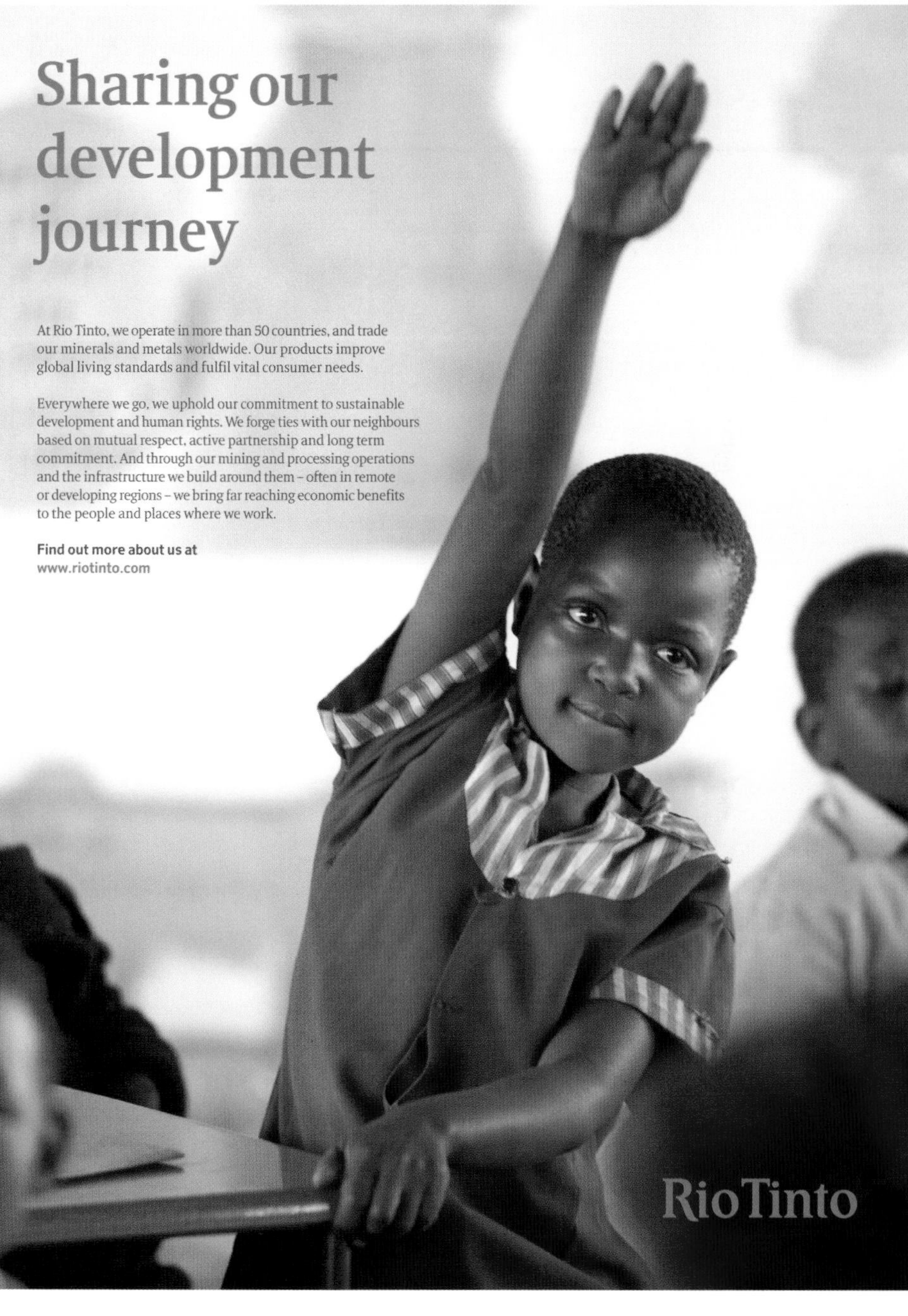

Austin Mitchell

Great Grimsby (returning MP)

Boundary changes

Tel: 020 7219 4559
E-mail: mitchellav@parliament.uk
Website: www.austinmitchell.org

Labour

Date of birth: 19 September 1934; Son of Richard Vernon and Ethel Mary Mitchell

Education: Woodbottom Council School; Bingley Grammar School, Yorkshire; Manchester University (BA history 1956, MA 1957); Nuffield College, Oxford (MA, DPhil 1963); Married Patricia Dorothea Jackson (divorced) (2 daughters); married Linda Mary McDougall (1 son 1 daughter)

Non-political career: Lecturer in history, Otago University, Dunedin, New Zealand 1959-63; Senior lecturer in politics, University of Canterbury, Christchurch, NZ 1963-67; Official fellow, Nuffield College, Oxford 1967-69; Journalist: Yorkshire Television 1969-71, BBC 1972, Yorkshire Television 1973-77; Programme controller Penine Radio 1975-77; Political commentator, Sky Television's Target programme 1989-98; Associate editor, *The House Magazine*; GMB, NUJ

Political career: Member for Grimsby 1977-83, for Great Grimsby 1983-2010, for Great Grimsby (revised boundary) since 6 May 2010 general election; PPS to John Fraser as Minister of State for Prices and Consumer Protection 1977-79; Opposition Whip 1979-85; Opposition Spokesperson for Trade and Industry 1988-89; Member, Public Accounts Commission 1997-; *Select Committees:* Member: Agriculture 1997-2001, Environment, Food and Rural Affairs 2001-05, Public Accounts 2005-10, Yorkshire and the Humber 2009-10; Vice-chair Labour Campaign for Electoral Reform; Chair: Labour Euro-Safeguards Campaign, Labour Economic Policy Group

Political interests: Economics, media, fishing industry, agriculture, poverty, accountancy, legal reform, European Union, electoral reform, constitutional reform, small businesses; Canada, Iceland, New Zealand, France, Germany, China, Hong Kong, Nigeria

Other organisations: Vice-Chair, Hansard Society; Member: Advisory Council, National Fishing Heritage Centre, Hairdressing Council 1979-; Vice-President, Federation of Economic Development Authorities (FEDA); President, Debating Group; Chair Yorkshire and Humber Seafood Group 2007-; Member, Royal Institute of International Affairs; Fellow Industry and Parliament Trust; Order of New Zealand 2001; *Publications:* New Zealand Politics in Action (1962); Government by Party (1966); Whigs in Opposition, 1815-30 (1969); Politics and People in New Zealand (1970); Half Gallon Quarter Acre Pavlova – Paradise (1974); Can Labour Win Again (1979); Yes Maggie there is an Alternative; Westminster Man (1982); The Case for Labour (1983); Four Years in the Death of the Labour Party (1983); Yorkshire Jokes (1988); Teach Thissen Tyke (1988); Britain, Beyond the Blue Horizon (1989); Competitive Socialism (1989); Accounting for Change (1993); Election '45 (1995); Corporate Governance Matters (1996); The Common Fisheries Policy, End or Mend? (1996); Co-author Last Time: Labour's Lessons from the Sixties (1997); Farewell My Lords (1999); Co-author Parliament in Pictures (1999); Pavlova Paradise Revisited (2002); Yorkshire Sayings (2005)

Recreations: Photography, contemplating exercise

Austin Mitchell MP, House of Commons, London SW1A 0AA
Tel: 020 7219 4559 Fax: 020 7219 4843
E-mail: mitchellav@parliament.uk
Constituency: 13 Bargate, Grimsby, Humberside DN34 4SS
Tel: 01472 342145 Fax: 01472 251484
Website: www.austinmitchell.org

GENERAL ELECTION RESULT

		%
Mitchell, A. (Lab)*	10,777	32.7
Ayling, V. (Con)	10,063	30.5
De Freitas, A. (Lib Dem)	7,388	22.4
Hudson, H. (UKIP)	2,043	6.2
Fyfe, S. (BNP)	1,517	4.6
Brown, E. (Ind)	835	2.5
Howe, A. (PNDP)	331	1.0
Majority	714	2.17
Electorate	61,229	
Turnout	32,954	53.82

**Member of last parliament*

CONSTITUENCY SNAPSHOT

From 1959 to 1977 this was the seat of Labour's foremost thinker of his age, Anthony Crosland. His sudden death in office as Foreign Secretary in 1977 prompted a by-election in which young former history lecturer and the television presenter, Austin Mitchell was elected.

Mitchell has represented the seat ever since. He has enjoyed comfortable margins here since 1987. Mitchell's majority topped 16,000 in 1997, but had shrunk to 7,654 by 2005. In 2010 Mitchell's majority was decimated to 714; in comparison, his 1983 majority was 731.

Grimsby's deep-sea fishing fleet has been almost wiped out, but the North East Lincolnshire town remains a major container port and one of Europe's leading food processing centres. Youngs, Heinz and Baxters are among the famous names to have factories here and the market, now dealing mainly in imported fish, is expanding and sells throughout the country.

Many people work in the oil refineries and chemical plants on the Humber estuary. Marine engineering is another important industry.

The modernisation of the area's industries has made them more hi-tech and therefore less labour-intensive, and Grimsby remains an unemployment black spot.

Madeleine Moon

Bridgend (returning MP)

Boundary changes

Tel: 020 7219 4417
E-mail: moonm@parliament.uk
Website: www.madeleinemoonmp.com

Labour

Date of birth: 27 March 1950; Daughter of Albert Edward and Hilda Ironside

Education: Whinney Hill School; Durham Girls Grammar School; Madeley College, Staffordshire (Cert Ed 1971); Keele University (BEd 1972); Cardiff University (CQSW, Dip SW 1980); Married Stephen John Moon 1983 (1 son)

Non-political career: Social services directorate Mid Glamorgan County Council 1980-86; Contracting officer City and County of Swansea and senior social work practitioner 1996-2002; Residential care home inspector Care Standards Inspectorate for Wales 2002-05; GMB, Unison; Porthcawl Town Council 1990-2000: Councillor, Mayor 1992-93, 1995-96; Councillor Bridgend Borough Council 1991-2004; Bridgend representative: Sports Council for Wales, Tourism South and West Wales; Chair British Resorts Association 1999-2001

Political career: Member for Bridgend 2005-10, for Bridgend (revised boundary) since 6 May 2010 general election; PPS: to Jim Knight as Minister of State, Department for Children, Schools and Families 2007-08, to Lord Hunt of Kings Heath as Minister of State, Department of Energy and Climate Change 2009-10; *Select Committees:* Member: Environment, Food and Rural Affairs 2005-07, Welsh Affairs 2005-06, Defence 2009-10

Political interests: Environment, health and social welfare, care for people with disabilities and old people, education, police, prisons, suicide, defence, women's role in public life; China, Israel, Palestinian Territories, Pakistan

Recreations: Theatre, film, reading, walking my dog

Madeleine Moon MP, House of Commons, London SW1A 0AA
Tel: 020 7219 4417 Fax: 020 7219 6488
E-mail: moonm@parliament.uk
Constituency: 47 Nolton Street, Bridgend,
Vale of Glamorgan CF31 3AA Tel: 01656 750002 Fax: 01656 660081
Website: www.madeleinemoonmp.com

GENERAL ELECTION RESULT

		%
Moon, M. (Lab)*	13,931	36.3
Baker, H. (Con)	11,668	30.4
Morgan, W. (Lib Dem)	8,658	22.6
Thomas, N. (PIC)	2,269	5.9
Urch, B. (BNP)	1,020	2.7
Fulton, D. (UKIP)	801	2.1
Majority	2,263	5.90
Electorate	58,700	
Turnout	38,347	65.33

**Member of last parliament*

CONSTITUENCY SNAPSHOT

When this seat was created in 1983 it fell to the Conservatives. However, since 1987 it has been in Labour hands, represented by Win Griffiths until 2005 and by Madeleine Moon since then.

There was a partial recovery by the Conservatives in 2005, though this was due in part to the Liberal Democrat vote share increasing. This, coupled with the removal of the incumbent's personal vote, reduced the Labour majority for new MP Madeleine Moon to 6,523. This seat was safe Labour but the Conservatives gained a 6 per cent swing in 2010 to put them within 2,263 votes of winning.

Bridgend lost Aberkenfig and Cefn Cribwr to Ogmore, while St Bride's Major, Wick and Ewenny went to Vale of Glanmorgan. Situated in South Wales, at the edge of the Vale of Glamorgan, the seat contains two major towns in Porthcawl and Bridgend itself.Heavy industry has dominated the economy. Though the coalmines and quarries have largely gone, they have been successfully replaced, most notably by Ford, which has a considerable presence in Bridgend. Porthcawl has a number of retirement homes and is a popular holiday destination. There are also a number of golf courses.

General economic growth has been aided by excellent transport links, in particular the M4.

Michael Moore

Berwickshire, Roxburgh and Selkirk *(returning MP)*

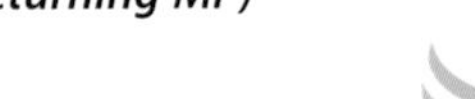

No boundary changes

Tel: 020 7219 2236
E-mail: michaelmooremp@parliament.uk
Website: www.michaelmoore.org.uk

Date of birth: 3 June 1965; Son of Reverend W. Haisley Moore, Church of Scotland minister, and Jill Moore, physiotherapist

Education: Strathallan School; Jedburgh Grammar School; Edinburgh University (MA politics and modern history 1987); Married Alison Louise Hughes 2004 (1 daughter)

Non-political career: Research assistant to Archy Kirkwood MP 1987-88; Coopers and Lybrand, Edinburgh 1988-97: Manager, Corporate Finance Practice 1993-97

Political career: Member for Tweeddale, Ettrick and Lauderdale 1997-2005, for Berwickshire, Roxburgh and Selkirk since 5 May 2005 general election; Liberal Democrat: Spokesperson for: Scotland 1997-99, Transport 1999-2001, Scotland 2001; Shadow Minister for Foreign Affairs 2001-05; Shadow Secretary of State for: Defence 2005-06, Foreign and Commonwealth Affairs 2006-07, International Development 2007-10, Northern Ireland and Scotland 2008; Secretary of State for Scotland (and provides ministerial support to Deputy Prime Minister) 2010-; *Select Committees:* Member: Scottish Affairs 1997-99, Armed Forces Bill 2005-06; Campaign Chair, 1999 and 2003 Scottish Parliament elections; Parliamentary Group Convener 2000-01; Scottish MP representative Liberal Democrat Policy Committee 2001-02; Deputy Leader, Scottish Liberal Democrats 2002-; Acting Leader, Scottish Liberal Democrats 2008

Political interests: Transport, textiles, Europe, corporate social responsibility, foreign affairs, defence, international development; Afghanistan, Kosovo

Other organisations: Member Amnesty International; Governor and Vice-chair Westminster Foundation for Democracy 2002-05; Board Member Scotland in Europe 2003-; Council member Royal Institute of International Affairs 2004-; Member Advisory Council of British Council 2005-; Parliamentary Visiting Fellow, St Anthony's College, Oxford 2003-04; Member Advisory Council John Smith Memorial Trust 2007-; Institute of Chartered Accountants of Scotland 1991; Jed-Forest Rugby Club

Recreations: Rugby, hill-walking, music, films

Michael Moore MP, House of Commons, London SW1A 0AA
Tel: 020 7219 2236 Fax: 020 7219 0263
E-mail: michaelmooremp@parliament.uk
Constituency: Parliamentary Office, 11 Island Street, Galashiels, Borders TD1 1NZ Tel: 01896 663650 Fax: 01896 663655
Website: www.michaelmoore.org.uk

GENERAL ELECTION RESULT

		%	+/-
Moore, M. (Lib Dem)*	22,230	45.4	3.6
Lamont, J. (Con)	16,555	33.8	5.0
Miller, I. (Lab)	5,003	10.2	-5.6
Wheelhouse, P. (SNP)	4,497	9.2	0.6
Fowler, S. (UKIP)	595	1.2	-0.1
Black, C. (SJP)	134	0.3	
Majority	5,675	11.58	
Electorate	73,826		
Turnout	49,014	66.39	

**Member of last parliament*

CONSTITUENCY SNAPSHOT

This seat was created in 2005 from the old Roxburgh and Berwickshire seat with the addition of ten wards from Tweeddale, Ettrick and Lauderdale. Lib Dem Archy Kirkwood had held Roxburgh and Berwickshire since its creation in 1983.

At the general election Lib Dem Michael Moore (moving across from Tweeddale, Ettrick and Lauderdale) won the new seat with a 5,901 majority. Moore's majority fell slightly in 2010 despite increasing his vote-share.

This is a predominantly rural constituency which includes the Border towns of Hawick, Jedburgh, Melrose and Kelso, equally famous for their ancient abbeys and their more modern rugby teams.

During the industrial revolution the local cottage weaving industry metamorphosed into the thriving centre of Scottish tweed production, now past its heyday. However, the tweed, cashmere and knitwear industries are still significant.

The even older industries of agriculture, forestry and fishing remain important to the local economy, with one of the highest proportions of people employed in the sector in the UK.

Robert the Bruce's heart is buried in Melrose Abbey. Tourists are also attracted to fish in the swirling rivers in the Border region.

About one in five constituents commute out of the Borders to work (usually to Edinburgh) and plans to re-open the Edinburgh-Borders line (closed since the 1960s) should improve transport links. The new line is due to be built from 2011, with completion expected in 2014.

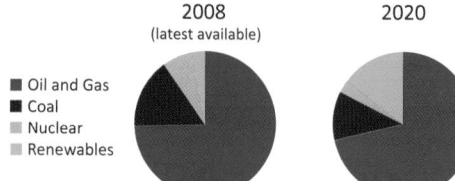

Penny Mordaunt

Portsmouth North

Boundary changes

Tel: 020 7219 3000
E-mail: penny.mordaunt.mp@parliament.uk
Website: www.pennymordaunt.com

Conservative

Date of birth: 1973

Education: Oaklands RC Comprehensive School; Reading University (philosophy) (President Students' Union)

Non-political career: Magician's assistant to Will Ayling, President of Magic Circle; Head of foreign press, George W Bush's presidential campaign 2000; Former communications director: London Borough of Kensington and Chelsea Council, Freight Transport Association, National Lottery; Director of strategy, policy and partnerships, Diabetes UK; Associate, Hanover

Political career: Contested Portsmouth North 2005 general election. Member for Portsmouth North since 6 May 2010 general election; Deputy Chair (political), Portsmouth North Conservatives; Head of Youth, Conservative Party; Head of Broadcasting, Conservative Party

Political interests: Care of the elderly, healthcare

Recreations: Painting, astronomy, crosswords

Penny Mordaunt MP, House of Commons, London SW1A 0AA
Tel: 020 7219 3000 E-mail: penny.mordaunt.mp@parliament.uk
Constituency: Portsmouth North Conservatives, 19 South Street, Portsmouth, Hampshire PO9 1BU Tel: 023 9248 4794
Website: www.pennymordaunt.com

GENERAL ELECTION RESULT

		%
Mordaunt, P. (Con)	19,533	44.3
McCarthy-Fry, S. (Lab/Co-op)*	12,244	27.8
Sanders, D. (Lib Dem)	8,874	20.1
Fitzgerald, M. (UKIP)	1,812	4.1
Knight, D. (England)	1,040	2.4
Maclennan, I. (Green)	461	1.0
Tosh, M. (TUSC)	154	0.4
Majority	7,289	16.52
Electorate	70,329	
Turnout	44,118	62.73

**Member of last parliament*

CONSTITUENCY SNAPSHOT

In the 1970s this was one of only two Labour seats on the whole of the South Coast, but it fell to the Conservatives in 1979. It was not until 1997 that Syd Rapson won the seat for Labour with a majority of 4,323. Rapson held the seat in 2001 with an increased majority.

Syd Rapson retired in 2005 and was replaced by Sarah McCarthy-Fry, an experienced local politician, who lost nearly 10 per cent of the vote-share, but retained the seat with a reduced majority of 1,139.

McCarthy-Fry was defeated in 2010 with a 8.6 per cent swing to the Conservative candidate, Penny Mordaunt.

Boundary changes were minimal.

The modern naval dockyard is a major employer, with large numbers of people also working in private-sector defence industries such as Lockheed Martin, Marconi-GEC, and BAe Systems.

The expanding and highly successful council-owned continental ferry port, just outside the constituency, employs around 2,000 people directly, and is responsible for a significant number of jobs through suppliers and servicing industries.

Jessica Morden

Newport East (returning MP)

No boundary changes

Tel: 020 7219 6135
E-mail: mordenj@parliament.uk
Website: www.jessicamorden.com

Date of birth: 29 May 1968; Daughter of Mick and Margaret Morden

Education: Croesyceiliog Comprehensive School; Birmingham University (BA history 1989); Partner Sion Ffrancon Jones (1 daughter, 1 son)

Non-political career: Labour Party organiser; Political assistant to Llew Smith MEP; Constituency assistant to Huw Edwards MP; General Secretary, Welsh Labour Party 1999-2005; Member GMB

Political career: Member for Newport East since 5 May 2005 general election; PPS to Secretaries of State for Wales: Peter Hain 2007-08, Paul Murphy 2008-09, Peter Hain 2009-10; *Select Committees:* Member: Constitutional Affairs/Justice 2005-10, Modernisation of the House of Commons 2005-06, Welsh Affairs 2005-07

Political interests: Anti-social behaviour, electoral issues

Recreations: Cinema, gym

Jessica Morden MP, House of Commons, London SW1A 0AA
Tel: 020 7219 6135 Fax: 020 7219 6196
E-mail: mordenj@parliament.uk
Constituency: Suite 5, 1st Floor, Clarence House, Clarence Place, Newport, Monmouthshire NP19 7AA Tel: 01633 841726
Fax: 01633 841727 Website: www.jessicamorden.com

GENERAL ELECTION RESULT

		%	+/-
Morden, J. (Lab)*	12,744	37.0	-8.1
Townsend, E. (Lib Dem)	11,094	32.2	8.5
Parry, D. (Con)	7,918	23.0	19.2
Jones, K. (BNP)	1,168	3.4	
Cross, F. (PIC)	724	2.1	
Rowlands, D. (UKIP)	677	2.0	-1.0
Screen, L. (SLP)	123	0.4	-0.5
Majority	1,650	4.79	
Electorate	54,437		
Turnout	34,448	63.28	

**Member of last parliament*

CONSTITUENCY SNAPSHOT

Since its creation in 1983, formed from the abolished Newport constituency, Newport East has been held by Labour. Roy Hughes was first elected to the seat, and was followed by Alan Howarth, known for defecting from the Conservatives to Labour in 1995, who retained the seat for Labour in 1997 with over 50 per cent of the vote.

Current MP Jessica Morden continued for Labour after winning at the at the 2005 general election with a reduced percentage majority. The Liberal Democrats came from third place to whittle down Labour MP Jessica Morden's majority to just 1,650 in 2010.

Transport links are good here, with the M4 motorway and national rail connections. Its location as the gateway to Wales has encouraged companies to build large facilities here, such as Wilkinson's distribution centre near Magor.

The University of Wales, Newport was granted full university status in 2002. Newport hosts the Ryder Cup golf tournament in 2010. The Celtic Manor Resort (where the event takes place) increasingly attracts major conferences and has hosted a number of high profile events such as the All Star Cup as dress rehearsals for the Ryder Cup.

Nicky Morgan

Loughborough

Boundary changes

Tel: 020 7219 3000
E-mail: nicky.morgan.mp@parliament.uk

Date of birth: 10 October 1972

Education: Surbiton High School, Kingston-upon-Thames; St Hugh's College, Oxford (BA law 1993, MA); Legal Practice Course 1994; Married Jonathan Morgan 2000 (1 son)

Non-political career: Trainee/assistant solicitor, Theodore Goddard 1994-97; Assistant solicitor, Allen & Overy 1998-2002; Corporate professional support lawyer, Travers Smith 2002-

Political career: Contested Islington South and Finsbury 2001 and Loughborough 2005 general elections. Member for Loughborough since 6 May 2010 general election; Chair, Wessex Young Conservatives 1995-97; Vice-chair, Battersea Conservatives 1997-99

Political interests: Business, financial services, housing, education, economy, higher education, mental health

Other organisations: Founder, Bluelist Organisation 2002-04; Member: Centre for Policy Studies, The Bow Group; Carlton

Recreations: Choral singing, cookery, reading, theatre, cinema, running

Nicky Morgan MP, House of Commons, London SW1A 0AA
Tel: 020 7219 3000 E-mail: nicky.morgan.mp@parliament.uk
Constituency: Loughborough Conservatives, 42 Station Road, Quorn, Leicestershire LE12 8BS Tel: 01509 415852 Fax: 01509 415126
Website: www.loughboroughconservatives.com

GENERAL ELECTION RESULT

		%
Morgan, N. (Con)	21,971	41.6
Reed, A. (Lab/Co-op)*	18,227	34.5
Willis, M. (Lib Dem)	9,675	18.3
Stafford, K. (BNP)	2,040	3.9
Foden, J. (UKIP)	925	1.8
Majority	3,744	7.09
Electorate	77,502	
Turnout	52,838	68.18

**Member of last parliament*

CONSTITUENCY SNAPSHOT

Stephen Dorrell held the seat for the Conservatives until 1997, but after boundary changes the seat fell to Labour's Andy Reed with a 5,712 majority.

A 5 per cent swing to the Conservatives in 2005 cut Reed's majority to 1,996. The Conservatives seized the seat from Andy Reed in 2010 with Nicky Morgan securing a majority of 3,744.

Boundary changes were slight, Quorn and Mountsorrel Castle ward is now entirely within the seat's boundaries.

Loughborough is a large town in north Leicestershire, between Leicester and Nottingham. The seat includes the town and its university as well as the surrounding small rural towns.

The local economy is dominated by education, pharmaceuticals, research and engineering. The area is quite typical of the East Midlands, with a skilled and educated working population, but has suffered a decline in the manufacturing industry common to the area during the 1980s and 1990s.

Investment has been attracted to Loughborough in recent years, notably from the Swedish pharmaceutical firm AstraZeneca as well as from the research headquarters of Advantica.

Loughborough has also become a key student town, and its university is the home of the county's first dedicated science park and is famous as a sporting university.

Graeme Morrice

Livingston

No boundary changes

Tel: 020 7219 3000
E-mail: graeme.morrice.mp@parliament.uk
Website: www.graememorrice.com

Date of birth: 23 February 1959

Education: Broxburn Academy; Napier University

Non-political career: West Lothian District Council: Councillor 1987-, Council Leader 1995-2007, Leader, Labour Group 2007-; Executive Spokesperson for Resources and Capacity, Convention of Scottish Local Authorities (COSLA)

Political career: Member for Livingston since 6 May 2010 general election

Political interests: Social justice, equality of opportunity, peace, solidarity, education, NHS

Graeme Morrice MP, House of Commons, London SW1A 0AA
Tel: 020 7219 3000 E-mail: graeme.morrice.mp@parliament.uk
Website: www.graememorrice.com

GENERAL ELECTION RESULT

		%	+/-
Morrice, G. (Lab)	23,215	48.5	-2.5
Bardell, L. (SNP)	12,424	25.9	4.4
Dundas, C. (Lib Dem)	5,316	11.1	-4.3
Adamson-Ross, A. (Con)	5,158	10.8	0.6
Orr, D. (BNP)	960	2.0	
Forrest, A. (UKIP)	443	0.9	
Hendry, A. (SSP)	242	0.5	-1.3
Slavin, J. (Ind)	149	0.3	
Majority	10,791	22.52	
Electorate	75,924		
Turnout	47,907	63.10	

CONSTITUENCY SNAPSHOT

Labour's Robin Cook became Livingston's first MP in 1983, after his old Edinburgh Central constituency had been substantially altered by boundary changes.

Livingston was enlarged with Oatbridge, Blackburn and Fauldhouse wards from Linlithgow in 2005, but they did not substantially alter the character of the seat. Despite a notional swing of 1.2 per cent to the SNP, Cook polled 51 per cent of the vote, returning to Westminster with a majority of 13,097.

Robin Cook died while walking in the Scottish hills in August 2005. His election agent Jim Devine held the seat for Labour, albeit with a majority reduced to 2,680. Jim Devine was barred from standing as Labour candidate here in 2010. Despite this, Graeme Morrice won easily for the Party with a 10,791 majority.

Livingston stretches from the western outskirts of Edinburgh to the Pentland Hills in the south, up to a small area of ex-mining towns just north of the M8.

The new town of Livingston is the largest town in the West Lothian region. Hi-tech companies manufacturing electronics and communications products have helped the town grow.

The old Lothians industrial heartland has benefited significantly from the burgeoning economy of Edinburgh compared with the old industrial towns in the west.

Anne-Marie Morris

Newton Abbot

New constituency

Conservative

Tel: 020 7219 3000
E-mail: annemarie.morris.mp@parliament.uk
Website: www.annemariemorris.co.uk

Date of birth: 1957

Education: Hertford College, Oxford (BA jurisprudence 1980); College of Law, London (Law Society finals 1981); Open University (MBA 1997); Harvard University (leadership programme 2004); School of Coaching, Strathclyde University (Diploma executive coaching 2007); Partner Roger

Non-political career: Trainee solicitor, Withers, London 1981-83; Corporate finance lawyer, Norton Rose, London 1983-85; Corporate commercial banking lawyer, Crossman Block, London 1985; Asset finance lawyer, Sinclair Roche & Temerley, Singapore 1986-88; Allen & Overy, London: Corporate finance lawyer 1988-90, Head of education and training 1990-93; Director of professional and business development, Baker & McKenzie 1993-95; Director of marketing and business development, Simmons & Simmons 1995-97; Marketing director, tax and legal services, PricewaterhouseCoopers 1997-99; Global marketing director: Ernst & Young 1999-2002, Linklaters 2002-05; Managing director, Manteion Ltd 2005-; Councillor, West Sussex County Council 2005-07; Governor: Rydon Primary School, Kingsteignton, Newton Abbot College

Political career: Member for Newton Abbot since 6 May 2010 general election; Secretary, Bolney branch, Arundel and South Downs Conservative Association 2003

Political interests: Health, education, NHS

Other organisations: Fellow, Royal Society of Arts 2000; Member, Campaign to Protect Rural England

Anne-Marie Morris MP, House of Commons, London SW1A 0AA
Tel: 020 7219 3000 E-mail: annemarie.morris.mp@parliament.uk
Constituency: Templer House, Sandford Orleigh, Newton Abbot, Devon TQ12 2SQ Tel: 01626 368277
Website: www.annemariemorris.co.uk

GENERAL ELECTION RESULT

		%
Morris, A. (Con)	20,774	43.0
Younger-Ross, R. (Lib Dem)*	20,251	41.9
Canavan, P. (Lab)	3,387	7.0
Hooper, J. (UKIP)	3,088	6.4
Lindsey, C. (Green)	701	1.5
Sharp, K. (Ind)	82	0.2
Majority	523	1.08
Electorate	69,343	
Turnout	48,283	69.63

**Member of last parliament*

CONSTITUENCY SNAPSHOT

The new constituency of Newton Abbot is essentially the same as Teignbridge but without the northern and western wards of Bovey, Chudleigh, Haytor, Kenn Valley, Moorland, Teignbridge North, and Teign Valley, which are now in the new Central Devon seat.

Teignbridge had been a Tory seat until 2001 when Richard Younger-Ross took the seat for the Liberal Democrats with a majority of more than 3,000. In 2005 Richard Younger-Ross doubled his majority over the Conservatives to 6,215. The Liberal Democrats lost to Conservative Anne-Marie Morris, who eked out a 523 majority following a notional 5.8 per cent swing in this new constituency.

The constituency consists of rolling Devon countryside, from the granite tors on Dartmoor to the long stretches of sandy beach by the coastal towns of Dawlish and Teignmouth.

The centre of this constituency is the small market town of Newton Abbot, while the northern three-quarters consists of rural villages. It is a sparsely populated region.

From Starcross to Shaldon the coast provides important additional income, attracting many tourists, especially walkers enjoying the South West Coastal Path, which runs over 650 miles from Minehead in Somerset to Poole in Dorset.

David Morris

Morecambe and Lunesdale

Boundary changes

Tel: 020 7219 3000
E-mail: david.morris.mp@parliament.uk

Divorced (2 sons)

Political career: Contested Blackpool South 2001 and Carmarthen West and South Pembrokeshire 2005 general elections. Member for Morecambe and Lunesdale since 6 May 2010 general election

David Morris MP, House of Commons, London SW1A 0AA
Tel: 020 7219 3000 E-mail: david.morris.mp@parliament.uk
Constituency: c/o Morecambe and Lunesdale Conservative Association, 1a Ellis Drive, Bare, Morecambe, Lancashire LA4 6DW
Tel: 01524 411059 Fax: 01524 831587

GENERAL ELECTION RESULT

		%
Morris, D. (Con)	18,035	41.5
Smith, G. (Lab)*	17,169	39.5
Jones, L. (Lib Dem)	5,791	13.3
Knight, M. (UKIP)	1,843	4.2
Coates, C. (Green)	598	1.4
Majority	866	1.99
Electorate	69,965	
Turnout	43,436	62.08

**Member of last parliament*

CONSTITUENCY SNAPSHOT

The seat was held by Sir Mark Lennox-Boyd from 1979 for the Conservatives until their crushing national defeat in 1997, when it was taken by Labour's Geraldine Smith. Her majority fell steadily since then and was 4,768 in 2005.

Smith was defeated in 2010 by the Conservative candidate, David Morris who secured a small majority of 866.

The seat lost Lower Lune Valley to Lancaster and Fleetwood, it had previously been shared between the two seats.

The seat contains the rural northern parts of Lancashire that borders Cumbria along with the seaside resort of Morecambe. Its two piers have both disappeared: one in a fire, the other a storm.

Morecambe and Lunesdale's local economy includes a fairly large construction industry. However, it has adapted to the service industry as well.

Revitalising tourism has been a positive way for the area to increase its income, and Morecambe is welcoming more tourists in recent years.

Grahame Morris

Easington

Boundary changes

Tel: 020 7219 3000
E-mail: grahame.morris.mp@parliament.uk
Website: grahamemorris.com

Date of birth: 13 March 1961; Son of late Richard Morris, colliery electrician, and Constance Morris, pit canteen worker

Education: Peterlee Howletch Secondary School; Newcastle College (BTEC Ordinary National Certificate); Newcastle Polytechnic (BTEC Higher National Certificate medical laboratory sciences); Married Michelle Hughes 1985 (2 sons)

Non-political career: Medical laboratory scientific officer, Sunderland Royal Infirmary 1980-87; Researcher and constituency caseworker to John Cummings MP 1987-2010; Member, GMB; Councillor, Easington District Council 1987-2003; Non-executive director, City Hospitals Sunderland NHS Trust 1997-2005

Political career: Member for Easington since 6 May 2010 general election; Member, Labour Party 1976-; Secretary, Easington Constituency Labour Party 1996-2006

Political interests: Health, local government, economic regeneration, tackling anti-social behaviour; China, Cuba, Czech Republic, Slovakia

Other organisations: Parliamentary officer, National Association of Councillors 2000-04; Southside Social Club, Easington village; Peterlee Labour Club; Murton Victoria (CIU); Easington Colliery Workingmen's Club CIU

Grahame Morris MP, House of Commons, London SW1A 0AA
Tel: 020 7219 3000 E-mail: grahame.morris.mp@parliament.uk
Constituency: Labour Campaign Office, The Glebe Centre Avenue, Durham Place, Murton, Seaham, Co Durham SR7 9BX
Tel: 0191-526 2828 Website: grahamemorris.com

GENERAL ELECTION RESULT

		%
Morris, G. (Lab)	20,579	58.9
Saville, T. (Lib Dem)	5,597	16.0
Harrison, R. (Con)	4,790	13.7
Dunn, C. (BNP)	2,317	6.6
Aiken, M. (UKIP)	1,631	4.7
Majority	14,982	42.91
Electorate	63,873	
Turnout	34,914	54.66

CONSTITUENCY SNAPSHOT

Ramsay MacDonald, Labour's first Prime Minister, became MP for Easington on the seat's creation in 1950, representing it for some 30 years.

John Cummings was first elected in 1987. In 1997 he had one of Labour's largest majorities at over 30,000. His margin has fallen since but still represents an absolute majority at 58.4 per cent in 2005. A solid Labour seat gave new MP Grahame Morris almost 60 per cent of the vote and a 14,982 majority.

Easington gained Hutton Henry from Sedgefield; it was previously shared between the two seats.

This coastal County Durham constituency includes Seaham Harbour, as well as large ex-coal mining villages such as Horden, Murton and Easington, and the new town of Peterlee.

The breakdown of the mining industry has had a highly detrimental effect on Easington's local economy. Attempts to diversify the economy include greater investment to attract more tourism in the area. Key employers in the constituency include Walkers Snackfoods, Metromail, NSK Bearings and Caterpillar.

A £50 million private sector investment helped create a retail centre at Dalton Park while the Whitehouse Industrial Park in Peterlee South West Industrial Estate continues to attract new business and bring jobs into the area.

James Morris

Halesowen and Rowley Regis

Boundary changes

Tel: 020 7219 3000
E-mail: james.morris.mp@parliament.uk
Website: www.jamesmorris4halesowenandrowleyregis.com

Conservative

Education: Nottingham High School; Birmingham University (English literature); Oxford University (Postgraduate Research); Cranfield School Management (MBA); Married (1 son 1 daughter)

Non-political career: Director, Mind the Gap 2003-08; Chief executive officer, Localis 2008-

Political career: Member for Halesowen and Rowley Regis since 6 May 2010 general election

Recreations: Cricket, family, theatre, music

James Morris MP, House of Commons, London SW1A 0AA
Tel: 020 7219 3000 E-mail: james.morris.mp@parliament.uk
Constituency: Halesowen and Rowley Regis Conservative Association, Church Chambers, High Street, Halesowen B63 3BB
Website: www.jamesmorris4halesowenandrowleyregis.com

GENERAL ELECTION RESULT

		%
Morris, J. (Con)	18,115	41.2
Hayman, S. (Lab)	16,092	36.6
Tibbetts, P. (Lib Dem)	6,515	14.8
Baddeley, D. (UKIP)	2,824	6.4
Thompson, D. (Ind)	433	1.0
Majority	2,023	4.60
Electorate	63,693	
Turnout	43,979	69.05

CONSTITUENCY SNAPSHOT

In 1997 the swing away from the Tories here was 10.7 per cent, enough for Labour's Sylvia Heal to win with a 10,337 majority. In 2001 Sylvia Heal's share remained above the 50 per cent mark. In 2005 Heal was re-elected but with a reduced majority of 4,337.

James Morris took the seat for the Conservatives in 2010 with a 2,023 majority on a 7 per cent swing.

Boundary changes moved parts of Langley to Warley, part of Cradley and Foxcote to Stourbridge, and part of Tividale to West Bromwich West. Belle Vale, Blackheath and Rowley were consolidated fully into this seat.

Halesowen and Rowley Regis is situated on the south-western fringes of the West Midlands conurbation. Halesowen is a prosperous town that benefited from a great deal of residential expansion during the 1980s.

While the seat does not have many professional or managerial workers, a very high proportion of residents are employed in skilled manual work. Manufacturing was the traditional staple here, centred on metal works.

There are two NHS trusts within striking distance of the constituency: Sandwell and West Birmingham NHS Trust, which comprises City Hospital in Birmingham, Sandwell General Hospital in West Bromwich and Rowley Regis Community Hospital in Rowley Regis (the only facility inside the constituency itself), and the Dudley Group of Hospitals NHS Trust.

Stephen Mosley

City of Chester

Boundary changes

Tel: 020 7219 3000
E-mail: stephen.mosley.mp@parliament.uk
Website: www.chestermp.com

Conservative

Date of birth: 22 June 1972

Education: King Edward's School, Birmingham; Nottingham University (BSc chemistry 1993); Married Caroline Smith 1997 (1 son 1 daughter)

Non-political career: IBM (UK) Ltd 1993-97; Director: Weblong Ltd 1997-2010, Streamfolder Ltd 2004-10, Severn Industrial Estates Ltd 2004-10; Chester City Council: Councillor 2000-, Council Deputy Leader 2007-09; Governor: Queens Park High School, Chester 2001-06, Overleigh St Mary's CoE Primary School, Chester 2005-; Councillor, Cheshire County Council 2005-09; Member, Cheshire Fire and Rescue Authority 2008-09

Political career: Member for City of Chester since 6 May 2010 general election

Political interests: Local government, science and technology, business; Central and Southern Africa

Stephen Mosley MP, House of Commons, London SW1A 0AA
Tel: 020 7219 3000 E-mail: stephen.mosley.mp@parliament.uk
Constituency: City of Chester Conservative Association, Unionist Buildings, Nicholas Street, Chester CH1 2NX Tel: 01224 322732
Website: www.chestermp.com

GENERAL ELECTION RESULT

		%
Mosley, S. (Con)	18,995	38.2
Russell, C. (Lab)*	16,412	33.0
Jewkes, E. (Lib Dem)	8,930	17.9
Weddell, A. (UKIP)	1,225	2.5
Abrams, E. (England)	594	1.2
Barker, T. (Green)	535	1.1
Whittingham, J. (Ind)	99	0.2
Majority	2,583	5.52
Electorate	68,874	
Turnout	46,790	67.94

**Member of last parliament*

CONSTITUENCY SNAPSHOT

In 1997 the Conservative Gyles Brandreth lost to Labour's Christine Russell. It was the first time that the Tories had lost the city since before the First World War. Christine Russell took the seat with a 10,553 majority on an 11.5 per cent swing.

In 2005, with a 6.7 per cent Russell's majority was slashed, falling to just 915.

Russell was defeated in the 2010 general election with a 3.9 per cent swing to the Conservative candidate, Stephen Mosley.

The seat lost Tattenhall and Waverton part-wards Eddisbury and Elton part-ward to Ellesmere Port and Neston.

Apart from the historic walled city, the constituency includes smaller outlying areas including Mollington, Saughall and Aldford. The urban population tends to be employed in the professional or managerial sectors but Chester's Roman heritage means that tourism is also a major industry.

The excavation of the Roman amphitheatre has been a work in progress since 2003, and will take over a decade to complete. The project will attract an estimated extra 40,000 visitors to the site and boost the local economy by £5 million annually.

The Garden Lane area of Chester that fronts the Shropshire Union Canal at Tower Wharf has recently been regenerated, with waterside restaurants, offices, new apartments and town houses.

David Mowat

Warrington South

Boundary changes

Tel: 020 7219 3000
E-mail: david.mowat.mp@parliament.uk

Date of birth: 20 February 1957

Education: Lawrence Sheriff Grammar School, Rugby; Imperial College, London (civil engineering 1978); Married Veronica 1983 (1 son 3 daughters)

Non-political career: Chartered accountant, Arthur Andersen; Accenture 1981-2005: Various roles, Global industrry managing partner – energy 2000-06; Councillor, Macclesfield Borough Council 2007-08

Political career: Member for Warrington South since 6 May 2010 general election; Treasurer, Tatton constituency Association

Other organisations: Member, Politea 2005-08; Warrington club

Recreations: Golf, chess, rugby, sailing

David Mowat MP, House of Commons, London SW1A 0AA
Tel: 020 7219 3000 E-mail: david.mowat.mp@parliament.uk
Constituency: Warrington South Conservative Association, 1 Stafford Road, Warrington WA4 6RP
Website: www.warringtonsouthconservatives.com

GENERAL ELECTION RESULT

		%
Mowat, D. (Con)	19,641	35.8
Bent, N. (Lab)	18,088	33.0
Crotty, J. (Lib Dem)	15,094	27.5
Ashington, J. (UKIP)	1,624	3.0
Davies, S. (Green)	427	0.8
Majority	1,553	2.83
Electorate	80,506	
Turnout	54,874	68.16

CONSTITUENCY SNAPSHOT

For decades this constituency sent Conservative members to Parliament. Mark Carlisle held the seat for 23 years from 1964, with healthy majorities. However, in 1992 Labour defeated Carlisle's successor, the one-term Tory MP Chris Butler, by just 200 votes. The Labour victor, Mike Hall, was leader of the local council. Mike Hall moved to Weaver Vale in 1997.

In 1997 Helen Southworth won the Labour nomination after significant boundary changes and was elected with a majority of 10,807, which fell to 7,397 in 2001. Southworth's majority was halved in 2005.

Labour was defeated in 2010 as the Conservative candidate, David Mowat took the seat with a majority of 1,553.

The seat gained the part-wards of Bewsey and Whitecross and Whittle Hall from Warrington North, in exchange for Fairfield and Howley part-ward; they had previously been shared between the two seats.

This Cheshire constituency is the more affluent of the Warrington two. There is some industry in the seat, mainly chemical and service industries, but it generally consists of quiet residential areas. High-income families narrowly outnumber traditional blue-collar workers.

The area benefits from good transport links, sited at the crossroads of the M6 and M62 motorways, midway between the cities of Manchester and Liverpool and on the route of the West Coast Main Line. The canals now support the leisure and tourism industry rather than the industries they were built for.

George Mudie

Leeds East (returning MP)

Boundary changes

Tel: 020 7219 5889
E-mail: mudieg@parliament.uk

Date of birth: 6 February 1945

Education: Local state schools; Married (2 children)

Non-political career: Trade Union Official; Former Leader, Leeds City Council

Political career: Member for Leeds East 1992-2010, for Leeds East (revised boundary) since 6 May 2010 general election; Opposition Whip 1994-97; Pairing and Accommodation Whip 1995-97; Deputy Chief Whip 1997-98; Parliamentary Under-Secretary of State, Department for Education and Employment (Lifelong Learning) 1998-99; Assistant Government Whip 2009-10; *Select Committees:* Member: Accommodation and Works 1992-98, Public Accounts 1994-95, Selection 1995-97, Selection 1997-98, Finance and Services 1997-98, Finance and Services 1998-99, Selection 1998-99, Treasury (Treasury Sub-Committee) 2001-, Treasury 2001-09, Joint Committee on Tax Law Rewrite Bills 2009

Other organisations: Harehills Labour

Recreations: Watching football

George Mudie MP, House of Commons, London SW1A 0AA
Tel: 020 7219 5889 E-mail: mudieg@parliament.uk
Constituency: 242 Brooklands Avenue, Leeds LS14 6NW
Tel: 0113-232 3266

GENERAL ELECTION RESULT

		%
Mudie, G. (Lab)*	19,056	50.4
Anderson, B. (Con)	8,763	23.2
Tear, A. (Lib Dem)	6,618	17.5
Brown, T. (BNP)	2,947	7.8
Davies, M. (Green Soc)	429	1.1
Majority	10,293	27.22
Electorate	65,067	
Turnout	37,813	58.11

**Member of last parliament*

CONSTITUENCY SNAPSHOT

Denis Healey won South East Leeds at a by-election in February 1952 and after the seat became Leeds East in 1955 Healey's majority rarely dropped below the 7,199 he gained in the by-election, even keeping above 6,000 in 1983, when more than a quarter of the voters backed the Liberal/SDP Alliance.

When Healey retired in 1992 his successor George Mudie increased the Labour majority to 12,697. A further swing in 1997 increased it to more than 17,000.

In 2005 there was a 5.5 per cent swing to the Lib Dems, who moved into second spot. This election left Labour with a 11,578 majority. Mudie held the seat with a reduced majority of 10,293 in 2010.

The seat exchanged six part-wards with other Leeds constituencies. The eastern Leeds division stretches out from Harehills to Temple Newsam.

This was once the centre of the Leeds clothing trade and the site of Montagu Burton's biggest factory. But foreign competition has killed the trade. Now the biggest single employers are the local authority and the health service, with Seacroft Hospital inside the constituency and St James's just outside.

The constituency benefits from good transport links with the A1/M1 link, and there are employment opportunities at the Osthorpe Business Park and the Aire Valley Regeneration Area with its IT centre.

Greg Mulholland

Leeds North West (returning MP)

Boundary changes

Tel: 020 7219 3833
E-mail: mulhollandg@parliament.uk
Website: www.gregmulholland.org

Date of birth: 31 August 1970; Son of John and Maureen Mulholland

Education: St Ambrose College, Altrincham; York University (BA politics 1991, MA public administration and public policy 1995); Married Raegan Hatton 2004 (1 daughter)

Non-political career: Account handler (sales promotion and events), several leading agencies 1997-2002; Councillor Leeds City Council 2003-05: Leeds District Spokesperson METRO (West Yorkshire Passenger Transport Authority) 2004-05

Political career: Member for Leeds North West 2005-10, for Leeds North West (revised boundary) since 6 May 2010 general election; Liberal Democrat Shadow Minister for: International Development 2005-06, Schools 2006-07, Health 2007-10; *Select Committees:* Member: Work and Pensions 2005-10; Executive member, Edinburgh Central 2001; Vice-chair Leeds North West 2003-05

Political interests: Education, higher education, international development, public transport, work and pensions, social care; Developing world, USA, Norway

Other organisations: Member, Amnesty International; Supporter: CAFOD, TIDAL (Trade Injustice Debt Action Leeds); Adel War Memorial Association

Recreations: Hillwalking, watching football and rugby league, skiing, travel, real ale, fitness

Greg Mulholland MP, House of Commons, London SW1A 0AA
Tel: 020 7219 3833 Fax: 020 7219 2510
E-mail: mulhollandg@parliament.uk
Constituency: Wainwright House, 12 Holt Park Centre, Holt Road, Leeds LS16 7SR Tel: 0113-226 6519 Fax: 0113-226 2237
Website: www.gregmulholland.org

GENERAL ELECTION RESULT

		%
Mulholland, G. (Lib Dem)*	20,653	47.5
Mulligan, J. (Con)	11,550	26.6
Blake, J. (Lab)	9,132	21.0
Bulmer, G. (BNP)	766	1.8
Thackray, M. (UKIP)	600	1.4
Hemingway, M. (Green)	508	1.2
Procter, A. (England)	153	0.4
Bavage, T. (Green Soc)	121	0.3
Majority	9,103	20.93
Electorate	65,399	
Turnout	43,483	66.49

**Member of last parliament*

CONSTITUENCY SNAPSHOT

From its creation in 1950 until 1997 this was a Conservative seat.

In 1992 Labour edged to a fraction behind the Lib Dems in third place, and it was they who benefited in 1997 when Harold Best won the seat on a swing of 11.8 per cent. Best improved his position with a further swing in 2001. However, Best's retirement in 2005 allowed the Liberal Democrat Greg Mulholland to leapfrog both the Tories and Labour to win the seat with a 1,877 majority on a 9.6 per cent swing.

In 2010 Mulholland was re-elected with a strong 9,103 majority and a 47.5 per cent share of the vote.

The seat lost part-wards to four of the other Leeds' seats, while it gained one part-ward from Pudsey, meaning all the Otley and Yeadon ward is now in the constituency.

This constituency takes in some of the middle-class residential areas of the city, radiating from Headingley to the outer suburbs and on into Wharfedale.

This area does not face the same unemployment issues as other Leeds divisions. Much of the city's professional classes live in this seat.

Headingley has become almost a student town within Leeds. As well as housing a hall of residence, up to half the houses are now multiple occupancy.

Rt Hon **David Mundell**

Dumfriesshire, Clydesdale and Tweeddale ***(returning MP)***

No boundary changes

Tel: 020 7219 4895
E-mail: mundelld@parliament.uk
Website: www.davidmundell.com

Conservative

Date of birth: 27 May 1962; Son of Dorah Mundell, hotelier

Education: Lockerbie Academy; Edinburgh University (LLB 1984); Strathclyde University Business School (MBA 1991); Married Lynda Carmichael 1987 (separated) (2 sons 1 daughter)

Non-political career: Solicitor Maxwell Waddell 1987-89; Corporate lawyer, Biggart Baillie & Gifford, Glasgow 1989-91; BT Scotland: Group legal adviser 1991-98, Head of national affairs 1998-99; Councillor: Annandale and Eskdale District Council 1984-86, Dumfries and Galloway Council 1986-87

Political career: Member for Dumfrieshire, Clydesdale and Tweeddale since 5 May 2005 general election; Shadow Secretary of State for Scotland 2005-10; Parliamentary Under-Secretary of State, Scotland Office 2010-; *Select Committees:* Member: Scottish Affairs 2005-10; Scottish Parliament: Contested Dumfries constituency 1999 and 2003 Scottish Parliament elections. MSP for South of Scotland region 1999-2005

Political interests: Business, commerce, rural affairs; USA

Other organisations: Member: Dyspraxia Foundation, Law Society of Scotland 1986-, Law Society 1992-; PC 2010

Rt Hon David Mundell MP, House of Commons, London SW1A 0AA
Tel: 020 7219 4895 Fax: 020 7219 2707
E-mail: mundelld@parliament.uk
Constituency: 2 Holm Street, Moffat,
Dumfries and Galloway DG10 9EB Tel: 01683 222746
Fax: 01683 222796 Website: www.davidmundell.com

GENERAL ELECTION RESULT

		%	+/-
Mundell, D. (Con)*	17,457	38.0	1.9
Beamish, C. (Lab/Co-op)	13,263	28.9	-3.3
Bhatia, C. (Lib Dem)	9,080	19.8	-0.5
Orr, A. (SNP)	4,945	10.8	1.7
McKeane, S. (UKIP)	637	1.4	0.4
Ballance, A. (Green)	510	1.1	
Majority	4,194	9.14	
Electorate	66,627		
Turnout	45,892	68.88	

**Member of last parliament*

CONSTITUENCY SNAPSHOT

This seat was created by the 2005 boundary review. It was made up of just over 50 per cent of the old Dumfries division, 21 per cent from Tweeddale, Ettrick and Lauderdale, 15 per cent from Clydesdale with the remainder coming from Galloway and Upper Nithsdale.

Labour had a 12 per cent notional majority to defend. However, the constituency became the Conservatives' only gain in Scotland and (with the loss of Dumfries and Galloway to Labour) their only Scottish seat. David Mundell won with a majority of 1,738. Mundell held on to the prize with an improved majority of 4,194.

The seat combines the rural parts of Dumfriesshire with the Clydesdale area of south Lanarkshire and the Tweeddale parts of the Scottish Borders. Most people live in small towns and villages surrounded by large areas of farmland.

The M74 bisects the constituency and two of its largest towns, Lockerbie and Moffat, lie close to the only motorway running from Scotland to England.

The west of the seat still has ties to mining and industry, and opencast mining continues to provide jobs. Knitwear manufacturing is also a dwindling industry.

Tourism is also important to the area and the Old Blacksmith's Shop and Centre at Gretna Green is one of Scotland's most visited free attractions with its history of runaway weddings from England.

Meg Munn

Sheffield Heeley ***(returning MP)***

Boundary changes

Tel: 020 7219 8316
E-mail: munnm@parliament.uk
Website: www.megmunnmp.org.uk

Labour/Co-operative

Date of birth: 24 August 1959; Daughter of late Reginald Edward Munn, representative and Lillian Munn, née Seward, retired nurse tutor

Education: Rowlinson Comprehensive School, Sheffield; York University (BA languages 1981); Nottingham University (MA social work 1986); Certificate of Qualification in social work 1986; Certificate in management studies 1995; Open University (Diploma management studies 1997); Married Dennis Bates 1989

Non-political career: Social work assistant, Berkshire County Council 1981-84; Nottinghamshire County Council: Social worker 1986-90, Senior social worker 1990-92; District manager, Barnsley Metropolitan Council 1992-96; Children's services manager, Wakefield Metropolitan District Council 1996-99; Assistant Director, City of York Council 1999-2000; Unison and its predecessor 1981-96; GMB 1997-; USDAW 2004-; Councillor Nottingham City Council 1987-91

Political career: Member for Sheffield Heeley 2001-10, for Sheffield Heeley (revised boundary) since 6 May 2010 general election; Team PPS Department for Education and Skills 2003-04; PPS to Margaret Hodge as Minister of State, Department for Education and Skills 2004-05; Parliamentary Under-Secretary of State: Department of Trade and Industry 2005-06, Department for Communities and Local Government (Women and Equality) 2006-07, Foreign and Commonwealth Office 2007-08; *Select Committees:* Member: Procedure 2001-02, Education and Skills 2001-03; Member Co-operative Party 1975-; Chair Co-operative Parliamentary Group 2004-05; Labour chair Westminster Foundation for Democracy 2008-

Political interests: Social welfare, social affairs, co-operative issues, European affairs, small businesses

Recreations: Tennis, swimming, reading

Meg Munn MP, House of Commons, London SW1A 0AA
Tel: 020 7219 8316 Fax: 020 7219 1793
E-mail: munnm@parliament.uk
Constituency: PO Box 4333, Sheffield, South Yorkshire S8 2EY
Tel: 0114-258 2010 Fax: 0114-258 6622
Website: www.megmunnmp.org.uk

GENERAL ELECTION RESULT

		%
Munn, M. (Lab/Co-op)*	17,409	42.6
Clement-Jones, S. (Lib Dem)	11,602	28.4
Crampton, A. (Con)	7,081	17.3
Beatson, J. (BNP)	2,260	5.5
Arnott, C. (UKIP)	1,530	3.7
Roberts, G. (Green)	989	2.4
Majority	5,807	14.21
Electorate	65,869	
Turnout	40,871	62.05

**Member of last parliament*

CONSTITUENCY SNAPSHOT

Sir Peter Roberts held this seat for the Tories until 1966, when Labour's Frank Hooley defeated him. John Spence won the seat back for the Tories by just 713 votes in 1970, only to lose again to Hooley in 1974.

In 1983 Hooley was deselected in favour of Bill Michie. Michie held the seat with a majority of more than 8,000.

By 1987 the majority was back in five figures, and continued to climb in 1992. In 1997 Michie's majority topped 17,000. Michie retired in 2001 and was replaced for Labour by Meg Munn. She won a 11,370 majority in 2005. Munn's majority was halved in 2010 to 5,807.

Boundary changes swapped a number of part-wards between the seat and the other Sheffield divisions.

This largely residential southern part of Sheffield is a wedge-shaped area stretching from the centre to the edge of the city and the Derbyshire border.

Housing is mixed with massive tower blocks and leafy suburbs. Owner-occupancy is generally low with a large percentage living in council accommodation, the majority in low-rise houses.

The seat is socially diverse, with a workforce made up of people in managerial jobs and in manual employment. As the area is largely residential, most people commute to work in the city centre and elsewhere. There are large numbers of public sector workers.

Tessa Munt

Wells

Boundary changes

Tel: 020 7219 3000
E-mail: tessa.munt.mp@parliament.uk

Date of birth: 16 October 1959

Education: Reigate County School for Girls; Sutton High School; Married Martin Munt 1992 (1 son 1 daughter 1 step-daughter)

Non-political career: Lecturer, South East Essex College of Arts and Technology 1992-94; Administrator, Holiday Explorers 1994; Supply teacher, Samuel Ward Upper School, Haverhill 1994-95; Community resource unit manager, Suffolk social services 1994-96; Personal assistant to Phil Edmonds 1996-98; Fee-earner: Francs Charlesly and Co 1996-98, Jay Benning and Pelts 1998-99, Forsters 1999-

Political career: Contested South Suffolk 2001 general election, Ipswich 2001 by-election and Wells 2005 general election. Member for Wells since 6 May 2010 general election; Vice-chair, Parliamentary Candidates Association 2003-

Political interests: Education, prison service, domestic violence, children and families, planning, the environment

Other organisations: Member: Greenpeace, Friends of the Earth, IFAW, CND, EIA; Wells Twinning Association; Burnham on Sea Twinning Association; Street Society; Shepton Mallet Society

Recreations: Listening to music, East African history, cinema, reading, cooking for friends

Tessa Munt MP, House of Commons, London SW1A 0AA
Tel: 020 7219 3000 E-mail: tessa.munt.mp@parliament.uk
Constituency: Yarrow Orchard, Yarrow Road, Mark, Highbridge, Somerset TA9 4LW Tel: 01278 641494 Fax: 07714 599669
Website: www.wellslibdems.org.uk

GENERAL ELECTION RESULT

		%
Munt, T. (Lib Dem)	24,560	44.0
Heathcoat-Amory, D. (Con)*	23,760	42.5
Merryfield, A. (Lab/Co-op)	4,198	7.5
Baynes, J. (UKIP)	1,711	3.1
Boyce, H. (BNP)	1,004	1.8
Briton, C. (Green)	631	1.1
Majority	800	1.43
Electorate	72,058	
Turnout	55,864	77.53

**Member of last parliament*

CONSTITUENCY SNAPSHOT

Wells (and its predecessor seat) has been in Conservative hands since 1945. David Heathcoat-Amory is the current Conservative incumbent and has represented the seat since 1983. In 1997 Heathcoat-Amory's majority was reduced to 528.

The Conservatives increased their majority in 2001 to 2,796 and increased it to 3,040 in 2005. After almost 30 years in parliament, Conservative David Heathcoat-Amory lost to Liberal Democrat Tessa Munt by just 800 votes in 2010.

Boundary changes were minimal and relate only to three wards that overlapped Wells and Somerton and Frome. The ward of Ashwick, Chilcompton and Stratton is now completely within the seat's boundaries, while the other two wards are now entirely within Somerton and Frome.

The Somerset city of Wells, after which the constituency is named, is England's smallest city. The constituency also lays claim to Glastonbury, and the burial site of King Arthur and Guinevere, said to be in the grounds of the ruined Glastonbury Abbey.

Given its scenic environs, including the Mendip Hills, the Cheddar Gorge and the Somerset Levels, as well as its historically significant buildings, and Glastonbury, home of the world-renowned music festival, tourism is the major employer in the constituency.

This is closely followed by agriculture, which despite the recent economic downturn, remains a vital aspect of the constituency.

Conor Murphy

Newry and Armagh ***(returning MP)***

No boundary changes

Sinn Féin

Tel: 020 7219 8534
E-mail: murphyc@parliament.uk

Date of birth: 10 July 1963

Education: St Colman's College, Newry; Ulster University (BA humanities); Queen's University, Belfast (MA); Married Catherine (1 son 1 daughter)

Non-political career: Councillor, Newry and Mourne District Council 1989-97

Political career: Contested Newry and Armagh 2001 general election. Member for Newry and Armagh since 5 May 2005 general election; Northern Ireland Assembly: MLA for Newry and Armagh 1998-, Member, Preparation for Government Committee 2006-07; Minister for Regional Development 2007-

Other organisations: Manages Cumann Na Meirleach Ard Mhaca Theas, project for ex-prisoners, South Armagh

Conor Murphy MP, House of Commons, London SW1A 0AA
Tel: 020 7219 8534 Fax: 020 7219 6107
E-mail: murphyc@parliament.uk
Constituency: 1 Kilmorey Terrace, Patrick Street, Newry, Co Down BT35 6DW Tel: 028 3026 1693 Fax: 028 3026 8283

GENERAL ELECTION RESULT

		%	+/-
Murphy, C. (Sinn Féin)*	18,857	42.0	1.1
Bradley, D. (SDLP)	10,526	23.4	-1.4
Kennedy, D. (UCUNF)	8,558	19.1	
Irwin, W. (DUP)	5,764	12.8	
Frazer, W. (Ind)	656	1.5	
Muir, A. (All)	545	1.2	
Majority	8,331	18.55	
Electorate	74,308		
Turnout	44,906	60.43	

**Member of last parliament*

CONSTITUENCY SNAPSHOT

A split nationalist vote enabled the UUP's Jim Nicholson to hold the constituency in the 1980s but after resigning his seat in protest at the Anglo Irish Agreement in 1985 he failed to hold it in the subsequent by-election, losing out to Seamus Mallon of the SDLP. Mallon held the seat until his retirement in 2005.

At the 2005 general election Sinn Féin's Conor Murphy defeated the SDLP's Dominic Bradley to succeed Mallon, securing over 40 per cent of the vote. In 2010 Murphy retained the seat with an 8,331 majority.

This is a large constituency between Belfast and the border with the Republic. It covers the whole of Armagh and most of Newry and Mourne district councils. It is dominated by the two cities that give it its name.

Armagh is the ecclesiastical capital of Ireland and is home to the heads of both the Catholic Church and the Anglican Church of Ireland.

Newry attained city status in 2002. It has enjoyed something of a boom status in the years since and has enjoyed a period of relative prosperity as its proximity to the Republic's border led shoppers from south of the border to spend the Euro in the city.

Rt Hon **Jim Murphy**

East Renfrewshire (returning MP)

No boundary changes

Tel: 020 7219 4615
E-mail: jimmurphymp@parliament.uk
Website: www.jimmurphymp.com

Date of birth: 23 August 1967; Son of Jim Murphy, pipe-fitter, and Anne Murphy, secretary

Education: Bellarmine Secondary School, Glasgow; Milnerton High School, Cape Town; Married Claire Cook (1 daughter 2 sons)

Non-political career: President: NUS (Scotland) 1992-94, NUS 1994-96; Director, Endsleigh Insurance 1994-96; Project Manager, Scottish Labour Party 1996-97; Member, GMB

Political career: Member for Eastwood/East Renfrewshire (renamed 2005) since 1 May 1997 general election; PPS to Helen Liddell as Secretary of State for Scotland 2001-02; Assistant Government Whip 2002-03; Government Whip 2003-05; Parliamentary Secretary, Cabinet Office 2005-06; Minister of State: Department for Work and Pensions (Employment and Welfare Reform) 2006-07, Foreign and Commonwealth Office (Europe) 2007-08; Secretary of State for Scotland 2008-10; Shadow Secretary of State for Scotland 2010-; *Select Committees:* Member: Public Accounts 1999-2001; Vice-chair, Labour Friends of Israel 1997-01, Chair 2001-02; Member, Co-operative Party

Political interests: Economy, employment, international affairs, defence, consumer issues, sport; Southern Africa, Middle East

Other organisations: PC 2008; *House Magazine* Commons Minister of the Year 2008; Bonnington Golf

Recreations: Football, travelling in Scotland and Ireland, cinema, horse-racing, golf

Rt Hon Jim Murphy MP, House of Commons, London SW1A 0AA
Tel: 020 7219 4615 Fax: 020 7219 5657
E-mail: jimmurphymp@parliament.uk
Constituency: 2 Stewart Drive, Clarkston, East Renfrewshire G76 7EZ
Tel: 0141-621 2080 Fax: 0141-621 2081
Website: www.jimmurphymp.com

GENERAL ELECTION RESULT

		%	+/-
Murphy, J. (Lab)*	25,987	50.8	6.9
Cook, R. (Con)	15,567	30.4	0.6
MacDonald, G. (Lib Dem)	4,720	9.2	-9.0
Archer, G. (SNP)	4,535	8.9	2.0
MacKay, D. (UKIP)	372	0.7	
Majority	10,420	20.36	
Electorate	66,249		
Turnout	51,181	77.26	

**Member of last parliament*

CONSTITUENCY SNAPSHOT

East Renfrewshire is the new name for the old Eastwood seat. Allan Stewart became Tory MP in 1979. In 1997 Stewart stood down and Paul Cullen was selected as the Conservative candidate, but the seat fell to Labour's Jim Murphy, on a swing of 14.3 per cent. Murphy trebled his majority in 2001.

There were no boundary changes in 2005, making the seat one of only three Scottish constituencies to escape the review unaltered, though its name was changed to East Renfrewshire. Jim Murphy's majority fell to 6,657 on a 2.6 per cent swing to the Conservatives. Murphy was re-elected in 2010 with a 10,420 majority.

This constituency includes several middle-class commuter towns in the far south of the Glasgow conurbation. It takes in a large rural area to the south and west.

Barrhead is the exception to the general prosperity. Overall, it is well-educated and the vast majority of the workforce is employed in non-manual positions.

Attractions in the area include a number of reservoirs, Rouken Glen, and the new Dams to Darnley Country Park.When completed in 2009, Whitelee Wind Farm became Europe's largest onshore wind farm.

Rt Hon **Paul Murphy**

Torfaen (returning MP)

No boundary changes

Tel: 020 7219 3463
E-mail: hunta@parliament.uk
Website: www.paulmurphymp.co.uk

Date of birth: 25 November 1948; Son of late Ronald and late Marjorie Murphy

Education: St Francis School, Abersychan; West Monmouth School, Pontypool; Oriel College, Oxford (MA modern history 1970); Single

Non-political career: Management trainee, CWS 1970-71; Lecturer in government, Ebbw Vale College of Further Education 1971-87; Visiting Parliamentary Fellow, St Anthony's College, Oxford 2006-07; Member, TGWU; Torfaen Borough Council: Councillor 1973-87, Chair, Finance Committee 1976-86

Political career: Contested Wells 1979 general election. Member for Torfaen since 11 June 1987 general election; Opposition Spokesman on: Welsh Affairs 1988-94, Northern Ireland 1994-95, Foreign Affairs 1995, Defence, Disarmament and Arms Control 1995-97; Minister of State, Northern Ireland Office (Minister for Political Development) 1997-99; Secretary of State: for Wales 1999-2002, for Northern Ireland 2002-05; Chairman, Intelligence and Security Committee 2005-08; Secretary of State for Wales 2008-09; *Select Committees:* Member: Joint Committee on National Security Strategy 2010; Secretary, Torfaen Constituency Labour Party 1971-87; Chair, Welsh Group of Labour MPs 1996-97

Political interests: Local and regional government, wales, education, housing, foreign affairs; Northern Ireland

Other organisations: Former Treasurer, Anglo-Austrian Society; Knight of St Gregory (Papal Award); PC 1999; KCMCO; Hon. Fellow, Oriel College, Oxford 2001; Parliamentary Visiting Fellow, St Antony's College, Oxford 2006-07; Hon. Fellow, Glyndŵr University, Wrexham 2009-; Oxford and Cambridge Club

Recreations: Classical music, cooking

Rt Hon Paul Murphy MP, House of Commons, London SW1A 0AA
Tel: 020 7219 3463 Fax: 020 7219 3819
E-mail: hunta@parliament.uk
Constituency: 73 Upper Trosnant Street, Pontypool, Torfaen, Gwent NP4 8AU Tel: 01495 750078 Fax: 01495 752584
Website: www.paulmurphymp.co.uk

GENERAL ELECTION RESULT

		%	+/-
Murphy, P. (Lab)*	16,847	44.8	-12.0
Burns, J. (Con)	7,541	20.0	4.3
Morgan, D. (Lib Dem)	6,264	16.6	0.9
ab Elis, R. (PIC)	2,005	5.3	-0.9
Wildgust, F. (Ind)	1,419	3.8	
Dunn, G. (UKIP)	862	2.3	-0.9
Turner-Thomas, R. (Ind)	607	1.6	-0.5
Clarke, O. (Green)	438	1.2	
Majority	9,306	24.72	
Electorate	61,178		
Turnout	37,640	61.53	

**Member of last parliament*

CONSTITUENCY SNAPSHOT

Leo Abse held the seat for over 20 years until his former agent Paul Murphy's election in 1987. By the 1997 general election Murphy had built his majority to 24,536. Since the Labour landslide of 1997 Murphy's majority has been reduced, but at the 2005 general election it was still 14,791. Murphy won again in 2010 with a 9,306 majority.

This Gwent Valley's seat includes the towns of Cwmbran and Pontypool and a number of smaller villages up to Blaenavon in the north. The seat has coterminous boundaries with the Torfaen local authority area.

This is largely former mining territory though the new town Cwmbran has excellent transport links and a mixed industrial economy.

It was at Blaenavon in 1878 that the Bessemer process of making fine steel was invented. The town's industrial heritage has placed it on the tourist map. It is now a World Heritage Site and also houses the National Coal Museum.

Pontypool grew around a 180-acre park owned by the Hanbury family. It is now largely a dormitory town for commuters and enjoys excellent links to the M4.

Ian Murray

Edinburgh South

No boundary changes

Tel: 020 7219 3000
E-mail: ian.murray.mp@parliament.uk
Website: www.murray4south.co.uk

Date of birth: 1976

Education: Wester Hailes Education Centre; Edinburgh University (social policy and law); Partner Hannah

Non-political career: Financial services, Royal Blind Asylum; Internet TV station; Partner, Alibi Bar; Managing director, 100mph Events Ltd; Member, USDAW; Councillor, Edinburgh City Council 2003-

Political career: Member for Edinburgh South since 6 May 2010 general election; Member: Labour Party, Co-operative Party; Campaign manager, Edinburgh Pentlands, 1997 and 2001 general election

Political interests: Education, services for disabled people, social justice, equal opportunities, environment, conservation

Other organisations: Member, Fabian Society; Trustee, Great War Memorial Committee

Ian Murray MP, House of Commons, London SW1A 0AA
Tel: 020 7219 3000 E-mail: ian.murray.mp@parliament.uk
Constituency: 31 Minto Street, Edinburgh EH9 2BT
Tel: 0131-667 7148 Website: www.murray4south.co.uk

GENERAL ELECTION RESULT

		%	+/-
Murray, I. (Lab)	15,215	34.7	1.6
Mackintosh, F. (Lib Dem)	14,899	34.0	1.8
Hudson, N. (Con)	9,452	21.6	-2.5
Howat, S. (SNP)	3,354	7.7	1.5
Burgess, S. (Green)	881	2.0	-1.2
Majority	316	0.72	
Electorate	59,354		
Turnout	43,801	73.80	

CONSTITUENCY SNAPSHOT

Sir William Darling held this seat for the Conservatives from 1945 until his resignation in 1957. (Sir William's great-nephew is the Labour MP Alistair Darling). Michael Hutchison replaced Darling at the resulting by-election, and held the seat until his retirement in 1979 when Michael Ancram, the son of the 12th Marquess of Lothian, retained the constituency for the Conservatives.

Michael Ancram lost the seat at the 1987 general election to Labour's Nigel Griffiths. By 1997 Labour's majority had risen to 11,452.

In 2001 Griffiths's majority fell by more than half as the Liberal Democrats took second position. Nigel Griffiths stood down in 2010 and Labour's Ian Murray won with a wafer thin Labour majority of 316.

The Liberal Democrats vote was boosted by the addition of South Morningside and Fairmilehead from Edinburgh Pentlands in 2005. However, Griffiths was returned by 405 votes.

Like the other Edinburgh seats, this is a constituency of contrasts. It contains some of the city's best housing stock, including the desirable residential areas of Marchmont, Merchiston, Morningside and Newington. Morningside has one of the highest concentrations of millionaires in the UK.

The seat is mostly affluent and more than half of all workers are managers or professionals or in associate managerial or professional occupations. Unemployment tends to be lower than in the rest of Edinburgh.

Sheryll Murray

South East Cornwall

Boundary changes

Tel: 020 7219 3000
E-mail: sheryll.murray.mp@parliament.uk
Website: www.sheryllmurray.com

Education: Torpoint Comprehensive School; Married Neil (1 son 1 daughter)

Non-political career: Former councillor, Cornwall County Council; Caradon District Council: Councillor, Leader Conservative group

Political career: Member for South East Cornwall since 6 May 2010 general election

Political interests: Environment, tourism

Sheryll Murray MP, House of Commons, London SW1A 0AA
Tel: 020 7219 3000 E-mail: sheryll.murray.mp@parliament.uk
Constituency: 21 Victoria Commercial Centre, Station Approach, Victoria, Roche, St Austell, Cornwall PL26 8LG Tel: 01726 891541
Fax: 01726 891708 Website: www.sheryllmurray.com

GENERAL ELECTION RESULT

		%
Murray, S. (Con)	22,390	45.1
Gillard, K. (Lib Dem)	19,170	38.6
Sparling, M. (Lab)	3,507	7.1
McWilliam, S. (UKIP)	3,083	6.2
Creagh-Osborne, R. (Green)	826	1.7
Holmes, R. (Meb Ker)	641	1.3
Majority	3,220	6.49
Electorate	72,237	
Turnout	49,617	68.69

CONSTITUENCY SNAPSHOT

Since 1945 this seat was held by both the Tories and the Liberals alternatively, although the Conservatives established themselves here from 1970 until 1997 when the Liberal Democrat Colin Breed won the seat. Colin Breed retained his seat in 2001 with a majority of 5,375.

Unlike in neighbouring North Cornwall, Liberal Democrat support remained solid here in the 2005 general election, with Colin Breed's vote majority increasing to just over 6,500. Conservative Sheryll Murray gained the seat from the Liberal Democrats following Colin Breed's retirement in 2010.

Boundary changes moved Fowey and Tywardreath, and St Blaise wards to St Austell and Newquay, whilst Stokeclimsland moved to North Cornwall.

The attractive rural constituency of South East Cornwall has many small ports, and a thriving tourism industry. Like most South Coast locations, it also has a high proportion of retired people.

The three main towns are Saltash, Torpoint and Liskeard, but most of the population live in the numerous small villages and former fishing ports spread out across the region.

The local economy is based to a considerable extent on tourism, although creative industries are growing exponentially. There are also considerable numbers involved in retail and manufacturing. Farming also plays a significant role here.

Dr **Andrew Murrison**

South West Wiltshire (returning MP)

New constituency

Tel: 020 7219 8128
E-mail: murrisona@parliament.uk
Website: www.andrewmurrison.co.uk

Conservative

Date of birth: 24 April 1961; Son of William Murrison and Marion, née Horn

Education: Harwich High School; The Harwich School; Bristol University medicine: (MB CHB 1984), (MD 1995); Cambridge University medicine (DPH 1996); Married Jennifer Jane Munden 1994 (5 daughters)

Non-political career: Surgeon Commander Royal Navy 1981-2000; Royal Naval Reserve 2000-: Served in Iraq (Operation Telic II) 2003; Principal Medical Officer HM Naval Base Portsmouth 1996-99; Staff Officer, Commander-In-Chief Fleet 1999-2000; Locum Consultant Occupational Physician Gloucestershire Royal Hospital and GP 2000-01

Political career: Member for Westbury 2001-10, for South West Wiltshire since 6 May 2010 general election; Shadow Minister for: Public Services, Health and Education 2003-04, Health 2004-07, Defence 2007-10; *Select Committees:* Member: Science and Technology 2001-05

Political interests: Health, defence; Morocco, Iraq

Other organisations: Royal British Legion; Lions 2001-; Gilbert Blane Medal 1994; MFOM 1994; Warminster Conservative Club, Royal British Legion, Warminster Branch, Vice-president, Trowbridge White Ensign Association, Westbury Lions; *Publications:* Investors in Communities (Bow Group, 2000)

Recreations: Sailing, skiing

Dr Andrew Murrison MP, House of Commons, London SW1A 0AA
Tel: 020 7219 8128 Fax: 020 7219 1944
E-mail: murrisona@parliament.uk
Constituency: Lovemead House, Roundstone Street, Trowbridge, Wiltshire BA14 8DG Tel: 01225 358584 Fax: 01225 358583
Website: www.andrewmurrison.co.uk

GENERAL ELECTION RESULT

		%
Murrison, A. (Con)*	25,321	51.7
Carbin, T. (Lib Dem)	14,954	30.5
Rennison, R. (Lab)	5,613	11.5
Cuthbert-Murray, M. (UKIP)	2,684	5.5
Black, C. (Ind)	446	0.9
Majority	10,367	21.15
Electorate	71,645	
Turnout	49,018	68.42

**Member of last parliament*

CONSTITUENCY SNAPSHOT

This new seat consists primarily of the Westbury seat minus its northernmost wards. There are three towns on the Wiltshire plains, plus Mere in the Salisbury district, the military town of Warminster, and the county town of Trowbridge plus Westbury itself. Westbury, a market town on the western edge of Salisbury Plain, is famed for its White Horse.

The Conservatives have held the Westbury area continually since the 1920s. It has been represented since the Second World War by a total of four MPs. Sir Robert Grimston was the MP until 1964 and he was followed by Sir Dennis Walters, who held the division continuously until 1992 when David Faber took the reins. Faber represented the constituency for nine years before being replaced by Andrew Murrison in 2001.

Murrison held a 5,000 plus majority in both 2001 and 2005. He won this new seat in 2010 for the Conservatives with a 10,367 majority.

There is a history of military establishments in the Warminster and Westbury areas; Warminster in particular is very much an army town.

The constituency is helped in maintaining its low unemployment and attracting inward investment by the fact that the town of Trowbridge as the county town is the main administrative headquarters for both the district and county councils.

Lisa Nandy

Wigan

Boundary changes

Tel: 020 7219 3000
E-mail: lisa.nandy.mp@parliament.uk
Website: www.lisanandy.co.uk

Date of birth: 9 August 1979

Education: Parrs Wood Comprehensive School, Manchester; Holy Cross Sixth Form College, Bury; Newcastle University (BA politics 2001); Birkbeck University, London (MSc government, policy and politics 2005)

Non-political career: Parliamentary assistant to Neil Gerrard MP 2001-03; Policy researcher, Centrepoint 2003-05; Policy adviser, Children's Society 2005-10; Member, Unite; London Borough of Hammersmith and Fulham Council: Councillor 2006-10, Shadow Cabinet Member for Housing and Regeneration; Governor, Brackenbury Primary School 2002-

Political career: Member for Wigan since 6 May 2010 general election; Member, Wigan Labour Party

Political interests: Children's issues

Other organisations: Director, Lyric Theatre, Hammersmith 2006-; Member, Amnesty International; Chair, Refugee Children's Consortium

Recreations: Watching and playing all sport, theatre and the arts

Lisa Nandy MP, House of Commons, London SW1A 0AA
Tel: 020 7219 3000 E-mail: lisa.nandy.mp@parliament.uk
Constituency: The Bricklayers, 29 Hallgate, Wigan WN1 1LR
Tel: 01942 826905 Website: www.lisanandy.co.uk

GENERAL ELECTION RESULT

		%
Nandy, L. (Lab)	21,404	48.5
Winstanley, M. (Con)	10,917	24.7
Clayton, M. (Lib Dem)	6,797	15.4
Freeman, A. (UKIP)	2,516	5.7
Mather, C. (BNP)	2,506	5.7
Majority	10,487	23.76
Electorate	75,564	
Turnout	44,140	58.41

CONSTITUENCY SNAPSHOT

There has been Labour representation here since 1918 and in some parts of the constituency, as early as 1906. After the death of incumbent Roger Stott in 1999, the Liberal Democrats cut the Labour majority after a 6 per cent swing. Labour candidate Neil Turner was elected with a majority of almost 7,000. He was re-elected in 2001 and 2005, receiving a five-figure majority on both occasions.

Turner retired at the 2010 general election. Lisa Nandy held the seat for Labour with a majority of 10,487.

The seat gained five part-wards from Makerfield, and the part-ward of Ince from Leigh.

Wigan is mainly urban, but the constituency is more than the town itself: on the constituency's northern edge, former pit villages such as Crooke, Standish and Haigh are surrounded by wonderful countryside.

After the post-Second World War boom of the 1950s and 1960s the coal and cotton industries declined; that decline became precipitous in the 1980s and the economy has only just begun to recover.

The council has made efforts to attract new industries into the town. Wigan has the Tidy Britain national group and the Tote. It also has Millikens, an American carpet company that brought to Britain cutting-edge computer technology for the carpet industry.

Pamela Nash

Airdrie and Shotts

No boundary changes

Tel: 020 7219 3000
E-mail: pamela.nash.mp@parliament.uk

Education: St Margaret's School, Airdrie; Glasgow University

Non-political career: Boots plc; Parliamentary researcher to John Reid MP

Political career: Member for Airdrie and Shotts since 6 May 2010 general election; Former member, Scottish Youth Parliament

Pamela Nash MP, House of Commons, London SW1A 0AA
Tel: 020 7219 3000 E-mail: pamela.nash.mp@parliament.uk

GENERAL ELECTION RESULT

		%	+/-
Nash, P. (Lab)	20,849	58.2	-0.7
Coyle, S. (SNP)	8,441	23.6	7.1
Whitfield, R. (Con)	3,133	8.7	-1.1
Love, J. (Lib Dem)	2,898	8.1	-3.3
McGeechan, J. (Ind)	528	1.5	
Majority	12,408	34.61	
Electorate	62,364		
Turnout	35,849	57.48	

CONSTITUENCY SNAPSHOT

Helen Liddell won Monklands East at a by-election caused by the death of then Labour Leader John Smith in 1994. She held the seat for Labour by 1,640 votes. In 1997, with the seat redrawn and renamed Airdrie and Shotts, Liddell's majority grew to over 15,000 votes and she increased her majority by a further 1.5 per cent in 2001.

In 2005 Liddell was appointed High Commissioner for Australia, passing her now enlarged, seat to John Reid whose Hamilton North and Bellshill seat was abolished. Reid increased his share of the vote to 59 per cent, giving Labour a majority of over 14,000. Reid retired in 2010 and the Party's Pamela Nash won the seat with almost 60 per cent of the vote.

Airdrie is the dominant town and commercial centre. The district general hospital, Monklands, is located in the town. Shotts is home to a high-security prison.

The area has suffered from the loss of traditional industries such as coal and steel. Mining and mineral extraction industries have left their mark on the landscape and architecture of the area. Shotts and the rural communities which surround it are pockmarked by large-scale quarrying, mining and landfill activities.

New industries are replacing the old with call centres and research facilities among the modern businesses locating in this part of Lanarkshire.The construction of the Airdrie - Bathgate rail link provides a new through route between Edinburgh and Glasgow.

Robert Neill

Bromley and Chislehurst ***(returning MP)***

Boundary changes

Tel: 020 7219 8471
E-mail: neillb@parliament.uk
Website: www.bobneillmp.co.uk

Conservative

Date of birth: 24 June 1952; Son of John Neill and Elsie Neill, née Coombs

Education: Abbs Cross School, Havering, Essex; London School of Economics (LLB law 1973); Married Daphne White 2009

Non-political career: Trainee dealer London Stock Exchange 1974; Barrister in private practice (specialising in criminal law) 1975-2006; Called to the Irish Bar 1990; London Borough of Havering: Councillor 1974-90, Chief whip and chairman of Environment and Social Services Committees; GLC Councillor for Romford 1985-86; Leader, London Fire and Civil Defence Authority 1985-87; Member GLA May 2000-08; Non-Executive Board Director, North-East London Strategic Health Authority 2002-06; Board Member, London Regional Arts Council 2003-07

Political career: Contested Dagenham 1983 and 1987 general elections. Member for Bromley and Chislehurst 29 June 2006 by-election to 2010, for Bromley and Chislehusrt (revised boundary) since 6 May 2010 general election; Shadow Minister for Communities and Local Government 2007-10 (Local Government 2009-10); Parliamentary Under-Secretary of State, Department for Communities and Local Government 2010-; *Select Committees:* Member: Constitutional Affairs/Justice 2006-10; Greater London Conservatives: Deputy chair 1993-96, Chair 1996-99; Leader GLA Conservative group 2000-02; Deputy chairman (local government) Conservative Party 2008-

Political interests: Policing and criminal justice, local government, environment, arts; Austria, France, Italy, Spain, Switzerland

Other organisations: Member: Royal Opera House Trust, Friends of English National Opera; Member, Committee of the Regions 2002-08; St Stephens Constitutional

Recreations: Theatre, travel, opera, sailing

Robert Neill MP, House of Commons, London SW1A 0AA
Tel: 020 7219 8471 Fax: 020 7219 8089
E-mail: neillb@parliament.uk
Constituency: Bromley and Chislehurst Conservative Association, 5 White Horse Hill, Chislehurst, Kent BR7 6DG Tel: 020 8295 2639
Website: www.bobneillmp.co.uk

GENERAL ELECTION RESULT

		%
Neill, R. (Con)*	23,569	53.5
Webber, S. (Lib Dem)	9,669	22.0
Kirby, C. (Lab)	7,295	16.6
Jenner, E. (UKIP)	1,451	3.3
Savage, R. (BNP)	1,070	2.4
Robertson, R. (Green)	607	1.4
Cheeseman, J. (England)	376	0.9
Majority	13,900	31.56
Electorate	65,427	
Turnout	44,037	67.31

**Member of last parliament*

CONSTITUENCY SNAPSHOT

Bromley was represented after the Second World War by One Nation Tories, the most notable of whom was Harold Macmillan, MP for Bromley from 1945 to 1964.

In 1997 the Conservative Eric Forth won a majority of 11,118 despite a 12 per cent swing to Labour.

In 2005 was re-elected with a 13,342 majority. Following Forth's death in 2006, the Conservative candidate Bob Neill held the seat at the by-election by 633 votes. Bob Neill held on to this safe Conservative seat with a 5 per cent swing away from the Lib Dems and an increased 13,900 majority.

The seat gained Cray Valley West ward from Orpington as well as the part of Bromley Town ward that was in Beckenham. Three part-wards were lost to Beckenham.

Containing the town of Bromley and the wealthy residential area of Chislehurst, this is as close to a traditional suburb as can be found in London. While the seat is within the London Borough of Bromley, it feels very much a part of Kent.

Bromley has become a more modern and upmarket area. New blocks of flats have sprung up among the inter-war semi-detached houses and an increasing number of young professionals, especially those with families, have moved to Bromley.

Brooks Newmark

Braintree (returning MP)

Boundary changes

Tel: 020 7219 3464
E-mail: newmarkb@parliament.uk
Website: www.brooksnewmark.com

Conservative

Date of birth: 8 May 1958; Son of late Howard and Gilda Newmark

Education: Bedford School; Harvard College, Harvard University, USA (BA history 1980); Worcester College, Oxford (politics post-graduate research 1980-82); Harvard Business School (MBA finance 1984); Married Lucy Keegan 1985 (4 sons 1 daughter)

Non-political career: Vice-president Shearson Lehman Brothers Inc 1984-87; Director: Newmark Brothers Ltd 1987-92, Stellican Ltd 1992-98; Partner Apollo Management LP 1998-2005

Political career: Contested Newcastle upon Tyne Central 1997 and Braintree 2001 general elections. Member for Braintree 2005-10, for Braintree (revised boundary) since 6 May 2010 general election; Opposition Whip 2007-10; Government Whip 2010-; *Select Committees:* Member: Science and Technology 2005-07, Treasury 2006-07, Finance and Services 2009-10; Chair, Southwark and Bermondsey Conservative Association 1990-93, Co-chair women2win 2006-

Political interests: Economic policy, special needs education, poverty reduction and international development, foreign policy, women's issues; China, India, Middle East, USA

Other organisations: Director Harvard University Alumni Association 2005-; Beefsteak, Boodle's, Cresta, White's

Recreations: Football (Newcastle United supporter), running, skiing

Brooks Newmark MP, House of Commons, London SW1A 0AA
Tel: 020 7219 3464 Fax: 020 7219 5245
E-mail: newmarkb@parliament.uk
Constituency: Avenue Lodge, The Avenue, Witham, Essex CM8 2DL
Tel: 01376 512386 Fax: 01376 516475
Website: www.brooksnewmark.com

GENERAL ELECTION RESULT

		%
Newmark, B. (Con)*	25,901	52.6
Edwards, B. (Lab)	9,780	19.9
Jarvis, S. (Lib Dem)	9,247	18.8
Ford, M. (UKIP)	2,477	5.0
Hooks, P. (BNP)	1,080	2.2
Blench, D. (Green)	718	1.5
Majority	16,121	32.76
Electorate	71,162	
Turnout	49,203	69.14

**Member of last parliament*

CONSTITUENCY SNAPSHOT

From the creation of the seat in 1974 until 1997 Braintree was represented in Parliament by Tory Tony Newton. His majority of 13,338 was wiped out with a swing to Labour of almost 13 per cent that elected Labour's Alan Hurst, with a majority of 1,451.

A swing of almost 1 per cent to the Conservatives in 2001 reduced Mr Hurst's majority to just 358. However, in 2005 the seat returned to the Tories as a 4 per cent swing elected Brooks Newmark with a 3,893 majority. The seat was held by Newmark with a 16,121 majority in 2010.

Boundary changes transferred nine wards in the southern part of the constituency to the new Witham constituency. The new boundary extends further north and includes eight wards and two part-wards from Saffron Walden.

Braintree lies in north Essex on the Roman road which links Colchester with St Albans, close to Stansted airport. Apart from the market towns of Braintree and Halstead the constituency has a rural flavour.

Braintree is a relatively prosperous and affluent constituency. Services are the largest employment sector, although Braintree district has a higher than average percentage of employees in manufacturing industries. There is also a small tourist industry, and many residents commute into London.

Sarah Newton

Truro and Falmouth

New constituency

Tel: 020 7219 3000
E-mail: sarah.newton.mp@parliament.uk
Website: www.sarahnewton.info

Conservative

Education: Falmouth School; Married Alan (1 son 2 daughters)

Non-political career: Marketing, Citibank then American Express; Former councillor, London Borough of Merton Council

Political career: Member for Truro and Falmouth since 6 May 2010 general election; Former vice-chair and chair, Wimbledon Conservative Association

Political interests: Agriculture, rural affairs, the elderly

Other organisations: Director, International Longevity Centre; Fellow, Royal Society of Arts

Recreations: Sailing, skiing, bee-keeping

Sarah Newton MP, House of Commons, London SW1A 0AA
Tel: 020 7219 3000 E-mail: sarah.newton.mp@parliament.uk
Constituency: Cornwall Conservatives, The Coach House, Parc Bracket, Tehidy Road, Camborne, Cornwall TR14 8TB
Tel: 01209 713355 Fax: 01209 716944
Website: www.sarahnewton.info

GENERAL ELECTION RESULT

		%
Newton, S. (Con)	20,349	41.7
Teverson, T. (Lib Dem)	19,914	40.8
Mackenzie, C. (Lab)	4,697	9.6
Blakeley, H. (UKIP)	1,911	3.9
Rich, L. (Meb Ker)	1,039	2.1
Wright, I. (Green)	858	1.8
Majority	435	0.89
Electorate	70,598	
Turnout	48,768	69.08

CONSTITUENCY SNAPSHOT

As Truro and St Austell, this seat has had a mixed parliamentary history over the last 60 years. It was Tory until 1974, when it changed to the Liberals, who have held on to it ever since. Matthew Taylor won the seat in 1987. He was elected in 2005 with a 7,403 majority.

Falmouth and Camborne has been represented by Liberal Democrat Julia Goldsworthy since 2005. Before that the seat had been held by both the Conservatives and Labour. Conservative Sarah Newton narrowly won a 435 majority over Liberal Democrat Terrye Teverson.

Boundary changes merged Truro and Falmouth and St Austell and Newquay to create the new seat of Truro and Falmouth. The seat contains all the wards from Carrick District Council.

The seat is be based around the River Fal, with main points of interest being the cathedral city of Truro, the idyllic Roseland Peninsula and the historic packet ship port of Falmouth.

Once well known for its tin mining, the main industry is now tourism, with jobs in distribution, hotels, and restaurants accounting for almost half of all employment.

Caroline Nokes

Romsey and Southampton North

New constituency

Tel: 020 7219 3000
E-mail: caroline.nokes.mp@parliament.uk

Date of birth: 26 June 1972; Daughter of Roy Perry, former MEP, and Veronica Haswell

Education: La Sagesse Convent, Romsey; Peter Symonds' College, Winchester; Sussex University (BA government and politics 1994); Married Marc Anthony Nokes 1995 (1 daughter)

Non-political career: Political researcher to Roy Perry MEP 1994-2004; Consultant Euro/Arab affairs 2004; Chief executive, National Pony Society -2009; Test Valley Borough Council: Councillor 1999-, Leisure portfolio holder 2001-

Political career: Contested Southampton Itchen 2001 and Romsey 2005 general elections. Member for Romsey and Southampton North since 6 May 2010 general election; Chair, Romsey Conservatives 2002-05

Political interests: Education

Other organisations: Carlton

Recreations: Travel, skiing, riding

Caroline Nokes MP, House of Commons, London SW1A 0AA
Tel: 020 7219 3000 E-mail: caroline.nokes.mp@parliament.uk
Constituency: Romsey Conservatives, Romsey Working Men's Club, 13 Market Place, Romsey SO51 8NA Tel: 01794 512132; 07811 189257
Website: www.romseyconservatives.co.uk

GENERAL ELECTION RESULT

		%
Nokes, C. (Con)	24,345	49.8
Gidley, S. (Lib Dem)*	20,189	41.3
Beg, A. (Lab)	3,116	6.4
Meropoulos, J. (UKIP)	1,289	2.6
Majority	4,156	8.49
Electorate	66,901	
Turnout	48,939	73.15

**Member of last parliament*

CONSTITUENCY SNAPSHOT

The new seat comprises most of the wards from the old Romsey constituency, with the exception of three wards and a part-ward lost to Winchester.

The Liberal Democrats gained Romsey in May 2000, when Sandra Gidley achieved a 12.6 per cent swing from the Conservatives at the by-election following the death of the sitting Conservative MP, Michael Colvin.

Gidley retained the seat, with a reduced majority of 2,370, at the general election a year later. A 2.3 per cent swing back to the Conservatives in 2005 cut Gidley's majority to just 125.

Gidley was defeated at the 2010 general election with a 4.5 per cent swing to the Conservative candidate, Caroline Nokes.

Romsey is a well-preserved medieval town, which attracts tourists to its abbey and the nearby country house of Broadlands. The landscape of the seat as a whole is typified by high-quality agricultural land, picture postcard villages, and affluent Southampton suburbs.

The prosperous wool trade declined during the 19th century but was followed by a thriving brewing industry. The swift flowing streams of the Test have provided a source of energy utilised throughout its history.

Siemens is one of the largest local employers. Commuters are well served by the M27 and M3, as well as train links to London and the Portsmouth to Cardiff rail service.

Dr **Jesse Norman**

Hereford and South Herefordshire

New constituency

Tel: 020 7219 3000
E-mail: jesse.norman.mp@parliament.uk
Website: www.jessenorman.com

Conservative

Education: Oxford University (BA); University College, London (MPhil; PhD); Married Kate 1992 (2 sons 1 daughter)

Non-political career: Ran educational project 1988-91; Director, Barclays 1991-97; Research academic, University College London; Executive director, Policy Exchange 2005; Policy adviser to George Osborne MP; Former school governor

Political career: Member for Hereford and South Herefordshire since 6 May 2010 general election; Chair, Conservative Co-operative Movement

Political interests: Public services

Other organisations: Founder, schoolsfirst.org.uk; *Publications:* Author: The Achievement of Michael Oakeshott (Gerald Duckworth & Co 1993), After Euclid (2005), Compassionate Conservatism (Policy Exchange 2006)

Dr Jesse Norman MP, House of Commons, London SW1A 0AA
Tel: 020 7219 3000 E-mail: jesse.norman.mp@parliament.uk
Constituency: Hereford Conservative Association, Grove Mill, Wormelow, Herefordshire HR2 8EG Tel: 01981 541085
Website: www.jessenorman.com

GENERAL ELECTION RESULT

		%
Norman, J. (Con)	22,366	46.2
Carr, S. (Lib Dem)	19,885	41.1
Roberts, P. (Lab)	3,506	7.3
Smith, V. (UKIP)	1,638	3.4
Oliver, J. (BNP)	986	2.0
Majority	2,481	5.13
Electorate	71,435	
Turnout	48,381	67.73

CONSTITUENCY SNAPSHOT

Paul Keetch won Hereford for the Liberal Democrats in 1997 with a 12.6 per cent majority. This was the first time a centre party had won the constituency since 1929.

Keetch only just held onto the seat in 2005 with 968 votes. In 2010 the Lib Dems were defeated by a 3.8 per cent swing to the Conservative candidate, Jesse Norman who secured a majority of 2,481.

Although a new constituency in name, Hereford and South Herefordshire remains extremely similar to the old Hereford constituency. The gain of a small part of Golden Valley North and the loss of part of Backbury and Old Gore to North Herefordshire are the extent of the changes.

It remains a rural constituency dominated in the west by the foothills of the Black Mountains on the Welsh border and in the south by the Wye Valley, with the city of Hereford at its heart. Sparsely-populated villages intermingle with arable and livestock farming, and a healthy tourist industry.

Hereford acts as the administrative, commercial, and retail hub for the large amount of surrounding rural countryside.

Light industry makes up much of the economy and the city is home to both a famous cattle market and the largest cider maker in the world.

The seat has an above average number of small employers. There are a large number of people in semi-routine occupations, demonstrating the importance of agricultural and manufacturing sectors.

David Nuttall

Bury North

Boundary changes

Tel: 020 7219 3000
E-mail: david.nuttall.mp@parliament.uk

Date of birth: 25 March 1962; Son of Roy Nuttall and late Kathleen Nuttall

Education: Aston Comprehensive School, Rotherham; London University external student (LLB law 1987); Law Society Finals Qualified Solicitor 1990; Notarial Examinations Qualified Notary 1998; Married Susan Smith 2004

Non-political career: Taylor Son & Co/Taylors: Trainee legal executive 1980-90, Qualified solicitor 1990, Partner 1990-98, Senior partner 1998-2006; Solicitor, Nuttalls Notaries 2006-; Rotherham Metropolitan Borough Council: Councillor 1992-96, 2004-06, Opposition leader 1995-96

Political career: Contested Sheffield Hillsborough 1997, Morecambe and Lunesdale 2001 and Bury North 2005 general elections. Member for Bury North since 6 May 2010 general election; Contested Yorkshire and the Humber 1999 European Parliament election; Member, Conservative Party 1980-; Chair, South Yorkshire Conservatives 2001-04

Political interests: Home affairs, law and order, small business

Other organisations: Salisbury Conservative Club, Bury; Yorkshire County Cricket Club; Ramsbottom Cricket Club

Recreations: Walking, watching sport especially football and cricket, bird-watching

David Nuttall MP, House of Commons, London SW1A 0AA
Tel: 020 7219 3000 E-mail: david.nuttall.mp@parliament.uk
Constituency: 21A Bolton Street, Bury, Lancashire BL9 0EY
Tel: 0161-764 4548 Fax: 0161-763 9620
Website: www.burynorthconservatives.com

GENERAL ELECTION RESULT

		%
Nuttall, D. (Con)	18,070	40.2
Khan, M. (Lab)	15,827	35.2
Baum, R. (Lib Dem)	7,645	17.0
Maude, J. (BNP)	1,825	4.1
Evans, S. (UKIP)	1,282	2.9
Brison, B. (Ind)	181	0.4
Lambert, G. (Pirate)	131	0.3
Majority	2,243	4.99
Electorate	66,759	
Turnout	44,961	67.35

CONSTITUENCY SNAPSHOT

After the constituency had swung between the Conservatives and Labour throughout the 1960s, 1970s and 1980s, Alastair Burt, now MP for North East Bedfordshire, held on to Bury North for the Tories from 1983 until 1997.

In 1997 David Chaytor, who now has a majority of 2,926, gained the seat for Labour. At the 2005 election Chaytor's majority fell by more than half.

David Nuttall seized the seat for the Conservatives with a majority of 2,243 in 2010.

Boundary changes were minimal. Church and Unsworth wards straddled the two divisions: the former ward is now entirely within the North's boundaries, while the latter is in Bury South.

Bury is one of the more relatively prosperous former textile towns in Lancashire, bolstered by alternative industries, and now part of the Manchester commuter belt.

The seat includes the small towns to the north of the town centre, such as Tottington and Ramsbottom, as well as Bury itself.

Bury has reinvented itself as a Manchester commuter dormitory. Bury was able to remain prosperous despite the decline of textiles, because it had other industries like paper-making, heavy and light engineering, and chemicals to fall back on.

Tourism has come to the area since the opening of the East Lancashire Railway, which features steam and diesel preservation and runs along the Irwell Valley.

Stephen O'Brien

Eddisbury (returning MP)

Boundary changes

Tel: 020 7219 6315
E-mail: obriens@parliament.uk
Website: www.stephenobrien.org.uk

Date of birth: 1 April 1957; Son of David O'Brien, retired businessman and Rothy O'Brien, retired shopowner and nurse

Education: Loretto School, Mombasa, Kenya; Handbridge School, Chester; Sedbergh School, Cumbria (music scholar); Emmanuel College, Cambridge (BA law 1979, MA); College of Law, Chester (Professional Qualification 1980); Married Gemma Townshend 1986 (2 sons 1 daughter)

Non-political career: Armed Forces Parliamentary Scheme (Army) 2001-03, 2005-; Articles, Freshfields, London 1981-83, Senior Managing Solicitor 1983-88; Redland plc 1988-98: Group secretary and director, Strategy and Corporate Affairs, Director of UK and overseas operations, Member, Group Executive Committee, Deputy chairman, Redland Tile and Brick (Northern Ireland 1995-98), Executive Director, Redland Clay Tile (Mexico 1994-98); International business consultant 1998-; Parliamentary Adviser to: Institute of Chartered Secretaries and Administrators 2000-, Manufacturing Technologies Association 2005-

Political career: Member for Eddisbury 22 July 1999 by-election to 2010, for Eddisbury (revised boundary) since 6 May 2010 general election; Private Member's Bill, Honesty in Food Labelling 1999-2000, re-introduced 2002-03; PPS to Michael Ancram as Chairman of the Conservative Party 2000-01; Opposition Whip 2001-02; Shadow: Financial Secretary to the Treasury 2002, Paymaster General 2002-03, Secretary of State for Industry 2003-05, Minister for: Education and Skills 2005, Health 2005-10; Parliamentary Under-Secretary of State, Department for International Development 2010-; *Select Committees:* Member: Education and Employment 1999-2001, Education and Employment (Education Sub-Committee) 1999-2001; Chairman, Chichester Conservative Association 1998-99; Executive committee member, Westminster Candidates Association 1998-99; Special adviser, Conservative Business Liaison Unit (construction sector) 1998-2001; Member, National Membership Committee of the Conservative Party 1999-2001

Political interests: Economy, trade and industry, agriculture and the rural economy, health, housing, infrastructure, transport, Northern Ireland, foreign affairs, education, constitutional affairs; Australia, China, Ireland, Latin America, Sub-Saharan Africa, USA

Other organisations: Non-executive director, City of London Sinfonia 2001-; Board Trustee, Liverpool School of Tropical Medicine 2006-; Non-executive director Small Business Research Trust 2006-08; Chairman Malaria Consortium (UK) 2007-; Board Trustee, Innovative Vector Control Consortium 2008-; Member, Law Society; Member: British-Irish Inter-Parliamentary Body 2000-, International Parliamentary Union 2006-, Commonwealth Parliamentary Association 1999-; FCIS; Winsford Constitutional and Conservative, Cheshire Pitt Club; Vice-chairman, Ebernoe cricket club

Recreations: Music (piano), fell-walking

Stephen O'Brien MP, House of Commons, London SW1A 0AA
Tel: 020 7219 6315 Fax: 020 7219 0584
E-mail: obriens@parliament.uk
Constituency: Eddisbury Conservative Association, 4 Church Walk, High Street, Tarporley, Cheshire CW6 0AJ Tel: 01829 733243
Fax: 01829 733243 Website: www.stephenobrien.org.uk

GENERAL ELECTION RESULT

		%
O'Brien, S. (Con)*	23,472	51.7
Thompson, R. (Lib Dem)	10,217	22.5
Merrick, P. (Lab)	9,794	21.6
Dodman, C. (UKIP)	1,931	4.3
Majority	13,255	29.19
Electorate	65,306	
Turnout	45,414	69.54

**Member of last parliament*

CONSTITUENCY SNAPSHOT

Conservative since its 1983 creation, Alastair Goodlad secured victory that year and Stephen O'Brien won at the 1999 by-election (when Goodlad took up the position of Australian High Commissioner).

Goodlad's majority shrank between 1987 and 1997. In the 1999 by-election O'Brien posted a majority of 1,606. In 2005 O'Brien was elected with an increased majority of 6,195.

In 2010 the Conservatives retained the seat with 23,472 votes giving O'Brien a majority of 13,255.

The seat gained two part-wards from the City of Chester, two from Crewe and Natwich and one from Ellesmere Port and Neston, while losing one part-ward to Crewe and Nantwich and two part-wards to Weaver Vale.

Eddisbury is a largely rural seat in Cheshire, in which Winsford is the only sizeable town. Eddisbury once thrived on salt-mining and sand-quarrying, but is developing a service sector.

It has a diverse employment base and has become an important administrative centre with the Vale Royal Borough Council's HQ and Cheshire Fire Service HQ; Cheshire Police moved its HQ to the town's Woodford Park in 2006.

Boasting several sites of natural beauty, this picturesque seat is also a popular tourist destination. The sandstone ridge and the dark woodland of Delamere Forest, together with peaceful canals, rivers and meres, overlook lush valleys and there is a recently restored canal boat system.

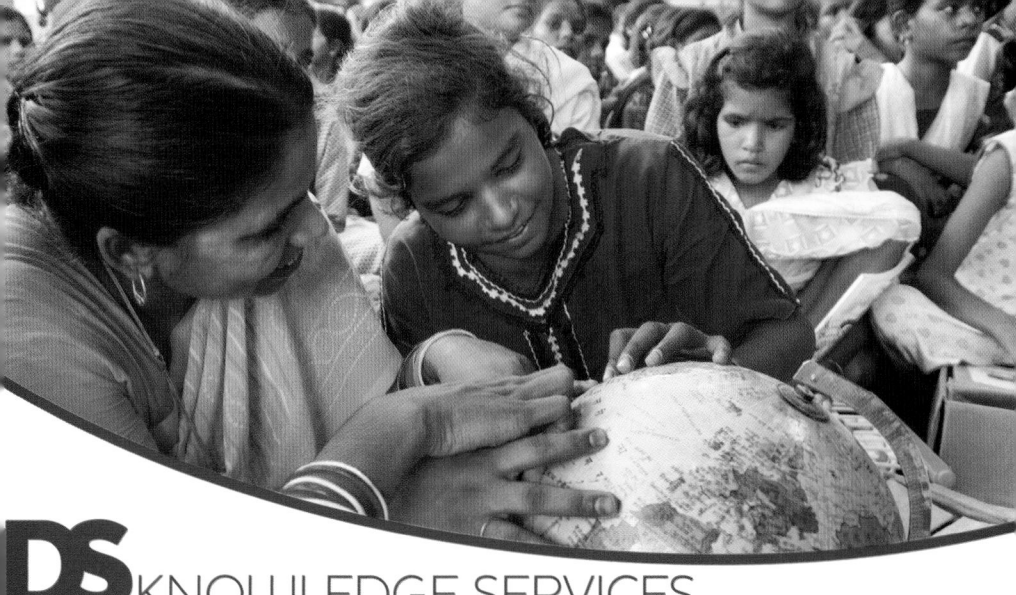

Fiona O'Donnell

East Lothian

No boundary changes

Tel: 020 7219 7059
E-mail: fiona.odonnell.mp@parliament.uk

Date of birth: 27 January 1960; Daughter of Gladys and Patrick Kenny

Education: Lochaber High School; Divorced (3 sons including twins and 1 daughter)

Non-political career: Voluntary sector – mental health, housing, disability, children and families; Public policy; Campaigner and development officer, Scottish Labour Party -2010; Member, GMB; Former: School board member, Community councillor, Scone

Political career: Member for East Lothian since 6 May 2010 general election; Member, Co-operative Party

Political interests: Education, carers, social inclusion

Other organisations: Member, RSPB

Fiona O'Donnell MP, House of Commons, London SW1A 0AA
Tel: 020 7219 7059 E-mail: fiona.odonnell.mp@parliament.uk
Constituency: 65 High Street, Tranent, East Lothian EH33 1LN
Tel: 07986 420421

GENERAL ELECTION RESULT

		%	+/-
O'Donnell, F. (Lab)	21,919	44.6	3.2
Veitch, M. (Con)	9,661	19.7	3.7
Ritchie, S. (Lib Dem)	8,288	16.9	-7.9
Sharp, A. (SNP)	7,883	16.0	3.0
Mackenzie, J. (Green)	862	1.8	-0.7
Lloyd, J. (UKIP)	548	1.1	0.4
Majority	12,258	24.93	
Electorate	73,438		
Turnout	49,161	66.94	

CONSTITUENCY SNAPSHOT

Before 1983 East Lothian was paired with Conservative Berwickshire, and switched between the Conservatives and Labour. In 1983 the new East Lothian seat returned Labour's John Home Robertson. The seat gained Lothian wards in 1997 while losing Musselburgh.

John Home Robertson retired from Westminster in 2001 and the new Labour candidate Anne Picking finished 11,000 votes ahead of the Conservatives.

In 2005 Musselburgh was returned to the seat. East Lothian's boundaries are now coterminous with the council's. Anne Picking (reverting to her maiden name of Moffat soon after the election) held the seat with a majority of nearly 8,000. The local CLP deselected Anne Moffat in early 2010 and Fiona O'Donnell's won the seat for the Party with a majority of 12,258.

This seat takes in the whole of the East Lothian council area to the east of Edinburgh on the Firth of Forth. It takes in Musselburgh in the west and Dunbar in the east. Musselburgh serves as a commuter town for the city's white-collar workers.

The area's economy was built on farming, fishing, coal mining and general manufacturing. Agriculture remains important, but traditional inshore fishing is now only a small-scale industry. The area's principal sources of employment are now in modern industries such as electronics, chemical research and printing.

There are a number of golf courses, including Musselburgh Links (the oldest golf course in the world) and Muirfield; Musselburgh is one of Scotland's three major racecourses.

Matthew Offord

Hendon

Boundary changes

Tel: 020 7219 3000
E-mail: matthew.offord.mp@parliament.uk
Website: www.matthewofford.co.uk

Conservative

Education: Amery Hill School, Alton; Nottingham Trent University (BA photography 1992); Lancaster University (MA environment, culture and society 2000)

Non-political career: Media analyst, Medialink Communications 1995-96; Political adviser: Conservative Central Office 1996-97, Local Government Association 1997; Political analyst, BBC; London Borough of Barnet Council: Councillor 2002-, Council deputy leader, Cabinet member for: Environment and Transport, Community Safety, Community Engagement

Political career: Contested Barnsley East and Mexborough 2001 general election. Member for Hendon since 6 May 2010 general election; Chair, Hendon Conservative Association 2004-

Other organisations: Fellow, Royal Geographical Society; Welsh Harp's Seahorse Sailing Club

Recreations: Sailing, scuba diving

Matthew Offord MP, House of Commons, London SW1A 0AA
Tel: 020 7219 3000 E-mail: matthew.offord.mp@parliament.uk
Constituency: 212 Ballards Lane, Finchley, London N3 2LX
Tel: 020 8445 0702 Website: www.matthewofford.co.uk

GENERAL ELECTION RESULT

		%
Offord, M. (Con)	19,635	42.3
Dismore, A. (Lab)*	19,529	42.1
Harris, M. (Lib Dem)	5,734	12.4
Lambert, R. (UKIP)	958	2.1
Newby, A. (Green)	518	1.1
Majority	106	0.23
Electorate	78,923	
Turnout	46,374	58.76

**Member of last parliament*

CONSTITUENCY SNAPSHOT

As North Hendon, this constituency was held by the Conservatives' Sir Ian Orr-Ewing from 1950 to 1970 and Sir John Gorst from 1970 to 1997.

When North Hendon was abolished in 1997, Sir John Gorst lost against Labour's Andrew Dismore in the bid for the newly-created Hendon on a 16 per cent swing. Dismore won with a majority of 6,155. While he increased his majority in 2001 to 7,417, his majority was cut to 2,699 in 2005. A wafer thin majority of 106 for new Conservative MP Matthew Offord, who defeated his Labour rival Andrew Dismore in a hostile campaign.

Hendon lost three part-wards (Finchley Church End, Garden Suburb and Golders Green) to Finchley and Golders Green and one part-ward (Underhill) to Chipping Barnet. It gained Mill Hill part-ward from Finchley and Golders Green.

This urban north-west London constituency is one of contrasts. Expensive houses in Edgware and the rural environs of Mill Hill stand in stark contrast to the pockets of council estates of Colindale and West Hendon.

The constituency has a sizeable ethnic community with one of Barnet's largest Jewish communities and large Asian and black communities.

Hendon is home to Middlesex University, the RAF Museum, the Hendon Police Training College, and the National Public Health Laboratory Service which provide significant employment.

The £40 million Edgware Community Hospital is now a flagship NHS facility.

Eric Ollerenshaw

Lancaster and Fleetwood

New constituency

Tel: 020 7219 3000
E-mail: eric.ollerenshaw.mp@parliament.uk

Date of birth: 26 March 1950

Non-political career: Former history teacher; Greater London Assembly: Member 2000-04, Leader, Conservative group; Former member: Metropolitan Police Authority, Great Ormond Street Hospital Board

Political career: Contested Heywood and Middleton 1992 general election. Member for Lancaster and Fleetwood since 6 May 2010 general election; Head, Cities and Diversity section, Conservative Party 2005-

Other organisations: OBE

Recreations: Reading, keeping fit, listening to music

Eric Ollerenshaw MP, House of Commons, London SW1A 0AA
Tel: 020 7219 3000 E-mail: eric.ollerenshaw.mp@parliament.uk
Constituency: NLCCC, The Village Centre, 59 High Street,
Great Eccleston, Lancashire PR3 0YB Tel: 01995 672977
Website: www.lancasterandfleetwoodconservatives.com

GENERAL ELECTION RESULT

		%
Ollerenshaw, E. (Con)	15,404	36.1
Grunshaw, C. (Lab)	15,071	35.3
Langhorn, S. (Lib Dem)	8,167	19.1
Dowding, G. (Green)	1,888	4.4
McGlade, F. (UKIP)	1,020	2.4
Kent, D. (BNP)	938	2.2
Riley, K. (Ind)	213	0.5
Majority	333	0.78
Electorate	69,908	
Turnout	42,701	61.08

CONSTITUENCY SNAPSHOT

The two parliamentary constituencies from which this new seat has been created were represented by different parties. Lancaster and Wyre was represented by Ben Wallace for the Conservatives, but he has chosen to fight the new Wyre and Preston North seat at the next election. Joan Humble held Blackpool North and Fleetwood for Labour from 1997 before retiring in 2010.

In 2010 Eric Ollerenshaw took the new seat for the Conservatives with a small majority of 333.

This new seat comprises most of the wards from Lancaster and Wyre, five wards from Blackpool North and Fleetwood seat and a part-ward from Morecambe and Lunesdale.

The seat combines the historic town of Lancaster with the coastal town of Fleetwood.

Lancaster University is a major employer in the constituency, with over 2,000 staff. The university is vital for the local economy. There is also the economic contribution of 17,000 students attending the University with many living in the constituency.

The town of Fleetwood has profited from an increase in tourism in recent years after the massive regeneration of the promenade and market areas. It also has a pier which overlooks the Irish Sea and a long coastline.

Chi Onwurah

Newcastle upon Tyne Central

Boundary changes

Tel: 020 7219 3000
E-mail: chi.onwurah.mp@parliament.uk
Website: www.chi4central.com

Date of birth: 12 April 1965

Education: Kenton School; Imperial College, London (BEng electrical engineering 1987); Manchester Business School (MBA)

Non-political career: Nortel 1987-95; Cable & Wireless 1995-99; Director of product strategy, Global Telesystems UK 1999-2000; Director of market development, Teligent 2000-01; Partner, Hammatan Ventures 2001-04; Head of telecoms technology, OFCOM 2004-; Member, Unite

Political career: Member for Newcastle upon Tyne Central since 6 May 2010 general election; Member, Labour Party 1981-

Political interests: Education, technology, manufacturing, international development

Other organisations: Former national executive member: Anti-Apartheid Movement, Action for South Africa (ACTSA); Member: International Advisory Board, Open University Business School, Chatham House

Recreations: Reading, music, country walks

Chi Onwurah MP, House of Commons, London SW1A 0AA
Tel: 020 7219 3000 E-mail: chi.onwurah.mp@parliament.uk
Constituency: c/o Labour North, Eldon House, Regent Centre, Gosforth, Newcastle upon Tyne NE3 3PW
Website: www.chi4central.com

GENERAL ELECTION RESULT

		%
Onwurah, C. (Lab)	15,692	45.9
Kane, G. (Lib Dem)	8,228	24.1
Holder, N. (Con)	6,611	19.4
Booth, K. (BNP)	2,302	6.7
Davies, M. (UKIP)	754	2.2
Pearson, J. (Green)	568	1.7
Majority	7,464	21.85
Electorate	60,507	
Turnout	34,155	56.45

CONSTITUENCY SNAPSHOT

Labour's Jim Cousins has held the seat since 1987. There was a swing of 11 per cent to the Liberal Democrats in the 2005 general election and Jim Cousins' majority was cut from 11,605 in 2001, to just 3,982 in 2005. Chi Onwurah won for Labour with a comfortable 7,466 majority.

Newcastle Upon Tyne Central underwent considerable boundary changes losing North Jesmond, Ouseburn and South Jesmond wards to Newcastle upon Tyne East. The seat also exchanged a number of part-wards with the North division.

Newcastle upon Tyne Central does not in fact encompass the true city centre, for although it includes Newcastle's lively East Quayside area, the majority of the constituency covers the land surrounding the large open space of Town Moor to the north.

This seat has a strong sense of identity defined in no small part by its football club Newcastle United.

Newcastle upon Tyne Central is a relatively middle-class, white-collar constituency. The number of professionals living in the seat is almost twice the average, while the number of constituents in managerial and technical jobs is also above average.

The seat is home to no heavy industry and very few industrial or manufacturing workers live in the constituency.

Guy Opperman

Hexham

Boundary changes

Tel: 020 7219 3000
E-mail: guy.opperman.mp@parliament.uk
Website: www.guyopperman.blogspot.com

Date of birth: 18 May 1965; Son of Michael and Julie Opperman

Education: Harrow; Lille University, France (Diploma 1984); Buckingham University (LLB 1986); Partner Karen

Non-political career: Farmer in Africa 1987-88; Director, TD Chrome Ltd (family engineering business); Called to the Bar 1989; Barrister, 3 Paper Buildings 1989-2010; Councillor, Wiltshire 1995-99

Political career: Contested North Swindon 1997 and Caernarfon 2005 general elections. Member for Hexham since 6 May 2010 general election; Adviser to Michael Ancram MP as Shadow Secretary of State for Foreign and Commonwealth Affairs

Political interests: Prison reform, health, education, foreign policy

Other organisations: Member, Countryside Alliance; Bar Pro Bono Award for Services to the Community 2007; Albert Edward Club, Hexham

Recreations: Cricket, amateur steeplechase jockey

Guy Opperman MP, House of Commons, London SW1A 0AA
Tel: 020 7219 3000 E-mail: guy.opperman.mp@parliament.uk
Constituency: Hexham Conservatives, 1 Meal Market, Hexham, Northumberland NE46 1NF Tel: 01434 603777 Fax: 01434 601659
Website: www.guyopperman.blogspot.com

GENERAL ELECTION RESULT

		%
Opperman, G. (Con)	18,795	43.2
Duffield, A. (Lib Dem)	13,007	29.9
Tinnion, A. (Lab)	8,253	19.0
Ford, S. (Ind)	1,974	4.5
Hawkins, Q. (BNP)	1,205	2.8
Moss, C. (Ind)	249	0.6
Majority	5,788	13.31
Electorate	61,375	
Turnout	43,483	70.85

CONSTITUENCY SNAPSHOT

Hexham has been in Conservative hands since 1924. For 21 years, until 1987 Tory Sir Geoffrey Rippon held the seat.

His successor, Alan Amos, withdrew just before the 1992 election. His hastily chosen successor Peter Atkinson increased the Conservative vote, bucking the national trend. His majority grew to more than 13,000.

In 1997 a swing of nearly 14 per cent cut the Conservative vote from its highest to its lowest point, and the Labour candidate Ian McMinn came within 222 votes of winning. In 2005 Peter Atkinson's majority doubled to 5,020. Peter Atkinson retired in 2010 and Guy Opperman held the seat for the Tories by 5,788 votes.

There were minimal boundary changes.

Hexham stretches, across 1,100 square miles of sparsely populated countryside from Hadrian's Wall to the Durham, Cumbrian and Scottish borders. Tourism plays a large part in the local economy: half of the Northumberland National Park lies within the constituency.

Most of the population live in three main centres: the historic market town of Hexham itself, the former mining town of Prudhoe, and the large commuter suburb around the old village of Ponteland.

Farming and related industries are in decline, though Hexham's auction mart is an important centre. There is little industry within the constituency, a paper mill at Prudhoe and a chipboard mill at Hexham.

Rt Hon **George Osborne**

Tatton (returning MP)

Boundary changes

Tel: 020 7219 8214
E-mail: osborneg@parliament.uk
Website: www.georgeosborne4tatton.com

Conservative

Date of birth: 23 May 1971; Son of Sir Peter George Osborne Bt, founder and chairman Osborne and Little plc, and Felicity Alexandra Osborne, née Loxton-Peacock

Education: St Paul's School, London; Davidson College, North Carolina USA (Dean Rusk Scholarship) 1990; Magdalen College, Oxford (Scholarship, BA modern history 1993, MA); Married Frances Victoria Howell 1998 (1 son 1 daughter)

Non-political career: Freelance journalist *Sunday* and *Daily Telegraph* 1993; Head of political section Conservative Research Department 1994-95; Special adviser Ministry of Agriculture, Fisheries and Food 1995-97; Political Office, 10 Downing Street 1997; Secretary Shadow Cabinet 1997-2001; Political secretary to William Hague MP as Leader of Opposition 1997-2001

Political career: Member for Tatton 2001-10, for Tatton (revised boundary) since 6 May 2010 general election; Member Public Accounts Commission 2002-05; Opposition Whip 2003; Shadow: Minister for Economic Affairs 2003-04, Chief Secretary of the Treasury 2004-05, Chancellor of the Exchequer 2005-10; Chancellor of the Exchequer 2010-; *Select Committees:* Member: Public Accounts 2001-04, Transport 2002-03; General election campaign co-ordinator 2007-

Other organisations: Vice-president East Cheshire Hospice; Panellist Atlantic Partnership; Honorary President British Youth Council; Governor European Investment Bank 2010-; PC 2010

Recreations: Cinema, theatre, walking, observing American politics

Rt Hon George Osborne MP, House of Commons, London SW1A 0AA Tel: 020 7219 8214 Fax: 020 7219 6372
E-mail: osborneg@parliament.uk
Constituency: Tatton Conservative Association, Manchester Road, Knutsford, Cheshire WA16 0LT Tel: 01565 632181
Fax: 01565 632182 Website: www.georgeosborne4tatton.com

GENERAL ELECTION RESULT

		%
Osborne, G. (Con)*	24,687	54.6
Lomax, D. (Lib Dem)	10,200	22.6
Jackson, R. (Lab)	7,803	17.3
Flannery, S. (Ind)	2,243	5.0
Gibson, M. (True English)	298	0.7
Majority	14,487	32.03
Electorate	65,689	
Turnout	45,231	68.86

**Member of last parliament*

CONSTITUENCY SNAPSHOT

From its creation in 1983 up to 1997, Tatton was Conservative territory. In 1992 incumbent Neil Hamilton won by almost 16,000 votes.

In 1997 the former war correspondent Martin Bell stood as an independent candidate. The local Conservative Association backed Neil Hamilton amid allegations of corruption, despite opposition from Central Office, while Labour and the Liberal Democrats withdrew their candidates. Bell won with a 60.2 per cent share of the vote, the first independent elected to Westminster for 50 years. He honoured his pledge to sit for only one term.

Tatton returned to the Conservative fold in 2001, electing George Osborne. In 2005 Osborne increased his majority to 11,731. In 2010 Osborne was re-elected with a 54.6 per cent vote-share.

The seat gained the part-ward of Rudheath and South Witton from Weaver Vale, and lost Henbury part-ward to Macclesfield.

In rural Cheshire, south west of Manchester, Tatton is a prosperous constituency comprising the commuter and market towns of Wilmslow, Knutsford and Alderley Edge, as well as more rural settlements.

The single most distinctive feature of the residents of this constituency is their affluence: more than a third of households can be categorised as high-income families.

Alderley Edge has been dubbed 'millionaire's village', home to footballers and celebrities. A major employer is the research laboratory of Astra Zeneca. The constituency contains Styal Prison, the largest female prison outside London.

Sandra Osborne

Ayr, Carrick and Cumnock ***(returning MP)***

No boundary changes

Tel: 020 7219 6402
E-mail: osbornes@parliament.uk
Website: www.epolitix.com/Sandra-Osborne

Labour

Date of birth: 23 February 1956; Daughter of Thomas Clark, labourer, and Isabella Clark, shop worker, meat factory worker, cleaner and laundry worker

Education: Camphill Senior Secondary, Paisley; Anniesland College; Jordanhill College (Diploma community education 1990); Strathclyde University (Diploma equality and discrimination 1991, MSc equality and discrimination 1992); Married Alastair Osborne 1982 (2 daughters)

Non-political career: Counsellor with Women's Aid 1983-94; TGWU: Member, Former Branch Secretary; Councillor, Kyle and Carrick District Council 1990-95; South Ayrshire Council: Councillor 1995-97, Convener, Community Services (Housing and Social Work) 1996-97

Political career: Member for Ayr 1997-2005, for Ayr, Carrick and Cumnock since 5 May 2005 general election; PPS: to Ministers of State for Scotland: Brian Wilson 1999-2001, George Foulkes 2001-02, to Helen Liddell as Secretary of State for Scotland 2002-03; *Select Committees:* Member: Information 1997-2000, Scottish Affairs 1998-99, European Scrutiny 2004-10, Foreign Affairs 2005-10

Political interests: Women, housing, poverty

Other organisations: Women's Aid

Recreations: Reading and television

Sandra Osborne MP, House of Commons, London SW1A 0AA
Tel: 020 7219 6402 E-mail: osbornes@parliament.uk
Constituency: 139 Main Street, Ayr KA8 8BX Tel: 01292 262906
Fax: 01292 885661 Website: www.epolitix.com/Sandra-Osborne

GENERAL ELECTION RESULT

		%	+/-
Osborne, S. (Lab)*	21,632	47.1	1.8
Grant, W. (Con)	11,721	25.5	2.4
Brodie, C. (SNP)	8,276	18.0	4.9
Taylor, J. (Lib Dem)	4,264	9.3	-4.8
Majority	9,911	21.60	
Electorate	73,320		
Turnout	45,893	62.59	

**Member of last parliament*

CONSTITUENCY SNAPSHOT

George Foulkes held this seat's predecessor Carrick, Cumnock and Doon Valley from 1979 (when it was named South Ayrshire).

The seat was redrawn in 2005. It includes nine of the 20 wards from Carrick, Cumnock and the Doon Valley, centred on Cumnock and the ex-mining villages of the Doon and Afton Valleys; and seven of the 18 wards from the old Ayr constituency, in and around Ayr itself.

In 2005 George Foulkes was elevated to the peerage. Sandra Osborne, previously MP for Ayr, held this seat for Labour with a reduced majority of 9997. Osborne won 47 per cent of the vote in 2010 and a 9,911 majority.

This seat takes up a large swathe of south Ayrshire in the west of Scotland. It is a former mining area. Ayr itself is an attractive port town on the Firth of Clyde. It is an important commercial and retail centre for the south of Scotland.

Alloway is a magnet for cultural tourists as the birthplace of Robert Burns and the setting for his poem Tam o' Shanter.

Many constituents work at nearby Prestwick airport (in neighbouring Central Ayrshire) and the attached aerospace industry, which has grown substantially in the past decades. The seat contains the Hadyard Hill wind farm, which was Britain's most powerful onshore wind farm when it was commissioned in 2006.

Richard Ottaway

Croydon South (returning MP)

Boundary changes

Tel: 020 7219 6392
E-mail: ottawayr@parliament.uk
Website: www.richardottaway.com

Conservative

Date of birth: 24 May 1945; Son of late Professor Christopher Ottaway and of Grace Ottaway

Education: Backwell School, Somerset; Bristol University (LLB 1974); Married Nicola Kisch 1982

Non-political career: Royal Navy Officer 1961-70; Admitted solicitor 1977, specialising in international, maritime and commercial law; Partner, William A. Crump & Son 1981-87; Director, Coastal States Petroleum (UK) Ltd 1988-95

Political career: Member for Nottingham North 1983-87. Contested Nottingham North 1987 general election. Member for Croydon South 1992-2010, for Croydon South (revised boundary) since 6 May 2010 general election; PPS: to Ministers of State, Foreign and Commonwealth Office 1985-87, to Michael Heseltine: as President of the Board of Trade and Secretary of State for Trade and Industry 1992-95, as Deputy Prime Minister and First Secretary of State 1995; Government Whip 1995-97; Opposition Whip June-November 1997; Opposition Spokesperson for: Local Government and London 1997-99, Defence 1999-2000, Treasury 2000-01; Shadow Secretary of State for the Environment 2004; Member, Intelligence and Security Committee 2005-; *Select Committees:* Member: Procedure 1996-97, Standards and Privileges 2001-04, Foreign Affairs 2003-04, Defence 2004-05; Vice-chair Conservative Party (with responsibility for local government) 1998-99; Chair Executive Committee, Society of Conservative Lawyers 2000-03; Vice-chair 1922 Committee 2005-, Member of Board Conservative Party 2006-

Political interests: Defence, industry, commerce, world population; Malaysia, Singapore; *Publications:* Papers on international and maritime law, global pollution, London, privatisation, debt and international fraud

Recreations: Yacht racing, jazz

Richard Ottaway MP, House of Commons, London SW1A 0AA
Tel: 020 7219 6392 Fax: 020 7219 2256
E-mail: ottawayr@parliament.uk
Constituency: Croydon South Conservative Association, 36 Brighton Road, Purley, Surrey CR8 2LG Tel: 020 8660 0491
Fax: 020 8763 9686 Website: www.richardottaway.com

GENERAL ELECTION RESULT

		%
Ottaway, R. (Con)*	28,684	50.9
Rix, S. (Lib Dem)	12,866	22.8
Avis, J. (Lab)	11,287	20.0
Bolter, J. (UKIP)	2,504	4.5
Ross, G. (Green)	981	1.7
Majority	15,818	28.08
Electorate	81,301	
Turnout	56,322	69.28

**Member of last parliament*

CONSTITUENCY SNAPSHOT

Croydon South is the most prosperous and least urban of the three Croydon constituencies. In 1966 Labour won the seat with a majority of 81. This change was brief and Labour's David Winnick lost the seat again in 1970.

By 1983 the Conservative majority reached nearly 30,000. In 1992 Richard Ottaway, a Nottingham MP from 1983 to 1987, inherited the seat and won with a majority of over 20,000.

In 1997 Labour cut Ottaway's majority by nearly half, however, it had recovered to 13,528 by 2005. Conservative Richard Ottaway held on to this suburban seat with an increased majority of 15,818.

Croham, and Selsdon and Ballards are now entirely within the Central division, having previously been shared between the two seats.

The seat includes the suburbs of Purley, Coulsdon, Sanderstead and Selsdon.

Croydon's transport links with central London make it a popular home for commuters on the edge of London but the borough's status as a centre for business and retail also means it is a hub of employment for surrounding suburban areas.

With a large number of commuters and local congestion trouble spots, transport is an important local issue. As part of the regeneration of the town centre, a relief road around Coulsdon has taken around 80 per cent of the traffic from the town centre.

Albert Owen

Ynys Môn (returning MP)

No boundary changes

Tel: 020 7219 8415
E-mail: owena@parliament.uk
Website: www.epolitix.com/mpwebsites/mpwebsitepage/mpsite/albert-owen-mp

Labour

Date of birth: 10 August 1959; Son of late William Owen and Doreen, née Wood

Education: Holyhead County Comprehensive School, Anglesey; Coleg Harlech (Diploma industrial relations 1994); York University (BA politics 1997); Married Angela Margaret Magee 1983 (2 daughters)

Non-political career: Merchant seafarer 1976-92; Welfare rights and employment adviser 1995-97; Centre manager Isle of Anglesey County Council 1997-2001; RMT 1976-92: Health and safety officer 1985-87, Ferry sector national panel 1987-92; NUS 1992-97: Welfare officer 1992-94; UNISON 1997-2001; Councillor Holyhead Town Council 1997-99

Political career: Member for Ynys Môn since 7 June 2001 general election; *Select Committees:* Member: Welsh Affairs 2001-05, 2006-10, Accommodation and Works 2001-05; Contested Ynys Môn constituency 1999 National Assembly for Wales election; Constituency Labour Party: Treasurer 1991-92, Vice-chair 1992-96; Press officer 1996-2000

Political interests: Welsh affairs, welfare, economic development; Ireland, Cyprus. Malta/Gozo

Other organisations: Director Homeless project 1998-; Member: Institute of Welsh Affairs 1999-2001, Management committee WEA North Wales 1999-2001; Chair Anglesey Regeneration Partnership 2000-01; Holyhead Sailing Club

Recreations: Cycling, walking, cooking, gardening

Albert Owen MP, House of Commons, London SW1A 0AA
Tel: 020 7219 8415 Fax: 020 7219 1951
E-mail: owena@parliament.uk
Constituency: 18 Thomas Street, Holyhead, Anglesey LL65 1RR
Tel: 01407 765750 Fax: 01407 764336 Website: www.epolitix.com/mpwebsites/mpwebsitepage/mpsite/albert-owen-mp

GENERAL ELECTION RESULT

		%	+/-
Owen, A. (Lab)*	11,490	33.4	-1.2
Rees, D. (PlC)	9,029	26.2	-4.9
Ridge-Newman, A. (Con)	7,744	22.5	11.5
Wood, M. (Lib Dem)	2,592	7.5	0.7
Rogers, P. (Ind)	2,225	6.5	-8.2
Gill, E. (UKIP)	1,201	3.5	2.5
Owen, D. (Christian)	163	0.5	
Majority	2,461	7.14	
Electorate	50,075		
Turnout	34,444	68.78	

**Member of last parliament*

CONSTITUENCY SNAPSHOT

Ynys Môn (previously Anglesey) was held from 1951 until 1979 by Cledwyn Hughes for Labour, until Keith Best captured it for the Conservatives in 1979. The Tories retained the seat in 1983, although Plaid Cymru had by that time emerged as the main challenger.

Following a share scandal, Tory MP Keith Best allowed Plaid Cymru's Ieuan Wyn Jones to win the renamed seat of Ynys Môn in 1987. Labour reclaimed the seat from Plaid Cymru at the 2001 general election by a majority of 800. Labour's Albert Owen increased his majority in 2005 to 1,242. Owen was re-elected in 2010 with a majority of just 2,461.

Ynys Môn is the largest island off the coast of England and Wales. The constituency also includes the smaller Holy Island. Separated by the Menai Strait from the coast of North Wales, it is linked by two historic bridges to the mainland.

The main town is Holyhead, which is a major port for transport across the Irish Sea.

Anglesey Aluminium was the largest manufacturing employer on the island until it closed in 2009. Tourism is an important industry. Most of the 125 miles of coastline is designated as an Area of Outstanding Natural Beauty or Heritage Coast.

Jim Paice

South East Cambridgeshire (returning MP)

Boundary changes

Tel: 020 7219 4101
E-mail: paicejet@parliament.uk
Website: www.jimpaice.com

Conservative

Date of birth: 24 April 1949; Son of late Edward Paice and of Winifred Paice

Education: Framlingham College, Suffolk; Writtle Agricultural College (National Diploma Agriculture 1970); Married Ava Patterson 1973 (2 sons)

Non-political career: Farm manager 1970-73; Farmer and contractor 1973-79; Training manager, later general manager, Framlingham Management and Training Services Ltd 1979-87, Non-executive director 1987-89; Director United Framlingham Farmers Ltd 1989-94; Suffolk Coastal District Council: Councillor 1976-87, Chair 1982-83

Political career: Contested Caernarvon 1979 general election. Member for South East Cambridgeshire 1987-2010, for South East Cambridgeshire (revised boundary) since 6 May 2010 general election; PPS: to Baroness Trumpington as Minister of State, Ministry of Agriculture, Fisheries and Food 1989-90, to John Selwyn Gummer: as Minister of Agriculture, Fisheries and Food 1990-93, as Secretary of State for the Environment 1993-94; Parliamentary Under-Secretary of State: Department of Employment 1994-95, Department for Education and Employment 1995-97; Opposition Spokesperson for: Agriculture, Fisheries and Food 1997-2001, Home Affairs 2001-03; Shadow Minister for: Home, Constitutional and Legal Affairs 2003-04, Home Affairs 2004; Shadow: Secretary of State for Agriculture, Fisheries and Food 2004-05, Minister for Agriculture 2005-10, and Rural Affairs 2006-10; Minister of State for Agriculture and Food, Department for Environment, Food and Rural Affairs 2010-

Political interests: Small businesses, employment, agriculture, rural affairs, training, waste management; Europe, New Zealand

Other organisations: Member Council of Ely Cathedral 2002-; UK delegate, EEC Council of Young Farmers 1974-78; Fellow Industry and Parliament Trust 1990; Trustee Game Conservancy Trust 2003-07, 2008-; Fellow, Writtle University College

Recreations: Shooting, conservation

Jim Paice MP, House of Commons, London SW1A 0AA
Tel: 020 7219 4101 Fax: 020 7219 3804
E-mail: paicejet@parliament.uk
Constituency: 153 St Neots Road, Hardwick, Cambridge CB3 7QJ
Tel: 01954 211444 Fax: 01954 212455 Website: www.jimpaice.com

GENERAL ELECTION RESULT

		%
Paice, J. (Con)*	27,629	48.0
Chatfield, J. (Lib Dem)	21,683	37.6
Cowan, J. (Lab)	4,380	7.6
Monk, A. (UKIP)	2,138	3.7
Sedgwick-Jell, S. (Green)	766	1.3
Woollard, G. (Ind)	517	0.9
Bell, D. (CPA)	489	0.9
Majority	5,946	10.32
Electorate	83,068	
Turnout	57,602	69.34

**Member of last parliament*

CONSTITUENCY SNAPSHOT

Since 1950 the seat has been held by the Tories despite numerous boundary changes. Gerald Howard represented Cambridgeshire, as the constituency was then known, from 1970 until 1981. The seat was renamed South East Cambridgeshire in 1983 when it was won by Francis Pym. He retired in 1987 and was replaced by James Paice who has held the seat ever since.

Support for the Conservatives in South East Cambridgeshire appears to have peaked in the 1992 general election, when Paice received a majority of 20,863; in 2005 it was 8,624. Paice held the seat in 2010 with a reduced majority of 5,946.

Boundary changes moved The Abingtons and Cottenham wards completely within South Cambridgeshire's boundaries.

The constituency of South East Cambridgeshire is large and sparsely populated. It is a mixture of suburban and rural areas. Agriculture is a key economic activity of the constituency, which is largely arable.

The seat runs from east of Cambridge to east of Newmarket, though excludes the horse-racing town itself, which a large kink in the Suffolk border punches through to seize. The ancient fen capital Ely is at its northern border.

Ian Paisley Jnr

North Antrim

Boundary changes

Tel: 020 7219 3000
Website: www.ipjr.net

Date of birth: 12 December 1966; Son of the Rt Hon Rev Dr Ian Paisley, MP, MLA, and Eileen Paisley (née Cassells), now Baroness Paisley of St George's

Education: Shaftesbury House College; Methodist College, Belfast; Queen's University, Belfast (BA modern history 1989; MSc Irish politics 1992); Married Fiona Currie 1990 (2 daughters 2 sons)

Non-political career: Researcher, author and political assistant; Lay visitor, Police Holding Centres for the Police Authority 1996-2001; Member, Northern Ireland Policing Board 2001-07, 2008-

Political career: Member for North Antrim since 6 May 2010 general election; Member Northern Ireland Forum for Political Dialogue 1996-98; MLA for North Antrim since 25 June 1998: Member, Preparation for Government Committee 2006-07; Junior Minister, Office of First and Deputy First Minister 2007-08

Political interests: Justice, Europe, agriculture; Africa, China, USA

Other organisations: British Motorcycle Federation; Trustee: Dan Winter Heritage Trust, Assembly Business Trust; Royal Humane Society for Life Saving 1999; Fellow, University of Maryland School of Leadership, Washington DC, USA; *Publications:* Reasonable Doubt – The Case for the UDR4; Echoes; Peace Deal; Ian Paisley – A Life in Photographs

Recreations: Rugby, reading, motor racing, collector of 19th century cartoons and political caricatures, motorcycling

Ian Paisley Jnr MP, House of Commons, London SW1A 0AA
Tel: 020 7219 3000
Constituency: 9-11 Church Street, Ballymena BT43 6DD
Tel: 028 2564 1421 Fax: 028 2564 7296 E-mail: info@ipjr.net
Website: www.ipjr.net

GENERAL ELECTION RESULT

		%
Paisley Jnr, I. (DUP)	19,672	46.4
Allister, J. (TUV)	7,114	16.8
McKay, D. (Sinn Féin)	5,265	12.4
Armstrong, I. (UCUNF)	4,634	10.9
O'Loan, D. (SDLP)	3,738	8.8
Dunlop, J. (All)	1,368	3.2
Cubitt, L. (Ind)	606	1.4
Majority	12,558	29.62
Electorate	73,338	
Turnout	42,397	57.81

CONSTITUENCY SNAPSHOT

From 1970 North Antrim provided the electoral base of the legendary and controversial Dr Ian Paisley, who founded both his own party, the Democratic Unionist Party, and church, the Free Presbyterian Church, and led both until 2008.

He confounded his critics when he entered Northern Ireland's power sharing as First Minister alongside Sinn Féin's Martin McGuinness. Paisley's majority in 2005 was a substantial 17,965. He retired in 2010.

Ian Paisley Jr succeeded his father in 2010 with a majority of 12,558, giving the DUP a comfortable 46 per cent vote-share.

The constituency lost three Moyle council wards: Glenaan, Glenariff and Glendum to East Antrim in the boundary review.

The mainly rural constituency of North Antrim in the north-east of Ulster covers most of Moyle as well as the whole of Ballymoney and Ballymena district councils.

It is world famous for the spectacular Giant's Causeway. These unique rock formations have for millions of years stood as a natural rampart against the unbridled ferocity of Atlantic storms.

This is one of Ulster's most fertile and prosperous farming regions. There is also a strong manufacturing industry base, including textiles, around Ballymena. It is fairly centrally situated with good road and rail links.

Neil Parish

Tiverton and Honiton

Boundary changes

Tel: 020 7219 3000
E-mail: neil.parish.mp@parliament.uk
Website: www.neilparish.co.uk

Date of birth: 26 May 1956

Education: Brymore School; Taunton College; Married Sue Edwards 1981 (1 son 1 daughter)

Non-political career: Former farmer and businessman; Sedgemoor District Counci: Councillor 1983-95, Deputy Leader 1989-95; Councillor, Somerset County Council 1989-93

Political career: Member for Tiverton and Honiton since 6 May 2010 general election; MEP for South West 1999-2009: Conservative agriculture spokesperson; President, Animal Welfare Intergroup; Agriculture and Rural Development Committee: Member 1999-2007, Chair 2007-09; Member: Foot and Mouth Temporary Committee 2002-04, Israel Delegation 2002-04, Fisheries Committee 2004-07; Australia and New Zealand Delegation: Chair 2004-07, Member 2007-08; Member: Conference of Delegation Chairmen 2004-07, Crisis of the Equitable Life Assurance Society Temporary Committee 2006-07, Conference of Committee Chairmen 2007-08, People's Republic of China Delegation 2008-09; Chair, Bridgwater Conservative Assocation 1997-99

Political interests: Regional policy, animal welfare, agriculture, EU enlargement

Recreations: Swimming, music, country life, Brains Trust, debating

Neil Parish MP, House of Commons, London SW1A 0AA
Tel: 020 7219 3000 E-mail: neil.parish.mp@parliament.uk
Constituency: 9C Mill Park Industrial Estate, White Cross Road, Woodbury Salterton, Exeter, Devon EX5 1EL Tel: 01278 691717
Fax: 01278 691717 Website: www.neilparish.co.uk

GENERAL ELECTION RESULT

		%
Parish, N. (Con)	27,614	50.3
Underwood, J. (Lib Dem)	18,294	33.3
Whitlock, V. (Lab)	4,907	8.9
Stanbury, D. (UKIP)	3,277	6.0
Connor, C. (Green)	802	1.5
Majority	9,320	16.98
Electorate	76,810	
Turnout	54,894	71.47

CONSTITUENCY SNAPSHOT

This seat has been Consevative all throughout all the post-Second World War years. Sir Robin Maxwell-Hyslop represented what was then called Tiverton for 32 years between 1960 and 1992.

He was replaced by Angela Browning who held the renamed seat in 1997 and increased her vote-share in 2001.

In 2005 Angela Browning almost doubled her majority to 11,051. New Tory candidate Neil Parish won a 9,320 majority in this safe seat, taking 50 per cent of the vote.

Under boundary changes the seat lost a number of wards to both East and Central Devon, while gaining the wards of Axminster Rural, Axminster Town, Beer and Branscombe, Coly Valley, Newbridges, Otterhead, Seaton, Trinity, and Yarty from East Devon.

Tiverton and Honiton are the largest towns in a vast area of rolling rural landscape in mid and east Devon. The countryside is interspersed with smaller country villages.

The countryside comprises a mix of tenant and non-tenant farmers on upland and lowland farms.

There is a shortage of affordable housing and public transport issues affect the whole community.

Priti Patel

Witham

New constituency

Tel: 020 7219 3000
E-mail: priti.patel.mp@parliament.uk
Website: www.priti4witham.com

Date of birth: 29 March 1972

Education: Westfield, Watford; Keele University (BA economics 1994); Essex University (Diploma British government and politics 1995); Married Alex Sawyer

Non-political career: Head of press office, Referendum Party 1995-97; Conservative Research Department 1997; Deputy press secretary to William Hague MP 1997-2000; Responsible drinking and corporate relations manager, Diageo 2003-08; Director, Weber Shandwick 2007-

Political career: Contested Nottingham North 2005 general election. Member for Witham since 6 May 2010 general election

Political interests: Law and order, the elderly, the euro

Recreations: Horse racing, cricket, travel

Priti Patel MP, House of Commons, London SW1A 0AA
Tel: 020 7219 3000 E-mail: priti.patel.mp@parliament.uk
Constituency: Witham Conservatives, Avenue Lodge, The Avenue, Witham, Essex CM8 2DL Tel: 01376 520649 Fax: 01376 516475
Website: www.priti4witham.com

GENERAL ELECTION RESULT

		%
Patel, P. (Con)	24,448	52.2
Phelps, M. (Lib Dem)	9,252	19.8
Spademan, J. (Lab)	8,656	18.5
Hodges, D. (UKIP)	3,060	6.5
Abbott, J. (Green)	1,419	3.0
Majority	15,196	32.45
Electorate	66,750	
Turnout	46,835	70.16

CONSTITUENCY SNAPSHOT

The new seat or Witham bears no close resemblance to any particular former constituency. Primarily Witham is made up of wards from seats that have strong Conservative histories: Braintree, North Essex and Maldon and East Chelmsford. Stanway ward was added from Colchester, which has been held by the Lib Dems since 1997.

In 2010 Priti Patel was elected for the Tories with 24,448 votes, securing a majority of 15,196.

This new seat is centred on the town of Witham in Essex. Outside the one main town it covers a largely rural area of mid-Essex bordering on the larger towns of Colchester, Braintree and Maldon.

This is a largely prosperous area, although with some wide variations between town and country.

Witham is home to several industrial estates, and the small town of Tiptree is famous for jam-making. Agriculture and tourism are important, with some marine and sailing activity in settlements on the Blackwater estuary. Coggeshall was a well-known antiques centre, but that is now in decline.

Rt Hon **Owen Paterson**

North Shropshire (returning MP)

No boundary changes

Tel: 020 7219 5185
E-mail: patersono@parliament.uk
Website: www.epolitix.com/Owen-Paterson

Date of birth: 24 June 1956; Son of late Alfred Dobell Paterson and Cynthia Marian Paterson

Education: Radley College; Corpus Christi College, Cambridge (MA history 1978); Married Hon. Rose Ridley 1980 (2 sons 1 daughter)

Non-political career: British Leather Co Ltd: Sales director 1985-93, Managing director 1993-99

Political career: Contested Wrexham 1992 general election. Member for North Shropshire since 1 May 1997 general election; Opposition Whip 2000-01; PPS to Iain Duncan Smith as Leader of the Opposition 2001-03; Shadow: Minister for: Environment, Food and Rural Affairs 2003-05, Transport 2005-07, Secretary of State for Northern Ireland 2007-10; Secretary of State for Northern Ireland 2010-; *Select Committees:* Member: Welsh Affairs 1997-2001, European Standing Committee A 1998-2001, Welsh Grand Committee 1998-2000 European Scrutiny 1999-2000, Agriculture 2000-01; Member: 92 Group 1997-, Conservative Friends of Israel 1997-, Conservative Way Forward 1997-, Conservative 2000 1997-; Vice-President, Conservatives Against a Federal Europe 1998-2001, Member, No Turning Back Group 1998-; Executive Member 1922 Committee 2000

Political interests: Trade, industry, agriculture, foreign affairs; Western and Eastern Europe, USA, China, India

Other organisations: Director, Orthopaedic Institute Ltd, Oswestry; Member, Countryside Alliance; President, Cotance (European Tanners' Confederation) 1996-98; Member: Inter-Parliamentary Union 1997-, Commonwealth Parliamentary Association 1997-; Member, Advisory Board, European Foundation 1998-; PC 2010; Liveryman, Leathersellers' Company; Patron, Oswestry Cricket Club; Member, Shropshire Cricket Club

Rt Hon Owen Paterson MP, House of Commons, London SW1A 0AA Tel: 020 7219 5185 Fax: 020 7219 3955
E-mail: patersono@parliament.uk
Constituency: No constituency office publicised Tel: 01978 710073 Fax: 01978 710667 Website: www.epolitix.com/Owen-Paterson

GENERAL ELECTION RESULT

		%	+/-
Paterson, O. (Con)*	26,692	51.5	2.2
Croll, I. (Lib Dem)	10,864	21.0	1.3
McLaughlan, I. (Lab)	9,406	18.1	-7.6
List, S. (UKIP)	2,432	4.7	-0.1
Reddall, P. (BNP)	1,667	3.2	
Boulding, S. (Green)	808	1.6	
Majority	15,828	30.52	
Electorate	78,926		
Turnout	51,869	65.72	

**Member of last parliament*

CONSTITUENCY SNAPSHOT

John Biffen held North Shropshire for the Conservatives from 1961 until 1997. Owen Paterson succeeded him in 1997 with a 2,195 majority.

Paterson increased his majority to 6,241 in 2001, and almost doubled it in 2005. The Conservatives held the seat with a majority of 15,828 in 2010.

Stretching across the entire width of Shropshire, this seat borders Stone in Staffordshire to the East, Eddisbury in Cheshire to the north, Clywd South to the west and Shrewsbury to the south.

It includes the towns of Wem, Whitchurch, Oswestry, and Market Drayton as well as a very large rural area.

North Shropshire consists of a chunk of rural countryside speckled with small towns and villages. Punctuated by green pastures, ancient woodlands and sandstone hills, the area has been dubbed one of England's only three remaining rural idylls by the Council for the Protection of Rural England.

The market towns of Oswestry and Market Drayton account for well over a third of the seat's population. The seat contains some former mining communities, but agriculture, tourism and light industry make up the largest sectors of the economy here and many of the constituency's firms are family-owned and relatively small.

Mark Pawsey

Rugby

New constituency

Tel: 020 7219 3000
E-mail: mark.pawsey.mp@parliament.uk
Website: www.markpawsey.org.uk

Conservative

Date of birth: 16 January 1957; Son of James Pawsey, MP for Rugby 1979-83, Rugby and Kenilworth 1983-97, and Cynthia Pawsey

Education: Lawrence Sheriff School, Rugby; Reading University (estate management 1978); Married Tracy Sara Harris 1984 (2 sons 2 daughters)

Non-political career: Trainee surveyor, Strutt and Parker 1978-79; Account manager, Autobar Vending Supplies Ltd 1979-82; Managing director, Central Catering Supplies Ltd 1982-; Councillor, Rugby Borough Council 2002-07

Political career: Contested Nuneaton 2005 general election. Member for Rugby since 6 May 2010 general election

Political interests: Planning, environment, local government, trade

Other organisations: Old Laurentian R.F.C

Recreations: Village life, rugby, wine appreciation

Mark Pawsey MP, House of Commons, London SW1A 0AA
Tel: 020 7219 3000 E-mail: mark.pawsey.mp@parliament.uk
Constituency: Rugby Conservative Association, Albert Buildings, 2 Castle Mews, Rugby CV21 2XL Tel: 01788 542677
Fax: 01788 569735 Website: www.markpawsey.org.uk

GENERAL ELECTION RESULT

		%
Pawsey, M. (Con)	20,901	44.0
King, A. (Lab)	14,901	31.4
Roodhouse, J. (Lib Dem)	9,434	19.9
Badrick, M. (BNP)	1,375	2.9
Sandison, R. (Green)	451	1.0
Milford, B. (UKIP)	406	0.9
Majority	6,000	12.64
Electorate	68,914	
Turnout	47,468	68.88

CONSTITUENCY SNAPSHOT

The 1979 election brought in the Tories' James Pawsey. He recorded victories of over 10,000 throughout the 1980s and early 1990s.

The election of Labour's Andy King in 1997 indicated the tide turned against the Conservatives that year. Andy King won by just 495 votes. In 2001 King secured a small swing in his favour increasing his majority to 2,877.

The Conservatives improved markedly in 2005, under the new candidate Jeremy Wright, when a 4 per cent swing gave them control of the seat with a 1,628 majority. The Conservative candidate, Mark Pawsey won his father's former seat in 2010 with a majority of 6,000. Jeremy Wright moved to the new seat of Kenilworth and Southam.

Following the Boundary Commission's review, Rugby was reconstituted to form a single constituency out of the former Rugby and Kenilworth.

This West Midlands seat has a diverse make up with a mix of industrial working class and more affluent rural areas.

Rugby is also a diverse town; the north and centre are industrial and working class. In these areas lies the railway line on which the town's past prosperity was built as well as the heavy engineering firms through which its present prosperity is maintained.

The south of the town and the rural areas is more middle-class and affluent. Notable companies in Rugby include GEC-Alsthom and Peugeot-Talbot. Dairy farming is also important to the rural areas.

Teresa Pearce

Erith and Thamesmead

Boundary changes

Tel: 020 7219 3000
E-mail: teresa.pearce.mp@parliament.uk
Website: teresapearce.co.uk

Labour

Date of birth: 1 February 1955; Daughter of Arthur Farrington, shoe repairer, and Josephine Farrington, book-keeper/clerk

Education: St Thomas More; Divorced (2 daughters)

Non-political career: Senior manager, PriceWaterhouseCoopers 1999-2009; Member, GMB; Councillor, London Borough of Bexley Council 1998-2002

Political career: Member for Erith and Thamesmead since 6 May 2010 general election; Member, National Constitutional Committee 1996-2008

Political interests: Tax reform, children in care

Recreations: Cinema, reading, travel

Teresa Pearce MP, House of Commons, London SW1A 0AA
Tel: 020 7219 3000 E-mail: teresa.pearce.mp@parliament.uk
Website: teresapearce.co.uk

GENERAL ELECTION RESULT

		%
Pearce, T. (Lab)	19,068	44.9
Bloom, C. (Con)	13,365	31.5
Cunliffe, A. (Lib Dem)	5,116	12.0
Saunders, K. (BNP)	2,184	5.1
Perrin, P. (UKIP)	1,139	2.7
Williams, L. (England)	465	1.1
Akinoshun, A. (Ind)	438	1.0
Cordle, S. (CPA)	379	0.9
Powley, M. (Green)	322	0.8
Majority	5,703	13.43
Electorate	69,918	
Turnout	42,476	60.75

CONSTITUENCY SNAPSHOT

The seat was created in 1997 from roughly equal numbers of voters from Woolwich, Erith and Crayford. The merger of the two seats produced a notional Labour majority approaching 6,000, and Erith and Crayford's MP David Evennett moved to neighbouring Bexleyheath and Crayford. Labour's John Austin-Walker went on to win a majority of 17,424.

In 2001 John Austin had dropped Walker, the name of his ex-wife; his majority decreased, but still took nearly 60 per cent of the vote. Austin increased his majority slightly in 2005 to 11,500. Labour's Teresa Pearce held onto this seat by 5,703 votes in the face of a substantial 6.3 per cent swing to the Conservatives.

All of Lesnes Abbey, Belvedere, Erith and Northumberland Heath Wards will now be in Erith and Thamesmead having previously been shared with neighbouring seats.

The 'new town' of Thamesmead, built on reclaimed marshland in the 1960s, is the largest conurbation.

The Royal Arsenal on the edge of the constituency was once the biggest employer in the area. The ordnance factory closed in 1967, but the site is enjoying a new lease of life as a museum and commercial and housing development.

The DLR has been extended to Woolwich Arsenal and Crossrail will pass through Abbey Wood for Thamesmead.

Mike Penning

Hemel Hempstead ***(returning MP)***

Boundary changes

Tel: 020 7219 8398
E-mail: penningm@parliament.uk
Website: www.penning4hemel.com

Conservative

Date of birth: 28 September 1957; Son of Freda and Brian Penning

Education: Appleton Comprehensive School, Benfleet, Essex; King Edmund Comprehensive School, Rochford, Essex; Married Angela Louden 1988 (2 daughters)

Non-political career: Soldier, Grenadier Guards 1974-80; Royal Army Medical Corps (RAMC) 1980-81; Fire officer, Essex Fire and Rescue Services 1982-88; Freelance political journalist, Express Newspapers and News International 1988-92; Politics and journalism lecturer, UK and USA 1992-2005; Journalist and media adviser to six Shadow Cabinet members 1996-2004; Deputy chief press spokesperson, Conservative Central Office 2000-04; Member FBU 1982-

Political career: Contested Thurrock 2001 general election. Member for Hemel Hempstead 2005-10, for Hemel Hemstead (revised boundary) since 6 May 2010 general election; Shadow Minister for Health 2007-10; Parliamentary Under-Secretary of State, Department for Transport 2010-; *Select Committees:* Member: Health 2005-07; Director, Conservatives Against a Federal Europe 1995; General election campaign manager, Rochford and Southend East 1997; Member Executive 1922 Committee 2006-07

Political interests: Constitution, single currency (against), health, home affairs, defence; Gibraltar

Other organisations: British Legion

Recreations: Rugby Union, Football

Mike Penning MP, House of Commons, London SW1A 0AA
Tel: 020 7219 8398 Fax: 020 7219 4759
E-mail: penningm@parliament.uk
Constituency: Hamilton House, 111 Marlowes, Hemel Hempstead, Hertfordshire HP1 1BB Tel: 01442 450444 Fax: 01442 450445
Website: www.penning4hemel.com

GENERAL ELECTION RESULT

		%
Penning, M. (Con)*	24,721	50.0
Grayson, R. (Lib Dem)	11,315	22.9
Orhan, A. (Lab)	10,295	20.8
Price, J. (BNP)	1,615	3.3
Alexander, D. (UKIP)	1,254	2.5
Young, M. (Ind)	271	0.6
Majority	13,406	27.10
Electorate	72,754	
Turnout	49,471	68.00

**Member of last parliament*

CONSTITUENCY SNAPSHOT

In 1997 a strong local campaign, combined with a 12.1 per cent regional swing to Labour, won the seat for Labour's Tony McWalter. McWalter increased his majority to 3,742 in 2001.

However, in 2005 McWalter could not hold off the Conservatives again. The Tory vote increased by only 1.8 per cent, but this was enough to allow Conservative candidate Mike Penning to take the seat with a majority of just under 500. McWalter's vote had fallen by 7.3 per cent.

In 2010 Penning retained the seat for the Conservatives with a strong 13,406 majority.

The seat lost its part of the Bovingdon, Flaunden and Chipperfield ward to South West Hertfordshire.

In the heart of the Hertfordshire commuter belt, the new town of Hemel Hempstead is more than just a convenient dormitory for affluent city workers. The inclusion of villages such as Kings Langley in the south make this constituency a pleasant mix of rural and urban Hertfordshire.

Hemel Hempstead is affluent, but not massively so. The town's enterprises have a high-tech character, and they include Dixons, BP, BT, the FI group, the British Standards Institute, and Kodak.

John Penrose

Weston-Super-Mare (returning MP)

Boundary changes

Tel: 020 7219 2385
E-mail: daviesbe@parliament.uk
Website: www.johnpenrose.co.uk

Date of birth: 22 June 1964; Son of late David Penrose and Anna Jill now Lawrie

Education: Ipswich School, Suffolk; Downing College, Cambridge (BA law 1986); Columbia University, USA (MBA 1991); Married Diana (Dido) Mary Harding 1995 (2 daughters)

Non-political career: Risk manager JP Morgan 1986-90; Management consultant McKinsey and Company 1992-94; Commercial director academic books division, Thomson Publishing 1995-96; Managing director schools publishing, Europe, Pearson PLC 1996-2000; Non-executive director Logotron Ltd 2008-

Political career: Contested Ealing Southall 1997 and Weston-Super-Mare 2001 general elections. Member for Weston-Super-Mare 2005-10, for Weston-Super-Mare (revised boundary) since 6 May 2010 general election; Shadow Minister for: Business, Enterprise and Regulatory Reform 2009, Business 2009-10; Parliamentary Under-Secretary of State (Minister for Tourism and Heritage), Department for Culture, Media and Sport 2010-; *Select Committees:* Member: Work and Pensions 2005-09, Regulatory Reform 2009-10; Treasurer Leyton and Wanstead Conservative Association 1993-95; Research secretary, The Bow Group 1998-99; PPS to Oliver Letwin as Chair Conservative Policy Review 2006-09

Political interests: Drug addiction, pensions, environment, education, international development

Other organisations: President: Weston YMCA, Weston Abbeyfields Nursing (charity), Winscombe and District Senior Citizens Forum; *Publications:* Members' Rights (The Bow Group) 1997

Recreations: Fishing, beekeeping

John Penrose MP, House of Commons, London SW1A 0AA
Tel: 020 7219 2385 E-mail: daviesbe@parliament.uk
Constituency: 24-26 Alexandra Parade, Weston-Super-Mare, Somerset BS23 1QX Tel: 01934 622894 Fax: 01934 632955
Website: www.johnpenrose.co.uk

GENERAL ELECTION RESULT

		%
Penrose, J. (Con)*	23,356	44.3
Bell, M. (Lib Dem)	20,665	39.2
Bradley, D. (Lab)	5,772	11.0
Spencer, P. (UKIP)	1,406	2.7
Parsons, P. (BNP)	1,098	2.1
Peverelle, J. (England)	275	0.5
Satch, S. (Ind)	144	0.3
Majority	2,691	5.10
Electorate	78,487	
Turnout	52,716	67.17

**Member of last parliament*

CONSTITUENCY SNAPSHOT

In the decades following the Second World War Weston-Super-Mare was a Conservative seat. From 1969 to 1997 the seat was held by Sir Jerry Wiggin. Sir Jerry's tenure witnessed the decline of the Tory vote in Weston-Super-Mare. In 1979 his majority was 32 per cent, which was nearly halved in 1983. By 1992 it had been halved again.

In 1997 Brian Cotter ended the 74-year Tory reign and captured the seat for the Liberal Democrats. His margin of victory was just 388 in 2001, and in 2005, John Penrose reclaimed the seat for the Conservatives with a majority of 2,079. Penrose won re-election with a majority of 2,691 in 2010.

Boundary changes were negligible. Wrington ward, which was previously shared between Weston-Super-Mare and Woodspring, moves in its entirety to the new seat of North Somerset.

This affluent constituency lies along the west coast, south-west of Bristol, and runs from the Severn estuary in the north to the Mendip Hills in the south. The constituency centres on the town of Weston-Super-Mare and includes surrounding villages such as Churchill, Winscombe and Sandford.

The town of Weston-Super-Mare is a major tourist destination renowned for its beaches, picturesque architecture and long promenade.

A variety of industries have based themselves in the area including GKN Westlands, Brymon Airways, Clarks, and First Group.

Andrew Percy

Brigg and Goole

Boundary changes

Tel: 020 7219 3000
E-mail: andrew.percy.mp@parliament.uk

Education: York University

Non-political career: History teacher; MP's researcher; Part-time primary teacher; Member, National Association of Schoolmasters Union of Woman Teachers (NASUWT); School governor

Political career: Member for Brigg and Goole since 6 May 2010 general election

Political interests: Education

Other organisations: Supporter: Countryside Alliance, Campaign Against Political Correctness

Andrew Percy MP, House of Commons, London SW1A 0AA
Tel: 020 7219 3000 E-mail: andrew.percy.mp@parliament.uk
Constituency: Brigg and Goole Conservative Association, Main Street, Normanby, Scunthorpe, North Lincolnshire DN15 9HS
Tel: 01724 720800
Website: www.brigg-gooleconservatives.co.uk; www.andrewpercy.org

GENERAL ELECTION RESULT

		%
Percy, A. (Con)	19,680	44.9
Cawsey, I. (Lab)*	14,533	33.1
Nixon, R. (Lib Dem)	6,414	14.6
Wright, N. (UKIP)	1,749	4.0
Ward, S. (BNP)	1,498	3.4
Majority	5,147	11.73
Electorate	67,345	
Turnout	43,874	65.15

**Member of last parliament*

CONSTITUENCY SNAPSHOT

The seat was created in 1997 from parts of Boothferry, Glanford and Scunthorpe, and Brigg and Cleethorpes. Brigg and Goole had a notional Conservative majority of more than 7,000. Ian Cawsey, achieved a swing of nearly 14 per cent to win for Labour with a majority of more than 6,000.

Small swings in the two subsequent elections reduced the Labour majority and in 2005 Cawsey retained the seat by a margin of 2,894. In 2010 Cawsey was defeated by the Conservatives. Andrew Percy was elected with a 5,147 majority.

The formerly split Ridge ward moved completely within Scunthorpe's boundaries.

Brigg and Goole crosses ancient county boundaries to link the North Lincolnshire market town of Brigg and the working-class port of Goole in the East Riding of Yorkshire.

The inland port of Goole (the main inland port in the east of England) is a major employer, exporting much of Yorkshire's produce, and many people work in other businesses along the marshy banks of the Rivers Ouse and Trent. But much of the constituency is rural and agriculture is important here.

A large proportion of employment in the seat is of a manual nature. As well as farming, there are also a number of steelworkers.

Toby Perkins

Chesterfield

Boundary changes

Tel: 020 7219 3000
E-mail: toby.perkins.mp@parliament.uk
Website: www.tobyperkins.org.uk

Labour

Date of birth: 12 August 1970; Son of V.F Perkins and late Teresa Perkins, both university lecturers

Education: Trinity School, Leamington Spa; Silverdale School, Sheffield; Married Susan Francis 1996 (1 son 1daughter)

Non-political career: Telephone sales, CCS Media 1991-95; Recruitment consultant/area manager, Prime Time Recruitment 1995-2002; Business owner, Club Rugby (internet sports firm) 2005-; Member, Amicus/Unite 2005-; Councillor, Chesterfield Borough Council 2003-; Director, Birdholme Childrens Centre Nursery

Political career: Member for Chesterfield since 6 May 2010 general election

Political interests: Sport and youth involvement, healthy eating, crime, jobs and regeneration

Other organisations: Former player, Chesterfield Rugby Club; Coach, Sheffield Tigers Rugby Club

Recreations: Rugby (qualified coach)

Toby Perkins MP, House of Commons, London SW1A 0AA
Tel: 020 7219 3000 E-mail: toby.perkins.mp@parliament.uk
Constituency: 21 Westbrook Drive, Chesterfield, Derbyshire S40 3PQ
Tel: 01246 566166 Website: www.tobyperkins.org.uk

GENERAL ELECTION RESULT

		%
Perkins, T. (Lab)	17,891	39.0
Holmes, P. (Lib Dem)*	17,342	37.8
Abbott, C. (Con)	7,214	15.7
Phillips, D. (UKIP)	1,432	3.1
Jerram, I. (England)	1,213	2.7
Kerr, D. (Green)	600	1.3
Daramy, J. (Ind)	147	0.3
Majority	549	1.20
Electorate	71,878	
Turnout	45,839	63.77

**Member of last parliament*

CONSTITUENCY SNAPSHOT

Labour polled five-figure majorities here up until 1979. Eric Varley, MP from 1964, suddenly left politics for a senior job with Coalite in 1984. At the by-election, Tony Benn, ejected from Bristol in 1983, won comfortably by more than 6,000 votes.

Benn retired from Parliament in 2001 and Labour's selection of the former London MP Reg Race was contentious with allegations of vote rigging. Paul Holmes captured the seat for the Liberal Democrats with a swing of 8.5 per cent, to become the first Liberal MP for the seat since 1924. In 2005 the Lib Dems held on again with an increased majority of 3,045.

Labour seized the seat from the Lib Dems in 2010 with Toby Perkins securing a majority of 549.

Boundary changes were relatively minor, with part-wards transferred between the seat and North East Derbyshire.

Chesterfield is a sub-regional centre, providing a range of functions for the surrounding area, including the main office locations for both Chesterfield Borough Council and North East Derbyshire District Council. Public service sectors are one of the main sources of employment in the borough.

The decline of heavy industry as well as the loss of the coal industry has produced a more diverse economy. New business parks and innovation centres have been developed on former industrial sites.

Claire Perry

Devizes

Boundary changes

Tel: 020 7219 3000
E-mail: claire.perry.mp@parliament.uk
Website: www.claireperry.org.uk

Conservative

Date of birth: 3 April 1964; Daughter of Joanna and David Richens, both retired

Education: Nailsea Comprehensive School; Oxford University (BA geography 1985); Harvard Business School (MBA 1990); Married Clayton Perry 1996 (1 son 2 daughters)

Non-political career: Analyst, Bank of America 1985-88; Consultant, McKinsey and Company 1990-94; Various roles, Credit Suisse First Boston 1994-2000; Volunteer fundraiser 2002-04; Former policy adviser to George Osborne MP 2007-09

Political career: Member for Devizes since 6 May 2010 general election; Member, Conservative Party 2006-

Political interests: Economy, education

Recreations: Reading, walking, cycling, gardening

Claire Perry MP, House of Commons, London SW1A 0AA
Tel: 020 7219 3000 E-mail: claire.perry.mp@parliament.uk
Constituency: Devizes Conservative Association, 116 High Street, Marlborough, Wiltshire SN8 1LZ Tel: 01672 512675
Fax: 01672 515682 Website: www.claireperry.org.uk

GENERAL ELECTION RESULT

		%
Perry, C. (Con)	25,519	55.1
Hornby, F. (Lib Dem)	12,514	27.0
Ali, J. (Lab)	4,711	10.2
Bryant, P. (UKIP)	2,076	4.5
Fletcher, M. (Green)	813	1.8
Houlden, M. (Ind)	566	1.2
Coome, N. (Libertarian)	141	0.3
Majority	13,005	28.06
Electorate	67,374	
Turnout	46,340	68.78

CONSTITUENCY SNAPSHOT

Devizes has returned Conservative MPs since 1945, often with majorities of well over 15,000. Michael Ancram held the seat for the Tories from 1992 until retiring in 2010. He had been re-elected in 2005 with a 13,194 majority. Ancram's successor Claire Perry won a 13,005 majority in this safe Conservative seat.

Boundary changes brought Bulford and Durrington wards into the seat from Salisbury, while four West Wiltshire wards move to Chippenham, and nine North Wiltshire wards move to North Wiltshire.

The Wiltshire constituency of Devizes has a multitude of pre-historic sites, barrows and white chalk horses. The Vale of Pewsey is perhaps the best example of the nature of the constituency and, along with the small market towns, is one of the major tourist attractions in the area.

The constituency has no large towns and is a predominantly rural area. Devizes itself is the home of the Wadworth's brewery. Otherwise, the economy is based on light industry and some agriculture. Tourism is also important.

In keeping with the rural nature of the constituency, routine and semi-routine workers make up a higher percentage of the workforce.

Stephen Phillips

Sleaford and North Hykeham

Boundary changes

Tel: 020 7219 3000
E-mail: stephen.phillips.mp@parliament.uk
Website: www.stephenphillips.org.uk

Date of birth: 9 March 1970; Son of Stewart Phillips, civil servant, and Janice Phillips

Education: Canford School, Dorset; Oriel College, Oxford (BCL law 1991; MA 1992); Married Fiona Parkin 1998 (1 son 2 daughters)

Non-political career: 2nd Lt, 14/20th King's Hussars, subsequently Welsh Guards 1988-91; Called to the Bar, Lincoln's Inn 1993; Barrister, 7 King's Bench Walk, London 1993-; QC 2009; Recorder, South East Circuit 2009-; Chair, board of governors, Frank Barnes School for Deaf Children

Political career: Member for Sleaford and North Hykeham since 6 May 2010 general election; Member, Conservative Party 1988-

Political interests: Foreign affairs, defence, education

Other organisations: Cavalry and Guards

Recreations: Getting muddy

Stephen Phillips MP, House of Commons, London SW1A 0AA
Tel: 020 7219 3000 E-mail: stephen.phillips.mp@parliament.uk
Constituency: Sleaford and North Hykham Conservatives, 6 Market Place, Sleaford, Lincolnshire NG34 7SD Tel: 01529 419000
Fax: 01529 419019 Website: www.stephenphillips.org.uk

GENERAL ELECTION RESULT

		%
Phillips, S. (Con)	30,719	51.6
Harding-Price, D. (Lib Dem)	10,814	18.2
Normington, J. (Lab)	10,051	16.9
Overton, M. (Ind)	3,806	6.4
Doughty, R. (UKIP)	2,163	3.6
Clayton, M. (BNP)	1,977	3.3
Majority	19,905	33.44
Electorate	85,550	
Turnout	59,530	69.59

CONSTITUENCY SNAPSHOT

The old Grantham seat has long been Conservative, and had been represented by Douglas Hogg from 1979 until his retirement in 2010. The 1997 boundary changes removed the town of Grantham itself and added North Hykeham, Skellingthorpe and Waddington. Hogg was defending a notional majority of nearly 20,000, but he was left with an actual majority of just 5,123.

Hogg's majority recovered and was 12,705 in 2005. In 2010 Stephen Phillips retained the seat for the Tories with a majority of 19,905.

Boundary changes moved Skellingthorpe and part-ward Bracebridge Heath and Waddington East to Lincoln, while Barrowby, Peascliffe and part-wards Heighington and Washingborough, Witham Valley, and Ermine moved into this seat.

This is a largely rural constituency of villages, suburbs and small towns. Sleaford is the largest town. This area has long been dependent on farming and market gardening on its rich land, much of it reclaimed from the marshes.

Though agriculture has declined, many people still work in related, and dependent, businesses, including the manufacture of trailers and agricultural equipment. Another source of local employment is the RAF, with its staff college at Cranwell and important bases at Digby and Waddington.

Bridget Phillipson

Houghton and Sunderland South

New constituency

Tel: 020 7219 3000
E-mail: bridget.phillipson.mp@parliament.uk
Website: www.bridgetphillipson.co.uk

Date of birth: 19 December 1983; Daughter of Claire Phillipson, director of domestic violence charity

Education: St Robert of Newminster School and Sixth Form College, Washington; Hertford College, Oxford (BA modern history 2005); Married Lawrence Dimery 2009

Non-political career: Sunderland City Council 2005-07; Women's refuge manager, Wearside Women in Need 2007-; Member, GMB 2005-

Political career: Member for Houghton and Sunderland South since 6 May 2010 general election; Member, Labour Party 1998-; Former chair, Oxford University Labour Club; North East representative, National Policy Forum

Political interests: Housing, armed forces, families and older people, votes at 16

Recreations: Dog walking, reading, history, music

Bridget Phillipson MP, House of Commons, London SW1A 0AA
Tel: 020 7219 3000 E-mail: bridget.phillipson.mp@parliament.uk
Constituency: West View, North Road, Hetton le Hole,
Tyne and Wear DH5 9JU Website: www.bridgetphillipson.co.uk

GENERAL ELECTION RESULT

		%
Phillipson, B. (Lab)	19,137	50.3
Oliver, R. (Con)	8,147	21.4
Boyle, C. (Lib Dem)	5,292	13.9
Wakefield, C. (Ind)	2,462	6.5
Allen, K. (BNP)	1,961	5.2
Elvin, R. (UKIP)	1,022	2.7
Majority	10,990	28.91
Electorate	68,729	
Turnout	38,021	55.32

CONSTITUENCY SNAPSHOT

The new constituency includes Copt Hill, Hetton, Houghton, and Shiney Row wards from Houghton and Washington East, and St Chad's and Sandhill from Sunderland South.

Both the seats which created the new constituency return Labour members. In Sunderland South the 2005 general election returned Chris Mullin MP with a majority of 11,059 votes. Houghton and Washington East re-elected Fraser Kemp with a majority of 16,065 in 2005. A new constituency but a familiar vote-share for the Labour Party with Bridget Phillipson winning a 10,990 majority.

This area formerly famed for its heavy industry has undergone dramatic social and economic changes and is now reliant on the service industry for much of its employment.

Throughout the 1980s Sunderland was particularly badly affected by the decline of the manufacturing industry, being at the heart of the coal and ship-building industries.

T-Mobile and Northern Electric have both located their call-centres in this seat. This is reflected in the large percentage of this population that works in service industries. At the Doxford International Business Park there are 7,000 jobs that did not exist a decade ago.

The Nissan plant (in neighbouring Washington and Sunderland West) is a major source of jobs for this region, and over 30 per cent work in the construction industry.

Rt Hon **Eric Pickles**

Brentwood and Ongar ***(returning MP)***

Boundary changes

Tel: 020 7219 4428
E-mail: picklese@parliament.uk
Website: www.ericpickles.com

Conservative

Date of birth: 20 April 1952; Son of late Jack and Constance Pickles

Education: Greenhead Grammar School, Keighley, Yorkshire; Leeds Polytechnic; Married Irene 1976

Non-political career: Bradford Metropolitan District Council: Councillor 1979-91, Leader Conservative Group 1987-91; Member Yorkshire Regional Health Authority 1982-90

Political career: Member for Brentwood and Ongar 1992-2010, for Brentwood and Ongar (revised boundary) since 6 May 2010 general election; Opposition Spokesperson for Social Security 1998-2001; Shadow: Minister for Transport 2001-02, Secretary of State for: Local Government and the Regions 2002-03, Local Government 2003-05, Minister for Local Government 2005-07, Secretary of State for Communities and Local Government 2007-09; Secretary of State for Communities and Local Government 2010-; *Select Committees:* Member: Environment, Transport and Regional Affairs 1997-98, Environment, Transport and Regional Affairs (Transport Sub-Committee) 1997-98; Member, Conservative Party National Union Executive Committee 1975-97; National Chairman, Young Conservatives 1980-81; Member, Conservative Party National Local Government Advisory Committee 1985-; Local Government Editor, Newsline 1990-; Deputy Leader, Conservative Group on Association of Metropolitan Authorities 1989-91; Vice-Chairman Conservative Party 1993-97; Deputy chairman (local government) Conservative Party 2005-07; Chairman Conservative Party 2009-10

Political interests: Housing, health, social services, local and regional government; Eastern Europe, India, Poland, USA

Other organisations: Chair, National Local Government Advisory Committee 1992-95; Member, One Nation Forum 1987-91; Chair Joint Committee Against Racism 1982-87; PC 2010; Carlton

Recreations: Films, opera, serious walking, golf

Rt Hon Eric Pickles MP, House of Commons, London SW1A 0AA
Tel: 020 7219 4428 Fax: 020 7219 2783
E-mail: picklese@parliament.uk
Constituency: 19 Crown Street, Brentwood, Essex CM14 4BA
Tel: 01277 210725 Fax: 01277 202221 Website: www.ericpickles.com

GENERAL ELECTION RESULT

		%
Pickles, E. (Con)*	28,792	56.9
Kendall, D. (Lib Dem)	11,872	23.5
Benzing, H. (Lab)	4,992	9.9
McGough, M. (UKIP)	2,037	4.0
Morris, P. (BNP)	1,447	2.9
Barnecutt, J. (Green)	584	1.2
Tilbrook, R. (England)	491	1.0
Sapwell, J. (Ind)	263	0.5
Attfield, D. (Ind)	113	0.2
Majority	16,920	33.44
Electorate	73,224	
Turnout	50,591	69.09

**Member of last parliament*

CONSTITUENCY SNAPSHOT

Represented by the Conservative Sir Robert McCrindle from the seat's creation in 1974 until 1992, Brentwood and Ongar is currently represented by the party's Eric Pickles.

Eric Pickles's 1992 majority of 15,175 was reduced in 1997, but Brentwood and Ongar did not experience the same fall in Tory fortunes as happened elsewhere in Essex. Mr Pickles was re-elected with a majority of almost 10,000.

Following allegations that the Peniel Pentecostal Church had taken over the local Conservative Party, Martin Bell threw his hat into the ring in 2001. All three major parties suffered losses to Mr Bell, who polled 31 per cent of the vote, but it was not enough to unseat Mr Pickles, whose majority was reduced to 2,821.

In 2005 with no challenge from Martin Bell, Pickles increased his majority to 11,612. He increased his winning margin to 16,920 in 2010.

Boundary changes were minimal.

Just outside Greater London, in a relatively rural corner of Essex, the seat takes its name from Brentwood, the largest town in the area, and the small town of Chipping Ongar to the north of the constituency.

The Ford Motor Company has a large headquarters in the constituency. Over 50 per cent of the borough's population commute, mostly to London.

Christopher Pincher

Tamworth

No boundary changes

Tel: 020 7219 3000
E-mail: christopher.pincher.mp@parliament.uk

Date of birth: 24 September 1969

Education: Ounsdale School, Staffordshire; London School of Economics (government and history 1991); Single

Non-political career: Manager, Accenture 1993-

Political career: Contested Warley 1997 and Tamworth 2005 general elections. Member for Tamworth since 6 May 2010 general election; Member, Conservative Party 1987-

Political interests: Home affairs, defence, education

Other organisations: Travellers' Club

Recreations: Literature and biography, golf, the turf

Christopher Pincher MP, House of Commons, London SW1A 0AA
Tel: 020 7219 3000 E-mail: christopher.pincher.mp@parliament.uk
Constituency: Tamworth Conservative Association, 23 Albert Road, Tamworth, Staffordshire B79 7JS Tel: 01827 571156
Fax: 01827 706610 Website: www.tamworthconservatives.com

GENERAL ELECTION RESULT

		%	+/-
Pincher, C. (Con)	21,238	45.8	8.9
Jenkins, B. (Lab)*	15,148	32.7	-10.1
Pinkett, J. (Lib Dem)	7,516	16.2	2.2
Smith, P. (UKIP)	2,253	4.9	2.1
Detheridge, C. (Christian)	235	0.5	
Majority	6,090	13.13	
Electorate	72,693		
Turnout	46,390	63.82	

*Member of last parliament

CONSTITUENCY SNAPSHOT

Tamworth has its own place in political history, being associated with Sir Robert Peel's 1834 Tamworth Manifesto, the first statement of principles ever issued by a political party.

Before 1983 the seat was called Lichfield and Tamworth before being redrawn as Staffordshire South East. David Lightbown was returned with a majority of almost 11,000 for the Tories in 1983.

He died in 1996 and at the by-election, held not long before the general election, Brian Jenkins secured the win for Labour with a 22 per cent swing. The following year the seat disappeared and Tamworth was created. Jenkins polled 25,808 votes, almost 52 per cent of the votes cast. He held the seat in 2005 with a reduced majority of 2,569.

Jenkins was defeated in 2010 with a 9.5 per cent swing to the Conservative Christopher Pincher.

A constituency in the south-east of Staffordshire about 15 miles north-east of Birmingham, Tamworth comprises the town and some rural areas to its north and west.

The town centre has a quarter of historic buildings, which are now something of an oasis, dwarfed by the tower blocks which sprang up to accommodate its burgeoning population.

It is one of Birmingham's congested satellite towns, nestling in the crook of the M42/A5 interchange, and its rural hinterland stretches to the north and west. Key businesses include Britvic, AAH Pharmaceuticals, Heidelberg, Swish Products and Percy Lane Ltd.

Dr **Daniel Poulter**

Central Suffolk and North Ipswich

Boundary changes

Tel: 020 7219 3000
E-mail: daniel.poulter.mp@parliament.uk
Website: www.drdanielpoulter.com

Conservative

Date of birth: 30 October 1978

Education: Bristol University (LLB); St Thomas' School of Medicine (MBBS); Engaged to Joanna

Non-political career: Doctor, Ipswich Hospital: Speciality registrar, obstetrics and gynaecology 2008-10; Locum doctor, Suffolk 2010-; Councillor, Hastings Borough Council 2006-07; Deputy Leader, Reigate and Banstead Council 2008-10

Political career: Member for Central Suffolk and North Ipswich since 6 May 2010 general election; Conservative Medical Society

Political interests: Health, rural affairs, pensions, older people, voluntary sector

Other organisations: Guys Hospital Rugby Club; *Publications:* Published author in field of women's health

Recreations: Cricket, rugby, golf, fishing

Dr Daniel Poulter MP, House of Commons, London SW1A 0AA
Tel: 020 7219 3000 E-mail: daniel.poulter.mp@parliament.uk
Constituency: 19 The Business Centre, Earl Soham, Suffolk IP13 7SA
Tel: 01728 685148 Website: www.drdanielpoulter.com

GENERAL ELECTION RESULT

		%
Poulter, D. (Con)	27,125	50.8
Aalders-Dunthorne, A. (Lib Dem)	13,339	25.0
Joshi, B. (Lab)	8,636	16.2
Philpot, R. (UKIP)	2,361	4.4
Stringer, A. (Green)	1,452	2.7
Trevitt, M. (Ind)	389	0.7
Vass, R. (NP)	118	0.2
Majority	13,786	25.81
Electorate	75,848	
Turnout	53,420	70.43

CONSTITUENCY SNAPSHOT

The Conservatives have held this region of Suffolk since 1951. Sir Michael Lord held the seat from its formation in 1983 until retiring in 2010. His majority grew from 14,781 in 1983 to 18,006 in 1992.

There was a swing of 14.2 per cent in 1997 to Labour, though Sir Michael once again emerged victorious with a majority of 3,538. In 2001 his majority fell by 69 votes. His majority more than doubled in 2005 to 7,856.

The seat was held by Daniel Poulter for the Conservatives in 2010 with a 13,786 majority.

Central Suffolk and North Ipswich lost the part-ward Stowupland to Bury St Edmunds and three other part-wards to Ipswich; it gained Whitton and Kesgrave East part-wards from Ipswich and Suffolk Central respectively.

The most rural of the Suffolk constituencies, with over two thirds of the population living in villages and rural areas, Central Suffolk and North Ipswich is a largely prosperous region of golden cornfields, commuter homes and picturesque retirement residences.

The economic pursuits are mainly agricultural, and associated industries can be found in the towns of the region, such as Framlingham, Wickham Market and, just outside the constituency, Needham Market.

The area houses a large commuter population, serving Ipswich, Bury St Edmunds and Norwich.

Stephen Pound

Ealing North (returning MP)

Boundary changes

Tel: 020 7219 4312
E-mail: stevepoundmp@parliament.uk
Website: www.stevepound.org.uk

Date of birth: 3 July 1948; Son of late Pelham Pound, journalist, and late Dominica Pound, teacher

Education: Hertford Grammar School; London School of Economics (Diploma industrial relations 1979, BSc economics 1982) (Sabbatical President of Union 1981-82); Married Maggie Griffiths 1976 (1 son 1 daughter)

Non-political career: Armed Forces Parliamentary Scheme (Navy); Seaman 1964-66; Bus conductor 1966-68; Hospital porter 1969-79; Student 1979-84; Housing officer 1984-97; Branch Secretary, 640 Middlesex Branch, COHSE 1975-79; Branch Officer, TGWU (ACTS) 1990-96; Councillor, London Borough of Ealing 1982-98: Mayor 1995-96

Political career: Member for Ealing North 1997-2010, for Ealing North (revised boundary) since 6 May 2010 general election; PPS to Hazel Blears: as Minister of State, Home Office 2005-06, as Minister without Portfolio 2006-07, to Stephen Timms: as Minister of State, Department for Business, Enterprise and Regulatory Reform 2007-08, as Minister of State, Department for Work and Pensions 2008, as Financial Secretary, HM Treasury 2008-09, to Sadiq Khan as Minister of State, Department for Transport 2009, to Stephen Timms as Financial Secretary, HM Treasury 2010; *Select Committees:* Member: Broadcasting 1997-2001, Northern Ireland Affairs 1999-2010, Standards and Privileges 2003-05

Political interests: Armenia, Assyria, Ireland, Poland, Ukraine

Other organisations: St Joseph's Catholic Social, Hanwell; Fulham FC Supporters Club

Recreations: Watching football, playing cricket, snooker, jazz, gardening, collecting comics

Stephen Pound MP, House of Commons, London SW1A 0AA
Tel: 020 7219 4312 Fax: 020 7219 5982
E-mail: stevepoundmp@parliament.uk
Website: www.stevepound.org.uk

GENERAL ELECTION RESULT

		%
Pound, S. (Lab)*	24,023	50.4
Gibb, I. (Con)	14,722	30.9
Lucas, C. (Lib Dem)	6,283	13.2
Furness, D. (BNP)	1,045	2.2
De Wulverton, I. (UKIP)	685	1.4
Warleigh-Lack, C. (Green)	505	1.1
Ljubisic, P. (Christian)	415	0.9
Majority	9,301	19.51
Electorate	67,902	
Turnout	47,678	70.22

**Member of last parliament*

CONSTITUENCY SNAPSHOT

William Molloy represented the seat for Labour from 1964 until it fell into the hands of Tory Harry Greenway in 1979.

Mr Greenway represented the seat until 1997 when Stephen Pound MP won the seat for Labour by a margin of over 9,000 votes. Pound held onto the seat in 2001 and again in 2005, although his majority was cut to 7,059. Long serving Labour MP Stephen Pound gained just over 50 per cent of the vote and a 9,301 majority despite Tory advances elsewhere in West London.

The seat gained parts of Greenford Broadway and Hobbayne wards from Ealing Southall and lost parts of Domers Wells, Ealing Broadway and Hangar Hill to Ealing Southall and Ealing Central and Acton.

This is a constituency of broad ethnic diversity with established Asian, Irish and Polish communities.

Heathrow Airport now provides much of the employment for residents of Ealing North. Manufacturing is still important. There has been an increase in warehousing and distribution industries, which are helped by the good communication links.

Rt Hon **Dawn Primarolo**

Bristol South (returning MP)

Boundary changes

Tel: 020 7219 4343
E-mail: primarolod@parliament.uk

Date of birth: 2 May 1954

Education: Thomas Bennett Comprehensive School, Crawley; Bristol Polytechnic (BA social science 1984); Née Gasson: married Michael Primarolo 1972 (divorced) (1 son); married Thomas Ducat 1990

Non-political career: Secretary 1972-73; Secretary and advice worker, Law Centre, East London; Secretary, Avon County Council 1975-78; Voluntary work 1978-81; Mature student 1981-87; Member Unison; Councillor, Avon County Council 1985-87

Political career: Member for Bristol South 1987-2010, for Bristol South (revised boundary) since 6 May 2010 general election; Opposition Spokesperson for: Health 1992-94, Treasury and Economic Affairs 1994-97; HM Treasury: Financial Secretary 1997-99, Paymaster General 1999-2007; Minister of State: for Public Health, Department of Health 2007-09, for Children, Young People and Families, Department for Children, Schools and Families 2009-10; Shadow Minister for Children 2010-; *Select Committees:* Member: Public Accounts 1997-98

Political interests: Education, housing, social security, health, economic policy, equal opportunities

Other organisations: PC 2002

Rt Hon Dawn Primarolo MP, House of Commons, London SW1A 0AA Tel: 020 7219 4343 E-mail: primarolod@parliament.uk
Constituency: PO Box 1002, Bristol, Gloucestershire BS99 1WH
Tel: 0117-909 0063 Fax: 0117-909 0064
Website: www.dawnprimarolo.co.uk

GENERAL ELECTION RESULT

		%
Primarolo, D. (Lab)*	18,600	38.5
Wright, M. (Lib Dem)	13,866	28.7
Lloyd Davies, M. (Con)	11,086	22.9
Chidsey, C. (BNP)	1,739	3.6
McNamee, C. (UKIP)	1,264	2.6
Bolton, C. (Green)	1,216	2.5
Clarke, C. (England)	400	0.8
Baldwin, T. (TUSC)	206	0.4
Majority	4,734	9.79
Electorate	78,579	
Turnout	48,377	61.56

**Member of last parliament*

CONSTITUENCY SNAPSHOT

Unlike the other constituencies of south west England, Bristol South has remained supportive of the Labour Party throughout the post-Second World War period. In fact, Bristol South was the only seat Labour retained in the south west at the 1983 general election.

Lone-surviving MP Michael Cocks held the seat from 1970 to 1987, when he was deselected, and succeeded by Dawn Primarolo. From 1997 to 2005 she has secured majorities of over 20 per cent. Primarolo's majority fell to 4,734 in 2010 following a 7.5 per cent swing to the Liberal Democrats.

Boundary changes were minimal.

The northern half of the constituency, close to the river, is characterised by Victorian and Edwardian terraced housing, and is largely owner-occupied. Far more populous, however, is the southern part of the constituency, which is dominated by large, modern council estates.

Of the four urban Bristol constituencies, Bristol South is the most working-class, with relatively low proportions of managerial class employees.

Mark Prisk

***Hertford and Stortford** (returning MP)*

Boundary changes

Tel: 020 7219 6358
E-mail: hunterj@parliament.uk
Website: www.markprisk.com

Conservative

Date of birth: 12 June 1962; Son of Michael Raymond, chartered surveyor, and Irene June, née Pearce

Education: Truro School, Cornwall; Reading University (BSc land management 1983); Married Lesley Jane Titcomb 1989

Non-political career: Graduate surveyor Knight Frank 1983-85; Derrick Wade & Waters 1985-91: Senior surveyor 1985-89, Director 1989-91; Principal: The Mark Prisk Connection 1991-97, mp², consultancy 1997-2001

Political career: Contested Newham North West 1992 and Wansdyke 1997 general elections. Member for Hertford and Stortford 2001-10, for Hertford and Stortford (revised boundary) since 6 May 2010 general election; Shadow: Financial Secretary 2002-03, Paymaster General 2003-04; Opposition Whip 2004-05; Shadow Minister for: Business and Enterprise 2005-09, Business 2009-10; Minister of State for Business and Enterprise, Department for Business, Innovation and Skills 2010-; *Select Committees:* Member: Welsh Affairs 2001-05, Regulatory Reform 2008-09; Chair Reading University Conservatives 1981-82; National vice-chair Federation of Conservative Students 1982-83; Deputy chair Hertfordshire Area 1999-2000; Member Conservative Business Relations Board 2006-

Political interests: Defence, education, planning, development, small businesses; China, Italy, Russia, USA

Other organisations: Member Prince's Trust; Founding chair Youth For Peace Through NATO 1983-86; Founder East Hertfordshire Business Forum; Chair Hertfordshire Countryside Partnership; Creator Charter for Hertfordshire's Countryside; Parliamentary Chairman, First Defence 2002-04; Vice-President First Defence 2004-; Trustee Industry and Parliamentary Trust 2007-; Member Royal Institute of Chartered Surveyors; *Publications:* Eternal Vigilance, The Defence of a Free Society, First Defence, 2003

Recreations: Music, piano, rugby, cricket, theatre, architecture, choral singing (vice-chair Parliamentary Choir 2008-)

Mark Prisk MP, House of Commons, London SW1A 0AA
Tel: 020 7219 6358 Fax: 020 7219 3826
E-mail: hunterj@parliament.uk
Constituency: Hertford and Stortford Conservatives, Unit 4, Swains Mill, Crane Mead, Ware, Hertfordshire SG12 9PY
Tel: 01920 462 182 Fax: 01920 485 805
Website: www.markprisk.com

GENERAL ELECTION RESULT

		%
Prisk, M. (Con)*	29,810	53.8
Lewin, A. (Lib Dem)	14,373	26.0
Terry, S. (Lab)	7,620	13.8
Sodey, D. (UKIP)	1,716	3.1
Harris, R. (BNP)	1,297	2.3
Xenophontos, L. (Ind)	325	0.6
Adams, M. (Ind)	236	0.4
Majority	15,437	27.88
Electorate	78,459	
Turnout	55,377	70.58

**Member of last parliament*

CONSTITUENCY SNAPSHOT

In 1997 there was a 13.5 per cent swing to Labour, reducing Conservative Bowen Wells's majority of over 17,500 to one of 6,885.

He retired in 2001 and was replaced by Mark Prisk who was elected with a majority of just over 5,500. In 2005 the challenge to the Conservatives receded, with Mark Prisk polling more than 50 per cent of the vote and being returned to Parliament with a majority of more than 13,000.

Prisk increased his majority to 15,437 at the 2010 general election.

Boundary changes were minor.

Set in the south-east corner of Hertfordshire, bordering Essex, the constituency is named after the towns of Hertford and Bishop's Stortford. The other main towns are Ware and Sawbridgeworth.

The constituency is affluent, having considerably more professional and managerial workers than the national average.

The major sources of employment for people living here are found in London. But the pharmaceutical industry is also an important provider of jobs locally with Merck Sharp & Dohme on the seat's southern border and GlaxoSmithKline in Harlow and Ware.

Mark Pritchard

The Wrekin (returning MP)

Boundary changes

Tel: 020 7219 8494
E-mail: pritchardm@parliament.uk
Website: www.markpritchard.com

Conservative

Date of birth: 22 November 1966; Son of late Frank Pritchard and of Romona Pritchard

Education: Afan Comprehensive School, Cymmer, Glamorgan; Aylestone School, Hereford; Regents Theological College (Cert theological and pastoral studies); London Guildhall University (MA marketing management); post-graduate diploma (marketing); Married Sondra Janae Spaeth 1997

Non-political career: Parliamentary researcher 1993-05; Director and founder 1998-2005: Pritchard Communications Ltd, Next Steps Market Research Ltd -2006; Councillor: Harrow Council 1993-94, Woking Borough Council 2000-03

Political career: Contested Warley 2001 general election. Member for The Wrekin 2005-10, for The Wrekin (revised boundary) since 6 May 2010 general election; *Select Committees:* Member: Environmental Audit 2005-07, Work and Pensions 2006-09, Welsh Affairs 2007-10, Transport 2009-10; Bow Group Council 1994; National Board Member Conservative Councillors Association 2002; Conservative Party Human Rights Commission 2006-

Political interests: Rural affairs, defence, education, cyber-security, homeland security, foreign relations; Africa, Argentina, India, Israel, Latin America, Philippines, USA

Other organisations: Member Miniature Schnauzer Club of Great Britain

Recreations: Walking, skiing, dogs, writing, animal welfare

Mark Pritchard MP, House of Commons, London SW1A 0AA
Tel: 020 7219 8494 Fax: 020 7219 5969
E-mail: pritchardm@parliament.uk
Constituency: 25 Church Street, Wellington, Shropshire TF1 1DG
Tel: 01952 256080 Fax: 01952 256080
Website: www.markpritchard.com

GENERAL ELECTION RESULT

		%
Pritchard, M. (Con)*	21,922	47.7
Kalinauckas, P. (Lab)	12,472	27.1
Daw, A. (Lib Dem)	8,019	17.4
Hurst, M. (UKIP)	2,050	4.5
Harwood, S. (BNP)	1,505	3.3
Majority	9,450	20.56
Electorate	65,544	
Turnout	45,968	70.13

**Member of last parliament*

CONSTITUENCY SNAPSHOT

Today's constituency bears little resemblance to The Wrekin that existed before 1997. That seat changed hands no fewer than 13 times between 1918 and 1987.

In 1997 Peter Bradley managed a narrow Labour win. In 2001 the Conservatives' choice of Old Etonian Jacob Rees-Mogg saw a 1 per cent swing to Labour, increasing Bradley's majority to 3,587.

However, a 3.5 per cent increase in vote-share for the Conservatives' Mark Pritchard was enough to give him the seat in 2005 with a majority of 942. In 2010 Pritchard was re-elected with a much-increased majority of 9,450.

Minor boundary changes see little change to the make-up of the constituency.

The Wrekin consists of a horseshoe-shaped area of Shropshire that curves around the new town of Telford.

The seat includes some of the northern areas of Telford, the market towns of Wellington and Newport, the old mining towns of Hadley and Donnington, and Wolverhampton commuter towns of Shifnal and Albrighton in the south east. It is a semi-rural seat, geographically dominated by The Wrekin, whose summit commands a view of 12 counties.

The area is diverse: it slips from factory to farmland, from hamlet to housing estate, and from foundry to business park. There is also a substantial military presence in the area, with RAF Cosford situated close to Wolverhampton.

Dr **John Pugh**

Southport (returning MP)

No boundary changes

Tel: 020 7219 8318
E-mail: pughj@parliament.uk
Website: www.johnpugh.org.uk

Date of birth: 28 June 1948; Son of James and Patricia Pugh

Education: Prescott Grammar School; Maidstone Grammar School; Durham University (BA philosophy 1971); Liverpool University (MA logic 1974, MEd 1981); Nottingham University (MPhil theology 1984); Manchester University (PhD logic 1995); Married Annette Sangar 1971 (1 son 3 daughters)

Non-political career: Head of social studies Salesian High School, Bootle 1972-83; Head of philosophy and religious studies Merchant Taylors' Boys' School, Crosby 1983-2001: Teacher, head of philosophy; Councillor, Sefton Metropolitan Borough Council 1987-2001: Former member Merseyside Police Authority; Member: North West Arts Board, Merseyside Partnership

Political career: Member for Southport since 7 June 2001 general election; Liberal Democrat: Spokesperson for Education 2002-05, Shadow Minister for: Transport 2005-06, Health 2006-07, Treasury 2008-10, Health 2009-10; *Select Committees:* Member: Transport, Local Government and the Regions 2001-02, Transport, Local Government and the Regions (Transport Sub-Committee) 2001-02, Transport, Local Government and the Regions (Urban Affairs Sub-Committee) 2001-02, ODPM/Communities and Local Government 2002-03, ODPM/Communities and Local Government (Urban Affairs Sub-Committee) 2003, ODPM/Communities and Local Government 2005-10, Crossrail Bill 2006-07, Public Accounts 2006-10; Chair Southport Liberal Democrat Association 1984-87

Political interests: Local and regional government, elderly, education, transport, health; *Publications:* Christian Understanding of God, 1990

Recreations: Philosophy society Liverpool University, weightlifting, reading, football, computers

Dr John Pugh MP, House of Commons, London SW1A 0AA
Tel: 020 7219 8318 Fax: 020 7219 1794
E-mail: pughj@parliament.uk
Constituency: 35 Shakespeare Street, Southport, Lancashire PR8 5AB
Tel: 01704 533555 Fax: 01704 884160
Website: www.johnpugh.org.uk

GENERAL ELECTION RESULT

		%	+/-
Pugh, J. (Lib Dem)*	21,707	49.6	3.3
Porter, B. (Con)	15,683	35.8	-1.1
Conalty, J. (Lab)	4,116	9.4	-3.4
Durrance, T. (UKIP)	2,251	5.1	3.3
Majority	6,024	13.77	
Electorate	67,202		
Turnout	43,757	65.11	

**Member of last parliament*

CONSTITUENCY SNAPSHOT

The Liberal Democrats won Southport in 1987, 1997, 2001 and 2005 but lost it in 1992 to the Conservatives.

John Pugh replaced Ronnie Fearn in 2001 with a reduced majority.

Pugh slightly increased his share of the vote in 2005 and his majority rose to 3,838.

In 2010 Pugh's majority increased to 6,024.

Situated on the north west coast of England, the seat of Southport is west of Manchester and north of Liverpool. After boundary changes in the 1970s it moved into Merseyside from Lancashire. Tourism is the main focus for this seaside town.

The social make-up of the constituency gravitates towards managers and skilled non-manual workers.

Given the large numbers of elderly people who live in the constituency, issues such as free personal care, the provision of pensions during hospital stays, perceived age discrimination, and free bus passes are all politically salient issues for the older voters of Southport.

Yasmin Qureshi

Bolton South East

Boundary changes

Tel: 020 7219 3000
E-mail: yasmin.qureshi.mp@parliament.uk
Website: www.yasminqureshi.org.uk

Labour

Date of birth: 5 July 1963; Daughter of Mohammad Qureshi, civil engineer, and Sakina Beg, primary school teacher

Education: Westfield School; South Bank Polytechnic, London (BA law 1984); Council of Legal Education (Barrister Exams 1985); University College, London (Masters law); Married Nadeem Ashraf Butt 2008

Non-political career: Called to the Bar, Lincoln's Inn 1985; Barrister 1987-: Crown prosecutor, Crown Prosecution Service 1987-2000; United Nations Mission in Kosovo, Judicial Affairs Department Co-ordinator, Criminal Law Unit 2000-01, Department director 2001-02; Crown prosecutor, Crown Prosecution Service 2004-08; Human rights adviser to Mayor of London, Ken Livingstone 2004-08; Barrister: 2 Kings Bench Walk Chambers, London 2004-08, Kenworthy's Chambers 2008-; Member: First Division Association, Union of Shop, Distributive and Allied Workers (USDAW), GMB

Political career: Contested Brent East 2005 general election. Member for Bolton South East since 6 May 2010 general election; Labour Party: Watford Constituency Labour Party: Secretary, Treasurer, Regional delegate to area, Delegate to Labour group

Political interests: Crime, education, young people

Other organisations: Former chair, Human Rights and Civil Liberties Working Group, Association of Muslim Lawyers; Former president, Pakistan Club (UK); British Institute of Human Rights; Society of Labour Lawyers; Fabian Society: Member, Former chair, Watford and District branch; Bolton Labour Socialist Club

Recreations: Reading

Yasmin Qureshi MP, House of Commons, London SW1A 0AA
Tel: 020 7219 3000 E-mail: yasmin.qureshi.mp@parliament.uk
Constituency: c/o Bolton Labour Party, 60 St Georges Road, Bolton, Lancashire BL1 2DD Tel: 01204 371202
Website: www.yasminqureshi.org.uk

GENERAL ELECTION RESULT

		%
Qureshi, Y. (Lab)	18,782	47.4
Morgan, A. (Con)	10,148	25.6
O'Hanlon, D. (Lib Dem)	6,289	15.9
Spink, S. (BNP)	2,012	5.1
Sidaway, I. (UKIP)	1,564	4.0
Johnson, A. (Green)	614	1.6
Syed, N. (CPA)	195	0.5
Majority	8,634	21.80
Electorate	69,928	
Turnout	39,604	56.64

CONSTITUENCY SNAPSHOT

The seat was created in 1983 and until 1997 this was the only one of Bolton borough's three constituent seats that was held by Labour. In 1997 Labour took control of all three Bolton seats.

Dr Brian Iddon was first elected in 1997, augmenting the outgoing David Young's (notional) majority by 10,000. Bolton South East is still the safest of the three by some margin. Brian Iddon retired in 2010 and the Labour candidate, Yasmin Qureshi held the seat with a majority of 8,634.

Boundary changes exchanged five part-wards between the three Bolton divisions.

Bolton, north west of Manchester, is an industrial town founded on textile manufacture and mining, although it is engineering that now bolsters the local economy.

The public sector is a major employer, especially the Royal Bolton Hospital. A strong service industry sector is being developed and the area has one of the best shopping centres in the North West.

Within the orbit of the M61 motorway, the seat benefits from commuter rail services to Manchester Piccadilly and Victoria. There are also regular services to Preston, Blackpool and the Lake District.

Dominic Raab

Esher and Walton

No boundary changes

Tel: 020 7219 3000
E-mail: dominic.raab.mp@parliament.uk
Website: www.dominicraab.com

Date of birth: 25 February 1974

Education: Dr Challoner's Grammar School, Amersham; Lady Margaret Hall, Oxford (law); Jesus College, Cambridge (Master's law); Married Erika

Non-political career: Lawyer, Linklaters; Foreign and Commonwealth Office 2000-06: The Hague 2003-06; Chief of staff to: David Davis MP 2006-08, Dominic Grieve MP 2008-10

Political career: Member for Esher and Walton since 6 May 2010 general election

Political interests: Civil liberties, human rights; Middle East

Other organisations: Clive Parry Prize for international law; *Publications:* Author, The Assault on Liberty (Fourth Estate, 2009)

Recreations: Travel, karate, thai boxing, theatre

Dominic Raab MP, House of Commons, London SW1A 0AA
Tel: 020 7219 3000 E-mail: dominic.raab.mp@parliament.uk
Constituency: c/o Esher and Walton Conservative Association, 3 Bridle Close, Kingston on Thames, Surrey KT1 2JW
Website: www.dominicraab.com

GENERAL ELECTION RESULT

		%	+/-
Raab, D. (Con)	32,134	58.9	13.4
Blackman, L. (Lib Dem)	13,541	24.8	-4.6
Eldergill, F. (Lab)	5,829	10.7	-8.7
Collignon, B. (UKIP)	1,783	3.3	
Popham, T. (Ind)	378	0.7	
Chinnery, J. (Loony)	341	0.6	-0.6
Kearsley, M. (England)	307	0.6	
Lear, A. (Best)	230	0.4	
Majority	18,593	34.09	
Electorate	75,338		
Turnout	54,543	72.40	

CONSTITUENCY SNAPSHOT

The Conservative tendencies of Esher and Walton are not out of place in Surrey as a whole. Even in the otherwise disastrous 1997 election for the Tories, the county returned nothing but Tory MPs. Ian Taylor was first elected in 1987. His majority in 1997 was 14,528. Since then, however, his majority fell - to 11,538 in 2001 and to 7,727 in 2005.

Taylor retired in 2010 and the seat was held by Dominic Raab with a 18,593 majority.

In the 1530s Archbishop Wolsey decided to build his Hampton Court Palace here, sitting just inside the constituency's northern boundary. Bordering greater London to the south west, nowadays this Surrey constituency must be classed as one of the most exclusive of the stockbroker commuter belt.

In addition to the two eponymous towns, this seat contains Burwood Park, Oxshott, Cobham, Hinchley Wood, and Stoke D'Abernon.

It has a close proximity to Greater London with the direct access to the City via London Waterloo.

Rt Hon **John Randall**

Uxbridge and South Ruislip ***(returning MP)***

New constituency

Tel: 020 7219 3400
E-mail: randallj@parliament.uk
Website: www.johnrandallmp.com

Conservative

Date of birth: 5 August 1955; Son of late Alec Albert Randall, company director, and Joyce Margaret, neé Gore

Education: Merchant Taylor's School, Northwood; School of Slavonic and East European Studies, London University (BA Serbo-Croat 1979); Married Katherine Frances Gray 1986 (2 sons 1 daughter)

Non-political career: Randall's of Uxbridge: Sales assistant 1973-79, Buyer 1979, Director 1980-, Managing director 1988-97; Tour leader, Birdquest Holidays and Limosa Holidays as specialist ornithologist 1986-97

Political career: Member for Uxbridge 31 July 1997 by-election to 2010, for Uxbridge and South Ruislip since 6 May 2010 general election; Opposition Whip 2000-03, 2003-05; Opposition Assisant Chief Whip 2005-10; Deputy Chief Whip (Treasurer of HM Household) 2010-; *Select Committees:* Member: Deregulation 1997-2001, Environment, Transport and Regional Affairs 1998-2000, Environment, Transport and Regional Affairs (Environment Sub-Committee) 1998-2000, Transport 2003-05, Finance and Services 2005-06, Selection 2005-07, Administration 2007-09, Members' Allowances 2009-10; Hon. Treasurer, Uxbridge Conservative Association 1994, Chairman 1994-97

Political interests: Environment, trade and industry, foreign affairs, transport; Balkans, Caucasus, Russia

Other organisations: Chair Uxbridge Retailers' Association -1997; PC 2010; Uxbridge Conservative; Member: Uxbridge Cricket Club, Uxbridge Rugby Football Club, Saracens Rugby Football Club, Middlesex County Cricket Club

Recreations: Local history, ornithology, theatre, opera, travel, music (plays piano), cricket, football, rugby

Rt Hon John Randall MP, House of Commons, London SW1A 0AA
Tel: 020 7219 3400 Fax: 020 7219 2590
E-mail: randallj@parliament.uk
Constituency: 36 Harefield Road, Uxbridge, Middlesex UB8 1PH
Tel: 01895 239465 Fax: 01895 253105
Website: www.johnrandallmp.com

GENERAL ELECTION RESULT

		%
Randall, J. (Con)*	21,758	48.3
Garg, S. (Lab)	10,542	23.4
Cox, M. (Lib Dem)	8,995	20.0
Neal, D. (BNP)	1,396	3.1
Wadsworth, G. (UKIP)	1,234	2.7
Harling, M. (Green)	477	1.1
Cooper, R. (England)	403	0.9
McAllister, F. (NF)	271	0.6
Majority	11,216	24.88
Electorate	71,168	
Turnout	45,076	63.34

**Member of last parliament*

CONSTITUENCY SNAPSHOT

Between 1945 and 1970 the seat was held by Labour. Since then, however, Uxbridge has been represented by Conservative MPs including Charles Curran (1970-72) and Sir Michael Shersby (1972-97), whose death shortly after his re-election in 1997 triggered a by-election which resulted in the election of the seat's current MP, John Randall.

Randall was re-elected in 2005 with a majority of 6,171. He held on to the new seat with a 11,216 majority and over 48 per cent of the vote.

This new constituency includes the wards of Brunel, Cavendish, Hillingdon East, Manor, South Ruislip, Uxbridge North, Uxbridge South and Yiewsley, from the old seats of Uxbridge, and Ruislip Northwood.

On the western edge of Greater London just north of Heathrow, Uxbridge is a relatively affluent, residential constituency with patches of industrial activity.

The constituency is home to the Uxbridge campus of Brunel University, which not only is a large local employer, but whose students contribute to the local economy.

Heathrow is also a major local employer, and plans for expansion of the airport can only increase job opportunities in the area, where most employment is predominantly non-manual.

RAF Northolt, home to the Royal Squadron which is responsible for VIP transport of the royal family, senior government ministers and senior military officers, is now situated in the constituency.

Rt Hon **Nick Raynsford**

***Greenwich and Woolwich** (returning MP)*

Boundary changes

Tel: 020 7219 2773
E-mail: raynsfordn@parliament.uk
Website: www.nickraynsford.org.uk

Date of birth: 28 January 1945; Son of late Wyvill and Patricia Raynsford

Education: Repton School, Derbyshire; Sidney Sussex College, Cambridge (BA history 1966, MA); Chelsea School of Art (diploma in art and design 1972); Married Anne Jelley 1968 (separated 2007) (3 daughters)

Non-political career: Director: SHAC, the London Housing Aid Centre 1976-86, Raynsford and Morris 1987-92; Member GMB; Councillor London Borough of Hammersmith and Fulham 1971-75

Political career: Member for Fulham 1986 by-election to 1987, for Greenwich 1992-97, and for Greenwich and Woolwich 1997-2010, for Greenwich and Woolwich (revised boundary) since 6 May 2010 general election; PPS to Roy Hattersley as Deputy Leader Labour Party 1986-87; Opposition Spokesperson for: Transport and London 1993-94, Housing, Construction and London 1994-97; Department of the Environment, Transport and the Regions 1997-2001: Parliamentary Under-Secretary of State 1997-99, Minister of State (Housing and Planning) 1999-2001; Minister of State Department for Transport, Local Government and the Regions (Local Government and the Regions) 2001-02; Minister of State: Office of the Deputy Prime Minister 2002-05: (Local Government and the Regions 2002-03, Local and Regional Government 2003-05)

Political interests: Housing, social policy, transport, environment; Europe

Other organisations: Chair Centre for Public Scrutiny 2007-; President Youthbuild UK 2008-; Trustee London Open House 2009-; PC 2001; *Publications:* A Guide to Housing Benefit (1982); Contributor to journals including Building, Housing and Roof

Recreations: Photography, walking, golf

Rt Hon Nick Raynsford MP, House of Commons, London SW1A 0AA Tel: 020 7219 2773 Fax: 020 7219 2619
E-mail: raynsfordn@parliament.uk
Constituency: 32 Woolwich Road, London SE10 0JU
Website: www.nickraynsford.org.uk

GENERAL ELECTION RESULT

		%
Raynsford, N. (Lab)*	20,262	49.2
Drury, S. (Con)	10,109	24.5
Lee, J. (Lib Dem)	7,498	18.2
Rustem, L. (BNP)	1,151	2.8
Hewett, A. (Green)	1,054	2.6
Adeleye, E. (Christian)	443	1.1
Wresniwiro, T. (England)	339	0.8
Kasab, O. (TUSC)	267	0.7
Alingham, T. (Ind)	65	0.2
Majority	10,153	24.65
Electorate	65,489	
Turnout	41,188	62.89

**Member of last parliament*

CONSTITUENCY SNAPSHOT

After the Second World War the Greenwich seat was held by Labour. However, Labour's Guy Barnett began to see his lead reducing in the late 1970s and early 1980s.

The seat fell to the SDP's Rosie Barnes at a by-election in 1987. Labour reclaimed both the Greenwich and Woolwich seats in 1992. When boundaries were redrawn in 1997 to create the current seat, Nick Raynsford's majority increased to 18,128. Raynsford has since managed to maintain a five-figure majority. Nick Raynsford retained this seat for Labour with a 10,153 majority despite a 5.1 per cent swing to the Conservatives.

The seat lost four part-wards to Eltham, while gaining Glyndon ward and that part of Woolwich Common that was in Eltham.

The constituency is home to Greenwich Park, Royal Naval College, Royal Observatory and National Maritime Museum and the Millennium Dome.

Jobs in the manufacturing and transport industries are in long-term decline and retail and tourism struggle to replace them. The Millennium Dome and its rebranding as the O2 Arena in 2007, has established itself as one of the capital's primary concert venues.

The constituency will play host to a number of events at the 2012 London Olympics:

Greenwich Park will host equestrian events, the Royal Artillery shooting events, and the O2 Arena gymnastics and basketball.

Mark Reckless

Rochester and Strood

New constituency

Tel: 020 7219 3000
E-mail: mark.reckless.mp@parliament.uk
Website: www.markreckless.com

Date of birth: 1970

Education: Oxford University (philosophy, politics and economics); Columbia Business School, New York USA (MBA); College of Law (LLB); Single

Non-political career: Economist, Booz Allen Hamilton -2004; Called to the Bar, Lincoln's Inn 2007; Councillor, Medway Council 2007-; Member, Kent Police Authority 2007-

Political career: Contested Medway 2001 and 2005 general elections. Member for Rochester and Strood since 6 May 2010 general election

Political interests: Airport expansion, law and order, health, transport

Other organisations: Top three economists, *Sunday Times* and *Institutional Investor* 1996 and 1997; *Publications:* The Euro: Bad for Business 1998

Recreations: Walking, running

Mark Reckless MP, House of Commons, London SW1A 0AA
Tel: 020 7219 3000 E-mail: mark.reckless.mp@parliament.uk
Constituency: 4B High Street, Rochester ME1 1PT Tel: 01634 833335
Website: www.markreckless.com

GENERAL ELECTION RESULT

		%
Reckless, M. (Con)	23,604	49.2
Murray, T. (Lab)	13,651	28.5
Juby, G. (Lib Dem)	7,800	16.3
Sands, R. (England)	2,182	4.6
Marchant, S. (Green)	734	1.5
Majority	9,953	20.75
Electorate	73,882	
Turnout	47,971	64.93

CONSTITUENCY SNAPSHOT

This new seat is mainly comprised of wards from the old Medway seat with a part-ward each from and Chatham and Aylesford and Gillingham.

The area has moved with the political tide since the 1950s, almost always following the national trend and electing a member of the governing party. Bob Marshall-Andrews won the seat for Labour in 1997 with a majority of 5,354. He was re-elected in 2001 with a reduced majority of 3,780. Marshall-Andrews was returned in 2005 with a reduced majority of 213.

The Conservatives won the new seat in 2010 with 23,604 votes giving Mark Reckless a majority of 9,953.

A largely industrial seat in the conurbation of Medway in Kent, the constituency is geographically the largest of the Medway seats, taking in not just Rochester and Strood but also the expanse of the Hoo peninsula between the estuaries of the Thames and Medway.

The peninsula and the Isle of Grain are largely marshland and an important site for wild birds. The south of the peninsula is industrial, and includes a major container port, a gas import plant and two power stations.

The village of Borstal in the West of Rochester was the site of the original borstal and still hosts HMP Rochester.

Rt Hon **John Redwood**

Wokingham (returning MP)

Boundary changes

Tel: 020 7219 4205
E-mail: redwoodj@parliament.uk
Website: www.johnredwood.com

Date of birth: 15 June 1951; Son of William Redwood and Amy, neé Champion

Education: Kent College, Canterbury; Magdalen College, Oxford (BA modern history 1971, MA); St Antony's College, Oxford (DPhil modern history 1975); Married Gail Felicity Chippington 1974 (divorced 2004) (1 son 1 daughter)

Non-political career: Fellow, All Souls College, Oxford 1972-87, 2003-05, 2007-; Tutor and lecturer 1972-73; Investment analyst, Robert Fleming & Co. 1974-77; N. M. Rothschild: Bank clerk 1977-78, Manager 1978-79, Assistant director 1979-80, Director, investment division 1980-83, Overseas corporate finance director and head of international (non-UK) privatisation 1986-87; Norcros plc: Director 1985-89, Chair 1987-89; Chair, Hare Hatch Holdings 1999-2008; Visiting professor Middlesex University Business School 2000-; Chair, Concentric PLC 2003-08; Non Executive Chairman, Evercore Pan-Asset Management Ltd, 2008-present; Councillor, Oxfordshire County Council 1973-77

Political career: Contested Southwark Peckham 1981 by-election. Member for Wokingham 1987-2010, for Wokingham (revised boundary) since 6 May 2010 general election; Department of Trade and Industry: Parliamentary Under-Secretary of State for Corporate Affairs 1989-90, Minister of State 1990-92; Minister for Local Government 1992-93; Secretary of State for Wales 1993-95; Member Shadow Cabinet 1997-2000: Shadow Secretary of State for: Trade and Industry 1997-99, Environment, Transport and the Regions 1999-2000; Member, Shadow Cabinet 2004-05: Shadow Secretary of State for Deregulation 2004-05; Contested Leadership of Conservative Party 1995 and 1997; Chair: No Turning Back Group 2001-, Policy Review on Economic Competitiveness 2005-

Political interests: Popular capitalism, European affairs, constitution, Euro, transport, economy; USA, China, India

Other organisations: Governor Oxford Polytechnic 1973-77; Investment Committee All Souls College, Oxford; Adviser, Treasury and Civil Service Select Committee 1981; Head, Prime Minister's policy unit 1983-85; PC 1993; Lords and Commons Cricket; *Publications:* Reason, Ridicule and Religion (Thames & Hudson, 1976); Public Enterprise in Crisis (Blackwell, 1980); Going for Broke (Blackwell, 1984); Popular Capitalism (Routledge, 1987); The Global Marketplace (HarperCollins, 1993); Our Currency, Our Country (Penguin, 1997); Several books and articles, especially on wider ownership and popular capitalism; The Death of Britain (Macmillan, 1999); Stars and Strife (Macmillan, 2001); Just Say No (Politicos, 2001); Third Way Which Way? (Middlesex, 2002); Singing the Blues (Politicos, 2004); Superpower Struggles (Palgrave, 2005); I Want To Make A Difference, But I Don't Like Politics (Politicos, 2006); After the Credit Crisis (Middlesex, 2009)

Recreations: Village cricket, water sports

Rt Hon John Redwood MP, House of Commons, London SW1A 0AA
Tel: 020 7219 4205 Fax: 020 7219 0377
E-mail: redwoodj@parliament.uk
Constituency: 30 Rose Street, Wokingham, Berkshire RG40 3SU
Tel: 0118-962 9501 Fax: 0118-962 9323
Website: www.johnredwood.com

GENERAL ELECTION RESULT

		%
Redwood, J. (Con)*	28,754	52.7
Bray, P. (Lib Dem)	15,262	28.0
Davidson, G. (Lab)	5,516	10.1
Ashwell, M. (Ind)	2,340	4.3
Zebedee, A. (UKIP)	1,664	3.1
Bisset, M. (Green)	567	1.0
Owen, P. (Loony)	329	0.6
Smith, R. (Ind)	96	0.2
Majority	13,492	24.74
Electorate	76,219	
Turnout	54,528	71.54

**Member of last parliament*

CONSTITUENCY SNAPSHOT

Wokingham has had three MPs since the constituency was established in 1950. All of them have been Conservatives.

Peter Remnant was elected in 1950 and held the seat for nine years. His replacement was Sir William Van Straubenzee who represented Wokingham for 28 years until 1987.

John Redwood won with a majority of over 20,000 in 1987. He maintained his majority in the 1992 general election. Redwood was re-elected with 50.1 per cent of the vote in 1997. His 2001 majority fell to 5,994 but was restored in 2005 to 7,240.

Redwood retained the seat in 2010 with a majority of 13,492.

Boundary changes were minimal.

Wokingham is a sprawling constituency south of the Thames in Berkshire, containing the historic market town of Wokingham and a wide area to the south-east of Reading.

In addition to the large number of constituents who commute into London, many people in Wokingham work for large hi-tech employers in the surrounding area, including Microsoft, IBM and Hewlett Packard.

The majority of jobs are firmly rooted in the service sector but the economic base of the district has broadened through the growth of new business developments such as Winnersh Triangle.

Jamie Reed

Copeland (returning MP)

Boundary changes

Tel: 020 7219 4706
E-mail: reedjr@parliament.uk

Date of birth: 4 August 1973; Son of Ronald and Gloria Reed

Education: Whitehaven School; Manchester Metropolitan University (BA English 1994); Leicester University (MA mass communication 2000); Married (3 sons)

Non-political career: Researcher European Parliament 1995-97; Adviser Labour Group Cumbria County Council 1997-2000; Manager TU and Community Sellafield Campaign 2000-01; Public affairs BNFL 2001-05; GMB

Political career: Member for Copeland 2005-10, for Copeland (revised boundary) since 6 May 2010 general election; PPS: to Tony McNulty as Minister of State, Home Office 2006-08, to Harriet Harman as Leader of the House of Commons 2008-10; *Select Committees:* Member: Environment, Food and Rural Affairs 2005-07, Regulatory Reform 2005-10

Political interests: Energy, climate change, local economic regeneration, Anglo-American relations; USA, EU, Israel/Palestine, Middle East

Recreations: American literature, modern history, football, fell walking, Whitehaven RLFC

Jamie Reed MP, House of Commons, London SW1A 0AA
Tel: 020 7219 4706 Fax: 020 7219 4870
E-mail: reedjr@parliament.uk
Constituency: Phoenix Enterprise Centre, Phoenix House, Jacktrees Road, Cleator Moor, Cumbria CA25 5BD Tel: 01946 816723
Fax: 01946 816743

GENERAL ELECTION RESULT

		%
Reed, J. (Lab)*	19,699	46.0
Whiteside, C. (Con)	15,866	37.1
Hollowell, F. (Lib Dem)	4,365	10.2
Jefferson, C. (BNP)	1,474	3.4
Caley-Knowles, E. (UKIP)	994	2.3
Perry, J. (Green)	389	0.9
Majority	3,833	8.96
Electorate	63,291	
Turnout	42,787	67.60

**Member of last parliament*

CONSTITUENCY SNAPSHOT

The seat was represented by Labour's Joseph Symonds between 1959 and 1970. Dr Jack Cunningham took over from 1970 until 2005. His majority fluctuated throughout his term as MP, and it was at its lowest in 1983 when he won by just 1,837 votes.

Labour's majority increased at the 2005 election under new MP Jamie Reed. Although almost half of the 11,996 majority Labour achieved in 1997, his majority of 6,320 was an increase of 4.4 per cent on 2001.

Reed was re-elected with a majority of 3,833 in 2010, there was a 2.1 per cent swing to the Conservatives.

The seat gained the wards of Crummock, Dalton, Derwent Valley and Keswick from Workington.

A coastal seat in western Cumbria, Copeland includes the southern tip of the Cumbrian Mountains and is mainly rural; there are urban areas on the coastline, such as the town of Whitehaven, which is a major fishing port.

Copeland also includes spectacular Lake District scenery, England's deepest lake and tallest mountain, and controversially, BNFL's plant at Sellafield.

Around two-fifths of the population are employed in the nuclear industry and other manufacturing, much higher than the national average. With the gradual decommissioning of the Sellafield nuclear facility the area is attempting to diversify and encourage tourism.

Jacob Rees-Mogg

North East Somerset

New constituency

Tel: 020 7219 3000
E-mail: jacob.reesmogg.mp@parliament.uk
Website: www.telljacob.com

Conservative

Date of birth: 1969; Son of William Rees-Mogg (now Lord Rees-Mogg) and Gillian Rees-Mogg (née Morris)

Education: Eton College; Trinity College, Oxford (BA history); Married Helena de Chair 2007 (1 son 1 daughter)

Non-political career: *Daily Telegraph* 1989; Conservative Central Office Research Department 1990; J. Rothschild 1991-93; Director, Lloyd George Management 1993-2003; Somerset Capital Management

Political career: Contested Central Fife 1997 and the Wrekin 2001 general elections. Member for North East Somerset since 6 May 2010 general election; President Oxford University Conservative Association 1990; Cities of London and Westminster Conservative Association: Treasurer 1997-, Chair

Recreations: History, cricket

Jacob Rees-Mogg MP, House of Commons, London SW1A 0AA
Tel: 020 7219 3000 E-mail: jacob.reesmogg.mp@parliament.uk
Constituency: North East Somerset Conservative Association, Rear of 16 High Street, Keynsham, Bristol BS31 1DQ Tel: 0117-987 2313
Fax: 0117-987 2322 Website: www.telljacob.com

GENERAL ELECTION RESULT

		%
Rees-Mogg, J. (Con)	21,130	41.3
Norris, D. (Lab)*	16,216	31.7
Coleshill, G. (Lib Dem)	11,433	22.3
Sandell, P. (UKIP)	1,754	3.4
Jay, M. (Green)	670	1.3
Majority	4,914	9.60
Electorate	67,412	
Turnout	51,203	75.96

**Member of last parliament*

CONSTITUENCY SNAPSHOT

North East Somerset is a new seat consisting essentially of the old Wansdyke seat, minus the South Gloucestershire wards, which are now in Kingswood.

Wansdyke and Woodsping were created in 1983 out of the old North Somerset constituency. Conservative Jack Aspinnall held Wansdyke from its creation until 1997. A swing of nearly 15 per cent to Labour elected the party's Dan Norris to Parliament with a majority of nearly 5,000.

Norris increased his majority to 5,613 in 2001. However, a 3.85 per cent swing to the Tories in 2005 slashed his majority to just 1,839. A notional Conservative majority of just 212 was converted into a 4,914 lead by the party's Jacob Rees-Mogg in 2010.

Bordering both Bristol in the west and Bath in the east, the seat is evenly split between rural and urban areas. Given its strategic location, the seat is an ideal commuter area for both Bristol and Bath, and this gives it a residential and moderately affluent character.Many workers in the constituency commute to either Bath or Bristol.

Tourism provides a major source of revenue for local businesses. In decades past coal and agriculture were the overwhelmingly dominant industries. Farming continues, but there has been no coalmining since 1973, when the Somerset coalfield at Midsomer Norton closed.

Simon Reevell

Dewsbury

Boundary changes

Tel: 020 7219 3000
E-mail: simon.reevell.mp@parliament.uk

Conservative

Education: Economics degree; Married Louise

Non-political career: Former army officer; Called to the Bar, Lincoln's Inn 1990; Barrister, 39 Park Square Chambers, Leeds

Political career: Member for Dewsbury since 6 May 2010 general election; Chair, Beverley and Holderness Conservative Association; Regional deputy chair (political), Yorkshire and the Humber Conservatives 2008-

Recreations: Tennis

Simon Reevell MP, House of Commons, London SW1A 0AA
Tel: 020 7219 3000 E-mail: simon.reevell.mp@parliament.uk
Constituency: Dewsbury Conservatives, Spring Villa, 16 Church Lane, Brighouse, West Yorkshire HD6 1AT Tel: 01484 717959

GENERAL ELECTION RESULT

		%
Reevell, S. (Con)	18,898	35.0
Malik, S. (Lab)*	17,372	32.2
Hutchinson, A. (Lib Dem)	9,150	16.9
Iqbal, K. (Ind)	3,813	7.1
Roberts, R. (BNP)	3,265	6.1
Cruden, A. (Green)	849	1.6
Felse, M. (England)	661	1.2
Majority	1,526	2.83
Electorate	78,901	
Turnout	54,008	68.45

**Member of last parliament*

CONSTITUENCY SNAPSHOT

David Ginsburg held the seat for Labour from 1959-81, when he defected to the SDP. Fighting the 1983 election for the SDP, he took more than a quarter of the vote and Labour dropped by nearly 12 points, enough to hand victory to the Conservative John Whitfield.

Ann Taylor recaptured Dewsbury for the Labour party in 1987 and won again in 1992 with slim majorities both times. She converted a notional majority of 3,500 into one of more than 8,000 in 1997.

Taylor stood down in 2005 and new Labour candidate Shahid Malik's majority fell to 4,615 due largely to the BNP. Malik was defeated in the 2010 general election by the Conservative Simon Reevell on a 5.9 per cent swing.

The redrawn constituency was extended southwards, gaining the rural wards of Kirkburton and Denby Dale from Wakefield, with three part-wards moving to Batley and Spen.

This West Yorkshire seat, south of Leeds, is based on the town of Dewsbury. The constituency spreads to the south and west and also takes in the town of Mirfield and villages in the more rural Kirkburton and Denby Dale.

Once at the centre of the wool weaving industry, Dewsbury and its smaller towns to the south and west still have remnants of the trade, now largely confined to the high quality end of the market.

Rachel Reeves

Leeds West

Boundary changes

Tel: 020 7219 3000
E-mail: rachel.reeves.mp@parliament.uk
Website: www.rachelreeves.net

Labour

Date of birth: 13 February 1979; Daughter of Graham and Sally Reeves, both teachers

Education: Cator Park School; New College, Oxford (BA philosophy, politics and economics 2000); London School of Economics (MSc economics 2004)

Non-political career: Economist: Bank of England 2000-02; British Embassy, Washington DC 2002-03; Bank of England 2004-06, Halifax Bank of Scotland 2006-; Amicus/MSF/Unite: Member 1998-; Youth representative, Southern Region 1999-2000, Political representative, Southern Region 2001-02, National political committee 2004-06, Yorkshire political committee 2006-; Governor: Kirkstall Valley Primary School 2006-, West Leeds High School 2007-

Political career: Contested Bromley and Chislehurst 2005 general election and 2006 by-election. Member for Leeds West since 6 May 2010 general election

Political interests: Economy, education, foreign affairs; China, USA

Other organisations: Amnesty International 1996-; Fawcett Society 1998-; Fabian Society 1998-; *Publications:* How do financial markets react to central bank communication?, Journal of Political Economy (2006)

Recreations: Tennis, swimming, cycling, reading

Rachel Reeves MP, House of Commons, London SW1A 0AA
Tel: 020 7219 3000 E-mail: rachel.reeves.mp@parliament.uk
Constituency: 1 Monkswood, Vesper Road, Leeds LS5 3QZ
Tel: 07788 441345 Website: www.rachelreeves.net

GENERAL ELECTION RESULT

		%
Reeves, R. (Lab)	16,389	42.3
Coleman, R. (Lib Dem)	9,373	24.2
Marjoram, J. (Con)	7,641	19.7
Beverley, J. (BNP)	2,377	6.1
Blackburn, D. (Green)	1,832	4.7
Miles, J. (UKIP)	1,140	2.9
Majority	7,016	18.10
Electorate	67,453	
Turnout	38,752	57.45

CONSTITUENCY SNAPSHOT

The seat was held by Labour from the Second World War until 1983, when the Liberal Michael Meadowcroft went from third place to wipe out Joe Dean's majority of nearly 13,000 with a swing of more than 18 per cent.

Labour recovered and John Battle recaptured the seat in 1987. Battle's majority hit nearly 20,000 in 1997 and fell back only slightly as a percentage in 2001. In 2005 the Liberal Democrats increased their share of the vote and moved into second place, 12,810 votes behind John Battle.

Rachel Reeves held the seat for Labour with a majority of 7,016 in 2010.

Boundary changes have swapped part-wards between the seat and Pudsey and Leeds Central.

The western division of Leeds is a working-class area. There are few high earners in this part of the city and a large portion of the housing is let by the council. Terraced houses are the main feature of the landscape in west Leeds, where back-to-backs are still to be found.

Many people still work in manufacturing, with engineering, textiles and printing the predominant industries, but all have declined. There are a number of small and medium-sized employers including warehousing and transport firms, some new technology companies and even a factory making organ pipes.

Alan Reid

Argyll and Bute ***(returning MP)***

No boundary changes

Tel: 020 7219 8127
E-mail: reida@parliament.uk

Date of birth: 7 August 1954; Son of James Reid and Catherine, née Steele

Education: Prestwick Academy; Ayr Academy; Strathclyde University (BSc maths 1975); Jordanhill College (teacher training qualification 1976); Bell College (computer data processing 1979); Single

Non-political career: Maths teacher 1976-77; Computer programmer Strathclyde Regional Council 1977-85; Computer project programmer Glasgow University 1985-; EIS 1976-77; NALGO 1977-85; AUT 1985-2001; Renfrew District Council 1988-96: Councillor, Group secretary

Political career: Contested Paisley South 1990 by-election, 1992 general election, Dumbarton 1997 general election. Member for Argyll and Bute 2001-05, for Argyll and Bute (revised boundary) since 5 May 2005 general election; Liberal Democrat: Whip 2002-05, Spokesperson for Scotland 2004-05, Shadow Minister for: Trade and Industry 2005-06, Information Technology 2005-06, Northern Ireland 2006-10, Scotland 2007-10, Whip 2009-10; *Select Committees:* Member: Broadcasting 2001-05; Scottish Liberal Democrats 1981-: Vice-convener 1994-98, Member executive committee; Election agent George Lyon Scottish Parliament election 1999

Political interests: Environment, employment, fuel tax, health, fishing industry, local issues, elderly, farming, rural development, international affairs

Recreations: Chess, football, walking, reading, television

Alan Reid MP, House of Commons, London SW1A 0AA
Tel: 020 7219 8127 Fax: 020 7219 1737
E-mail: reida@parliament.uk
Constituency: 95 Alexandra Parade, Dunoon, Argyll PA23 8AL
Tel: 01369 704840 Fax: 01369 701212
Website: www.argyllandbute-libdems.org.uk

GENERAL ELECTION RESULT

		%	+/-
Reid, A. (Lib Dem)*	14,292	31.6	-4.8
Mulvaney, G. (Con)	10,861	24.0	0.6
Graham, D. (Lab)	10,274	22.7	0.4
McKenzie, M. (SNP)	8,563	18.9	3.4
Morrison, E. (Green)	789	1.8	
Doyle, G. (Ind)	272	0.6	
Black, J. (SJP)	156	0.4	
Majority	3,431	7.59	
Electorate	67,165		
Turnout	45,207	67.31	

**Member of last parliament*

CONSTITUENCY SNAPSHOT

In February 1974 the SNP's Iain MacCormick gained the Argyll seat from the Tories. In 1979 John MacKay won back Argyll for the Conservatives, and held it in 1983 (when the island of Bute was added to the constituency, giving the seat its current name) before being defeated by Liberal Democrat Ray Michie in 1987. By 1997 Michie had trebled her majority to nearly 6,000.

In 2001 Ray Michie retired and her successor, Alan Reid, was elected with a reduced majority of 1,653.

Boundary changes in 2005 enlarged Argyll and Bute with all ten wards from Dumbarton which fall within the Argyll and Bute council area. Reid was elected with an increased majority of 5,636 over the Conservatives. His majority fell to 3,431 in 2010.

Argyll and Bute is vast, remote and beautiful. It comprises 26 inhabited islands off the west coast of Scotland, including Iona, Islay, Jura, Mull and Tiree, as well as a great swathe of the mainland from the Kintyre Peninsula to the moors of Argyll in the remote north, including the commuter town of Helensburgh.

Renewable energy is a growth industry and more traditional occupations include forestry, fishing and farming and the distillation of whisky. Tourism is also very important.

Most of the constituency's problems stem from its sheer size and its inaccessibility, hampering the provision of local services.

Argyll and Bute is the home to the Clyde Naval Base at Faslane.

Emma Reynolds

Wolverhampton North East

Boundary changes

Tel: 020 7219 3000
E-mail: emma.reynolds.mp@parliament.uk
Website: www.emmareynolds.org.uk

Date of birth: 2 November 1977

Education: Perton Middle School; Codsall High School; Wulfrun College; Wedham College, Oxford (BA politics, philosophy and economics 2000)

Non-political career: Intern, British High Commission, Pakistan summer 1999; English teacher, France, Spain and Argentina; Information officer, Enlargement Information Centre, European Commission 2000-01; Policy researcher, Small Business Europe, Brussels 2001-04; Political adviser, Party of European Socialists, Brussels 2004-06; Special adviser to Geoff Hoon MP as: Minister for Europe 2006-07, Chief-Whip 2007-08; Senior consultant (part-time), Cogitamus Ltd 2009-10; Member, GMB 2002

Political career: Member for Wolverhampton North East since 6 May 2010 general election

Political interests: Foreign affairs, public services, economy, welfare state, manufacturing, skills; EU, India, Latin America, Pakistan, USA

Recreations: Running, cinema, reading, swimming, tennis

Emma Reynolds MP, House of Commons, London SW1A 0AA
Tel: 020 7219 3000 E-mail: emma.reynolds.mp@parliament.uk
Constituency: 492A Stafford Road, Wolverhampton,
West Midlands WV10 6AN Tel: 01902 784697
Website: www.emmareynolds.org.uk

GENERAL ELECTION RESULT

		%
Reynolds, E. (Lab)	14,448	41.4
Rook, J. (Con)	11,964	34.3
Ross, C. (Lib Dem)	4,711	13.5
Patten, S. (BNP)	2,296	6.6
Valdmanis, P. (UKIP)	1,138	3.3
Bhatoe, S. (SLP)	337	1.0
Majority	2,484	7.12
Electorate	59,324	
Turnout	34,894	58.82

CONSTITUENCY SNAPSHOT

This seat was Labour for years, represented by Renee Short, but in the 1980s the Conservatives' advance in the Midlands cut her majority down to 214 votes. With Short standing down in 1987, Maureen Hicks took the seat for the Conservatives. The Tories then lost the seat again to Labour's Ken Purchase in 1992.

In the landslide of 1997 Labour's majority grew to 12,987. In 2005 the Labour share of the vote fell by 5.8 per cent, however, this still left Labour with a comfortable 25 per cent majority.

In 2010 Emma Reynolds held the seat for Labour at her first election here with a majority of 2,484 despite a 9 per cent swing to the Tories.

Boundary changes saw Wolverhampton South West lose parts of three wards to its northern neighbour: Bushbury South and Low Hill, Heath Town, and Oxley. In return, this seat lost a significant tranche of territory in St Peter's on its western border.

Wolverhampton North East is at the northern end of the industrial conurbation of the West Midlands, a traditional Labour stronghold.

Major employers in the constituency include Goodrich Actuation Systems (formerly Lucas Aerospace), Smiths (formerly Dowty) Aerospace and Corus. Retail and construction are also large-scale employers, boosted by city regeneration and business investment schemes.

Jonathan Reynolds

Stalybridge and Hyde

Boundary changes

Tel: 020 7219 3000
E-mail: jonathan.reynolds.mp@parliament.uk
Website: www.jonathanreynolds.org.uk

Education: Houghton Kepier Comprehensive School; Sunderland City College; Manchester University (BA politics and modern history); BPP Law School, Manchester; Married Claire (1 son)

Non-political career: Former political assistant to James Purnell MP; Trainee solicitor, Addleshaw Goddard, Manchester; Columnist, Progress online magazine; Unite (Amicus sector): Member, Secretary, Manchester One Branch; Tameside Council: Councillor 2007-, Cabinet Secretary Without Portfolio, Deputy chair, Longdendale and Hattersley District Assembly; Governor: Hollingworth Primary School, Longdendale Language College

Political career: Member for Stalybridge and Hyde since 6 May 2010 general election; Member: National Executive Committee, Labour Party 2003-05, Co-operative Party

Recreations: Football, history, music

Jonathan Reynolds MP, House of Commons, London SW1A 0AA
Tel: 020 7219 3000 E-mail: jonathan.reynolds.mp@parliament.uk
Constituency: Hyde Town Hall, Market Street, Hyde SK14 1AL
Tel: 0161-367 8077 Website: www.jonathanreynolds.org.uk

GENERAL ELECTION RESULT

		%
Reynolds, J. (Lab/Co-op)	16,189	39.6
Adlard, R. (Con)	13,445	32.9
Potter, J. (Lib Dem)	6,965	17.0
Jones, A. (BNP)	2,259	5.5
Cooke, J. (UKIP)	1,342	3.3
Bergan, R. (Green)	679	1.7
Majority	2,744	6.71
Electorate	69,037	
Turnout	40,879	59.21

CONSTITUENCY SNAPSHOT

Labour has won the seat since the Second World War. Labour's improvement here in 1997 was less than its national average. For the mainstream parties, the election results in 2005 differed very little from the previous election. Labour's James Purnell was re-elected with a majority of 8,348, just 500 fewer votes than in 2001.

Purnell retired from Parliament in 2010. The Labour candidate, Jonathan Reynolds held the seat with a majority of 2,744.

Boundary changes moved two part-wards, which were previously shared with Denton and Reddish, completely within the seat's boundaries. Likewise, Mossley and Stalybridge North wards are now also entirely in the seat, having been shared with Ashton-under-Lyne.

The constituency lies on the eastern outskirts of Manchester, at the foot of the Pennines and includes some areas of moorland. This mainly residential seat is made up of a number of towns and villages that nestle along the Pennine belt, as well as the old towns of Hyde and Stalybridge.

The single biggest demographic group is that of blue-collar workers. Despite the closures of mills over the years, the constituency has retained one of the highest rates of manufacturing employment in the North West.

Millions of pounds of private and public sector money has been spent on the regeneration of Stalybridge town centre with the primary aim of making it a more desirable place to live.

Rt Hon Sir **Malcolm Rifkind**

Kensington ***(returning MP)***

New constituency

Tel: 020 7219 5683
E-mail: shaylorc@parliament.uk
Website: www.malcolmrifkind.co.uk

Conservative

Date of birth: 21 June 1946

Education: George Watson's College, Edinburgh; Edinburgh University (LLB law 1966; MSc 1970); Married Edith Amalia Steinberg 1970 (1 son 1 daughter)

Non-political career: Lecturer, University College of Rhodesia 1967-68; Called to the Scottish Bar 1970; QC (Scotland) 1985; Member Edinburgh Town Council 1970-74

Political career: Contested Edinburgh Central 1970 general election. Member for Edinburgh Pentlands 1974-97. Contested Edinburgh Pentlands 1997 and 2001 general elections. Member for Kensington and Chelsea 2005-10, for Kensington since 6 May 2010 general election; Opposition front bench spokesperson for Scottish Affairs 1975-76; Minister for Home Affairs and the Environment, Scottish Office 1979-82; Foreign and Commonwealth Office: Parliamentary Under-Secretary of State 1982-83, Minister of State 1983-86; Secretary of State for: Scotland 1986-90, Transport 1990-92, Defence 1992-95, Foreign and Commonwealth Affairs 1995-97; Shadow Secretary of State for Work and Pensions 2005 Member, Speaker's Committee for the Independent Parliamentary Standards Authority 2010-; *Select Committees:* Member: Joint Committee on Conventions 2006; Chair: Standards and Privileges 2009-10; Member: Liaison 2010, Joint Committee on National Security Strategy 2010; Hon president, Scottish Young Conservatives 1976-77; Hon secretary, Federation of Conservative Students 1977-79; President Scottish Conservative Party 1997-2002

Other organisations: Member Queen's Bodyguard for Scotland, Royal Company of Archers 1993; Hon Colonel, 162 Movement Control Regiment, RLC (V); Privy Counsellor 1986; KCMG 1997; New Club, Pratt's, White's

Recreations: Field sports

Rt Hon Sir Malcolm Rifkind KCMG MP, House of Commons, London SW1A 0AA Tel: 020 7219 5683 Fax: 020 7219 4213
E-mail: shaylorc@parliament.uk
Constituency: 1A Chelsea Manor Street, London SW3 5RP
Tel: 020 7352 0102 Fax: 020 7351 5885
Website: www.malcolmrifkind.co.uk

GENERAL ELECTION RESULT

		%
Rifkind, M. (Con)*	17,595	50.1
Gurney, S. (Lab)	8,979	25.5
Meltzer, R. (Lib Dem)	6,872	19.6
Pearson, C. (UKIP)	754	2.2
Ebrahimi-Fardouee, M. (Green)	753	2.1
Adams, E. (Green Soc)	197	0.6
Majority	8,616	24.51
Electorate	65,961	
Turnout	35,150	53.29

**Member of last parliament*

CONSTITUENCY SNAPSHOT

Kensington and Chelsea is one of the strongest local Conservative associations in the country, selecting Alan Clarke, Michael Portillo and Malcolm Rifkind to fight the seat. Rifkind, was elected in 2005 with a 12,418 majority.

Regent's Park and Kensington North has a more mixed electoral history. From 1979 until the 1997 Labour victory, the seat was held by the Tory Sir John Wheeler. Karen Buck has held the seat for Labour ever since, although her majority has fallen at each subsequent election. In 2005 her majority almost halved to 6,131. Former Foreign Secretary Malcolm Rifkind was elected to this safe Tory seat with an 8,616 majority in 2010.

The seat was formed from wards from Regent's Park and Kensington North, and Kensington and Chelsea. Kensington constituency comprises Earl's Court, South Kensington, High Street Kensington and Holland Park, with Ladbroke Grove and Notting Hill in the north.

The five most expensive streets in the UK are within the constituency.

Uniquely for the country, more than half of the children in the borough attended independent schools, a mark of the great disparity of wealth within the LEA area.

Linda Riordan

Halifax (returning MP)

Boundary changes

Tel: 020 7219 5399
E-mail: riordanl@parliament.uk
Website: www.lindariordanmp.co.uk

Date of birth: 31 May 1953; Daughter of John Foulds and Alice Haigh

Education: J.H.Whitley Secondary Modern School, Illingworth, Yorkshire; Bradford University (BA politics/history 1997); Married Alan Riordan 1979 (died 2007)

Non-political career: Midland Bank; Private secretary to Alice Mahon MP 2001-05; Unite; Councillor Calderdale Metropolitan Borough Council 1995-2006

Political career: Member for Halifax 2005-10, for Halifax (revised boundary) since 6 May 2010 general election; *Select Committees:* Member: Environmental Audit 2005-, Crossrail Bill 2006-07, Procedure 2006-10, Justice 2008-10

Political interests: Transport, culture, media and sport, justice; Kashmir

Recreations: Reading, swimming, theatre

Linda Riordan MP, House of Commons, London SW1A 0AA
Tel: 020 7219 5399 Fax: 020 7219 1513
E-mail: riordanl@parliament.uk
Constituency: 2-4 Shaw Lodge House, Halifax,
West Yorkshire HX3 9ET Tel: 01422 251800 Fax: 01422 251888
Website: www.lindariordanmp.co.uk

GENERAL ELECTION RESULT

		%
Riordan, L. (Lab/Co-op)*	16,278	37.4
Allott, P. (Con)	14,806	34.0
Wilson, E. (Lib Dem)	8,335	19.1
Bates, T. (BNP)	2,760	6.3
Park, D. (Ind)	722	1.7
Sangha, J. (UKIP)	654	1.5
Majority	1,472	3.38
Electorate	70,380	
Turnout	43,555	61.89

**Member of last parliament*

CONSTITUENCY SNAPSHOT

Labour held the seat from 1964 until losing to the Tories in 1983. Alice Mahon won it back for Labour with a majority of 1,212 in 1987.

In 1997 there was a big swing to Labour, which was enough to give Mahon a majority of 11,000. The Labour vote dropped back again in 2001.

Mahon stood down in 2005 and her Labour replacement, Linda Riordan, held the seat, though Labour's majority fell to 3,417. Riordan was re-elected in 2010 with a reduced majority of 1,472.

There have been minor boundary changes, consisting of an exchange of part-wards with Calder Valley, and the Tory-voting wards of Northowram and Shelf, and Sowerby Bridge moving entirely within Halifax's boundaries.

This seat is based on the Yorkshire Pennines' former wool town which gives it its name. The constituency also stretches beyond the town to take in Ovenden Moor to the north as well as the rural space between Halifax and Bradford including the large village of Shelf.

In recent years the town has been dominated by its bank. The town's wool manufacturing industry is largely dead. However some textiles and carpet-making remain, mostly small firms supplying niche markets.

Margaret Ritchie

South Down

Boundary changes

Tel: 020 7219 3000
E-mail: margaret.ritchie.mp@parliament.uk

Social Democratic and Labour Party

Date of birth: 25 March 1958; Daughter of late John Ritchie and late Rose Ritchie (née Drumm)

Education: St Mary's High School; Queen's University Belfast (BA geography and political science 1979); Post-graduate qualification, administrative management; Single

Non-political career: Assistant to Eddie McGrady MP 1987-2003; Down District Council: Councillor 1985-2009, Chair 1993-94; SDLP Group Whip

Political career: Member for South Down since 6 May 2010 general election; Member, Northern Ireland Forum 1996; MLA for South Down since 26 November 2003; SDLP Spokesperson for Regional Development 2003-07; Minister for Social Development 2007-10; Social Democratic and Labour Party: Member 1980-, Member General Council, International Secretary -2007, Leader 2010-

Political interests: Health, environment, Europe, provision facilities for the young, economy, regional development; Belgium, France

Other organisations: Board member, St Patrick's Centre; Alternate Member, Committee of the Regions -2005

Recreations: Walking, reading

Margaret Ritchie MP, House of Commons, London SW1A 0AA
Tel: 020 7219 3000 E-mail: margaret.ritchie.mp@parliament.uk
Constituency: 5-7 Irish Street, Downpatrick BT30 6BN
Tel: 028 4461 6887 Fax: 028 4461 6116

GENERAL ELECTION RESULT

		%
Ritchie, M. (SDLP)	20,648	48.5
Ruane, C. (Sinn Féin)	12,236	28.7
Wells, J. (DUP)	3,645	8.6
McCallister, J. (UCUNF)	3,093	7.3
McConnell, I. (TUV)	1,506	3.5
Enright, C. (Green)	901	2.1
Griffin, D. (All)	560	1.3
Majority	8,412	19.75
Electorate	70,784	
Turnout	42,589	60.17

CONSTITUENCY SNAPSHOT

Ex-Conservative Minister Enoch Powell held South Down for the Ulster Unionists for 13 years from 1974. In 1987 the SDLP's Eddie McGrady finally entered Parliament at his fourth attempt when he beat Powell and he held the seat through four further general election victories.

In 2001 his majority reached 13,858 before Sinn Féin clawed slightly closer in 2005; Catriona Ruane reduced McGrady's majority to 9,140. Margaret Ritchie, leader of the SDLP, retained the seat for the Party with a majority of 8,412 at the 2010 general election.

Boundary changes switch the Down District Council wards around Ballynahinch to neighbouring Strangford.

This is a sprawling rural and coastal constituency in the south east corner of Northern Ireland. It stretches from Downpatrick and Strangford Lough in the east, to the edge of Newry and Carlingford Lough in the west.

The main town, Downpatrick, is famous as the burial place of St Patrick. Its best known natural features are the Mountains of Mourne. Downpatrick serves as an administrative centre for the area and is home to the new Downe hospital.

Agriculture is important to South Down, as well as the fishing industry. The constituency contains the busy fishing ports Ardglass and Kilkeel. The port at Warrenpoint is both a seaside resort and contains a ferry port, which serves Newry.

Tourism is increasingly important to the area and attractions include the Murlough Nature Reserve and Downpatrick racecourse.

Andrew Robathan

South Leicestershire ***(returning MP)***

New constituency

Tel: 020 7219 3459
E-mail: thompsondm@parliament.uk

Conservative

Date of birth: 17 July 1951; Son of late Douglas and Sheena Robathan (née Gimson)

Education: Merchant Taylors' School, Northwood; Oriel College, Oxford (BA modern history 1973, MA); RMA, Sandhurst; Army Staff College (psc 1984); Married Rachael Maunder 1991 (1 son 1 daughter)

Non-political career: Regular Army officer, Coldstream Guards and SAS 1974-89; Rejoined Army for Gulf War January-April 1991; BP 1991-92; Councillor, London Borough of Hammersmith and Fulham 1990-92

Political career: Member for Blaby 1992-2010, for South Leicestershire since 6 May 2010 general election; PPS to Iain Sproat as Minister of State, Department of National Heritage 1995-97; Shadow Minister for: Trade and Industry 2002-03, International Development 2003, Defence 2004-05; Opposition Deputy Chief Whip 2005-10; Parliamentary Under-Secretary of State, Ministry of Defence 2010-; *Select Committees:* Member: International Development 1997-2002, International Development 2003-04, Administration 2005-07, Selection 2006-10; Member 1922 Committee Executive 2001-02, 2003-04

Political interests: International development, environment, transport, defence, Northern Ireland; Africa, Indian Sub Continent, Middle East

Other organisations: Chair Halo Trust 2003-06; Freeman, Merchant Taylors Company; Freeman, City of London; Special Forces Club, Pratts

Recreations: Mountain walking, skiing, wild life, shooting

Andrew Robathan MP, House of Commons, London SW1A 0AA
Tel: 020 7219 3459 Fax: 020 7219 0096
E-mail: thompsondm@parliament.uk
Constituency: 51 Main Street, Broughton Astley,
Leicestershire LE9 6RE Tel: 01455 283594 Fax: 01455 286159

GENERAL ELECTION RESULT

		%
Robathan, A. (Con)*	27,000	49.5
Ayesh, A. (Lib Dem)	11,476	21.0
Gimson, S. (Lab)	11,392	20.9
Preston, P. (BNP)	2,721	5.0
Williams, J. (UKIP)	1,988	3.6
Majority	15,524	28.44
Electorate	76,639	
Turnout	54,577	71.21

**Member of last parliament*

CONSTITUENCY SNAPSHOT

This new seat is effectively the old Blaby seat less part of Bosworth ward which is now in Harborough.

For 18 years after its creation in 1974, Blaby was held by the Conservatives' Nigel Lawson. In 1992 former army officer Andrew Robathan took the reins and has won with ease ever since. However, his majorities have not been nearly as large as Lawson's, or even his own 25,000 majority in 1992. In 1997 he won by 6,474 votes, by 6,209 in 2001 and by 7,873 in 2005.

Robathan retained the seat in 2010 with a majority of 15,524.

Blaby is a small village on the outskirts of Leicester and the constituency also includes a section of the Harborough council areas as well as Braunstone, Narborough and Countesthorpe.

Consisting, as it does, mainly of small dormitory villages and rural space, South Leicestershire had little economic activity of its own and is mainly home to commuters to Leicester.

The seat is particularly popular with families and older workers, drawn to the area by the green space, low crime and the excellent transport links provided by the M1 and M69 motorways.

Angus Robertson

Moray (returning MP)

No boundary changes

Tel: 020 7219 8259
E-mail: robertsona@parliament.uk
Website: www.moraymp.org

SNP

Scottish National Party

Date of birth: 28 September 1969

Education: Broughton High School, Edinburgh; Aberdeen University (MA politics and international relations 1991); Married Carron Anderson 2006

Non-political career: News editor Austrian Broadcasting Corporation 1991-99; Reporter BBC Austria 1992-99; Contributor: National Public Radio USA, Radio Telefís Eireann, Ireland, Deutsche Welle, Germany; Consultant in media skills, presentation skills and political affairs with Communications Skills International (CSI) 1994-2001; NUJ

Political career: Member for Moray 2001-05, for Moray (revised boundary) since 5 May 2005 general election; SNP Spokesperson for: Foreign Affairs and for Defence 2001-, Europe and for Office of the Deputy Prime Minister 2005-07; SNP Westminster Group: Deputy Leader 2005-07, Leader 2007-; *Select Committees:* Member: European Scrutiny 2001-10; Contested Midlothian 1999 Scottish Parliament election; Member National Executive Young Scottish Nationalists 1986; National organiser Federation of Student Nationalists 1988; Member SNP International Bureau; Deputy SNP spokesperson for Constitutional and External Affairs 1998-99; European policy adviser SNP Group Scottish Parliament

Political interests: Scottish independence, international and European affairs, defence, whisky, oil, fishing, sustainable development and youth issues; Austria, Germany, Norway, Ireland, USA, Armenia, Azerbaijan, Georgia

Recreations: Sport, current affairs, history, travel, socialising, cinema, whisky tasting

Angus Robertson MP, House of Commons, London SW1A 0AA
Tel: 020 7219 8259 Fax: 020 7219 1781
E-mail: robertsona@parliament.uk
Constituency: Moray Parliamentary Office, 9 Wards Road, Elgin, Morayshire IV30 1NL Tel: 01343 551 111 Fax: 01343 556 355
Website: www.moraymp.org

GENERAL ELECTION RESULT

		%	+/-
Robertson, A. (SNP)*	16,273	39.7	3.2
Ross, D. (Con)	10,683	26.1	4.1
Green, K. (Lab)	7,007	17.1	-3.3
Paterson, J. (Lib Dem)	5,956	14.5	-4.7
Gatt, D. (UKIP)	1,085	2.7	
Majority	5,590	13.63	
Electorate	65,925		
Turnout	41,004	62.20	

**Member of last parliament*

CONSTITUENCY SNAPSHOT

Before 1983 this seat was known as Moray and Nairn and until 1974 returned Conservative MPs. Winnie Ewing won the seat for the SNP in 1974, but lost it by 420 votes to Alexander Pollock in 1979. Her daughter-in-law Margaret Ewing recaptured Moray in 1983.

Margaret Ewing stood down from the Commons in 2001. Her successor Angus Robertson had his majority reduced by two-thirds.

In 2005 he increased his vote-share by 7 per cent, returning to Westminster with a majority of 5,676. Robertson held this safe seat with a 5,590 majority in 2010.

This constituency covers the Moray council area between Aberdeenshire and The Highlands in north east Scotland. It has spectacular coastline on the Moray Firth. The population is sprinkled between numerous small fishing and farming towns, of which Elgin, Keith and Buckie are the largest.

The area is home to some of the finest distilleries in Scotland, producing well-known labels as Glenlivet and Glenfiddich. Whisky represents a quarter of all the UK's food and drink exports and is vital to the local economy.

The largest single employer is the RAF, which has bases at Lossiemouth and Kinloss. Kinloss is the base for the new Nimrod MRA4 and Lossiemouth hosts the £10 billion joint strike fighter jet.

The local geography lends itself to renewable energy. One of the largest proposed schemes is the sitting of many wind turbines in the Moray Firth.

Hugh Robertson

Faversham and Mid Kent ***(returning MP)***

Boundary changes

Tel: 020 7219 2643
E-mail: robertsonh@parliament.uk
Website: www.hughrobertson.org.uk

Conservative

Date of birth: 9 October 1962; Son of George Patrick Robertson, headmaster, and June Miller, née McBryde

Education: King's School, Canterbury; Reading University (BSc land management 1985); Royal Military Academy Sandhurst (Commissioned 1986); Married Anna Copson 2002 (1 son)

Non-political career: Army officer Life Guards, serving in Northern Ireland, Gulf War and Bosnia 1985-95; Schroder Investment Management 1995-2001: Assistant director 1999-2001; Special adviser on security to Shadow Northern Ireland Secretary 1998-2001

Political career: Member for Faversham and Mid Kent 2001-10, for Faversham and Mid Kent (revised boundary) since 6 May 2010 general election; Opposition Whip 2002-04; Opposition Spokesperson for Sport 2004-05; Shadow Minister for Sport and for Olympics 2005-10; Parliamentary Under-Secretary of State (Minister for Sport and the Olympics), Department for Culture, Media and Sport 2010-

Political interests: Defence, foreign affairs, fruit farming, sport, Olympics; Balkans, Middle East, Syria

Other organisations: Governor Westminster Foundation for Democracy 2005-08; Sultan of Brunei's Personal Order of Merit 1992; Armourers and Brasiers Prize 1986; Fellow Royal Geographical Society; Cavalry and Guards; Pratts; MCC (playing member); Playing Member MCC, Member Chelsea FC

Recreations: Cricket, hockey, skiing

Hugh Robertson MP, House of Commons, London SW1A 0AA
Tel: 020 7219 2643 Fax: 020 7219 1765
E-mail: robertsonh@parliament.uk
Constituency: 8 Faversham Road, Lenham, Kent ME17 2PN
Tel: 01622 851616 Fax: 01622 850294
Website: www.hughrobertson.org.uk

GENERAL ELECTION RESULT

		%
Robertson, H. (Con)*	26,250	56.2
Naghi, D. (Lib Dem)	9,162	19.6
Rehal, A. (Lab)	7,748	16.6
Larkins, S. (UKIP)	1,722	3.7
Valentine, T. (Green)	890	1.9
Kemp, G. (NF)	542	1.2
Davidson, H. (Loony)	398	0.9
Majority	17,088	36.58
Electorate	68,858	
Turnout	46,712	67.84

**Member of last parliament*

CONSTITUENCY SNAPSHOT

Faversham and Mid Kent has had a short and unvaried electoral history, created in 1997. Andrew Rowe took the seat for the Conservatives with a majority of 4,173. Mr Rowe, having represented in the old Mid Kent seat since the 1980s, did not run for another term.

His replacement, Hugh Robertson, increased the majority by 10 votes to 4,183 in 2001. In 2005 the incumbent more than doubled his majority to 8,720.

Robertson held the seat with 26,250 votes giving him a majority of 17,088 at the 2010 general election.

Faversham and Mid Kent gained a ward and a part-ward from Maidstone and the Weald, while losing a part-ward to both Maidstone and the Weald and Sittingbourne and Sheppey.

The region has a long pedigree in fruit farming and this is the only seat left in England where it is the predominant agricultural type, particularly around the medieval market town of Faversham where the majority of fruit farms are based.

Larger local firms such as Faversham-based Shepherd Neame, the oldest family-owned brewery in England.

John Robertson

Glasgow North West ***(returning MP)***

No boundary changes

Tel: 020 7219 6964
E-mail: robertsonjo@parliament.uk
Website: www.johnrobertsonmp.co.uk

Labour

Date of birth: 17 April 1952; Son of Charles Robertson and Agnes Millen, née Webster

Education: Shawlands Academy; Langside College (ONC electrical engineering 1983); Stow College (HNC electrical engineering 1985); Married Eleanor Wilkins Munro 1973 (3 daughters)

Non-political career: GPO/ Post Office/ British Telecom/ BT 1969-2000: technical officer 1973-87, special faults investigation officer 1987-91, customer service manager 1991-95, field manager 1995-99, local customer manager 1999-2000; Member: NCU/POEU/CWU 1969-90, STE/Connect 1991-; CWU/NCU: political and education officer, Glasglow Branch 1986-90; Connect: chair West of Scotland 1997-2000; Member: AMICUS 2004-

Political career: Member for Glasgow Anniesland 23 November 2000 by-election to 2005, for Glasgow North West since 5 May 2005 general election; PPS: to Kim Howells as Minister of State, Foreign and Commonwealth Office 2005-08, to Yvette Cooper: as Chief Secretary to the Treasury 2008-09, as Secretary of State for Work and Pensions 2009-10; *Select Committees:* Member: Scottish Affairs 2001-05, European Scrutiny 2003-05, Energy and Climate Change 2009-10; Election agent to Donald Dewar MP, MSP 1993-2000; Chair Anniesland constituency Labour party 1995-2000; Secretary: Glasgow Group of MPs 2001-06, Scottish Parliamentary Labour Party 2004-

Political interests: International development, defence, work and pensions, Scottish affairs, communications, foreign affairs, music, nuclear energy; Australia, Iran, Japan, Nigeria, USA, Mexico, Angola

Other organisations: Member: Commonwealth Parliamentary Association 2000-, International Parliamentary Union 2000-; Cambus Athletic Football Club, Garrowhill Cricket Club, Old Kilpatrick Bowling Club

Recreations: Reading, music, football, cricket, golf

John Robertson MP, House of Commons, London SW1A 0AA
Tel: 020 7219 6964 Fax: 020 7219 1096
E-mail: robertsonjo@parliament.uk
Constituency: 131 Dalsetter Avenue, Drumchapel, Glasgow G15 8TE
Tel: 0141-944 7298 Fax: 0141-944 7121
Website: www.johnrobertsonmp.co.uk

GENERAL ELECTION RESULT

		%	+/-
Robertson, J. (Lab)*	19,233	54.1	5.0
McKee, N. (Lib Dem)	5,622	15.8	-3.7
Park, M. (SNP)	5,430	15.3	1.6
Sullivan, R. (Con)	3,537	9.9	0.4
Crawford, M. (Green)	882	2.5	-1.4
McLean, S. (BNP)	699	2.0	
Livingstone, M. (Comm)	179	0.5	
Majority	13,611	38.25	
Electorate	60,968		
Turnout	35,582	58.36	

**Member of last parliament*

CONSTITUENCY SNAPSHOT

Glasgow North West has been part of several constituencies. Its core, around Drumchapel, was the centre of the old Glasgow Garscadden seat. However, Drumchapel was substantially depopulated and 12,000 voters were added from Kelvindale and Jordanhill to create Glasgow Anniesland.

Donald Dewar was elected in Garscadden in 1978, in a by-election caused by the death of William Small. In 1999 Dewar was also elected to the Scottish Parliament and became Scotland's first ever First Minister. Dewar died in October 2000. Labour's John Robertson won the by-election with 52 per cent of the vote.

In the 2005 boundary changes much of Glasgow Anniesland was incorporated into Glasgow North West, although Kelvindale was lost to Glasgow North. John Robertson won the new seat with a majority of 10,093. John Robertson has won a 13,611 majority for Labour in 2010.

The constituency fans out from Partick along the Clyde to Yoker and extends north to take in the huge Drumchapel estate. The estate is one of the largest social housing projects in Scotland.

The area has suffered from Clydeside industrial decline but is home to one of Glasgow's last remaining shipyards at Scotstoun on the Clyde. Two new aircraft carriers will be built in-part at Scotstoun, ensuring the future of the shipyard until at least 2016.

Laurence Robertson

Tewkesbury ***(returning MP)***

Boundary changes

Tel: 020 7219 4196
E-mail: robertsonl@parliament.uk

Conservative

Date of birth: 29 March 1958; Son of James Robertson, former colliery electrician, and Jean Robertson, neé Larkin

Education: St James' Church of England Secondary School; Farnworth Grammar School; Bolton Institute of Higher Education (Diploma management services); Married Susan Lees 1989 (2 step-daughters)

Non-political career: Warehouse assistant 1976-77; Work study engineer 1977-83; Industrial management consultant 1983-89; Factory owner 1987-88; Charity fundraising, public relations and special events consultant 1988-

Political career: Contested Makerfield 1987, Ashfield 1992 general elections. Member for Tewkesbury 1997-2010, for Tewkesbury (revised boundary) since 6 May 2010 general election; Opposition Whip 2001-03; Shadow Minister for: Trade and Industry 2003, Economic Affairs 2003-05, Northern Ireland 2005-10; *Select Committees:* Member: Environmental Audit 1997-99, Joint Committee on Consolidation of Bills Etc 1997-2001, Social Security 1999-2001, European Scrutiny 1999-2002, Education and Skills 2001; Former Member: Conservative 2000 Foundation, Conservative Way Forward; Vice-chair, Association of Conservative Clubs (ACC) 1997-2000

Political interests: Overseas aid, constitution, European affairs, education, economic policy, law and order, countryside, Northern Ireland; UK, USA, Ethiopia, other African countries

Other organisations: Fellow Industry and Parliament Trust 2001; *Publications:* Europe: The Case Against Integration (1991); The Right Way Ahead (1995)

Recreations: Horses and horseracing, golf, other sports (completed 6 marathons), reading, writing, countryside

Laurence Robertson MP, House of Commons, London SW1A 0AA
Tel: 020 7219 4196 Fax: 020 7219 2325
E-mail: robertsonl@parliament.uk
Constituency: 22 High Street, Tewkesbury, Gloucestershire GL20 5AL
Tel: 01684 291640 Fax: 01684 291759

GENERAL ELECTION RESULT

		%
Robertson, L. (Con)*	25,472	47.2
Cameron, A. (Lib Dem)	19,162	35.5
Emmerson, S. (Lab)	6,253	11.6
Jones, B. (UKIP)	2,230	4.1
Sidford, M. (Green)	525	1.0
Ridgeon, G. (Loony)	319	0.6
Majority	6,310	11.69
Electorate	76,655	
Turnout	53,961	70.39

**Member of last parliament*

CONSTITUENCY SNAPSHOT

Both Tewkesbury and its predecessor constituency, Cirencester and Tewkesbury, have returned Conservative MPs throughout the post-Second World War period.

Nicholas Ridley retired after 33 years in 1992 and was replaced by the Eton-educated Geoffrey Clifton-Brown (the seventh member of his family to sit in the Commons since the 1800s), who moved on to represent the new Cotswold seat in 1997. Since 1997 Laurence Robertson has held Tewkesbury for the Conservatives. In 2005 Robertson was returned with majority of 9,892. He was re-elected in 2010 despite a 4 per cent swing to the Liberal Democrats.

Boundary changes moved part-wards Leckhampton, Oakley, Up Hatherley, and Warden Hill to Cheltenham, whilst Longlevens ward and part-wards Prestbury and Swindon Village move into the seat.

This seat contains a mix of suburban and rural territory, and lies to the north of Gloucestershire. Though a considerable distance apart, the large and expanding cities of Cheltenham and Gloucester are linked by a sprawl of suburban development which occupies the southern half of the Tewkesbury seat.

Tewkesbury is an historic market town which, with over 400 listed buildings, is very popular with tourists. Its imposing 12th century Abbey of St Mary is particularly popular.

A large proportion of constituents commute to Cheltenham and Gloucester.

Geoffrey Robinson

Coventry North West (returning MP)

Boundary changes

Tel: 020 7219 4504
E-mail: robinsong@parliament.uk
Website: www.epolitix.com/geoffrey-robinson

Labour

Date of birth: 25 May 1938; Son of late Robert Norman Robinson and late Dorothy Jane, née Skelly

Education: Emanuel School, London; Clare College, Cambridge; Yale University, USA; Married Marie Elena Giorgio 1967 (1 daughter 1 son)

Non-political career: Labour Party research assistant 1965-68; Senior executive Industrial Reorganisation Corporation 1968-70; Financial controller British Leyland 1970-72; Managing director Leyland Innocenti 1972-73; Chief executive Jaguar Cars Coventry 1974-75; Chief executive (unpaid) Triumph Motorcycles (Meriden) Ltd 1978-80; Director West Midlands Enterprise Board 1982-85; Chief executive TransTec plc 1986-97; Member, T&G

Political career: Member for Coventry North West 4 March 1976 by-election to 2010, for Coventry North West (revised boundary) since 6 May 2010 general election; Opposition Frontbench Spokesperson for: Science 1982-83, Trade and Industry and Regional Affairs 1983-87; Paymaster General, HM Treasury 1997-98

Political interests: Industry, economic policy, new technology; France, Germany, Italy, USA; *Publications:* The Unconventional Minister: My Life in New Labour

Recreations: Motorcars, gardens, architecture, football

Geoffrey Robinson MP, House of Commons, London SW1A 0AA
Tel: 020 7219 4504 Fax: 020 7219 0984
E-mail: robinsong@parliament.uk
Constituency: Transport House, Short Street, Coventry, Warwickshire CV1 2LS Tel: 024 7625 7870 Fax: 024 7625 7813
Website: www.epolitix.com/geoffrey-robinson

GENERAL ELECTION RESULT

		%
Robinson, G. (Lab)*	19,936	42.8
Ridley, G. (Con)	13,648	29.3
McKee, V. (Lib Dem)	8,344	17.9
Sheppard, E. (BNP)	1,666	3.6
Nattrass, M. (UKIP)	1,295	2.8
Clarke, J. (Ind)	640	1.4
Wood, J. (Green)	497	1.1
Downes, N. (SAP)	370	0.8
Sidhu, W. (CMGB)	164	0.4
Majority	6,288	13.51
Electorate	72,871	
Turnout	46,560	63.89

**Member of last parliament*

CONSTITUENCY SNAPSHOT

The Labour party has held the seat since the Second World War. In 1976 Geoffrey Robinson won the by-election following the death of Maurice Edelman with a majority of 3,694.

Robinson went on to consolidate his majority in the 1980s and 1990s. In 1997 his majority was 16,601. However, in 2005 the Tory vote increased, contributing to a slightly reduced majority for Robinson of 9,315. Robinson was re-elected with a majority of 6,288 in 2010.

This seat lost only small segments of wards which had previously been inside its boundaries - parts of Earlsdon were lopped off the south-western corner, to the west a segment of Westwood went to Coventry South, and a part of Longford went to Coventry North East.

Coventry North West fans out from the inner city Radford ward to suburbs in the west and north of the city.

Coventry was a centre of the British motor industry. Jaguar-Daimler's large factories traditionally made them the constituency's largest employer, but the closure of the plant hit the area hard.

The seat combines a low proportion of professional and managerial level employees with large numbers of skilled and semi-skilled workers. Bablake contains some of the most desirable areas, while deprivation rates are higher in the more inner-city wards of Radford and Holbrook.

Dan Rogerson

North Cornwall (returning MP)

Boundary changes

Tel: 020 7219 4707
E-mail: rogersond@parliament.uk
Website: www.danrogerson.org

Date of birth: 23 July 1975; Son of Stephen John and Patricia Rogerson

Education: St Mary's School, Bodmin; Bodmin College, Cornwall; University of Wales, Aberystwyth (BSc politics 1996); Married Heidi Lee Purser 1999 (2 sons 1 daughter)

Non-political career: Research assistant Bedford Borough Council 1996-98; Administrative officer De Montfort University 1998-2002; Campaigns officer (Devon and Cornwall) Liberal Democrats 2002-04; UNISON 1996-97; Bedford Borough Council: Councillor 1999-2002, Deputy Group Leader 2000-02

Political career: Contested North East Bedfordshire 2001 general election. Member for North Cornwall 2005-10, for North Cornwall (revised boundary) since 6 May 2010 general election; Liberal Democrat: Shadow Minister for: Environment, Food and Rural Affairs 2005-06, Office of the Deputy Prime Minister/Communities and Local Government 2006-07, Whip 2007-10, Shadow Minister for: the Arts, Culture and Heritage 2007, Communities and Local Government 2007-10; *Select Committees:* Member: Environment, Food and Rural Affairs 2005-10; Member Association of Liberal Democrat Councillors 1998-

Political interests: Fighting post office closures, local services, local taxation, minority languages, housing, dairy industry, waste, muscular dystrophy

Other organisations: Camelford Liberal; St Lawrence's Social

Recreations: Blues music, collecting books of Liberal historical interest, reading

Dan Rogerson MP, House of Commons, London SW1A 0AA
Tel: 020 7219 4707 Fax: 020 7219 1018
E-mail: rogersond@parliament.uk
Constituency: 4 Tower Street, Launceston, Cornwall PL15 8BQ
Tel: 01566 777123 Fax: 01566 772122
Website: www.danrogerson.org

GENERAL ELECTION RESULT

		%
Rogerson, D. (Lib Dem)*	22,512	48.1
Flynn, S. (Con)	19,531	41.7
O'Connor, M. (UKIP)	2,300	4.9
Hulme, J. (Lab)	1,971	4.2
Willett, J. (Meb Ker)	530	1.1
Majority	2,981	6.36
Electorate	68,662	
Turnout	46,844	68.22

**Member of last parliament*

CONSTITUENCY SNAPSHOT

The seat has swung back and forth between the three main parties until the Liberal Democrats, represented by Paul Tyler, were able to secure the seat in 1992.

Tyler held the seat for three terms, increasing his majority to 9,832 in 2001. He stood down in 2005 and his successor, Dan Rogerson, was unable to prevent 9.5 per cent of Liberal Democrat support switching sides at the 2005 election. Rogerson emerged with a much more slender-looking 3,076 majority. Despite the Liberal Democrats losing half their seats in Cornwall in 2010, Dan Rogerson has held on with a steady majority of 2,981.

Boundary changes moved the wards Edgcumbe North, Edgcumbe South, Gannel, Rialton, Rock, St Columb, St Enoder to St Austell and Newquay, while the seat gained Stokeclimsland from South East Cornwall.

The key towns in North Cornwall are Launceston and Bodmin and the seaside towns of Newquay, Padstow and Bude. Although tourism is what this part of Cornwall is particularly famous for, the seat also has an above average number of people involved in farming and agriculture.

The population profile of this constituency is similar to all of Cornwall, in that there is a heavy demographic bias towards the over-65s, with over a quarter more retired people here than the national average.

Andrew Rosindell

Romford (returning MP)

Boundary changes

Tel: 020 7219 8475
E-mail: rosindella@parliament.uk
Website: www.andrew.rosindell.com

Date of birth: 17 March 1966; Son of Frederick William Rosindell, tailor and Eileen Rosina Clark, pianist

Education: Marshalls Park Comprehensive School, Romford; Single

Non-political career: Central Press Features London 1984-86; Freelance journalist 1986-97; Parliamentary researcher to Vivian Bendall MP 1986-97; Director and international director European Foundation 1997-2001; London Borough of Havering: Councillor 1990-2002, Alderman 2007-; Chairman North Romford Community Area Forum 1998-2002

Political career: Contested Glasgow Provan 1992 and Thurrock 1997 general elections. Member for Romford 2001-10, for Romford (revised boundary) since 6 May 2010 general election; Opposition Whip 2005-07; Shadow Minister for Home Affairs (Animal Welfare) 2007-10; *Select Committees:* Member: Regulatory Reform 2001-05, Joint Committee on Statutory Instruments 2002-03, Constitutional Affairs 2004-05; Chair: Greater London Young Conservatives 1987-88, National Young Conservatives 1993-94, Romford Conservative Association 1998-2001; International secretary Young Conservatives United Kingdom 1991-98; Member National Union Executive Committee Conservative Party 1986-88, 1992-94; Chairman Conservative Friends of Gibraltar 2002-; Member: Conservative Christian Fellowship; Vice-chairman (Campaigning) Conservative Party 2004-05

Political interests: Foreign and international relations, European affairs, law and order, defence, local and regional government, animal welfare, Gibraltar; Australia, Canada, Crown Dependencies, Eastern Europe, Gulf States, New Zealand, Nordic countries, UK Overseas Territories, USA

Other organisations: Chairman European Young Conservatives 1993-97; International Democrat Union Executive member 1994-2002, Chairman International Young Democrat Union 1998-2002; Romford Conservative and Constitutional; Royal Air Forces Association; Romford Royal British Legion; *Publications:* Co-author Defending Our Great Heritage, 1993

Recreations: Staffordshire bull terrier Buster

Andrew Rosindell MP, House of Commons, London SW1A 0AA
Tel: 020 7219 8475 Fax: 020 7219 1960
E-mail: rosindella@parliament.uk
Constituency: 85 Western Road, Romford, Essex RM1 3LS
Tel: 01708 766700 Fax: 01708 707163
Website: www.andrew.rosindell.com

GENERAL ELECTION RESULT

		%
Rosindell, A. (Con)*	26,031	56.0
Voller, R. (Lab)	9,077	19.5
Duffett, H. (Lib Dem)	5,572	12.0
Bailey, R. (BNP)	2,438	5.3
Batten, G. (UKIP)	2,050	4.4
Thorogood, P. (England)	603	1.3
Haines, G. (Green)	447	1.0
Hyde, P. (Ind)	151	0.3
Sturman, D. (Ind)	112	0.2
Majority	16,954	36.48
Electorate	71,193	
Turnout	46,481	65.29

**Member of last parliament*

CONSTITUENCY SNAPSHOT

From 1974 to 1997 the Conservative MP, Sir Michael Neubert, served this constituency. In 1997 Labour's candidate Eileen Gordon took the seat with a three-figure majority.

In response the Conservatives brought in Andrew Rosindell. He was brought up in Romford and served as a local councillor.

He took Romford back for the Tories in 2001 and his gain was the biggest swing for the Tories that year. He increased his share of the vote to nearly 60 per cent in 2005. Rosindell has gradually increased his majority since he was first elected, achieving 16,954 and 56 per cent of the vote in 2010.

Romford gained Hyland ward from the old Hornchurch constituency and lost part-wards to the new Hornchurch and Upminster seat.

Romford is in north east London and is seen as a traditional market town, with the market first established here in 1247. It is an important office and shopping centre for north-east London and Essex and the administrative centre of Havering.

There has been much growth in Romford town centre in the last five years, with a number of housing and retail developments.

The new Crossrail service will stop at Romford, due to enter service in 2017.

The new Queen's hospital opened in Romford in 2006, to replaced Oldchurch hospital, which has been demolished and the site redeveloped for housing.

Steve Rotheram

Liverpool Walton

Boundary changes

Tel: 020 7219 3000
E-mail: steve.rotheram.mp@parliament.uk
Website: www.steve4walton.co.uk

Date of birth: 4 November 1961; Son of Dorothy and Harry Rotheram

Education: Ruffwood Comprehensive; Kirkby Further Education College (building studies 1995); Studying for MA in contemporary urban renaissance; Married Sandra 1989 (1 son 2 daughters)

Non-political career: Construction sector 1978-89; Instructor 1989-2001; Director: SIP Property Development LLP, SPR Consultants, LIPA; Member, UCATT (UCATT-supported MP); Councillor, Liverpool City Council 2002-; Former Lord Mayor of Liverpool

Political career: Member for Liverpool Walton since 6 May 2010 general election; Member, Association of Labour Councillors

Other organisations: Member: St George's Hall Trust, Liverpool Institute of Performing Arts, Fazakerley 9/10 Credit Union, The Social Academy, St George's Hall Trust

Recreations: Football (Liverpool FC season ticket holder), theatre

Steve Rotheram MP, House of Commons, London SW1A 0AA
Tel: 020 7219 3000 E-mail: steve.rotheram.mp@parliament.uk
Constituency: 69-71 County Road, Walton, Liverpool L4 3QD
Website: www.steve4walton.co.uk

GENERAL ELECTION RESULT

		%
Rotheram, S. (Lab)	24,709	72.0
Moloney, P. (Lib Dem)	4,891	14.2
Marsden, A. (Con)	2,241	6.5
Stafford, P. (BNP)	1,104	3.2
Nugent, J. (UKIP)	898	2.6
Manwell, J. (CPA)	297	0.9
Ireland, D. (TUSC)	195	0.6
Majority	19,818	57.72
Electorate	62,612	
Turnout	34,335	54.84

CONSTITUENCY SNAPSHOT

Sir Kenneth Thompson held the seat for the Tories until 1964 when Eric Heffer won the seat he was to serve until his death in 1991. He was succeeded at the by-election by Peter Kilfoyle.

In 2001 Kilfoyle's majority fell to 17,996 and by a further 2,000 votes at the 2005 general election. In 2010 Kilfoyle retired and Steve Rotheram held the seat for Labour with a majority of 19,818.

The seat gained four part-wards from Liverpool West Derby, and a part-ward each from Liverpool Riverside and Liverpool Wavertree. It lost a part-ward to Liverpool Riverside and two part-wards to Liverpool West Derby.

This is the northernmost seat in Liverpool and is home to the iconic football grounds of Liverpool (Anfield) and Everton (Goodison Park). Both Everton and Liverpool football clubs have ambitious redevelopment plans, the former seeking to move out of the city centre altogether to the neighbouring borough of Knowsley whilst the latter has publicised plans for a 71,000 seat stadium which the club's owners would like to see built by 2011.

Apart from the two football clubs, the biggest employers in the constituency are the two large prisons, Altcourse Prison and HMP Liverpool (Walton). Walton's economic past was based on the maritime success of the city as a whole.

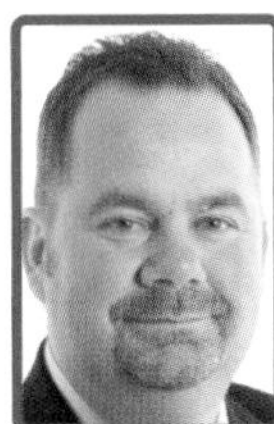

Frank Roy

Motherwell and Wishaw ***(returning MP)***

No boundary changes

Tel: 020 7219 6467
E-mail: royf@parliament.uk
Website: www.frankroy.org.uk

Labour

Date of birth: 29 August 1958; Son of late James Roy, settler manager, and Esther McMahon, home-help

Education: St Joseph's High School, Motherwell; Our Lady's High School, Motherwell; Motherwell College (HNC marketing 1994); Glasgow Caledonian University (BA consumer and management studies 1994); Married Ellen Foy 1977 (1 son 1 daughter)

Non-political career: Steelworker Ravenscraig 1977-91; Personal assistant to Helen Liddell MP 1994-97; Member, GMB; Shop steward, ISTC 1983-90

Political career: Member for Motherwell and Wishaw 1997-2005, for Motherwell and Wishaw (revised boundary) since 5 May 2005 general election; PPS: to Helen Liddell as Minister of State, Scottish Office 1998-99, to Secretaries of State for Scotland: Dr John Reid 1999-2001, Helen Liddell 2001; Sponsor Aviation Offences Act 2003; Assistant Government Whip 2005-06; Government Whip 2006-10; *Select Committees:* Member: Social Security 1997-98, Defence 2001-05, Selection 2008-10

Political interests: Employment, social welfare; Europe, USA

Other organisations: Parliamentary election agent to Dr Jeremy Bray 1987-92; Vice-President, Federation of Economic Development Authorities (FEDA)

Recreations: Football, reading, music

Frank Roy MP, House of Commons, London SW1A 0AA
Tel: 020 7219 6467 Fax: 020 7219 6866 E-mail: royf@parliament.uk
Constituency: 265 Main Street, Wishaw, Lanarkshire ML2 7NE
Tel: 01698 303040 Fax: 01698 303060 Website: www.frankroy.org.uk

GENERAL ELECTION RESULT

		%	+/-
Roy, F. (Lab)*	23,910	61.1	3.7
Fellows, M. (SNP)	7,104	18.2	1.7
Douglas, S. (Lib Dem)	3,840	9.8	-2.2
Gilroy, P. (Con)	3,660	9.4	0.1
Gunnion, R. (Solidarity)	609	1.6	
Majority	16,806	42.96	
Electorate	66,918		
Turnout	39,123	58.46	

**Member of last parliament*

CONSTITUENCY SNAPSHOT

Dr Robert McIntyre became the SNP's first ever MP when he won the Motherwell by-election in April 1945. However, at the July 1945 general election Alexander Anderson won the seat back for Labour, and the Party has held it ever since. Dr Jeremy Bray held the renamed Motherwell and Wishaw from October 1974, through its renaming once again in 1983 as Motherwell South, before returning to its old name of Motherwell and Wishaw by the time Bray retired in 1997. His successor Frank Roy maintained Bray's majority.

Motherwell and Wishaw was relatively unscathed by the 2005 boundary review. Frank Roy was returned with a majority of 15,222. Roy was re-elected in 2010 with over 60 per cent of the vote.

This constituency is in the Clyde Valley, to the south-east of Glasgow and part of the North Lanarkshire council area. The area is still dominated by its social housing estates.

Centred on the towns of Motherwell and Wishaw, the seat's industrial character is leavened by Strathclyde County Park. Employers include the whisky distillers William Grant & Sons.

Years after the closure of Ravenscraig steelworks the site still dominated the landscape. A £1.2 billion transformation of the former steelworks began in 2006. The 20-year redevelopment project will create a new town. It is hoped that 8,000 jobs will eventually be created under a regeneration that is larger than anything since the post-war New Towns were built in Scotland.

Lindsay Roy

Glenrothes (returning MP)

No boundary changes

Tel: 020 7219 8273
E-mail: royl@parliament.uk

Date of birth: 19 January 1949; Son of John, railway signalman, and Margaret Roy, nurse

Education: Perth Academy; Edinburgh University (BSc geography 1970); Married Irene Elizabeth 1972 (1 daughter 2 sons)

Non-political career: Teacher, then principal teacher of modern studies, Queen Anne High School, Dunfermline, Fife 1972-83; Assistant rector Kircaldy High School, Fife 1983-86; Depute rector Glenwood High School, Glenrothes, Fife 1986-89; Rector: Inverkeithing High School, Fife 1989-2007, Kirkcaldy High School 2008-; Associate assessor HM Inspectorate of Education 1996-2008

Political career: Member for Glenrothes since 6 November 2008 by-election; PPS to Tessa Jowell as Minister for the Cabinet Office and Paymaster General 2009-10; *Select Committees:* Member: Scottish Affairs 2009-10

Political interests: Education, health and welfare, economy, foreign policy, international development; New Zealand, South Africa, Finland, Argentina, Thailand, China, Uganda

Other organisations: Management board member, Carnegie College 1997-2006; Church Elder, St Columba's Church, Glenrothes; CBE 2004; Fellow, Royal Society for the Arts 2004

Recreations: Five-a-side football, mountain biking, mountain climbing, angling, reading

Lindsay Roy MP, House of Commons, London SW1A 0AA
Tel: 020 7219 8273 E-mail: royl@parliament.uk
Constituency: 1 Newark Road South, Glenrothes, Fife KY7 4NS
Website: www.fifelabour.org.uk

GENERAL ELECTION RESULT

		%	+/-
Roy, L. (Lab)*	25,254	62.3	10.5
Alexander, D. (SNP)	8,799	21.7	-1.6
Wills, H. (Lib Dem)	3,108	7.7	-5.0
Low, S. (Con)	2,922	7.2	0.1
Seunarine, K. (UKIP)	425	1.1	-0.1
Majority	16,455	40.62	
Electorate	67,893		
Turnout	40,508	59.66	

**Member of last parliament*

CONSTITUENCY SNAPSHOT

In 1987 Henry McLeish inherited the then Fife Central seat from Willie Hamilton, which he retained with more than half the vote in both 1992 and 1997.

In 2001 McLeish was succeeded by John MacDougall. The current Glenrothes seat includes the whole of Central Fife along with additional wards from Dunfermline East and Kirkcaldy. At the 2005 general election John MacDougall won with a majority of 10,664.

John MacDougall died in August 2008 after a long illness. In the subsequent by-election in November, Lindsay Roy held off the SNP challenge winning with a majority of 6,737. Lindsay Roy was re-elected for this solid Labour seat with a 16,448 majority.

This Fife seat is centred on the new town of Glenrothes and includes the industrial ports of Leven and Methil. Parts of the constituency have serious deprivation problems, in particular the Methil area.

The main industries were once coal and linoleum, but diversification has made Glenrothes a centre for the electronics industry.

Glenrothes is the administrative capital of Fife and there are many local authority jobs. The town is well-kept and the standard of housing is high.

Chris Ruane

Vale of Clwyd (returning MP)

Boundary changes

Labour

Tel: 020 7219 6378
E-mail: ruanec@parliament.uk

Date of birth: 18 July 1958; Son of late Michael Ruane, labourer, and Esther Ruane

Education: Blessed Edward Jones Comprehensive, Rhyl; University College of Wales, Aberystwyth (BSc (Econ) history and politics 1979); Liverpool University (PGCE 1980); Married Gill Roberts 1994 (2 daughters)

Non-political career: Primary school teacher Ysgol Mair, Rhyl 1982-97, Deputy head 1991-97; National Union of Teachers: School Rep 1982-97, President, West Clwyd 1991, Vale of Clwyd 1997; Councillor, Rhyl Town Council 1988-99

Political career: Contested Clwyd North West 1992 general election. Member for Vale of Clwyd 1997-2010, for Vale of Clwyd (revised boundary) since 6 May 2010 general election; PPS: to Peter Hain as Secretary of State for Wales 2002-07, to Caroline Flint: as Minister of State, Department for Work and Pensions 2007-08, as Minister for Housing, Department for Communities and Local Government 2008, to David Miliband as Foreign Secretary 2009-10; *Select Committees:* Member: Welsh Affairs 1999-2002, Joint Committee on Statutory Instruments and Commons Committee on Statutory Instruments 2009-10; Member Labour Group of Seaside MPs 1997-; Chair, North Wales Group of Labour MPs 2002-

Political interests: Anti-poverty, education, environment, safe communities, regeneration of seaside towns; Belize

Other organisations: Member Steering Group forming Vale of Clwyd Credit Union; Founder Member: Rhyl Anti Apartheid 1987, Rhyl Environmental Association 1988, President, Rhyl and District Amnesty International Group 1989; Chair Rhyl City Strategy Consortium; President North Wales Ramblers Association 2008-; Fellow Industry and Parliament Trust 2001

Recreations: Cooking, walking, reading, humour

Chris Ruane MP, House of Commons, London SW1A 0AA
Tel: 020 7219 6378 Fax: 020 7219 6090
E-mail: ruanec@parliament.uk
Constituency: 25 Kinmel Street, Rhyl, Clwyd LL18 1AH
Tel: 01745 354626 Fax: 01745 334827

GENERAL ELECTION RESULT

		%
Ruane, C. (Lab)*	15,017	42.3
Wright, M. (Con)	12,508	35.2
Penlington, P. (Lib Dem)	4,472	12.6
Wyn-Jones, C. (PIC)	2,068	5.8
Si'Ree, I. (BNP)	827	2.3
Turner, T. (UKIP)	515	1.5
Butler, M. (Green Soc)	127	0.4
Majority	2,509	7.06
Electorate	41,198	
Turnout	35,534	86.25

**Member of last parliament*

CONSTITUENCY SNAPSHOT

The Vale of Clwyd constituency came into existence in 1997, formed from parts of the former Clwyd North West and Delyn constituencies. Historically Clwyd North West was a Tory seat and they had also held Delyn until 1992. Despite this, Labour's Chris Ruane won Vale of Clwyd in 1997 by a majority of 8,955.

Successive small swings to the Conservatives in 2001 and 2005 reduced Ruane's majority to 4,669. Ruane won re-election for Labour but his majority was reduced to just 2,509.

Boundary changes have moved the third of Llandyrnog that had been in Clwyd West into this seat.

This North Wales constituency takes in the coastal resorts of Rhyl and Prestatyn as well as much of Denbighshire including the town of Denbigh itself. The seaside resorts both have a high proportion of retired people.

Inland, the comparatively prosperous Vale of Clwyd has some of the best farming land in Wales and has a higher proportion of Welsh speakers than found in the coastal resorts.

Agriculture and tourism are key employment sectors, although both have declined in recent years.

A number of light industrial estates have sprung up in Rhyl and Denbigh, including the St Asaph Business Park.

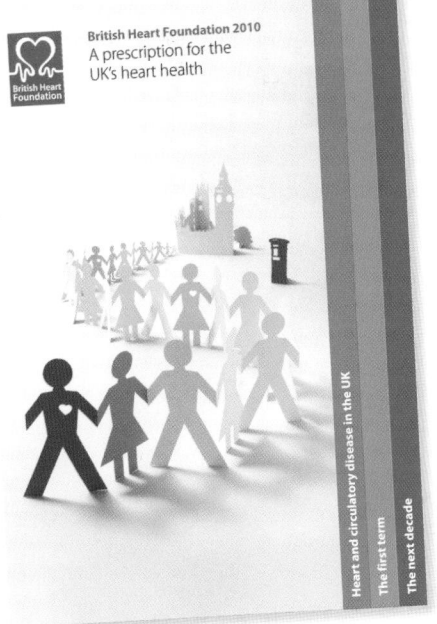

Amber Rudd

Hastings and Rye

Boundary changes

Tel: 020 7219 3000
E-mail: amber.rudd.mp@parliament.uk
Website: www.amberrudd.co.uk

Date of birth: 16 August 1963

Education: Queen's College, London; Edinburgh University (MA Hons history 1986); Divorced (1 son 1 daughter)

Non-political career: JPMorgan, London 1986-87; Director, Lawnstone Ltd 1988-97; Director, MacArthur and Co 1997-99; Chief executive officer, Investors Noticeboard Ltd 1999-2001; Consultant, I-Search Ltd 2001-03; Columnist, *Corporate Financier* 2003-; Managing director and senior consultant, Lawnstone Ltd 2003-

Political career: Contested Liverpool Garston 2005 general election. Member for Hastings and Rye since 6 May 2010 general election

Political interests: Defence, foreign policy, welfare

Recreations: Theatre, cinema

Amber Rudd MP, House of Commons, London SW1A 0AA
Tel: 020 7219 3000 E-mail: amber.rudd.mp@parliament.uk
Constituency: 383 Battle Road, St Leonards on Sea,
East Sussex TN37 7BE Tel: 01424 850828 Fax: 01424 853994
Website: www.amberrudd.co.uk

GENERAL ELECTION RESULT

		%
Rudd, A. (Con)	20,468	41.1
Foster, M. (Lab)*	18,475	37.1
Perry, N. (Lib Dem)	7,825	15.7
Smith, A. (UKIP)	1,397	2.8
Prince, N. (BNP)	1,310	2.6
Bridger, R. (England)	339	0.7
Majority	1,993	4.00
Electorate	78,000	
Turnout	49,814	63.86

**Member of last parliament*

CONSTITUENCY SNAPSHOT

In 1997 sitting Tory MP, Jacqui Lait, was beaten by Labour's Michael Foster on a 18.7 per cent swing. Labour went from third place to victory by a margin of 2,560 votes. Foster became Hasting's first non-Tory MP for 95 years; the previous non-Tory Member was a Liberal. Michael Foster's 2005 majority was 2,026.

Foster was defeated in the 2010 general election with a 3.3 per cent swing to the Conservative candidate, Amber Rudd, who secured a 1,993 majority.

Brede Valley ward was added from Bexhill and Battle. It lost Rother Levels ward to Bexhill and Battle, which had previously been shared between both seats.

Alongside the towns of Hastings and Rye, this characterful and historic Sussex constituency takes in the smaller Cinque Port of Winchelsea.

As well as miles of coastline, the gently undulating countryside encompasses a series of small towns and villages, extending as far as the Kent border.

Some 2,000 people are employed locally in the call-centre industry alone, and there are a number of language schools teaching English to foreign visitors. The local fishing industry remains significant. Hastings still has the biggest beach-launched fleet in Europe. Rye also has a thriving port.

The resort village of Camber Sands, with its caravans and miles of golden beach, is a particularly notable centre of the constituency's tourist industry.

Rt Hon **Joan Ruddock**

Lewisham Deptford (returning MP)

Boundary changes

Tel: 020 7219 4513
E-mail: ruddockj@parliament.uk
Website: www.joanruddock.org.uk

Date of birth: 28 December 1943; Daughter of late Kenneth Anthony and Eileen Anthony

Education: Pontypool Grammar School for Girls; Imperial College, London University (BSc botany 1965); Married Keith Ruddock 1963 (separated 1990, he died 1996); partner Frank Doran MP

Non-political career: Director: research and publications, Shelter, National Campaign for Homeless 1968-73, Oxford Housing Aid Centre 1973-77; Special programmes officer (Manpower Services Commission) for unemployed young people, Berkshire County Council 1977-79; Manager, Citizens Advice Bureau, Reading 1979-86; Member, UNITE

Political career: Contested Newbury 1979 general election. Member for Lewisham Deptford 1987-2010, for Lewisham Deptford (revised boundary) since 6 May 2010 general election; Private Member's Bill on flytipping – Control of Pollution Act (amendment) 1989; Opposition Spokesperson for: Transport 1989-92, Home Affairs 1992-94, Environmental Protection 1994-97; Parliamentary Under-Secretary of State for Women 1997-98; Promoted: Ten-Minute Rule Bill 1999, Prophylactic Mastectomy Registry Presentation Bill 1999, Organic Food and Farming Targets Bill 1999, Ten-Minute Rule Bill 2000, Sex Discrimination (Amendment) No. 2, Ten-Minute Rule Bill 2002, Waste Bill, Private Member's Bill – Municipal Waste, Recycling Bill 2003, (Household Waste Recycling Act 2003); Parliamentary Under-Secretary of State: Department for Environment, Food and Rural Affairs 2007-08, Department of Energy and Climate Change (DECC) 2008-09; Minister of State, DECC 2009-10; *Select Committees:* Member: Modernisation of the House of Commons 2001-05, Environment, Food and Rural Affairs 2003-05, International Development 2005-07

Political interests: Environment, Women, Foreign Affairs; Afghanistan, Palestine

Other organisations: Chair, CND 1981-85; Member, British Delegation to Council of Europe and Western European Union 1988-89; Inter-Parliamentary Union 2001-; PC 2010; Hon. Fellow: Goldsmith's College, London University; Laban, London; ARCS (1965)

Recreations: Travel, music, gardening

Rt Hon Joan Ruddock MP, House of Commons, London SW1A 0AA
Tel: 020 7219 4513 Fax: 020 7219 6045
E-mail: ruddockj@parliament.uk
Constituency: Suite 201, Astra House, Arklow Road, London SE14 6EB
Tel: 020 8691 5992 Fax: 020 8691 8242
Website: www.joanruddock.org.uk

GENERAL ELECTION RESULT

		%
Ruddock, J. (Lab)*	22,132	53.7
Langley, T. (Lib Dem)	9,633	23.4
Townsend, G. (Con)	5,551	13.5
Johnson, D. (Green)	2,772	6.7
Page, I. (SAP)	645	1.6
Martin, M. (CPA)	487	1.2
Majority	12,499	30.32
Electorate	67,058	
Turnout	41,220	61.47

**Member of last parliament*

CONSTITUENCY SNAPSHOT

The Labour vote has rarely dropped below 50 per cent. Joan Ruddock inherited the constituency following her predecessor John Silkin's death in 1987.

In 1997 Ruddock was re-elected with a massive 18,878 majority. Her winning margin shrunk in 2001 and 2005 but was still in five figures. Former Climate Change minister Joan Ruddock held the seat with a majority of 12,499 and over 53 per cent of the vote.

The seat gained the Crofton Park and Lewisham Central part-wards from Lewisham West and Lewisham Central respectively. It lost Rushey Green to Lewisham East.

With the River Thames as its northernmost boundary, Lewisham Deptford's wards range from inner city wards to the somewhat leafier Brockley. The area is close to central London, the City and Docklands.

There is a sizeable student population, due to Goldsmiths College being in the heart of the seat.

There has been millions of pounds of investment in the Silwood Estate, which spans the Deptford-Southwark border, and in the New Cross Gate area through the Single Regeneration Budget and the New Deal for Communities budget.

David Ruffley

Bury St Edmunds ***(returning MP)***

Boundary changes

Tel: 020 7219 2880
E-mail: ruffleyd@parliament.uk
Website: www.davidruffleymp.com

Conservative

Date of birth: 18 April 1962; Son of Jack Laurie Ruffley solicitor and Yvonne Grace, neé Harris

Education: Bolton Boys' School; Queens' College, Cambridge (BA law 1985); Single

Non-political career: Clifford Chance Solicitors, London 1985-91; Special adviser to Ken Clarke, MP as: Secretary of State for Education and Science 1991-92, Home Secretary 1992-93, Chancellor of the Exchequer 1993-96; Strategic Economic Consultant to the Conservative Party 1996-97; Member, Advisory Council of the Centre for Policy Studies 2003-

Political career: Member for Bury St Edmunds 1997-2010, for Bury St Edmonds (revised boundary) since 6 May 2010 general election; Opposition Whip 2004-05; Shadow Minister for: Work and Pensions 2005-07, Home Affairs 2007-10; *Select Committees:* Member: Public Administration 1997-99, Treasury 1998-2004, Treasury (Treasury Sub-Committee) 1999-2004, Treasury 2005-06; Member 1922 Committee Executive 2003-04

Political interests: Treasury, welfare reform; USA, China, France, Central Asia, Middle East

Other organisations: Patron: West Suffolk Voluntary Association for the Blind, Bury and District Football League, Alzheimer's Society West Suffolk Branch; Unpaid adviser to Grant Maintained Schools Foundation 1996-97; Fellow, British American Project 2002-; USA Department of State International Visitor Programme, Trade and Economic Development 2003; Patron, Bury St Edmunds Town Trust; Farmers' (Bury St Edmunds); Bury St Edmunds Golf Club

Recreations: Football, cinema, golf, thinking

David Ruffley MP, House of Commons, London SW1A 0AA
Tel: 020 7219 2880 Fax: 020 7219 3998
E-mail: ruffleyd@parliament.uk
Constituency: 1B Woolpit Business Park, Woolpit, Bury St Edmunds, Suffolk IP30 9UP Tel: 01359 244199 Fax: 01359 245002
Website: www.davidruffleymp.com

GENERAL ELECTION RESULT

		%
Ruffley, D. (Con)*	27,899	47.5
Chappell, D. (Lib Dem)	15,519	26.4
Hind, K. (Lab)	9,776	16.7
Howlett, J. (UKIP)	3,003	5.1
Ereira-Guyer, M. (Green)	2,521	4.3
Majority	12,380	21.08
Electorate	84,727	
Turnout	58,718	69.30

**Member of last parliament*

CONSTITUENCY SNAPSHOT

After extensive boundary changes to the Conservative Bury St Edmunds in 1997, the Labour vote increased by 11.2 per cent at the general election. After two recounts, the Conservative candidate, David Ruffley, was announced as the winner by just 368 votes.

In 2001 Ruffley extended his majority to 2,503 and a 6.9 per cent swing to the Tories in 2005, left him with a comfortable majority of 9,930. Ruffley's majority increased to 12,380 in 2010.

The constituency gained one part-ward from Central Suffolk and North Ipswich and gained and lost two part-wards from and to West Suffolk.

Bury St Edmunds encompasses the eponymous town of Bury St Edmunds and a number of rural communities and market towns in northern Suffolk.

The local economy largely revolves around farming and refinement of agricultural produce. The town of Bury St Edmunds has the largest sugar beet factory in the country, run by British Sugar, and is home to the nation's largest malt extract manufacturer. Greene King owns a large brewery in the town.

There is a presence of a number of specialist technology companies: W Vinten manufactures reconnaissance systems and its sister company makes televisual apparatus, Herga Electric makes fibre-optic sensors, while BT also has its regional office in the area.

Bob Russell

Colchester (returning MP)

Boundary changes

Tel: 020 7219 5150
E-mail: brooksse@parliament.uk
Website: www.bobrussell.org.uk

Date of birth: 31 March 1946; Son of late Ewart Russell and late Muriel Russell (neé Sawdy)

Education: St Helena Secondary Boys, Colchester; North-East Essex Technical College (Proficiency Certificate, National Council for the Training of Journalists 1966); Married Audrey Blandon 1967 (twin sons 1 daughter 1 daughter deceased)

Non-political career: Trainee reporter, *Essex County Standard* and *Colchester Gazette* 1963-66; News editor, *Braintree and Witham Times* 1966-68; Editor, *Maldon and Burnham Standard* 1968-69; Sub-editor: London *Evening News* 1969-72, London *Evening Standard* 1972-73; Press officer, BT Eastern Region 1973-85; Publicity information officer, Essex University 1986-97; Branch secretary, North-Essex, National Union of Journalists 1967-68; Councillor, Colchester Borough Council 1971-2002: Mayor 1986-87, Council Leader 1987-91

Political career: Member for Colchester 1997-2010, for Colchester (revised boundary) since 6 May 2010 general election; Liberal Democrat: Spokesperson for: Home and Legal Affairs 1997-99, Sport 1999-2005; Whip 1999-2002, 2003-06, Shadow Minister for Defence 2005-10, Whip 2006-10; *Select Committees:* Member: Home Affairs 1998-2005, 2006-10 Catering 2000-01, Regulatory Reform 2005-06, Armed Forces Bill 2005-06, Chairmen's Panel 2009-10; Member: Labour Party 1966, SDP May 1981, Liberal Democrats since formation

Political interests: Environment, local and regional government, sport, transport, animal welfare, voluntary sector, youth organisations, defence; St Helena

Other organisations: Member: Oxfam, East of England Co-operative Society, Colchester Credit Union, Scout Association; Fellow Industry and Parliament Trust 2005; Honorary Alderman of Colchester 2002; Journalists Prize, NEETC 1965; Colchester United Football Club

Recreations: Local history, walking, camping, watching Colchester Utd FC

Bob Russell MP, House of Commons, London SW1A 0AA
Tel: 020 7219 5150 Fax: 020 7219 2365
E-mail: brooksse@parliament.uk
Constituency: Magdalen Hall, Wimpole Road, Colchester, Essex C01 2DE Tel: 01206 506600 Fax: 01206 506610
Website: www.bobrussell.org.uk

GENERAL ELECTION RESULT

		%
Russell, B. (Lib Dem)*	22,151	48.0
Quince, W. (Con)	15,169	32.9
Newell, J. (Lab)	5,680	12.3
Pitts, J. (UKIP)	1,350	2.9
Chaney, S. (BNP)	705	1.5
Lynn, P. (Green)	694	1.5
Bone, E. (England)	335	0.7
Noble, G. (Essex)	35	0.1
Shaw, P. (Ind)	20	0.0
Majority	6,982	15.13
Electorate	74,062	
Turnout	46,139	62.30

**Member of last parliament*

CONSTITUENCY SNAPSHOT

In 1983 the town was divided between two constituencies, Colchester North and Colchester South and Maldon. Both seats returned Tory MPs.

Major boundary changes in 1995 re-united the town as a single constituency, and the Conservative Stephen Shakespeare finished 1,581 votes behind Lib Dem Bob Russell, who won the seat with 34.4 per cent of the vote.

Russell was re-elected in 2001, boosting his majority over the Conservatives by nearly 4,000. Russell increased his majority once again in 2005, to 6,277. The Lib Dems retained the seat with 22,151 votes giving Russell a majority of 6,982.

There were minor boundary changes to the seat.

Colchester, in Essex, is Britain's earliest recorded town, the Roman Camulodunum.

Colchester has a mixed economy, with little heavy industry, but two successful industrial parks. Among the largest employers are Essex University, which contributes about £60 million a year to the local economy, and the army garrison, with about 5,000 direct jobs. Redevelopment of the garrison has created a new urban village with 2,600 homes and community facilities.

David Rutley

Macclesfield

Boundary changes

Tel: 020 7219 3000
E-mail: david.rutley.mp@parliament.uk
Website: www.davidrutley.org.uk

Conservative

Date of birth: 7 March 1961

Education: Lewes Priory School; London School of Economics (BSc Econ 1985); Harvard Business School (MBA 1989); Married Rachel (4 children)

Non-political career: Business development director, PepsiCo International 1991-94; Special adviser 1994-96: Cabinet office, Ministry of Agriculture, HM Treasury; Director of business effectiveness, Safeway Stores 1996-2000; ASDA stores 2000-05: Director of Financial Services, Director of E-commerce; Sales and marketing director, Halifax General Insurance 2005-07; Barclays Bank 2008-10: Business consultant 2008-09, Marketing director 2009-10

Political career: Contested St Albans 1997 general election. Member for Macclesfield since 6 May 2010 general election

Political interests: Rural affairs, local economy, anti-social behaviour; China, Denmark, USA

Recreations: Walking in the Peak District, fishing, ornithology, mountaineering

David Rutley MP, House of Commons, London SW1A 0AA
Tel: 020 7219 3000 E-mail: david.rutley.mp@parliament.uk
Constituency: Macclesfield Conservative Association, West Bank Road, Macclesfield, Cheshire SK10 3BT Tel: 01625 617066
Fax: 01625 617066 Website: www.davidrutley.org.uk

GENERAL ELECTION RESULT

		%
Rutley, D. (Con)	23,503	47.0
Barlow, R. (Lib Dem)	11,544	23.1
Heald, A. (Lab)	10,164	20.3
Murphy, B. (Mac Ind)	2,590	5.2
Smith, J. (UKIP)	1,418	2.8
Knight, J. (Green)	840	1.7
Majority	11,959	23.89
Electorate	73,417	
Turnout	50,059	68.18

CONSTITUENCY SNAPSHOT

Macclesfield has been Conservative since the decline of the old Liberal party in the early 20th century. The seat has been represented by only three MPs since the Second World War. Nicholas Winterton replaced Sir Arthur Harvey at the 1971 by-election.

In 2001 his majority fell after a decline in turnout, but rose to 9,401 in 2005, albeit slightly short of the five-figures he achieved before 1997.

In 2010 David Rutley replaced Winterton and held the seat for the Conservatives with a majority of 11,959.

The seat gained the Henbury part-ward from Tatton.

Previously a centre for silk manufacturing, Macclesfield has always been one of the more upmarket former textile towns in the North West, including Tytherington and Bollingbrook in the north of the town, together with the more rural areas north of the town, comprising the commuter belt of Disley, Poynton, Bollington and Prestbury.

The silk trade has long given way to predominantly service sector employment, particularly financial and business services. However, manufacturing underpins the local economy, represented by the seat's largest employer, pharmaceutical giant AstraZeneca situated just outside Macclesfield.

Macclesfield's hinterland continues to be an important farming area, with dairy, beef and sheep predominating.

Adrian Sanders

Torbay (returning MP)

Boundary changes

Tel: 020 7219 6304
E-mail: sandersa@parliament.uk
Website: www.adriansanders.org

Date of birth: 25 April 1959; Son of late John Sanders, insurance official and Helen, nurse

Education: Torquay Boys' Grammar School; Married Alison Nortcliffe 1992

Non-political career: Parliamentary officer, Liberal Democrat Whips' Office 1989-90; Association of Liberal Democrat Councillors 1990-92; Policy officer, National Council for Voluntary Organisations 1992-93; Assistant to Paddy Ashdown MP, Liberal Democrat Party Leader 1992-93 Southern Association of Voluntary Action Groups for Europe 1993-97; Councillor, Torbay Borough Council 1984-86

Political career: Contested Torbay 1992 general election. Member for Torbay 1997-2010, for Torbay (revised boundary) since 6 May 2010 general election; Liberal Democrat: Whip 1997-2001, Spokesperson for: Housing 1997-2001, Environment, Transport, the Regions and Social Justice 1999-2001, Transport, Local Government and the Regions (Local Government) 2001-02, Tourism 2002-05, Whip 2006-10: Deputy Chief Whip 2006-10; *Select Committees:* Member: Joint Committee on Consolidation of Bills Etc 1997-2001, Office of the Deputy Prime Minister 2003-05, Office of the Deputy Prime Minister (Urban Affairs Sub-Committee) 2003-05, Culture, Media and Sport 2005-10, Selection 2006-10, Modernisation of the House of Commons 2006-08; Contested Devon and East Plymouth 1994 European Parliament election; Vice-President, National League of Young Liberals 1985; Political secretary, Devon and Cornwall Regional Liberal Party 1983-84; Information officer, Association of Liberal Councillors 1986-89

Political interests: Local and regional government, voluntary sector, tourism; USA

Other organisations: Member: CPA 1997-, IPU 1997-, British American Parliamentary Group 1997-

Recreations: Football

Adrian Sanders MP, House of Commons, London SW1A 0AA
Tel: 020 7219 6304 Fax: 020 7219 3963
E-mail: sandersa@parliament.uk
Constituency: 69 Belgrave Road, Torquay, Devon TQ2 5HZ
Tel: 01803 200036 Fax: 01803 200031
Website: www.adriansanders.org

GENERAL ELECTION RESULT

		%
Sanders, A. (Lib Dem)*	23,126	47.0
Wood, M. (Con)	19,048	38.7
Pedrick-Friend, D. (Lab)	3,231	6.6
Parrott, J. (UKIP)	2,628	5.3
Conway, A. (BNP)	709	1.4
Moss, S. (Green)	468	1.0
Majority	4,078	8.29
Electorate	76,151	
Turnout	49,210	64.62

**Member of last parliament*

CONSTITUENCY SNAPSHOT

Torbay was a Tory seat from 1945 to 1997, when the Liberal Democrats' Adrian Sanders took the seat in 1997 by a majority of just 12 votes.

However, the Liberal Democrats consolidated their position in 2001, polling over 50 per cent of the total votes. In 2005 Sanders retained the seat with a much reduced majority of 2,029. The Liberal Democrat vote fell by almost 10 per cent. Adrian Sanders won the revised seat for the Lib Dems in 2010 with a 4,078 vote lead.

Boundary changes were minimal.

The coastal towns which make up the Devon constituency of Torbay are known as the 'English Riviera', and tourism is certainly a major industry here.

Torbay is a small constituency centred on Torquay and most of Paignton. This is an urban seat, and the third most densely populated area in the South West.

This is a huge retirement area and so there are vast numbers of over 65s here

Low incomes reflect a labour market with an abundance of constituents employed in sectors such as hotel and catering, retail and health and social services.

Laura Sandys

South Thanet

Boundary changes

Tel: 020 7219 3000
E-mail: laura.sandys.mp@parliament.uk
Website: www.telllaura.org.uk

Conservative

Daughter of Lord Duncan-Sandys; Married Randolph Kent

Non-political career: Senior research associate, Centre for Defence Studies, King's College, London

Political career: Member for South Thanet since 6 May 2010 general election; Member, Quality of Life Taskforce, Conservative Party

Political interests: Small businesses, care of the elderly, education, defence policy

Other organisations: Deputy chair, Civic Trust; Trustee, Open University; Chair, Open Democracy

Laura Sandys MP, House of Commons, London SW1A 0AA
Tel: 020 7219 3000 E-mail: laura.sandys.mp@parliament.uk
Constituency: c/o Conservative Office, 7-9 Kings Street, Ramsgate CT11 8NN Tel: 01843 595258
Website: www.telllaura.org.uk

GENERAL ELECTION RESULT

		%
Sandys, L. (Con)	22,043	48.0
Ladyman, S. (Lab)*	14,426	31.4
Bucklitsch, P. (Lib Dem)	6,935	15.1
Shonk, T. (UKIP)	2,529	5.5
Majority	7,617	16.58
Electorate	71,596	
Turnout	45,933	64.16

**Member of last parliament*

CONSTITUENCY SNAPSHOT

South Thanet was a Conservative seat until 1997. The Tories regularly polled over 50 per cent of the vote. This was the seat of Jonathan Aitken who at the time of the 1997 election was facing the allegations which eventually resulted in his being jailed for perjury. Aitken had represented South Thanet for 25 years, and in 1997 he defended a 11,513 majority but Labour's Dr Stephen Ladyman took the seat with a majority of 2,878.

In 2001 his majority slipped to 1,792 and he held the seat in 2005 by just 664 votes. Laura Sandys won the seat for the Conservatives in 2010 with a 7,617 majority.

The seat gained a part-ward from Dover and two wards from North Thanet, while losing one part-ward to each of those seats. To find out what might have happened had this boundary change been in force at the last election, see a notional - or estimated - result below.

South Thanet sits in the north-east corner of Kent and includes the coastal resorts of Broadstairs and Ramsgate plus the Port of Sandwich.

The largest employer is Pfizer but other large employers include Sericol and Kent International Airport, which is owned by Infratil.

The new high-speed rail service introduced in 2009 has significantly cut the journey time into St Pancras International.

Anas Sarwar

Glasgow Central

No boundary changes

Tel: 020 7219 3000
E-mail: anas.sarwar.mp@parliament.uk
Website: www.sarwar4glasgow.com

Date of birth: 14 March 1983; Son of Mohammed Sarwar, MP 1997-2010, and Perveen Sarwar

Education: Hutchesons' Grammar School; Glasgow University; Married Furheen (1 son)

Non-political career: Dentist, NHS, Glasgow

Political career: Member for Glasgow Central since 6 May 2010 general election; Contested Glasgow region (1) 2007 Scottish Parliament election; Member, Labour Party 1999-

Political interests: Foreign policy, international development

Other organisations: Founder and co-ordinator, Y-Vote

Anas Sarwar MP, House of Commons, London SW1A 0AA
Tel: 020 7219 3000 E-mail: anas.sarwar.mp@parliament.uk
Constituency: Campaign Centre, 9 Scotland Street, Glasgow G5 8NB
Tel: 07527 291898 Website: www.sarwar4glasgow.com

GENERAL ELECTION RESULT

		%	+/-
Sarwar, A. (Lab)	15,908	52.0	4.0
Saeed, O. (SNP)	5,357	17.5	2.8
Young, C. (Lib Dem)	5,010	16.4	-1.3
Bradley, J. (Con)	2,158	7.1	0.8
Whitelaw, A. (Green)	800	2.6	-2.3
Holt, I. (BNP)	616	2.0	-0.4
Nesbitt, J. (SSP)	357	1.2	-2.8
Urquhart, R. (UKIP)	246	0.8	
Archibald, F. (Pirate)	120	0.4	
Majority	10,551	34.51	
Electorate	60,062		
Turnout	30,572	50.90	

CONSTITUENCY SNAPSHOT

The 2005 boundary review cut the 10 Glaswegian seats to seven. This division contains wards from five of the previous Glasgow seats, the bulk formed by combining the central wards of the old Govan, Kelvin and Shettleston seats, which used to divide the city centre.

Mohammad Sarwar won in 2005 with a 13,518 majority. Notionally, this represented a 6.5 per cent reduction in Labour's share of the vote which was consistent with the regional swing against the party. New MP Anas Sarwar took 52 per cent of the vote to succeed his father in this safe Labour seat in 2010.

This constituency straddles the river Clyde and contains many of Glasgow's best-known landmarks including Glasgow Central railway station and the cathedral.

The cityscape includes some architecturally significant tenement properties as well as Victorian town houses and the Merchant City. The Merchant City has been rejuvenated in recent decades with luxury apartments, boutique shops and a number of smart bars and restaurants.

Glasgow was awarded the 2014 Commonwealth Games in November 2007. The seat is to be the home of the athletes' village, which will be built by the river in Dalmarnock at the seat's border with the eastern division. After the Games the homes will be sold or socially rented, giving the area some much-needed rejuvenation.

Lee Scott

Ilford North (returning MP)

Boundary changes

Tel: 020 7219 8326
E-mail: scottle@parliament.uk
Website: www.leescott.co.uk

Conservative

Date of birth: 6 April 1956; Son of late Sydney and Renne Scott

Education: Clarks College, Ilford, Essex; College of Distributive Trades, London; Married Estelle Doreen Dombey, née King 1987 (3 daughters 2 sons)

Non-political career: Director, Scott and Fishell 1972-1982; Selfridges 1975-80; Tatung 1980-82; Sales executive: Toshiba 1982-84, ITT 1984-86, NKR 1986-88; Campaign director/provincial director, United Jewish Israel Appeal 1988-98; Director, Scott Associates 1998-; London Borough of Redbridge: Councillor 1998-2006, Cabinet member for regeneration and the community 2002

Political career: Contested Waveney 2001 general election. Member for Ilford North 2005-10, for Ilford North (revised boundary) since 6 May 2010 general election; *Select Committees:* Member: Transport 2005-08, Health 2007-10; Deputy chair (political), Ilford North CC 1998-99; Essex area chairman, Conservative Friends of Israel 2001-

Political interests: Middle East affairs, trade and industry, community issues, transport

Other organisations: Committee member Victim Support Redbridge 1999-

Recreations: Music, reading, sport

Lee Scott MP, House of Commons, London SW1A 0AA
Tel: 020 7219 8326 Fax: 020 7219 0970
E-mail: scottle@parliament.uk
Constituency: 9 Sevenways Parade, Gants Hill, Ilford, Essex IG2 6XH
Tel: 020 8551 4107 Fax: 020 8551 4801 Website: www.leescott.co.uk

GENERAL ELECTION RESULT

		%
Scott, L. (Con)*	21,506	45.8
Klein, S. (Lab)	16,102	34.3
Berhanu, A. (Lib Dem)	5,924	12.6
Warville, D. (BNP)	1,545	3.3
Van Der Stighelen, H. (UKIP)	871	1.9
Allen, C. (Green)	572	1.2
Hampson, R. (Christian)	456	1.0
Majority	5,404	11.50
Electorate	71,995	
Turnout	46,976	65.25

**Member of last parliament*

CONSTITUENCY SNAPSHOT

The constituency has been mainly dominated by the Conservatives since 1945. Linda Perham won the seat for Labour in 1997 with a 3,224 majority. It fell at subsequent elections and in 2005 the Conservatives' Lee Scott was returned to the Commons with a majority of 1,653. Scott held the seat in 2010 with an increased majority of 5,404.

The seats lost Snaresbrook and Wanstead part-wards wards to Leyton and Wanstead.

This mostly residential constituency of Ilford North is typical commuter land on the north-eastern outskirts of Greater London.

Although it is within the M25, demographically the constituency resembles Essex commuter towns which lie to its north-east. Most constituents work in finance, distribution or manufacturing and the majority commute into central London.

The constituency is served by National Express rail services and the London Underground's central line, and the M11 links it to Stansted airport and Cambridge.

The new Queen's hospital in Romford should help to reduce the pressure on the King George and Whipps Cross hospitals which serve the constituency.

Green-belt development is a significant concern. Roding Valley Park, Hainault Forest, Fairlop Plane and Claybury Forest all provide valued green space.

Alison Seabeck

Plymouth, Moor View ***(returning MP)***

New constituency

Tel: 020 7219 6431
E-mail: seabecka@parliament.uk
Website: www.alisonseabeckmp.org.uk

Date of birth: 20 January 1954; Daughter of Lilian née Lomas and late Michael John Ward (former MP for Peterborough)

Education: Harold Hill Grammar School, Romford, Essex; North East London Polytechnic (general studies); Married Denis George Seabeck 1975 (divorced 2007) (2 daughters)

Non-political career: Various posts including Marks and Spencer management trainee, employment consultant, PA to college of further education principal; Parliamentary assistant to Roy Hattersley MP 1987-92; Adviser to Nick Raynsford MP 1992-2005; UNITE-Amicus; Member, Secretary of South Thames community branch

Political career: Member for Plymouth Devonport 2005-10, for Plymouth, Moor View since 6 May 2010 general election; PPS to Geoff Hoon as Minister of State for Europe 2006-07; Assistant Government Whip 2007-08; PPS to Geoff Hoon as Secretary of State for Transport 2008-09; *Select Committees:* Member: ODPM/Communities and Local Government 2005-06, Regulatory Reform 2005-07, Communities and Local Government 2009-10; Chair: South West 2009-10; Member: Labour Women's Network, South London Co-operative Party 2001-06, SW Co-operative Party 2006-

Political interests: Local government, construction, housing, defence; Europe, Australia, India and Pakistan

Other organisations: Member Fawcett Society; Parliamentary convener London Housing Group 2006-07; Patron Devon Lupus Group 2006-

Recreations: Travelling, swimming, reading, gardening, photography

Alison Seabeck MP, House of Commons, London SW1A 0AA
Tel: 020 7219 6431 Fax: 020 7219 0883
E-mail: seabecka@parliament.uk
Constituency: None publicised Tel: 01752 365617 Fax: 01752 364325
Website: www.alisonseabeckmp.org.uk

GENERAL ELECTION RESULT

		%
Seabeck, A. (Lab)*	15,433	37.2
Groves, M. (Con)	13,845	33.3
Bonar, S. (Lib Dem)	7,016	16.9
Wakeham, B. (UKIP)	3,188	7.7
Cook, R. (BNP)	1,438	3.5
Miller, W. (Green)	398	1.0
Marchesi, D. (SLP)	208	0.5
Majority	1,588	3.82
Electorate	67,261	
Turnout	41,526	61.74

**Member of last parliament*

CONSTITUENCY SNAPSHOT

There is little difference between Plymouth Moor View and its predecessor. Ham is now entirely within the seat's boundaries, whilst part-wards Devonport and Stoke moved entirely into Plymouth Sutton and Devonport.

As Plymouth Devonport, the seat has had some notable MPs, including Michael Foot for a decade after the Second World War, and Social Democrat founder and leader David Owen. Owen was able to hold his seat from 1974 until his party dwindled to extinction in 1990. He stood down in 1992 leaving Labour's David Jamieson to poll a majority of more than 7,000, increasing this to more than 19,000 in 1997. A 7.8 per cent swing to the Conservatives didn't stop Labour's Alison Seabeck winning the new seat in 2010 with a majority of 1,588.

Jamieson retired in 2005 and the Labour vote fell by 14 per cent, leaving Alison Seabeck with a morority of 8,103.

Comprising the northern part of the famous naval city, Plymouth Moor View has a largely urban working-class feel.

Although HMS Devonport Dockyard is no longer in the seat, most constituents are nonetheless employed in related industries such as electronics, engineering and boat building, defence and public administration.

There is a huge manufacturing base here, making products ranging from the high technology at British Aerospace to Wrigley's chewing gum.

Andrew Selous

South West Bedfordshire (returning MP)

No boundary changes

Tel: 020 7219 8134
E-mail: selousa@parliament.uk
Website: www.andrewselous.org.uk

Conservative

Date of birth: 27 April 1962; Son of Commander Gerald Selous, and Miranda Selous, née Casey

Education: Eton College; London School of Economics (BSc Econ industry and trade 1984); Married Harriet Victoria Marston 1993 (3 daughters)

Non-political career: TA officer Honourable Artillery Company, Royal Regiment of Fusiliers 1981-94; Director CNS Electronics Ltd 1988-94; Underwriter Great Lakes Re (UK) plc 1991-2001

Political career: Contested Sunderland North 1997 general election. Member for South West Bedfordshire since 7 June 2001 general election; PPS to Michael Ancram as Shadow Foreign Secretary 2004; Opposition Whip 2004-06; Shadow Minister for Work and Pensions 2006-10; *Select Committees:* Member: Work and Pensions 2001-05; Chairman Conservative Christian Fellowship 2001-06

Political interests: Trade and industry, social affairs, families, defence, homelessness

Other organisations: ACII 1993; Chartered Insurer 1998; Leighton Buzzard Conservative, Dunstable Conservative

Recreations: Family, walking, tennis, bridge

Andrew Selous MP, House of Commons, London SW1A 0AA
Tel: 020 7219 8134 Fax: 020 7219 1297
E-mail: selousa@parliament.uk
Constituency: 6c Princes Street, Dunstable, Bedfordshire LU6 3AX
Tel: 01582 662 821 Fax: 01582 476 619
Website: www.andrewselous.org.uk

GENERAL ELECTION RESULT

		%	+/-
Selous, A. (Con)*	26,815	52.8	4.7
Cantrill, R. (Lib Dem)	10,166	20.0	3.2
Bone, J. (Lab)	9,948	19.6	-10.4
Newman, M. (UKIP)	2,142	4.2	
Tolman, M. (BNP)	1,703	3.4	
Majority	16,649	32.79	
Electorate	76,559		
Turnout	50,774	66.32	

**Member of last parliament*

CONSTITUENCY SNAPSHOT

In 1992 Conservative Sir David Madel was re-elected with a 21,273 majority. This was slashed to just 132 in 1997.

On Sir David's retirement in 2001 current Tory MP Andrew Selous slightly increased the Tory majority to 776.

In 2005 Mr Selous presided over an 8.2 per cent swing from Labour to the Conservatives, enough to give the Tories a 8,277 majority. The Conservatives doubled their majority in 2010 to 16,649.

This constituency of South West Bedfordshire is situated west across the M1 from Luton. The main centres of population in the constituency are Leighton Buzzard, Dunstable and Houghton Regis.

Leighton Buzzard to the north and west has jobs in light industry and distribution and its proximity to the M1, A5 and good rail links to London and Milton Keynes make both towns natural commuter territory.

Tourism is an important local money-earner, with the Chiltern hills, stately homes and Whipsnade Zoo among the attractions. The expansion of Luton Airport and regeneration projects in Luton following the closure of Vauxhall Motors have also brought more job opportunities to the constituency.

Jim Shannon

Strangford

Boundary changes

Tel: 020 7219 3000
E-mail: jim.shannon.mp@parliament.uk

Date of birth: 25 March 1955; Son of Richard James Shannon, retired, and Moira Rebecca Rhoda Shannon, retired

Education: Ballywalter Primary School; Coleraine Academical Institution (1971); Married Sandra George 1987 (3 sons)

Non-political career: Ulster Defence Regiment 1973-75, 1976-77; Royal Artillery TA 1977-88; Self-employed pork retailer 1985-; Member: Mid Ards Branch, Ulster Farmers' Union, Transport and General Workers' Union (TGWU) 1976-85; Ards Borough Council: Councillor 1985-, Mayor 1991-92

Political career: Member for Strangford since 6 May 2010 general election; Member Northern Ireland Forum for Political Dialogue 1996-; MLA for Strangford since 25 June 1998; Democratic Unionist Party

Political interests: Farming, fishing, environment, Ulster-Scots; Scotland, USA

Other organisations: Secretary, Loyal Orange Institution, Kircubbin LOL 1900; Registrar, Royal Black Perceptory Ballywater No 675; Comber, Apprentice Boys of Derry; Member: British Association Shooting and Conservation, Countryside Alliance NI, Royal British Legion, Greyabbey Branch, National Trust; General Service Medal, Ulster Defence Regiment; Carrowdore Shooting Club

Recreations: Fieldsports, football

Jim Shannon MP, House of Commons, London SW1A 0AA
Tel: 020 7219 3000 E-mail: jim.shannon.mp@parliament.uk

GENERAL ELECTION RESULT

		%
Shannon, J. (DUP)	14,926	45.9
Nesbitt, M. (UCUNF)	9,050	27.8
Girvan, D. (All)	2,828	8.7
Hanna, C. (SDLP)	2,164	6.7
Williams, T. (TUV)	1,814	5.6
Coogan, M. (Sinn Féin)	1,161	3.6
Haig, B. (Green)	562	1.7
Majority	5,876	18.08
Electorate	60,539	
Turnout	32,505	53.69

CONSTITUENCY SNAPSHOT

John D Taylor, a former UUP security minister in the old Northern Ireland parliament, survived an attempted assassination and kept this seat for 18 years from 1983, despite latterly being strongly opposed by the DUP.

Taylor declined to stand in the 2001 general election and his UUP successor David McNarry was defeated by the DUP's Iris Robinson. At the 2005 general election Robinson increased her majority to 13,049. Robinson stood down in January 2010. In the 2010 general election Jim Shannon held the seat for the DUP with 14,926 votes.

As well as gaining two Down District Council wards, Strangford lost a significant lump of its Castlereagh wards (essentially the suburb of Dundonald) to East Belfast.

The constituency surrounds Strangford Lough and dominates the Ards Peninsula. The main town is Newtownards, overlooked by the Scrabo Tower.

Just over an eighth of the population is Catholic. The Presbyterian community is dominant in this part of Northern Ireland. The workforce is largely engaged in non-manual work with a relatively small manufacturing base.

The industries are farming, fishing and tourism. Attractions include the Castle Espie wetland nature reserve.

Rt Hon **Grant Shapps**

Welwyn Hatfield (returning MP)

No boundary changes

Tel: 020 7219 8497
E-mail: shappsg@parliament.uk
Website: www.shapps.com

Conservative

Date of birth: 14 September 1968; Son of Tony and Beryl Shapps

Education: Watford Boys Grammar School; Cassio College, Watford (OND business and finance 1987) Manchester Polytechnic (HND business and finance 1989); Married Belinda Goldstone 1997 (1 son twin son and daughter)

Non-political career: Sales executive Nashua Gestetner 1989-90; Founder Printhouse Corporation 1990-: Chairman 2000-

Political career: Contested North Southwark and Bermondsey 1997 and Welwyn Hatfield 2001 general elections. Member for Welwyn Hatfield since 5 May 2005 general election; Shadow Minister for Housing (attending Shadow Cabinet) 2007-10; Minister of State for Housing and Local Government, Department for Communities and Local Government 2010-; *Select Committees:* Member: Public Administration 2005-07; Branch chair Barnhill, Brent North 1995-99; Member: Conservative Friends of Israel 1995, Selsdon Group 1996, Conservative Foreign Affairs Forum 1996; Vice-president North Southwark and Bermondsey Association 1997; Vice-chairman (Campaigning) Conservative Party 2005-09

Political interests: Health, education, home affairs, foreign affairs

Other organisations: PC 2010; *Publications:* What's Right for 21st Century (Printhouse Publishing, 2001)

Rt Hon Grant Shapps MP, House of Commons, London SW1A 0AA
Tel: 020 7219 8497 Fax: 020 7219 0659
E-mail: shappsg@parliament.uk
Constituency: Welwyn Hatfield Conservative Association, Maynard House, The Common, Hatfield, Hertfordshire AL10 0NF
Tel: 01707 262632 Fax: 01707 263892 Website: www.shapps.com

GENERAL ELECTION RESULT

		%	+/-
Shapps, G. (Con)*	27,894	57.0	7.5
Hobday, M. (Lab)	10,471	21.4	-14.8
Zukowskyj, P. (Lib Dem)	8,010	16.4	2.3
Platt, D. (UKIP)	1,643	3.4	
Weston, J. (Green)	796	1.6	
Parker, N. (Ind)	158	0.3	
Majority	17,423	35.58	
Electorate	72,058		
Turnout	48,972	67.96	

**Member of last parliament*

CONSTITUENCY SNAPSHOT

In 1997 Labour's Melanie Johnson defeated the Tories' David Evans in Welwyn Hatfield after ten years' incumbency with a majority of 5,595 on an 11 per cent swing.

By 2001 this majority had become just 1,196. In 2005 continued success at a local level translated into a parliamentary gain for the Tories. A larger than average 8 per cent swing in their favour was enough to hand Grant Shapps the seat with a 5,956 majority.

Shapps was re-elected with 27,894 votes in 2010 giving the Conservatives a 17,423 majority.

Created out of two towns, Welwyn and Hatfield, the constituency contains the New Town and Garden City as well as Brookmans Park.

The pharmaceutical sector is now the major industry here with many large firms such as Roche, GlaxoSmithKline and Schering Plough situated in Welwyn Garden City. Hi-tech firms such as T-Mobile and ComputaCentre have also moved to the constituency.

The area previously occupied by British Aerospace was redeveloped and used as the campus for the University of Hertfordshire, which has become one of the region's largest employers, with over 2,500 staff.

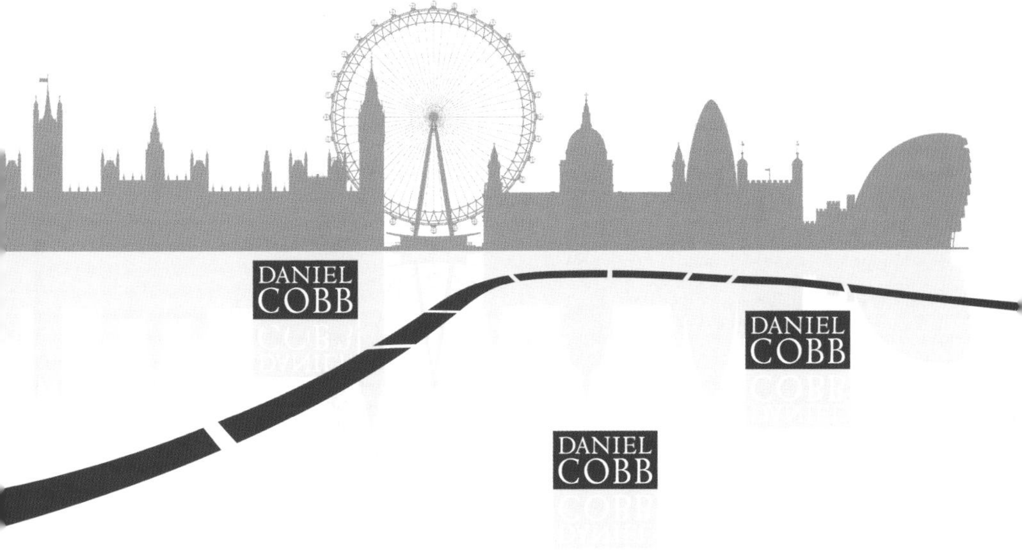

Alok Sharma

Reading West

Boundary changes

Tel: 020 7219 3000
E-mail: alok.sharma.mp@parliament.uk
Website: www.aloksharma.co.uk

Conservative

Date of birth: 7 September 1967

Education: Blue Coat School, Reading; Salford University (BSc applied physics with electronics 1988); Married (2 daughters)

Non-political career: Chartered accountant; Accountancy and corporate finance advice; School governor

Political career: Member for Reading West since 6 May 2010 general election; Member, Conservative Party 1978-

Political interests: Trade, industry, finance; India, Pakistan, Sweden

Other organisations: Former chair, economic affairs committee, Bow Group; Fellow, Royal Society for the encouragement of Arts, Manufacturing and Commerce

Alok Sharma MP, House of Commons, London SW1A 0AA
Tel: 020 7219 3000 E-mail: alok.sharma.mp@parliament.uk
Constituency: 16C Upton Road, Tilehurst, Reading,
Berkshire RG30 4BJ Tel: 0118-945 4881
Website: www.aloksharma.co.uk

GENERAL ELECTION RESULT

		%
Sharma, A. (Con)	20,523	43.2
Sarkar, N. (Lab)	14,519	30.6
Benson, D. (Lib Dem)	9,546	20.1
Hay, B. (UKIP)	1,508	3.2
Thomas, H. (CSP)	852	1.8
Windisch, A. (Green)	582	1.2
Majority	6,004	12.63
Electorate	72,118	
Turnout	47,530	65.91

CONSTITUENCY SNAPSHOT

Before 1997 Conservative MP Sir Anthony Durant had represented Reading West for more than 20 years. In the three general elections between 1983 and 1992 he consistently polled over 50 per cent of the vote.

In 1997 the Conservative candidate Nicholas Bennett's inherited share of the vote fell to 38.9 per cent, while Labour's grew to 45.1 per cent. A 15 per cent swing to Labour gave their candidate Martin Salter a 2,997 majority. In 2001 Salter nearly tripled his majority to 8,894 votes, however, this fell to 4,682 in 2001.

Salter retired in 2010 and the Labour candidate lost the seat to Conservative Alok Sharma following a 12.1 per cent swing.

The seat gained the part-wards of Battle and Whitley from Reading East.

Reading is the county town of Berkshire, where the river Kennet joins the Thames. Reading West is larger than its eastern counterpart, covering territory further to the west in the Newbury district, with its more affluent residential areas in a rural setting alongside the Thames.

The M25 is close by and the M4 passes near the constituency and the town's proximity to London have attracted national companies to set up headquarters and manufacture hi-tech products, particularly computers.

First Great Western operates the London to Cardiff/Swansea line that runs through Reading station, providing alternative links along the M4 corridor.

Virendra Sharma

Ealing Southall (returning MP)

Boundary changes

Tel: 020 7219 6080
E-mail: sharmav@parliament.uk

Date of birth: 5 April 1947

Education: London School of Economics (MA 1979); Married Nirmala (1 son 1 daughter)

Non-political career: Day services manager, London Borough of Hillingdon 1996-2007; Member, Transport and General Workers' Union (TGWU); Councillor London Borough of Ealing 1982-: Former Mayor

Political career: Member for Ealing Southall 17 July 2007 by-election to 2010, Ealing Southall (revised boundary) since 6 May 2010 general election; PPS to Phil Woolas as Minister of State, Home Office and HM Treasury 2008-09; *Select Committees:* Member: Joint Committee on Human Rights 2007-10, Justice 2007-09, International Development 2009-10; Labour Party National Ethnic Minorities Officer 1986-92

Other organisations: Member, Indian Workers Association

Virendra Sharma MP, House of Commons, London SW1A 0AA
Tel: 020 7219 6080 Fax: 020 7219 3969
E-mail: sharmav@parliament.uk
Constituency: 112A The Green, Southall, Middlesex UB2 4BQ
Tel: 020 8571 1003 Fax: 020 8571 1003

GENERAL ELECTION RESULT

		%
Sharma, V. (Lab)*	22,024	51.5
Singh, G. (Con)	12,733	29.8
Bakhai, N. (Lib Dem)	6,383	14.9
Basu, S. (Green)	705	1.7
Anil, M. (Christian)	503	1.2
Chaggar, S. (England)	408	1.0
Majority	9,291	21.73
Electorate	60,379	
Turnout	42,756	70.81

**Member of last parliament*

CONSTITUENCY SNAPSHOT

Labour MPs have represented the area for well over half a century. Sydney Bidwell held the seat for 26 years from 1966. He retired in 1992 and was replaced by Piara Khabra, who became the first Asian MP to represent the seat.

Khabra was re-elected in 2001 with a majority of 13,683. Khabra increased his vote by almost 700 votes in the 2005 election, although his actual majority fell.

Khabra was the oldest Member of Parliament when he died in June 2007 at the age of 82. At the by-election Virenda Sharma retained the seat for Labour, though with a reduced majority. Sharma held the seat for Labour with an increased share of the vote and a majority of 9,291.

Boundary changes have moved Ealing Broadway, Walpole, and Ealing Common wards to the new Ealing Central and Acton seat, while Hobbayne and Greenford Broadway ward is now entirely within Ealing North's boundaries. Dormers Wells ward is completely in the seat's boundaries, having previously been shared with the North division.

Southall is well known for having the largest Asian shopping centre in the capital, alongside restaurants offering authentic Asian cuisine.

Many constituents are employed in the service industries and various shops and restaurants. Heathrow Airport has a huge impact on this constituency. More residents in this constituency work in or around Heathrow than any other.

Barry Sheerman

Huddersfield (returning MP)

Boundary changes

Tel: 020 7219 5037
E-mail: sheermanb@parliament.uk
Website: www.barrysheerman.org.uk

Labour/Co-operative

Date of birth: 17 August 1940; Son of late Albert William Sheerman and Florence, née Pike

Education: Hampton Grammar School; Kingston Technical College (economics and politics); London School of Economics (BSc economics 1965); London University (MSc political sociology 1967); Married Pamela Elizabeth Brenchley 1965 (1 son 3 daughters)

Non-political career: Lecturer, University College of Wales, Swansea 1966-79; Member: AUT, Amicus; Councillor Loughor and Lliw Valley Unitary District Council 1972-79-

Political career: Contested Taunton October 1974 general election. Member for Huddersfield East 1979-83, for Huddersfield 1983-2010, for Huddersfield (revised boundary) since 6 May 2010 general election; Opposition Spokesperson for: Employment and Education 1983-88, Home Affairs 1988-92, Disabled People's Rights 1992-94; *Select Committees:* Chair: Education and Employment (Education Sub-Committee) 1999-2001; Member: Liaison 1999-2010, Education and Employment (Employment Sub-Committee) 2000-01; Chair: Education and Skills/Children, Schools and Families 2001-10; Member: Liaison (Liaison Sub-Committee) 2002-10; Member, Co-operative Party; Chair, Labour Forum for Criminal Justice

Political interests: Trade, industry, finance, further education, education, economy, social enterprise and entrepreneurship; European Union, South America, USA, Kenya

Other organisations: Chair: Parliamentary Advisory Council on Transport Safety 1981-, Urban Mines 1995-, Networking for Industry/Policy Connect 1995-; Governor, London School of Economics 1995-; Chair, Cross-Party Advisory Group on Preparation for EMU 1998-; Vice-Chair, Joint Pre-Legislative Committee Investigating the Financial Services and Markets Bill 1998-; Chair, Cross-Party Advisory Group to Chancellor of the Exchequer on European Economic Reform; World Bank Business Partnership for Development Global Road Safety Partnership (GRSP); Chair National Educational Research and Development Trust; Fellow Industry and Parliament Trust 1982, 1996; Director and Trustee National Children's Centre; Chair John Clare Education and Environment Trust 2004-; Two honorary doctorates; FRSA, FRGS, City and Guilds Institute; Member, Royal Commonwealth Club; *Publications:* Co-author Harold Laski: A Life on the Left (1993)

Recreations: Walking, biography, films, social entrepreneurship

Barry Sheerman MP, House of Commons, London SW1A 0AA
Tel: 020 7219 5037 Fax: 020 7219 2404
E-mail: sheermanb@parliament.uk
Constituency: Labour Party, 6 Cross Church Street, Huddersfield, West Yorkshire HD1 2PT Tel: 01484 451382 Fax: 01484 451334
Website: www.barrysheerman.org.uk

GENERAL ELECTION RESULT

		%
Sheerman, B. (Lab/Co-op)*	15,725	38.8
Tweed, K. (Con)	11,253	27.8
Blanchard, J. (Lib Dem)	10,023	24.7
Cooper, A. (Green)	1,641	4.1
Firth, R. (BNP)	1,563	3.9
Cooney, P. (TUSC)	319	0.8
Majority	4,472	11.04
Electorate	66,316	
Turnout	40,524	61.11

**Member of last parliament*

CONSTITUENCY SNAPSHOT

Joseph Mallalieu held for Labour in 1945 and then sat for Huddersfield East for Labour for nearly 30 years from 1950, when the town was divided between two seats.

Mallalieu retired in 1979, to be succeeded by Barry Sheerman. The seat was recast as Huddersfield in 1983 and Sheerman won a majority of nearly 4,000. He increased his majority in subsequent elections and in 1997 achieved a lead of 15,848.

In 2005 there was a significant 7.1 per cent swing to the Lib Dems, who assumed second place but remained 8,351 behind Labour. Sheerman was re-elected with a majority of 4,472 in 2010.

Boundary changes removed the splitting of wards between Colne Valley and Dewsbury.

This seat is based on the West Yorkshire town of the same name. Once a highly prosperous town in the heyday of the woollen textile trade, Huddersfield still retains some industry such as precision engineering, chemicals and high quality textiles.

The biggest single employer, aside from the local authority and health service, is the town's university.

Huddersfield railway station is a grade one listed building and was described by John Betjeman as 'the most splendid station facade in England'. St George's Square, in which the station stands, won the Europa Nostra award for European architecture.

Alec Shelbrooke

Elmet and Rothwell

New constituency

Tel: 020 7219 3000
E-mail: alec.shelbrooke.mp@parliament.uk

Conservative

Date of birth: 10 January 1976

Education: St George's CoE Comprehensive School, Gravesend; Brunel University (mechanical engineering 1998)

Non-political career: Project administrator, Nanofactory, Leeds University 1999-; Member, MSF/Unite 1999-; Councillor, Leeds City Council 2004-

Political career: Contested Wakefield 2005 general election. Member for Elmet and Rothwell since 6 May 2010 general election; Deputy Chair, Elmet Conservative Association 2001-04

Political interests: Foreign affairs, transport, education

Recreations: Footbal, motor racing, cricket and music

Alec Shelbrooke MP, House of Commons, London SW1A 0AA
Tel: 020 7219 3000 E-mail: alec.shelbrooke.mp@parliament.uk
Constituency: Elmet and Rothwell Conservatives, 17 High Street, Tadcaster LS24 9AP Tel: 01937 838080
Website: www.elmetandrothwell.com

GENERAL ELECTION RESULT

		%
Shelbrooke, A. (Con)	23,778	42.6
Lewis, J. (Lab)	19,257	34.5
Golton, S. (Lib Dem)	9,109	16.3
Clayton, S. (BNP)	1,802	3.2
Oddy, D. (UKIP)	1,593	2.9
Nolan, C. (Ind)	250	0.5
Majority	4,521	8.10
Electorate	77,724	
Turnout	55,789	71.78

CONSTITUENCY SNAPSHOT

The predecessor Elmet constituency was formed in 1983 and was won quite comfortably for the Tories by Spencer Batiste in that year. He held it for the next 14 years, with a fairly consistent 47 per cent of the vote.

Colin Burgon won for Labour in 1997, when a swing of nearly 11 per cent landed him a majority of nearly 9,000. The Conservatives cut Burgon's majority in 2001 but failed to make any headway in 2005 and Labour's majority remained over 4,000.

Labour was defeated in the 2010 general election with a 9.8 per cent swing going to the Conservative candidate, Alec Shelbrooke.

The new constituency retained much of the Elmet seat and gained the small town of Rothwell.

This new West Yorkshire seat is a mixture of rural communities and small towns stretching round the east of Leeds.

Rothwell is the main market town in the former mining area south and east of Leeds which also includes the smaller Garforth and Swillington. These are all now primarily commuter towns for Leeds. Though all the mines are gone many former miners still live in the vicinity with associated health problems.

The A1-M1 link passing through the constituency was the first major private sector road project in the country.

Richard Shepherd

Aldridge-Brownhills (returning MP)

Boundary changes

Tel: 020 7219 5004
E-mail: shepherdr@parliament.uk

Conservative

Date of birth: 6 December 1942; Son of late Alfred Shepherd and Davida Sophia, neé Wallace

Education: Isleworth Grammar School, Middlesex; London School of Economics (BSc 1964; MSc 1967); John Hopkins School of Advanced International Studies (Diploma economics 1965)

Non-political career: Director, retail food business in London; Underwriter, Lloyd's 1974-94; Personal assistant to Edward Taylor MP (Glasgow Cathcart) October 1974 general election

Political career: Contested Nottingham East February 1974 general election. Member for Aldridge-Brownhills 1979-2010, for Aldridge-Brownhills (revised boundary) since 6 May 2010 general election; Introduced four Private Member's Bills: The Crown Immunity Bill 1986, Protection of Official Information Bill 1988, The Referendum Bill 1992, Public Interest Disclosure Bill; *Select Committees:* Member: Modernisation of the House of Commons 1997-2010, Public Administration 1997-2000, Joint Committee on Human Rights 2001-10

Other organisations: Co-Chair, Campaign for Freedom of Information; Member, South East Economic Planning Council 1970-74; *The Spectator*: Backbencher of the Year 1987, Parliamentarian of the Year 1995; Campaign for Freedom of Information 1988; Beefsteak, Chelsea Arts

Richard Shepherd MP, House of Commons, London SW1A 0AA
Tel: 020 7219 5004 Fax: 020 7219 0083
E-mail: shepherdr@parliament.uk
Constituency: 82 Walsall Road, Aldridge, Walsall,
West Midlands WS9 0JW Tel: 01922 451449 Fax: 01922 458078

GENERAL ELECTION RESULT

		%
Shepherd, R. (Con)*	22,913	59.3
Hussain, A. (Lab)	7,657	19.8
Jenkins, I. (Lib Dem)	6,833	17.7
Macnaughton, K. (Green)	847	2.2
Gray, S. (Christian)	394	1.0
Majority	15,256	39.48
Electorate	59,355	
Turnout	38,644	65.11

**Member of last parliament*

CONSTITUENCY SNAPSHOT

Aldridge-Brownhills was created in 1974, largely from the former mining constituencies of Brownhills, Pelsall and Walsall Wood. Labour's Geoffrey Edge took the seat in the two general elections of that year. His majority in February 1974 was 366 votes.

The Conservative victory of 1979 gave the seat to Richard Shepherd with over 50 per cent of the vote and he consolidated his lead through the 1980s with a margin of over 10,000 votes. In 2005 he was returned with a 5,508 majority. In 2010 Shepherd was re-elected with a much-increased majority of 15,256.

The seat gained the parts of two wards that were in Walsall North in exchange for the parts of Blakenall and St Matthew's wards that went to the north and south divisions respectively.

Aldridge-Brownhills is a predominantly middle-class, residential seat that sits just outside the northern fringes of the West Midlands conurbation among the suburbs of Walsall.

The constituency has two halves. Aldridge is predominantly a residential community, while Brownhills is an ex-mining and industrial town.

Jim Sheridan

Paisley and Renfrewshire North (returning MP)

No boundary changes

Tel: 020 7219 8314
E-mail: sheridanj@parliament.uk
Website: www.james-sheridan-mp.org.uk

Labour

Date of birth: 24 November 1952

Education: St Pius Secondary School; Married Jean McDowell 1977 (1 son 1 daughter)

Non-political career: Print room assistant Beaverbrook Newspapers 1967-70; Semi-skilled painter Barcley Curle 1970-74; M/C operator Bowater Containers 1974-79; Semi-skilled painter Yarrow Shipbuilders 1982-84; Material handler Pilkington Optronics 1984-99; TGWU 1984-: Convener 1984-99, Stand down official 1998-99; Renfrewshire Council: Councillor 1999-2003, Chair Scrutiny Board

Political career: Member for West Renfrewshire 2001-05, for Paisley and Renfrewshire North since 5 May 2005 general election; Team PPS Ministry of Defence 2005-06 (resigned over Lebanon conflict); *Select Committees:* Member: Information 2001-04, Broadcasting 2003-05, Public Accounts 2003-05, Armed Forces Bill 2005-06, International Development 2007-09, Chairmen's Panel 2009-10

Political interests: Foreign affairs, defence, employment, welfare, social affairs; Nigeria, Saudi Arabia

Other organisations: Inchinnan Community Association

Recreations: Keep fit, golf, football

Jim Sheridan MP, House of Commons, London SW1A 0AA
Tel: 020 7219 8314 E-mail: sheridanj@parliament.uk
Constituency: Mirren Court Three, Ground Floor, 123 Renfrew Road, Paisley, Renfrewshire PA3 4EA Tel: 0141-847 1457; 0141-847 1458
Fax: 0141-847 1395 Website: www.james-sheridan-mp.org.uk

GENERAL ELECTION RESULT

		%	+/-
Sheridan, J. (Lab)*	23,613	54.0	8.4
MacLaren, M. (SNP)	8,333	19.1	0.3
Campbell, A. (Con)	6,381	14.6	1.0
Dobson, R. (Lib Dem)	4,597	10.5	-7.7
Pearson, G. (Ind)	550	1.3	
Rollo, C. (SSP)	233	0.5	-1.1
Majority	15,280	34.96	
Electorate	63,704		
Turnout	43,707	68.61	

**Member of last parliament*

CONSTITUENCY SNAPSHOT

Paisley has been in Labour hands since 1924, gaining an extra MP in 1983 when boundary changes created Paisley North and Paisley South. The MPs for both (Allen Adams and Norman Buchan) died in the same month, and both by-elections were held in November 1990. Labour's Irene Adams was selected to succeed her late husband in Paisley North. She retired in 2005.

The seat was enlarged in 2005 when 12 of the 16 wards from Paisley North were combined with eight West Renfrewshire wards to form Paisley and Renfrewshire North. Jim Sheridan, previously MP for Renfrewshire West won the new seat with a majority of 11,001. He increased his majority to 15,280 in 2010.

The constituency occupies a stretch of the south bank of the river Clyde from Finlaystone to the edge of Glasgow. Paisley is industrial, but the west of the seat is more suburban, including areas such as Bishopton and Bridge of Weir. Linwood and Renfrew are in the east.

Renfrew was a shipbuilding centre and was the county town of Renfrewshire but Paisley has been the area's admin HQ for many years. Main employers are now found at the Braehead development as well as boiler firm Doosan Babcock.

Glasgow Airport is in this constituency just east of the M8. It is the largest private employer in the area. The airport has been expanded with the building of a new 'skyhub'. The £30 million development extends the main terminal building as well as building a new security area.

Gavin Shuker

Luton South

Boundary changes

Tel: 020 7219 3000
E-mail: gavin.shuker.mp@parliament.uk
Website: www.gavinshuker.org

Labour/Co-operative

Date of birth: 10 October 1981

Education: Icknield High School; Luton Sixth Form College; Girton College, Cambridge (BA social and political science 2003); Married Lucie 2007

Non-political career: Associate pastor, City Life Church, Cambridge 2003-06; Charity worker, Fusion UK 2003-08; Endis Ltd 2008-10; Church leader, City Life Church, Luton 2006-; Member, Unite

Political career: Member for Luton South since 6 May 2010 general election

Political interests: Political engagement, electoral reform, child poverty, student funding, transport policy (especially rail), international development, debt reduction, civil liberties; Bangladesh, India, Ireland, Pakistan, Poland, Portugal

Recreations: Cooking, real ale, church, formula one

Gavin Shuker MP, House of Commons, London SW1A 0AA
Tel: 020 7219 3000 E-mail: gavin.shuker.mp@parliament.uk
Constituency: c/o Luton Labour Party, 3 Union Street, Luton, Bedfordshire LU1 3AN Tel: 01582 730764
Website: www.gavinshuker.org

GENERAL ELECTION RESULT

		%
Shuker, G. (Lab/Co-op)	14,725	34.9
Huddleston, N. (Con)	12,396	29.4
Hussain, Q. (Lib Dem)	9,567	22.7
Rantzen, E. (Ind)	1,872	4.4
Blakey, T. (BNP)	1,299	3.1
Lawman, C. (UKIP)	975	2.3
Rhodes, S. (Ind)	463	1.1
Scheimann, M. (Green)	366	0.9
Hall, J. (Ind)	264	0.6
Choudhury, F. (Ind)	130	0.3
Lathwell, S. (Ind)	84	0.2
Sweeney, F. (WRP)	75	0.2
Majority	2,329	5.52
Electorate	59,962	
Turnout	42,216	70.40

CONSTITUENCY SNAPSHOT

The Conservatives lost the seat to Labour's Margaret Moran in 1997 with a swing of 11 per cent, giving her a majority of 23.5 per cent. There was a further small swing to Labour in 2001, increasing her majority to 10,133.

As in neighbouring Luton North, the Labour majority was considerably reduced in 2005. Margaret Moran was returned with a 5,650 majority. Despite Moran's expenses revelations Gavin Shuker held the seat for Labour with a majority of 2,329 in 2010.

The seat gained the part-ward of Biscot from Luton North, and lost its share of the Barnfield and Saints wards.

This constituency has more industry than its neighbour, Luton North, and incorporates the largest local shopping area, the Mall Arndale. The Capability Green development has also brought in major new investment from large companies such as Astra Zeneca, Barclays, and Ernst and Young. Luton South also includes the rapidly expanding international airport.

The local economy is aided by the fact that the transport and communication links are excellent. The M1 runs across the west of the seat and the Thameslink rail service takes commuters directly into London. Its location between Oxford and Cambridge on the west/east axis and between Birmingham and London north/south offers is ideal for many national and international investors.

Mark Simmonds

Boston and Skegness ***(returning MP)***

Boundary changes

Tel: 020 7219 8143
E-mail: simmondsm@parliament.uk
Website: www.marksimmondsmp.org

Conservative

Date of birth: 12 April 1964; Son of Neil Mortlock Simmonds, teacher, and Mary Griffith Simmonds, née Morgan, teacher

Education: Worksop College, Nottinghamshire; Trent Polytechnic (BSc urban estate surveying 1986); Married Lizbeth Josefina Hanomancin-Garcia 1994 (2 daughters 1 son)

Non-political career: Surveyor Savills 1986-88; Partner Strutt and Parker 1988-96; Director Hillier Parker 1997-99; Chairman Mortlock Simmonds Brown 1999-; London Borough of Wandsworth 1990-94: Councillor, Chairman: Property Committee 1991-92, Housing Committee 1992-94

Political career: Contested Ashfield 1997 general election. Member for Boston and Skegness 2001-10, for Boston and Skegness (revised boundary) since 6 May 2010 general election; Shadow Minister for: Public Services, Health and Education 2003-04, Education 2004, Foreign Affairs 2004-05, International Development 2005-07, Health 2007-10; *Select Committees:* Member: Environmental Audit 2001-03, Education and Skills 2001-03

Political interests: Economy, education, agriculture, foreign affairs, health; Latin America

Other organisations: Naval and Military; Honky Tonk Cricket

Recreations: Reading, history, rugby, tennis, family

Mark Simmonds MP, House of Commons, London SW1A 0AA
Tel: 020 7219 8143 Fax: 020 7219 1746
E-mail: simmondsm@parliament.uk
Constituency: The Conservative Association, Main Ridge West, Boston, Lincolnshire PE21 6QQ Tel: 01205 751414
Fax: 01205 751414 Website: www.marksimmondsmp.org

GENERAL ELECTION RESULT

		%
Simmonds, M. (Con)*	21,325	49.5
Kenny, P. (Lab)	8,899	20.6
Smith, P. (Lib Dem)	6,371	14.8
Pain, C. (UKIP)	4,081	9.5
Owens, D. (BNP)	2,278	5.3
Wilson, P. (Ind)	171	0.4
Majority	12,426	28.81
Electorate	70,529	
Turnout	43,125	61.15

**Member of last parliament*

CONSTITUENCY SNAPSHOT

The old constituency of Holland-with-Boston had been Conservative for a number of years before Boston and Skegness was created in 1997.

Sir Richard Body had represented the area since 1996. In 1997 his notional 11,000 majority did not materialise, as a 10.6 per cent swing to Labour reduced his majority to just 647. Sir Richard retired in 2001.

There was no Tory revival in 2001 for new MP Mark Simmonds, who won a slender 515-vote majority. However, in 2005 Simmonds was re-elected with a higher majority of 5,907. In 2010 Simmonds held the seat with a majority of 12,426.

Boundary changes moved the wards of Croft and Stickney entirely within the seat; previously they were shared with Louth and Horncastle.

Skegness and the other east-coast resorts added in 1995 are havens for retirement. However, contrary to the stereotype of seaside retirees, many people have retired to their seaside bungalows here from the industrial areas of the North and East Midlands.

Half a million people flock to the coast for their holidays, and the coastal strip has Europe's biggest concentration of caravans.

Aside from tourism, the local economy depends on agriculture and its associated industries, such as road haulage and food-packaging houses. Boston, the third largest town in the county, has a more mixed economy, with some light industry.

David Simpson

Upper Bann (returning MP)

No boundary changes

Tel: 020 7219 8533
E-mail: simpsond@parliament.uk

Date of birth: 16 February 1959

Education: Killicomaine High School; College of Business Studies, Belfast; Married Elaine Elizabeth (1 adopted son 2 adopted daughters)

Non-political career: Food manufacturing industry; Senior partner, Universal Meat Company; Craigavon Borough Council: Councillor 2001-, Deputy mayor 2003-04, Mayor 2004-05; Member, Northern Ireland Policing Board 2007-

Political career: Member for Upper Bann since 5 May 2005 general election; DUP Spokesperson for: Trade and Industry 2005-07, Young People 2007-, Transport 2007-09, International Development 2007-, Business, Innovation and Skills 2009-; *Select Committees:* Member: Joint Committee on Statutory Instruments and Commons Committee on Statutory Instruments 2006-09, Transport 2007-09, Northern Ireland Affairs 2009-10; Northern Ireland Assembly: MLA for Upper Bann 2003-; DUP: Vice-President; Vice-Chairman: Victims Committee, Council Association; Chairman, Upper Bann Constituency Association

Other organisations: Deputy Master, Loughall District Loyal Orange Order

David Simpson MP, House of Commons, London SW1A 0AA
Tel: 020 7219 8533 Fax: 020 7219 2347
E-mail: simpsond@parliament.uk
Constituency: 13 Thomas Street, Portadown BT62 3NP
Tel: 028 3833 2234 Fax: 028 3833 2123

GENERAL ELECTION RESULT

		%	+/-
Simpson, D. (DUP)*	14,000	33.8	-3.4
Hamilton, H. (UCUNF)	10,639	25.7	
O'Dowd, J. (Sinn Féin)	10,237	24.7	4.0
Kelly, D. (SDLP)	5,276	12.8	-0.1
Heading, B. (All)	1,231	3.0	0.8
Majority	3,361	8.12	
Electorate	74,732		
Turnout	41,383	55.38	

**Member of last parliament*

CONSTITUENCY SNAPSHOT

The constituency was created in 1983 and first held by UUP deputy leader Harold McCusker, who died in 1990. He was succeeded by David Trimble, who went on to lead the party and sign the Good Friday Agreement in 1998.

Trimble's majority was slashed to 2,058 in 2001. In the 2005 general election Trimble was beaten by the DUP's David Simpson, who secured a majority of 5,398. Simpson retained the seat for the DUP with 14,000 votes at the 2010 general election.

This seat is situated in the middle of Northern Ireland south of Lough Neagh.

The northern part of the seat takes in Lurgan and Portadown, along with the new town of Craigavon which takes up much of the space between the two.

The manufacturing sector in Craigavon is the strongest in Northern Ireland outside Belfast.

Banbridge to the south is growing rapidly and the town centre features 'The Cut' one of the first underpasses, completed in 1834.

The biggest attractions for tourists are Lough Neagh and the river Bann, which are well-known for coarse fishing along with the Oxford Island Nature Reserve.

Keith Simpson

Broadland (returning MP)

New constituency

Tel: 020 7219 4053
E-mail: keithsimpsonmp@parliament.uk
Website: www.keithsimpson.com

Conservative

Date of birth: 29 March 1949; Son of Harry Simpson and Jean Betty, neé Day

Education: Thorpe Grammar School, Norfolk; Hull University (BA history 1970); King's College, University of London; Married Pepita Hollingsworth 1984 (1 son)

Non-political career: Honorary Colonel Royal Military Police TA 1998-2007; Senior lecturer in war studies RMA Sandhurst 1973-86; Head of foreign affairs and defence section Conservative Research Department 1987-88; Special adviser to George Younger MP and Tom King MP as Secretaries of State for Defence 1988-90; Director Cranfield Security Studies Institute, Cranfield University 1991-97; Member: Royal United Services Institute for Defence Studies, British Commission for Military History, Lord Chancellor's Advisory Panel on the National Archives; Parliamentary Commissioner Commonwealth War Graves Commission 2008-

Political career: Contested Plymouth Devonport 1992 general election. Member for Mid Norfolk 1997-2010, for Broadland since 6 May 2010 general election; Opposition Spokesperson for Defence 1998-99; Opposition Whip 1999-2001; Opposition Spokesperson for Environment, Food and Rural Affairs 2001-02; Shadow Minister for: Defence 2002-05, Foreign Affairs 2005-10; *Select Committees:* Member: European Standing Committee A 1998, Environment, Food and Rural Affairs 2001-02; National vice-chair Federation of Conservative Students 1971-72; Chairman Conservative History Group 2003-

Political interests: Foreign affairs, defence, education, farming, countryside; France, Germany, Gulf States, Israel, Jordan, Poland, Saudi Arabia, Syria, USA

Other organisations: Council Member SSAFA 1997-2002; Trustee, History of Parliament Trust 2005-; *Publications:* The Old Contemptibles (1981); Joint Editor A Nations in Arms (1985); History of the German Army (1985); Editor The War the Infantry Knew 1914-1919 (1986)

Recreations: Stroking cats, reading, restaurants, cinema, malt whiskies, observing ambitious people

Keith Simpson MP, House of Commons, London SW1A 0AA
Tel: 020 7219 4053 Fax: 020 7219 0975
E-mail: keithsimpsonmp@parliament.uk
Constituency: Mid Norfolk Conservative Association, The Stable, Church Farm, Attlebridge, Norfolk NR9 5ST Tel: 01603 865763
Fax: 01603 865762 Website: www.keithsimpson.com

GENERAL ELECTION RESULT

		%
Simpson, K. (Con)*	24,338	46.2
Roper, D. (Lib Dem)	17,046	32.4
Barron, A. (Lab)	7,287	13.8
Agnew, S. (UKIP)	2,382	4.5
Crowther, E. (BNP)	871	1.7
Curran, S. (Green)	752	1.4
Majority	7,292	13.84
Electorate	73,168	
Turnout	52,676	71.99

**Member of last parliament*

CONSTITUENCY SNAPSHOT

Broadland is a new constituency. It replaces the now abolished Mid Norfolk seat and also includes part of the North Norfolk and Norwich North seats.

The Conservatives held Mid Norfolk from its creation in 1983 when Richard Ryder won the seat. He retired in 1997 and was replaced by Keith Simpson with a majority of 1,336. He increased his majority in both 2001 and 2005.

Simpson won the new seat with 24,338 votes, giving the Conservatives a majority of 7,292 at the 2010 general election.

Broadland spans from the northern suburbs of Norwich to the north parts of the city, including market towns such as Wroxham and Wensum.

The new constituency is a mainly residential area. The wards inherited from Mid Norfolk have a prevalence of seasonal work that is tied to the cycles of agriculture and tourism.

Many of the constituents in the Broadland area commute into Norwich. The area is relatively wealthy; there is a combination of young professionals who work in the city and a large proportion of pensioner constituents.

Aylsham and Acle are two market towns important for their connections with food processing and food production.

Marsha Singh

Bradford West (returning MP)

Boundary changes

Tel: 020 7219 4516
E-mail: singhm@parliament.uk

Date of birth: 11 October 1954; Son of Harbans Singh and late Kartar Kaur

Education: Belle Vue Boys Upper School; Loughborough University (BA languages, politics and economics of modern Europe 1976); Married Sital Kaur 1971 (widowed 2001) (1 son 1 daughter); married Kuldip Mann 2006 (1 stepson 1 stepdaughter)

Non-political career: Senior development manager, Bradford Community Health 1990-97; Member, Unison

Political career: Member for Bradford West since 1 May 1997 general election; PPS to Phil Woolas as Minister of State, Home Office and HM Treasury 2009-10; *Select Committees:* Member: Home Affairs 1997-05, International Development 2005-10; Chair: Bradford West Labour Party 1986-91, 1996-97, District Labour Party 1992

Political interests: European Union, health, education, small businesses; Pakistan/Kashmir, Palestine, India, Middle East, Europe

Recreations: Chess, bridge, reading

Marsha Singh MP, House of Commons, London SW1A 0AA
Tel: 020 7219 4516 Fax: 020 7219 0965
E-mail: singhm@parliament.uk
Constituency: Bradford West Constituency Office, 2nd Floor, 76 Kirkgate, Bradford, West Yorkshire BD1 1HZ Tel: 01274 402220
Fax: 01274 402211

GENERAL ELECTION RESULT

		%
Singh, M. (Lab)*	18,401	45.4
Iqbal, Z. (Con)	12,638	31.2
Hall-Matthews, D. (Lib Dem)	4,732	11.7
Sampson, J. (BNP)	1,370	3.4
Ali, A. (Respect)	1,245	3.1
Ford, D. (Green)	940	2.3
Smith, J. (UKIP)	812	2.0
Craig, N. (DN)	438	1.1
Majority	5,763	14.20
Electorate	62,519	
Turnout	40,576	64.90

**Member of last parliament*

CONSTITUENCY SNAPSHOT

Edward Lyons won the seat from the Conservatives for Labour in February 1974 and increased his majority in 1979, but defected to the Social Democrats in 1981. In 1983 the left-winger Max Madden won the seat for Labour. Madden steadily increased his margin over the next two elections. In 1992 he had a majority of nearly 10,000.

Max Madden was replaced by Marsha Singh as Labour candidate and won seat in 1997 with a reduced majority of 3,877.

In 2005 support for both Labour and the Conservatives fell while the Liberal Democrats and the BNP both increased their share of the vote, reducing Labour's majority to 3,026. Singh retained the seat with an increased majority of 5,763 at the 2010 general election.

Bradford West lost part-wards to Bradford East, Bradford South and Shipley, while gaining part-wards from Bradford South, Bradford North and Shipley.

The wards within the seat contain some major contrasts. The seat stretches west from the less affluent Manningham area near the city centre to the leafy, hilly suburbs of Clayton and Thornton.

Bradford has declined as a centre of textile manufacturing. This seat suffers very high unemployment. However, it also has a higher proportion of professional workers than Bradford East or South. The seat also has the lowest proportion of council tenants.

Chris Skidmore

Kingswood

Boundary changes

Tel: 020 7219 3000
E-mail: chris.skidmore.mp@parliament.uk
Website: www.chrisskidmore.com

Conservative

Date of birth: 17 May 1981

Education: Bristol Grammar School; Oxford University (history)

Non-political career: *Western Daily Press*; *People* magazine; Researcher, *Great Tales of English History*

Political career: Member for Kingswood since 6 May 2010 general election; Conservative Party: Member 1996-, Adviser on education, Director, Public Services Improvement Group

Other organisations: Chair, Bow Group; *Publications:* Author, Edward VI: The Lost King (Weidenfeld 2007)

Chris Skidmore MP, House of Commons, London SW1A 0AA
Tel: 020 7219 3000 E-mail: chris.skidmore.mp@parliament.uk
Constituency: c/o Bristol and South Gloucestershire Conservatives, 5 Westfield Park, Bristol BS6 6LT Tel: 0117-973 6811
Fax: 0117-923 8153 Website: www.chrisskidmore.com

GENERAL ELECTION RESULT

		%
Skidmore, C. (Con)	19,362	40.4
Berry, R. (Lab)*	16,917	35.3
FitzHarris, S. (Lib Dem)	8,072	16.9
Dowdney, N. (UKIP)	1,528	3.2
Carey, M. (BNP)	1,311	2.7
Foster, N. (Green)	383	0.8
Blundell, M. (England)	333	0.7
Majority	2,445	5.10
Electorate	66,361	
Turnout	47,906	72.19

**Member of last parliament*

CONSTITUENCY SNAPSHOT

Kingswood was carved out of Bristol South East and Wansdyke in 1974. The seat alternated between Labour and the Conservatives between 1974 and 1992. A Labour victory in 1992 saw Dr Roger Berry win by more than 2,000 votes. Despite the removal of the St George wards in 1995, and the substitution of areas of Wansdyke in their place, Berry was able to increase his majority to nearly 24 per cent in 1997. In 2005, Berry's vote fell however, he was still re-elected with a majority of 7,873. Berry was defeated in 2010 by Conservative Chris Skidmore with a 2,445 majority on a 9.4 per cent swing.

The seat gained Oldland Common ward from Wansdyke and three wards that were previously shared between the seat and Wansdyke and now entirely within Kingswood's boundaries. Two wards were lost to Bristol East as well as two wards and a part-ward to Filton and Bradley Stoke.

Kingswood profits directly from its proximity to Bristol, and from an economic perspective is an integral part of the greater Bristol area. Most residents work outside the constituency.

The largest private sector employers in the area are Rolls-Royce and British Aerospace Systems. Other large-scale employers include Royal Mail, Bendix Engineering and Sun Life.

Smaller-scale local industries and older manufacturing enterprises have been in decline in recent decades.

Dennis Skinner

Bolsover (returning MP)

Boundary changes

Tel: 020 7219 5107
E-mail: skinnerd@parliament.uk

Date of birth: 11 February 1932; Son of Edward Skinner

Education: Tupton Hall Grammar School, Clay Cross, Derbyshire; Ruskin College, Oxford; Married Mary Parker 1960 (died) (1 son 2 daughters)

Non-political career: Miner 1949-70; President, Derbyshire Miners 1966-70; Councillor: Clay Cross UDC 1960-70, Derbyshire County Council 1964-70; Former President, Derbyshire UDC Association

Political career: Member for Bolsover 1970-2010, for Bolsover (revised boundary) since 6 May 2010 general election; President, North East Derbyshire Constituency Labour Party 1968-71; Member, Labour Party National Executive Committee 1978-92, 1994-98, 1999-; Vice-Chair, Labour Party 1987-88, Chair 1988-89

Political interests: Inland waterways, energy, economic policy, environment, anti-Common Market, Third World

Recreations: Cycling, tennis, athletics (watching)

Dennis Skinner MP, House of Commons, London SW1A 0AA
Tel: 020 7219 5107 Fax: 020 7219 0028
E-mail: skinnerd@parliament.uk
Constituency: 1 Elmhurst Close, South Normanton, Alfreton, Derbyshire DE55 3NF Tel: 01773 581027

GENERAL ELECTION RESULT

		%
Skinner, D. (Lab)*	21,994	50.0
Rowley, L. (Con)	10,812	24.6
Hawksworth, D. (Lib Dem)	6,821	15.5
Radford, M. (BNP)	2,640	6.0
Calladine, R. (UKIP)	1,721	3.9
Majority	11,182	25.42
Electorate	72,766	
Turnout	43,988	60.45

**Member of last parliament*

CONSTITUENCY SNAPSHOT

Bolsover has been Labour since its creation in 1950, and has only ever had two MPs, both miners. Harold Neal had already been MP for the predecessor seat Clay Cross since a by-election in 1944. He represented the area for 25 years before handing over to Dennis Skinner in 1970.

His majority has never fallen below five figures, and no other party can hope to mount a credible challenge. Skinner's majority increased at every general election before 2001, in 1997 reaching 57 per cent and topping 27,000 votes. In 2005 his majority was a very safe 18,437.

Skinner held the seat with 21,994 votes giving Labour a majority of 11,182 at the 2010 general election.

Boundary changes have been slight, with the gain of Holmwood and Heath ward from North East Derbyshire.

Bolsover stretches 20 miles north to south on either side of the M1 motorway. The constituency used to have one of the biggest concentrations of coal mines in the country. That and the associated heavy industry, hydraulics and engineering dominated the local economy, but the last pit closed in 1994.

Manufacturing still accounted for almost double the national average of employees, but diversification has placed great emphasis on the retail and service sectors. The biggest single employer is the McArthur-Glen designer outlet at South Normanton.

Andy Slaughter

Hammersmith (returning MP)

New constituency

Tel: 020 7219 4990
E-mail: slaughtera@parliament.uk
Website: www.andyslaughter.com

Date of birth: 29 September 1960; Son of Alfred Frederick and Marie Frances Slaughter

Education: Latymer Upper School, London; Exeter University (BA English 1982); Single

Non-political career: Barrister specialising in housing and personal injury law 1993-; GMB; Unite; Governor William Morris Sixth Form 1994-; London Borough of Hammersmith and Fulham: Councillor 1986-2006, Council leader 1996-2005

Political career: Contested Uxbridge 1997 by-election. Member for Ealing, Acton and Shepherd's Bush 2005-10, for Hammersmith since 6 May 2010 general election; PPS: to Stephen Ladyman as Minister of State, Department for Transport 2005-07, to Lord Jones of Birmingham as Minister of State, Foreign and Commonwealth Office and Department for Business, Enterprise and Regulatory Reform 2007-08, to Lord Malloch-Brown as Minister of State, Foreign and Commonwealth Office 2007-09; *Select Committees:* Member: Regulatory Reform 2005-07, Children, Schools and Families 2007-09, Court of Referees 2007-10, Communities and Local Government 2009-10, London 2009-10

Political interests: International affairs, housing, education, health, transport; Carribean, EU, Somalia, Spain, Palestine

Other organisations: Management committee, Hammersmith and Fulham Community Law Centre 1990-

Andy Slaughter MP, House of Commons, London SW1A 0AA
Tel: 020 7219 4990 Fax: 020 7381 5074
E-mail: slaughtera@parliament.uk
Constituency: 28 Greyhound Road, London W6 8NX
Tel: 020 7610 1950 Fax: 020 7219 6775
Website: www.andyslaughter.com

GENERAL ELECTION RESULT

		%
Slaughter, A. (Lab)*	20,810	43.9
Bailey, S. (Con)	17,261	36.4
Emerson, M. (Lib Dem)	7,567	16.0
Miles, R. (Green)	696	1.5
Crichton, V. (UKIP)	551	1.2
Searle, J. (BNP)	432	0.9
Brennan, S. (Ind)	135	0.3
Majority	3,549	7.48
Electorate	72,348	
Turnout	47,452	65.59

**Member of last parliament*

CONSTITUENCY SNAPSHOT

This new seat combines the northern half of the old Hammersmith and Fulham seat with the Hammersmith and Fulham Borough wards from the old Ealing, Acton and Shepherd's Bush seat.

Hammersmith and Fulham had changed hands a number of times over the decades but was a Labour seat from 1997 until Greg Hands won the seat for the Tories in 2005 with a 7.3 per cent swing. Ealing, Acton and Shepherd's Bush has also switched between Labour and the Conservatives, but had been held by Labour since 1997, and present incumbent Andy Slaughter, since 2005. A shock result as Conservative Shaun Bailey was heavily tipped to win - Labour's Andrew Slaughter earned a respectable 3,549 majority.

In the south of the seat there are terraces of stylish single residences and high-income family housing. Moving north towards Shepherd's Bush there are larger ethnic communities and council estates like the White City and the Edward Woods Estate.

The northern part of the seat also includes the famous Wormwood Scrubs prison and the BBC television studios.

The seat's excellent transport connections have made its picturesque riverside residential areas extremely desirable to many professionals. The constituency is also just outside the congestion charging zone.

Rt Hon **Andrew Smith**

Oxford East (returning MP)

Boundary changes

Tel: 020 7219 4512
E-mail: smithad@parliament.uk
Website: www.andrewsmithmp.org.uk

Date of birth: 1 February 1951; Son of late David E. C. Smith and Georgina H. J. Smith

Education: Reading Grammar School; St John's College, Oxford (BA economics, politics 1972, BPhil sociology 1974); Married Valerie Lambert 1976 (1 son)

Non-political career: Member relations officer Oxford and Swindon Co-op Society 1979-87; Member, Union Shop, Distributive and Allied Workers; Councillor Oxford City Council 1976-87

Political career: Oxford East 1983. Member for Oxford East 1987-2010, for Oxford East (revised boundary) since 6 May 2010 general election; Opposition Spokesperson for Education 1988-92; Opposition Frontbench Spokesperson for Treasury and Economic Affairs 1992-96; Shadow Chief Secretary to the Treasury 1994-96; Shadow Secretary of State for Transport 1996-97; Minister of State, Department for Education and Employment (Minister for Employment, Welfare to Work and Equal Opportunities) 1997-99; Chief Secretary to the Treasury 1999-2002; Secretary of State for Work and Pensions 2002-04; *Select Committees:* Member: South East 2009-10

Political interests: Car industry, education, retail industry, housing, employment

Other organisations: Chair of governors, Oxford Polytechnic/Oxford Brookes University 1987-93; PC 1997; Hon. Doctorate, Oxford Brookes University; Blackbird Leys Community Association; President Blackbird Leys Boys and Girls Football Club

Recreations: Gardening, walking, windsurfing

Rt Hon Andrew Smith MP, House of Commons, London SW1A 0AA
Tel: 020 7219 4512 E-mail: smithad@parliament.uk
Constituency: Unit 1, Newtec Place, Magdalen Road,
Oxford OX4 1RE Tel: 01865 305080 Fax: 01865 305089
Website: www.andrewsmithmp.org.uk

GENERAL ELECTION RESULT

		%
Smith, A. (Lab)*	21,938	42.5
Goddard, S. (Lib Dem)	17,357	33.6
Argar, E. (Con)	9,727	18.8
Dhall, S. (Green)	1,238	2.4
Gasper, J. (UKIP)	1,202	2.3
O'Sullivan, D. (SEP)	116	0.2
Crawford, R. (EPA)	73	0.1
Majority	4,581	8.87
Electorate	81,886	
Turnout	51,651	63.08

**Member of last parliament*

CONSTITUENCY SNAPSHOT

Conservative Steve Norris took the seat in 1983 but was defeated by Labour's Andrew Smith in 1987. The Liberal Democrats became the second party in 2001 Smith's support peaked in 1997 in line with the national swing to Labour.

In 2005 Labour's majority was cut to 963. The 12.5 per cent drop in support for Labour was the largest fall suffered by any party in the region. Smith held the seat with a majority of 4,581 at the 2010 general election.

The seat gained five part-wards from Oxford West and Abingdon.

The constituency of Oxford East comprises most of the city of Oxford, including Cowley, Headington and the peripheral housing estates of Blackbird Leys, Rose Hill and Barton.

Ethnic communities contribute to the vibrant independence of the Cowley Road Area.

Major employers are the teaching hospitals, Oxford Brookes University, pharmaceutical, bio-technology, light engineering, printing and publishing companies. The Oxford Science Park and the business park at Cowley have also attracted many successful companies, including the European headquarters of Harley Davidson.

Angela Smith

Penistone and Stocksbridge ***(returning MP)***

New constituency

Tel: 020 7219 6713
E-mail: smithac@parliament.uk
Website: www.angelasmith-mp.org.uk

Date of birth: 16 August 1961; Daughter of Tom and Pat Smith

Education: Toll Bar Secondary School, Waltham; Nottingham University (BA English studies 1990); Newnham College, Cambridge (PhD 1994); Married Steven Wilson 2005 (1 stepson 1 stepdaughter)

Non-political career: Medical secretary, National Health Service 1979-84; Secretary, Barclays Bank 1984-87; Lecturer in English, Dearne Valley College, 1994-2003; UNISON; Councillor, Sheffield City Council 1996-2005; Member Regional Education and Skills Commission 2002-05; Chair 14-19 Board, Sheffield First for Learning and Work 2002-05

Political career: Member for Sheffield Hillsborough 2005-10, for Penistone and Stocksbridge since 6 May 2010 general election; PPS to Yvette Cooper: as Minister of State, ODPM/Department for Communities and Local Government 2005-08, as Chief Secretary to the Treasury 2008; *Select Committees:* Member: Regulatory Reform 2005-07, Court of Referees 2007-10, Transport 2009-10

Political interests: Education, pensions, skills agenda, environment and conservation

Recreations: Hill-walking, cooking

Angela Smith MP, House of Commons, London SW1A 0AA
Tel: 020 7219 6713 Fax: 020 7219 8598
E-mail: smithac@parliament.uk
Constituency: The Arc, Town Hall, Manchester Road, Stocksbridge, Sheffield, South Yorkshire S36 2DT Tel: 0114-283 1855
Fax: 0114-283 1850 Website: www.angelasmith-mp.org.uk

GENERAL ELECTION RESULT

		%
Smith, A. (Lab)*	17,565	37.8
Pitfield, S. (Con)	14,516	31.2
Cuthbertson, I. (Lib Dem)	9,800	21.1
James, P. (BNP)	2,207	4.7
French, G. (UKIP)	1,936	4.2
McEnhill, P. (England)	492	1.1
Majority	3,049	6.55
Electorate	68,501	
Turnout	46,516	67.91

**Member of last parliament*

CONSTITUENCY SNAPSHOT

The new constituency covers a similar area to the historic Penistone constituency with the western wards of Barnsley now combining with the northern wards of the old Sheffield Hillsborough constituency.

Both the Barnsley West and Penistone and Sheffield Hillsborough constituencies have been historically held by Labour.

Predominantly a mining seat, Barnsley West and Penistone returned former miners with five-figure majorities. In 2005 Michael Clapham secured a 11,314 majority for Labour.

Likewise, Sheffield Hillsborough has consistently returned Labour members. Angela C Smith has represented the seat since 2005 when she was returned with a 11,243-vote majority.

At the 2010 general election Smith was elected to the new seat with a majority of 3,049.

This predominantly semi-rural seat in South Yorkshire is a mixture of the west of Barnsley and the Pennine moorlands, with the northern edge of Sheffield.

Stretching from the urban north of Sheffield to include a number of towns and vast acres of Pennine moorland, Penistone and Stocksbridge is a highly diverse area. The constituency has most of its countryside and more prosperity in the west, with more deprivation to the east, while the Sheffield wards are largely suburban.

The traditional industries of coal mining and steel-making have declined, and the economy is now more diversified. Engineering and pipe-making continue but the service industries are expanding. Farming and business in Penistone is also important.

Chloe Smith

***Norwich North** (returning MP)*

Boundary changes

Tel: 020 7219 8449
E-mail: smithc@parliament.uk
Website: www.chloesmith.org.uk

Conservative

Date of birth: 17 May 1982; Daughter of David, furniture designer and maker, and Claire, teacher

Education: Methwold High School, Norfolk; Swaffham Sixth Form College, Norfolk; York University (BA English literature 2004)

Non-political career: Former constituency assistant to Gillian Shephard MP and Bernard Jenkin MP; Business consultant Deloitte 2004-09; Parliamentary assistant to James Clappison MP; Governor, Swaffham School

Political career: Member for Norwich North 23 July 2009 by-election to 2010, for Norwich North (revised boundary) since 6 May 2010 general election; Assistant Government Whip 2010-; *Select Committees:* Member: Work and Pensions 2009-10; Member: Conservative Friends of Israel 2001-, Conservative Party Implementation Team 2008-09, Tory Reform Group 2009-

Political interests: Work and pensions, public services, machinery of government

Recreations: Arts, including theatre and drawing; sports, including cycling, badminton

Chloe Smith MP, House of Commons, London SW1A 0AA
Tel: 020 7219 8449 E-mail: smithc@parliament.uk
Constituency: Norwich North Conservatives, Christ Church Centre, Magdalen Road, Norwich NR3 4LA Tel: 01603 414774
Fax: 01603 414774 Website: www.chloesmith.org.uk

GENERAL ELECTION RESULT

		%
Smith, C. (Con)*	17,280	40.6
Cook, J. (Lab/Co-op)	13,379	31.4
Stephen, D. (Lib Dem)	7,783	18.3
Tingle, G. (UKIP)	1,878	4.4
Goldfinch, J. (Green)	1,245	2.9
Richardson, T. (BNP)	747	1.8
Holden, B. (Ind)	143	0.3
Holland, A. (Christian)	118	0.3
Majority	3,901	9.16
Electorate	65,258	
Turnout	42,573	65.24

**Member of last parliament*

CONSTITUENCY SNAPSHOT

Norwich North consistently returned Labour MPs from 1950 until 1983. The seat went to the Conservatives' Patrick Thompson at the 1983 general election. With significant boundary changes and a 10.6 per cent swing to Labour, Ian Gibson secured a majority of 9,470 in 1997.

In 2005 Dr Gibson's vote decreased again, though he was re-elected with a majority of 5,459. Gibson resigned from Parliament in 2009 and at the by-election Conservative Chloe Smith took the seat with a 7,438 majority. Smith was re-elected at the general election with a 3,901 majority.

Norwich North lost four wards to Broadland and one part-ward to Norwich South and gained two part-wards.

Norwich North is less urban than the seat covering the southern half of the city. As well as containing a considerable amount of council housing in the Mousehold area of Norwich, the constituency takes in the suburbs of Sprowston and the rural area to the north surrounding Norwich airport.

The seat skirts the city centre, following the loop of the river Yare. The majority of the city's large firms lie south of this division in the Norwich South constituency, but many of Norwich North's inhabitants are employed in the city's major industries: insurance, financial services, media and in the manufacturing sector.

Henry Smith

Crawley

No boundary changes

Tel: 020 7219 3000
E-mail: henry.smith.mp@parliament.uk

Conservative

Date of birth: 14 May 1969; Son of late John Edwin Smith and Josephine Ann Smith

Education: Frensham Heights, Farnham; University College London (BA philosophy 1991); Married Jennifer Lois Ricks 1994 (1 son 1 daughter)

Non-political career: Property investment business; West Sussex County Council: Councillor 1997-, Council leader 2003-; Councillor, Crawley Borough Council 2002-04

Political career: Contested Crawley 2001 and 2005 general elections. Member for Crawley since 6 May 2010 general election

Political interests: Local government, foreign policy; USA

Other organisations: Crawley Conservative Club; Flag Institute; *Publications:* Co-author, Direct Democracy: An Agenda for a New Model Party (2005)

Recreations: Vexillology, skiing

Henry Smith MP, House of Commons, London SW1A 0AA
Tel: 020 7219 3000 E-mail: henry.smith.mp@parliament.uk
Constituency: Crawley Conservative Association, Crawley Conservative Club, Jubilee Walk, Three Bridges, Crawley, West Sussex RH10 1LQ
Tel: 07899 800037 Website: www.crawleyconservatives.org.uk

GENERAL ELECTION RESULT

		%	+/-
Smith, H. (Con)	21,264	44.8	36.8
Oxlade, C. (Lab)	15,336	32.3	-6.7
Vincent, J. (Lib Dem)	6,844	14.4	-1.0
Trower, R. (BNP)	1,672	3.5	0.5
French, C. (UKIP)	1,382	2.9	0.7
Smith, P. (Green)	598	1.3	
Khan, A. (JP)	265	0.6	0.1
Hubner, A. (Ind)	143	0.3	
Majority	5,928	12.48	
Electorate	72,781		
Turnout	47,504	65.27	

CONSTITUENCY SNAPSHOT

Crawley was created from part of the constituency of Horsham in 1983, consisting of an urban core surrounded by a rural fringe. The MP from 1983 until 1997 was the Conservative Nicholas Soames, grandson of Winston Churchill; in 1992 he had a majority of 12.5 per cent over Labour.

Labour's Laura Moffat won the seat in 1997 on a swing of 13.4 per cent with a majority of 23 per cent, in their first ever win in West Sussex.

Moffatt held onto the seat in 2001 but with a reduced majority of 6,770. In 2005 there was a 8.5 per cent swing to the Conservatives. After three recounts Moffatt won by just 37 votes.

Labour was defeated in the 2010 general election with a 6.3 per cent swing to the Conservative Henry Smith, who secured a 5,928 majority.

Despite a history going back to the Bronze Age, Crawley was designated a new town in 1946.

The town is divided into a series of residential neighbourhoods around the town centre, each with its own schools, shops and community facilities.

It grew rapidly during the 1960s and 1970s in line with the growth of its major employer, Gatwick airport, together with 300 associated businesses.

Julian Smith

Skipton and Ripon

Boundary changes

Tel: 020 7219 3000
E-mail: julian.smith.mp@parliament.uk
Website: www.votejuliansmith.com

Conservative

Date of birth: 1971

Education: Millfield School, Somerset; Balfon High School; Birmingham University (English and history 1993); Married Amanda

Non-political career: Squash coach, Perpignan; Landscape Promotions 1993-94; The Bird Moore Partnership 1994-99; Founder and managing director, Arq International, London 1999-

Political career: Member for Skipton and Ripon since 6 May 2010 general election; Deputy chair, Bethnal Green and Bow Conservatives 2008-09

Political interests: Business, education, welfare, universities and skills, agriculture

Other organisations: Junior international squash player

Recreations: Violin and piano

Julian Smith MP, House of Commons, London SW1A 0AA
Tel: 020 7219 3000 E-mail: julian.smith.mp@parliament.uk
Constituency: Skipton and Ripon Conservative Association, Churchill House, 19 Otley Street, Skipton BD23 1DY Tel: 01756 792092
Fax: 01756 798742 Website: www.votejuliansmith.com

GENERAL ELECTION RESULT

		%
Smith, J. (Con)	27,685	50.6
Flynn, H. (Lib Dem)	17,735	32.4
Hazelgrove, C. (Lab)	5,498	10.1
Mills, R. (UKIP)	1,909	3.5
Allen, B. (BNP)	1,403	2.6
Bell, R. (Ind)	315	0.6
Gilligan, D. (Youth)	95	0.2
Leakey, R. (Currency)	84	0.2
Majority	9,950	18.18
Electorate	77,381	
Turnout	54,724	70.72

CONSTITUENCY SNAPSHOT

Skipton and Ripon was formed in 1983 out of the two seats named after their respective towns, both Conservative for most of their history.

In 1983, while Ripon and Skipton both lost wards, Skipton kept its MP, Conservative John Watson. David Curry took over from Watson in 1987. He polled large majorities over the Liberals throughout his tenure and in 2005 had a lead of 11,620. Curry retired in 2010 and Julian Smith held the seat for the Conservatives with a majority of 9,950.

Boundary changes have been minimal.

This is a largely rural constituency taking in a swathe of land in the south west of North Yorkshire. As well as the two named towns, it includes much of the Yorkshire Dales.

The attractive cathedral city of Ripon and the Pennine town of Skipton, with its ancient castle and market, draw tourists and ramblers from all over the country. Other attractions in the area include the stunning World Heritage Site Fountains Abbey as well as Bolton Abbey and Malham Tarn.

There is some light industry around the two main towns and some small hi-tech business parks including one set around the country mansion Broughton Hall. The biggest single private sector employer is the Skipton Building Society.

Nick Smith

Blaenau Gwent

Boundary changes

Tel: 020 7219 3000
E-mail: nick.smith.mp@parliament.uk
Website: www.nick-smith.net

Date of birth: 14 January 1960

Education: Tredegar Comprehensive School; Coventry University (BA history, politics and international relations 1981); Birkbeck College, London (MSc economic change 1991); Divorced (2 daughters)

Non-political career: Constituency organiser to Frank Dobson MP 1989-91; Organiser, Wales Labour Party 1991-93; Head of membership development, Labour Party 1993-98; Consultant, international campaining 1998-2000; Campaign manager, public policy, NSPCC 2000-04; Secretary general, European Parliamentary Labour Party 2005-06; Director, policy and partnerships, Royal College of Speech and Language Therapists 2006-; AEEU; Transport and General Workers' Union; GMB; Community; Unite; London Borough of Camden Council: Former councillor, Member, then executive member, Education 2003-05; Governor, nursery school

Political career: Member for Blaenau Gwent since 6 May 2010 general election; Election agent to Emily Thornberry MP 2005

Political interests: Economic development, health, children

Other organisations: Member: Aneurin Bevan Society, Tribune, Fabian Society; Fellow, Royal Geographical Society

Recreations: Hiking, singing, reading, chess

Nick Smith MP, House of Commons, London SW1A 0AA
Tel: 020 7219 3000 E-mail: nick.smith.mp@parliament.uk
Website: www.nick-smith.net

GENERAL ELECTION RESULT

		%
Smith, N. (Lab)	16,974	52.4
Davies, D. (Ind)*	6,458	19.9
Smith, M. (Lib Dem)	3,285	10.1
Stevenson, L. (Con)	2,265	7.0
Davies, R. (PIC)	1,333	4.1
King, A. (BNP)	1,211	3.7
Kocan, M. (UKIP)	488	1.5
O'Connell, A. (SLP)	381	1.2
Majority	10,516	32.46
Electorate	52,438	
Turnout	32,395	61.78

**Member of last parliament*

CONSTITUENCY SNAPSHOT

Created in 1983, this constituency is the successor to the famous Ebbw Vale seat, represented by Aneurin Bevan from 1929 to 1960. He was succeeded by Michael Foot.

After Foot's retirement in 1992, Llewellyn Smith kept the seat in Labour hands.

Labour's dominance evaporated after Llew Smith's decision to stand down in 2005. Maggie Jones was selected from an all-women shortlist but the majority of local party members didn't attend the selection meeting, with a protest being held outside. Local Assembly Member, Peter Law, resigned from the Labour Party to stand against Ms Jones. He beat her with a 9,121 majority.

Peter Law died in 2006. Labour failed to regain the seat and Dai Davies, Law's election agent, held on with a majority of 2,484. Labour won back this normally safe seat from Dai Davies, with a massive 29.2 per cent swing and a 10,516 majority.

This valley's constituency in South Wales includes the towns of Ebbw Vale and Tredegar.

The towns that make up the seat were built on coal and steel. Ebbw Vale was famous for its now closed steelworks. A diverse industrial base has replaced much of the traditional heavy industry and the profile of businesses spans sectors such as pharmaceuticals, food processing, electronics and high-tech engineering.

One major project is the £300 million regeneration of the former steelworks. The project includes residential buildings, recreational facilities, a new school, a theatre and a new hospital.

Owen Smith

Pontypridd

Boundary changes

Tel: 020 7219 3000
E-mail: owen.smith.mp@parliament.uk

Education: Sussex University (history and French); Married Liz (2 sons 1 daughter)

Non-political career: Producer, BBC Wales -2002; Special Adviser to Paul Murphy MP as: Secretary of State for Wales 2002, Secretary of State for Northern Ireland 2002-05; Director, policy and communications, Pfizer 2005; Corporate affairs director, Amgen UK

Political career: Contested Blaenau Gwent 2006 by-election. Member for Pontypridd since 6 May 2010 general election

Owen Smith MP, House of Commons, London SW1A 0AA
Tel: 020 7219 3000 E-mail: owen.smith.mp@parliament.uk

GENERAL ELECTION RESULT

		%
Smith, O. (Lab)	14,220	38.8
Powell, M. (Lib Dem)	11,435	31.2
Gonzalez, L. (Con)	5,932	16.2
Bellin, I. (PIC)	2,673	7.3
Bevan, D. (UKIP)	1,229	3.4
Parsons, S. (SLP)	456	1.2
Watson, D. (Christian)	365	1.0
Matthews, J. (Green)	361	1.0
Majority	2,785	7.59
Electorate	58,219	
Turnout	36,671	62.99

CONSTITUENCY SNAPSHOT

Dr Kim Howells was first elected at the by-election in 1989 following the death of Brynmor John, who had represented the seat since 1970. Howells saw off the Plaid Cymru challenge with a majority of 10,794.

Dr Howells built his majority to a 1997 peak of 23,129. His majority has declined since then but his majority in 2005 was a still large 13,191. Despite a 13.3 per cent swing to the Liberal Democrats, Labour's Owen Smith held the seat for the party with a majority of 2,785.

Boundary changes here are just about the biggest in South Wales: over 12,000 electors have been removed, Cilfyndd and Glynoch have moved to Cynon Valley while Pentyrch and Creigiaw/St Fagans are now in Cardiff West.

Based around the market town of Pontypridd, the constituency includes former mining villages on the periphery of the valleys towards the outskirts of Cardiff.

Pontypridd and Tonyrefail in the north are old mining and commercial towns.

The Royal Mint is also located here at Llantrisant and provides employment for the area as does the Dewi Sant Hospital.

There are also a sizeable number of commuters to Cardiff, and a notable student population due to the large University of Glamorgan campus at Treforest.

Sir **Robert Smith**

West Aberdeenshire and Kincardine ***(returning MP)***

No boundary changes

Tel: 020 7219 3531
E-mail: robert.smith.mp@parliament.uk
Website: www.libdems.org.uk/party/people/sir-robert-smith.0110.html

Date of birth: 15 April 1958; Son of late Sir (William) Gordon Smith, Bt, VRD, and of Diana Lady Smith

Education: Merchant Taylors' School, Northwood; Aberdeen University (BSc); Married Fiona Anne Cormack MD 1993 (3 daughters)

Non-political career: Family estate manager until 1997; Councillor, Aberdeenshire Council 1995-97; JP 1997

Political career: Contested (SDP/Liberal Alliance) Aberdeen North 1987 general election. Member for West Aberdeenshire and Kincardine 1997-2005, for West Aberdeenshire and Kincardine (revised boundary) since 5 May 2005 general election; Liberal Democrat: Whip 1999-2001, Spokesperson for: Scotland 1999-2001, Trade and Industry 2005-06, Energy 2005-06, Deputy Chief Whip 2001-06, Deputy Shadow Leader of the House 2007-10; Whip 2008-10; *Select Committees:* Member: Scottish Affairs 1999-2001, European Standing Committee A 2000-01, Procedure 2001-10, Trade and Industry 2001-05, Unopposed Bills (Panel) 2001-10, Standing Orders 2001-10, Accommodation and Works 2003-05, International Development 2007-09, Energy and Climate Change 2009-10

Political interests: Electoral reform, offshore oil and gas industry, rural affairs

Other organisations: General Council Assessor, Aberdeen University 1994-98; Director, Grampian Transport Museum 1995-97; Vice-convener, Grampian Joint Police Board 1995-97; Member, Electoral Reform Society; Royal Yacht Squadron, Royal Thames Yacht

Recreations: Hill-walking, sailing

Sir Robert Smith Bt MP, House of Commons, London SW1A 0AA
Tel: 020 7219 3531 Fax: 020 7219 4526
E-mail: robert.smith.mp@parliament.uk
Constituency: 6 Dee Street, Banchory, Kincardineshire AB31 5ST
Tel: 01330 820330 Fax: 01330 820338
Website: www.libdems.org.uk/party/people/sir-robert-smith.0110.html

GENERAL ELECTION RESULT

		%	+/-
Smith, R. (Lib Dem)*	17,362	38.4	-7.8
Johnstone, A. (Con)	13,678	30.3	1.9
Robertson, D. (SNP)	7,086	15.7	4.4
Williams, G. (Lab)	6,159	13.6	0.5
Raikes, G. (BNP)	513	1.1	
Atkinson, A. (UKIP)	397	0.9	
Majority	3,684	8.15	
Electorate	66,110		
Turnout	45,195	68.36	

**Member of last parliament*

CONSTITUENCY SNAPSHOT

Tory Alick Buchanan-Smith was MP in this area from 1964 until his death in 1991. Nicol Stephen won the Kincardine and Deeside by-election for the Liberal Democrats, but his tenure was short-lived and George Kynoch won back the seat for the Conservatives in 1992.

The seat got its current name for the 1997 election at which Kynoch was defeated by Liberal Democrat Sir Robert Smith. In 2001 Sir Robert nearly doubled his majority.

In the 2005 boundary changes West Aberdeenshire and Kincardine was largely left together. Its northern boundary was tidied up and some wards from Gordon were added. At the general election Smith increased his majority to 7,471. Robert Smith's majority was halved to 3,684 in 2010.

This seat has a mixture of farming land, commuter towns such as Portlethen and tourist areas on the coast at Stonehaven and in the Upper Deeside area around the Queen's holiday home of Balmoral.

The rich farmland of the Mearns forms the backdrop to Lewis Grassic Gibbon's famous A Scots Quair. It is a prosperous area, with high-levels of home ownership as well as large landowner estates.

The well-paid jobs in Scotland's richest city and the low unemployment rate have attracted inward migration of working-age people and their families over the past two decades. The constituency's population is relatively youthful with a higher proportion of children and a lower proportion of pensioners than in the rest of the region.

Hon **Nicholas Soames**

Mid Sussex (returning MP)

Boundary changes

Tel: 020 7219 4143
E-mail: soamesn@parliament.uk
Website: www.nicholassoames.org.uk

Conservative

Date of birth: 12 February 1948; Son of late Baron and Lady Soames

Education: Eton College; Mons Officer Cadet School 1966; Married Catherine Weatherall 1981 (divorced 1988) (1 son); married Serena Smith 1993 (1 daughter 1 son)

Non-political career: Lieutenant, 11th Hussars 1967-72; Equerry to Prince of Wales 1970-72; Stockbroker 1972-74; PA to: Sir James Goldsmith 1974-76, US Senator Mark Hatfield 1976-78; Assistant director, Sedgwick Group 1979-81; Senior Vice President, MARSH; Member Council of RUSI

Political career: Contested Dumbartonshire Central 1979 general election. Member for Crawley 1983-97, for Mid Sussex 1997-2010, for Mid Sussex (revised boundary) since 6 May 2010 general election; PPS: to John Gummer as Minister of State for Employment and Chairman of the Conservative Party 1984-86, to Nicholas Ridley as Secretary of State for the Environment 1987-89; Joint Parliamentary Secretary, Ministry of Agriculture, Fisheries and Food 1992-94; Minister of State for the Armed Forces, Ministry of Defence 1994-97; Shadow Secretary of State for Defence 2003-05: Member Shadow Cabinet 2004-05; *Select Committees:* Member: Public Administration 1999, Joint Committee on Consolidation of Bills Etc 2001-10, Standards and Privileges 2006-10; Member 1922 Committee Executive 2000-03, 2005-06

Political interests: Defence, foreign affairs, trade and industry, aerospace, aviation, agriculture and countryside matters

Other organisations: Amber Foundation; Member Council National Trust; White's, Turf, Pratt's

Recreations: Country pursuits, racing

Hon Nicholas Soames MP, House of Commons, London SW1A 0AA
Tel: 020 7219 4143 Fax: 020 7219 2998
E-mail: soamesn@parliament.uk
Constituency: 5 Hazelgrove Road, Haywards Heath,
West Sussex RH16 3PH Tel: 01444 452590 Fax: 01444 415766
Website: www.nicholassoames.org.uk

GENERAL ELECTION RESULT

		%
Soames, N. (Con)*	28,329	50.7
Tierney, S. (Lib Dem)	20,927	37.5
Boot, D. (Lab)	3,689	6.6
Montgomery, M. (UKIP)	1,423	2.6
Brown, P. (Green)	645	1.2
Minihane, S. (BNP)	583	1.0
Thunderclap, B. (Loony)	259	0.5
Majority	7,402	13.25
Electorate	77,182	
Turnout	55,855	72.37

**Member of last parliament*

CONSTITUENCY SNAPSHOT

Tim Renton held the seat for the Conservatives in the 1980s and 90s. He was replaced by Nicholas Soames, Winston Churchill's grandson, in 1997 with a majority of 6,854. In 2001 Soames improved his majority with a 1.1% swing. Soames' majority fell to 5,890 in 2005.

The Conservatives retained the seat in 2010 with 28,329 votes giving Soames a majority of 7,402.

The seat gained four part-wards from Arundel and South Downs, two part-wards from Horsham and lost a part-ward to each of those seats.

Mid Sussex has a healthy and vibrant economy. The service sector accounts for around 70 per cent of employment, with around a third of people in managerial positions. Many of Mid Sussex's residents commute each day to London, Brighton, Crawley or Gatwick, especially from Haywards Heath.

The three major towns in Mid Sussex have their own particular economic features. Burgess Hill is an important office and manufacturing centre, particularly well known for its high-tech telecommunication and pharmaceutical companies. East Grinstead contains a number of regional headquarters in the finance, travel and general office sectors as well as leading companies in the industrial sector. Finally, Haywards Heath is a major centre for the banking, insurance and finance sectors.

Anna Soubry

Broxtowe

Boundary changes

Tel: 020 7219 3000
E-mail: anna.soubry.mp@parliament.uk

Conservative

Date of birth: 7 December 1956

Education: Hartland Comprehensive School, Worksop; Birmingham University (law); Bar Finals

Non-political career: Trainee reporter, Alloa; Presenter and reporter, *North Tonight*, Grampian TV; Presenter and reporter, Central TV: *Central News East, Central Weekend, Heart of the Country*; Barrister 1995-; Former Shop Steward, National Union of Journalists

Political career: Contested Gedling 2005 general election. Member for Broxtowe since 6 May 2010 general election; Member, Conservatives 2002-

Other organisations: Rector, Stirling University

Recreations: Gardening, cooking

Anna Soubry MP, House of Commons, London SW1A 0AA
Tel: 020 7219 3000 E-mail: anna.soubry.mp@parliament.uk
Constituency: Broxtowe Conservatives, Conservative HQ, King Edward Court, King Edward Street, Nottingham NG1 1EW
Tel: 0115-948 4576 Fax: 0115-948 3392
Website: www.broxtoweconservatives.com

GENERAL ELECTION RESULT

		%
Soubry, A. (Con)	20,585	39.0
Palmer, N. (Lab)*	20,196	38.3
Watts, D. (Lib Dem)	8,907	16.9
Shore, M. (BNP)	1,422	2.7
Cobb, C. (UKIP)	1,194	2.3
Mitchell, D. (Green)	423	0.8
Majority	389	0.74
Electorate	72,042	
Turnout	52,727	73.19

**Member of last parliament*

CONSTITUENCY SNAPSHOT

Broxtowe was recreated in 1983 and after a 28-year absence and was a traditional Conservative stronghold. However, in 1997 Labour's Dr Nick Palmer overturned a majority of nearly 10,000 to win the seat. Palmer then went on to increase his vote in 2001, with a majority of nearly 6,000. However, in 2005 the Labour vote in the area mirrored national trends, and Palmer's majority was more than halved to 2,296.

Palmer was defeated in 2010 with a 2.6 per cent swing to the Conservative Candidate, Anna Soubry.

Boundary changes were minimal.

Covering the western fringes of the west and north west of Nottingham, Broxtowe has changed significantly politically and socially since the early 1990s.

A predominantly middle-class constituency containing a mix of open countryside and more built-up suburbs, Broxtowe largely escaped the economic turmoil of the 1980s and early 90s that beset neighbouring constituencies more reliant on mining and manufacturing.

Boots, based in the east of the constituency, remains the major employer in the area. The service industry has now taken over manufacturing as the largest source of employment, with a number of call-centres opening throughout the area.

Sir **Peter Soulsby**

Leicester South ***(returning MP)***

Boundary changes

Tel: 020 7219 8332
E-mail: soulsbyp@parliament.uk
Website: www.petersoulsby.org

Date of birth: 27 December 1948; Son of Robert Soulsby and Mary, née Reed

Education: Minchenden School, Southgate, London; City of Leicester College (BEd 1973); Married Alison Prime 1969 (3 daughters)

Non-political career: Special educational needs teacher 1973-90; British Waterways: Board member 1998-2004, Vice-chair 2000-04; Unite; Leicester City Council: Councillor 1973-2003, Council leader 1981-94, 1995-99; Chaired Leicester City Challenge Project 1994-98; Member Audit Commission 1993-99

Political career: Contested Harborough 1979 general election, Leicester South 2004 by-election. Member for Leicester South 2005-10, for Leicester South (revised boundary) since 6 May 2010 general election; *Select Committees:* Member: Environment, Food and Rural Affairs 2005-10, Crossrail Bill 2006-07, Modernisation of the House of Commons 2007-10, Procedure 2009-10, Transport 2009-10, East Midlands 2009-10; Election agent to Jim Marshall in 1997 and 2001 general elections

Political interests: Local government, environment, transport

Other organisations: Convenor National Executive Committee, Unitarian and Free Christian Churches 2006-; Kt 1999

Recreations: Inland waterways

Sir Peter Soulsby MP, House of Commons, London SW1A 0AA
Tel: 020 7219 8332 Fax: 020 7219 0983
E-mail: soulsbyp@parliament.uk
Constituency: 60 Charles Street, Leicester LE1 1FB
Tel: 0116-251 1927 Website: www.petersoulsby.org

GENERAL ELECTION RESULT

		%
Soulsby, P. (Lab)*	21,479	45.6
Gill, P. (Lib Dem)	12,671	26.9
Grant, R. (Con)	10,066	21.4
Waudby, A. (BNP)	1,418	3.0
Dixey, D. (Green)	770	1.6
Lucas, C. (UKIP)	720	1.5
Majority	8,808	18.69
Electorate	77,175	
Turnout	47,124	61.06

**Member of last parliament*

CONSTITUENCY SNAPSHOT

At the 1983 election Labour's James Marshall lost by just seven votes to the Conservative Derek Spencer. Similar to Leicester East which also fell to the Tories in 1983, Marshall regained the seat for Labour in 1987 and had steadily built his majority until his death in 2004. In 1997 his majority stood at 16,000 but was reduced to 13,243 in 2001.

Parmjit Singh Gill won a 2004 by-election for the Lib Dems but it was a short-lived victory as Peter Soulsby won the seat back for Labour in 2005 with a 3,717 majority. In 2010 Soulsby held the seat with a majority of 8,808.

Boundary changes were negligible: Castle ward is now entirely within the seat having previously been shared with Leicester West.

This constituency falls in a mixed, residential part of Leicester. Like the eastern division, Leicester South has a large Asian community.

Leicester is one of the most culturally diverse cities. Leicester has the second largest Hindu population of any city outside India, after Cape Town in South Africa. The city's Diwali celebrations are the largest outside India.

More than half the workforce is employed in manual occupations. However, it also includes middle-class housing along the A6 to the south east, especially in Knighton.

Rt Hon **John Spellar**

Warley (returning MP)

Boundary changes

Tel: 020 7219 0674
E-mail: spellarj@parliament.uk
Website: www.johnspellar.labour.co.uk

Date of birth: 5 August 1947; Son of late William David Spellar, and of Phyllis Kathleen Spellar

Education: Dulwich College, London; St Edmund's Hall, Oxford (BA philosophy, politics and economics 1969); Married Anne Rosalind Wilmot 1981 (died 2003) (1 daughter)

Non-political career: National Officer, Electrical, Electronic, Telecommunication and Plumbing Union 1969-97

Political career: Contested Bromley 1970 general election. Member for Birmingham Northfield 28 October 1982 by-election to June 1983. Contested Birmingham Northfield 1987 general election. Member for Warley West 1992-97, for Warley 1997-2010, for Warley (revised boundary) since 6 May 2010 general election; Opposition Whip 1992-94; Opposition Spokesperson for: Northern Ireland 1994-95, Defence, Disarmament and Arms Control 1995-97; Ministry of Defence: Parliamentary Under-Secretary of State 1997-99, Minister of State for the Armed Forces 1999-2001; Minister for Transport: Department of Transport, Local Government and the Regions 2001-02, Department for Transport 2002-03; Minister of State, Northern Ireland Office 2003-05; Government Whip 2008-10; *Select Committees:* Member: Joint Committee on Conventions 2006, Finance and Services 2009-10

Political interests: Energy, electronics industry, motor industry, construction industry, defence; Australia, Israel, USA

Other organisations: PC 2001; Rowley Regis and Blackheath Labour; Brand Hall Labour

Recreations: Gardening

Rt Hon John Spellar MP, House of Commons, London SW1A 0AA
Tel: 020 7219 0674 Fax: 020 7219 2113
E-mail: spellarj@parliament.uk
Constituency: Brandhall Labour Club, Tame Road, Oldbury, West Midlands B68 0JT Tel: 0121-423 2933 Fax: 0121-423 2933
Website: www.johnspellar.labour.co.uk

GENERAL ELECTION RESULT

		%
Spellar, J. (Lab)*	20,240	52.9
Parmar, J. (Con)	9,484	24.8
Keating, E. (Lib Dem)	5,929	15.5
Harvey, N. (UKIP)	2,617	6.8
Majority	10,756	28.11
Electorate	63,106	
Turnout	38,270	60.64

**Member of last parliament*

CONSTITUENCY SNAPSHOT

Warley replaced the old Warley East seat in 1997, and before that the constituency was known as Smethwick, which in 1964 gained notoriety when Conservative Peter Griffiths defeated the incumbent Labour MP. The seat has remained with Labour since 1966. The current MP is Labour's John Spellar, here since 1997.

Spellar was re-elected in 2010 with a 10,756 majority and 52.9 per cent share of the vote.

Boundary changes mean the new seat sees Old Warley, St Pauls, Langley and Smethwick wards consolidated in this seat. The acquisition of all of St Pauls and Langley has extended Warley fairly substantially in its north-western corner. Meanwhile, chunks of Oldbury went to West Bromwich West, and Blackheath to Halesowen and Rowley Regis.

Warley is on the western outskirts of Birmingham. The area now has a multi-racial population.

Just outside Birmingham, Warley is very similar to the constituencies it borders within the city. It is an economically deprived area.

There are significant numbers of ethnic communities, a large number of whom are from the Indian subcontinent.

Rt Hon **Caroline Spelman**

Meriden (returning MP)

Boundary changes

Tel: 020 7219 4189
E-mail: spelmanc@parliament.uk
Website: www.carolinespelman.com

Conservative

Date of birth: 4 May 1958; Daughter of late Marshall and Helen Margaret Cormack

Education: Herts and Essex Grammar School for Girls, Bishops Stortford; Queen Mary College, London (BA European studies 1980); Married Mark Spelman 1987 (2 sons 1 daughter)

Non-political career: Sugar beet commodity secretary, National Farmers Union 1981-84; Deputy director, International Confederation of European Beetgrowers, Paris 1984-89; Research fellow, Centre for European Agricultural Studies 1989-93; Director, Spelman, Cormack and Associates, Food and Biotechnology Consultancy 1989-

Political career: Contested Bassetlaw 1992 general election. Member for Meriden 1997-2010, for Meriden (revised boundary) since 6 May 2010 general election; Opposition Whip 1998-99; Opposition Spokesperson for: Health 1999-2001, Women's Issues 1999; Shadow: Secretary of State for International Development 2001-03, Minister for Women 2001-04, Secretary of State for: the Environment 2003-04, Local and Devolved Government Affairs 2004-05, Office of the Deputy Prime Minister/Communities and Local Government 2005-07, 2009-10; Secretary of State for Environment, Food and Rural Affairs 2010-; *Select Committees:* Member: Science and Technology 1997-98; Co-opted member executive committee Conservative Women's National Council; Member: Board of directors governing council Conservative Christian Fellowship, Advisory Board for Women2Win; Chairman Conservative Party 2007-09

Political interests: Environment, agriculture, international development; France, Germany, India, Malawi, Pakistan

Other organisations: Board Member, Parliamentary Office of Science and Technology (POST) 1997-2001; Trustee Snowdon Awards Scheme for Disabled; PC 2010; Parliamentary Choir; Member: Lords and Commons Ski Club, Lords and Commons Tennis Club; *Publications:* A Green and Pleasant Land (Bow Group, 1994); The non-food uses of agricultural raw materials (CABI, 1991)

Recreations: Tennis, skiing, cooking, gardening

Rt Hon Caroline Spelman MP, House of Commons, London SW1A 0AA Tel: 020 7219 4189 Fax: 020 7219 0378
E-mail: spelmanc@parliament.uk
Constituency: 2 Manor Road, Solihull, West Midlands B91 2BH
Tel: 0121-711 2955 Fax: 0121-711 4322
Website: www.carolinespelman.com

GENERAL ELECTION RESULT

		%
Spelman, C. (Con)*	26,956	51.7
Williams, E. (Lab)	10,703	20.5
Slater, S. (Lib Dem)	9,278	17.8
O'Brien, F. (BNP)	2,511	4.8
Allcock, B. (UKIP)	1,378	2.6
Stanton, E. (Green)	678	1.3
Sinclaire, N. (SMRA)	658	1.3
Majority	16,253	31.16
Electorate	83,826	
Turnout	52,162	62.23

**Member of last parliament*

CONSTITUENCY SNAPSHOT

Labour won in 1955, 1964 and 1966, punctuated by a Conservative victory in 1959. In 1968 the Tories retook the seat at a by-election and held it in 1970. John Tomlinson won for Labour in both 1974 elections but lost in 1979. Over the next three general elections Conservative MP Ian Mills built up his majority.

Ian Mills died shortly before the 1997 election. His successor, Caroline Spelman won with a margin of 582. By 2005 this had increased to a healthy 7,009. Spelman more than doubled her majority in 2010 to 16,253.

Meriden lost parts of Elmdon and St Alphege wards to Solihull, but gain parts of Bickenhall and Blythe wards. Its south-west corner will extend further west, absorbing what was Solihull's part of Bickenhill ward.

Situated in the commuter belt between Birmingham and Coventry, Meriden claims to be the geographical heart of England.

Meriden is at the centre of England's transport system, the home of Birmingham International Airport, the intersection of the M6 and M42 and rail links through Birmingham. It contains some of the most affluent residential areas in the West Midlands in the southern half of the seat around Knowle and Dorridge.

The transformation of Solihull town centre helped bolster retail employment, while the Blyth Valley Business Park created employment opportunities.

Mark Spencer

Sherwood

Boundary changes

Tel: 020 7219 3000
E-mail: mark.spencer.mp@parliament.uk

Conservative

Date of birth: 20 January 1970; Son of Cyril and Dorothy Spencer

Education: Colonel Frank Seeley School, Calverton; Shuttleworth Agricultural College, Bedfordshire (farming course; National Certificate agriculture); Married Claire (1 son 1 daughter)

Non-political career: Farmer; Proprietor: Spring Lane Farm Shop, Floralands Garden Village, Lambley; Councillor, Gedling District Council 2003-; Nottinghamshire County Council: Councillor 2005-, Shadow spokesman for community safety and partnerships 2006-; Governor, Woodborough Woods Foundation School; Member, East Midlands Regional Assembly 2009-10

Political career: Member for Sherwood since 6 May 2010 general election

Political interests: Rural affairs, education, health, employment, business; UK

Other organisations: National Federation of Young Farmers' Clubs: Chair 2000, Member; Royal Agricultural Society of England: Trustee, Associate 2005, Honorary show director 2007-09, Fellow 2010; Trustee, The Core Centre, Calverton

Recreations: Family, farming, socialising

Mark Spencer MP, House of Commons, London SW1A 0AA
Tel: 020 7219 3000 E-mail: mark.spencer.mp@parliament.uk
Constituency: c/o Sherwood Conservative Association, Sherwood House, 99 Main Street, Calverton, Nottingham NG14 6FG
Tel: 0115-965 4867 Website: www.sherwoodconservatives.com

GENERAL ELECTION RESULT

		%
Spencer, M. (Con)	19,211	39.2
Oldknow, E. (Lab)	18,997	38.8
Moore, K. (Lib Dem)	7,283	14.9
North, J. (BNP)	1,754	3.6
Parker, M. (UKIP)	1,490	3.0
Swan, R. (Ind)	219	0.5
Majority	214	0.44
Electorate	71,043	
Turnout	48,954	68.91

CONSTITUENCY SNAPSHOT

Sherwood was formed in 1983 with parts of the Newark, Ashfield and Gedling constituencies. Conservative Andrew Stewart won that year by just 658 votes, but increased his majority in 1987.

In the midst of the collapse of the area's mining industry in 1992 Paddy Tipping won Sherwood for the Labour party with a majority of 2,910. In 1997 he increased this to a massive 16,812. While dipping since then, Tipping's lead in 2001 and 2005 was 9,373 and 6,652 respectively.

In 2010 Mark Spencer took the seat for the Conservatives with a small majority of 214.

Boundary changes were minimal: the seat gained four part-wards from Gedling while losing one part-ward to both Newark and Gedling.

Sherwood covers the central part of Nottinghamshire, and contains the former mining communities of Hucknall, Ravenshead, Ollerton and Calverton.

Sherwood's economy was devastated by the pit closures of the 1980s and early 1990s. The town of Ollerton, in particular, was almost completely reliant on the local pit. The constituency used to have seven pits - it now has none.

The textiles industry was one of the largest employers of women. While this industry has not declined as sharply as mining, there have been job losses.

The area has slowly attracted other forms of investment such as smaller manufacturing firms, light engineering and distribution plants.

Rt Hon Sir **John Stanley**

Tonbridge and Malling (returning MP)

No boundary changes

Tel: 020 7219 4506

Conservative

Date of birth: 19 January 1942

Education: Repton School, Derby; Lincoln College, Oxford; Married Susan Giles 1968 (1 son 1 daughter 1 son deceased)

Non-political career: Conservative Research Department 1967-68; Research Associate, Institute for Strategic Studies 1968-69; Rio Tinto-Zinc Corp. Ltd 1969-79

Political career: Contested Newton 1970 general election. Member for Tonbridge and Malling since 28 February 1974 general election; PPS to Margaret Thatcher as Leader of the Opposition 1976-79; Minister for Housing and Construction 1979-83; Minister for the Armed Forces 1983-87; Minister of State, Northern Ireland Office 1987-88; *Select Committees:* Member: Foreign Affairs 1992-, Quadripartite (Committees on Strategic Export Controls)/Arms Export Controls 2006-10

Other organisations: Commonwealth Parliamentary Association (CPA): UK Branch: Member, Executive Committee 1999-, Hon Treasurer 2007-10; PC 1984; Knighted 1988

Recreations: Music and the arts, sailing

Rt Hon Sir John Stanley MP, House of Commons, London SW1A 0AA Tel: 020 7219 4506
Constituency: 91 High Street, West Malling, Maidstone, Kent ME19 6NA Tel: 01732 842794 Fax: 01732 873960
E-mail: contact@tcconservatives.com

GENERAL ELECTION RESULT

		%	+/-
Stanley, J. (Con)*	29,723	57.9	5.2
Simpson, L. (Lib Dem)	11,545	22.5	3.1
Griffiths, D. (Lab)	6,476	12.6	-11.2
Waller, D. (UKIP)	1,911	3.7	
Dawe, S. (Green)	764	1.5	
Easter, M. (NF)	505	1.0	
Rogers, L. (England)	390	0.8	
Majority	18,178	35.43	
Electorate	71,790		
Turnout	51,314	71.48	

**Member of last parliament*

CONSTITUENCY SNAPSHOT

Sir John Stanley has represented this seat since 1974 with mostly five-figure majorities and around 50 per cent of the vote.

At the 1997 general election he was returned with a majority of 10,230. In 2001 Stanley's majority was reduced to 8,250. This returned to 13,352 at the 2005 election.

In 2010 Stanley secured a majority of 18,178.

Within the boundaries of this constituency, which stretches across a wide expanse of west Kent, there are numerous towns and villages including Edenbridge, East and West Peckham, East and West Malling, as well as Tonbridge itself.

The River Medway flows in a north easterly direction through Tonbridge towards the Medway Gap in the North Downs on its way to the sea.

Tonbridge and Malling is a fairly diverse constituency, home to commuters, light industry, high-tech development, and there is still a strong if reduced farming community.

Tonbridge is midway between London and the south coast. Road links are good, and the constituency is close to the Channel Tunnel and Ashford International and Ebbsfleet railway stations. Tourism is an important industry for Kent and this area is no exception.

Andrew Stephenson

Pendle

No boundary changes

Tel: 020 7219 3000
E-mail: andrew.stephenson.mp@parliament.uk

Conservative

Date of birth: 17 February 1981

Education: Poynton County High School; Royal Holloway, University of London (BSc business management 2002)

Non-political career: Partner, Stephenson and Threader 2002-; Councillor, Macclesfield Borough Council 2003-07

Political career: Member for Pendle since 6 May 2010 general election; National deputy chair, Conservative Future 2001-02; Chair, Tatton Conservative Association 2006

Political interests: Environment, small business, education, health, economy, local government

Other organisations: Member, SELRAP (Skipton East Lancashire Railway Action Partnership); Colne British Legion, Earby Conservative Club, Barnoldswick Conservative Club

Recreations: Manchester City FC, walking, food and drink

Andrew Stephenson MP, House of Commons, London SW1A 0AA
Tel: 020 7219 3000 E-mail: andrew.stephenson.mp@parliament.uk
Constituency: 9 Cross Street, Nelson, Lancashire BB9 7EN
Tel: 01282 614748 Website: www.pendleconservatives.com

GENERAL ELECTION RESULT

		%	+/-
Stephenson, A. (Con)	17,512	38.9	7.3
Prentice, G. (Lab)*	13,927	30.9	-5.9
Anwar, A. (Lib Dem)	9,095	20.2	-2.8
Jackman, J. (BNP)	2,894	6.4	0.3
Cannon, G. (UKIP)	1,476	3.3	1.5
Masih, R. (Christian)	141	0.3	
Majority	3,585	7.96	
Electorate	66,417		
Turnout	45,045	67.82	

**Member of last parliament*

CONSTITUENCY SNAPSHOT

The seat was created in 1983 and replaced the almost identical Lancashire seat of Nelson and Colne.

Labour's Gordon Prentice first won the seat in 1992 from the Conservative John Lee. Gordon Prentice's majority has fallen since the high-point of 1997, standing at just 2,180 in 2005.

Prentice was defeated in 2010. The seat was taken by the Conservative candidate, Andrew Stephenson who secured a majority of 3,585.

Pendle is situated on the east of Lancashire bordering North and West Yorkshire. The area itself has a population of about 90,000 and covers the towns of Nelson and Colne, bordering Burnley to the west.

Pendle is a relatively socially-mixed constituency. As is common among old Lancashire towns, terraced housing covers much of the area.

Manufacturing is healthy here, employing about a third of the workforce. Many of these jobs are provided by employers such as Rolls-Royce and Silentnight beds.

There is also a small tourist trade in this area, as the beautiful countryside provides an idyllic setting. The famous Pendle witches add a further interest for visitors.

John Stevenson

Carlisle

Boundary changes

Tel: 020 7219 3000
E-mail: john.stevenson.mp@parliament.uk
Website: johnstevenson-conservative.co.uk

Conservative

Date of birth: 1963

Education: Dundee University (BA history and politics); College of Law, Chester

Non-political career: Trainee solicitor, Dickinson Dees, Newcastle upon Tyne 1990; Solicitor, now partner, Bendles, Carlisle; Councillor, Carlisle City Council 1999-

Political career: Member for Carlisle since 6 May 2010 general election; Chair: Carlisle Conservative Association, Penrith and the Border Conservative Association, North Cumbria Conservatives

Other organisations: Committee member, Chatsworth Tennis Club

Recreations: Golf, running, sport

John Stevenson MP, House of Commons, London SW1A 0AA
Tel: 020 7219 3000 E-mail: john.stevenson.mp@parliament.uk
Constituency: 31 Chiswick Street, Carlisle CA1 1HJ Tel: 01228 521192
Fax: 01228 512066 Website: johnstevenson-conservative.co.uk

GENERAL ELECTION RESULT

		%
Stevenson, J. (Con)	16,589	39.3
Boaden, M. (Lab)	15,736	37.3
Hughes, N. (Lib Dem)	6,567	15.6
Stafford, P. (BNP)	1,086	2.6
Owen, M. (UKIP)	969	2.3
Reardon, J. (Green)	614	1.5
Metcalfe, J. (TUSC)	376	0.9
Howe, P. (Ind)	263	0.6
Majority	853	2.02
Electorate	65,263	
Turnout	42,200	64.66

CONSTITUENCY SNAPSHOT

In 1964 the Labour candidate Ron Lewis was elected, ousting the incumbent Independent Conservative Donald Johnson. Eric Martlew was first elected in 1987.

Labour won 57 per cent of the vote in 1997. Results in 2005 differed very little from 2001: Eric Martlew's majority held firm at 5,695, decreasing by only seven votes since 2001.

Martlew retired in 2010 and John Stevenson took the seat for the Conservatives with a 7.7 per cent swing giving him a small majority of 853.

Carlisle gained Stanwix Urban part-ward and Wetheral ward from Penrith and the Border.

Carlisle is a predominantly urban constituency comprising the city itself, as well as outlying rural towns. Industry within the seat is focused on food manufacturing, with agriculture playing a role in the lives of many inhabitants. Tourism is also important with much historical interest attached to the city's Roman heritage, notably Hadrian's World.

United Biscuits and Northern Foods employ around 2,000 workers each. The area also acts as a centre for local government and the retail industry.

Carlisle's strategic position has also ensured its growth as a communication centre, firstly as a railway centre with the main West Coast line from London to Glasgow and the scenic Carlisle to Settle railway, and secondly as the crossing point of the M6/A74 north-south motorway and A69 east-west trunk road.

Bob Stewart

Beckenham

Boundary changes

Tel: 020 7219 3000
E-mail: bob.stewart.mp@parliament.uk

Conservative

Date of birth: 7 July 1949; Son of Jock Stewart MC and Joan Stewart

Education: Chigwell School; Royal Military Academy Sandhurst 1969; Wales University (international politics 1977); Married Claire Podbielski 1994 (4 children; 2 children from first marriage)

Non-political career: British Army, Cheshire Regiment 1969-96: Served in Northern Ireland, British UN Commander, Bosnia 1992-93, Policy chief, Supreme HQ Allied Powers Europe, Belgium –1996; Senior consultant, Hill & Knowlton 1997-98; Managing director, WorldSpace 1999-2001; Freelance writer and lecturer 2002-

Political career: Member for Beckenham since 6 May 2010 general election

Political interests: Defence, veteran service personnel, disabled children; Eastern Europe, Middle East, Northern Ireland

Other organisations: President, Action for Armed Forces; Vice-president, UKNDA; Distinguished Service Order 1993; Army and Navy; *Publications:* Broken Lives 1993; Leadership Under Pressure 2009

Bob Stewart MP, House of Commons, London SW1A 0AA
Tel: 020 7219 3000 E-mail: bob.stewart.mp@parliament.uk
Constituency: Beckenham Conservative Association, 31 Beckenham Road, Beckenham, Kent BR3 4PR Tel: 07771 863894
Website: www.beckenhamconservatives.com

GENERAL ELECTION RESULT

		%
Stewart, B. (Con)	27,597	57.9
Jenkins, S. (Lib Dem)	9,813	20.6
Egan, D. (Lab)	6,893	14.5
Brolly, O. (UKIP)	1,551	3.3
Tonks, R. (BNP)	1,001	2.1
Garrett, A. (Green)	608	1.3
Eastgate, D. (England)	223	0.5
Majority	17,784	37.29
Electorate	66,219	
Turnout	47,686	72.01

CONSTITUENCY SNAPSHOT

As part of the Bromley seat before 1948 and then as Beckenham, this area has always been represented by the Conservatives. The seat was made safer for the Tories with the addition of West Wickham when the Ravensbourne constituency was abolished in 1997.

Between 1992 and 1997 the seat was represented by Conservative Piers Merchant. Shortly after the election, Merchant resigned and a by-election was won by the Conservative Jacqui Lait, who retained the seat for the Tories with a majority of 1,227.

Lait consolidated her majority of in 2001 and 2005 before retiring in 2010. Bob Stewart held this ultra-safe Conservative seat with a 3.2 per cent swing in his favour and a 17,784 majority.

Boundary changes transferred the Crystal Palace and Penge and Cator wards to Lewisham West and Penge. Beckenham gained two wards from Bromley and Chislehurst.

Almost three-quarters of housing in Beckenham is owner-occupied. Residences are dominated by 1930s suburban semis and detached houses in Beckenham, Shortlands and Kelsey Park.

A new hospital in Farnborough, to the south of Beckenham, opened in 2003, providing better facilities for Beckenham and taking pressure off the smaller health facilities within the seat.

Many people in Beckenham depend on trains to commute into central London, with a number of overland stations within the constituency travelling to London Bridge, London Waterloo and London Victoria.

Iain Stewart

Milton Keynes South

New constituency

Tel: 020 7219 3000
E-mail: iain.stewart.mp@parliament.uk
Website: www.ias4mks.com

Conservative

Date of birth: 18 September 1972; Son of James Stewart and Leila Stewart

Education: Hutchesons' Grammar School, Glasgow; Exeter University (BA politics 1993) Chartered Management Institute (Diploma management 2006)

Non-political career: Trainee chartered accountant, Coopers and Lybrand 1993-1994; Head of research, Scottish Conservative Party 1994-98; Parliamentary Resources Unit, House of Commons: Deputy director 1998-2001, Director 2001-06; Associate, Odgers, Ray and Berndtson 2006-; Councillor, Shenley Brook End and Tattenhoe Parish Council 2005-

Political career: Contested Milton Keynes South West 2001 and 2005 general elections. Member for Milton Keynes South since 6 May 2010 general election; Contested Glasgow Rutherglen constituency 1999 Scottish Parliament election

Political interests: Constitution, economy, transport, energy security

Other organisations: Founder member, Atlantic Bridge 1999; Bletchley Conservative; President, Stony Stratford Conservative 2007-; *Publications:* It's Our Money! Who Spends it? (London Scottish Tory Club 2004) The Scottish Constituition – In Search of a New Settlement (Policy Institute 2007)

Recreations: Opera, good food, wine and whisky, gym, running marathons

Iain Stewart MP, House of Commons, London SW1A 0AA
Tel: 020 7219 3000 E-mail: iain.stewart.mp@parliament.uk
Constituency: Milton Keynes South West Conservatives, 105 Queensway, Bletchley, Milton Keynes, Buckinghamshire MK2 2DN
Tel: 01908 372038 Fax: 01908 375982 Website: www.ias4mks.com

GENERAL ELECTION RESULT

		%
Stewart, I. (Con)	23,034	41.6
Starkey, P. (Lab)*	17,833	32.2
Jones, P. (Lib Dem)	9,787	17.7
Pinto, P. (UKIP)	2,074	3.8
Tait, M. (BNP)	1,502	2.7
Deacon, K. (Green)	774	1.4
Nti, S. (CPA)	245	0.4
Worth, J. (NRP)	84	0.2
Majority	5,201	9.40
Electorate	90,487	
Turnout	55,333	61.15

**Member of last parliament*

CONSTITUENCY SNAPSHOT

Dr Phyllis Starkey won Labour the seat from the Tories in 1997 with a swing of nearly 15 per cent. Her majority fell in both 2001 and 2005 to 6,978 and 4,010 respectively.

Starkey was defeated in the new seat at the 2010 general election with a 6.2 per cent swing to the Conservative candidate, Iain Stewart, who secured a 5,201 general election.

Milton Keynes South is made up predominantly from wards from the old Milton Keynes South West seat. However, the new seat now includes all of Bletchley and Fenny Stratford, and Walton Park wards, which were previously shared with Milton Keynes North East.

As well as some of the new town areas in Milton Keynes, this seat encompasses the old railway towns of Bletchley (famous for its Second World War code-breaking activities), Stony Stratford and Fenny Stratford.

The largest employer in the constituency is the Open University. Otherwise employment, interest and money are represented by a host of enterprises, with the accent on information technology, design and engineering, and call-centres.

The Milton Keynes Partnership is aiming to build 2,000 new homes per year. Debates continue on how the necessary physical and social infrastructure can be built in parallel with this development.

Rory Stewart

Penrith and The Border

Boundary changes

Tel: 020 7219 3000
E-mail: rory.stewart.mp@parliament.uk
Website: www.rorystewart.co.uk

Conservative

Date of birth: 1973

Education: Eton College; Balliol College, Oxford (politics, philosophy and economics)

Non-political career: Officer, Black Watch; Foreign and Commonwealth Office: British Embassy, Indonesia, British Representative, Montenegro -2000; Walked across Pakistan, Iran, Afghanistan, India and Nepal 2000-02; Provincial governor, Maysan and Dhi Qar provinces, Iraq 2003; Founder and chief executive, Turquoise Mountain 2006-08; Ryan Family professor, practice of human rights and director, Carr Centre for Human Rights Policy, Harvard University 2009-

Political career: Member for Penrith and The Border since 6 May 2010 general election

Political interests: Agriculture, armed forces, rural affairs; Afghanistan

Other organisations: OBE 2004; Royal Society of Literature Ondaatje Award 2004; Radio France award 2009; *Publications:* Author: The Places in Between (Picador 2004), The Prince of the Marshes (Harcourt 2006), Occupational Hazards: My Time Governing in Iraq (Picador 2006)

Rory Stewart MP, House of Commons, London SW1A 0AA
Tel: 020 7219 3000 E-mail: rory.stewart.mp@parliament.uk
Constituency: Penrith and The Border Conservative Association, 31 Chiswick Street, Carlisle, Cumbria CA1 1HJ Tel: 01228 521192
Website: www.rorystewart.co.uk

GENERAL ELECTION RESULT

		%
Stewart, R. (Con)	24,071	53.4
Thornton, P. (Lib Dem)	12,830	28.5
Cannon, B. (Lab)	5,834	12.9
Stanyer, J. (UKIP)	1,259	2.8
Davidson, C. (BNP)	1,093	2.4
Majority	11,241	24.93
Electorate	64,548	
Turnout	45,087	69.85

CONSTITUENCY SNAPSHOT

Conservative David Maclean was first elected in July 1983 when he won the by-election caused by the elevation to the peerage of William Whitelaw, who had been MP here since 1955.

On that occasion the voters gave Maclean a majority of just over 500. By 2001 Maclean's majority was 14,677.

Despite a strong Lib Dem challenge in 2005, there was little change to David Maclean's share of the vote: he polled over 51 per cent, losing just 256 votes from the 2001 election, with a majority of 11,904.

David Maclean retired in 2010 and was succeeded by Rory Stewart who won the seat with a majority of 11,241.

Boundary changes were minimal.

This massive northern Cumbrian constituency stretches from the Solway Firth to the Yorkshire Dales, from the Scottish border at Gretna Green to Helvellyn in the heart of the Lakes. The only towns of note are Penrith and Appleby.

Penrith and the Border is sparsely populated and an economy predominately based in agriculture. Lakes, forests and fells combine to offer some of the country's most beautiful scenery and tourism is a major industry.

The M6 motorway and the West Coast main railway pass through the constituency between Scotland and the South. The scenic Carlisle-Settle railway provides access to Leeds and Yorkshire.

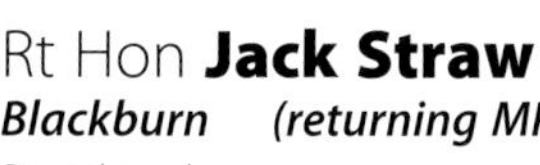

Rt Hon **Jack Straw**

Blackburn (returning MP)

Boundary changes

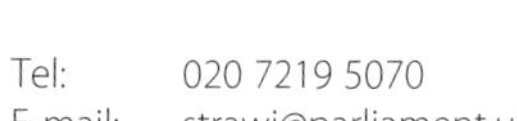

Tel: 020 7219 5070
E-mail: strawj@parliament.uk

Date of birth: 3 August 1946; Son of late Walter Arthur Straw, insurance clerk, and Joan Sylvia Straw, nursery teacher

Education: Brentwood School; Leeds University (LLB 1967); Inns of Court School of Law 1972; Married Anthea Weston (divorced 1978) (1 daughter deceased); married Alice Perkins 1978 (1 son 1 daughter)

Non-political career: President, National Union of Students 1969-71; Called to the Bar, Inner Temple 1972; Practised as Barrister 1972-74; Special adviser: to Barbara Castle as Secretary of State for Social Services 1974-76, to Peter Shore as Secretary of State for the Environment 1976-77; Member, staff of Granada Television *World in Action* 1977-79; Master of Bench of Inner Temple 1997; Member, GMB; Councillor, Islington Borough Council 1971-78; ILEA: Member 1971-74, Deputy Leader 1973

Political career: Contested Tonbridge and Malling February 1974 general election. Member for Blackburn 1979-2010, for Blackburn (revised boundary) since 6 May 2010 general election; Opposition Spokesperson for: Treasury and Economic Affairs 1980-83, Environment 1983-87; Shadow: Education Secretary 1987-92, Environment Secretary 1992-94, Home Secretary 1994-97; Home Secretary 1997-2001; Foreign Secretary 2001-06; Leader of the House of Commons 2006-07; Member House of Commons Commission 2006-07; Lord Chancellor and Secretary of State for Justice 2007-10; Shadow Lord Chancellor and Secretary of State for Justice 2010-; *Select Committees:* Chair: Modernisation of the House of Commons 2006-07; Member, Labour Party National Executive Committee 1994-95

Political interests: Education, taxation, economic policy, local and regional government, police, foreign affairs, European Union

Other organisations: Member of Council Lancaster University 1989-92; Governor: Blackburn College 1990-, Pimlico School 1994-2000, Chair 1995-98; Member Speaker's Committee on the Electoral Commission; PC 1997; *House Magazine* Minister of the Year 2006; Fellow, Royal Statistical Society 1995- Hon LLD Leeds University 1999; Hon LLD Brunel University 2007; Visiting fellow, Nuffield College, Oxford 1990-98; Hon Vice-President Blackburn Rovers FC 1998; *Publications:* Policy and Ideology, 1993

Recreations: Cooking, walking, music, watching Blackburn Rovers

Rt Hon Jack Straw MP, House of Commons, London SW1A 0AA
Tel: 020 7219 5070 Fax: 020 7219 8079
E-mail: strawj@parliament.uk
Constituency: Richmond Chambers, Richmond Road, Blackburn, Lancashire BB1 7AS Tel: 01254 52317 Fax: 01254 682213

GENERAL ELECTION RESULT

		%
Straw, J. (Lab)*	21,751	47.8
Law-Riding, M. (Con)	11,895	26.1
English, P. (Lib Dem)	6,918	15.2
Evans, R. (BNP)	2,158	4.7
Irfanullah, B. (Ind)	1,424	3.1
Anwar, B. (UKIP)	942	2.1
Astley, G. (Ind)	238	0.5
Sharp, J. (Ind)	173	0.4
Majority	9,856	21.66
Electorate	72,331	
Turnout	45,499	62.90

**Member of last parliament*

CONSTITUENCY SNAPSHOT

Jack Straw, the incumbent member for Blackburn, has been the member since 1979 and succeeded Labour's Barbara Castle who held the seat for 24 years, from its creation.

In 1983 Straw's majority was as low was 3,055; however, by 1992 it had almost doubled to 6,027. While, as in many other seats, the majority increased in 1997, to 14,451, this has not been maintained in subsequent elections with his majority currently standing at 8,009.

Straw was re-elected in 2010 with a majority of 9,856 which gave Labour a 47.8 per cent share of the vote.

Boundary changes were minimal: three part-wards moved to Rossendale and Darwen.

Blackburn in Lancashire was once renowned as the weaving capital of the world, experiencing massive growth during the nineteenth century with the population growing five-fold to 100,000.

Blackburn suffered the same reverse of fortunes that all Lancashire cottons towns did post-First World War. A large manufacturing base has remained since then, though most of the jobs are now provided by the service industry.

Gary Streeter

South West Devon (returning MP)

Boundary changes

Tel: 020 7219 4070
E-mail: deans@parliament.uk
Website: www.garystreeter.co.uk

Date of birth: 2 October 1955; Son of Kenneth Victor, farmer, and Shirley Streeter

Education: Tiverton Grammar School; King's College, London (LLB 1977); Married Janet Vanessa Stevens 1978 (1 son 1 daughter)

Non-political career: Solicitor; Partner, Foot and Bowden, Plymouth, (specialist in company and employment law) 1984-98; Plymouth City Council: Councillor 1986-92, Chair Housing Committee 1989-91

Political career: Member for Plymouth Sutton 1992-97, for South West Devon 1997-2010, for South West Devon (revised boundary) since 6 May 2010 general election; PPS: to Sir Derek Spencer as Solicitor General 1993-95, to Sir Nicholas Lyell as Attorney-General 1994-95; Assistant Government Whip 1995-96; Parliamentary Secretary, Lord Chancellor's Department 1996-97; Opposition Spokesperson for: Foreign Affairs 1997-98, Europe 1997-98; Shadow Secretary of State for International Development 1998-2001; Shadow Minister for Foreign Affairs 2003-04; *Select Committees:* Member: Office of the Deputy Prime Minister 2002-04, Office of the Deputy Prime Minister (Urban Affairs Sub-Committee) 2003-04, Home Affairs 2005-10, Chairmen's Panel 2009-10; Chair board of directors governing council Conservative Christian Fellowship; Vice-chair Conservative Party 2001-02; Chair Conservative Party: Human Rights Commission 2005-07, International Office 2005-08

Political interests: Law and order, family moral and social affairs, developing world; North Korea, Middle East

Other organisations: Member Speaker's Committee on the Electoral Commission

Recreations: Watching cricket and rugby, family

Gary Streeter MP, House of Commons, London SW1A 0AA
Tel: 020 7219 4070 Fax: 020 7219 2414
E-mail: deans@parliament.uk
Constituency: Old Newnham Farm, Plymouth, Devon PL7 5BL
Tel: 01752 335666 Fax: 01752 338401
Website: www.garystreeter.co.uk

GENERAL ELECTION RESULT

		%
Streeter, G. (Con)*	27,908	56.0
Pascoe, A. (Lib Dem)	12,034	24.1
Pollard, L. (Lab)	6,193	12.4
Williams, H. (UKIP)	3,084	6.2
Brean, V. (Green)	641	1.3
Majority	15,874	31.84
Electorate	70,059	
Turnout	49,860	71.17

**Member of last parliament*

CONSTITUENCY SNAPSHOT

The seat has been Conservative for over 20 years, with the late Alan Clark representing Plymouth Sutton from 1983 to 1992 when Gary Streeter took over. Major boundary changes in 1997 transferred 60 per cent of Sutton's electors to the new seat of South West Devon, with the remainder coming from South Hams. At the general election Streeter was elected to the new seat with a 7,397 majority. The Conservatives held the seat at the 2001 general election with a similarly sized majority of 7,144. In 2005 Gary Streeter was returned with a 10,141 majority. Streeter held this safe Conservative seat in 2010 with 56 per cent of the vote and a majority of 15,874.

Boundary changes moved Buckland Monachorum and Walkham part-ward to Torridge and West Devon.

This is a varied constituency that incorporates part of the Devon city of Plymouth, part rural land and part coast.

There are many affluent small towns and villages in the more highly populated areas of Plympton and Plymstock on the outskirts of Plymouth, but otherwise the region has a very low average density of people.

Surprisingly for this coastal constituency, significantly lower than usual numbers work in the hotel and catering industries. There is a small, but significant farming community here, and agricultural issues remain important.

Mel Stride

Central Devon

New constituency

Tel: 020 7219 3000
E-mail: mel.stride.mp@parliament.uk

Date of birth: 30 September 1961

Education: Portsmouth Grammar School; St Edmund Hall, Oxford (BA politics, philosophy and economics 1984) (President Oxford Union 1984); Married Michelle King Hughes 2006 (2 daughters)

Non-political career: Founder and ex-director, Venture Marketing Group 1987-2007; Member, Amicus 2006-

Political career: Member for Central Devon since 6 May 2010 general election; Oxford University Conservative Association: Member 1981-84, President 1982

Political interests: Education, welfare reform, health, social justice

Other organisations: Commission for Social Justice Working Group 2006-07; Pilot's licence 1990; Registered blue badge guide 2005; Guide of the Year 2005; Carlton

Recreations: History, walking, spending time with family

Mel Stride MP, House of Commons, London SW1A 0AA
Tel: 020 7219 3000 E-mail: mel.stride.mp@parliament.uk
Constituency: Central Devon Conservative Association Office, 2A Manaton Court, Manaton Close, Matford Business Park, Exeter EX2 8PF Tel: 01392 823336 Fax: 01392 823306

GENERAL ELECTION RESULT

		%
Stride, M. (Con)	27,737	51.5
Hutty, P. (Lib Dem)	18,507	34.4
Macdonald, M. (Lab)	3,715	6.9
Edwards, R. (UKIP)	2,870	5.3
Matthews, C. (Green)	1,044	1.9
Majority	9,230	17.13
Electorate	71,204	
Turnout	53,873	75.66

CONSTITUENCY SNAPSHOT

Central Devon is predominantly comprised of wards from three constituencies: Tiverton and Honiton; Torridge and West Devon; and Teignbridge. Two wards are from North Devon. Tiverton and Honiton has always been represented by the Conservatives; Torridge and West Devon has been mainly held by the Conservatives, but had been held by the Lib Dems for a decade until the 2005 general election when the Tories took the seat back. Likewise, Teignbridge has been held by the Conservatives and Liberal Democrats since its inception in 1983. The Conservative Mel Stride took this new seat with over 50 per cent of the vote and a majority of 9,230 in 2010.

Much of the seat is based around the North of Dartmoor National Park, and the seat overall is predominantly rural, apart from the town of Okehampton and some smaller towns.

This is a sparsely populated seat, with a significant agricultural industry and some light industry in the smaller market towns. Tourism contributes to the local economy through Dartmoor National Park.

The substantial army training camp on Dartmoor is reached via Okehampton, and is referred to as 'Okehampton Camp'. It is managed by the Defence Training Estate, and used by a variety of military units, predominantly the Commando Training Centre Royal Marines.

Graham Stringer

Blackley and Broughton ***(returning MP)***

New constituency

Tel: 020 7219 5235
E-mail: stringerg@parliament.uk

Date of birth: 17 February 1950; Son of late Albert Stringer, railway clerk, and Brenda Stringer, shop assistant

Education: Moston Brook High School; Sheffield University (BSc chemistry 1971); Married Kathryn Carr 1999 (1 son 1 stepson 1 stepdaughter)

Non-political career: Analytical chemist; Chair of Board, Manchester Airport plc 1996-97; Branch officer and shop steward, MSF; Member AMICUS/Unite; Councillor, Manchester City Council 1979-98, Leader 1984-96

Political career: Member for Manchester Blackley 1997-2010, for Blackley and Broughton since 6 May 2010 general electionn; Parliamentary Secretary, Cabinet Office 1999-2001; Government Whip 2001-02; *Select Committees:* Member: Environment, Transport and Regional Affairs 1997-99, Environment, Transport and Regional Affairs (Transport Sub-Committee) 1997-99, Transport 2002-10, Modernisation of the House of Commons 2006, Science and Technology 2006-07, Innovation, Universities[, Science] and Skills 2007-10

Political interests: Urban regeneration, House of Lords reform, revitalising local democracy, aviation and airports, bus regulation

Other organisations: Hon. RNCM; Member: Manchester Tennis and Racquet Club, Cheetham Hill Cricket Club

Recreations: Real tennis, squash

Graham Stringer MP, House of Commons, London SW1A 0AA
Tel: 020 7219 5235 E-mail: stringerg@parliament.uk
Constituency: North Manchester Sixth Form College, Rochdale Road, Manchester M9 4AF Tel: 0161-202 6600 Fax: 0161-202 6626

GENERAL ELECTION RESULT

		%
Stringer, G. (Lab)*	18,563	54.3
Edsberg, J. (Con)	6,260	18.3
Hobhouse, W. (Lib Dem)	4,861	14.2
Adams, D. (BNP)	2,469	7.2
Phillips, K. (Respect)	996	2.9
Willescroft, B. (UKIP)	894	2.6
Zaman, S. (Christian)	161	0.5
Majority	12,303	35.97
Electorate	69,489	
Turnout	34,204	49.22

**Member of last parliament*

CONSTITUENCY SNAPSHOT

This is essentially the old Manchester Blackley seat, with two wards from Salford, but it has lost Lost Moston ward and City Centre part-ward to Manchester Central.

Manchester Blackley typifies the post-Second World War decline of the Conservative Party in the North's city-centre seats. Blackley had been a Conservative seat until the Second World War; thereafter it traditionally swung with the country. Since 1964 Labour has successively entrenched itself and Blackley has ceased to be a national weather-vane of political opinion.

Current incumbent Graham Stringer has received large majorities since he was first elected to parliament in 1997. In 2005 his majority was down slightly but still a safe 12,027. In 2010 Stringer won the new seat with a 12,303 majority despite a 6.7 per cent swing to the Tories.

Blackley and Broughton covers the northern wards of Manchester. The constituency is mainly a residential area of recently declining suburbs and has comparatively low levels of owner-occupation.

Blackley's schools have enjoyed major investment and improvements. In Cheetham the new Temple School has been built with private finance initiative funding. The seat also contains King David's School, a predominantly Jewish institution that regularly ranks as one of the best performers in the country.

Gisela Stuart

Birmingham, Edgbaston ***(returning MP)***

Boundary changes

Tel: 020 7219 5051
E-mail: stuartg@parliament.uk
Website: www.giselastuartmp.co.uk

Date of birth: 26 November 1955; Daughter of late Martin Gschaider and Liane Krompholz

Education: Staatliche Realschule, Vilsbiburg, Bavaria; Manchester Polytechnic (businesss studies 1979); London University (LLB 1992); Married Robert Scott Stuart 1980 (divorced 2000) (2 sons)

Non-political career: Deputy director London Book Fair 1983; Translator; Lawyer and lecturer Worcester College of Technology and Birmingham University 1992-97; Member, AMICUS

Political career: Member for Birmingham Edgbaston 1997-2010, for Birmingham, Edgbaston (revised boundary) since 6 May 2010 general election; PPS to Paul Boateng as Minister of State, Home Office 1998-99; Parliamentary Under-Secretary of State, Department of Health 1999-2001; Parliamentary representative Convention on Future of Europe 2002-04; *Select Committees:* Member: Social Security 1997-98, Foreign Affairs 2001-10, Joint Committee on Conventions 2006

Political interests: Pension law, constitutional reform, European Union

Other organisations: Member: Advisory Board Birmingham University Business School, Board of the External System London University; Trustee: Westminster Foundation of Democracy, Henry Jackson Society; Fellow Industry and Parliament Trust 2002; *Publications:* The Making of Europe's Constitution (Fabian Society, 2003); Editor *The House Magazine* 2005-

Gisela Stuart MP, House of Commons, London SW1A 0AA
Tel: 020 7219 5051 E-mail: stuartg@parliament.uk
Constituency: Tel: 0121-454 5430 Fax: 0121-454 3167
Website: www.giselastuartmp.co.uk

GENERAL ELECTION RESULT

		%
Stuart, G. (Lab)*	16,894	40.6
Alden, D. (Con)	15,620	37.6
Harmer, R. (Lib Dem)	6,387	15.4
Lloyd, T. (BNP)	1,196	2.9
Warwick, G. (UKIP)	732	1.8
Simpson, P. (Green)	469	1.1
Takhar, H. (Impact)	146	0.4
Fernando, C. (Christian)	127	0.3
Majority	1,274	3.06
Electorate	68,573	
Turnout	41,571	60.62

**Member of last parliament*

CONSTITUENCY SNAPSHOT

Before the 1997 Labour general election victory, no Labour candidate had ever won here. The constituency had been in Conservative hands since 1885 and had been represented by a single MP, Dame Jill Knight, for the previous 31 years.

Gisela Stuart's victory in 1997 continued the constituency's record for the longest run of women serving as MPs, the first being Dame Edith Pitt in 1953. In 2010 Stuart was re-elected against the odds with a 40.6 per cent share of the vote and a majority of 1,274.

Boundary changes moved Bartley Green and Harborne wards entirely within this seat, having formerly been shared with Birmingham Northfield and Ladywood. The gain of the Harborne ward stretches the old constituency boundaries to the north, and Bartley Green gains from Birmingham Northfield add a chunk in the south; the loss of a Selly Oak ward fragment in the south is relatively minor.

Birmingham Edgbaston represents a sizeable part of the western side of Britain's second largest city.

The seat houses Birmingham University and Edgbaston cricket ground, home to Warwickshire County Cricket Club. The two largest employers are Birmingham University and the University Hospital Trust, both based in the Edgbaston division.

Graham Stuart

Beverley and Holderness ***(returning MP)***

Boundary changes

Tel: 020 7219 4340
E-mail: stuartgc@parliament.uk
Website: www.grahamstuart.com

Conservative

Date of birth: 12 March 1962; Son of late Dr Peter Stuart and of Joan Stuart

Education: Glenalmond College, Perthshire; Selwyn College, Cambridge (BA law/philosophy 1985); Married Anne Crawshaw 1989 (2 daughters)

Non-political career: Sole proprietor Go Enterprises 1984-; Director CSL Publishing Ltd 1987-; Cambridge City Council: Councillor 1998-2004, Leader Conservative Group 2000-04

Political career: Contested Cambridge 2001 general election. Member for Beverley and Holderness 2005-10, for Beverley and Holderness (revised boundary) since 6 May 2010 general election; *Select Committees:* Member: Environmental Audit 2006-10, Joint Committee on the Draft Climate Change Bill 2007, Education and Skills/Children, Schools and Families 2007-10; Chairman Cambridge University Conservative Association 1985; Member Conservative Party Board 2006-

Political interests: Older people, mental health, welfare, economics, community hospitals, climate change, education

Other organisations: Chair: CHANT (Community Hospitals Acting Nationally Together) 2005-, East Riding Health Action Group 2007-

Recreations: Rowing, cricket, motor cycling

Graham Stuart MP, House of Commons, London SW1A 0AA
Tel: 020 7219 4340 Fax: 020 7219 6925
E-mail: stuartgc@parliament.uk
Constituency: 9 Cross Street, Beverley, East Yorkshire HU17 9AX
Tel: 01482 881316 Fax: 01482 861667
Website: www.grahamstuart.com

GENERAL ELECTION RESULT

		%
Stuart, G. (Con)*	25,063	47.1
Dobson, C. (Lib Dem)	12,076	22.7
Saunders, I. (Lab)	11,224	21.1
Whitelam, N. (BNP)	2,080	3.9
Horsfield, A. (UKIP)	1,845	3.5
Rigby, B. (Green)	686	1.3
Hughes, R. (Ind)	225	0.4
Majority	12,987	24.41
Electorate	79,611	
Turnout	53,199	66.82

**Member of last parliament*

CONSTITUENCY SNAPSHOT

This seat was created in 1997 with parts taken from the old Beverley, Bridlington and Boothferry constituencies. In that year the Tories had a notional majority of nearly 16,000, however, a swing of 16 per cent reduced James Cran's majority to 1,211.

There was a further small swing to Labour in 2001 but in 2005 Graham Stuart increased the Tory majority from 781 to 2,580. In 2010 Stuart held the seat with a 12,987 majority.

Boundary changes moved Beverley Rural ward fully into the constituency, while Cottingham North and East Wolds and Coastal are now entirely within the boundaries of Haltemprice and Howden and East Yorkshire respectively.

This East Yorkshire seat takes in large stretches of country and coast on the remote Holderness peninsula, including the seaside towns of Hornsea and Withernsea. It also includes the East Riding's county town, Beverley.

Farming remains important in this rural area. There are industrial estates around Beverley, a BP chemical refinery at Salt End on the Humber estuary, and much of the UK's natural gas is brought ashore at Easington. Tourism is important in the seaside towns, and Holderness is a magnet for birdwatchers. Many of the workers in the constituency are commuters working in Hull.

A £30 million southern relief by-pass and park-and ride scheme for Beverley got planning permission in early 2010. Beverley is rapidly becoming congested as a result of Hull commuters.

Andrew Stunell

Hazel Grove ***(returning MP)***

Boundary changes

Tel: 020 7219 5136
E-mail: stunella@parliament.uk
Website: www.andrewstunell.org.uk

Date of birth: 24 November 1942; Son of late Robert George Stunell and Trixie Stunell

Education: Surbiton Grammar School; Manchester University (architecture RIBA Pt. II exemption 1963); Liverpool Polytechnic; Married Gillian Chorley 1967 (3 sons 2 daughters)

Non-political career: Architectural assistant: CWS Manchester 1965-67, Runcorn New Town 1967-81; Freelance architectural assistant 1981-85; Various posts including political secretary, Association of Liberal Democrat Councillors (ALDC) 1985-97, Head of Service 1989-96; Member, NALGO: New Towns Whitley Council 1977-81; Councillor: Chester City Council 1979-90, Cheshire County Council 1981-91, Stockport Metropolitan Borough Council 1994-2002; Vice-chair Association of County Councils 1985-90; Vice-president Local Government Association 1997-

Political career: Contested City of Chester 1979, 1983, 1987, Hazel Grove 1992 general elections. Member for Hazel Grove 1997-2010, for Hazel Grove (revised boundary) since 6 May 2010 general election; Liberal Democrat: Spokesperson for Energy 1997-2005, Deputy Chief Whip 1997-2001, Chief Whip 2001-06, Shadow Secretary of State for Office of the Deputy Prime Minister/Communities and Local Government 2006-07; Parliamentary Under-Secretary of State, Department for Communities and Local Government 2010-; *Select Committees:* Member: Broadcasting 1997-2000, Modernisation of the House of Commons 1997-2006, Procedure 1997-2001, Unopposed Bills (Panel) 1997-2001, Standing Orders 1998-2001, Finance and Services 2001-06, Selection 2001-06, International Development 2009-10, Arms Export Controls 2009-10; Member: Liberal Democrat Federal Executive Committee 2001-06, Liberal Democrat Federal Conference Committee 2001-06; Chair Local Election Campaign 2007-

Political interests: Local democracy and regional devolution, Third World, race relations, energy, climate change

Other organisations: Member United Nations Association 1959-; President, Goyt Valley Rail Users Association; Vice-president Macclesfield Canal Society 1998-; NW Constitutional Convention 1999-; Fellow Industry and Parliament Trust 2000; OBE 1995; *Publications:* Life In The Balance (1986); Budgeting For Real (1984, 1994, 1999); Thriving In The Balance (1995); Open Active & Effective (1995); Local Democracy Guaranteed (1996); Energy – Clean and Green to 2050 (1999); Nuclear Waste – Cleaning up the Mess (2001)

Recreations: Theoretical astronomy, camping, table tennis

Andrew Stunell OBE MP, House of Commons, London SW1A 0AA
Tel: 020 7219 5136 Fax: 020 7219 2302
E-mail: stunella@parliament.uk
Constituency: Liberal Democrat HQ, 68A Compstall Road, Romiley, Stockport, Cheshire SK6 4DE Tel: 0161-406 7070
Fax: 0161-494 2425 Website: www.andrewstunell.org.uk

GENERAL ELECTION RESULT

		%
Stunell, A. (Lib Dem)*	20,485	48.8
Abercorn, A. (Con)	14,114	33.6
Scorer, R. (Lab)	5,234	12.5
Whittaker, J. (UKIP)	2,148	5.1
Majority	6,371	15.18
Electorate	63,074	
Turnout	41,981	66.56

**Member of last parliament*

CONSTITUENCY SNAPSHOT

In 1966 Cheadle, from which the seat of Hazel Grove was to be carved, was won by Liberal Dr Michael Winstanley. It returned to the Tories in 1970. The seat was split in February 1974 and Winstanley won it at its inception only to lose to the Tories in October.

Thereafter, with the exception of the 1979 general election, Liberal Sir Tom Arnold won the seat with slender margins until he retired in 1997. Andrew Stunell's 1997 winning margin of 11,814 has fallen in the three subsequent elections. Stunnell's 2010 majority was 6,371 following a 2.4 per cent swing to the Conservatives.

The seat swapped one part-ward with Cheadle and two part-wards with Stockport.

This commuter dormitory to the south-east of Stockport and Manchester is mainly middle-class and heavily residential. It contains a number of suburban communities including Bredbury, Romiley, and Marple beyond which moors and farms run into the Pennine foothills. The traditional cotton industry has been replaced with light industry and office-based employment.

Unemployment is historically low, and light industry and office-based employment is prevalent throughout the seat. A significant number commute to work in the financial and service sectors found predominantly in Manchester and Stockport.

Julian Sturdy

York Outer

New constituency

Tel: 020 7219 3000
E-mail: julian.sturdy.mp@parliament.uk
Website: www.juliansturdy.co.uk

Date of birth: 1971; Son of Robert Sturdy MEP and Elizabeth Hommes

Education: Harper Adams University (agriculture); Married Victoria (1 son 1 daughter)

Non-political career: Farming and property business; Councillor, Harrogate Borough Council 2002-07; Governor, educational foundation of local school

Political career: Contested Scunthorpe 2005 general election. Member for York Outer since 6 May 2010 general election

Other organisations: Director, Harrogate District Community Transport

Julian Sturdy MP, House of Commons, London SW1A 0AA
Tel: 020 7219 3000 E-mail: julian.sturdy.mp@parliament.uk
Constituency: York Conservatives, 1 Ash Street, York YO26 4ZB
Tel: 01904 788355 Website: www.juliansturdy.co.uk

GENERAL ELECTION RESULT

		%
Sturdy, J. (Con)	22,912	43.0
Kirk, M. (Lib Dem)	19,224	36.1
Alexander, J. (Lab)	9,108	17.1
Morris, J. (UKIP)	1,100	2.1
Smurthwaite, C. (BNP)	956	1.8
Majority	3,688	6.92
Electorate	74,965	
Turnout	53,300	71.10

CONSTITUENCY SNAPSHOT

York Outer is a new constituency that is an amalgamation of wards from four disappearing seats: City of York, Vale of York, Ryedale and Selby. The new seat was created when the boundary commission opted to allocate two seats to the City of York council area. This seat is a doughnut shape surrounding the City of York seat.

The City of York has been held by Labour since 1992 while the other three seats have been in Tory hands in recent years.

Conservative candidate, Julian Sturdy took the new seat in 2010 securing 22,912 votes and a majority of 3,688.

Heslington is home to York University, one of the top research universities in the country. It was ranked the 11th best university in The Times 2010 league table. There is also the University College of Ripon and York.

Not only do the universities themselves employ more than 3,000 people, they have attracted half as many again to a major bioscience research industry, the largest in the country. The Department for Environment, Food and Rural Affairs has its research laboratory here and York was the UK's founding National Science City.

The seat comprises the historic villages of Osbaldwick and Fulford, with the former playing host to the successful park-and-ride scheme at Grimston Bar - helping to reduce congestion in York city centre.

Gerry Sutcliffe

Bradford South (returning MP)

Boundary changes

Tel: 020 7219 3247
E-mail: sutcliffeg@parliament.uk
Website: www.gerrysutcliffe.org.uk

Labour

Date of birth: 13 May 1953; Son of Henry and Margaret Sutcliffe

Education: Cardinal Hinsley Grammar School, Bradford; Married Maria Holgate 1972 (3 sons)

Non-political career: Salesperson 1969-72; Display advertising, *Bradford Telegraph and Argus* 1972-75; Field printers, Bradford 1975-80; Deputy Branch Secretary, SOGAT/GPMU 1980-94; Member: Yorkshire and Humberside Trade Union Friends of Labour, Regional TUC; Bradford City Council: Councillor 1982-94, Leader 1992-94

Political career: Member for Bradford South 9 June 1994 by-election to 2010, for Bradford South (revised boundary) since 6 May 2010 general election; PPS: to Harriet Harman as Secretary of State for Social Security and Minister for Women 1997-98, to Stephen Byers as: Chief Secretary, HM Treasury July-December 1998, Secretary of State for Trade and Industry 1999; Assistant Government Whip 1999-2001; Government Whip 2000-03; Parliamentary Under-Secretary of State: Department of Trade and Industry 2003-06: (Employment Relations, Competition and Consumers 2003-04, Employment Relations, Consumers and Postal Services 2004-05, Employment Relations and Consumer Affairs 2005-06), Home Office/Ministry of Justice (Criminal Justice and Offender Management) 2006-07, Department for Culture, Media and Sport (Minister for Sport) 2007-10; *Select Committees:* Member: Public Accounts 1996-98, Unopposed Bills (Panel) 1997-99, Selection 2001-03

Political interests: Employment, local and regional government; Pakistan, Bangladesh, India, European Union

Other organisations: Patron: Catholic Housing Aid (CHAS), Bradford City Football in the Community

Recreations: Sport, music

Gerry Sutcliffe MP, House of Commons, London SW1A 0AA
Tel: 020 7219 3247 Fax: 020 7219 1227
E-mail: sutcliffeg@parliament.uk
Constituency: 3rd Floor, 76 Kirkgate, Bradford,
West Yorkshire BD1 1SZ Tel: 01274 400007 Fax: 01274 400020
Website: www.gerrysutcliffe.org.uk

GENERAL ELECTION RESULT

		%
Sutcliffe, G. (Lab)*	15,682	41.3
Palmer, M. (Con)	11,060	29.1
Griffiths, A. (Lib Dem)	6,948	18.3
Sutton, S. (BNP)	2,651	7.0
Illingworth, J. (UKIP)	1,339	3.5
Lewthwaite, J. (DN)	315	0.8
Majority	4,622	12.16
Electorate	63,580	
Turnout	37,995	59.76

**Member of last parliament*

CONSTITUENCY SNAPSHOT

In 1970 Labour's majority was under 2,000. It rose in subsequent elections but the Liberal-SDP Alliance doubled their vote in 1983 and Labour won by just 110 votes.

There was another tight result in 1987 when Bob Cryer won by just 309 votes. He increased his majority in 1992, but was killed in a car crash in 1994.

In the by-election Labour's Gerry Sutcliffe was elected with a majority of nearly 10,000. He suffered only a tiny swing against him in 2001 and 2005 when he won a 9,167 majority.

In 2010 Sutcliffe held the seat with a reduced majority of 4,622.

Great Horton, Queensbury, and Tong ward are now entirely in the seat; while Clayton and Fairweather Green, and Little Horton wards are now completely within Bradford West and the new Bradford East respectively.

Bradford South stretches from Queensbury in the west to the pretty village of Tong in the east.

This is a solidly working-class constituency. Manual work is far more prevalent here than the national average. Owner-occupancy is quite high but many live in council accommodation.

The city has suffered from a decline in its traditional textiles industry. However, this seat has suffered proportionally less than the other Bradford seats.

Ian Swales

Redcar

Boundary changes

Tel: 020 7219 3000
E-mail: ian.swales.mp@parliament.uk

Date of birth: 5 April 1953

Education: Manchester University (BSc chemical engineering); FCCA 1977; Married Pat (3 children)

Non-political career: Yorkshire Electricity; Various roles, to Global Head of Leadership Development, ICI 1978-99; Training and consultancy business

Political career: Contested Redcar 2005 general election. Member for Redcar since 6 May 2010 general election; Member SDP/Liberal Democrats 1981-

Other organisations: Member: British Humanist Association, Menieres Society

Recreations: Walking, reading, travel

Ian Swales MP, House of Commons, London SW1A 0AA
Tel: 020 7219 3000 E-mail: ian.swales.mp@parliament.uk
Constituency: 39 Coast Road, Redcar, Cleveland TS10 3NN
Tel: 01642 477838 Website: www.redcarlibdems.org.uk

GENERAL ELECTION RESULT

		%
Swales, I. (Lib Dem)	18,955	45.2
Baird, V. (Lab)*	13,741	32.8
Mastin, S. (Con)	5,790	13.8
Bulmer, M. (UKIP)	1,875	4.5
Broughton, K. (BNP)	1,475	3.5
Walter, H. (TUSC)	127	0.3
Majority	5,214	12.43
Electorate	67,125	
Turnout	41,963	62.51

**Member of last parliament*

CONSTITUENCY SNAPSHOT

In Labour hands since its creation in 1974, Redcar has only ever had three MPs. James Tinn served for three terms, as did his successor Mo Mowlam from 1987. Mowlam bequeathed a sizable majority to her successor, the QC Vera Baird.

Vera Baird polled 3,000 fewer votes in 2005, taking 51 per cent of the vote, but her majority fell by only 1,327 to 12,116, a consequence of the Conservatives dropping into third place. Baird suffered expenses outrage and the largest swing away from Labour (21.4 per cent), the beneficiary being Liberal Democrat Ian Swales.

Boundary changes moved part-ward Saltburn to Middlesbrough South and East Cleveland while part-ward St Germains becomes fully incorporated within the seat.

A coastal constituency, Redcar includes the eponymously named seaside resort. It is sandwiched in between Middlesbrough to the south and Hartlepool and Stockton to the north.

The constituency is dominated by the heavy industry of south Teesside. As with so many northern areas built on heavy industry Redcar has suffered for the past few decades from the decline of traditional employment.

The biggest employer is the troubled Corus steelworks. The other major employers are the former ICI Wilton chemical complex and Teesport, the second largest docks complex in Britain, part of which falls within the constituency.

Desmond Swayne

New Forest West *(returning MP)*

Boundary changes

Tel: 020 7219 4886
E-mail: swayned@parliament.uk
Website: www.desmondswaynemp.com

Conservative

Date of birth: 20 August 1956; Son of George Joseph Swayne and Elisabeth McAlister Swayne, neé Gibson

Education: Bedford School; St Mary's College, St Andrews University (MA theology 1980); Married Moira Cecily Teek 1987 (1 son 2 daughters)

Non-political career: Major, Territorial Army; Schoolmaster A-level economics: Charterhouse 1980-81, Wrekin College 1982-87; Manager risk management systems Royal Bank of Scotland 1988-96

Political career: Contested Pontypridd 1987, West Bromwich West 1992 general elections. Member for New Forest West 1997-2010, for New Forest West (revised boundary) since 6 May 2010 general election; Opposition Whip 2002-03; Opposition Spokesperson for: Health 2001, Defence 2001-02; Shadow Minister for: International Affairs 2003-04, Northern Ireland 2004; PPS to Leaders of the Opposition: Michael Howard 2004-05, David Cameron 2005-10; PPS to David Cameron as Prime Minister 2010-; *Select Committees:* Member: Scottish Affairs 1997-2001, Social Security 1999-2001, Procedure 2002-05, Defence 2005-06, Ecclesiastical Committee

Other organisations: Member Countryside Alliance; TD; Cavalry and Guards; Serpentine Swimming Club

Recreations: Territorial Army

Desmond Swayne MP, House of Commons, London SW1A 0AA
Tel: 020 7219 4886 Fax: 020 7219 0901
E-mail: swayned@parliament.uk
Constituency: 4 Cliff Crescent, Marine Drive, Barton-on-Sea, New Milton, Hampshire BH25 7EB Tel: 01425 629844
Fax: 01425 621898 Website: www.desmondswaynemp.com

GENERAL ELECTION RESULT

		%
Swayne, D. (Con)*	27,980	58.8
Plummer, M. (Lib Dem)	11,084	23.3
Hurne, J. (Lab)	4,666	9.8
Lyon, M. (UKIP)	2,783	5.9
Richards, J. (Green)	1,059	2.2
Majority	16,896	35.52
Electorate	68,332	
Turnout	47,572	69.62

**Member of last parliament*

CONSTITUENCY SNAPSHOT

Desmond Swayne has held New Forest West since its creation in 1997. He held the seat comfortably that year and increased his majority at the two subsequent elections. In 2005 it stood at 17,285.

The seat was held by Swayne in 2010 with a 16,896 majority.

The seat lost part of the Boldre and Sway ward to New Forest East.

This seat contains the more affluent and populous areas of the Forest, in the towns of Lymington, Ringwood and New Milton. Forestry, farming and market gardening are prominent in much of the seat, with many market towns and villages scattered through the area.

The Forest itself, established as a hunting ground by William the Conqueror in 1079, dominates the constituency both geographically and economically, drawing around seven million tourists every year and providing employment opportunities.

Farming and market gardening continue as the mainstays of the rural economy, and there is a fair amount of light industry, especially manufacturing and engineering.

Jo Swinson

East Dunbartonshire ***(returning MP)***

No boundary changes

Tel: 020 7219 8088
E-mail: swinsonj@parliament.uk
Website: www.joswinson.org.uk

Liberal Democrat

Date of birth: 5 February 1980; Daughter of Peter and Annette Swinson

Education: Douglas Academy, Milngavie, Glasgow; London School of Economics (BSc management 2000); Single

Non-political career: Marketing executive and manager Emap's Viking FM 2000-02; Marketing manager Spaceandpeople Ltd 2002-04; Development officer UK Public Health Association Scotland 2004-05

Political career: Contested Hull East 2001 general election. Member for East Dunbartonshire since 5 May 2005; Liberal Democrat: Spokesperson for Culture, Media and Sport 2005-06, Whip 2005-06, Shadow: Secretary of State for Scotland 2006-07, Minister for Women and Equalities 2007, Minister for Foreign and Commonwealth Office 2008-10; *Select Committees:* Member: Environmental Audit 2007-10; Contested Strathkelvin and Bearsden 2003 Scottish Parliament election; Liberal Democrat Youth and Students (LDYS): Secretary 1998-99, Vice-chair 1999-2000, Vice-chair campaigns 2000-01; Vice-chair Haltemprice and Howden Liberal Democrats 2000, Member Federal Executive 2002; Vice-chair Gender Balance Taskforce 2003-06, Chair, Campaign for Gender Balance 2007-08

Political interests: Corporate social responsibility, equality, political engagement, quality of life and wellbeing, climate change, allergy; India, Romania, Sierra Leone

Other organisations: Member: Amnesty International 1998-, New Economics Foundation 2003-, New Politics Network 2004-; Friends of the Earth, Unlock Democracy

Recreations: Hiking, gym, reading, running

Jo Swinson MP, House of Commons, London SW1A 0AA
Tel: 020 7219 8088 Fax: 020 7219 0555
E-mail: swinsonj@parliament.uk
Constituency: 4 Springfield House, Emerson Road, Bishopbriggs, Glasgow G64 1QE Tel: 0141-762 2209 Fax: 0141-762 5604
Website: www.joswinson.org.uk

GENERAL ELECTION RESULT

		%	+/-
Swinson, J. (Lib Dem)*	18,551	38.7	-3.1
Galbraith, M. (Lab)	16,367	34.1	1.1
Nolan, M. (Con)	7,431	15.5	-1.0
White, I. (SNP)	5,054	10.5	4.7
Beeley, J. (UKIP)	545	1.1	
Majority	2,184	4.55	
Electorate	63,795		
Turnout	47,948	75.16	

**Member of last parliament*

CONSTITUENCY SNAPSHOT

In 1983 Michael Hirst won Strathkelvin and Bearsden for the Conservatives before losing to Labour's Sam Galbraith in 1987. Galbraith increased his majority in 1992 and in 1997.

Sam Galbraith retired in 2001 and John Lyons succeeded him as Labour MP.

Following boundary changes in 2005 most constituents were included in the new seat of East Dunbartonshire. The new seat also included voters from the eastern wards of Clydebank and Milngavie, and from Coatbridge and Chryston. These electors boosted the Liberal Democrat vote and Jo Swinson took the seat from Labour. Swinson retained the seat with a 2,184 majority.

East Dunbartonshire is situated to the north east of Glasgow. Most of its residential areas are commuter dormitories with much of the population travelling into Glasgow for work.

Bearsden began as a Roman fort on the short-lived Antonine Wall, which was the northernmost boundary of the Roman Empire.

Bishopbriggs was a quarrying, mining and manufacturing area. Since the end of quarrying and the decline of heavy industry the town grew as a housing area outside Glasgow.

Milngavie was a small industrial town based on the water-powered mills on the River Allander. Most industry has disappeared and it too is now primarily a Glasgow commuter area.

The coalmines and many of the mills and large-scale employers have closed. The constituency's major employer is now the large Stobhill Hospital.

A new prison near Bishopbriggs replacing the old HMP Low Moss is due to open in 2011.

Hugo Swire

East Devon (returning MP)

Boundary changes

Tel: 020 7219 8163
E-mail: swireh@parliament.uk
Website: www.hugoswiremp.org.uk

Conservative

Date of birth: 30 November 1959; Son of late H R Swire and of Marchioness Townshend, neé Montgomerie

Education: Eton College; St Andrews University (1979 only); Royal Military Academy Sandhurst; Married Sasha Nott 1996 (2 daughters)

Non-political career: Commissioned 1st Battalion Grenadier Guards 1980-83; Joint managing director International News Services and Prospect Films 1983-85; Financial consultant Streets Financial Ltd 1985-87; Head of development National Gallery 1988-92; Sotheby's: Deputy director 1992-97, Director 1997-2003

Political career: Contested Greenock and Inverclyde 1997 general election. Member for East Devon 2001-10, for East Devon (revised boundary) since 6 May 2010 general election; PPS to Theresa May as chairman of the Conservative Party 2003; Opposition Whip 2003-04; Shadow: Minister for the Arts 2004-05, Secretary of State for Culture, Media and Sport 2005-07; Minister of State, Northern Ireland Office 2010-; *Select Committees:* Member: Northern Ireland Affairs 2002-05; Secretary Conservative Middle East Council

Political interests: Arts, tourism, sport, agriculture, architectural heritage, defence, foreign affairs, rural affairs, housing; United Arab Emirates, Lebanon, Oman, Slovenia, Bosnia

Other organisations: Charity auctioneer and fundraiser for numerous charities; Fundraising committee member University of St Andrews; Chair Speakers' Advisory Committee on Works of Art 2005-; Fund for Refugees in Slovenia; Fellow Royal Society of Arts 1993; White's, Pratt's, Beefsteak

Recreations: Showing pig

Hugo Swire MP, House of Commons, London SW1A 0AA
Tel: 020 7219 8163 Fax: 020 7219 1895
E-mail: swireh@parliament.uk
Constituency: 9C Mill Road Industrial Estate, White Cross Road, Woodbury Salterton, Exeter, Devon EX5 1EL Tel: 01395 233503
Fax: 01395 233903 Website: www.hugoswiremp.org.uk

GENERAL ELECTION RESULT

		%
Swire, H. (Con)*	25,662	48.3
Robathan, P. (Lib Dem)	16,548	31.2
Manson, G. (Lab)	5,721	10.8
Amor, M. (UKIP)	4,346	8.2
Pavey, S. (Green)	815	1.5
Majority	9,114	17.17
Electorate	73,109	
Turnout	53,092	72.62

**Member of last parliament*

CONSTITUENCY SNAPSHOT

The Conservatives have held this seat continuously since 1945. In the 1997 general election the long-serving Sir Peter Emery polled 44 per cent while Rachel Tretheway for the Liberal Democrats gained nearly 30 per cent. Hugo Swire became MP in 2001 when Sir Peter stepped down after 34 years.

In 2005 the Conservative vote fell slightly while the Liberal Democrat vote increased fractionally but Hugo Swire was still re-elected with a majority of 7,936. Swire increased his majority to 9,114 in 2010.

The seat gained five wards from Tiverton and Honiton and two wards from Exeter, while losing eight wards and one part-ward to Tiverton and Honiton.

The small strip of land on the coast to the east of Exeter makes up the affluent constituency of East Devon.

The constituency is geared to older people and their housing and social needs. As in all Devon constituencies, the proportion of non-white people is low.

The constituency tends to be white-collar workers, farmers or people involved in the retail or tourist industries.

Robert Syms

Poole (returning MP)

Boundary changes

Tel: 020 7219 4601
E-mail: edwardsn@parliament.uk

Date of birth: 15 August 1956; Son of Raymond Syms, builder, and Mary Syms, teacher

Education: Colston's School, Bristol; Married Nicola Guy 1991 (divorced 1999); married Fiona Mellersh 2000 (separated 2007) (1 daughter 1 son)

Non-political career: Director, family building, plant hire and property group, Chippenham, Wiltshire 1978-; Councillor: North Wiltshire District Council 1983-87, Wiltshire County Council 1985-97; Member, Wessex Regional Health Authority 1988-90

Political career: Contested Walsall North 1992 general election. Member for Poole 1997-2010, for Poole (revised boundary) since 6 May 2010 general election; PPS to Michael Ancram as Chair Conservative Party 1999-2000; Opposition Spokesperson for Environment, Transport and Regions 1999-2001; Opposition Whip 2003; Shadow Minister for: Local and Devolved Government Affairs 2003-05, Local Government 2005-07; *Select Committees:* Member: Health 1997-2000, 2007-10, Procedure 1998-99, Transport 2002-03; North Wiltshire Conservative Association: Treasurer 1982-84, Deputy Chair 1983-84, Chair 1984-86; Vice-Chair Conservative Party 2001-03

Political interests: Economic policy, constitution, local and regional government; USA, most of English speaking world

Other organisations: Member, North Wiltshire Enterprise Agency 1986-90; Member, Calne Development Project Trust 1986-97; Fellow of the Chartered Institute of Building (FCIOB)

Recreations: Reading, music

Robert Syms MP, House of Commons, London SW1A 0AA
Tel: 020 7219 4601 Fax: 020 7219 6867
E-mail: edwardsn@parliament.uk
Constituency: Poole Conservative Association, 38 Sandbanks Road, Poole, Dorset BH14 8BX Tel: 01202 739922 Fax: 01202 739944

GENERAL ELECTION RESULT

		%
Syms, R. (Con)*	22,532	47.5
Eades, P. (Lib Dem)	14,991	31.6
Sanderson, J. (Lab)	6,041	12.7
Wellstead, N. (UKIP)	2,507	5.3
Holmes, D. (BNP)	1,188	2.5
Northover, I. (Ind)	177	0.4
Majority	7,541	15.90
Electorate	64,661	
Turnout	47,436	73.36

**Member of last parliament*

CONSTITUENCY SNAPSHOT

Since 1950 this seat has known only Conservative MPs, with incumbent Robert Syms serving as MP here since 1997. He was first elected on a majority just short of 5,300, less than his predecessor's majority of 12,981 in 1992. However, in 2001 the Conservatives gained back some ground they lost in 1997, increasing their share of the vote by 3 per cent, while in 2005 Robert Syms was returned again with a majority of 5,988. Syms won an improved majority of 7,541 in 2010.

Boundary changes moved Branksome East ward and Alderney part-ward to Bournemouth West, while Creekmoor part-ward will be fully contained within Poole.

Set on the north bank of Poole harbour, the second largest natural harbour in the world, Poole is an affluent and economically secure seat, from Sandbanks, which has some of the highest residential land-value in Britain, to the town's many new industrial developments.

Once the town was known for fishing, boat-building, and pottery, but now chemical, pharmaceutical, electronic and engineering industries are the notable employers in the area.

Tourism is also important to the local economy, with many visitors drawn to the seaside and many yacht clubs based in Poole harbour.

Mark Tami

Alyn and Deeside (returning MP)

No boundary changes

Tel: 020 7219 8174
E-mail: tamim@parliament.uk
Website: www.marktami.co.uk

Labour

Date of birth: 3 October 1962; Son of Michael John Tami and Patricia Tami

Education: Enfield Grammar School; Swansea University (BA history 1985); Married Sally Ann Daniels 1994 (2 sons)

Non-political career: AEEU: Head of research and communications 1992-99, Head of policy 1999-2001; Member: AEEU Amicus 1986-, TUC General Council 1999-2001

Political career: Member for Alyn and Deeside since 7 June 2001 general election; PPS to John Healey as Financial Secretary to the Treasury 2005-06; Assistant Government Whip 2007-10; *Select Committees:* Member: Northern Ireland Affairs 2001-05, European Standing Committee B 2003-05, Joint Committee on Tax Law Rewrite Bills 2005-07, Joint Committee on Human Rights 2007; Treasurer, Labour Friends of Australia

Political interests: Manufacturing, aerospace, animal welfare

Other organisations: Glamorgan County Cricket

Recreations: Football (Norwich City), cricket, fishing, antiques

Mark Tami MP, House of Commons, London SW1A 0AA
Tel: 020 7219 8174 Fax: 020 7219 1943
E-mail: tamim@parliament.uk
Constituency: Deeside Enterprise Centre, Rowleys Drive, Shotton, Deeside, Clwyd CH5 1PP Tel: 01244 819854 Fax: 01244 823548
Website: www.marktami.co.uk

GENERAL ELECTION RESULT

		%	+/-
Tami, M. (Lab)*	15,804	39.6	-9.2
Gallagher, W. (Con)	12,885	32.3	7.1
Brighton, P. (Lib Dem)	7,308	18.3	1.0
Jones, M. (PIC)	1,549	3.9	0.2
Walker, J. (BNP)	1,368	3.4	
Howson, J. (UKIP)	1,009	2.5	-0.1
Majority	2,919	7.31	
Electorate	60,931		
Turnout	39,923	65.52	

**Member of last parliament*

CONSTITUENCY SNAPSHOT

The Westminster constituency was created in 1983 and has been in Labour hands since. The party's vote-share declined slightly in 2001, probably due to the retirement of the long-serving MP Barry Jones, who had held the seat from which most of Alyn and Deeside was created, East Flint, since 1970.

His replacement as the Labour candidate was Mark Tami, whose majority was cut to 9,222.

Tami's majority was cut further in 2005 to 8,378. Tami is now looking vulnerable to the Tories who achieved an 8.1 per cent swing and reduced his majority to 2,919.

Situated in north-east Wales, on the English border, some of the outlying localities of this seat are practically suburbs of Chester.

Despite the decline of the local steelworks, the constituency still has a manufacturing and industrial economic base and is somewhat dependent on the huge Airbus aerospace factory at Broughton. Toyota also maintains a large factory in the constituency.

Another major development has been the creation and expansion of Broughton Shopping Park, the biggest retail centre in North Wales.

The high-tech employment sector has become increasingly important.

Sir **Peter Tapsell**

Louth and Horncastle ***(returning MP)***

Boundary changes

Conservative

Tel: 020 7219 4409

Date of birth: 1 February 1930; Son of late Eustace Tapsell and late Jessie, neé Hannay

Education: Tonbridge School; Merton College, Oxford (BA modern history 1953, MA; Diploma economics 1954); Married The Hon. Cecilia Hawke, daughter of 9th Baron Hawke 1963 (divorced 1971) (1 son deceased); married Gabrielle Mahieu 1974

Non-political career: Subaltern Army national service in Middle East 1948-50; Royal Sussex Regiment; Conservative research department 1954-57; Personal assistant to Anthony Eden as Prime Minister 1955; Partner, James Capel and Co (stockbrokers) 1957-90; Adviser to central banks and international companies 1960-; Member Trilateral Commission 1979-98

Political career: Contested Wednesbury February 1957 by-election. Member for Nottingham West 1959-64, for Horncastle 1966-83, for Lindsey East 1983-97, for Louth and Horncastle 1997-2010, for Louth and Horncastle (revised boundary) since 6 May 2010 general election; Opposition Frontbench Spokesperson for: Foreign and Commonwealth Affairs 1976-77, Treasury and Economic Affairs 1977-78; *Select Committees:* Member: Unopposed Bills (Panel) 2004-10

Political interests: Foreign affairs, economics and finance; Third World

Other organisations: Chair British-Caribbean Association 1963-64; Vice-President Tennyson Society 1966-; Council member: Institute of Fiscal Studies 1983-2005, Business Advisory Committee of UN; Longest serving Conservative MP; Member: Business Advisory Council of the UN, International Investment Advisory Board to Brunei Government 1976-83; Hon Deputy Chair, Mitsubishi Trust Oxford Foundation 1988-; Trustee Oxford Union Society 1985-93; Brunei Dato 1971; Hon Life Member 6th Squadron RAF 1971; Knighted 1985; *Spectator*: Backbencher of the Year 1993, Parliamentarian of the Year 2004; Hon Postmaster, Merton College, Oxford 1953; Hon Fellow, Merton College, Oxford 1989; Athenaeum, Carlton, Hurlingham

Recreations: Overseas travel, walking in mountains, reading history

Sir Peter Tapsell MP, House of Commons, London SW1A 0AA
Tel: 020 7219 4409 Fax: 020 7219 0976
Constituency: Cannon Street House, Cannon Street, Louth, Lincolnshire LN11 9NL Tel: 01507 609840 Fax: 01507 608091

GENERAL ELECTION RESULT

		%
Tapsell, P. (Con)*	25,065	49.6
Martin, F. (Lib Dem)	11,194	22.2
Mountain, P. (Lab)	8,760	17.4
Green, J. (BNP)	2,199	4.4
Nurse, P. (UKIP)	2,183	4.3
Simpson, D. (Ind)	576	1.1
Mair, C. (England)	517	1.0
Majority	13,871	27.47
Electorate	77,650	
Turnout	50,494	65.03

**Member of last parliament*

CONSTITUENCY SNAPSHOT

Louth and Horncastle were separate constituencies until 1983, and most of the present seat was known as East Lindsey from 1983 to 1997. Tory Peter Tapsell, held the seat as East Lindsey and has continued to do so in its current incarnation.

In 1997 Labour claimed second place cutting Sir Peter's majority to 6,900. In 2001 the Conservatives recovered their vote-share, slightly increasing their majority. Tapsell's majority increased to 9,896 in 2005.

Tapsell held the seat for the Tories with a majority of 13,871 at the 2010 general election.

Boundary changes moved part-wards Croft and Stickney to Boston and Skegness, whilst part-wards Binbrook, Ludford, and Roughton will be fully incorporated into this seat. All wards had previously been shared between the two seats.

This is a large rural and seaside constituency in the north-east of the county of Lincolnshire.

This former sheep farming country now produces a multitude of crops with the help of modern fertilisers. Even more fertile is the flat country to the south which produces the biggest tonnage of cereals per hectare in Europe.

Half a million people flock to the east coast for their holidays, particularly Mablethorpe and Sutton-on-Sea.

Sarah Teather

Brent Central ***(returning MP)***

New constituency

Tel: 020 7219 2284
E-mail: teathers@parliament.uk
Website: www.sarahteather.org.uk

Date of birth: 1 June 1974

Education: Leicester Grammar School; St John's College, Cambridge (BA pharmacology 1996)

Non-political career: Science policy officer Royal Society 1998-2001; Science policy consultant Technopolis Ltd 2001-02; Policy analyst Macmillan Cancer Relief 2002-03; Councillor, London Borough of Islington 2002-03

Political career: Contested Finchley and Golders Green 2001 general election. Member for Brent East 18 September 2003 by-election-2010, for Brent Central since 6 May 2010 general election; Liberal Democrat: Spokesperson for: Health 2003-04, London 2004-05 Shadow: Minister for Communities and Local Government 2005, to Office of the Deputy Prime Minister 2005-06, Secretary of State for Education and Skills/Innovation, Universities and Skills 2006-07, Secretary of State for Business, Enterprise and Regulatory Reform 2007-08, Minister for Housing 2008-10; Minister of State for Children and Families, Department for Education 2010-

Political interests: Health, housing, Middle East, Guantanamo Bay, civil liberties

Other organisations: Patron: PLIAS, Silver Star

Sarah Teather MP, House of Commons, London SW1A 0AA
Tel: 020 7219 2284 Fax: 020 7219 0041
E-mail: teathers@parliament.uk
Constituency: 1 High Road, Willesden Green, London NW10 2TE
Tel: 020 8459 0455 Fax: 020 8830 3280
Website: www.sarahteather.org.uk

GENERAL ELECTION RESULT

		%
Teather, S. (Lib Dem)*	20,026	44.2
Butler, D. (Lab)*	18,681	41.2
Rajput, S. (Con)	5,068	11.2
Ali, S. (Green)	668	1.5
Williams, E. (Christian)	488	1.1
Duale, A. (Respect)	230	0.5
McCastree, D. (Ind)	163	0.4
Majority	1,345	2.97
Electorate	74,076	
Turnout	45,324	61.19

**Member of last parliament*

CONSTITUENCY SNAPSHOT

Brent Central has been created to take in parts of the abolished Brent East and Brent South seats. The new seat takes in nine wards from across the London Borough of Brent spanning from Dollis Hill in the north to Queen's Park in the south.

Brent East was previously a Labour seat held by Ken Livingstone until 2001. His replacement, Paul Daisley, died in 2003. Labour lost its first by-election in 15 years when Sarah Teather won with a 29 per cent swing to the Liberal Democrats. In 2005 she consolidated her hold, winning a 2,712 majority.

Brent South was a Labour seat represented by Paul Boateng between 1987 and 2005. Labour had a 17,380 majority in 2001. The Lib Dems made gains in 2005 but were still over 11,000 votes behind Dawn Butler.

Liberal Democrat Sarah Teather managed to hold onto this new seat with a slim 1,345 majority despite a strong Labour challenge from Dawn Butler.

Housing ranges from council estates in Stonebridge to detached family homes in Mapesbury. The constituency is home to Neasden Temple, the largest Hindu temple in the country, which serves Brent's large Hindu community.

The £757 million Wembley Stadium, Conference Centre and Empire Pool are within the constituency, along the boundary with Brent North. The stadium opened in 2007, providing an economic boost with thousands of new jobs. Facilities will be used at the 2012 London Olympics.

Gareth Thomas

Harrow West ***(returning MP)***

Boundary changes

Tel: 020 7219 4243
E-mail: thomasgr@parliament.uk

Labour/Co-operative

Date of birth: 15 July 1967

Education: Hatch End High School; Lowlands College; University College of Wales, Aberystwyth (BSc (Econ) politics 1988); University of Greenwich (PGCE 1992); King's College, London (MA imperial and Commonwealth studies 1996)

Non-political career: Member, AMICUS; Councillor London Borough of Harrow 1990-97: Labour Group Whip 1996-96

Political career: Member for Harrow West 1997-2010, for Harrow West (revised boundary) since 6 May 2010 general election; PPS to Charles Clarke: as Minister of State, Home Office 1999-2001, as Minister without Portfolio and Party Chair 2001-02, Secretary of State for Education and Skills 2002-03; Sponsored Private Member's Bill, Industrial and Provident Societies Act 2002; Parliamentary Under-Secretary of State: Department for International Development 2003-08, Department for Business, Enterprise and Regulatory Reform (Trade and Consumer Affairs) 2007-08; Minister of State (Trade, Investment and Consumer Affairs/Trade, Development and Consumer Affairs), Departments for: Business, Enterprise and Regulatory Reform 2008-09, International Development 2008-10; *Select Committees:* Member: Environmental Audit 1997-99; Member: Fabian Society, SERA; Chair Co-operative Party 2000-

Political interests: Energy, mutuals, health, environment; Europe, Norway, India, Sri Lanka, Pakistan

Other organisations: Vice-Chair, Association of Local Government Social Services Committee; Fellow Industry and Parliament Trust 2003; United Services Club, Pinner; *Publications:* At the Energy Crossroads Policies for a Low Carbon Economy (Fabian Society 2001); From Margins to Mainstream – Making Social Resposibility Part of Corporate Culture (2002)

Recreations: Canoeing, running, rugby union

Gareth Thomas MP, House of Commons, London SW1A 0AA
Tel: 020 7219 4243 Fax: 020 7219 1154
E-mail: thomasgr@parliament.uk
Constituency: 132 Blenheim Road, West Harrow, Middlesex HA2 7AA
Tel: 020 8861 6300 Fax: 020 8861 6414

GENERAL ELECTION RESULT

		%
Thomas, G. (Lab/Co-op)*	20,111	43.6
Joyce, R. (Con)	16,968	36.8
Noyce, C. (Lib Dem)	7,458	16.2
Crossman, H. (UKIP)	954	2.1
Langley, R. (Green)	625	1.4
Majority	3,143	6.82
Electorate	71,510	
Turnout	46,116	64.49

**Member of last parliament*

CONSTITUENCY SNAPSHOT

For decades this was one of the safer Tory seats in London, first held by Norman Bower from 1945-51, followed by Sir Alfred Braithwaite who held the seat until 1960. Sir Alfred's successor was Sir John Page, who remained the local MP until 1987, when he was succeeded by Robert Hughes, former chairman of the Young Conservatives.

Hughes' parliamentary career came to an end in 1997 when Labour's Gareth Thomas's took the seat on a 17.5 per cent swing. Thomas's majority increased in 2001 to over 6,000 votes, but fell to 2,028 in 2005. Thomas managed to hold on with a majority of 3,143 despite a 5.7 per cent swing to the Conservatives.

Harrow West gained Harrow on the Hill part-ward and the wards of Greenhill and Marlborough from Harrow East. Hatch End, Pinner, and Pinner South were transferred to the new constituency of Ruislip, Northwood and Pinner.

Harrow is a culturally, ethnically and economically diverse place, with around a third of its population being Asian.

At just over three-quarters, Harrow West has one of the highest concentrations of owner-occupiers in the country.

Harrow residents have access to some of the best primary and secondary schools in the country. Edgware Hospital was closed in 2002.

Emily Thornberry

Islington South and Finsbury ***(returning MP)***

No boundary changes

Tel: 020 7219 5676
E-mail: thornberrye@parliament.uk
Website: www.emilythornberry.com

Date of birth: 27 July 1960; Daughter of late Sallie Thornberry and Cedric Thornberry

Education: Church of England Secondary Modern, Guildford; Burlington Danes, Shepherd's Bush, London; Kent University, Canterbury (BA law 1982); Married Christopher Nugee 1992 (1 daughter 2 sons)

Non-political career: Member Mike Mansfield's Chambers: Tooks Court 1985; Member Unite (TGWU sector) 1985-

Political career: Member for Islington South and Finsbury since 5 May 2005 general election; PPS to Joan Ruddock as Minister of State, Department of Energy and Climate Change 2009-10; *Select Committees:* Member: Environmental Audit 2005-07, Joint Committee on the Draft Legal Services Bill 2006, Communities and Local Government 2006-09

Political interests: Housing, environment, poverty and disadvantage; Middle East

Other organisations: Society of Labour Lawyers 1983; Friends of the Earth 1990; Friends and Family of Shiraz Miah 1995

Recreations: Family, cycling, travel

Emily Thornberry MP, House of Commons, London SW1A 0AA
Tel: 020 7219 5676 Fax: 020 7219 5955
E-mail: thornberrye@parliament.uk
Constituency: 65 Barnsbury Street, Islington, London N1 1EJ
Tel: 020 7697 9307 Fax: 020 7697 4587
Website: www.emilythornberry.com

GENERAL ELECTION RESULT

		%	+/-
Thornberry, E. (Lab)*	18,407	42.3	2.5
Fox, B. (Lib Dem)	14,838	34.1	-4.1
Cox, A. (Con)	8,449	19.4	4.6
Humphreys, J. (Green)	710	1.6	-3.1
McDonald, R. (UKIP)	701	1.6	0.1
Dodds, J. (England)	301	0.7	
Deboo, R. (AC)	149	0.3	
Majority	3,569	8.19	
Electorate	67,649		
Turnout	43,555	64.38	

**Member of last parliament*

CONSTITUENCY SNAPSHOT

This seat has been Labour since the Second World War. In 1983 Labour's Chris Smith won by a majority of 363 votes and also won in 1987 with a similar majority.

However, in 1992 the Labour lead increased to over 10,000 and by 1997 Smith polled over 60 per cent. Emily Thornberry was first elected in 2005 with a majority of just 484. Thornberry was re-elected with an improved vote-share and much-increased majority of 3,569.

Islington is known for its coffee shops, wine bars and restaurants on Upper Street and around Angel.

Islington South is more affluent than its northern counterpart, with slightly lower unemployment and fewer people with no qualifications.

The main political issues in the seat are a lack of affordable housing, youth provision, a greener Islington, and the closure of post offices.

John Thurso

***Caithness, Sutherland and Easter Ross** (returning MP)*

No boundary changes

Tel: 020 7219 1752
E-mail: thursoj@parliament.uk
Website: www.johnthurso.org.uk

Liberal Democrat

Date of birth: 10 September 1953; Son of late Robin, 2nd Viscount Thurso and Margaret, née Robertson; succeeded his father 1995 as 3rd Viscount Thurso and 6th Bt of Ulbster

Education: Eton College; Westminster Technical College (HCIMA membership exam 1974); Married Marion Ticknor, née Sage 1976 (2 sons 1 daughter)

Non-political career: Director: Lancaster Hotel 1981-85, Cliveden House Ltd 1985-93; Non-executive director Savoy Hotel plc 1993-98; Managing director Fitness and Leisure Holdings Ltd 1995-2001; Chair: Thurso Fisheries Ltd 1995-, Scrabster Harbour Trust 1996-2001; Director: Profile Recruitment and Management Ltd 1996-2002, Walker Greenbank plc 1997-2002, Anton Mosiman Ltd 1997-2002; Chairman International Wine and Spirit Competition 1999-; Deputy Chairman Millennium and Copthorn's Hotels plc 2002-09

Political career: Member for Caithness, Sutherland and Easter Ross 2001-05, for Caithness, Sutherland and Easter Ross (revised boundary) since 5 May 2005 general election; Liberal Democrat Whip 2001-02; Scottish Liberal Democrat Spokesperson for Tourism 2001-05; Liberal Democrat: Spokesperson for Scotland 2001-06, Shadow Secretary of State for: Transport 2003-05, Scotland 2003-06, Business, Enterprise and Regulatory Reform 2008-09, Business, Innovation and Skills 2009-10; *Select Committees:* Member: Culture, Media and Sport 2001-05, Administration 2005-10, Treasury 2006-10; Liberal Democrat Lords spokesperson for: Tourism 1996-99, Food 1998-99; Member Liberal Democrat Party Federal Policy Committee 1999-2001

Political interests: Tourism, House of Lords reform

Other organisations: Chair: Bucks Game Conservancy 1990-92, BHA Clubs Panel 1992-1996, Master Innholders Association 1995-97; President Licensed Victuallers Schools 1996-97; President and Fellow, Tourism Society 1999-; Patron: Hotel Catering and International Management Association 1997-2003, Institute of Management Services 1998-; President Academy of Food and Wine Service 1998-; Chair UK Springboard Festival Year 2000; First former hereditary member of House of Lords to become an MP; FHCIMA 1991; FInstD 1997; Liveryman Innholders' Company 1997; Freeman City of London 1991; Brook's, New Edinburgh; *Publications:* Tourism Tomorrow (1998)

John Thurso MP, House of Commons, London SW1A 0AA
Tel: 020 7219 1752 Fax: 020 7219 3797
E-mail: thursoj@parliament.uk
Website: www.johnthurso.org.uk

GENERAL ELECTION RESULT

		%	+/-
Thurso, J. (Lib Dem)*	11,907	41.4	-9.0
MacKay, J. (Lab)	7,081	24.6	3.7
Urquhart, J. (SNP)	5,516	19.2	5.9
Graham, A. (Con)	3,744	13.0	2.8
Campbell, G. (Ind)	520	1.8	
Majority	4,826	16.78	
Electorate	47,257		
Turnout	28,768	60.88	

**Member of last parliament*

CONSTITUENCY SNAPSHOT

Robert Maclennan was Labour MP for Caithness and Sutherland from 1966. In 1981 he joined the SDP, and held the seat for the SDP/Liberal Alliance in 1983 and 1987. He went on to win the seat as a Lib Dem in 1992 and won the enlarged Caithness, Sutherland and Easter Ross seat in 1997.

Maclennan retired in 2001. His replacement, (Viscount) John Thurso, became the first hereditary peer to lose his seat in the Lords and gain one in the Commons.

In 2005 Thurso increased his majority to 8,168. He held the seat in 2010 with a reduced majority of 4,826.

This northern tip of the British mainland stretches over 100 kilometres from the Cromarty Firth to John o' Groats, and its most populous part is southerly Easter Ross, especially Invergordon which depends on oil-related industries.

The huge wilderness to the north, rising through Sutherland to Caithness, is sparsely populated, with the exception of Thurso and Wick, which are local hubs for the area's scattered farming and fishing communities.

Around half the workforce has non-manual jobs, and a significant minority of the population work as farmers, crofters and fishermen. However, tourism is becoming increasingly important.

The £2.9 billion clean-up operation at Dounreay, the former fast-breeder reactor plant, was expected to be completed in 2033. This has since been brought forward to 2025. The area will lose one of its largest employers when the process is completed.

Rt Hon **Stephen Timms**

East Ham (returning MP)

Boundary changes

Tel: 020 7219 4000
E-mail: timmss@parliament.uk
Website: www.stephentimms.org.uk

Date of birth: 29 July 1955; Son of late Ronald James Timms, engineer, and Margaret Joyce Timms, retired school teacher

Education: Farnborough Grammar School, Hampshire; Emmanuel College, Cambridge (MA mathematics 1977, MPhil operational research 1978); Married Hui-Leng Lim 1986

Non-political career: Computer and telecommunications industry; Logica Ltd 1978-86; Ovum Ltd 1986-94; Member Unite; London Borough of Newham: Councillor 1984-97, Leader of the Council 1990-94; Board Member, East London Partnership (now East London Business Alliance) 1990-2006; Stratford Development Partnership 1992-94

Political career: Member for Newham North East from 9 June 1994 by-election to 1997, for East Ham 1997-2010, for East Ham (revised boundary) since 6 May 2010 general election; PPS to Andrew Smith as Minister of State, Department for Education and Employment 1997-98; Joint PPS to Marjorie Mowlam as Secretary of State for Northern Ireland 1998; Department of Social Security 1998-99: Parliamentary Under-Secretary of State 1998-99, Minister of State 1999; Financial Secretary, HM Treasury 1999-2001; Minister of State: Department for Education and Skills (School Standards) 2001-02, Department of Trade and Industry (Energy, E-Commerce and Postal Services) 2002-04; Financial Secretary, HM Treasury 2004-05; Minister of State Department for Work and Pensions (Pensions Reform) 2005-06; Chief Secretary to the Treasury 2006-07; Minister of State (Competitiveness), Department for Business, Enterprise and Regulatory Reform 2007-08; Minister of State, Department for Work and Pensions 2008; Financial Secretary, HM Treasury 2008-10; Parliamentary Under-Secretary of State, Department for Business, Innovation and Skills (Digital Britain) 2009-10; *Select Committees:* Member: Treasury 1996-97, Public Accounts 2004-05, Joint Committee on Tax Law Rewrite Bills 2009-10; Joint vice-chair, Christian Socialist Movement 1995-98

Political interests: Economic policy, urban regeneration, telecommunications, employment, Christian socialism

Other organisations: Fellow Industry and Parliament Trust 1997; PC 2006; Honorary doctorate; *Publications:* Broadband Communications: The Commercial Impact (1987)

Rt Hon Stephen Timms MP, House of Commons, London SW1A 0AA Tel: 020 7219 4000 Fax: 020 7219 2949
E-mail: timmss@parliament.uk
Website: www.stephentimms.org.uk

GENERAL ELECTION RESULT

		%
Timms, S. (Lab)*	35,471	70.4
Shea, P. (Con)	7,645	15.2
Brice, C. (Lib Dem)	5,849	11.6
O'Connor, B. (England)	822	1.6
Maciejowska, J. (Green)	586	1.2
Majority	27,826	55.24
Electorate	90,675	
Turnout	50,373	55.55

**Member of last parliament*

CONSTITUENCY SNAPSHOT

Ron Leighton represented this seat in Westminster for Labour from 1979 until his death in 1994. Stephen Timms won the by-election.

In the 1997 election Labour's majority more than doubled from 9,461 in 1992 to 19,538. Timms has retained the seat since: in 2001 his share of the vote increased to 73.1 per cent, but his majority in the 2005 election was cut to 13,155 as Respect polled 8,171 votes to take second place from the Tories. Timms built on his huge popularity to secure over 70 per cent of the vote, helped by a 7.7 per cent swing away from the Tories.

East Ham has gained part-wards Beckton and Royal Docks from Poplar and Canning Town and part of Boleyn from West Ham, and has lost its part of Custom House ward to West Ham.

The constituency contains the King George V and the Royal Albert docks, City airport and Green Street, the UK's most successful Asian shopping street.

The ExCel exhibition centre at the Royal Docks attracts thousands of visitors, and is providing the impetus for the building of seven new international hotels in its immediate vicinity.

The Silvertown Quays redevelopment project close to the Royal Victoria Dock will be developed in four phases into the 2020s. Projects under way for the 2012 Olympics should help significantly regenerate the Lea Valley area, of which the constituency is a part.

Edward Timpson

Crewe and Nantwich (returning MP)

Boundary changes

Tel: 020 7219 8027
E-mail: timpsone@parliament.uk
Website: www.edwardtimpsonmp.com

Date of birth: 26 December 1973; Son of William John Anthony Timpson and Alexandra Winkfield Timpson

Education: Uppingham School, Rutland; Durham University (BA politics 1996); Law conversion; College of Law, London (LLB 1997); Married Julia Helen Still 2002 (1 son 2 daughters)

Non-political career: Called to the Bar 1999; Practises family law

Political career: Member for Crewe and Nantwich 22 May 2008 by-election to 2010, for Crewe and Nantwich (revised boundary) since 6 May 2010 general election; *Select Committees:* Member: Children, Schools and Families 2008-10, Joint Committee on Human Rights 2008-10; Campaign co-ordinator, Eddisbury Conservative Association 2006-07

Political interests: Crime, family, education; *Publications:* Author of children's book

Recreations: Marathons, travel, writing, cricket, football

Edward Timpson MP, House of Commons, London SW1A 0AA
Tel: 020 7219 8027 Fax: 020 7219 2868
E-mail: timpsone@parliament.uk
Website: www.edwardtimpsonmp.com

GENERAL ELECTION RESULT

		%
Timpson, E. (Con)*	23,420	45.9
Williams, D. (Lab)	17,374	34.0
Wood, R. (Lib Dem)	7,656	15.0
Clutton, J. (UKIP)	1,414	2.8
Williams, P. (BNP)	1,043	2.0
Parsons, M. (Ind)	177	0.4
Majority	6,046	11.84
Electorate	77,460	
Turnout	51,084	65.95

**Member of last parliament*

CONSTITUENCY SNAPSHOT

Between 1945 and 2008 Crewe was represented by just two MPs, both of them Labour. Schofield Allen held the seat until 1974 and was succeeded by Gwyneth Dunwoody.

This seat was formed in 1983 from the Labour seat of Crewe and the Tory wards of Nantwich. Despite a swing of almost 4 per cent to the Conservatives in 2005, her majority remained 7,000. She died in April 2008 and the by-election was won by Conservative Edward Timpson, the first time the Tories had won a Labour seat at a by-election since 1978.

In 2010 Timpson held the seat and secured a majority of 6,046.

The seat lost two part-wards to Eddisbury, and gained one in return.

Crewe is a working-class enclave in the middle-class county of Cheshire. It is famous for the quality of its engineering works and major railway junction: the West Coast mainline splits at Crewe.

Crewe Business Park is home to several national and international companies including Bentley, Adtranz, Fujitsu and Osmetech. Manchester Metropolitan University has a large campus outside the town. Nantwich is a traditional market town, famous for its Tudor buildings, antique shops and smaller enterprises, including cheesemaking.

Crewe town centre and the railway and bus stations are to be redeveloped in a £100 million project that will also provide new residential and office space.

Justin Tomlinson

North Swindon

Boundary changes

Tel: 020 7219 3000
E-mail: justin.tomlinson.mp@parliament.uk

Date of birth: 5 November 1976

Education: Harry Cheshire High School, Kidderminster; Oxford Brookes University (BA business and marketing 1999); Married Halina Roberts 2005

Non-political career: Sales and marketing manager, First Leisure 1999-2000; Marketing executive, Point to Point 2000; Director, TB Marketing Solutions Ltd 2000-; Swindon Borough Council: Councillor 2000-, Cabinet member 2003-

Political career: Contested North Swindon 2005 general election. Member for North Swindon since 6 May 2010 general election; Chair, Oxford Brookes University Conservative Students' Association 1995-99; Deputy chair, North Swindon Conservative Association 2000-04; National chair, Conservative Future 2002-03

Other organisations: Committee member, Bracknell Town FC 2003-05

Recreations: Football, cricket

Justin Tomlinson MP, House of Commons, London SW1A 0AA
Tel: 020 7219 3000 E-mail: justin.tomlinson.mp@parliament.uk
Constituency: Swindon Conservative Association, Unit 17, Dorcan Business Village, Murdock Road, Swindon SN3 5HY
Tel: 01793 522123 Website: www.swindonconservatives.com

GENERAL ELECTION RESULT

		%
Tomlinson, J. (Con)	22,408	44.6
Agarwal, V. (Lab)	15,348	30.5
Lock, J. (Lib Dem)	8,668	17.2
Halden, S. (UKIP)	1,842	3.7
Bates, R. (BNP)	1,542	3.1
Hughes, B. (Green)	487	1.0
Majority	7,060	14.04
Electorate	78,391	
Turnout	50,295	64.16

CONSTITUENCY SNAPSHOT

In the 1997 general election Michael Wills was selected by Labour as their candidate and won the seat with a 7 per cent swing and a majority of 7,688. He successfully defended the seat in 2001. However, in 2005 Wills's support fell, losing him more than 9 per cent of his vote, leaving him with a majority of 2,571.

The Conservatives and Liberal Democrat votes declined between 1997 and 2001, but they both picked up supporters in 2005. Swindon was a Labour bastion in a sea of Tory blue, but Conservative Justin Tomlinson took the seat in 2010 with a 10.1 per cent swing.

The seat lost Cricklade ward to North Wiltshire whilst Blunsdon and Convingham and Nythe are now entirely within the seat's boundaries, having previously been shared with South Swindon

Swindon is situated in north Wiltshire between London and Bristol and linked to both by major motorway and rail routes. Its accessibility has turned it into a centre for business, shopping, and increasingly, tourism. The Great Western Designer Outlet Village shopping centre in Swindon is now one of the town's biggest attractions.

Manufacturing companies, such as GEC Plessey, are based here, as is one of Honda's major UK factories.

David Tredinnick

Bosworth (returning MP)

Boundary changes

Tel: 020 7219 4474
E-mail: tredinnickd@parliament.uk

Date of birth: 19 January 1950; Son of Stephen Victor Tredinnick and Evelyn Mabel, neé Wates

Education: Eton College; Mons Officer Cadet School; Graduate School of Business Cape Town University (MBA 1975); St John's College, Oxford (MLitt 1987); Married Rebecca Shott 1983 (Divorced 2008) (1 son 1 daughter)

Non-political career: 2nd Lieutenant Grenadier Guards 1968-71; Trainee, E. B. Savory Milln & Co. (Stockbrokers) 1972-73; Account executive, Quadrant Int. 1974; Salesman, Kalle Infotech UK 1976; Sales manager, Word Right Word Processing 1977-78; Consultant, Baird Communications NY 1978-79; Marketing manager, QI Europe Ltd 1979-81; Manager, Malden Mitcham Properties 1981-87

Political career: Contested Cardiff South and Penarth 1983 general election. Member for Bosworth 1987-2010, for Bosworth (revised boundary) since 6 May 2010 general election; PPS to Sir Wyn Roberts as Minister of State, Welsh Office 1991-94; *Select Committees:* Member: Liaison 1997-2005; Chair: Joint Committee on Statutory Instruments 1997-2005; Member Executive 1922 Committee 2002-05

Political interests: Complementary and alternative medicine, health care, diet and nutrition, foreign affairs, home affairs, police, law and order, environment; Eastern Europe

Other organisations: Chair British Atlantic Group of Young Politicians 1989-91; Future of Europe Trust 1991-95

Recreations: Golf, skiing, tennis, windsurfing, sailing

David Tredinnick MP, House of Commons, London SW1A 0AA
Tel: 020 7219 4474 Fax: 020 7219 4901
E-mail: tredinnickd@parliament.uk
Constituency: Bosworth Conservative Association, 10a Priory Walk, Hinckley, Leicestershire LE10 1BZ Tel: 01455 635741
Fax: 01455 612023

GENERAL ELECTION RESULT

		%
Tredinnick, D. (Con)*	23,132	42.6
Mullaney, M. (Lib Dem)	18,100	33.4
Palmer, R. (Lab)	8,674	16.0
Ryde, J. (BNP)	2,458	4.5
Veldhuizen, D. (UKIP)	1,098	2.0
Lampitt, J. (England)	615	1.1
Brooks, M. (Science)	197	0.4
Majority	5,032	9.27
Electorate	77,296	
Turnout	54,274	70.22

**Member of last parliament*

CONSTITUENCY SNAPSHOT

The seat was a Labour stronghold following the Second World War; however, Labour's dominance ended in 1970 when Adam Butler snatched a narrow victory for the Tories.

The Conservatives' lead was slight throughout the 1970s, but the party built up a safe majority by the mid-1980s. David Tredinnick took over the seat in 1987 but he only held on by 1,027 votes in 1997. Tredinnick's majority increased in 2005 to 5,319. In 2010 Tredinnick retained the seat for the Conservatives with a 5,032 majority.

Boundary changes were negligible: two wards that straddled the seat with neighbouring Charnwood are now completely within Bosworth's boundaries.

The constituency is largely rural. The town of Bosworth only makes up a small part, with Hinckley being the largest town.

The old Leicestershire coalfield once dominated the local economy, and its closure led to significant unemployment. Manufacturing industries have been a consistent presence since the beginning of the industrial revolution, though the local textiles, clothing and footwear plants seem to be in terminal decline. However, the industry still employs around a quarter of constituents.

The other traditional occupation is farming. Pigs, beef and dairy farming have been the traditional focus in the seat, though some have diversified to ride out the national agricultural downturn.

Jon Trickett

Hemsworth (returning MP)

Boundary changes

Tel: 020 7219 5074
E-mail: trickettj@parliament.uk
Website: www.jontrickett.org.uk

Date of birth: 2 July 1950; Son of Laurence and Rose Trickett

Education: Roundhay School, Leeds; Hull University (BA politics); Leeds University (MA political sociology); Married Sarah Balfour 1993 (1 son 2 daughters)

Non-political career: Plumber/builder 1974-86; Member: GMB, RMT Parliamentary Campaigning Group 2002-; Leeds City Council: Councillor 1984-96, Leader of the Council 1989-96

Political career: Member for Hemsworth 1 February 1996 by-election to 2010, for Hemsworth (revised boundary) since 6 May 2010 general election; PPS to Peter Mandelson: as Minister without Portfolio 1997-98, as Secretary of State for Trade and Industry July-December 1998, to Gordon Brown as Prime Minister 2008-10; *Select Committees:* Member: Unopposed Bills (Panel) 1997-2010, Education and Employment 2001, Education and Employment (Employment Sub-Committee) 2001, Public Accounts 2001-06

Political interests: Economic policy, finance, industry, sport; Middle East, France, USA

Other organisations: British Cycling Federation; Member: British Cycling Federation, West Riding Sailing Club; Hon Life Member, Cyclists' Touring Club

Recreations: Cycle racing, windsurfing

Jon Trickett MP, House of Commons, London SW1A 0AA
Tel: 020 7219 5074 Fax: 020 7219 2133
E-mail: trickettj@parliament.uk
Constituency: 1a Highfield Road, Hemsworth, Pontefract,
West Yorkshire WF9 4DP Tel: 01977 722290 Fax: 01977 722290
Website: www.jontrickett.org.uk

GENERAL ELECTION RESULT

		%
Trickett, J. (Lab)*	20,506	46.8
Myatt, A. (Con)	10,662	24.3
Belmore, A. (Lib Dem)	5,667	12.9
Womersley, I. (Ind)	3,946	9.0
Kitchen, I. (BNP)	3,059	7.0
Majority	9,844	22.45
Electorate	72,552	
Turnout	43,840	60.43

**Member of last parliament*

CONSTITUENCY SNAPSHOT

Hemsworth has often seen large Labour majorities. In 1987 their majority was above 20,000. George Buckley died in 1991 and at the by-election the seat went to Derek Enright. He then died in 1995, and his successor in that by-election was Jon Trickett.

In 1997 Trickett's majority was nearly 24,000. There was a slight swing to the Conservatives in 2001, and a further swing to them in 2005. However, Trickett's majority was still 13,481. In 2010 Trickett was re-elected with a majority of 9,844.

Hemsworth has gained part-wards from both Normanton and Wakefield while two part-wards have been lost to the new seat of Normanton, Pontefract and Castleford.

A former mining constituency Hemsworth in West Yorkshire covers much of the semi-rural land to the south and east of Wakefield which is covered by the city council boundaries.

At one time this area had 40 pits, the biggest concentration of mines in the country after Bolsover. Now there are none left.

This dependence on coal meant that the demise of the industry in the 1980s and early 1990s was an even greater disaster here than elsewhere in the coalfields. There was virtually no other industry, communities were isolated and the motorways, great engines of inward investment, skirt round the outside. As a result, regeneration here has been slow. Though there is now some warehousing and distribution industry.

Elizabeth Truss

South West Norfolk

Boundary changes

Tel: 020 7219 3000
E-mail: elizabeth.truss.mp@parliament.uk
Website: www.elizabethtruss.com

Conservative

Date of birth: 26 July 1975; Daughter of John Truss and Priscilla Truss

Education: Roundhay School, Leeds; Merton College, Oxford (BA philosophy, politics and economics 1996); Married Hugh O'Leary 2000 (2 daughters)

Non-political career: Commercial analyst, Shell International 1996-2000; Commercial manager, Cable and Wireless 2000-05; Managing director, political division, Communication Group 2006-07; Deputy director, Reform 2007-09; Councillor, London Borough of Greenwich Council 2006-10

Political career: Contested Hemsworth 2001 and Calder Valley 2005 general elections. Member for South West Norfolk since 6 May 2010 general election; Member, Conservative Party 1996-; Chair, Lewisham Deptford Conservative Association 1998-2000

Political interests: Conservation, economy, education, food

Recreations: Film, food, design

Elizabeth Truss MP, House of Commons, London SW1A 0AA
Tel: 020 7219 3000 E-mail: elizabeth.truss.mp@parliament.uk
Constituency: South West Norfolk Conservatives, Shirley House, 23 London Street, Swaffham, Norfolk PE37 7DP Tel: 01760 721241
Website: www.elizabethtruss.com

GENERAL ELECTION RESULT

		%
Truss, E. (Con)	23,753	48.3
Gordon, S. (Lib Dem)	10,613	21.6
Smith, P. (Lab)	9,119	18.6
Hipsey, K. (UKIP)	3,061	6.2
Pearce, D. (BNP)	1,774	3.6
Allen, L. (Green)	830	1.7
Majority	13,140	26.73
Electorate	74,298	
Turnout	49,150	66.15

CONSTITUENCY SNAPSHOT

Between 1945 and 1966 the seat produced three-figure majorities at seven of the eight general elections. Since 1964 the Conservatives have represented the constituency: Paul Hawkins held the seat for 23 years from 1964, building his majority to 14,910 at his final election.

Gillian Shephard replaced Paul Hawkins in 1987. She never beat her initial majority of 20,436 but held the seat in 1992 by nearly 17,000 votes.

In 1997 Shephard's majority was cut to 2,464 but increased in 2001. She retired in 2005 and was succeeded by Chris Fraser who won with a majority of 10,086. Elizabeth Truss held the seat for the Tories in 2010 with a 13, 140 majority.

The seat gained four wards from North West Norfolk but lost nine to Mid Norfolk.

South West Norfolk encompasses many rural communities, such as Wissey, as well as large market towns like Thetford and Swaffham.

The majority of employment is in the areas from Downham Market in the west to Thetford, the seat's largest town, in the south. Industry outside these centres is primarily in agricultural production and in the provision of services to the area's numerous rural communities. Industry tends towards light manufacturing, engineering and distribution.

Andrew Turner

Isle of Wight (returning MP)

No boundary changes

Tel: 020 7219 8490
Website: www.islandmp.com

Conservative

Date of birth: 24 October 1953; Son of Eustace Albert Turner, schoolmaster, and Joyce Mary Turner, née Lowe, schoolmistress

Education: Rugby School; Keble College, Oxford (BA geography 1976, MA 1981); Birmingham University (PGCE 1977); Henley Management College; Single

Non-political career: Teacher economics and geography, comprehensive schools 1977-84; Conservative Research Department specialist: education, trade and industry 1984-86; Special Adviser to Secretary of State for Social Services Norman Fowler 1986-88; Director, Grant-Maintained Schools Foundation 1988-97; Education consultant 1997-2001; Deputy director, Education Unit, Institute of Economic Affairs 1998-2000; Head of policy and resources, education department, London Borough of Southwark 2000-01; Councillor Oxford City Council 1979-96; Sheriff of Oxford 1994-95

Political career: Contested Hackney South and Shoreditch 1992 and Isle of Wight 1997 general elections. Member for Isle of Wight since 7 June 2001 general election; Sponsored Animal Welfare (Journey to Slaughter) Bill 2001; Shadow Minister for Charities 2005-06; *Select Committees:* Member: Education and Skills 2001-05, Justice 2008-10; Contested Birmingham East 1994 European Parliament election; Appointee party education policy groups for general elections: 1987, 1992, 2001; Member Executive 1922 Committee 2001-03, 2006-; Vice-president Association of Conservative Clubs 2002-05; Vice-chairman (Campaigning) Conservative Party 2003-05

Political interests: Education, social services, economy, constitution

Other organisations: Fellow, Royal Society of Arts

Recreations: Walking, old movies, avoiding gardening

Andrew Turner MP, House of Commons, London SW1A 0AA
Tel: 020 7219 8490 Fax: 020 7219 0174
Constituency: 24 The Mall, Carisbrooke Road, Newport IW PO30 1BW
Tel: 01983 530808 E-mail: mail@islandmp.com
Website: www.islandmp.com

GENERAL ELECTION RESULT

		%	+/-
Turner, A. (Con)*	32,810	46.7	-2.1
Wareham, J. (Lib Dem)	22,283	31.7	2.3
Chiverton, M. (Lab)	8,169	11.6	-5.5
Tarrant, M. (UKIP)	2,435	3.5	
Clynch, G. (BNP)	1,457	2.1	
Dunsire, I. (England)	1,233	1.8	
Keats, B. (Green)	931	1.3	
Martin, P. (MEP)	616	0.9	
Harris, P. (Ind)	175	0.3	
Randle-Jolliffe, P. (Ind)	89	0.1	
Corby, E. (Ind)	66	0.1	-0.7
Majority	10,527	14.98	
Electorate	109,966		
Turnout	70,264	63.90	

**Member of last parliament*

CONSTITUENCY SNAPSHOT

The seat has a history of being closely contested, and since the 1970s has been traded between the Liberals/Liberal Democrats and the Conservatives. The Liberals took the seat in 1974, the Tories won it back in 1987 and ten years later in 1997, the seat reverted to the Liberal Democrats. They held on for only four years until the Conservatives won back the seat in 2001. The Tories consolidated their position in 2005, giving Andrew Turner a majority of 12,978.

Turner retained the seat with 32,810 votes giving him a majority of 10,527at the 2010 general election.

The Island boasts a diverse geographical landscape which attracts tourists by the thousand. The Island is also well known for its three prisons, Parkhurst, Albany and Camp Hill as well as the Cowes Week regatta.

The Island is predominantly rural inland. Nearly half of its total area is designated an Area of Outstanding Natural Beauty.

Most people live in the coastal towns and resorts, which include Newport, Cowes, Ryde, Ventnor, Sandown and Shanklin.

The main industries are tourism, agriculture, boat building and marine engineering. Agriculture includes sheep and dairy farming, and arable crops. Major employers include AMS (formerly BAE), GKN, the county council, and the health authority. Parkhurst, Albany and Camp Hill prisons are also an important source of local employment.

Karl Turner

Kingston upon Hull East

Boundary changes

Tel: 020 7219 3000
E-mail: karl.turner.mp@parliament.uk
Website: www.easthull.org.uk

Date of birth: 15 April 1971; Son of Ken Turner, trade unionist, and Pat Turner

Education: Bransholme High School; Hull College; Hull University (law 2004)

Non-political career: Youth training scheme, Hull City Council; Self-employed antiques dealer; Called to the Bar, Middle Temple 2005; Barrister: Max Gold Partnership, Hull 2005-09, Wilberforce Chambers, Hull 2009-; Member: Unison, GMB

Political career: Member for Kingston upon Hull East since 6 May 2010 general election

Karl Turner MP, House of Commons, London SW1A 0AA
Tel: 020 7219 3000 E-mail: karl.turner.mp@parliament.uk
Constituency: 430 Holderness Road, Hull HU9 3DW
Tel: 07730 499461 Website: www.easthull.org.uk

GENERAL ELECTION RESULT

		%
Turner, K. (Lab)	16,387	47.9
Wilcock, J. (Lib Dem)	7,790	22.8
Mackay, C. (Con)	5,667	16.6
Hookem, M. (UKIP)	2,745	8.0
Uttley, J. (NF)	880	2.6
Burton, M. (England)	715	2.1
Majority	8,597	25.15
Electorate	67,530	
Turnout	34,184	50.62

CONSTITUENCY SNAPSHOT

John Prescott first won the seat in 1970, taking over from Harry Pursey who had held the seat since 1945. Apart from a blip in 1983, Prescott regularly racked up absolute majorities.

The Liberal Democrats moved into a distant second place in 2001 on the back of a 5.9 per cent swing and consolidated that position in 2005 with a further 7 per cent swing in their favour. However, this still left Prescott with a 11,747 vote majority. Prescott retired in 2010 and Karl Turner was elected for Labour with a majority of 8,597.

The Hull seats were redrawn so that the constituency boundaries coincide with the local government wards. As a result, this seat trades part wards with Hull North, gaining parts of Sutton and Holderness wards and losing part of Bransholme West.

The east end of this East Yorkshire city is largely an area of docks, terraced streets and housing estates.

This is the most working-class seat in a working-class city.

Major employers include the thriving docks themselves, the BP refinery on the estuary and Reckitt Benckiser, the descendant of the firm founded in Hull in 1840.

There is a large-scale programme of new building projects taking place on the waterside in Hull. The Deep, Sir Terry Farrell's futuristic 'submarium', is located at the mouth of the Hull.

Derek Twigg

Halton (returning MP)

Boundary changes

Tel: 020 7219 1039
E-mail: twiggd@parliament.uk
Website: www.derektwigg.org.uk

Labour

Date of birth: 9 July 1959; Son of Kenneth and Irene Twigg

Education: Bankfield High School, Widnes; Halton College of Further Education; Married Mary Cassidy 1988 (1 son 1 daughter)

Non-political career: Civil servant, Department for Education and Employment 1975-96; Member GMB; Councillor: Cheshire County Council 1981-85; Halton Borough Council 1983-97

Political career: Member for Halton 1997-2010, for Halton (revised boundary) since 6 May 2010 general election; PPS: to Helen Liddell: as Minister of State, Department of the Environment, Transport and the Regions 1999, as Minister of State, Department of Trade and Industry 1999-2001, to Stephen Byers as Secretary of State for Transport, Local Government and the Regions 2001-02; Assistant Government Whip 2002-03, Government Whip 2003-04; Parliamentary Under-Secretary of State: Department for Education and Skills 2004-05, Department for Transport 2005-06, Ministry of Defence (Minister for Veterans) 2006-08; *Select Committees:* Member: Public Accounts 1998-99, Children, Schools and Families 2009-10

Political interests: Economy, education, health and poverty, housing

Recreations: Various sporting activities, hill walking, military history

Derek Twigg MP, House of Commons, London SW1A 0AA
Tel: 020 7219 1039 Fax: 020 7219 3642
E-mail: twiggd@parliament.uk
Constituency: F2 Moor Lane Business Centre, Moor Lane, Widnes, Cheshire WA8 7AQ Tel: 0151-424 7030 Fax: 0151-495 3800
Website: www.derektwigg.org.uk

GENERAL ELECTION RESULT

		%
Twigg, D. (Lab)*	23,843	57.7
Jones, B. (Con)	8,339	20.2
Harasiwka, F. (Lib Dem)	5,718	13.8
Taylor, A. (BNP)	1,563	3.8
Moore, J. (UKIP)	1,228	3.0
Craig, J. (Green)	647	1.6
Majority	15,504	37.51
Electorate	68,884	
Turnout	41,338	60.01

*Member of last parliament

CONSTITUENCY SNAPSHOT

Halton was first created in 1983 from Widnes and Runcorn, on opposite sides of the Mersey and of the political divide. Labour won Widnes comfortably at every general election after 1945, while Runcorn was Tory.

Labour won the new seat in 1983 by 7,000 votes, and then doubled their lead in 1987. In 1997 Derek Twigg was elected with a majority of 23,650. His majority fell at the two subsequent elections and was 14,606 in 2005.

In 2010 Labour held the seat with 23,843 votes giving Twigg a majority of 15,504.

The seat gained three part-wards from Weaver Vale.

Although part of Cheshire since the 1970s, Halton is very much a Merseyside seat, comprising the towns of Widnes and Runcorn on the north banks of the river Mersey, historically dominated by the chemicals industry.

Runcorn, originally developed as a canal port, is more modern than Widnes, and houses a large Liverpool overspill population.

Widnes is best known for its chemical industry and rugby league team. One of the starker creations of the industrial revolution, the town has retained a distinctly Lancastrian ambience.

Runcorn is dominated by mainly chemicals-based heavy industry. A huge INEOS chemicals plant is based there, the seat's second-largest employer.

Stephen Twigg

Liverpool West Derby

Boundary changes

Tel: 020 7219 3000
E-mail: stephen.twigg.mp@parliament.uk

Labour/Co-operative

Date of birth: 25 December 1966; Son of Ian David Twigg and late Jean Barbara Twigg

Education: Southgate Comprehensive; Balliol College, Oxford (BA politics and economics 1988); Single

Non-political career: Former President, National Union of Students; Former Parliamentary Officer: Amnesty International UK, NCVO; Former Research Assistant to Margaret Hodge, MP for Barking; Former Political Consultant, Rowland Sallingbury Casey; General Secretary, Fabian Society 1996-97; Director: Foreign Policy Centre 2005-, Special projects, Aegis Trust 2005-; Member, AMICUS-MSF; London Borough of Islington Council: Councillor 1992-97, Chief Whip 1994-96, Deputy Leader 1996

Political career: Member for Enfield Southgate 1997-2005, for Liverpool West Derby since 6 May 2010 general election; Parliamentary Secretary, Privy Council Office 2001-02; Department for Education and Skills 2002-05: Parliamentary Under-Secretary of State 2002-04: for Young People and Learning 2002, for Schools 2002-04, Minister of State 2004-05; *Select Committees:* Member: Modernisation of the House of Commons 1998-2000, Education and Employment 1999-2001, Education and Employment (Employment Sub-Committee) 1999-2001; Chair: Labour Campaign for Electoral Reform -2001, Labour Friends of Israel -2001

Political interests: Education, electoral reform, local and regional government, foreign affairs; Cyprus, Israel

Other organisations: General Secretary, Fabian Society 1996-97; Member: Amnesty International, Stonewall, League Against Cruel Sports; Governor: Merryhills Primary School, Southgate School, Middlesex University Court; Principal Patron, Theatre Company; Hon President, British Youth Council; Patron, Principal Theatre Co; Member, Holocaust Educational Trust; National Liberal; Southgate Cricket; *Publications:* Co-author, The Cross We Bear: Electoral Reform in Local Government (1997)

Stephen Twigg MP, House of Commons, London SW1A 0AA
Tel: 020 7219 3000 E-mail: stephen.twigg.mp@parliament.uk

GENERAL ELECTION RESULT

		%
Twigg, S. (Lab/Co-op)	22,953	64.1
Twigger, P. (Lib Dem)	4,486	12.5
Radford, S. (Lib)	3,327	9.3
Hall, P. (Con)	3,311	9.3
Jones, H. (UKIP)	1,093	3.1
Andersen, K. (SLP)	614	1.7
Majority	18,467	51.61
Electorate	63,082	
Turnout	35,784	56.73

CONSTITUENCY SNAPSHOT

Bob Wareing represented the seat from 1983 when he successfully challenged the incumbent Eric Ogden, who defected to the SDP in 1981.

The biggest challenge that Wareing faced at the 2001 general election was from his own selection panel. Once he had survived deselection by four votes, he triumphed with a majority of over 15,225.

Wareing was deselected in September 2007 in favour of Stephen Twigg, who ousted Tory Cabinet Minister Michael Portillo in 1997, to lose, Enfield Southgate in 2005. In 2010 Twigg was elected with a majority of 18,467.

The seat gained four part-wards from Liverpool Wavertree and two part-wards from Liverpool Walton. It loses four part-wards to Liverpool Walton and two part-wards to Liverpool Wavertree.

This residential seat to the north-east of Liverpool is made up of both inner-city and suburban areas.

The seat is one of contrasts. Europe's largest private housing estate, Croxteth County Park Estate has been constructed around the perimeters of the stately Croxteth Hall and County Park, the Croxteth County Park.

While most jobs are in the public sector, other notable employers include Littlewood's Pools on Walton Hall Avenue, and Gillmoss Trading Estate that contains numerous small businesses.

Andrew Tyrie

Chichester (returning MP)

Boundary changes

Tel: 020 7219 6371
E-mail: tyriea@parliament.uk

Conservative

Date of birth: 15 January 1957; Son of the late Derek and Patricia Tyrie

Education: Felstead School, Essex; Trinity College, Oxford (BA philosophy, politics and economics 1979, MA); College of Europe, Bruges (Diploma in economics 1980); Wolfson College, Cambridge (MPhil international relations 1981)

Non-political career: Group head office, British Petroleum 1981-83; Adviser to Chancellors of the Exchequer: Nigel Lawson 1986-89, John Major 1989-90; Fellow, Nuffield College, Oxford 1990-91; Senior economist, European Bank for Reconstruction and Development 1992-97

Political career: Contested Houghton and Washington 1992 general election. Member for Chichester since 1 May 1997 general election; Member, Public Accounts Commission 1997-; Shadow: Financial Secretary 2003-04, Paymaster General 2004-05; *Select Committees:* Member: Joint Committee on Consolidation of Bills Etc 1997-2001, Public Administration 1997-2001, Treasury (Treasury Sub-Committee) 2001-04, Treasury 2001-03, Constitutional Affairs/Justice 2005-10, Joint Committee on Conventions 2006, Treasury 2009-10, Reform of the House of Commons 2009-10, Joint Committee on Tax Law Rewrite Bills 2009-10: Chair 2010; Member Executive 1922 Committee 2005-06

Political interests: European Union, economic policy, constitutional reform, international affairs

Other organisations: Member, Inter-Parliamentary Union 1999-; MCC, RAC, Chichester Yacht Club, Goodwood Golf and Country Clubs, The Garrick; *Publications:* Various works on economic and monetary union in Europe and other European issues; The Prospects for Public Spending (1996); Reforming the Lords: a Conservative Approach (1998); Sense on EMU (1998); Co-author Leviathan at Large: The New Regulator for the Financial Markets (2000); Mr Blair's Poodle: An Agenda for Reviving the House of Commons (2000); Back from the Brink (2001); Co-author Statism by Stealth: New Labour, New Collectivism (2002); Axis of Instability: America, Britain and the New World Order after Iraq (2003); Mr Blair's Poodle goes to War: The House of Commons, Congress and Iraq (2004); Pruning the Politicians: The Case for a smaller House of Commons (2004); The Conservative Party's proposals for the funding of political parties (2006); One Nation Again (2006)

Recreations: Golf, walking

Andrew Tyrie MP, House of Commons, London SW1A 0AA
Tel: 020 7219 6371 Fax: 020 7219 0625
E-mail: tyriea@parliament.uk
Constituency: Chichester Conservative Association, 145 St Pancras, Chichester, West Sussex PO19 4LH Tel: 01243 783519
Fax: 01243 536848

GENERAL ELECTION RESULT

		%
Tyrie, A. (Con)*	31,427	55.3
Lury, M. (Lib Dem)	15,550	27.4
Holland, S. (Lab)	5,937	10.5
Moncrieff, A. (UKIP)	3,873	6.8
Majority	15,877	27.96
Electorate	81,462	
Turnout	56,787	69.71

**Member of last parliament*

CONSTITUENCY SNAPSHOT

Chichester has elected Conservative MPs since 1924, including the famous athlete Chris Chataway (1969-74) and Anthony Nelson (1974-97). Nelson enjoyed majorities of around 20,000.

He was succeeded in 1997 by Andrew Tyrie when the Conservative majority was cut by almost half with a 7.7 per cent swing to the Liberal Democrats.

In the 2001 general election there was a small swing back to the Conservatives, giving Tyrie a five-figure majority. Tyrie added another percentage point in 2005.

Tyrie retained the seat with a majority of 15,877 at the 2010 general election.

Chichester gained part of the Plaistow ward from Horsham, while losing the part-wards of Bury and Petworth and to Arundel and South Downs.

The western-most constituency in West Sussex is largely rural, stretching north from the coast across the South Downs to the borders of Hampshire and Surrey. The cathedral city and county town of Chichester was the Roman Noviomagus, and its street plan and Roman walls are still largely intact.

There are also a number of stately homes such as Goodwood with its racecourse and famous racing circuit, and Cowdray Park, the international polo venue.

Employment is predominantly in the service sector. Rolls-Royce has built their new £60 million factory and headquarters at Goodwood. Tourism is also important to the area.

Chuka Umunna

Streatham

Boundary changes

Tel: 020 7219 3000
E-mail: chuka.umunna.mp@parliament.uk
Website: www.streathamlabour.org.uk

Date of birth: 17 October 1978

Education: St Dunstam's College, Catford; Manchester University (LLB English and French law 2001); Nottingham Law School 2002

Non-political career: Trainee solicitor/solicitor, Herbert Smith LLP 2002-06; Solicitor, Rochman Landau 2006-; Member: GMB, Unite; Governor, Sunnyhill Primary School, Streatham; Board member, Sunnyhill Children's Centre

Political career: Member for Streatham since 6 May 2010 general election; Member, Labour Party 1997-; Vice-chair, Streatham Labour Party 2004-08; Member, BAME Labour 2006-

Political interests: Economy, employment, equality, education, home affairs and justice, climate change, community and youth engagement

Other organisations: Member, Fabian Society 1998-; Management committee member, Compass 2003-; Trustee, Generation Next Foundation; *Publications:* Founder and former editor, TMP Online 2007-08

Chuka Umunna MP, House of Commons, London SW1A 0AA
Tel: 020 7219 3000 E-mail: chuka.umunna.mp@parliament.uk
Constituency: Streatham Labour Party, PO Box 59960,
London SW16 9AA Tel: 020 7501 4111
Website: www.streathamlabour.org.uk

GENERAL ELECTION RESULT

		%
Umunna, C. (Lab)	20,037	42.8
Nicholson, C. (Lib Dem)	16,778	35.8
Bhansali, R. (Con)	8,578	18.3
Findlay, R. (Green)	861	1.8
Macharia, G. (Christian)	237	0.5
Polenceus, J. (England)	229	0.5
Lepper, P. (WRP)	117	0.3
Majority	3,259	6.96
Electorate	74,531	
Turnout	46,837	62.84

CONSTITUENCY SNAPSHOT

From 1918 until 1992 Streatham returned only Conservative MPs. However, in 1992 Keith Hill became its first ever Labour MP defeating Sir William Shelton with a majority of 2,317.

Labour were aided by boundary changes in 1997, which moved the northern edge of this constituency to include the inner-city neighbourhoods near the heart of Brixton. In 2005 the Liberal Democrats took over 10 per cent off Labour's vote-share, although Keith Hill still had a majority of 7,456. Keith Hill retired in 2010 and Chuka Umunna held this seat for Labour with a 3,259 majority despite a 5 per cent swing to the Liberal Democrats.

The seat lost three part-wards to Dulwich and West Norwood.

This south London constituency is a seat of some contrasts. From the leafier suburbs in Streatham, to Clapham, via Balham and Brixton, this is a culturally and ethnically diverse constituency.

With its short journey times into the West End and the City on the Northern Line, Clapham is a desirable place for young professionals to live.

Ethnically and culturally, Streatham is one of the most diverse communities in the UK.

Lambeth LEA caters for a highly diverse population with around 150 languages being spoken in its school.

Paul Uppal

Wolverhampton South West

Boundary changes

Tel: 020 7219 3000
E-mail: paul.uppal.mp@parliament.uk
Website: www.pauluppal.wordpress.com

Conservative

Date of birth: 14 June 1967

Education: Harborne Hill Comprehensive; Warwick University 1989; Married (3 children)

Non-political career: Runs own business

Political career: Contested Birmingham Yardley 2005 general election. Member for Wolverhampton South West since 6 May 2010 general election

Political interests: Crime

Paul Uppal MP, House of Commons, London SW1A 0AA
Tel: 020 7219 3000 E-mail: paul.uppal.mp@parliament.uk
Constituency: Wolverhampton Conservative Association, Carver Building, Neachells Lane, Wolverhampton,
West Midlands WV11 3QQ Tel: 01902 866355; 07950 985886
Website: www.pauluppal.wordpress.com

GENERAL ELECTION RESULT

		%
Uppal, P. (Con)	16,344	40.7
Marris, R. (Lab)*	15,653	39.0
Lawrence, R. (Lib Dem)	6,430	16.0
Mobberley, A. (UKIP)	1,487	3.7
Barry, R. (EPA)	246	0.6
Majority	691	1.72
Electorate	59,160	
Turnout	40,160	67.88

**Member of last parliament*

CONSTITUENCY SNAPSHOT

Wolverhampton South West's most noteworthy representative to date is Enoch Powell, the incumbent between 1950 and 1974. Powell left the Tories in 1974 to become an Ulster Unionist when the Heath government joined the European Community, leaving the seat for Nicholas Budgen. Budgen polled over 50 per cent of the vote in the 1979, 1983 and 1987 elections. In 1992 his vote remained stable, but by now the opposition realignment had allowed Labour to cut the Tory majority to just under 6,000.

In 1997 Jenny Jones took the seat for Labour on a 10 per cent swing. After Jones stood down in 2001 Rob Marris held the seat for Labour. Conservative Paul Uppal defeated Marris in 2010, securing a small majority of 691.

The constituency has been scaled down to the benefit of its north-easterly neighbour, Wolverhampton South West, losing parts of three wards - Oxley, Heath Town, and Bushbury South and Low Hill - in its north-eastern corner. The seat consolidated the whole of St Peter's ward within its boundaries.

This seat is the most prosperous of the three Wolverhampton seats, stretching out from the city centre into the residential, predominantly middle-class south-west part of the city.

Fewer people work in manufacturing than in the other Wolverhampton seats. The constituency being the home of the principal Wolverhampton University campus, a large student population resides here.

Hon **Ed Vaizey**

Wantage (returning MP)

Boundary changes

Tel: 020 7219 6350
E-mail: vaizeye@parliament.uk
Website: www.vaizey.com

Conservative

Date of birth: 5 June 1968; Son of late Lord Vaizey of Greenwich and of Marina Vaizey

Education: St Paul's School, London; Merton College, Oxford (BA modern history 1989, MA); City University (Diploma law 1992); Inns of Court School of Law; Married Alexandra Mary Jane Holland 2005 (1 son 1 daughter)

Non-political career: Desk officer Conservative Research Department 1989-91; Called to the Bar, Middle Temple 1993; Barrister specialising in family law and child care 1994-96; Director: Public Policy Unit 1996-97, Politics International 1997-98; Director and partner Consolidated Communications 1998-2003; Freelance journalist 2001-; Speechwriter to Michael Howard as Leader of the Opposition 2004

Political career: Contested Bristol East 1997 general election. Member for Wantage 2005-10, for Wantage (revised boundary) since 6 May 2010 general election; Shadow Minister for the Arts 2006-10; Parliamentary Under-Secretary of State (Minister for Culture, Communications and Creative Industries), Departments for Business, Innovation and Skills and Culture, Media and Sport 2010-; *Select Committees:* Member: Modernisation of the House of Commons 2005-07, Environmental Audit 2006-07; Election aide to Iain Duncan Smith MP 2001 general election; Deputy chair Conservative Globalisation and Global Poverty Policy Group 2006-

Political interests: Arts, architecture, energy, science and technology, environment; India, Israel, Middle East, USA; *Publications:* Editor: A Blue Tomorrow (Politicos, 2001), The Blue Book on Health (Politicos, 2002), The Blue Book on Transport (Politicos, 2002)

Recreations: Horse riding, football

Hon Ed Vaizey MP, House of Commons, London SW1A 0AA
Tel: 020 7219 6350 Fax: 020 7219 2718
E-mail: vaizeye@parliament.uk
Constituency: Oxfordshire Conservatives, 8 Gorwell, Watlington, Oxfordshire OX49 5QE Tel: 01491 612852 Fax: 01491 612001
Website: www.vaizey.com

GENERAL ELECTION RESULT

		%
Vaizey, E. (Con)*	29,284	52.0
Armitage, A. (Lib Dem)	15,737	27.9
Mitchell, S. (Lab)	7,855	13.9
Jones, J. (UKIP)	2,421	4.3
Twine, A. (Green)	1,044	1.9
Majority	13,547	24.04
Electorate	80,456	
Turnout	56,341	70.03

**Member of last parliament*

CONSTITUENCY SNAPSHOT

A Conservative has represented this seat ever since the Second World War. Robert Jackson consistently polled over 50 per cent of the vote between 1983 and 1992 and still had comfortable majority in 1997.

Robert Jackson defected to Labour in 2004 and new MP, Ed Vaizey was elected with a 8,017 majority. He held the seat in 2010 with a 13,547 majority.

The seat gained the part-ward of Marcham and Shippon from Oxford West and Abingdon, in exchange for the part-wards of Appleton and Cumnor and Sunningwell and Wootton.

This seat covers the south-western quarter of Oxfordshire, between Oxford and Swindon. The main towns are Didcot, Wallingford, Faringdon and Wantage.

Didcot is a famous railway junction, while Wantage is a market town south east of Oxford lies at the foot of the Downs, and there are numerous racing stables in surrounding villages.

The town's buildings are mostly 17th and 18th century with narrow cobbled streets and passages. The main towns in the constituency have thriving shopping centres and regular market days.

Wantage is in the heart of an area full of high technology companies. The constituency also includes pretty upper Thames riverside villages and small towns occupied by well-off M4/M40 commuters and second-homers.

Shailesh Vara

North West Cambridgeshire ***(returning MP)***

Boundary changes

Tel: 020 7219 6050
E-mail: varas@parliament.uk
Website: www.shaileshvara.com

Conservative

Date of birth: 4 September 1960; Son of Lakhman Arjan Vara and Savita, neé Gadher

Education: Aylesbury Grammar School; Brunel University (LLB); Married Beverley Fear 2002 (2 sons)

Non-political career: Articled: Richards Butler 1988-90 (in Hong Kong 1989-90), Solicitor: Crossman Block 1991-92, Payne Hicks Beach 1992-93, CMS Cameron McKenna 1994-2001

Political career: Contested Birmingham Ladywood 1997 and Northampton South 2001 general elections. Member for North West Cambridgeshire 2005-10, for North West Cambridgeshire (revised boundary) since 6 May 2010 general election; Shadow Deputy Leader of the House 2006-10; Assistant Government Whip 2010-; *Select Committees:* Member: Environment, Food and Rural Affairs 2005-06; Society of Conservative Lawyers: Treasurer 2001-04, Vice-chair Executive Committee 2006-; Vice-chair Conservative Party 2001-05

Other organisations: Vice-President Small Business Bureau 1998-, Governor Westminster Kingsway College 2002-05; Member executive committee Great Fen Project 2005-

Recreations: Cricket, theatre, tae kwon do

Shailesh Vara MP, House of Commons, London SW1A 0AA
Tel: 020 7219 6050 Fax: 020 7219 1183 E-mail: varas@parliament.uk
Constituency: North West Cambridgeshire Conservative Association, The Barn, Hawthorn Farm, Ashton, Stamford, Lincolnshire PE9 3BA
Tel: 01733 239467 Fax: 01780 783770
Website: www.shaileshvara.com

GENERAL ELECTION RESULT

		%
Vara, S. (Con)*	29,425	50.5
Wilkins, K. (Lib Dem)	12,748	21.9
York, C. (Lab)	9,877	17.0
Brown, R. (UKIP)	4,826	8.3
Goldspink, S. (England)	1,407	2.4
Majority	16,677	28.61
Electorate	88,857	
Turnout	58,283	65.59

**Member of last parliament*

CONSTITUENCY SNAPSHOT

The first MP for North West Cambridgeshire was Sir Brian Mawhinney, who had represented Peterborough from 1979 to 1997. In 2005 Mawhinney was replaced by Shailesh Vara as the Conservative candidate for the general election. Although the Tory vote dipped by 4 per cent the Labour vote dropped further and Vara was elected with a majority of 9,833.

Vara held the seat with a majority of 16,677 at the 2010 general election.

Boundary changes were minor.

Bisected north to south by the busy A1, the seat contains a mix of suburban land around the city of Peterborough and a large expanse of rural land that stops just short of Stamford in the north.

The Peterborough wards are generally incongruous with the rest of the constituency. They comprise some of the poorest areas of the Peterborough unitary authority, and have higher concentrations of residents in receipt of public funds, and higher levels of council tenancies than the rest of the city.

The remainder of the constituency is far more affluent and characterised by small towns, private housing estates and rural areas.

There is also a varied manufacturing sector consisting mainly of small- and medium-sized firms. Electronics enterprises, hi-tech firms and the defence industry are important employers, though the last of these is in decline.

Rt Hon **Keith Vaz**

Leicester East (returning MP)

Boundary changes

Tel: 020 7219 4605
E-mail: vazk@parliament.uk
Website: www.keithvazmp.com

Date of birth: 26 November 1956; Son of late Merlyn Verona Vaz, teacher, and late Anthony Xavier Vaz

Education: St Joseph's Convent, Aden; Latymer Upper School, Hammersmith; Gonville and Caius College, Cambridge (BA law 1979, MA, MCFI 1988); College of Law, London; Married Maria Fernandes 1993 (1 son 1 daughter)

Non-political career: London Borough of (LB) Richmond: Articled Clerk 1980-82, Solicitor 1982; Senior solicitor LB Islington 1982-85; Solicitor: Highfields and Belgrave Law Centre 1985-87, North Leicester Advice Centre 1986-87; Member UNISON 1985-; Vice-chair British Council 1998-99

Political career: Contested Richmond and Barnes 1983 general election. Member for Leicester East 1987-2010, for Leicester East (revised boundary) since 6 May 2010 general election; Opposition Front Bench Spokesperson for the Environment 1992-97; PPS: to John Morris as Attorney General 1997-99, to Solicitors General Lord Falconer of Thoroton 1997-98, Ross Cranston 1998-99; Parliamentary Secretary, Lord Chancellor's Department 1999; Minister of State, Foreign and Commonwealth Office (Minister for Europe) 1999-2001; *Select Committees:* Member: Home Affairs 1987-92, Constitutional Affairs 2003-07; Chair: Home Affairs 2003-10; Member: Liaison 2007-10, Joint Committee on National Security Strategy 2010; Contested Surrey West 1984 and 1994 European Parliament elections; Chair: Labour Party Race Action Group 1983-2000 (Patron 2000-), Unison Group 1990-99; Vice-chair Tribune Group 1992; Labour Party Regional Executive 1994-96; Chairman National Ethnic Minority Taskforce 2006-; Member Labour Party National Executive Committee 2007-; Vice-chair Women's, Race and Equality Committee; Trustee Labour Party Pensions Regulator 2008

Political interests: Education, legal services, local and regional government, race relations, urban policy, small businesses; India, Pakistan, Yemen, Bangladesh, Oman

Other organisations: President, Leicester and South Leicestershire RSPCA 1988-99; Member, National Advisory Committee, Crime Concern 1989-93; Patron, Gingerbread 1990-; Joint patron, UN Year of Tolerance 1995; Founder patron, Naz Project, London 1999-; Patron, Asian Donors Appeal 2000-; Founder patron: Next Steps Foundation 2003, Silver Star Appeal 2006; Promoter, Race Relations Remedies Act 1994; Governor, Commonwealth Institute 1998-99; Member, Executive Committee Inter-Parliamentary Union 1993-94; EU Ambassador for Year of Inter Cultural Dialogue 2008; Fellow Industry and Parliament Trust 1993; Medal of Honour, President of Yemen on behalf of the people of Yemen 2004; PC 2006; EU Ambassador Year of Intercultural Dialogue 2008; Safari (Leicester); *Publications:* Columnist: Tribune, Catholic Herald; Co-author Law Reform Now (1996)

Recreations: Tennis

Rt Hon Keith Vaz MP, House of Commons, London SW1A 0AA
Tel: 020 7219 4605 Fax: 020 7219 3922 E-mail: vazk@parliament.uk
Constituency: 144 Uppingham Road, Leicester LE5 0QF
Tel: 0116-212 2028 Fax: 0116-212 2121
Website: www.keithvazmp.com

GENERAL ELECTION RESULT

		%
Vaz, K. (Lab)*	25,804	53.8
Hunt, J. (Con)	11,722	24.4
Asghar, A. (Lib Dem)	6,817	14.2
Gilmore, C. (BNP)	1,700	3.5
Taylor, M. (Green)	733	1.5
Ransome, F. (UKIP)	725	1.5
Sadiq, A. (Unity)	494	1.0
Majority	14,082	29.34
Electorate	72,986	
Turnout	47,995	65.76

**Member of last parliament*

CONSTITUENCY SNAPSHOT

Leicester East had been a Labour seat for decades until the sitting MP Tom Bradley defected to the Social Democrat Party on its creation in 1981. He may have come third when he fought the seat for his new party two years later at the general election, but it split the Labour vote enough to let in Tory Peter Bruinvels.

With no SDP candidate in 1987 Keith Vaz regained the seat for Labour and has held it ever since. With a lead in 1992 of 11,316 he increased his majority yet further in 1997 to 18,422. By 2005 Vaz's majority had fallen to 15,876.

Despite a 4.8 per cent swing to the Conservatives, Vaz held the seat in 2010 with a comfortable majority of 14,082.

Boundary changes were minimal and relate to two wards that overlapped the seat and Leicester West. Latimer ward is now entirely within Leicester East, while Abbey ward has moved to the western division.

Hosiery, textiles, knitwear and engineering are the biggest industries in the constituency. Around half of the workforce is a skilled or partly skilled manual worker. Some 30 per cent work in the manufacturing industry. Fewer than one-fifth of the labour force work in managerial, professional and skilled technical jobs.

Valerie Vaz

Walsall South

Boundary changes

Tel: 020 7219 7176
E-mail: valerie.vaz.mp@parliament.uk
Website: www.valerie-vaz4walsall-south.org.uk

Labour

Daughter of late Merlyn Verona Vaz, teacher, and late Anthony Xavier Vaz

Education: Twickenham County Grammar School; Bedford College, London University (BSc biochemistry 1978); Sidney Sussex College, Cambridge (Research animal nutrition); College of Law, London (common professional examination 1981; solicitors final examination 1982); Married Paul Townsend 1992 (1 daughter)

Non-political career: Trainee solicitor, Herbert Smith; Lawyer: London Borough of Brent, London Borough of Hammersmith and Fulham; Presenter, Network East, BBC; Townsend Vaz Solicitors; Deputy district judge (part-time), Midlands and Oxford Circuits; Solicitor, Government Legal Service, HM Treasury 2001-10: On secondment, Ministry of Justice 2008-09; Member: MSF 1987-2001, FDA 2001-10, Equity; School governor 1986-90; London Borough of Ealing Council: Councillor 1986-90, Deputy Council Leader 1988-89; Member, Ealing Health Authority 1986-89

Political career: Contested Twickenham 1987 general election. Member for Walsall South since 6 May 2010 general election; Contested East Midlands 1999 European Parliament election

Political interests: Constitutional affairs, international development, science and technology; India, Kashmir, Pakistan

Other organisations: Member: Lay Advisory Panel, College of Optometrists, National Trust; Premier Friend, Kew Gardens

Recreations: Music – play piano, gardening

Valerie Vaz MP, House of Commons, London SW1A 0AA
Tel: 020 7219 7176 E-mail: valerie.vaz.mp@parliament.uk
Website: www.valerie-vaz4walsall-south.org.uk

GENERAL ELECTION RESULT

		%
Vaz, V. (Lab)	16,211	39.7
Hunt, R. (Con)	14,456	35.4
Sinha, M. (Lib Dem)	5,880	14.4
Bennett, D. (UKIP)	3,449	8.4
Khan, G. (Christian)	482	1.2
Mulla, M. (Ind)	404	1.0
Majority	1,755	4.29
Electorate	64,830	
Turnout	40,882	63.06

CONSTITUENCY SNAPSHOT

Labour held on to Walsall South through tight election contests, notably 1983 when the Conservatives were only 703 votes short of taking the seat from Bruce George. After 1983 George increased his share of the vote, reaching a high of 59 per cent in 2001.

George was re-elected in 2005 with a majority of 7,946. Bruce George retired in 2010 and Valerie Vaz held the seat for Labour with a majority of 1,755.

Boundary changes saw an extensive Walsall South-North swap of part-wards. The seat gained Pleck, Darlaston South, and Bentley and Darlaston North, but ceded Blakenall, Birchills Leamore, and Willenhall South. All of St Matthew's ward is now within the seat, having previously been shared with Aldridge-Brownhills.

The decline of mining and restructuring in manufacturing hit Walsall's economy hard and it is only just recovering. This is a multi-ethnic seat, with Indian and Pakistani communities.

Walsall Council approved a £140 million project to redevelop Walsall Manor Hospital with state-of-the-art facilities in 2007.

Martin Vickers

Cleethorpes

Boundary changes

Tel: 020 7219 3000
E-mail: martin.vickers.mp@parliament.uk
Website: www.vickers4cleethorpes.net

Conservative

Date of birth: 13 September 1950

Education: Havelock School; Grimsby College; Lincoln University (BA politics 2004); Married Ann (1 daughter)

Non-political career: Printing industry; Retail industry; Constituency agent to Edward Leigh MP 1994-; North East Lincolnshire Council: Councillor, Former Cabinet Member for Environmental Services

Political career: Contested Cleethorpes 2005 general election. Member for Cleethorpes since 6 May 2010 general election

Recreations: Reading, football, cricket, travel, railways, music

Martin Vickers MP, House of Commons, London SW1A 0AA
Tel: 020 7219 3000 E-mail: martin.vickers.mp@parliament.uk
Constituency: 179 Grimsby Road, Cleethorpes DN35 7DJ
Tel: 01472 602325 Website: www.vickers4cleethorpes.net

GENERAL ELECTION RESULT

		%
Vickers, M. (Con)	18,939	42.1
McIsaac, S. (Lab)*	14,641	32.6
Morland, M. (Lib Dem)	8,192	18.2
Harness, S. (UKIP)	3,194	7.1
Majority	4,298	9.56
Electorate	70,214	
Turnout	44,966	64.04

**Member of last parliament*

CONSTITUENCY SNAPSHOT

The seat in was created in 1997, based on the Brigg and Cleethorpes division, which had been Conservative territory since its own creation in 1983.

Michael Brown polled large majorities in the old seat. But in 1997 his new Cleethorpes seat lost 16,000 voters to Brigg and Goole, reducing the notional Tory majority to under 6,500. However, a 15 per cent swing to Labour's Shona McIsaac gave her a majority of 9,176.

There was a small swing to the Tories in 2001 and a larger one in 2005, leaving Labour with a 2,642 majority. In 2010 Martin Vickers, the Conservative candidate, was elected with a swing of 7.8 per cent.

Boundary changes were minimal.

This seat centres on the Humber resort itself and curls around Grimsby on three sides, taking in Barton-on-Humber, the port of Immingham and a handful of Wolds villages to the south.

Cleethorpes combines rural and coastal resort areas close to heavy industry. The gas industries, chemical factories and refineries on the Humber bank provide much of the employment.

Food processing and cold storage are important, as is the deep-water container port of Immingham. The Kimberly-Clark paper products plant at Barton-on Humber is an important employer.

Cleethorpes itself is still popular with day trippers. Attractions include Cleethorpes Pier and the Pleasure Island theme park.

Rt Hon **Theresa Villiers**

Chipping Barnet ***(returning MP)***

Boundary changes

Tel: 020 7219 3000
E-mail: villierst@parliament.uk
Website: www.theresavilliers.co.uk

Conservative

Date of birth: 5 March 1968; Daughter of George and Virginia Villiers

Education: Francis Holland School, London; Bristol University (LLB 1990); Jesus College, Oxford University (BCL 1991); Inns of Court School of Law (1992); Married Sean Wilken 1999 (divorced)

Non-political career: Barrister Lincoln's Inn 1994-95; Lecturer in law King's College, London University 1995-99

Political career: Member for Chipping Barnet 2005-10, for Chipping Barnet (revised boundary) since 6 May 2010 general election; Shadow: Chief Secretary to the Treasury 2005-07, Secretary of State for Transport 2007-10; Minister of State, Department for Transport 2010-; *Select Committees:* Member: Environmental Audit 2005-06; European Parliament: MEP for London 1999-2005: Deputy leader Conservatives in the European Parliament 2001-02; Vice-president: Conservative Future, Association of Conservative Candidates

Political interests: Transport, economic policy, business, deregulation, information technology, animal welfare, Cyprus, financial services, environment; Cyprus, Israel

Other organisations: President: Friends of Barnet Hospital, London Green Belt Council, Barnet Borough Talking Newspaper; PC 2010; *Publications:* European Tax harmonisation: The Impending Threat; Co-author Waiver, Variation and Estoppel (Chancery Wiley Law Publications 1998)

Rt Hon Theresa Villiers MP, House of Commons, London SW1A 0AA Tel: 020 7219 3000 E-mail: villierst@parliament.uk
Constituency: 163 High Street, Barnet, Hertfordshire EN5 5SU
Tel: 020 8449 7345 Fax: 020 8449 7346
Website: www.theresavilliers.co.uk

GENERAL ELECTION RESULT

		%
Villiers, T. (Con)*	24,700	48.8
Welfare, D. (Lab)	12,773	25.2
Barber, S. (Lib Dem)	10,202	20.2
Fluss, J. (UKIP)	1,442	2.9
Tansley, K. (Green)	1,021	2.0
Clayton, P. (Ind)	470	0.9
Majority	11,927	23.57
Electorate	77,798	
Turnout	50,608	65.05

**Member of last parliament*

CONSTITUENCY SNAPSHOT

Chipping Barnet has been a Conservative seat since 1950 when the seat was won by Reginald Maudling. On Maudling's death in 1979 Sir Sydney Chapman took over and held the seat through six general elections.

Sir Sydney retained the seat for the Tories in 1997, seeing the lowest swing against the Tories of all the north London seats. On Sir Sydney's retirement in 2005 Theresa Villiers was elected with a 5,960 majority. Conservative rising star Theresa Villiers doubled her majority to 11,927 on a 5.8 per cent swing away from Labour.

The seat gained two part-wards (Coppetts from Finchley and Golders Green and Underhill from Hendon) and lost Woodhouse ward to Finchley and Golders Green.

An affluent part of London's northern stockbroker belt, Chipping Barnet lies within the most rural, north-easterly part of the borough of Barnet, on the boundary with Hertfordshire. It contains the old market town of Barnet in the north and the shopping area of North Finchley in the south.

The seat is largely upper-middle class suburbia with many desirable residential areas. The High Barnet branch of the Northern line terminates in the seat, providing good transport links to central London for the seat's many commuters. The Piccadilly line terminates just outside the seat.

There is little industry within the seat, but many constituents are employed in the retail industry.

Charles Walker

Broxbourne (returning MP)

No boundary changes

Tel: 020 7219 0338
E-mail: walkerc@parliament.uk
Website: www.charleswalker.org

Conservative

Date of birth: 11 September 1967; Son of Carola Chataway, née Ashton, and late Timothy Walker

Education: American School of London; University of Oregon, USA (BSc politics and American history 1990); Married Fiona Jane Newman 1995 (1 daughter 2 sons)

Non-political career: Communications director CSG (Corporate Services Group) Plc 1997-2001; Director: Blue Arrow Ltd 1999-2001, LSM Processing Ltd 2002-04, Debitwise 2004; Amicus; Councillor Wandsworth Borough Council 2002-06

Political career: Contested Ealing North 2001 general election. Member for Broxbourne since 5 May 2005 general election; *Select Committees:* Member: Scottish Affairs 2005-10, Public Administration 2007-10; Vice chairman: Lewisham East Conservatives 1992-93, Battersea Conservatives 2002-03; 1922 Committee: Member Executive 2006-10, Vice-chair 2010-

Political interests: Employment, taxation, the economy, mental health

Other organisations: Patron Isabelle Hospice

Recreations: Fishing, watching cricket

Charles Walker MP, House of Commons, London SW1A 0AA
Tel: 020 7219 0338 Fax: 020 7219 0505
E-mail: walkerc@parliament.uk
Constituency: 76 High Street, Hoddesdon, Hertfordshire EN11 8ET
Tel: 01992 479972 Fax: 01992 479973
Website: www.charleswalker.org

GENERAL ELECTION RESULT

		%	+/-
Walker, C. (Con)*	26,844	58.8	5.1
Watson, M. (Lab)	8,040	17.6	-7.9
Witherick, A. (Lib Dem)	6,107	13.4	1.2
McCole, S. (BNP)	2,159	4.7	
Harvey, M. (UKIP)	1,890	4.1	0.5
Lemay, D. (England)	618	1.4	
Majority	18,804	41.18	
Electorate	71,391		
Turnout	45,658	63.95	

**Member of last parliament*

CONSTITUENCY SNAPSHOT

Broxbourne is safe Tory territory. In 1997 Dame Marion Rose (MP since 1983) was re-elected with a majority of over 6,600. She increased this to 8,993 in 2001 before retiring in 2005. Charles Walker held the seat for the Tories in 2005. He was elected with a safe 11,509 majority.

Walker retained the seat in 2010 with a 18,804 majority after a 6.4 per cent swing to the Conservatives.

In the heart of the Lea valley, Broxbourne lies in a predominantly urban corner of south-east Hertfordshire. Most of its population are based in a thin strip of commuter towns and villages running up the western side of the river Lea, and the seat includes places such as Waltham Cross, Cheshunt, Wormley, Broxbourne itself, Hoddesdon and Rye Park.

The seat's good transport links and its proximity to London make it popular with business and commuters alike.

Major employers in the constituency include the headquarters of Tesco and the pharmaceutical company Merck Sharpe & Dohme. Small businesses are, however, the biggest source of employment and the constituency is home to a number of computer and light manufacturing industries.

Robin Walker

Worcester

No boundary changes

Tel: 020 7219 3000
E-mail: robin.walker.mp@parliament.uk
Website: www.walker4worcester.com

Conservative

Date of birth: 12 April 1978; Son of Peter Walker, former MP now Lord Walker of Worcester, and Tessa Pout

Education: St Paul's School, London; Balliol College, Oxford (BA ancient and modern history 2000)

Non-political career: Intern, Office of the chairman of the House Ways and Means Committee, Washington DC, September 2000; Chief executive, Property Map Ltd 2000-01; Research executive, i-Search Ltd 2001-03; Finsbury Group: Executive 2003-04, Senior executive 2004-06, Associate partner 2006-09, Partner 2009-

Political career: Member for Worcester since 6 May 2010 general election; Parliamentary assistant to Stephen Powell MP, general election campaign 1997; Volunteer assistant to Worcester Conservative Association, general election campaign 2001; Press officer to Oliver Letwin MP April-May 2005

Political interests: Education, health, police, foreign affairs, defence, business

Other organisations: Member, TRG 1997-; Carlton Club: Member, Member and deputy treasurer, Political Committee 2000-04; Member, Young Members Committee 2004-07

Recreations: Walking, reading, travel, writing, watching, cricket and rugby

Robin Walker MP, House of Commons, London SW1A 0AA
Tel: 020 7219 3000 E-mail: robin.walker.mp@parliament.uk
Constituency: Worcester Conservatives, Churchill House, 15 Sansome Place, Worcester WR1 1UA Tel: 01905 24058 Fax: 01905 330075
Website: www.walker4worcester.com

GENERAL ELECTION RESULT

		%	+/-
Walker, R. (Con)	19,358	39.5	4.6
Foster, M. (Lab)*	16,376	33.4	-8.3
Alderson, J. (Lib Dem)	9,525	19.5	3.2
Bennett, J. (UKIP)	1,360	2.8	0.4
Kirby, S. (BNP)	1,219	2.5	0.4
Stephen, L. (Green)	735	1.5	-0.5
Robinson, A. (Pirate)	173	0.4	
Nielsen, P. (Ind)	129	0.3	
Christian-Brookes, A. (Ind)	99	0.2	
Majority	2,982	6.09	
Electorate	72,831		
Turnout	48,974	67.24	

**Member of last parliament*

CONSTITUENCY SNAPSHOT

Historically a Conservative seat, Labour reduced the Conservative majority to only 6,152 in 1992. The combination of Labour's 1997 national victory and boundary changes, which took the majority of rural voters to the new seat of Mid Worcestershire, allowed Michael John Foster to win the seat for Labour with a majority of almost 7,500.

Despite a low turnout in 2001 Foster was re-elected, albeit with a reduced majority of some 5,700. In 2005 the 3.2 per cent swing from Labour to the Conservatives (much in line with the national trend) left Labour with a majority of 3,144.

Foster was defeated at the 2010 general election with a 6.4 per cent swing to the Conservative candidate, Robin Walker. Walker secured a majority of 2,982.

Worcester is a cathedral city and covers the city of Worcester and the surrounding area, including the cathedral, the Guildhall and Worcester racecourse.

The majority of the population has come from Birmingham, with the M5/M42/M6 motorway box making commuting far easier.

The numbers in business and real estate are small but there is a particularly high number employed in wholesale and retail. The city is also home to the Royal Worcester porcelain factory and the associated gift shops and museums, and the Three Choirs festival held triennially.

Ben Wallace

Wyre and Preston North ***(returning MP)***

New constituency

Tel: 020 7219 5804
E-mail: wallaceb@parliament.uk
Website: www.benwallacemp.com

Date of birth: 15 May 1970

Education: Millfield School, Somerset; Royal Military Academy, Sandhurst (Commission 1991); Married Liza Cooke 2001 (1 son 1 daughter)

Non-political career: Army officer, Scots Guards 1991-98: Service in Northern Ireland, Central America, Cyprus, Germany; Intelligence 1994-95; RGS&H advertising agency, Boston, USA 1988; Ski instructor, Austrian National Ski School 1988-89; EU and overseas director, Qinetiq 2003-05

Political career: Member for Lancaster and Wyre 2005-10, for Wyre and Preston North since 6 May 2010 general election; Shadow Minister for Scotland 2007-10; PPS to Kenneth Clarke as Lord Chancellor and Secretary of State for Justice 2010-; *Select Committees:* Member: Scottish Affairs 2005-10; Contested West Aberdeenshire and Kincardine constituency 1999 Scottish Parliament election. MSP for North East Scotland region1999-2003: Conservative Party Health Spokesperson

Political interests: Foreign policy, intelligence, home affairs, health, security, sport; Italy, Middle East, Romania, Russia, USA

Other organisations: Member Queen's Bodyguard of Scotland, the Royal Archers 2007-; Mentioned in despatches 1991

Recreations: Sailing, skiing, racing, motorsport

Ben Wallace MP, House of Commons, London SW1A 0AA
Tel: 020 7219 5804 Fax: 020 7219 5901
E-mail: wallaceb@parliament.uk
Constituency: North Lancashire Conservative Campaign Centre, Great Eccleston Village Centre, 59 High Street, Great Eccleston, Lancashire PR3 0YB Tel: 01995 672977
Website: www.benwallacemp.com

GENERAL ELECTION RESULT

		%
Wallace, B. (Con)*	26,877	52.3
Gallagher, D. (Lib Dem)	11,033	21.5
Smith, C. (Lab)	10,932	21.3
Cecil, N. (UKIP)	2,466	4.8
Majority	15,844	30.84
Electorate	71,201	
Turnout	51,380	72.16

**Member of last parliament*

CONSTITUENCY SNAPSHOT

This new seat combines wards from five Lancashire constituencies, but predominantly Lancaster and Wyre. The seat stretches up to the Stania and Carleton wards in the north and round to the Brock and Great Eccleston wards in the south west.

Ben Wallace entered parliament after the 2005 general election, defeating Labour's Hilton Dawson. Dawson had a majority of 741 before the election and Wallace won with a clear majority of 4,171.

Wallace won the new seat in 2010 with a majority of 15,844.

The seat takes in the rural areas of the city of Preston and many of the small Wyre villages.

The constituency is fairly rural, with the largest towns Poulton-Le-Fylde and Thornton. Thornton will benefit in increased tourism from the extra funding for the Blackpool tramway system. The tramway service provides visitors an accessible route to Thornton where they give the local economy a much-needed boost.

The majority of the people in the area work in the services industry, with a particularly high number in public administration. Manufacturing in this part of Lancashire is less prevalent than elsewhere in the county as it does not cover any of the major cotton mill towns.

Joan Walley

Stoke-on-Trent North ***(returning MP)***

Boundary changes

Tel: 020 7219 4524
E-mail: walleyj@parliament.uk
Website: www.joanwalleymp.org.uk

Labour

Date of birth: 23 January 1949; Daughter of late Arthur and late Mary Emma Walley

Education: Biddulph Grammar School, Staffordshire; Hull University (BA social administration 1970); University College of Wales, Swansea (Diploma in community work development); Married Jan Ostrowski 1981 (2 sons)

Non-political career: Alcoholics recovery project 1970-73; Local government officer: Swansea City Council 1974-78, Wandsworth Council 1978-79; NACRO development officer 1979-82; Member: UNISON, UNITY; Lambeth Council: Councillor 1981-85, Chair, Health and Consumer Services Committee

Political career: Member for Stoke-on-Trent North 1987-2010, for Stoke-on-Trent North (revised boundary) since 6 May 2010 general election; Opposition Spokesperson on: Environmental Protection and Development 1988-90, Transport 1990-95; *Select Committees:* Member: Trade and Industry 1995-97, Trade and Industry 1997-98, Environmental Audit 1997-2010, Chairmen's Panel 2008-10, West Midlands 2009-10; Member: SERA, SEA

Political interests: Environment, health, small businesses; Eastern Europe

Other organisations: Vice-President, Institute Environmental Health Officers; President: West Midlands Home and Water Safety Council, City of Stoke on Trent Primary School Sports Association; Member, Armed Forces Parliamentary Scheme (RAF); Fellow Industry and Parliament Trust 1990; Fegg Hayes Sports and Social

Recreations: Walking, swimming, music, football

Joan Walley MP, House of Commons, London SW1A 0AA
Tel: 020 7219 4524 Fax: 020 7219 4397
E-mail: walleyj@parliament.uk
Constituency: Unit 5, Burslem Enterprise Centre, Moorland Road, Burslem, Stoke-on-Trent, Staffordshire ST6 1JN Tel: 01782 577900
Fax: 01782 836462 Website: www.joanwalleymp.org.uk

GENERAL ELECTION RESULT

		%
Walley, J. (Lab)*	17,815	44.3
Large, A. (Con)	9,580	23.8
Fisher, J. (Lib Dem)	7,120	17.7
Baddeley, M. (BNP)	3,196	8.0
Locke, G. (UKIP)	2,485	6.2
Majority	8,235	20.49
Electorate	72,052	
Turnout	40,196	55.79

**Member of last parliament*

CONSTITUENCY SNAPSHOT

The vast majority of the residents of Stoke-on-Trent have voted Labour for generations. Like its neighbours, the northern division has returned the party's candidates since before 1945; even in 1983 Labour was over 15 per cent clear of the Conservatives in second place. Since then Labour has routinely taken well over 50 per cent of the vote share. In 2005 Joan Walley was returned with a majority of 10,036.

Walley was re-elected in 2010 with a reduced majority of 8,235 following a 8.8 per cent swing to the Conservatives.

The seat lost of the more rural Brown Edge and Endon and Stanley wards and gained the urban town of Kidsgrove.

Stoke-on-Trent North comprises the Potteries towns of Burslem and Turnstall. Burslem was the birthplace of Josiah Wedgwood and is the mother town of the Potteries.

Earthenware is still the town's speciality and pottery factories cluster around its civic buildings and shops: notable companies here include Royal Doulton and Moorland Pottery. Tunstall is the northernmost of the towns and stands on a ridge surrounded by old tile and brickmaking sites; pottery and tile making are also still a major activity here.

Employment is still weighted towards manufacturing.

Robert Walter

North Dorset (returning MP)

Boundary changes

Tel: 020 7219 6981
E-mail: walterr@parliament.uk
Website: www.bobwaltermp.com

Conservative

Date of birth: 30 May 1948

Education: Lord Weymouth School, Warminster; Aston University, Birmingham (BSc 1971); Married Sally Middleton 1970 (died 1995) (2 sons 1 daughter); married Barbara Gorna 2000 (divorced 2005)

Non-political career: Former Farmer; Sheep farm, South Devon; Director and Vice-President, Aubrey G Lanston and Co 1986-97; Member, London Stock Exchange 1983-86; Visiting lecturer in East-West trade, Westminster University

Political career: Contested Bedwelty 1979 general election. Member for North Dorset 1997-2010, for North Dorset (revised boundary) since 6 May 2010 general election; Opposition Spokesperson for Constitutional Affairs (Wales) 1999-2001; *Select Committees:* Member: Unopposed Bills (Panel) 1997-2010, Health 1997-99, European Standing Committee B 1998-2005, European Scrutiny 1999, International Development 2001-03, Treasury 2003-05, Treasury (Treasury Sub-Committee) 2004-10; Chair: Aston University Conservative Association 1967-69, Westbury Constituency Young Conservative 1973-76, Conservative Foreign Affairs Forum 1986-88, Member: Carlton Club Political Committee 1991-99, National Union Executive Committee 1992-95, Conservative Group for Europe: Chair 1992-95, Vice-President 1997-2000; Member Executive 1922 Committee 2002-05

Political interests: Agriculture, health

Other organisations: Founder Chair, Wiltshire Europe Society; Member: National Farmers Union, National Sheep Association, Royal Agricultural Society of England; Former Chairman, European Democrat Forum; Member British-Irish Inter-Parliamentary Body 1997-: Chair European Affairs Committee 2006-; Member Assembly of Western European Union 2001-: President Federated Group of Christian Democrats and European Democrats, Chair Defence Committee; Member Parliamentary Assembly of Council of Europe 2001-: Chair Media Sub-committee, Political officer European Democrat Group; Liveryman, Worshipful Company of Needlemakers 1983; Freeman, City of London 1983

Recreations: Sailing

Robert Walter MP, House of Commons, London SW1A 0AA
Tel: 020 7219 6981 Fax: 020 7219 2608
E-mail: walterr@parliament.uk
Constituency: The Stables, White Cliff Gardens, Blandford Forum, Dorset DT11 7BU Tel: 0845 123 2785 Fax: 01258 459 614
Website: www.bobwaltermp.com

GENERAL ELECTION RESULT

		%
Walter, R. (Con)*	27,640	51.1
Gasson, E. (Lib Dem)	20,015	37.0
Bunney, M. (Lab)	2,910	5.4
Nieboer, J. (UKIP)	2,812	5.2
Hayball, A. (Green)	546	1.0
Monksummers, R. (Loony)	218	0.4
Majority	7,625	14.08
Electorate	73,698	
Turnout	54,141	73.46

**Member of last parliament*

CONSTITUENCY SNAPSHOT

Between 1945 and 1950 this seat was represented by the Liberal Frank Byers. Since 1950, however, it has been represented uninterruptedly by Tory MPs. During the Thatcher and Major years the constituency was held by Nicholas Baker, but he made way in 1997 Robert Walter.

In 2005 Walter was re-elected with a reduced majority of 2,274 over the Liberal Democrats. Walter won in 2010 with a 7,625 lead over the Liberal Democrats.

Boundary changes for the election were minimal.

Set in the Dorset countryside to the north of Poole, the constituency includes the Dorset Downs and Cranbourne Chase, designated areas of outstanding beauty. It is home to the small market towns of Gillingham, Blandford Forum, and Shaftesbury, the latter notable for the remains of Edward the Martyr and as the final resting place of King Canute.

Farming is a significant part of the local economy, but there are also a large number of commuter villagers, and an above average number of constituents are employed in managerial and technical jobs.

The area benefits economically from the headquarters of the Royal Corps of Signals, which is based at Blandford army camp in the constituency, and also from its areas of outstanding natural beauty and historical importance, which attract many tourists.

David Ward

Bradford East

New constituency

Tel: 020 7219 3000
E-mail: david.ward.mp@parliament.uk
Website: davidward4bradford.org.uk

Date of birth: 24 June 1953

Education: Boston Grammar School; North Kesteven Grammar School; Trent Polytechnic (accountancy 1977); Bradford University (MBA 1981; MPhil 1984); Leicester University (MSc 1986); Married Jacqueline Ann 1984 (2 sons)

Non-political career: Accountant, Lincolnshire County Council 1971-79; Leeds Metropolitan University: Principal lecturer 1985-2004, Bradford sports partnership manager (on secondment) 2004-; UNISON (NALGO): Member 1971-79, Branch treasurer 1977-79; Member, NAFTHE 1985-; Bradford Metropolitan District Council: Councillor 1984-, Education portfolio holder 2000-04, Deputy Leader, Liberal Democrat Group 2004-, Chair, Bradford North Area Committee 2005-

Political career: Contested Bradford North 1990 by-election and 1992, 2001 and 2005 general elections. Member for Bradford East since 6 May 2010 general election

Political interests: Education, community cohesion

Other organisations: Director, Inspired Futures 2008-

Recreations: Football

David Ward MP, House of Commons, London SW1A 0AA
Tel: 020 7219 3000 E-mail: david.ward.mp@parliament.uk
Constituency: 23 Clara Road, Wrose, Bradford,
West Yorkshire BD2 1QE Tel: 01274 787959 Fax: 01274 407240
Website: davidward4bradford.org.uk

GENERAL ELECTION RESULT

		%
Ward, D. (Lib Dem)	13,637	33.7
Rooney, T. (Lab)*	13,272	32.8
Riaz, M. (Con)	10,860	26.8
Poynton, N. (BNP)	1,854	4.6
Hussain, R. (Ind)	375	0.9
Shields, P. (Ind)	237	0.6
Robinson, G. (NF)	222	0.6
Majority	365	0.90
Electorate	65,116	
Turnout	40,457	62.13

**Member of last parliament*

CONSTITUENCY SNAPSHOT

The new seat of Bradford East is mainly made up of wards from the old Bradford North seat, with part-wards coming from the other Bradford divisions as well as Shipley.

Bradford North was won by Labour's Ben Ford in 1964 and he represented the seat for nearly 20 years. When Ford was deselected in favour of Pat Wall in 1983 he stood as an independent, splitting the vote, allowing the Conservative Geoffrey Lawler to win.

In 1987 Wall narrowly won the seat back for Labour, but he died in 1990. At the by-election Terry Rooney won with a majority of more than 9,500.

He increased his majority to nearly 13,000 in 1997. In 2005 Labour's lead fell to 3,511 after a 9.8 per cent swing to the Liberal Democrats. However, in 2010 David Ward won for the Lib Dems with a majority of 365, defeating Labour with a 7.6 per cent swing.

Bradford East consists of mixed housing and a relatively high level of owner-occupancy; from the slightly more middle-class neighbourhoods in the north to the typical Victorian terraced streets and council estates nearer the city centre.

As the centre of the Yorkshire woollen industry, Bradford once processed two-thirds of the nation's wool and the main industries are still textiles and engineering, mostly by small firms.

There is a large non-white majority; with Sikhs, Hindus and Pakistani and Bangladeshi Muslims in roughly equal numbers.

Angela Watkinson

Hornchurch and Upminster ***(returning MP)***

New constituency

Tel: 020 7219 8470
E-mail: watkinsona@parliament.uk
Website: www.angelawatkinsonmp.com

Conservative

Date of birth: 18 November 1941; Daughter of Edward John Ellicott and Maisie Eileen, née Thompson

Education: Wanstead County High School; Anglia University (HNC public administration 1989); Married Roy Michael Watkinson 1961 (divorced) (1 son 2 daughters)

Non-political career: Bank of New South Wales 1958-64; Family career break 1964-76; Special school secretary Essex County Council 1976-88; London Borough of Barking and Dagenham Council: Clerk to school governing bodies 1988, Committee clerk 1988-89; Committee manager Basildon District Council 1989-94; Councillor, Group secretary, Committee chair: London Borough of Havering 1994-98, Essex County Council 1997-2001

Political career: Member for Upminster 2001-10, for Hornchurch and Upminster since 6 May 2010 general election; Opposition Whip 2002-04; Shadow Minister for: Health and Education 2004, Education 2004-05, Local Government Affairs and Communities 2005; Opposition Whip 2005-10; Government Whip 2010-; *Select Committees:* Member: Home Affairs 2001-02, European Scrutiny 2002-03; Vice-president Billericay Conservative Association 1999-; Member: Monday Club 1996-2001, Conservative Way Forward Group 1998-, Conservative Christian Fellowship 1999-, Conservative Friends of Israel 2001-

Political interests: Education, law and order, families, European affairs, constitution, local and regional government, sustainable resources, dance; Egypt, Korea, Qatar, Sweden, USA

Other organisations: Patron Romford Autistic Group Support 2007; Ambassador for Guiding

Recreations: Working, family, travel, reading, music, dining, crosswords, sudoku, visiting stately homes and gardens, animal sanctuaries

Angela Watkinson MP, House of Commons, London SW1A 0AA
Tel: 020 7219 8470 Fax: 020 7219 1957
E-mail: watkinsona@parliament.uk
Constituency: 23 Butts Green Road, Hornchurch, Essex RM11 2JS
Tel: 01708 475252 Fax: 01708 470495
Website: www.angelawatkinsonmp.com

GENERAL ELECTION RESULT

		%
Watkinson, A. (Con)*	27,469	51.5
McGuirk, K. (Lab)	11,098	20.8
Chilvers, K. (Lib Dem)	7,426	13.9
Whelpley, W. (BNP)	3,421	6.4
Webb, L. (UKIP)	2,848	5.3
Collins, M. (Green)	542	1.0
Durant, D. (Ind)	305	0.6
Olukotun, J. (Christian)	281	0.5
Majority	16,371	30.66
Electorate	78,487	
Turnout	53,390	68.02

**Member of last parliament*

CONSTITUENCY SNAPSHOT

The new constituency comprises wards from the old seats of Hornchurch and Upminster.

Alan Lee Williams won Hornchurch for Labour in 1974, but was defeated in the 1979 elections by the Conservative Robin Squire who held the seat until he was defeated by Labour's John Cryer in 1997. He lost the seat by 480 votes to the Tory James Brokenshire in 2005.

Between 1974 and 1997 Upminster had been represented only by Conservative MPs, but in 1997 Keith Darvill gained it for Labour. Conservative Angela Watkinson the seat back in 2001 with a majority of just 1,241, but increased her majority to 6,042 in 2005. Angela Watkinson took this new seat as expected, with a 16,371 majority and over 50 per cent of the vote.

This suburban area in north east London has more in common with Essex than with metropolitan London. Countryside and commuter suburbs mingle in the prosperous Cranham and Emerson Park areas of the seat, contrasting with the large council estate in Harold Hill.

Industry and commerce range from manufacturing to retail and financial services. Good transport links support the constituency's employment dependence on central London: the City itself is 12 miles to the west.

The council has been vigilant about preserving the ample supply of green space within the borough.

Tom Watson

West Bromwich East (returning MP)

Boundary changes

Tel: 020 7219 8335
E-mail: watsont@parliament.uk
Website: www.tom-watson.co.uk

Date of birth: 8 January 1967; Son of Anthony Watson, trade union official, and Linda Watson, née Pearce, social worker

Education: King Charles I School, Kidderminster; Married Siobhan Corby 2000 (1 son 1 daughter)

Non-political career: Marketing officer Save the Children 1987-88; Account executive advertising agency 1988-90; Development officer, Labour Party 1993-97; Political Officer AEEU 1997-2001; Member AEEU 1995-

Political career: Member for West Bromwich East 2001-10, for West Bromwich East (revised boundary) since 6 May 2010 general election; PPS to Dawn Primarolo as Paymaster General, HM Treasury 2003-04; Assistant Government Whip 2004-05; Government Whip 2005-06; Parliamentary Under-Secretary of State, Ministry of Defence (Minister for Veterans) 2006; Assistant Government Whip 2007-08; Parliamentary Secretary, Cabinet Office 2008-09; *Select Committees:* Member: Home Affairs 2001-03, Culture, Media and Sport 2009-10; National Development Officer (Youth) Labour Party 1993-97

Political interests: Industry, manufacturing, law and order, small businesses, defence, technology; USA, Japan, Australia

Other organisations: Fellow Industry and Parliament Trust 2006; West Bromwich Labour, Friar Park Labour; *Publications:* Co-author Votes for All, Fabian Society pamphlet 2000

Recreations: Supporter West Bromwich Albion FC, gardening, film

Tom Watson MP, House of Commons, London SW1A 0AA
Tel: 020 7219 8335 Fax: 020 7219 1943
E-mail: watsont@parliament.uk
Constituency: 1 Thomas Street, West Bromwich,
West Midlands B70 6NT Tel: 0121-569 1904 Fax: 0121-553 1898
Website: www.tom-watson.co.uk

GENERAL ELECTION RESULT

		%
Watson, T. (Lab)*	17,657	46.5
Thompson, A. (Con)	10,961	28.9
Garrett, I. (Lib Dem)	4,993	13.2
Lewin, T. (BNP)	2,205	5.8
Cowles, M. (England)	1,150	3.0
Grey, S. (UKIP)	984	2.6
Majority	6,696	17.64
Electorate	62,824	
Turnout	37,950	60.41

**Member of last parliament*

CONSTITUENCY SNAPSHOT

Labour has won West Bromwich East since its creation in 1974. By 1992 the Party's majority had increased to 2,813. They took 47.9 per cent of the vote that year. In 1997 Labour won 57.2 per cent of the vote and a 13,584 majority when their candidate, Tom Watson, replaced former minister Peter Snape.

In the 2005 general election West Bromwich East was one of only a handful of seats nationally to register a swing in favour of the Labour Party. In 2010 Watson was re-elected with a majority of 6,696 despite a swing of 7.7 per cent to the Tories.

Boundary changes were minimal.

West Bromwich is a populous area lying between Wednesbury and Handsworth in the Black Country.

No replacement has yet been found for manufacturing as the dominant employment sector. As in many parts of the West Midlands, economic restructuring away from manufacturing favours services and retail.

David Watts

St Helens North (returning MP)

Boundary changes

Tel: 020 7219 6325
E-mail: wattsd@parliament.uk

Date of birth: 26 August 1951; Son of Leonard and Sarah Watts

Education: Seel Road Secondary Modern School; Married Avril Davies 1972 (2 sons)

Non-political career: Labour Party organiser; Research assistant to: Angela Eagle MP 1992-93, John Evans MP 1993-97; Shop steward, United Biscuits AEU; St Helens MBC: Councillor 1979-97, Leader 1993-97; Vice-chair Association of Metropolitan Authorities

Political career: Member for St Helens North 1997-2010, for St Helens North (revised boundary) since 6 May 2010 general election; PPS: to John Spellar: as Minister of State, Ministry of Defence 1999-2001, as Minister of Transport, Department for Transport, Local Government and the Regions 2001-02, as Minister of State, Department for Transport 2002-03, to John Prescott as Deputy Prime Minister 2003-05; Government Whip 2005-10; *Select Committees:* Member: Finance and Services 1997-2001, 2005-06; Chair PLP North West Regional Group 2000-01

Political interests: Regional policy, education, training

Other organisations: UK President, Euro Group of Industrial Regions 1989-93

Recreations: Watching football and rugby, reading

David Watts MP, House of Commons, London SW1A 0AA
Tel: 020 7219 6325 Fax: 020 7219 0913
E-mail: wattsd@parliament.uk
Constituency: 1st Floor, Century House, Hardshaw Street, St Helens, Merseyside WA10 1QU Tel: 01744 21336 Fax: 01744 21343

GENERAL ELECTION RESULT

		%
Watts, D. (Lab)*	23,041	51.7
Greenall, P. (Con)	9,940	22.3
Beirne, J. (Lib Dem)	8,992	20.2
Robinson, G. (UKIP)	2,100	4.7
Whatham, S. (SLP)	483	1.1
Majority	13,101	29.40
Electorate	74,985	
Turnout	44,556	59.42

**Member of last parliament*

CONSTITUENCY SNAPSHOT

Labour's John Evans was first elected to Parliament in 1974 as the MP for Newton. Newton disappeared in 1983 and John Evans was elected for the new seat of St Helens North, which he held from 1983 to 1997.

David Watts was returned for the Party with a 23,417 majority in 1997. At the 2005 general election he was returned with a reduced majority of 13,962.

Watts was re-elected in 2010 with a majority of 13,101, there was a 4.6 per cent swing to the Tories.

The seat gained the part-wards of Parr and Windle from St Helens South.

The slightly more affluent of the St Helens constituencies, St Helens North, like its neighbour, is a mainly industrial seat, built on the back of the coal, glass and chemical industries. It is famous for its glass technology, its Beecham's powders and, of course, its rugby team. The area is also home to the Haydock racecourse.

Economic development is an important issue following the decline of traditional industries. Much hope is pinned on the development of trading links with Europe in the form of a direct rail freight line from the North West.

This is rugby league territory and the local club St Helens is hugely popular. Their new stadium is expected to be completed by 2011 and is part of a larger regeneration project for the whole town.

Mike Weatherley

Hove

Boundary changes

Tel: 020 7219 3000
E-mail: mike.weatherley.mp@parliament.uk
Website: www.mikeweatherley.org.uk

Conservative

Date of birth: 2 July 1957

Education: Kent College, Canterbury; South Bank Polytechnic (BA business studies 1979); Married Adriana Alves 2003 (2 sons 1 daughter)

Non-political career: Group finance and administration director, Cash Bases Group Ltd 1994-2000; Group finance controller, Pete Waterman Ltd 2000-05, Vice-president, Finance and Administration (Europe), Motion Picture Licensing Company Ltd 2007-; Councillor, Crawley Borough Council 2006-07

Political career: Contested Barking 2001 and Brighton Pavilion 2005 general elections. Member for Hove since 6 May 2010 general election

Political interests: Music, transport, manufacturing, film; Brazil, Europe

Recreations: Skiing, football (qualified referee), rock music

Mike Weatherley MP, House of Commons, London SW1A 0AA
Tel: 020 7219 3000 E-mail: mike.weatherley.mp@parliament.uk
Constituency: Hove and Portslade Conservatives, 66A Boundary Road, Hove BN3 5TD Tel: 01273 411844
Website: www.mikeweatherley.org.uk

GENERAL ELECTION RESULT

		%
Weatherley, M. (Con)	18,294	36.7
Barlow, C. (Lab)*	16,426	33.0
Elgood, P. (Lib Dem)	11,240	22.6
Davey, I. (Green)	2,568	5.2
Perrin, P. (UKIP)	1,206	2.4
Ralfe, B. (Ind)	85	0.2
Majority	1,868	3.75
Electorate	71,708	
Turnout	49,819	69.47

**Member of last parliament*

CONSTITUENCY SNAPSHOT

Until 1997 Hove was Conservative territory, having returned Conservative MPs since 1950, often with around 60 per cent of the vote. This changed, however, in 1997 when Ivor Caplin became the first-ever Labour MP for Hove, capturing the seat with a 3,959 majority.

Caplin retired in 2005 and was replaced by Celia Barlow who retained the seat by a margin of 420 votes ahead of the Tories. Barlow was defeated in the 2010 general election with a 2.4 per cent swing to the Conservative candidate, Mike Weatherley.

Boundary changes moved Goldsmid and Brunswick and Adelaide wards entirely within the seat's boundaries; the wards had previously been shared between the seat and Brighton Pavilion.

Hove's Regency terraces, wide tree-lined avenues, bowling greens, golf courses and 'pleasure grounds' make it one of the South East's most desirable places to live.

The constituency contains the district of Portslade, the entrance to Shoreham Harbour, and the southernmost reaches of the South Downs.

The major employers are the local government bodies and civic infrastructure. The Legal and General insurance company is also a major employer.

Hove acts as a dormitory town for Brighton and London, with the majority of constituents employed in managerial and skilled non-manual work.

Prof **Steve Webb**

Thornbury and Yate ***(returning MP)***

New constituency

Tel: 020 7219 6557
E-mail: webbs@parliament.uk
Website: www.stevewebb.org.uk

Date of birth: 18 July 1965; Son of Brian and Patricia Webb

Education: Dartmouth High School, Birmingham; Hertford College, Oxford (BA philosophy, politics and economics 1983); Married Helen Edwards 1993 (1 daughter 1 son)

Non-political career: Researcher then programme director, Institute for Fiscal Studies 1986-95; University of Bath: Professor of social policy 1995-, Visiting professor 1997-

Political career: Member for Northavon 1997-2010, for Thornbury and Yate since 6 May 2010 general election; Liberal Democrat: Spokesperson for Social Security and Welfare (Pensions) 1997-99, Principal Spokesperson for Social Security 1999-2001, Shadow Secretary of State for: Work and Pensions 2001-05, Health 2005-06; Chair of the Election Manifesto Team 2006-07; Shadow Secretary of State for Environment, Food and Rural Affairs 2007-08; Shadow Minister for Countryside 2008; Shadow Secretary of State for: Energy and Climate Change 2008-09, for Work and Pensions 2009-10; Minister of State, Department for Work and Pensions 2010-; *Select Committees:* Member: Ecclesiastical Committee; Member Liberal Democrat: Costings Group, Policy Committee, Manifesto Committee, Economic Recovery Group

Political interests: Social affairs, welfare, Third World, internet

Other organisations: Member: Oxfam, Amnesty International, World Development Movement; Member, Commission on Social Justice; Special Adviser to Social Security Select Committee 1986-95; *Publications:* Include: Beyond The Welfare State (1990), Co-author For Richer, For Poorer (1994), Inequality in the UK (1997)

Recreations: Internet, occasional church organist, armchair supporter of West Bromwich Albion

Prof Steve Webb MP, House of Commons, London SW1A 0AA
Tel: 020 7219 6557 Fax: 020 7219 1110
E-mail: webbs@parliament.uk
Constituency: Poole Court, Poole Court Drive, Yate, Bristol, Gloucestershire BS37 5PP Tel: 01454 322100 Fax: 01454 866515
Website: www.stevewebb.org.uk

GENERAL ELECTION RESULT

		%
Webb, S. (Lib Dem)*	25,032	51.9
Riddle, M. (Con)	17,916	37.2
Egan, R. (Lab)	3,385	7.0
Knight, J. (UKIP)	1,709	3.5
Beacham, T. (Ind Fed UK)	126	0.3
Clements, A. (Ind)	58	0.1
Majority	7,116	14.76
Electorate	64,092	
Turnout	48,226	75.24

**Member of last parliament*

CONSTITUENCY SNAPSHOT

This seat was once effectively the South Gloucestershire constituency, until it changed its name in 1974 to Northavon, following the creation of Avon county.

The Tory vote here was relatively secure until 1997, when they were defeated by the Liberal Democrat Steve Webb. Webb more than quadrupled his majority over the Tories to 9,877 in 2001. He strengthened his position further in 2005, securing a majority of 11,033. Webb was elected to this new seat with over 50 per cent of the vote and a 7,116 majority.

Thornbury and Yate is essentially the Northavon seat, but without Almondsbury, and Pilning and Severn Beach wards, and part-wards Bradley Stoke Bowsland and Winterbourne, which are now in Filton and Bradley Stoke.

Thornbury and Yate is a mixture of suburbs and small towns, and covers a large geographical area.

Much of the workforce in this middle-class, suburban constituency is employed in what is known as the 'north fringe' of Bristol. High-tech industries based outside the constituency but attracting much of its labour include BAE Systems, the Defence Procurement Agency, and Airbus.

The UK headquarters for the mobile telephone company Orange is situated in the south of the constituency and is a major employer. Other large employers in the financial services and insurance sectors include Sun Life and AXA.

Mike Weir

Angus (returning MP)

No boundary changes

Tel: 020 7219 8125
E-mail: weirm@parliament.uk
Website: www.angussnp.org

Date of birth: 24 March 1957; Son of James Gordon Weir, electrician, and Elizabeth Mary, née Fraser, hospital cook

Education: Arbroath High School; Aberdeen University (LLB 1979); Married Anne Elizabeth Jack 1985 (2 daughters)

Non-political career: Solicitor: Charles Wood and Son 1981-83, Myers and Wills 1983-84; Solicitor and partner J and DG Shiell 1984-2001; Angus District Council 1984-88: Councillor, Convener General Purposes Committee 1984-88

Political career: Contested Aberdeen South 1987 general election. Member for Angus 2001-05, for Angus (revised boundary) since 5 May 2005 general election; SNP Spokesperson for: Trade and Industry 2004, Health 2004, Environment 2004, Work and Pensions 2005-07, Trade, Industry and Energy 2005-, Environment 2007-; *Select Committees:* Member: Scottish Affairs 2001-05, Trade and Industry/Business, Enterprise and Regulatory Reform/Business and Enterprise 2005-09, Chairmen's Panel 2005-10, Energy and Climate Change 2009-10

Political interests: Disability, European affairs, rural affairs, international and sustainable development, climate change, environment, energy, industry/business

Other organisations: Law Society of Scotland 1981

Recreations: History, organic gardening

Mike Weir MP, House of Commons, London SW1A 0AA
Tel: 020 7219 8125 Fax: 020 7219 1746
E-mail: weirm@parliament.uk
Constituency: 10A George Street, Montrose DD10 8EN
Tel: 01674 675743, 16 Brothock Bridge, Arbroath, Angus DD11 1AT
Tel: 01241 874522, 2 Grampion Park, Forfar DD8 1DD
Tel: 01307 463475 Website: www.angussnp.org

GENERAL ELECTION RESULT

		%	+/-
Weir, M. (SNP)*	15,020	39.6	6.0
Costa, A. (Con)	11,738	30.9	1.5
Hutchens, K. (Lab/Co-op)	6,535	17.2	-0.7
Samani, S. (Lib Dem)	4,090	10.8	-6.7
Gray, M. (UKIP)	577	1.5	
Majority	3,282	8.65	
Electorate	62,863		
Turnout	37,960	60.39	

**Member of last parliament*

CONSTITUENCY SNAPSHOT

Andrew Welsh won the Angus East seat for the SNP in 1987. In 1997 Angus East became Angus and SNP support was supplemented by boundary changes; Welsh increased his majority to over 10,000.

Welsh stood down from Westminster in 2001 to concentrate on work in the Scottish Parliament. Michael Weir held the seat for the SNP.

In 2005 the seat lost the SNP strongholds of Monifieth and Carnoustie (which went on to help the SNP gain Dundee East). The re-drawn seat had a slender notional majority of 1.5 per cent. However, the Conservative vote share fell by 2.1 per cent and Mike Weir was re-elected with a majority of 1,601. Mike Weir doubled his majority to 3,282 from 1,590 in 2005.

Situated in the north-east of Scotland, Angus is a large rural seat dominated by farmland, but also includes the coastal towns of Montrose and Arbroath. The towns of Brechin, Forfar and Kirriemuir were added to the seat in 2005.

Arbroath was where Scotland's first declaration of independence was signed in 1320. It is also renowned for producing the famous Arbroath smokie. The town has been home to the Royal Marines' elite 45 Commando Unit since 1971.

Historically the area was a centre for manufacturing, with half the working population employed in factories. There are still a large number of engineering companies although manufacturing has declined.

The oil industry has generated jobs in Montrose, compensating for the decline in employment in fishing and agriculture in recent years.

James Wharton

Stockton South

Boundary changes

Tel: 020 7219 3000
E-mail: james.wharton.mp@parliament.uk
Website: www.jameswharton.co.uk

Date of birth: 16 February 1984

Education: Yarm School; Durham University (LLB law 2005)

Non-political career: Works for a North East law firm

Political career: Member for Stockton South since 6 May 2010 general election; Constituency chairman 2002-06

Political interests: Education, young people, law and order

Other organisations: United club, Cecil club

Recreations: Countryside, walking, eating out, friends and family

James Wharton MP, House of Commons, London SW1A 0AA
Tel: 020 7219 3000 E-mail: james.wharton.mp@parliament.uk
Constituency: Stockton Conservatives, Suite 29 DTV Business Centre, Orde Wingate Way, Stockton on Tees TS19 0GD Tel: 01642 636235 Fax: 01642 636234 Website: www.jameswharton.co.uk

GENERAL ELECTION RESULT

		%
Wharton, J. (Con)	19,577	38.9
Taylor, D. (Lab)*	19,245	38.3
Bell, J. (Lib Dem)	7,600	15.1
Sinclair, N. (BNP)	1,553	3.1
Braney, P. (UKIP)	1,471	2.9
Hossack, Y. (Ind)	536	1.1
Strike, T. (Christian)	302	0.6
Majority	332	0.66
Electorate	74,552	
Turnout	50,284	67.45

**Member of last parliament*

CONSTITUENCY SNAPSHOT

In 1997, Labour's Dari Taylor was able to win the seat with a majority of 11,585, representing a 16 per cent swing from Conservative to Labour. This was the first time Labour had taken the seat since its creation. Like neighbouring Stockton North, there was a swing of just over 3 per cent to the Conservatives in 2005. However, unlike that seat, the Conservatives managed to improve on their 2001 standing here, gaining just over 1,000 votes. Dari Taylor's majority fell by almost 3,000 votes, leaving her a margin of 6,139. Tory James Wharton won the seat from Labour with a tiny majority of 332 on a 7 per cent swing, giving his party its second North East seat.

Boundary changes moved part-ward Bishopsgarth and Elm Tree entirely within this seat, whilst part-wards Newtown, Stockton Town centre, and Western Parishes moved to Stockton North.

Unlike many of its North East counterparts, Stockton South is generally a middle-class seat and does not share many of the problems of Stockton North.

The service industry is the largest employer in the area: this half of Stockton contains the town centre, which is a focal point for shoppers from the surrounding region. The suburbs of Stockton South house many commuters from Middlesbrough, who are attracted to the more refined and rural nature of this area.

Heather Wheeler

South Derbyshire

Boundary changes

Tel: 020 7219 3000
E-mail: heather.wheeler.mp@parliament.uk
Website: www.heatherwheeler.co.uk

Conservative

Date of birth: 14 May 1959; Daughter of Mr CPC Wilkinson, retired civil servant, and Mrs FM Wilkinson, retired primary teacher

Education: Grey Coat Hospital Secondary School, London; City of London Polytechnic (1985); Married Bob Wheeler 1986 (1 daughter)

Non-political career: Manager, Rics Ins Brokers 1979-87; Company secretary and director, Bretby Inns Ltd 1997-; Councillor, London Borough of Wandsworth Council 1982-86; South Derbyshire District Council: Councillor 1995-, Leader, Conservative group 2002-, Council Leader 2007-

Political career: Contested Coventry South 2001 and 2005 general elections. Member for South Derbyshire since 6 May 2010 general election; Various posts, Putney and South Derbyshire Conservative Association 1976-99

Political interests: Affordable housing, economic regeneration

Recreations: Family, watching sport, DIY, the Archers

Heather Wheeler MP, House of Commons, London SW1A 0AA
Tel: 020 7219 3000 E-mail: heather.wheeler.mp@parliament.uk
Constituency: South Derbyshire Conservative Association, The Nissen Hut, Church Street, Swadlincote, Derbyshire DE11 8LF
Tel: 01283 224969 Website: www.heatherwheeler.co.uk

GENERAL ELECTION RESULT

		%
Wheeler, H. (Con)	22,935	45.5
Edwards, M. (Lab)	15,807	31.4
Diouf, A. (Lib Dem)	8,012	15.9
Jarvis, P. (BNP)	2,193	4.4
Swabey, C. (UKIP)	1,206	2.4
Liversuch, P. (SLP)	266	0.5
Majority	7,128	14.14
Electorate	70,610	
Turnout	50,419	71.40

CONSTITUENCY SNAPSHOT

South Derbyshire was created in 1983, largely drawn from the old Belper division. Belper was dominated for 25 years after the Second World War by Labour's George Brown.

After Mr Brown's departure in 1970 the seat passed to the Conservatives and has since been won by the governing party. Edwina Currie was first elected in 1983 and held the seat for 14 years, before losing to Labour in 1997.

Mark Todd won a 13,967 majority in 1997, which fell at the two subsequent elections and was just 4,495 in 2005. Tory Heather Wheeler took the seat from Labour with a majority of 7,128 in 2010.

Boundary changes were minimal.

This seat is both rural and industrial. A third of the National Forest is in South Derbyshire.

Industry once revolved around coal and clay, but both have now all but disappeared. The market for skilled labour recovered relatively well due largely to the presence of Toyota's car assembly plant at Burnaston.

As the largest population centre, Swadlincote is also the administrative and business heart of the constituency. Small-scale farming continues to play a significant role in the local economy, though the profitability of agricultural activities, in line with national trends, is in serious decline.

Chris White

Warwick and Leamington

Boundary changes

Tel: 020 7219 3000
E-mail: chris.white.mp@parliament.uk
Website: www.white4warwickandleamington.com

Conservative

Non-political career: MG Rover, Longbridge; Freelance public relations consultant; Councillor, Warwick District Council 2007-; Governor, Myton School

Political career: Contested Birmingham Hall Green 2001 and Warwick and Leamington 2005 general elections. Member for Warwick and Leamington since 6 May 2010 general election

Chris White MP, House of Commons, London SW1A 0AA
Tel: 020 7219 3000 E-mail: chris.white.mp@parliament.uk
Constituency: Warwick and Leamington Conservatives, PO Box 2036, Leamington Spa, Warwickshire CV32 5ZY Tel: 01926 400359
Website: www.white4warwickandleamington.com

GENERAL ELECTION RESULT

		%
White, C. (Con)	20,876	42.6
Plaskitt, J. (Lab)*	17,363	35.4
Beddow, A. (Lib Dem)	8,977	18.3
Lenton, C. (UKIP)	926	1.9
Davison, I. (Green)	693	1.4
Cullinane, J. (Ind)	197	0.4
Majority	3,513	7.16
Electorate	58,030	
Turnout	49,032	84.49

**Member of last parliament*

CONSTITUENCY SNAPSHOT

The Conservatives' hold on Warwick and Leamington ran from 1945 to 1997. For 12 of those years Warwick and Leamington was represented by Prime Minister Sir Anthony Eden. Subsequently, the seat returned Sir John Hobson for nine years, then Sir Dudley Smith from 1968 to 1997.

In 1997, with a swing of 10.2 per cent to Labour, James Plaskitt turned Sir Dudley's five-figure majority into a 3,398 one of his own.

Labour retained the seat with an increased majority of 5,953 in 2001, however, Labour's majority was reduced to 266 votes in 2005 and Plaskitt was finally defeated in 2010. Chris White took the seat for the Conservatives securing a majority of 3,513.

Boundary changes mean the new seat will remain much the same.

This prosperous constituency is situated to the south east of Birmingham and includes the towns of Warwick and Leamington Spa as well as surrounding villages.

As the name suggests, Leamington has benefited from the presence of saline springs in the area. Their discovery transformed what was then a small village to a popular resort. Warwick still preserves its medieval core, surrounded by the open spaces of the common and racecourse, the grounds of the Priory, St Nicholas Meadow and the river Avon.

Warwick and Leamington has a more diverse economy than some of its neighbours. Specialist and games software and research and design are all important sectors in the area's economy.

Dr **Eilidh Whiteford**

Banff and Buchan

No boundary changes

Tel: 020 7219 7005
E-mail: eilidh.whiteford.mp@parliament.uk
Website: www.eilidhwhiteford.info

SNP Scottish National Party

Date of birth: 24 April 1969; Daughter of Douglas Whiteford and Kathleen MacLeod

Education: Banff Academy; Glasgow University (MA Hons English and Scottish literature 1991; PhD Scottish literature 1998); Guelph University, Ontario (MA English language and literature 1994)

Non-political career: Assistant to Alex Salmond MP 1992; Tutor in Scottish studies, Newbattle Abbey College 1995-97; Part-time lecturer, Scottish literature, Glasgow University 1995-97; Assistant to: Allan MacCartney MEP 1998, Ian Hudghton MEP 1998-99, Irene McGugan MSP 1999; Academic development officer and lecturer, Scottish literature, Glasgow University and Newbattle Abbey College 1999-2001; Co-ordinator, Scottish Carers' Alliance 2001-03; Scottish campaign manager, Oxfam Scotland 2003-09

Political career: Member for Banff and Buchan since 6 May 2010 general election; Member, SNP 1986-

Political interests: Social policy, agriculture and fisheries, international development

Recreations: Music, reading

Dr Eilidh Whiteford MP, House of Commons, London SW1A 0AA
Tel: 020 7219 7005 E-mail: eilidh.whiteford.mp@parliament.uk
Constituency: c/o Banff and Buchan SNP, 19 Maiden Street, Peterhead, Aberdeenshire AB42 1EE
Website: www.eilidhwhiteford.info

GENERAL ELECTION RESULT

		%	+/-
Whiteford, E. (SNP)	15,868	41.3	-9.9
Buchan, J. (Con)	11,841	30.8	11.4
Reynolds, G. (Lab)	5,382	14.0	2.0
Milne, G. (Lib Dem)	4,365	11.4	-1.9
Payne, R. (BNP)	1,010	2.6	
Majority	4,027	10.47	
Electorate	64,300		
Turnout	38,466	59.82	

CONSTITUENCY SNAPSHOT

Formerly known as Aberdeenshire East, the SNP gained the seat in February 1974 when Douglas Henderson defeated Tory incumbent Patrick Wolrige-Gordon. Henderson's tenure was brief as Albert McQuarrie won the seat back for the Conservatives in 1979 and held it (renamed Banff and Buchan) in 1983. However, in 1987 Alex Salmond won the seat for the SNP and has increased his majority at every subsequent election.

In 2005 Banff and Buchan was enlarged with four wards from the Gordon constituency. Salmond improved on his notional majority by 2.3 per cent, polling more than 50 per cent of the vote. First Minister Alex Salmond stood down in 2010. Eilidh Whitford is now flying the SNP flag with a 4,027 majority.

This predominantly rural seat stretches from Portsoy, along the north-east coast of Scotland to the ports of Fraserburgh and Peterhead, down as far as Cruden Bay, and inland to Pitsligo and Mintlaw.

The constituency has traditionally relied on farming and fishing and still contains one of the highest proportions of people engaged in food production in the UK.

Since the early 1970s the constituency's coastal settlements have benefited from the North Sea oil industry. The major ports at Peterhead and Fraserburgh depend on the oil boom, supplying maintenance and service industries.

The area is also likely to increase in importance as a centre for renewable energy after Peterhead was named as one of the hubs for the development of offshore renewable energy.

Dr **Alan Whitehead**

Southampton Test (returning MP)

Boundary changes

Tel: 020 7219 5517
E-mail: whiteheada@parliament.uk
Website: www.alan-whitehead.org.uk

Date of birth: 15 September 1950

Education: Isleworth Grammar School, Isleworth, Middlesex; Southampton University (BA politics and philosophy 1973, PhD political science 1976); Married Sophie Wronska 1979 (1 son 1 daughter)

Non-political career: Outset: Deputy director 1976-79, Director 1979-83; Director BIIT 1983-92; Professor of public policy Southampton Institute 1992-97; Member, Unison (formerly NUPE); Southampton City Council: Councillor 1980-92, Leader 1984-92

Political career: Contested Southampton Test 1983, 1987 and 1992 general elections. Member for Southampton Test 1997-2010, for Southampton Test (revised boundary) since 6 May 2010 general election; Joint PPS to David Blunkett as Secretary of State for Education and Employment 1999-2000; PPS to Baroness Blackstone as Minister for Education and Employment 1999-2001; Parliamentary Under-Secretary of State, Department for Transport, Local Government and the Regions 2001-02; *Select Committees:* Member: Environment, Transport and Regional Affairs 1997-99, Environment, Transport and Regional Affairs (Environment Sub-Committee) 1997-99, Constitutional Affairs/Justice 2003-10, Standards and Privileges 2005-10, Joint Committee on the Draft Climate Change Bill 2007, Energy and Climate Change 2009-10; Member Labour Party National Policy Forum 1999-2001; Chair Manifesto Group Local Government 2007-

Political interests: Environment, local and regional government, higher education, education, constitution, transport, energy; France, Lithuania, Poland

Other organisations: Director/Board Member: Southampton Environment Centre, Southampton Sustainable Energy Ltd; Visiting professor, Southampton Institute 1997-

Recreations: Football (playing and watching), writing, tennis

Dr Alan Whitehead MP, House of Commons, London SW1A 0AA
Tel: 020 7219 5517 Fax: 020 7219 0918
E-mail: whiteheada@parliament.uk
Constituency: 20-22 Southampton Street, Southampton, Hampshire SO15 1ED Tel: 02380 231942 Fax: 02380 231943
Website: www.alan-whitehead.org.uk

GENERAL ELECTION RESULT

		%
Whitehead, A. (Lab)*	17,001	38.5
Moulton, J. (Con)	14,588	33.0
Callaghan, D. (Lib Dem)	9,865	22.3
Hingston, P. (UKIP)	1,726	3.9
Bluemel, C. (Green)	881	2.0
Sanderson, C. (Ind)	126	0.3
Majority	2,413	5.46
Electorate	71,931	
Turnout	44,187	61.43

**Member of last parliament*

CONSTITUENCY SNAPSHOT

Dr Alan Whitehead won this seat for Labour in 1997 from the Conservative Sir James Hill, who had held it since 1979. Dr Whitehead was returned in 1997 a 13,684 majority. Dr Whitehead's majority in 2005 was 7,018.

Labour held the seat in 2010 with 17,001 votes giving Whitehead a majority of 2,413.

The seat gained two part-wards from Southampton Itchen, and lost two part-wards to Romsey and Southampton North.

The seat covers the western part of the City of Southampton, and is named after the river Test, the larger of the city's two rivers.

It extends through the leafy northern suburbs and the western port areas as well as the council-housing estates of the western fringes including the Redbridge ward on the edge of the city.

Southampton's livelihood has come largely from its position as a thriving seaport and employs a large number of constituents, even though this half of the city contains little of the dockyards.

Major employers in the area are the city council, Southampton University, the Southampton Institute and the NHS Hospital Trusts. Students make up a significant element of the city's population.

Southampton Test hosts one of the UK's largest geothermal and combined heat and power systems, which is providing cheap and reliable heat and energy to the area.

Craig Whittaker

Calder Valley

Boundary changes

Tel: 020 7219 3000
E-mail: craig.whittaker.mp@parliament.uk

Conservative

Date of birth: 30 August 1962

Education: Belmont High School, New South Wales, Australia; Tighes Hill College, New South Wales, Australia; Divorced (1 son 2 daughters)

Non-political career: Director, Kezdem PTY Ltd, New South Wales, Australia 1991; Branch manager, Wilkinsons Home and Garden Stores 1992-98; General manager, PC World Dixons Store Group 1998-; Councillor, Heptonstall Parish Council 1998-2003; Calderdale Metropolitan Borough Council: Councillor 2003-04, 2007-, Cabinet member, Children and Young Peoples Services 2007-

Political career: Member for Calder Valley since 6 May 2010 general election; Constituency agent 2005 general election; Chair, Calder Valley Conservative Association 2005-06

Political interests: Education, children, aged care

Other organisations: Tormorden Conservative Club; Carlton Club

Recreations: Sailing, reading

Craig Whittaker MP, House of Commons, London SW1A 0AA
Tel: 020 7219 3000 E-mail: craig.whittaker.mp@parliament.uk
Constituency: Calderdale and Kirklees Campaign Centre, Spring Villa, 16 Church Lane, Brighouse, West Yorkshire HD6 1AT
Tel: 01484 717959; 0798 4717282
Website: www.caldervalleyconservatives.com

GENERAL ELECTION RESULT

		%
Whittaker, C. (Con)	20,397	39.4
Booth, S. (Lab)	13,966	27.0
Myers, H. (Lib Dem)	13,037	25.2
Gregory, J. (BNP)	1,823	3.5
Burrows, G. (UKIP)	1,173	2.3
Sweeny, K. (Green)	858	1.7
Cole, T. (Ind)	194	0.4
Greenwood, B. (Ind)	175	0.3
Rogan, P. (England)	157	0.3
Majority	6,431	12.42
Electorate	76,903	
Turnout	51,780	67.33

CONSTITUENCY SNAPSHOT

Christine McCafferty won the seat for Labour in 1997 with a swing of 9.5 per cent. The Tories managed a 2.3 per cent swing back in 2001, and a further 1.8 per cent swing in 2005 when Labour's majority fell to 1,367.

Labour was defeated in 2010 following a 7.6 per cent swing to the Conservative candidate, Craig Whittaker.

Very slight boundary changes resulted in the exchange of part-wards with Halifax due to realignment of local government boundaries.

Winding round Halifax and up onto the remote Pennines, this large West Yorkshire seat includes the smaller Calderdale towns and villages.

The largest town is Brighouse, a former textile mill town. The seat also includes Todmorden, a market town that sits on the historic Yorkshire/Lancashire border, Elland, a small town between Halifax and Huddersfield and the small former textile town Hebden Bridge.

By most measures this is a modestly prosperous constituency with a large percentage of households owner-occupied, with few renting from the local authority.

The Calder Valley was a traditionally working-class industrial area of small settlements, heavily dominated by the woollen industry. Manual workers still make up much of the workforce and there is still some textile activity, but the wool mills are long gone.

John Whittingdale

Maldon (returning MP)

New constituency

Tel: 020 7219 3557
E-mail: whittingdalej@parliament.uk
Website: www.johnwhittingdale.org.uk

Date of birth: 16 October 1959; Son of late John Whittingdale and Margaret Whittingdale

Education: Winchester College; University College, London (BSc economics 1982); Married Ancilla Murfitt 1990 (divorced 2008) (1 son 1 daughter)

Non-political career: Head of political section Conservative Research Department 1982-84; Special adviser to Secretaries of State for Trade and Industry Norman Tebbit, Leon Brittan and Paul Channon 1984-87; Manager N M Rothschild & Sons 1987; Political secretary to Margaret Thatcher as Prime Minister 1988-90; Private secretary to Margaret Thatcher MP 1990-92

Political career: Member for South Colchester and Maldon 1992-97, for Maldon and Chelmsford East 1997-2010, for Maldon since 6 May 2010 general election; PPS to Eric Forth as Minister of State for: Education 1994-95, Education and Employment 1994-96; Opposition Whip 1997-98; Opposition Spokesperson for the Treasury 1998-99; Parliamentary private secretary to William Hague as Leader of Opposition 1999-2001; Shadow Secretary of State for: Trade and Industry 2001-02, Culture, Media and Sport 2002-03, Agriculture, Fisheries and Food 2003-04, Culture, Media and Sport 2004-05; *Select Committees:* Member: Health 1993-97, Information 1997-98, Trade and Industry 2001; Chair: Culture, Media and Sport 2005-10; Member: Liaison 2005-10; Member: 92 Group, No Turning Back Group; Member executive Conservative Way Forward 2005-; 1922 Committee: Member Executive 2005-06, Vice-chair 2006-; Member Conservative Party Board 2006-

Political interests: Broadcasting and media; China, Israel, Japan, Korea, Malaysia, Russia, USA

Other organisations: Fellow Royal Society of Arts 2008-; Council member Freedom Association 2008-; Fellow Industry and Parliament Trust 1996; OBE 1990; Essex; *Publications:* New Policies for the Media (1995)

Recreations: Cinema, music

John Whittingdale OBE MP, House of Commons, London SW1A 0AA Tel: 020 7219 3557 Fax: 020 7219 2522
E-mail: whittingdalej@parliament.uk
Constituency: Maldon and East Chelmsford Conservative Association, 19 High Street, Maldon, Essex CM9 5PE Tel: 01621 855663
Fax: 01621 855217 Website: www.johnwhittingdale.org.uk

GENERAL ELECTION RESULT

		%
Whittingdale, J. (Con)*	28,661	59.8
Tealby-Watson, E. (Lib Dem)	9,254	19.3
Nandanwar, S. (Lab)	6,070	12.7
Pryke, J. (UKIP)	2,446	5.1
Blain, L. (BNP)	1,464	3.1
Majority	19,407	40.52
Electorate	68,861	
Turnout	47,895	69.55

**Member of last parliament*

CONSTITUENCY SNAPSHOT

Maldon was created in the main from Maldon and East Chelmsford. It also includes the town of South Woodham Ferrers. The more urban parts of Chelmsford borough moved to Chelmsford, and areas north of the Blackwater estuary are now in Witham.

Tom Driberg sat as MP for Maldon as an Independent during the Second World War and for Labour from 1945 to 1955. He was to be the seats' last Labour MP. In 1983 it became South Colchester and Maldon. John Whittingdale was first elected to the seat in 1992.

The strength of the Conservative position here was highlighted in 1997 when, despite a swing to Labour of 15.6 per cent, Whittingdale was returned to the new seat Maldon and Chelmsford East with a majority of 10,000.

In 2005 the Tory MP was re-elected with an increased majority of 12,573. Whittingdale won the new seat with a majority of 19,407 at the 2010 general election.

This Essex constituency is mostly rural or coastal, combining the estuary towns of Maldon and Burnham-on-Crouch with much more sparsely-populated rural areas.

Traditional businesses such as agriculture, salt-making, barge repairing and oyster-fishing continue along the estuary but tourism plays an important role and the area has begun to attract high-tech industries.

Rt Hon **Malcolm Wicks**

Croydon North ***(returning MP)***

Boundary changes

Tel: 020 7219 4418
E-mail: wicksm@parliament.uk
Website: www.malcolmwicks.labour.co.uk

Labour

Date of birth: 1 July 1947; Son of late Arthur Wicks and Daisy, neé Hunt

Education: Elizabeth College, Guernsey; North West London Polytechnic; London School of Economics (BSc sociology); Married Margaret Baron 1968 (1 son 2 daughters)

Non-political career: Fellow, Department of Social Administration, York University 1968-70; Research worker, Centre for Environmental Studies 1970-72; Lecturer in social administration, Brunel University 1970-74; Social policy analyst, Urban Deprivation Unit, Home Office 1974-77; Lecturer in social policy, Civil Service College 1977-78; Research director and secretary, Study Commission on the Family 1978-83; Director, Family Policy Studies Centre 1983-92; TGWU

Political career: Contested Croydon North West 1987 general election. Member for Croydon North West 1992-97, for Croydon North 1997-2010, for Croydon North (revised boundary) since 6 May 2010 general election; Opposition Spokesperson for Social Security 1995-97; Parliamentary Under-Secretary of State (Lifelong Learning), Department for Education and Employment 1999-2001; Department for Work and Pensions 2001-05: Parliamentary Under-Secretary of State (Work) 2001-03, Minister of State (Pensions) 2003-05; Minister of State: Department of Trade and Industry 2005-07 (Energy 2005-06, Science and Innovation 2006-07), Department for Business, Enterprise and Regulatory Reform (Energy) 2007-08; *Select Committees:* Member: Social Security 1994-96, 1997-98, Liaison 1998-99; Chair: Education and Employment (Education Sub-Committee) 1998-99

Political interests: Social policy, welfare state, education; Australia, Europe, New Zealand

Other organisations: Vice-president: Alzheimer's Society, Carer to Carer; Chair Renewables Advisory Board -2008; PC 2008; Ruskin House Labour (Croydon); *Publications:* Several publications and articles on social policy and welfare including: Old and Cold: hypothermia and social policy (1978); Co-author Government and Urban Poverty (1983); A Future for All: do we need a welfare state? (1987); Co-author Family Change and Future Policy (1990); A New Agenda (IPPR 1993)

Recreations: Music, walking, gardening, very occasional white water rafting

Rt Hon Malcolm Wicks MP, House of Commons, London SW1A 0AA
Tel: 020 7219 4418 Fax: 020 7219 2795
E-mail: wicksm@parliament.uk
Constituency: 84 High Street, Thornton Heath, Croydon, Surrey CR7 8LF Tel: 020 8665 1214 Fax: 020 8683 0179
Website: www.malcolmwicks.labour.co.uk

GENERAL ELECTION RESULT

		%
Wicks, M. (Lab)*	28,949	56.0
Hadden, J. (Con)	12,466	24.1
Jerome, G. (Lib Dem)	7,226	14.0
Khan, S. (Green)	1,017	2.0
Serter, J. (UKIP)	891	1.7
Williams, N. (Christian)	586	1.1
Shaikh, M. (Respect)	272	0.5
Stevenson, B. (Comm)	160	0.3
Seyed Mohamed, M. (Ind)	111	0.2
Majority	16,483	31.90
Electorate	85,212	
Turnout	51,678	60.65

**Member of last parliament*

CONSTITUENCY SNAPSHOT

Before 1992 the Conservatives typically held the advantage throughout the borough. When Labour's Malcolm Wicks won the seat in 1992 he was only the second Labour candidate to win a Croydon seat since 1918. In 1997 the seat was reformed as Croydon North and Wicks's majority grew to 18,398.

In 2005 both Labour and the Conservatives' share of the vote dipped but polling almost 14,000 more votes than the Tories. Wicks was re-elected by a comfortable margin. Former Energy minister Malcolm Wicks defied the national trend with a 16,483 majority for Labour and increased his share of the vote to 56 per cent.

Broad Green and South Norwood wards are now entirely within the seat having previously been shared with Croydon Central.

This is the most urban of the three Croydon constituencies. Selhurst Park, home to Crystal Palace FC, is the prominent landmark of this seat and the area's burgeoning local economy is built on retail and businesses exploiting its good transport links with Gatwick airport and central London.

High-profile companies in the borough include Nestlé, British Telecom and Vodafone alongside various financial and insurance companies, typical of well-connected areas on the edge of London.

The constituency will benefit from extensions to the East London Tube line, which will link West Croydon station and Crystal Palace to the centre of London.

Bill Wiggin

North Herefordshire (returning MP)

New constituency

Tel: 020 7219 1777
E-mail: wigginb@parliament.uk
Website: www.billwiggin.com

Date of birth: 4 June 1966; Son of Sir Jerry Wiggin and Mrs Rosie Dale Harris

Education: Eton College; University College of North Wales (BA economics 1988); Married Camilla Chilvers 1999 (2 sons 1 daughter)

Non-political career: Trader UBS 1991-93; Associate director currency options sales Dresdner Kleinwort Benson 1994-98; Manager structured products Commerzbank 1998-2001

Political career: Contested Burnley 1997 general election. Member for Leominster 2001-10, for North Herefordshire since 6 May 2010 general election; Shadow: Minister for Environment, Food and Rural Affairs 2003, Secretary of State for Wales 2003-05, Minister for Environment, Food and Rural Affairs 2005-09; Opposition Whip 2009-10; Assistant Government Whip 2010-; *Select Committees:* Member: Welsh Affairs 2001-03, Transport, Local Government and the Regions 2001-02, Environment, Food and Rural Affairs 2002-05; Contested North West region 1999 European Parliament election; Vice-chair Hammersmith and Fulham Conservative Association 1995-97; Member 1922 Committee Executive 2002-03

Political interests: Defence, agriculture, Treasury, environment

Other organisations: Governor Hammersmith and West London College 1995-98; Trustee Violet Eveson Charitable Trust; Freeman of City of London; Goldsmiths Company; Hurlingham, Annabels, Pratt's

Recreations: Motorcycles, country sports, Hereford cattle

Bill Wiggin MP, House of Commons, London SW1A 0AA
Tel: 020 7219 1777 Fax: 020 7219 1893
E-mail: wigginb@parliament.uk
Constituency: 8 Corn Square, Leominster, Herefordshire HR6 8LR
Tel: 01568 612565 Fax: 01568 610320 Website: www.billwiggin.com

GENERAL ELECTION RESULT

		%
Wiggin, B. (Con)*	24,631	51.8
Hurds, L. (Lib Dem)	14,744	31.0
Sabharwal, N. (Lab)	3,373	7.1
Oakton, J. (UKIP)	2,701	5.7
Norman, F. (Green)	1,533	3.2
King, J. (Ind)	586	1.2
Majority	9,887	20.78
Electorate	66,525	
Turnout	47,568	71.50

**Member of last parliament*

CONSTITUENCY SNAPSHOT

North Herefordshire has not elected a non-Tory since 1906. Peter Temple-Morris held the seat from 1974 to 2001. In November 1997 the Conservative Party removed the party whip from him. After a short time as an Independent, Temple-Morris crossed the floor and joined the Labour benches before standing down in 2001.

The Conservative Bill Wiggin took the seat. In 2005 he increased his majority to 13,187. Wiggin was re-elected with a majority of 9,887 following a 3.8 per cent swing to the Lib Dems.

The new seat of North Herefordshire lies entirely within Herefordshire unitary authority. North Herefordshire is largely equivalent to the previous Leominster constituency, but without its previous wards in Worcestershire. It is therefore solely made up of the northern half of the county of Herefordshire and is one of the largest constituencies in England.

The seat comprises the market towns of Leominster, Kington, Bromyard and Ledbury, as well as great swathes of surrounding countryside. Leominster is the largest town, with a population of about 10,000.

The town contains the constituency's only real industry and its specialities include the wool trade and the export of the famous Hereford breed of cattle.

Rt Hon **David Willetts**

Havant (returning MP)

Boundary changes

Tel: 020 7219 4570
E-mail: willettsd@parliament.uk
Website: www.davidwilletts.org.uk

Conservative

Date of birth: 9 March 1956; Son of John and Hilary Willetts

Education: King Edward's School, Birmingham; Christ Church, Oxford (BA philosophy, politics and economics 1978); Married Hon. Sarah Butterfield 1986 (1 son 1 daughter)

Non-political career: HM Treasury 1978-84: Private secretary to Nicholas Ridley MP as Financial Secretary 1981-82, Principal, Monetary Policy Division 1982-84; Prime Minister's Downing Street Policy Unit 1984-86; Director of Studies, Centre for Policy Studies 1987-92; Consultant director, Conservative Research Department 1987-92; Director: Retirement Security Ltd 1988-94, Electra Corporate Ventures Ltd 1988-94; Governor, Ditchley Foundation 1998-; Visiting Fellow, Nuffield College, Oxford 1999-2006; Member, Global Commission on Ageing 2000-; Visiting Fellow, Cass Business School 2004-; Member: Lambeth and Lewisham Family Practitioners' Committee 1987-90, Parkside Health Authority 1988-90, Social Security Advisory Committee 1989-92

Political career: Member for Havant 1992-2010, for Havant (revised boundary) since 6 May 2010 general election; PPS to Sir Norman Fowler as Chairman of Conservative Party 1993-94; Assistant Government Whip 1994-95; Government Whip July-November 1995; Parliamentary Secretary, Office of Public Service 1995-96; Paymaster General, Office of Public Service July-December 1996; Opposition Spokesman for Employment 1997-98; Shadow Secretary of State for: Education and Employment 1998-99, Social Security 1999-2001, Work and Pensions 2001-05, and Welfare Reform 2004-05, Trade and Industry 2005, Education and Skills/Innovation, Universities and Skills 2005-09; Shadow Minister for Universities and Skills 2009-10; Minister of State for Universities and Science, Department for Business, Innovation and Skills 2010-; *Select Committees:* Member: Social Security 1992-93; Chair, Conservative Research Department 1997; Member Conservative Policy Board 2001-; Head of Policy Co-ordination Conservative Party 2003-04

Political interests: Economic policy, health, social security, education; USA, Germany

Other organisations: PC 2010; Hurlingham; *Publications:* Modern Conservatism, 1992; Civic Conservatism, 1994; Blair's Gurus, 1996; Why Vote Conservative, 1997; Welfare to Work, 1998; After the Landslide, 1999; Browned-off: What's Wrong with Gordon Brown's Social Policy 2000; Co-author Tax Credits: Do They Add Up? 2002; Left Out, Left Behind, 2003; Old Europe? Demographic Change and Pension Reform, 2003

Recreations: Swimming, reading, cycling

Rt Hon David Willetts MP, House of Commons, London SW1A 0AA
Tel: 020 7219 4570 Fax: 020 7219 2567
E-mail: willettsd@parliament.uk
Constituency: c/o Havant Conservative Association, 19 South Street, Havant, Hampshire PO9 1BU Tel: 02392 499746 Fax: 02392 498753
Website: www.davidwilletts.org.uk

GENERAL ELECTION RESULT

		%
Willetts, D. (Con)*	22,433	51.1
Payton, A. (Lib Dem)	10,273	23.4
Smith, R. (Lab)	7,777	17.7
Keiran, G. (UKIP)	2,611	6.0
Addams, F. (England)	809	1.8
Majority	12,160	27.70
Electorate	69,712	
Turnout	43,903	62.98

**Member of last parliament*

CONSTITUENCY SNAPSHOT

From 1974 to 1992 Havant returned Conservative Sir Ian Lloyd. His popularity peaked in 1987 with a majority of 14,169. He was replaced by David Willets, another Conservative, in 1992.

David Willett's majority fell from 17,584 in 1992 to 3,729 in 1997. However, Willetts improved his majority in 2001 and again in 2005.

The seat was held by Willett in 2010 with a 12,160 majority.

The seat lost part of the Waterloo ward to the Meon Valley.

Coastal Havant is adjacent to Portsmouth North. Leigh Park council estate is balanced by private estates in Purbrook and Stakes, and an elderly population on Hayling Island.

Havant has a similar socio-economic profile to the neighbouring maritime seats of Portsmouth North and Gosport. Hayling Island accounts for many retirees, who take advantage of the mild climate.

As in much of Hampshire, the production and construction industries are vital. Manufacturing, including pharmaceuticals, kitchen equipment and toys, is an important sector. The constituency is also strongly represented in mechanical, electrical and instrument engineering, as well as in high-technology work.

A lack of open spaces encourages local opposition to many new developments.

CIENCE AND THE NEW PARLIAMENT

e new Parliament faces major new challenges.

 great global issues of our time – climate ıange, food security, water, energy and health – ll interconnected.

:annot tackle one in isolation from the other.

 single Member of the new Parliament – ther newly-elected or newly re-elected – will be ved in one way or another in these issues.

ce, engineering and technology [SET] are at eart of many of the scientific challenges which ıew Parliament now faces – and SET underpins of the solutions.

what are these challenges?

Royal Society of Chemistry [RSC] has identified n areas where science – and the chemical ces in particular – can make a real difference. ce is not just the way forward out of the sion. It is the key to new challenges such as:

rgy
d
ıre Cities
nan Health
style & Recreation
 Material & Feedstocks
er & Air

at will this mean in practice?

gy
ing and securing environmentally sustainable gy supplies, and improving efficiency of power ration, transmission and use.

ing and securing a safe, environmentally dly, diverse and affordable food supply.

re Cities
oping cities to meet the emergent needs of izens.

an Health
oving and maintaining accessible health, ding disease prevention.

style & Recreation
ding a sustainable route for people to live r and more varied lives.

er & Air
ing the sustainable management of water and ıality, and addressing the societal impact on resources (quality and availability).

SC | Advancing the Chemical Sciences

How can we deliver change?

These big global challenges can only be addressed if we provide an excellent, diverse and well maintained science base, a good supply of well trained individuals and an innovative climate from which good ideas can be exploited and flourish.

A diverse, highly skilled and technically innovative workforce is fundamental to developing and applying new technologies.

This begins in schools where young children are first given the opportunity to experience the excitement of science and this should be nurtured through their entire education experience.

Raising students' interest and curiosity in the sciences will hopefully stimulate their interest in pursuing a career in science or engineering.

As well as education institutions, industry has a vital role to play in the continuing development of the workforce. Investment in one-the-job training and lifelong learning will help to develop the skills required to adapt to technological advances and ensure that the sciences remain competitive.

We cannot afford a skills shortage, which could leave the next generation ill-equipped to tackle major scientific and technological challenges.

The Role of the New Parliament

The composition of the new Parliament is very different from the old. Its way of working may well be different. But Parliament's central role should be as important as ever.

The role of MPs in this new Parliament is vital – and it is up to them to ensure that they now have access to the best possible scientific advice.

That is why this Parliament will need a strong Select Committee on Science and Technology – in both Houses.

And there are now real opportunities for newly-elected MPs to take a leading role in debating science issues of all kinds.

For its part the scientific and engineering community will work together – building links with all MPs – to provide Parliament with the best possible scientific advice.

Parliamentary Links Day

The Largest Science Event in the House

Each year the scientific and engineering community joins together in the Royal Society of Chemistry's Parliamentary Links Day. It is the largest science gathering held in Parliament. It is dedicated to helping all MPs – especially new MPs – to understand the issues that we face and how science & engineering can help. It's on **Tuesday 22nd June from 10.30am** in the **Attlee Suite Portcullis House**. Put the date in your diary now.

That's why the RSC is here to help.

Science is the solution.

Science is the key to the future.

Science matters.

A little bit of Parliamentary history was made at the Royal Society of Chemistry's Parliamentary Links Day on 24 June 2009 when the new Speaker of the House of Commons the Rt Hon John Bercow MP welcomed the science and community to Parliament on his first public engagement outside the Chamber.

Hywel Williams

Arfon (returning MP)

New constituency

Tel: 020 7219 8150
E-mail: williamshy@parliament.uk
Website: www.hywelwilliams.plaidcymru.org

Plaid Cymru

Date of birth: 14 May 1953; Son of Robert Williams and Jennie Page Williams, shopkeepers

Education: Glan y Môr School, Pwllheli; University of Wales: Cardiff (BSc psychology 1974), Bangor (CQSW social work 1979); Divorced (3 daughters)

Non-political career: Social worker: Mid Glamorgan County Council 1974-76, Gwynedd County Council 1976-84; North Wales Social Work Practice Centre, University of Wales, Bangor 1985-94: Project worker 1985-94, Head of centre 1991-94; Freelance lecturer consultant and author social work and social policy 1994-2001; NALGO 1974-84; NUPE 1974-84; UCAC 1984-94

Political career: Member for Caernarfon 2001-10, for Arfon since 6 May 2010 general election; Plaid Cymru Spokesperson for: Work and Pensions 2001-, Health 2001-, Disability 2001-05, International Development 2004-, Culture, Media and Sport 2005-06, Education and Skills/Children, Schools and Families 2005-10, Treasury 2006-07, Defence 2007-09, Transport 2007-09, Cabinet Office 2010-, Energy and Climate Change 2010-, Education 2010-; *Select Committees:* Member: European Standing Committee B 2002-04, Welsh Affairs 2004-05, Chairmen's Panel 2005-10; Contested Clwyd South 1999 constituency National Assembly for Wales election; Policy developer Social security and policy for older people Plaid Cymru 1999-2001; Plaid Cymru policy cabinet 1999-2001

Political interests: Social affairs, social security, social work, language issues, Kurdish issues, international development; Turkey

Other organisations: Member Welsh Committee Central Council for Education and Training in Social Work; *Publications:* Geirfa Gwaith Cymdeithasol/ A Social Work Vocabulary (University of Wales Press [UWP], 1988); General editor Geirfa Gwaith Plant/ Child Care Terms (UWP, 1993); Gwaith Cymdeithasol a'r Iaith Gymraeg/ Social Work and the Welsh Language (UWP/CCETSW); Llawlyfr Hyfforddi a Hyfforddwyr/ An Index of Trainers and Training (AGWC, 1994); Gofal – Pecyn Adnoddau a Hyfforddi Gofal yn y Gymuned yng Nghymru/ A Training and Resource Pack for Community Care in Wales (CCETSW Cymru, 1998)

Recreations: Reading, cinema, walking, kite flying

Hywel Williams MP, House of Commons, London SW1A 0AA
Tel: 020 7219 8150 Fax: 020 7219 3705
E-mail: williamshy@parliament.uk
Constituency: 8 Castle Street, Caernarfon, Gwynedd LL55 1SE
Tel: 01286 672 076 Fax: 01286 672 003
Website: www.hywelwilliams.plaidcymru.org

GENERAL ELECTION RESULT

		%
Williams, H. (PlC)*	9,383	36.0
Pugh, A. (Lab)	7,928	30.4
Millar, R. (Con)	4,416	16.9
Green, S. (Lib Dem)	3,666	14.1
Williams, E. (UKIP)	685	2.6
Majority	1,455	5.58
Electorate	41,198	
Turnout	26,078	63.30

**Member of last parliament*

CONSTITUENCY SNAPSHOT

Located in the uppermost reaches of North West Wales, the new Arfon seat combines the town and the area around Caernarfon, including Bangor and its University.

The seat's most famous member was Liberal Prime Minister, David Lloyd George who held the seat from 1890 until 1945, becoming the first Welsh constituency to be represented by a serving Prime Minster.

At the general election in February 1974, Plaid Cymru's Dafydd Wigley won the seat and was member until he stood down 2001.

In 2001 Plaid Cymru retained the seat when Hywel Williams succeeded Wigley. In 2005 Mr Williams obtained a majority of 5,209. This new seat could easily have gone Labour, but Plaid Cymru's Hywel Williams won with a 1,455 majority.

Replacing the seat of Caernarfon, Arfon looks out over the coast towards Ynys Môn. To the South, the seat includes a portion of Snowdonia National Park. Snowdon itself is on the south-easterly border with Dwyfor Meirionnydd.

As efforts to conserve the Welsh language have become prominent, Caernarfon has become a centre for Welsh media. The constituency also includes Bangor University.

Tourism and farming are the mainstays of the local economy. Apart from Snowdonia, other attractions in the area include Caernarfon Castle (the site of Price Charles' investiture as the Price of Wales in 1969), parts of the Castles and Town Walls of Kind Edward in Gwynedd World Heritage site.

Mark Williams

Ceredigion (returning MP)

Boundary changes

Tel: 020 7219 8469
E-mail: williamsmf@parliament.uk
Website: www.markwilliams.org.uk

Date of birth: 24 March 1966; Son of Ronald and Pauline Williams

Education: Richard Hale School, Hertford; University College of Wales, Aberystwyth (BSc politics and economics 1987); Plymouth University (PGCE primary education 1993); Married Helen Refna Wyatt 1997 (2 daughters and twin son and daughter)

Non-political career: Primary school teacher: Madron Daniel School, Cornwall 1993-96, Forches Cross School, Barnstaple, Devon 1996-2000; Deputy head teacher, Llangors Church in Wales School, nr Brecon 2000-05; Member, National Association of Schoolmasters/Union of Women Teachers (NASUWT) 1993

Political career: Contested Monmouth 1997 general election, Ceredigion 2000 by-election and 2001 general election. Member for Ceredigion 2005-10, for Ceredigion (revised boundary) since 6 May 2010 general election; Liberal Democrat Shadow Minister for: Education 2005-06, Wales 2006-10, Innovation, Universities and Skills 2007; *Select Committees:* Member: Welsh Affairs 2005-10; Research assistant, Liberal/Liberal Democrat Peers 1987-92; Member, Welsh Liberal Democrats Executive 1991-92; Constituency assistant, Geraint Howells MP 1987-92; President, Ceredigion Liberal Democrats 1998-2000; Member, Welsh Liberal Democrats Campaign Committee 2000

Political interests: Education, rural affairs

Other organisations: Member: Greenpeace, Countryside Alliance

Recreations: Reading, political biographies, gardening, fresh air

Mark Williams MP, House of Commons, London SW1A 0AA
Tel: 020 7219 8469 E-mail: williamsmf@parliament.uk
Constituency: 32 North Parade, Aberystwyth, Ceredigion SY23 2NF
Tel: 01970 615880 Website: www.markwilliams.org.uk

GENERAL ELECTION RESULT

		%
Williams, M. (Lib Dem)*	19,139	50.0
James, P. (PIC)	10,815	28.3
Evetts, L. (Con)	4,421	11.6
Boudier, R. (Lab)	2,210	5.8
Williams, E. (UKIP)	977	2.6
Kiersch, L. (Green)	696	1.8
Majority	8,324	21.76
Electorate	59,043	
Turnout	38,258	64.80

**Member of last parliament*

CONSTITUENCY SNAPSHOT

Apart from an eight-year period between 1966 and 1974 when Labour's Erlystan Morgan represented Ceredigion, this seat was held by the Liberals from the end of the Second World War until 1992 when Plaid Cymru won the seat. Plaid Cymru solidified their lead in 1997.

In 2000 Cynog Dafis resigned his seat and on 3 February 2000 the first of three electoral battles between Simon Thomas for Plaid Cymru and Mark Williams for the Liberal Democrats was held. Simon Thomas won the by-election. He went on to hold the seat at the 2001 general election.

A disappointing Plaid Cymru performance in 2005, coupled with a general upswing for the Liberal Democrats, was enough for Mark Williams to take the seat with a wafer-thin majority of 219. Williams increased his majority to 8,324 in 2010 on a 10.6 per cent swing.

Boundary changes to the seat were negligible.

This constituency in west Wales has the same boundaries as the county of the same name. The constituency stretches from Aberystwyth on the coast, south to Cardigan and inland to Lampeter. It is a largely rural area.

Rural west Wales is the area where Welsh survived the strongest and around half the population of this seat can speak the language.

This seat is home to two of Wales' universities: Aberystwyth and Lampeter.

Roger Williams

Brecon and Radnorshire ***(returning MP)***

No boundary changes

Tel: 020 7219 8145
E-mail: williamsr@parliament.uk
Website: www.rogerwilliams.org.uk

Date of birth: 22 January 1948; Son of Morgan Glyn and Eirlys Williams

Education: Christ College, Brecon, Powys; Selwyn College, Cambridge University (BA agriculture 1969); Married Penelope James 1973 (1 daughter 1 son)

Non-political career: Farmer 1969-; Former chair Brecon and Radnorshire NFU; Member Farmers Union of Wales; Councillor Powys County Council 1981-2001; Member Development Board for Rural Wales 1989-97; Chair Mid Wales Agri-Food Partnership; Member Country Landowners and Business Association; Chair Brecon Beacons National Park 1991-95

Political career: Member for Brecon and Radnorshire since 7 June 2001 general election; Liberal Democrat: Spokesperson/Shadow Minister for Rural Affairs 2002-05, 2006-10, Whip 2004-07, Shadow Secretary of State for Wales 2007-10, Whip 2008-10; *Select Committees:* Member: Welsh Affairs 2001-05, Environment, Food and Rural Affairs 2005-10; Contested Carmarthen West and South Pembrokeshire 1999 National Assembly for Wales election

Political interests: Agriculture, education, economic development; Afghanistan

Other organisations: Lay school inspector

Recreations: Sport, walking, nature conservation

Roger Williams MP, House of Commons, London SW1A 0AA
Tel: 020 7219 8145 Fax: 020 7219 1747
E-mail: williamsr@parliament.uk
Constituency: 4 Watergate, Brecon, Powys LD3 9AN
Tel: 01874 625 739 Fax: 01874 625 635
Website: www.rogerwilliams.org.uk

GENERAL ELECTION RESULT

		%	+/-
Williams, R. (Lib Dem)*	17,929	46.2	1.4
Davies, S. (Con)	14,182	36.5	1.9
Lloyd, C. (Lab)	4,096	10.5	-4.4
Davies, J. (PIC)	989	2.6	-1.1
Easton, C. (UKIP)	876	2.3	0.4
Robinson, D. (Green)	341	0.9	
Green, J. (Christian)	222	0.6	
Offa, L. (Loony)	210	0.5	
Majority	3,747	9.65	
Electorate	53,589		
Turnout	38,845	72.49	

**Member of last parliament*

CONSTITUENCY SNAPSHOT

Between 1938 and 1979 the main part of this seat had been held continuously by Labour. Tom Hooson won for the Tories in 1979 and was able to increase his 1983 majority to 8,784.

Hooson's sudden death in 1985 led to a by-election that was won by the Alliance's Richard Livsey. Livsey held the seat until 1992 when he was unseated by Conservative Jonathan Evans with a majority of 130. Richard Livsey regained the seat in 1997 with a majority of 5,097.

In the 2001 general election the new Liberal Democrat candidate, Roger Williams, had his majority cut to 751. In 2005 he solidified his position to with a majority of 3,905. Williams won a 3,747 majority in 2010.

The largest seat in Wales geographically, making up the southern part of the large county of Powys.

As a rural seat, farming is important to the local economy. Tourism is also important, particularly in the Brecon Beacons. Indeed, many farms have tried to combine the two key industries under the Farm Tourism Scheme.

It is a very beautiful constituency, containing the Brecon Beacons National Park, market towns Brecon, Builth Wells and Radnor and the spa town Llandrindod Wells.

The scenic nature of the seat makes it an attractive place for people to retire to and the seat has one of the highest proportions of pensioners age in Wales.

Stephen Williams

Bristol West (returning MP)

Boundary changes

Tel: 020 7219 8416
E-mail: stephenwilliamsmp@parliament.uk
Website: www.bristolwest-libdems.org.uk

Date of birth: 11 October 1966; Son of late Malcolm Williams, road worker, and Diana Williams (née Evans), school dinner lady, waitress

Education: Mountain Ash Comprehensive School; Bristol University (BA history 1988); Single

Non-political career: Graduate trainee up to supervisor, Coopers and Lybrand, Bristol 1988-95; Tax manager: Kraft Jacobs Suchard Ltd, Cheltenham Head Office 1995, Grant Thornton, Cheltenham Head Office 1996-98, Grant Thornton, Bristol Office 1998-2001, Orange plc 2001-02, Wincanton plc 2002-03, RAC plc 2004-05; Deputy Leader/Group Chair Liberal Democrat Group, Avon Council 1993-96; Bristol City Council: Councillor 1995-99, Leader Liberal Democrat Group/Shadow Council Leader 1995-97

Political career: Contested Bristol South 1997 and Bristol West 2001 general elections. Member for Bristol West 2005-10, for Bristol West (revised boundary) since 6 May 2010; Liberal Democrat: Shadow Minister for: Health 2005-06, Further and Higher Education 2006-07, Children, Schools and Families 2007, Shadow Secretary of State for Innovation, Universities and Skills 2007-10; *Select Committees:* Member: Education and Skills/Children, Schools and Families 2005-08, Public Accounts 2005-06; Chair, Bristol University SDP/Liberal Club 1986-87; Constituency secretary, Cynon Valley SDP 1986-88

Political interests: Taxation, education, preventive health care, transport, civil rights, arts, Europe

Recreations: Art galleries, historic sites, theatre, cinema, eating out, playing pool, postcard collecting, genealogy

Stephen Williams MP, House of Commons, London SW1A 0AA
Tel: 020 7219 8416 Fax: 020 7219 4802
E-mail: stephenwilliamsmp@parliament.uk
Constituency: PO Box 2500, Bristol, Gloucestershire BS6 9AH
Tel: 0117-942 3494 Fax: 0117-942 6925
Website: www.bristolwest-libdems.org.uk

GENERAL ELECTION RESULT

		%
Williams, S. (Lib Dem)*	26,593	48.1
Smith, P. (Lab)	15,227	27.5
Yarker, N. (Con)	10,169	18.4
Knight, R. (Green)	2,090	3.8
Lees, C. (UKIP)	655	1.2
Kushlick, D. (Ind)	343	0.6
Baker, J. (England)	270	0.5
Majority	11,366	20.54
Electorate	82,728	
Turnout	55,347	66.90

**Member of last parliament*

CONSTITUENCY SNAPSHOT

In the decades following the Second World War Bristol West was held by the Conservatives, remaining even when the other Tory seats in the city, Bristol East and Bristol North West, fell to Labour. Valerie Davey took the seat for Labour in the 1997 general election.

Davey held the seat in 2001 with a 4,426-vote majority, but in a three-way contest in 2005 Stephen Williams won Bristol West for the Liberal Democrats, securing a majority of 5,128. Williams doubled his majority to 11,366 in 2010.

Boundary changes moved three wards and three part-wards to Bristol North West, while the wards of Easton and Lawrence Hill come into the seat from Bristol East.

In many ways Bristol West might be considered the most diverse of the city's constituencies, with its unusual mix of students, ethnic minorities, and wealthy professionals.

The character of the constituency is quite diverse. Areas such as Cotham, Redland and Clifton are popular with the upper middle classes, whereas Ashley, Easton and Lawrence Hill are more working-class and ethnically diverse.

The major employers in the constituency are the two universities, Bristol University and the University of the West of England. Bristol West is said to have the highest concentration of residents with doctoral degrees of any constituency in the UK.

Chris Williamson

Derby North

Boundary changes

Tel: 020 7219 3000
E-mail: chris.williamson.mp@parliament.uk
Website: chriswilliamsonlabourleader.blogspot.com

Non-political career: Bricklayer 1973-78; Market trader 1978-79; Social worker 1981-87; Welfare rights officer 1987-2002; Derby City Council: Councillor 1991-, Council Leader; Member: General Assembly, Local Government Association 2006-, State of the City Forum, Derby City Partnership 2009-

Political career: Member for Derby North since 6 May 2010 general election; Member, Labour Party 1976-

Political interests: Poverty, animal welfare, urban regeneration, environment, climate change, local government community empowerment

Other organisations: League Against Cruel Sports: Member 1976-, Chair 1984-94, Trustee

Chris Williamson MP, House of Commons, London SW1A 0AA
Tel: 020 7219 3000 E-mail: chris.williamson.mp@parliament.uk
Constituency: Derby Labour Party, 2A Wentworth House, Vernon gate, Derby DE1 1UR Tel: 01332 345636
Website: chriswilliamsonlabourleader.blogspot.com

GENERAL ELECTION RESULT

		%
Williamson, C. (Lab)	14,896	33.0
Mold, S. (Con)	14,283	31.7
Care, L. (Lib Dem)	12,638	28.0
Cheeseman, P. (BNP)	2,000	4.4
Ransome, E. (UKIP)	829	1.8
Gale, D. (Ind)	264	0.6
Geraghty, D. (Pirate)	170	0.4
Majority	613	1.36
Electorate	71,484	
Turnout	45,080	63.06

CONSTITUENCY SNAPSHOT

Labour held the seat for most of the post-Second World War period. But this was brought to an abrupt end in 1983 as the Conservative Greg Knight gained a 10 per cent swing to unseat the incumbent Philip Whitehead. Mr Knight went on to win two elections before being defeated by Labour in 1997.

In 1997 Bob Laxton secured a sizable majority for Labour. He managed to poll over half the vote in 2001, but in 2005 his vote-share fell and he was returned with a reduced 3,757 majority.

In 2010 the seat was held by Chris Williamson for Labour with a majority of 613.

The seat gained Littleover ward from Derby South as well as four other wards that were previously shared between the two divisions. Allestree and Oakwood wards and a part-ward moved to Mid Derbyshire, while the seat also lost a part-ward to Derby South.

With the aerospace and rail industries dominating the labour market, this is an area with relatively few managerial and professional workers.

Although manufacturing accounts for an above average of employees, higher percentages work in finance, IT and other business activities and public administration, education and health.

Gavin Williamson

South Staffordshire

Boundary changes

Tel: 020 7219 3000
E-mail: gavin.williamson.mp@parliament.uk

Date of birth: 1976; Married Joanne (2 daughters)

Non-political career: Businessman; Managing director, architecture design company; Councillor, North Yorkshire County Council 2001-05

Political career: Contested Blackpool North and Fleetwood 2005 general election. Member for South Staffordshire since 6 May 2010 general election; Former chair, Conservative Students; Deputy chair, Staffordshire Conservatives; Chair, Stoke-on-Trent Conservative Association; Vice-chair, Derbyshire Dales Conservative Association

Gavin Williamson MP, House of Commons, London SW1A 0AA
Tel: 020 7219 3000 E-mail: gavin.williamson.mp@parliament.uk
Constituency: South Staffordshire Conservative Association, The Firs, Station Road, Codsall, Wolverhampton, West Midlands WV8 1BX
Tel: 01902 844985 Fax: 01902 844967

GENERAL ELECTION RESULT

		%
Williamson, G. (Con)	26,834	53.2
McElduff, K. (Lab)	10,244	20.3
Fellows, S. (Lib Dem)	8,427	16.7
Nattrass, M. (UKIP)	2,753	5.5
Bradnock, D. (BNP)	1,928	3.8
Morris, A. (Ind)	254	0.5
Majority	16,590	32.89
Electorate	73,390	
Turnout	50,440	68.73

CONSTITUENCY SNAPSHOT

Formerly know as Staffordshire South West, this constituency was formed in 1974 when Cannock was split. Sir Patrick Cormack won Cannock from Nye Bevan's widow Jennie Lee in 1970, but he moved to the new seat on its creation and represented it until 2010. Through the years Cormack returned majorities of around 20,000 in the 1980s and 1990s. In 1997, with boundary changes he was still returned with a 7,821 majority.

In 2005 the death of the Lib Dem candidate during the election campaign caused the poll to be postponed until June. Cormack was re-elected with a majority of 8,847.

The Conservatives held the seat with a majority of 16,590 in 2010. New MP Gavin Williamson secured 26,834 votes.

Boundary changes have been minimal.

South Staffordshire is a prosperous rural seat that curls around the western and northern fringes of the West Midlands, particularly Wolverhampton.

The seat contains no major towns, but neither is it wholly rural. Large suburban villages such as Codsall, Perton and Wombourne serve as commuter dormitories for Wolverhampton and Dudley.

There are more agricultural and mining and quarrying jobs in South Staffordshire than the national average. However, South Staffordshire is mainly home to those in managerial and professional occupations.

Jenny Willott

Cardiff Central (returning MP)

No boundary changes

Tel: 020 7219 8418
E-mail: willottj@parliament.uk
Website: www.jennywillott.com

Date of birth: 29 May 1974; Daughter of Brian and Alison Willott

Education: Wimbledon High School; Uppingham School; St Mary's College, Durham (BA classics 1996); London School of Economics (MSc Econ development studies 1997); Married Andrew Poole 2009

Non-political career: Researcher and proposal writer, Adithi NGO, Bihar, India 1995; Head of office, Lembit Öpik MP 1997-2000; Researcher, Lib Dem group, National Assembly for Wales 2000-01; Project administrator, Barnado's, Derwen project 2001; Head of advocacy, UNICEF UK 2001-03; Head of Victim Support South Wales 2003-05; Councillor London Borough of Merton 1998-2000

Political career: Contested Cardiff Central 2001 general election. Member for Cardiff Central since 5 May 2005 general election; Liberal Democrat: Shadow Minister for Youth Affairs 2006-07, Whip 2006-08: Deputy Chief Whip 2006-08, Shadow: Minister for Justice 2008, Secretary of State for Work and Pensions 2008-09, Chancellor of the Duchy of Lancaster 2009-10; PPS to Chris Huhne as Secretary of State for Energy and Climate Change 2010-; *Select Committees:* Member: Work and Pensions 2005-10, Public Administration 2005-10

Political interests: International development, foreign affairs, children's issues, crime and disorder; India

Recreations: Travelling, music, reading

Jenny Willott MP, House of Commons, London SW1A 0AA
Tel: 020 7219 8418 Fax: 020 7219 0694
E-mail: willottj@parliament.uk
Constituency: 99 Woodville Road, Cathays, Cardiff CF24 4DY
Tel: 029 2066 8558 Fax: 029 2066 5760
Website: www.jennywillott.com

GENERAL ELECTION RESULT

		%	+/-
Willott, J. (Lib Dem)*	14,976	41.4	-8.2
Rathbone, J. (Lab)	10,400	28.8	-5.5
Robson, K. (Con)	7,799	21.6	12.4
Williams, C. (PIC)	1,246	3.5	-0.1
Davies, S. (UKIP)	765	2.1	1.1
Coates, S. (Green)	575	1.6	
Saunders, R. (TUSC)	162	0.5	
Beech, M. (Loony)	142	0.4	
Mathias, A. (Ind)	86	0.2	
Majority	4,576	12.66	
Electorate	61,162		
Turnout	36,151	59.11	

**Member of last parliament*

CONSTITUENCY SNAPSHOT

At its creation for the 1983 general election, the new seat of Cardiff Central was won by Conservative Ian Grist. Labour broke through here in 1992 when Jon Owen Jones won the Cardiff Central seat at his second attempt.

Jones increased his majority in 1997 to 7,923 as the Conservatives' vote fell and the Liberal Democrats moved into second place. The Liberal Democrats continued to advance and in 2001 cut his majority from 7,923 to just 659.

In 2005 Jenny Willott achieved an 8.7 per cent swing for the Liberal Democrats to take the seat with a convincing 5,593 majority over Labour. Willott won re-election with a 4,576 majority in 2010.

This seat in the city centre includes the castle, the university, the City Hall, the law courts, the National Museum, Cardiff Royal Infirmary and a large shopping area.

Cardiff is a major sporting venue. This seat includes the Millennium Stadium and a revamped Sophia Gardens cricket ground which has become an international venue.

The city has enjoyed growth as a regional, commercial and administrative centre. Consequently it has a high proportion of employees in the service sector.

There is a huge student population resulting in the seat having the lowest proportion of home-owners after Swansea West, also a student area.

Phil Wilson

Sedgefield (returning MP)

Boundary changes

Tel: 020 7219 4966
E-mail: wilsonphil@parliament.uk

Date of birth: 31 May 1959; Son of Ivy and Bernard Wilson

Education: Trimdon Secondary Modern; Sedgefield Comprehensive School; Partner Margaret Brown since 1999 (2 children, 3 stepchildren)

Non-political career: Shop assistant; Civil Service clerical worker; Aide to Tony Blair MP 1987-94; Researcher to Stephen Hughes MEP 1989; Labour Party organiser and assistant general secretary 1994-99; Public relations consultant: Brunswick 1999-2002, Fellows Associates 2002-07; Member: USDAW 1977-78, CPSA 1978-87, TGWU 1986-, GMB 1994-

Political career: Member for Sedgefield 19 July 2007 by-election to 2010, for Sedgefield (revised boundary) since 6 May 2010 general election; PPS: to Vernon Coaker as Minister of State: Home Office 2008-09, Department for Children, Schools and Families 2009, to Andy Burnham as Secretary of State for Health 2009-10; *Select Committees:* Member: Public Accounts 2007-10, Regulatory Reform 2007-10, North East 2009-10

Political interests: Regional development, sustainable communities, education; USA

Recreations: Reading, jazz, history

Phil Wilson MP, House of Commons, London SW1A 0AA
Tel: 020 7219 4966 Fax: 020 7219 0639
E-mail: wilsonphil@parliament.uk
Constituency: 4 Beveridge Walkway, Newton Aycliffe,
Co Durham DL5 4EE Tel: 01325 321603 Fax: 01325 321603
Website: www.philwilsonmp.co.uk

GENERAL ELECTION RESULT

		%
Wilson, P. (Lab)*	18,141	45.1
Mahapatra, N. (Con)	9,445	23.5
Thompson, A. (Lib Dem)	8,033	20.0
Gregory, B. (UKIP)	4,179	10.4
Walker, M. (BNP)	2,075	5.2
Gittins, P. (Ind)	1,049	2.6
Majority	8,696	21.62
Electorate	64,727	
Turnout	40,222	62.14

**Member of last parliament*

CONSTITUENCY SNAPSHOT

Sedgefield was created in 1983. Former Prime Minister Tony Blair won the seat that year with a majority over 8,000. A swing of nearly 10 per cent in 1997 sent the Labour majority above 25,000, and the seat's MP to Downing Street.

Tony Blair resigned as both Prime Minister and MP on 29 June 2007 and the by-election was held on 19 July. Eleven candidates stood and Labour's Phil Wilson held the seat with a majority of 6,956, half that of Blair in 2005. Wilson was returned in 2010 with 8,696 majority.

The seat lost part-ward Faverdale and Harrowgate Hill to Darlington, and Hutton Henry to Easington.

Sedgefield constituency almost completely surrounds Darlington on the southern edge of County Durham, and takes in former colliery villages in the north east, the new town of Newton Aycliffe and Sedgefield itself.

Once heavily industrial, Sedgefield's economy is now diversifying into light engineering, distributive trades and the service sector.

Newton Aycliffe is the main centre of employment, along with both Spennymoor and Peterlee, which fall just outside the constituency boundaries. All three have big industrial estates.

Some people commute into Darlington and the other big centres of Teesside. There has been inward investment from Japanese companies such at Fujitsu and Nippon Silica Glass.

Robert Wilson

Reading East (returning MP)

Boundary changes

Tel: 020 7219 6519
E-mail: robwilsonmp@parliament.uk
Website: www.robwilsonmp.com

Conservative

Date of birth: 4 January 1965

Education: Wallingford School, Oxfordshire; Reading University (BA history); Married Jane (4 children)

Non-political career: Entrepreneur in health and telecommunications; Councillor Reading Borough Council 1992-96, 2003-06

Political career: Contested Bolton North East 1997 general election. Member for Reading East 2005-10, for Reading East (revised boundary) since 6 May 2010 general election; Shadow Minister for Higher Education 2007-09; Opposition Whip 2009-10; *Select Committees:* Member: Education and Skills 2005-07, Procedure 2005-08, Innovation, Universities[, Science] and Skills/Science and Technology 2007-10

Political interests: Crime, education, immigration

Recreations: Cricket, family

Robert Wilson MP, House of Commons, London SW1A 0AA
Tel: 020 7219 6519 Fax: 020 7219 0847
E-mail: robwilsonmp@parliament.uk
Constituency: 12a South View Park, Marsack Street, Reading, Berkshire RG4 5AF Tel: 0118-375 9785
Website: www.robwilsonmp.com

GENERAL ELECTION RESULT

		%
Wilson, R. (Con)*	21,269	42.6
Epps, G. (Lib Dem)	13,664	27.3
Dodds, A. (Lab)	12,729	25.5
Pitfield, A. (UKIP)	1,086	2.2
White, R. (Green)	1,069	2.1
Lloyd, J. (Ind)	111	0.2
Turberville, M. (Ind)	57	0.1
Majority	7,605	15.21
Electorate	74,922	
Turnout	49,985	66.72

**Member of last parliament*

CONSTITUENCY SNAPSHOT

Reading East had just one Conservative MP from the 1970s until 1997, Sir Gerard Vaughan. Vaughan polled over 50 per cent of the vote in the four general elections from 1979 to 1992.

In 1997 Sir Gerard retired and his nominated successor lost to Labour's Jane Griffiths by 3,795 votes. Griffiths was re-elected in 2001 with an increased majority of 5,595.

Griffiths retired in 2005 and was replaced as candidate by Tony Page who lost the seat in 2005, when the party's vote-share fell by 10.5 per cent. The Conservative Rob Wilson won with a majority of 475.

The Conservatives retained the seat in 2010 with 21,269 votes giving Wilson a majority of 7,605.

The formerly divided wards of Battle and Whitley were moved fully into Reading West. The part-ward of Maiden Erlegh ward was lost to Wokingham. The seat gained the part-ward of Loddon from Maidenhead.

Reading lies at the heart of the Thames Valley, one of the most prosperous areas of the UK. Reading East contains all the town centre and the more commercial and business-orientated parts.

Reading's Oracle Shopping and Leisure Destination, provides some 4,000 jobs. The town has attracted several major international IT companies, including Microsoft, Compaq and the Oracle Corporation. It is also the national headquarters of companies including Prudential, Thames Water and Yellow Pages.

Sammy Wilson

East Antrim (returning MP)

Boundary changes

Tel: 020 7219 8523
E-mail: lewisp@parliament.uk
Website: www.sammywilson.org

Date of birth: 4 April 1953; Son of Alexander and Mary Wilson

Education: Methodist College, Belfast; Queen's University, Belfast (BA economics and politics 1975); Stranmillis College, Belfast (DipEd 1976)

Non-political career: Head of economics, Grosvenor Grammar School, Belfast 1975-83; East Belfast City Council: Councillor 1981-2010, Lord Mayor 1986-87, 2000-01; Member, Northern Ireland Policing Board 2001-06

Political career: Contested Strangford 1992 and East Antrim 2001 general elections. Member for East Antrim 2005-10, for East Antrim (revised boundary) since 6 May 2010 general election; DUP Spokesperson for: Education and Skills 2003-07, Housing 2005-07, Communities and Local Government 2007-09, Children, Schools and Families 2007-, Innovation, Universities and Skills 2007-09, Treasury 2009-; *Select Committees:* Member: Northern Ireland Affairs 2005-09, Transport 2009; Northern Ireland Assembly: Member Northern Ireland Forum for Political Dialogue 1996, MLA for Belfast East 1998-2003, and for East Antrim 2003-: Minister of: Environment 2008-09, Finance and Personnel 2009-; DUP press officer 1982-96

Political interests: Social issues, policing, education; *Publications:* The Carson Trail (1982); The Unionist Case – The Forum Report Answered (1984); Data Response Questions in Economics (1995)

Recreations: Gardening, motorbikes

Sammy Wilson MP, House of Commons, London SW1A 0AA
Tel: 020 7219 8523 Fax: 020 7219 3671
E-mail: lewisp@parliament.uk
Constituency: East Antrim DUP, 116 Main Street, Larne,
Co Antrim BT40 1RG Tel: 028 2826 7722 Fax: 028 2826 9922
Website: www.sammywilson.org

GENERAL ELECTION RESULT

		%
Wilson, S. (DUP)*	13,993	45.9
McCune, R. (UCUNF)	7,223	23.7
Lynch, G. (All)	3,377	11.1
McMullan, O. (Sinn Féin)	2,064	6.8
McCamphill, J. (SDLP)	2,019	6.6
Morrison, S. (TUV)	1,826	6.0
Majority	6,770	22.20
Electorate	60,204	
Turnout	30,502	50.66

**Member of last parliament*

CONSTITUENCY SNAPSHOT

The UUP's Roy Beggs, who is a former DUP member, won this seat for the Ulster Unionists in 1983. He was defeated by his former party in 2005.

He had only narrowly retained the seat in 2001. The DUP had drafted in former Lord Mayor of Belfast, Sammy Wilson, who increased the DUP vote by 16.5 per cent. Wilson achieved a swing of 11.5 per cent in 2005, winning with a margin of 7,304. Wilson held the seat in 2010 with a reduced majority of 6,770.

Boundary changes have added two wards to the seat from North Antrim.

This largely urban constituency nestles on the north eastern coast of Ireland between the Antrim Hills and Belfast Lough.

The constituency is dominated by the port of Larne. Given its easy access to sea and airports, the seat contains an above average percentage of distribution operators including Famac, a world-wide courier service, and the Belfast Co-operative Society Distribution Centre, a major grocery retail supplier in Northern Ireland.

The constituency's large heavy industry sector was reduced by the closure of the ICI and Courtaulds plants in Carrickfergus in the 1980s, but still retains the large power station at Ballylumford. The seat also contains the Kilroot dual-fired power station.

David Winnick

Walsall North (returning MP)

Boundary changes

Tel: 020 7219 5003
E-mail: winnickd@parliament.uk
Website: www.epolitix.com/David-Winnick

Labour

Date of birth: 26 June 1933; Son of late Eugene and Rose Winnick

Education: London School of Economics (Diploma social administration 1974); 1 son; Married Bengisu Rona 1968 (divorced)

Non-political career: Association of Professional, Executive, Clerical & Computer Staff (APEX): Member Executive Council 1978-88, Vice-President 1983-88; Councillor, London Borough of: Willesden Council 1959-64, Brent Council 1964-66

Political career: Contested Harwich 1964 general election. Member for Croydon South 1966-70. Contested Croydon Central October 1974 general election and Walsall North 1976 by-election. Member for Walsall North 1979-2010, for Walsall North (revised boundary) since 6 May 2010 general election; *Select Committees:* Member: Procedure 1989-97, Home Affairs 1997-2010

Other organisations: Chair, United Kingdom Immigrants Advisory Service 1984-90; British Co-Chair, British-Irish Inter-Parliamentary Body 1997-2005

Recreations: Reading, theatre, films, walking

David Winnick MP, House of Commons, London SW1A 0AA
Tel: 020 7219 5003 E-mail: winnickd@parliament.uk
Constituency: 45 Field Road, Bloxwich, Walsall,
West Midlands WS3 3JD Tel: 01922 492084 Fax: 01922 408307
Website: www.epolitix.com/David-Winnick

GENERAL ELECTION RESULT

		%
Winnick, D. (Lab)*	13,385	37.0
Clack, H. (Con)	12,395	34.3
Fazal, N. (Lib Dem)	4,754	13.1
Woodall, C. (BNP)	2,930	8.1
Hazell, E. (UKIP)	1,737	4.8
Smith, P. (Dem Lab)	842	2.3
Shakir, B. (Christian)	144	0.4
Majority	990	2.74
Electorate	65,183	
Turnout	36,187	55.52

**Member of last parliament*

CONSTITUENCY SNAPSHOT

Walsall North has been a Labour seat for a number of years. Between 1950 and 1974 William Wells held the seat and the voters elected his successor John Stonehouse in 1974. However, Stonehouse was convicted of fraud and disappeared in a bizarre political drama, leaving a pile of clothes on a beach in an attempt to fake his own death. He eventually served three years in prison.

At the subsequent by-election in 1976 Robin Hodgson won the seat for the Conservatives. David Winnick won the seat back in 1979 for Labour and has held it ever since. In the 2005 general election Labour secured a 6,640 majority, his majority was a much-reduced majority 990 in 2010.

Boundary changes mean the new seat brings in all of Blakenall, Birchill Leamore and Willenhall South. Several part-wards went to Aldridge-Brownhills and Walsall South in exchange.

Walsall North is one of the two constituencies that make up the historic town on the north edge of the West Midlands conurbation.

The industrial revolution transformed Walsall and left behind foundries, mines and ironworks. Metalwork was the core local industry and bits, stirrups, buckles and spurs are still made locally. Today investment has brought new jobs in the service sector.

Rt Hon **Rosie Winterton**

Doncaster Central ***(returning MP)***

Boundary changes

Tel: 020 7219 0925
E-mail: wintertonr@parliament.uk
Website: www.rosiewinterton.co.uk

Labour

Date of birth: 10 August 1958; Daughter of late Gordon and Valerie Winterton, teachers

Education: Doncaster Grammar School; Hull University (BA history 1979)

Non-political career: Constituency personal assistant to John Prescott, MP 1980-86; Parliamentary officer: Southwark Council 1986-88, Royal College of Nursing 1988-90; Managing Director, Connect Public Affairs 1990-94; Head of private office of John Prescott as Deputy Leader of Labour Party 1994-97; Branch Officer, TGWU 1998-99; Member: NUJ, TGWU

Political career: Member for Doncaster Central 1997-2010, for Doncaster Central (revised boundary) since 6 May 2010 general election; Member, Intelligence and Security Committee January 2000-; Parliamentary Secretary, Lord Chancellor's Department 2001-03; Minister of State: Department of Health 2003-07, Department for Transport 2007-08; Minister for Yorkshire and the Humber 2008-10; Minister of State: (Pensions and the Ageing Society), Department for Work and Pensions 2008-09, (Regional Economic Development and Co-ordination) Departments for Business, Innovation and Skills and for Communities and Local Government 2009-10; Shadow Leader of the House of Commons and Lord Privy Seal 2010-; Member, Labour Party Strategic Campaign Committee; Representative, PLP on the National Policy Forum of the Labour Party

Political interests: Regional policy, employment, transport, housing, home affairs

Other organisations: Member, Amnesty International; Leader, Leadership Campaign Team 1998-99; Chair, Transport and General Workers' Parliamentary Group 1998-99; Member Standing Committees: Transport Bill January 2000, Finance Bill April 2000; Member Speaker's Committee on the Electoral Commission 2009-; PC 2006; Doncaster Trades and Labour, Intake Social, Doncaster Catholic

Recreations: Sailing, reading

Rt Hon Rosie Winterton MP, House of Commons, London SW1A 0AA Tel: 020 7219 0925 Fax: 020 7219 2811
E-mail: wintertonr@parliament.uk
Constituency: Doncaster Trades, 19 South Mall, Frenchgate, Doncaster, South Yorkshire DN1 1LL Tel: 01302 326297
Fax: 01302 342921 Website: www.rosiewinterton.co.uk

GENERAL ELECTION RESULT

		%
Winterton, R. (Lab)*	16,569	39.7
Davies, G. (Con)	10,340	24.8
Wilson, P. (Lib Dem)	8,795	21.1
Parramore, L. (England)	1,816	4.4
Bettney, J. (BNP)	1,762	4.2
Andrews, M. (UKIP)	1,421	3.4
Pickles, S. (Ind)	970	2.3
Williams, D. (CURE)	72	0.2
Majority	6,229	14.92
Electorate	75,207	
Turnout	41,757	55.52

**Member of last parliament*

CONSTITUENCY SNAPSHOT

Anthony Barber held the seat for the Conservatives for 13 years from 1951. Then in 1964 Harold Walker won for Labour and was MP here for 33 years. In 1983 his majority was only 2,508, however, it had increased to 10,682 by 1992.

Sir Harold retired in 1997. A swing of more than 10 per cent gave Labour's Rosie Winterburn a majority of 18,000.

Despite convictions of Labour councillors following the Donnygate investigation, the swing against Labour in 2001 was below 3 per cent. The Liberal Democrats vote grew by ten points in 2005 leaving Winterton with a 9,802 majority. In 2010 Winterton was re-elected with a reduced majority of 6,229.

Boundary changes were minimal.

Although at one time surrounded by pit villages, Doncaster was never in itself a mining town. Rail and engineering were the two major industries in the town, and although hit by recession in the 1990s, both still survive, now often as parts of multinationals. A large new industrial site is situated just outside the town.

The constituency has its better-heeled areas around the racecourse, famous for the classic St Leger.

The excellent road and rail links fuel the growing distribution economy. IKEA has a huge distribution centre here. There are also large industrial sites near the motorways.

Peter Wishart

Perth and North Perthshire (returning MP)

No boundary changes

Tel: 020 7219 8303
E-mail: wishartp@parliament.uk

Date of birth: 9 March 1962; Son of late Alex Wishart, former dockyard worker and Nan Irvine, retired teacher

Education: Queen Anne High School, Dunfermline, Fife; Moray House College of Education (Dip CommEd 1984); Married Carrie Lindsay 1990 (separated 2003) (1 son)

Non-political career: Musician Big Country 1981; Community worker Central Region 1984-85; Musician Runrig 1985-2001; Musicians Union 1985-

Political career: Member for North Tayside 2001-05, for Perth and North Perthshire since 5 May 2005 general election; SNP Chief Whip 2001-07; SNP Spokesperson for: Transport 2001-05, Rural Affairs 2001-05, Culture, Media and Sport 2001-, Constitution 2005-07, Overseas Aid 2005-07, Home Affairs 2007-, Justice 2007-, International Development 2007-; *Select Committees:* Member: Catering 2004-05, Administration 2005-08, Scottish Affairs 2009-10; Member: National Council 1997-, NEC 1999-2006; Executive vice-convener fundraising SNP 1999-2001

Political interests: Arts and culture, international development, justice and equality; Scandinavia, Germany, Southern Africa

Other organisations: Director Fast Forward Positive Lifestyle 1992-2001; Campaign Committee Scotland Against Drugs 1997-99

Recreations: Music, hillwalking, travel

Peter Wishart MP, House of Commons, London SW1A 0AA
Tel: 020 7219 8303 E-mail: wishartp@parliament.uk
Constituency: 35 Perth Street, Blairgowrie, Perthshire PH10 6DL
Tel: 01250 876 576 Fax: 01250 876 991, 9 York Place, Perth, Perthshire PH2 8EP Tel: 01738 639598 Fax: 01738 587637

GENERAL ELECTION RESULT

		%	+/-
Wishart, P. (SNP)*	19,118	39.6	6.0
Lyburn, P. (Con)	14,739	30.5	0.2
Glackin, J. (Lab)	7,923	16.4	-2.3
Barrett, P. (Lib Dem)	5,954	12.3	-3.8
Taylor, D. (Trust)	534	1.1	
Majority	4,379	9.07	
Electorate	72,141		
Turnout	48,268	66.91	

**Member of last parliament*

CONSTITUENCY SNAPSHOT

Perthshire was very safe for the Conservatives for the majority of the 20th century. However, the SNP captured Perth and Kinross at the by-election following Nicholas Fairbairn's death in 1995, and North Tayside in 1997. The Party held the seat in 2001 with Annabelle Ewing representing Perth and Peter Wishart in North Tayside.

Boundary changes in 2005 merged North Tayside, Perth, and Ochil into two new constituencies: Perth and North Perthshire and Ochil and South Perthshire. While Annabelle Ewing narrowly lost to Labour in Ochil and South Perthshire, Pete Wishart was returned with a majority of 1,521. This seat was a key Tory target in 2010, but Wishart held on with an increased majority of 4,739.

Framed by the Grampian Mountains in the north-west and the Firth of Tay in the south-west, Perth and North Perthshire includes a series of idyllic towns in Highland Perthshire as well as Lochs Tay, Tummel and Rannoch.

Around half of the electorate resides in the prosperous town of Perth, but the seat also includes some of the most fertile farming land in Scotland. Both Scottish and Southern Energy and Stagecoach, based in Perth, are major employers.

At the heart of the constituency lies the picturesque town of Pitlochry, as well as nearby Killiecrankie, Birnam Wood (made famous by Shakespeare's Macbeth) and the historic town of Scone, once home of the Stone of Destiny.

Dr **Sarah Wollaston**

Totnes

Boundary changes

Tel: 020 7219 3000
E-mail: sarah.wollaston.mp@parliament.uk
Website: www.drsarah.org.uk

Conservative

Date of birth: 1962

Education: Tal Handaq Service Children's School, Malta; Watford Grammar School for Girls; Guys Hospital Medical School (BSc pathology 1983; MB 1986); Married Adrian (1 son 2 daughters)

Non-political career: Forensic medical examiner, police 1996-2001; GP, Chagford Health Centre 1999-; Trainer, Peninsula Medical School 2001-; Teacher, Exeter Postgraduate Centre -2010; Examiner, Royal College of General Practitioners

Political career: Member for Totnes since 6 May 2010 general election

Political interests: NHS, alcohol related problems, bovine TB, rural communities

Recreations: Cross-country running, tandeming

Dr Sarah Wollaston MP, House of Commons, London SW1A 0AA
Tel: 020 7219 3000 E-mail: sarah.wollaston.mp@parliament.uk
Constituency: South Devon Conservatives, Station Road, Totnes, Devon TQ9 5HW Tel: 01803 866069 Fax: 01803 867286
Website: www.drsarah.org.uk

GENERAL ELECTION RESULT

		%
Wollaston, S. (Con)	21,940	45.9
Brazil, J. (Lib Dem)	17,013	35.6
Whitty, C. (Lab)	3,538	7.4
Beer, J. (UKIP)	2,890	6.0
Somerville, L. (Green)	1,181	2.5
Turner, M. (BNP)	624	1.3
Drew, S. (Ind)	390	0.8
Hopwood, S. (Ind)	267	0.6
Majority	4,927	10.30
Electorate	67,937	
Turnout	47,843	70.42

CONSTITUENCY SNAPSHOT

Totnes has been a Tory seat for the past 60 years. Anthony Steen was the MP for Totnes from 1983 until his retirement in 2010. Before that, the area was represented by Ray Mawby for 28 years.

In 2001 Steen polled an increased majority of 3,597, while the Labour vote fell to just over 12%. In 2005 the Liberal Democrats won back some of the support they lost in 2001, but it was not enough to defeat Anthony Steen, who was returned with a reduced majority of 1,947. Steen was forced into retirement in 2010 by the expenses scandal, but his replacement Sarah Wollaston has doubled the party's majority to 4,927.

There were minor boundary changes to this seat.

Situated on the south Devon coast Totnes takes in Dartmouth on the coast and Dartmoor further inland.

Tourism makes up the majority of the constituency's income supported by fishing and farming.

Totnes lies in the centre of the constituency surrounded by many other small towns and villages such as South Brent. There is a considerable amount of agricultural land here, with coastal towns stretching right down to Bigbury in the south and Brixham in the north.

The South West Coast Path has proved to be a particular tourist attraction.

Mike Wood

Batley and Spen ***(returning MP)***

Boundary changes

Tel: 020 7219 4125
E-mail: woodm@parliament.uk
Website: www.mikewood.org.uk

Labour

Date of birth: 3 March 1946; Son of late Rowland L. Wood, foundry worker, and late Laura M. Wood, retired cleaner

Education: Nantwich and Acton Grammar School, Nantwich, Cheshire; Salisbury/Wells Theological College (Cert Theol 1974); Leeds University (CQSW 1981); Leeds Polytechnic (BA history and politics 1989); Married 2nd Christine O'Leary 1999 (1 son 1 daughter from previous marriage; 2 stepdaughters)

Non-political career: Probation officer, social worker, community worker 1965-97; Member GMB; Kirklees Metropolitan District Council: Councillor 1980-88, Deputy Leader 1986-87

Political career: Contested Hexham 1987 general election. Member for Batley and Spen 1997-2010, for Batley and Spen (revised boundary) since 6 May 2010 general election; *Select Committees:* Member: Broadcasting 1997-98; Member, Labour Friends of India 1997-

Political interests: Poverty, housing, transport, environmental issues and world development, small businesses; France, Indian Sub-continent

Recreations: Sport, music, ornithology, walking

Mike Wood MP, House of Commons, London SW1A 0AA
Tel: 020 7219 4125 Fax: 020 7219 2861
E-mail: woodm@parliament.uk
Constituency: Tom Myer's House, 9 Cross Crown Street, Cleckheaton, West Yorkshire BD19 3HW Tel: 01274 335233 Fax: 01274 335235
Website: www.mikewood.org.uk

GENERAL ELECTION RESULT

		%
Wood, M. (Lab)*	21,565	41.5
Small, J. (Con)	17,159	33.0
Bentley, N. (Lib Dem)	8,925	17.2
Exley, D. (BNP)	3,685	7.1
Blakeley, M. (Green)	605	1.2
Majority	4,406	8.48
Electorate	76,732	
Turnout	51,939	67.69

**Member of last parliament*

CONSTITUENCY SNAPSHOT

The seat was won by the Conservative Elizabeth Peacock by just 870 votes in 1983. Peacock improved her lead in 1987, and in 1992 she held on against the odds.

But in 1997 Labour's Mike Wood won with the biggest majority the seat had known, although the swing to Labour here was only just over 7 per cent, well below the national average. Labour was left with a majority of 5,788 in 2005. Wood held the seat for Labour in 2010 with a 4,406 majority.

Boundary changes moved the wards of Batley East, Heckmondwike, and Liversedge and Gomersal entirely into the seat, while both Dewsbury East and West moved completely into Dewsbury.

This is a largely urban West Yorkshire seat, which includes the textiles town of Batley and smaller villages in-between.

This is a predominantly working-class manufacturing seat with a diverse economy. It was once a coal-mining era, but the last pits closed in the 1970s.

Textile manufacturing continues in small companies, but many of the heavy wool mills are now silent. As in some other areas within commuting distance of Leeds, there is a large amount of new building, extensions and conversion of old mills into upmarket accommodation.

John Woodcock

Barrow and Furness

Boundary changes

Tel: 020 7219 3000
E-mail: john.woodcock.mp@parliament.uk
Website: www.john-woodcock-for-furness.org

Labour/Co-operative

Married Mandy Telford (1 daughter)

Non-political career: Head, safeguarding vulnerable people, Crime and Policing Group, Home Office 2003-07; Special Adviser to: John Hutton as: Chancellor of the Duchy of Lancaster and Minister for the Cabinet Office 2005, Secretary of State for Work and Pensions 2005-07, Secretary of State for Business, Enterprise and Regulatory Reform 2007-08, Gordon Brown MP as Prime Minister on political press issues 2009; Governor, Walney School

Political career: Member for Barrow and Furness since 6 May 2010 general election

Political interests: Civil nuclear power, manufacturing industry

John Woodcock MP, House of Commons, London SW1A 0AA
Tel: 020 7219 3000 E-mail: john.woodcock.mp@parliament.uk
Constituency: Barrow and Furness PPC, 22 Hartington Street, Barrow-in-furness, Cumbria LA14 5SL Tel: 01229 820025
Website: www.john-woodcock-for-furness.org

GENERAL ELECTION RESULT

		%
Woodcock, J. (Lab/Co-op)	21,226	48.1
Gough, J. (Con)	16,018	36.3
Rabone, B. (Lib Dem)	4,424	10.0
Smith, J. (UKIP)	841	1.9
Ashburner, M. (BNP)	840	1.9
Loynes, C. (Green)	530	1.2
Greaves, B. (Ind)	245	0.6
Majority	5,208	11.80
Electorate	68,758	
Turnout	44,124	64.17

CONSTITUENCY SNAPSHOT

Barrow-in-Furness was for many years a Labour seat, but Barrow's association with the defence industry may have helped the Conservatives to win the seat in 1983 and 1987. Labour returned in 1992 when John Hutton was elected MP for Barrow and Furness. In the 1997 national victory, Hutton increased his majority to 14,497. However, his majority was cut to 9,889 in 2001.

Hutton's majority fell again in 2005 to 6,037. Hutton stood down in 2010 but the seat was held by the Labour candidate, John Woodcock who secured a majority of 5,208.

Broughton and Crake Valley wards extended the seat to the north.

Barrow and Furness lies in Cumbria, north of the Lake District, across the bay from Morecambe. The seat takes in lush farmland and the small town of Ulverston as well as the port of Barrow, best known as a shipbuilding centre.

Barrow-in-Furness still relies heavily on submarine building, together with other naval and commercial shipbuilding.

Key employers in the area include BAE Defence Systems, which provide around 4,000 defence-related jobs within the constituency. The pharmaceutical industry has become increasingly important, with GlaxoSmithKline being another major employer.

Rt Hon **Shaun Woodward**

St Helens South and Whiston ***(returning MP)***

New constituency

Tel: 020 7219 2680
E-mail: woodwardsh@parliament.uk
Website: www.shaunwoodward.com

Labour

Date of birth: 26 October 1958; Son of Dennis George Woodward and Joan Lillian, neé Nunn

Education: Bristol Grammar School; Jesus College, Cambridge (MA English literature); Married Camilla Davan Sainsbury 1987 (1 son 3 daughters)

Non-political career: BBC TV News and Current Affairs 1982-98; Director of communications, Conservative Party 1991-92; Member, Amicus; Member Foundation Board, RSC 1998-2002; Director: English National Opera 1998-2001, Marine Stewardship Council 1998-2001

Political career: Member for Witney 1997-2001 (Conservative May 1997 to December 1999, Labour December 1999 to June 2001), for St Helens South 2001-10, for St Helens South and Whiston since 6 May 2010 general election; Conservative Opposition Spokesperson for Environment, Transport and the Regions 1999; Parliamentary Under-Secretary of State: Northern Ireland Office 2005-06, Department for Culture, Media and Sport (Minister for Creative Industries and Tourism) 2006-07; Secretary of State for Northern Ireland 2007-10; Shadow Secretary of State for Northern Ireland 2010-; *Select Committees:* Member: Broadcasting 1997-99, European Scrutiny 1998-99, Foreign Affairs 1999, Broadcasting 2000-01, Joint Committee on Human Rights 2001-05

Political interests: Finance, environment, education, culture, children's issues, European affairs, race relations and civil rights, regeneration, international development, works of art; USA, France, Germany, Italy, China and Australia

Other organisations: Trustee, Childline -2005; Vice-President, St Helens District Council for Voluntary Service; Honorary President, St Helens Millennium Centre; PC 2007; Visiting professor, Queen Mary and Westfield College, London University; Visiting fellow, John F. Kennedy School of Government, Harvard University; *Publications:* Co-author: Tranquillisers (1983), Ben: The Story of Ben Hardwick (1984), Drugwatch (1985)

Recreations: Opera, tennis, reading, gardening, architecture

Rt Hon Shaun Woodward MP, House of Commons, London SW1A 0AA Tel: 020 7219 2680 Fax: 020 7219 0979
E-mail: woodwardsh@parliament.uk
Constituency: 1st Floor, Century House, Hardshaw Street, St Helens, Merseyside WA10 1QW Tel: 01744 24226 Fax: 01744 24306
Website: www.shaunwoodward.com

GENERAL ELECTION RESULT

		%
Woodward, S. (Lab)*	24,364	52.9
Spencer, B. (Lib Dem)	10,242	22.2
Allen, V. (Con)	8,209	17.8
Winstanley, J. (BNP)	2,040	4.4
Sumner, J. (UKIP)	1,226	2.7
Majority	14,122	30.65
Electorate	77,975	
Turnout	46,081	59.10

**Member of last parliament*

CONSTITUENCY SNAPSHOT

This seat is formed from three wards from the Knowsley South and seven from the St Helens South.

Since 2001 Shaun Woodward has been the MP for St Helens South. Woodward's selection was controversial, particularly as no local candidates were put on the shortlist, and as a result labour's level of support fell dramatically.

Labour voters returned to the fold in 2005 Shaun Woodward increased his share of the vote and majority, although it was by only 324 votes to 9,309. He was returned to the new seat with a majority of 14,122 in 2010.

Famous for its successful rugby league team and the giant Pilkington glass factory, there are also a number of other manufacturing industries in the town.

Regeneration is important here. The town has benefited from funding for improvements of the St Helens central station, the canal, and north to the Transco gas depot.

This is rugby league territory. The local club, St Helens, is probably the single most important institution in the town. The club has received planning permission for a major redevelopment of the derelict 46-acre former United Glass site into a £25 million, 18,000-capacity stadium for the Saints and a multi-million pound Tesco Extra. Work should be finished on the development by 2011.

Phil Woolas

Oldham East and Saddleworth *(returning MP)*

Boundary changes

Tel: 020 7219 1149
E-mail: woolasp@parliament.uk

Date of birth: 11 December 1959; Son of Dennis and Maureen Woolas

Education: Nelson Grammar School; Walton Lane High School; Nelson and Colne College; Manchester University (BA philosophy 1981); Married Tracey Allen 1988 (2 sons)

Non-political career: President National Union of Students 1984-86; Producer: BBC *Newsnight* 1988-90, Channel 4 News 1990; Head of communication GMB 1991-97; Member, GMB

Political career: Contested Littleborough and Saddleworth 1995 by-election. Member for Oldham East and Saddleworth 1997-2010, Oldham East and Saddleworth (revised boundary) since 6 May 2010 general election; PPS to Lord Macdonald of Tradeston as Minister for Transport, Department of the Environment, Transport and the Regions 1999-2001; Assistant Government Whip 2001-02; Government Whip 2002-03; Deputy Leader of the House of Commons 2003-05; Minister of State: Office of the Deputy Prime Minister/Department for Communities and Local Government (Minister for Local Government) 2005-07, Department for Environment, Food and Rural Affairs 2007-08, Home Office (Borders and Immigration) and HM Treasury 2008-10; Minister for the North West 2009-10; *Select Committees:* Member: Environmental Audit 2008-09; Chair, Tribune Newspaper 1997-2001; Deputy Leader, Leadership Campaign Team 1997-99

Political interests: Employment, economics, media, trade and industry; Kashmir and Jammu

Other organisations: RTS Award for Political Coverage 1990; Lancashire County Cricket Club, Manchester United Football Club

Recreations: Photography

Phil Woolas MP, House of Commons, London SW1A 0AA
Tel: 020 7219 1149 Fax: 020 7219 0992
E-mail: woolasp@parliament.uk
Constituency: 11 Church Lane, Oldham,
Greater Manchester OL1 3AN Tel: 0161-624 4248
Fax: 0161-626 8572

GENERAL ELECTION RESULT

		%
Woolas, P. (Lab)*	14,186	31.9
Watkins, E. (Lib Dem)	14,083	31.6
Ali, K. (Con)	11,773	26.4
Stott, A. (BNP)	2,546	5.7
Bentley, D. (UKIP)	1,720	3.9
Nazir, G. (Christian)	212	0.5
Majority	103	0.23
Electorate	72,765	
Turnout	44,520	61.18

**Member of last parliament*

CONSTITUENCY SNAPSHOT

The Conservatives' Geoffrey Dickens held Littleborough and Saddleworth from 1983, however, the Liberal Democrat Chris Davies took the seat at the by-election following Dickens's death in 1995. In 1997 Chris Davies lost the seat to his 1995 by-election Labour opponent, Phil Woolas.

In the 2001 general election there was very little change to the relative positions of the three main parties. In 2005 Phil Woolas, increased his majority to 3,590. Woolas was re-elected in 2010 with a small majority of 103.

The seat gained the part-wards of Alexandra and St Mary's from Oldham West and Royton, in return for the part-wards of Medlock Vale and Royton South. It also lost all Rochdale borough wards to Rochdale.

Despite its name, the seat contains little of the town of Oldham. Situated to the south of Rochdale and on the eastern edge of Greater Manchester, the overwhelming part of the seat's geographical area is in the Saddleworth region, the umbrella name for a group of commuter villages in the south Pennines including Diggle, Uppermill and Delph.

Saddleworth is one of the most middle-class parts of the North West and houses prosperous commuters to Manchester.

David Wright

Telford (returning MP)

Boundary changes

Tel: 020 7219 8331
E-mail: wrightda@parliament.uk
Website: www.davidwrightmp.org.uk

Date of birth: 22 December 1966; Son of Kenneth William Wright and Heather Wright, neé Wynn

Education: Wrockwardine Wood Comprehensive School, Telford, Shropshire; New College, Telford, Shropshire; Wolverhampton Polytechnic (BA humanities 1988); Married Lesley Insole 1996

Non-political career: Housing strategy manager Sandwell Metropolitan Borough Council 1988-2001; Member TGWU 1988-; Councillor Wrekin District Council 1989-97; Oakengates Town Council 1989-2000: Councillor, Former chair

Political career: Member for Telford 2001-10, for Telford (revised boundary) since 6 May 2010 general election; PPS: to Rosie Winterton as Minister of State, Department of Health 2004-05, to David Miliband as: Minister of Communities and Local Government 2005-06, Secretary of State for Environment, Food and Rural Affairs 2006, to John Hutton as Secretary of State for Work and Pensions 2006, to Jane Kennedy as Financial Secretary to the Treasury 2007-08; Assistant Government Whip 2009-10; *Select Committees:* Member: Administration 2001-02, Environmental Audit 2001-05, Procedure 2001-05, Communities and Local Government 2007, 2009

Political interests: Housing and regeneration, regional development, sports development, hunting with dogs (against), poverty; France, USA

Other organisations: Member Chartered Institute of Housing (MCIH); Member: Wrockwardine Wood and Trench Labour, Dawley Social

Recreations: Football (Telford United), local history, visiting medieval towns

David Wright MP, House of Commons, London SW1A 0AA
Tel: 020 7219 8331 Fax: 020 7219 1979
E-mail: wrightda@parliament.uk
Constituency: 35B High Street, Dawley, Telford, Shropshire TF4 2EX
Tel: 01952 507747 Fax: 01952 506064
Website: www.davidwrightmp.org.uk

GENERAL ELECTION RESULT

		%
Wright, D. (Lab)*	15,977	38.7
Biggins, T. (Con)	14,996	36.3
Bennion, P. (Lib Dem)	6,399	15.5
Allen, D. (UKIP)	2,428	5.9
Spencer, P. (BNP)	1,513	3.7
Majority	981	2.37
Electorate	65,061	
Turnout	41,313	63.50

**Member of last parliament*

CONSTITUENCY SNAPSHOT

Telford is unusual in a rural county like Shropshire, as it is a centrally planned new town, with a large urban sprawl. The town was formerly included in the old Wrekin seat, which had swung between Labour and Conservative no fewer than seven times since 1945.

The Labour majority has fallen from 11,290 in 1997 under long-time Wrekin MP Bruce Grocott, to 8,383 in 2001, when David Wright took the reins, and fell again to 5,406 in 2005.

Wright was re-elected in 2010 with a small majority of 981 after a 6.3 per cent swing to the Conservatives.

Boundary changes mean parts of several more rural wards move into Wrekin.

Telford in the West Midlands was designated as a new town in 1946, but only really developed from 1968. While most of the seat is centred on Telford, it also includes the picturesque gorge town of Ironbridge, a birth place for the Industrial Revolution.

The population has grown steadily from 75,000 in 1961 to 160,000 in 2001, exceeding both central and local government predictions.

Telford's economy supports a mixture of medium-sized companies, particularly in the service sector. The four biggest companies are GKN Sankey, Epson, Denso Manufacturing, and EDS.

Several new developments have been underway in the Telford area, including a multi-million revamp on the Madeley Centre, the town's central indoor shopping centre.

Iain Wright

Hartlepool (returning MP)

No boundary changes

Tel: 020 7219 5587
E-mail: wrighti@parliament.uk
Website: www.iainwrightmp.org.uk

Labour

Date of birth: 9 May 1972; Son of Mervyn Wright, factory shift manager and Linda Wright, née Harland, hairdresser

Education: Manor Comprehensive School, Hartlepool; Hartlepool Sixth Form College, Hartlepool; University College, London (BA history 1994, MA 1995); Married Tiffiny Lee Shanley 1995 (3 sons 1 daughter)

Non-political career: Audit manager Enterprise Risk Services Deloitte & Touche 1996-2003; Governance manager OneNorthEast (Regional Development Agency) 2003-04; Member GMB; Councillor Hartlepool Borough Council 2002-04: Cabinet member for performance management 2003-04

Political career: Member for Hartlepool since 30 September 2004 by-election; PPS to Rosie Winterton as Minister of State, Department of Health 2005-06; Parliamentary Under-Secretary of State: Department for Communities and Local Government 2007-09, Department for Children, Schools and Families (14-19 Reform and Apprenticeships) 2009-10; *Select Committees:* Member: European Standing Committee A 2004-05, Public Administration 2005-06, Modernisation of the House of Commons 2006-08, Public Accounts 2007; Treasurer Hartlepool CLP 2002-04; Board member Labour North 2003-04; Chair Labour Friends of Israel 2005-06

Political interests: Economics, regeneration; Middle East, China, Latin America

Recreations: Music, history, Hartlepool United Football Club

Iain Wright MP, House of Commons, London SW1A 0AA
Tel: 020 7219 5587 Fax: 020 7219 2811
E-mail: wrighti@parliament.uk
Constituency: 23 South Road, Hartlepool, Cleveland TS26 9HD
Tel: 01429 224403 Fax: 01429 864775
Website: www.iainwrightmp.org.uk

GENERAL ELECTION RESULT

		%	+/-
Wright, I. (Lab)*	16,267	42.5	-8.8
Wright, A. (Con)	10,758	28.1	16.7
Clark, R. (Lib Dem)	6,533	17.1	-13.2
Allison, S. (UKIP)	2,682	7.0	3.5
Bage, R. (BNP)	2,002	5.2	
Majority	5,509	14.41	
Electorate	68,923		
Turnout	38,242	55.49	

**Member of last parliament*

CONSTITUENCY SNAPSHOT

In 1964 Labour ended what was a period of Conservative dominance when Ted Leadbitter won the seat. The party has held the seat since then. Peter Mandelson succeeded Leadbitter in 1992, and five years later a swing of more than 11 per cent gave him more than 60 per cent of the votes cast and a five-figure majority.

Peter Mandelson gave up his seat in Hartlepool in August 2004 to accept EU Commissioner, triggering a by-election that was won by the Labour candidate Iain Wright. In 2005 Iain Wright improved on his by-election performance, increasing his majority to 7,478. However, his majority was half that of Mandelson's in 2001. Iain Wright won a comfortable majority of 5,509 in 2010.

The constituency includes the town and old port of Hartlepool itself plus the surrounding coastal area. Some of the coast is attractive, but most is dominated by the giant chemical factories that are part of the North East industrial tradition.

There is still a chemical plant at Seal Sands, and the nuclear power station at Seaton Carew employs 500 staff.

Moves to smarten up the town and its image include the Historic Quay, a heritage development recreating the 18th century port, with a museum, marina, shopping and leisure facilities.

Jeremy Wright

Kenilworth and Southam (returning MP)

New constituency

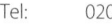

Tel: 020 7219 8299
E-mail: wrightjp@parliament.uk
Website: www.jeremywright.co.uk

Conservative

Date of birth: 24 October 1972; Son of John and Audrey Wright

Education: Taunton School, Somerset; Trinity School, New York City, USA; Exeter University (LLB law 1995); Inns of Court School of Law (Bar vocational course 1996); Married Yvonne Annette Salter 1998 (1 daughter)

Non-political career: Barrister, specialising in criminal law 1996-

Political career: Member for Rugby and Kenilworth 2005-10, for Kenilworth and Southam since 6 May 2010 general election; Opposition Whip 2007-10; Government Whip 2010-; *Select Committees:* Member: Constitutional Affairs 2005-07; Chairman, Warwick and Leamington Conservative Association 2002-03

Political interests: Criminal justice, education, foreign affairs; USA

Other organisations: Trustee Community Development Foundation; Fellow Industry and Parliament Trust 2007

Recreations: Travel, golf, James Bond films

Jeremy Wright MP, House of Commons, London SW1A 0AA
Tel: 020 7219 8299 Fax: 020 7219 0024
E-mail: wrightjp@parliament.uk
Constituency: Wilton House, Southbank Road, Kenilworth, Warwickshire CV8 1LA Tel: 01926 853650 Fax: 01926 854615
Website: www.jeremywright.co.uk

GENERAL ELECTION RESULT

		%
Wright, J. (Con)*	25,945	53.6
Rock, N. (Lib Dem)	13,393	27.7
Milton, N. (Lab)	6,949	14.4
Moore, J. (UKIP)	1,214	2.5
Harrison, J. (Green)	568	1.2
Rukin, J. (Ind)	362	0.8
Majority	12,552	25.92
Electorate	59,630	
Turnout	48,431	81.22

**Member of last parliament*

CONSTITUENCY SNAPSHOT

The Conservative James Pawsey MP sat here from 1979 and recorded majorities of over 10,000 throughout the 1980s and early 1990s.

In 1997 Labour's Andy King won with a margin of 495 votes. He increased this to 2,877 in 2001.

However, 2005 Tory Jeremy Wright secured a 4.1 per cent swing which was enough to win the seat with 1,628 votes. Wright was re-elected with a majority of 12,552 in 2010.

Kenilworth and Southam, a new seat and the successor to Rugby and Kenilworth, is an affluent large curved seat taking in the rural commuter villages that lie between Rugby, Warwick and Coventry including rural parts of Stratford-on-Avon.

Kenilworth is the largest town in the constituency and accounts for approximately one-third of the electorate. The rest of the constituency is made up of semi-rural villages.

Despite being a rural area, agriculture provides little employment. Many residents commute to work in Birmingham, Coventry, Banbury and Solihull.

The constituency boasts several centres of excellence including Warwick University, the National Agricultural Centre, Ryton Organic Gardens, and major motor industry facilities, including Ford at Gaydon.

The town benefits from good transport links, including Birmingham International Airport as well as the M6, M42 and M40 motorways.

Simon Wright

Norwich South

Boundary changes

Tel: 020 7219 3000
E-mail: simon.wright.mp@parliament.uk
Website: www.simonwright.org.uk

Date of birth: 15 September 1979

Education: Dereham Neatherd High School; Imperial College, London (BSc mathematics); Kings College, London (PGCE); Married Rosalind

Non-political career: Former maths teacher; Campaigns and communications officer to Norman Lamb MP; Former Councillor, North Norfolk District Council

Political career: Member for Norwich South since 6 May 2010 general election; Agent to Norman Lamb MP 2005 general election

Recreations: Music

Simon Wright MP, House of Commons, London SW1A 0AA
Tel: 020 7219 3000 E-mail: simon.wright.mp@parliament.uk
Constituency: 9 Europa Way, Norwich NR1 2EN
Website: www.simonwright.org.uk

GENERAL ELECTION RESULT

		%
Wright, S. (Lib Dem)	13,960	29.4
Clarke, C. (Lab)*	13,650	28.7
Little, A. (Con)	10,902	22.9
Ramsay, A. (Green)	7,095	14.9
Emmens, S. (UKIP)	1,145	2.4
Heather, L. (BNP)	697	1.5
Polley, G. (WRP)	100	0.2
Majority	310	0.65
Electorate	73,649	
Turnout	47,549	64.56

**Member of last parliament*

CONSTITUENCY SNAPSHOT

Electorally predictable between 1950 and 1974 as a Conservative seat, Norwich South has latterly become a Labour seat. Labour MP John Garrett held the seat from 1974 until 1983 when he lost to Tory John Powly by 1,712 votes.

John Garrett regained the seat by 336 votes in 1987. A swing of 10 per cent Labour in 1997 elected the new Labour candidate, Charles Clarke to Parliament with a majority of 14,239.

In 2005 Charles Clarke's majority was cut to 3,653. The Liberal Democrats closed the gap on Labour, moving into second place. Charles Clarke was defeated in 2010 when the Liberal Democrats' Simon Wright secured a small margin of 310 votes.

Norwich South gained two part-wards and lost two part-wards.

Norwich South takes in the majority of the city centre and its historical features including its Norman castle and cathedral. The seat also includes sizeable residential and industrial areas in the south and west of the city. The University of East Anglia is situated on the western edge of the city.

The city is a regional financial centre. Norwich Union, Norwich's largest employer, has been based here for 200 years.

The manufacturing industry has declined since the early 1990s. Local engineering firms have weathered the storm well and Colman's - the mustard manufacturer - still has a major plant in the city.

Tim Yeo

South Suffolk (returning MP)

Boundary changes

Tel: 020 7219 6353
E-mail: timyeomp@parliament.uk
Website: www.epolitix.com/Tim-Yeo

Conservative

Date of birth: 20 March 1945; Son of late Dr Kenneth John Yeo and Norah Margaret Yeo

Education: Charterhouse, Godalming, Surrey; Emmanuel College, Cambridge (MA history 1968); Married Diane Helen Pickard 1970 (1 son 1 daughter)

Non-political career: Assistant treasurer, Bankers Trust Company 1970-73; Director: Worcester Engineering Co. Ltd 1975-86; Chief executive, Spastics Society 1980-83; Chair, Univent plc 1995-, Genus plc 2002-04; Columnist, *Financial Times* 2004-08; Director, ITI Energy Ltd 2006-; Chair: AFC Energy plc 2007-, Eco City Vehicles plc 2007-; Director, Groupe Eurotunnel SA 2007-

Political career: Contested Bedwelty February 1974 general election. Member for South Suffolk 1983-2010, for South Suffolk (revised boundary) since 6 May 2010 general election; PPS to Douglas Hurd: as Home Secretary 1988-89, as Foreign and Commonwealth Secretary 1989-90; Joint Parliamentary Under-Secretary of State: Department of the Environment 1990-92, Department of Health 1992-93; Minister of State, Department of the Environment 1993-94; Opposition Spokesperson for Environment, Transport and the Regions 1997-98; Shadow Minister of Agriculture, Fisheries and Food 1998-2001; Shadow Secretary of State for: Culture, Media and Sport 2001-02, Trade and Industry 2002-03, Public Services, Health and Education 2003-04, Environment and Transport 2004-05; *Select Committees:* Member: Treasury 1996-97, Culture, Media and Sport 2005-06; Chair: Environmental Audit 2005-10; Member: Liaison 2006-10, Joint Committee on the Draft Climate Change Bill 2007; Vice-chair, Conservative Party (with responsibility for Local Government) 1998

Political interests: Health, economic policy, environment, charity reform, rural affairs

Other organisations: Chair, Charities VAT Reform Group 1981-88; President, Charities Tax Reform Group 1988-90; Vice-President, International Voluntary Service 1984; Trustee Tanzania Development Trust 1980-97; Fellow Industry and Parliament Trust 1985; Royal St George's (Sandwich), Royal and Ancient Golf Club of St Andrews, MCC, Sunningdale Golf; *Publications:* Public Accountancy and Aquisition of Charities (1983); Golf correspondent *Country Life* 1994-2006

Recreations: Golf, skiing

Tim Yeo MP, House of Commons, London SW1A 0AA
Tel: 020 7219 6353 Fax: 020 7219 4857
E-mail: timyeomp@parliament.uk
Constituency: 43 High Street, Hadleigh, Suffolk IP7 5AB
Tel: 01473 823435 Fax: 01473 823536 Website: www.epolitix.com/Tim-Yeo

GENERAL ELECTION RESULT

		%
Yeo, T. (Con)*	24,550	47.8
Bennett, N. (Lib Dem)	15,861	30.9
Bishton, E. (Lab)	7,368	14.3
Campbell Bannerman, D. (UKIP)	3,637	7.1
Majority	8,689	16.90
Electorate	72,498	
Turnout	51,416	70.92

**Member of last parliament*

CONSTITUENCY SNAPSHOT

The Conservative Tim Yeo began his tenure as MP for Suffolk South in 1983 after a selection battle with the sitting Tory MP Keith Stainton. Stainton had represented the seat under previous boundaries for 20 years, but Yeo emerged victorious at the general election of 1983 and won a majority of 11,269.

At the 1997 election Yeo emerged with a much-reduced majority of 4,175. Nevertheless, this gave Suffolk South the largest Conservative majority of any seat in the county.

Yeo's majority has since recovered and was 6,606 in 2005. At the 2010 general election Yeo held the seat with a 8,689 majority.

Cavendish ward is now entirely within the seat, having previously been shared with West Norfolk.

Suffolk South is a rural seat centred around Sudbury, the area's largest town. It takes in the scenic area around the river Stour popularly known as 'Constable country' and runs along much of the Essex boundary.

The area is famous for its picturesque villages, which have attracted affluent second-home buyers, and is home for commuters to Ipswich, Cambridge and London.

Sudbury is home to Delphi Automotive Systems and Reliant Cars are made in the town.

Rt Hon Sir **George Young**

North West Hampshire (returning MP)

Boundary changes

Tel: 020 7219 6665
E-mail: youngg@parliament.uk
Website: www.sirgeorgeyoung.org.uk

Conservative

Date of birth: 16 July 1941; Son of late Sir George Young, 5th Bt, CMG, and Elizabeth Young, neé Knatchbull-Hugessen

Education: Eton College; Christ Church, Oxford (BA philosophy, politics and economics 1963, MA); Surrey University (MPhil economics 1971); Married Aurelia Nemon-Stuart 1964 (2 sons 2 daughters)

Non-political career: Economic adviser Post Office 1969-74; Councillor: London Borough of Lambeth 1968-71, GLC 1970-73

Political career: Member for Ealing Acton 1974-97, for North West Hampshire 1997-2010, for North West Hampshire (revised boundary) since 6 May 2010 general election; Opposition Whip 1976-79; Parliamentary Under-Secretary of State: Department of Health and Social Services 1979-81, Department of Environment 1981-86; Government Whip 1990; Department of Environment: Minister for Housing and Planning 1990-93, Minister for Housing, Inner Cities and Construction 1993-94; Financial Secretary, HM Treasury 1994-95; Secretary of State for Transport 1995-97; Member Shadow Cabinet 1997-2000: Shadow: Secretary of State for Defence 1997-98, Leader of the House of Commons 1998-99, Chancellor of the Duchy of Lancaster 1998-99, Leader of the House of Commons and Constitutional Affairs 1999-2000, Leader of the House of Commons 2009-10; Member: House of Commons Commission 2009-, Speaker's Committee for the Independent Parliamentary Standards Authority 2009-; Leader of the House of Commons, Lord Privy Seal 2010-; *Select Committees:* Member: Public Accounts 1994-95, Modernisation of the House of Commons 1998-2000, Selection 2001-09; Chair: Standards and Privileges 2001-09; Member: Liaison 2001-09, Liaison (Liaison Sub-Committee) 2002-09, Reform of the House of Commons 2009

Political interests: Housing, disability, health education, constitutional reform

Other organisations: 6th Baronet, created 1813, succeeded his father 1960; Trustee: Guinness Trust 1986-90, Foundations Independent Living Trust, 2002-; PC 1993; *Publications:* Tourism – Blessing or Blight (1970)

Recreations: Bicycling, opera

Rt Hon Sir George Young MP, House of Commons, London SW1A 0AA Tel: 020 7219 6665 Fax: 020 7219 2566
E-mail: youngg@parliament.uk
Constituency: 2 Church Close, Andover, Hampshire SP10 1DP
Tel: 01264 401401 Fax: 01264 391155
Website: www.sirgeorgeyoung.org.uk

GENERAL ELECTION RESULT

		%
Young, G. (Con)*	31,072	58.3
McCann, T. (Lib Dem)	12,489	23.4
Evans, S. (Lab)	6,980	13.1
Oram, S. (UKIP)	2,751	5.2
Majority	18,583	34.87
Electorate	76,040	
Turnout	53,292	70.08

**Member of last parliament*

CONSTITUENCY SNAPSHOT

This has always been Tory seat. First elected as MP for Hampshire North West in 1997, Sir George Young took over this seat with a five-figure majority after it was vacated by Sir David Mitchell.

He increased his share of the vote in 2001 and again in 2005 when his majority was 13,264. In 2010 Young retained the seat with a strong 18,583 majority.

The seat lost the part-wards of Hatch Warren and Beggarwood, Popley West, and Rooksdown to Basingstoke and the part-ward of Sherborne St John to North East Hampshire.

North West Hampshire covers the northern part of the Test Valley, whose largest community is Andover, and includes scores of picturesque hamlets and a generous acreage of rolling Hampshire countryside.

The industrial parks on its outskirts, largely the result of overspill from London in the early 1960s, have not detracted significantly from the market town atmosphere of present day Andover.

Agricultural and manufacturing industries are both relatively strong here, as is the financial services industry with Lloyds TSB and Scottish Widows among those providing many of the plentiful service sector jobs.

Representing the armed forces, which makes a significant contribution to the local economy in most Hampshire constituencies, is the Defence Logistics Organisation.

Nadhim Zahawi

Stratford-on-Avon

Boundary changes

Tel: 020 7219 3000
E-mail: nadhim.zahawi.mp@parliament.uk
Website: www.zahawi.com

Conservative

Date of birth: 2 June 1967

Education: King's College School, Wimbledon; University College, London (BSc chemical engineering); Married Lana (2 sons)

Non-political career: European marketing director, Smith and Brooks Ltd; Co-founder and chief executive officer, YouGov 2000-10; Councillor, London Borough of Wandsworth Council 1994-2006; Governor: Chartfield Delicate School 2002-04, Brandlehow Primary School

Political career: Contested Erith and Thamesmead 1997 general election. Member for Stratford-on-Avon since 6 May 2010 general election

Other organisations: Chair, Police Consultative Committee, Putney

Recreations: Horseriding and show jumping

Nadhim Zahawi MP, House of Commons, London SW1A 0AA
Tel: 020 7219 3000 E-mail: nadhim.zahawi.mp@parliament.uk
Constituency: Stratford Conservatives, 3 Trinity Street,
Stratford-upon-Avon, Warwickshire CV37 6BL Tel: 01789 292723
Website: www.zahawi.com

GENERAL ELECTION RESULT

		%
Zahawi, N. (Con)	26,052	51.6
Turner, M. (Lib Dem)	14,706	29.1
Johnston, R. (Lab)	4,809	9.5
Parsons, B. (UKIP)	1,846	3.7
Jones, G. (BNP)	1,097	2.2
Basnett, N. (Ind)	1,032	2.0
Varga, K. (Green)	527	1.0
Bishop, F. (England)	473	0.9
Majority	11,346	22.45
Electorate	69,516	
Turnout	50,542	72.71

CONSTITUENCY SNAPSHOT

Stratford has a long history of support for the Conservatives and after the 2001 and 2005 general elections the seat remains one of the party's safest. Before 1997 the seat was home to Alan Howarth, who defected from the Tories to Labour in October 1995, having held the seat since 1983. Previously, the seat was home to the War Secretary John Profumo.

John Maples held the seat from 1997 until retiring in 2010. Nadhim Zahawi held the seat for the Conservatives at his first election with 26,052 votes, giving him a majority of 11,346.

Boundary changes were minor.

Famous as the birthplace of William Shakespeare, Stratford-on-Avon as a constituency is spread over the southern half of Warwickshire. The historical connections of the town and natural beauty of the countryside draw millions of visitors each year.

With the exception of the town of Stratford, the seat is largely rural. The seat has a higher than average proportion of professional and management workers, with many of them commuting to nearby Birmingham and Coventry.

Big employers in the town of Stratford include the headquarters of NFU Mutual Insurance, Intrum Justitia, a debt recovery company and the telemarketing firm Sitel.

NEW MPs

(232 MPs who did not serve in the 2005 Parliament, 5 of whom had been MPs in earlier Parliaments)

ADAMS, Nigel	*Con*	Selby and Ainsty	28
ALDOUS, Peter	*Con*	Waveney	31
ALEXANDER, Heidi	*Lab*	Lewisham East	35
ALI, Rushanara	*Lab*	Bethnal Green and Bow	36
ANDREW, Stuart	*Con*	Pudsey	40
BAGSHAWE, Louise	*Con*	Corby	44
BAKER, Steve	*Con*	Wycombe	48
BALDWIN, Harriett	*Con*	West Worcestershire	50
BARCLAY, Steve	*Con*	North East Cambridgeshire	55
BARWELL, Gavin	*Con*	Croydon Central	60
BEBB, Guto	*Con*	Aberconwy	62
BERGER, Luciana	*Lab/Co-op*	Liverpool Wavertree	73
BERRY, Jake	*Con*	Rossendale and Darwen	74
BINGHAM, Andrew	*Con*	High Peak	76
BIRTWISTLE, Gordon	*Lib Dem*	Burnley	78
BLACKMAN, Bob	*Con*	Harrow East	79
BLACKWOOD, Nicola	*Con*	Oxford West and Abingdon	81
BLENKINSOP, Tom	*Lab*	Middlesbrough South and East Cleveland	83
BLOMFIELD, Paul	*Lab*	Sheffield Central	84
BOLES, Nicholas	*Con*	Grantham and Stamford	87
BRADLEY, Karen	*Con*	Staffordshire Moorlands	90
BRAY, Angie	*Con*	Ealing Central and Acton	94
BRIDGEN, Andrew	*Con*	North West Leicestershire	97
BRINE, Steve	*Con*	Winchester	98
BRUCE, Fiona	*Con*	Congleton	106
BUCKLAND, Robert	*Con*	South Swindon	110
BURLEY, Aidan	*Con*	Cannock Chase	112
BURNS, Conor	*Con*	Bournemouth West	114
BYLES, Dan	*Con*	North Warwickshire	123
CAIRNS, Alun	*Con*	Vale of Glamorgan	128
CARMICHAEL, Neil	*Con*	Stroud	137
CHAPMAN, Jenny	*Lab*	Darlington	141
CHISHTI, Rehman	*Con*	Gillingham and Rainham	142
COFFEY, Therese	*Con*	Suffolk Coastal	156
COLLINS, Damian	*Con*	Folkestone and Hythe	157
COLVILE, Oliver	*Con*	Plymouth, Sutton and Devonport	158
CREASY, Stella	*Lab/Co-op*	Walthamstow	167
CROCKART, Mike	*Lib Dem*	Edinburgh West	168
CROUCH, Tracey	*Con*	Chatham and Aylesford	169
CRYER, John*	*Lab*	Leyton and Wanstead	171
CUNNINGHAM, Alex	*Lab*	Stockton North	172
CURRAN, Margaret	*Lab*	Glasgow East	175
DAKIN, Nic	*Lab*	Scunthorpe	176
DANCZUK, Simon	*Lab*	Rochdale	177
DAVIES, Geraint*	*Lab/Co-op*	Swansea West	183

** MP in earlier Parliament*

DAVIES, Glyn	*Con*	Montgomeryshire	184
DE BOIS, Nick	*Con*	Enfield North	187
DE PIERO, Gloria	*Lab*	Ashfield	189
DINENAGE, Caroline	*Con*	Gosport	190
DOCHERTY, Thomas	*Lab*	Dunfermline and West Fife	194
DOYLE, Gemma	*Lab/Co-op*	West Dunbartonshire	203
DOYLE-PRICE, Jackie	*Con*	Thurrock	204
DRAX, Richard	*Con*	South Dorset	205
DROMEY, Jack	*Lab*	Birmingham, Erdington	206
DUGHER, Michael	*Lab*	Barnsley East	208
EDWARDS, Jonathan	*PlC*	Carmarthen East and Dinefwr	217
ELLIOTT, Julie	*Lab*	Sunderland Central	219
ELLIS, Michael	*Con*	Northampton North	220
ELLISON, Jane	*Con*	Battersea	221
ELPHICKE, Charlie	*Con*	Dover	224
ESTERSON, Bill	*Lab*	Sefton Central	226
EUSTICE, George	*Con*	Camborne and Redruth	227
EVANS, Christopher	*Lab/Co-op*	Islwyn	228
EVANS, Graham	*Con*	Weaver Vale	229
EVANS, Jonathan*	*Con*	Cardiff North	230
FOVARGUE, Yvonne	*Lab*	Makerfield	245
FREEMAN, George	*Con*	Mid Norfolk	249
FREER, Mike	*Con*	Finchley and Golders Green	250
FULLBROOK, Lorraine	*Con*	South Ribble	251
FULLER, Richard	*Con*	Bedford	252
GARNIER, Mark	*Con*	Wyre Forest	257
GILBERT, Stephen	*Lib Dem*	St Austell and Newquay	262
GILMORE, Sheila	*Lab*	Edinburgh East	265
GLASS, Patricia	*Lab*	North West Durham	266
GLEN, John	*Con*	Salisbury	267
GLINDON, Mary	*Lab*	North Tyneside	268
GOLDSMITH, Zac	*Con*	Richmond Park	271
GRAHAM, Richard	*Con*	Gloucester	276
GRANT, Helen	*Con*	Maidstone and The Weald	277
GREATREX, Tom	*Lab/Co-op*	Rutherglen and Hamilton West	280
GREEN, Kate	*Lab*	Stretford and Urmston	282
GREENWOOD, Lilian	*Lab*	Nottingham South	284
GRIFFITHS, Andrew	*Con*	Burton	287
GUMMER, Ben	*Con*	Ipswich	288
GYIMAH, Sam	*Con*	East Surrey	290
HALFON, Robert	*Con*	Harlow	295
HAMES, Duncan	*Lib Dem*	Chippenham	296
HANCOCK, Matt	*Con*	West Suffolk	303
HARRINGTON, Richard	*Con*	Watford	311
HARRIS, Rebecca	*Con*	Castle Point	312
HART, Simon	*Con*	Carmarthen West and South Pembrokeshire	314
HEATON-HARRIS, Christopher	*Con*	Daventry	325
HENDERSON, Gordon	*Con*	Sittingbourne and Sheppey	327

HILLING, Julie	*Lab*	Bolton West	339
HINDS, Damian	*Con*	East Hampshire	340
HOLLINGBERY, George	*Con*	Meon Valley	347
HOPKINS, Kris	*Con*	Keighley	352
HUNT, Tristram	*Lab*	Stoke-on-Trent Central	364
HUPPERT, Julian	*Lib Dem*	Cambridge	366
JAMES, Margot	*Con*	Stourbridge	372
JAMIESON, Cathy	*Lab/Co-op*	Kilmarnock and Loudoun	374
JAVID, Sajid	*Con*	Bromsgrove	375
JOHNSON, Gareth	*Con*	Dartford	379
JOHNSON, Jo	*Con*	Orpington	380
JONES, Andrew	*Con*	Harrogate and Knaresborough	381
JONES, Graham	*Lab*	Hyndburn	383
JONES, Marcus	*Con*	Nuneaton	386
JONES, Susan Elan	*Lab*	Clwyd South	387
KELLY, Chris	*Con*	Dudley South	394
KENDALL, Liz	*Lab*	Leicester West	395
KIRBY, Simon	*Con*	Brighton Kemptown	398
KWARTENG, Kwasi	*Con*	Spelthorne	400
LATHAM, Pauline	*Con*	Mid Derbyshire	406
LAVERY, Ian	*Lab*	Wansbeck	407
LEADSOM, Andrea	*Con*	South Northamptonshire	410
LEE, Jessica	*Con*	Erewash	411
LEE, Phillip	*Con*	Bracknell	412
LEFROY, Jeremy	*Con*	Stafford	414
LESLIE, Charlotte	*Con*	Bristol North West	416
LESLIE, Chris*	*Lab/Co-op*	Nottingham East	417
LEWIS, Brandon	*Con*	Great Yarmouth	419
LLOYD, Stephen	*Lib Dem*	Eastbourne	425
LONG, Naomi	*All*	Belfast East	428
LOPRESTI, Jack	*Con*	Filton and Bradley Stoke	429
LORD, Jonathan	*Con*	Woking	430
LUCAS, Caroline	*Green*	Brighton Pavilion	433
LUMLEY, Karen	*Con*	Redditch	436
McCANN, Michael	*Lab*	East Kilbride, Strathaven and Lesmahagow	438
McCARTNEY, Jason	*Con*	Colne Valley	440
McCARTNEY, Karl	*Con*	Lincoln	441
McCLYMONT, Gregg	*Lab*	Cumbernauld, Kilsyth and Kirkintilloch East	442
McGOVERN, Alison	*Lab*	Wirral South	448
McKINNELL, Catherine	*Lab*	Newcastle upon Tyne North	454
MACLEOD, Mary	*Con*	Brentford and Isleworth	455
McPARTLAND, Stephen	*Con*	Stevenage	458
McVEY, Esther	*Con*	Wirral West	461
MAHMOOD, Shabana	*Lab*	Birmingham, Ladywood	463
MAYNARD, Paul	*Con*	Blackpool North and Cleveleys	470
MEARNS, Ian	*Lab*	Gateshead	473
MENZIES, Mark	*Con*	Fylde	474
METCALFE, Steve	*Con*	South Basildon and East Thurrock	476

** MP in earlier Parliament*

MILLS, Nigel	*Con*	Amber Valley	484
MORDAUNT, Penny	*Con*	Portsmouth North	492
MORGAN, Nicky	*Con*	Loughborough	494
MORRICE, Graeme	*Lab*	Livingston	495
MORRIS, Anne-Marie	*Con*	Newton Abbot	496
MORRIS, David	*Con*	Morecambe and Lunesdale	497
MORRIS, Grahame	*Lab*	Easington	498
MORRIS, James	*Con*	Halesowen and Rowley Regis	499
MOSLEY, Stephen	*Con*	City of Chester	500
MOWAT, David	*Con*	Warrington South	501
MUNT, Tessa	*Lib Dem*	Wells	506
MURRAY, Ian	*Lab*	Edinburgh South	510
MURRAY, Sheryll	*Con*	South East Cornwall	511
NANDY, Lisa	*Lab*	Wigan	513
NASH, Pamela	*Lab*	Airdrie and Shotts	514
NEWTON, Sarah	*Con*	Truro and Falmouth	517
NOKES, Caroline	*Con*	Romsey and Southampton North	518
NORMAN, Jesse	*Con*	Hereford and South Herefordshire	519
NUTTALL, David	*Con*	Bury North	520
O'DONNELL, Fiona	*Lab*	East Lothian	524
OFFORD, Matthew	*Con*	Hendon	525
OLLERENSHAW, Eric	*Con*	Lancaster and Fleetwood	526
ONWURAH, Chi	*Lab*	Newcastle upon Tyne Central	527
OPPERMAN, Guy	*Con*	Hexham	528
PAISLEY JNR, Ian	*DUP*	North Antrim	536
PARISH, Neil	*Con*	Tiverton and Honiton	537
PATEL, Priti	*Con*	Witham	538
PAWSEY, Mark	*Con*	Rugby	540
PEARCE, Teresa	*Lab*	Erith and Thamesmead	541
PERCY, Andrew	*Con*	Brigg and Goole	544
PERKINS, Toby	*Lab*	Chesterfield	545
PERRY, Claire	*Con*	Devizes	546
PHILLIPS, Stephen	*Con*	Sleaford and North Hykeham	547
PHILLIPSON, Bridget	*Lab*	Houghton and Sunderland South	548
PINCHER, Christopher	*Con*	Tamworth	550
POULTER, Daniel	*Con*	Central Suffolk and North Ipswich	551
QURESHI, Yasmin	*Lab*	Bolton South East	558
RAAB, Dominic	*Con*	Esher and Walton	559
RECKLESS, Mark	*Con*	Rochester and Strood	562
REES-MOGG, Jacob	*Con*	North East Somerset	565
REEVELL, Simon	*Con*	Dewsbury	566
REEVES, Rachel	*Lab*	Leeds West	567
REYNOLDS, Emma	*Lab*	Wolverhampton North East	569
REYNOLDS, Jonathan	*Lab/Co-op*	Stalybridge and Hyde	570
RITCHIE, Margaret	*SDLP*	South Down	573
ROTHERAM, Steve	*Lab*	Liverpool Walton	582
RUDD, Amber	*Con*	Hastings and Rye	588
RUTLEY, David	*Con*	Macclesfield	592

SANDYS, Laura	*Con*	South Thanet	594
SARWAR, Anas	*Lab*	Glasgow Central	595
SHANNON, Jim	*DUP*	Strangford	599
SHARMA, Alok	*Con*	Reading West	602
SHELBROOKE, Alec	*Con*	Elmet and Rothwell	605
SHUKER, Gavin	*Lab/Co-op*	Luton South	608
SKIDMORE, Chris	*Con*	Kingswood	613
SMITH, Henry	*Con*	Crawley	619
SMITH, Julian	*Con*	Skipton and Ripon	620
SMITH, Nick	*Lab*	Blaenau Gwent	621
SMITH, Owen	*Lab*	Pontypridd	622
SOUBRY, Anna	*Con*	Broxtowe	625
SPENCER, Mark	*Con*	Sherwood	630
STEPHENSON, Andrew	*Con*	Pendle	632
STEVENSON, John	*Con*	Carlisle	633
STEWART, Bob	*Con*	Beckenham	634
STEWART, Iain	*Con*	Milton Keynes South	635
STEWART, Rory	*Con*	Penrith and The Border	636
STRIDE, Mel	*Con*	Central Devon	639
STURDY, Julian	*Con*	York Outer	644
SWALES, Ian	*Lib Dem*	Redcar	646
TOMLINSON, Justin	*Con*	North Swindon	659
TRUSS, Elizabeth	*Con*	South West Norfolk	662
TURNER, Karl	*Lab*	Kingston upon Hull East	664
TWIGG, Stephen*	*Lab/Co-op*	Liverpool West Derby	666
UMUNNA, Chuka	*Lab*	Streatham	668
UPPAL, Paul	*Con*	Wolverhampton South West	669
VAZ, Valerie	*Lab*	Walsall South	674
VICKERS, Martin	*Con*	Cleethorpes	675
WALKER, Robin	*Con*	Worcester	679
WARD, David	*Lib Dem*	Bradford East	683
WEATHERLEY, Mike	*Con*	Hove	687
WHARTON, James	*Con*	Stockton South	690
WHEELER, Heather	*Con*	South Derbyshire	691
WHITE, Chris	*Con*	Warwick and Leamington	692
WHITEFORD, Eilidh	*SNP*	Banff and Buchan	693
WHITTAKER, Craig	*Con*	Calder Valley	695
WILLIAMSON, Chris	*Lab*	Derby North	706
WILLIAMSON, Gavin	*Con*	South Staffordshire	707
WOLLASTON, Sarah	*Con*	Totnes	715
WOODCOCK, John	*Lab/Co-op*	Barrow and Furness	717
WRIGHT, Simon	*Lib Dem*	Norwich South	723
ZAHAWI, Nadhim	*Con*	Stratford-on-Avon	726

** MP in earlier Parliament*

DEFEATED MPs

76: 51 Labour, 6 Lab/Co-op, 2 Conservative, 9 Lib Dem, 4 Ind, 1 DUP, 1 SNP, 1 Ind KHHC, 1 Respect

AINGER, Nick	*Lab*	Carmarthen West and South Pembrokeshire
ANDERSON, Janet	*Lab*	Rossendale and Darwen
ATKINS, Charlotte	*Lab*	Staffordshire Moorlands
BAIRD, Vera	*Lab*	Redcar
BARLOW, Celia	*Lab*	Hove
BERRY, Roger	*Lab*	Kingswood
BLIZZARD, Bob	*Lab*	Waveney
BORROW, David	*Lab*	South Ribble
BUTLER, Dawn	*Lab*	Brent Central
CAWSEY, Ian	*Lab*	Brigg and Goole
CLARK, Paul	*Lab*	Gillingham and Rainham
CLARKE, Charles	*Lab*	Norwich South
COOK, Frank	*Ind*	Stockton North
DAVIES, Dai	*Ind*	Blaenau Gwent
DHANDA, Parmjit	*Lab*	Gloucester
DISMORE, Andrew	*Lab*	Hendon
DREW, David	*Lab/Co-op*	Stroud
FOSTER, Michael Jabez	*Lab*	Hastings and Rye
FOSTER, Michael John	*Lab*	Worcester
GALLOWAY, George	*Respect*	Poplar and Limehouse
GIDLEY, Sandra	*Lib Dem*	Romsey and Southampton North
GILROY, Linda	*Lab/Co-op*	Plymouth, Sutton and Devonport
GOLDSWORTHY, Julia	*Lib Dem*	Camborne and Redruth
HALL, Patrick	*Lab*	Bedford
HARRIS, Evan	*Lib Dem*	Oxford West and Abingdon
HEATHCOAT-AMORY, David	*Con*	Wells
HOLMES, Paul	*Lib Dem*	Chesterfield
HOPE, Phil	*Lab/Co-op*	Corby
JENKINS, Brian	*Lab*	Tamworth
KEEBLE, Sally	*Lab*	Northampton North
KEEN, Ann	*Lab*	Brentford and Isleworth
KIDNEY, David	*Lab*	Stafford
KNIGHT, Jim*	*Lab*	South Dorset
KRAMER, Susan	*Lib Dem*	Richmond Park
LADYMAN, Stephen	*Lab*	South Thanet
LINTON, Martin	*Lab*	Battersea
McCARTHY-FRY, Sarah	*Lab/Co-op*	Portsmouth North
McISAAC, Shona	*Lab*	Cleethorpes
McNULTY, Tony	*Lab*	Harrow East
MALIK, Shahid	*Lab*	Dewsbury
MALLABER, Judy	*Lab*	Amber Valley
MARRIS, Rob	*Lab*	Wolverhampton South West
MASON, John	*SNP*	Glasgow East
MERRON, Gillian	*Lab*	Lincoln
MOLE, Chris	*Lab*	Ipswich

** Awarded life peerage in dissolution honours*

MORGAN, Julie	*Lab*	Cardiff North
NORRIS, Dan	*Lab*	North East Somerset
O'BRIEN, Mike	*Lab*	North Warwickshire
ÖPIK, Lembit	*Lib Dem*	Montgomeryshire
PALMER, Nick	*Lab*	Broxtowe
PELLING, Andrew	*Ind*	Croydon Central
PLASKITT, James	*Lab*	Warwick and Leamington
PRENTICE, Gordon	*Lab*	Pendle
PROSSER, Gwyn	*Lab*	Dover
RAMMELL, Bill	*Lab*	Harlow
REED, Andy	*Lab/Co-op*	Loughborough
RENNIE, Willie	*Lib Dem*	Dunfermline and West Fife
ROBINSON, Peter	*DUP*	Belfast East
ROONEY, Terry	*Lab*	Bradford East
ROWEN, Paul	*Lib Dem*	Rochdale
RUSSELL, Christine	*Lab*	City of Chester
RYAN, Joan	*Lab*	Enfield North
SHAW, Jonathan	*Lab*	Chatham and Aylesford
SMITH, Angela E*	*Lab/Co-op*	South Basildon and East Thurrock
SMITH, Geraldine	*Lab*	Morecambe and Lunesdale
SMITH, Jacqui	*Lab*	Redditch
SNELGROVE, Anne	*Lab*	South Swindon
SPINK, Bob	*Ind*	Castle Point
STARKEY, Phyllis	*Lab*	Milton Keynes South
TAYLOR, Dari	*Lab*	Stockton South
TAYLOR, Richard	*Ind KHHC*	Wyre Forest
WALTHO, Lynda	*Lab*	Stourbridge
WARD, Claire	*Lab*	Watford
WATERSON, Nigel	*Con*	Eastbourne
WRIGHT, Anthony David	*Lab*	Great Yarmouth
YOUNGER-ROSS, Richard	*Lib Dem*	Newton Abbot

RETIRED MPs

(148, of whom 20 given life peerages)

AINSWORTH, Peter	*Con*	East Surrey
ANCRAM, Michael	*Con*	Devizes
ARMSTRONG, Hilary*	*Lab*	North West Durham
ATKINSON, Peter	*Con*	Hexham
AUSTIN, John	*Lab*	Erith and Thamesmead
BARRETT, John	*Lib Dem*	Edinburgh West
BATTLE, John	*Lab*	Leeds West
BLACKMAN, Liz	*Lab*	Erewash
BOSWELL, Timothy*	*Con*	Daventry
BREED, Colin	*Lib Dem*	South East Cornwall
BROWNE, Des*	*Lab*	Kilmarnock and Loudoun
BROWNING, Angela*	*Con*	Tiverton and Honiton
BURGON, Colin	*Lab*	Elmet

* *Awarded life peerage in dissolution honours*

BUTTERFILL, John	*Con*	Bournemouth West
BYERS, Stephen	*Lab*	North Tyneside
CABORN, Richard	*Lab*	Sheffield Central
CHALLEN, Colin	*Lab*	Morley and Rothwell
CHAPMAN, Ben	*Lab*	Wirral South
CHAYTOR, David	*Ind*	Bury North
CLAPHAM, Michael	*Lab*	Barnsley West and Penistone
CLELLAND, David	*Lab*	Tyne Bridge
COHEN, Harry	*Lab*	Leyton and Wanstead
CONWAY, Derek	*Ind*	Old Bexley and Sidcup
CORMACK, Patrick	*Con*	South Staffordshire
COUSINS, Jim	*Lab*	Newcastle upon Tyne Central
CRYER, Ann	*Lab*	Keighley
CUMMINGS, John	*Lab*	Easington
CURRY, David	*Con*	Skipton and Ripon
CURTIS-THOMAS, Claire	*Lab*	Crosby
DAVIES, Quentin*	*Lab*	Grantham and Stamford
DEAN, Janet	*Lab*	Burton
DEVINE, Jim	*Ind*	Livingston
ETHERINGTON, Bill	*Lab*	Sunderland North
FISHER, Mark	*Lab*	Stoke-on-Trent Central
FOLLETT, Barbara	*Lab*	Stevenage
FRASER, Christopher	*Con*	South West Norfolk
GEORGE, Bruce	*Lab*	Walsall South
GERRARD, Neil	*Lab*	Walthamstow
GOODMAN, Paul	*Con*	Wycombe
GREENWAY, John	*Con*	Ryedale
GRIFFITHS, Nigel	*Lab*	Edinburgh South
GROGAN, John	*Lab*	Selby
GUMMER, John*	*Con*	Suffolk Coastal
HALL, Mike	*Lab*	Weaver Vale
HEAL, Sylvia	*Lab*	Halesowen and Rowley Regis
HENDERSON, Doug	*Lab*	Newcastle upon Tyne North
HEPPELL, John	*Lab*	Nottingham East
HESFORD, Stephen	*Lab*	Wirral West
HEWITT, Patricia	*Lab*	Leicester West
HILL, Keith	*Lab*	Streatham
HOGG, Douglas	*Con*	Sleaford and North Hykeham
HOON, Geoffrey	*Lab*	Ashfield
HORAM, John	*Con*	Orpington
HOWARD, Michael*	*Con*	Folkestone and Hythe
HOWARTH, David	*Lib Dem*	Cambridge
HOWELLS, Kim	*Lab*	Pontypridd
HUGHES, Beverley*	*Lab*	Stretford and Urmston
HUMBLE, Joan	*Lab*	Blackpool North and Fleetwood
HUTTON, John*	*Lab*	Barrow and Furness
IDDON, Brian	*Lab*	Bolton South East
INGRAM, Adam	*Lab*	East Kilbride, Strathaven and Lesmahagow

** Awarded life peerage in dissolution honours*

JACK, Michael	*Con*	Fylde
JONES, Lynne	*Lab*	Birmingham Selly Oak
JONES, Martyn	*Lab*	Clwyd South
KEETCH, Paul	*Lib Dem*	Hereford
KELLY, Ruth	*Lab*	Bolton West
KEMP, Fraser	*Lab*	Houghton and Washington East
KENNEDY, Jane	*Lab*	Liverpool Wavertree
KEY, Robert	*Con*	Salisbury
KILFOYLE, Peter	*Lab*	Liverpool Walton
KIRKBRIDE, Julie	*Con*	Bromsgrove
LAIT, Jacqui	*Con*	Beckenham
LAXTON, Bob	*Lab*	Derby North
LEPPER, David	*Lab/Co-op*	Brighton Pavilion
LEVITT, Tom	*Lab*	High Peak
LORD, Michael	*Con*	Central Suffolk and North Ipswich
McAVOY, Thomas*	*Lab/Co-op*	Rutherglen and Hamilton West
McCAFFERTY, Christine	*Lab*	Calder Valley
McCARTNEY, Ian	*Lab*	Makerfield
McFALL, John*	*Lab/Co-op*	West Dunbartonshire
McGRADY, Eddie	*SDLP*	South Down
MACKAY, Andrew	*Con*	Bracknell
McKENNA, Rosemary	*Lab*	Cumbernauld, Kilsyth and Kirkintilloch East
MACKINLAY, Andrew	*Lab*	Thurrock
MACLEAN, David	*Con*	Penrith and The Border
MALINS, Humfrey	*Con*	Woking
MAPLES, John*	*Con*	Stratford-on-Avon
MARSHALL-ANDREWS, Robert	*Lab*	Medway
MARTLEW, Eric	*Lab*	Carlisle
MATES, Michael	*Con*	East Hampshire
MILBURN, Alan	*Lab*	Darlington
MOFFAT, Anne	*Lab*	East Lothian
MOFFATT, Laura	*Lab*	Crawley
MORAN, Margaret	*Lab*	Luton South
MORLEY, Elliot	*Ind*	Scunthorpe
MOSS, Malcolm	*Con*	North East Cambridgeshire
MOUNTFORD, Kali	*Lab*	Colne Valley
MULLIN, Chris	*Lab*	Sunderland South
MURPHY, Denis	*Lab*	Wansbeck
NAYSMITH, Doug	*Lab/Co-op*	Bristol North West
OATEN, Mark	*Lib Dem*	Winchester
O'HARA, Edward	*Lab*	Knowsley South
OLNER, Bill	*Lab*	Nuneaton
PAISLEY, Ian*	*DUP*	North Antrim
PEARSON, Ian	*Lab*	Dudley South
POPE, Greg	*Lab*	Hyndburn
PRENTICE, Bridget	*Lab*	Lewisham East
PRESCOTT, John*	*Lab*	Hull East
PRICE, Adam	*PlC*	Carmarthen East and Dinefwr

** Awarded life peerage in dissolution honours*

PURCHASE, Ken	*Lab/Co-op*	Wolverhampton North East
PURNELL, James	*Lab*	Stalybridge and Hyde
REID, John*	*Lab*	Airdrie and Shotts
SALMOND, Alex	*SNP*	Banff and Buchan
SALTER, Martin	*Lab*	Reading West
SARWAR, Mohammad	*Lab*	Glasgow Central
SHORT, Clare	*Ind*	Birmingham Ladywood
SIMON, Siôn	*Lab*	Birmingham Erdington
SIMPSON, Alan	*Lab*	Nottingham South
SMITH, John	*Lab*	Vale of Glamorgan
SOUTHWORTH, Helen	*Lab*	Warrington South
SPICER, Michael*	*Con*	West Worcestershire
SPRING, Richard	*Con*	West Suffolk
STEEN, Anthony	*Con*	Totnes
STEWART, Ian	*Lab*	Eccles
STOATE, Howard	*Lab*	Dartford
STRANG, Gavin	*Lab*	Edinburgh East
TAYLOR, Ian	*Con*	Esher and Walton
TAYLOR, Matthew*	*Lib Dem*	Truro and St Austell
TIPPING, Paddy	*Lab*	Sherwood
TODD, Mark	*Lab*	South Derbyshire
TOUHIG, Don*	*Lab/Co-op*	Islwyn
TRUSWELL, Paul	*Lab*	Pudsey
TURNER, Des	*Lab*	Brighton Kemptown
TURNER, Neil	*Lab*	Wigan
USSHER, Kitty	*Lab*	Burnley
VIGGERS, Peter	*Con*	Gosport
VIS, Rudi	*Lab*	Finchley and Golders Green
WAREING, Robert	*Ind*	Liverpool West Derby
WIDDECOMBE, Ann	*Con*	Maidstone and The Weald
WILLIAMS, Alan	*Lab*	Swansea West
WILLIAMS, Betty	*Lab*	Conwy
WILLIS, Phil*	*Lib Dem*	Harrogate and Knaresborough
WILLS, Michael*	*Lab*	North Swindon
WILSHIRE, David	*Con*	Spelthorne
WINTERTON, Ann	*Con*	Congleton
WINTERTON, Nicholas	*Con*	Macclesfield
WRIGHT, Tony Wayland	*Lab*	Cannock Chase
WYATT, Derek	*Lab*	Sittingbourne and Sheppey

** Awarded life peerage in dissolution honours*

WOMEN MPs (143)

Name	Party	Page
ABBOTT, Diane	*Lab*	26
ALEXANDER, Heidi	*Lab*	35
ALI, Rushanara	*Lab*	36
BAGSHAWE, Louise	*Con*	44
BALDWIN, Harriett	*Con*	50
BECKETT, Margaret	*Lab*	63
BEGG, Anne	*Lab*	64
BERGER, Luciana	*Lab/Co-op*	73
BLACKMAN-WOODS, Roberta	*Lab*	80
BLACKWOOD, Nicola	*Con*	81
BLEARS, Hazel	*Lab*	82
BRADLEY, Karen	*Con*	90
BRAY, Angie	*Con*	94
BROOKE, Annette	*Lib Dem*	100
BROWN, Lyn	*Lab*	102
BRUCE, Fiona	*Con*	106
BUCK, Karen	*Lab*	109
BURT, Lorely	*Lib Dem*	122
CHAPMAN, Jenny	*Lab*	141
CLARK, Katy	*Lab*	146
CLWYD, Ann	*Lab*	153
COFFEY, Ann	*Lab*	155
COFFEY, Therese	*Con*	156
COOPER, Rosie	*Lab*	160
COOPER, Yvette	*Lab*	161
CREAGH, Mary	*Lab*	166
CREASY, Stella	*Lab/Co-op*	167
CROUCH, Tracey	*Con*	169
CURRAN, Margaret	*Lab*	175
DE PIERO, Gloria	*Lab*	189
DINENAGE, Caroline	*Con*	190
DORRIES, Nadine	*Con*	201
DOYLE, Gemma	*Lab/Co-op*	203
DOYLE-PRICE, Jackie	*Con*	204
EAGLE, Angela	*Lab*	215
EAGLE, Maria	*Lab*	216
ELLIOTT, Julie	*Lab*	219
ELLISON, Jane	*Con*	221
ELLMAN, Louise	*Lab/Co-op*	222
ENGEL, Natascha	*Lab*	225
FEATHERSTONE, Lynne	*Lib Dem*	237
FLINT, Caroline	*Lab*	242
FOVARGUE, Yvonne	*Lab*	245
FULLBROOK, Lorraine	*Con*	251
GILDERNEW, Michelle	*Sinn Féin*	263
GILLAN, Cheryl	*Con*	264
GILMORE, Sheila	*Lab*	265
GLASS, Patricia	*Lab*	266
GLINDON, Mary	*Lab*	268
GOODMAN, Helen	*Lab*	272
GRANT, Helen	*Con*	277
GREEN, Kate	*Lab*	282
GREENING, Justine	*Con*	283
GREENWOOD, Lilian	*Lab*	284
GRIFFITH, Nia	*Lab*	286
HARMAN, Harriet	*Lab*	308
HARRIS, Rebecca	*Con*	312
HERMON, Sylvia	*Ind*	336
HILLIER, Meg	*Lab/Co-op*	338
HILLING, Julie	*Lab*	339
HODGE, Margaret	*Lab*	344
HODGSON, Sharon	*Lab*	345
HOEY, Kate	*Lab*	346
JACKSON, Glenda	*Lab*	370
JAMES, Margot	*Con*	372
JAMES, Siân	*Lab*	373
JAMIESON, Cathy	*Lab/Co-op*	374
JOHNSON, Diana	*Lab*	378
JONES, Helen	*Lab*	384
JONES, Susan Elan	*Lab*	387
JOWELL, Tessa	*Lab*	388
KEELEY, Barbara	*Lab*	392
KENDALL, Liz	*Lab*	395
LAING, Eleanor	*Con*	401
LATHAM, Pauline	*Con*	406
LEADSOM, Andrea	*Con*	410
LEE, Jessica	*Con*	411
LESLIE, Charlotte	*Con*	416
LONG, Naomi	*All*	428
LUCAS, Caroline	*Green*	433
LUMLEY, Karen	*Con*	436
McCARTHY, Kerry	*Lab*	439
McDONAGH, Siobhain	*Lab*	444
McGOVERN, Alison	*Lab*	448
McGUIRE, Anne	*Lab*	451
McINTOSH, Anne	*Con*	452
McKECHIN, Ann	*Lab*	453
McKINNELL, Catherine	*Lab*	454
MACLEOD, Mary	*Con*	455
MACTAGGART, Fiona	*Lab*	460
McVEY, Esther	*Con*	461
MAHMOOD, Shabana	*Lab*	463
MAIN, Anne	*Con*	464
MAY, Theresa	*Con*	468

MILLER, Maria	*Con*	482
MILTON, Anne	*Con*	485
MOON, Madeleine	*Lab*	489
MORDAUNT, Penny	*Con*	492
MORDEN, Jessica	*Lab*	493
MORGAN, Nicky	*Con*	494
MORRIS, Anne-Marie	*Con*	496
MUNN, Meg	*Lab/Co-op*	505
MUNT, Tessa	*Lib Dem*	506
MURRAY, Sheryll	*Con*	511
NANDY, Lisa	*Lab*	513
NASH, Pamela	*Lab*	514
NEWTON, Sarah	*Con*	517
NOKES, Caroline	*Con*	518
O'DONNELL, Fiona	*Lab*	524
ONWURAH, Chi	*Lab*	527
OSBORNE, Sandra	*Lab*	532
PATEL, Priti	*Con*	538
PEARCE, Teresa	*Lab*	541
PERRY, Claire	*Con*	546
PHILLIPSON, Bridget	*Lab*	548
PRIMAROLO, Dawn	*Lab*	553
QURESHI, Yasmin	*Lab*	558
REEVES, Rachel	*Lab*	567
REYNOLDS, Emma	*Lab*	569
RIORDAN, Linda	*Lab/Co-op*	572
RITCHIE, Margaret	*SDLP*	573
RUDD, Amber	*Con*	588
RUDDOCK, Joan	*Lab*	589
SANDYS, Laura	*Con*	594
SEABECK, Alison	*Lab*	597
SMITH, Angela	*Lab*	617
SMITH, Chloe	*Con*	618
SOUBRY, Anna	*Con*	625
SPELMAN, Caroline	*Con*	628
STUART, Gisela	*Lab*	641
SWINSON, Jo	*Lib Dem*	648
TEATHER, Sarah	*Lib Dem*	653
THORNBERRY, Emily	*Lab*	655
TRUSS, Elizabeth	*Con*	662
VAZ, Valerie	*Lab*	674
VILLIERS, Theresa	*Con*	676
WALLEY, Joan	*Lab*	681
WATKINSON, Angela	*Con*	684
WHEELER, Heather	*Con*	691
WHITEFORD, Eilidh	*SNP*	693
WILLOTT, Jenny	*Lib Dem*	708
WINTERTON, Rosie	*Lab*	713
WOLLASTON, Sarah	*Con*	715

MPs BY AGE

Ages as at 1st May 2010

James Wharton	26	*Con*	690
Bridget Phillipson	26	*Lab*	548
Anas Sarwar	27	*Lab*	595
Chloe Smith	27	*Con*	618
Gavin Shuker	28	*Lab/Co-op*	608
Chris Skidmore	28	*Con*	613
Andrew Stephenson	29	*Con*	632
Alison McGovern	29	*Lab*	448
Tom Blenkinsop	29	*Lab*	83
Jo Swinson	30	*Lib Dem*	648
Nicola Blackwood	30	*Con*	81
Simon Wright	30	*Lib Dem*	723
Lisa Nandy	30	*Lab*	513
Rachel Reeves	31	*Lab*	567
Aidan Burley	31	*Con*	112
Jake Berry	31	*Con*	74
Chris Kelly	31	*Con*	394
Daniel Poulter	31	*Con*	551
Chuka Umunna	31	*Lab*	668
Rehman Chishti	31	*Con*	142
Matt Hancock	31	*Con*	303
Charlotte Leslie	31	*Con*	416
Julian Huppert	31	*Lib Dem*	366
Robin Walker	32	*Con*	679
Ben Gummer	32	*Con*	288
Stella Creasy	32	*Lab/Co-op*	167
Emma Reynolds	32	*Lab*	569
Duncan Hames	32	*Lib Dem*	296
Jessica Lee	33	*Con*	411
Ian Murray	33	*Lab*	510
Gavin Williamson	33	*Con*	707
Stephen Gilbert	33	*Lib Dem*	262
Justin Tomlinson	33	*Con*	659
Sam Gyimah	33	*Con*	290
Stephen McPartland	33	*Con*	458
Jonathan Edwards	34	*PlC*	217
Alec Shelbrooke	34	*Con*	605
Paul Maynard	34	*Con*	470
Elizabeth Truss	34	*Con*	662
Tracey Crouch	34	*Con*	169
Dan Rogerson	34	*Lib Dem*	580
Kwasi Kwarteng	34	*Con*	400
Michael Dugher	35	*Lab*	208
Heidi Alexander	35	*Lab*	35
Zac Goldsmith	35	*Con*	271
Tom Greatrex	35	*Lab/Co-op*	280
Dan Byles	35	*Con*	123
Andrew Gwynne	35	*Lab*	289
Sarah Teather	35	*Lib Dem*	653
Tristram Hunt	35	*Lab*	364
Jenny Willott	35	*Lib Dem*	708
Marcus Jones	36	*Con*	386
John Glen	36	*Con*	267
Dominic Raab	36	*Con*	559
Damian Collins	36	*Con*	157
Steve Brine	36	*Con*	98
Penny Mordaunt	36	*Con*	492
Rory Stewart	36	*Con*	636
Edward Timpson	36	*Con*	658
Jenny Chapman	36	*Lab*	141
Jamie Reed	36	*Lab*	564
Stephen Crabb	37	*Con*	164
Steve Barclay	37	*Con*	55
Willie Bain	37	*Lab*	46
Jeremy Wright	37	*Con*	722
Nicky Morgan	37	*Con*	494
Conor Burns	37	*Con*	114
Iain Stewart	37	*Con*	635
David Lammy	37	*Lab*	403
Chris Leslie	37	*Lab/Co-op*	417
Caroline Nokes	37	*Con*	518
Stephen Mosley	37	*Con*	500
Danny Alexander	37	*Lib Dem*	32
Iain Wright	37	*Lab*	721
Priti Patel	38	*Con*	538
Daniel Kawczynski	38	*Con*	391
Philip Davies	38	*Con*	185
Louise Bagshawe	38	*Con*	44
Jo Johnson	38	*Con*	380
Liz Kendall	38	*Lab*	395
Mark Menzies	38	*Con*	474
Julian Smith	38	*Con*	620
Julian Sturdy	38	*Con*	644
Naomi Long	38	*All*	428
Stuart Andrew	38	*Con*	40
Therese Coffey	38	*Con*	156
Caroline Dinenage	38	*Con*	190
David Gauke	38	*Con*	258
James Duddridge	38	*Con*	207
Brandon Lewis	38	*Con*	419
Steve Baker	38	*Con*	48
George Osborne	38	*Con*	530
Douglas Carswell	38	*Con*	138
Karl Turner	39	*Lab*	664
John Leech	39	*Lib Dem*	413
Charlie Elphicke	39	*Con*	224
Mark Reckless	39	*Con*	562
Andrew Griffiths	39	*Con*	287
Sadiq Khan	39	*Lab*	397
Liam Byrne	39	*Lab*	124
Phillip Lee	39	*Con*	412
Greg Mulholland	39	*Lib Dem*	503
Toby Perkins	39	*Lab*	545
Alun Cairns	39	*Con*	128
David Davies	39	*Con*	182
Angus MacNeil	39	*SNP*	457
Tim Farron	39	*Lib Dem*	236
Jeremy Browne	39	*Lib Dem*	105
Ben Wallace	39	*Con*	680
Mark Lancaster	39	*Con*	404
Michelle Gildernew	40	*Sinn Féin*	263
Karen Bradley	40	*Con*	90
Stephen Phillips	40	*Con*	547
Mark Harper	40	*Con*	310

Mark Spencer	40	*Con*	630
Andy Burnham	40	*Lab*	113
Jack Lopresti	40	*Con*	429
Ed Miliband	40	*Lab*	480
Sajid Javid	40	*Con*	375
Damian Hinds	40	*Con*	340
Gareth Johnson	40	*Con*	379
Angus Robertson	40	*SNP*	575
Christopher Pincher	40	*Con*	550
Jackie Doyle-Price	40	*Con*	204
David Burrowes	40	*Con*	116
Jacob Rees-Mogg	40	*Con*	565
Henry Smith	40	*Con*	619
Justine Greening	41	*Con*	283
Eilidh Whiteford	41	*SNP*	693
Robert Halfon	41	*Con*	295
Yvette Cooper	41	*Lab*	161
Meg Hillier	41	*Lab/Co-op*	338
Karl McCartney	41	*Con*	441
Guto Bebb	41	*Con*	62
Robert Buckland	41	*Con*	110
Grant Shapps	41	*Con*	600
Ed Vaizey	41	*Con*	670
Susan Elan Jones	41	*Lab*	387
Jessica Morden	41	*Lab*	493
Theresa Villiers	42	*Con*	676
Jason McCartney	42	*Con*	440
James Brokenshire	42	*Con*	99
Rebecca Harris	42	*Con*	312
Mary Creagh	42	*Lab*	166
Christopher Heaton-Harris	42	*Con*	325
Michael Ellis	42	*Con*	220
Douglas Alexander	42	*Lab*	34
Esther McVey	42	*Con*	461
Charles Walker	42	*Con*	678
Alok Sharma	42	*Con*	602
Greg Clark	42	*Con*	145
Michael Gove	42	*Con*	274
Jim Murphy	42	*Lab*	508
Gareth Thomas	42	*Lab/Co-op*	654
George Freeman	42	*Con*	249
Katy Clark	42	*Lab*	146
Paul Uppal	42	*Con*	669
Nadhim Zahawi	42	*Con*	726
Graham Brady	42	*Con*	92
Natascha Engel	43	*Lab*	225
Ivan Lewis	43	*Lab*	420
Ed Balls	43	*Lab/Co-op*	52
Tom Watson	43	*Lab*	685
Nick Clegg	43	*Lib Dem*	150
Stephen Twigg	43	*Lab/Co-op*	666
David Wright	43	*Lab*	720
Ian Paisley Jnr	43	*DUP*	536
Nigel Adams	43	*Con*	28
Mark Pritchard	43	*Con*	556
Jeremy Hunt	43	*Con*	362
Bill Esterson	43	*Lab*	226
Simon Danczuk	43	*Lab*	177
Stephen Williams	43	*Lib Dem*	705
David Cameron	43	*Con*	130

Tobias Ellwood	43	*Con*	223
David Cairns	43	*Lab*	129
Diana Johnson	43	*Lab*	378
Bill Wiggin	43	*Con*	698
Sharon Hodgson	44	*Lab*	345
Lilian Greenwood	44	*Lab*	284
Mark Williams	44	*Lib Dem*	703
Andrew Rosindell	44	*Con*	581
Gregory Barker	44	*Con*	56
Robert Flello	44	*Lab*	241
Steve Metcalfe	44	*Con*	476
Edward Davey	44	*Lib Dem*	179
David Laws	44	*Lib Dem*	408
Greg Hands	44	*Con*	305
Nicholas Boles	44	*Con*	87
Mark Francois	44	*Con*	248
Adam Afriyie	44	*Con*	29
Adam Holloway	44	*Con*	349
Steve Webb	44	*Lib Dem*	688
Alistair Carmichael	44	*Lib Dem*	136
David Miliband	44	*Lab*	478
Jonathan Djanogly	44	*Con*	191
Michael Moore	44	*Lib Dem*	490
Guy Opperman	44	*Con*	528
Chi Onwurah	45	*Lab*	527
Kerry McCarthy	45	*Lab*	439
Pat McFadden	45	*Lab*	447
Ian Austin	45	*Lab*	42
Stewart Jackson	45	*Con*	371
Robert Wilson	45	*Con*	710
Jane Ellison	45	*Con*	221
Simon Kirby	45	*Con*	398
Philip Hollobone	45	*Con*	348
Andrew Bridgen	45	*Con*	97
Mark Field	45	*Con*	239
John Penrose	45	*Con*	543
Kevan Jones	46	*Lab*	385
Mark Simmonds	46	*Con*	609
John Cryer	46	*Lab*	171
Claire Perry	46	*Con*	546
Mark Hoban	46	*Con*	342
Karen Lumley	46	*Con*	436
Maria Miller	46	*Con*	482
Tom Harris	46	*Lab*	313
Michael McCann	46	*Lab*	438
Julie Elliott	46	*Lab*	219
Kris Hopkins	46	*Con*	352
John Stevenson	46	*Con*	633
Andrew Jones	46	*Con*	381
Graham Evans	46	*Con*	229
George Hollingbery	46	*Con*	347
Amber Rudd	46	*Con*	588
Simon Hart	46	*Con*	314
Conor Murphy	46	*Sinn Féin*	507
Yasmin Qureshi	46	*Lab*	558
Andrea Leadsom	46	*Con*	410
Nick Herbert	47	*Con*	334
Mark Garnier	47	*Con*	257
Huw Irranca-Davies	47	*Lab*	369
John Bercow	47	*Speaker*	71

Stewart Hosie	47	*SNP*	354
Sarah Wollaston	47	*Con*	715
Jeffrey Donaldson	47	*DUP*	197
Richard Bacon	47	*Con*	43
Martin Horwood	47	*Lib Dem*	353
Hugh Robertson	47	*Con*	576
Mark Tami	47	*Lab*	651
Craig Whittaker	47	*Con*	695
Andrew Bingham	47	*Con*	76
Mark Prisk	47	*Con*	554
Tim Loughton	47	*Con*	431
David Mundell	47	*Con*	504
Paul Burstow	47	*Lib Dem*	118
Nick Hurd	47	*Con*	367
Tom Brake	47	*Lib Dem*	93
Andrew Selous	48	*Con*	598
David Ruffley	48	*Con*	590
Jon Cruddas	48	*Lab*	170
Chris Grayling	48	*Con*	279
David Nuttall	48	*Con*	520
Graham Stuart	48	*Con*	642
Peter Wishart	48	*SNP*	714
Paul Farrelly	48	*Lab*	235
Stephen Hammond	48	*Con*	302
Chris Bryant	48	*Lab*	108
Neil Carmichael	48	*Con*	137
Steve Rotheram	48	*Lab*	582
Mel Stride	48	*Con*	639
Helen Grant	48	*Con*	277
Liam Fox	48	*Con*	246
Caroline Flint	48	*Lab*	242
Peter Aldous	48	*Con*	31
Angela Smith	48	*Lab*	617
Nick Harvey	48	*Lib Dem*	316
Khalid Mahmood	48	*Lab*	462
Andrew Murrison	49	*Con*	512
Ann McKechin	49	*Lab*	453
William Hague	49	*Con*	292
Grahame Morris	49	*Lab*	498
David Rutley	49	*Con*	592
Angela Eagle	49	*Lab*	215
Maria Eagle	49	*Lab*	216
Caroline Lucas	49	*Green*	433
Richard Benyon	49	*Con*	70
Eric Joyce	49	*Lab*	389
Andy Slaughter	49	*Lab*	615
Ian Lucas	49	*Lab*	434
Shailesh Vara	49	*Con*	672
Nick Gibb	49	*Con*	260
Ben Bradshaw	49	*Lab*	91
Emily Thornberry	49	*Lab*	655
Crispin Blunt	49	*Con*	86
Mark Durkan	49	*SDLP*	214
Geraint Davies	49	*Lab/Co-op*	183
Harriett Baldwin	49	*Con*	50
Kate Green	49	*Lab*	282
Geoffrey Cox	50	*Con*	163
Lyn Brown	50	*Lab*	102
John Hemming	50	*Lib Dem*	326
Siobhain McDonagh	50	*Lab*	444
John Healey	50	*Lab*	323
Fiona O'Donnell	50	*Lab*	524
Nick Smith	50	*Lab*	621
John Mann	50	*Lab*	465
Lorraine Fullbrook	50	*Con*	251
Phil Woolas	50	*Lab*	719
Stephen Hepburn	50	*Lab*	332
Hugo Swire	50	*Con*	649
Charles Kennedy	50	*Lib Dem*	396
Kevin Brennan	50	*Lab*	96
Tessa Munt	50	*Lib Dem*	506
John Whittingdale	50	*Con*	696
Oliver Colvile	50	*Con*	158
Meg Munn	50	*Lab/Co-op*	505
Albert Owen	50	*Lab*	534
Derek Twigg	50	*Lab*	665
Siân James	50	*Lab*	373
John Baron	50	*Con*	58
Phil Wilson	50	*Lab*	709
Jeremy Lefroy	50	*Con*	414
Heather Wheeler	50	*Con*	691
Charles Hendry	50	*Con*	330
Adrian Sanders	51	*Lib Dem*	593
Bernard Jenkin	51	*Con*	376
Nick de Bois	51	*Con*	187
Ian Liddell-Grainger	51	*Con*	422
Graeme Morrice	51	*Lab*	495
David Simpson	51	*DUP*	610
Andrew George	51	*Lib Dem*	259
Margaret Curran	51	*Lab*	175
Mark Hendrick	51	*Lab/Co-op*	328
Shaun Woodward	51	*Lab*	718
Karen Buck	51	*Lab*	109
Frank Roy	51	*Lab*	583
Nigel Dodds	51	*DUP*	195
Philip Dunne	51	*Con*	213
Rosie Winterton	51	*Lab*	713
Chris Ruane	51	*Lab*	586
Clive Efford	51	*Lab*	218
John Hayes	51	*Con*	320
Brooks Newmark	51	*Con*	516
Caroline Spelman	51	*Con*	628
Robert Smith	52	*Lib Dem*	623
Richard Graham	52	*Con*	276
Laurence Robertson	52	*Con*	578
Margaret Ritchie	52	*SDLP*	573
Eleanor Laing	52	*Con*	401
Richard Drax	52	*Con*	205
Helen Goodman	52	*Lab*	272
Anne-Marie Morris	52	*Con*	496
Patrick McLoughlin	52	*Con*	456
Nigel Evans	52	*Con*	231
Richard Harrington	52	*Con*	311
Mike Penning	52	*Con*	542
Norman Lamb	52	*Lib Dem*	402
Roberta Blackman-Woods	52	*Lab*	80
Norman Baker	52	*Lib Dem*	47
Mark Hunter	52	*Lib Dem*	365
Alan Campbell	52	*Lab*	132
David Hanson	52	*Lab*	306

Mike Weatherley	52	*Con*	687
Wayne David	52	*Lab*	180
Stephen Lloyd	52	*Lib Dem*	425
Lindsay Hoyle	52	*Lab*	358
Nadine Dorries	52	*Con*	201
Anne Main	52	*Con*	464
Ian Mearns	53	*Lab*	473
Stephen O'Brien	53	*Con*	522
Alan Duncan	53	*Con*	210
Mike Weir	53	*SNP*	689
Barry Gardiner	53	*Lab*	255
David Mowat	53	*Con*	501
Mark Pawsey	53	*Con*	540
Andrew Tyrie	53	*Con*	667
Mary Glindon	53	*Lab*	268
Robert Goodwill	53	*Con*	273
Andrew Lansley	53	*Con*	405
Anna Soubry	53	*Con*	625
Nia Griffith	53	*Lab*	286
Yvonne Fovargue	53	*Lab*	245
Keith Vaz	53	*Lab*	673
Jim McGovern	53	*Lab*	449
Cathy Jamieson	53	*Lab/Co-op*	374
Theresa May	53	*Con*	468
James Clappison	53	*Con*	144
Desmond Swayne	53	*Con*	647
Robert Syms	53	*Con*	650
David Lidington	53	*Con*	423
Patrick Mercer	53	*Con*	475
Owen Paterson	53	*Con*	539
Neil Parish	53	*Con*	537
Dominic Grieve	53	*Con*	285
Oliver Letwin	53	*Con*	418
Hazel Blears	53	*Lab*	82
Bob Blackman	54	*Con*	79
Lee Scott	54	*Con*	596
Andrew Mitchell	54	*Con*	486
David Willetts	54	*Con*	700
Sandra Osborne	54	*Lab*	532
Damian Green	54	*Con*	281
Anne Begg	54	*Lab*	64
Philip Hammond	54	*Con*	300
Gisela Stuart	54	*Lab*	641
Anne Milton	54	*Con*	485
Gary Streeter	54	*Con*	638
Sylvia Hermon	54	*Ind*	336
John Randall	54	*Con*	560
Steve McCabe	54	*Lab*	437
Stephen Timms	54	*Lab*	657
John Howell	54	*Con*	357
Gordon Banks	54	*Lab*	54
Alistair Burt	54	*Con*	120
Alex Cunningham	54	*Lab*	172
Fabian Hamilton	55	*Lab*	298
Eric Illsley	55	*Ind*	368
Henry Bellingham	55	*Con*	67
Jim Shannon	55	*DUP*	599
Peter Luff	55	*Con*	435
Teresa Pearce	55	*Lab*	541
Helen Jones	55	*Lab*	384
Oliver Heald	55	*Con*	322
James Gray	55	*Con*	278
Marsha Singh	55	*Lab*	612
Anne McIntosh	55	*Con*	452
Lorely Burt	55	*Lib Dem*	122
Richard Burden	55	*Lab*	111
Alan Reid	55	*Lib Dem*	568
Chris Huhne	55	*Lib Dem*	360
Dawn Primarolo	55	*Lab*	553
Iain Duncan Smith	56	*Con*	212
David Heath	56	*Lib Dem*	324
Alison Seabeck	56	*Lab*	597
David Anderson	56	*Lab*	39
Alistair Darling	56	*Lab*	178
Gordon Marsden	56	*Lab*	466
Hilary Benn	56	*Lab*	68
Andrew Turner	56	*Con*	663
Angie Bray	56	*Con*	94
Diane Abbott	56	*Lab*	26
Fiona Mactaggart	56	*Lab*	460
John Thurso	56	*Lib Dem*	656
Mark Lazarowicz	56	*Lab/Co-op*	409
Julian Brazier	56	*Con*	95
John Denham	56	*Lab*	188
Francis Maude	56	*Con*	467
David Ward	56	*Lib Dem*	683
Vernon Coaker	56	*Lab*	154
Paul Goggins	56	*Lab*	270
Linda Riordan	56	*Lab/Co-op*	572
Hywel Williams	56	*PlC*	702
Gerry Sutcliffe	56	*Lab*	645
Ian Swales	57	*Lib Dem*	646
Sammy Wilson	57	*DUP*	711
Geoffrey Clifton-Brown	57	*Con*	152
Gregory Campbell	57	*DUP*	133
Graham Allen	57	*Lab*	37
Jim Sheridan	57	*Lab*	607
Edward Garnier	57	*Con*	256
Peter Bone	57	*Con*	88
Tony Cunningham	57	*Lab*	174
Simon Burns	57	*Con*	115
Mike Gapes	57	*Lab/Co-op*	254
James Arbuthnot	57	*Con*	41
Robert Neill	57	*Con*	515
Bob Ainsworth	57	*Lab*	30
Michael Fallon	57	*Con*	234
Cheryl Gillan	58	*Con*	264
Eric Pickles	58	*Con*	549
John Robertson	58	*Lab*	577
Jim Fitzpatrick	58	*Lab*	240
David Amess	58	*Con*	38
Barbara Keeley	58	*Lab*	392
Stephen Dorrell	58	*Con*	200
David Jones	58	*Con*	382
Hugh Bayley	58	*Lab*	61
Lynne Featherstone	58	*Lib Dem*	237
Julian Lewis	58	*Con*	421
Elfyn Llwyd	58	*PlC*	427
Russell Brown	58	*Lab*	104
John McDonnell	58	*Lab*	446

David Watts	58	*Lab*	686
Andrew Robathan	58	*Con*	574
Martin Caton	58	*Lab*	140
John Redwood	58	*Con*	563
Simon Hughes	58	*Lib Dem*	359
Jim Dowd	59	*Lab*	202
Gordon Brown	59	*Lab*	101
Andrew Smith	59	*Lab*	616
David Hamilton	59	*Lab*	297
Alan Whitehead	59	*Lab*	694
Martin Vickers	59	*Con*	675
Ian Davidson	59	*Lab/Co-op*	181
Rosie Cooper	59	*Lab*	160
Harriet Harman	59	*Lab*	308
Edward Leigh	59	*Con*	415
Tony Baldry	59	*Con*	49
Jon Trickett	59	*Lab*	661
Nick Brown	59	*Lab*	103
Michael Fabricant	59	*Con*	233
Jonathan Evans	59	*Con*	230
Martin McGuinness	59	*Sinn Féin*	450
Alan Johnson	59	*Lab*	377
Madeleine Moon	60	*Lab*	489
Eric Ollerenshaw	60	*Con*	526
Tony Lloyd	60	*Lab*	426
Graham Stringer	60	*Lab*	640
Peter Hain	60	*Lab*	294
Dai Havard	60	*Lab*	319
David Tredinnick	60	*Con*	660
Clive Betts	60	*Lab*	75
Alasdair McDonnell	60	*SDLP*	445
Alan Meale	60	*Lab*	472
Bob Stewart	60	*Con*	634
George Howarth	60	*Lab*	355
David Evennett	60	*Con*	232
Jeremy Corbyn	60	*Lab*	162
Anne McGuire	60	*Lab*	451
Jim Paice	61	*Con*	535
Frank Doran	61	*Lab*	199
Greg Knight	61	*Con*	399
Keith Simpson	61	*Con*	611
Andrew Miller	61	*Lab*	481
Andy Love	61	*Lab/Co-op*	432
Joan Walley	61	*Lab*	681
Lindsay Roy	61	*Lab*	584
Peter Soulsby	61	*Lab*	626
David Davis	61	*Con*	186
Paul Murphy	61	*Lab*	509
Gerry Adams	61	*Sinn Féin*	27
Jack Dromey	61	*Lab*	206
Brian Donohoe	61	*Lab*	198
William McCrea	61	*DUP*	443
Stephen Pound	61	*Lab*	552
John Pugh	61	*Lib Dem*	557
Robert Walter	61	*Con*	682
Denis MacShane	61	*Lab*	459
Jim Hood	61	*Lab*	350
Nicholas Soames	62	*Con*	624
Pauline Latham	62	*Con*	406
Gordon Henderson	62	*Con*	327

Roger Williams	62	*Lib Dem*	704
Tessa Jowell	62	*Lab*	388
Gerald Howarth	62	*Con*	356
Michael Connarty	62	*Lab*	159
John Spellar	62	*Lab*	627
Malcolm Wicks	62	*Lab*	697
Annette Brooke	62	*Lib Dem*	100
David Blunkett	62	*Lab*	85
Christopher Chope	62	*Con*	143
Virendra Sharma	63	*Lab*	603
Don Foster	63	*Lib Dem*	244
Kevin Barron	63	*Lab*	59
Ann Coffey	63	*Lab*	155
Jack Straw	63	*Lab*	637
Roger Godsiff	63	*Lab*	269
Kate Hoey	63	*Lab*	346
Malcolm Rifkind	63	*Con*	571
David Crausby	63	*Lab*	165
Hywel Francis	63	*Lab*	247
Mike Hancock	64	*Lib Dem*	304
Paul Beresford	64	*Con*	72
David Heyes	64	*Lab*	337
Bob Russell	64	*Lib Dem*	591
Mike Wood	64	*Lab*	716
Adrian Bailey	64	*Lab/Co-op*	45
Louise Ellman	64	*Lab/Co-op*	222
Pat Doherty	64	*Sinn Féin*	196
Richard Ottaway	64	*Con*	533
Tim Yeo	65	*Con*	724
George Mudie	65	*Lab*	502
Nick Raynsford	65	*Lab*	561
Malcolm Bruce	65	*Lib Dem*	107
Margaret Hodge	65	*Lab*	344
Peter Bottomley	65	*Con*	89
Glyn Davies	66	*Con*	184
Joan Ruddock	66	*Lab*	589
Gordon Birtwistle	66	*Lib Dem*	78
Peter Lilley	66	*Con*	424
Alun Michael	66	*Lab/Co-op*	477
Roger Gale	66	*Con*	253
Ronnie Campbell	66	*Lab*	135
Vincent Cable	66	*Lib Dem*	126
Alan Beith	67	*Lib Dem*	65
Margaret Beckett	67	*Lab*	63
Richard Shepherd	67	*Con*	606
Andrew Stunell	67	*Lib Dem*	643
Frank Field	67	*Lab*	238
Brian Binley	68	*Con*	77
John Stanley	68	*Con*	631
Angela Watkinson	68	*Con*	684
Kelvin Hopkins	68	*Lab*	351
George Young	68	*Con*	725
Jim Dobbin	68	*Lab/Co-op*	192
Menzies Campbell	68	*Lib Dem*	134
James Cunningham	69	*Lab*	173
Tom Clarke	69	*Lab*	148
Barry Sheerman	69	*Lab/Co-op*	604
Kenneth Clarke	69	*Con*	147
William Cash	69	*Con*	139
Frank Dobson	70	*Lab*	193

Michael Meacher	70	*Lab*	471
Geoffrey Robinson	71	*Lab*	579
Stuart Bell	71	*Lab*	66
Alan Keen	72	*Lab/Co-op*	393
Alan Haselhurst	72	*Con*	318
Ann Clwyd	73	*Lab*	153
Glenda Jackson	73	*Lab*	370
Paul Flynn	75	*Lab*	243
Austin Mitchell	75	*Lab*	488
Joe Benton	76	*Lab*	69
David Winnick	76	*Lab*	712
Dennis Skinner	78	*Lab*	614
Gerald Kaufman	79	*Lab*	390
Peter Tapsell	80	*Con*	652

MPs BY PARTY

CONSERVATIVE

LABOUR

LABOUR/CO-OPERATIVE

LIBERAL DEMOCRAT

DEMOCRATIC UNIONIST PARTY

SCOTTISH NATIONAL PARTY

SINN FÉIN

PLAID CYMRU

EDWARDS, Jonathan	217	WILLIAMS, Hywel	702
LLWYD, Elfyn	427		

SOCIAL DEMOCRATIC AND LABOUR PARTY

DURKAN, Mark	214	RITCHIE, Margaret	573
McDONNELL, Alasdair	445		

INDEPENDENT

HERMON, Sylvia	336	ILLSLEY, Eric	368

ALLIANCE

LONG, Naomi	428

GREEN PARTY

LUCAS, Caroline	433

GENERAL ELECTION

PARTIES WITH SEATS IN THE HOUSE OF COMMONS

Con	Conservative
Lab	Labour
Lib Dem	Liberal Democrat
DUP	Democratic Unionist Party
SNP	Scottish National Party
SF	Sinn Féin
PlC	Plaid Cymru
SDLP	Social Democratic and Labour Party
Ind	Independent
All	Alliance
Green	Green
Speaker	Speaker

PARTIES WITH CANDIDATES IN THE GENERAL ELECTION

AC Animal's Court; **Animal** The Animal Protection Party; **Apol** Dem Apolitical Democrats; **ATSP** All The South Party; **AWL** Alliance for Workers' Liberty; **AWP** Anticapitalists – Workers Power; **BCM** Basingstoke Common Man; **Beer** Reduce Tax on Beer; **BEP** Blue Environment Party; **Best** Best of a Bad Bunch; **Better Britain** A Better Britain For All; **BNP** British National Party; **Brent North Ind** Brent North Needs An Independent MP; **Brom Ind Con** Bromsgrove Independent Conservative; **Bus-Pass** Bus-Pass Elvis Party; **Christian** Christian Party; **CIP** Campaign for Independent Politicians; **Clause 28** Clause 28 Children's Protection Christian Democrats; **CMGB** Christian Movement for Great Britain; **CNBPG** Community Need Before Private Greed; **Comm** Communist Party; **Comm GB** Communist Party of Great Britain; **Comm League** Communist League; **Common Good** The Common Good; **Corn Dem** Cornish Democats; **CPA** Christian People's Alliance; **CSP** Common Sense Party; **CURE** Citizens for Undead Rights and Equality; **Currency Virtue** Currency Cognitive Appraisal Party; **Deficit Cut** The Deficit Party; **Dem Lab** Democratic Labour Party; **DN** Democratic Nationalists; **EIP** English Independence Party; **England** English Democrats – Putting England First; **EPA** Equal Parenting Alliance; **Essex** Peoples Party Essex; **Expense** A Vote Against MP Expense Abuse; **FDP** Fancy Dress Party; **FR** for Freedom and Responsibility; **GMVY** Go Mad and Vote for Yourself; **Green Soc** Alliance for Green Socialism; **Humanity** Humanity; **Impact** Impact Party; **Ind** Independent; **Ind EACPS** Independent Ealing Acton Communities Public Services; **Ind Fed** UK Independents Federation UK; **Ind KHHC** Independent Kidderminster Hospital and Health Concern; **Integrity** Integrity UK; **IZB** Islam Zinda Baad Platform; **JACP** Justice and Anti-Corruption Party; **JOT** The Joy of Talk; **JP** Justice Party; **Land Power** Land is Power; **Lib** Liberal; **Libertarian** Libertarian Party; **Lincs Ind** Lincolnshire Independents; **LLPBPP** Local Liberals People Before Politics Party; **Loony** Official Monster Raving Loony Party; **LTT** Lawfulness Trustworthiness and Transparency; **Mac Ind** Macclesfield Independent; **Magna Carta** The Magna Carta Party; **MCCP** Magna Carta Conservation Party Great Britain; **Meb Ker** Mebyon Kernow (The Party for Cornwall); **Medway** Medway Independent Party; **MEP** Middle England Party; **MRP** Money Reform Party; **NCDMV** No Candidate Deserves My Vote; **NF** National Front; **NICCF** New Independent Conservative Chelsea and Fulham; **NLP** National Liberal Party; **NMB** New Millennium Bean Party; **Nobody** Nobody Party; **NP** The New Party; **NRP** Nationwide Reform Party; **NSOPS** Northampton – Save Our Public Services; **Pirate** Pirate Party; **PNDP** Peoples National Democratic Party; **Reform 2000** Reform 2000; **Respect** Respect – The Unity Coalition; **Restoration** Restoration Party; **RRG** Radical Reform Group; **SACL** Scotland Against Crooked Lawyers; **SAP** Socialist Alternative Party; **Science** Science Party; **Scrap** Scrap Members Allowances; **SDP** Social Democratic Party; **SEP** Socialist Equality Party; **SIG** Staffordshire Independent Group; **SJP** Scottish Jacobite Party; **SKGH** Save King George Hospital; **SLP** Socialist Labour Party; **SMRA** Solihull and Meriden Residents Association; **Socialist** Socialist; **Solidarity** Solidarity – Scotland's Socialist Movement; **SOTBTH** Support Our Troops Bring Them Home; **SSP** Scottish Socialist Party; **Tamsin** Tamsin Omond to the Commons; **Tendring** Tendring First; **TPP** The Peace Party – non-violence, justice, environment; **True English** The True English (Poetry) Party; **Trust** The Trust Party; **TUSC** Trade Unionist and Socialist Coalition; **TUV** Traditional Unionist Voice; **UCUNF** Ulster Conservatives and Unionists – New Force; **UKIP** UK Independence Party; **Unity** Unity For Peace And Socialism; **UV** United Voice; **WCP** Welsh Christian Party; **Wessex Reg** Wessex Regionalists; **WRP** Workers' Revolutionary Party; **You** You Party; **Youth** The Youth Party; **YRDPL** Your Right to Democracy Party Limited.

STATE OF THE PARTIES

	2010 General Election	2005 General Election
Conservative	306	198
Labour*	258	355
Liberal Democrat	57	62
Democratic Unionist Party	8	9
Scottish National Party	6	6
Sinn Féin	5	5
Social Democratic Labour Party	3	3
Plaid Cymru	3	3
Alliance	1	2
Green	1	0
Independent	1	0
Ulster Unionist Party	0	1
Respect	0	1
The Speaker	1	1
Total	**650**	**646**

**Includes Labour/Co-operative MPs. These figures represent the election result and as such include Eric Illsley as a Labour member, however, he now sits as an Independent.*

SHARE OF THE VOTE

	Total Seats	Total Votes	% of votes
Con	306	10,703,864	36.1
Lab	258	8,609,462	29.0
Lib Dem	57	6,836,761	23.0
UKIP	0	921,913	3.1
BNP	0	552,305	1.9
SNP	6	491,386	1.7
Green	1	285,616	1.0
Ind	1	231,870	0.8
Sinn Féin	5	171,942	0.6
DUP	8	168,216	0.6
PIC	3	165,394	0.6
SDLP	3	110,970	0.4
UCUNF	0	102,361	0.3
England	0	64,826	0.2
All	1	42,762	0.1
Respect	0	33,251	0.1
TUV	0	26,300	0.1
Speaker	1	22,860	0.1
Other	0	142,490	0.5
TOTAL	**650**	**29,684,549**	**65.1**

SHARE OF THE VOTE BY REGION

ENGLAND

EASTERN

	Total Seats	Total Votes	% of Votes
Con	52	1,356,739	47.12
Lib Dem	4	692,932	24.07
Lab	2	564,581	19.61
UKIP	0	123,437	4.29
BNP	0	59,505	2.07
Green	0	42,677	1.48
Ind	0	26,108	0.91
England	0	8,390	0.29
Tendring	0	1,078	0.04
CPA	0	862	0.03
Christian	0	635	0.02
Loony	0	548	0.02
TUSC	0	362	0.01
NCDMV	0	327	0.01
YRDPL	0	264	0.01
Animal	0	181	0.01
WRP	0	175	0.01
Beer	0	153	0.01
NP	0	118	0.00
CURE	0	108	0.00
LTT	0	100	0.00
Essex	0	35	0.00
TOTAL	**58**	**2,879,315**	**67.3**

EAST MIDLANDS

	Total Seats	Total Votes	% of Votes
Con	31	915,933	41.18
Lab	15	661,813	29.76
Lib Dem	0	462,988	20.82
UKIP	0	72,659	3.27
BNP	0	69,706	3.13
Ind	0	16,680	0.75
Green	0	11,667	0.52
England	0	8,641	0.39
Lincs Ind	0	929	0.04
Loony	0	712	0.03
Unity	0	494	0.02
TUSC	0	406	0.02
NSOPS	0	325	0.01
Pirate	0	283	0.01

SLP	0	266	0.01
Christian	0	223	0.01
Science	0	197	0.01
Bus-Pass	0	112	0.01
Scrap	0	59	0.00
Humanity	0	50	0.00
TOTAL	**46**	**2,224,143**	**67.00**

LONDON

	Total Seats	Total Votes	% of Votes
Lab	38	1,245,637	36.62
Con	28	1,174,568	34.53
Lib Dem	7	751,561	22.10
UKIP	0	59,452	1.75
Green	0	54,316	1.60
BNP	0	45,902	1.35
Respect	0	17,368	0.51
Ind	0	14,590	0.43
England	0	9,076	0.27
Christian	0	8,272	0.24
NF	0	2,825	0.08
CPA	0	2,794	0.08
TUSC	0	1,603	0.05
Loony	0	858	0.03
SKGH	0	746	0.02
SAP	0	645	0.02
Lib	0	539	0.02
WRP	0	502	0.01
Reform 2000	0	379	0.01
Brent North Ind	0	333	0.01
CNBPG	0	332	0.01
Pirate	0	303	0.01
UV	0	209	0.01
Green Soc	0	197	0.01
NICCF	0	196	0.01
Ind EACPS	0	190	0.01
SLP	0	184	0.01
Comm	0	160	0.00
AC	0	149	0.00
Socialist	0	143	0.00
Tamsin	0	123	0.00
Comm League	0	110	0.00
AWP	0	109	0.00
Ind Fed UK	0	99	0.00
Animal	0	96	0.00

LONDON *cont.*

	Total Seats	Total Votes	% of Votes
CURE	0	76	0.00
AWL	0	75	0.00
Magna Carta	0	66	0.00
Restoration	0	45	0.00
Libertarian	0	41	0.00
Better Britain	0	35	0.00
BEP	0	17	0.00
TOTAL	**73**	**3,394,921**	**64.60%**

NORTH EAST

	Total Seats	Total Votes	% of Votes
Lab	25	518,261	43.55
Con	2	282,347	23.72
Lib Dem	2	280,468	23.57
BNP	0	51,940	4.36
UKIP	0	34,896	2.93
Ind	0	15,669	1.32
Green	0	3,787	0.32
LLPBPP	0	1,964	0.17
England	0	1,456	0.12
NF	0	599	0.05
Christian	0	575	0.05
TUSC	0	393	0.03
Comm GB	0	177	0.01
TOTAL	**29**	**1,192,532**	**61**

NORTH WEST

	Total Seats	Total Votes	% of Votes
Lab	47	1,292,978	39.47
Con	22	1,038,967	31.71
Lib Dem	6	707,716	21.60
UKIP	0	103,782	3.17
BNP	0	70,032	2.14
Ind	0	20,188	0.62
Green	0	17,046	0.52
England	0	4,533	0.14
Lib	0	3,327	0.10
NF	0	3,298	0.10
Mac Ind	0	2,590	0.08
Respect	0	2,398	0.07
TUSC	0	2,378	0.07
SLP	0	1,450	0.04
Christian	0	1,355	0.04

CPA	0	1,287	0.04
IZB	0	545	0.02
Pirate	0	367	0.01
CSP	0	321	0.01
You	0	319	0.01
True English	0	298	0.01
Impact	0	243	0.01
Integrity	0	230	0.01
Clause 28	0	217	0.01
Loony	0	198	0.01
WRP	0	59	0.00
SEP	0	54	0.00
TOTAL	**75**	**3,276,176**	**62.40**

SOUTH EAST

	Total Seats	Total Votes	% of Votes
Con	74	2,118,035	49.32
Lib Dem	4	1,124,777	26.19
Lab	4	697,495	16.24
UKIP	0	177,269	4.13
Green	1	62,124	1.45
BNP	0	30,618	0.71
Ind	0	26,865	0.63
Speaker	1	22,860	0.53
England	0	15,442	0.36
Loony	0	3,315	0.08
Trust	0	2,699	0.06
Christian	0	2,104	0.05
NF	0	1,690	0.04
CSP	0	852	0.02
EIP	0	803	0.02
TPP	0	737	0.02
TUSC	0	692	0.02
CPA	0	651	0.02
MEP	0	616	0.01
Expense	0	475	0.01
Best	0	474	0.01
JACP	0	427	0.01
Animal	0	398	0.01
FR	0	270	0.01
RRG	0	266	0.01
JP	0	265	0.01
BCM	0	247	0.01
FDP	0	207	0.00
MRP	0	173	0.00

SOUTH EAST *cont.*

	Total Seats	Total Votes	% of Votes
CIP	0	167	0.00
SLP	0	148	0.00
SEP	0	116	0.00
Medway	0	109	0.00
Deficit	0	107	0.00
Apol Dem	0	95	0.00
Pirate	0	94	0.00
NLP	0	93	0.00
NRP	0	84	0.00
EPA	0	73	0.00
Wessex Reg	0	62	0.00
CURE	0	61	0.00
Scrap	0	60	0.00
MCCP	0	44	0.00
TOTAL	**84**	**4,294,159**	**67.98**

SOUTH WEST

	Total Seats	Total Votes	% of Votes
Con	36	1,187,637	42.82
Lib Dem	15	962,954	34.72
Lab	4	426,910	15.39
UKIP	0	123,910	4.47
Green	0	31,517	1.14
BNP	0	20,866	0.75
Ind	0	6,135	0.22
Meb Ker	0	5,379	0.19
England	0	3,277	0.12
Lib	0	1,108	0.04
Loony	0	1,030	0.04
Christian	0	743	0.03
SLP	0	499	0.02
Corn Dem	0	396	0.01
TUSC	0	390	0.01
GMVY	0	233	0.01
Libertarian	0	141	0.01
Ind Fed UK	0	126	0.00
Comm GB	0	96	0.00
ATSP	0	31	0.00
TOTAL	**55**	**2,773,378**	**69.25**

WEST MIDLANDS

	Total Seats	Total Votes	% of Votes
Con	33	1,044,081	39.54
Lab	24	808,114	30.61
Lib Dem	2	540,160	20.46
UKIP	0	106,273	4.02
BNP	0	72,806	2.76
Ind KHHC	0	16,150	0.61
Green	0	14,996	0.57
Respect	0	12,240	0.46
Ind	0	8,676	0.33
Christian	0	2,366	0.09
England	0	2,289	0.09
Brom Ind Con	0	2,182	0.08
SAP	0	1,962	0.07
SIG	0	1,208	0.05
SMRA	0	977	0.04
SLP	0	864	0.03
Dem Lab	0	842	0.03
TUSC	0	824	0.03
NF	0	751	0.03
SDP	0	637	0.02
CMGB	0	598	0.02
Common Good	0	305	0.01
EPA	0	246	0.01
Impact	0	234	0.01
Loony	0	179	0.01
Pirate	0	173	0.01
Nobody	0	73	0.00
TOTAL	**59**	**2,640,206**	**64.75**

YORKSHIRE AND THE HUMBER

	Total Seats	Total Votes	% of Votes
Lab	32	826,537	34.35
Con	19	790,062	32.83
Lib Dem	3	552,570	22.96
BNP	0	104,177	4.33
UKIP	0	67,322	2.80
Ind	0	21,032	0.87
Green	0	20,824	0.87
England	0	11,722	0.49
TUSC	0	2,047	0.09
Lib	0	1,418	0.06
Green Soc	0	1,257	0.05
Respect	0	1,245	0.05

YORKSHIRE AND THE HUMBER *cont.*

	Total Seats	Total Votes	% of Votes
NF	0	1,237	0.05
SLP	0	957	0.04
SDP	0	914	0.04
DN	0	753	0.03
PNDP	0	331	0.01
Loony	0	318	0.01
Christian	0	250	0.01
Comm GB	0	139	0.01
Youth	0	95	0.00
Currency	0	84	0.00
CURE	0	72	0.00
TOTAL	**54**	**2,405,363**	**62.94**

NORTHERN IRELAND

	Total Seats	Total Votes	% of Votes
Sinn Féin	5	171,942	25.52
DUP	8	168,216	24.96
SDLP	3	110,970	16.47
UCUNF	0	102,361	15.19
Ind	1	47,778	7.09
All	1	42,762	6.35
TUV	0	26,300	3.90
Green	0	3,542	0.53
TOTAL	**18**	**673,871**	**57.64**

SCOTLAND

	Total Seats	Total Votes	% of Votes
Lab	41	1,035,535	42.00
SNP	6	491,386	19.93
Lib Dem	11	465,471	18.88
Con	1	412,765	16.74
UKIP	0	17,223	0.70
Green	0	16,827	0.68
BNP	0	8,910	0.36
Ind	0	6,479	0.26
SSP	0	3,157	0.13
TUSC	0	2,217	0.09
SLP	0	1,673	0.07
Solidarity	0	1,126	0.05
Christian	0	835	0.03
Trust	0	534	0.02
Lib	0	389	0.02

SJP	0	290	0.01
Comm	0	179	0.01
SACL	0	138	0.01
Pirate	0	120	0.00
JOT	0	93	0.00
Land Power	0	57	0.00
Comm League	0	48	0.00
TOTAL	**59**	**2,465,452**	**63.95**

WALES

	Total Seats	Total Votes	% of Votes
Lab	26	531,601	36.24
Con	8	382,730	26.09
Lib Dem	3	295,164	20.12
PIC	3	165,394	11.28
UKIP	0	35,690	2.43
Ind	0	21,670	1.48
BNP	0	17,843	1.22
Green	0	6,293	0.43
SOTBTH	0	3,588	0.24
Christian	0	1,408	0.10
SLP	0	1,155	0.08
NMB	0	558	0.04
WCP	0	539	0.04
NF	0	384	0.03
Loony	0	352	0.02
TUSC	0	341	0.02
Comm	0	196	0.01
Green Soc	0	127	0.01
TOTAL	**40**	**1,465,033**	**65.73**

SEATS WHICH CHANGED PARTIES

Changes are based on notional election results, thus Solihull is shown as changing parties even though its MP represented the predecessor seat in the 2005 parliament. In addition, as changes are based on notional 2005 general election results, Norwich North is shown as changing parties, although the Conservatives gained it from Labour in a by-election; similarly Glasgow East does not appear as a change in party as a by-election gain was reversed at the general election. North Down is listed as the sitting MP changed her party during the course of the last parliament.

	2005	2010
Aberconwy*	Lab	Con
Amber Valley*	Lab	Con
Arfon*	Lab	PIC
South Basildon and East Thurrock*	Lab/Co-op	Con
Battersea*	Lab	Con
Bedford*	Lab	Con

**Notional holder after boundary changes*

	2005	2010
Belfast East*	DUP	Alliance
Bethnal Green and Bow*	Respect	Lab
Blackpool North and Cleveleys*	Lab	Con
Blaenau Gwent*	Ind	Lab
Bradford East*	Lab	Lib Dem
Brent Central*	Lab	Lib Dem
Brentford and Isleworth*	Lab	Con
Brigg and Goole*	Lab	Con
Brighton Pavilion*	Lab	Green
Bristol North West*	Lab	Con
Broxtowe*	Lab	Con
Burnley	Lab	Lib Dem
Burton*	Lab	Con
Bury North*	Lab	Con
Calder Valley*	Lab	Con
Camborne and Redruth*	Lib Dem	Con
Cannock Chase*	Lab	Con
Cardiff North	Lab	Con
Carlisle*	Lab	Con
Carmarthen West and South Pembrokeshire*	Lab	Con
Chatham and Aylesford*	Lab	Con
City of Chester*	Lab	Con
Chesterfield*	Lib Dem	Lab
Cleethorpes*	Lab	Con
Colne Valley*	Lab	Con
Corby	Lab/Co-op	Con
South East Cornwall*	Lib Dem	Con
Crawley	Lab	Con
Crewe and Nantwich*	Lab	Con
Darford*	Lab	Con
South Derbyshire*	Lab	Con
Dewsbury*	Lab	Con
South Dorset	Lab	Con
Dover*	Lab	Con
North Down	UUP	Ind
Dudley South*	Lab	Con
Ealing Central and Acton*	Lab	Con
Eastbourne*	Con	Lib Dem
Elmet and Rothwell*	Lab	Con
Enfield North*	Lab	Con
Erewash*	Lab	Con
Filton and Bradley Stoke*	Lab	Con
Finchley and Golders Green*	Lab	Con
Gillingham and Rainham*	Lab	Con

**Notional holder after boundary changes*

	2005	2010
Gloucester*	Lab	Con
Great Yarmouth	Lab	Con
Halesowen and Rowley Regis*	Lab	Con
Harlow*	Lab	Con
Harrow East*	Lab	Con
Hastings and Rye*	Lab	Con
Hendon*	Lab	Con
Hereford and South Herefordshire*	Lib Dem	Con
High Peak*	Lab	Con
Hove*	Lab	Con
Hyndburn*	Lab	Con
Ipswich*	Lab	Con
Keighley*	Lab	Con
Kingswood*	Lab	Con
Lancaster and Fleetwood*	Lab	Con
North West Leicestershire	Lab	Con
Lincoln*	Lab	Con
Loughborough*	Lab/Co-op	Con
Milton Keynes North*	Lab	Con
Milton Keynes South*	Lab	Con
Montgomeryshire*	Lib Dem	Con
Morecambe and Lunesdale*	Lab	Con
Newton Abbot*	Lib Dem	Con
Northampton North*	Lab	Con
Northampton South*	Lab	Con
Norwich North*	Lab	Con
Norwich South*	Lab	Lib Dem
Nuneaton*	Lab	Con
Oxford West and Abingdon*	Lib Dem	Con
Pendle	Lab	Con
Plymouth, Sutton and Devonport*	Lab/Co-op	Con
Portsmouth North*	Lab/Co-op	Con
Pudsey*	Lab	Con
Reading West*	Lab	Con
Redcar*	Lab	Lib Dem
Redditch*	Lab	Con
South Ribble*	Lab	Con
Richmond Park*	Lib Dem	Con
Romsey and Southampton North*	Lib Dem	Con
Rossendale and Darwen*	Lab	Con
Rugby*	Lab	Con
Sherwood*	Lab	Con
Stafford *	Lab	Con
Staffordshire Moorlands*	Lab	Con

**Notional holder after boundary changes*

	2005	2010
Stevenage*	Lab	Con
Stockton South*	Lab	Con
Stourbridge*	Lab	Con
Stroud*	Lab/Co-op	Con
North Swindon*	Lab	Con
South Swindon*	Lab	Con
Tamworth*	Lab	Con
South Thanet*	Lab	Con
Thurrock*	Lab	Con
Truro and Falmouth*	Lib Dem	Con
Warrington South*	Lab	Con
Warwick and Leamington*	Lab	Con
North Warwickshire*	Lab	Con
Watford*	Lab	Con
Waveney*	Lab	Con
Weaver Vale*	Lab	Con
Wells*	Con	Lib Dem
Winchester*	Lib Dem	Con
Wolverhampton South West*	Lab	Con
Worcester	Lab	Con
Wyre Forest*	Ind KHHC	Con
York Outer*	Lib Dem	Con

**Notional holder after boundary changes*

RESULTS IN VULNERABLE CONSERVATIVE SEATS

	% majority 2005	Result	Swing
Sittingbourne and Sheppey*	0.05	Con hold	12.7% from Lab to Con
Clwyd West*	0.14	Con hold	8.4% from Lab to Con
Guildford*	0.17	Con hold	6.9% from Lib Dem to Con
Solihull*	0.25	Lib Dem gain	0.3% from Con to Lib Dem
Hemel Hempstead*	0.36	Con hold	1.9% from Lib Dem to Con
Kettering*	0.39	Con hold	9.4% from Lab to Con
North East Somerset*	0.46	Con hold	4.6% from Lab to Con
Croydon Central*	0.72	Con hold	3.3% from Lab to Con
Shipley*	0.97	Con hold	9.6% from Lab to Con
Rochester and Strood*	1.14	Con hold	9.8% from Lab to Con
Wellingborough*	1.25	Con hold	10.8% from Lab to Con
Eastbourne*	1.41	Lib Dem gain	4% from Con to Lib Dem
Gravesham	1.45	Con hold	9.1% from Lab to Con
Wirral West*	1.51	Con hold	2.3% from Lab to Con
Preseli Pembrokeshire*	1.53	Con hold	5% from Lab to Con
Reading East*	1.71	Con hold	2% from Lib Dem to Con

**Notional majority following boundary change*

South Thanet*	1.76	Con hold	7.4% from Lab to Con
Scarborough and Whitby	2.65	Con hold	6.9% from Lab to Con
Enfield Southgate*	2.72	Con hold	7.2% from Lab to Con
The Wrekin*	2.85	Con hold	8.9% from Lab to Con
St Albans*	2.94	Con hold	3.7% from Con to Lib Dem
Shrewsbury and Atcham	3.59	Con hold	0.1% from Lib Dem to Con
Staffordshire Moorlands*	3.86	Con hold	5.7% from Lab to Con
Dumfriesshire, Clydesdale and Tweeddale	3.89	Con hold	2.6% from Lab to Con
Ilford North*	4.14	Con hold	3.7% from Lab to Con
Weston-Super-Mare*	4.26	Con hold	0.4% from Lib Dem to Con
Forest of Dean	4.3	Con hold	9.2% from Lab to Con
Selby and Ainsty*	4.31	Con hold	9.7% from Lab to Con
Ludlow	4.36	Con hold	7.8% from Lib Dem to Con
West Dorset	4.62	Con hold	1.1% from Lib Dem to Con
Putney*	4.8	Con hold	9.9% from Lab to Con
Meon Valley*	4.91	Con hold	9.4% from Lib Dem to Con
Central Devon*	4.99	Con hold	6.1% from Lib Dem to Con
Torridge and West Devon*	5.37	Con hold	No swing
Wimbledon*	5.69	Con hold	0.4% from Lib Dem to Con
Wells*	5.74	Lib Dem gain	3.6% from Con to Lib Dem
Totnes*	5.76	Con hold	2.3% from Lib Dem to Con
West Worcestershire*	6.03	Con hold	3.3% from Lib Dem to Con
Beverley and Holderness*	6.23	Con hold	1.6% from Lib Dem to Con
Basingstoke*	6.27	Con hold	4.6% from Lib Dem to Con

RESULTS IN VULNERABLE LABOUR SEATS

	% majority 2005	**Result**	**Swing**
Gillingham and Rainham*	0.03	Con gain	9.3% from Lab to Con
Crawley	0.09	Con gain	6.3% from Lab to Con
Rochdale*	0.35	Lab hold	0.8 from Lib Dem to Lab
Harlow*	0.58	Con gain	5.9% from Lab to Con
Finchley and Golders Green*	0.7	Con gain	5.8% from Lab to Con
Oxford East*	0.73	Lab hold	4.1% from Lib Dem to Lab
Portsmouth North*	0.77	Con gain	8.6% from Lab to Con
Battersea*	0.81	Con gain	6.5% from Lab to Con
Edinburgh South	0.95	Lab hold	0.1% from Lab to Lib Dem
Hove*	1	Con gain	2.4% from Lab to Con
Hampstead and Kilburn*	1.14	Lab hold	6.7% from Lab to Con
Ochil and South Perthshire	1.47	Lab hold	4.4% from SNP to Lab
Islington South and Finsbury	1.56	Lab hold	3.3% from Lib Dem to Lab
Filton and Bradley Stoke*	1.58	Con gain	6.4% from Lab to Con
Milton Keynes North*	1.71	Con gain	9.2% from Lab to Con
Arfon*	1.82	PlC gain	3.7% from Lab to PlC

**Notional majority following boundary change*

Labour *cont.*	% majority 2005	Result	Swing
Stroud*	1.85	Con gain	2% from Lab to Con
Dartford*	1.9	Con gain	11.6% from Lab to Con
South Basildon and East Thurrock*	2.14	Con gain	7.5% from Lab to Con
Ealing Central and Acton*	2.16	Con gain	5% from Lab to Con
City of Chester*	2.2	Con gain	3.9% from Lab to Con
Watford*	2.33	Con gain	6.1% from Lab to Con
Enfield North*	2.35	Con gain	0.7% from Lab to Con
Colne Valley*	2.51	Con gain	6.5% from Lib Dem to Con
Cardiff North	2.53	Con gain	6.5% from Lab to Con
Hastings and Rye*	2.54	Con gain	3.3% from Lab to Con
Calder Valley*	2.73	Con gain	7.6% from Lab to Con
Stourbridge*	2.92	Con gain	6.9% from Lab to Con
Milton Keynes South*	3.04	Con gain	6.2% from Lab to Con
Corby	3.13	Con gain	3.4% from Lab to Con
Aberdeen South	3.24	Lab hold	2.5% from Lib Dem to Lab
Vale of Glamorgan*	3.37	Con gain	6.1% from Lab to Con
South Swindon*	3.5	Con gain	5.5% from Lab to Con
Ynys Môn	3.5	Lab hold	1.8% from PIC to Lab
South Dorset	3.73	Con gain	9.3% from Lab to Con
Northampton South*	3.78	Con gain	9.6% from Lab to Con
High Peak*	3.8	Con gain	6.5% from Lab to Con
Loughborough*	3.88	Con gain	5.5% from Lab to Con
Aberconwy*	3.93	Con gain	7.6% from Lab to Con
Birmingham Edgbaston*	4.01	Lab hold	0.5% from Lab to Con

RESULTS IN VULNERABLE LIBERAL DEMOCRAT SEATS

	% majority 2005	Result	Swing
York Outer*	0.44	Con gain	3.7% from Lib Dem to Con
Romsey and Southampton North*	0.46	Con gain	4.5% from Lib Dem to Con
Ceredigion*	0.61	Lib Dem hold	10.6% from PIC to Lib Dem
Cheltenham*	0.66	Lib Dem hold	4.3% from Con to Lib Dem
Eastleigh*	1.12	Lib Dem hold	3% from Con to Lib Dem
Somerton and Frome*	1.12	Lib Dem hold	0.9% from Con to Lib Dem
Manchester Withington*	1.39	Lib Dem hold	1.4% from Lab to Lib Dem
Westmorland and Lonsdale*	1.7	Lib Dem hold	11.1% from Con to Lib Dem
Hereford and South Herefordshire*	2.39	Con gain	3.8% from Lib Dem to Con
Bristol West*	2.55	Lib Dem hold	9% from Lab to Lib Dem
Carshalton and Wallington *	2.93	Lib Dem hold	4.3% from Con to Lib Dem
Taunton Deane*	3.3	Lib Dem hold	1.8% from Con to Lib Dem
Chippenham*	4.7	Lib Dem hold	No swing
Leeds North West*	4.96	Lib Dem hold	5.4% from Con to Lib Dem

**Notional majority following boundary change*

Hornsey and Wood Green	5.06	Lib Dem hold	3.7% from Lab to Lib Dem
Torbay*	6.01	Lib Dem hold	1.1% from Con to Lib Dem
Sutton and Cheam*	6.22	Lib Dem hold	1.5% from Lib Dem to Con
Chesterfield*	6.36	Lab gain	3.8% from Lib Dem to Lab
North Cornwall*	6.87	Lib Dem hold	0.3% from Lib Dem to Con

RESULT IN VULNERABLE SDLP SEAT

	% majority 2005	**Result**	**Swing**
Belfast South*	0.5	SDLP hold	8.4% from DUP to SDLP

RESULTS IN VULNERABLE SNP SEATS

	% majority 2005	**Result**	**Swing**
Dundee East	0.97	SNP hold	1.8% from Lab to SNP
Perth and North Perthshire	3.31	SNP hold	2.9% from Con to SNP
Angus	4.2	SNP hold	2.2% from Con to SNP

RESULT IN VULNERABLE RESPECT SEAT

	% majority 2005	**Result**	**Swing**
Bethnal Green and Bow*	2.1	Lab gain	14.1% from Respect to Lab

**Notional majority following boundary change*

SEATS BY PERCENTAGE MAJORITY

				%	Majority
1	Steve Rotheram	*Lab*	Liverpool Walton	57.72	19,818
2	George Howarth	*Lab*	Knowsley	57.53	25,690
3	Stephen Timms	*Lab*	East Ham	55.24	27,826
4	Gerry Adams	*Sinn Féin*	Belfast West	54.71	17,579
5	Willie Bain	*Lab*	Glasgow North East	54.21	15,942
6	Stephen Twigg	*Lab/Co-op*	Liverpool West Derby	51.61	18,467
7	Alistair Carmichael	*Lib Dem*	Orkney and Shetland	51.32	9,928
8	Joe Benton	*Lab*	Bootle	51.31	21,181
9	Gordon Brown	*Lab*	Kirkcaldy and Cowdenbeath	50.24	23,009
10	Tom Clarke	*Lab*	Coatbridge, Chryston and Bellshill	49.75	20,714
11	Lyn Brown	*Lab*	West Ham	47.99	22,534
12	Ian Davidson	*Lab/Co-op*	Glasgow South West	46.16	14,671
13	Tom Greatrex	*Lab/Co-op*	Rutherglen and Hamilton West	44.70	21,002
14	William Hague	*Con*	Richmond (Yorkshire)	43.69	23,336
15	John Hayes	*Con*	South Holland and The Deepings	43.60	21,880
16	Frank Roy	*Lab*	Motherwell and Wishaw	42.96	16,806
17	Grahame Morris	*Lab*	Easington	42.91	14,982
18	Sylvia Hermon	*Ind*	North Down	42.90	14,364
19	Frank Field	*Lab*	Birkenhead	42.78	15,195
20	Mark Francois	*Con*	Rayleigh and Wickford	42.68	22,338
21	Greg Hands	*Con*	Chelsea and Fulham	41.96	16,722
22	David Lammy	*Lab*	Tottenham	41.61	16,931
23	Douglas Alexander	*Lab*	Paisley and Renfrewshire South	41.54	16,614
24	Dominic Grieve	*Con*	Beaconsfield	41.50	21,782
25	Gemma Doyle	*Lab/Co-op*	West Dunbartonshire	41.19	17,408
26	Charles Walker	*Con*	Broxbourne	41.18	18,804
27	Lindsay Roy	*Lab*	Glenrothes	40.62	16,455
28	John Whittingdale	*Con*	Maldon	40.52	19,407
29	Richard Shepherd	*Con*	Aldridge-Brownhills	39.48	15,256
30	Maria Eagle	*Lab*	Garston and Halewood	39.41	16,877
31	David Cameron	*Con*	Witney	39.36	22,740
32	David Cairns	*Lab*	Inverclyde	38.43	14,416
33	Adam Afriyie	*Con*	Windsor	38.42	19,054
34	John Robertson	*Lab*	Glasgow North West	38.25	13,611
35	Huw Irranca-Davies	*Lab*	Ogmore	38.23	13,246
36	Nick Hurd	*Con*	Ruislip, Northwood and Pinner	37.96	19,060
37	Martin McGuinness	*Sinn Féin*	Mid Ulster	37.62	15,363
38	Charles Kennedy	*Lib Dem*	Ross, Skye and Lochaber	37.52	13,070

				%	Majority
39	Derek Twigg	*Lab*	Halton	37.51	15,504
40	Bob Stewart	*Con*	Beckenham	37.29	17,784
41	James Clappison	*Con*	Hertsmere	37.24	17,605
42	Chris Bryant	*Lab*	Rhondda	37.18	11,553
43	Christopher Heaton-Harris	*Con*	Daventry	37.06	19,188
44	Harriet Harman	*Lab*	Camberwell and Peckham	36.84	17,187
45	Margaret Curran	*Lab*	Glasgow East	36.81	11,840
46	Hugh Robertson	*Con*	Faversham and Mid Kent	36.58	17,088
47	Louise Ellman	*Lab/Co-op*	Liverpool Riverside	36.53	14,173
48	Margaret Hodge	*Lab*	Barking	36.51	16,555
49	Andrew Rosindell	*Con*	Romford	36.48	16,954
50	Graham Stringer	*Lab*	Blackley and Broughton	35.97	12,303
51	Hywel Francis	*Lab*	Aberavon	35.66	11,039
52	Grant Shapps	*Con*	Welwyn Hatfield	35.58	17,423
53	Desmond Swayne	*Con*	New Forest West	35.52	16,896
54	Michael Fallon	*Con*	Sevenoaks	35.45	17,515
55	John Stanley	*Con*	Tonbridge and Malling	35.43	18,178
56	Christopher Evans	*Lab/Co-op*	Islwyn	35.21	12,215
57	Jo Johnson	*Con*	Orpington	35.17	17,200
58	James Arbuthnot	*Con*	North East Hampshire	35.13	18,597
59	David Blunkett	*Lab*	Sheffield, Brightside and Hillsborough	35.03	13,632
60	Jim Sheridan	*Lab*	Paisley and Renfrewshire North	34.96	15,280
61	George Young	*Con*	North West Hampshire	34.87	18,583
62	James Brokenshire	*Con*	Old Bexley and Sidcup	34.86	15,857
63	Pamela Nash	*Lab*	Airdrie and Shotts	34.61	12,408
64	Anas Sarwar	*Lab*	Glasgow Central	34.51	10,551
65	Michael Fabricant	*Con*	Lichfield	34.29	17,683
66	Philip Hammond	*Con*	Runnymede and Weybridge	34.29	16,509
67	Andrea Leadsom	*Con*	South Northamptonshire	34.19	20,478
68	Alistair Burt	*Con*	North East Bedfordshire	34.10	18,942
69	Dominic Raab	*Con*	Esher and Walton	34.09	18,593
70	Andrew Mitchell	*Con*	Sutton Coldfield	33.61	17,005
71	Eric Pickles	*Con*	Brentwood and Ongar	33.44	16,920
72	Stephen Phillips	*Con*	Sleaford and North Hykeham	33.44	19,905
73	Gregg McClymont	*Lab*	Cumbernauld, Kilsyth and Kirkintilloch East	33.43	13,755
74	Meg Hillier	*Lab/Co-op*	Hackney South and Shoreditch	33.34	14,288
75	Stephen Hepburn	*Lab*	Jarrow	33.28	12,908
76	Siân James	*Lab*	Swansea East	33.17	10,838
77	John Healey	*Lab*	Wentworth and Dearne	33.06	13,920
78	Gavin Williamson	*Con*	South Staffordshire	32.89	16,590

				%	Majority
79	Ian Mearns	*Lab*	Gateshead	32.80	12,549
80	Andrew Selous	*Con*	South West Bedfordshire	32.79	16,649
81	Brooks Newmark	*Con*	Braintree	32.76	16,121
82	Eleanor Laing	*Con*	Epping Forest	32.48	15,131
83	Nick Smith	*Lab*	Blaenau Gwent	32.46	10,516
84	Priti Patel	*Con*	Witham	32.45	15,196
85	Tony Baldry	*Con*	Banbury	32.41	18,227
86	Ann Clwyd	*Lab*	Cynon Valley	32.19	9,617
87	George Osborne	*Con*	Tatton	32.03	14,487
88	Malcolm Wicks	*Lab*	Croydon North	31.90	16,483
89	Cheryl Gillan	*Con*	Chesham and Amersham	31.86	16,710
90	Gary Streeter	*Con*	South West Devon	31.84	15,874
91	Michael Gove	*Con*	Surrey Heath	31.81	17,289
92	Andy Burnham	*Lab*	Leigh	31.71	15,011
93	Tom Harris	*Lab*	Glasgow South	31.57	12,658
94	Robert Neill	*Con*	Bromley and Chislehurst	31.56	13,900
95	Patrick Mercer	*Con*	Newark	31.53	16,152
96	Mark Hoban	*Con*	Fareham	31.45	17,092
97	Steve Barclay	*Con*	North East Cambridgeshire	31.43	16,425
98	Damian Green	*Con*	Ashford	31.34	17,297
99	Charles Hendry	*Con*	Wealden	31.25	17,179
100	Theresa May	*Con*	Maidenhead	31.22	16,769
101	Roger Gale	*Con*	North Thanet	31.21	13,528
102	Siobhain McDonagh	*Lab*	Mitcham and Morden	31.20	13,666
103	Christopher Chope	*Con*	Christchurch	31.18	15,410
104	Caroline Spelman	*Con*	Meriden	31.16	16,253
105	Peter Luff	*Con*	Mid Worcestershire	31.15	15,864
106	Diane Abbott	*Lab*	Hackney North and Stoke Newington	31.13	14,461
107	John Howell	*Con*	Henley	30.99	16,588
108	Henry Bellingham	*Con*	North West Norfolk	30.98	14,810
109	Greg Clark	*Con*	Tunbridge Wells	30.95	15,576
110	Sam Gyimah	*Con*	East Surrey	30.88	16,874
111	Ben Wallace	*Con*	Wyre and Preston North	30.84	15,844
112	Caroline Dinenage	*Con*	Gosport	30.71	14,413
113	Sharon Hodgson	*Lab*	Washington and Sunderland West	30.69	11,458
114	Angela Watkinson	*Con*	Hornchurch and Upminster	30.66	16,371
115	Shaun Woodward	*Lab*	St Helens South and Whiston	30.65	14,122
116	Owen Paterson	*Con*	North Shropshire	30.52	15,828
117	David Miliband	*Lab*	South Shields	30.42	11,109
118	Joan Ruddock	*Lab*	Lewisham Deptford	30.32	12,499

				%	Majority
119	Mark Menzies	*Con*	Fylde	30.18	13,185
120	Oliver Heald	*Con*	North East Hertfordshire	30.13	15,194
121	Phillip Lee	*Con*	Bracknell	30.12	15,704
122	Iain Duncan Smith	*Con*	Chingford and Woodford Green	30.07	12,963
123	Mark Field	*Con*	Cities of London and Westminster	29.99	11,076
124	Eric Illsley	*Ind*	Barnsley Central	29.98	11,093
125	Nick Clegg	*Lib Dem*	Sheffield Hallam	29.89	15,284
126	Nick Herbert	*Con*	Arundel and South Downs	29.81	16,691
127	John Baron	*Con*	Basildon and Billericay	29.78	12,398
128	Patrick McLoughlin	*Con*	Derbyshire Dales	29.64	13,866
129	Ian Paisley Jnr	*DUP*	North Antrim	29.62	12,558
130	Anne McIntosh	*Con*	Thirsk and Malton	29.52	11,281
131	Kevan Jones	*Lab*	North Durham	29.48	12,076
132	Kenneth Clarke	*Con*	Rushcliffe	29.45	15,811
133	David Watts	*Lab*	St Helens North	29.40	13,101
134	Chris Grayling	*Con*	Epsom and Ewell	29.36	16,134
135	Keith Vaz	*Lab*	Leicester East	29.34	14,082
136	Stephen O'Brien	*Con*	Eddisbury	29.19	13,255
137	Jim Hood	*Lab*	Lanark and Hamilton East	28.95	13,478
138	Bridget Phillipson	*Lab*	Houghton and Sunderland South	28.91	10,990
139	Michael Dugher	*Lab*	Barnsley East	28.89	11,090
140	Mark Simmonds	*Con*	Boston and Skegness	28.81	12,426
141	Paul Beresford	*Con*	Mole Valley	28.81	15,653
142	Jeffrey Donaldson	*DUP*	Lagan Valley	28.70	10,486
143	Pat Doherty	*Sinn Féin*	West Tyrone	28.67	10,685
144	Shailesh Vara	*Con*	North West Cambridgeshire	28.61	16,677
145	Yvonne Fovargue	*Lab*	Makerfield	28.53	12,490
146	Jeremy Hunt	*Con*	South West Surrey	28.50	16,318
147	Michael McCann	*Lab*	East Kilbride, Strathaven and Lesmahagow	28.47	14,503
148	Hilary Benn	*Lab*	Leeds Central	28.47	10,645
149	Andrew Robathan	*Con*	South Leicestershire	28.44	15,524
150	Khalid Mahmood	*Lab*	Birmingham, Perry Barr	28.32	11,908
151	Nigel Evans	*Con*	Ribble Valley	28.25	14,769
152	Shabana Mahmood	*Lab*	Birmingham, Ladywood	28.20	10,105
153	William Cash	*Con*	Stone	28.14	13,292
154	John Spellar	*Lab*	Warley	28.11	10,756
155	Richard Ottaway	*Con*	Croydon South	28.08	15,818
156	Nicholas Boles	*Con*	Grantham and Stamford	28.08	14,826
157	Stephen Dorrell	*Con*	Charnwood	28.07	15,029
158	Claire Perry	*Con*	Devizes	28.06	13,005

				%	Majority
159	Alan Haselhurst	*Con*	Saffron Walden	28.00	15,242
160	Douglas Carswell	*Con*	Clacton	27.99	12,068
161	Andrew Tyrie	*Con*	Chichester	27.96	15,877
162	Peter Lilley	*Con*	Hitchin and Harpenden	27.91	15,271
163	Denis MacShane	*Lab*	Rotherham	27.89	10,462
164	Nick Gibb	*Con*	Bognor Regis and Littlehampton	27.88	13,063
165	Mark Prisk	*Con*	Hertford and Stortford	27.88	15,437
166	Jeremy Corbyn	*Lab*	Islington North	27.83	12,401
167	Wayne David	*Lab*	Caerphilly	27.80	10,755
168	Mary Glindon	*Lab*	North Tyneside	27.76	12,884
169	David Willetts	*Con*	Havant	27.70	12,160
170	Nadine Dorries	*Con*	Mid Bedfordshire	27.60	15,152
171	Peter Tapsell	*Con*	Louth and Horncastle	27.47	13,871
172	Brian Donohoe	*Lab*	Central Ayrshire	27.34	12,007
173	George Freeman	*Con*	Mid Norfolk	27.29	13,856
174	George Mudie	*Lab*	Leeds East	27.22	10,293
175	Crispin Blunt	*Con*	Reigate	27.19	13,591
176	Matt Hancock	*Con*	West Suffolk	27.14	13,050
177	Bob Ainsworth	*Lab*	Coventry North East	27.14	11,775
178	Mike Penning	*Con*	Hemel Hempstead	27.10	13,406
179	Elizabeth Truss	*Con*	South West Norfolk	26.73	13,140
180	Cathy Jamieson	*Lab/Co-op*	Kilmarnock and Loudoun	26.59	12,378
181	James Duddridge	*Con*	Rochford and Southend East	26.54	11,050
182	David Hamilton	*Lab*	Midlothian	26.37	10,349
183	Peter Hain	*Lab*	Neath	26.33	9,775
184	Greg Knight	*Con*	East Yorkshire	26.31	13,486
185	Damian Hinds	*Con*	East Hampshire	26.30	13,497
186	Ed Miliband	*Lab*	Doncaster North	26.30	10,909
187	David Gauke	*Con*	South West Hertfordshire	26.29	14,920
188	Tony Lloyd	*Lab*	Manchester Central	26.15	10,439
189	Andrew Gwynne	*Lab*	Denton and Reddish	26.12	9,831
190	Maria Miller	*Con*	Basingstoke	26.01	13,176
191	Stuart Bell	*Lab*	Middlesbrough	25.97	8,689
192	Jeremy Wright	*Con*	Kenilworth and Southam	25.92	12,552
193	John Bercow	*Speaker*	Buckingham	25.92	12,529
194	Daniel Poulter	*Con*	Central Suffolk and North Ipswich	25.81	13,786
195	Gordon Henderson	*Con*	Sittingbourne and Sheppey	25.49	12,383
196	Dennis Skinner	*Lab*	Bolsover	25.42	11,182
197	John McDonnell	*Lab*	Hayes and Harlington	25.39	10,824
198	Clive Betts	*Lab*	Sheffield South East	25.37	10,505

				%	Majority
199	Alan Duncan	*Con*	Rutland and Melton	25.35	14,000
200	Don Foster	*Lib Dem*	Bath	25.24	11,883
201	Karl Turner	*Lab*	Kingston upon Hull East	25.15	8,597
202	Rory Stewart	*Con*	Penrith and The Border	24.93	11,241
203	Fiona O'Donnell	*Lab*	East Lothian	24.93	12,258
204	John Randall	*Con*	Uxbridge and South Ruislip	24.88	11,216
205	John Redwood	*Con*	Wokingham	24.74	13,492
206	Paul Murphy	*Lab*	Torfaen	24.72	9,306
207	Kate Hoey	*Lab*	Vauxhall	24.66	10,651
208	Justine Greening	*Con*	Putney	24.65	10,053
209	Nick Raynsford	*Lab*	Greenwich and Woolwich	24.65	10,153
210	Malcolm Rifkind	*Con*	Kensington	24.51	8,616
211	Graham Stuart	*Con*	Beverley and Holderness	24.41	12,987
212	Michael Connarty	*Lab*	Linlithgow and East Falkirk	24.40	12,553
213	Liam Byrne	*Lab*	Birmingham, Hodge Hill	24.28	10,302
214	Stephen Hammond	*Con*	Wimbledon	24.07	11,408
215	Ed Vaizey	*Con*	Wantage	24.04	13,547
216	David Evennett	*Con*	Bexleyheath and Crayford	23.95	10,344
217	David Rutley	*Con*	Macclesfield	23.89	11,959
218	Peter Bottomley	*Con*	Worthing West	23.88	11,729
219	Pauline Latham	*Con*	Mid Derbyshire	23.85	11,292
220	Tim Farron	*Lib Dem*	Westmorland and Lonsdale	23.82	12,264
221	David Davis	*Con*	Haltemprice and Howden	23.81	11,602
222	Andy Love	*Lab/Co-op*	Edmonton	23.81	9,613
223	Mark Hendrick	*Lab/Co-op*	Preston	23.79	7,733
224	Lisa Nandy	*Lab*	Wigan	23.76	10,487
225	Yvette Cooper	*Lab*	Normanton, Pontefract and Castleford	23.74	10,979
226	Graham Allen	*Lab*	Nottingham North	23.74	8,138
227	David Lidington	*Con*	Aylesbury	23.73	12,618
228	Nigel Adams	*Con*	Selby and Ainsty	23.71	12,265
229	George Hollingbery	*Con*	Meon Valley	23.66	12,125
230	David Heyes	*Lab*	Ashton under Lyne	23.66	9,094
231	Gregory Barker	*Con*	Bexhill and Battle	23.60	12,880
232	Theresa Villiers	*Con*	Chipping Barnet	23.57	11,927
233	Graham Brady	*Con*	Altrincham and Sale West	23.47	11,595
234	Geoffrey Clifton-Brown	*Con*	The Cotswolds	23.46	12,864
235	Norman Lamb	*Lib Dem*	North Norfolk	23.41	11,626
236	Bernard Jenkin	*Con*	Harwich and North Essex	23.36	11,447
237	Stella Creasy	*Lab/Co-op*	Walthamstow	23.12	9,478
238	Sheila Gilmore	*Lab*	Edinburgh East	23.03	9,181

				%	Majority
239	Tim Loughton	*Con*	East Worthing and Shoreham	22.95	11,105
240	Peter Bone	*Con*	Wellingborough	22.82	11,787
241	Rushanara Ali	*Lab*	Bethnal Green and Bow	22.82	11,574
242	David Laws	*Lib Dem*	Yeovil	22.81	13,036
243	Mark Harper	*Con*	Forest of Dean	22.69	11,064
244	Julian Lewis	*Con*	New Forest East	22.60	11,307
245	Menzies Campbell	*Lib Dem*	North East Fife	22.58	9,048
246	Graeme Morrice	*Lab*	Livingston	22.52	10,791
247	Nadhim Zahawi	*Con*	Stratford-on-Avon	22.45	11,346
248	Jon Trickett	*Lab*	Hemsworth	22.45	9,844
249	David Davies	*Con*	Monmouth	22.41	10,425
250	Sammy Wilson	*DUP*	East Antrim	22.20	6,770
251	Frank Doran	*Lab*	Aberdeen North	22.18	8,361
252	Mike Gapes	*Lab/Co-op*	Ilford South	22.06	11,297
253	Elfyn Llwyd	*PlC*	Dwyfor Meirionnydd	22.03	6,367
254	Sajid Javid	*Con*	Bromsgrove	21.90	11,308
255	Chi Onwurah	*Lab*	Newcastle upon Tyne Central	21.85	7,464
256	Yasmin Qureshi	*Lab*	Bolton South East	21.80	8,634
257	Michael Meacher	*Lab*	Oldham West and Royton	21.79	9,352
258	Mark Williams	*Lib Dem*	Ceredigion	21.76	8,324
259	Virendra Sharma	*Lab*	Ealing Southall	21.73	9,291
260	Jack Straw	*Lab*	Blackburn	21.66	9,856
261	Phil Wilson	*Lab*	Sedgefield	21.62	8,696
262	Sandra Osborne	*Lab*	Ayr, Carrick and Cumnock	21.60	9,911
263	Katy Clark	*Lab*	North Ayrshire and Arran	21.46	9,895
264	Edward Leigh	*Con*	Gainsborough	21.44	10,559
265	Gareth Johnson	*Con*	Dartford	21.22	10,628
266	Kwasi Kwarteng	*Con*	Spelthorne	21.18	10,019
267	Andrew Murrison	*Con*	South West Wiltshire	21.15	10,367
268	David Ruffley	*Con*	Bury St Edmunds	21.08	12,380
269	Chris Leslie	*Lab/Co-op*	Nottingham East	21.05	6,969
270	Greg Mulholland	*Lib Dem*	Leeds North West	20.93	9,103
271	Richard Benyon	*Con*	Newbury	20.90	12,248
272	Bill Wiggin	*Con*	North Herefordshire	20.78	9,887
273	Mark Reckless	*Con*	Rochester and Strood	20.75	9,953
274	Mark Pritchard	*Con*	The Wrekin	20.56	9,450
275	Stephen Williams	*Lib Dem*	Bristol West	20.54	11,366
276	Francis Maude	*Con*	Horsham	20.52	11,460
277	Joan Walley	*Lab*	Stoke-on-Trent North	20.49	8,235
278	Angela Eagle	*Lab*	Wallasey	20.42	8,507

				%	Majority
279	Jim Murphy	*Lab*	East Renfrewshire	20.36	10,420
280	Vincent Cable	*Lib Dem*	Twickenham	20.33	12,140
281	David Anderson	*Lab*	Blaydon	20.30	9,117
282	Philip Davies	*Con*	Shipley	20.12	9,944
283	Philip Dunne	*Con*	Ludlow	20.01	9,749
284	Jonathan Djanogly	*Con*	Huntingdon	19.94	10,819
285	Kate Green	*Lab*	Stretford and Urmston	19.90	8,935
286	Richard Bacon	*Con*	South Norfolk	19.89	10,940
287	Steve Baker	*Con*	Wycombe	19.85	9,560
288	Margaret Ritchie	*SDLP*	South Down	19.75	8,412
289	Adam Holloway	*Con*	Gravesham	19.69	9,312
290	Jim McGovern	*Lab*	Dundee West	19.60	7,278
291	Stephen Pound	*Lab*	Ealing North	19.51	9,301
292	Tessa Jowell	*Lab*	Dulwich and West Norwood	19.42	9,365
293	Philip Hollobone	*Con*	Kettering	19.21	9,094
294	Damian Collins	*Con*	Folkestone and Hythe	19.17	10,122
295	Simon Hughes	*Lib Dem*	Bermondsey and Old Southwark	19.10	8,530
296	Pat McFadden	*Lab*	Wolverhampton South East	19.03	6,593
297	Luciana Berger	*Lab/Co-op*	Liverpool Wavertree	18.90	7,167
298	Peter Soulsby	*Lab*	Leicester South	18.69	8,808
299	Danny Alexander	*Lib Dem*	Inverness, Nairn, Badenoch and Strathspey	18.61	8,765
300	Paul Goggins	*Lab*	Wythenshawe and Sale East	18.59	7,575
301	Alistair Darling	*Lab*	Edinburgh South West	18.58	8,447
302	Rehman Chishti	*Con*	Gillingham and Rainham	18.55	8,680
303	Conor Murphy	*Sinn Féin*	Newry and Armagh	18.55	8,331
304	Ian Lavery	*Lab*	Wansbeck	18.37	7,031
305	Alan Johnson	*Lab*	Kingston upon Hull West and Hessle	18.22	5,740
306	Frank Dobson	*Lab*	Holborn and St Pancras	18.19	9,942
307	Julian Smith	*Con*	Skipton and Ripon	18.18	9,950
308	Rachel Reeves	*Lab*	Leeds West	18.10	7,016
309	Jim Shannon	*DUP*	Strangford	18.08	5,876
310	Edward Garnier	*Con*	Harborough	18.00	9,877
311	Anne McGuire	*Lab*	Stirling	17.85	8,354
312	Tom Watson	*Lab*	West Bromwich East	17.64	6,696
313	Tobias Ellwood	*Con*	Bournemouth East	17.55	7,728
314	Gerald Kaufman	*Lab*	Manchester Gorton	17.49	6,703
315	Kelvin Hopkins	*Lab*	Luton North	17.48	7,520
316	Patricia Glass	*Lab*	North West Durham	17.37	7,612
317	Ann Coffey	*Lab*	Stockport	17.34	6,784
318	Alasdair McDonnell	*SDLP*	Belfast South	17.33	5,926

			%	Majority
319 Ronnie Campbell	*Lab*	Blyth Valley	17.29	6,668
320 David Burrowes	*Con*	Enfield Southgate	17.19	7,626
321 Hugo Swire	*Con*	East Devon	17.17	9,114
322 Tristram Hunt	*Lab*	Stoke-on-Trent Central	17.14	5,566
323 Mel Stride	*Con*	Central Devon	17.13	9,230
324 Neil Parish	*Con*	Tiverton and Honiton	16.98	9,320
325 Ian Liddell-Grainger	*Con*	Bridgwater and West Somerset	16.97	9,249
326 Rebecca Harris	*Con*	Castle Point	16.95	7,632
327 Tim Yeo	*Con*	South Suffolk	16.90	8,689
328 Alex Cunningham	*Lab*	Stockton North	16.90	6,676
329 David Jones	*Con*	Clwyd West	16.84	6,419
330 John Thurso	*Lib Dem*	Caithness, Sutherland and Easter Ross	16.78	4,826
331 David Amess	*Con*	Southend West	16.67	7,270
332 Mark Lancaster	*Con*	Milton Keynes North	16.63	8,961
333 Therese Coffey	*Con*	Suffolk Coastal	16.63	9,128
334 Laura Sandys	*Con*	South Thanet	16.58	7,617
335 John Mann	*Lab*	Bassetlaw	16.57	8,215
336 Penny Mordaunt	*Con*	Portsmouth North	16.52	7,289
337 Robert Goodwill	*Con*	Scarborough and Whitby	16.50	8,130
338 John Cryer	*Lab*	Leyton and Wanstead	15.98	6,416
339 Robert Syms	*Con*	Poole	15.90	7,541
340 Julie Elliott	*Lab*	Sunderland Central	15.76	6,725
341 Adrian Bailey	*Lab/Co-op*	West Bromwich West	15.62	5,651
342 Eric Joyce	*Lab*	Falkirk	15.45	7,843
343 Brian Binley	*Con*	Northampton South	15.40	6,004
344 James Gray	*Con*	North Wiltshire	15.37	7,483
345 Barry Gardiner	*Lab*	Brent North	15.35	8,028
346 Helen Jones	*Lab*	Warrington North	15.32	6,771
347 Gregory Campbell	*DUP*	East Londonderry	15.32	5,355
348 Karen Bradley	*Con*	Staffordshire Moorlands	15.27	6,689
349 Norman Baker	*Lib Dem*	Lewes	15.27	7,647
350 Robert Wilson	*Con*	Reading East	15.21	7,605
351 Andrew Stunell	*Lib Dem*	Hazel Grove	15.18	6,371
352 Bob Russell	*Lib Dem*	Colchester	15.13	6,982
353 Andrew Turner	*Con*	Isle of Wight	14.98	10,527
354 Daniel Kawczynski	*Con*	Shrewsbury and Atcham	14.98	7,944
355 Rosie Winterton	*Lab*	Doncaster Central	14.92	6,229
356 Heidi Alexander	*Lab*	Lewisham East	14.90	6,216
357 Margaret Beckett	*Lab*	Derby South	14.86	6,122
358 Richard Drax	*Con*	South Dorset	14.79	7,443

				%	Majority
359	Steve Webb	*Lib Dem*	Thornbury and Yate	14.76	7,116
360	Andrew Bridgen	*Con*	North West Leicestershire	14.46	7,511
361	Iain Wright	*Lab*	Hartlepool	14.41	5,509
362	Jack Lopresti	*Con*	Filton and Bradley Stoke	14.31	6,914
363	Russell Brown	*Lab*	Dumfries and Galloway	14.28	7,449
364	Meg Munn	*Lab/Co-op*	Sheffield Heeley	14.21	5,807
365	Marsha Singh	*Lab*	Bradford West	14.20	5,763
366	Heather Wheeler	*Con*	South Derbyshire	14.14	7,128
367	Robert Walter	*Con*	North Dorset	14.08	7,625
368	Justin Tomlinson	*Con*	North Swindon	14.04	7,060
369	Anne Milton	*Con*	Guildford	14.00	7,782
370	Fiona Bruce	*Con*	Congleton	13.91	7,063
371	Hugh Bayley	*Lab*	York Central	13.88	6,451
372	Tracey Crouch	*Con*	Chatham and Aylesford	13.85	6,069
373	Keith Simpson	*Con*	Broadland	13.84	7,292
374	Malcolm Bruce	*Lib Dem*	Gordon	13.83	6,748
375	Hazel Blears	*Lab*	Salford and Eccles	13.78	5,725
376	John Pugh	*Lib Dem*	Southport	13.77	6,024
377	Angus Robertson	*SNP*	Moray	13.63	5,590
378	Liam Fox	*Con*	North Somerset	13.57	7,862
379	Julian Huppert	*Lib Dem*	Cambridge	13.55	6,792
380	Geoffrey Robinson	*Lab*	Coventry North West	13.51	6,288
381	Teresa Pearce	*Lab*	Erith and Thamesmead	13.43	5,703
382	Conor Burns	*Con*	Bournemouth West	13.40	5,583
383	Guy Opperman	*Con*	Hexham	13.31	5,788
384	Andrew Lansley	*Con*	South Cambridgeshire	13.27	7,838
385	Nicholas Soames	*Con*	Mid Sussex	13.25	7,402
386	Edward Davey	*Lib Dem*	Kingston and Surbiton	13.24	7,560
387	Karen Lumley	*Con*	Redditch	13.22	5,821
388	Ann McKechin	*Lab*	Glasgow North	13.16	3,898
389	Christopher Pincher	*Con*	Tamworth	13.13	6,090
390	Jim Dobbin	*Lab/Co-op*	Heywood and Middleton	12.95	5,971
391	Jim Dowd	*Lab*	Lewisham West and Penge	12.94	5,828
392	Jim Fitzpatrick	*Lab*	Poplar and Limehouse	12.91	6,030
393	Steve Metcalfe	*Con*	South Basildon and East Thurrock	12.90	5,772
394	Jonathan Lord	*Con*	Woking	12.90	6,807
395	Angus MacNeil	*SNP*	Na h-Eileanan An Iar	12.81	1,885
396	Mark Durkan	*SDLP*	Foyle	12.73	4,824
397	Helen Goodman	*Lab*	Bishop Auckland	12.68	5,218
398	Jenny Willott	*Lib Dem*	Cardiff Central	12.66	4,576

				%	Majority
399	Andrew Griffiths	*Con*	Burton	12.65	6,304
400	Mark Pawsey	*Con*	Rugby	12.64	6,000
401	Dai Havard	*Lab*	Merthyr Tydfil and Rhymney	12.64	4,056
402	Alok Sharma	*Con*	Reading West	12.63	6,004
403	Mike Hancock	*Lib Dem*	Portsmouth South	12.60	5,200
404	Harriett Baldwin	*Con*	West Worcestershire	12.59	6,804
405	Nia Griffith	*Lab*	Llanelli	12.55	4,701
406	Kevin Barron	*Lab*	Rother Valley	12.54	5,866
407	Lynne Featherstone	*Lib Dem*	Hornsey and Wood Green	12.49	6,875
408	Henry Smith	*Con*	Crawley	12.48	5,928
409	Ian Swales	*Lib Dem*	Redcar	12.43	5,214
410	Craig Whittaker	*Con*	Calder Valley	12.42	6,431
411	Alan Meale	*Lab*	Mansfield	12.42	6,012
412	Mike Freer	*Con*	Finchley and Golders Green	12.32	5,809
413	Gerald Howarth	*Con*	Aldershot	12.31	5,586
414	John Glen	*Con*	Salisbury	12.31	5,966
415	Julian Brazier	*Con*	Canterbury	12.29	6,048
416	Jane Ellison	*Con*	Battersea	12.25	5,977
417	Gerry Sutcliffe	*Lab*	Bradford South	12.16	4,622
418	Helen Grant	*Con*	Maidstone and The Weald	12.04	5,889
419	Edward Timpson	*Con*	Crewe and Nantwich	11.84	6,046
420	John Woodcock	*Lab/Co-op*	Barrow and Furness	11.80	5,208
421	Nick Brown	*Lab*	Newcastle upon Tyne East	11.77	4,453
422	Andrew Percy	*Con*	Brigg and Goole	11.73	5,147
423	Laurence Robertson	*Con*	Tewkesbury	11.69	6,310
424	Tony Cunningham	*Lab*	Workington	11.65	4,575
425	Stephen Crabb	*Con*	Preseli Pembrokeshire	11.63	4,605
426	Kevin Brennan	*Lab*	Cardiff West	11.60	4,750
427	Michael Moore	*Lib Dem*	Berwickshire, Roxburgh and Selkirk	11.58	5,675
428	Fiona Mactaggart	*Lab*	Slough	11.57	5,523
429	Lee Scott	*Con*	Ilford North	11.50	5,404
430	Tom Brake	*Lib Dem*	Carshalton and Wallington	11.46	5,260
431	Guto Bebb	*Con*	Aberconwy	11.34	3,398
432	Nick Harvey	*Lib Dem*	North Devon	11.34	5,821
433	Robert Halfon	*Con*	Harlow	11.22	4,925
434	Liz Kendall	*Lab*	Leicester West	11.21	4,017
435	Thomas Docherty	*Lab*	Dunfermline and West Fife	11.18	5,470
436	Ian Lucas	*Lab*	Wrexham	11.09	3,658
437	Barry Sheerman	*Lab/Co-op*	Huddersfield	11.04	4,472
438	Margot James	*Con*	Stourbridge	10.93	5,164

				%	Majority
439	Alan Campbell	*Lab*	Tynemouth	10.90	5,739
440	Jeremy Lefroy	*Con*	Stafford	10.87	5,460
441	Stewart Jackson	*Con*	Peterborough	10.82	4,861
442	Lorraine Fullbrook	*Con*	South Ribble	10.79	5,554
443	Alun Michael	*Lab/Co-op*	Cardiff South and Penarth	10.61	4,709
444	Charlie Elphicke	*Con*	Dover	10.47	5,274
445	Eilidh Whiteford	*SNP*	Banff and Buchan	10.47	4,027
446	Barbara Keeley	*Lab*	Worsley and Eccles South	10.40	4,337
447	Robert Flello	*Lab*	Stoke-on-Trent South	10.36	4,130
448	Jim Paice	*Con*	South East Cambridgeshire	10.32	5,946
449	Sarah Wollaston	*Con*	Totnes	10.30	4,927
450	Gordon Banks	*Lab*	Ochil and South Perthshire	10.28	5,187
451	Chris Kelly	*Con*	Dudley South	10.10	3,856
452	Brandon Lewis	*Con*	Great Yarmouth	9.93	4,276
453	Dawn Primarolo	*Lab*	Bristol South	9.79	4,734
454	Andrew Miller	*Lab*	Ellesmere Port and Neston	9.79	4,331
455	Roger Williams	*Lib Dem*	Brecon and Radnorshire	9.65	3,747
456	Jacob Rees-Mogg	*Con*	North East Somerset	9.60	4,914
457	Alan Keen	*Lab/Co-op*	Feltham and Heston	9.60	4,658
458	Martin Vickers	*Con*	Cleethorpes	9.56	4,298
459	Fabian Hamilton	*Lab*	Leeds North East	9.56	4,545
460	Jake Berry	*Con*	Rossendale and Darwen	9.53	4,493
461	David Crausby	*Lab*	Bolton North East	9.45	4,084
462	Iain Stewart	*Con*	Milton Keynes South	9.40	5,201
463	Simon Burns	*Con*	Chelmsford	9.36	5,110
464	Martin Horwood	*Lib Dem*	Cheltenham	9.32	4,920
465	Andrew Bingham	*Con*	High Peak	9.29	4,677
466	David Tredinnick	*Con*	Bosworth	9.27	5,032
467	Jack Dromey	*Lab*	Birmingham, Erdington	9.22	3,277
468	Chloe Smith	*Con*	Norwich North	9.16	3,901
469	Jonathan Edwards	*PIC*	Carmarthen East and Dinefwr	9.16	3,481
470	David Mundell	*Con*	Dumfriesshire, Clydesdale and Tweeddale	9.14	4,194
471	Peter Wishart	*SNP*	Perth and North Perthshire	9.07	4,379
472	Jamie Reed	*Lab*	Copeland	8.96	3,833
473	Rosie Cooper	*Lab*	West Lancashire	8.96	4,343
474	Paul Flynn	*Lab*	Newport West	8.92	3,544
475	Andrew Smith	*Lab*	Oxford East	8.87	4,581
476	Alun Cairns	*Con*	Vale of Glamorgan	8.85	4,307
477	Jason McCartney	*Con*	Colne Valley	8.75	4,837
478	Mike Weir	*SNP*	Angus	8.65	3,282

			%	Majority
479 Caroline Nokes	*Con*	Romsey and Southampton North	8.49	4,156
480 Mike Wood	*Lab*	Batley and Spen	8.48	4,406
481 Simon Hart	*Con*	Carmarthen West and South Pembrokeshire	8.45	3,423
482 James Cunningham	*Lab*	Coventry South	8.37	3,845
483 Adrian Sanders	*Lib Dem*	Torbay	8.29	4,078
484 Caroline Flint	*Lab*	Don Valley	8.28	3,595
485 Kerry McCarthy	*Lab*	Bristol East	8.27	3,722
486 Emily Thornberry	*Lab*	Islington South and Finsbury	8.19	3,569
487 Mike Crockart	*Lib Dem*	Edinburgh West	8.19	3,803
488 Susan Elan Jones	*Lab*	Clwyd South	8.17	2,834
489 Anne Begg	*Lab*	Aberdeen South	8.15	3,506
490 Robert Smith	*Lib Dem*	West Aberdeenshire and Kincardine	8.15	3,684
491 David Simpson	*DUP*	Upper Bann	8.12	3,361
492 Alec Shelbrooke	*Con*	Elmet and Rothwell	8.10	4,521
493 Stephen McPartland	*Con*	Stevenage	8.01	3,578
494 Bill Esterson	*Lab*	Sefton Central	7.97	3,862
495 Andrew Stephenson	*Con*	Pendle	7.96	3,585
496 Jenny Chapman	*Lab*	Darlington	7.90	3,388
497 Angie Bray	*Con*	Ealing Central and Acton	7.87	3,716
498 Roger Godsiff	*Lab*	Birmingham, Hall Green	7.80	3,799
499 Catherine McKinnell	*Lab*	Newcastle upon Tyne North	7.77	3,414
500 Owen Smith	*Lab*	Pontypridd	7.59	2,785
501 Alan Reid	*Lib Dem*	Argyll and Bute	7.59	3,431
502 Robert Buckland	*Con*	South Swindon	7.52	3,544
503 Steve McCabe	*Lab*	Birmingham, Selly Oak	7.48	3,482
504 Andy Slaughter	*Lab*	Hammersmith	7.48	3,549
505 John Hemming	*Lib Dem*	Birmingham, Yardley	7.35	3,002
506 Mark Tami	*Lab*	Alyn and Deeside	7.31	2,919
507 Graham Jones	*Lab*	Hyndburn	7.24	3,090
508 Chris Huhne	*Lib Dem*	Eastleigh	7.20	3,864
509 Chris White	*Con*	Warwick and Leamington	7.16	3,513
510 Albert Owen	*Lab*	Ynys Môn	7.14	2,461
511 Emma Reynolds	*Lab*	Wolverhampton North East	7.12	2,484
512 Bob Blackman	*Con*	Harrow East	7.09	3,403
513 Nicky Morgan	*Con*	Loughborough	7.09	3,744
514 Chris Ruane	*Lab*	Vale of Clwyd	7.06	2,509
515 Aidan Burley	*Con*	Cannock Chase	7.01	3,195
516 Alan Beith	*Lib Dem*	Berwick-upon-Tweed	7.00	2,690
517 Chuka Umunna	*Lab*	Streatham	6.96	3,259
518 Julian Sturdy	*Con*	York Outer	6.92	3,688

				%	Majority
519	Zac Goldsmith	*Con*	Richmond Park	6.90	4,091
520	Nic Dakin	*Lab*	Scunthorpe	6.88	2,549
521	Jeremy Browne	*Lib Dem*	Taunton Deane	6.87	3,993
522	Oliver Letwin	*Con*	West Dorset	6.84	3,923
523	Ivan Lewis	*Lab*	Bury South	6.82	3,292
524	Gareth Thomas	*Lab/Co-op*	Harrow West	6.82	3,143
525	Jonathan Reynolds	*Lab/Co-op*	Stalybridge and Hyde	6.71	2,744
526	Richard Burden	*Lab*	Birmingham, Northfield	6.65	2,782
527	Roberta Blackman-Woods	*Lab*	City of Durham	6.63	3,067
528	Stephen Lloyd	*Lib Dem*	Eastbourne	6.59	3,435
529	Angela Smith	*Lab*	Penistone and Stocksbridge	6.55	3,049
530	Charlotte Leslie	*Con*	Bristol North West	6.50	3,274
531	Sheryll Murray	*Con*	South East Cornwall	6.49	3,220
532	Martin Caton	*Lab*	Gower	6.44	2,683
533	Dan Rogerson	*Lib Dem*	North Cornwall	6.36	2,981
534	Mark Hunter	*Lib Dem*	Cheadle	6.23	3,272
535	Esther McVey	*Con*	Wirral West	6.19	2,436
536	Kris Hopkins	*Con*	Keighley	6.16	2,940
537	David Hanson	*Lab*	Delyn	6.14	2,272
538	Robin Walker	*Con*	Worcester	6.09	2,982
539	Nigel Dodds	*DUP*	Belfast North	6.01	2,224
540	Gavin Barwell	*Con*	Croydon Central	5.97	2,969
541	Jon Cruddas	*Lab*	Dagenham and Rainham	5.95	2,630
542	Madeleine Moon	*Lab*	Bridgend	5.90	2,263
543	Hywel Williams	*PlC*	Arfon	5.58	1,455
544	Stephen Mosley	*Con*	City of Chester	5.52	2,583
545	Gavin Shuker	*Lab/Co-op*	Luton South	5.52	2,329
546	Alan Whitehead	*Lab*	Southampton Test	5.46	2,413
547	Steve Brine	*Con*	Winchester	5.45	3,048
548	Karen Buck	*Lab*	Westminster North	5.37	2,126
549	Geoffrey Cox	*Con*	Torridge and West Devon	5.35	2,957
550	Paul Maynard	*Con*	Blackpool North and Cleveleys	5.30	2,150
551	Gordon Marsden	*Lab*	Blackpool South	5.26	1,852
552	Jessica Lee	*Con*	Erewash	5.25	2,501
553	Lindsay Hoyle	*Lab*	Chorley	5.21	2,593
554	Ben Bradshaw	*Lab*	Exeter	5.21	2,721
555	Natascha Engel	*Lab*	North East Derbyshire	5.20	2,445
556	Mark Garnier	*Con*	Wyre Forest	5.19	2,643
557	Jesse Norman	*Con*	Hereford and South Herefordshire	5.13	2,481
558	Chris Skidmore	*Con*	Kingswood	5.10	2,445

				%	Majority
559	John Penrose	*Con*	Weston-Super-Mare	5.10	2,691
560	David Nuttall	*Con*	Bury North	4.99	2,243
561	Sadiq Khan	*Lab*	Tooting	4.98	2,524
562	Michael Ellis	*Con*	Northampton North	4.81	1,936
563	Jessica Morden	*Lab*	Newport East	4.79	1,650
564	Richard Graham	*Con*	Gloucester	4.77	2,420
565	Duncan Hames	*Lib Dem*	Chippenham	4.72	2,470
566	Marcus Jones	*Con*	Nuneaton	4.63	2,069
567	James Morris	*Con*	Halesowen and Rowley Regis	4.60	2,023
568	Jo Swinson	*Lib Dem*	East Dunbartonshire	4.55	2,184
569	Stewart Hosie	*SNP*	Dundee East	4.49	1,821
570	Naomi Long	*All*	Belfast East	4.45	1,533
571	Ben Gummer	*Con*	Ipswich	4.43	2,079
572	Anne Main	*Con*	St Albans	4.36	2,305
573	Lilian Greenwood	*Lab*	Nottingham South	4.34	1,772
574	Gordon Birtwistle	*Lib Dem*	Burnley	4.34	1,818
575	Valerie Vaz	*Lab*	Walsall South	4.29	1,755
576	John Leech	*Lib Dem*	Manchester Withington	4.10	1,850
577	Amber Rudd	*Con*	Hastings and Rye	4.00	1,993
578	Clive Efford	*Lab*	Eltham	3.96	1,663
579	Vernon Coaker	*Lab*	Gedling	3.86	1,859
580	Alison Seabeck	*Lab*	Plymouth, Moor View	3.82	1,588
581	Nick de Bois	*Con*	Enfield North	3.81	1,692
582	Mike Weatherley	*Con*	Hove	3.75	1,868
583	Andrew George	*Lib Dem*	St Ives	3.74	1,719
584	Mary Macleod	*Con*	Brentford and Isleworth	3.64	1,958
585	Mark Lazarowicz	*Lab/Co-op*	Edinburgh North and Leith	3.64	1,724
586	Tom Blenkinsop	*Lab*	Middlesbrough South and East Cleveland	3.63	1,677
587	Mary Creagh	*Lab*	Wakefield	3.63	1,613
588	Louise Bagshawe	*Con*	Corby	3.60	1,951
589	Paul Farrelly	*Lab*	Newcastle-under-Lyme	3.59	1,552
590	Glyn Davies	*Con*	Montgomeryshire	3.50	1,184
591	William McCrea	*DUP*	South Antrim	3.48	1,183
592	Stuart Andrew	*Con*	Pudsey	3.38	1,659
593	Linda Riordan	*Lab/Co-op*	Halifax	3.38	1,472
594	Paul Burstow	*Lib Dem*	Sutton and Cheam	3.31	1,608
595	Simon Kirby	*Con*	Brighton Kemptown	3.11	1,328
596	Gisela Stuart	*Lab*	Birmingham, Edgbaston	3.06	1,274
597	Richard Fuller	*Con*	Bedford	3.00	1,353
598	David Heath	*Lib Dem*	Somerton and Frome	3.00	1,817

				%	Majority
599	Sarah Teather	*Lib Dem*	Brent Central	2.97	1,345
600	Simon Reevell	*Con*	Dewsbury	2.83	1,526
601	David Mowat	*Con*	Warrington South	2.83	1,553
602	Stephen Gilbert	*Lib Dem*	St Austell and Newquay	2.78	1,312
603	David Winnick	*Lab*	Walsall North	2.74	990
604	Oliver Colvile	*Con*	Plymouth, Sutton and Devonport	2.62	1,149
605	Richard Harrington	*Con*	Watford	2.58	1,425
606	Caroline Lucas	*Green*	Brighton Pavilion	2.42	1,252
607	David Wright	*Lab*	Telford	2.37	981
608	Karl McCartney	*Con*	Lincoln	2.31	1,058
609	Graham Evans	*Con*	Weaver Vale	2.25	991
610	Ed Balls	*Lab/Co-op*	Morley and Outwood	2.25	1,101
611	Neil Carmichael	*Con*	Stroud	2.24	1,299
612	Austin Mitchell	*Lab*	Great Grimsby	2.17	714
613	John Stevenson	*Con*	Carlisle	2.02	853
614	David Morris	*Con*	Morecambe and Lunesdale	1.99	866
615	Andrew Jones	*Con*	Harrogate and Knaresborough	1.96	1,039
616	Simon Danczuk	*Lab*	Rochdale	1.94	889
617	Diana Johnson	*Lab*	Kingston upon Hull North	1.93	641
618	Paul Uppal	*Con*	Wolverhampton South West	1.72	691
619	Ian Austin	*Lab*	Dudley North	1.68	649
620	Peter Aldous	*Con*	Waveney	1.50	769
621	Tessa Munt	*Lib Dem*	Wells	1.43	800
622	Geraint Davies	*Lab/Co-op*	Swansea West	1.42	504
623	Chris Williamson	*Lab*	Derby North	1.36	613
624	Alison McGovern	*Lab*	Wirral South	1.33	531
625	Toby Perkins	*Lab*	Chesterfield	1.20	549
626	Nigel Mills	*Con*	Amber Valley	1.17	536
627	Anne-Marie Morris	*Con*	Newton Abbot	1.08	523
628	David Ward	*Lib Dem*	Bradford East	0.90	365
629	Sarah Newton	*Con*	Truro and Falmouth	0.89	435
630	Eric Ollerenshaw	*Con*	Lancaster and Fleetwood	0.78	333
631	Anna Soubry	*Con*	Broxtowe	0.74	389
632	Ian Murray	*Lab*	Edinburgh South	0.72	316
633	James Wharton	*Con*	Stockton South	0.66	332
634	Simon Wright	*Lib Dem*	Norwich South	0.65	310
635	Annette Brooke	*Lib Dem*	Mid Dorset and North Poole	0.57	269
636	Mark Spencer	*Con*	Sherwood	0.44	214
637	John Denham	*Lab*	Southampton Itchen	0.43	192
638	Jonathan Evans	*Con*	Cardiff North	0.41	194

				%	Majority
639	Gloria De Piero	*Lab*	Ashfield	0.40	192
640	Paul Blomfield	*Lab*	Sheffield Central	0.40	165
641	Lorely Burt	*Lib Dem*	Solihull	0.32	175
642	Nicola Blackwood	*Con*	Oxford West and Abingdon	0.31	176
643	Matthew Offord	*Con*	Hendon	0.23	106
644	Phil Woolas	*Lab*	Oldham East and Saddleworth	0.23	103
645	Jackie Doyle-Price	*Con*	Thurrock	0.20	92
646	Julie Hilling	*Lab*	Bolton West	0.19	92
647	George Eustice	*Con*	Camborne and Redruth	0.16	66
648	Dan Byles	*Con*	North Warwickshire	0.11	54
649	Glenda Jackson	*Lab*	Hampstead and Kilburn	0.08	42
650	Michelle Gildernew	*Sinn Féin*	Fermanagh and South Tyrone	0.01	4

SEATS BY PERCENTAGE MAJORITY BY PARTY

CONSERVATIVE

			%	Majority
1	William Hague	Richmond (Yorkshire)	43.69	23,336
2	John Hayes	South Holland and The Deepings	43.60	21,880
3	Mark Francois	Rayleigh and Wickford	42.68	22,338
4	Greg Hands	Chelsea and Fulham	41.96	16,722
5	Dominic Grieve	Beaconsfield	41.50	21,782
6	Charles Walker	Broxbourne	41.18	18,804
7	John Whittingdale	Maldon	40.52	19,407
8	Richard Shepherd	Aldridge-Brownhills	39.48	15,256
9	David Cameron	Witney	39.36	22,740
10	Adam Afriyie	Windsor	38.42	19,054
11	Nick Hurd	Ruislip, Northwood and Pinner	37.96	19,060
12	Bob Stewart	Beckenham	37.29	17,784
13	James Clappison	Hertsmere	37.24	17,605
14	Christopher Heaton-Harris	Daventry	37.06	19,188
15	Hugh Robertson	Faversham and Mid Kent	36.58	17,088
16	Andrew Rosindell	Romford	36.48	16,954
17	Grant Shapps	Welwyn Hatfield	35.58	17,423
18	Desmond Swayne	New Forest West	35.52	16,896
19	Michael Fallon	Sevenoaks	35.45	17,515
20	John Stanley	Tonbridge and Malling	35.43	18,178
21	Jo Johnson	Orpington	35.17	17,200
22	James Arbuthnot	North East Hampshire	35.13	18,597
23	George Young	North West Hampshire	34.87	18,583
24	James Brokenshire	Old Bexley and Sidcup	34.86	15,857
25	Michael Fabricant	Lichfield	34.29	17,683
26	Philip Hammond	Runnymede and Weybridge	34.29	16,509
27	Andrea Leadsom	South Northamptonshire	34.19	20,478
28	Alistair Burt	North East Bedfordshire	34.10	18,942
29	Dominic Raab	Esher and Walton	34.09	18,593
30	Andrew Mitchell	Sutton Coldfield	33.61	17,005
31	Eric Pickles	Brentwood and Ongar	33.44	16,920
32	Stephen Phillips	Sleaford and North Hykeham	33.44	19,905
33	Gavin Williamson	South Staffordshire	32.89	16,590
34	Andrew Selous	South West Bedfordshire	32.79	16,649
35	Brooks Newmark	Braintree	32.76	16,121
36	Eleanor Laing	Epping Forest	32.48	15,131
37	Priti Patel	Witham	32.45	15,196

			%	Majority
38	Tony Baldry	Banbury	32.41	18,227
39	George Osborne	Tatton	32.03	14,487
40	Cheryl Gillan	Chesham and Amersham	31.86	16,710
41	Gary Streeter	South West Devon	31.84	15,874
42	Michael Gove	Surrey Heath	31.81	17,289
43	Robert Neill	Bromley and Chislehurst	31.56	13,900
44	Patrick Mercer	Newark	31.53	16,152
45	Mark Hoban	Fareham	31.45	17,092
46	Steve Barclay	North East Cambridgeshire	31.43	16,425
47	Damian Green	Ashford	31.34	17,297
48	Charles Hendry	Wealden	31.25	17,179
49	Theresa May	Maidenhead	31.22	16,769
50	Roger Gale	North Thanet	31.21	13,528
51	Christopher Chope	Christchurch	31.18	15,410
52	Caroline Spelman	Meriden	31.16	16,253
53	Peter Luff	Mid Worcestershire	31.15	15,864
54	John Howell	Henley	30.99	16,588
55	Henry Bellingham	North West Norfolk	30.98	14,810
56	Greg Clark	Tunbridge Wells	30.95	15,576
57	Sam Gyimah	East Surrey	30.88	16,874
58	Ben Wallace	Wyre and Preston North	30.84	15,844
59	Caroline Dinenage	Gosport	30.71	14,413
60	Angela Watkinson	Hornchurch and Upminster	30.66	16,371
61	Owen Paterson	North Shropshire	30.52	15,828
62	Mark Menzies	Fylde	30.18	13,185
63	Oliver Heald	North East Hertfordshire	30.13	15,194
64	Phillip Lee	Bracknell	30.12	15,704
65	Iain Duncan Smith	Chingford and Woodford Green	30.07	12,963
66	Mark Field	Cities of London and Westminster	29.99	11,076
67	Nick Herbert	Arundel and South Downs	29.81	16,691
68	John Baron	Basildon and Billericay	29.78	12,398
69	Patrick McLoughlin	Derbyshire Dales	29.64	13,866
70	Anne McIntosh	Thirsk and Malton	29.52	11,281
71	Kenneth Clarke	Rushcliffe	29.45	15,811
72	Chris Grayling	Epsom and Ewell	29.36	16,134
73	Stephen O'Brien	Eddisbury	29.19	13,255
74	Mark Simmonds	Boston and Skegness	28.81	12,426
75	Paul Beresford	Mole Valley	28.81	15,653
76	Shailesh Vara	North West Cambridgeshire	28.61	16,677
77	Jeremy Hunt	South West Surrey	28.50	16,318

			%	Majority
78	Andrew Robathan	South Leicestershire	28.44	15,524
79	Nigel Evans	Ribble Valley	28.25	14,769
80	William Cash	Stone	28.14	13,292
81	Richard Ottaway	Croydon South	28.08	15,818
82	Nicholas Boles	Grantham and Stamford	28.08	14,826
83	Stephen Dorrell	Charnwood	28.07	15,029
84	Claire Perry	Devizes	28.06	13,005
85	Alan Haselhurst	Saffron Walden	28.00	15,242
86	Douglas Carswell	Clacton	27.99	12,068
87	Andrew Tyrie	Chichester	27.96	15,877
88	Peter Lilley	Hitchin and Harpenden	27.91	15,271
89	Nick Gibb	Bognor Regis and Littlehampton	27.88	13,063
90	Mark Prisk	Hertford and Stortford	27.88	15,437
91	David Willetts	Havant	27.70	12,160
92	Nadine Dorries	Mid Bedfordshire	27.60	15,152
93	Peter Tapsell	Louth and Horncastle	27.47	13,871
94	George Freeman	Mid Norfolk	27.29	13,856
95	Crispin Blunt	Reigate	27.19	13,591
96	Matt Hancock	West Suffolk	27.14	13,050
97	Mike Penning	Hemel Hempstead	27.10	13,406
98	Elizabeth Truss	South West Norfolk	26.73	13,140
99	James Duddridge	Rochford and Southend East	26.54	11,050
100	Greg Knight	East Yorkshire	26.31	13,486
101	Damian Hinds	East Hampshire	26.30	13,497
102	David Gauke	South West Hertfordshire	26.29	14,920
103	Maria Miller	Basingstoke	26.01	13,176
104	Jeremy Wright	Kenilworth and Southam	25.92	12,552
105	Daniel Poulter	Central Suffolk and North Ipswich	25.81	13,786
106	Gordon Henderson	Sittingbourne and Sheppey	25.49	12,383
107	Alan Duncan	Rutland and Melton	25.35	14,000
108	Rory Stewart	Penrith and The Border	24.93	11,241
109	John Randall	Uxbridge and South Ruislip	24.88	11,216
110	John Redwood	Wokingham	24.74	13,492
111	Justine Greening	Putney	24.65	10,053
112	Malcolm Rifkind	Kensington	24.51	8,616
113	Graham Stuart	Beverley and Holderness	24.41	12,987
114	Stephen Hammond	Wimbledon	24.07	11,408
115	Ed Vaizey	Wantage	24.04	13,547
116	David Evennett	Bexleyheath and Crayford	23.95	10,344
117	David Rutley	Macclesfield	23.89	11,959

			%	Majority
118	Peter Bottomley	Worthing West	23.88	11,729
119	Pauline Latham	Mid Derbyshire	23.85	11,292
120	David Davis	Haltemprice and Howden	23.81	11,602
121	David Lidington	Aylesbury	23.73	12,618
122	Nigel Adams	Selby and Ainsty	23.71	12,265
123	George Hollingbery	Meon Valley	23.66	12,125
124	Gregory Barker	Bexhill and Battle	23.60	12,880
125	Theresa Villiers	Chipping Barnet	23.57	11,927
126	Graham Brady	Altrincham and Sale West	23.47	11,595
127	Geoffrey Clifton-Brown	The Cotswolds	23.46	12,864
128	Bernard Jenkin	Harwich and North Essex	23.36	11,447
129	Tim Loughton	East Worthing and Shoreham	22.95	11,105
130	Peter Bone	Wellingborough	22.82	11,787
131	Mark Harper	Forest of Dean	22.69	11,064
132	Julian Lewis	New Forest East	22.60	11,307
133	Nadhim Zahawi	Stratford-on-Avon	22.45	11,346
134	David Davies	Monmouth	22.41	10,425
135	Sajid Javid	Bromsgrove	21.90	11,308
136	Edward Leigh	Gainsborough	21.44	10,559
137	Gareth Johnson	Dartford	21.22	10,628
138	Kwasi Kwarteng	Spelthorne	21.18	10,019
139	Andrew Murrison	South West Wiltshire	21.15	10,367
140	David Ruffley	Bury St Edmunds	21.08	12,380
141	Richard Benyon	Newbury	20.90	12,248
142	Bill Wiggin	North Herefordshire	20.78	9,887
143	Mark Reckless	Rochester and Strood	20.75	9,953
144	Mark Pritchard	The Wrekin	20.56	9,450
145	Francis Maude	Horsham	20.52	11,460
146	Philip Davies	Shipley	20.12	9,944
147	Philip Dunne	Ludlow	20.01	9,749
148	Jonathan Djanogly	Huntingdon	19.94	10,819
149	Richard Bacon	South Norfolk	19.89	10,940
150	Steve Baker	Wycombe	19.85	9,560
151	Adam Holloway	Gravesham	19.69	9,312
152	Philip Hollobone	Kettering	19.21	9,094
153	Damian Collins	Folkestone and Hythe	19.17	10,122
154	Rehman Chishti	Gillingham and Rainham	18.55	8,680
155	Julian Smith	Skipton and Ripon	18.18	9,950
156	Edward Garnier	Harborough	18.00	9,877
157	Tobias Ellwood	Bournemouth East	17.55	7,728

			%	Majority
158	David Burrowes	Enfield Southgate	17.19	7,626
159	Hugo Swire	East Devon	17.17	9,114
160	Mel Stride	Central Devon	17.13	9,230
161	Neil Parish	Tiverton and Honiton	16.98	9,320
162	Ian Liddell-Grainger	Bridgwater and West Somerset	16.97	9,249
163	Rebecca Harris	Castle Point	16.95	7,632
164	Tim Yeo	South Suffolk	16.90	8,689
165	David Jones	Clwyd West	16.84	6,419
166	David Amess	Southend West	16.67	7,270
167	Mark Lancaster	Milton Keynes North	16.63	8,961
168	Therese Coffey	Suffolk Coastal	16.63	9,128
169	Laura Sandys	South Thanet	16.58	7,617
170	Penny Mordaunt	Portsmouth North	16.52	7,289
171	Robert Goodwill	Scarborough and Whitby	16.50	8,130
172	Robert Syms	Poole	15.90	7,541
173	Brian Binley	Northampton South	15.40	6,004
174	James Gray	North Wiltshire	15.37	7,483
175	Karen Bradley	Staffordshire Moorlands	15.27	6,689
176	Robert Wilson	Reading East	15.21	7,605
177	Andrew Turner	Isle of Wight	14.98	10,527
178	Daniel Kawczynski	Shrewsbury and Atcham	14.98	7,944
179	Richard Drax	South Dorset	14.79	7,443
180	Andrew Bridgen	North West Leicestershire	14.46	7,511
181	Jack Lopresti	Filton and Bradley Stoke	14.31	6,914
182	Heather Wheeler	South Derbyshire	14.14	7,128
183	Robert Walter	North Dorset	14.08	7,625
184	Justin Tomlinson	North Swindon	14.04	7,060
185	Anne Milton	Guildford	14.00	7,782
186	Fiona Bruce	Congleton	13.91	7,063
187	Tracey Crouch	Chatham and Aylesford	13.85	6,069
188	Keith Simpson	Broadland	13.84	7,292
189	Liam Fox	North Somerset	13.57	7,862
190	Conor Burns	Bournemouth West	13.40	5,583
191	Guy Opperman	Hexham	13.31	5,788
192	Andrew Lansley	South Cambridgeshire	13.27	7,838
193	Nicholas Soames	Mid Sussex	13.25	7,402
194	Karen Lumley	Redditch	13.22	5,821
195	Christopher Pincher	Tamworth	13.13	6,090
196	Steve Metcalfe	South Basildon and East Thurrock	12.90	5,772
197	Jonathan Lord	Woking	12.90	6,807

			%	Majority
198	Andrew Griffiths	Burton	12.65	6,304
199	Mark Pawsey	Rugby	12.64	6,000
200	Alok Sharma	Reading West	12.63	6,004
201	Harriett Baldwin	West Worcestershire	12.59	6,804
202	Henry Smith	Crawley	12.48	5,928
203	Craig Whittaker	Calder Valley	12.42	6,431
204	Mike Freer	Finchley and Golders Green	12.32	5,809
205	Gerald Howarth	Aldershot	12.31	5,586
206	John Glen	Salisbury	12.31	5,966
207	Julian Brazier	Canterbury	12.29	6,048
208	Jane Ellison	Battersea	12.25	5,977
209	Helen Grant	Maidstone and The Weald	12.04	5,889
210	Edward Timpson	Crewe and Nantwich	11.84	6,046
211	Andrew Percy	Brigg and Goole	11.73	5,147
212	Laurence Robertson	Tewkesbury	11.69	6,310
213	Stephen Crabb	Preseli Pembrokeshire	11.63	4,605
214	Lee Scott	Ilford North	11.50	5,404
215	Guto Bebb	Aberconwy	11.34	3,398
216	Robert Halfon	Harlow	11.22	4,925
217	Margot James	Stourbridge	10.93	5,164
218	Jeremy Lefroy	Stafford	10.87	5,460
219	Stewart Jackson	Peterborough	10.82	4,861
220	Lorraine Fullbrook	South Ribble	10.79	5,554
221	Charlie Elphicke	Dover	10.47	5,274
222	Jim Paice	South East Cambridgeshire	10.32	5,946
223	Sarah Wollaston	Totnes	10.30	4,927
224	Chris Kelly	Dudley South	10.10	3,856
225	Brandon Lewis	Great Yarmouth	9.93	4,276
226	Jacob Rees-Mogg	North East Somerset	9.60	4,914
227	Martin Vickers	Cleethorpes	9.56	4,298
228	Jake Berry	Rossendale and Darwen	9.53	4,493
229	Iain Stewart	Milton Keynes South	9.40	5,201
230	Simon Burns	Chelmsford	9.36	5,110
231	Andrew Bingham	High Peak	9.29	4,677
232	David Tredinnick	Bosworth	9.27	5,032
233	Chloe Smith	Norwich North	9.16	3,901
234	David Mundell	Dumfriesshire, Clydesdale and Tweeddale	9.14	4,194
235	Alun Cairns	Vale of Glamorgan	8.85	4,307
236	Jason McCartney	Colne Valley	8.75	4,837
237	Caroline Nokes	Romsey and Southampton North	8.49	4,156

			%	Majority
238	Simon Hart	Carmarthen West and South Pembrokeshire	8.45	3,423
239	Alec Shelbrooke	Elmet and Rothwell	8.10	4,521
240	Stephen McPartland	Stevenage	8.01	3,578
241	Andrew Stephenson	Pendle	7.96	3,585
242	Angie Bray	Ealing Central and Acton	7.87	3,716
243	Robert Buckland	South Swindon	7.52	3,544
244	Chris White	Warwick and Leamington	7.16	3,513
245	Bob Blackman	Harrow East	7.09	3,403
246	Nicky Morgan	Loughborough	7.09	3,744
247	Aidan Burley	Cannock Chase	7.01	3,195
248	Julian Sturdy	York Outer	6.92	3,688
249	Zac Goldsmith	Richmond Park	6.90	4,091
250	Oliver Letwin	West Dorset	6.84	3,923
251	Charlotte Leslie	Bristol North West	6.50	3,274
252	Sheryll Murray	South East Cornwall	6.49	3,220
253	Esther McVey	Wirral West	6.19	2,436
254	Kris Hopkins	Keighley	6.16	2,940
255	Robin Walker	Worcester	6.09	2,982
256	Gavin Barwell	Croydon Central	5.97	2,969
257	Stephen Mosley	City of Chester	5.52	2,583
258	Steve Brine	Winchester	5.45	3,048
259	Geoffrey Cox	Torridge and West Devon	5.35	2,957
260	Paul Maynard	Blackpool North and Cleveleys	5.30	2,150
261	Jessica Lee	Erewash	5.25	2,501
262	Mark Garnier	Wyre Forest	5.19	2,643
263	Jesse Norman	Hereford and South Herefordshire	5.13	2,481
264	Chris Skidmore	Kingswood	5.10	2,445
265	John Penrose	Weston-Super-Mare	5.10	2,691
266	David Nuttall	Bury North	4.99	2,243
267	Michael Ellis	Northampton North	4.81	1,936
268	Richard Graham	Gloucester	4.77	2,420
269	Marcus Jones	Nuneaton	4.63	2,069
270	James Morris	Halesowen and Rowley Regis	4.60	2,023
271	Ben Gummer	Ipswich	4.43	2,079
272	Anne Main	St Albans	4.36	2,305
273	Amber Rudd	Hastings and Rye	4.00	1,993
274	Nick de Bois	Enfield North	3.81	1,692
275	Mike Weatherley	Hove	3.75	1,868
276	Mary Macleod	Brentford and Isleworth	3.64	1,958
277	Louise Bagshawe	Corby	3.60	1,951

			%	Majority
278	Glyn Davies	Montgomeryshire	3.50	1,184
279	Stuart Andrew	Pudsey	3.38	1,659
280	Simon Kirby	Brighton Kemptown	3.11	1,328
281	Richard Fuller	Bedford	3.00	1,353
282	Simon Reevell	Dewsbury	2.83	1,526
283	David Mowat	Warrington South	2.83	1,553
284	Oliver Colvile	Plymouth, Sutton and Devonport	2.62	1,149
285	Richard Harrington	Watford	2.58	1,425
286	Karl McCartney	Lincoln	2.31	1,058
287	Graham Evans	Weaver Vale	2.25	991
288	Neil Carmichael	Stroud	2.24	1,299
289	John Stevenson	Carlisle	2.02	853
290	David Morris	Morecambe and Lunesdale	1.99	866
291	Andrew Jones	Harrogate and Knaresborough	1.96	1,039
292	Paul Uppal	Wolverhampton South West	1.72	691
293	Peter Aldous	Waveney	1.50	769
294	Nigel Mills	Amber Valley	1.17	536
295	Anne-Marie Morris	Newton Abbot	1.08	523
296	Sarah Newton	Truro and Falmouth	0.89	435
297	Eric Ollerenshaw	Lancaster and Fleetwood	0.78	333
298	Anna Soubry	Broxtowe	0.74	389
299	James Wharton	Stockton South	0.66	332
300	Mark Spencer	Sherwood	0.44	214
301	Jonathan Evans	Cardiff North	0.41	194
302	Nicola Blackwood	Oxford West and Abingdon	0.31	176
303	Matthew Offord	Hendon	0.23	106
304	Jackie Doyle-Price	Thurrock	0.20	92
305	George Eustice	Camborne and Redruth	0.16	66
306	Dan Byles	North Warwickshire	0.11	54

LABOUR

			%	Majority
1	Steve Rotheram	Liverpool Walton	57.72	19,818
2	George Howarth	Knowsley	57.53	25,690
3	Stephen Timms	East Ham	55.24	27,826
4	Willie Bain	Glasgow North East	54.21	15,942
5	Joe Benton	Bootle	51.31	21,181
6	Gordon Brown	Kirkcaldy and Cowdenbeath	50.24	23,009
7	Tom Clarke	Coatbridge, Chryston and Bellshill	49.75	20,714
8	Lyn Brown	West Ham	47.99	22,534

			%	Majority
9	Frank Roy	Motherwell and Wishaw	42.96	16,806
10	Grahame Morris	Easington	42.91	14,982
11	Frank Field	Birkenhead	42.78	15,195
12	David Lammy	Tottenham	41.61	16,931
13	Douglas Alexander	Paisley and Renfrewshire South	41.54	16,614
14	Lindsay Roy	Glenrothes	40.62	16,455
15	Maria Eagle	Garston and Halewood	39.41	16,877
16	David Cairns	Inverclyde	38.43	14,416
17	John Robertson	Glasgow North West	38.25	13,611
18	Huw Irranca-Davies	Ogmore	38.23	13,246
19	Derek Twigg	Halton	37.51	15,504
20	Chris Bryant	Rhondda	37.18	11,553
21	Harriet Harman	Camberwell and Peckham	36.84	17,187
22	Margaret Curran	Glasgow East	36.81	11,840
23	Margaret Hodge	Barking	36.51	16,555
24	Graham Stringer	Blackley and Broughton	35.97	12,303
25	Hywel Francis	Aberavon	35.66	11,039
26	David Blunkett	Sheffield, Brightside and Hillsborough	35.03	13,632
27	Jim Sheridan	Paisley and Renfrewshire North	34.96	15,280
28	Pamela Nash	Airdrie and Shotts	34.61	12,408
29	Anas Sarwar	Glasgow Central	34.51	10,551
30	Gregg McClymont	Cumbernauld, Kilsyth and Kirkintilloch East	33.43	13,755
31	Stephen Hepburn	Jarrow	33.28	12,908
32	Siân James	Swansea East	33.17	10,838
33	John Healey	Wentworth and Dearne	33.06	13,920
34	Ian Mearns	Gateshead	32.80	12,549
35	Nick Smith	Blaenau Gwent	32.46	10,516
36	Ann Clwyd	Cynon Valley	32.19	9,617
37	Malcolm Wicks	Croydon North	31.90	16,483
38	Andy Burnham	Leigh	31.71	15,011
39	Tom Harris	Glasgow South	31.57	12,658
40	Siobhain McDonagh	Mitcham and Morden	31.20	13,666
41	Diane Abbott	Hackney North and Stoke Newington	31.13	14,461
42	Sharon Hodgson	Washington and Sunderland West	30.69	11,458
43	Shaun Woodward	St Helens South and Whiston	30.65	14,122
44	David Miliband	South Shields	30.42	11,109
45	Joan Ruddock	Lewisham Deptford	30.32	12,499
46	Kevan Jones	North Durham	29.48	12,076
47	David Watts	St Helens North	29.40	13,101
48	Keith Vaz	Leicester East	29.34	14,082

			%	Majority
49	Jim Hood	Lanark and Hamilton East	28.95	13,478
50	Bridget Phillipson	Houghton and Sunderland South	28.91	10,990
51	Michael Dugher	Barnsley East	28.89	11,090
52	Yvonne Fovargue	Makerfield	28.53	12,490
53	Michael McCann	East Kilbride, Strathaven and Lesmahagow	28.47	14,503
54	Hilary Benn	Leeds Central	28.47	10,645
55	Khalid Mahmood	Birmingham, Perry Barr	28.32	11,908
56	Shabana Mahmood	Birmingham, Ladywood	28.20	10,105
57	John Spellar	Warley	28.11	10,756
58	Denis MacShane	Rotherham	27.89	10,462
59	Jeremy Corbyn	Islington North	27.83	12,401
60	Wayne David	Caerphilly	27.80	10,755
61	Mary Glindon	North Tyneside	27.76	12,884
62	Brian Donohoe	Central Ayrshire	27.34	12,007
63	George Mudie	Leeds East	27.22	10,293
64	Bob Ainsworth	Coventry North East	27.14	11,775
65	David Hamilton	Midlothian	26.37	10,349
66	Peter Hain	Neath	26.33	9,775
67	Ed Miliband	Doncaster North	26.30	10,909
68	Tony Lloyd	Manchester Central	26.15	10,439
69	Andrew Gwynne	Denton and Reddish	26.12	9,831
70	Stuart Bell	Middlesbrough	25.97	8,689
71	Dennis Skinner	Bolsover	25.42	11,182
72	John McDonnell	Hayes and Harlington	25.39	10,824
73	Clive Betts	Sheffield South East	25.37	10,505
74	Karl Turner	Kingston upon Hull East	25.15	8,597
75	Fiona O'Donnell	East Lothian	24.93	12,258
76	Paul Murphy	Torfaen	24.72	9,306
77	Kate Hoey	Vauxhall	24.66	10,651
78	Nick Raynsford	Greenwich and Woolwich	24.65	10,153
79	Michael Connarty	Linlithgow and East Falkirk	24.40	12,553
80	Liam Byrne	Birmingham, Hodge Hill	24.28	10,302
81	Lisa Nandy	Wigan	23.76	10,487
82	Yvette Cooper	Normanton, Pontefract and Castleford	23.74	10,979
83	Graham Allen	Nottingham North	23.74	8,138
84	David Heyes	Ashton under Lyne	23.66	9,094
85	Sheila Gilmore	Edinburgh East	23.03	9,181
86	Rushanara Ali	Bethnal Green and Bow	22.82	11,574
87	Graeme Morrice	Livingston	22.52	10,791
88	Jon Trickett	Hemsworth	22.45	9,844

			%	Majority
89	Frank Doran	Aberdeen North	22.18	8,361
90	Chi Onwurah	Newcastle upon Tyne Central	21.85	7,464
91	Yasmin Qureshi	Bolton South East	21.80	8,634
92	Michael Meacher	Oldham West and Royton	21.79	9,352
93	Virendra Sharma	Ealing Southall	21.73	9,291
94	Jack Straw	Blackburn	21.66	9,856
95	Phil Wilson	Sedgefield	21.62	8,696
96	Sandra Osborne	Ayr, Carrick and Cumnock	21.60	9,911
97	Katy Clark	North Ayrshire and Arran	21.46	9,895
98	Joan Walley	Stoke-on-Trent North	20.49	8,235
99	Angela Eagle	Wallasey	20.42	8,507
100	Jim Murphy	East Renfrewshire	20.36	10,420
101	David Anderson	Blaydon	20.30	9,117
102	Kate Green	Stretford and Urmston	19.90	8,935
103	Jim McGovern	Dundee West	19.60	7,278
104	Stephen Pound	Ealing North	19.51	9,301
105	Tessa Jowell	Dulwich and West Norwood	19.42	9,365
106	Pat McFadden	Wolverhampton South East	19.03	6,593
107	Peter Soulsby	Leicester South	18.69	8,808
108	Paul Goggins	Wythenshawe and Sale East	18.59	7,575
109	Alistair Darling	Edinburgh South West	18.58	8,447
110	Ian Lavery	Wansbeck	18.37	7,031
111	Alan Johnson	Kingston upon Hull West and Hessle	18.22	5,740
112	Frank Dobson	Holborn and St Pancras	18.19	9,942
113	Rachel Reeves	Leeds West	18.10	7,016
114	Anne McGuire	Stirling	17.85	8,354
115	Tom Watson	West Bromwich East	17.64	6,696
116	Gerald Kaufman	Manchester Gorton	17.49	6,703
117	Kelvin Hopkins	Luton North	17.48	7,520
118	Patricia Glass	North West Durham	17.37	7,612
119	Ann Coffey	Stockport	17.34	6,784
120	Ronnie Campbell	Blyth Valley	17.29	6,668
121	Tristram Hunt	Stoke-on-Trent Central	17.14	5,566
122	Alex Cunningham	Stockton North	16.90	6,676
123	John Mann	Bassetlaw	16.57	8,215
124	John Cryer	Leyton and Wanstead	15.98	6,416
125	Julie Elliott	Sunderland Central	15.76	6,725
126	Eric Joyce	Falkirk	15.45	7,843
127	Barry Gardiner	Brent North	15.35	8,028
128	Helen Jones	Warrington North	15.32	6,771

			%	Majority
129	Rosie Winterton	Doncaster Central	14.92	6,229
130	Heidi Alexander	Lewisham East	14.90	6,216
131	Margaret Beckett	Derby South	14.86	6,122
132	Iain Wright	Hartlepool	14.41	5,509
133	Russell Brown	Dumfries and Galloway	14.28	7,449
134	Marsha Singh	Bradford West	14.20	5,763
135	Hugh Bayley	York Central	13.88	6,451
136	Hazel Blears	Salford and Eccles	13.78	5,725
137	Geoffrey Robinson	Coventry North West	13.51	6,288
138	Teresa Pearce	Erith and Thamesmead	13.43	5,703
139	Ann McKechin	Glasgow North	13.16	3,898
140	Jim Dowd	Lewisham West and Penge	12.94	5,828
141	Jim Fitzpatrick	Poplar and Limehouse	12.91	6,030
142	Helen Goodman	Bishop Auckland	12.68	5,218
143	Dai Havard	Merthyr Tydfil and Rhymney	12.64	4,056
144	Nia Griffith	Llanelli	12.55	4,701
145	Kevin Barron	Rother Valley	12.54	5,866
146	Alan Meale	Mansfield	12.42	6,012
147	Gerry Sutcliffe	Bradford South	12.16	4,622
148	Nick Brown	Newcastle upon Tyne East	11.77	4,453
149	Tony Cunningham	Workington	11.65	4,575
150	Kevin Brennan	Cardiff West	11.60	4,750
151	Fiona Mactaggart	Slough	11.57	5,523
152	Liz Kendall	Leicester West	11.21	4,017
153	Thomas Docherty	Dunfermline and West Fife	11.18	5,470
154	Ian Lucas	Wrexham	11.09	3,658
155	Alan Campbell	Tynemouth	10.90	5,739
156	Barbara Keeley	Worsley and Eccles South	10.40	4,337
157	Robert Flello	Stoke-on-Trent South	10.36	4,130
158	Gordon Banks	Ochil and South Perthshire	10.28	5,187
159	Dawn Primarolo	Bristol South	9.79	4,734
160	Andrew Miller	Ellesmere Port and Neston	9.79	4,331
161	Fabian Hamilton	Leeds North East	9.56	4,545
162	David Crausby	Bolton North East	9.45	4,084
163	Jack Dromey	Birmingham, Erdington	9.22	3,277
164	Jamie Reed	Copeland	8.96	3,833
165	Rosie Cooper	West Lancashire	8.96	4,343
166	Paul Flynn	Newport West	8.92	3,544
167	Andrew Smith	Oxford East	8.87	4,581
168	Mike Wood	Batley and Spen	8.48	4,406

			%	Majority
169	James Cunningham	Coventry South	8.37	3,845
170	Caroline Flint	Don Valley	8.28	3,595
171	Kerry McCarthy	Bristol East	8.27	3,722
172	Emily Thornberry	Islington South and Finsbury	8.19	3,569
173	Susan Elan Jones	Clwyd South	8.17	2,834
174	Anne Begg	Aberdeen South	8.15	3,506
175	Bill Esterson	Sefton Central	7.97	3,862
176	Jenny Chapman	Darlington	7.90	3,388
177	Roger Godsiff	Birmingham, Hall Green	7.80	3,799
178	Catherine McKinnell	Newcastle upon Tyne North	7.77	3,414
179	Owen Smith	Pontypridd	7.59	2,785
180	Steve McCabe	Birmingham, Selly Oak	7.48	3,482
181	Andy Slaughter	Hammersmith	7.48	3,549
182	Mark Tami	Alyn and Deeside	7.31	2,919
183	Graham Jones	Hyndburn	7.24	3,090
184	Albert Owen	Ynys Môn	7.14	2,461
185	Emma Reynolds	Wolverhampton North East	7.12	2,484
186	Chris Ruane	Vale of Clwyd	7.06	2,509
187	Chuka Umunna	Streatham	6.96	3,259
188	Nic Dakin	Scunthorpe	6.88	2,549
189	Ivan Lewis	Bury South	6.82	3,292
190	Richard Burden	Birmingham, Northfield	6.65	2,782
191	Roberta Blackman-Woods	City of Durham	6.63	3,067
192	Angela Smith	Penistone and Stocksbridge	6.55	3,049
193	Martin Caton	Gower	6.44	2,683
194	David Hanson	Delyn	6.14	2,272
195	Jon Cruddas	Dagenham and Rainham	5.95	2,630
196	Madeleine Moon	Bridgend	5.90	2,263
197	Alan Whitehead	Southampton Test	5.46	2,413
198	Karen Buck	Westminster North	5.37	2,126
199	Gordon Marsden	Blackpool South	5.26	1,852
200	Lindsay Hoyle	Chorley	5.21	2,593
201	Ben Bradshaw	Exeter	5.21	2,721
202	Natascha Engel	North East Derbyshire	5.20	2,445
203	Sadiq Khan	Tooting	4.98	2,524
204	Jessica Morden	Newport East	4.79	1,650
205	Lilian Greenwood	Nottingham South	4.34	1,772
206	Valerie Vaz	Walsall South	4.29	1,755
207	Clive Efford	Eltham	3.96	1,663
208	Vernon Coaker	Gedling	3.86	1,859

			%	Majority
209	Alison Seabeck	Plymouth, Moor View	3.82	1,588
210	Tom Blenkinsop	Middlesbrough South and East Cleveland	3.63	1,677
211	Mary Creagh	Wakefield	3.63	1,613
212	Paul Farrelly	Newcastle-under-Lyme	3.59	1,552
213	Gisela Stuart	Birmingham, Edgbaston	3.06	1,274
214	David Winnick	Walsall North	2.74	990
215	David Wright	Telford	2.37	981
216	Austin Mitchell	Great Grimsby	2.17	714
217	Simon Danczuk	Rochdale	1.94	889
218	Diana Johnson	Kingston upon Hull North	1.93	641
219	Ian Austin	Dudley North	1.68	649
220	Chris Williamson	Derby North	1.36	613
221	Alison McGovern	Wirral South	1.33	531
222	Toby Perkins	Chesterfield	1.20	549
223	Ian Murray	Edinburgh South	0.72	316
224	John Denham	Southampton Itchen	0.43	192
225	Gloria De Piero	Ashfield	0.40	192
226	Paul Blomfield	Sheffield Central	0.40	165
227	Phil Woolas	Oldham East and Saddleworth	0.23	103
228	Julie Hilling	Bolton West	0.19	92
229	Glenda Jackson	Hampstead and Kilburn	0.08	42

LABOUR/CO-OPERATIVE

			%	Majority
1	Stephen Twigg	Liverpool West Derby	51.61	18,467
2	Ian Davidson	Glasgow South West	46.16	14,671
3	Tom Greatrex	Rutherglen and Hamilton West	44.70	21,002
4	Gemma Doyle	West Dunbartonshire	41.19	17,408
5	Louise Ellman	Liverpool Riverside	36.53	14,173
6	Christopher Evans	Islwyn	35.21	12,215
7	Meg Hillier	Hackney South and Shoreditch	33.34	14,288
8	Cathy Jamieson	Kilmarnock and Loudoun	26.59	12,378
9	Andy Love	Edmonton	23.81	9,613
10	Mark Hendrick	Preston	23.79	7,733
11	Stella Creasy	Walthamstow	23.12	9,478
12	Mike Gapes	Ilford South	22.06	11,297
13	Chris Leslie	Nottingham East	21.05	6,969
14	Luciana Berger	Liverpool Wavertree	18.90	7,167
15	Adrian Bailey	West Bromwich West	15.62	5,651
16	Meg Munn	Sheffield Heeley	14.21	5,807

			%	Majority
17	Jim Dobbin	Heywood and Middleton	12.95	5,971
18	John Woodcock	Barrow and Furness	11.80	5,208
19	Barry Sheerman	Huddersfield	11.04	4,472
20	Alun Michael	Cardiff South and Penarth	10.61	4,709
21	Alan Keen	Feltham and Heston	9.60	4,658
22	Gareth Thomas	Harrow West	6.82	3,143
23	Jonathan Reynolds	Stalybridge and Hyde	6.71	2,744
24	Gavin Shuker	Luton South	5.52	2,329
25	Mark Lazarowicz	Edinburgh North and Leith	3.64	1,724
26	Linda Riordan	Halifax	3.38	1,472
27	Ed Balls	Morley and Outwood	2.25	1,101
28	Geraint Davies	Swansea West	1.42	504

LIBERAL DEMOCRAT

			%	Majority
1	Alistair Carmichael	Orkney and Shetland	51.32	9,928
2	Charles Kennedy	Ross, Skye and Lochaber	37.52	13,070
3	Nick Clegg	Sheffield Hallam	29.89	15,284
4	Don Foster	Bath	25.24	11,883
5	Tim Farron	Westmorland and Lonsdale	23.82	12,264
6	Norman Lamb	North Norfolk	23.41	11,626
7	David Laws	Yeovil	22.81	13,036
8	Menzies Campbell	North East Fife	22.58	9,048
9	Mark Williams	Ceredigion	21.76	8,324
10	Greg Mulholland	Leeds North West	20.93	9,103
11	Stephen Williams	Bristol West	20.54	11,366
12	Vincent Cable	Twickenham	20.33	12,140
13	Simon Hughes	Bermondsey and Old Southwark	19.10	8,530
14	Danny Alexander	Inverness, Nairn, Badenoch and Strathspey	18.61	8,765
15	John Thurso	Caithness, Sutherland and Easter Ross	16.78	4,826
16	Norman Baker	Lewes	15.27	7,647
17	Andrew Stunell	Hazel Grove	15.18	6,371
18	Bob Russell	Colchester	15.13	6,982
19	Steve Webb	Thornbury and Yate	14.76	7,116
20	Malcolm Bruce	Gordon	13.83	6,748
21	John Pugh	Southport	13.77	6,024
22	Julian Huppert	Cambridge	13.55	6,792
23	Edward Davey	Kingston and Surbiton	13.24	7,560
24	Jenny Willott	Cardiff Central	12.66	4,576
25	Mike Hancock	Portsmouth South	12.60	5,200

			%	Majority
26	Lynne Featherstone	Hornsey and Wood Green	12.49	6,875
27	Ian Swales	Redcar	12.43	5,214
28	Michael Moore	Berwickshire, Roxburgh and Selkirk	11.58	5,675
29	Tom Brake	Carshalton and Wallington	11.46	5,260
30	Nick Harvey	North Devon	11.34	5,821
31	Roger Williams	Brecon and Radnorshire	9.65	3,747
32	Martin Horwood	Cheltenham	9.32	4,920
33	Adrian Sanders	Torbay	8.29	4,078
34	Mike Crockart	Edinburgh West	8.19	3,803
35	Robert Smith	West Aberdeenshire and Kincardine	8.15	3,684
36	Alan Reid	Argyll and Bute	7.59	3,431
37	John Hemming	Birmingham, Yardley	7.35	3,002
38	Chris Huhne	Eastleigh	7.20	3,864
39	Alan Beith	Berwick-upon-Tweed	7.00	2,690
40	Jeremy Browne	Taunton Deane	6.87	3,993
41	Stephen Lloyd	Eastbourne	6.59	3,435
42	Dan Rogerson	North Cornwall	6.36	2,981
43	Mark Hunter	Cheadle	6.23	3,272
44	Duncan Hames	Chippenham	4.72	2,470
45	Jo Swinson	East Dunbartonshire	4.55	2,184
46	Gordon Birtwistle	Burnley	4.34	1,818
47	John Leech	Manchester Withington	4.10	1,850
48	Andrew George	St Ives	3.74	1,719
49	Paul Burstow	Sutton and Cheam	3.31	1,608
50	David Heath	Somerton and Frome	3.00	1,817
51	Sarah Teather	Brent Central	2.97	1,345
52	Stephen Gilbert	St Austell and Newquay	2.78	1,312
53	Tessa Munt	Wells	1.43	800
54	David Ward	Bradford East	0.90	365
55	Simon Wright	Norwich South	0.65	310
56	Annette Brooke	Mid Dorset and North Poole	0.57	269
57	Lorely Burt	Solihull	0.32	175

DEMOCRATIC UNIONIST PARTY

			%	Majority
1	Ian Paisley Jnr	North Antrim	29.62	12,558
2	Jeffrey Donaldson	Lagan Valley	28.70	10,486
3	Sammy Wilson	East Antrim	22.20	6,770
4	Jim Shannon	Strangford	18.08	5,876
5	Gregory Campbell	East Londonderry	15.32	5,355

			%	Majority
6	David Simpson	Upper Bann	8.12	3,361
7	Nigel Dodds	Belfast North	6.01	2,224
8	William McCrea	South Antrim	3.48	1,183

SCOTTISH NATIONAL PARTY

			%	Majority
1	Angus Robertson	Moray	13.63	5,590
2	Angus MacNeil	Na h-Eileanan An Iar	12.81	1,885
3	Eilidh Whiteford	Banff and Buchan	10.47	4,027
4	Peter Wishart	Perth and North Perthshire	9.07	4,379
5	Mike Weir	Angus	8.65	3,282
6	Stewart Hosie	Dundee East	4.49	1,821

SINN FÉIN

			%	Majority
1	Gerry Adams	Belfast West	54.71	17,579
2	Martin McGuinness	Mid Ulster	37.62	15,363
3	Pat Doherty	West Tyrone	28.67	10,685
4	Conor Murphy	Newry and Armagh	18.55	8,331
5	Michelle Gildernew	Fermanagh and South Tyrone	0.01	4

PLAID CYMRU

			%	Majority
1	Elfyn Llwyd	Dwyfor Meirionnydd	22.03	6,367
2	Jonathan Edwards	Carmarthen East and Dinefwr	9.16	3,481
3	Hywel Williams	Arfon	5.58	1,455

SOCIAL DEMOCRATIC AND LABOUR PARTY

			%	Majority
1	Margaret Ritchie	South Down	19.75	8,412
2	Alasdair McDonnell	Belfast South	17.33	5,926
3	Mark Durkan	Foyle	12.73	4,824

INDEPENDENT

			%	Majority
1	Sylvia Hermon	North Down	42.90	14,364
2	Eric Illsley	Barnsley Central	29.98	11,093

ALLIANCE

			%	Majority
1	Naomi Long	Belfast East	4.45	1,533

GREEN PARTY

			%	Majority
1	Caroline Lucas	Brighton Pavilion	2.42	1,252

THE SPEAKER

			%	Majority
1	John Bercow	Buckingham	25.92	12,529

THE COALTION PROGRAMME FOR GOVERNMENT

BANKING

In recent years, we have seen a massive financial meltdown due to over-lending, over-borrowing and poor regulation. The Government believes that the current system of financial regulation is fundamentally flawed and needs to be replaced with a framework that promotes responsible and sustainable banking, where regulators have greater powers to curb unsustainable lending practices and we take action to promote more competition in the banking sector. In addition, we recognise that much more needs to be done to protect taxpayers from financial malpractice and to help the public manage their own debts.

- We will reform the banking system to avoid a repeat of the financial crisis, to promote a competitive economy, to sustain the recovery and to protect and sustain jobs.
- We will introduce a banking levy and seek a detailed agreement on implementation.
- We will bring forward detailed proposals for robust action to tackle unacceptable bonuses in the financial services sector; in developing these proposals, we will ensure they are effective in reducing risk.
- We want the banking system to serve business, not the other way round. We will bring forward detailed proposals to foster diversity in financial services, promote mutuals and create a more competitive banking industry.
- We will develop effective proposals to ensure the flow of credit to viable SMEs. This will include consideration of both a major loan guarantee scheme and the use of net lending targets for the nationalised banks.
- We will take steps to reduce systemic risk in the banking system and will establish an independent commission to investigate the complex issue of separating retail and investment banking in a sustainable way; while recognising that this will take time to get right, the commission will be given an initial time frame of one year to report.
- We will reform the regulatory system to avoid a repeat of the financial crisis. We will bring forward proposals to give the Bank of England control of macro-prudential regulation and oversight of micro-prudential regulation.
- We rule out joining or preparing to join the European Single Currency for the duration of this agreement.
- We will work with the Bank of England to investigate how the process of including housing costs in the CPI measure of inflation can be accelerated.
- We will create Britain's first free national financial advice service, which will be funded in full from a new social responsibility levy on the financial services sector.
- We take white collar crime as seriously as other crime, so we will create a single agency to take on the work of tackling serious economic crime that is currently done by, among others, the Serious Fraud Office, Financial Services Authority and Office of Fair Trading.

BUSINESS

The Government believes that business is the driver of economic growth and innovation, and that we need to take urgent action to boost enterprise, support green growth and build a new and more responsible economic model. We want to create a fairer and more balanced economy, where we are not so dependent on a narrow range of economic sectors, and where new businesses and economic opportunities are more evenly shared between regions and industries.

- We will cut red tape by introducing a 'one-in, one-out' rule whereby no new regulation is brought in without other regulation being cut by a greater amount.

- We will end the culture of 'tick-box' regulation, and instead target inspections on high-risk organisations through co-regulation and improving professional standards.
- We will impose 'sunset clauses' on regulations and regulators to ensure that the need for each regulation is regularly reviewed.
- We will review IR 35, as part of a wholesale review of all small business taxation, and seek to replace it with simpler measures that prevent tax avoidance but do not place undue administrative burdens or uncertainty on the self-employed, or restrict labour market flexibility.
- We will find a practical way to make small business rate relief automatic.
- We will reform the corporate tax system by simplifying reliefs and allowances, and tackling avoidance, in order to reduce headline rates. Our aim is to create the most competitive corporate tax regime in the G20, while protecting manufacturing industries.
- We will seek to ensure an injection of private capital into Royal Mail, including opportunities for employee ownership. We will retain Post Office Ltd in public ownership.
- We will seek to ensure a level playing field between small and large retailers by enabling councils to take competition issues into account when drawing up their local plans to shape the direction and type of new retail development.
- We will give the public the opportunity to challenge the worst regulations.
- We will review employment and workplace laws, for employers and employees, to ensure they maximise flexibility for both parties while protecting fairness and providing the competitive environment required for enterprise to thrive.
- We will make it easier for people to set up new enterprises by cutting the time it takes to start a new business. Our ambition is to make the UK one of the fastest countries in the world to start up a new business. We will reduce the number of forms needed to register a new business, and move towards a 'one-click' registration model.
- We will end the ban on social tenants starting businesses in their own homes.
- We will promote small business procurement, in particular by introducing an aspiration that 25% of government contracts should be awarded to small and medium-sized businesses and by publishing government tenders in full online and free of charge.
- We will consider the implementation of the Dyson Review to make the UK the leading hi-tech exporter in Europe, and refocus the research and development tax credit on hi-tech companies, small firms and start-ups.
- We will review the range of factors that can be considered by regulators when takeovers are proposed.
- We will reinstate an Operating and Financial Review to ensure that directors' social and environmental duties have to be covered in company reporting, and investigate further ways of improving corporate accountability and transparency.
- We will ensure that Post Offices are allowed to offer a wide range of services in order to sustain the network, and we will look at the case for developing new sources of revenue, such as the creation of a Post Office Bank.
- We will end the so-called 'gold-plating' of EU rules, so that British businesses are not disadvantaged relative to their European competitors.
- We will support the creation of Local Enterprise Partnerships - joint local authority-business bodies brought forward by local authorities themselves to promote local economic development - to replace Regional Development Agencies (RDAs). These may take the form of the existing RDAs in areas where they are popular.
- We will take steps to improve the competitiveness of the UK tourism industry, recognising the important part it plays in our national economy.

CIVIL LIBERTIES

We will be strong in defence of freedom. The Government believes that the British state has become too authoritarian, and that over the past decade it has abused

and eroded fundamental human freedoms and historic civil liberties. We need to restore the rights of individuals in the face of encroaching state power, in keeping with Britain's tradition of freedom and fairness.

- We will implement a full programme of measures to reverse the substantial erosion of civil liberties and roll back state intrusion.
- We will introduce a Freedom Bill.
- We will scrap the ID card scheme, the National Identity register and the ContactPoint database, and halt the next generation of biometric passports.
- We will outlaw the finger-printing of children at school without parental permission.
- We will extend the scope of the Freedom of Information Act to provide greater transparency.
- We will adopt the protections of the Scottish model for the DNA database.
- We will protect historic freedoms through the defence of trial by jury.
- We will restore rights to non-violent protest.
- We will review libel laws to protect freedom of speech.
- We will introduce safeguards against the misuse of anti-terrorism legislation.
- We will further regulate CCTV.
- We will end the storage of internet and email records without good reason.
- We will introduce a new mechanism to prevent the proliferation of unnecessary new criminal offences.
- We will establish a Commission to investigate the creation of a British Bill of Rights that incorporates and builds on all our obligations under the European Convention on Human Rights, ensures that these rights continue to be enshrined in British law, and protects and extends British liberties. We will seek to promote a better understanding of the true scope of these obligations and liberties.

COMMUNITIES AND LOCAL GOVERNMENT

The Government believes that it is time for a fundamental shift of power from Westminster to people. We will promote decentralisation and democratic engagement, and we will end the era of top-down government by giving new powers to local councils, communities, neighbourhoods and individuals.

- We will promote the radical devolution of power and greater financial autonomy to local government and community groups. This will include a review of local government finance.
- We will rapidly abolish Regional Spatial Strategies and return decision-making powers on housing and planning to local councils, including giving councils new powers to stop 'garden grabbing'.
- In the longer term, we will radically reform the planning system to give neighbourhoods far more ability to determine the shape of the places in which their inhabitants live, based on the principles set out in the Conservative Party publication *Open Source Planning*.
- We will abolish the unelected Infrastructure Planning Commission and replace it with an efficient and democratically accountable system that provides a fast-track process for major infrastructure projects.
- We will publish and present to Parliament a simple and consolidated national planning framework covering all forms of development and setting out national economic, environmental and social priorities.
- We will maintain the Green Belt, Sites of Special Scientific Interest (SSSIs) and other environmental protections, and create a new designation - similar to SSSIs - to protect green areas of particular importance to local communities.
- We will abolish the Government Office for London and consider the case for abolishing the remaining Government Offices.
- We will provide more protection against aggressive bailiffs and unreasonable charging orders, ensure that courts have the power to insist that repossession is always a last resort, and ban orders for sale on unsecured debts of less than £25,000.

- We will explore a range of measures to bring empty homes into use.
- We will promote shared ownership schemes and help social tenants and others to own or part-own their home.
- We will promote 'Home on the Farm' schemes that encourage farmers to convert existing buildings into affordable housing.
- We will create new trusts that will make it simpler for communities to provide homes for local people.
- We will phase out the ring-fencing of grants to local government and review the unfair Housing Revenue Account.
- We will freeze Council Tax in England for at least one year, and seek to freeze it for a further year, in partnership with local authorities.
- We will create directly elected mayors in the 12 largest English cities, subject to confirmatory referendums and full scrutiny by elected councillors.
- We will give councils a general power of competence.
- We will ban the use of powers in the Regulation of Investigatory Powers Act (RIPA) by councils, unless they are signed off by a magistrate and required for stopping serious crime.
- We will allow councils to return to the committee system, should they wish to.
- We will abolish the Standards Board regime.
- We will stop the restructuring of councils in Norfolk, Suffolk and Devon, and stop plans to force the regionalisation of the fire service.
- We will impose tougher rules to stop unfair competition by local authority newspapers.
- We will introduce new powers to help communities save local facilities and services threatened with closure, and give communities the right to bid to take over local state-run services.
- We will implement the Sustainable Communities Act, so that citizens know how taxpayers' money is spent in their area and have a greater say over how it is spent.
- We will cut local government inspection and abolish the Comprehensive Area Assessment.
- We will require continuous improvements to the energy efficiency of new housing.
- We will provide incentives for local authorities to deliver sustainable development, including for new homes and businesses.
- We will review the effectiveness of the raising of the stamp duty threshold for first-time buyers.
- We will give councillors the power to vote on large salary packages for unelected council officials.

CONSUMER PROTECTION

The Government believes that action is needed to protect consumers, particularly the most vulnerable, and to promote greater competition across the economy. We need to promote more responsible corporate and consumer behaviour through greater transparency and by harnessing the insights from behavioural economics and social psychology.

- We will give regulators new powers to define and ban excessive interest rates on credit and store cards; and we will introduce a seven-day cooling-off period for store cards.
- We will oblige credit card companies to provide better information to their customers in a uniform electronic format that will allow consumers to find out whether they are receiving the best deal.
- We will introduce stronger consumer protections, including measures to end unfair bank and financial transaction charges.
- We will take forward measures to enhance customer service in the private and public sectors.
- We will introduce, as a first step, an Ombudsman in the Office of Fair Trading who can proactively enforce the Grocery Supply Code of Practice and curb abuses of power, which undermine our farmers and act against the long-term interest of consumers.
- We will introduce honesty in food labelling so that consumers can be confident about where their food comes from and its environmental impact.

- We will increase households' control over their energy costs by ensuring that energy bills provide information on how to move to the cheapest tariff offered by their supplier, and how each household's energy usage compares to similar households.
- We will give Post Office Card account holders the chance to benefit from direct debit discounts and ensure that social tariffs offer access to the best prices available.
- We will seek to extend protection and support to 'off-grid' energy consumers.

CRIME AND POLICING

The Government believes that we need radical action to reform our criminal justice system. We need police forces that have greater freedom from Ministerial control and are better able to deal with the crime and anti-social behaviour that blights people's lives, but which are much more accountable to the public they serve.

- We will reduce time-wasting bureaucracy that hampers police operations, and introduce better technology to make policing more effective while saving taxpayers' money.
- We will amend the health and safety laws that stand in the way of common sense policing.
- We will seek to spread information on which policing techniques and sentences are most effective at cutting crime across the Criminal Justice System.
- We will have a full review of the terms and conditions for police officer employment.
- We will introduce measures to make the police more accountable through oversight by a directly elected individual, who will be subject to strict checks and balances by locally elected representatives.
- We will oblige the police to publish detailed local crime data statistics every month, so the public can get proper information about crime in their neighbourhoods and hold the police to account for their performance.
- We will require police forces to hold regular 'beat meetings' so that residents can hold them to account.
- We will make hospitals share non-confidential information with the police so they know where gun and knife crime is happening and can target stop-and-search in gun and knife crime hot spots.
- We will give people greater legal protection to prevent crime and apprehend criminals.
- We will ensure that people have the protection that they need when they defend themselves against intruders.
- We will ban the sale of alcohol below cost price.
- We will review alcohol taxation and pricing to ensure it tackles binge drinking without unfairly penalising responsible drinkers, pubs and important local industries.
- We will overhaul the Licensing Act to give local authorities and the police much stronger powers to remove licences from, or refuse to grant licences to, any premises that are causing problems.
- We will allow councils and the police to shut down permanently any shop or bar found to be persistently selling alcohol to children.
- We will double the maximum fine for under-age alcohol sales to £20,000.
- We will permit local councils to charge more for late-night licences to pay for additional policing.
- We will promote better recording of hate crimes against disabled, homosexual and transgender people, which are frequently not centrally recorded.
- We will introduce a system of temporary bans on new 'legal highs' while health issues are considered by independent experts. We will not permanently ban a substance without receiving full advice from the Advisory Council on the Misuse of Drugs.
- We will review the operation of the Extradition Act - and the US/UK extradition treaty - to make sure it is even-handed.

CULTURE, OLYMPICS, MEDIA AND SPORT

The Government believes that a vibrant cultural, media and sporting sector is crucial for our well-being and quality of life. We need to promote excellence in these fields, with government funding used where appropriate to encourage philanthropic and corporate investment.

- We will maintain the independence of the BBC, and give the National Audit Office full access to the BBC's accounts to ensure transparency.
- We will enable partnerships between local newspapers, radio and television stations to promote a strong and diverse local media industry.
- We will maintain free entry to national museums and galleries, and give national museums greater freedoms.
- We will work with the Scottish Government to deliver a successful Commonwealth Games in Glasgow in 2014, and ensure that the 2013 Rugby League and the 2015 Rugby Union World Cups are successful. We will strongly support the England 2018 World Cup bid.
- We will work with the Mayor of London to ensure a safe and successful Olympic and Paralympic Games in London in 2012, and urgently form plans to deliver a genuine and lasting legacy.
- We will examine the case for moving to a 'gross profits tax' system for the National Lottery, and reform the National Lottery so that more money goes into sport, the arts and heritage.
- We will stop wasteful spending by National Lottery distributors by banning lobbying activities and restricting administration costs to 5% of total income.
- We will use cash in dormant betting accounts to improve local sports facilities and support sports clubs.
- We will encourage the reform of football governance rules to support the co-operative ownership of football clubs by supporters.
- We will support the creation of an annual Olympic-style schools sport event to encourage competitive sport in schools, and we will seek to protect school playing fields.
- We will cut red tape to encourage the performance of more live music.
- We will introduce measures to ensure the rapid roll-out of superfast broadband across the country. We will ensure that BT and other infrastructure providers allow the use of their assets to deliver such broadband, and we will seek to introduce superfast broadband in remote areas at the same time as in more populated areas. If necessary, we will consider using the part of the TV licence fee that is supporting the digital switchover to fund broadband in areas that the market alone will not reach.

DEFENCE

The Government believes that we need to take action to safeguard our national security at home and abroad. We also recognise that we need to do much more to ensure that our Armed Forces have the support they need, and that veterans and their families are treated with the dignity that they deserve.

- We will maintain Britain's nuclear deterrent, and have agreed that the renewal of Trident should be scrutinised to ensure value for money. Liberal Democrats will continue to make the case for alternatives. We will immediately play a strong role in the Nuclear Non-Proliferation Treaty Review Conference, and press for continued progress on multilateral disarmament.
- We will aim to reduce Ministry of Defence running costs by at least 25%.
- We will work to rebuild the Military Covenant by:
    - ensuring that Service personnel's rest and recuperation leave can be maximised;
    - changing the rules so that Service personnel only have to register once on the Service register;
    - exploring the potential for including Service children as part of our proposals for a pupil premium;

- providing university and further education scholarships for the children of Servicemen and women who have been killed on active duty since 1990;
- providing support for ex-Service personnel to study at university,
- creating a new programme, 'Troops for Teachers', to recruit ex-Service personnel into the teaching profession;
- providing extra support for veteran mental health needs; and
- reviewing the rules governing the awarding of medals.

- We will double the operational allowance for Armed Forces personnel serving in Afghanistan, and include Armed Forces pay in our plans for a fair pay review.
- We will ensure that injured personnel are treated in dedicated military wards.
- We will look at whether there is scope to refurbish Armed Forces' accommodation from efficiencies within the Ministry of Defence.
- We will support defence jobs through exports that are used for legitimate purposes, not internal repression, and will work for a full international ban on cluster munitions.

DEFICIT REDUCTION

The Government believes that it is the most vulnerable who are most at risk from the debt crisis, and that it is deeply unfair that the Government could have to spend more on debt interest payments than on schools. So we need immediate action to tackle the deficit in a fair and responsible way, ensure that taxpayers' money is spent responsibly, and get the public finances back on track.

- We recognise that deficit reduction, and continuing to ensure economic recovery, is the most urgent issue facing Britain.
- We will significantly accelerate the reduction of the structural deficit over the course of a Parliament, with the main burden of deficit reduction borne by reduced spending rather than increased taxes.
- We will introduce arrangements that will protect those on low incomes from the effect of public sector pay constraint and other spending constraints.
- We will protect jobs by stopping the proposed jobs tax.
- We will set out a plan for deficit reduction in an emergency budget. We have created an independent Office for Budget Responsibility to make new forecasts of growth and borrowing for this emergency budget.
- We will make modest cuts of £6 billion to non-front-line services within the financial year 2010/11, subject to advice from the Treasury and the Bank of England on their feasibility and advisability. A proportion of these savings can be used to support jobs.
- We will hold a full Spending Review reporting this autumn, following a fully consultative process involving all tiers of government and the private sector.
- We will reduce spending on the Child Trust Fund and tax credits for higher earners.
- We will create strong financial discipline at all levels of government and place an obligation on public servants to manage taxpayers' money wisely.
- We will reduce the number and cost of quangos.

ENERGY AND CLIMATE CHANGE

The Government believes that climate change is one of the gravest threats we face, and that urgent action at home and abroad is required. We need to use a wide range of levers to cut carbon emissions, decarbonise the economy and support the creation of new green jobs and technologies. We will implement a full programme of measures to fulfil our joint ambitions for a low carbon and eco-friendly economy.

- We will push for the EU to demonstrate leadership in tackling international climate change, including by supporting an increase in the EU emission reduction target to 30% by 2020.

- We will seek to increase the target for energy from renewable sources, subject to the advice of the Climate Change Committee.
- We will continue public sector investment in carbon capture and storage (CCS) technology for four coal-fired power stations.
- We will establish a smart grid and roll out smart meters.
- We will establish a full system of feed-in tariffs in electricity - as well as the maintenance of banded Renewables Obligation Certificates.
- We will introduce measures to promote a huge increase in energy from waste through anaerobic digestion.
- We will create a green investment bank.
- We will retain energy performance certificates while scrapping HIPs.
- We will introduce measures to encourage marine energy.
- We will establish an emissions performance standard that will prevent coal-fired power stations being built unless they are equipped with sufficient carbon capture and storage to meet the emissions performance standard.
- We will cancel the third runway at Heathrow.
- We will refuse permission for additional runways at Gatwick and Stansted.
- We will replace Air Passenger Duty with a per-flight duty.
- We will introduce a floor price for carbon, and make efforts to persuade the EU to move towards full auctioning of ETS permits.
- Through our 'Green Deal', we will encourage home energy efficiency improvements paid for by savings from energy bills. We will also take measures to improve energy efficiency in businesses and public sector buildings. We will reduce central government carbon emissions by 10% within 12 months.
- We will reform energy markets to deliver security of supply and investment in low carbon energy, and ensure fair competition including a review of the role of Ofgem.
- We will instruct Ofgem to establish a security guarantee of energy supplies.
- We will give an Annual Energy Statement to Parliament to set strategic energy policy and guide investment.
- We will deliver an offshore electricity grid in order to support the development of a new generation of offshore wind power.
- We will encourage community-owned renewable energy schemes where local people benefit from the power produced. We will also allow communities that host renewable energy projects to keep the additional business rates they generate.
- As part of the creation of a green investment bank, we will create green financial products to provide individuals with opportunities to invest in the infrastructure needed to support the new green economy.
- We will work towards an ambitious global climate deal that will limit emissions and explore the creation of new international sources of funding for the purpose of climate change adaptation and mitigation.
- Liberal Democrats have long opposed any new nuclear construction. Conservatives, by contrast, are committed to allowing the replacement of existing nuclear power stations provided that they are subject to the normal planning process for major projects (under a new National Planning Statement), and also provided that they receive no public subsidy.
- We will implement a process allowing the Liberal Democrats to maintain their opposition to nuclear power while permitting the Government to bring forward the National Planning Statement for ratification by Parliament so that new nuclear construction becomes possible. This process will involve:
    - the Government completing the drafting of a national planning statement and putting it before Parliament;
    - specific agreement that a Liberal Democrat spokesperson will speak against the Planning Statement, but that Liberal Democrat MPs will abstain; and
    - clarity that this will not be regarded as an issue of confidence.

ENVIRONMENT, FOOD AND RURAL AFFAIRS

The Government believes that we need to protect the environment for future generations, make our economy more environmentally sustainable, and improve our quality of life and well-being. We also believe that much more needs to be done to support the farming industry, protect biodiversity and encourage sustainable food production.

- We will introduce measures to make the import or possession of illegal timber a criminal offence.
- We will introduce measures to protect wildlife and promote green spaces and wildlife corridors in order to halt the loss of habitats and restore biodiversity.
- We will launch a national tree planting campaign.
- We will review the governance arrangements of National Parks in order to increase local accountability.
- We will work towards full compliance with European Air Quality standards.
- We will take forward the findings of the Pitt Review to improve our flood defences, and prevent unnecessary building in areas of high flood risk.
- We will examine the conclusions of the Cave and Walker Reviews, and reform the water industry to ensure more efficient use of water and the protection of poorer households.
- We will work towards a 'zero waste' economy, encourage councils to pay people to recycle, and work to reduce littering.
- We will reduce the regulatory burden on farmers by moving to a risk-based system of regulation, and will develop a system of extra support for hill farmers.
- We will investigate ways to share with livestock keepers the responsibility for preparing for and dealing with outbreaks of disease.
- We will take forward the Marine and Coastal Access Act and ensure that its conservation measures are implemented effectively.
- As part of a package of measures, we will introduce a carefully managed and science-led policy of badger control in areas with high and persistent levels of bovine tuberculosis.
- We will promote high standards of farm animal welfare. We will end the testing of household products on animals and work to reduce the use of animals in scientific research. We will promote responsible pet ownership by introducing effective codes of practice under the Animal Welfare Act, and will ensure that enforcement agencies target irresponsible owners of dangerous dogs.
- We will ensure that food procured by government departments, and eventually the whole public sector, meets British standards of production wherever this can be achieved without increasing overall cost.
- We will investigate measures to help with fuel costs in remote rural areas, starting with pilot schemes.
- We will create a presumption in favour of sustainable development in the planning system.
- We oppose the resumption of commercial whaling, will press for a ban on ivory sales, and will tackle the smuggling and illegal trade on wildlife through our new Border Police Force.
- We will bring forward a motion on a free vote enabling the House of Commons to express its view on the repeal of the Hunting Act.

EQUALITIES

The Government believes that there are many barriers to social mobility and equal opportunities in Britain today, with too many children held back because of their social background, and too many people of all ages held back because of their gender, race, religion or sexuality. We need concerted government action to tear down these barriers and help to build a fairer society.

- We will promote equal pay and take a range of measures to end discrimination in the workplace.

- We will extend the right to request flexible working to all employees, consulting with business on how best to do so.
- We will undertake a fair pay review in the public sector to implement our proposed '20 times' pay multiple.
- We will look to promote gender equality on the boards of listed companies.
- We will promote improved community relations and opportunities for Black, Asian and Minority Ethnic (BAME) communities, including by providing internships for underrepresented minorities in every Whitehall department and funding a targeted national enterprise mentoring scheme for BAME people who want to start a business.
- We will stop the deportation of asylum seekers who have had to leave particular countries because their sexual orientation or gender identification puts them at proven risk of imprisonment, torture or execution.
- We will use our relationships with other countries to push for unequivocal support for gay rights and for UK civil partnerships to be recognised internationally.

EUROPE

The Government believes that Britain should play a leading role in an enlarged European Union, but that no further powers should be transferred to Brussels without a referendum. This approach strikes the right balance between constructive engagement with the EU to deal with the issues that affect us all, and protecting our national sovereignty.

- We will ensure that the British Government is a positive participant in the European Union, playing a strong and positive role with our partners, with the goal of ensuring that all the nations of Europe are equipped to face the challenges of the 21st century: global competitiveness, global warming and global poverty.
- We will ensure that there is no further transfer of sovereignty or powers over the course of the next Parliament. We will examine the balance of the EU's existing competences and will, in particular, work to limit the application of the Working Time Directive in the United Kingdom.
- We will amend the 1972 European Communities Act so that any proposed future treaty that transferred areas of power, or competences, would be subject to a referendum on that treaty - a 'referendum lock'. We will amend the 1972 European Communities Act so that the use of any passerelle would require primary legislation.
- We will examine the case for a United Kingdom Sovereignty Bill to make it clear that ultimate authority remains with Parliament.
- We will ensure that Britain does not join or prepare to join the Euro in this Parliament.
- We will strongly defend the UK's national interests in the forthcoming EU budget negotiations and agree that the EU budget should only focus on those areas where the EU can add value.
- We will press for the European Parliament to have only one seat, in Brussels.
- We will approach forthcoming legislation in the area of criminal justice on a case-by-case basis, with a view to maximising our country's security, protecting Britain's civil liberties and preserving the integrity of our criminal justice system. Britain will not participate in the establishment of any European Public Prosecutor.
- We support the further enlargement of the EU.

FAMILIES AND CHILDREN

The Government believes that strong and stable families of all kinds are the bedrock of a strong and stable society. That is why we need to make our society more family friendly, and to take action to protect children from excessive commercialisation and premature sexualisation.

- We will maintain the goal of ending child poverty in the UK by 2020.

- We will reform the administration of tax credits to reduce fraud and overpayments.
- We will bring forward plans to reduce the couple penalty in the tax credit system as we make savings from our welfare reform plans.
- We support the provision of free nursery care for pre-school children, and we want that support to be provided by a diverse range of providers, with a greater gender balance in the early years workforce.
- We will take Sure Start back to its original purpose of early intervention, increase its focus on the neediest families, and better involve organisations with a track record of supporting families. We will investigate ways of ensuring that providers are paid in part by the results they achieve.
- We will refocus funding from Sure Start peripatetic outreach services, and from the Department of Health budget, to pay for 4,200 extra Sure Start health visitors.
- We will investigate a new approach to helping families with multiple problems.
- We will publish serious case reviews, with identifying details removed.
- We will review the criminal records and vetting and barring regime and scale it back to common sense levels.
- We will crack down on irresponsible advertising and marketing, especially to children. We will also take steps to tackle the commercialisation and sexualisation of childhood.
- We will encourage shared parenting from the earliest stages of pregnancy - including the promotion of a system of flexible parental leave.
- We will put funding for relationship support on a stable, long-term footing, and make sure that couples are given greater encouragement to use existing relationship support.
- We will conduct a comprehensive review of family law in order to increase the use of mediation when couples do break up, and to look at how best to provide greater access rights to non-resident parents and grandparents.

FOREIGN AFFAIRS

The Government believes that Britain must always be an active member of the global community, promoting our national interests while standing up for the values of freedom, fairness and responsibility. This means working as a constructive member of the United Nations, NATO and other multilateral organisations including the Commonwealth; working to promote stability and security; and pushing for reform of global institutions to ensure that they reflect the modern world.

- We will take forward our shared resolve to safeguard the UK's national security and support our Armed Forces in Afghanistan and elsewhere.
- We will push for peace in the Middle East, with a secure and universally recognised Israel living alongside a sovereign and viable Palestinian state.
- We will work to establish a new 'special relationship' with India and seek closer engagement with China, while standing firm on human rights in all our bilateral relationships.
- We will maintain a strong, close and frank relationship with the United States.
- We want to strengthen the Commonwealth as a focus for promoting democratic values and development.
- We will work to promote stability in the Western Balkans.
- We will support concerted international efforts to prevent Iran from obtaining a nuclear weapon.
- We support reform of the UN Security Council, including permanent seats for Japan, India, Germany, Brazil and African representation.
- We will work to intensify our cultural, educational, commercial and diplomatic links with many nations beyond Europe and North America to strengthen the UK's relations with the fastest-growing areas of the world economy.
- We will never condone the use of torture.

GOVERNMENT TRANSPARENCY

The Government believes that we need to throw open the doors of public bodies, to enable the public to hold politicians and public bodies to account. We also recognise that this will help to deliver better value for money in public spending, and help us achieve our aim of cutting the record deficit. Setting government data free will bring significant economic benefits by enabling businesses and non-profit organisations to build innovative applications and websites.

- We will require public bodies to publish online the job titles of every member of staff and the salaries and expenses of senior officials paid more than the lowest salary permissible in Pay Band 1 of the Senior Civil Service pay scale, and organograms that include all positions in those bodies.
- We will require anyone paid more than the Prime Minister in the centrally funded public sector to have their salary signed off by the Treasury.
- We will regulate lobbying through introducing a statutory register of lobbyists and ensuring greater transparency.
- We will also pursue a detailed agreement on limiting donations and reforming party funding in order to remove big money from politics.
- We will strengthen the powers of Select Committees to scrutinise major public appointments.
- We will introduce new protections for whistleblowers in the public sector.
- We will take steps to open up government procurement and reduce costs; and we will publish government ICT contracts online.
- We will create a level playing field for opensource software and will enable large ICT projects to be split into smaller components.
- We will require full, online disclosure of all central government spending and contracts over £25,000.
- We will create a new 'right to data' so that government-held datasets can be requested and used by the public, and then published on a regular basis.
- We will require all councils to publish meeting minutes and local service and performance data.
- We will require all councils to publish items of spending above £500, and to publish contracts and tender documents in full.
- We will ensure that all data published by public bodies is published in an open and standardised format, so that it can be used easily and with minimal cost by third parties.

IMMIGRATION

The Government believes that immigration has enriched our culture and strengthened our economy, but that it must be controlled so that people have confidence in the system. We also recognise that to ensure cohesion and protect our public services, we need to introduce a cap on immigration and reduce the number of nonEU immigrants.

- We will introduce an annual limit on the number of non-EU economic migrants admitted into the UK to live and work. We will consider jointly the mechanism for implementing the limit.
- We will end the detention of children for immigration purposes.
- We will create a dedicated Border Police Force, as part of a refocused Serious Organised Crime Agency, to enhance national security, improve immigration controls and crack down on the trafficking of people, weapons and drugs.
- We will work with police forces to strengthen arrangements to deal with serious crime and other cross-boundary policing challenges, and extend collaboration between forces to deliver better value for money.
- We support E-borders and will reintroduce exit checks.

- We will apply transitional controls as a matter of course in the future for all new EU Member States.
- We will introduce new measures to minimise abuse of the immigration system, for example via student routes, and will tackle human trafficking as a priority.
- We will explore new ways to improve the current asylum system to speed up the processing of applications.

INTERNATIONAL DEVELOPMENT

The Government believes that even in these difficult economic times, the UK has a moral responsibility to help the poorest people in the world. We will honour our aid commitments, but at the same time will ensure much greater transparency and scrutiny of aid spending to deliver value for money for British taxpayers and to maximise the impact of our aid budget.

- We will honour our commitment to spend 0.7% of GNI on overseas aid from 2013, and to enshrine this commitment in law.
- We will encourage other countries to fulfil their aid commitments.
- We will support actions to achieve the Millennium Development Goals. In particular, we will prioritise aid spending on programmes to ensure that everyone has access to clean water, sanitation, healthcare and education; to reduce maternal and infant mortality; and to restrict the spread of major diseases like HIV/ AIDS, TB and malaria.
- We will recognise the vital role of women in development, promote gender equality and focus on the rights of women, children and disabled people to access services.
- We will use the aid budget to support the development of local democratic institutions, civil society groups, the media and enterprise; and support efforts to tackle corruption.
- We will introduce full transparency in aid and publish details of all UK aid spending online. We will push for similarly high levels of transparency internationally.
- We will create new mechanisms to give British people a direct say in how an element of the aid budget is spent.
- We will keep aid untied from commercial interests, and will maintain DfID as an independent department focused on poverty reduction.
- We will stick to the rules laid down by the OECD about what spending counts as aid.
- We will push hard in 2010 to make greater progress in tackling maternal and infant mortality.
- We will work to accelerate the process of relieving Heavily Indebted Poor Countries of their debt.
- We will support efforts to establish an International Arms Trade Treaty to limit the sales of arms to dangerous regimes.
- We will support pro-development trade deals, including the proposed Pan-African Free Trade Area.
- We will support innovative and effective smaller British non-governmental organisations that are committed to tackling poverty.
- We will explore ways of helping the very poorest developing countries to take part in international climate change negotiations.
- We will ensure that UK Trade and Investment and the Export Credits Guarantee Department become champions for British companies that develop and export innovative green technologies around the world, instead of supporting investment in dirty fossil-fuel energy production.
- We will provide a more integrated approach to post-conflict reconstruction where the British military is involved - building on the Stabilisation Unit in Whitehall and creating a new Stabilisation and Reconstruction Force to bridge the gap between the military and the reconstruction effort.
- We will review what action can be taken against 'vulture funds'.
- We will support reform of global financial institutions such as the World Bank and the International Monetary Fund in order to increase the involvement of developing nations.

JOBS AND WELFARE

The Government believes that we need to encourage responsibility and fairness in the welfare system. That means providing help for those who cannot work, training and targeted support for those looking for work, but sanctions for those who turn down reasonable offers of work or training.

- We will end all existing welfare to work programmes and create a single welfare to work programme to help all unemployed people get back into work.
- We will ensure that Jobseeker's Allowance claimants facing the most significant barriers to work are referred to the new welfare to work programme immediately, not after 12 months as is currently the case. We will ensure that Jobseeker's Allowance claimants aged under 25 are referred to the programme after a maximum of six months.
- We will realign contracts with welfare to work service providers to reflect more closely the results they achieve in getting people back into work.
- We will reform the funding mechanism used by government to finance welfare to work programmes to reflect the fact that initial investment delivers later savings through lower benefit expenditure, including creating an integrated work programme with outcome funding based upon the DEL/AME switch.
- We will ensure that receipt of benefits for those able to work is conditional on their willingness to work.
- We support the National Minimum Wage because of the protection it gives lowincome workers and the incentives to work it provides.
- We will re-assess all current claimants of Incapacity Benefit for their readiness to work. Those assessed as fully capable for work will be moved onto Jobseeker's Allowance.
- We will support would-be entrepreneurs through a new programme - Work for Yourself - which will give the unemployed access to business mentors and start-up loans.
- We will draw on a range of Service Academies to offer pre-employment training and work placements for unemployed people.
- We will develop local Work Clubs - places where unemployed people can gather to exchange skills, find opportunities, make contacts and provide mutual support.
- We will investigate how to simplify the benefit system in order to improve incentives to work.

JUSTICE

The Government believes that more needs to be done to ensure fairness in the justice system. This means introducing more effective sentencing policies, as well as overhauling the system of rehabilitation to reduce reoffending and provide greater support and protection for the victims of crime.

- We will introduce a 'rehabilitation revolution' that will pay independent providers to reduce reoffending, paid for by the savings this new approach will generate within the criminal justice system.
- We will conduct a full review of sentencing policy to ensure that it is effective in deterring crime, protecting the public, punishing offenders and cutting reoffending. In particular, we will ensure that sentencing for drug use helps offenders come off drugs.
- We will explore alternative forms of secure, treatment-based accommodation for mentally ill and drugs offenders.
- We will implement the Prisoners' Earnings Act 1996 to allow deductions from the earnings of prisoners in properly paid work to be paid into the Victims' Fund.
- We will consider how to use proceeds from the Victim Surcharge to deliver up to 15 new rape crisis centres, and give existing rape crisis centres stable, long-term funding.
- We will carry out a fundamental review of Legal Aid to make it work more efficiently.

- We will change the law so that historical convictions for consensual gay sex with over16s will be treated as spent and will not show up on criminal records checks.
- We will extend anonymity in rape cases to defendants.
- We will introduce effective measures to tackle anti-social behaviour and low-level crime, including forms of restorative justice such as Neighbourhood Justice Panels.

NATIONAL SECURITY

The Government believes that its primary responsibility is to ensure national security. We need a coherent approach to national security issues across government, and we will take action to tackle terrorism, and its causes, at home and abroad.

- We have established a National Security Council and appointed a National Security Adviser.
- We have commenced a Strategic Defence and Security Review, commissioned and overseen by the National Security Council, with strong Treasury involvement. We will also develop and publish a new National Security Strategy.
- We will urgently review Control Orders, as part of a wider review of counter-terrorist legislation, measures and programmes. We will seek to find a practical way to allow the use of intercept evidence in court.
- We will deny public funds to any group that has recently espoused or incited violence or hatred. We will proscribe such organisations, subject to the advice of the police and security and intelligence agencies.
- We believe that Britain should be able to deport foreign nationals who threaten our security to countries where there are verifiable guarantees that they will not be tortured. We will seek to extend these guarantees to more countries.

NHS

The Government believes that the NHS is an important expression of our national values. We are committed to an NHS that is free at the point of use and available to everyone based on need, not the ability to pay. We want to free NHS staff from political micromanagement, increase democratic participation in the NHS and make the NHS more accountable to the patients that it serves. That way we will drive up standards, support professional responsibility, deliver better value for money and create a healthier nation.

- We will guarantee that health spending increases in real terms in each year of the Parliament, while recognising the impact this decision will have on other departments.
- We will stop the top-down reorganisations of the NHS that have got in the way of patient care. We are committed to reducing duplication and the resources spent on administration, and diverting these resources back to front-line care.
- We will significantly cut the number of health quangos.
- We will cut the cost of NHS administration by a third and transfer resources to support doctors and nurses on the front line.
- We will stop the centrally dictated closure of A&E and maternity wards, so that people have better access to local services.
- We will strengthen the power of GPs as patients' expert guides through the health system by enabling them to commission care on their behalf.
- We will ensure that there is a stronger voice for patients locally through directly elected individuals on the boards of their local primary care trust (PCT). The remainder of the PCT's board will be appointed by the relevant local authority or authorities, and the Chief Executive and principal officers will be appointed by the Secretary of State on the advice of the new independent NHS board. This will ensure the right balance between locally accountable individuals and technical expertise.

- The local PCT will act as a champion for patients and commission those residual services that are best undertaken at a wider level, rather than directly by GPs. It will also take responsibility for improving public health for people in their area, working closely with the local authority and other local organisations.
- If a local authority has concerns about a significant proposed closure of local services, for example an A&E department, it will have the right to challenge health organisations, and refer the case to the Independent Reconfiguration Panel. The Panel would then provide advice to the Secretary of State for Health.
- We will give every patient the right to choose to register with the GP they want, without being restricted by where they live.
- We will develop a 24/7 urgent care service in every area of England, including GP out-ofhours services, and ensure every patient can access a local GP. We will make care more accessible by introducing a single number for every kind of urgent care and by using technology to help people communicate with their doctors.
- We will renegotiate the GP contract and incentivise ways of improving access to primary care in disadvantaged areas.
- We will make the NHS work better by extending best practice on improving discharge from hospital, maximising the number of day care operations, reducing delays prior to operations, and where possible enabling community access to care and treatments.
- We will help elderly people live at home for longer through solutions such as home adaptations and community support programmes.
- We will prioritise dementia research within the health research and development budget.
- We will seek to stop foreign healthcare professionals working in the NHS unless they have passed robust language and competence tests.
- Doctors and nurses need to be able to use their professional judgement about what is right for patients and we will support this by giving front-line staff more control of their working environment.
- We will strengthen the role of the Care Quality Commission so it becomes an effective quality inspectorate. We will develop Monitor into an economic regulator that will oversee aspects of access, competition and price-setting in the NHS.
- We will establish an independent NHS board to allocate resources and provide commissioning guidelines.
- We will enable patients to rate hospitals and doctors according to the quality of care they received, and we will require hospitals to be open about mistakes and always tell patients if something has gone wrong.
- We will measure our success on the health results that really matter - such as improving cancer and stroke survival rates or reducing hospital infections.
- We will publish detailed data about the performance of healthcare providers online, so everyone will know who is providing a good service and who is falling behind.
- We will put patients in charge of making decisions about their care, including control of their health records.
- We will create a Cancer Drugs Fund to enable patients to access the cancer drugs their doctors think will help them, paid for using money saved by the NHS through our pledge to stop the rise in Employer National Insurance contributions from April 2011.
- We will reform NICE and move to a system of value-based pricing, so that all patients can access the drugs and treatments their doctors think they need.
- We will introduce a new dentistry contract that will focus on achieving good dental health and increasing access to NHS dentistry, with an additional focus on the oral health of schoolchildren.
- We will provide £10 million a year beyond 2011 from within the budget of the Department of Health to support children's hospices in their vital work. And so that proper support for the most sick children and adults can continue in the setting of their choice, we will introduce a new per-patient funding system for all hospices and providers of palliative care.

- We will encourage NHS organisations to work better with their local police forces to clamp down on anyone who is aggressive and abusive to staff.
- We are committed to the continuous improvement of the quality of services to patients, and to achieving this through much greater involvement of independent and voluntary providers.
- We will give every patient the power to choose any healthcare provider that meets NHS standards, within NHS prices. This includes independent, voluntary and community sector providers.

PENSIONS AND OLDER PEOPLE

The Government believes that people deserve dignity and respect in old age, and that they should be provided with the support they need. That means safeguarding key benefits and pensions, and taking action to make it easier for older people to work or volunteer.

- We will restore the earnings link for the basic state pension from April 2011, with a 'triple guarantee' that pensions are raised by the higher of earnings, prices or 2.5%.
- We will commit to establishing an independent commission to review the longterm affordability of public sector pensions, while protecting accrued rights.
- We will phase out the default retirement age and hold a review to set the date at which the state pension age starts to rise to 66, although it will not be sooner than 2016 for men and 2020 for women. We will end the rules requiring compulsory annuitisation at 75.
- We will implement the Parliamentary and Health Ombudsman's recommendation to make fair and transparent payments to Equitable Life policy holders, through an independent payment scheme, for their relative loss as a consequence of regulatory failure.
- We will explore the potential to give people greater flexibility in accessing part of their personal pension fund early.
- We will protect key benefits for older people such as the winter fuel allowance, free TV licences, free bus travel, and free eye tests and prescriptions.
- We will simplify the rules and regulations relating to pensions to help reinvigorate occupational pensions, encouraging companies to offer high-quality pensions to all employees, and we will work with business and the industry to support auto enrolment.

POLITICAL REFORM

The Government believes that our political system is broken. We urgently need fundamental political reform, including a referendum on electoral reform, much greater co-operation across party lines, and changes to our political system to make it far more transparent and accountable.

- We will establish five-year fixed-term Parliaments. We will put a binding motion before the House of Commons stating that the next general election will be held on the first Thursday of May 2015. Following this motion, we will legislate to make provision for fixed-term Parliaments of five years. This legislation will also provide for dissolution if 55% or more of the House votes in favour.
- We will bring forward a Referendum Bill on electoral reform, which includes provision for the introduction of the Alternative Vote in the event of a positive result in the referendum, as well as for the creation of fewer and more equal sized constituencies. We will whip both Parliamentary parties in both Houses to support a simple majority referendum on the Alternative Vote, without prejudice to the positions parties will take during such a referendum.
- We will bring forward early legislation to introduce a power of recall, allowing voters to force a by-election where an MP is found to have engaged in serious wrongdoing and having had a petition calling for a by-election signed by 10% of his or her constituents.
- We will establish a committee to bring forward proposals for a wholly or mainly elected upper chamber on the basis of proportional representation. The committee will come forward with a draft motion by December 2010. It is likely that this will advocate single long terms of office. It is also likely

that there will be a grandfathering system for current Peers. In the interim, Lords appointments will be made with the objective of creating a second chamber that is reflective of the share of the vote secured by the political parties in the last general election.

- We will bring forward the proposals of the Wright Committee for reform to the House of Commons in full - starting with the proposed committee for management of backbench business. A House Business Committee, to consider government business, will be established by the third year of the Parliament.
- We will reduce electoral fraud by speeding up the implementation of individual voter registration.
- We will establish a commission to consider the 'West Lothian question'.
- We will prevent the possible misuse of Parliamentary privilege by MPs accused of serious wrongdoing.
- We will cut the perks and bureaucracy associated with Parliament.
- We will consult with the Independent Parliamentary Standards Authority on how to move away from the generous final-salary pension system for MPs.
- We will fund 200 all-postal primaries over this Parliament, targeted at seats which have not changed hands for many years. These funds will be allocated to all political parties with seats in Parliament that they take up, in proportion to their share of the total vote in the last general election.
- We will ensure that any petition that secures 100,000 signatures will be eligible for formal debate in Parliament. The petition with the most signatures will enable members of the public to table a bill eligible to be voted on in Parliament.
- We will introduce a new 'public reading stage' for bills to give the public an opportunity to comment on proposed legislation online, and a dedicated 'public reading day' within a bill's committee stage where those comments will be debated by the committee scrutinising the bill.
- We will improve the civil service, and make it easier to reward the best civil servants and remove the least effective.
- We will reform the Civil Service Compensation Scheme to bring it into line with practice in the private sector.
- We will put a limit on the number on Special Advisers.
- We will introduce extra support for people with disabilities who want to become MPs, councillors or other elected officials.
- We will open up Whitehall recruitment by publishing central government job vacancies online.
- We will publish details of every UK project that receives over £25,000 of EU funds.
- We will give residents the power to instigate local referendums on any local issue.
- We will stop plans to impose supplementary business rates on firms if a majority of the firms affected do not give their consent.
- We will give residents the power to veto excessive council tax increases.
- We will continue to promote peace, stability and economic prosperity in Northern Ireland, standing firmly behind the agreements negotiated and institutions they establish. We will work to bring Northern Ireland back into the mainstream of UK politics, including producing a government paper examining potential mechanisms for changing the corporation tax rate in Northern Ireland.
- We will implement the proposals of the Calman Commission and introduce a referendum on further Welsh devolution.
- We will review the control and use of accumulated and future revenues from the Fossil Fuel Levy in Scotland.
- We recognise the concerns expressed by the Holtham Commission on the system of devolution funding. However, at this time, the priority must be to reduce the deficit and therefore any change to the system must await the stabilisation of the public finances. Depending on the outcome of the forthcoming referendum, we will establish a process similar to the Calman Commission for the Welsh Assembly. We will take forward the Sustainable Homes Legislative Competence Order.
- We will make the running of government more efficient by introducing enhanced Departmental Boards which will form collective operational leadership of government departments.

PUBLIC HEALTH

The Government believes that we need action to promote public health, and encourage behaviour change to help people live healthier lives. We need an ambitious strategy to prevent ill-health which harnesses innovative techniques to help people take responsibility for their own health.

- We will give local communities greater control over public health budgets with payment by the outcomes they achieve in improving the health of local residents.
- We will give GPs greater incentives to tackle public health problems.
- We will investigate ways of improving access to preventative healthcare for those in disadvantaged areas to help tackle health inequalities.
- We will ensure greater access to talking therapies to reduce long-term costs for the NHS.

SCHOOLS

The Government believes that we need to reform our school system to tackle educational inequality, which has widened in recent years, and to give greater powers to parents and pupils to choose a good school. We want to ensure high standards of discipline in the classroom, robust standards and the highest quality teaching. We also believe that the state should help parents, community groups and others come together to improve the education system by starting new schools.

- We will promote the reform of schools in order to ensure that new providers can enter the state school system in response to parental demand; that all schools have greater freedom over the curriculum; and that all schools are held properly to account.
- We will fund a significant premium for disadvantaged pupils from outside the schools budget by reductions in spending elsewhere.
- We will give parents, teachers, charities and local communities the chance to set up new schools, as part of our plans to allow new providers to enter the state school system in response to parental demand.
- We will support Teach First, create Teach Now to build on the Graduate Teacher Programme, and seek other ways to improve the quality of the teaching profession.
- We will reform the existing rigid national pay and conditions rules to give schools greater freedoms to pay good teachers more and deal with poor performance.
- We will help schools tackle bullying in schools, especially homophobic bullying.
- We will simplify the regulation of standards in education and target inspection on areas of failure.
- We will give anonymity to teachers accused by pupils and take other measures to protect against false accusations.
- We will seek to attract more top science and maths graduates to be teachers.
- We will publish performance data on educational providers, as well as past exam papers.
- We will create more flexibility in the exams systems so that state schools can offer qualifications like the IGCSE.
- We will reform league tables so that schools are able to focus on, and demonstrate, the progress of children of all abilities.
- We will give heads and teachers the powers they need to ensure discipline in the classroom and promote good behaviour.
- We believe the most vulnerable children deserve the very highest quality of care. We will improve diagnostic assessment for schoolchildren, prevent the unnecessary closure of special schools, and remove the bias towards inclusion.
- We will improve the quality of vocational education, including increasing flexibility for 14-19 year olds and creating new Technical Academies as part of our plans to diversify schools provision.
- We will keep external assessment, but will review how Key Stage 2 tests operate in future.

- We will ensure that all new Academies follow an inclusive admissions policy. We will work with faith groups to enable more faith schools and facilitate inclusive admissions policies in as many of these schools as possible.

SOCIAL ACTION

The Government believes that the innovation and enthusiasm of civil society is essential in tackling the social, economic and political challenges that the UK faces today. We will take action to support and encourage social responsibility, volunteering and philanthropy, and make it easier for people to come together to improve their communities and help one another.

- We will support the creation and expansion of mutuals, co-operatives, charities and social enterprises, and enable these groups to have much greater involvement in the running of public services.
- We will give public sector workers a new right to form employee-owned co-operatives and bid to take over the services they deliver. This will empower millions of public sector workers to become their own boss and help them to deliver better services.
- We will train a new generation of community organisers and support the creation of neighbourhood groups across the UK, especially in the most deprived areas.
- We will take a range of measures to encourage charitable giving and philanthropy.
- We will introduce National Citizen Service. The initial flagship project will provide a programme for 16 year olds to give them a chance to develop the skills needed to be active and responsible citizens, mix with people from different backgrounds, and start getting involved in their communities.
- We will use funds from dormant bank accounts to establish a 'Big Society Bank', which will provide new finance for
- neighbourhood groups, charities, social enterprises and other non-governmental bodies.
- We will take a range of measures to encourage volunteering and involvement in social action, including launching a national day to celebrate and encourage social action, and make regular community service an element of civil service staff appraisals.

SOCIAL CARE AND DISABILITY

The Government believes that people needing care deserve to be treated with dignity and respect. We understand the urgency of reforming the system of social care to provide much more control to individuals and their carers, and to ease the cost burden that they and their families face.

- We will establish a commission on long-term care, to report within a year. The commission will consider a range of ideas, including both a voluntary insurance scheme to protect the assets of those who go into residential care, and a partnership scheme as proposed by Derek Wanless.
- We will break down barriers between health and social care funding to incentivise preventative action.
- We will extend the greater roll-out of personal budgets to give people and their carers more control and purchasing power.
- We will use direct payments to carers and better community-based provision to improve access to respite care.
- We will reform Access to Work, so disabled people can apply for jobs with funding already secured for any adaptations and equipment they will need.

TAXATION

The Government believes that the tax system needs to be reformed to make it more competitive, simpler, greener and fairer. We need to take action to ensure that the tax framework better reflects the values of this Government.

- We will increase the personal allowance for income tax to help lower and middle income earners. We will announce in the first Budget a substantial increase in the personal allowance from April 2011, with the benefits focused on those with lower and middle incomes. This will be funded with the money that would have been used to pay for the increase in employee National Insurance thresholds proposed by the Conservative Party, as well as revenues from increases in Capital Gains Tax rates for non-business assets as described below. The increase in employer National Insurance thresholds proposed by the Conservatives will go ahead in order to stop the planned jobs tax.
- We will further increase the personal allowance to £10,000, making real terms steps each year towards meeting this as a longerterm policy objective. We will prioritise this over other tax cuts, including cuts to Inheritance Tax.
- We will also ensure that provision is made for Liberal Democrat MPs to abstain on budget resolutions to introduce transferable tax allowances for married couples without prejudice to the coalition agreement.
- We will reform the taxation of air travel by switching from a per-passenger to a per-plane duty, and will ensure that a proportion of any increased revenues over time will be used to help fund increases in the personal allowance.
- We will seek ways of taxing non-business capital gains at rates similar or close to those applied to income, with generous exemptions for entrepreneurial business activities.
- We will make every effort to tackle tax avoidance, including detailed development of Liberal Democrat proposals.
- We will increase the proportion of tax revenue accounted for by environmental taxes.
- We will take measures to fulfil our EU treaty obligations in regard to the taxation of holiday letting that do not penalise UK-based businesses.
- We will review the taxation of non-domiciled individuals.

TRANSPORT

The Government believes that a modern transport infrastructure is essential for a dynamic and entrepreneurial economy, as well as to improve well-being and quality of life. We need to make the transport sector greener and more sustainable, with tougher emission standards and support for new transport technologies.

- We will mandate a national recharging network for electric and plug-in hybrid vehicles.
- We will grant longer rail franchises in order to give operators the incentive to invest in the improvements passengers want - like better services, better stations, longer trains and better rolling stock.
- We will reform the way decisions are made on which transport projects to prioritise, so that the benefits of low carbon proposals (including light rail schemes) are fully recognised.
- We will make Network Rail more accountable to its customers.
- We will establish a high speed rail network as part of our programme of measures to fulfil our joint ambitions for creating a low carbon economy. Our vision is of a truly national high speed rail network for the whole of Britain. Given financial constraints, we will have to achieve this in phases.
- We support Crossrail and further electrification of the rail network.
- We will turn the rail regulator into a powerful passenger champion.
- We will support sustainable travel initiatives, including the promotion of cycling and walking, and will encourage joint working between bus operators and local authorities.
- We are committed to fair pricing for rail travel.
- We will work towards the introduction of a new system of HGV road user charging to ensure a fairer arrangement for UK hauliers.
- We will stop central government funding for new fixed speed cameras and switch to more effective ways of making our roads safer, including authorising 'drugalyser' technology.
- We will tackle rogue private sector wheel clampers.

UNIVERSITIES AND FURTHER EDUCATION

The Government believes that our universities are essential for building a strong and innovative economy. We will take action to create more college and university places, as well as help to foster stronger links between universities, colleges and industries.

- We will seek ways to support the creation of apprenticeships, internships, work pairings, and college and workplace training places as part of our wider programme to get Britain working.
- We will set colleges free from direct state control and abolish many of the further education quangos. Public funding should be fair and follow the choices of students.
- We will await Lord Browne's final report into higher education funding, and will judge its proposals against the need to:
  - increase social mobility;
  - take into account the impact on student debt;
  - ensure a properly funded university sector;
  - improve the quality of teaching;
  - advance scholarship; and
  - attract a higher proportion of students from disadvantaged backgrounds.
- If the response of the Government to Lord Browne's report is one that Liberal Democrats cannot accept, then arrangements will be made to enable Liberal Democrat MPs to abstain in any vote.
- We will review support for part-time students in terms of loans and fees.
- We will publish more information about the costs, graduate earnings and student satisfaction of different university courses.
- We will ensure that public funding mechanisms for university research safeguard its academic integrity.

The deficit reduction programme takes precedence over any of the other measures in this agreement, and the speed of implementation of any measures that have a cost to the public finances will depend on decisions to be made in the Comprehensive Spending Review.

The Government fully supports the devolution of powers to Northern Ireland, Scotland and Wales. As a result of devolution, many decisions made by UK Ministers or in the Westminster Parliament now apply to England only. The Northern Ireland Executive, the Scottish Executive and the Welsh Assembly Government make their own policy on their devolved issues. This document therefore sets out the agreed priorities for the Coalition Government in Westminster.

NAME INDEX

INDEX BY CONSTITUENCY

INDEX BY COI REGION

EAST MIDLANDS

EASTERN

LONDON

NORTH EAST

NORTH WEST

SOUTH EAST

SOUTH WEST

WEST MIDLANDS

YORKSHIRE AND HUMBERSIDE

NORTHERN IRELAND

SCOTLAND

WALES

INDEX BY PARTY

CONSERVATIVE

LABOUR

LABOUR/CO-OPERATIVE

LIBERAL DEMOCRAT

DEMOCRATIC UNIONIST PARTY

SCOTTISH NATIONAL PARTY

SINN FÉIN

PLAID CYMRU

SOCIAL DEMOCRATIC AND LABOUR PARTY

INDEPENDENT

ALLIANCE

GREEN PARTY

THE SPEAKER

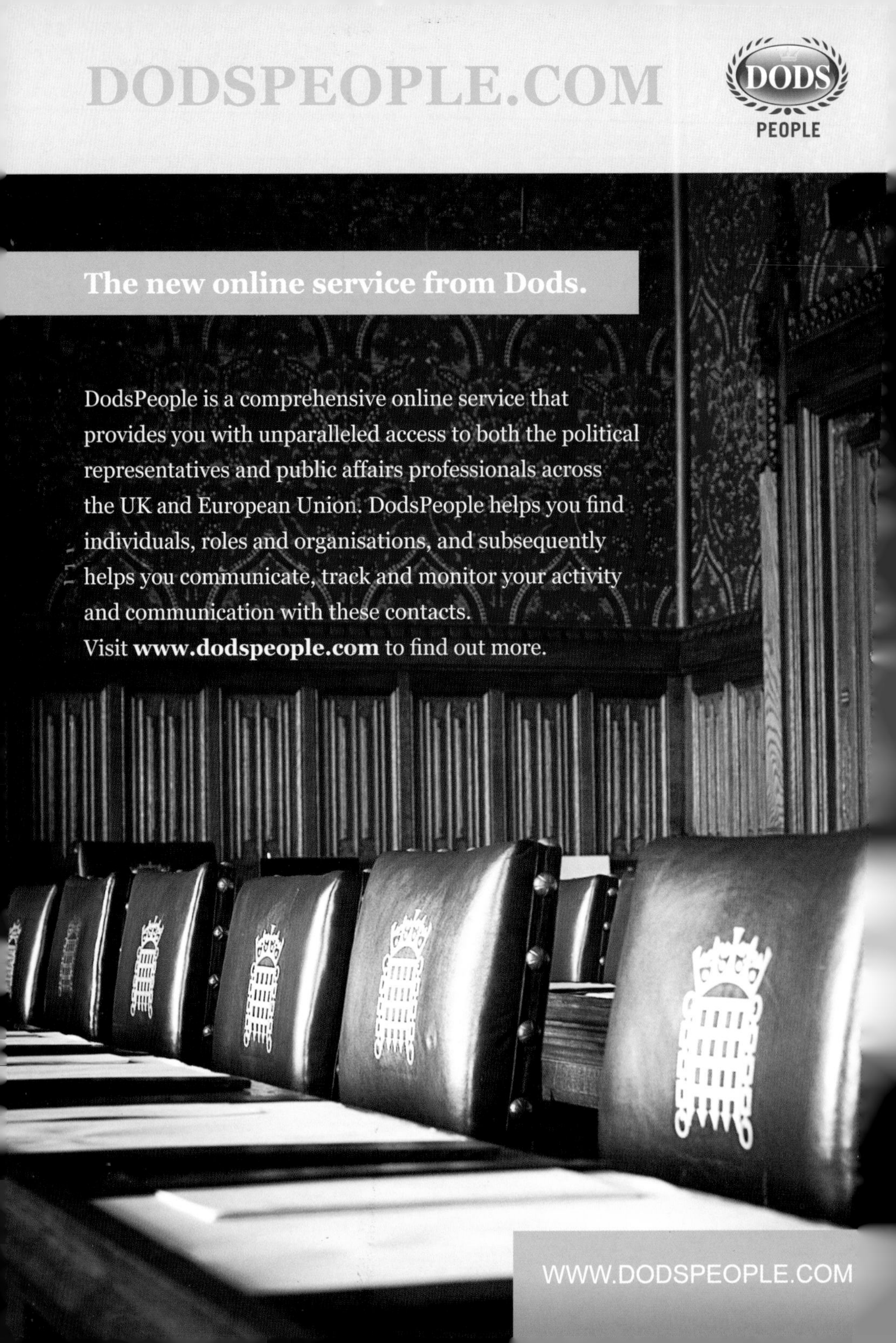